Contents

Welcome to the AA Restaurant Guide

Welcome to the 24th edition of The AA Restaurant Guide. Our hotel and restaurant inspectors have been travelling up and down the country, making anonymous visits to hundreds of establishments and they've awarded the coveted AA Rosettes to the best places to eat. See pages 8–9 for more details on how the Rosettes are awarded.

Multi-Rosette quality and new venues

The quality of the UK dining scene just keeps getting better and better – this year's guide includes 13 five-Rosette, 39 four-Rosette and 202 three-Rosette restaurants.

There are also more than 180 new venues in the guide. In England, they include The Knife and Cleaver in Bedford and the enigmatically named The Man Behind the Curtain in Leeds. The Scotland pages welcome The Falls of Feugh Restaurant in Banchory, Aberdeenshire and Andy Murray's new venture in the shape of Cromlix and Chez Roux in Dunblane, Stirling. The Wales pages say hello to Bryn Williams at Porth Eirias, Colwyn Bay and, in the north, Château Rhianta on Anglesey.

Award winners

Our award winners are a particularly strong group of places, chosen as best in class by our hospitality awards panel. The Restaurants of the Year for each of the home nations represent that crucial juncture where a distinctive concept meets the finest cooking with an emphasis this year on international influences.

Likewise, our individual award winners are all highly experienced; from the AA Chef of the Year, whose career has benefited from the tutelage of some of the industry's best known names (see page 10) to the Lifetime Achievement Award recipient whose career spans much of the postwar British dining scene (page 12). The Food Service Award winner, although a venue, has a particular global view, welcoming travellers from all over the globe on a daily, if not hourly, basis (page 13).

Raise a glass

The AA Wine Awards (see page 17) single out three restaurants that our inspectors feel have shown a real passion for and knowledge of wine. This year, multi-Rosette restaurants play all the star roles. We've also highlighted notable wine lists throughout the guide – so look out for NOTABLE WINE LIST.

Look to the future

It's not just the established and experienced venues that are celebrated in the AA Restaurant Guide. This year sees the first AA College Restaurant of the Year award, which is designed to mirror the main Rosette award process by highlighting the best catering college teams. In partnership with People 1st, the AA has awarded College Rosettes in relation to food, service and kitchen management. Read more about the bright young future of the hospitality industry on pages 20–23, including the announcement of the College Restaurant of the Year winner.

Change and change again

The transient nature of the hospitality industry means that chefs move around all the time, and restaurants may change ownership. As any change at the multi-Rosette level requires a new inspection to verify their award, some of these restaurants appear in the guide with their Rosette level unconfirmed.

Our inspections are ongoing throughout the year however, so once their award is confirmed it will be published at www.theaa.com/restaurant-and-pub.

Tell us what you think

We welcome your feedback about the restaurants included in this guide, and the guide itself. A readers' report form appears at the back of the book, so please write in, or email us at **AA.Restaurants@theAA.com**.

The restaurants also feature on **theAA.com** and you can follow us on twitter **@TheAA_Lifestyle** or 'like' the AA on facebook at **www.facebook.com/TheAAUK**.

Using the guide

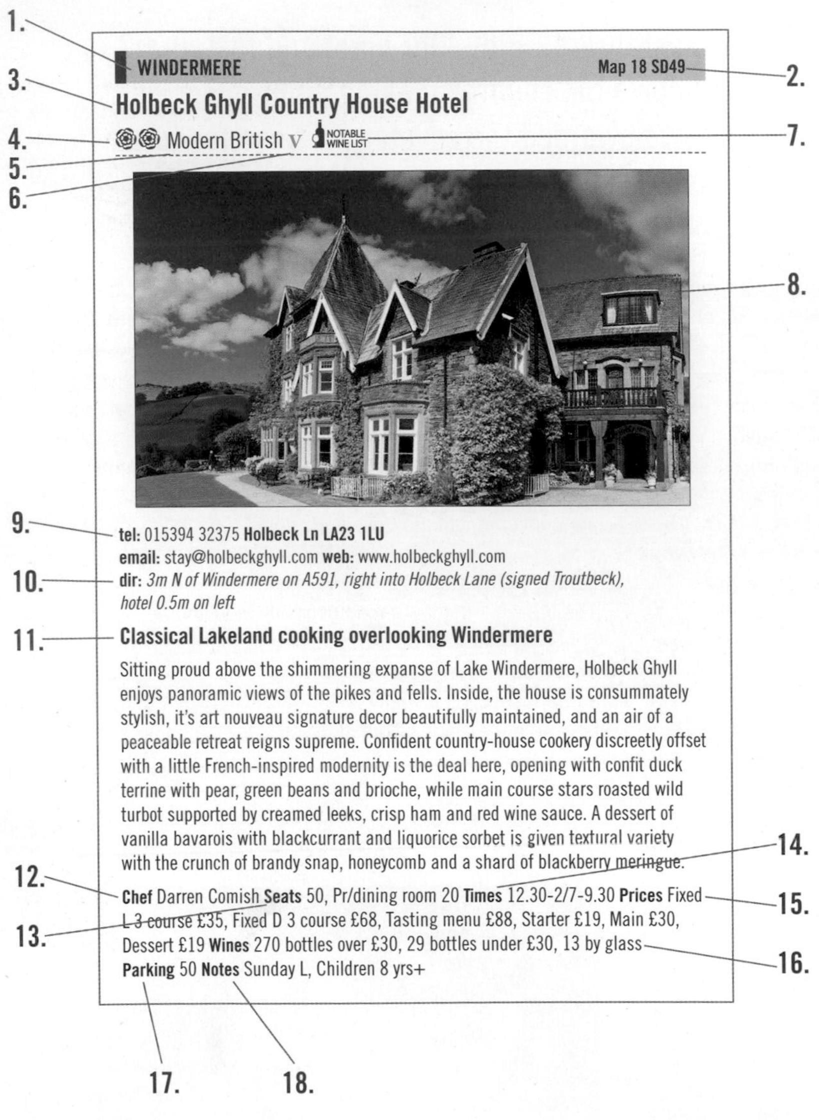

WINDERMERE Map 18 SD49

Holbeck Ghyll Country House Hotel

Modern British V NOTABLE WINE LIST

tel: 015394 32375 **Holbeck Ln LA23 1LU**
email: stay@holbeckghyll.com **web:** www.holbeckghyll.com
dir: *3m N of Windermere on A591, right into Holbeck Lane (signed Troutbeck), hotel 0.5m on left*

Classical Lakeland cooking overlooking Windermere

Sitting proud above the shimmering expanse of Lake Windermere, Holbeck Ghyll enjoys panoramic views of the pikes and fells. Inside, the house is consummately stylish, it's art nouveau signature decor beautifully maintained, and an air of a peaceable retreat reigns supreme. Confident country-house cookery discreetly offset with a little French-inspired modernity is the deal here, opening with confit duck terrine with pear, green beans and brioche, while main course stars roasted wild turbot supported by creamed leeks, crisp ham and red wine sauce. A dessert of vanilla bavarois with blackcurrant and liquorice sorbet is given textural variety with the crunch of brandy snap, honeycomb and a shard of blackberry meringue.

Chef Darren Comish **Seats** 50, Pr/dining room 20 **Times** 12.30-2/7-9.30 **Prices** Fixed L 3 course £35, Fixed D 3 course £68, Tasting menu £88, Starter £19, Main £30, Dessert £19 **Wines** 270 bottles over £30, 29 bottles under £30, 13 by glass **Parking** 50 **Notes** Sunday L, Children 8 yrs+

1. Location

Restaurants in the guide are listed in country and county order, then by town and then alphabetically within the town. There is an index by restaurant at the back of the guide and a similar one for Central & Greater London at the start of that section.

2. Map reference

Each town or village is given a map reference – the map page number and a two-figure reference based on the National Grid. For example:

Map 18 SD49

18 refers to the page number of the map section at the back of the guide

SD is the National Grid lettered square (representing 100,000 sq metres) in which the location will be found

4 is the figure reading across the top and bottom of the map page

9 is the figure reading down at each side of the map page. For Central London and Greater London, there is a map section starting on page 222.

3. Restaurant name

A name in italics indicates where an establishment has not supplied us with up-to-date information. The paragraph of details that follows the description will also be omitted where this is the case.

4. AA Rosette award

Restaurants are awarded one or more Rosettes, up to a maximum of five. See pages 8–9 for details.

5. Food style

A summary of the main cuisine type(s).

6. Vegetarian menu

V Indicates a vegetarian menu. Restaurants with some vegetarian dishes available are indicated under Notes (see 18, below).

7. Notable wine list

NOTABLE WINE LIST This symbol, where present, indicates a notable wine list (see pages 17–19).

8. Photograph(s)

Restaurants are invited to enhance their entry with up to two photographs.

9. Contact details

10. Directions

Short directions are given. London locations give the nearest station.

11. Description

Description of the restaurant and food.

12. Chef(s)

The names of the chef(s) are as up-to-date as possible at the time of going to press, but changes in personnel often occur, and may affect both the style and quality of the restaurant.

13. Number of seats

Number of seats in the restaurant, followed by private dining room (Pr/dining room).

14. Daily opening and closing times

Daily opening and closing times, the days of the week when closed and seasonal closures. Some restaurants offer all-day dining. Note that opening times are liable to change without notice. It is always wise to telephone in advance.

15. Prices

Prices are for fixed lunch (2 courses) and dinner (3 courses) and à la carte dishes. Note: Prices quoted are an indication only, and are subject to change. Service charges are not included here and may vary depending on the size of the party. Most restaurants will have some form of service charge.

16. Number of wines

Number of wines under and over £30, and available by the glass.

17. Parking details

On site parking or nearby parking.

18. Notes

Additional information as supplied by the restaurants including, for example, availability of vegetarian dishes (not a full menu, see 6, above), Sunday lunch prices and policy towards children.

FURTHER INFORMATION

Food allergies

From December 2014, an EU regulation came into force making it easier for those with food allergies to make safer food choices when eating out. There are 14 allergens listed in the regulation, and restaurants are required to list any of these that are used in the dishes they offer. These may be highlighted on the menus or customers can ask staff for full information. Remember, if you are allergic to a food and are in any doubt speak to a member of the restaurant's staff. For further information see: www.food.gov.uk/science/allergy-intolerance

Smoking regulations

From July 2007 smoking was banned in all enclosed public places in the United Kingdom and Ireland. Internal communal areas must be smoke-free.

Facilities for disabled guests

The Equality Act 2010 provides legal rights for disabled people including access to goods, services and facilities, and means that service providers may have to consider making adjustments to their premises. For more information about the Act see www.gov.uk/government/policies/creating-a-fairer-and-more-equal-society or www.gov.uk/definition-of-disability-under-equality-act-2010.

The establishments in this guide should be aware of their obligations under the Act. We recommend that you phone in advance to ensure that the establishment you have chosen has appropriate facilities.

How the AA assesses for Rosette Awards

First introduced in 1956, the AA's Rosette Award scheme was the first nationwide scheme for assessing the quality of food served by restaurants and hotels.

A consistent approach

The Rosette scheme is an award, not a classification, and although there is necessarily an element of subjectivity when it comes to assessing taste, we aim for a consistent approach throughout the UK. Our awards are made solely on the basis of a meal visit or visits by one or more of our hotel and restaurant inspectors, who have an unrivalled breadth and depth of experience in assessing quality. Essentially it's a snapshot, whereby the entire meal including ancillary items (when served) are assessed. Of all the restaurants across the UK, approximately 10 per cent are of a standard which is worthy of 1 Rosette and above.

What makes a restaurant worthy of a Rosette award?

For AA inspectors, the top and bottom line is the food. The taste of a dish is what counts, and whether it successfully delivers to the diner the promise of the menu. A restaurant is only as good as its worst meal. Although presentation and competent service should be appropriate to the style of the restaurant and the quality of the food, they cannot affect the Rosette assessment as such, either up or down. The summaries below indicate what our inspectors look for, but are intended only as guidelines. The AA is constantly reviewing its award criteria, and competition usually results in an all-round improvement in standards, so it becomes increasingly difficult for restaurants to reach an award level.

The next level

Achieving a Rosette is a huge achievement and something not to be underestimated. We are often asked by chefs and proprietors: "What is the difference between 1 and 5 Rosettes and how can I get to the next level?" We answer that it's how well a chef manages to apply advanced technique while retaining maximum flavour, and assuming an appropriate quality of source ingredients.

While we endeavour to work with the industry and promote great cooking across the UK, it's of paramount importance for chefs to always serve their market first. We recommend they don't chase awards, but see them as something to celebrate when they come along. Where, however, the winning of Rosettes is an aspiration, the simple guidelines, shown opposite, may help. Experiencing AA food tastings, enhanced food tastings or signing up to one of the AA Rosette Academies can also give further insight and guidance, but these are separate from the awards process and do not influence any assessments.

✪ One Rosette

These restaurants will be achieving standards that standout in their local area, featuring:

- food prepared with care, understanding and skill
- good quality ingredients

The same expectations apply to hotel restaurants where guests should be able to eat in with confidence and a sense of anticipation.

Around 45% of restaurants/hotels in this guide have one Rosette.

✪✪ Two Rosettes

The best local restaurants, which aim for and achieve:

- higher standards
- better consistency
- greater precision is apparent in the cooking
- obvious attention to the selection of quality ingredients

Around 45% of restaurants/hotels in this guide have two Rosettes.

✪✪✪ Three Rosettes

Outstanding restaurants that achieve standards that demand national recognition well beyond their local area. The cooking will be underpinned by:

- the selection and sympathetic treatment of the highest quality ingredients
- timing, seasoning and the judgment of flavour combinations will be consistently excellent

These virtues will tend to be supported by other elements such as intuitive service and a well-chosen wine list.

Around 10% of the restaurants/hotels in this guide have three Rosettes and above.

✪✪✪✪ Four Rosettes

Among the top restaurants in the UK where the cooking demands national recognition. These restaurants will exhibit:

- intense ambition
- a passion for excellence
- superb technical skills
- remarkable consistency
- an appreciation of culinary traditions combined with a passionate desire for further exploration and improvement

39 restaurants in this guide have four Rosettes.

✪✪✪✪✪ Five Rosettes

The pinnacle, where the cooking compares with the best in the world. These restaurants will have:

- highly individual voices
- exhibit breathtaking culinary skills and set the standards to which others aspire to, yet few achieve

13 restaurants in this guide have five Rosettes.

Announcements of awards

One and two Rosettes are awarded at the time of inspection. Three and four Rosette awards are announced twice during the year, but never at the time of inspection. Five Rosettes are awarded just the once during a year and never at the time of inspection.

Suspension of Multi-Rosettes (3, 4, 5 Rosettes)

When a chef holds 3, 4 or 5 Rosettes and moves from one establishment to another, the award is suspended at the hotel/restaurant he/she has just left. The award does not follow the chef automatically either. We therefore recommend that when a change of chef occurs, establishments let us know as soon as possible in order for us to schedule forthcoming inspections.

AA Chef of the Year 2016–17

Simon Rogan

Since he opened his flagship restaurant, L'Enclume, inside an 800-year-old smithy in the Cumbrian village of Cartmel, Simon Rogan has achieved phenomenal success and international acclaim. A chef who has worked at an unprecedented level of innovation and technical skill for the past 15 years, Rogan continues to strive for perfection, pushing the boundaries and exploring tastes and textures.

Rogan is one of the most creative and dynamic chefs working in the UK today and the food at L'Enclume has made an indelible impression on the country's food scene, his influence is far-reaching.

With his use of edible flowers and subtle Alpine herbs – much of it foraged or grown on the restaurant's abundant 12-acre farm, alongside the fruit and vegetables – Rogan continues to create striking and complex signature dishes like venison leg cooked in hay with roast celeriac and braised red cabbage, and poached pears, atsina cress snow, sweet cheese ice cream and rosehip syrup.

Trained classically at Southampton Technical College, Rogan secured an apprenticeship at Rhinefield House Hotel in Hampshire at the age of 17, where he remained for five years.

Joining chef Jean-Christophe Novelli in 1988 at the Geddes restaurant in Southampton, he rose to the position of sous chef. Rogan worked on and off for Novelli for eight years, including at both The Maltster's Arms in Tuckenhay, Devon (at the time owned by Keith Floyd with Novelli as head chef), and at Gordleton Mill, in Hampshire.

During this period, he also worked under culinary giants Marco Pierre White and John Burton-Race, before spending two years in Paris under chef Alain Senderens at Lucas Carton – an experience Rogan refers to as his finishing school.

Rogan and his partner Penny Tapsell opened their Lake District restaurant-with-rooms L'Enclume in 2002, followed six years later by the more informal Rogan & Company, also in the village of Cartmel.

In 2013, Rogan expanded his empire by opening two restaurants at The Midland Hotel in Manchester, followed the year after by Fera at Claridge's in Mayfair, London.

The son of a greengrocer working at Southampton fruit and vegetable market, Rogan's earliest taste of kitchen life was at the age of 14 when he worked in his local Greek restaurant, although his first love was football. A talented teenage player, he had trials at Chelsea and was offered a contract with Fulham before deciding to take a position at catering college instead. Football's loss is very much cooking's gain.

On the menu

Duck gizzard,
whey onions, Tunworth

Brill in poultry juices,
celeriac, yeast flakes,
fermented mushroom

Woodruff, apple sorrel
and yoghurt

Previous winners

Daniel Clifford
Midsummer House,
Cambridge,
Cambridgeshire

Nathan Outlaw
Restaurant Nathan Outlaw,
Port Isaac, Cornwall

Tom Kerridge
The Hand and Flowers,
Marlow, Buckinghamshire

Chris and Jeff Galvin
Galvin La Chapelle,
London E1

Michael Caines
Gidleigh Park,
Chagford, Devon

Andrew Fairlie
Andrew Fairlie@Gleneagles,
Auchterarder,
Perth & Kinross

Germain Schwab

Raymond Blanc
Belmond Le Manoir aux
Quat' Saisons, Great Milton,
Oxfordshire

Shaun Hill
Walnut Tree Inn,
Abergavenny, Monmouthshire

Heston Blumenthal
The Fat Duck, Bray, Berkshire

Jean-Christophe Novelli

Gordon Ramsay
Restaurant Gordon Ramsay,
London SW3

Rick Stein
The Seafood Restaurant,
Padstow, Cornwall

Marco Pierre White

Kevin Viner

Philip Howard
The Square, London W1

Marcus Wareing
Marcus, The Berkeley,
London SW1

Martin Wishart
Restaurant Martin Wishart,
Leith, Edinburgh

Pierre Koffmann
Koffmann's, London SW1

AA Lifetime Achievement Award 2016–17

Pierre Koffmann

French chef Pierre Koffmann has been one of the undisputed heavyweights of the British restaurant scene since he arrived in England in the early 1970s.

Born in Tarbes, Gascony in 1948, the young Koffmann spent childhood holidays with his maternal grandparents, Camille and Marcel, on their farm at Saint Puy, a small village near Tarbes. Although Koffmann's mother was a good cook, it was his grandmother who inspired him the most. Living off the land and cooking as the seasons dictated on a big open fire, Camille used every part of the animals and it shaped Koffmann's love of cooking seasonal ingredients.

Leaving school at 14, Koffmann tried for jobs with the post office and French railway, but eventually opted for the local cookery school. Arriving in London at the age of 22, his original plan was only to stay for six months, but he quickly found a job working for Michel and Albert Roux at Le Gavroche. Within six months he had been promoted to sous chef and was soon appointed head chef at the Roux Brothers' Waterside Inn at Bray, where he stayed for five years. In 1977, Koffmann and his first wife, Annie, opened their first restaurant, La Tante Claire, in Chelsea and it quickly gained a reputation as one of the best dining experiences in London. Two decades later, Koffmann took up residency in the Berkeley Hotel in Knightsbridge, where he continued to cook until he decided to hang up his apron in 2003. However, his retirement was short-lived.

In 2009, Koffmann made a high-profile comeback running a pop-up version of La Tante Claire on the roof of Selfridges. The original one-week event sold out immediately and it continued for two months, during which time he served up 3,200 plates of his signature dish of pig's trotters stuffed with chicken mousseline, sweetbreads and morel mushrooms.

The huge success of the Koffman pop-up inspired him to make an unexpected return to The Berkeley Hotel, where he opened Koffmann's, a restaurant offering a relaxed, informal style with classic provincial French cuisine inspired by the food enjoyed as a child in rural Gascony.

During his career, he has trained a number of chefs including Gordon Ramsay, Marco Pierre White, Marcus Wareing and Jason Atherton. With so many culinary giants working under him over the years, Koffmann's ongoing influence on the British restaurant scene is immeasurable.

AA Food Service Award 2016–17

The Ritz, London W1

Opened in 1906 by César Ritz, The Ritz is one of the finest hotels in the world and remains a bastion of classical service, thanks to skilled staff providing the highest personal care and attention to detail.

Refurbished and painstakingly restored in recent years by owners Sir David Barclay and Sir Frederick Barclay, The Ritz is the epitome of luxury and style, an iconic hotel that remains timeless but contemporary at the same time.

Executive chef John Williams has overseen The Ritz's stunning restaurant for more than a decade and the dining room has a reverential air that's entirely in keeping with the top-flight haute cuisine being served.

Established by influential chef Auguste Escoffier, The Ritz restaurant is widely regarded as one of the most stunning dining rooms in the world. Towering marble columns, neo-classical statues, ceiling frescoes and a magnificent chandelier, it's a room that screams opulence and it provides a stunning backdrop for the classical French cooking, with many dishes inspired by the original Escoffier recipes.

Whether it's a meal in the restaurant, an indulgent afternoon tea in the Palm Court or expertly crafted cocktails in the Rivoli Bar, all Ritz employees demonstrate exceptional customer service skills and a professional, friendly attitude. Employees are offered a variety of training and development opportunities and the hotel strives to create a motivating and rewarding environment for staff at every level.

The Ritz has long been associated with food service of the highest international standard, something which has lead the hotel to receiving a Royal Warrant for Banqueting and Catering Services – the first hotel to have been honoured with this prestigious award.

More than 110 years since it first opened, The Ritz provides a food service benchmark by which other hotels are measured.

Inspector comments:

This iconic London hotel always offered high international standards and it retains much of its historic splendour. This year, these standards did not disappoint. The entire team (not just the food and beverage team) displayed great guest focus, and intuitive hospitality was perfectly gauged. Delivery across all areas remains. Polished and professional, and nothing is too much trouble for the dynamic team.

In addition, the food and beverage teams offered memorable, welcoming and engaging hospitality with excellent guest name use, too.

Service delivery is always polished, professional and fluent, and true theatre can be seen in the Rivoli Bar, Ritz Restaurant, during breakfast and even in-room dining.

AA Restaurants of the Year 2016–17

ENGLAND

LUMIÈRE ®®®

CHELTENHAM page 147

Located in the centre of Cheltenham, close to the Regency spa town's bustling Promenade, Jon and Helen Howe have been running Lumière since 2009 and it has gradually grown to become a well-supported neighbourhood restaurant. Its unassuming, easy-to-miss façade belies an elegant and welcoming interior, with Helen and her small team running things out front as husband Jon cooks in the tiny, but efficiently run, kitchen at the back. Prior to Lumière, Jon honed his skills under industry giants such as Heston Blumenthal and John Campbell and he is committed to using fresh, seasonal produce, much of it local from named suppliers including fruit and veg from the garden of Helen's parents. The modern, innovative cooking has a global influence with exacting flavours and contemporary twists in dishes like Wiltshire ham hock terrine, smoked eel, pineapple and gingerbread, and duck, pak choi, sesame, plum, maple and lime. Rhubarb, white chocolate, thyme, hibiscus and honeycomb is a typical dessert. It's all backed up with slick service and a superb, carefully considered wine list.

LONDON

SOSHARU ®®®

LONDON EC1 page 240

Close to Farringdon tube station in the heart of Clerkenwell, Jason Atherton's latest opening is a restaurant inspired by a Japanese-style sharing plate concept. Translated as 'social', Sosharu is based on the informal Izakaya restaurants of Japan and it's a buzzy place with casually dressed staff and a separate cocktail bar and private dining area where groups of ten can enjoy a bespoke menu chosen by the chef. With an open pass between the kitchen and main restaurant, diners can watch as the chefs cook small plates of beautifully crafted Japanese specialties, including sashimi, tempura and dishes cooked on the hibachi grill. From the cold section of the menu, scallop tartare with fresh peas, sesame and lemon purée is one enticing starter, perhaps followed by grilled lamb cutlets, roasted onion and sesame and red miso. Sukiyaki Wagyu beef, glass noodles, young leeks and shiitake mushrooms is one main course inspired by the classics. The pedigree wine list has been designed with food matching in mind and there is also an excellent selection of saki.

Potential Restaurants of the Year are nominated by our team of full-time inspectors based on their routine visits. We are looking for somewhere that is exceptional in its chosen area of the market. While the Rosette awards are based on the quality of the food alone, Restaurant of the Year takes into account all aspects of the dining experience.

SCOTLAND

INVER RESTAURANT ®®

STRACHUR page 503

The setting, on the shores of Loch Fyne on Scotland's west coast, is enviable enough, but chef Pam Brunton and partner Rob Latimer have created something quite special since opening in spring 2015. The pair previously worked at a number of notable places in Europe including the world-famous Noma restaurant in Denmark and they follow a similar Scandinavian philosophy of using the freshest local produce from sea and land in the seasonal menus at Inver. From bread and butter to ice cream and preserves, everything here is made from scratch on the premises and the dishes display a clarity of flavours. Techniques such as preserving and fermenting are used with great skill in dishes like fresh Loch Fyne crab, fennel cream, rye and fennel seed crisps, which might be followed by a main course of rack and shoulder of Isle of Bute lamb, ewes milk yogurt, grilled leek and wild garlic. Sorrel sorbet and damson vodka is one of the inspired desserts, while the concise but lively wine list draws its inspiration from Europe.

WALES

RESTAURANT JAMES SOMMERIN ®®®

PENARTH page 582

Right on the esplanade at Penarth, overlooking the Bristol Channel, James Sommerin's eponymous restaurant with rooms is worthy of a detour. Previously at the Crown at Whitebrook (and no stranger to the TV cameras thanks to the *Great British Menu*), Sommerin is cooking up a storm in this contemporary sea-facing restaurant with its gorgeous views over the Severn estuary. With its white walls decorated with vibrant artwork from local artists, the bright and airy dining room has a viewing window into the kitchen, where there is also a chef's table for those who want to dine even closer to the action. The food is highly accomplished, with top drawer ingredients conjured into memorable dishes like a starter of scallops, Jerusalem artichoke, mushroom and fennel seed. Next up, a confit leg of Gressingham duck might be teamed with salt-baked swede, dates and spices or local cod served with squid ink, samphire and potato. The appealing combinations of flavours and textures continue through to a dessert of treacle, raspberry, rosemary and olive oil.

AA Wine Awards 2016–17

The annual AA Wine Awards, sponsored by Matthew Clark Wines, attracted a huge response from our AA recognised restaurants with over 1,300 wine lists submitted for judging. Three national winners were chosen – Sketch (Lecture Room & Library), London for England and the Overall Winner; The Kitchen, Edinburgh for Scotland; and The Whitebrook, Monmouthshire for Wales (see overleaf for details).

All 2,000 Rosetted restaurants in last year's guide were invited to submit their wine lists. From these the panel selected a shortlist of over 260 establishments who are highlighted in the guide with the Notable Wine List symbol.

The shortlisted establishments were asked to choose wines from their list (within a budget of £80 per bottle) to accompany a menu designed by last year's winner The Sun Inn, Dedham.

The final judging panel included Piers Baker, Proprietor of The Sun Inn, Nick Zalinski, Business Director, Matthew Clark Wines (our sponsor) and Paul Hackett, AA Hotel Services. The judges' comments are shown under the award winners overleaf.

They also felt the wine list from Donnington Valley Hotel and Spa, Newbury, was worthy of commendation and this has been highlighted on its entry on page 40.

What makes a wine list notable?

We are looking for high-quality wines, with diversity across grapes and/or countries and style, the best individual growers and vintages. The list should be well presented, ideally with some helpful notes and, to reflect the demand from diners, a good choice of wines by the glass.

Things that disappoint the judges are spelling errors on the lists, wines under incorrect regions or styles, split vintages (which are still far too common), lazy purchasing (all wines from a country from just one grower or negociant) and confusing wine list layouts. Sadly, many restaurants still do not pay much attention to wine, resulting in ill-considered lists.

The AA Wine Awards are sponsored by Matthew Clark, Whitchurch Lane, Bristol, BS14 0JZ Tel: 01275 891400
email: enquiries@matthewclark.co.uk web: www.matthewclark.co.uk

To reach the final shortlist, we look for a real passion for wine, which should come across to the customer, a fair pricing policy (depending on the style of the restaurant), interesting coverage (not necessarily a large list), which might include areas of specialism, perhaps a particular wine area, sherries or larger formats such as magnums.

Sketch (Lecture Room & Library) – the winning wine selection

Menu	Wine Selection
Canapés – Crab crostino, fennel powder; stuffed artichokes with breadcrumbs & olives; roast Crown Prince squash with lardo	NV Roederer, Quartet, California
Pasta course – Panzotti with Swiss chard, buffalo ricotta, fresh walnut sauce.	2013 Gavi, Alborina, Castello di Tassarolo
Fish course – Roast tranche of turbot, violetta artichokes, samphire, girolles, beurre blanc	2010 Chablis, Butteaux, Montmains, George
Meat course – Roast grouse with thyme, Chianti Classico, potato & porcini 'al forno', sage, pancetta, watercress	2005 Coteaux du Languedoc, Mas Julien
Cheese – Montgomery's Cheddar, Stichelton and Wigmore served with pear and date chutney, grapes and flatbread	2001 Château La Grande Clotte, Lussac Saint-Emilion
Pudding course – Hendrick's gin pannacotta, cucumber spaghetti, mint syrup	Domaine Laurent Cazottes Goutte de Poire William Passerillee

AA Wine Awards – the winners

WINNER FOR ENGLAND AND OVERALL WINNER

SKETCH (LECTURE ROOM & LIBRARY) @@@@@

LONDON W1 page 310

Visionary Algerian-born restaurateur Mourad Mazouz transformed the former headquarters of Christian Dior into a suitably opulent and grand dining experience when he teamed up with the French master chef Pierre Gagnaire to create Sketch. Walk through the discreet entrance flanked by doormen and you enter a multi-faceted place where food, art and music combine to create a unique experience for the senses. In the fine-dining Lecture Room & Library with its ornate high ceilings, warm Middle Eastern colours and ivory walls of studded leather, the modern French cooking showcases great technical know-how in complex dishes delivering memorable flavours and textures. The extensive and detailed wine list featuring more than 700 bottles is easy to navigate and covers both Old and New Worlds, including an impressive selection of Champagnes and wines from Morocco.

Judging observations: A real wine lover's treat with real quality in evidence, bags of interest and a few quirks too. A very extensive yet accessible list which is clearly laid-out and feels totally hand-selected. Unusually for a restaurant with a team of sommeliers ready to provide guidance, the list features detailed and beautifully researched tasting notes throughout, which capture the individual characteristics of every bottle and genuinely honours the wine. Particular highlights include an excellent selection by the glass, a mind-blowing Champagne selection and the scope of exclusive Cuvées is highly impressive. To conclude, a tome which oozes class on every page and a list you just want to keep on reading.

WINNER FOR SCOTLAND

THE KITCHIN ◎◎◎◎◎

EDINBURGH page 515

Opposite the offices of the Scottish Government on the waterfront at Leith, Tom Kitchin's eponymous restaurant was once a bonded warehouse storing whisky, although since it opened in 2006, it's the wine rather than Scotch that has created the most interest. Kitchin's 'from nature to plate' cooking philosophy combines finely-honed technical skills with hyper-local raw materials. Based on solid French technique, the dynamic cooking is modern British and the tranquil dining room reflects the dockland building's heritage via various textures of wool, wood, stone and glass. The conscientiously curated wine list includes many classic Old World wines from France, but it also keeps things fresh with bottles from contemporary wine makers from newer territories, with plenty by the glass to encourage food pairing. Kitchin's impeccable desserts are enhanced further by an impressive selection of 'stickies'.

Judging observations: A beautiful list with a fine and varied selection by the glass, showing a good spread of styles across both the Old and New World. Well-laid out and clear to navigate across its regional and global structure. Look out for a well-chosen range of Champagne and stickies too. All in all, this is a well balanced, highly personal list where the well-known 'big guns' sit side by side with newer trailblazers.

WINNER FOR WALES

THE WHITEBROOK ◎◎◎◎

MONMOUTHSHIRE page 571

Since they took over at the end of 2013, Chris Harrod and his wife, Kirsty, have drawn diners from all over Wales and the southwest to their classy 32-cover restaurant-with-rooms. Always cooking at the fine-dining end of the spectrum, Chris previously worked at The Lanesborough and L'Ortolan, but it was his three years under Raymond Blanc at Belmond Le Manoir aux Quat'Saison that really set him up for his first solo venture. Overlooking the Wye Valley, the restaurant makes good use of the locality for its produce, particularly wild herbs and local pork (suckling pig with pine nut, artichokes and hop shoots is a signature dish), and fish arrives daily from Cornwall. The well-judged and eclectic wine list features many small producers and includes bottles from Croatia and Corsica.

Judging observations: A lovely list which goes to great lengths to engage and guide the customer. The selection is arranged by drinking style, with brief but helpful headings which aids selection and makes the list accessible; there is a useful vintage guide. The by-the-glass section is punchy, varied and appealing. We loved the section 'a little different from around the world', which highlighted a personal selection of wines across the list. There's good value to be found across the varied price points, so all pockets are catered for.

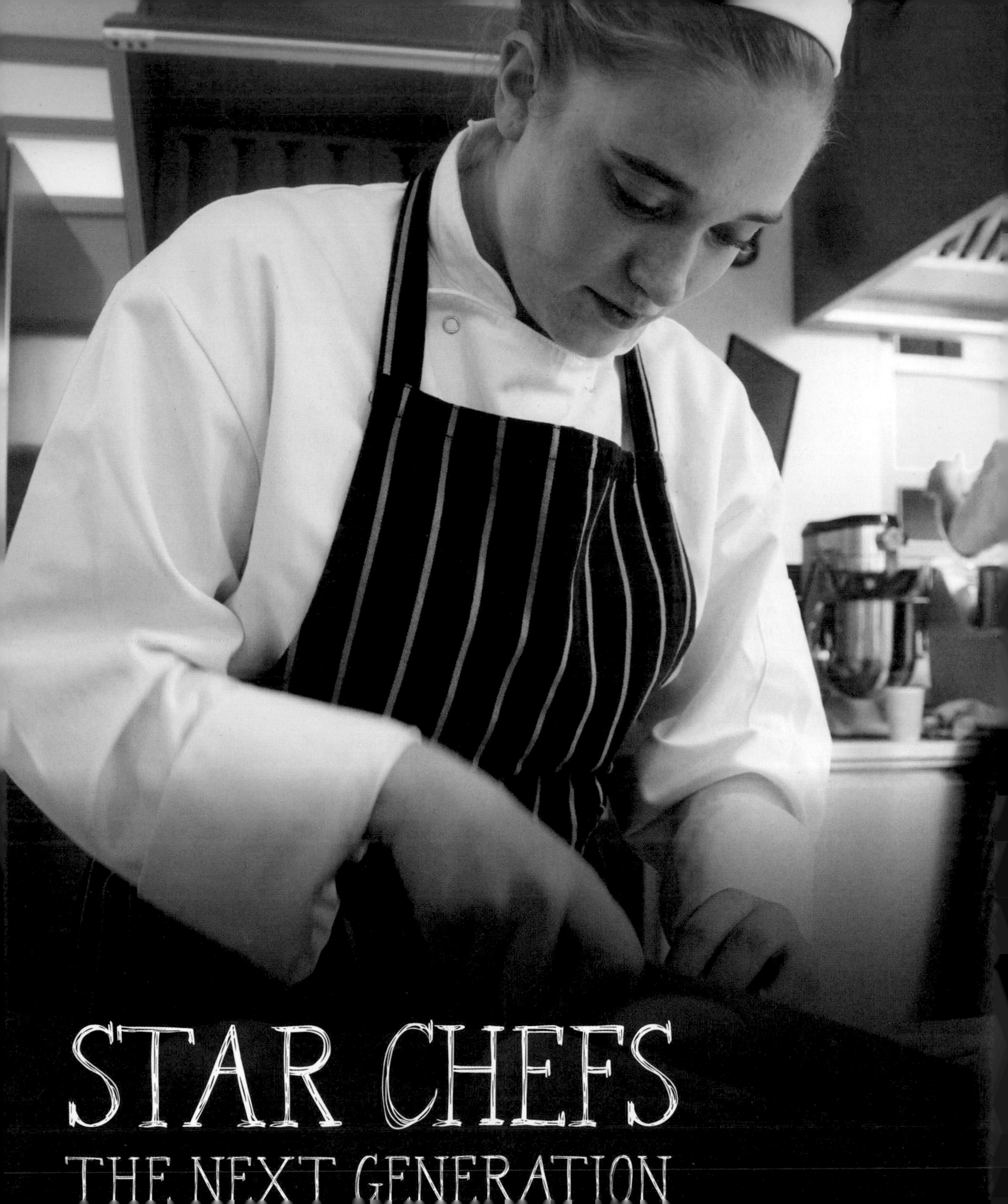

STAR CHEFS

THE NEXT GENERATION

College restaurants are no longer the best kept secrets in their local community and are growing in reputation all the time. Mike Pedley takes a look at the AA's College Rosette scheme and new College Restaurant of the Year award and what it means for the future of the industry.

Foodies in the know have long been aware of the remarkably good food and value for money to be found at some of the UK's catering college restaurants, where the meals are prepared by professional cookery students under the guidance of experienced chef-lecturers. The restaurants are run and managed with a similar level of expertise and professionalism. After all, what's the point of great food if the front-of-house team – a vital element of the whole experience – aren't hitting the heights? It's a win-win deal: the lucky diners get high quality food and service at bargain basement prices and students develop invaluable hands-on experience. In addition, customers' feedback helps students to hone their skills, expand knowledge and improve confidence.

It's vital that students studying for professional qualifications in the hospitality and food and beverage world learn the skills that will be the bedrock of their working lives, and college training restaurants provide that invaluable experience of preparing and serving food for paying customers in realistic working environments.

Among the ranks of this next generation of budding chefs are the Athertons, Rogans, Outlaws and Kitchins of the future, so the AA College Rosette scheme has been set up to nurture the talented individuals who will one day become household names, and whose restaurants will in due course stake their claim to a place on the UK's foodie map. The new AA College Restaurant of the Year award will help flag up some of these rising stars destined for high-flying culinary careers.

Industry recognition

Launched in March 2016, the AA College Restaurant of the Year award seeks to uncover and reward the hard work of chef -lecturers and student brigades that run college restaurants. It is open to colleges that have been awarded an AA College Rosette and those that have been accredited by People 1st, the workforce development experts. The scheme is endorsed by a group of leading hospitality employers, including Starwood Capital, Exclusive Hotels and Whitbread, and is a 'stamp of approval' that recognises colleges and training providers offering exceptional hospitality training.

Given the current chef shortage and the food industry's target to recruit 11,000 chefs by 2022, the accreditation scheme can help hospitality businesses find quality colleges and work-based providers who will then support them with recruitment and training and development.

"It's fundamental to recognise our future hospitality industry..."

Garry Baldwin, senior hotel and restaurant inspector, and the man in charge of the new award initiative for AA Hotel Services says "It's fundamental to recognise our future hospitality industry. This assessment promotes standards at grass roots level and raises awareness of AA Hotel Services within the industry. Building on the relationship that we have established with People 1st in the development of the AA College Rosette, we can't wait to congratulate the first AA College Restaurant of the Year award winner in 2016. This award will allow them to really promote and showcase themselves."

Putting people first

Martine Pullen, director of membership at People 1st, comments: "As part of the Accreditation Scheme, People 1st has partnered with AA Hotel Services to carry out assessment visits. To support these visits, AA Hotel Services is providing an inspector who will tour the facilities, inspect the college

◁ A young chef hard at work

The AA College Rosette scheme

The AA College Rosette Scheme is designed to recognise the efforts of students, both front and back of house who are the future of the hospitality industry. The college accreditation process, provided by People 1st, recognises colleges offering exceptional hospitality training, and those that perform above and beyond as centres of excellence in a specialist field.

The AA is the only nationwide assessment organisation and as a leader in the field it makes sense to become part of such an initiative. The AA offers an industry skill set, paired with the heritage of the brand and, of course, the Star rating and Rosette schemes. The following provides a guide to what the three levels of The AA College Rosette scheme mean:

Entry Level – Recommended

Establishments will have a clear and recognised commitment to students and the industry. The restaurant will have had an inspection as part of the scheme, however they must demonstrate greater strength and confidence before an award can be given. The restaurant will be working towards either the Level 1 or 2 award.

Level 1 – Award

Restaurants serving food prepared with care, understanding and skill, using good quality ingredients. These restaurants will be achieving standards that standout in their local area and within the currently benchmarked colleges. Diners at these restaurants should be able to order with both confidence and a sense of anticipation, for a meal prepared and served with care and attention to detail.

Level 2 – Highly Commended

In addition to the criteria at Entry level and Level 1, restaurants at Level 2 will show confidence and clear structure. The learning environment, in addition to the facility, will at its very best, and above all, be appropriate to target markets. Restaurants will have an excellent grasp of commercial acumen and can operate well within a genuine restaurant setting. Restaurants at this level are likely to have a clear brand and excellent links to the hospitality industry which will serve to benefit the students. Service levels are highly polished, there is clear support from the lecturers and notable peer-to-peer learning and training.

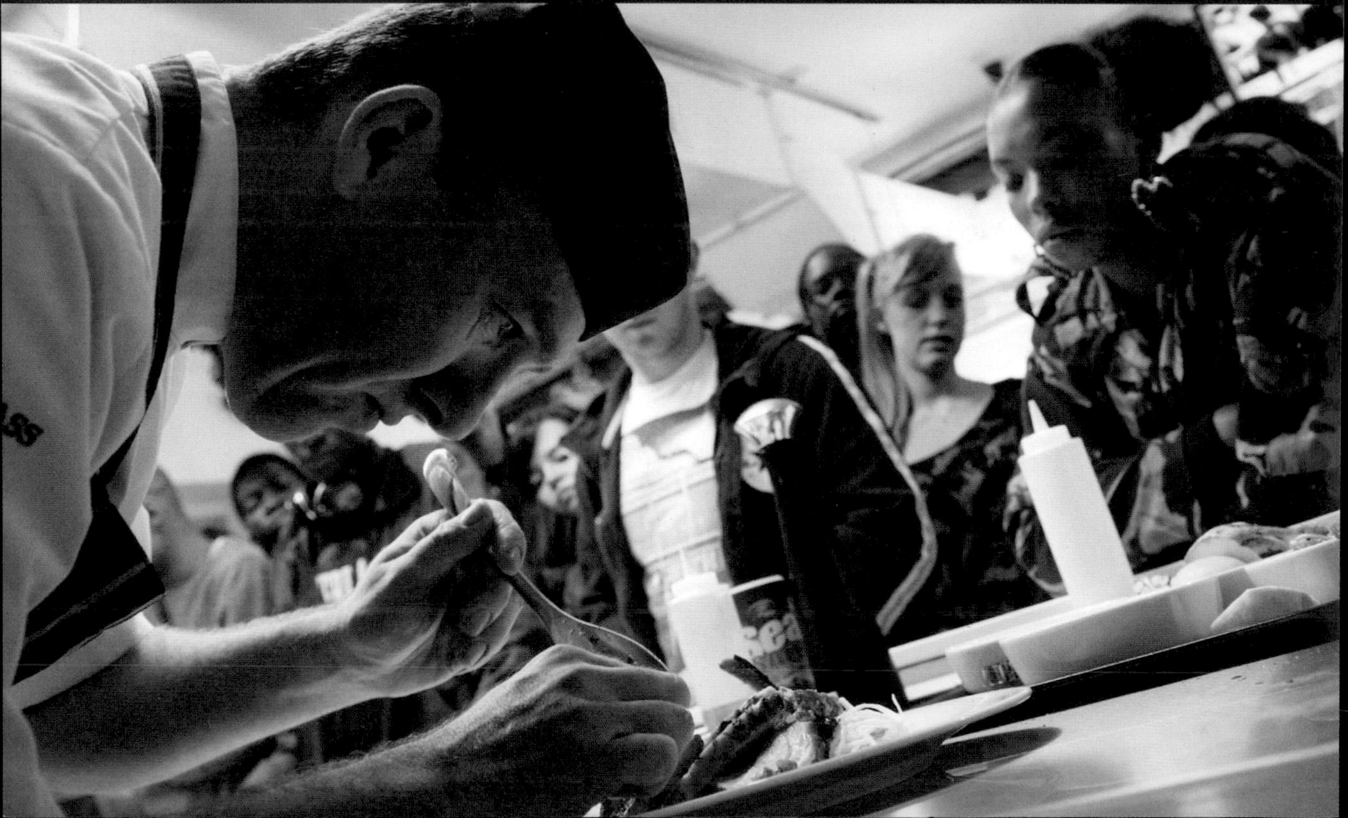

restaurant and speak to learners about their experience. People 1st has also worked with AA Hotel Services to develop a Rosette system, which recognises college restaurants for the quality of the food produced and the level of service delivered. We are delighted to further develop our partnership with the AA and sponsor the AA College Restaurant of the Year Award. The new award gives our accredited colleges an additional opportunity to be recognised for the excellent work of their restaurants and reward the dedication of the lecturer and student teams that run them."

The initiative has been warmly welcomed by colleges too. Dave Thomas, programme area manager for hospitality and food at Leicester College adds: "We are really excited that People 1st and AA Hotel Services have started this competition. It builds on the fantastic recognition that our restaurant has gained since being awarded our Rosette and as a team of lecturers and students, it gives us the chance to stand amongst our industry peers as an award winner."

An inspector calls

The inspection visits were very positive, with the inspection team's tours noting impressive facilities, cuisine and service, and clear focus on key areas such as the quality of ingredients used and the menu composition. The lecturers' support within the dining environments has been consistently good, with clear and relevant detail given during restaurant operations.

Highlights include the sort of things you would expect to see in top-drawer restaurants: a chef's table, television links between the kitchen and restaurant, as well as the use of iPads for wine lists and training development for example, backed by some excellent kitchen facilities, and warmth and hospitality from students. All of which shows a clear drive for excellent standards in delivering some rather enjoyable meals. Finally, there's no point setting up a brilliant operation if it goes bust very quickly, so inspectors have also been pleased to see a clear business focus, whatever the operation, be it a bakery, a food boutique, a coffee shop and, in some cases, development of catering services in other parts of the college.

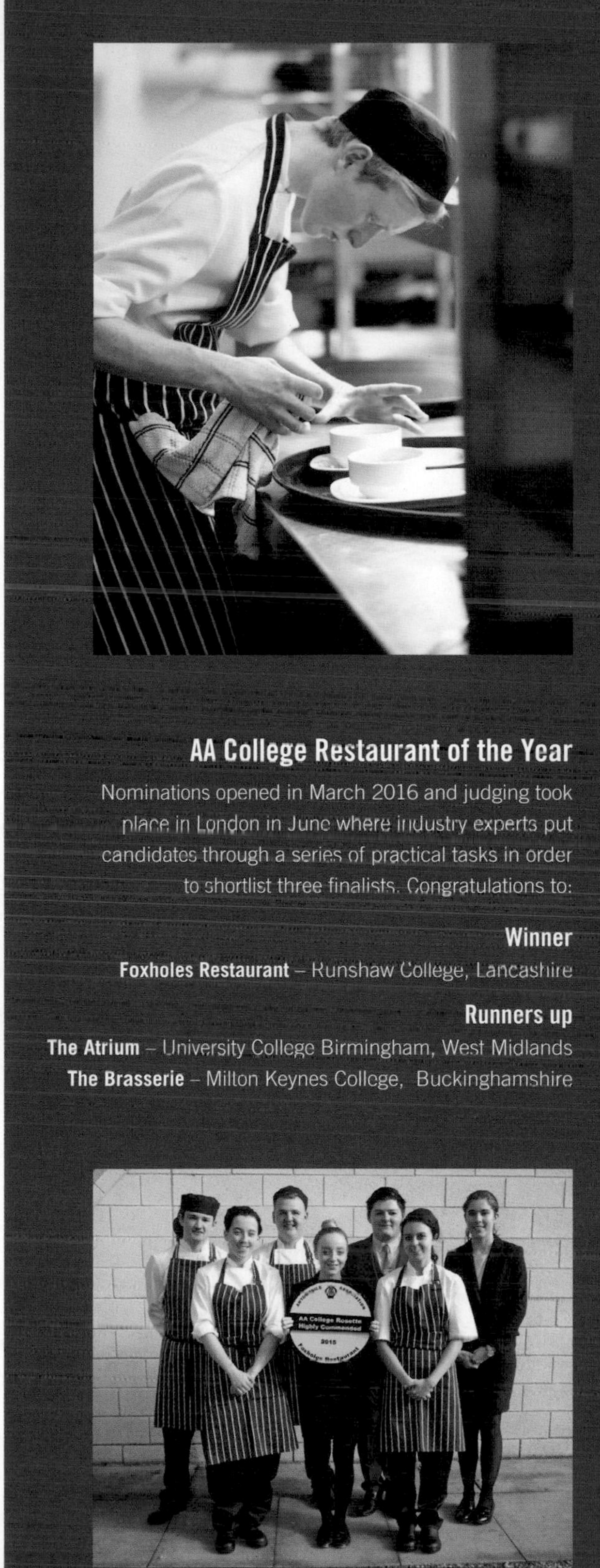

AA College Restaurant of the Year

Nominations opened in March 2016 and judging took place in London in June where industry experts put candidates through a series of practical tasks in order to shortlist three finalists. Congratulations to:

Winner

Foxholes Restaurant – Runshaw College, Lancashire

Runners up

The Atrium – University College Birmingham, West Midlands

The Brasserie – Milton Keynes College, Buckinghamshire

◁ Getting it right and striving for perfection

Foxholes Restaurant – Runshaw College, AA College Restaurant of the Year, pictured above, and right with their Highly Commended award

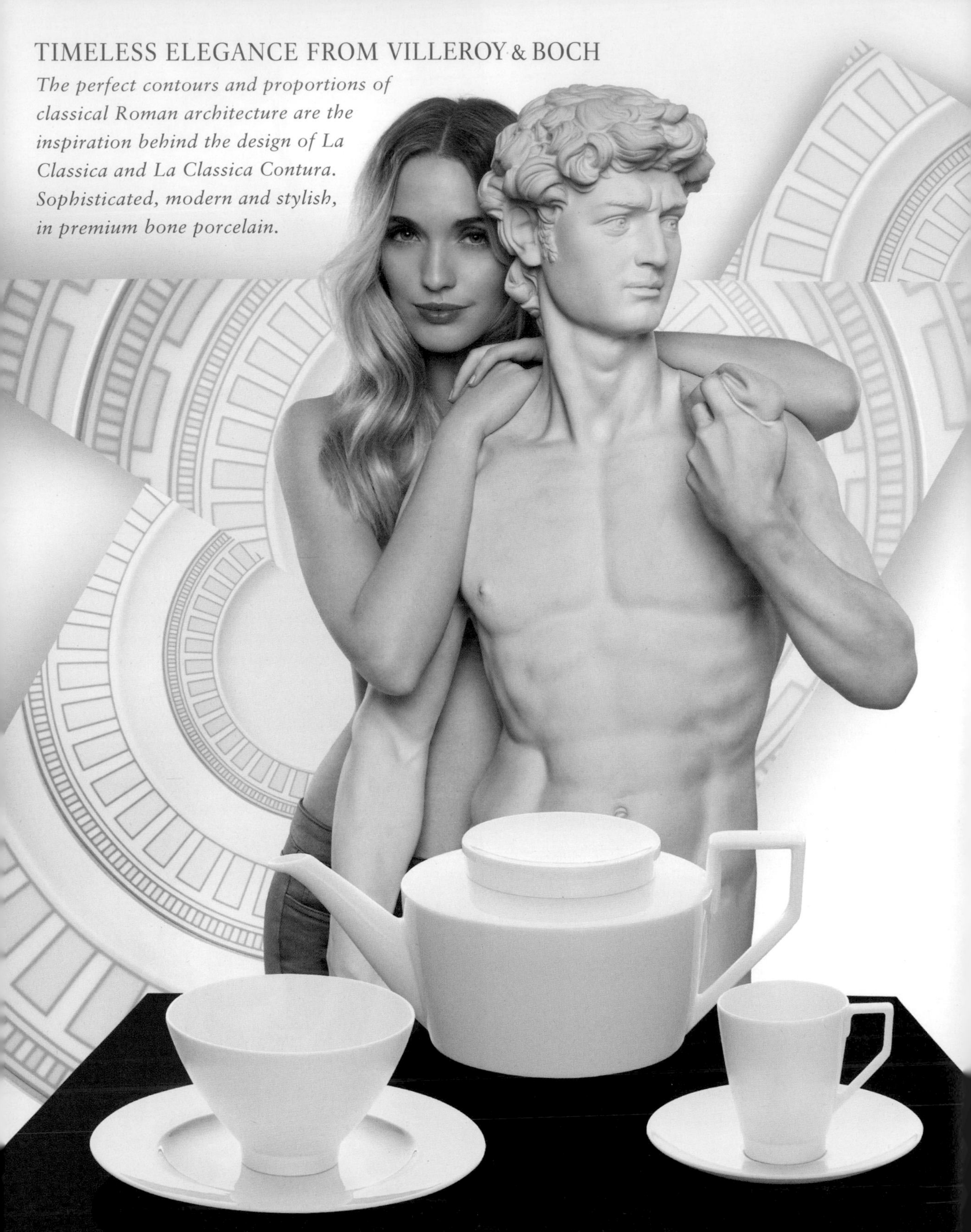
TIMELESS ELEGANCE FROM VILLEROY & BOCH
The perfect contours and proportions of classical Roman architecture are the inspiration behind the design of La Classica and La Classica Contura. Sophisticated, modern and stylish, in premium bone porcelain.

Top Restaurants 2016–17

Each year all the restaurants in the AA Restaurant Guide are awarded a specially commissioned plate that marks their achievement in gaining one or more AA Rosettes. The plates represent a partnership between the AA and Villeroy & Boch – two quality brands working together to recognise high standards in restaurant cooking.

Restaurants awarded three, four or five AA Rosettes represent the top ten per cent of the restaurants in this guide. The pages that follow list those establishments that have attained this special status.

5 ROSETTES

LONDON

Hélène Darroze at The Connaught, W1

Hibiscus, W1

Marcus, SW1

Pollen Street Social, W1

Restaurant Story, SE1

Sketch (Lecture Room & Library), W1

ENGLAND

BERKSHIRE
The Fat Duck, Bray

BRISTOL
Casamia Restaurant, Bristol

CAMBRIDGESHIRE
Midsummer House Restaurant, Cambridge

CUMBRIA
L'Enclume, Cartmel

NOTTINGHAMSHIRE
Restaurant Sat Bains with Rooms, Nottingham

OXFORDSHIRE
Belmond Le Manoir aux Quat'Saisons, Great Milton

SCOTLAND

CITY OF EDINBURGH
The Kitchin, Edinburgh

4 ROSETTES

LONDON

Alain Ducasse at The Dorchester, W1

Alyn Williams at The Westbury, W1

Chapter One, Bromley, Greater London

Fera at Claridge's, W1

The Five Fields, SW3

Le Gavroche Restaurant, W1

The Greenhouse, W1

The Ledbury, W11

Murano, W1

Seven Park Place by William Drabble, SW1

Texture Restaurant, W1

ENGLAND

BERKSHIRE

The Waterside Inn, Bray

BUCKINGHAMSHIRE

The Hand & Flowers, Marlow

CHESHIRE

Simon Radley at The Chester Grosvenor, Chester

CORNWALL & ISLES OF SCILLY

Paul Ainsworth at No. 6, Padstow

Restaurant Nathan Outlaw, Port Isaac

GLOUCESTERSHIRE

Le Champignon Sauvage, Cheltenham

GREATER MANCHESTER

The French by Simon Rogan, Manchester

Manchester House Bar & Restaurant, Manchester

LANCASHIRE

Northcote, Langho

LINCOLNSHIRE

Winteringham Fields, Winteringham

MERSEYSIDE

Fraiche, Oxton

OXFORDSHIRE

Orwells, Henley-on-Thames

RUTLAND

Hambleton Hall, Oakham

SURREY

Stovell's, Chobham

WEST MIDLANDS

Hampton Manor, Solihull

WILTSHIRE

Whatley Manor Hotel and Spa, Malmesbury

YORKSHIRE, NORTH

The Black Swan at Oldstead, Oldstead

CHANNEL ISLANDS

JERSEY

Bohemia Restaurant, St Helier

Ocean Restaurant at The Atlantic Hotel, St Brelade

SCOTLAND

CITY OF EDINBURGH

Number One, The Balmoral, Edinburgh

Restaurant Martin Wishart, Edinburgh

21212, Edinburgh

HIGHLAND

Boath House, Nairn

PERTH & KINROSS

Andrew Fairlie@Gleneagles, Auchterarder

WALES

CEREDIGION

Gareth Ward at Ynyshir Hall, Eglwys Fach

MONMOUTHSHIRE

The Whitebrook, Whitebrook

REPUBLIC OF IRELAND

DUBLIN

Restaurant Patrick Guilbaud, Dublin

COUNTY WATERFORD

Cliff House Hotel, Ardmore

3 ROSETTES

LONDON

Amaya, SW1

Ametsa with Arzak Instruction, SW1

Arbutus Restaurant, W1

L'Atelier de Joël Robuchon, WC2

Avista, W1

A. Wong, SW1

La Belle Époque, Hounslow, Greater London

Bingham, Richmond Upon Thames, Greater London

Bulgari Hotel, London, SW7

Chez Bruce, SW17

City Social, EC2

Clos Maggiore, WC2

The Clove Club, EC1

Club Gascon, EC1

Corrigan's Mayfair, W1

CUT at 45 Park Lane, W1

Dabbous, W1

Dinner by Heston Blumenthal, SW1

Galvin at Windows Restaurant & Bar, W1

Galvin La Chapelle, E1

Gauthier Soho, W1

The Gilbert Scott, NW1

The Glasshouse, Kew, Greater London

The Goring, SW1

Hakkasan Mayfair, W1

Hedone, W4

HKK, EC2

Kitchen Table, W1

Kitchen W8, W8

Koffmann's, SW1

Little Social, W1

Locanda Locatelli, W1

Medlar Restaurant, SW10

Merchants Tavern, EC2

Min Jiang, W8

The Ninth, W1

Odette's, NW1

One-O-One, SW1

Orrery, W1

Outlaw's at The Capital, SW3

Pied à Terre, W1

Portland, W1

Rasoi Restaurant, SW3

3 ROSETTES

continued

The Rib Room Bar and Restaurant, SW1

The Ritz Restaurant, W1

The River Café, W6

Roka Charlotte Street, W1

Roka Mayfair, W1

Roux at Parliament Square, SW1

Sketch (The Gallery), W1

Social Eating House, W1

Sosharu, EC1

Thirty Six by Nigel Mendham at Dukes London, SW1

Trinity Restaurant, SW4

Typing Room, E2

Umu, W1

Wild Honey, W1

ENGLAND

BEDFORDSHIRE
Paris House Restaurant, Woburn

BERKSHIRE
Hinds Head, Bray

L'Ortolan, Shinfield

The Royal Oak Paley Street, Maidenhead

The Vineyard, Newbury

BUCKINGHAMSHIRE
André Garrett at Cliveden, Taplow

The Artichoke, Amersham

The Coach, Marlow

Humphry's at Stoke Park, Stoke Poges

The Pointer, Brill

The Riverside Restaurant, Marlow

CAMBRIDGESHIRE
Restaurant Alimentum, Cambridge

CHESHIRE
The Alderley Restaurant, Alderley Edge

The Lord Clyde, Macclesfield

1851 Restaurant at Peckforton Castle, Peckforton

CORNWALL & ISLES OF SCILLY
Driftwood, Portscatho

Hell Bay, Bryher

Hotel Tresanton, St Mawes

The Seafood Restaurant, Padstow

CUMBRIA
The Cottage in the Wood, Braithwaite

Forest Side, Ambleside

Gilpin Hotel & Lake House, Windermere

Hipping Hall, Kirkby Lonsdale

Lake Road Kitchen, Ambleside

Rogan & Company Restaurant, Cartmel

The Samling, Windermere

DERBYSHIRE
Fischer's Baslow Hall, Baslow

The Peacock at Rowsley, Rowsley

DEVON
The Old Inn, Drewsteignton

DORSET
Summer Lodge Country House Hotel, Restaurant & Spa, Evershot

COUNTY DURHAM
The Orangery, Darlington

GLOUCESTERSHIRE
The Beaufort Dining Room Ellenborough Park, Cheltenham

Buckland Manor, Buckland

The Dial House, Bourton-on-the-Water

The Feathered Nest Country Inn, Nether Westcote

Lords of the Manor, Upper Slaughter

Lumière, Cheltenham

The Slaughters Manor House, Lower Slaughter

HAMPSHIRE
Avenue Restaurant at Lainston House Hotel, Winchester

Cambium, Brockenhurst

Hartnett Holder & Co, Lyndhurst

JSW, Petersfield

The Montagu Arms Hotel, Beaulieu

36 on the Quay, Emsworth

HERTFORDSHIRE
Colette's at The Grove, Chandler's Cross

KENT
Thackeray's, Royal Tunbridge Wells

The West House, Biddenden

LANCASHIRE
The Freemasons at Wiswell, Whalley

LINCOLNSHIRE
Harry's Place, Grantham

MERSEYSIDE
The Lawns Restaurant at Thornton Hall, Thornton Hough

NORFOLK
Morston Hall, Blakeney

The Neptune Restaurant with Rooms, Hunstanton

Roger Hickman's Restaurant, Norwich

Titchwell Manor Hotel, Titchwell

NORTHAMPTONSHIRE
Rushton Hall Hotel and Spa, Kettering

OXFORDSHIRE
The Kingham Plough, Kingham

The Lamb Inn, Burford

Restaurant 56, Faringdon

Shaun Dickens at The Boathouse, Henley-on-Thames

The Sir Charles Napier, Chinnor

The Wild Rabbit, Kingham

SHROPSHIRE
Fishmore Hall, Ludlow

Old Downton Lodge, Ludlow

SOMERSET
Allium Restaurant at The Abbey Hotel, Bath

The Bath Priory Hotel, Restaurant & Spa, Bath

The Dower House Restaurant, Bath

Little Barwick House, Yeovil

The Olive Tree at the Queensberry Hotel, Bath

STAFFORDSHIRE
Swinfen Hall Hotel, Lichfield

SUFFOLK
Lavenham Great House 'Restaurant with Rooms', Lavenham

SURREY
Langshott Manor, Horley

Matt Worswick at The Latymer, Bagshot

The Tudor Room, Egham

SUSSEX, EAST
The Little Fish Market, Hove

SUSSEX, WEST
Amberley Castle, Amberley

Gravetye Manor Hotel, West Hoathly

The Lickfold Inn, Lickfold

Restaurant Tristan, Horsham

TYNE & WEAR
House of Tides, Newcastle upon Tyne

Jesmond Dene House, Newcastle upon Tyne

WEST MIDLANDS
Adam's, Birmingham

Purnell's, Birmingham

Simpsons, Birmingham

Turners, Birmingham

WILTSHIRE
The Bybrook at The Manor House, Castle Combe

The Harrow at Little Bedwyn, Little Bedwyn

The Park Restaurant, Colerne

Red Lion Freehouse, Pewsey

WORCESTERSHIRE
Brockencote Hall Country House Hotel, Chaddesley Corbett

YORKSHIRE, NORTH
The Angel Inn, Hetton

Black Swan Hotel, Helmsley

The Grand Hotel & Spa, York, York

The Hare Inn, Scawton

The Park Restaurant, York

Samuel's at Swinton Park, Masham

Yorebridge House, Bainbridge

YORKSHIRE, WEST
Box Tree, Ilkley

The Man Behind the Curtain, Leeds

CHANNEL ISLANDS

JERSEY
Longueville Manor Hotel, St Saviour

Ormer, St Helier

Restaurant Sirocco@The Royal Yacht, St Helier

Tassili, St Helier

SCOTLAND

ANGUS
Airds Hotel and Restaurant, Port Appin

Gordon's, Inverkeilor

DUMFRIES & GALLOWAY
Knockinaam Lodge, Portpatrick

DUNBARTONSHIRE, WEST
Martin Wishart at Loch Lomond, Balloch

CITY OF EDINBURGH
Castle Terrace Restaurant, Edinburgh

Norton House Hotel & Spa, Edinburgh

Ondine Restaurant, Edinburgh

Pompadour by Galvin, Edinburgh

Restaurant Mark Greenaway, Edinburgh

Timberyard, Edinburgh

FIFE
The Cellar, Anstruther

The Peat Inn, Peat Inn

Road Hole Restaurant, St Andrews

Rocca Restaurant, St Andrews

CITY OF GLASGOW
Cail Bruich, Glasgow

The Gannet, Glasgow

Hotel du Vin at One Devonshire Gardens, Glasgow

HIGHLAND
The Cross, Kingussie

Inverlochy Castle Hotel, Fort William

Station Road, Fort Augustus

The Torridon, Torridon

PERTH & KINROSS
Fonab Castle Hotel & Spa, Pitlochry

SOUTH AYRSHIRE
Glenapp Castle, Ballantrae

Lochgreen House Hotel, Troon

STIRLING
Cromlix and Chez Roux, Dunblane

Roman Camp Country House Hotel, Callander

SCOTTISH ISLANDS

ISLE OF SKYE
Kinloch Lodge, Isleornsay

The Three Chimneys & The House Over-By, Colbost

Ullinish Country Lodge, Struan

WALES

ANGLESEY, ISLE OF
The Bull - Beaumaris, Beaumaris

Sosban & The Old Butcher's Restaurant, Menai Bridge

CONWY
Bodysgallen Hall and Spa, Llandudno

MONMOUTHSHIRE
Walnut Tree Inn, Abergavenny

NEWPORT
The Epicure Experience by Richard Davies, Newport

PEMBROKESHIRE
Grove, Narberth

POWYS
Llangoed Hall, Llyswen

VALE OF GLAMORGAN
Restaurant James Sommerin, Penarth

NORTHERN IRELAND

COUNTY ANTRIM
Galgorm Resort & Spa, Ballymena

BELFAST
Deanes EIPIC, Belfast

COUNTY DOWN
The Boathouse Restaurant, Bangor

COUNTY FERMANAGH
Lough Erne Resort, Enniskillen

REPUBLIC OF IRELAND

COUNTY CLARE
Gregans Castle, Ballyvaughan

COUNTY KILKENNY
The Lady Helen Restaurant, Thomastown

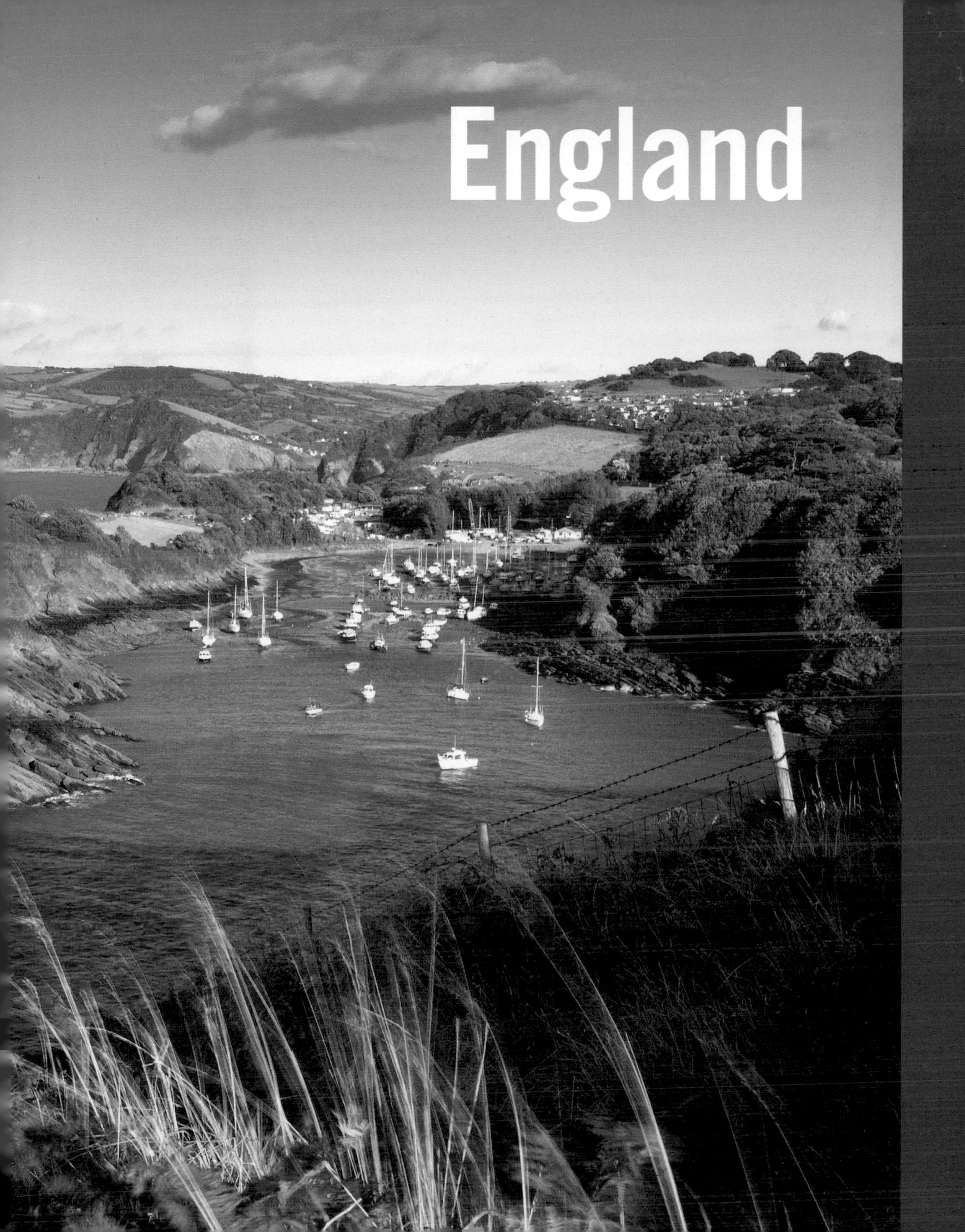

England

BEDFORDSHIRE

BEDFORD — Map 12 TL04

Barns Hotel

Modern British

tel: 01234 270044 **Cardington Rd MK44 3SA**
email: reservations@barnshotelbedford.co.uk **web:** www.barnshotelbedford.co.uk
dir: *M1 junct 13, A421, approx 10m to A603 Sandy/Bedford exit, hotel on right at 2nd rdbt*

Modern brasserie-style dining by the river

Occupying a lovely riverside location within landscaped gardens, Samuel Whitbread of brewing fame was born here in the 18th century. The hotel's WineGlass Restaurant is the main dining option with a bright and contemporary conservatory-style dining room that opens onto a terrace. The menu favours feel-good modern British combinations, so there might be a herb-crusted Brixworth chicken liver pâté served with grape chutney to kick things off. Main courses such as cottage pie, cabbage and bacon show good sense and sound execution. To finish, try the strawberry millefeuille with Chantilly cream. The wine list offers plenty by the glass.

The Bedford Swan Hotel

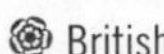 British

tel: 01234 346565 **The Embankment MK40 1RW**
email: info@bedfordswanhotel.co.uk **web:** www.bedfordswanhotel.co.uk
dir: *M1 junct 13, take A421 following signs to city centre (one way system). Turn left to The Embankment, car park on left after Swan statue*

Re-modelled 18th-century riverside hotel with inventive menu

Part of the town since the 18th century, the Bedford Swan now puts on a contemporary show after a swish makeover. Exposed stone walls and burnished wooden tables make an appealing setting for hearty British cooking with a creative edge. Scallops and pork are matched with andouille sausage, fiery harissa aïoli and sakura shoots to get things off the mark, ahead of a meaty combo involving lamb (cannon, grilled cutlets and confit pressed shoulder) with sautéed celeriac, shallot purée and minted red wine jus. Fish fans might find pan-fried stone bass with golden beetroot risotto and watercress 'bubbles'. For afters, honey adds richness to a crème brûlée with buttery shortbread.

The Knife and Cleaver

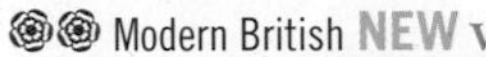 Modern British NEW v

tel: 01234 930789 & 07554 790103 **The Grove, Houghton Conquest MK45 3LA**
email: info@theknifeandcleaver.com **web:** www.theknifeandcleaver.com
dir: *S of Bedford on A6, turn right to Houghton Conquest. Over rdbt, pass post office, right at next rdbt. Left to The Knife and Cleaver*

Stylish roadside inn with contemporary dining

The red-brick pub has been extended over the centuries, but still looks the part of an old roadside inn, with nine bedrooms out back in converted stables. Original beams, painted panels and smart patterned seats and banquettes create a stylish, traditional tone. Dining is a big part of the attraction, with the kitchen turning out contemporary-inflected stuff such as a pretty terrine inspired by a classic ploughman's, served with piccalilli and Guinness loaf, followed by Cotswold chicken with white onion purée and morels, or a veggie beetroot tarte Tatin. The menu changes with the seasons and local supply lines are well used.

Chef Graham Roe, Terry Stewart **Seats** 40, Pr/dining room 28 **Times** 12-3/6-9, Closed 1 Jan **Prices** Fixed L 2 course £22, Fixed D 3 course £28, Starter £6-£10, Main £13-£17, Dessert £7-£8 **Wines** 6 bottles over £30, 30 bottles under £30, 21 by glass **Parking** 20 **Notes** Sunday L £13-£24, Children welcome

BOLNHURST — Map 12 TL05

The Plough at Bolnhurst

Modern British

tel: 01234 376274 **Kimbolton Rd MK44 2EX**
email: reservations@bolnhurst.com **web:** www.bolnhurst.com
dir: *A14/A421 onto B660 for approx 5m to Bolnhurst village*

Classy modern seasonal menu in a lively Tudor pub

The Plough is a whitewashed 15th-century country inn with a full quota of beams and timbers, stone walls, tiny windows and welcoming fires in its cosy bars. The restaurant is a striking contrast: the airy extension features lofty oak-beamed ceilings while full-length windows flood the room with light. Top-quality produce is transformed into big-flavoured modern dishes on daily-changing menus that may open with a terrine of ham, chicken and foie gras with rhubarb and ginger chutney, followed by grilled Dover sole with herb butter. Steaks from the Josper grill are a speciality, and for pudding there might be pear frangipane tart with cinnamon ice cream.

Chef Martin Lee **Seats** 96, Pr/dining room 32 **Times** 12-2/6.30-9, Closed 27 Dec-14 Jan, Mon, D Sun **Prices** Fixed L 2 course fr £19, Fixed D 3 course fr £23, Starter £4.60-£11, Main £16.95-£23.95, Dessert £5.25-£8.95 **Wines** 56 bottles over £30, 78 bottles under £30, 15 by glass **Parking** 30 **Notes** Sunday L £17.95-£28, Vegetarian available, Children welcome

FLITWICK — Map 11 TL03

Hallmark Hotel Flitwick Manor

British, Modern European

tel: 01525 712242 **Church Rd MK45 1AE**
email: flitwick@hallmarkhotels.co.uk **web:** www.hallmarkhotels.co.uk
dir: *M1 junct 12, follow Flitwick after 1m turn left into Church Rd. Manor 200 yds on left*

Classic British dishes in modern European style

A Georgian house in its own wooded parkland, classic British dishes with modern European influence are the stock-in-trade at Flitwick. Making a strong impact are a starter of braised pig's cheek scattered with dried grapefruit and crumbled walnuts, alongside silky parsnip purée. Look out for a main of seasonal grouse, the breast and leg bursting with gamey flavour, with caramelised roasted onion, sliced pear and yogurt, the whole topped with delicate onion rings, while fish may be cod with butternut squash, Savoy cabbage and spring onion. At dessert, it's hard to resist a snowball of banana parfait with chocolate mousse, chunks of peanut brittle and a ribbon of caramel.

Chef Steve Barringer **Seats** 30, Pr/dining room 60 **Times** 12-2/7-9.30 **Prices** Fixed L 2 course fr £24.50, Fixed D 3 course fr £35 **Wines** 16 bottles over £30, 12 bottles under £30, 8 by glass **Parking** 75 **Notes** Sunday L, Vegetarian available, Children welcome

HENLOW Map 12 TL13

The Crown

Modern British

tel: 01462 812433 **2 High St SG16 6BS**
email: info@thecrownpub.co.uk **web:** www.crownpub.co.uk
dir: *A1 junct 10, A507 for 7m, rdbt A507/A659, turn right into Henlow. On right*

Modernised village pub with inventive cooking

The busy pub on the main road through the village functions as a quintessential rural hostelry, full of enthusiastic local custom in both bar and dining room. Despite modernisation it retains its pub ethos, and boasts a young, classically-trained chef. A typical starter might be hazelnut-crumbed pigeon breast with peppered goats' cheese mousse and beetroot textures, while main courses take a more traditional tack with meats such as herb-crusted rack of lamb and wild mushrooms, or maintain the inventive pace for fish, perhaps sea trout with crabmeat sauce, braised fennel and clams. Finish, perhaps, with roasted pear in puff pastry and tarragon cream.

Chef Karl Jaques **Seats** 80, Pr/dining room 24 **Times** 7.30am-9.30pm, All-day dining, Closed 25 Dec **Prices** Prices not confirmed **Wines** 13 bottles over £30, 28 bottles under £30, 15 by glass **Parking** 60 **Notes** Sunday L, Vegetarian available, Children welcome

LUTON Map 6 TL02

Adam's Brasserie at Luton Hoo Hotel, Golf & Spa

Modern British

tel: 01582 734437 & 698888 **Luton Hoo Hotel, Golf & Spa, The Mansion House LU1 3TQ**
email: reservations@lutonhoo.co.uk
dir: *M1 junct 10a, A1081 towards Harpenden/St Albans. Hotel less than a mile on left*

Brasserie cooking in smartened-up stables

The extensive Luton Hoo Estate, with its golf course and magnificent gardens, is home to this luxe spa hotel. Adam's Brasserie, in the former stables, operates as a country club and an alternative to the more formal Wernher Restaurant. High ceilings and large windows give a sense of space, and booth seating boosts the brasserie vibe. The menu is a roster of feel-good dishes, such as duck rillettes with spicy plum and ginger chutney, followed by fillet of sea bass with parsnip purée, roast swede, broccoli and lemon jus, or perhaps a steak or spiced pork fillet from the grill. Finish with bread-and-butter pudding and custard.

Chef Will Hughes **Seats** 90, Pr/dining room 290 **Times** 12-3/6-10, Closed D Sun **Prices** Starter £6.50-£9.95, Main £13.95-£24.95, Dessert £6.75-£9.75 **Wines** 32 bottles over £30, 13 bottles under £30, 12 by glass **Parking** 100 **Notes** Pre-open air cinema menu 2 course £19.50 (Aug-Sep), Sunday L £38.50, Vegetarian available, Children welcome

See advert below

Paris House Restaurant

WOBURN **Map 11 SP93**

Modern British V

tel: 01525 290692 **London Rd, Woburn Park MK17 9QP**
email: info@parishouse.co.uk **web:** www.parishouse.co.uk
dir: *M1 junct 13. From Woburn take A4012 Hockliffe, 1m out of Woburn village on left*

Impeccable contemporary cooking in a reassembled timbered house

Reached along a tree-lined drive through 22 acres of deer park, Paris House is an ornately detailed Tudor manor built in the mid-Victorian era for the Paris Exposition, and shipped back to Bedfordshire in 19th-century flat-pack format for reassembling. Inside, despite the mullioning of the windows, the decorative scheme is rather more in the now, with modernist light fittings and abstract glass ornaments in the private dining space, contrasting with lightly worn traditionalism in the main room. Phil Fanning's culinary production is full of ingeniously fresh fusion ideas, bringing Asian influences to bear on a modern British base. Menus are headed in Roman numerals by their numbers of courses, starting with a fairly leisurely VI at lunch, and extending into the full bells-and-whistles VIII and X at dinner. A Thai excursion might open the itinerary, with a pork gyoza dumpling in tom yum, along with pork cheek and squid noodles, before king crab turns up in malt and avocado dressing. Duck liver is pointed with fruity notes from sour cherry and blood orange, prior to a fish dish that might gather turbot, crayfish and clams for a kind of marine pot au feu. The main meat dish builds continuities with that duck liver dish, offering the breast now with red miso and mushrooms. A cheese dish that segues into desserts has become a popular mode, so expect something like beetroot Fourme d'Ambert and chocolate, ahead of a brace of dessert courses, perhaps an east Asian take on boozy trifle with mandarin, black beans, coriander and sake, before a pumpkin creation arrives with preserved grapes and apple to close the show. The attention to detail throughout is astonishing, and the wine flights worth the extra for a carefully-selected roll call of matching flavours.

Chef Phil Fanning **Seats** 37, Pr/dining room 14
Times 12-2/7-9, Closed Xmas, Mon-Tue, D Sun **Prices** Tasting menu £43-£195 **Wines** 99 bottles over £30, 3 bottles under £30, 13 by glass **Parking** 24 **Notes** D 6/8/10 course, L 6 course, Sunday L £63, Children welcome

LUTON *continued*

Wernher Restaurant at Luton Hoo Hotel, Golf & Spa

@@ Modern European

tel: 01582 734437 & 698888 **The Mansion House LU1 3TQ**
email: reservations@lutonhoo.co.uk **web:** www.lutonhoo.co.uk
dir: *M1 junct 10a, A1081 towards Harpenden/St Albans. Hotel less than a mile on left*

Magnificent country estate with sharp modern cooking

When only the full stately-home extravaganza will do – the sort of place where the chaps are required to sport jacket and tie at dinner – the magnificent Wernher in Luton Hoo is hard to top, with its marble panelling, ornate chandeliers and opulent fabrics. The kitchen's bright modern dishes are built on top-class ingredients, starting with a pressing of ham hock with pumpkin remoulade, green tea gel and pistachio bread. Main courses are equally well conceived: baked sea bream is matched with herb crushed potatoes, courgette, mange-tout and dill butter, and for dessert, rum and raisin iced parfait comes with orange sponge and gel.

Chef Will Hughes **Seats** 80, Pr/dining room 290 **Times** 12.30-2/7-10, Closed Jan, Mon-Tue **Prices** Fixed L 2 course £25, Fixed D 3 course £42.50-£55, Tasting menu £67.50-£105 **Wines** 231 bottles over £30, 2 bottles under £30, 13 by glass **Parking** 316 **Notes** Speciality menu, 'Ladies Hoo Lunch' Wed with wine, Sunday L £38.50, Vegetarian available, Children welcome

See advert on page 33

WOBURN Map 11 SP93

Paris House Restaurant

@@@ – *see opposite*

The Woburn Hotel

@@ Modern British, French

tel: 01525 290441 **George St MK17 9PX**
email: info@thewoburnhotel.co.uk **web:** www.thewoburnhotel.co.uk
dir: *5 mins from M1 junct 13. Follow signs to Woburn. In town centre at x-rds, parking to rear via Park St*

High-impact French cooking on the Woburn Estate

Olivier Bertho's cooking is rooted in the great French traditions but is very much of the present, so roast cod fillet, for instance, is served with brandade and chorizo and bean cassoulet. Combinations in dishes intrigue without seeming wacky, as seen in a palate-pleasing starter of a pan-fried scallop with lime syrup, crab cannelloni and crispy squid with garlic and chilli. Meat dishes are just as well thought out: pan-fried braised lamb with pistachio pesto, redcurrant jus and spices, say, or roast breast of guinea fowl with creamy mushroom sauce, thyme-flecked sweet potato purée and Savoy cabbage. Dessert might be strawberry trifle with sparkling wine jelly and elderflower syllabub cream.

Chef Olivier Bertho **Seats** 40, Pr/dining room 90 **Times** 12-2/6.30-9.30 **Prices** Starter £5.50-£10.25, Main £13.50-£19.95, Dessert £7.25-£8.50 **Wines** 28 bottles over £30, 21 bottles under £30, 20 by glass **Parking** 80 **Notes** Sunday L £20-£25, Vegetarian available, Children welcome

BERKSHIRE

ASCOT Map 6 SU96

The Barn at Coworth

@ British

tel: 01344 876600 **Blacknest Rd SL5 7SE**
email: restaurants.CPA@dorchestercollection.com
dir: *M25 junct 13 onto A30 signed Egham/Bagshot until Wentworth Golf Club. Right at lights onto Blacknest Rd (A329) Hotel on left*

Converted barn with a local flavour

There's a fine-dining restaurant at this lavish country hotel, plus this converted barn where you can tuck into classy brasserie-style food. It looks great with its open-to-view kitchen, unbuttoned vibe and cheerful service team sporting orange polo tops, and there's a fabulous terrace, too, with gorgeous views over the grounds. Local ingredients feature on the menu, such as trout from the River Test, potted and served with horseradish crème fraîche and lamb's lettuce, or main-course Bramble Farm chicken with creamed potatoes, New Forest mushrooms, cabbage and bacon. There're also a posh burger and fish and chips. Among desserts, free-range egg custard tart might come with Yorkshire rhubarb in season.

ASCOT ***continued***

Bluebells Restaurant & Garden Bar

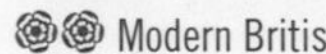 Modern British

tel: 01344 622722 **Shrubbs Hill, London Rd, Sunningdale SL5 OLE**
email: info@bluebells-restaurant.co.uk
dir: *From M25 junct 13, A30 towards Bagshot. Restaurant between Wentworth & Sunningdale*

Stylish setting for ambitious contemporary cooking

Bluebells stands out from the crowd with its sleek modern looks and upbeat, buzzy ambience. The kitchen works a modern British groove, allowing that old stager, chicken liver parfait, to get a kick from red Muscadet wine jelly, quince chutney, poached pear and toasted hazelnuts. A meticulously sourced main course partners Blythburgh pork tenderloin with crispy pig's head, wilted kale, roasted garlic foam and potato fritters. Or you might opt for fish, with a cassoulet uniting monkfish with mussels, white beans, chorizo and saffron. Service remains expert and relaxed all the way through to a finale of vanilla and praline crème brûlée with chestnut ice cream and vanilla macaroons.

Chef Tamas Baranyai **Seats** 90, Pr/dining room 14
Times 12-2.30/6.30-9.45, Closed 25-26 Dec, 1-11 Jan, BHs, Mon, D Sun **Prices** Fixed L 2 course fr £20, Fixed D 3 course fr £37 **Wines** 74 bottles over £30, 30 bottles under £30, 12 by glass **Parking** 100 **Notes** Sunday L £22-£29, Vegetarian available, Children welcome

Macdonald Berystede Hotel & Spa

British, European

tel: 01344 623311 **Bagshot Rd, Sunninghill SL5 9JH**
email: general.berystede@macdonald-hotels.co.uk **web:** www.berystede.com
dir: *M3 junct 3/A30, A322 then left onto B3020 to Ascot or M25 junct 13, follow signs for Bagshot. At Sunningdale turn right onto A330*

Ambitious brasserie cooking near Legoland and the racing

The Berystede is a handsome red-brick Victorian mansion handy for the racing at Ascot. Curvy banquettes and gleaming contemporary cutlery and glassware set the scene for inventive, up-to-date brasserie dishes that can look a little busy but deliver on flavour. Pan-fried scallops with black pudding, lardo, Brussels sprouts and chestnuts might start you off. Go on to something like wild turbot fillet with squid ink gnocchi, roasted salsify, samphire and smoked mussels, or onion ash-rolled venison loin with venison faggot, ceps, grelot onions and venison jus. Desserts are no less labour intensive, as in chocolate and peanut butter mousse with peanut butter and caramel ice cream and salted chocolate popcorn.

Restaurant Coworth Park

Modern British NOTABLE WINE LIST

tel: 01344 876600 & 756784 **London Rd SL5 7SE**
email: restaurants.CPA@dorchestercollection.com **web:** www.coworthpark.com
dir: *M25 junct 13 onto A30 signed Egham/Bagshot until Wentworth Golf Club. Right at lights onto Blacknest Rd (A329) Hotel on left*

Modern classic dishes in a gleaming-white hotel

A gleaming-white balustraded Georgian house near the racecourse, Coworth is part of the Dorchester Collection. The kitchen's output is forward-thinking, with a plethora of modern classic dishes produced with scrupulous attention to detail. The now inseparable pairing of scallops and black pudding offers caramelised shellfish, texturally echoed by silky shallot purée, as an alternative to lightly spiced duck breast with beetroot and salt-baked turnips. Then perhaps a fish dish such as roasted turbot with bacon, mushrooms and red wine, or else Scottish beef fillet with oxtail suet pudding and watercress purée. Yorkshire rhubarb with blood orange, cheesecake cream and a scattering of crumbs makes a simple enough deconstruction to finish.

Chef Herbert Brindle **Seats** 66, Pr/dining room 16
Times 12.30-3/6.30-9.30, Closed Mon-Tue, D Sun **Prices** Fixed L 2 course £25, Fixed D 3 course £40-£70, Tasting menu £95 **Wines** 600+ bottles over £30, 4 bottles under £30, 18 by glass **Parking** 100 **Notes** Fixed L Tue-Sat, D Tue-Thu, Tasting menu 7 course, Sunday L £39-£45, Vegetarian available, Children 8 yrs+ D

BRAY **Map 6 SU97**

Caldesi in Campagna

Traditional Italian

tel: 01628 788500 **Old Mill Ln SL6 2BG**
email: campagna@caldesi.com
dir: *M4 junct 8/9, at rdbt exit A308 Bray/Windsor. Continue for 0.5m, left B3028 Bray village, right Old Mill Lane, restaurant in 400yds on right*

Refined Italian eatery with a smart patio garden

Here, in an immaculate house on the edge of Bray, expect classic Italian stuff made with (mostly) British ingredients. Among antipasti, deep-fried courgette flowers are filled with ricotta and basil, seared Scottish scallops arrive with a Jerusalem artichoke cream, pancetta and some slivers of black truffle, and cured hams are shipped over from the motherland. Pasta courses include tagliolini with Cornish crab, and pappardelle with duck and a rich red wine and tomato ragù. Follow on with a classic cacciucco – seafood casserole – with squid, gurnard, clams and mussels, or pan-fried calves' liver with sage and an olive oil mash. Traditional desserts might include Sicilian lemon tart.

Chef Gregorio Piazza **Seats** 50, Pr/dining room 12
Times 12-2.30/6.30-10, Closed Xmas for approx 5 days, Mon, D Sun **Prices** Fixed L 2 course £19.50, Starter £12.50-£16, Main £24.50-£29.50, Dessert £8.50-£9.50 **Wines** 110 bottles over £30, 15 bottles under £30, 18 by glass **Parking** 8 **Notes** Sunday L £32.50-£38.50, Vegetarian available, Children welcome

The Crown

British

tel: 01628 621936 & 788545 **High St SL6 2AH**
email: reservations@thecrownatbray.co.uk
dir: *M4 junct 8/9, follow signs for Maidenhead/Windsor. At rdbt take 3rd exit to Windsor, then left into Bray. 100mtrs on left after bridge*

Heston's proper pub

Devotees of the British pub know the Crown is safe in Heston Blumenthal's hands. His third address in the village, this 16th-century inn offers real ales, a well-constructed wine list and a menu that owes much to pub traditions while displaying the quality that goes with the Blumenthal name. King prawn cocktail is a classy version served with rye bread, Cornish mussels are flavoured by garlic, apple and cider, and if you just fancy a sandwich, try an open salt beef version with dill pickles and shallots. Main courses might include fish and chips, or free-range pork belly with castelluccio lentils and hispi cabbage. Finish with rhubarb and custard.

The Fat Duck

– see opposite

The Fat Duck

BRAY **Map 6 SU97**

Modern British V

tel: 01628 580333 **High St SL6 2AQ**

dir: *M4 junct 8/9 (Maidenhead) take A308 towards Windsor, turn left into Bray. Restaurant in centre of village on right*

Mind-boggling culinary creations at Heston HQ

You don't just book a table, you buy a ticket. For this is a journey and, as the man himself says, expect a 'memorable day out'. Since its revamp in 2015, when the restaurant was decamped to Australia and the original premises got done up from top to bottom, there's a sense that Heston Blumenthal has completed a journey himself, the restaurant now able to reflect his sense of adventure and discovery better than ever before. A visit feels like a day out, for even lunch is a four- or five-hour affair (good job the striking leather chairs are so darn comfortable). The front-of-house team are more integral to proceedings than ever before, delivering the multiple courses with style and a naturalness that is to be commended. The whole experience is theatrical, even a trip to the loo, and The Fat Duck offers the most singularly exciting, stimulating and invigorating dining experience in the UK. Each stage of the journey has a theme and tiny dish descriptions are read with the aid of a magnifying glass to enhance the sense of wonder. 'The day before we go: Are we nearly there yet?' kicks off with the lightest aerated macaroon you'll come across, bursting with beetroot flavour and tempered with a delicate horseradish cream. 'Just the tonic' is a welcome 'drink' – choose from a Paloma or Piña Colada, and revel in the theatre as liquid nitrogen does its stuff. 'Morning: rise and shine, it's breakfast time' is a simply inspired feat of interaction between kitchen and customer where we play our part in the construction of the dish by choosing a 'variety pack' carton. The mini iPod is one of the elements that has had a lot of press, and there's no doubt 'Sound of the Sea' is a signature dish worthy of the name – the seafood seemingly washed up on the beach full of flavour, texture and balance. Recollections of rock pooling days results in Cornish crab, smoked caviar and golden trout roe matched with velouté of white chocolate and sea vegetables in an absolute stunner, the white chocolate looking for all the world like the shell of a crab, and melting into the dish as a mussel broth is poured over – a belter. 'Evening are you ready for dinner' is a four-course meal in itself, recalling the flavours of gourmet meals of old, and involving so much work for the kitchen it is quite staggering. Among sweet courses, 'And then to dream' is a virtual sweet shop delivered to your table. The wine list is a bit of a journey too, a five-star trip with most time spent in the top regions of France.

Chef Heston Blumenthal, Jonny Lake **Seats** 42
Times 12-2/7-9, Closed 2 wks at Xmas, Sun-Mon **Prices** Tasting menu £255 **Wines** 500 bottles over £30 **Parking** Two village car parks **Notes** Tasting menu only, Children welcome

BRAY *continued*

Hinds Head

British NOTABLE WINE LIST

tel: 01628 626151 **High St SL6 2AB**
email: info@hindsheadbray.com
dir: *M4 junct 8/9, at rdbt take exit to Maidenhead Central, next rdbt take exit Bray & Windsor, after 0.5m take B3028 to Bray*

Heston's modern take on old-English fare with bang-on flavours

A beamed ceiling, panelled walls, a brick fireplace and plain wooden furniture are all in place, as expected in a 15th-century inn at the heart of this well-manicured village. It might be under the aegis of Heston Blumenthal, but don't expect this to be an adjunct of his Fat Duck with its culinary pyrotechnics. The intention here is to offer traditional British fare in keeping with the building's style, and Heston has worked closely with the Tudor kitchen at Hampton Court Palace to re-introduce historical dishes like snail hash and oxtail and kidney suet pudding. It's possible to pop in for a glass of wine or a pint with a snack like a Scotch egg, but most people are here for a meal. The kitchen marries solid techniques with a British larder, producing commendable results. Start with the earthy flavours of venison carpaccio with horseradish and turnips and a shallot and caper dressing, or voguish-sounding pan-fried scallops with celery, walnuts, monk's beard, compressed apple and langoustine oil. Main courses include familiar chicken, ham and leek pie with mustard cream and mash, and the stimulating combination of plaice fillet with chard, confit fennel, salmon roe and cidery butter sauce. Like everything else, desserts are exemplary: try rhubarb trifle or quaking pudding.

Chef Janos Veres **Seats** 100, Pr/dining room 22
Times 12-2.30/6.15-9.15, Closed 25 Dec, D 1 Jan, BHs, Sun **Prices** Starter £7.95-£15.50, Main £19.25-£35, Dessert £7.95-£9.50 **Wines** 65 bottles over £30, 11 bottles under £30, 11 by glass **Parking** 40 **Notes** Fixed L 4 course £47.50, Private dining 3/5 course £52/£65, Sunday L £20.95-£25.50, Vegetarian available, Children welcome

The Riverside Brasserie

Modern European

tel: 01628 780553 **Bray Marina, Monkey Island Ln SL6 2EB**
email: info@riversidebrasserie.co.uk
dir: *Off A308, signed Bray Marina*

Accomplished cooking by the Thames

Tucked away beside the Thames in Bray Marina, this waterside restaurant oozes understated class and an easygoing ambience. Full-length glass doors mean the river views are still there whether you dine inside or alfresco on the decked area, while the chefs in the open-to-view kitchen turn out unfussy yet skilfully-cooked brasserie food. Deep-fried baby squid with aïoli is one classic starter, while whole baked sea bass with sautéed potatoes and cherry tomatoes is an uncomplicated main course. Apple and apricot crumble with good quality vanilla ice cream is one way to round things off.

The Waterside Inn

– see below

The Waterside Inn

BRAY **Map 6 SU97**

French
tel: 01628 620691 **Ferry Rd SL6 2AT**
email: reservations@waterside-inn.co.uk
dir: *M4 junct 8/9, A308 (Windsor) then B3028 to Bray. Restaurant clearly signed*

The Roux family's riverside restaurant four and a half decades on

The Roux brothers' first foray out of London in 1972 brought them to an old inn on the upper reaches of the Thames. It still looks the part from outside – timbered, low-roofed – although presumably nobody parked your car for you when it was just a pub. Inside is an affable cocoon of old-school civility, the dining room opening up to the little jetty and the soothing plash of the river in summer. Under Alain Roux and his team leader Diego Masciaga, the place trades in transcendent classical French gastronomy. How else to explain the careful shoehorning of braised snails, mushroom duxelle and sauce béarnaise into little choux buns, or the gilding of flaked crabmeat with Oscietra caviar? Many of the dishes have earned their places on the various menus through time-hallowed tradition, such that regulars would revolt at their removal. Main courses such as poached sole fillet with crayfish and morels in basil sauce, or rabbit with chestnuts in Armagnac sauce, undergird the whole experience, but there are peripheral hints of what's au courant elsewhere, as when the glorious Challandais duck comes with celeriac and peanut purée in a sauce of grapes. The French and English cheeses are sublime, but don't shun the dessert menu, which is probably the most experimental phase of the whole meal, producing Norwegian blood orange and ginger omelette with bourbon parfait, or honey cream cheese mousse, garnished with gariguette strawberries and vanilla sorbet. An extra whip-round may be needed to make a start on the monumental wine list.

Chef Alain Roux **Seats** 75, Pr/dining room 8 **Times** 12-2/7-10, Closed 26 Dec-1 Jan, Mon-Tue **Prices** Fixed L 2 course £49.50, Starter £37-£60, Main £53-£66, Dessert £31-£41 **Wines** 1000+ bottles over £30, 1 bottle under £30, 14 by glass **Parking** 20 **Notes** Tasting menu 7 course, 6 course D £160, Sunday L £160, Vegetarian available, Children 12 yrs+

CHIEVELEY Map 5 SU47

Crab & Boar

Modern British

tel: 01635 247550 **Wantage Rd RG20 8UE**
email: info@crabandboar.com **web:** www.crabandboar.com
dir: *M4 junct 13, towards Chieveley. Left into School Rd, right at T-junct, 0.5m on right. Follow brown tourist signs*

Singular seafood – and more – in rural Berkshire

The Crab & Boar has had a stylish refurb: walls in the interconnecting rooms are decorated in muted tones, with exposed beams, while bare wooden tables are smartly set and chairs are a mixed bag, all presenting a refined ambience. The kitchen still concentrates on exploiting the freshness and vitality of seafood. Start with seared scallops with cauliflower, vanilla purée and orange and proceed to lemon sole accompanied simply by samphire and tomato beurre blanc. Carnivores are well served too – perhaps pressed ham hock with sweetcorn relish, then pork loin and belly with peach, hispi cabbage and a chorizo potato cake. Finish with passionfruit cheesecake.

Chef Tom Scade **Seats** 120, Pr/dining room 14 **Times** 12-2.30/6-9.30, Closed D 25 Dec **Prices** Starter £7.50-£10, Main £13-£26, Dessert £5.50-£8 **Wines** 52 bottles over £30, 26 bottles under £30, 24 by glass **Parking** 80 **Notes** Sunday L £14-£16.50, Vegetarian available, Children welcome

COOKHAM Map 6 SU88

The White Oak

European, British

tel: 01628 523 043 **The Pound SL6 9QE**
email: info@thewhiteoak.co.uk
dir: *M4 junct 8/9 onto A308(M) towards Maidenhead Central, continue towards Marlow. Right at lights Switchback Road South to Gardener Road. At rdbt 1st exit B4447 Switchback Road North to Cookham, right at mini-rdbt to The Pound*

Versatile dining pub in Stanley Spencer country

The team behind the White Oak reopened it in 2008 as a modern dining pub. Set in Stanley Spencer's beloved Cookham, it has splashy contemporary artwork, bare tables and generous washes of natural light from a skylight and patio doors. The core of the operation is traditional pub cooking, including a Monday steak night, but with some latter-day technical ambition. That comes off well in gin and tonic salmon with lime, cucumber and treacle granola, followed perhaps by rump and sweetbreads of Welsh lamb with artichoke purée and shimejis. Gird your loins at pudding stage for carrot cake with sweet-pickled sultanas, cream cheese and walnuts.

Chef Adam Hague **Seats** 80, Pr/dining room 14 **Times** 12-2.30/6.30-9.30, Closed D Sun (winter) **Prices** Fixed L 2 course fr £12, Fixed D 3 course £19, Starter £5.50-£9, Main £13.50-£26, Dessert £6-£9 **Wines** 26 bottles over £30, 29 bottles under £30, 13 by glass **Parking** 32 **Notes** Tasting menu 5-7 course, Sunday L £13.50-£18, Vegetarian available, Children welcome

FRILSHAM Map 5 SU57

The Pot Kiln

British, European

tel: 01635 201366 **RG18 0XX**
email: info@potkiln.org
dir: *From Yattendon follow Pot Kiln signs, cross over motorway. Continue for 0.25m pub on right*

Confident country cooking in rural inn

This rural red-brick country inn is worth tracking down for its proper pubby vibe and unpretentious approach to modern British cooking. The owners, Mike and Katie Robinson, source their produce with care, but what makes the Pot Kiln stand out from the herd is its passion for game. Start with a classic chicken liver and foie gras parfait with toasted brioche and chutney, or get stuck straight into a wild venison Scotch egg from the bar menu. Main-course beef cheeks are braised for 10 hours and served with mash, black cabbage and slow-cooked shallots, or there may be pan-fried hake with fennel rösti, roasted vine tomatoes, spinach and basil.

Chef Mike Robinson **Seats** 48 **Times** 12-2.30/7-9.30, Closed 25 Dec, D Sun **Prices** Prices not confirmed **Wines** 45 bottles over £30, 17 bottles under £30, 12 by glass **Parking** 70 **Notes** Monthly food event nights, Sunday L, Vegetarian available, Children welcome

HUNGERFORD Map 5 SU36

Littlecote House Hotel

Modern European

tel: 01488 682509 **Chilton Foliat RG17 0SU**
web: www.warnerleisurehotels.co.uk
dir: *M4 junct 14, A338/A4 Hungerford, follow brown signs*

Appealing modern menu in an historic house

Littlecote has history: there's the remains of a Roman settlement in the grounds, and Cromwell's soldiers were billeted here in the Civil War. In its top restaurant, Oliver's Bistro, we fast-forward to the 21st century: the kitchen turns out resolutely up-to-date, creative ideas that showcase local suppliers, all supported by a globetrotting wine list. Confit duck terrine looks pretty as a picture on a black slate, together with fig sorbet and cubes of brioche, while main-course confit pork belly comes with fondant potato, cauliflower purée, pancetta and Granny Smith apple. For pudding, try a simple but highly effective pairing of chocolate fondant with peanut ice cream and brittle.

Chef Philip O'Hagan **Seats** 40, Pr/dining room 8 **Times** 6.30-9, Closed Mon, L all week **Prices** Starter £6.50-£7.50, Main £16.50-£22, Dessert £7-£8.50 **Wines** 3 bottles over £30, 23 bottles under £30, 14 by glass **Parking** 200 **Notes** Sunday L, Vegetarian available, No children

HURLEY Map 5 SU88

The Olde Bell Inn

 Modern British

tel: 01628 825881 **High St SL6 5LX**
email: oldebellreception@coachinginn.co.uk **web:** www.theoldebell.co.uk
dir: *M4 junct 8/9 follow signs for Henley. At rdbt take A4130 to Hurley, turn right to Hurley Village, 800yds on right*

Classy, creative cooking in a smartly revamped coaching inn

You'll find plenty of period character at the Olde Bell – dating in part to the 12th century, it's cool and elegant, with loads of original features. There are six acres of grounds to explore, including a kitchen garden. The kitchen serves up some smart dishes that show sound technical knowledge. You might start with chicken liver and port pâté, while a main course rump of English lamb, nicely timed and rested, is served with Provençal vegetables and dauphinoise, or there's fillet of sea bass accompanied by sweet chilli escabèche, roast potatoes and chorizo. Save room for the light, moist sticky toffee pudding.

MAIDENHEAD Map 6 SU88

Boulters Riverside Brasserie

Modern British

tel: 01628 621291 **Boulters Lock Island SL6 8PE**
email: info@boultersrestaurant.co.uk
dir: *M4 junct 7 onto A4 towards Maidenhead, cross Maidenhead bridge, right at rdbt. Restaurant 0.5m on right*

Modern brasserie dining by the river

One very good reason to head to this buzzy, contemporary brasserie is the Thames-side location overlooking Boulters Lock, where the river ambles past Maidenhead Bridge. Glass walls separate diners from the river, while the ground-floor brasserie is flooded with light and looks stylishly neutral with its bare darkwood tables and wooden floors. The food doesn't take a back seat, though: expect well-executed contemporary dishes along the lines of wild mushroom risotto with caramelised Jerusalem artichoke and truffle cream, while main course could be splendidly fresh hake fillet with a hazelnut crust, creamed leek, oxtail croustade and fondant potato.

Chef Daniel Woodhouse **Seats** 70, Pr/dining room 12 **Times** 12-9.30, All-day dining, Closed D Sun **Prices** Fixed L 2 course £15.95-£19.95, Starter £6.95-£8.50, Main £12.95-£24, Dessert £5.50-£9.95 **Wines** 33 bottles over £30, 30 bottles under £30, 18 by glass **Parking** 15, Public car park **Notes** Brunch, Sunday L £15.95, Vegetarian available, Children welcome

Fredrick's Hotel and Spa

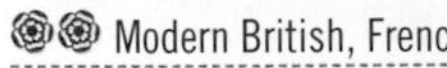 Modern British, French

tel: 01628 581000 **Shoppenhangers Rd SL6 2PZ**
email: reservations@fredricks-hotel.co.uk **web:** www.fredricks-hotel.co.uk
dir: *From M4 junct 8/9 take A404(M), then turning (junct 9a) for Cox Green/White Waltham. Left on to Shoppenhangers Rd, restaurant 400 mtrs on right*

Modern dining at a classy spa hotel

Last year saw new ownership, but nobody is really able to see the join. The kitchen team continue to produce assiduously researched contemporary cooking. Home-smoked salmon tian comes with potato galette and dill pickle, and pork is put to good use in rillettes and crackling salad with pickled apple. Meats come in pairs at main course: loin and belly of lamb, fillet and cheek of pork, breast and confit leg of duck, the last with Swiss chard, rhubarb and gingered mash. A trio of traditional grills offers the extra treat of duck-fat roasties. Populist desserts include chocolate fondant with salted caramel and yogurt sorbet.

Chef Charlie Murray **Seats** 60, Pr/dining room 120 **Times** 7-9.30, Closed L all week **Prices** Fixed D 3 course fr £39, Tasting menu fr £55 **Wines** 25 bottles over £30, 11 bottles under £30, 7 by glass **Parking** 80 **Notes** ALC menu 1/2/3 course £28/£35/£42, Vegetarian available, Children welcome

The Royal Oak Paley Street

– see opposite

NEWBURY Map 5 SU46

HIGHLY COMMENDED IN THE AA WINE AWARDS 2016–17

Donnington Valley Hotel & Spa

Modern British V NOTABLE WINE LIST

tel: 01635 551199 **Old Oxford Rd, Donnington RG14 3AG**
email: general@donningtonvalley.co.uk **web:** www.donningtonvalley.co.uk
dir: *M4 junct 13, A34 towards Newbury. Take immediate left signed Donnington Hotel. At rdbt take right, at 3rd rdbt take left, follow road for 2m, hotel on right*

Engaging modern cooking in a golfing and spa hotel

A likeable, informal sort of place, not least the Wine Press restaurant: a light-filled, raftered room on two levels. There's much to like on the menu too, with up-to-the-minute dishes alongside more conventional British fare. Pan-fried scallops partner tomato and bean cassoulet, white pudding and pancetta crisps, before a main course of braised blade of beef with pancetta dauphinoise, wild mushrooms and fine beans. Pickled cucumber gives a welcome smack of acidity to poached salmon and herb roulade, and orange jus is a traditional contrast to confit duck leg with buttery mash and stem broccoli. Finish with warm milk chocolate fondant with dark chocolate ganache and triple chocolate ice cream.

Chef Kelvin Johnson **Seats** 120, Pr/dining room 130 **Times** 12-2/7-10, Closed L 1 Jan, Sat **Prices** Fixed D 3 course fr £28, Starter £8-£12, Main £17-£24, Dessert £8-£10 **Wines** 321 bottles over £30, 49 bottles under £30, 36 by glass **Parking** 150 **Notes** Sunday L £19-£22, Children welcome

Regency Park Hotel

Modern European

tel: 01635 871555 **Bowling Green Rd, Thatcham RG18 3RP**
email: info@regencyparkhotel.com **web:** www.regencyparkhotel.co.uk
dir: *M4 junct 13, follow A339 to Newbury for 2m, then take the A4 (Reading), the hotel is signed*

Good cooking in a modern spa hotel

Not far from Highclere Castle, better known as *Downton Abbey*, the Regency Park is a modern spa hotel in pleasant grounds. A spacious dining room with one whole wall of glass looking out on a garden cascade, the Watermark's dimmed lights and piped music bring soothing balm in the evenings. The cooking delivers with dishes that hit the spot; pinkly roasted wood-pigeon salad with quail's eggs, Parma ham, pine nuts and raisins for example. Main course could be precisely timed sea bass in saffron velouté, served with both herb gnocchi and spring onion risotto, and the star finisher is rich vanilla pannacotta with mulled winter fruits and a caramel biscuit.

The Royal Oak Paley Street

MAIDENHEAD **Map 6 SU88**

Modern British NOTABLE WINE LIST

tel: 01628 620541 **Paley St, Littlefield Green SL6 3JN**
email: reservations@theroyaloakpaleystreet.com
web: www.theroyaloakpaleystreet.com
dir: *M4 junct 8/9. Take A308 towards Maidenhead Central, then A330 to Ascot. After 2m, turn right onto B3024 to Twyford. Second pub on left*

First-class modern British cooking in a spruced-up country pub

The Parkinson family's whitewashed 17th-century country pub might look a little unassuming, but the food brings in foodies from far and wide, and the place hasn't lost sight of the village hostelry's primary duty, which is pumping a good pint of cask-conditioned ale to order. Outside, the attractive gardens run to an ornamental waterfall, while the interiors have been appealingly designed to retain the character of an oak-beamed main bar with a real fire. A more modern tone prevails in the dining area, where flagstone and wood floors, high-backed leather chairs, unclothed tables and striking contemporary artworks brighten a scene that is classy but not over-dressed, and retains a relaxed feel. Here, friendly, efficient staff deliver on-trend plates of finely worked, high-impact modern cooking, opening with a sheer raviolo filled with smoked herring on an Indian-spiced leek bed, topped with luscious chilli jam, or there might be roast quail supported by braised chicory and a hazelnut and pear salad. Next up, the rich spring flavours of rump and shoulder of South Downs lamb are offset with capers, kale and carrots, or a Spanish mélange of stone bass, chorizo, mussels and samphire in paimpol bean stew might catch the eye. For dessert, there could be skilfully reworked rhubarb and custard with orange shortbread and rhubarb sorbet, or apricot and pistachio tart with milk ice cream, or go for a savoury finish with well-kept British and Irish cheeses. If you're not up for a full meal, snacks such as Scotch egg, spiced aubergine and houmous, or mini fishcakes with tartare deliver the same punchy flavours and excellent ingredients. The icing on the cake is a cracking list of over 500 wines with a good choice by the glass.

Chef James Bennett **Seats** 80, Pr/dining room 20 **Times** 12-2.30/6.30-9.30, Closed D Sun **Prices** Fixed L 2 course £25, Starter £6-£8, Main £16-£28, Dessert £5-£7 **Wines** 400 bottles over £30, 80 bottles under £30, 20 by glass **Parking** 70 **Notes** Sunday L fr £19.50, Vegetarian available, Children welcome

NEWBURY *continued*

The Vineyard

Modern French V NOTABLE WINE LIST

tel: 01635 528770 **Stockcross RG20 8JU**
email: general@the-vineyard.co.uk **web:** www.the-vineyard.co.uk
dir: *From M4 take A34 towards Newbury, exit at 3rd junct for Speen. Right at rdbt then right again at 2nd rdbt*

World-class wines and modern French cuisine in five-star splendour

A modest entrance off a narrow road between Newbury and Stockcross leads to the ranch-style hotel with its works of contemporary sculpture in the grounds. The whole experience is enhanced by striking modern design, with a split-level dining room connected by a staircase bounded by a representation of trellised vines. In early 2016, Robbie Jenks took up the reins in the kitchen, maintaining the highly stylised modern cuisine for which the place is noted. First up might be velvet-centred Label Rouge foie gras in textured crumb with aged grapes and hazelnuts in verjus, a dish fit for a vineyard if ever there was. Longhorn beef tartare might be counter-intuitively matched with sea rosemary and sorrel granita, before mains bring on further dazzle in the shape of carefully-torched halibut fillet, alongside crab tortellini, pickled kohlrabi and samphire in shellfish bisque. Pasta has a habit of inveigling its way into different dishes: there's ingenious cannelloni with the Middlewhite pork, as well as asparagus and wild garlic. To finish, two might share an ample coconut éclair, served with praline, mango and passionfruit. An enormous wine list completes the deal, its star offerings being bottles from the owner's estate in the Knights Valley district of Sonoma County, California.

Chef Robbie Jenks **Seats** 86, Pr/dining room 140 **Times** 12-2/7-9.30 **Prices** Fixed L 3 course £29, Tasting menu £89-£99 **Wines** 2500 bottles over £30, 60 bottles under £30, 100 by glass **Parking** 100 **Notes** L 4 course £39, D 4/5 course £65/£75, Sunday L £39, Children welcome

The Woodspeen – Restaurant and Cookery School

Modern British

tel: 01635 265070 **Lambourn Rd RG20 8BN**
email: hello@thewoodspeen.com
dir: *Phone for directions*

Unfussy modern food from a master practitioner

The Woodspeen is a restaurant with a swanky new cookery school attached. The building has been expanded with a natty glass-fronted extension that has a touch of Scandinavian style about it, complete with a soaring blond wood ceiling. Start with Cornish mackerel with beetroots (golden and ruby) and horseradish in a fashionable partnership, or a simple wild mushroom risotto with aged parmesan. Follow with local venison of the highest order, or a halibut and chorizo dish that doesn't reach the same heights. There's plenty of talent in this kitchen, judging by a finisher of egg custard tart with clementine sorbet.

Chef John Campbell **Seats** 70, Pr/dining room 12 **Times** 12-2.30/6-9.30, Closed 26 Dec, Mon, D Sun **Prices** Prices not confirmed **Wines** 211 bottles over £30, 51 bottles under £30, 13 by glass **Parking** 30 **Notes** Pre-theatre menu 6-6.30pm, Sunday L, Vegetarian available, Children welcome

READING Map 5 SU77

The French Horn

Traditional French, British V

tel: 0118 969 2204 **Sonning RG4 6TN**
email: info@thefrenchhorn.co.uk **web:** www.thefrenchhorn.co.uk
dir: *From Reading take A4 E to Sonning. Follow B478 through village over bridge, hotel on right, car park on left*

Classical French dining by the Thames

The riverside setting is a treat, with the dining room opening on to a terrace, at the family-run French Horn, which is full of old-school charm with slick and well-managed service. The menu looks across the Channel for its inspiration, with a classically-based repertoire (and high prices). Foie gras terrine is given a modern twist from its accompaniment of spiced caramel, and crabmeat from pineapple compôte. They might be followed by poached fillets of Dover sole with clams, samphire and saffron sauce, or roast lamb fillet with hazelnut sauce, courgettes and polenta. Francophiles can end with crêpe Suzette or crème brûlée.

Chef J Diaga **Seats** 70, Pr/dining room 24 **Times** 12-2/7-9.30, Closed 1-4 Jan **Prices** Fixed L 2 course £21, Fixed D 3 course £28, Starter fr £8, Main £23-£36.50, Dessert £9-£13.50 **Wines** 400 bottles over £30, 8 bottles under £30, 14 by glass **Parking** 40 **Notes** Sunday L £58.50, Children welcome

Holiday Inn Reading M4 Jct 10

– see opposite

Malmaison Reading

Modern European, International

tel: 0118 956 2300 & 956 2302 **Great Western House, 18-20 Station Rd RG1 1JX**
email: reading@malmaison.com **web:** www.malmaison.com
dir: *Next to Reading station*

Enlivening brasserie cooking in a restyled railway hotel

By all accounts the oldest railway hotel in the world, the early Victorian property is a real charmer. Its historic past is recognised in some decorative touches, but this being a Mal, the overall finish is glamorous and stylish. Settle into the Malbar for a pre-dinner cocktail or head straight into the restaurant with its bare-brick walls and bench seating recalling the old railway couchettes. The brasserie-inspired menu traverses the globe in search of feel-good flavours; prawn cocktail to start, say, or tuna tartare with an Asian spin, or a classic moules marinière. Move on to a Black Angus steak cooked on the grill, porcini risotto or a blinged-up burger.

Holiday Inn Reading M4 Jct 10

Modern British, Indian

tel: 0118 944 0444 **Wharfedale Rd, Winnersh Triangle RG41 5TS**
email: reservations@hireadinghotel.com **web:** www.hireadinghotel.com
dir: *M4 junct 10/A329(M) towards Reading (E), 1st exit signed Winnersh. Left at lights into Wharfedale Rd. Hotel on left, adjacent to Winnersh Triangle Station*

Imaginative modern cooking in a smart Holiday Inn

This is a flagship for the group, designed with an impressive level of contemporary flair. Led by a chef with a solid country-house pedigree, the skilled kitchen team delivers well-thought-out menus of modern Mediterranean inflected ideas. Pan-fried king scallops with pea purée, pancetta and mint foam is the sort of dish you'd love to find all along the motorway network. Follow with a three-way serving of pork (pan-fried tenderloin, slow-cooked belly and braised cheeks) supported by baby turnips, sweet potato and cider sauce, or there could be monkfish with celeriac rösti, fennel, and tomato and star anise sauce. End with something like blackberry soufflé with clotted cream ice cream.

Holiday Inn Reading M4 Jct 10

Chef Graham Weston **Seats** 120, Pr/dining room 20 **Times** 12-11, All-day dining **Prices** Fixed L 2 course £20.95, Fixed D 3 course £24.95, Starter £7.25-£9.25, Main £16.50-£24.95, Dessert £7.25-£7.75 **Wines** 7 bottles over £30, 63 bottles under £30, 14 by glass **Parking** 132 **Notes** Afternoon tea £15 (with wine £17.50, with champagne £20), Sunday L £20.95-£24.95, Vegetarian available, Children welcome

See advert below

READING *continued*

Millennium Madejski Hotel Reading

British, International V

tel: 0118 925 3500 **Madejski Stadium RG2 OFL**
email: reservations.reading@millenniumhotels.co.uk **web:** www.millenniumhotels.co.uk
dir: *1m N from M4 junct 11. 2m S from Reading town centre*

Modern British dishes in a glam football hotel

The Madejski Stadium, base of Reading Football Club, shares an ultra-modern complex with this swishly smart hotel. There's a champagne bar on entry, while Cilantro is the fine-dining restaurant, its refined feel defined by a display of wines, neatly clothed tables and sharp service. Dishes tend to be straightforward, seen in succulent fillet of beef with a selection of vegetables, a rich port-based jus and a textbook béarnaise. Fish might be represented by braised brill with no more than cauliflower purée and glazed carrots, and bookending main courses may be scallop céviche and gravad lax with caviar and green beans with chives, and caramelised apple layers with vanilla ice cream.

Chef Denzil Newton **Seats** 55, Pr/dining room 20 **Times** 7-10, Closed 25 Dec, 1 Jan, BHs, Sun-Mon, L all week **Prices** Prices not confirmed **Wines** 12 by glass **Parking** 100 **Notes** Gourmand menu 7 course £49.50, Children 12 yrs+

Mya Lacarte

Modern British

tel: 0118 946 3400 **5 Prospect St, Caversham RG4 8JB**
email: eat@myalacarte.co.uk
dir: *M4 junct 10, continue onto A3290/A4 signed Caversham. At Crown Plaza Hotel continue over Caversham Bridge, restaurant 3rd left*

Carefully sourced British produce on the high street

Mya Lacarte sources materials as locally as possible. It's dedicated to healthy living, so the menu flags dairy- and gluten-free dishes as well as vegetarian, and the results on the plate are deeply satisfying. Starters can be as busy as pan-fried fillet of haddock with bubble-and-squeak, a poached egg, smoked bacon and pancetta and as simple as a pork Scotch egg with mustard mayonnaise. Choose from dishes of clearly defined flavours such as braised shin of beef with mustard-enhanced mash, baby vegetables and mushrooms, or a salad of roast winter vegetables with pine nuts, sunflower seeds, parmesan shavings and basil oil. Finish on deconstructed baked Alaska with basil ice cream.

Chef Aidan Channon, Josh Wimlett, Daniel Pocz-Nagy **Seats** 35, Pr/dining room 12 **Times** 12-3/5-10.30, Closed 25-26 Dec, 1 Jan, Sun (ex occasions & functions) **Prices** Fixed L 2 course £14.95, Fixed D 3 course £14.95-£18.95, Starter £5.95-£9, Main £13.95-£23, Dessert £3-£8 **Wines** 10 bottles over £30, 20 bottles under £30, 10 by glass **Parking** NCP **Notes** Vegetarian available, Children welcome

SHINFIELD **Map 5 SU76**

L'Ortolan

Modern French V NOTABLE WINE LIST

tel: 0118 988 8500 **Church Ln RG2 9BY**
email: info@lortolan.com **web:** www.lortolan.com
dir: *From M4 junct 11 take A33 towards Basingstoke. At 1st lights turn left, after garage turn left, 1m turn right at Six Bells pub. Restaurant 1st left (follow tourist signs)*

Consummate modern gastronomy in a former vicarage

The setting, in the countryside a little way out of Reading, and its clerical origins as a vicarage, may confer the slight air of an Anthony Trollope novel on L'Ortolan. This attractively faced red-brick building in pretty gardens has been home to outstanding dining for a number of years, and Tom Clarke has brought new energy and focus to the production here. At tables looking out over the lawns, or in the kitchen if that's your thing, you may well feel you have one of the vantage-points of modern British gastronomy. Harmoniously contrasting flavours are built up in elaborate dishes such as fried duck liver with matching parfait, smoked duck, pineapple and spiced meringue, or the sublimely earthy egg ravioli with trompettes and textured celeriac in truffle jus. Pedigree local meats are hunted down for mains like venison loin with purple pomme purée, blackberries and beetroot in juniper sauce, or there may be confidently presented fish such as stone bass with braised chicory and monk's beard in red wine jus. All the little extras are fitted around these inspired dishes, up to a fragrant finale of buttermilk pannacotta with poached rhubarb, gingerbread purée and rosemary ice cream. The Menu Gourmand offers a representative tour of the territory.

Chef Tom Clarke **Seats** 58, Pr/dining room 22 **Times** 12-2/7-9, Closed 2 wks Xmas-New Year, Sun-Mon **Prices** Prices not confirmed **Wines** 210 bottles over £30, 1 bottle under £30, 17 by glass **Parking** 30 **Notes** Chef's table, Children 3 yrs+

SLOUGH **Map 6 SU97**

Hilton London Heathrow Airport Terminal 5

British, International

tel: 01753 686860 **Poyle Rd, Colnbrook SL3 OFF**
email: heathrowairportterminal5.info@hilton.com **web:** www.heathrowt5.hilton.com
dir: *M25 junct 14, exit onto Horton Rd signed Poyle, Datchet. At 2nd rdbt exit onto Poyle Rd, Heathrow Terminal 5 is 400mtrs on left*

Global flavours at Terminal 5

Open all day and located on the mezzanine level of this hotel by Terminal 5, with views over the lobby, The Gallery's long, globally-inspired menu features dishes that recall an altogether more pastoral existence. 'From the Farm' comes classic Caesar salad and roast pork belly with crackling, a white pudding beignet, chilli jam, chorizo-mashed potato and green beans, while 'From the Field' there might be paneer makhani with basmati rice and mango chutney. The sea might be represented by crab and langoustine linguine, and starters include a salad of avocado, shrimps, smoked salmon and grapefruit. Finish with sticky toffee pudding with honeycomb ice cream.

Chef Jasbeer Dawar **Seats** 203 **Times** 6.30am-10.30pm, All-day dining **Prices** Fixed L 2 course fr £23.50, Fixed D 3 course fr £29.50, Starter £5.95-£12.95, Main £16.25-£34.95, Dessert £7.95-£15.95 **Wines** 18 bottles over £30, 18 bottles under £30, 14 by glass **Parking** 472 **Notes** Breakfast, Sunday L, Vegetarian available, Children welcome

Mr Todiwala's Kitchen

Modern Pan-Asian

tel: 01753 686860 & 766482 **Poyle Rd, Colnbrook SL3 OFF**
email: heathrowairportterminal5.info@hilton.com **web:** www.hilton.com/heathrowt5
dir: *M25 junct 14, exit onto Horton Rd signed Poyle, Datchet. At 2nd rdbt exit onto Poyle Rd, Heathrow Terminal 5 is 400mtrs on left*

Uplifting Pan-Indian cooking at Heathrow's newest terminal

Cyrus Todiwala (he of Café Spice Namaste) brings pan-Indian style to this airport hotel, in a clinically-white atmosphere of lime-washed floors and café-style furnishings. Highly spiced, vividly seasoned food is the perfect antidote to corporate anonymity, and appears in the form of prawns in a hot sweet-and-sour sauce, or masala dosai, followed by chicken tikka with steamed rice, or Keralan-style duck breast. Seafood might appear as Goan king prawn curry with organic red rice, or grilled halibut fillet in coconut curry sauce on garlic and chilli risotto. Vegetarian dishes include the croquette of spinach and split peas in rich coconut curry.

Chef Cyrus Todiwala, Arun Dev **Seats** 70 **Times** 6-10.30, Closed Xmas, Sun **Prices** Prices not confirmed **Wines** 10 bottles over £30, 11 bottles under £30, 10 by glass **Parking** 480 **Notes** Vegetarian available, Children welcome

THATCHAM Map 5 SU56

The Bunk Inn

Modern British, French NEW

tel: 01635 200400 **Curridge RG18 9DS**
email: info@thebunkinn.co.uk **web:** www.thebunkinn.co.uk
dir: *Phone for directions*

Characterful village inn serving modern British food

A short canter from Newbury Racecourse, this convivial village inn takes its name from locals from the nearby brickworks who used to 'bunk off' work early for a crafty pint. Still very much the village hub where locals prop up the bar by the open fire with a glass of ale and a packet of crisps, its confident modern cooking also attracts foodies. Start with crispy squid, pressed octopus, chorizo, sweetcorn and paprika and basil jus before moving on to smoked chicken schnitzel, fried duck egg, black pudding, treacle-cured bacon, braised gem and caper and lemon dressing.

Chef Lewis Spreadbury **Seats** 50, Pr/dining room 22 **Times** 12-2.30/6.30-9, Closed D 24-26 Dec, 1 Jan **Prices** Fixed L 2 course £17-£23, Tasting menu £40-£65, Starter £6.50-£12, Main £13.50-£22.25, Dessert £6.50-£8 **Wines** 17 bottles over £30, 26 bottles under £30, 12 by glass **Parking** 50 **Notes** Sunday L £13-£16.50, Vegetarian available, Children welcome

WHITE WALTHAM Map 5 SU87

The Beehive

British

tel: 01628 822877 **Waltham Rd SL6 3SH**
email: reservations@thebeehivewhitewaltham.com
web: www.thebeehivewhitewaltham.com
dir: *M4 junct 8/9, follow signs White Waltham. Located opposite cricket grounds*

Gimmick-free cooking in a village local

With the cricket ground opposite, The Beehive is the epitome of the English village pub. A bar menu, daily-changing lunch and dinner menus, and a specials board reveal season-driven, modern British dishes known for their gimmick-free, 'less is more' simplicity. If a starter of Dorset snails with garlic butter, Gorgonzola and grilled sourdough wouldn't be your choice, you'll easily find an alternative, such as English asparagus with poached egg, monk's beard, parmesan and pea shoots. Follow with calves' liver, cooked pink, with crisp bacon, soft and sweet melted onions and mash. Yorkshire rhubarb trifle topped with vanilla custard, cream, almonds and berries looks especially scrumptious in its glass tumbler.

Chef Dominic Chapman **Seats** 75 **Times** 12-2.30/6-9.30, Closed 25-26 Dec, D Sun **Prices** Starter £6.95-£10.95, Main £14.50-£24, Dessert £6.95-£8 **Wines** 29 bottles over £30, 14 bottles under £30, 14 by glass **Parking** 40 **Notes** Sunday L, Vegetarian available, Children welcome

WINDSOR Map 6 SU97

Castle Hotel Windsor MGallery by Sofitel

Modern British

tel: 01753 851557 **18 High St SL4 1LJ**
email: h6618@accor.com **web:** www.sofitel.com
dir: *M25 junct 13 take A308 towards town centre then onto B470 to High St. M4 junct 6 towards A332, at rdbt first exit into Clarence Rd, left at lights to High St*

British cooking in the vicinity of the Queen's residence

Sitting directly opposite the Royal Guildhall, with the Queen's Berkshire bolthole on hand, the hotel named after the latter could hardly be better positioned. It was originally a Tudor building with a balcony and patriotic flagpoles, but now a large dining room offering classic dishes from a traditional British menu, in the form of a Marco Pierre White Steakhouse Bar & Grill. Wash down a hearty grill dish with a wide variety of wines or choose a warming pie dish in the winter months. When you're done, retire to the Marco Pierre White bar for cocktails.

The Greene Oak

Modern British

tel: 01753 864294 **Oakley Green SL4 5UW**
email: info@thegreeneoak.co.uk
dir: *Phone for directions*

Modern pub dining in a welcoming country inn

Very much a dining pub, the Greene Oak is a charming old place with bright, homely decor and cheerful staff who keep it all ticking along nicely. The kitchen makes good use of local seasonal ingredients, focusing on gently contemporary British- and European-inspired ideas. A starter of salt-cod croquettes arrives in the company of pea purée, mint aïoli and a quail's egg, with main-course pan-roasted sea trout to follow, or a succulent confit pork belly in an earthy combo with trompette mushrooms and grain mustard sauce. End on a tropical note with coconut pannacotta, pineapple carpaccio and spiced pineapple sorbet. Terrace tables fill up fast on warm days.

The Oakley Court

 Modern British V

tel: 01753 609988 **Windsor Rd, Water Oakley SL4 5UR**
email: guestrelations@oakleycourthotel.co.uk **web:** www.oakleycourt.co.uk
dir: *M4 junct 6 to Windsor. At rdbt right onto A308. Hotel 2.5m on right*

Creative modern European cooking amid Gothic extravagance

With turrets, gables and 37 acres of well-tended grounds, Oakley Court is a prime example of a Victorian Gothic castle. As you would expect in a hotel of this standing, there's golf, tennis and swimming on tap, or pampering in the treatment rooms. The half-panelled dining room, with its crisply clothed tables and formal service, is the place to head for creative modern British cooking. An innovative pairing of celeriac, passionfruit, foie gras and coffee is one opener, perhaps before Balmoral estate venison, black garlic, shallots and Valrhona chocolate. Finish with heritage tomatoes, strawberries and black olives.

Chef Damian Broom **Seats** 28 **Times** 6.30-9.30, Closed Xmas, New Year, Sun-Mon, L all week **Wines** 29 bottles over £30, 14 bottles under £30, 10 by glass **Parking** 200 **Notes** Children 12 yrs+

WINDSOR *continued*

Scottish Steakhouse@Caleys

Scottish, Modern British

tel: 01753 483100 **Macdonald Windsor Hotel, 23 High St SL4 1LH**
email: gm.windsor@macdonaldwindsor.co.uk **web:** www.macdonaldhotels.co.uk
dir: *M4 junct 6 A355, take A332, rdbt 1st exit signed town centre. In 0.7m turn left into Bachelors Acre*

Scottish (and other) steak club opposite Windsor Castle

This contemporary townhouse hotel directly opposite the castle offers ringside views of the changing of the guard. The Scottish Steakhouse restaurant is a large room with polished dark wooden tables, where you can expect top-quality cuts cooked exactly as ordered on the Josper grill, with a choice of sauces. Elsewhere, the menu is surprisingly wide-ranging: starters take in squid tempura with Vietnamese dipping sauce, and main courses including sea bass fillet with crisp shaved fennel and chilli, lime and soy sauce as well as corned beef hash with a fried duck egg. To finish, go for brownies with marshmallow and honeycomb served with toffee ice cream.

Chef Emma Broom **Seats** 70, Pr/dining room 100 **Times** 7am-10pm, All-day dining **Prices** Fixed L 2 course fr £20, Starter fr £4.95, Main fr £14.95, Dessert fr £3 **Wines** 34 bottles over £30, 13 bottles under £30, 14 by glass **Parking** 30, Pre-booked and chargeable **Notes** ALC also Sun, Scottish Steakhouse menu, Sunday L, Vegetarian available, Children welcome

WOKINGHAM Map 5 SU86

Miltons Restaurant

Modern British, European V

tel: 0118 989 5100 & 989 5166 **Cantley House Hotel, Milton Rd RG40 1JY**
email: info@miltonsrestaurant.co.uk **web:** www.miltonsrestaurant.co.uk
dir: *Phone for directions*

Rustic chic setting for modern brasserie food

The Cantley House Hotel is a 17th-century barn, with a split-level dining space done in a rustic-chic manner, and modern brasserie food is the name of the game. Duck and bacon ballotine with seared foie gras and apple rösti is a well-conceived and well-executed starter. At main, precise timing and seasoning distinguishes a fried pavé of halibut with razor clams, crab and trompette mushrooms in a crème fraîche emulsion, or there may be cannon of lamb with a mini-shepherd's pie and roast vegetables in marjoram. For dessert, try runny-centred dark chocolate fondant comes with hazelnut cream for a satisfying finisher, or else go for the blue ribbon British cheeses.

Miltons Restaurant

Chef Andreas Barauskas **Seats** 60, Pr/dining room 34 **Times** 7-10, All-day dining, Closed Mon, D Sun **Prices** Fixed L 2 course £14.50-£17.50, Starter £6.50-£9.50, Main £16-£22.50, Dessert £4.50-£11 **Wines** 16 bottles over £30, 23 bottles under £30, 12 by glass **Parking** 70 **Notes** Sunday L, Children welcome

BRISTOL

BRISTOL Map 4 ST57

The Acorn Restaurant

British, International NEW

tel: 01454 771420 & 0844 815 9063 *(Calls cost 7p per minute plus your phone company's access charge)* **Mercure Bristol North, The Grange, Northwoods, Winterbourne BS36 1RP**
email: gm.mercurebristolnorthgrange@jupiterhotels.co.uk **web:** www.mercurebristol.co.uk
dir: *A38 towards Filton/Bristol. At rdbt 1st exit into Bradley Stoke Way, at lights 1st left into Woodlands Ln, at 2nd rdbt left into Trench Ln. In 1m left at T-junct, hotel 200yds on left*

Brasserie-style menu and contemporary swagger

A lick of Farrow & Ball paint and some bold artworks have created an appealing contemporary space, but it's still a warm and comfortable setting, even with a bit of glamour about it. The kitchen's populist brasserie-style menu offers broad appeal in the shape of burgers, pizza, steak and ale pie, and 21-day aged Cumbrian steaks served on a wooden board with a host of accompaniments. Start with a deliciously rich chicken liver parfait with apple and cider chutney, or calamari in tempura batter, and finish with sticky toffee pudding or a slate of British cheeses.

Chef Etienne Forget **Seats** 54, Pr/dining room 12 **Times** 12-2/6.30-10 **Prices** Starter £5.50-£6.95, Main £11-£23.50, Dessert £5.50-£8.75 **Wines** 1 bottle over £30, 16 bottles under £30, 17 by glass **Parking** 150 **Notes** Sunday L £12.95-£18.95, Vegetarian available, Children welcome

Casamia Restaurant

BRISTOL **Map 4 ST57**

Modern British V

tel: 0117 959 2884 **The General, Lower Guinea St BS1 6SY**
email: info@casamiarestaurant.co.uk
dir: *Phone for directions*

Exciting progressive cooking that follows the seasons

The restaurant world was shaken by the tragically early death of Jonray Sanchez-Iglesias in November 2015. A family affair from the very beginning – as its name attests – when brothers Peter and Jonray took over their parents' traditional Italian trattoria they began a transformation the likes of which has surely not been seen before. They created one of the very best restaurants in the country...or the world for that matter. A move from Westbury-on-Trym into the revamped waterside area around the old Bristol General Hospital signals a determination to continue to grow, develop and astound. The new area will also be home to a couple of new ventures from the Sanchez-Iglesias family – a tapas joint called Tapas and a pizzeria called Pizza. The new Casamia has a contemporary simplicity with natural shades, exposed brickwork, simply stylish tables, artworks that reflect the changing seasons (they literally change them to fit with the season), and an open kitchen that blends into the dining area to breakdown the divide between cooks and customers. The chefs work calmly and deliberately in their immaculate whites, and they join the waiters in taking turns to bring the dishes to the table – each element described with knowledge and passion. Ordering couldn't be easier as it's a fixed price and no decisions need to be made, apart from whether to go for the wine flight as well. The cost is high, but this is exceptional cooking, with set lunch the best option for anyone wanting to get the experience on a budget. As is the fashion at this level, it begins with a series of 'snacks' that set the pace; how about an iron skillet with a piece of artichoke and a generous grating of truffle? Perfect simplicity. There's drama and creativity all the way through, from a hay-lined box containing a ceramic egg shell filled with confit duck, an intense 'yolk' and the subtle flavours of cardamom, to a winter root vegetable salad made with the full armoury of contemporary techniques. The ingredients are exceptional, such as a fillet of rainbow trout that is cooked perfectly and arrives with cabbage leaves of varying forms and intensity of flavour, or the fallow deer that is cooked on the indoor barbecue. A variety of plates and bowls adds character to each course, while many of the dishes are tiny bites that disappear in a tantalising instant, such as the cheese course that precedes dessert – Cornish camembert sandwiched between two pieces of dried rhubarb, say. Among desserts, a clever passionfruit number is served in a dish resembling the fruit, and a 'variations of mandarin' is full of theatre. The classiest lollipop you'll ever eat sends you home with a smile on your face.

Chef Peter Sanchez-Iglesias **Seats** 40
Times 12-1.30/6-9.30, Closed Xmas, New Year, BHs, Sun-Tue
Prices Tasting menu £68-£88 **Wines** 74 bottles over £30, 19 bottles under £30, 11 by glass **Parking** Car park off Commercial Rd
Notes Fixed L 5 course £38, Tasting menu 10 course, Children welcome

BRISTOL *continued*

The Avon Gorge Hotel

Modern British

tel: 0117 973 8955 **Sion Hill, Clifton BS8 4LD**
email: rooms@theavongorge.com **web:** www.theavongorge.com
dir: *From S: M5 junct 19, A369 to Clifton Toll, over suspension bridge, 1st right into Sion Hill. From N: M5 junct 18A, A4 to Bristol, under suspension bridge, follow signs to bridge, exit Sion Hill*

Splendid Clifton location and modern British cooking

Fans of Brunel's landmark suspension bridge couldn't ask for a better vantage point to take in his handiwork than this Victorian hotel's Bridge Café. Burgers (lamb with tomato and rosemary focaccia and cucumber and harissa yogurt, anyone?) and steaks with béarnaise or venison steak glazed with port, juniper and redcurrant, and timeless ideas such as Butcombe beer-battered fish and chips, broaden the appeal of a broadly modern British menu that kicks off with smoked duck terrine with home-made chutney and toasted brioche. Main-course fish options deliver herb-crusted pollock fillet with crayfish and saffron risotto and lemon oil, and to finish, there's a retro classic in the form of peach Melba.

Chef Marcus Bradley **Seats** 50, Pr/dining room 20 **Times** 12-4/6-10 **Prices** Prices not confirmed **Wines** 16 bottles under £30, 19 by glass **Parking** 25 **Notes** Sunday L, Vegetarian available, Children welcome

Best Western Henbury Lodge Hotel

Modern British

tel: 0117 950 2615 **Station Rd, Henbury BS10 7QQ**
email: info@henburyhotel.com **web:** www.henburyhotel.com
dir: *M5 junct 17/A4018 towards city centre, 3rd rdbt right into Crow Ln. At end turn right, hotel 200mtrs on right*

Country-house style at Edmund Burke's old place

Henbury Lodge retains the feel of a Georgian country mansion, with its portico entrance, elegant interiors and a many-mirrored dining room, the Blaise restaurant, done in pale primrose. The cooking has more than a little of the country-house style about it. Start with a sauté of chicken livers and smoked bacon in a salad with caramelised hazelnuts, prior to a well-judged main course of crisp-skinned haddock with two-tone carrots (yellow and purple) or the signature rabbit leg filled with black pudding and apple, wrapped in Parma ham, on leeks in grain mustard sauce. For dessert, try luxuriously gooey treacle tart with mascarpone and an unusual but effective marmalade ice cream.

Chef Phil Hardwick **Seats** 22 **Times** 7-9, Closed Xmas-New Year, Sun, L all week **Prices** Starter £6-£8, Main £15-£21, Dessert £6-£8 **Wines** 1 bottle over £30, 17 bottles under £30, 7 by glass **Parking** 20 **Notes** Vegetarian available, Children welcome

Bordeaux Quay

Modern European

tel: 0117 943 1200 **V-Shed, Canons Way BS1 5UH**
email: info@bordeaux-quay.co.uk
dir: *Canons Rd off the A4, beyond Millennium Square car park*

Modern warehouse conversion covering all bases on the waterfront

This dynamic set up on Bristol's waterfront takes in a restaurant, brasserie, bar, deli, bakery and cookery school in a stylishly redeveloped dockland warehouse. The restaurant is on the first floor, with elegant table settings and fine wood alongside industrial pipe work, or you might opt for an alfresco meal on the terrace of the brasserie downstairs. Start with squid ink risotto with smoked haddock and a quail's egg, before salt marsh lamb (roasted and served with crispy bonbon, chermoula and fried polenta), or leek and saffron tart with Jerusalem artichokes, bitter leaves and toasted hazelnuts. To finish, pear tarte Tatin comes with star anise and molasses parfait.

Chef Alex Murray, Andy Pole **Seats** 90, Pr/dining room 28 **Times** 12-10.30, All-day dining, Closed Xmas **Prices** Fixed D 3 course £19.50-£30, Starter £5-£9.50, Main £9.50-£25, Dessert £5-£9.50 **Wines** 40 bottles over £30, 40 bottles under £30, 30 by glass **Parking** Millennium Sq **Notes** Breakfast, Sunday L £13.50-£23, Vegetarian available, Children welcome

Casamia Restaurant

– see page 47

Glass Boat Restaurant

Modern French

tel: 0117 929 0704 **Welsh Back BS1 4SB**
email: bookings@glassboat.co.uk
dir: *Moored below Bristol Bridge in the old centre of Bristol*

Modern bistro fare on a glamorous barge

This 1920s barge once earned its crust along the Severn Estuary but is now moored up in the heart of the city, converted to a decidedly handsome restaurant with walnut floors and a beautiful marble bar. The menu offers modern bistro fare with plenty of imagination, plying a course from chicken liver parfait with onion jam, or crispy frogs' legs with wild garlic risotto, to chicken suprême with celeriac, Savoy cabbage with lardons and honey-roasted swede. Seafood dishes are full of appeal too – perhaps a creamy bourride of monkfish and mussels. Finish with zesty lemon tart with crème fraîche. Theatre-goers can enjoy a good-value supper until 7pm.

Goldbrick House

Modern British

tel: 0117 945 1950 **69 Park St BS1 5PB**
email: info@goldbrickhouse.co.uk
dir: *M32, follow signs for city centre. Left side of Park St, going up the hill towards museum*

Modern brasserie cooking in an all-things-to-all-comers venue

In this converted pair of townhouses you'll find an all-day café-bar, a cocktail bar, a main restaurant, with chandeliers and gilt-framed mirrors, and the light-filled Orangery. The kitchen follows a modern brasserie route, turning out appealing and successful starters along the lines of smoked pork belly with quince, pecan granola and mead dressing, and cured sea trout with pickled fennel and blackened orange. No less original are main courses: perhaps poached sea bass fillet with salsify purée, chestnut and crab fricassee and smoked pancetta sauce, although there's usually a steak for diehards. Chocoholics could finish with a brownie with banana and honeycomb.

Hotel du Vin Bristol

French, British

tel: 0117 9255577 **The Sugar House, Narrow Lewins Mead BS1 2NU**
email: info.bristol@hotelduvin.com **web:** www.hotelduvin.com
dir: *From M4 junct 19, M32 into Bristol. At rdbt take 1st exit & follow main road to next rdbt. Turn onto other side of carriageway, hotel 200yds on right*

Simple and successful brasserie cooking with first-rate wines

In a former sugar warehouse close to the waterfront, the casual French-inspired bistro at the Bristol HdV is a buzzy and easy-going venue. Factor in the world-class wine list, and you've got a compelling package. The bilingual menu deals in classic stuff such as steak tartare or French onion soup, and the kitchen tackles a Comté soufflé with considerable success. Among main courses, moules et frites and calves' liver and bacon are straight-up options, with duck shepherd's pie offering something a little off-piste. Excellent pastry helps a treacle tart hit the spot, and the impressive wine list isn't all about France.

Chef Marcus Lang **Seats** 85, Pr/dining room 72 **Times** 12-2.30/5.30-10.30, Closed L 31 Dec **Prices** Fixed L 2 course £16.95-£19.59, Fixed D 2 course fr £39, Starter £5.50-£11.95, Main £15.50-£30, Dessert £5.50-£9.95 **Wines** 332 bottles over £30, 18 bottles under £30, 23 by glass **Parking** 8, NCP Rupert St **Notes** Sunday L, Vegetarian available, Children welcome

The Ox

Modern British

tel: 0117 922 1001 **The Basement, 43 Corn St BS1 1HT**
email: info@theoxbristol.com
dir: *Exit M32 towards City centre A38, Baldwin St B4053. Park at Princes St NCP. 100mtrs down from Bristol Register Office*

Steaks and more in an atmospheric basement

Head down to the basement – a one-time bank vault – and you'll find a restaurant that the old boys of yesteryear would have admired, with its oak panels, ox blood leather seats and murals. They'd have appreciated the red-blooded menu too, for the Ox focuses on steaks (rib-eye, sirloin, rib on the bone, fillet etc.) all served with triple-cooked chips and a choice of sauce. There's a lot more besides, including trendy small plates of hickory-smoked ribs and squid salad, plus a charcuterie board to share, and alternative main courses run to fishcakes and veggie cannelloni. Finish with warm caramelised rice pudding with boozy prunes and apple compôte.

Chef Todd Francis **Seats** 80 **Times** 12-2.30/5-10.30, Closed Xmas, L Sat, D Sun **Prices** Fixed L 2 course £14, Starter £6-£9.50, Main £12.50-£29.50, Dessert £6-£9.50 **Wines** 36 bottles over £30, 11 bottles under £30, 8 by glass **Parking** NCP Prince St, NCP Trenchard **Notes** Sharing menu £32-£35, Early bird steak & wine 5-7pm £14.50, Sunday L fr £17.50, Vegetarian available, Children welcome

The Pump House

Modern British NOTABLE WINE LIST

tel: 0117 927 2229 **Merchants Rd, Hotwells BS8 4PZ**
email: info@the-pumphouse.com **web:** www.the-pumphouse.com
dir: *A4 Clevedon to city centre, left before swing bridge*

Thriving dockside pub-restaurant with a serious approach to food

Chef-proprietor Toby Gritten has made great use of the hydraulic pumping station down on the waterside to create a buzzy gastropub and restaurant. Gritten likes to champion local produce, including foraged materials, and everything from bread to chutneys is made in-house. Depending on the season, you might start with seared Bath chap with apple, celeriac and a fried quail's egg, or game terrine with forced rhubarb and chicory. Main-course venison steak with root vegetables and smoked bone marrow is one way to go, but there's also the likes of roast gurnard with walnuts, parsley and brown shrimps. End with lemon croquette, kaffir lime leaves and sorbet, and toasted marshmallow.

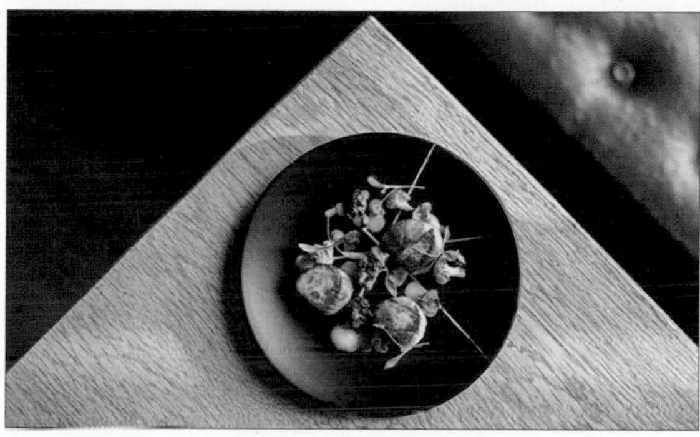

The Pump House

Chef Toby Gritten **Seats** 50 **Times** 12-3.30/6.30-9.30, Closed 25 Dec, Mon-Wed, L Thu, D Sun **Prices** Tasting menu £55, Starter £4-£10.50, Main £9.50-£25, Dessert £6-£8 **Wines** 138 bottles over £30, 47 bottles under £30, 24 by glass **Parking** 20 **Notes** Tasting menu 5/8 course, Sunday L £16-£18.50, Vegetarian available, Children welcome

riverstation

Modern European NOTABLE WINE LIST

tel: 0117 914 4434 & 914 5560 **The Grove BS1 4RB**
email: relax@riverstation.co.uk **web:** www.riverstation.co.uk
dir: *On harbour side in central Bristol between St Mary Redcliffe church & Arnolfini*

Buzzy riverside setting and switched-on brasserie food

This lively venue is glazed from top to bottom to make the most of its harbourside location, both from the ground-floor café-bar and the industrial-chic first-floor restaurant. Inspiration is drawn from far and wide to create bright, up-to-date dishes rooted in good culinary sense. Cauliflower and potato soup gets a kick of harissa oil, and confit duck is partnered by Wagyu beef and served with lomo, smoked pickled peach and chicory. They may precede chargrilled pork skirt with morcilla, panisse, greens and rhubarb or more familiar roast chicken breast with provençale sauce, mash and spring greens. Enterprising puddings include tarte de Santiago with orange ice cream and kumquats.

Chef Matt Hampshire **Seats** 120, Pr/dining room 30
Times 12-2.30/6-10.30, Closed 24-26 Dec, D Sun **Prices** Fixed L 2 course £13.50, Fixed D 3 course £18.50, Starter £5.50-£7.50, Main £16-£19.50, Dessert £6-£7.50 **Wines** 51 bottles over £30, 25 bottles under £30, 15 by glass **Parking** Pay & display, parking opposite (meter) **Notes** Pre-theatre £12 Mon-Fri 6-7.15pm. Fixed D 2/3 course Mon-Fri, Sunday L £19-£24, Vegetarian available, Children welcome

BRISTOL *continued*

Second Floor Restaurant

Modern European NOTABLE WINE LIST

tel: 0117 961 8898 **Harvey Nichols, 27 Philadelphia St, Quakers Friars BS1 3BZ**
email: reception.bristol@harveynichols.com
dir: *Phone for directions*

Vibrant modern cooking in stylish second-floor dining room

Overlooking the old Quakers Friars Dominican friary in the heart of Cabot Circus shopping quarter, this gold and beige-hued second-floor dining room is a supremely relaxing place. The kitchen turns out a menu of lively modern British European food. Seared scallops, chorizo, cuttlefish, orzo pasta and squid ink reduction makes an attention-seeking opener. Main course could be roast sirloin of beef, braised feather blade, smoked potato purée, baby onions, pancetta, mushrooms and parsley oil. Finish with pineapple and coconut cannelloni, passionfruit and coconut cream macaroon and rum ice cream. There are some interesting wines on offer too.

Chef Louise McCrimmon **Seats** 60, Pr/dining room 10 **Times** 12-3/6-10, Closed 25 Dec, 1 Jan, Etr Sun, D Sun-Mon **Prices** Fixed L 3 course £20, Starter £7.50-£10, Main £18-£25, Dessert £5.50-£8 **Wines** 310 bottles over £30, 40 bottles under £30, 21 by glass **Parking** NCP/Cabot Circus car park **Notes** Sun brunch, Afternoon tea, Vegetarian available, Children welcome

The Spiny Lobster

 Mediterranean, Seafood

tel: 0117 973 7384 **128 Whiteladies Rd, Clifton BS8 2RS**
email: enquiries@rockfishgrill.co.uk
dir: *From city centre follow signs for Clifton, restaurant halfway along Whiteladies Rd*

Fish and seafood presented fresh and simple

Rebranded from its former incarnation as the Rockfish Grill, Mitch Tonks' seafood brasserie and fish market maintains a rigorous commitment to freshness and simplicity, using fish and shellfish mostly landed by the Brixham boats. The refurbished room sports racing-green buttoned banquettes, linen-clothed tables and piscine artwork, and friendly staff make the formula a winning one. The simple approach with top-class materials slapped onto a charcoal-burning Josper grill works wonders with scallops roasted with citrus and cucumber, then mains such as hake served with romesco sauce, John Dory with tomato and basil, or lemon sole with anchovy and rosemary. Finish with the likes of chocolate tart with honey and crème fraîche.

Chef Neil Roach **Seats** 52 **Times** 12-2.30/6-10.30, Closed 25 Dec, 1 Jan, Sun-Mon **Prices** Fixed L 2 course fr £15, Fixed D 3 course fr £18, Starter £6.90-£12, Main £14-£28, Dessert £5.50-£12 **Wines** 21 bottles over £30, 15 bottles under £30, 12 by glass **Parking** On street **Notes** Fixed L 2 course menu before 7pm, Vegetarian available, Children welcome

The White Horse

European NEW

tel: 0117 329 4900 **24 High St, Westbury on Trym BS9 3DZ**
email: bookings@whitehorsebristol.co.uk
dir: *Phone for directions*

Revamped coaching inn with focus on food

This old coaching inn has been welcoming travellers and locals for a couple of hundred years, and continues to do so following a 21st-century makeover into a self-styled gastropub. The original charm of the place remains, while shades of grey and chunky wooden tables suit the mood of the times, and the bar is well stocked with real ales and artisan gins. The kitchen bakes its own bread and offers everything from populist burgers to roast hake with crab mash. Start with chicken liver and foie gras parfait with Muscat and apple jelly, and end on a creative note with baked figs with goats' cheese ice cream.

Chef Nigel Bisset **Seats** 40, Pr/dining room 12 **Times** 12-9.30, All-day dining **Prices** Fixed L 2 course fr £15, Starter £6-£10, Main £12-£23, Dessert £6-£9 **Wines** 10 bottles over £30, 18 bottles under £30, 12 by glass **Notes** Sunday L £12-£19, Vegetarian available, Children welcome

BUCKINGHAMSHIRE

AMERSHAM **Map 6 SU99**

The Artichoke

 *– see opposite*

The Crown

Modern British

tel: 01494 721541 **16 High St HP7 0DH**
email: reception@thecrownamersham.com **web:** www.thecrownamersham.com
dir: *M40 junct 2 onto A355, continue to Amersham. Onto Gore Hill, left into The Broadway*

Good eating in a modernised coaching inn

The 16th-century timber-framed coaching inn has brushed up nicely after a stylish makeover, and presents an eclectic rustic-chic look to its 21st-century visitors, mixing ancient period character with a clean-cut modern style. There are Tudor beams, inglenook fireplaces and sloping floors, offset by trendy fabrics and chunky bare wood tables. The unfussy cooking aims for big-hearted natural flavours, serving salmon rillettes as an opener with caviar crème fraîche and herb salad, or smoked chicken and ham terrine. Main course brings on seared trout with truffled pea purée and salsa verde, or duck breast and confit leg with ratatouille. Finish with warm chocolate and basil fondant.

Chef Kevin Hay **Seats** 24, Pr/dining room 36 **Times** 12-3/6-9.30 **Prices** Starter £5.50-£9.50, Main £17-£23, Dessert £5.95-£8.50 **Wines** 25 bottles over £30, 23 bottles under £30, 19 by glass **Parking** 35 **Notes** Afternoon tea, Healthy option menu, Sunday L, Vegetarian available, Children welcome

Gilbey's Restaurant

Modern British

tel: 01494 727242 **1 Market Square HP7 0DF**
email: oldamersham@gilbeygroup.com
dir: *M40 junct 2, A355 exit Beaconsfield/Amersham*

Imaginative modern cooking in a former school building

Low ceilings, wood flooring and cheerful art on sky-blue walls create an ambience of stylish, intimate rusticity at this former grammar school, while friendly staff contribute to the congenial atmosphere. The kitchen makes a virtue of simplicity, working an intelligent vein of appealing modern British ideas. Get going with duck liver parfait brûlée with kumquat compôte and cornichons and move on to fillet of stone bass imaginatively partnered by confit squid, risotto nero, charred leeks and saffron, or noisette and shoulder of lamb with aubergines, turnips and pressed new potatoes. To finish, lemon tart is served to good effect with orange sorbet and raspberries.

Chef Adam Whitlock **Seats** 50, Pr/dining room 12 **Times** 12-2.30/6-9.45, Closed 23-28 Dec, D Sun **Prices** Fixed L 2 course £17.50, Fixed D 3 course £22.50-£26.50, Starter £6.75-£13.95, Main £17.50-£29.75, Dessert £7.95-£12 **Wines** 23 bottles over £30, 16 bottles under £30, 8 by glass **Parking** On street & car park **Notes** Sunday L, Vegetarian available, Children welcome

The Artichoke

AMERSHAM Map 6 SU99

Modern European V 

tel: 01494 726611 **9 Market Square, Old Amersham HP7 0DF**
email: info@artichokerestaurant.co.uk
web: www.artichokerestaurant.co.uk
dir: *M40 junct 2. 1m from Amersham New Town*

Creative and technically impressive cooking with local flavour

Time was when the peaks of gastronomy used to be scaled only in grand hotel dining rooms and country houses. Today, they may just as easily crop up in a modest-looking building on a suburban square, albeit one with its gnarled and beamed roots in the Tudor period. Laurie and Jacqueline Gear have created one of the more exciting outposts of contemporary cuisine here, in no small measure deriving from a formative stint Laurie spent at René Redzepi's Noma in Copenhagen, one of the reference venues of Scandi modernism. The setting has an understated character, for all the depictions of artichokes in relief on the wall panels, the better to illuminate the senses by means of dynamically creative dishes. Individual components counterbalance each other cleverly in ideas such as smoked haddock with radishes and beetroot in horseradish cream, or the symmetrical alignment of roasted scallop and local ham with a pork and shellfish tarragon dressing. Each plate seems to teem with ingredients, as when roasted salsify turns up with golden enoki mushrooms, truffle gel, toasted hazelnut crumbs, sweet cicely and chervil emulsion. Different ethnic notes come and go, for example in a Thai-style coconut curry butter for the roast cod, or lightly spiced couscous for a winter roots dish with toasted pumpkin seeds on the veggie menu. Thoroughbred meats get their moment in the spotlight: Perthshire short rib; breast of locally-farmed duck; cheek, hock and belly of incomparable pork with Morteau sausage, pickled cabbage and apple caramel. Desserts maintain the pace for mandarin and rice pudding soufflé with brazil nut crumble and chocolate sorbet, or the reliably ambrosial Brillat-Savarin cheesecake with Poire Williams sorbet, chervil and granola. French and English artisan cheeses come with delicate hand-made crackers.

Chef Laurie Gear, Ben Jenkins **Seats** 48, Pr/dining room 16 **Times** 12-3/6.30-11, Closed 2 wks Xmas & Apr, 2 wks Aug/Sep, Sun-Mon **Prices** Fixed L 3 course £28, Fixed D 3 course £48, Tasting menu £38-£68, Starter £12.50-£14, Main £22.50-£25, Dessert £6.50-£8.50 **Wines** 246 bottles over £30, 5 bottles under £30, 13 by glass **Parking** On street, nearby car park **Notes** Tasting menu 7 course, L tasting menu 5 course £38, Children 8 yrs+ D

AYLESBURY Map 11 SP81

Hartwell House Hotel, Restaurant & Spa

Modern British NOTABLE WINE LIST

tel: 01296 747444 **Oxford Rd HP17 8NR**
email: info@hartwell-house.com **web:** www.hartwell-house.com
dir: *2m SW of Aylesbury on A418 (Oxford road)*

Ambitious country-house cooking in a rococo stately home

Within 90 acres of parkland in the Vale of Aylesbury, Hartwell House is a majestic property with enough pomp to have served as home to an exiled claimant to the French throne (Louis XVIII, no less). Seafood normally crops up among well-constructed starters – perhaps pan-fried fillet of red mullet with chorizo and cannellini bean cassoulet and creamed leeks. Everything looks good on the plate and flavours are nicely handled. Main-course slowly-braised ox cheek bourguignon with Savoy cabbage, winter vegetables, delmonico potatoes and braising juices, is a real seasonal warmer, while the estate's orchard and hives are behind apple mousse with honeycomb, apple jelly and cinnamon ice cream.

Chef Daniel Richardson **Seats** 56, Pr/dining room 36
Times 12.30-1.45/7.30-9.45, Closed L 31 Dec **Prices** Fixed L 2 course £25, Fixed D 3 course £36-£62 **Wines** 325 bottles over £30, 11 bottles under £30, 15 by glass **Parking** 50 **Notes** Sunday L £28-£36, Vegetarian available, Children 6 yrs+

BEACONSFIELD Map 6 SU99

Crazy Bear Beaconsfield

British, International

tel: 01494 673086 **75 Wycombe End, Old Town HP9 1LX**
email: enquiries@crazybear-beaconsfield.co.uk **web:** www.crazybeargroup.co.uk
dir: *M40 junct 2, 3rd exit from rdbt, next rdbt 1st exit. Over 2 mini-rdbts, on right*

Bright modern menus in flamboyant setting

The word 'restraint' was not in the designers' brief when they converted this 15th-century coaching inn into a flamboyant, English-themed restaurant (there's also a Thai option). It's a fun, high-energy place, with a menu that covers classics, chargrilled meats and some lively modern global ideas. The set-up has its own farm shop that supplies the black pudding and crispy Old Spot bacon to go with seared Lyme Bay scallops. Main course sees pan-fried sea bass fillet matched with Mediterranean vegetables, a soft-boiled quail's egg and black olive potatoes. Dessert gilds the lily somewhat, partnering a well-executed Madagascan vanilla crème brûlée with raspberry sorbet, jelly and shortbread.

Chef Martin Gallon **Seats** 75, Pr/dining room 22 **Times** 12-12, All-day dining **Prices** Prices not confirmed **Wines** 180 bottles over £30, 30 bottles under £30, 20 by glass **Parking** 20, On street **Notes** Sunday L, Vegetarian available, Children welcome

The Jolly Cricketers

Modern British

tel: 01494 676308 **24 Chalfont Rd, Seer Green HP9 2YG**
email: amanda@thejollycricketers.co.uk
dir: *M40 junct 2, take A355 N, at rdbt 1st exit onto A40, next rdbt 2nd exit onto A355, right into Longbottom Ln, left into School Ln & continue into Chalfont Rd*

Assured cooking in village pub with a cricketing theme

The Jolly Cricketers ticks all the boxes with its cosy, low-ceilinged bar, cricket-themed pictures, congenial atmosphere (four-legged friends are welcome too), range of real ales and a sensibly concise menu of crowd-pleasing modern dishes. Devilled Cornish crab with melba toast gets things off to a flying start, or you might go for rabbit and ham terrine with carrot and vanilla purée. A main course of Cornish hake baked with a lemon and parsley crust and served with potato gnocchi, chorizo and cucumber hits all the right notes, or perhaps pot-roasted rump of beef with carrots, pancetta and creamed potatoes. End with vanilla pannacotta with poached champagne rhubarb and rhubarb sorbet.

Chef Matt Lyons **Seats** 36, Pr/dining room 22 **Times** 12-2.30/6.30-9, Closed 25-26 Dec **Prices** Starter £6-£10.50, Main £14-£23.50, Dessert £6.50-£9.50 **Wines** 21 bottles over £30, 16 bottles under £30, 16 by glass **Parking** 10, On street **Notes** Sunday L, Vegetarian available, Children welcome

BRILL Map 11 SP61

The Pointer

Modern British

tel: 01844 238339 **27 Church St HP18 9RT**
email: info@thepointerbrill.co.uk **web:** www.thepointerbrill.co.uk
dir: *M40 junct 9, A41 Aylesbury, right onto B4011, left towards Brill, 20mtrs on left*

Prime local produce in a rustic-chic dining pub

Meat fans need look no further than this stylish pub and restaurant in a beautiful hilltop village. It's a tastefully renovated spot that's a long way removed from a pint-and-packet-of-crisps boozer, but nor is it a pretentious gastropub aimed at fat wallets. Diners walk past the action in the open kitchen on the way to the rustic-chic dining room, where the modern British line-up makes good use of the rare breed pigs and English Longhorn cattle that owner David Howden raises with a local farmer. For starters, Aylesbury duck liver parfait with red onion marmalade and warm brioche is a superlative version of an old favourite. Then main course might be faggots of local lamb with creamed potatoes, beetroot, hispi cabbage and rich lamby gravy. If you're up for a fishy alternative, wild Cornish black bream is timed just so, and accompanied by home-made pasta with sea herbs and vegetables, wild garlic and hazelnut pesto. For pudding, there's a vibrant Sicilian lemon posset with ruby grapefruit and mint ice cream, or good old treacle tart with buttermilk sorbet. If you're impressed by the meat you've just eaten, the butcher's shop next door will sort you out with supplies to take home.

Chef Mini Patel **Seats** 30 **Times** 12-2.30/6.30-9, Closed 1 wk Jan, Mon, D Sun **Prices** Fixed L 2 course £15, Starter £6-£12, Main £15-£30, Dessert £6-£12 **Wines** 61 bottles over £30, 18 bottles under £30, 13 by glass **Parking** 5 **Notes** Sunday L £18-£30, Vegetarian available, Children welcome

BUCKINGHAM Map 11 SP63

Buckingham Villiers Hotel

Modern British

tel: 01280 822444 **3 Castle St MK18 1BS**
email: reservations@villiershotels.com **web:** www.villiers-hotel.co.uk
dir: *M1 junct 13 N or junct 15 S follow signs to Buckingham. Castle St by Old Town Hall*

Straightforward brasserie cooking in the medieval quarter

The Villiers has a smartly kitted-out restaurant overlooking a courtyard and the kitchen concentrates on tried-and-tested dishes. Thus, pan-fried fillet of sea bass with potato purée and garden greens might be an alternative main course to pan-fried calves' liver with bubble-and-squeak, pancetta and mustard sauce. More innovative dishes are just as well handled, seen in a gently flavoured starter of mushroom, leek and spinach risotto with goats' cheese mousse and mushroom velouté, followed by slow-cooked breast of lamb with piperade, goats' curd, aubergine, polenta and pine nuts, all components adding up to a satisfying whole. End with one of the enjoyable puddings, such as pistachio baked Alaska with candied pistachios.

Chef Paul Stopps **Seats** 70, Pr/dining room 150 **Times** 12-2.30/6-9.30 **Prices** Fixed L 2 course £14-£18, Fixed D 3 course £23-£26, Starter £4.95-£7.50, Main £10.50-£20.95, Dessert £6.75-£7.95 **Wines** 17 bottles over £30, 32 bottles under £30, 13 by glass **Parking** 52 **Notes** Sunday L £18-£25, Vegetarian available, Children welcome

BURNHAM Map 6 SU98

Burnham Beeches Hotel

Modern British, European

tel: 01628 429955 **Grove Rd SL1 8DP**
email: burnhambeeches@corushotels.com **web:** www.corushotels.com
dir: *Off A355, via Farnham Royal rdbt*

Classically minded cooking in an early Georgian hotel

Close to Windsor, Burnham Beeches Hotel is an extended Georgian manor house set in 10 acres of attractive grounds and a popular choice as a wedding venue. Comprising two interconnecting rooms, the oak-panelled Gray's restaurant is a formal affair with white linen and views of the pretty garden. The gently contemporary dishes are based on classical themes and techniques. Start with pan-fried scallops, leek purée and herb oil before moving on to roasted duck breast, cavolo nero and pumpkin. Finish, if you're in the mood for dessert, with a perfectly caramelised apple tarte Tatin paired with apple and cinnamon sorbet.

Chef Rafal Wysocki **Seats** 70, Pr/dining room 120 **Times** 12-2/7-9.30 **Prices** Prices not confirmed **Wines** 28 bottles over £30, 17 bottles under £30, 9 by glass **Parking** 150 **Notes** Sunday L, Vegetarian available, Children welcome

CUBLINGTON Map 11 SP82

The Unicorn

Modern, Traditional British

tel: 01296 681261 **12 High St LU7 0LQ**
email: theunicornpub@btconnect.com **web:** www.theunicornpub.co.uk
dir: *2m N of A418 (between Aylesbury & Leighton Buzzard). In village centre*

The kind of pub every village should have

This 17th-century inn serves the local community. It has a shop, opens for coffee mornings and afternoon teas on Friday and Saturday and serves bar snacks all day. Interesting ways with seafood can be seen in crab cakes with mango salsa, pea shoots and beurre blanc, then pan-fried sea trout with ratatouille and saffron confit potatoes. Meat is deftly handled too: pheasant sausage with apricot and fig compôte and hazelnut emulsion, for example, followed by a duo of lamb (confit shoulder and rack) with fondant potato and pea and carrot purée. Don't pass on puddings such as chocolate marquise with caramelised oranges or plum frangipane tart with clotted cream.

Chef Christopher George **Seats** 60, Pr/dining room 30 **Times** 12-2.30/6.30-9, Closed D Sun **Prices** Fixed L 2 course £13.95-£18.95, Fixed D 3 course £16.95-£21.95, Starter £5-£7.50, Main £10.75-£24.50, Dessert £5-£8.50 **Wines** 3 bottles over £30, 25 bottles under £30, 10 by glass **Parking** 20 **Notes** Breakfast Sat, Sunday L £14.95-£21.95, Vegetarian available, Children welcome

GERRARDS CROSS Map 6 TQ08

The Bull Hotel

Modern British

tel: 01753 885995 **Oxford Rd SL9 7PA**
email: bull@sarova.co.uk **web:** www.sarova.com
dir: *M40 junct 2 follow Beaconsfield on A355. After 0.5m 2nd exit at rdbt signed A40 Gerrards Cross for 2m. The Bull on right*

Classy hotel restaurant on the high street

The old Bull started life in 1688, serving travellers on the road between London and Oxford, and is now a swish four-star hotel. Its Beeches restaurant has a smart contemporary look and a Mediterranean-accented menu. Consider ham hock terrine with home-made piccalilli, griddled sourdough bread and beetroot pearls to start. Follow with cod loin with Swiss chard, parsley purée, sautéed parsley root, beetroot carpaccio and chorizo crisp, or pork fillet and braised belly with black pudding, apple purée and red wine sauce. Puddings can be as true Brit as Cox's apple tart with rhubarb crumble ice cream and toffee apple, or as Gallic as chocolate fondant with Chantilly cream.

Chef Rao Matta **Seats** 110, Pr/dining room 150
Times 12.30-2.30/6.30-9.30, Closed L Sat, D Sun **Prices** Prices not confirmed
Wines 19 bottles over £30, 17 bottles under £30, 22 by glass **Parking** 100 **Notes** Live jazz Sun L 12.30-2.30, Vegetarian available, Children welcome

GREAT MISSENDEN Map 6 SP80

Nags Head Inn & Restaurant

British, French

tel: 01494 862200 & 862945 **London Rd HP16 0DG**
email: goodfood@nagsheadbucks.com **web:** www.nagsheadbucks.com
dir: *N from Amersham on A413 signed Great Missenden, left at Chiltern Hospital onto London Rd (1m S of Great Missenden)*

Charming pub with ambitious Anglo-French cooking

Dating from the 15th century, the Nags Head is now a stylishly modernised gastropub. Contemporary Anglo-French cuisine is the attraction, with the kitchen adding its own endlessly inventive – and totally persuasive – touches to dishes. Starters have taken in shrimp eggs Benedict on pea polenta, and duck liver parfait with pear chutney. Ever successful main courses follow a similar route, among them breast of guinea fowl with courgette and pepper purée and grape and brandy jus, and halibut meunière with smoked swordfish shavings and beetroot and pea beurre blanc. To end, pannacotta ice cream adds a diverting accompaniment to apple and rhubarb tart.

Chef Claude Paillet, Tom Bell **Seats** 60 **Times** 12-2.30/6.30-9.30, Closed 25 Dec **Prices** Fixed L 2 course £16.50, Fixed D 3 course £22, Starter £5.95-£13.95, Main £13.95-£24.95, Dessert £5.95-£7.45 **Wines** 95 bottles over £30, 31 bottles under £30, 19 by glass **Parking** 35 **Notes** Sunday L £14.95-£16.95, Vegetarian available, Children welcome

LONG CRENDON Map 5 SP60

The Angel Restaurant

Modern European, Mediterranean V NOTABLE WINE LIST

tel: 01844 208268 **47 Bicester Rd HP18 9EE**
email: info@angelrestaurant.co.uk
dir: *M40 junct 7, beside B4011, 2m NW of Thame*

Confident cooking in 16th-century coaching inn

A one-time coaching inn dating from the 16th century, the Angel retains plenty of period charm, though it's more restaurant with rooms than country pub these days. There's a cosy bar for a pre-dinner drink, dining areas filled with original features, and a smart conservatory. The cooking is modern European, with Asian influences sometimes to the fore. Daily specials appear on a blackboard and fish is a favoured offering. Begin with Thai-spiced tiger prawn risotto with parmesan and chilli crackling, before moving on to roast lamb chump on cassoulet in redcurrant and rosemary jus. Desserts bring on banana parfait with caramelised banana and chocolate sauce.

Chef Trevor Bosch **Seats** 75, Pr/dining room 14 **Times** 12-2.30/7-9.30, Closed 25 Dec, D Sun **Prices** Prices not confirmed **Wines** 60 bottles over £30, 40 bottles under £30, 12 by glass **Parking** 30 **Notes** Sunday L, Children welcome

MARLOW Map 5 SU88

The Coach

British, French

tel: 01628 483013 **3 West St SL7 2LS**
web: www.thecoachmarlow.co.uk
dir: *Phone for directions*

Big-hearted cooking in Tom Kerridge's second pub

Truly, Marlow is blessed. This younger sibling of the nearby Hand & Flowers is a timbered pub in the English period style with a hot-shot chef producing reference food for the 21st century. The surroundings banish all thought of ceremonious formality with embossed tiled walls, comfortable leather seating and a properly pubby ambience. There's no booking, so pitch up and take your chances, and you will be rewarded with beautifully-realised cooking from the modern demotic repertoire. The menu is constructed as an enticing jumble of meat and (more or less) non-meat options, with small and large plates jostled in together. Chicken Kiev and cauliflower cheese piles two of our favourite things on to one plate, while unexpected spins on bistro classics produce a version of chilli made with venison, chocolate, red wine and toasted rice cream. A rotisserie spins out anything from whole stuffed quail to vegetable sides like celeriac with honey-mustard glaze and veggie main dishes such as beetroot with feta, apple and horseradish. At the end, there are space-filling homely puddings – banana custard with dates and honeycomb, or rhubarb crumble and ginger ice cream. The cheese option could well be Lincolnshire Poacher served with crackers and grapes.

Chef Nick Beardshaw, Tom Kerridge **Seats** 40 **Times** 12-2.30/6-10.30, Closed 25 Dec **Prices** Starter £5-£12.50, Main £5.50-£12.50, Dessert £6.50 **Wines** 14 bottles over £30, 6 bottles under £30, 20 by glass **Notes** Breakfast, Sunday L, Vegetarian available, Children welcome

Danesfield House Hotel & Spa

Modern British NOTABLE WINE LIST

tel: 01628 891010 **Henley Rd SL7 2EY**
email: reservations@danesfieldhouse.co.uk **web:** www.danesfieldhouse.co.uk
dir: *M4 junct 4/A404 to Marlow. Follow signs to Medmenham and Henley. Hotel is 3m outside Marlow*

Classy, classical dining in a majestic house

Danesfield House is nothing short of magnificent: a 1901 white mansion with a castellated roof in beautifully-maintained grounds. The cooking comes out of the contemporary British mould. The odd luxury appears – lobster linguine with shellfish cream, say – but the kitchen generally takes a down-to-earth approach. Potted shrimps, game terrine and scallops with sauce vièrge might be followed by cod fillet with spicy lentils, fondant potato and meat jus, or, in season, pheasant breast saltimbocca with green beans, chestnut mash and sage jus. Pastry is clearly made by an expert, so focus on a tart for dessert: pear frangipane with matching purée, say, or lemon with blackberry sorbet.

Chef Billy Reid **Seats** 84, Pr/dining room 14 **Times** 12-2.30/6.30-9.30 **Prices** Fixed L 2 course £30, Starter £9.50-£17.50, Main £12.50-£30, Dessert £8.50-£13 **Wines** 235 bottles over £30, 15 bottles under £30, 30 by glass **Parking** 100 **Notes** Sunday L £30-£35, Vegetarian available, Children welcome

Glaze Restaurant

Modern British NEW

tel: 01628 496800 **Crowne Plaza Marlow, Field House Ln SL7 1GJ**
email: enquiries@cpmarlow.co.uk **web:** www.cpmarlow.co.uk
dir: *A404 exit to Marlow, left at mini rdbt, left into Fieldhouse Lane*

Classic and creative dining with lake views

The main restaurant in the swanky modern Crowne Plaza Marlow is an appropriately contemporary brasserie-style number in a large open-plan space with views over the lake. A vast wall of floor-to-ceiling glass opens onto the terrace. Kick off with simple feel-good stuff like asparagus with a runny egg and béarnaise sauce, or scallops with cauliflower purée and black pudding dressing, before the comfort of beer-battered cod with ace hand-cut chips. This kitchen can also turn its hand to 'signature dishes' such as pressed pork belly with sour apple foam, while the grill offers up steaks with a choice of sauces. Finish with chocolate brownie with pistachio ice cream.

Chef Stuart Hine **Seats** 150 **Times** 6.30-11 **Prices** Prices not confirmed **Wines** 15 bottles over £30, 19 bottles under £30, 21 by glass **Parking** 300 **Notes** Vegetarian available, Children welcome

The Hand & Flowers

 – *see below*

The Hand & Flowers

MARLOW **Map 5 SU88**

British, French
tel: 01628 482277 **126 West St SL7 2BP**
email: contact@thehandandflowers.co.uk
dir: *M40 junct 4/M4 junct 8/9 follow A404 to Marlow*

Big flavours in an outstanding gastro inn

For the past decade or so, the pub has been turning out food that has garnered praise, headlines and a host of awards, and ever since his triumph on the BBC's Great British Menu in 2010, Tom Kerridge has been a regular presence on TV, in print and in a slew of cookbooks. Kerridge honed his craft in some of the premier kitchens of the London dining scene before striking out on his own, and here he offers the culmination of that experience. There's a satisfying lack of pretension all round and, given the outstanding food on offer, the place is uncannily relaxed and friendly. Look a little closer and you'll notice the attention to detail that has gone into making it look so humble - interesting artworks, precise table settings and the professionalism underlying the cheerfulness of the service team. The kitchen produces dishes that are by turns straightforward and sophisticated. The lack of a pretentious tasting menu shows the direct and straight-talking nature of the place, with the à la carte menu supported by an amazingly good value no-choice set lunch option. Take a starter of salt-baked swede and haggis tart, for example, which comes with crispy lamb, 'Chantilly de chèvre' and raw mushroom, or another starter that partners pavé and parfait of salmon with black apple jelly, confit lemon, Avruga caviar and garlic bread. Among main courses, loin of venison with boudin noir purée, root vegetables, ragout pie and cow puff delivers powerful and complex layers of flavour, while the fish of the day could be matched with a crab pancake, bouillabaisse sauce and calcot onions. Finish with an exemplary vanilla crème brûlée or a banana soufflé with coffee syrup and caramelised walnut ice cream. In keeping with pub tradition, there's a Sunday lunch menu, which may prove to be the best you've ever had.

Chef Tom Kerridge **Seats** 54 **Times** 12-2.45/6.30-9.45, Closed 24-26 Dec, D Sun, 1 Jan **Prices** Fixed L 2 course £15, Starter £9.50-£16.50, Main £27-£38.50, Dessert £9.50-£12.50 **Wines** 107 bottles over £30, 16 bottles under £30, 17 by glass **Parking** 20 **Notes** Sunday L £28.50, Vegetarian available, Children welcome

MARLOW *continued*

The Riverside Restaurant

Modern British

tel: 01628 484444 **Macdonald Compleat Angler, Marlow Bridge SL7 1RG**
email: compleatangler@macdonald-hotels.co.uk
web: www.macdonaldhotels.co.uk/compleatangler
dir: *M4 junct 8/9 or M40 junct 4. A404 to rdbt, take Bisham exit, 1m to Marlow Bridge, hotel on right*

Bright, modern cooking by the river

The elegantly formal Riverside Restaurant serves up a magnificent view of the Thames, Marlow bridge and the church opposite from its conservatory dining room, while the service team, slick and professional, ensure there's nothing to detract from the occasion, be it a summer lunch or wintertime dinner. Tables on the outdoor terrace are a treat in warm weather, with candles adding to the special atmosphere in the evening. The kitchen's output draws on contemporary ideas without pushing the envelope too much, and high quality seasonal ingredients are the bedrock of the menu. 'Small plates' might include an impressive ham hock and foie gras terrine, with pea mousse and raisin purée, and scorched fillet of mackerel partnered with potato salad, truffle mayo and apple caramel. Among 'large plates', breast of duck is served with cider raisins and quince, sea trout keeps company with brown butter jus, and marinated rump steak comes with wild mushroom gratin and classic dauphinoise. To finish, brioche treacle slice is an indulgent treat, served with blackcurrant clotted cream ice cream, or go for a straight-up crème brûlée. Fit in some cheese from the passing trolley if you've room. The attention to detail extends to excellent home-made breads and creative amuse-bouche.

Chef Michael Lloyd **Seats** 90, Pr/dining room 100 **Times** 12-2.30/7-9.30 **Prices** Fixed L 2 course fr £18.50, Tasting menu £60, Starter £6-£17, Main £12-£26, Dessert £5-£13 **Wines** 78 bottles over £30, 18 bottles under £30, 25 by glass **Parking** 100 **Notes** Vegetarian available, Children welcome

Sindhu by Atul Kochhar

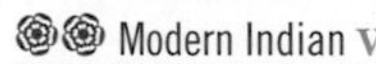
Modern Indian V

tel: 01628 405405 **Macdonald Compleat Angler, Marlow Bridge SL7 1RG**
email: info@sindhurestaurant.co.uk **web:** www.sindhurestaurant.co.uk
dir: *M4 junct 8/9 or M40 junct 4. A404 to rdbt, take Bisham exit, 1m to Marlow Bridge, hotel on right*

Indian cuisine with traditional roots and contemporary variations

This is Macdonald Hotels' second restaurant within its Compleat Angler on the River Thames by Marlow Weir. Atul is an acclaimed chef, renowned for his modern Indian cuisine and passion for sustainable fishing. To start, try karara kekda, a crisp soft-shelled crab with spiced squid and passionfruit chilli chutney. Highly recommended too is erachi Chettinad, tandoor-grilled rack of lamb with vegetable polenta and spices from Tamil Nadu. Equally desirable are murgh makhani, which is tandoor-smoked chicken with creamy tomato and fenugreek sauce, and pan-roasted stone bass with coconut meen moilee sauce and fork-crushed potato with mustard seeds. Desserts work well and bhapi doi, a rose yogurt cheesecake, is no exception.

Chef Gopal Krishnan **Seats** 58 **Times** 12-3/6-11 **Prices** Prices not confirmed **Wines** 40 bottles over £30, 20+ bottles under £30, 10 by glass **Parking** 100 **Notes** Sunday L, Children welcome

The Vanilla Pod

British, French V NOTABLE WINE LIST

tel: 01628 898101 **31 West St SL7 2LS**
email: contact@thevanillapod.co.uk
dir: *From M4 junct 8/9 or M40 junct 4 take A404, A4155 to Marlow. From Henley take A4155*

Intelligently constructed dishes in TS Eliot's old home

The culinary bar is set high in this stretch of the Thames Valley stockbroker belt, and The Vanilla Pod delivers a sure-footed take on modern British cooking, its roots clearly in the French classics. The setting is a handsome townhouse where TS Eliot once lived, thoroughly refurbished with a chic contemporary look in brown and cream. First out might be gin-cured salmon with pickled fennel, or butternut squash risotto. The kitchen then extracts clear, robust flavours from top-class ingredients in main courses such as lamb rump with orange and saffron cabbage, and puddings could take in coffee and orange pannacotta, or classic tarte Tatin.

Chef Michael Macdonald **Seats** 28, Pr/dining room 8 **Times** 12-2/7-10, Closed 24 Dec-3 Jan, Sun-Mon **Prices** Prices not confirmed **Wines** 80 bottles over £30, 12 bottles under £30, 10 by glass **Parking** West St car park **Notes** ALC 3 course £45, Tasting menu 8 course, Children welcome

MILTON KEYNES **Map 11 SP83**

Mercure Milton Keynes Parkside Hotel

Modern British NEW

tel: 01908 661919 **Newport Rd, Woughton on the Green MK6 3LR**
email: h6627-gm@accor.com **web:** www.mercure.com
dir: *M1 junct 14, A509 towards Milton Keynes. 2nd exit on H6 follow signs to Woughton on the Green*

Modernised traditional dishes in a sylish hotel

In the tranquil rural location of the Ouzel Valley Park, the Grade II listed white building has been made over in a slick boutique style. Simply laid, unclothed tables and a wall papered as a trompe l'oeil library set the tone in the restaurant, where the kitchen delivers confidently rendered favourites with a modern spin. One visually-attractive starter is cured salmon with fennel, orange, rye crisps and dill crème fraîche, all elements complementing each other. Excellently timed corn-fed chicken is an impressive main course, served with gnocchi, peas and chicken jus, and to finish there might be burnt cream with mixed berries.

Chef Harvey Lockwood **Seats** 46, Pr/dining room 100 **Times** 12-3/6.30-9.30, Closed D Sun **Prices** Fixed L 2 course £9.50, Fixed D 3 course £25, Tasting menu £55, Starter £7.50-£8.50, Main £15.50-£24, Dessert £6.50-£11.95 **Wines** 9 bottles over £30, 6 bottles under £30, 11 by glass **Parking** 70 **Notes** Sunday L, Vegetarian available, Children welcome

STOKE POGES **Map 6 SU98**

Humphry's at Stoke Park

– see opposite

Humphry's at Stoke Park

STOKE POGES **Map 6 SU98**

Modern British

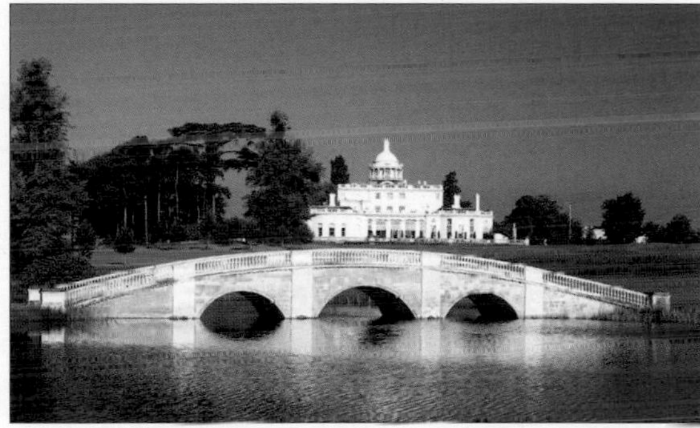

tel: 01753 717171 & 717172 **Park Rd SL2 4PG**
email: info@stokepark.com **web:** www.humphrysrestaurant.co.uk
dir: *M4 junct 6 or M40 junct 2, take A355 towards Slough, then B416. Stoke Park in 1.25m on right*

Innovative contemporary country-club cuisine

Stoke Park is a splendid white mansion with a dome and columns in 300 acres of parkland, lakes and gardens laid out by 'Capability' Brown and reworked by Humphry Repton. It's an estate of many parts, with a championship golf course, no fewer than 13 tennis courts (tournaments are held here), spa and leisure facilities, a gym and indoor pool. It has also served as the location for a number of films and pop concerts. The interior has original architectural features, oil paintings and all the swanky trappings expected in a luxury hotel. The cream of the three eating options is Humphry's, named after the landscape gardener who designed the bridge over the lake it overlooks. It is a magnificent room, with a marble fireplace, floor-to-ceiling windows, a corniced ceiling and a decor of golds and yellows. In charge of the kitchen is Chris Wheeler, a switched-on, innovative chef working around a tranche of contemporary ideas based on a foundation of pedigree ingredients. It's no surprise to find luxury items on the menus, among them lobster and beef tournedos, but the style is far from dyed in the wool, with plenty of exciting options. Among starters, crab goes into a tian with avocado and has accompaniments of cucumber jelly, a soft-boiled quail's egg and grapefruit salsa. Roast pheasant consommé is partnered by braised leg tortellini. Main courses illustrate the same attention to detail in such labour-intensive dishes as pan-fried halibut fillet with girolles, samphire, cracked pepper linguine and a langoustine bisque foam, and roast breast of duck with a cylinder of leg meat, textures of beetroot, a potato croquette and spicy jus. Puddings keep pace with the rest of the output, among them perhaps apricot soufflé with almond and Amaretto ice cream and apricot sauce.

Chef Chris Wheeler **Seats** 50, Pr/dining room 146
Times 12.30-2.30/7-10, Closed 24-26 Dec, 1st wk Jan, Mon-Tue, L Wed-Thu **Prices** Fixed L 2 course £25, Fixed D 3 course £68, Tasting menu £85-£130 **Wines** 90 bottles over £30, 4 bottles under £30, 12 by glass **Parking** 400 **Notes** ALC L only, Tasting menu 5/7 course also avail with wine, Sunday L £35, Vegetarian available, Children 12 yrs+ L

TAPLOW Map 6 SU98

André Garrett at Cliveden

 Modern British, French V 

tel: 01628 668561 **Cliveden Estate SL6 0JF**
email: info@clivedenhouse.co.uk **web:** www.clivedenhouse.co.uk
dir: *M4 junct 7, A4 towards Maidenhead, 1.5m, onto B476 towards Taplow, 2.5m, hotel on left*

Stunning dishes in a stately home

If you've left the city behind for a splendid day out, feel free to potter around the 376 acres surrounding the house. You won't get that in Shoreditch. Cliveden has been welcoming clientele since one of the Dukes of Buckingham had it built the year London burned down. The swagged and chandeliered dining room enjoys imperious views of the grounds, and makes a backdrop that would leave lesser chefs than André Garrett quailing, yet the cooking dazzles with creative opulence in the contemporary French style. There's more than a hint of bravado in pairing English rose veal and oyster in a tartare dabbed with Exmoor caviar, garnished with nasturtium blooms and sourdough melba toast. And there's real swagger in main courses such as roasted Red-legged partridge with salsify and walnut crumble in Muscat, or the sea-fresh turbot grenobloise with cockles, braised celery hearts and brioche butter. A tasting menu will be irresistible for the highest rollers, and desserts fully measure up to the foregoing with the likes of rice pudding soufflé, Seville orange marmalade and a scoop of ice cream made with 12-year-old Balvenie single malt.

Chef André Garrett **Seats** 78, Pr/dining room 60 **Times** 12.15-2.30/7-9.45 **Prices** Fixed L 3 course fr £33, Fixed D 3 course fr £72.50, Tasting menu fr £97.50 **Wines** 575 bottles over £30, 8 bottles under £30, 10 by glass **Parking** 60 **Notes** Tasting menu L £85, Sunday L, Children welcome

WADDESDON Map 11 SP71

The Five Arrows

 Modern British

tel: 01296 651727 **High St HP18 0JE**
email: reservations@thefivearrows.co.uk **web:** www.waddesdon.org.uk
dir: *On A41 in Waddesdon. Into Baker St for car park*

Contemporary dining on the Rothschild estate

Part of the Rothschild estate, this small Victorian hotel stands at the gates of Waddesdon Manor but has none of the airs and graces of the grand French château-style stately home. The relaxed restaurant sports a smart, contemporary look with wine-related prints on the walls. The repertoire displays a seasonal focus that delivers bright contemporary ideas, starting with bouillabaisse soup, roasted red peppers, fennel and saffron. Next up, pan-fried cannon of lamb and slow-cooked shoulder is paired with fregola, tapenade, baby gem, broad beans and rosemary jus. For pudding, there's caramelised lemon tart and raspberry sorbet.

Chef Karl Penny **Seats** 60, Pr/dining room 30 **Times** 12-2.15/6.30-9.15, Closed D 25-26 Dec, 1 Jan **Prices** Fixed L 2 course fr £15.50, Fixed D 3 course £32-£48, Starter £6.95-£7.95, Main £11.50-£24.95, Dessert £6.95-£8.50 **Wines** 56 bottles over £30, 41 bottles under £30, 18 by glass **Parking** 30, On street **Notes** Sunday L, Vegetarian available, Children welcome

WOOBURN COMMON Map 6 SU98

Chequers Inn

@@ British, French

tel: 01628 529575 **Kiln Ln, Wooburn HP10 0JQ**
email: info@chequers-inn.com **web:** www.chequers-inn.com
dir: *M40 junct 2, A40 through Beaconsfield Old Town towards High Wycombe. 2m from town left into Broad Ln. Inn 2.5m on left*

French-influenced modern cooking in an old coaching inn

A former 17th-century coaching inn, there's no denying that the Chequers has moved with the times. The Anglo-French cooking in its newly extended chic restaurant delivers compelling flavour combinations. A starter of cured mackerel, for example, is partnered with horseradish pannacotta and apple, radish and orange vinaigrette. A main course dish of lamb – saddle and crispy belly – arrives with pea relish, goats' cheese mash and mint jus, while a fishy main might be plaice with chargrilled baby gem, ricotta gnocchi, pickled black grapes and curry cream sauce. Desserts are no less creative: try blueberry cheesecake with confit lemon and crème fraîche sorbet.

Chef Pascal Lemoine **Seats** 60, Pr/dining room 60 **Times** 12-2.30/7-9.30, Closed D Sun, 25 Dec, 1 Jan **Prices** Starter £4.95-£9.95, Main £8.95-£26.95, Dessert £6.45 **Wines** 11 bottles over £30, 27 bottles under £30, 11 by glass **Parking** 50 **Notes** Afternoon tea £12.95, Sunday L, Vegetarian available, Children welcome

CAMBRIDGESHIRE

BALSHAM Map 12 TL55

The Black Bull Inn

@ Modern British

tel: 01223 893844 **27 High St CB21 4DJ**
email: info@blackbull-balsham.co.uk **web:** www.blackbull-balsham.co.uk
dir: *From S: M11 junct 9, A11 towards Newmarket, follow Balsham signs. From N: M11 junct 10, A505 signed Newmarket (A11), onto A11, follow Balsham signs*

Thatched country pub with creative team in the kitchen

Topped by a mop of thatch and with a fabulous garden and terrace, Balsham's village hostelry has its own-brewed real ale on tap and a choice of eating spaces from the tucked-away nooks around the bar to a barn with a lofty vaulted ceiling and chunky solid oak tables. Start, perhaps, with pan-fried pigeon breast with beetroot, lardons, pine nuts and balsamic-dressed rocket. Move on to braised lamb shank with Parmentier potatoes, pearl barley, root vegetables and mint jus, or pancetta-wrapped monkfish tail with curried clam cream and vanilla mashed potato. Finish with an inventive clementine and star anise tarte Tatin with pomegranate seeds and crème anglaise.

Chef Andrew Price **Seats** 60, Pr/dining room 60 **Times** 12-2/6.30-9 **Prices** Starter £5-£10, Main £10-£30, Dessert £5-£10 **Wines** 16 bottles over £30, 38 bottles under £30, 22 by glass **Parking** 20 **Notes** Tasting menu, Pudding Club, Sunday L £5-£35, Vegetarian available, Children welcome

CAMBRIDGE Map 12 TL45

Best Western Plus Cambridge Quy Mill Hotel

Modern European, British, French

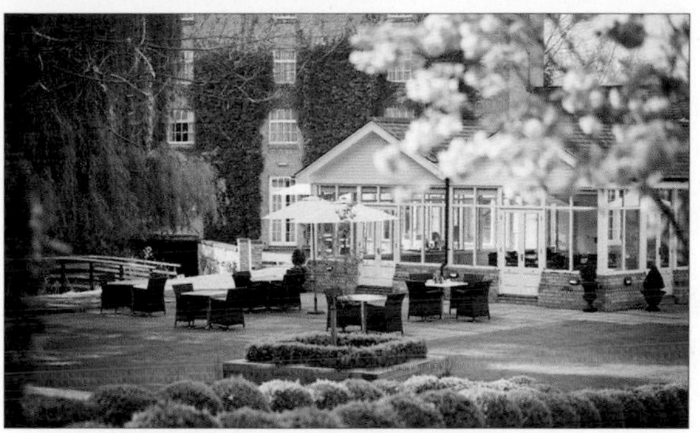

tel: 01223 293383 **Church Rd, Stow-Cum-Quy CB25 9AF**
email: info@cambridgequymill.co.uk **web:** www.cambridgequymill.co.uk
dir: *Exit A14 at junct 35, E of Cambridge, onto B1102 for 50yds. Entrance opposite church*

Confident cooking in a former watermill

Situated in the miller's house, and overlooking the waterwheel and mill race, the refurbished Mill House restaurant makes the most of this feature, while putting on a distinctly contemporary country inn look. By night it's an intimate place with open fires and candlelight, cool jazz floating in the background. The menu keeps an eye on the seasons, uniting roast venison with parsnip ketchup, apple and hazelnuts, while butter-poached pheasant breast might arrive with its slow-cooked leg, pumpkin, granola and pickled pear. Fishy ideas run to roasted halibut with baby gem, salt-baked shallots, wild mushrooms and bacon, and for dessert, perhaps plum, vanilla and almond tart with plum ripple ice cream.

Chef Gavin Murphy **Seats** 48, Pr/dining room 80 **Times** 12-2.30/7-9.45, Closed 25 Dec, L Mon-Fri **Prices** Fixed L 2 course £15, Starter £7.50-£12, Main £16-£30, Dessert £7.50-£12 **Wines** 11 bottles over £30, 24 bottles under £30, 14 by glass **Parking** 90 **Notes** Complimentary bread & amuse-bouche with all ALC, Brunch, Sunday L £15-£25, Vegetarian available, Children welcome

The Carpenters Arms

Modern British

tel: 01223 367050 **182-186 Victoria Rd CB4 3DZ**
email: hello@carpentersarmscambridge.co.uk **web:** www.carpentersarmscambridge.co.uk
dir: *Please phone for directions*

Refined modern dishes and pizza variations for all the family

The team behind the Carpenters makeover have maintained the pubby feel of the place, kept its heart and soul intact, and created a family-friendly place that serves the community. There's a small courtyard garden and a wood-fired oven installed to turn out the people's favourite, pizza. The menu offers some classic dishes, often with a twist or two (venison burger, for example), and some refinement in the execution. A starter of treacle-cured salmon with roast beetroot and balsamic glaze could be followed by a main course like confit duck leg on tomato and bean cassoulet with celeriac mash. Look to the specials board for dessert temptations.

Chef Marco Coelho **Seats** 40, Pr/dining room 25 **Times** 12-2.30/6-10 **Prices** Starter £4-£8, Main £9-£18, Dessert £5-£7 **Parking** 10 **Notes** Brunch Sat & Sun, Sunday L £11-£15, Vegetarian available, Children welcome

Hotel du Vin Cambridge

French Bistro

tel: 01223 227330 **15-19 Trumpington St CB2 1QA**
email: info.cambridge@hotelduvin.com **web:** www.hotelduvin.com
dir: *M11 junct 11 Cambridge S, pass Trumpington Park & Ride on left. Hotel 2m on right after double rdbt*

Classic bistro dining in the city centre

Hotel du Vin's Cambridge outpost is all reclaimed wooden floors, banquettes, unclothed wooden tables, candlelight, an open-to-view kitchen and references to wine all around. The place is normally humming, and well-drilled staff deliver authentic, well-executed bistro staples. Steak tartare, prawn cocktail, chicken liver parfait and scallops with sauce vierge – the list goes on – before main courses of roast chicken with pommes frites, moules frites or a steak from the grill: perhaps rib-eye or fillet. Good-quality rustic bread, served with unsalted butter, is part of the package, puddings run to rich chocolate mousse with Chantilly cream, or tarte au citron, and the wine list is outstanding.

Hotel Felix

Modern British, Mediterranean

tel: 01223 277977 **Whitehouse Ln, Huntingdon Rd CB3 0LX**
email: help@hotelfelix.co.uk **web:** www.hotelfelix.co.uk
dir: *M11 junct 13. From A1 N take A14 then A1307. At City of Cambridge sign turn left into Whitehouse Ln*

Inventive modern cooking in an elegant boutique hotel

Combining elegant period features with the contemporary, this Victorian mansion is now home to a sleek boutique hotel. The Graffiti restaurant sports abstract modern art, burnished darkwood floors, and unclothed tables, while the large terrace is a crowd puller for fair weather dining. The food is as vibrant as the decor, mixing modern British with plenty of sunny Mediterranean flavours. A meal might start with pan-fried scallops, truffle mash, pea velouté and pancetta before moving on to crispy pork belly, garlic crushed Jersey Royals, chargrilled baby gem and honey mustard sauce. Finish with chocolate and mixed berry iced parfait.

Chef Marcela Morales **Seats** 45, Pr/dining room 60 **Times** 12-2/6.30-10 **Prices** Fixed L 2 course £16.50, Starter £5.95-£8.25, Main £14.50-£21.95, Dessert £5.75-£9.75 **Wines** 35 bottles over £30, 21 bottles under £30, 29 by glass **Parking** 90 **Notes** Afternoon tea, Sunday L £22.50, Vegetarian available, Children welcome

Midsummer House

– *see page 60 and advert on page 61*

Midsummer House

CAMBRIDGE **Map 12 TL45**

Modern British V NOTABLE WINE LIST

tel: 01223 369299 **Midsummer Common CB4 1HA**
email: reservations@midsummerhouse.co.uk
web: www.midsummerhouse.co.uk
dir: *Park in Pretoria Rd, then walk across footbridge. Restaurant on left*

Stellar cooking from a chef at the top of his game

The Victorian villa on the edge of Midsummer Common, with cattle grazing on the lush green grass, and the River Cam flowing by, is certainly an idyllic tableau. It's been run since 1998 by chef Daniel Clifford, whose unwavering energy and enthusiasm has put Midsummer House well and truly on the gastronomic map. A good deal of TV exposure has certainly helped (Clifford was a winner in the BBC's *Great British Menu* in 2012 and 2013) and the restaurant is now unequivocally recognised as one of the country's A-list addresses. It is an exceedingly civilised series of spaces done out with good taste in fashionably neutral shades, enhanced by the service team who make a visit seamless, easy and fun. The conservatory looks over the pretty garden and there's a small bar upstairs with a terrace looking out over the River Cam. The menus are of the tasting variety – five-, seven-, eight- and ten-course options – with the shorter version offered at lunch in the week and in the rather swish private dining room. Clifford's background at the top end of classical dining, creative mind and astounding technical abilities, combine to deliver flavour combinations that hit the mark again and again, with outstanding ingredients and everything looking gorgeous on the plate. First up might be smoked haddock with potato, pickled onion and caviar in a clever partnership that brings the best out of the immaculate produce, followed by celeriac baked over hot coals and matched with hazelnut, hollandaise sauce, celery and wood sorrel. Subsequent courses could see braised brill matched with smoked bone marrow and mushroom conserve, or roast loin of pine-smoked venison with cannelloni, apple and elderberry purée. The sweet courses might include an intricate composition involving aerated pear, blueberry and white chocolate. The wine list is a fine piece of work too.

Chef Daniel Clifford **Seats** 45, Pr/dining room 16
Times 12-1.30/7-9, Closed 2 wks Xmas, Sun-Mon, L Tue
Prices Prices not confirmed **Wines** 759 bottles over £30, 23 bottles under £30, 21 by glass **Parking** On street **Notes** Tasting menu 5/7/10 course £47.50/£82.50/£105, Children welcome

MIDSUMMER HOUSE

Midsummer House is located in the heart of historic Cambridge. This Victorian Villa encapsulates Daniel Clifford's vision for culinary perfection and is home to some seriously stylish food.

Daniel Clifford's quest for culinary perfection has taken the restaurant to another level over the past 13 years; his cooking has a modern-focus which is underpinned by classical French technique offering seriously sophisticated food with dishes arriving dressed to thrill.

Upstairs there is a private dining room, and a sophisticated bar and terrace for alfresco drinks with river views. Our private dining room is the perfect location for small weddings, lavish birthday celebrations, simple family gatherings or corporate entertaining.

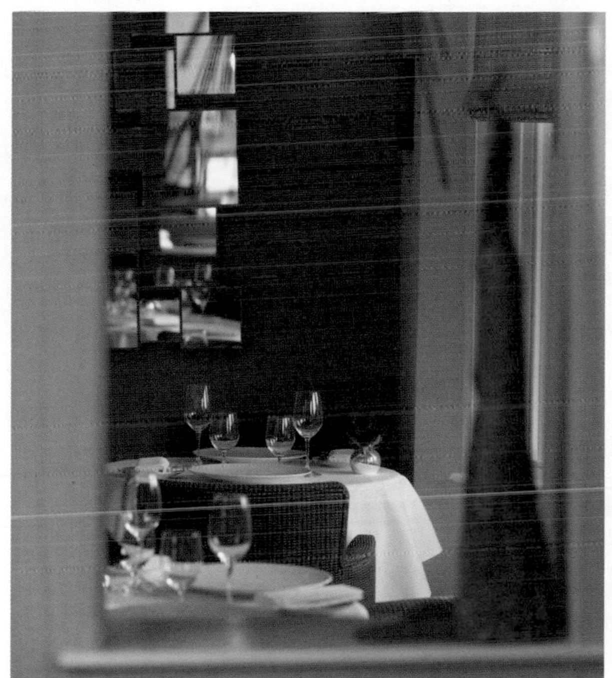

Midsummer Common, Cambridge CB4 1HA

Tel: 01223 369299 • **Fax:** 01223 302672

Website: www.midsummerhouse.co.uk • **Email:** reservations@midsummerhouse.co.uk

CAMBRIDGE *continued*

The Old Red Lion Inn

Modern, Traditional NEW

tel: 01223 892909 **Horseheath CB21 4QF**
email: info@theoldredlion.co.uk **web:** www.theoldredlion.co.uk
dir: *A11, Fourwentways junct, A1307 to Haverhill. After Linton, join dual carriageway. 200mtrs after Horseneath, hotel on left*

Revamped traditional inn offering modern dishes

A thoughtfully and stylishly modernised traditional inn, the Old Red Lion offers a comfortable bar/lounge and spacious outdoor patio as well as an elegant restaurant. On the seasonally-changing menu you'll find a good selection of modern British dishes, with the ingredients sourced from local farm and high-quality producers. Maybe start with confit duck leg terrine with chestnuts, prunes, and a wonderfully-sticky prune and onion chutney, before moving on to slow-cooked pork belly with fondant potato, cider jus, crackling and pan-fried tenderloin. Try the peanut butter chocolate brownie with peanut butter parfait and peanut praline to finish.

Chef Richard Spence **Seats** 50 **Times** 12-2.30/6-9, Closed 1 Jan, D Sun **Prices** Prices not confirmed **Wines** 2 bottles over £30, 18 bottles under £30, 8 by glass **Parking** 30 **Notes** Sunday L, Vegetarian available, Children 7.30 wknds

Restaurant Alimentum

– see opposite

Restaurant 22

Modern European

tel: 01223 351880 **22 Chesterton Rd CB4 3AX**
email: enquiries@restaurant22.co.uk
dir: *M11 junct 13 towards Cambridge, turn left at rdbt onto Chesterton Rd*

Accomplished cooking in an elegant little restaurant

The converted Victorian townhouse near Jesus Green conceals a discreetly elegant and comfortable dining room done out in shades of fawn, brown and beige. The menu follows a monthly changing, set-price formula of three courses with a sorbet following the starter, which might be duck liver pâté with spiced clementine jelly, roasted pears and brioche. The cooking is driven by market-fresh ingredients, and dishes are distinguished by a lack of frill and flounce. Consistently accomplished main courses include Scottish hake with salt-baked celeriac and pig's cheek bonbon, while to finish, iced candied fruit parfait comes with an espresso espuma.

Chef Chris Kipping **Seats** 26, Pr/dining room 14 **Times** 7-9.45, Closed 25 Dec & New Year, Sun-Mon, L all week **Prices** Prices not confirmed **Wines** 26 bottles over £30, 52 bottles under £30, 6 by glass **Parking** On street **Notes** Vegetarian available, Children 10 yrs+

ELY Map 12 TL58

The Anchor Inn

Modern British V

tel: 01353 778537 **Bury Ln, Sutton Gault, Sutton CB6 2BD**
email: anchorinn@popmail.bta.com **web:** www.anchor-inn-restaurant.co.uk
dir: *Signed off B1381 in Sutton village, 7m W of Ely via A142*

Local ingredients in Fen country

Right out in the sticks, a few miles from Ely, The Anchor was built more than 360 years back ago for workers digging the canals that drained the Fens. The heritage of the building looms large when you get inside, with oak panels, quarry tiles and hefty beams. Although very much a pub (with real ales), the contemporary British food is the star attraction, with the menu packed with regional ingredients. Kick off with cod cheeks and pea purée, served with Bloody Mary tomatoes, move on to Denham Estate venison steak with classic dauphinoise potatoes and venison croquette, or tuna steak with Niçoise salad including quail's egg and asparagus.

Chef Maciej Bilewski **Seats** 60 **Times** 12-2/7-9, Closed D 25-26 Dec **Prices** Fixed L 2 course £14.95, Starter £5.50-£12, Main £13-£25, Dessert £6-£7 **Wines** 19 bottles over £30, 26 bottles under £30, 11 by glass **Parking** 10 **Notes** Sunday L £12.95-£18.95, Children welcome

FORDHAM Map 12 TL67

The White Pheasant

British, European

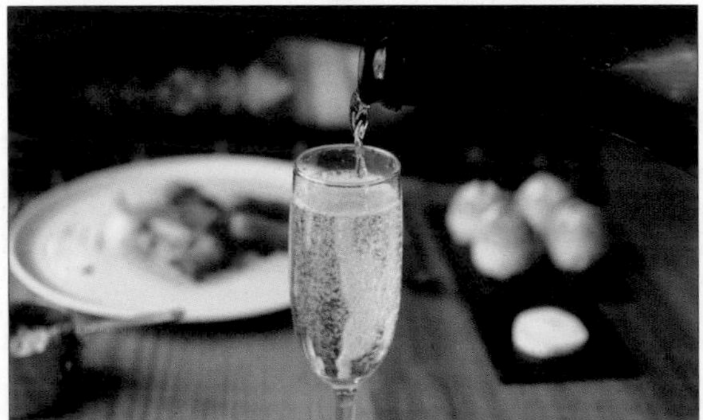

tel: 01638 720414 **21 Market St CB7 5LQ**
email: whitepheasant@live.com **web:** www.whitepheasant.com
dir: *A14 to Newmarket, A142 Ely junct, follow signs Fordham. Situated on rdbt, junct Station Rd*

Gastropub run by an accomplished chef

The White Pheasant is a modern foodie pub with simply decorated interior, log fires and plain wood tables, but chef-proprietor Calvin Holland's cooking sets it a cut above the average. The kitchen sources the best materials from local producers and has the technical nous to extract full-on flavours from it. Pork shoulder might provide the meat for a starter, served as a bonbon with burnt apple, cider sauce and pickled salad. Main course could see hake partnered with seared scallops, sweetcorn, potato dice and mushroom cream. Leave room for rhubarb Arctic roll and pistachio macaroon.

Chef Calvin Holland **Seats** 50 **Times** 12-2.30/6.30-9.30, Closed Mon, D Sun **Prices** Tasting menu £40-£65, Starter £7-£10, Main £16-£30, Dessert £6.95-£8.50 **Wines** 23 bottles over £30, 32 bottles under £30, 10 by glass **Parking** 25 **Notes** Tasting menu 5 course £79 for 2 people, Sunday L £15-£30, Vegetarian available, Children welcome

Restaurant Alimentum

CAMBRIDGE **Map 12 TL45**

Modern European NOTABLE WINE LIST

tel: 01223 413000 **152-154 Hills Rd CB2 8PB**
email: reservations@restaurantalimentum.co.uk
web: www.restaurantalimentum.co.uk
dir: *Opposite Cambridge Leisure Park*

Impeccable ingredients and classy cooking

Dropping the car off in the nearby multi-storey car park may not be the most auspicious start, but the rest of a trip to Alimentum is a journey of discovery in every sense. In an ambience of pared-back café tables and laminate floor, this is one of the central pillars of Cambridge's lively, spirited dining scene. Mark Poynton is in the culinary vanguard, sourcing ethically, subjecting less familiar cuts to today's slow cooking, partnering textures and flavours in surprising alignments, and blending recognisable ethnic references such as Japanese, Indian and ancestral French in among dishes that come from nowhere in particular other than the globalised brave new world. Where else to place a starter of smoked eel with fennel, grapes, almonds and buttermilk, or the fish dish of stone bass with langoustine, cauliflower, goats' cheese and PX sherry? When there is a recognisable compass point to a dish, it transmits its message with powerful articulacy, so curry-spiced scallops and apple with their cumin-booming dhal, coriander and yogurt is unmistakable in its orientation, and there's a world of Francophilia in a main course of beef short rib with Vacherin Mont d'Or, celeriac and garlic in red wine sauce. Seven- and ten-course tasters solve the problem of knowing where to choose, and every dish looks as diverting as can be, with artfully-composed assemblages of cubes, oblongs and smears. Desserts reach into the Scottish larder for a reworking of cranachan, all plump raspberries, oats, honey and lavender, or offer Battenberg cake its long-awaited makeover with pistachios, chocolate and cherry. Wines have been discriminatingly sourced from Europe and beyond, with many classy bottles to suit the enterprising style of the food.

Chef Mark Poynton **Seats** 62, Pr/dining room 30 **Times** 12-2.30/6-10, Closed 24-30 Dec, BHs, L 31 Dec **Prices** Fixed L 2 course £21, Fixed D 3 course £29, Tasting menu £75-£90, Starter £15, Main £35, Dessert £15 **Wines** 131 bottles over £30, 7 bottles under £30, 17 by glass **Parking** NCP Cambridge Leisure Centre (3 min walk) **Notes** Tasting menu 7/10 course, Sunday L, Vegetarian available, Children welcome

HINXTON Map 12 TL44

The Red Lion Inn

 Modern British

tel: 01799 530601 **32 High St CB10 1QY**
email: info@redlionhinxton.co.uk **web:** www.redlionhinxton.co.uk
dir: *M11 junct 10, at rdbt take A505 continue to A1301 signed Saffron Walden/Hinxton for 0.75m & follow signs for Hinxton. From S: M11 junct 9, towards A11, left onto A1301. Left to Hinxton*

Ambitious modern cooking in a Tudor village inn

With its timeless rustic cosiness – beams, bare brick-walls, Chesterfield sofas and a walk-in inglenook – the timbered Tudor Red Lion's bar is a great spot for classic pub grub, but seekers of contemporary British cuisine head for the airy, oak-raftered restaurant, where there's an eclectic carte pitched just right for the kitchen's ambitions. Pan-seared scallops open the show, together with truffle cornflower purée, poached radish and crispy mushrooms, while mains could bring slow-braised Denham Estate venison with dauphinoise potato, sautéed cavolo nero and black cherry jus. For balmy-day dining, there's a walled garden, where a dovecote and the village church clock tower add to the quintessentially English mood.

Chef Jiri Wolker **Seats** 60 **Times** 12-2/6.30-9 **Prices** Starter £5-£10, Main £10-£30, Dessert £5-£10 **Wines** 16 bottles over £30, 38 bottles under £30, 22 by glass **Parking** 43 **Notes** Pudding Club, Sunday L £5-£30, Vegetarian available, Children welcome

HUNTINGDON Map 12 TL27

The Abbot's Elm

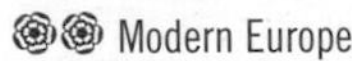 Modern European

tel: 01487 773773 **Abbots Ripton PE28 2PA**
email: info@theabbotselm.co.uk **web:** www.theabbotselm.co.uk
dir: *A1(M) junct 13 onto A14 towards Huntingdon. At 1st rdbt straight on (A141 Spittals Way). Left at 2nd rdbt signed Abbots Ripton. 3m in village centre*

Thatched inn with confident cooking

The interior of this 17th-century pub has acquired a bit of a contemporary sheen while retaining the soul of the place, with a lounge bar serving real ales and a cosy snug as well as a smart restaurant. Expect classy pub classics and sandwiches in the bar (or garden), while the restaurant ups the ante with the likes of mosaic of game with apple chutney, or Scotch egg with parsley aïoli. Successful main courses range from roast fillet of cod with saffron-infused shellfish chowder and baby winter vegetables, to chicken chablisiènne with mash and carrots, while among puddings may be lemon tart with cherry sorbet.

Chef Julia Abbey **Seats** 54 **Times** 12-2/6-9.30, Closed 2wks Jan, Mon (winter), D Sun **Prices** Starter £5.25-£9.50, Main £8-£26, Dessert £6.50-£6.95 **Wines** 30 bottles over £30, 23 bottles under £30, 28 by glass **Parking** 50 **Notes** Sunday L £19.95-£24.95, Vegetarian available, Children welcome

The Old Bridge Hotel

Modern British NOTABLE WINE LIST

tel: 01480 424300 **1 High St PE29 3TQ**
email: oldbridge@huntsbridge.co.uk **web:** www.huntsbridge.com
dir: *From A14 or A1 follow Huntingdon signs. Hotel visible from inner ring road*

Notable cooking and exceptional wines from an old favourite

Once a bank, this 18th-century townhouse is now a boutique hotel with a popular restaurant. Although the kitchen occasionally looks to the Far East for inspiration, the modern style is more influenced by British and Mediterranean flavours, with seasonality at the heart of the menu. Baked scallops with samphire and pancetta is one way to kick off a meal, perhaps followed by an accurately timed piece of slow-cooked belly of pork with perfect crackling, sage and onion mash, wilted spinach and apple sauce. A perfectly wobbly pannacotta with fresh raspberries is one of the simple desserts on offer.

Chef Jack Woolner **Seats** 100, Pr/dining room 60 **Times** 12-2/6.30-10 **Prices** Fixed L 2 course £19, Starter £7-£12, Main £14-£29, Dessert £6-£8 **Wines** 300 bottles over £30, 75 bottles under £30, 35 by glass **Parking** 60 **Notes** Sunday L, Vegetarian available, Children welcome

KEYSTON Map 11 TL07

Pheasant Inn

Modern British, European NOTABLE WINE LIST

tel: 01832 710241 **Loop Rd PE28 0RE**
email: info@thepheasant-keyston.co.uk
dir: *0.5m off A14, clearly signed, 10m W of Huntingdon, 14m E of Kettering*

European-influenced cooking full of fresh ideas

A whitewashed thatched village inn, the Pheasant maintains its centuries-old identity, with simple furniture under the oak beams. The dining room, done in hunting-print wallpaper with high-backed chairs at unclothed tables, plays host to European-influenced cooking that's full of fresh ideas. Crown Prince squash makes a hearty soup, garnished with a slick of crème fraîche. Main courses look to Italy for inspiration for the shellfish risotto and cavolo nero that accompany sea trout, or to France for a classically mandarin-sauced serving of duck breast and confit leg with rösti, red cabbage and beetroot. Finish with tremulous pannacotta, served with poached pear and rhubarb sorbet.

Chef Simon Cadge **Seats** 80, Pr/dining room 30 **Times** 12-2/6.30-9.30, Closed 2-15 Jan, Mon, D Sun **Prices** Fixed L 2 course £14.95, Fixed D 3 course £29.95, Starter £5.95-£9.95, Main £11.95-£21.95, Dessert £5.95-£7.95 **Wines** 50 bottles over £30, 25 bottles under £30, 12 by glass **Parking** 40 **Notes** Sunday L £15.95-£25, Vegetarian available, Children welcome

LITTLE WILBRAHAM Map 12 TL55

Hole in the Wall

Modern British

tel: 01223 812282 **2 High St CB21 5JY**
email: hello@holeinthewallcambridge.co.uk
dir: *A14 junct 35. A11 exit at The Wilbrahams*

Classic country inn with sound seasonal cooking

It's easy to see why this friendly and characterful 16th-century inn is so popular. The village setting is lovely and the cosmopolitan daily-changing menu features some very clever, innovative cooking that really hits the mark. A starter of chicken liver parfait comes with puréed rhubarb, puréed prune and tiny lapsang souchong jelly cubes, while beautifully cooked hake is accompanied by roast cauliflower and silky cauliflower purée, raisin agrodolce bringing a lovely acid note. The buttermilk pannacotta is a great finish, a simple dish elevated by the kick from a blood orange sorbet and a good hazelnut financier.

Chef Alex Rushmer **Seats** 75, Pr/dining room 40 **Times** 12-2/7-9, Closed 2 wks Jan, Mon, L Tue, D Sun **Prices** Prices not confirmed **Wines** 10 by glass **Parking** 30 **Notes** Sunday L, Vegetarian available, Children welcome

MELBOURN Map 12 TL34

The Sheene Mill

Modern, Traditional British

tel: 01763 261393 **39 Station Rd SG8 6DX**
email: reservations@sheenemill.com **web:** www.sheenemill.com
dir: *M11 junct 10 onto A505 towards Royston. Right to Melbourn, pass church on right, on left before old bridge*

Confident modern cooking in a stylish mill

The 16th-century mill house no longer works the River Mel, but the waterway and pond are reminders of its former life. Now, there are glorious gardens, a spa and stylish bedrooms, while the restaurant is watched over by an engaging service team. The kitchen takes a contemporary approach. Rock oyster beignets arrive as a starter with chilli and parsley salsa and cucumber jelly, for example, and mackerel cannelloni is a clever construction pointed up by home-made piccalilli. Slow-cooked belly of pork with braised Puy lentils, black pudding bonbon and sautéed wild mushrooms is a rustic-chic main course option, with pineapple and star anise tarte Tatin among some creative desserts.

Chef Lee Scott **Seats** 120, Pr/dining room 60 **Times** 12-3/6-9.30, Closed 26 Dec, 1 Jan **Prices** Fixed L 2 course £19, Starter £5-£12, Main £13-£28, Dessert £5-£8 **Wines** 31 bottles over £30, 18 bottles under £30, 11 by glass **Parking** 50 **Notes** Afternoon tea £18, Sunday L £18-£28, Vegetarian available, Children welcome

See advert on page 65

PETERBOROUGH Map 12 TL19

Best Western Plus Orton Hall Hotel & Spa

Modern British

tel: 01733 391111 **The Village, Orton Longueville PE2 7DN**
email: reception@ortonhall.co.uk **web:** www.bw-ortonhallhotel.co.uk
dir: *Off A605 E, opposite Orton Mere*

Grand old building with well-crafted menu

Once home to the Marquess of Huntly, the old hall doesn't lack for period charm, with the restaurant featuring burnished oak panels and mullioned windows. The 20-acre estate boasts a spa and there's an atmospheric pub, but the Huntly Restaurant is the place to eat. It's a refined room with smartly dressed tables and a formal service style. The cooking is broadly modern British, with traditional starters such as oak-smoked salmon and salmon mousse, followed by roasted duck breast with caramel orange sauce and excellent dauphinoise potatoes. Bring things to a close with iced Belgian chocolate and tangerine parfait.

Chef Kevin Wood **Seats** 34, Pr/dining room 40 **Times** 12.30-2/7-9.30, Closed 25 Dec, L Mon-Sat **Prices** Fixed D 3 course £30-£37 **Wines** 10 bottles over £30, 37 bottles under £30, 6 by glass **Parking** 200 **Notes** Sunday L, Vegetarian available, Children welcome

Bull Hotel

Modern European, British

tel: 01733 561364 **Westgate PE1 1RB**
email: rooms@bull-hotel-peterborough.com **web:** www.peelhotels.co.uk
dir: *Off A1, follow city centre signs. Hotel opposite Queensgate Shopping Centre. Car park on Broadway adjacent to library*

Modernised classic dishes in a Georgian coaching inn

From the outside, this 17th-century former coaching inn displays its period credentials but there's a contemporary swagger inside, not least in the brasserie-style restaurant out back. With cream-painted brickwork and darkwood tables, the vibe is informal and cheerful. The menu deals in classic flavours and combinations, with duck liver parfait, toasted brioche, apple and ginger compôte a typical first course. It could be followed by 21-day aged rib-eye steak, roasted cherry tomatoes, buttered mushrooms, triple-cooked chips and pink peppercorn sauce. Finish with sticky orange and poppy seed cake, lime curd and raspberry sorbet.

Chef Andrew Tedders **Seats** 80, Pr/dining room 200 **Times** 12-2/6.30-9.45, Closed L Sat **Prices** Prices not confirmed **Wines** 3 bottles over £30, 20 bottles under £30, 8 by glass **Parking** 100 **Notes** Brunch, Afternoon tea, Sunday L, Vegetarian available, Children welcome

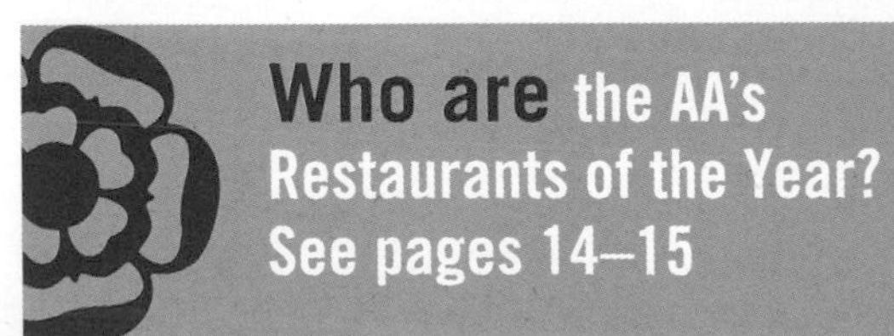

ST NEOTS Map 12 TL16

The George Hotel & Brasserie

Modern British

tel: 01480 812300 **High St, Buckden PE19 5XA**
email: mail@thegeorgebuckden.com **web:** www.thegeorgebuckden.com
dir: *Off A1, S of junct with A14*

Popular brasserie with well-judged dishes

The Furbank family brought this old coaching inn back to life in 2003 by creating a cool and contemporary venue and respecting the integrity of the old building. The menu delivers feel-good flavours based on quality ingredients (including some stuff they grow themselves). Smoked haddock risotto is helped along with a hint of curry spices and matched with cauliflower tempura, followed perhaps by a simple, comforting main of slow-cooked blade of beef with velvety mash, carrots and beans. Apple and frangipane tart with Calvados ice cream or morello cherry clafoutis with mascarpone cream end things indulgently.

Chef Benaissa El Akil **Seats** 60, Pr/dining room 30 **Times** 12-2.30/7-9.30, Closed D 25-26 Dec **Prices** Prices not confirmed **Wines** 42 bottles over £30, 70 bottles under £30, 18 by glass **Parking** 25 **Notes** Sunday L, Vegetarian available, Children welcome

STILTON Map 12 TL18

Bell Inn Hotel

British, European V

tel: 01733 241066 **Great North Rd PE7 3RA**
email: reception@thebellstilton.co.uk **web:** www.thebellstilton.co.uk
dir: *A1(M) junct 16, follow Stilton signs. Hotel in village centre*

Contemporary cooking in rambling old coaching inn

This coaching inn in a charming village may date from 1642 but its kitchen turns out bright ideas in the contemporary mode. Pulled pork and apple terrine with piccalilli and a deep-fried egg has a good balance of flavours among starters, or there might be broad bean risotto in garlic and parsley butter topped with seared scallops. Main courses run to roast chicken breast with tarragon sauce, baby vegetables and dauphinoise, or loin of cod on tomato and basil sauce with butternut squash risotto and wilted spinach. Presentation is a forte, seen in a dessert of peanut butter parfait with hot toffee sauce garnished with slices of marinated plums.

Chef David Hawkins **Seats** 60, Pr/dining room 20 **Times** 12-2/7-9.30, Closed 25 Dec, BHs, L Mon-Sat, D Sun **Prices** Fixed D 3 course £32-£37.85, Starter £5.55-£6.95, Main £9.95-£23.95, Dessert £5.75-£8.95 **Wines** 9 bottles over £30, 39 bottles under £30, 12 by glass **Parking** 30 **Notes** Sunday L £16.95-£19.95, Children welcome

WANSFORD Map 12 TL09

The Haycock Hotel

Modern British

tel: 01780 782223 & 781124 **London Rd PE8 6JA**
email: phil.brette@thehaycock.co.uk **web:** www.thehaycock.co.uk
dir: *In village centre accessible from A1/A47 intersection*

Bright, modern cooking in historic inn

This 16th-century coaching inn on the River Nene matches the period charm of days gone by with the usual modern touches, including a rather nifty dining option in a cosy room. The kitchen is not averse to the occasional contemporary touch and modern cooking technique, so carpaccio of venison might come with a horseradish pannacotta and parmesan wafer, and a main course fillet of beef is served with an oxtail barley risotto and merlot reduction. There's evident ambition on show, although not everything reaches the same heights. For dessert, chocolate and pear brûlée is served with a brandy snap biscuit.

WISBECH Map 12 TF40

Crown Lodge Hotel

Modern, Traditional

tel: 01945 773391 **Downham Rd, Outwell PE14 8SE**
email: office@thecrownlodgehotel.co.uk **web:** www.thecrownlodgehotel.co.uk
dir: *5m SE of Wisbech on A1122, 1m from junct with A1101, towards Downham Market*

Simple modern setting and a broad menu

A modern hotel kitted out to host conferences and meetings, Crown Lodge is a useful local resource. The flexible approach to dining means you can go for simple things like fish and chips or a burger, but there's also a more ambitious carte. This offers a starter of roast loin of lamb with sweetbreads and braised Puy lentils, and another that wraps local asparagus in filo pastry and dresses it with lemon and thyme. Move on to whole grilled plaice, or pan-fried kangaroo steak with wasabi-infused mash, and you'll find plenty of choice for dessert with everything from classic crème brûlée to hearty sticky toffee pudding up for grabs.

Chef Jamie Symons **Seats** 40, Pr/dining room 100 **Times** 12-2.30/6-10, Closed 25-26 Dec, 1 Jan **Prices** Prices not confirmed **Wines** 4 bottles over £30, 52 bottles under £30, 10 by glass **Parking** 50 **Notes** Sunday L, Vegetarian available, Children welcome

CHESHIRE

ALDERLEY EDGE Map 16 SJ87

The Alderley Restaurant

@@@ – see opposite

BROXTON Map 15 SJ45

Carden Park Hotel, Golf Resort & Spa

@ Modern British

tel: 01829 731000 **Carden Park CH3 9DQ**
web: www.cardenpark.co.uk
dir: *A41 signed Whitchurch to Chester, at Broxton rdbt turn on to A534 towards Wrexham. After 2m turn into Carden Park Estate*

Nostalgic country estate cooking

Carden Park is a lavishly scaled country estate not far from Chester. If you look hard, you'll see its Jacobean core, but the views from the formal gardens to the Welsh mountains beyond are enough to be going on with. Country-house cooking with a nostalgic air is the drill, embracing ginger-crumbed goats' cheese mousse with beetroot purée and a parmesan wafer, before a trio of lamb – a faggot of braised shoulder, roast rump and chargrilled cutlet – with sticky red cabbage, wilted spinach and fondant potato. Finish with flapjack-based coconut and raspberry delice with coconut ice cream and raspberry sauce, or tangerine tart and orange sorbet.

BURWARDSLEY Map 15 SJ55

The Pheasant Inn

@ British, European

tel: 01829 770434 **Higher Burwardsley CH3 9PF**
email: info@thepheasantinn.co.uk **web:** www.thepheasantinn.co.uk
dir: *A41 from Chester towards Whitchurch. After 6m turn left for Tattenhall. In village signs for Burwardsley. Top of hill left at PO*

Crowd-pleasing modern pub dining

Looking smart after a recent spruce up, The Pheasant's wide-ranging menu features a healthy showing of local produce and pleases both traditionalists seeking pub classics done well (home-made pies and gravy, or beer-battered haddock and chunky chips with mushy peas and tartare sauce, say) or those looking for more contemporary ideas. These include crispy ox cheek with celeriac and horseradish remoulade, candied beetroot and smoked bacon, ahead of pheasant 'saltimbocca' with sauerkraut, sweetcorn, and apple and sage fritters. Desserts deliver comfort in the form of sticky toffee pudding with salted caramel sauce and rum and raisin ice cream, or creamy rice pudding with lavender shortbread and blackberry jam.

Chef Matt Leech **Seats** 120 **Times** 12-9.30, All-day dining **Prices** Prices not confirmed **Wines** 13 bottles over £30, 27 bottles under £30, 12 by glass **Parking** 60 **Notes** Sunday L, Vegetarian available, Children welcome

CHESTER Map 15 SJ46

ABode Chester

@@ Modern British V

tel: 01244 405820 & 347000 **Grosvenor Rd CH1 2DJ**
email: restaurant@abodechester.co.uk **web:** www.abodechester.co.uk
dir: *Phone for directions*

Confident contemporary cooking and stellar views

The Cheshire outpost of the ABode hotel group occupies a shiny modern rotunda overlooking Chester racecourse. Its restaurant, the main dining option, is on the fifth floor, with stellar views over the castle and lush countryside. There's a contemporary finish to the space, with stylish fixtures and rather glam light fittings. The various menus take a classical approach with contemporary touches along the way. Roast quail comes with herb gnocchi and truffled egg yolk in tarragon jus, while main courses bring on salted cod with caramelised cauliflower and raisin vinaigrette in cumin velouté. Finish with lemon tart and confit lemon sorbet.

Chef Gareth Stevenson **Seats** 76, Pr/dining room 18 **Times** 12-2.30/6-9.45, Closed 26 Dec, 1 Jan, D 25 Dec **Prices** Fixed L 3 course £18, Fixed D 3 course £25, Tasting menu £65-£85, Starter £9.50-£16, Main £13.50-£24.50, Dessert £8.95 **Wines** 43 bottles over £30, 11 bottles under £30, 18 by glass **Parking** 36 **Notes** L 4 course £23, Race L 2/3 course £25/£30, Afternoon tea, Sunday L £18-£28, Children welcome

Best Western Premier Hallmark Queen Hotel

@@ British

tel: 01244 305000 **City Rd CH1 3AH**
email: queenhotel@feathers.uk.com **web:** www.feathers.uk.com
dir: *Follow signs for Railway Station. Hotel is opposite*

Modern brasserie style in an old railway hotel

The Queen, a Victorian railway hotel, has been given an eye-popping makeover to shake out any cobwebs, with much use of loudly patterned fabrics. There are three restaurants, the principal one being a sleek wood-floored space with kitchen views. The cooking style is modern brasserie, with quality ingredients treated with respect in vigorously flavoured dishes. A trio of scallops sitting on cushions of creamy brown shrimp risotto looks the part, and may be the curtain-raiser to herb-crusted lamb rump, served with champ in a forthright rosemary jus. Indulgence arrives in the finale of treacle frangipane tart with egg custard ice cream, made with eggs from a local Cheshire farm.

Chef Alan Davies **Seats** 54, Pr/dining room 16 **Times** 6-10 **Prices** Fixed D 3 course £30, Starter £6-£12, Main £16-£25, Dessert £6-£14 **Wines** 5 bottles over £30, 27 bottles under £30, 6 by glass **Parking** 153 **Notes** Vegetarian available, Children 8 yrs+

The Alderley Restaurant

ALDERLEY EDGE **Map 16 SJ87**

Modern British V

tel: 01625 583033 **Macclesfield Rd SK9 7BJ**
email: reservations@alderleyedgehotel.com
web: www.alderleyedgehotel.com
dir: *A538 to Alderley Edge, then B5087 Macclesfield Rd*

Dynamic modern cooking amid the Cheshire smart set

Imperiously enthroned on a wooded slope overlooking the village, the hotel started life in 1850 as a kind of Elizabethan Gothic Neverland for one of Manchester's industrial plutocracy. Over the ensuing century, it passed from one moneyed family to another, before being used as a billet for US servicemen during the war years. Despite its rather forbidding look, it makes an entirely apposite country-house hotel for the modern age, kitted out with all the facilities you would expect at this level, including a dining room, the Alderley, of surpassing magnificence, all crisply starched cloths and swagged drapes. The kitchen's approach is to take dishes that have recognisable origins in traditional British cooking, and subject them to productive glamorising, with fashionable ingredients and artful presentations to the fore. A reworked ploughman's lunch starter brings together a pork pie fritter, Montgomery cheddar and spiced beer and apple jelly, although the prawn cocktail does quite well without any extraneous sprucing up – it really is prawns, tomatoes, iceberg and Marie Rose dressing, with a poached Scottish langoustine watching over it. The lobster thermidor starter, served with lobster and salmon tortellini and sea veg, is a little more, well, Alderley Edge. At main course, you might delve into the regional cookbook for variations on lamb hotpot, made with Cumbrian fell-bred lamb and pickled red cabbage, or look to a slow-cooked fish dish of turbot and cockles, with textured artichoke, wild mushrooms and pommes Anna. Desserts to make you feel looked after include a liquid-centred white chocolate parfait with banana variations and toffee sauce, as well as Caribbean-themed coconut pannacotta with rum-poached pineapple, fragrant with lime and coriander. Then again, a wodge of apple pie with Calvados custard might do. The cheese menu is a treasure-trove of English artisan masterpieces, served with treacle, walnut and raisin bread.

Chef Sean Sutton **Seats** 80, Pr/dining room 130
Times 12-2/7-10, Closed 1 Jan, L 31 Dec, D 25-26 Dec **Wines** 300 bottles over £30, 19 bottles under £30, 16 by glass **Parking** 82
Notes Sunday L fr £27.95, Children welcome

CHESTER *continued*

La Brasserie at The Chester Grosvenor & Spa

 Modern European

tel: 01244 324024 & 895618 **Eastgate CH1 1LT**
email: restaurants@chestergrosvenor.co.uk
dir: *A56 follow signs for city centre hotels. On Eastgate St next to the Eastgate clock*

Top-end brasserie dining at landmark hotel

La Brasserie at the Grosvenor offers commendable support to its superstar sibling the Simon Radley restaurant. With all the swagger of an authentique Parisian outfit, it has black-leather banquettes, shimmering brass and a giant hand-painted skylight, plus a menu that builds confidently on classic ideas. A starter combines seared yellowfin tuna with a croustillade basket of salad Niçoise elements, and you could then venture south for Ibérico pork cutlet with buttered butterbeans, chorizo and lemon and chilli croquetas, or salmon with an anise-scented stew of mussels, potatoes and fennel tops. Dessert could be a terrific Valrhona chocolate bar with millionaire shortbread and banana ice cream.

Chef Simon Radley, Gareth Jones **Seats** 80 **Times** 12-2.30/5.30-10.30, Closed 25 Dec **Prices** Fixed D 3 course £25-£35, Starter £9.95-£13.95, Main £16.95-£29.95, Dessert £6.95-£10.95 **Wines** 13 bottles over £30, 18 bottles under £30, 31 by glass **Parking** NCP attached to hotel **Notes** Champagne Sun 3 course £35, All day menu Sat-Sun, Sunday L, Vegetarian available, Children welcome

The Chef's Table

 Modern British

tel: 01244 403040 **Music Hall Passage CH1 2EU**
email: info@chefstablechester.co.uk
dir: *M53 junct 12 onto A56 to city centre. Delamere St onto Northgate St then onto St Werburgh St. 500 yds to right is Music Hall passage*

Bold flavours and modern cooking close to the cathedral

At the end of a narrow alley between a dress shop and a coffee house, Chef's Table is the place for an all-day brunch, maybe an Isle of Man crab sandwich, a roast lamb rump salad or a Hebridean black pudding tattie scone. Two- or three-course, fixed-price lunches are served until 3pm. In the evening, start with clear-flavoured fresh squid in its own ink, saffron aïoli, chorizo purée and monk's beard, and follow with roast rack of lamb with pistachio, confit tomatoes, broad beans, oca du Peru, carrots and even nasturtiums. To finish, try poached rhubarb, rhubarb ripple and bubble gum ice cream, candyfloss and toasted almonds.

Chef Liam McKay **Seats** 24 **Times** 12-2.30/6-9, Closed Xmas, New Yr, Mon, D Sun **Prices** Fixed L 2 course £15 **Wines** 6 bottles over £30, 10 bottles under £30, 15 by glass **Parking** Chester Market NCP **Notes** Sunday L £18-£23, Vegetarian available, Children welcome

Simon Radley at The Chester Grosvenor

CHESTER **Map 15 SJ46**

Modern French V NOTABLE WINE LIST
tel: 01244 324024 & 895618 **Eastgate CH1 1LT**
email: hotel@chestergrosvenor.co.uk **web:** www.chestergrosvenor.co.uk
dir: *A56 follow signs for city centre hotels. On Eastgate St next to the Eastgate clock*

Cooking of grand excitement in Chester's crown jewel hotel

Traditional values and old-school formality are thriving at Chester's landmark hotel, where a luxurious finish and pin-sharp attention to detail combine to make The Chester Grosvenor one of the premier addresses in the Northwest. The Elizabethan frontage confirms the antiquity of the old girl, and, developed over the years by the richest landlord in the land (that would be the Duke of Westminster), today's hotel has a swish spa and a main restaurant that hits the heights. The Simon Radley dining room has all the decorum you might imagine, with everything in its place and formal service that suits the mood, and they like you to dress smartly. The man with his name above the door has struck a keen balance between contemporary tastes and classical values, delivering menus that reveal sound judgement and acute technical ability. Flamed mackerel arrives in the company of the fashionable sea buckthorn, with cobnuts and hazelnuts to provide a bit of textural excitement, and agnolotti get stuffed with creamy salt cod and are served with crispy cod skin, girolle ketchup and a warm (and deliciously runny) egg yolk. Next up, French rabbit gets a good work out, loin, kidney and liver, or go for the sweetly named 'cabbage patch' Yorkshire grouse with three brassicas, spiced-bread mousse and juniper jelly. Finish with a creative dessert fashioned around Swiss Tête de Moine cheese. The wine list is a fine piece of work with a wise sommelier on hand.

Chef Simon Radley, Ray Booker **Seats** 45, Pr/dining room 14 **Times** 6.30-9, Closed 25 Dec, 1 wk Jan, Sun-Mon, L all week (ex Dec) **Prices** Prices not confirmed **Wines** 819 bottles over £30, 41 bottles under £30, 24 by glass **Parking** Car park attached to hotel (£10 24hrs) **Notes** ALC £50-£75, Tasting menu (also vegetarian) 8 course, Children 12 yrs+

Grosvenor Pulford Hotel & Spa

Mediterranean, European

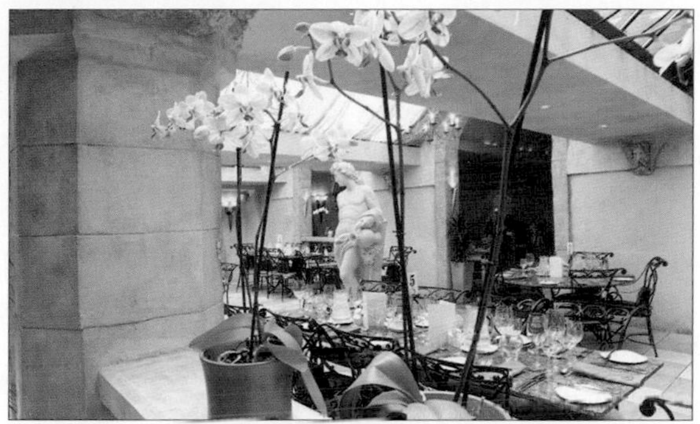

tel: 01244 570560 **Wrexham Rd, Pulford CH4 9DG**
email: enquiries@grosvenorpulfordhotel.co.uk **web:** www.grosvenorpulfordhotel.co.uk
dir: *M53/A55 at junct signed A483 Chester/Wrexham & North Wales. Left onto B5445, hotel 2m on right*

Flavours of the Med in a smart hotel

The sprawling red-brick hotel has a swish spa, luxe bedrooms, and pretty gardens, but the main dining option of Ciro's Brasserie stands out with its classical theme recalling ancient Rome via arches, murals and stucco paintwork. It's the setting for a broadly Mediterranean-inspired menu: prawns pil-pil, sizzled in olive oil, garlic and chilli, are one way to begin, or go for a pasta dish such as chorizo and mushroom tagliatelle. Main courses are equally well-crafted and well-considered: beef blade braised for eight hours with horseradish mash, or sea bass with squid-ink linguine. To finish, there's tiramisù, or lemon tart and cream.

Chef Richard Pierce **Seats** 120, Pr/dining room 200 **Times** 12-3/6-9.30 **Wines** 16 bottles over £30, 30 bottles under £30, 12 by glass **Parking** 200 **Notes** Afternoon tea £14.95, Sunday L £12.95, Vegetarian available, Children welcome

Restaurant 1539

Modern British

tel: 01244 304611 & 304610 **Chester Race Company Limited, The Racecourse CH1 2LY**
email: restaurant1539@chester-races.com
dir: *In Chester racecourse, access via main car park entrance or by foot from Nun's Road*

Brasserie cooking for racing enthusiasts

Part of the Chester racecourse complex, 1539 was given a cool half-million's worth of upgrade in 2014. The full-drop windows of the restaurant are still a major feature, and if your heart isn't given to equestrianism, swivel round for an ambient view into the kitchen. It produces up-to-the-minute brasserie cooking, ranging from ham hock terrine with crushed peas and bacon in mustard dressing, to mains like well-timed roast cod with a brown shrimp risotto in red wine reduction, or honey-roast breast and confit leg of duck with braised red cabbage in orange and port jus. Desserts court the popular vote with dark chocolate tart and salted caramel.

Simon Radley at The Chester Grosvenor

– see opposite

The Sticky Walnut

Modern European

tel: 01244 400400 **11 Charles St CH2 3AZ**
dir: *5 mins from Chester train station*

Well-presented high quality seasonal dishes and rustic charm

The Sticky Walnut is spread over two floors, with chunky wooden tables, blackboards and an open kitchen. First course chicken liver pâté with apple and pear chutney and buttery toasted focaccia delivers complementary flavours and shows refinement in its presentation. Or choose squab pigeon breast with quince, salsify, caraway and meat juices, before a main course of fillet of brill matched with pumpkin and parmesan risotto and sautéed wild mushrooms. Meaty mains bring full-bore flavours, perhaps braised beef shin with truffle chips and onion purée. With cracking desserts like a deconstructed lime cheesecake with pecan butter biscuits and chocolate sorbet, this is a kitchen that delivers real impact.

Chef Gary Usher **Seats** 50 **Times** 12-2.30/6-10, Closed 25-26 Dec **Prices** Prices not confirmed **Wines** 19 bottles over £30, 20 bottles under £30, 11 by glass **Parking** Car park nearby **Notes** Sunday L, Vegetarian available, Children welcome

CREWE Map 15 SJ75

Crewe Hall

Modern European

tel: 01270 253333 & 259319 **Weston Rd CW1 6UZ**
email: crewehall@qhotels.co.uk **web:** www.qhotels.co.uk
dir: *M6 junct 16 follow A500 to Crewe. Last exit at rdbt onto A5020. 1st exit next rdbt to Crewe. Crewe Hall 150yds on right*

Contemporary brasserie in a 17th-century stately home

Jacobean Crewe Hall is reminiscent of a grand stately home with magnificent interiors, but there's nothing stuffy about it, and that especially goes for the Brasserie, housed in a modern wing of the building, with its open-plan layout and buzzy atmosphere. There's tikka spicing in a first-course pressing of lamb belly (with Indian-inspired accompaniments), and soy and honey enriching slow-cooked onglet steak among main courses. There's simplicity in a fish dish of pan-fried stone bass with hollandaise sauce, a pasta option of home-made pappardelle with goats' cheese, and steaks cooked on the grill. Finish with a fashionably modern warm bitter chocolate construction with chocolate soil and yogurt sorbet.

Chef Daniel Richardson **Seats** 120 **Times** 12-3/6-10 **Prices** Prices not confirmed **Wines** 32 bottles over £30, 17 bottles under £30, 18 by glass **Parking** 500 **Notes** Sunday L, Vegetarian available, Children welcome

KNUTSFORD Map 15 SJ77

Belle Epoque

 Modern French

tel: 01565 633060 **60 King St WA16 6DT**
email: info@thebelleepoque.com **web:** www.thebelleepoque.com
dir: *Phone for directions*

Contemporary brasserie cooking in a characterful building

As its name suggests, this restaurant occupies a 1907 building full of period character. Run by the same family for over 40 years, supply lines to local farmers and artisan producers are well established. A starter of hot-smoked salmon comes with cauliflower purée, caviar and samphire, while main course stars lamb fillet and breast alongside celeriac purée, kale, parmesan crisps and fondant potatoes. Fish cookery is equally well executed, perhaps serving pan-fried skate wing with Morecambe Bay shrimps, fondant potatoes and brown butter sauce. At dessert, try a modern take on rhubarb and custard, the rhubarb served poached, as a sorbet, and a jelly 'cannelloni' wrapped around silky crème pâtissière.

Chef Paul Wright **Seats** 60, Pr/dining room 80 **Times** 5.30-9.30, Closed Sun-Mon, L all week **Prices** Prices not confirmed **Wines** 60 bottles over £30, 40 bottles under £30, 10 by glass **Parking** Car park nearby **Notes** Fixed D before 7.30pm, Tasting menu 5/8 course, Vegetarian available, Children 7 yrs+

Cottons Hotel & Spa

Modern British

tel: 01565 650333 **Manchester Rd WA16 OSU**
email: cottons.dm@shirehotels.com **web:** www.restaurant-and-bar.co.uk/knutsford/
dir: *On A50, 1m from M6 junct 19*

Appealing British menus in modern surroundings

A large, modern hotel at the edge of town, Cottons' menu is an appealing brasserie-style package. Start with oak-smoked Severn and Wye salmon, served with beetroot and horseradish crème fraîche, or share a 'taste of Cheshire' plate of cured meats and seasonal salads. Chargrilled steaks (aged for 28 days) come with confit tomato and fries, and sandwiches are up for grabs during the day. Among main courses, fish curry with a spicy coconut cream sauce arrives with basmati rice and naan bread, and Wainwright ale-battered haddock is served with thick-cut chips, mushy peas and tartare sauce. Comforting desserts include warm treacle tart with Pedro Ximénez and clotted cream.

Chef Adrian Sedden **Seats** 80, Pr/dining room 30 **Times** 11.30-9.30, All-day dining **Prices** Prices not confirmed **Wines** 15 bottles over £30, 34 bottles under £30, 18 by glass **Parking** 120 **Notes** Afternoon tea, Early bird menu, Supper events, Sunday L, Vegetarian available, Children welcome

Mere Court Hotel & Conference Centre

Modern Mediterranean

tel: 01565 831000 **Warrington Rd, Mere WA16 ORW**
email: sales@merecourt.co.uk **web:** www.merecourt.co.uk
dir: *A50, 1m W of junct with A556, on right*

Creative modern cooking in an Arts and Crafts house

With seven acres of beautiful gardens, Mere Court hotel has bags of appeal. Dating from the turn of the 20th century, this imposing Arts and Crafts house has plenty of period swagger. The oak-panelled Arboretum Restaurant is an elegant spot with lake views, and is the setting for upbeat European-inspired cooking. Fried duck egg with smoked goats' cheese, thyme and potato rösti and beetroot purée is one way to start, while main courses might include fillet of sea trout, mascarpone and mint spelt with shallot purée. Finish with chocolate and Cointreau orange mousse, orange jelly and chocolate soil.

Chef Mike Malbon **Seats** 40, Pr/dining room 150 **Times** 12-2/6.30-9.30 **Prices** Prices not confirmed **Wines** 4 by glass **Parking** 150 **Notes** Sunday L, Vegetarian available, Children welcome

The Mere Golf Resort & Spa

International

tel: 01565 830155 **Chester Rd, Mere WA16 6LJ**
email: reservations@themereresort.co.uk **web:** www.themereresort.co.uk
dir: *M6 junct 19 or M56 junct 7*

Modern Brit brasserie cooking at a Cheshire resort

The Mere is a must for Cheshire's fairways fans, plus it's a good location for accomplished brasserie dining in the open-plan Browns. Linen tablecloths and relatively formal service are slightly at odds with the overall tone, but the food makes some good modern statements. A robust opener is deeply-flavoured oxtail roulade with creamed parsnip, a prelude to the likes of well-seasoned grilled John Dory with apple, mussels and pancetta, or slow-cooked venison rump with baby turnips, spiced pear and carrot purée in redcurrant and rosemary sauce. Finish with sticky toffee pudding in butterscotch sauce with vanilla ice cream, or a selection of cheeses with tomato chutney.

LYMM Map 15 SJ68

The Church Green British Grill

Modern British

tel: 01925 752068 & 611771 **Higher Ln WA13 OAP**
email: reservations@thechurchgreen.co.uk
dir: *M6 junct 20 follow signs for Lymm along B5158 after 1.5m turn right at T-junct onto A56 towards Altrincham, on right after 0.5m*

A fresh take on traditional grill cookery in a Cheshire village

Chef-patron Aiden Byrne will be a familiar face to *MasterChef* fans, and known to anybody who has eaten recently at some of London's premier addresses. The focus is on traditional British grill cooking, with excellent prime materials and touches of modern technique. Pheasant breast is regally-partnered with smoked foie gras, charred kale and hazelnut risotto. Fish shows up well, as in olive-oiled salmon with a robust fresh Niçoise salad. Topping and tailing it all might be a serving of home-made black pudding with a crisply poached egg (quite a feat) and caper and rocket salad, and comfort-pud finales like Bakewell tart with black cherry and Amaretto ice cream.

Chef Aiden Byrne **Seats** 50 **Times** 12-9.30, All-day dining, Closed 25 Dec **Prices** Fixed D 3 course £27.50-£39.50, Starter £5-£11, Main £17.50-£21.50, Dessert £5-£7 **Wines** 27 bottles over £30, 31 bottles under £30, 15 by glass **Parking** 25 **Notes** Wknd brunch menu, Sunday L £12-£18, Vegetarian available, Children welcome

MACCLESFIELD Map 16 SJ97

The Lord Clyde

Modern British

tel: 01625 562123 **36 Clarke Ln, Kerridge SK10 5AH**
email: hello@thelordclyde.co.uk
dir: *A523 Silk Rd take B5090 Bollington Rd. 1st right onto Clarke Ln*

Brilliantly innovative country-pub food from a South African émigré

A stone-built inn on a Cheshire country lane seems a surprising destination for a Cape Towner whose culinary journey is via Copenhagen's Noma, Le Manoir aux Quat' Saisons and the Fat Duck. Meet Ernst van Zyl, a prodigiously talented chef spreading his wings here to dazzling effect. Against a contemporary rustic backdrop of chunky wood tables and a smattering of modern artwork, the Lord Clyde is both a local pub and a dining destination, with polished but engaging service in the restaurant. The distinctively presented dishes fizz with innovative energy. The first foray might be a roll of crabmeat and Pink Lady apple, garnished with pickled apple, avocado purée and crisped chicken skin, a plateful of consummate freshness and quality. Most dishes are conceived as two pairs, as though on a dance card, so a main course of venison haunch and toasted spelt, celeriac and kale, offers benchmark pinkly roasted meat with the spelt in a creamy 'risotto', as well as steamed and crisp-fried kale and salt-baked and puréed celeriac. Turbot might link up with chorizo, attended by white beans and broccoli in various textures. Ingenuity at dessert produces a disassembled Alaska of lemon drizzle sponge, mascarpone ice cream and sea buckthorn curd amid melting shards of meringue.

Chef Ernst van Zyl **Seats** 24 **Times** 12-2/6.30-9, Closed Mon, D Sun **Prices** Tasting menu £52.50-£125, Starter £7-£12, Main £16.50-£25, Dessert £6.50-£15 **Wines** 11 bottles over £30, 32 bottles under £30, 10 by glass **Parking** 7 **Notes** Tasting menu 7/10 course, Chef Table 7 course £115-£165, Sunday L, Vegetarian available, Children welcome

The Shrigley Hall Hotel, Golf & Country Club

Modern British

tel: 01625 575757 **Shrigley Park, Pott Shrigley SK10 5SB**
email: shrigleyhall@thehotelcollection.co.uk **web:** www.thehotelcollection.co.uk
dir: *Exit A523 at Legh Arms towards Pott Shrigley. Hotel 2m on left before village*

Modern British cooking in a stately Georgian hotel

With the Peaks as a backdrop beyond the grounds of this grand Georgian building, the elegant and spacious Oakridge dining room matches the classical culinary approach of the kitchen. Chicken liver parfait, pear and almond relish and toasted ciabatta is a well-executed classic and it might precede a more globally-influenced slow-cooked soy and honey belly pork, sweet potato mash, chilli roasted tender-stem broccoli and ginger jus. Pan-fried trout fillet with warm Niçoise salad, truffle potatoes and tartare cream is a more European route at main course. Finish with dark chocolate and mint marquise with grapefruit sorbet.

NANTWICH Map 15 SJ65

Rookery Hall Hotel & Spa

Modern British

tel: 01270 610016 **Main Rd, Worleston CW5 6DQ**
email: rookeryhall@handpicked.co.uk **web:** www.handpickedhotels.co.uk/rookeryhall
dir: *B5074 off 4th rdbt, on Nantwich by-pass. Hotel 1.5m on right*

Old-school comforts in an imposing Cheshire mansion

Rookery Hall was built in 1816 by the owner of a Jamaican sugar plantation whose wealth is evident in the sumptuous interior. Notable starters include crisp pork belly with pea purée, caramelised Granny Smiths and Maxim potatoes, and white crab meat with tomato confit, red pepper and avocado sorbet. Sound technique and accuracy are hallmarks of main courses too, seen in breast of Yorkshire grouse with creamed potato, bread purée, cabbage and bacon fricassée, watercress cream and wood sorrel, and monkfish in curry sauce with sauté potatoes, broccoli and crispy almond flakes. For pudding try prune and almond tart, its pastry lightly flaky, with Armagnac ice cream.

Chef Michael Batters **Seats** 90, Pr/dining room 160 **Times** 12-2/7-9.30, Closed L Mon-Sat **Wines** 81 bottles over £30, 9 bottles under £30, 12 by glass **Parking** 100 **Notes** Sunday L £24.95, Vegetarian available, Children welcome

PECKFORTON Map 15 SJ55

1851 Restaurant at Peckforton Castle

Modern British V

tel: 01829 260930 **Stone House Ln CW6 9TN**
email: info@peckfortoncastle.co.uk **web:** www.peckfortoncastle.co.uk
dir: *A49. At Beeston Castle pub right signed Peckforton Castle. Approx 2m, entrance on right*

An abundance of fresh, innovative energy

This place may look like a medieval castle, but the numeric in the restaurant's name denotes the year this mightily imposing building was finished, straight out of the imagination of a wealthy Victorian gent. Today's hotel and wedding venue does justice to the lofty ambition of its originator, with pampering treatments, events, luxe bedrooms and a host of outdoor activities on hand. The 1851 Restaurant has made the hotel a dining destination, too, with Mark Ellis bringing in passionate foodies for his pin-sharp contemporary cooking. The slick and stylish dining room matches the modern thinking in the kitchen, with a shimmering wall of wine bottles as you enter. There's a sense of fun in the naming of dishes – cheese on toast, for example, is a simple and clever construction of whipped Cheshire cheese, sourdough, grelot onions and a piquant brown sauce. Regional produce is used to good effect with Goosnargh chicken and local rabbit prime examples. Main course Hereford beef is a fine fillet, cooked just right, and served with rib pudding, or go for Loch Duart salmon cooked at 44° and cured in beetroot. Finish with a creative zesty lemon number, or a lasagne of Valrhona dark chocolate.

Chef Mark Ellis **Seats** 65, Pr/dining room 160 **Times** 12.30-3/6-9.30, Closed L Mon-Fri **Prices** Fixed L 2 course £19.95, Fixed D 3 course £25 **Wines** 15 bottles over £30, 30 bottles under £30, 12 by glass **Parking** 300 **Notes** D 5 course £45, Sunday L fr £19.95, Children welcome

PUDDINGTON Map 15 SJ37

Macdonald Craxton Wood Hotel

Modern British V

tel: 0151 347 4000 & 347 4016 **Parkgate Rd, Ledsham CH66 9PB**
email: events.craxton@macdonald-hotels.co.uk
web: www.macdonaldhotels.co.uk/craxtonwood
dir: *From M6 take M56 towards N Wales, then A5117/A540 to Hoylake. Hotel on left 200yds past lights*

Smart British cooking and top-notch ingredients

Set in 27 acres of peaceful woodland, this grand-looking hotel near Chester is a stylish and relaxed sort of place. Muted mauve colours and dining chairs in striped fabric add an elegance to the restaurant, where the Josper grill comes into its own for main-course meats such as rump of Highland lamb served with traditional accompaniments and a choice of sauces. The kitchen turns out some imaginative dishes, such as a starter of curried mackerel, cucumber textures and mint yogurt. Quality produce is seen in main courses of corn-fed chicken breast, Koffmann cabbage and fondant potato.

Chef Matthew Jencitis **Seats** 100, Pr/dining room 12 **Times** 12-3/6-9.30, Closed L Mon-Sat **Prices** Fixed L 2 course £15-£17.95, Fixed D 3 course £25-£35.50, Starter £6-£10, Main £15-£28, Dessert fr £6 **Wines** 32 bottles over £30, 28 bottles under £30, 12 by glass **Parking** 300 **Notes** Sunday L £21.95-£27.95, Children welcome

SANDIWAY Map 15 SJ67

Nunsmere Hall Hotel

British, European

tel: 01606 889100 **Tarporley Rd, Oakmere CW8 2ES**
email: reservations@nunsmere.co.uk **web:** www.nunsmere.co.uk
dir: *M6 junct 18, A54 to Chester, at x-rds with A49 turn left towards Tarporley, hotel 2m on left*

Traditional European cooking in the old Brocklebank place

Start with a drink in the Captain's Bar, then glide in state to a berth in the Crystal dining room, where pictures of polo-players adorn the walls. The cooking keeps things firmly anchored in European traditions, opening with crab salad on sun-dried tomato toast, or a blue cheese soufflé with poached pear in honey-mustard dressing. After this, beef arrives lavishly in two guises – slow-roast sirloin and braised shin-on green bean fricassée with wine-pickled shallots and fluffy chips. Salmon is cooked sous-vide and served with bok choy in port syrup, and bringing up the rear might be firm vanilla pannacotta with poached rhubarb, or lemon tart and raspberry sorbet.

Chef Craig Malone **Seats** 60, Pr/dining room 120 **Times** 12-2/7-9.30 **Wines** 66 bottles over £30, 32 bottles under £30, 15 by glass **Parking** 120 **Notes** Sunday L £29.50, Vegetarian available, Children welcome

TARPORLEY Map 15 SJ56

Macdonald Portal Hotel Golf & Spa

Modern British

tel: 01829 734100 **Cobblers Cross Ln CW6 0DJ**
email: general.portal@macdonald-hotels.co.uk
web: www.macdonaldhotels.co.uk/the portal
dir: *Off A49 in village of Tarporley*

Classic and modern cuisine amid three golf courses

The Portal's restaurant has panoramic views of its golf courses and the Cheshire countryside beyond. Comfortable leather banquette seating and unclothed tables make for an unfussy look, and the cooking follows suit with classic steaks and grills supporting forays into the modern British style. The repertoire takes in haggis fritter with a poached egg and hot-spiced tomato relish, and mains such as well-timed square-cut cod fillet in a herb crust with salty kale and samphire and puréed cauliflower, or honey-glazed duck breast with dauphinoise, roast pumpkin and pak choi in anise sauce. Finish with hot chocolate fondant, served with white chocolate mousse and banana ice cream.

WARMINGHAM Map 15 SJ76

The Bear's Paw

Modern European, British

tel: 01270 526317 **School Ln CW11 3QN**
email: info@thebearspaw.co.uk **web:** www.thebearspaw.co.uk
dir: *M6 junct 17, A534, A533 signed Middlewich & Northwich. Continue on A533, left into Mill Ln, left into Warmingham Ln. Right into Plant Ln, left into Green Ln*

North Western cooking in a modernised village pub

A Victorian pub given a modern makeover inside, with lots of light wood, and library shelves in the dining room. Local farmers supply the kitchen with quality North Western produce, with cheeses and ice creams also sourced from within a tight radius. It all ends up on a lengthy menu of modern country-inn cooking, taking in a generous fishcake of poached salmon and smoked haddock garnished with curly kale, beetroot purée and a soft-poached egg among beginners. This could be followed by the likes of calves' liver with crisp-fried haggis, caramelised onion purée, Chantenay carrots and creamy mash in an earthy lentil jus. Finish with Bakewell tart with blackcurrant sorbet.

Chef Scott Cunningham **Seats** 150 **Times** 12-9.30, All-day dining **Prices** Prices not confirmed **Wines** 17 bottles over £30, 26 bottles under £30, 12 by glass **Parking** 75 **Notes** Sunday L, Vegetarian available, Children welcome

WARRINGTON Map 15 SJ68

Best Western Hallmark Warrington Fir Grove

Modern British

tel: 01925 267471 **Knutsford Old Rd WA4 2LD**
email: firgrove@bestwestern.co.uk **web:** www.bw-firgrovehotel.co.uk
dir: *M6 junct 20, follow signs for A50 to Warrington for 2.4m, before swing bridge over canal, turn right & right again*

Opulent room for contemporary dining

There's an Italian theme going down at the Fir Grove hotel, with business facilities including the Venetian Conference Centre and the plush and elegant Capri Restaurant keeping to the theme. The kitchen does not show such obsession for Italy, though, but rather takes a contemporary Modern British approach, while there's a decidedly sunny, Mediterranean spin to the output. Duck terrine, poached rhubarb, gingerbread crumb is a thoroughly modern combination, followed by a well-timed cod loin with creamed potatoes and crispy pieces of chorizo. To finish, stem ginger and lime posset is served with a nicely crumbly piece of shortbread. Service is by a young and brisk team.

WILMSLOW Map 16 SJ88

The Stanneylands

Modern British

tel: 01625 525225 **Stanneylands Rd SK9 4EY**
email: sales@stanneylandshotel.co.uk **web:** www.stanneylands.co.uk
dir: *From M56 at airport turn off, follow signs to Wilmslow. Left into Station Rd, onto Stanneylands Rd. Hotel on right*

Modern cooking in a stylish Cheshire hotel

Despite being over the county border in Cheshire, Wilmslow has long been a gentrified refuge from nearby Manchester and the airport, which makes Stanneylands a good bet for the business traveller, as well as those seeking an escape from urban bustle. Way back in the 18th century, it was a simple farmhouse, but gradual evolution has transformed it into a stylish country hotel. The kitchen delivers a gently modern repertoire such as first-course pan-seared scallops with spiced squash purée and a tender piece of pork belly, followed by shoulder and rump of lamb matched with onion ketchup and, for dessert, blackberry bavarois.

Chef Richard Maun **Seats** 60, Pr/dining room 120 **Times** 12-3/7-10 **Prices** Fixed L 2 course £14.95-£16.95, Fixed D 3 course £31.95-£33.95, Tasting menu £50-£65, Starter £6.95-£9, Main £14.50-£25, Dessert £7.50-£9 **Wines** 66 bottles over £30, 32 bottles under £30, 15 by glass **Parking** 110 **Notes** Afternoon tea £16.95 (with champagne £24.95), Sunday L £24.95-£30, Vegetarian available, Children welcome

CORNWALL & ISLES OF SCILLY

BODMIN Map 2 SX06

Trehellas House Hotel & Restaurant

British, French

tel: 01208 72700 **Washaway PL30 3AD**
email: enquiries@trehellashouse.co.uk **web:** www.trehellashouse.co.uk
dir: *Take A389 from Bodmin towards Wadebridge. Hotel on right 0.5m beyond road to Camelford*

Bright Cornish cooking at an inn with a past

Trehellas House is a modern country hotel, its guest rooms spread between an old inn and coach house. Its beamed, slate-flagged dining room makes a homely setting for bright Cornish cooking that mixes innovation and tradition. Potted St Ives crab with gravad lax and melba toast might be the curtain-raiser for slow-roast lamb shank with crushed minted potatoes and ratatouille in thyme jus, or sea bass with spinach in caper butter sauce. Finish with nutty apple and apricot crumble, served with rhubarb ice cream, or a selection of local cheeses with celery, grapes and chutney. The hotel's proximity to Camel Valley makes that vineyard's benchmark Cornish fizz the obvious aperitif.

Chef Fabrice Gerardin **Seats** 40 **Times** 12-2/6.30-9 **Prices** Starter £6-£10, Main £13-£28, Dessert £7-£10 **Wines** 25 bottles under £30, 6 by glass **Parking** 30 **Notes** Sunday L £10-£18, Vegetarian available, Children welcome

BOSCASTLE Map 2 SX09

The Wellington Hotel

Modern British, French

tel: 01840 250202 **The Harbour PL35 0AQ**
email: info@wellingtonhotelboscastle.com **web:** www.wellingtonhotelboscastle.com
dir: *A30, A395 at Davidstowe follow Boscastle signs. B3266 to village. Right into Old Rd*

Creative contemporary cooking in popular fishing village

There's a traditional bar with real ales and blackboard menus and a charming restaurant with chandeliers at this 16th-century coaching inn with a castellated tower. The kitchen sources its materials from within the county and serves bright, modern ideas with their roots in the classics. The concise menu could kick off with mussels poached in cider finished with clotted cream, or ham terrine with pickles and honeycomb. Equally well conceived are main courses: perhaps roast rump of beef with chorizo, olives and spring vegetables, or grilled sea bass fillet with fennel, dill, French beans, potatoes and mustard. End with rice pudding with Baileys ice cream.

Chef Kit Davis **Seats** 25, Pr/dining room 20 **Times** 6-9, Closed Sun-Mon, L all week **Prices** Fixed D 3 course £37.50 **Wines** 10 bottles over £30, 25 bottles under £30, 7 by glass **Parking** 15 **Notes** Vegetarian available, Children welcome

BRYHER (ISLES OF SCILLY) Map 2 SV81

Hell Bay

Modern British V

tel: 01720 422947 **TR23 0PR**
email: contactus@hellbay.co.uk **web:** www.hellbay.co.uk
dir: *Access by boat from Penzance, plane from Exeter, Newquay or Land's End*

Assured cooking in a Scillies hideaway

Bryher is one of the more isolated of the Scillies, a tiny island that can be tramped on foot in not much more than a morning, following a ferry crossing from St Mary's or Tresco. Set amid gentle hillocks laden with gorse and stretching golden sands, Hell Bay is an evocatively misnamed location. The white hotel behind its picket fence looks unassuming enough, but is a beacon of culinary creativity, thanks to Richard Kearsley's assured, confident cooking. Naturally, fish is a big draw, from local mackerel with fennel pannacotta and gribiche, to mains such as the glorious seared turbot in bisque sauce, with balancing accompaniments of charred lettuce and luxurious lobster tortellini, its pasta shell of dim sum tenderness. Supplies can be pretty erratic on a small island, but West Country venison usually makes it here too, for a signature dish of the haunch in chocolate jus with turnip gratin and red cabbage. Finish with well-rendered prune and Armagnac soufflé with a rather shy Earl Grey ice cream, but good walnut and cranberry biscotti, or pineapple Tatin with coconut sorbet. Breakfasters may gather their own eggs if they wish from the chicken coop. Meanwhile, the menu on offer in the Crab Shack next door is simplicity itself – crab, scallops or mussels.

Chef Richard Kearsley **Seats** 70, Pr/dining room 12
Times 12-2/6.45-9.30, Closed 2 Nov-17 Mar **Prices** Fixed L 2 course £12-£30, Fixed D 3 course £45, Starter £6-£11, Main £9-£22, Dessert £5-£9 **Wines** 20 bottles over £30, 30 bottles under £30, 11 by glass **Parking** 5 **Notes** Children welcome

CALLINGTON Map 3 SX36

Langmans Restaurant

Modern British

tel: 01579 384933 **3 Church St PL17 7RE**
email: dine@langmansrestaurant.co.uk
dir: *From the direction of Plymouth into town centre, left at lights and second right into Church St*

Imaginative tasting menu using regional ingredients

This restaurant offers finely-crafted regional food in an unassuming venue between the moorlands of Bodmin and Dart. Start perhaps with a partridge breast on spelt risotto, followed by a bacon-enriched soup of butternut squash garnished with a scallop. Fish comes next, perhaps sea bass in a green array of samphire, spinach and fennel, and then a choice of main meats, fallow deer in red wine with dauphinoise, chanterelles and sprout-flowers, or sirloin in Madeira with grelots and smoked mash. A digestive pause will do nicely before Cornish and West Country cheeses appear, prior to two desserts. A chocolate version of the B52 cocktail shot might precede apple crumble and custard.

Chef Anton Buttery **Seats** 24 **Times** 7.30-close, Closed Sun-Wed, L all week
Prices Tasting menu £45 **Wines** 45 bottles over £30, 50 bottles under £30, 11 by glass **Parking** Town centre car park **Notes** Tasting menu 7 course, Vegetarian available

FALMOUTH Map 2 SW83

Falmouth Hotel

 British

tel: 01326 312671 **Castle Beach TR11 4NZ**
email: reservations@falmouthhotel.com **web:** www.falmouthhotel.com
dir: *A30 to Truro then A390 to Falmouth. Follow signs for beaches, hotel on seafront near Pendennis Castle*

Seasonal cooking in a great white seafront hotel

Nothing becomes a seaside town like a great white hotel, lording it over the waters from the headland. The elegant dining room has sweeping views over the bay and a menu that works its way round the seasonal calendar in both British and international modes. Many dishes come in two sizes, so that you might start imaginatively with roasted ling fillet wrapped in Parma ham in a sweetcorn and potato chowder with prawns and a near-bushel of fresh parsley. Main course might be a rump cut of superb local lamb on well-executed potato rösti. Good pastry is the hallmark of zesty lemon tart, served with raspberry coulis and clotted cream.

The Greenbank Hotel

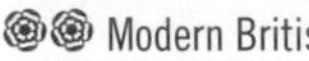 Modern British

tel: 01326 312440 **Harbourside TR11 2SR**
email: reception@greenbank-hotel.co.uk **web:** www.greenbank-hotel.co.uk
dir: *Approaching Falmouth from Penryn, take left along North Parade. Follow sign to Falmouth Marina and Greenbank Hotel*

Crowd-pleasing menu with panoramic estuary views

The house that became the Greenbank Hotel has occupied this spot since 1640, and in 2015 its restaurant received a top-to-toe facelift. A new head chef delivers a please-all roster of classics (fish and chips, burgers and steaks) and modern European dishes with Cornish produce as a starting point. Uncluttered starters include potted ham hock with home-made piccalilli, followed by fish from local day boats – pan-roasted hake fillet, say, with crab and chorizo risotto, samphire and pomegranate. If the mood calls for meat, braised beef cheeks come with celeriac dauphinoise, cauliflower and red wine sauce. Desserts include sticky toffee pudding with white chocolate fudge, toffee sauce and clotted cream.

Chef Nick Hodges **Seats** 80, Pr/dining room 16 **Times** 12-9.15, All-day dining **Prices** Prices not confirmed **Wines** 27 bottles over £30, 38 bottles under £30, 14 by glass **Parking** 60 **Notes** Afternoon tea, Sunday L, Vegetarian available, Children welcome

Merchants Manor

Modern British NEW

tel: 01326 211427 **1 Weston Manor TR11 4AJ**
email: info@merchantsmanor.com **web:** www.merchantsmanor.com
dir: *Phone for directions*

Cornish Riviera setting for modern British food

Built in 1913 for a local brewer, this turreted house was quickly nicknamed 'Screw Top Mansion' by locals when the brewery began using such beer bottles. Today's mature, sub-tropical gardens offer glimpses of the sea, from where The Brasserie's kitchen sources the key ingredients for pan-seared Cornish scallops, Falmouth Bay lobster and Manor fish pie. From Cornwall's terra firma comes attractively presented crispy chicken breast, confit leg and pressed skin with poached oyster, fried egg yolk and potato cake. Other possibilities include grilled steaks, and green garden herb and grain salad with oven-baked squash and roasted cauliflower. Round off with chocolate orange fondant and Cointreau ice cream.

Chef Dale McIntosh **Seats** Pr/dining room **Prices** Starter £6-£8.50, Main £12-£49.50, Dessert £5-£7 **Notes** Afternoon tea £15-£19, Vegetarian available

Oliver's Eatery

Modern, Traditional British NEW V

tel: 01326 218138 **33 High St, Town Centre TR11 2AD**
dir: *Phone for directions*

A kitchen with its heart in local produce

When the ingredients are either foraged or fresh from Falmouth harbour, you're off to a flying start at this relaxed and unassuming high-street venue run by a husband-and-wife team. The kitchen cuts no corners, making everything from scratch, starting with super-fresh, crispy-skinned mackerel with a vibrant salad and crème fraîche and chive dressing, then chicken escalope with roast tomatoes, wild asparagus and bacon and pomegranate molasses dressing. A well-made lemon tart with fresh raspberries, raspberry purée and lemon sorbet provides a zesty finish. The place is booked well in advance, showing it has a loyal local fan base.

Chef Ken Symons **Seats** 28 **Times** 12-2/7-9, Closed Sun-Mon **Prices** Fixed L 2 course fr £15, Tasting menu fr £45, Starter £5-£8.50, Main £14-£23.50, Dessert fr £6.50 **Wines** 7 bottles over £30, 16 bottles under £30, 12 by glass **Parking** NCP, on street **Notes** Children welcome

Penmorvah Manor

Modern British NEW

tel: 01326 250277 **Budock Water TR11 5ED**
email: reception@penmorvah.co.uk **web:** www.penmorvah.co.uk
dir: *A39 to Hillhead rdbt, take 2nd exit. Right at Falmouth Football Club, through Budock. Hotel opposite Penjerrick Gardens*

Modern brasserie cooking in Victorian gentility

The stone-built manor house has stood in its six acres of wooded gardens near Falmouth since 1872. The atmosphere is white-linened gentility, the culinary style is modern brasserie, with well turned-out dishes making an impact on both eye and palate. Chicken liver parfait comes with puréed cauliflower and red onion marmalade, an alternative to chargrilled mackerel and orange in horseradish cream. Mains bring on accurately seared brill with tiger prawns and garlic mash in celeriac velouté, or lamb rump with sweet potato dauphinoise in port and redcurrants. Lemon mousse in citrus syrup is a lively finish, or try white chocolate and banana parfait in butterscotch sauce.

Chef Jennifer Reed **Seats** 60, Pr/dining room 60 **Times** 12-2/6.45-9 **Prices** Fixed L 2 course fr £16.95, Fixed D 3 course £25-£27.50, Starter £5.95-£9, Main £15.50-£21, Dessert £6.50-£8 **Wines** 4 bottles over £30, 23 bottles under £30, 6 by glass **Parking** 80 **Notes** Afternoon tea £12.50, Sunday L £16.95-£19.95, Vegetarian available, Children welcome

The Royal Duchy Hotel

Modern British

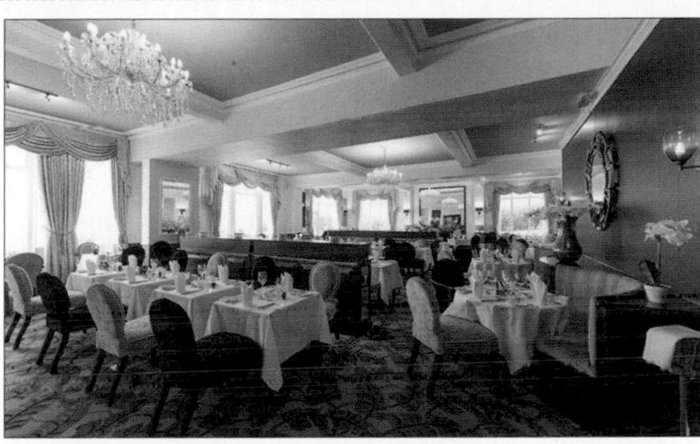

tel: 01326 313042 **Cliff Rd TR11 4NX**
email: reservations@royalduchy.co.uk **web:** www.brend-hotels.co.uk
dir: *On Cliff Rd, along Falmouth seafront*

Well-judged cooking and Falmouth Bay views

With palm trees framing splendid sea views across the bay from its alfresco terrace, the Royal Duchy Hotel certainly has that Riviera touch. Gently contemporary cooking is the order of the day, based on simple combinations that reflect the seasons. Thus a summer's meal sets out with ham hock terrine partnered by pea pannacotta and sweet mustard vinaigrette, followed by superb roast loin lamb of with new potatoes, seasonal vegetables and lamb nage. Fish lovers might be treated to pan-fried bream and scallops with olive crushed potatoes, ratatouille and sauce vièrge. For dessert, try warm ginger cake with candied carrot and mascarpone.

Chef John Mijatovic **Seats** 100, Pr/dining room 24 **Times** 12.30-2/6-9, Closed L Mon-Sat **Prices** Fixed D 3 course £39 **Wines** 62 bottles over £30, 65 bottles under £30, 16 by glass **Parking** 40 **Notes** Sunday L £18.95, Vegetarian available, Children welcome

St Michael's Hotel and Spa

Modern Mediterranean, British

tel: 01326 312707 **Gyllyngvase Beach, Seafront TR11 4NB**
email: info@stmichaelshotel.co.uk **web:** www.stmichaelshotel.co.uk
dir: *Follow signs for seafront & beaches*

Seductive sea views and compelling contemporary cooking

There's a stylishly upmarket vibe at this seaside hotel with its hip-looking bar and nautically-themed restaurant. The kitchen buys materials solely from local producers, and its passion for cooking is palpable in well-executed, succulent seared scallops, served with celeriac purée, delicate vanilla dressing and apple and hazelnut salad, and game and bacon terrine with pickled mushrooms and onion chutney. There's perfectly timed seared venison steak, with parsnips, red cabbage and silky mash, and a smoked haddock and mussel chowder for baked hake fillet. The momentum carries into desserts: perhaps peanut butter parfait with moreish chocolate sorbet and chunks of banana, and lemon and blackberry posset with mascarpone cream.

Chef James Knight-Pacheco **Seats** 80, Pr/dining room 25 **Times** 12-2.30/6.30-9.30 **Prices** Prices not confirmed **Wines** 14 bottles over £30, 32 bottles under £30, 17 by glass **Parking** 30 **Notes** Sunday L, Vegetarian available, Children welcome

FOWEY Map 2 SX15

Fowey Hall

@@ British NEW

tel: 01726 833866 **Hanson Dr PL23 1ET**
email: info@foweyhallhotel.co.uk **web:** www.foweyhallhotel.co.uk
dir: *Exit A30 Bodmin follow signs Lostwithiel. 1st left at T-junct. Follow signs Fowey. Right into Hansen Dr*

Stunning estuary views and family-friendly attitude

High above Fowey Estuary with views to inspire, the one-time grand Victorian house is now a stylish hotel with a family-friendly approach, including access for the youngers to its spa facilities. The dining options include a kid-friendly space and a wood-panelled restaurant which is just for grown-ups. The latter is the smart setting for some unpretentious food made from ingredients sourced from the region. Start with a full-flavoured Cornish fish soup with red mullet, rouille and croûtons, move on to organic Gelly Farm chicken or a steak cooked on the grill, and finish with a passionfruit cheesecake that gets the sweet and sharp balance spot on.

Chef James Parkinson **Seats** Pr/dining room 24 **Times** 12-2.30/6-9.15, Closed during exclusive use **Parking** 36, Public car park **Notes** Sunday L £16.50-£19.50, Vegetarian available, Children welcome

The Fowey Hotel

@@ Modern European

tel: 01726 832551 **The Esplanade PL23 1HX**
email: reservations@thefoweyhotel.co.uk **web:** www.richardsonhotels.co.uk
dir: *A30 to Okehampton, continue to Bodmin. Then B3269 to Fowey for 1m, on right bend left junct then right into Dagands Rd. Hotel 200mtrs on left*

Focused cooking and soothing harbour views

If you're ambling the town's narrow streets of crooked houses and shops tumbling towards the River Fowey estuary, look out for this handsome Victorian hotel. Its restaurant Spinnakers basks in those splendid briny vistas, while the kitchen delivers simple classic combinations. Fowey mussels in a creamy, saffron-infused fricassée with celeriac and tomato sets the ball rolling, followed by a three-way serving of West Country lamb, comprising seared loin, rolled breast and sweetbreads in the company of fondant potato, wilted greens, carrot purée, purple sprouting broccoli and a mint and balsamic jus. To finish, a correctly wobbly yogurt pannacotta is matched with poached rhubarb and its jelly, and orange syrup.

GOLANT Map 2 SX15

Cormorant Hotel & Restaurant

@@ Modern European

tel: 01726 833426 **PL23 1LL**
email: relax@cormoranthotel.co.uk **web:** www.cormoranthotel.co.uk
dir: *A390 onto B3269 signed Fowey. In 3m left to Golant, through village to end of road, hotel on right*

Mediterranean modernism on the Fowey estuary

The Cormorant occupies a roost above the estuary, as a seat on the sunny terrace confirms. A pastel-hued dining room with linen-clad tables is the setting for Mediterranean-style cooking such as chargrilled mackerel with pepper and fennel escabèche, prawn fritters and tomato gel, or chicken terrine with butternut purée, roasted hazelnuts and something the menu calls 'pickled smijis', possibly renamed shimeji mushrooms. Cornish produce is in evidence throughout, from glorious shellfish to pollock with lemon mash and sautéed bok choy, or a pork assiette comprising roast loin, confit belly and black pudding, served with sweet potato purée. At dessert, go Caribbean with pineapple Tatin and coconut ice cream.

Chef Dane Watkins **Seats** 30 **Times** 12-2/6.30-9.30, Closed L Nov-Feb (some days) **Prices** Fixed D 3 course £38, Tasting menu £55, Starter £6-£8, Main £14-£25, Dessert £5-£8 **Wines** 22 bottles over £30, 46 bottles under £30, 7 by glass **Parking** 20 **Notes** Tasting menu 6 course, Brasserie menu, Sunday L, Vegetarian available, Children 12 yrs+ D

HELSTON Map 2 SW62

New Yard Restaurant

@@ Modern English

tel: 01326 221595 **Trelowarren Estate, Mawgan TR12 6AF**
email: newyard@trelowarren.com **web:** www.newyardrestaurant.co.uk
dir: *5m from Helston*

Modern Cornish cooking on a historic estate

The New Yard Restaurant has been carved out of the former stable yard of the vast Trelowarren Estate. The interior has a distinctive look, sporting a chequered floor and arched windows, and its punchy, far-reaching menu ranges from tempura calamari with chilli jam to rump of lamb with spicy yogurt, sweet potato and baby carrots. Carpaccio with rocket and parmesan, or crab with pumpkin, macaroni and parmesan, is a prelude to pork belly, of superb quality, accompanied by smoked cheek in a subtle sauce, queen scallops, cauliflower and samphire. Puddings are worth exploring, judging by white chocolate mousse with a raspberry and lemon version of Eton Mess and raspberry sorbet.

Chef Chris Philliskirk **Seats** 50 **Times** 12-2.15/6.30-9, Closed Jan, Mon-Tue (end Sep-Spring BH), D Sun **Prices** Starter £6.50-£9, Main £14-£20, Dessert £4.50-£8.50 **Wines** 8 bottles over £30, 19 bottles under £30, 6 by glass **Parking** 20 **Notes** Breakfast Fri-Sun, Vegetarian menu on request, Sunday L fr £12.50, Children welcome

LIZARD Map 2 SW71

Housel Bay Hotel

@ Modern British, French V

tel: 01326 290417 & 290917 **Housel Cove TR12 7PG**
email: info@houselbay.com **web:** www.houselbay.com
dir: *A30 from Exeter, exit Truro and take A34/A394 to Helston & A3083 to Lizard*

Regional cooking on a Lizard clifftop

Perched on a blustery clifftop on the Lizard, Housel Bay is a late Victorian hotel that retains a generous complement of original features. The walls are crowded with pictures and ephemera and the kitchen does its bit with a modern British repertoire. Try a full-flavoured first course of oxtail ravioli with mushrooms and spinach, dressed in truffle oil and parmesan, or seared haddock with crayfish, pea purée and an underpowered beurre blanc. There may be slow-cooked shoulder of lamb with Greek salad, plus plenty of vegetarian choices, and to finish, orange and passionfruit tart, classic tiramisù, or a slate of regional cheeses.

Chef Lee Harris **Seats** 70 **Times** 12-2/6.45-9, Closed Xmas **Prices** Fixed L 2 course £19, Fixed D 3 course £25, Starter £5-£7.50, Main £12.50-£19.50, Dessert £5.50-£7.50 **Parking** 30 **Notes** Sunday L £16.50-£19.50, Children welcome

LOOE Map 2 SX25

Trelaske Hotel & Restaurant

Modern British

tel: 01503 262159 **Polperro Rd PL13 2JS**
email: info@trelaske.co.uk **web:** www.trelaske.co.uk
dir: *B252 signed Looe. Over Looe bridge signed Polperro. 1.9m, hotel signed on right*

Local produce in verdant Cornwall

In a rural location between Looe and Polperro, this small hotel is surrounded by four acres of grounds. Dishes are intelligently composed to allow flavours to sparkle. Take a starter of duck liver, fig and pistachio terrine, the hint of sweetness from the fruit a perfect foil for the bold meaty flavour, the nuts adding some crunch. An alternative might be crabmeat with pink grapefruit and rösti before beautifully timed roast salmon fillet with rolls of cucumber stuffed with a creamy mint and cumin filling, or loin of lamb with mint and lemon stuffing, ratatouille and lamb jus. Puddings hit the same high standards: perhaps vanilla pannacotta, or summer pudding.

Chef Ross Lewin **Seats** 40 **Times** 12-2/7-9, Closed Nov-Feb, L Mon-Sat **Prices** Fixed D 3 course £33.50 **Wines** 10 bottles over £30, 22 bottles under £30, 8 by glass **Parking** 60 **Notes** Sunday L £21.50, Vegetarian available, Children 5 yrs+

LOSTWITHIEL Map 2 SX15

Asquiths Restaurant

Modern British

tel: 01208 871714 **19 North St PL22 0EF**
email: info@asquithsrestaurant.co.uk
dir: *Opposite St Bartholomews church*

Minimal fuss, maximum flavours

Its black and white decor, smartly set tables and elegant staff create positive impressions of this restaurant opposite the church, where food is taken seriously. Confit duck and beetroot pastilla is teamed with silky pomegranate molasses and couscous, with an alternative perhaps of kedgeree with a Scotch egg and pea cream. Fish gets a decent showing, maybe a well-timed roast hake fillet given an Indian slant from curried cauliflower and a courgette bhaji along with potato purée. Or go for full-bodied haunch of venison with Puy lentils braised with smoked bacon, hogs pudding croquette and butternut squash purée. For pudding try caramelised stout pannacotta with cinnamon crumbs and apple cannoli.

Chef Graham Cuthbertson **Seats** 28, Pr/dining room 10 **Times** 7-9, Closed Xmas, Jan, Sun-Mon, L all week **Prices** Starter £6-£7, Main £14-£17, Dessert £6-£7.50 **Wines** 4 bottles over £30, 36 bottles under £30, 6 by glass **Parking** Car park at rear **Notes** Vegetarian available, Children welcome

MARAZION Map 2 SW53

Mount Haven Hotel & Restaurant

Modern British

tel: 01736 710249 **Turnpike Rd TR17 0DQ**
email: reception@mounthaven.co.uk **web:** www.mounthaven.co.uk
dir: *From centre of Marazion, up hill E, hotel 400yds on right*

Accomplished modern cooking in family-run hotel

St Michael's Mount forms a dramatic backdrop at this boutique hotel near the South West Coast Path. Panko-crusted ham hock and black pudding terrine, given a gentle punch from piccalilli, has been a deeply flavoured starter, with roast scallops with crisp pork belly and sweetcorn purée another thoughtfully-composed first course. Seafood is a strong suit among mains – perhaps roast hake fillet accompanied by crab risotto, or whole plaice with tartare sauce, herbed new potatoes and salad – while meat-eaters could choose perhaps pork chop with mustard mash, kale and caramelised onion jus. Properly wobbly pannacotta with caramelised figs is an effective finale, or go for treacle tart.

Chef Nathan Williams **Seats** 50 **Times** 12-2/6.30-8.30, Closed 19 Dec-8 Feb **Prices** Fixed L 2 course £14.50, Starter £5-£10, Main £10-£25, Dessert £1.50-£9 **Wines** 20 bottles over £30, 20 bottles under £30, 19 by glass **Parking** 32 **Notes** Sunday L £14.50-£18.50, Vegetarian available, Children welcome

MAWGAN PORTH Map 2 SW86

The Scarlet Hotel

 Modern European

tel: 01637 861800 **Tredragon Rd TR8 4DQ**
email: stay@scarlethotel.co.uk **web:** www.scarlethotel.co.uk
dir: *A39, A30 towards Truro. At Trekenning rdbt take A3059, follow Newquay Airport signs. Right after garage signed St Mawgan & Airport. Right after airport, right at T-junct signed Padstow (B3276). At Mawgan Porth left. Hotel 250yds on left*

Southwestern clifftop cooking in a soothing eco-hotel

The Scarlett has impeccable eco credentials, but first and foremost it's about hedonistic pleasures – wining, dining and some serious pampering. The kitchen team keep things focused on the West Country. Pan-fried gurnard rocks up with a jumble of stir-fried squid flavoured with chilli and ginger, while terrine of confit Cornish chicken comes in the company of celeriac remoulade and pickles. Next up, tender braised ox cheek forms the bedrock of an impressive main course (with potato and bacon terrine and white port sauce), and, to finish, white chocolate mousse is surrounded by a honeycomb shell, joined by pistachio cake and griottine cherries.

Chef Tom Hunter **Seats** 70, Pr/dining room 20 **Times** 12.30-2.15/7-9.30, Closed 2-27 Jan, L 25 & 31 Dec **Prices** Fixed L 3 course £23.50, Fixed D 3 course £44.50, Starter £8-£14, Main £14-£24, Dessert £6-£10 **Wines** 66 bottles over £30, 15 bottles under £30, 45 by glass **Parking** 37, In village **Notes** Sunday L £19.50, Vegetarian available, Children 13 yrs+

MAWNAN SMITH Map 2 SW72

Budock Vean – The Hotel on the River

Traditional British V

tel: 01326 250288 & 252100 **TR11 5LG**
email: relax@budockvean.co.uk **web:** www.budockvean.co.uk/food
dir: *From A39 follow tourist signs to Trebah Gardens. 0.5m to hotel*

On point flavours in a traditional country house

Cornwall's benign climate helped create the 65 acres of sub-tropical gardens that surround Budock Vean, but it is the inspired vision of the owners that made an organically-managed landscape of woodlands, gardens and golf course on the banks of the Helford River. The elegant restaurant is the setting for a menu in which high-quality Cornish produce is treated with simplicity and respect in dishes such as spiced West Country chicken breast with poached pear, followed by pan-fried fillet of John Dory (from local waters) with wild mushrooms and chive-butter sauce. A dessert of banoffee pie with chocolate ice cream and honeycomb hits the sweet spot.

Chef Darren Kelly **Seats** 100, Pr/dining room 40 **Times** 12-2.30/7-9, Closed 3 wks Jan, L Mon-Sat **Prices** Starter fr £8, Main fr £23, Dessert fr £6 **Wines** 41 bottles over £30, 49 bottles under £30, 7 by glass **Parking** 100 **Notes** 4 course D £41, Sunday L fr £21, Children welcome

MEVAGISSEY Map 2 SX04

Trevalsa Court Hotel

 Modern British

tel: 01726 842460 **School Hill, Polstreth PL26 6TH**
email: stay@trevalsa-hotel.co.uk **web:** www.trevalsa-hotel.co.uk
dir: *From St Austell take B3273 to Mevagissey. Pass sign to Pentewan. At top of hill left at x-rds. Hotel signed*

Clifftop hotel with a modern menu and excellent local seafood

Situated on a clifftop, there is a real sub-tropical feel to this handsome granite and slate house. When the sun shines, a table on the terrace with views across Mevagissey Bay is worth its weight in gold, but the view is pretty special from inside, too. What appears on the menu is grounded in the local environment, with a decent showing of seafood. Start with venison Wellington and pickled red cabbage before a main course John Dory, galette potatoes, clams, fennel, brown shrimp and pomegranate salsa. Coconut crème brûlée, banana bread and banana sorbet is a typical dessert.

MULLION Map 2 SW61

Mullion Cove Hotel

Modern British

tel: 01326 240328 **TR12 7EP**
email: enquiries@mullion-cove.co.uk **web:** www.mullion-cove.co.uk
dir: *A3083 towards The Lizard. Through Mullion towards Mullion Cove. Hotel in approx 1m*

Sea views and accomplished modern cooking

This solidly built white property on the Lizard Peninsula sits on the clifftop, giving uninterrupted sea and coast views. The kitchen is committed to local suppliers, with day boats providing seafood: perhaps whole grilled plaice with baby potatoes, seasonal greens and citrusy caper butter. Or there could be roast breast and confit leg of guinea fowl, the meat of superb quality and perfectly cooked, served with carrots, parsnip purée, kale and Calvados velouté. An international element is evident in some dishes, for example a flavourful starter of seafood laksa (clams, squid, mullet and prawns) with pickled vegetables. Puddings might be chocolate mousse with chocolate 'soil' and damson and liquorice sorbet.

Chef Paul Stephens **Seats** 60, Pr/dining room 20 **Times** 12-2/6.30-8.45, Closed L Mon-Sat **Prices** Fixed D 3 course £28-£35 **Wines** 51 bottles over £30, 44 bottles under £30, 14 by glass **Parking** 45 **Notes** Sunday L £19.95, Vegetarian available, Children 7 yrs+

The Restaurant at the Polurrian Bay Hotel

Modern NEW

tel: 01326 240421 **TR12 7EN**
email: info@polurrianhotel.com
dir: *A394 to Helston. Follow The Lizard & Mullion signs onto A3083. Approx 5m, right onto B3296 to Mullion. Follow one-way system to T-junct, left signed Mullion Cove. 0.5m right, follow hotel sign*

Creative cooking and coastal views

This one-time Victorian railway hotel has been reworked in smart contemporary style. From its perch on the cliffs of the Lizard Peninsula, the rather grand restaurant presents those wild coastal views as a backdrop to inventive modern cooking based on tip-top ingredients from local producers. Pork belly is neatly offset with fresh apple, caramelised apple purée and sage, with granola and crackling adding crunch. Next up, pan-fried monkfish and razor clams come with buttered spinach, fennel and a foam of Cornish distiller Curio's samphire gin. To finish, poached rhubarb arrives with green apple sorbet, home-made ginger sherbet and maple granola.

Chef Andrew Chan **Seats** 80, Pr/dining room 25 **Times** 12-2/6-9 **Prices** Fixed L 2 course fr £25, Fixed D 3 course fr £32, Starter £6-£8, Main £15-£28, Dessert fr £7 **Wines** 29 bottles over £30, 28 bottles under £30, 15 by glass **Parking** 55 **Notes** May close for private functions, Sunday L £16.95-£19.95, Vegetarian available, Children welcome

NEWQUAY Map 2 SW86

Headland Hotel

Modern British NEW

tel: 01637 872211 **Fistral Beach TR7 1EW**
email: reception@headlandhotel.co.uk **web:** www.headlandhotel.co.uk
dir: *A30 onto A392 towards Newquay, follow signs to Fistral Beach, hotel is adjacent*

Stunning views and stylish eating

You'll likely find yourself distracted by the incredible views from the Headland's elegant dining room when you should be perusing the menu – you might even spot dolphins out in the bay. Inside it's smart and sharp – crisp linens, formal service, and the style is modern British with a few nods to the past such as potted shrimps or Windsor brown soup. Contemporary dishes might include a foie gras torchon with Cornish cider brandy jelly, spiced poached apricots and toasted brioche. A main of sole fillets comes with kale and excellent salsify fritters. Finish with rhubarb gin jelly and vanilla meringue.

Chef Christopher Archambault **Seats** 150, Pr/dining room 100 **Times** 12.30-2.30/6.30-9, Closed L Mon-Sat **Prices** Fixed D 3 course fr £35, Starter £6-£11, Main £20-£39, Dessert £6-£7 **Wines** 74 bottles over £30, 24 bottles under £30, 11 by glass **Parking** 100 **Notes** Sunday L £19.95-£23.95, Vegetarian available, Children welcome

Silks Bistro and Champagne Bar

Modern British

tel: 01637 839048 & 872244 **Atlantic Hotel, Dane Rd TR7 1EN**
email: info@atlantichotelnewquay.co.uk **web:** www.atlantichotelnewquay.co.uk
dir: *From M5 southbound junct 31, take A30 at Newquay sign. Follow signs Fistral Beach. Hotel at top of Dane Rd*

Modern bistro cooking with a champagne bar attached

Although it was built in 1892 this is no gloomy Victorian haunt. Silks is bright and modern, with zebra-patterned bar stools, and sunburst-styled café chairs at linen-swathed tables. In the evenings, candlelight softens the scene. Starters such as ham hock and parsley terrine with home-made piccalilli or Newlyn crab cakes with lemon and sweet chilli mayo pave the way for comfort-oriented mains. There might be battered fish (whatever's fresh on the day) with proper chips, lemon and tartare sauce, or a hearty plate of confit belly pork with cassoulet and apple coulis.

Puddings are equally feel-good; try dark chocolate brownie with toffee sauce and vanilla ice cream.

Silks Bistro and Champagne Bar

Chef Aaron Janes **Seats** 100, Pr/dining room 24 **Times** 12-10, All-day dining **Prices** Prices not confirmed **Wines** 9 bottles over £30, 22 bottles under £30, 9 by glass **Parking** Car park adjacent **Notes** Sunday L, Vegetarian available, Children welcome

PADSTOW **Map 2 SW97**

The Metropole

Modern British

tel: 01841 532486 & 0800 005 2244 **Station Rd PL28 8DB**
email: reservations@the-metropole.co.uk **web:** www.the-metropole.co.uk
dir: *M5/A30 past Launceston, follow signs for Wadebridge and N Cornwall. Then take A39 and follow signs for Padstow*

Harbourside restaurant with an assured team in the kitchen

This Victorian hotel has commanding views over the foodie town and Camel Estuary, and where better to enjoy them but over a meal in the Harbour Restaurant. The kitchen is driven by local supplies, producing starters of seared scallops with celeriac, apple purée and hog's pudding alongside blue cheese and leek bread-and-butter pudding with apple, apricot and rocket. Salmon fillet stars in a main course with sauté potato, confit tomato, celeriac, fine beans and beurre blanc, or perhaps roast chicken breast with dauphinoise potatoes, Savoy cabbage, carrot purée and thyme jus. End in the comfort zone with lemon and thyme-glazed treacle tart with blackberries and lemon curd ice cream.

Chef Michael Corbin **Seats** 70, Pr/dining room 30 **Times** 12-2/6.30-9, Closed L Mon-Tue, Thu-Sat **Prices** Fixed L 2 course £11, Starter £6.50-£9.75, Main £17-£30, Dessert £6.50-£10 **Wines** 35 bottles over £30, 26 bottles under £30, 17 by glass **Parking** 50 **Notes** Sunday L £15-£18, Vegetarian available, Children welcome

Paul Ainsworth at No. 6

– see page 82

Rojano's in the Square

Italian, Mediterranean NEW

tel: 01841 532796 **9 Mill Square PL28 8AE**
dir: *In the centre of Padstow yards from the harbour*

The best of Cornwall and Italy

Italian cuisine and Cornish ingredients come together in this vibrant restaurant located a few steps from the harbour. A few tables out front and a first-floor balcony, complete with heaters and artificial grass, boosts the Med vibe. The menu extends to sourdough pizzas, classic pasta dishes, Cornish beef in a juicy burger, and a blackboard listing daily specials. Smoked Cornish mackerel stars in a pâté with chargrilled sourdough bread, and the calamari is second to none. Finish with proper gooey chocolate brownie with two ice creams – coconut and salted caramel. The wine list stays loyal to Italy, with good options by the glass.

Chef Paul Dodd **Seats** 72 **Times** 12-3/5-10, Closed 3 wks in Jan **Prices** Starter £4-£9.50, Main £12-£18.95, Dessert £6.50-£8.50 **Wines** 7 bottles over £30, 15 bottles under £30, 12 by glass **Parking** Harbour car park **Notes** Vegetarian available, Children welcome

St Petroc's & Bistro

Mediterranean, French

tel: 01841 532700 **4 New St PL28 8EA**
email: reservations@rickstein.com **web:** www.rickstein.com
dir: *From Lawns car park on New St, head down hill. Bistro 100yds on left*

Informal bistro dining from Rick Stein's stable

The bistro is an informal and relaxing sort of place, with simple tables and chairs on worn wooden floorboards, modern paintings on plain white walls, and professional service from attentive staff. There's a cosy bar and a pleasant lounge for pre-dinner drinks and a courtyard and garden for alfresco meals. With Rick Stein at the helm, seafood gets a decent showing, but the flavours of France and the broader Mediterranean dominate. Start with chargrilled sardines or warm salad of wood pigeon, before grilled hake with gnocchi and beurre rouge, or a steak cooked over charcoal and offered up with hand-cut chips.

Chef Nick Evans **Seats** 54, Pr/dining room 12 **Times** 12-2/6.30-9.30, Closed 25-26 Dec, D 24 Dec **Prices** Fixed L 2 course fr £15, Starter £5.95-£11, Main £15.95-£24, Dessert £6.75-£8.50 **Wines** 10 bottles over £30, 10 bottles under £30, 14 by glass **Parking** Lawns car park up hill **Notes** Vegetarian available, Children welcome

The Seafood Restaurant

International Seafood V NOTABLE WINE LIST

tel: 01841 532700 **Riverside PL28 8BY**
email: reservations@rickstein.com **web:** www.rickstein.com
dir: *Follow signs for Padstow town centre, onto Station Rd signed Harbour car park, restaurant opposite*

Padstein ahoy! Fishy delights from around the globe

Rick Stein's culinary globetrotting for the Beeb has certainly been good for business: perennially buzzing with life, the flagship is an expansive space of blond wood, white walls, colourful splashes of contemporary art, and linen-dressed tables spread around a central altar of shellfish and crustaceans. Global influences garnered from exploration of the world's cuisines all feed into the menu, providing a glow of the Med here, a hit of Asian fire and spice there, as well as classics that you just don't mess with – Dover sole, for example, grilled whole and served à la meunière with nutty brown beurre noisette. It's all built on piscine produce that's as good as it gets. A decadent starter of lobster and foie gras is leavened with crunchy green beans and avocado, and revved up with a zesty lemon dressing. Mains keep things pretty simple, too; witness braised fillet of brill with slivers of Wiltshire black truffle, potato ribbons, mushrooms and a sublime butter-rich sauce, or Stein's travels could be reflected in stir-fried Singapore crab with garlic, ginger, chilli and coriander. To finish, chocolate fondant is matched with salted caramel and toasted sesame ice cream. The wine list brings home good ideas from every continent, rather like the boss.

Chef Stephane Delourme **Seats** 120 **Times** 12-3/6.30-10, Closed 25-26 Dec, D 24 Dec **Prices** Fixed L 3 course £31-£40, Starter £11.50-£26.50, Main £19.50-£50, Dessert £8.90-£9.50 **Wines** 155 bottles over £30, 24 bottles under £30, 46 by glass **Parking** Pay & display opposite **Notes** 3 course summer/winter menu £40/£31, Children 3 yrs+

Paul Ainsworth at No. 6

PADSTOW **Map 2 SW97**

Modern British V NOTABLE WINE LIST

tel: 01841 532093 **6 Middle St PL28 8AP**
email: enquiries@number6inpadstow.co.uk
web: www.number6inpadstow.co.uk
dir: *A30 follow signs for Wadebridge then sign to Padstow*

Defining contemporary cooking in a pint-sized townhouse

Paul Ainsworth's is only the most recent Padstow career to have gone into orbit as a result of TV appearances and a growing presence in tourist Cornwall's favourite little town. If the swirling crowds can all get a bit much, his original venue (since joined by Rojano's and six suites in a nearby townhouse) remains a civilised sanctuary. Buried amid the narrow streets off the harbour front, it occupies a Georgian townhouse, with sleek contemporary dining spaces spread over two floors and eye-catching decorative touches including a stunning piece from sculptor Beth Cullen-Kerridge. Clued-up staff run the show. John Walton's kitchen produces impressive renditions of carefully-conceived modern dishes, often given to formal experimentation but with a strong supporting foundation of premium Cornish ingredients, with tongue-in-cheek appropriations from the world of haute cuisine. Fallow deer comes with a trio of cabbages, a little pig trotter sauce and a serving of 'pâté en waffle' for a main course that bursts with native wit as well as flavour. The opalescent cod, timed to the second, is ably served by local crab in mayonnaise, alongside the earthy texture of kohlrabi and a seasoning of fenugreek. Prior to those, there may be a reworked quiche lorraine made with smoked haddock, or a daring serving of sashimi scallop with kimchi and umami-drenched anchovy paste. Vegetarians may begin with a tangle of tagliatelle turnip with smoked Portobellos, proceeding to a botanical textbook main course of roots, alliums, tubers, brassicas and fungi. Desserts hark back to the golden days of trifle, albeit with rhubarb and saffron, and bread-and-butter pudding, as well as offering a tiramisù and chocolate tart fix with yogurt sorbet, while cheese – perhaps a mature Barkham Blue – comes in the Lancashire fashion with an Eccles cake and port.

Chef Paul Ainsworth, John Walton **Seats** 46, Pr/dining room 10 **Times** 12-2.30/6-10, Closed 24-26 Dec, 19 Jan-12 Feb, Sun-Mon (excl BH Sun) **Prices** Fixed L 2 course £19, Starter £12-£16, Main £30-£39, Dessert £11-£24 **Wines** 75 bottles over £30, 18 bottles under £30, 16 by glass **Parking** Harbour car park and on street **Notes** Children 4 yrs+

PADSTOW *continued*

Treglos Hotel

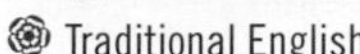

Traditional English V

tel: 01841 520727 **Constantine Bay PL28 8JH**
email: stay@treglosho tel.com **web:** www.treglosho tel.com
dir: *At St Merryn x-rds take B3276 towards Newquay. In 500mtrs right to Constantine Bay, follow brown signs*

Modern Cornish cooking at a smart family run hotel

A family-run hotel overlooking Constantine Bay near Padstow, this was converted from a Victorian house in the 1930s. Wallis Simpson stayed here before the abdication, and the smart interiors certainly look fitting for the glitterati. In a dining room done in maroon and leafy green, the menus take a modern approach, with specials built around a solid core repertoire. Proceedings might open with mackerel céviche, pickled cucumber and horseradish cream in apple vinaigrette, a curtain-raiser to pork three ways with apricot purée, date gel and five-spice veg. At the end comes a dome of 70% chocolate filled with praline mousse, served with toasted marshmallow.

Chef Gavin Hill **Seats** 100 **Times** 12-2.30/6.45-8.45, Closed 30 Nov-10 Feb **Prices** Prices not confirmed **Wines** 8 by glass **Parking** 40 **Notes** Sun L by arrangement £10/£30, Afternoon tea £5.25, Children 3 yrs+

PENZANCE Map 2 SW43

The Bay@Hotel Penzance

Modern British

tel: 01736 366890 & 363117 **Britons Hill TR18 3AE**
email: eat@thebaypenzance.co.uk **web:** www.thebaypenzance.co.uk
dir: *From A30 take exit to Penzance at Tesco rdbt. 3rd right onto Britons Hill. Hotel on right*

Appealing modern food, sea views and a stylish setting

Bay Brasserie's kitchen sources its materials from the West Country, with fresh fish and shellfish hauled in from Cornish ports to appear in mains such as roast cod fillet with squid and vegetable compôte and seaweed salsa, or grilled brill with brown shrimps, tomato and samphire. Cornish lobster comes grilled with garlic and herbs or thermidor sauce. Fans of local meat have plenty to get their teeth into – perhaps pan-fried pigeon breast with figs, chard and Pernod jus, while roast rump of lamb gets the support of onions and anchovy, smoked aubergine and potato cake. Baked dark chocolate and cardamom tart with crème fraîche sorbet could provide the finale.

Chef Ben Reeve **Seats** 60, Pr/dining room 12 **Times** 12-2.30/17-9.30, Closed 1st 2 wks Jan **Prices** Fixed L 2 course £15, Starter £6.95-£9.50, Main £14.50-£24, Dessert £7.25-£9.50 **Wines** 31 bottles over £30, 23 bottles under £30, 13 by glass **Parking** 12, On street **Notes** Sunday L £13.50-£23.50, Vegetarian available, Children welcome

Ben's Cornish Kitchen

British

tel: 01736 719200 **West End, Marazion TR17 0EL**
email: ben@benscornishkitchen.com
dir: *On coast road opposite St Michael's Mount*

Contemporary cooking on the Cornish coast

Seagulls wheel about the thriving little village of Marazion, just outside Penzance, in a coastal scene that may strike a chord with followers of *Doc Martin*. In starters, there's a dual role for cured and crisp-fried beef with watercress, pungent horseradish and a sourdough croûton, or a twice-baked cheese soufflé with soused pear and spiced pecans. Then mains bring on milky-textured cod with crushed root veg, mussels and spinach, or intensely flavoured braised lamb shoulder with frankly stunning pearl barley risotto and crunchy broccoli in salsa verde. Tropical elements add up to an irresistible dessert of coconut pannacotta with dried pineapple, lime-macerated mango, spiced caramel and mint sugar.

Chef Ben Prior **Seats** 35, Pr/dining room 20 **Times** 12-2/7-9, Closed Sun-Mon **Prices** Fixed L 2 course fr £17, Fixed D 3 course fr £29, Tasting menu fr £39 **Wines** 65 bottles over £30, 65 bottles under £30, 20 by glass **Parking** Across the road **Notes** Vegetarian available, Children welcome

Harris's Restaurant

British, French

tel: 01736 364408 **46 New St TR18 2LZ**
email: contact@harrissrestaurant.co.uk
dir: *Down narrow cobbled street opposite Lloyds Bank & the Humphry Davy statue on Market Jew St*

Clearly focused, unfussy food just off the high street

The Harris family have run their appealing restaurant on a cobbled side street in the town centre for over 30 years, offering professionally prepared and freshly cooked quality produce (local meats, seafood from Newlyn, for instance), with the kitchen taking an unshowy line. Seafood makes up the bulk of starters – crab Florentine topped with spinach and parmesan sauce, for example – with meat dishes getting a fair showing among mains: Creedy Carver duck comes with red cabbage spiked with star anise, red wine jus, green beans and sugarsnap peas. A textbook vanilla crème brûlée with fresh raspberries and a tuile biscuit provides a satisfying finish.

Chef Roger Harris **Seats** 40, Pr/dining room 20 **Times** 12-2/7-9.30, Closed 3 wks winter, 25-26 Dec, 1 Jan, Sun-Mon **Prices** Starter £7.50-£8.95, Main £19.50-£29.95, Dessert £6.50-£7.50 **Wines** 28 bottles over £30, 17 bottles under £30, 8 by glass **Parking** On street, local car park **Notes** Seasonal opening times, Vegetarian available, Children 5 yrs+

The Tolcarne Inn

Seafood NEW

tel: 01736 363074 **Newlyn TR18 5PR**
email: info@tolcarneinn.co.uk
dir: *Phone for directions*

Straight-talking seafood cooking next to the fish market

Only the high sea wall separates The Tolcarne Inn from the crashing waves on the other side, adding considerable charm to this traditional stone-built pub next to Newlyn's bustling fish market. Close links with local fishermen mean the day's catch dictates what appears on the chalkboard menu. Pan-fried fillet of mackerel turns up in a starter with fine beans and pickled mushrooms, followed perhaps by a juicy fillet of hake teamed with cavolo nero, roasted beetroot, creamed potato, smoked bacon and hazelnuts. Dessert could be strawberries Escoffier with lemon rosemary and mascarpone ice cream.

Chef Ben Tunnicliffe **Times** 12-2.15/7-close **Prices** Starter £5.75-£7.75, Main £9.50-£15.50, Dessert £5 **Notes** Sunday L

PORTHLEVEN Map 2 SW62

Kota Restaurant with Rooms

British, Pacific Rim

tel: 01326 562407 **Harbour Head TR13 9JA**
email: kota@btconnect.com **web:** www.kotarestaurant.co.uk
dir: *B3304 from Helston into Porthleven, Kota on harbour head opposite slipway*

Seafood-based fusion food on a Cornish harbour

Perched on the waterfront, Kota is named from the Maori word for seafood. In a spacious beamed room with tiled floor, an inspired spin on marine-based fusion food wins many converts. Lively openers such as mackerel tartare with beetroot, watercress aïoli and horseradish snow, or local mussels in leeks, saffron and cider, give way to generous main dishes like brill with crispy chicken wings, purple potato gnocchi, oyster mushrooms and romanesco in chicken jus. Finish with West Country cheeses and home-made chutneys, or dark chocolate tart with miso caramel, sesame praline and green tea ice cream. There's also a six-course tasting menu.

Chef Jude Kereama **Seats** 40 **Times** 6-9, Closed Jan-Feb, Sun-Mon, L all week **Prices** Fixed D 3 course fr £21, Starter £6.50-£10.50, Main £11.50-£21.50, Dessert £6.95-£9.50 **Wines** 7 bottles over £30, 30 bottles under £30, 13 by glass **Parking** On street **Notes** Tasting menu 6 course, Vegetarian available, Children welcome

PORT ISAAC Map 2 SW98

Outlaw's Fish Kitchen

Modern British, Seafood

tel: 01208 881183 & 880237 **1 Middle St PL29 3RH**
email: fishkitchen@outlaws.co.uk
dir: *Phone for directions*

Stunning seafood in a casual harbourside setting

Nathan Outlaw is a big fish in Cornwall with a number of restaurants across the county (plus one in London), the pick of which is Restaurant Nathan Outlaw itself. The Fish Kitchen is a rustic little place right on the harbour, with sea views, unclothed tables and an easy-going vibe. The menu is straight and true when it comes to the fruits of the sea – crab fritters turn up with curry mayonnaise before a perfectly timed John Dory fillet with saffron, mussel and cucumber sauce. For dessert, there is elderflower set cream, blueberry jelly and sugared pistachios.

Chef Tim Barnes, Dean Medlen, Ashley Outlaw **Seats** 25
Times 12-3/6-9.30, Closed Jan, Xmas, Sun-Mon (Oct-Jun) **Prices** Prices not confirmed **Wines** 13 bottles over £30, 6 bottles under £30, 6 by glass **Parking** 2 car parks at top of village **Notes** Set menu to share £42.50, Small plates menu £2-£12, Vegetarian available, Children welcome

Restaurant Nathan Outlaw

– see below

Restaurant Nathan Outlaw

PORT ISAAC Map 2 SW98

Modern British, Seafood V

tel: 01208 880896 **6 New Rd PL29 3SB**
email: rno@nathan-outlaw.com
dir: *M5/A30/A39 towards Wadebridge, B3267 through St Teath, B3267 on to Port Isacc*

Refined multi-course seafood dining from a modern master

Up on New Road with stunning views over the sea, Nathan Outlaw has found a home for his flagship restaurant that is both contemporary and, like the man himself, confidently understated. With a host of TV appearances under his belt, a number of fish-themed books, not to mention restaurants in London, Rock and a second place in Port Isaac, Nathan is the go-to-guy to deal with the fruits of the sea. There's no better way to get an idea of what Mr Outlaw is all about than to settle down in the simply soothing dining room with that sea view and Cornish artworks on the walls, and work your way through the Seafood Tasting Menu. The seafood is always the star of the show, but the acute technical skills of the kitchen team, some creative thinking, and informed, charming service create a memorable experience. Flavours are judged just right in an opening course of cured monkfish with ginger, fennel and lemon, followed by a daringly clever pairing of raw scallop and preserved herring with a hit of chilli and bacon. The journey through local waters continues with the arrival of lemon sole with wild garlic and a crispy oyster, gurnard in a crabby Porthilly sauce, and a fabulous piece of turbot partnered with spring vegetables and green dressing. Next up, a cheese course might be Cornish Jack with celery and walnuts, before the arrival of two sweet courses, the first of which could be a beautiful and clever affair with orange and rhubarb.

Chef Nathan Outlaw, Chris Simpson **Seats** 30, Pr/dining room 8
Times 12-2/7-9, Closed Xmas, Jan, Sun-Tue, L Wed-Thu **Prices** Tasting menu £119 **Wines** 163 bottles over £30, 1 bottle under £30, 16 by glass **Parking** Adjacent to restaurant **Notes** Fixed L 4 course £59, Children 10 yrs+

PORTLOE Map 2 SW93

The Lugger

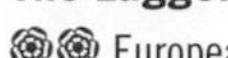 European

tel: 01872 501322 **TR2 5RD**
email: reservations.lugger@bespoke-hotels.com **web:** www.luggerhotel.com
dir: *A390 to Truro, B3287 to Tregony, A3078 (St Mawes Rd), left for Veryan, left for Portloe*

Enterprising cooking by the harbour

Dating from the 16th century, now a luxury hotel, The Lugger overlooks the sea and tiny harbour of a picturesque village on the Roseland Peninsula, with a terrace outside the smart, spacious restaurant for summer dining. Local ingredients are the kitchen's linchpin, particularly seafood, which might appear as crab soufflé with white crabmeat in chillied crab bisque. Elsewhere, look for contemporary treatments such as venison bresaola with sultana purée, pickled walnuts and gruyère, then turbot steamed over fruit tea with watercress gnocchi and candied shallots. Cornish cheeses are alternatives to afters like lemon tart brûlée with pistachio crumb and rose jelly.

Chef Jonathan Domé **Seats** 45 **Times** 12.30-2.30/7-9 **Prices** Prices not confirmed **Wines** 8 by glass **Parking** 25 **Notes** Tasting menu 6 course with wines, Sunday L, Vegetarian available, Children welcome

PORTSCATHO Map 2 SW83

Driftwood

@@@ Modern European

tel: 01872 580644 **Rosevine TR2 5EW**
email: info@driftwoodhotel.co.uk **web:** www.driftwoodhotel.co.uk
dir: *5m from St Mawes off the A3078, signed Rosevine*

Intelligent cooking in a stunning coastal setting

Perched on the clifftop above the rugged coastline around Gerrans Bay, this elegant boutique bolt-hole sits in seven acres of grounds with a wooded path winding down to its own beach. Framed by the restaurant's huge windows, those quintessentially Cornish vistas are the backdrop to a luminous white room done out in a beachcomber-chic look: pale wood floors, linen-draped tables, and bleached driftwood framing mirrors and artworks. Head chef Chris Eden is a Cornishman with a passion for the best his home territory can offer, and brings it together in intelligently-designed compositions. A starter of roast partridge with pumpkin, pickled elderberries, mead, spelt and pistachios shows flair in selecting ingredients for their striking originality, well-judged partnerships and how they work on the palate – it even comes with a crostini of wild garlic mousse, ceps and shaved truffle that could stand alone as a dish in its own right. The coastal vibes bring seafood to mind, so mains could be an equally well-constructed dish of sea-fresh roast cod, partnered by taramasalata, St Austell mussels and Avruga caviar, with kale crisps, sea purslane and broccoli to ring the textural changes. Finish with a carefully-constructed dessert of spiced pineapple with a toasted coconut meringue and a palate-cleansing lemongrass and lime sorbet.

Chef Christopher Eden **Seats** 34 **Times** 6.30-9.30, Closed early Dec-early Feb, L all week **Prices** Fixed D 3 course £60, Tasting menu £85-£110 **Wines** 60 bottles over £30, 9 bottles under £30, 7 by glass **Parking** 20 **Notes** Tasting menu 8/10 course, Vegetarian available, Children 6 yrs+

ST AUSTELL Map 2 SX05

Austell's

 Modern British

tel: 01726 813888 **10 Beach Rd PL25 3PH**
email: brett@austells.co.uk
dir: *From A390 towards Par, 0.5m after Charlestown rdbt at 2nd lights turn right. Left at rdbt. Restaurant 600yds on right*

Sophisticated dining near the beach

Austell's is a simple, uncluttered spot, with wooden floors and artwork on plain walls. Diners on the raised area see the team at work in the open-plan kitchen. Mediterranean accents enhance a menu of Cornish produce – local ham hock comes in a terrine with pea risotto, smoked Granny Smith apple purée, port and truffle dressing and a prmesan wafer, followed by pan-fried sea bass fillet and seared scallops with dauphinoise potato, carrot purée, green beans wrapped in pancetta, and a delightful pea velouté. For dessert, black cherry compôte is a perfect foil for a decadently gooey chocolate brownie, with honeycomb, frosted pecans and cherry ice cream adding further interest.

Boscundle Manor

@@ Modern British

tel: 01726 813557 **Boscundle PL25 3RL**
email: reservations@boscundlemanor.co.uk **web:** www.boscundlemanor.co.uk
dir: *Phone for directions*

Country hotel with a local flavour

Set in five acres of grounds and within easy reach of the Eden Project, this 18th-century manor offers spa treatments and indoor pool. The smart restaurant is a draw in its own right. The romantic dining room is candlelit and intimate, and everything is made in-house, from bread to ice cream. The à la carte is a satisfying blend of harmonious flavours, classical technique and contemporary touches. Start with twice-baked West Country cheese soufflé, perhaps, and move on to well-timed pan-fried cod with good crisp skin as a textural contrast, then finish with coconut pannacotta with intense coconut sorbet.

ST AUSTELL *continued*

Carlyon Bay Hotel

Modern, Traditional British

tel: 01726 812304 **Sea Rd, Carlyon Bay PL25 3RD**
email: reservations@carlyonbay.com **web:** www.carlyonbay.com
dir: *From St Austell, follow signs for Charlestown. Carlyon Bay signed on left, hotel at end of Sea Rd*

Simple traditions on the St Austell clifftop

Perched on a clifftop above St Austell, this large hotel, spa and golf course is an imposing presence above the bay. Taking care of the gastronomic side of things is the aptly-named Bay View Restaurant, where huge windows allow maximum exposure to the rugged Cornish coast views. The kitchen keeps things simple and relies on the quality and provenance of its ingredients. A traditional prawn cocktail is a good way to start, followed by roasted pork loin, spring onion and bacon mash, pear cider gravy and roasted pear. To finish, chocolate and tonka bean tart with vanilla ice cream.

The Cornwall Hotel, Spa & Estate

Modern British

tel: 01726 874050 & 874051 **Pentewan Rd, Tregorrick PL26 7AB**
email: enquiries@thecornwall.com **web:** www.thecornwall.com
dir: *A391 to St Austell then B3273 towards Mevagissey. Hotel approx 0.5m on right*

Enticing modern cooking in a stylish manor house

The Arboretum Restaurant in the old White House part of the hotel is a classy, contemporary space done out in a fashionably muted palette. The menu here treads an uncomplicated modern path, keeping step with the seasons and making good use of regional ingredients. Get things going with the timeless comfort of chicken liver parfait with fig chutney and brioche, followed by pan-roasted cod with crispy ham, crushed potatoes, mange-tout and white wine sauce. For more casual eating, there's Acorns Brasserie and the Parkland Terrace, whose views over the Pentewan Valley make it a fine spot for a pre-dinner cocktail.

ST IVES Map 2 SW54

Carbis Bay Hotel

International

tel: 01736 795311 **Carbis Bay TR26 2NP**
email: info@carbisbayhotel.co.uk **web:** www.carbisbayhotel.co.uk
dir: *A3074, through Lelant. 1m, at Carbis Bay 30yds before lights turn right into Porthrepta Rd to sea & hotel*

Contemporary cooking and panoramic views

The family that run the hotel also own the sandy beach that is only 90 seconds away, and the view over sand and sea is breathtaking. The Sands Restaurant with its glorious sea views and contemporary finish has plenty of seafood up for grabs with the likes of seared scallops with variations of apple or monkfish tails with crayfish fritter and crab remoulade, but meaty options hit the spot, too, such as a starter of chicken satay with sticky chilli peanuts and caramelised pineapple. Finish with dark chocolate mousse served with a cherry and Disaronno ice cream.

The Garrack

Modern European

tel: 01736 796199 **Burthallan Ln TR26 3AA**
email: garrackhotel@btconnet.com **web:** www.garrack.com
dir: *Exit A30 for St Ives, then from B3311 follow brown signs for Tate Gallery, then brown Garrack signs*

Enterprising menus and sea views

The restaurant offers sea views over St Ives and has a stylish contemporary look, with high-backed leather seats. Pan-fried scallops with crispy-coated black pudding, silky celeriac purée and roast pepper emulsion is a starter of vibrant, well-defined flavours. Follow with beautifully-cooked slow-roast belly pork with crisp crackling, bubble-and-squeak and thyme-speckled cider jus, with rhubarb compôte by way of counterpoint. Global cuisines add variety – tempura crayfish tails, say, with sweet chilli dipping sauce and mango and chilli salsa, then pink duck breast in an orange reduction with wontons, spiced pears and butternut squash roasted with beetroot. Pastry is consistently good, seen in pear frangipane tart with Amaretto ice cream.

Chef Tom Avery, Mark Forster **Seats** 52 **Times** 6-9 **Prices** Starter £4.50-£7.50, Main £12.50-£22, Dessert £5-£6.50 **Wines** 5 bottles over £30, 31 bottles under £30, 10 by glass **Parking** 20 **Notes** Sunday L £10.50-£18.95, Vegetarian available, Children welcome

Porthminster Beach Restaurant

Modern Mediterranean, Pacific Rim V

tel: 01736 795352 **TR26 2EB**
email: pminster@btconnect.com
dir: *On Porthminster Beach, beneath the St Ives Railway Station*

Seafood-led fusion cookery on the beach at St Ives

In a region with no shortage of places to eat with an accompanying sea view, the landmark white building surveying Porthminster Beach stands head and shoulders above much of the competition. Crispy-fried salt-and-spice squid is served with an Asian salad and a zippy citrus miso, while main-course John Dory fillets are pan fried and partnered with tempura prawns, jasmine rice, chilli ponzu and lime. There are good meat dishes too – Thai-style duck curry, perhaps, with aubergine, bok choy, crispy noodles and beansprout salad. To finish, poached pear cuts the richness of chocolate crème brûlée with chocolate cinder biscuit and lavender-scented white chocolate.

Chef Mick Smith, Ryan Venning **Seats** 60 **Times** 12-3.30/6-9.30, Closed 25 Dec, Mon (winter) **Prices** Starter £8-£12, Main £13-£40, Dessert £4-£10 **Wines** 16 bottles over £30, 26 bottles under £30, 9 by glass **Parking** 300yds (railway station) **Notes** Children welcome

The Queens

Modern British

tel: 01736 796468 **2 High St TR26 1RR**
email: info@queenshotelstives.com **web:** www.queenshotelstives.com
dir: *A3074 to town centre. With station on right, down hill to High St. On left opposite Boots*

Upmarket seasonal gastropub fare near the harbour

Behind the flower-planted frontage of this pub it's all quite trendy and modern while retaining a traditional feel, so all comers are happy, as they are with the appealingly interesting cooking. Ideas are plucked from a variety of sources, so fish goujons with taramasalata is as likely to feature among starters as crispy pork with a quail's egg and parsnip purée. Well-considered main courses are a forte, too: herb-roasted hake, flaky and moist, for instance, is served with tempura samphire, green bean and quinoa salad and crushed potatoes, and loin of lamb with shepherd's pie, greens and carrot purée. Don't pass on puddings, among them apple, raisin and cinnamon crumble.

Chef Chris Richards **Seats** 50 **Times** 12.30-2.30/6.30-9, Closed 25 Dec, L Mon (Nov-Mar) **Prices** Starter £5-£7, Main £9-£17, Dessert £5-£6 **Wines** 20 bottles under £30, 12 by glass **Parking** Station car park **Notes** L menu all mains £10 or under, Sunday L £11, Vegetarian available, Children welcome

Seagrass Restaurant

Modern Seafood

tel: 01736 793763 **Fish St TR26 1LT**
email: info@seagrass-stives.com
dir: *On Fish St opposite the Sloop pub*

Splendid seafood straight from the bay

Seagrass has made quite a splash with its modern seafood-orientated cooking. Tucked away just off the seafront, a secretive doorway leads up to the cool, stylish first-floor restaurant. The kitchen makes everything – breads, stocks, ice cream – from scratch, and strong supply lines with local fishermen ensure that the shellfish in the platters of fruits de mer are plucked fresh from the bay. Make a start with pan-fried Cornish scallops with cucumber, lime and avocado, then move on to salted cod loin, matched enterprisingly with seafood cannelloni, roast tomato velouté, peas, samphire and crispy sea lettuce, and round off with pink grapefruit tart with candied walnuts and crème fraîche.

ST MAWES **Map 2 SW83**

Hotel Tresanton

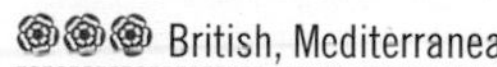

British, Mediterranean

tel: 01326 270055 **27 Lower Castle Rd TR2 5DR**
email: info@tresanton.com
dir: *On waterfront in town centre*

Bright modern cooking in super-stylish seafront hotel

An exquisite Cornish coastal spot is the setting for Olga Polizzi's celebrated seaside hotel, where undeniable class is combined with enduring style. The light, clean decor works as much for what has been left out as added in, and the place feels as though it breathes in the fresh southwestern air through every pore, all the action provided by the changing sea. A svelte dining room is crisply clothed and mosaic-floored, all cool blues and reassuring calm, and staff run it with approachable good humour. Paul Wadham achieves perfect harmony with the marine environment, and every element in each dish makes a meaningful contribution to the whole. A confident pairing of sea bass and nubbles of chorizo with sprouting broccoli, white beans and tomato makes an inspired main-course assemblage, or there could be whole Dover sole with samphire and tiny brown shrimps, or meaty monkfish with roast peppers and pesto. They might follow sardine crostini with anchovies and olives, or perhaps a textbook chicken liver and foie gras parfait with caramelised onions and toasted sourdough. The Mediterranean mood continues to the end with moist Tunisian orange cake, offset with gently sour yogurt sorbet, or for something lighter, look to crème caramel with raspberries and a poppy seed tuile.

Chef Paul Wadham **Seats** 60, Pr/dining room 45
Times 12.30-2.30/7-9.30, Closed 2 wks Jan **Prices** Fixed L 2 course £23, Starter £12-£16, Main £18-£40, Dessert £7-£9 **Wines** 61 bottles over £30, 14 bottles under £30, 11 by glass **Parking** 30 **Notes** Sunday L, Vegetarian available, Children 6 yrs+ D

ST MELLION **Map 3 SX36**

St Mellion International Resort

Modern International

tel: 01579 351351 **PL12 6SD**
email: stmellion@crown-golf.co.uk **web:** www.st-mellion.co.uk
dir: *On A388 about 4m N of Saltash*

Accomplished cosmopolitan cooking in large golfing resort

St Mellion's culinary focus is the An Boesti restaurant, a spacious room with a striking colour scheme of black and white. Beef Wellington is as likely to be on the menu as loin of lamb with rhubarb, garlic confit and potatoes mashed with rosemary, with a fish option of perhaps seared sea bass fillet with potato purée, samphire, courgettes and sultana beurre blanc. Roast chicken wings appear as a starter with Thai mushrooms, limed cucumber and butternut squash alongside ham hock terrine with coriander yogurt, pickled ginger and shallots. As well as a selection of Cornish cheeses, a pleasing conclusion may be cappuccino crème brûlée with cinnamon doughnuts.

Chef Mark Brankin **Seats** 60, Pr/dining room **Times** 6.30-9.30, Closed Xmas, New Year, Mon-Tue (off season), L all week **Prices** Prices not confirmed **Wines** 8 bottles over £30, 11 bottles under £30, 14 by glass **Parking** 750 **Notes** Vegetarian available, Children 4 yrs+

TALLAND BAY **Map 2 SX25**

Talland Bay Hotel

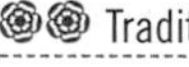

Traditional International

tel: 01503 272667 **Porthallow PL13 2JB**
email: info@tallandbayhotel.co.uk **web:** www.tallandbayhotel.co.uk
dir: *Signed from x-rds on A387 between Looe & Polperro*

Extensive menu and eccentric artefacts

The hotel named after the bay has bundles of boutique personality and an extensive menu to match. A crisped pork schnitzel with shaven fennel and apple purée in grain mustard dressing is a robust enough starter, or you could try salt-and-pepper squid in sweet chilli with peanuts. With the sea right before you, fish dishes are a strong suit, as is the case with crisp-grilled sea bass in orange and rosemary butter. A Greek theme brings on versions of kleftiko and moussaka, and desserts go for classic simplicity in the shape of thin-based lemon tart with intense blackcurrant sorbet, or a cheesecake take on Eton Mess.

Chef Nick Hawke **Seats** 40, Pr/dining room 24 **Times** 12-2.30/6.30-9.30 **Wines** 27 bottles over £30, 11 bottles under £30, 9 by glass **Parking** 23 **Notes** Afternoon tea, Sunday L £21.50-£25, Vegetarian available, Children welcome

TRESCO (ISLES OF SCILLY) Map 2 SV81

New Inn

Modern, Traditional

tel: 01720 422849 & 422867 **TR24 0QQ**
email: newinn@tresco.co.uk **web:** www.tresco.co.uk
dir: *Ferry or light plane from Land's End, Newquay or Exeter; 250yds from harbour (private island, contact hotel for details)*

Unfussy cooking in a lively pub

The waterside New Inn is right at the heart of this small community, where guests and islanders mix happily. The fine dining here is based around island produce (everything else has to be brought in by sea, don't forget). Kick off perhaps with crab on toast, datterini tomatoes, pistachio bread and pea shoots and then move on to a West Country pork belly with mash, Savoy cabbage, bacon, black pudding and cider jus or a chicken and root vegetable pie with mash and kale. There are daily specials too, and a good range of desserts.

Chef Sarah Skeate **Seats** 80, Pr/dining room 20 **Times** 12-2/6.30-9, Closed Mon-Tue (Nov-Feb) **Prices** Starter £7-£11, Main £14-£28, Dessert £7-£8 **Wines** 5 bottles over £30, 13 bottles under £30, 8 by glass **Parking** Car free island **Notes** Sunday L £10, Vegetarian available, Children welcome

TRURO Map 2 SW84

The Alverton Hotel

Modern British, European

tel: 01872 276633 **Tregolls Rd TR1 1ZQ**
web: www.thealverton.co.uk
dir: *From Truro bypass take A39 to St Austell. Just past church on left*

Grand hotel with upscale brasserie dining using local ingredients

Dating from 1830, The Alverton is an impressive granite building designed by the same chap who gave us nearby Truro Cathedral. Food and drink is a major part of the appeal, whether it's lunch, afternoon tea or an evening meal. There is plenty of period charm and a contemporary sheen to the smart, upmarket brasserie. The menu takes a modern European path with a good representation of Cornish ingredients. Start with pigeon, textures of beetroot, sautéed cabbage and charred pear before moving on to venison fillet, parsnip purée, celeriac and juniper jus. Finish with pear arlette and crème fraîche sorbet.

Hooked Restaurant & Bar

Modern British, Seafood

tel: 01872 274700 **Tabernacle St TR1 2EJ**
email: inthecity@hookedcornwall.com
dir: *100yds off Lemon Quay*

Lively spot for modern seafood cookery

Tucked away down a quiet street just off the city centre, there's a lively buzz about this smart modern brasserie. Uncovered tables, exposed brickwork and high ceilings with a sail loft feel add a seaside vibe, as do fish shoal lampshades. Seafood is the leading suit, with tapas dishes available daytime and evening. The main menu incorporates crab salad, mango, lime and cardamom salsa, which might lead on to monkfish Wellington wrapped in prosciutto with smoked garlic mash, scampi, pea velouté and crispy capers. Lemon tart with crème fraîche, meringue and blackberry sorbet is typical of the intricately worked desserts.

Chef Robert Duncan **Seats** 36, Pr/dining room 24
Times 12-2.30/5.30-9.30, Closed Sun **Prices** Fixed L 2 course fr £14.95, Starter £2.95-£8.95, Main £11.95-£23.95, Dessert £4.95-£7.50 **Wines** 6 bottles over £30, 24 bottles under £30, 12 by glass **Parking** Car park opposite **Notes** Pre-theatre menu 5.30-6.45 Mon-Sat 2/3 course £14.95/£17.95, Vegetarian available, Children welcome

Tabb's

 Modern European

tel: 01872 262110 **85 Kenwyn St TR1 3BZ**
email: n.tabb@tabbs.co.uk
dir: *Down hill past train station, right at mini rdbt, 200yds on left*

Skilful contemporary cooking a short stroll from the city centre

The recently refurbished Tabb's occupies a white corner building that looks for all the world like a private dwelling. The kitchen's a busy place, producing everything in-house. Pigeon breast is partnered by a soft-boiled egg, black pasta and sun-dried tomato dressing, and another starter might be rich smoked haddock chowder flavoured with lemongrass, ginger and chilli oil. Beautifully tender roast pork belly is accompanied by couscous gently spiked by harissa along with black olives, green lentils, battered courgettes and sauté potatoes, and grilled hake fillet by Provençal-style leeks and mushrooms and Jerusalem artichoke velouté. Puddings run to tonka bean pannacotta with strawberry sorbet given a kick of black pepper.

Chef Nigel Tabb **Seats** 28 **Times** 12-2/5.30-9.30, Closed 25 Dec, 1 Jan, 1 wk Jan, Mon, L Sat, D Sun **Prices** Fixed L 2 course £19.50, Fixed D 3 course £25, Starter £7.25-£10.50, Main £15.75-£20.50, Dessert £7.50 **Wines** 17 bottles over £30, 30 bottles under £30, 15 by glass **Parking** 200yds **Notes** Tapas L £12, Pre-theatre menu 5.30-6.45pm bookings only, Sunday L £19.50-£32.50, Vegetarian available, Children welcome

VERYAN Map 2 SW93

The Quarterdeck at The Nare

Traditional British

tel: 01872 500000 **Carne Beach TR2 5PF**
email: stay@narehotel.co.uk **web:** www.quarterdeckrestaurant.co.uk
dir: *From Tregony follow A3078 for approx 1.5m. Left at Veryan sign, through village towards sea & hotel*

Smart beachside setting for stylish modern food

The Quarterdeck is a shipshape, yachtie-themed setting of polished teak, gingham seats and square rails. The kitchen produces modern dishes bursting with bold flavours – pan-seared scallops are partnered with braised pork cheek, potato and truffle terrine, parsnip purée and sauced with a cider reduction, followed by a big, rich dish of roasted grouse matched with foie gras, creamy polenta, date purée, poached pear and caramelised shallots. Local fish and shellfish are a strong point too – perhaps a luxurious duo of pan-fried turbot and lobster medallion with carrot and lime purée, honeycomb and beurre blanc. A finale of apple pie millefeuille highlights strong technical skills.

Chef Richard James **Seats** 60 **Times** 12.30-2.30/7-9.30, Closed 25 Dec, D 31 Dec **Prices** Fixed L 2 course £27.50-£35, Starter £9.50-£12, Main £18-£55, Dessert £9.50-£11 **Wines** 150 bottles over £30, 50 bottles under £30, 19 by glass **Parking** 60 **Notes** Afternoon tea, Vegetarian available, Children welcome

WATERGATE BAY Map 2 SW86

Fifteen Cornwall

 Italian

tel: 01637 861000 **On The Beach TR8 4AA**
email: restaurant@fifteencornwall.co.uk
dir: *M5 to Exeter & join A30 westbound. Exit Highgate Hill junct, following signs to airport and at T-junct after airport, turn left & follow road to Watergate Bay*

Italian cooking, Jamie-style, on the beach

Floor-to-ceiling windows show off the ever-changing sea views from this large, contemporary space, but it's just as smart and welcoming after sunset. Jamie Oliver's guiding principle remains the same – to give young people a solid grounding in skills and experience, and the classy fixtures and fittings and not-so-low prices make this a destination eatery. You'll find proper Italian food on the menu, with porchetta, mackerel and crispy capers a good place to start, followed by a generous portion of wild garlic agnolotti with short rib ragù and horseradish. Lemon tart with Buttervilla's rhubarb and clotted cream rounds things off nicely.

Seats 120, Pr/dining room 10 **Times** 12-2.30/6.15-9.15 **Prices** Fixed L 3 course £32, Tasting menu £65-£85, Starter £14-£15, Main £21-£29, Dessert £6-£9 **Wines** 79 bottles over £30, 8 bottles under £30, 15 by glass **Parking** In front of restaurant & on site P&D **Notes** Tasting menu 5/7 course, ALC L only, Vegetarian available, Children 12 yrs+ D

CUMBRIA

ALSTON Map 18 NY74

Lovelady Shield Country House Hotel

Modern British

tel: 01434 381203 **CA9 3LF**
email: enquiries@lovelady.co.uk **web:** www.lovelady.co.uk
dir: *2m E of Alston, signed off A689 at junct with B6294*

Refined modern dining in intimate country house

A white Georgian property on the banks of the River Nent, eating here is a treat, with a wide-ranging menu that can set diners dithering. Starters might include saffron-infused crab arancini with tomato compôte and basil pesto. Main courses too are quite complex, bringing out layers of flavours and textures: duo of spring lamb, for instance, features a roast loin and a braised shoulder on crushed new potatoes with wild garlic and a mint and sun-blushed tomato sauce. Or there's the roast cod fillet in pancetta sauce, anchovy with lemon and thyme risotto. A skilled pastry cook is behind puddings such as tarte Tatin with ginger custard.

Chef Tom Orton **Seats** 30 **Times** 12-2/7-8.30, Closed L Mon-Sat **Prices** Tasting menu £59.50, Starter £11.50, Main £23.50, Dessert £12.50 **Wines** 100 bottles over £30, 50 bottles under £30, 11 by glass **Parking** 20 **Notes** D 4 course £49.50, Tasting D 7 course, Sunday L, Vegetarian available, Children 7 yrs+

AMBLESIDE Map 18 NY30

Forest Side

Modern British NEW V

tel: 015394 35250 **Keswick Rd, Grasmere LA22 9RN**
email: info@theforestside.com **web:** www.theforestside.com
dir: *Leave M6 at junct 36, take 1st exit at rdbt onto A590 to Grasmere. Take 2nd exit at mini-rdbt. Hotel is 0.5m on the right*

Inventive cooking from a rising star

A top-to-toe makeover has transformed this Victorian Gothic mansion into a stylish boutique bolthole designed to appeal to 21st-century pleasure-seekers. An important part of the package is the restaurant, where the old oak floors have been recycled into tables by a local craftsman. Forest Side's new kitchen sports a full arsenal of modern kit, and it's all in the hands of Kevin Tickle, a local lad who served time at Simon Rogan's L'Enclume, so you can expect imaginative ideas built on the finest local, sometimes foraged, produce, with goodies from the resurrected kitchen garden. The finely-tuned flavours of seaweed broth with clams, marsh herbs and kohlrabi make for a storming opener, followed by an immaculately handled slab of cod served with onion purée, brown shrimp butter and mollusc broth. The sheer quality of the raw materials speaks for itself in a dish showcasing pork two ways: loin and belly, accompanied by cultured pollen yogurt and a birch sap reduction from trees in the hotel's grounds. Next comes a crossover course, blending the sweet and savoury notes of sweet cheese parfait with a sea buckthorn biscuit and coltsfoot, while the finale stars forced Yorkshire rhubarb (poached, sorbet and gel) with burnt butter biscuit and sweet cicely.

Chef Kevin Tickle **Seats** 50, Pr/dining room 12 **Times** 12-2/7-9.30, Closed L Mon-Tue **Prices** Fixed L 2 course £25-£35, Fixed D 3 course £55, Tasting menu £60-£85 **Wines** 147 bottles over £30, 3 bottles under £30, 20 by glass **Parking** 44 **Notes** Children 8 yrs+

Lake Road Kitchen

Northern European NEW

tel: 015394 22012 **Lake Rd LA22 0AD**
email: info@lakeroadkitchen.co.uk
dir: *From S, M6 junct 36, follow A590. Take A591 towards Kendal & Windermere. Through Windermere then 3m to Ambleside*

Northern European seasonal food that rings the daily changes

The converted shop premises just off Ambleside's main street feature two broad windows that let passing strollers see what they are missing. James Cross styles the place a north European bistro, which gives some indication of his determination to work with the seasons and the climate, pickling and bottling for the winter months, foraging for summer berries and autumn mushrooms, as well as bringing in much fine Lakeland meat, supplemented by Cornish fish. The menu changes daily, and the hits just keep on coming. A spring meal opens with a vivid green stew of broad beans, peas and asparagus, including wild beach peas, while the colder end of autumn brings on a pair of scallops on tart apple purée dressed in dill oil. Butter-basted teal comes to table in the pan, the breast sliced on to an underlay of wild mushrooms, lingonberries and chard. In May, there may be flowering ramsons to garnish a serving of roast cod with razor clams and mash. Desserts mobilise excellent pastry work for a tarte fine of apple in Calvados sauce, garnished with some of last winter's blackberries pickled in booze, or a buckwheat tart of sea buckthorn custard in sharp orange, topped with scorched meringue. Home-baked breads include an exemplary sourdough with crunchy dark crust, served with hand-churned whey butter.

Chef James Cross **Seats** 28 **Times** 6-9, Closed 31 Jan-12 Feb, Mon-Tue **Prices** Prices not confirmed **Wines** 21 bottles over £30, 4 bottles under £30, 25 by glass **Parking** On street, car park **Notes** Vegetarian available, Children 12 yrs+

The Old Stamp House Restaurant

Modern British V

tel: 015394 32775 **Church St LA22 0BU**
email: oldstamphouse@outlook.com
dir: *Follow A591 into Ambleside from either direction & enter one way system. Church St accessed from Lake Rd, right after the Royal Oak*

Contemporary cooking in Wordsworth's old place

It's not widely known that William Wordsworth was Cumbria's 'Distributor of Stamps' back in 19th century, and this is where he plied his trade. The organic and foraged ingredients on show make this is a thoroughly modern sort of restaurant. Prices are fair given the craft and creativity, with the fixed-price lunch a veritable bargain. Things kick off with excellent bread before first-course smoked Furness wood pigeon with beetroot turned out fashionably in an array of textures, plus celeriac purée and pickled cherries. Next up, Whitehaven turbot, cooked just right, or Alston Moor red grouse with Scottish girolles and truffle jus. Finish with a dazzling Amaretto parfait.

Chef Ryan Blackburn **Seats** 30, Pr/dining room 8
Times 12.30-1.30/6-9, Closed Xmas, Sun-Mon, L Tue **Prices** Fixed L 2 course fr £20, Tasting menu fr £55, Starter £8-£14, Main £19-£27, Dessert £8-£10 **Wines** 25 bottles over £30, 15 bottles under £30, 6 by glass **Parking** On street **Notes** L tasting menu £35, Children welcome

AMBLESIDE *continued*

Rothay Manor

 Modern British NEW

tel: 01539 433605 **Rothay Bridge LA22 0EH**
email: hotel@rothaymanor.co.uk **web:** www.rothaymanor.co.uk
dir: *In Ambleside follow signs for Coniston (A593). Manor 0.25m SW of Ambleside opposite rugby pitch*

Refined Lakeland hotel with a loyal clientele

A great example of a traditional Lake District country-house hotel, whitewashed Rothay Manor stands in attractive landscaped gardens a short walk from bustling Ambleside. A Liverpool shipping merchant built it in 1823 and many Regency features are still much in evidence. Served by efficient and friendly staff, the Cumbria-influenced modern British food at dinner might comprise a starter of king scallops with smoked onion mayonnaise, smoked pancetta, caviar and parsley; followed by fir-infused fillet of Ambleside venison with Brussels sprouts, orange, celeriac and gin purée, and smoked pancetta. Madeira and Earl Grey pannacotta with home-made hobnob crumb and sorbet to finish.

Chef Brandon Shepherd **Seats** 40, Pr/dining room 20 **Times** 12-2/7-9, Closed 2-20 Jan **Prices** Fixed D 3 course fr £42.50 **Wines** 15 bottles over £30, 15 bottles under £30, 10 by glass **Notes** Sunday L £17.95-£24.95, Vegetarian available, Children welcome

Waterhead Hotel

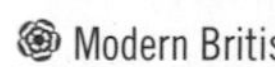

tel: 015394 32566 **Lake Rd LA22 0ER**
email: waterhead@englishlakes.co.uk **web:** www.englishlakes.co.uk
dir: *A591 into Ambleside, hotel opposite Waterhead Pier*

Vibrant brasserie cooking on the edge of Windermere

Just a short stroll from the bustle of Ambleside, the Waterhead sports a thoroughly modern boutique look with funky purple LED lighting to go with its up-to-date brasserie dishes. Start with duck liver parfait with red onion jelly and toasted treacle and walnut bread. Follow with pan-fried tuna steak with fondant potatoes, seasonal veggies and béarnaise sauce, or look to the grill for slabs of Cumbrian beef, or a trendy burger of pulled pork shoulder with honey and bourbon barbecue sauce, sweet potato wedges and crispy fried onions. Coconut and raspberry pannacotta with shaved coconut and raspberry purée is a good way to finish.

Chef Nick Martin **Seats** 70 **Times** 7-9.30, Closed Xmas, New Year (only open to residents), L all week **Prices** Starter £5.50-£9.95, Main £14.95-£26, Dessert £4.50-£9.95 **Wines** 25 bottles over £30, 41 bottles under £30, 11 by glass **Parking** 50, Nearby pay & display **Notes** Vegetarian available, Children welcome

APPLEBY-IN-WESTMORLAND **Map 18 NY62**

Appleby Manor Country House Hotel

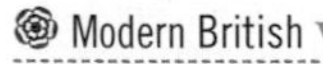

tel: 017683 51571 **Roman Rd CA16 6JB**
email: reception@applebymanor.co.uk **web:** www.applebymanor.co.uk
dir: *M6 junct 40/A66 towards Brough. Take Appleby turn, then immediately right. Continue for 0.5m*

Peaceful rural views and modern country-house cooking

The outlook over Appleby Castle and the Eden Valley is a pastoral treat, and this Victorian sandstone house was put up by someone with an eye for a view. The hotel's newest addition is a luxe garden spa. The 1871 Bistro delivers breezy feel-good dishes in a charming rustic room, while the main restaurant takes a more refined approach to proceedings. There's plenty of regional produce on the menu and the kitchen delivers smart, upscale food. Begin with breast of wood pigeon with caramelised pears and cider sauce, before Solway salmon three ways, or a haunch steak of Lakeland venison, and finish with sticky toffee pudding.

Chef Chris Thompson **Seats** 100, Pr/dining room 20 **Times** 12-2/7-9, Closed 24-26 Dec **Prices** Starter £6.95-£11, Main £14.95-£22, Dessert £5.95-£8.95 **Wines** 10 bottles over £30, 38 bottles under £30, 10 by glass **Parking** 60 **Notes** Sunday L £10-£25, Children welcome

BARROW-IN-FURNESS **Map 18 SD26**

Abbey House Hotel

Traditional British, French

tel: 01229 838282 & 0844 826 2091 *(Calls cost 7p per minute plus your phone company's access charge)* **Abbey Rd LA13 0PA**
email: enquiries@abbeyhousehotel.com **web:** www.abbeyhousehotel.com
dir: *From A590 follow signs for Furness General Hospital & Furness Abbey. Hotel approx 100yds on left*

Stylish spot for contemporary hotel dining

This grand red-brick house in 14 acres of countryside is home to the charming and gently contemporary Oscar's restaurant. There's nothing stuffy about the place, with a relaxed (but professional) approach all round. The kitchen turns out modern dishes based on a good amount of regional produce. Gravad lax is a simple enough starter, but here it is perked up with an oyster beignet, pickled beetroot and basil crème fraîche, while main-course cannon of lamb is tender and full of flavour. Finish with a decent version of tarte Tatin with home-made fig ice cream and cinnamon syrup. There's a stylish cocktail bar, too.

Chef James Lowery **Seats** 100, Pr/dining room 24 **Times** 10-10, All-day dining **Prices** Starter £4.95-£8.50, Main £12.95-£19.50, Dessert £6-£7.95 **Wines** 13 bottles over £30, 20 bottles under £30, 15 by glass **Parking** 200 **Notes** Sunday L £10.95-£18.95, Vegetarian available, Children welcome

Clarence House Country Hotel & Restaurant

British, International V

tel: 01229 462508 **Skelgate, Dalton-in-Furness LA15 8BQ**
email: clarencehsehotel@aol.com **web:** www.clarencehouse-hotel.co.uk
dir: *A590 through Ulverston & Lindal, 2nd exit at rdbt & 1st exit at next. Follow signs to Dalton, hotel at top of hill on right*

Lakeland cooking in a small-town hotel

There is indeed a country feel to this pleasant, white-painted hotel on the edge of a small south Lakes town. Its Victorian-orangery-style dining room looks out over well-tended gardens, and tables on the terrace bask in the afternoon sun. Nearby is the beautiful St Thomas's Valley, while further west are the dune-fringed beaches of Furness. Internationally influenced, the largely British menu offers starters of baked scallops with cauliflower purée, marinated raisins and crispy Parma ham, or heritage tomato and mozzarella salad with home-made pesto. Roast grouse with bubble-and-squeak galette, blackberries and whisky jus is a characteristic main, others being fell-bred beef, Cumbrian lamb and grills.

Chef Andrew Hill **Seats** 100, Pr/dining room 14 **Times** 12-2/7-9, Closed D Sun **Prices** Prices not confirmed **Wines** 28 bottles over £30, 35 bottles under £30, 8 by glass **Parking** 40 **Notes** Fri D carvery £29.95, Sunday L, Children welcome

BASSENTHWAITE Map 18 NY23

Armathwaite Hall Hotel and Spa

◎◎ British, French V

tel: 017687 76551 **CA12 4RE**
email: reservations@armathwaite-hall.com **web:** www.armathwaite-hall.com
dir: *From M6 junct 40/A66 to Keswick then A591 towards Carlisle. Continue for 7m and turn left at Castle Inn*

Fine dining with lake views

Standing in 400 acres of grounds bordering Bassenthwaite, Armathwaite Hall has rich fabrics and acres of oak panelling, as well as all the present-day amenities. The Lake View Restaurant is a lovely high-ceilinged room in rich golds and reds with comfortable chairs at formally-laid tables. The kitchen steers a course to keep traditionalists and modernists happy, sending out starters like marinated Shetland scallops with ham hock, avocado and ginger. Main course might be loin and braised shoulder of Cartmel venison with poached pear and parsleyed bulgar wheat, while the signature dessert is apple and cinnamon spring roll with yogurt sorbet and figs.

Chef Kevin Dowling **Seats** 80, Pr/dining room **Times** 12.30-1.45/7.30-9 **Prices** Prices not confirmed **Wines** 6 by glass **Parking** 100 **Notes** Fixed D 5 course £46.95, Sunday L, Children welcome

The Pheasant

◎ Modern British

tel: 017687 76234 **CA13 9YE**
email: info@the-pheasant.co.uk **web:** www.the-pheasant.co.uk
dir: *M6 junct 40, take A66 (Keswick and North Lakes). Continue past Keswick towards Cockermouth. Signed from A66*

Contemporary classic cooking led by Cumbrian ingredients

Dating from the 17th century, this long, low-slung building has a charming, atmospheric bar and a beamed bistro as well as the more formal Fell Restaurant. The kitchen relies on local sources for its ingredients and, while its roots may lie in the great classical techniques and repertoire, it keeps a finger on the contemporary pulse. Start with twice-baked Swiss cheese soufflé, leek velouté and parmesan, as a prelude to tender Gressingham duck breast in port and cherry jus with granola, parsnip and beetroot. A trip down memory lane at dessert turns up a reworking of sponge-and-ice-cream Arctic roll made with pistachios and griottines.

Ravenstone Lodge

◎ British

tel: 01768 776629 **CA12 4QG**
email: enquiries@ravenstonelodge.co.uk **web:** www.ravenstonelodge.co.uk
dir: *5m N of Keswick on A591*

Unfussy but imaginative country-house cooking

Enjoying an enviable position near Bassenthwaite Lake, this country-house hotel has plenty going on, including a bar and bistro in the former stables. The Coach House restaurant is smartly turned out and the team in the kitchen takes quality regional ingredients and doesn't muck about with them too much. Start with a twice-baked Appleby cheese soufflé, glazed with parmesan before moving on to roast Cumbrian pork belly, fondant potato, braised red cabbage, apple sauce and red wine jus. Warm pear and almond tart with toffee sauce and vanilla ice cream is a fine way to round off a meal.

Chef James Cooper **Seats** 26 **Times** 6.30-9 **Prices** Starter £5-£10, Main £15-£25, Dessert £5-£8 **Wines** 10 bottles over £30, 20 bottles under £30, 12 by glass **Parking** 15 **Notes** Vegetarian available, Children 8 yrs+

BORROWDALE Map 18 NY21

Borrowdale Gates Hotel

◎ British, French

tel: 017687 77204 **CA12 5UQ**
email: hotel@borrowdale-gates.com **web:** www.borrowdale-gates.com
dir: *B5289 from Keswick, after 4m turn right over bridge to Grange. Hotel 400yds on right*

Skilful modern country-house dining with Lakeland views

In an area of the Borrowdale Valley hailed by Wainwright as one of the most picturesque in the Lake District, this classic Lakeland country house is set in the heart of prime walking territory. The kitchen has ramped up its efforts since the hotel's recent refurbishment, turning out a confident take on modern British dishes cooked with skill. Start with pan-seared Scottish scallops, smoked black pudding, apple and raisin purée, and salsify crisps, and proceed to breast and crispy leg of corn-fed chicken, baby leeks, thyme gnocchi and wilted kale. End with blackberry pannacotta, apple tart and green apple sorbet.

Chef Christopher Standhaven **Seats** 50 **Times** 12-3/6-10, Closed Jan **Prices** Fixed D 3 course fr £41, Starter £5.50-£12.50, Main £12.50-£26 **Wines** 24 bottles over £30, 31 bottles under £30, 18 by glass **Parking** 25 **Notes** Light L only Mon-Sat, Sunday L fr £23.50, Vegetarian available, Children welcome

Hazel Bank Country House

◎ British

tel: 017687 77248 **Rosthwaite CA12 5XB**
email: info@hazelbankhotel.co.uk **web:** www.hazelbankhotel.co.uk
dir: *A66 Keswick, follow B5289 signed Borrowdale, turn left before Rosthwaite over humpback bridge*

Daily-changing set menu in gorgeous Lakeland valley

This classic stone-built Lakeland house sits amid four acres in the village of Rosthwaite in the gorgeous Borrowdale Valley. The drill is a daily-changing four-course menu, with a cheeseboard as optional extra. Spring might bring on a short-pastried warm goats' cheese tart with caramelised red onion marmalade to begin, followed by a tranche of seared monkfish in lemon oil with minted peas. Then comes Lakeland beef for main, served with charlottes roasted in the skins, and parsnip purée topped with smoked black pudding crumble, in thyme-scented red wine jus. Things come to rest with a featherlight chocolate brownie, Belgian truffle and white chocolate ice cream.

Chef David Jackson **Seats** 20 **Times** 7-8, Closed Dec-Jan, L all week **Prices** Fixed D 3 course £29-£39 **Wines** 25 bottles over £30, 55 bottles under £30, 10 by glass **Parking** 12 **Notes** Vegetarian available, Children 14 yrs+

BORROWDALE *continued*

Leathes Head Hotel

British

tel: 017687 77247 **CA12 5UY**
email: reservations@leatheshead.co.uk **web:** www.leatheshead.co.uk
dir: *3.75m S of Keswick on B5289, set back on the left*

Modern country-house cooking and glorious views

Tucked away in the heart of the beautiful Borrowdale Valley, the Leathes Head's chef, shows real passion for locally-grown and reared produce in daily-changing menus. Ham hock terrine is pointed up with mustard mayonnaise, sherry vinegar jelly and a crispy deep-fried quail's egg, while local Herdwick hogget is showcased in a main course involving cutlets, roasted shoulder and kidney with white bean purée, fondant potato and a glossy rosemary jus. Fish-wise, there might be sea trout with smoked crushed potatoes, purple sprouting broccoli and wild garlic mayonnaise. For dessert, citrussy lemon parfait is counterpointed with the intensity of praline and caramelised popcorn.

Chef Daniel Hopkins **Seats** 24 **Times** 6.30-8.30, Closed mid Nov-mid Feb **Prices** Prices not confirmed **Wines** 23 bottles over £30, 31 bottles under £30, 10 by glass **Parking** 15 **Notes** Fixed D 4 course £39.50, Vegetarian available, Children 9 yrs+

Lodore Falls Hotel

Modern British V

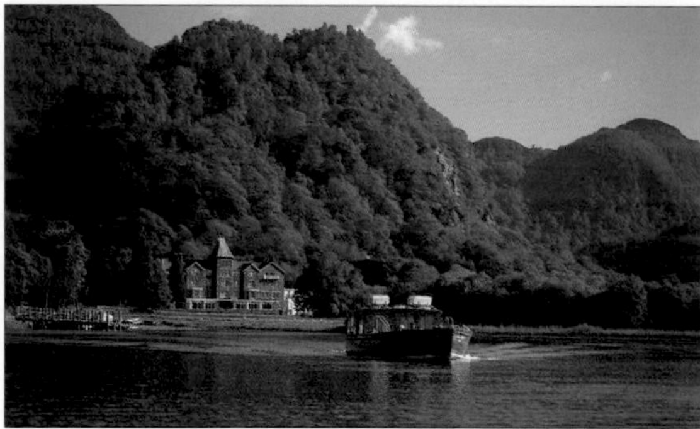

tel: 017687 77285 & 0800 840 1246 **CA12 5UX**
email: lodorefalls@lakedistricthotels.net **web:** www.lakedistricthotels.net/lodorefalls
dir: *M6 junct 40, A66 to Keswick, B5289 to Borrowdale. Hotel on left*

Plush lakeside dining using local ingredients

The Lake View Restaurant has plush, traditional furnishings and pristine white tablecloths, and is the setting for some good modern dishes. Opening the batting could be a brilliantly crisp-skinned fillet of gilt head bream on soba noodles, seasoned with wasabi and yuzu. A sorbet, perhaps pink champagne, precedes the main course, which may be breast of locally-shot pheasant with wilted Savoy cabbage, a loose carrot and swede purée and thyme-roasted potatoes, in a rich jus boosted with port, or sea bass with crushed potato and crab in brandied lobster cream sauce. A fine dark chocolate fondant with crushed pistachios and whisky marmalade ice cream is well worth the wait.

Chef Shane Hamilton **Seats** 120, Pr/dining room 24 **Times** 12-2/6.30-9.15 **Prices** Fixed L 2 course £15.95, Fixed D 3 course £35 **Wines** 32 bottles over £30, 73 bottles under £30, 17 by glass **Parking** 90 **Notes** Pudding Club 2nd Thu of month D 5 course £42.50, Sunday L £14.95-£19.95, Children welcome

BRAITHWAITE — Map 18 NY22

The Cottage in the Wood

Modern British V

tel: 017687 78409 **Whinlatter Pass CA12 5TW**
email: relax@thecottageinthewood.co.uk **web:** www.thecottageinthewood.co.uk
dir: *M6 junct 40, A66 signed Keswick. 1m after Keswick take B5292 signed Braithwaite, hotel in 2m*

Stunning views and accomplished cooking

Described as England's only true mountain forest, Whinlatter is home to the aptly named Cottage in the Wood, where soaring trees and a spectacular view down the valley make for a captivating setting. The former 17th-century coaching inn is now a slick boutique restaurant with rooms, and its semi-circular dining room serves up the scenery in all its glory (a second area lacks the view but has a roaring log fire), while a table on the terrace puts you right among the trees. The contemporary finish of the interior is matched by the dynamic cooking of Chris Archer, who turns regional produce into one of the area's most memorable culinary experiences. The kitchen's beautifully-crafted output begins with impressive amuse-bouche (a stunning cucumber and horseradish gazpacho, say), before a terrine of smoked duck breast and confit leg arrives wrapped in local air-dried ham, pointed up with apricot purée and served with a pistachio biscotti. Next up, Tony Cresswell's Lorton Lop gets a thorough work-out in a technically-accomplished dish, or go for Cornish sea bream with wild garlic and brown shrimps. To finish, a classic Opera gâteau is flavoured with burnt orange. There's a tasting menu with an optional artisan cheese plate, while the canny wine list has plenty of options by the glass.

Chef Christopher Archer **Seats** 40 **Times** 12.30-2/6-9, Closed Jan, Sun-Mon, L Tue-Wed **Prices** Prices not confirmed **Wines** 40 bottles over £30, 12 bottles under £30, 8 by glass **Parking** 16 **Notes** Fixed D 4 course £55 (groups of 6+), Children 10 yrs+ D

CARLISLE — Map 18 NY35

Crown Hotel

Modern British

tel: 01228 561888 **Station Rd, Wetheral CA4 8ES**
email: info@crownhotelwetheral.co.uk **web:** www.crownhotelwetheral.co.uk
dir: *M6 junct 42, B6263 to Wetheral, right at village shop, car park at rear of hotel*

Modern British cooking in a village hotel

The white Georgian hotel is in a picturesque village a few miles out of Carlisle, close to Hadrian's Wall. Its Conservatory restaurant overlooks the landscaped gardens, and has a striking raftered ceiling and red quarry tiles on the floor. The kitchen favours a largely modern British approach, giving dishes their own distinctive identity. Twice-baked goats' cheese soufflé comes tricked out with balsamic red onions, pomegranate seeds and pickled walnuts. Comforting ways with main courses include baked cod with Morecambe Bay shrimps, buttered kale and parsleyed mash, and for pudding, look no further than flawlessly caramelised tarte Tatin with vanilla ice cream.

Chef Paul Taylor **Seats** 80, Pr/dining room 120 **Times** 12-2.30/7-9.30, Closed L Sat **Prices** Prices not confirmed **Wines** 8 bottles over £30, 36 bottles under £30, 14 by glass **Parking** 70 **Notes** Sunday L, Vegetarian available, Children welcome

L'Enclume

CARTMEL **Map 18 SD37**

Modern British V NOTABLE WINE LIST

tel: 015395 36362 **Cavendish St LA11 6PZ**
email: info@lenclume.co.uk **web:** www.lenclume.co.uk
dir: *Follow signs for A590 W, turn left for Cartmel before Newby Bridge*

A world-class dining experience by the AA's Chef of the Year

Most chefs these days claim to supply their kitchens from the local larder, but few control their ingredients' provenance in the way that Simon Rogan achieves here: much of what's on your plate will have been picked a short while ago at his 12-acre organic farm nearby, or foraged from the local countryside. What he doesn't produce himself is sourced with diligence, usually from trusted local suppliers, so the cooking has deep roots in the Lake District countryside – the very definition of 'cuisine de terroir'. And that sense of being in tune with the landscape extends to the village surroundings: L'Enclume looks at first sight like the solid 700-year-old blacksmith's forge it once was (the name is French for 'anvil'). Thanks to Rogan's efforts and unique creativity it has morphed into a world-class culinary destination whose interior has an almost Scandinavian sparseness, all whitewashed walls with minimal adornment, polished stone floors and unclothed tables. If you want to put up for the night (so you can go for broke with the impressive wine list and revelatory wine flights, perhaps), the operation comprises classy bedrooms in three buildings around the village. The multi-course (we're talking double figures here) menus, including a veggie version, are interpreted by on-the-ball serving staff, which is essential when you consider that a meal here is a succession of dishes intricately constructed from multiple, often unusual, components. With inventive cooking of this ilk, the kitchen needs its high-tech gadgets, but everything is done here for a reason rather than empty effect, and respect for the produce remains paramount. These days, the Rogan empire extends to the The Midland Hotel in Manchester, where there's a brace of dining options – The French and Mr Cooper's House and Garden – and southwards to Fera within that grandest of old dames, Claridge's, so the business of delivering the goods on a day-to-day basis is in the talented hands of head chef Tom Barnes. Expect fun and technical brilliance from the off in the canapés: 'oyster pebbles' are soft meringues filled with oyster cream, while smoked eel with ham fat arrives surrounded by hay under a smoke-filled cloche. The meal proper starts with artichoke broth with Westcombe cheddar and hen of the woods mushrooms. Elsewhere, lightly-smoked venison comes with crystallised balls of charcoal oil, mustard mayonnaise and strands of fennel, while brill is poached in poultry juices and matched with celeriac, yeast flakes and fermented mushroom. Sweet courses might deliver caramelised pumpkin with brown butter and almond, or a thought-provoking ensemble of woodruff, apple, sorrel and yogurt. The sommelier team approach the tricky challenge of matching wine to off-the-wall flavours with passion, championing lesser-seen grape varieties, biodynamic wines, and always keen to support English producers.

Chef Simon Rogan, Tom Barnes, Marcus Noack **Seats** 50, Pr/dining room 6 **Times** 12-1.30/6.30-9.30, Closed 25-26 Dec, 2-16 Jan, Mon **Prices** Prices not confirmed Tasting menu £130 **Wines** 290 bottles over £30, 30 by glass **Parking** 7, On street **Notes** Fixed L 6 course £49, Tasting menu L/D 18-20 course, Children 10 yrs+ D

CARTMEL Map 18 SD37

Aynsome Manor Hotel

Modern, Traditional British

tel: 015395 36653 **LA11 6HH**
email: aynsomemanor@btconnect.com **web:** www.aynsomemanorhotel.co.uk
dir: *M6 junct 36, A590 signed Barrow-in-Furness towards Cartmel. Left at end of road, hotel before village*

Traditional country-house dining with a daily-changing menu

A charming small country-house hotel in the untouched Vale of Cartmel with views south to the Norman priory, meadows and woods. The cooking shows accurate timings, judiciously considered combinations and clear flavours, seen in starters of guinea fowl and leek terrine wrapped in Cumbrian ham served with apricot and sultana chutney, and mussels steamed with garlic, parsley, cream and white wine. Main courses on the short, daily-changing menus might include rich, gamey venison loin in damson and gin jus plated with a sage and onion-flavoured polenta cake. Seasonal vegetables are served separately, and classic lemon tart with whipped cream and fruit compôte is a memorable finish.

Chef Gordon Topp **Seats** 28 **Times** 7-8.30, Closed 25-26 Dec, 2-28 Jan, L Mon-Sat **Prices** Fixed D 3 course £29.50-£31 **Wines** 20 bottles over £30, 45 bottles under £30, 6 by glass **Parking** 20 **Notes** Sunday L £18.95-£21, Vegetarian available, Children 5 yrs+

L'Enclume

– see page 93

Rogan & Company Restaurant

Modern British

tel: 015395 35917 **The Square LA11 6QD**
email: reservations@roganandcompany.co.uk
dir: *From M6 junct 36 follow signs for A590. Turn off at sign for Cartmel village*

Reimagined dishes from the Rogan repertoire

With Simon Rogan's name above the door and the flagship L'Enclume just up the road, you expect good things at this clean-lined, rustic-chic restaurant in a Lakeland stone house with Cartmel Priory an impressive backdrop and a cracking riverside location. Rogan is not at the stoves of course, but the food bears his stamp, albeit in a more stripped-back and accessible style, and the same supremely good produce lies at the heart of everything (much of it sourced from his farm down the valley). It is dynamic, contemporary stuff, starting with a deeply muttony croquette of lamb belly pointed up with piquant capers, cornichons and shallots and partnered with creamed potato, caramelised onion and watercress – a case of simplicity done with style. More big, bold flavours arrive at main course stage: hake fillet is butter-poached, then roasted and served with confit potatoes, wild garlic oil, silky celeriac purée, crispy chicken skin and hazelnut. Meatier appetites could try Cumbrian rib steak with truffle pudding, purple potato latkas, shallots and parsley. Desserts are no less enticing judging by the caramel tart, which arrives with candied lemon and mascarpone ice cream, or there could be a comforting baked rice pudding with blackberries, pear and almond.

Chef Simon Rogan, Lee Bird **Seats** 40, Pr/dining room 10 **Times** 12-2.30/6.30-9, Closed 1st wk Jan, L Mon, D Sun **Prices** Fixed L 2 course £18, Starter £7-£8, Main £13-£24.50, Dessert £7.50 **Wines** 26 bottles over £30, 6 bottles under £30, 13 by glass **Parking** On street **Notes** Sunday L £20-£30, Vegetarian available, Children welcome

CROSTHWAITE Map 18 SD49

The Punchbowl Inn at Crosthwaite

Modern British

tel: 015395 68237 **Lyth Valley LA8 8HR**
email: info@the-punchbowl.co.uk **web:** www.the-punchbowl.co.uk
dir: *A590 then A5074 signed Bowness/Crosthwaite. Inn within 4.5m on right next to St Mary's Church*

Fashion-conscious Cumbrian dishes in the damson-rich Lyth Valley

A small country house in the verdant Lyth Valley, The Punchbowl is one of Lakeland's homelier places, run with great civility by the hands-on team. A slate-topped bar and modern rustic furniture give the place a fresh look, and the substantial menu shows plenty of fashion-conscious technique. Seared wood pigeon, for instance, is accompanied by celeriac, blueberries, pear and chocolate. That might be followed by spot-on pan-fried salmon, bursting with flavour, with curried chickpeas, white crabmeat, pak choi and amaretti, or an equally well-composed dish of roast saddle of rabbit with crayfish mousse, apricots and potato purée. Vibrant combinations extend to puddings, seen in vanilla crème brûlée with Lyth Valley damsons, lavender and shortbread.

Chef Scott Fairweather **Seats** 50, Pr/dining room 16 **Times** 12-9, All-day dining **Prices** Starter £4.95-£8.50, Main £13.50-£19.95, Dessert £6.95-£9.95 **Wines** 68 bottles over £30, 30 bottles under £30, 12 by glass **Parking** 40 **Notes** Sunday L £14.95, Vegetarian available, Children welcome

GLENRIDDING Map 18 NY31

Inn on the Lake

Modern European V

tel: 017684 82444 **Lake Ullswater CA11 0PE**
email: innonthelake@lakedistricthotels.net **web:** www.lakedistricthotels.net
dir: *M6 junct 40, A66 Keswick, A592 Windermere*

Modern cooking on the shore of Ullswater

In 15 acres of grounds surrounding Ullswater, this hotel's main culinary action takes place in its Lake View Restaurant, the elegant dining room decorated with shades of lilac and fawn. The kitchen makes good use of regional ingredients to produce dishes of modernity and creativity. First course seared king scallops, for example (cooked just right), arrive in the company of textures of cauliflower and black pudding fritter, dressed with a pancetta foam, and there's an Asian spin to a main course of cured salmon with crispy salt-and-pepper squid and Thai broth. Desserts include dark chocolate delice or a tarte Tatin made with Cox's apples.

Inn on the Lake

Chef Mark Harris **Seats** 100, Pr/dining room 40 **Times** 12-2/7-9 **Prices** Fixed D 3 course £34 **Wines** 20 bottles over £30, 35 bottles under £30, 8 by glass **Parking** 100 **Notes** ALC 3 course £44, Sunday L fr £20.95, Children welcome

GRANGE-OVER-SANDS **Map 10 SD47**

Clare House

Modern British

tel: 015395 33026 **Park Rd LA11 7HQ**
email: info@clarehousehotel.co.uk **web:** www.clarehousehotel.co.uk
dir: *Off A590 onto B5277, through Lindale into Grange, keep left, hotel 0.5m on left past Crown Hill & St Paul's Church*

Long-established, elegant and tranquil sea-facing hotel

The Read family has owned this traditional hotel with secluded gardens overlooking Morecambe Bay since the 1960s, and their passionate care is evident wherever you look. In the two-roomed dining area, well-spaced tables dressed in crisp linen are attended by smartly turned-out, loyally long-serving staff. No-nonsense modern British cooking offers bay-caught shrimp risotto finished with butter and parmesan, as well as pulled belly pork enhanced by black pudding, fine beans, sautéed potatoes, apple purée, herb sauce and, last but definitely not least, crisp crackling. To finish, consider a well-executed sticky toffee chocolate pudding with home-made butterscotch ice cream and toffee sauce.

Chef Andrew Read, Mark Johnston **Seats** 36 **Times** 12-2.30/6.30-7.30, Closed mid Dec-end Mar **Wines** 1 bottle over £30, 26 bottles under £30, 3 by glass **Parking** 16 **Notes** Fixed D 5 course £38, Light L menu Mon-Sat, Sunday L £24, Vegetarian available, Children welcome

GRASMERE **Map 18 NY30**

The Daffodil Hotel & Spa

Modern NEW

tel: 015394 63550 **Keswick Rd LA22 9PR**
email: stay@daffodilhotel.com **web:** www.daffodilhotel.com
dir: *M6 junct 36 then A591 for 24m past Windermere & Ambleside. Hotel on left on entering Grasmere*

Modern cooking with a lake view

Made of local stone and with a prime spot by Grasmere, The Daffodil enjoys a fine Lakeland vista, and sensibly the restaurant is up on the first floor to make the best of it. The contemporary finish within – from the bedrooms to the swish spa – extends to the restaurant with its darkwood tables and chairs and arty photos of celebrities on the walls. The kitchen makes excellent use of local ingredients and delivers first course Asian-spiced monkfish or whipped goats' cheese with pickled beetroots and toasted walnuts, followed by free-range pork belly with traditional flavours delivered in a modern way.

Chef Graham Harrower **Seats** Pr/dining room **Times** 6-9 **Prices** Starter £6.95-£9.50, Main £9.95-£25.95, Dessert £6.95-£7.95 **Wines** 12 bottles over £30, 24 bottles under £30, 12 by glass **Notes** Afternoon tea fr £12.95, Vegetarian available

The Dining Room

Modern British

tel: 015394 35217 **Oak Bank Hotel, Broadgate LA22 9TA**
email: info@lakedistricthotel.co.uk **web:** www.lakedistricthotel.co.uk
dir: *N'bound: M6 junct 36 onto A591 to Windermere, Ambleside, then Grasmere. S'bound: M6 junct 40 onto A66 to Keswick, A591 to Grasmere*

Stylish modern cooking in Lakeland country house

With pretty gardens running down to the River Rothay, the Victorian Oak Bank Hotel has plenty of Lakeland charm. The comfortable and refined Dining Room restaurant is the setting for some ambitious, creative food and the kitchen clearly has an eye for presentation and enticing combinations. A first course, for example, might consist of pan-seared pigeon, with roast celeriac, pickled mushroom and a warm dashi broth. Next up, beef fillet, oxtail, skirlie mash, spring cabbage and smoked aubergine purée. For dessert, try the rhubarb and custard comprising rhubarb, parfait, poached, sorbet, gel and vanilla anglaise, or maybe chocolate and rapeseed oil delice with caramelised white chocolate.

Seats 30 **Times** 12.30-1.30/6.30-8.30, Closed 18-26 Dec, 2-19 Jan **Prices** Fixed L 2 course £21.95-£25.95, Tasting menu £60 **Wines** 14 bottles over £30, 47 bottles under £30, 7 by glass **Parking** 14 **Notes** Fixed D menu 4 course £40-£49, Sunday L £21.95-£29, Vegetarian available, Children 10 yrs+

Rothay Garden Hotel

Modern British V

tel: 01539 435334 **Broadgate LA22 9RJ**
email: stay@rothaygarden.com **web:** www.rothaygarden.com
dir: *From N: M6 junct 40, A66 to Keswick, then S on A591 to Grasmere. From S: M6 junct 36 take A591 through Windermere/Ambleside to Grasmere. At N end of village adjacent to park*

Well-balanced modern dishes in a contemporary conservatory

On the edge of Grasmere, this refurbished Victorian hotel sits in riverside gardens, with the panoramic sweep of the Lakeland fells as background. A starter of seared scallops and barbecued pork belly is enhanced by sweet potato purée and piquant spiced apple, or there could be grilled sea bass with shellfish risotto, lemongrass foam and leek julienne. Next up, the focus is on Lakeland lamb, served as roast rump and shepherd's pie with carrot purée, parsnip and potato rösti, green beans and rosemary jus, or roast venison with dauphinoise potato, Drambuie jus, braised red cabbage and roast pear. The finishing flourish is a well-risen raspberry soufflé with crème anglaise.

Chef Andrew Burton, A Kneeshaw **Seats** 60 **Times** 12-1.30/7-9 **Prices** Fixed L 3 course £21.50, Fixed D 3 course £39.50 **Wines** 140 bottles over £30, 52 bottles under £30, 12 by glass **Parking** 38 **Notes** Sunday L, No children

GRASMERE *continued*

The Wordsworth Hotel & Spa

⊛ Modern British

tel: 015394 35592 **Stock Ln LA22 9SW**
email: enquiry@thewordsworthhotel.co.uk **web:** www.thewordsworthhotel.co.uk
dir: *Off A591 centre of village adjacent to St Oswald's Church*

Creative country-house cooking in the heart of the Lakes

Set in two acres of riverside gardens with breathtaking Grasmere views, this was once the hunting lodge for the Earl of Cadogan. These days, this plush hotel offers cutting-edge cooking in the Signature Restaurant. With atmospheric lighting and an airy conservatory, the dining room makes for an elegant setting for modern interpretations of classic flavour combinations. Start with pan-fried scallops, apple, pancetta and cauliflower, before moving on to Herdwick lamb rump, crispy belly, cabbage, carrots, creamed haggis and barbecue gel. End with 'tea and coffee' an inventive dessert of coffee cheesecake, Earl Grey bonbons and Amaretto jellies.

Chef Jaid Smallman **Seats** 65, Pr/dining room 18 **Times** 12.30-2/6.30-9.30 **Prices** Fixed L 2 course fr £22.95, Fixed D 3 course fr £40, Tasting menu fr £75 **Wines** 40 bottles over £30, 12 bottles under £30, 10 by glass **Parking** 50 **Notes** Sunday L, Vegetarian available, Children 5 yrs+

HAWKSHEAD **Map 18 SD39**

The Queen's Head Inn & Restaurant

⊛ British NEW

tel: 01539 436271 **Main St LA22 0NS**
email: info@queensheadhawkshead.co.uk **web:** www.queensheadhawkshead.co.uk
dir: *Phone for directions*

Classic inn serving modern food

The black-and-white timbered facade of this classic Lakeland inn has been rooted into Hawkshead life since the 17th century. Inside, there's a lively buzz and the timeless charm of head-skimming oak beams, panelled walls and wood and flagstone floors. The food comes from the distinctly modern end of the spectrum, and it's all built on prime local materials. Start with beetroot-cured salmon with beetroot purée, horseradish mayonnaise and watercress, and follow with wild duck breast, the skin nicely crisped, with carrot and orange purée, fennel, and red wine and orange jus. For pudding, there's a coconut and tonka bean pannacotta with pistachio crumb and meringue.

Chef Ken Clarke **Times** 12-3/6-9 **Prices** Starter £5.95-£10.95, Main £10.95-£22.95, Dessert £5.50-£6.50 **Notes** Sunday L £13.95, Vegetarian available, Children welcome

IRTHINGTON **Map 21 NY56**

The Golden Fleece

⊛ Modern British

tel: 01228 573686 **Rule Holme CA6 4NF**
email: info@thegoldenfleececumbria.co.uk **web:** www.thegoldenfleececumbria.co.uk
dir: *M6 junct 44 onto A689 signed Brampton. 1m past airport on left*

Upgraded old inn with polished gastropub cooking

Refurbishment has transformed this white two-storey inn into the eye-catching combination of bar and restaurant with rooms it is today. The menu neatly encapsulates both pub elements and more refined offerings. Ale-battered cod and chips, lamb hotpot and chargrilled steaks are all possibilities, alongside tender pink slices of loin of venison on rösti with a copper pot of game casserole, red wine jus and seasonal vegetables, or roast monkfish tail in Thai-style broth with jasmine rice. Topping and tailing these are light-textured cheese soufflé with a refreshing herb salad, and burnt Cambridge cream (a precursor of crème brûlée) with berry compôte and amaretti biscuit.

Chef Robert Cowan **Seats** 70, Pr/dining room 30 **Times** 12-9, All-day dining, Closed 1-8 Jan, L Mon-Fri (Nov-Mar) **Prices** Prices not confirmed **Wines** 2 bottles over £30, 33 bottles under £30, 12 by glass **Parking** 100 **Notes** Nov-Mar Mon-Fri open 4-9pm, Sunday L, Vegetarian available, Children welcome

KENDAL **Map 18 SD59**

Castle Green Hotel in Kendal

⊛⊛ Modern British

tel: 01539 734000 **Castle Green Ln LA9 6RG**
email: reception@castlegreen.co.uk **web:** www.castlegreen.co.uk
dir: *M6 junct 37, A684 towards Kendal. Hotel on right in 5m*

Innovative Cumbrian cooking with views of the fells

The Greenhouse restaurant at this charming country house, now a spa hotel, benefits from great natural daylight shining through large windows that showcase panoramic views over the fells. Innovative cooking showcasing fine Cumbrian produce is the deal. Seared scallops with pork belly, lentils, cauliflower and sultanas is a well-balanced starter, and there may be roast quail with red wine sauce, sweetcorn and asparagus. Continue with something like fillet of cod spiced by ras el hanout with samphire, mussels and crushed potatoes, or slow-cooked beef cheek with shallots, barley and sloe gin, and end with an array of miniature desserts.

Chef Justin Woods **Seats** 80, Pr/dining room 250 **Times** 12-2/6-10 **Prices** Fixed D 3 course £28, Tasting menu £45, Starter £6-£8.50, Main £16-£23.50, Dessert £6-£8.50 **Wines** 3 bottles over £30, 20 bottles under £30, 7 by glass **Parking** 200 **Notes** Tasting menu 5 course, Afternoon tea, Vegetarian available, Children welcome

KESWICK **Map 18 NY22**

Brossen Steakhouse

⊛ Modern British NEW

tel: 01768 773333 **Inn on the Square, Main St CA12 5JF**
email: innonthesquare@lakedistricthotels.net **web:** www.innonthesquare.co.uk/brossen
dir: *A66 to Keswick centre then follow signs to Bell Close car park. Rear entrance to hotel can be accessed from the car park.*

28-day hung steaks in modern setting

The Inn on the Square is a revamped hotel with a contemporary edge and a restaurant that is all about prime protein cooked over coals. The dining room is light, bright and casual, with a view into the kitchen and murals depicting where on the beast the cuts of meat come from. There's ambition in the delivery of first course caramelised scallops with 'textures' of cauliflower, shards of maple-cured bacon and cider reduction, while the steaks are served straight up and cooked just right (apparently they're cooked in the water bath before being finished on the grill). Rotisserie chicken and salmon with brown shrimps are alternatives to the red meat.

Chef Kyle Bowman **Seats** 64, Pr/dining room 40 **Times** 12-2.30/6-9.30 **Prices** Starter £5.50-£9.95, Main £11-£50, Dessert £4.95-£9.95 **Wines** 14 bottles over £30, 36 bottles under £30, 19 by glass **Parking** Bell Close car park **Notes** Sunday L £15.95-£18.50, Vegetarian available, Children welcome

Morrels

Modern British

tel: 017687 72666 **34 Lake Rd CA12 5DQ**
email: info@morrels.co.uk
dir: *Between market square & Keswick Theatre by the lake*

Light-filled modern brasserie

A Victorian house between the Theatre by the Lake and Keswick Market boasting a contemporary restaurant where, in a light-filled space, a menu of modern brasserie cooking is offered. Fishcakes of Cajun-style blackened salmon and chorizo, dressed with mint and dill yogurt, is a palate-priming starter, as is haggis spring rolls with hoisin dip. Mains offer plenty of Lakeland meats – sizable sirloins with chunky chips and sauce Diane, fell-bred lamb with bubble-and-squeak – as well as forthright fish preparations such as monkfish in prosciutto with tomato, clam and garlic linguine. Finish with a raspberry ripple-themed Eton Mess, or a warm chocolate brownie served with white chocolate and marshmallow sauce.

Chef Karl Link, David Lamont **Seats** 56 **Times** 5.30-close, Closed 5-16 Jan, Mon, L all week **Prices** Fixed D 3 course £21.95, Starter £4.50-£8.50, Main £12-£19.50, Dessert £6-£7 **Wines** 8 bottles over £30, 28 bottles under £30, 9 by glass **Notes** Sun D 2/3 course £14.50/£17.95, Vegetarian available, Children 5 yrs+

KIRKBY LONSDALE **Map 18 SD67**

Carters at the Sun Inn

Modern British V

tel: 015242 71965 **6 Market St LA6 2AU**
email: email@sun-inn.info **web:** www.sun-inn.info
dir: *From A65 follow signs to town centre. Inn on main street*

Friendly old inn with local ingredients and plenty of flavour

Anyone with foodie inclinations should visit the white-painted 17th-century Sun Inn, a proper pub with oak beams, log fires and real ales in the convivial bar, and a smart contemporary dining room. Reliable hands in the kitchen conjure up full-flavoured dishes using the best local ingredients. Start with suckling pig pointed up with blood orange gel, caramelised red chicory, deep-fried black pudding and crispy crackling, followed by a bouillabaisse-style fish stew of gurnard, squid, home-smoked mussels and fennel, all topped with croûtons and a punchy red pepper rouille. To finish, a chocolate and mint-themed workout delivers a diverting array of textures including mousse, gel, foam and chocolate Genoise cake.

Chef Sam Carter **Seats** 40 **Times** 12-3/6.30-9, Closed 25 Dec, L Mon **Prices** Fixed L 2 course £18.90-£21.95, Fixed D 3 course £28.95-£33.95, Starter £7, Main £20.95, Dessert £7 **Wines** 23 bottles over £30, 31 bottles under £30, 8 by glass **Parking** On street & nearby car park **Notes** Sunday L £13.95-£22.95, Children welcome

Hipping Hall

Modern British V 

tel: 015242 71187 **Cowan Bridge LA6 2JJ**
email: info@hippinghall.com **web:** www.hippinghall.com
dir: *8.5m E of M6 junct 36 on A65*

Accomplished modern cooking with national parks on either hand

The hall takes its name from the hipping, or stepping, stones crossing the little stream that runs past the old wash house of this three-storey stone property in mature gardens between the Lake District and the Yorkshire Dales. Smartly furnished and decorated with guests' comfort in mind, it's a great place to get away from it all. The restaurant provides a stylish environment, with its boarded floor, high-backed upholstered chairs at generously spaced tables and a cracking log fire. Oli Martin is a sure-footed chef with bags of flair, creating daily-changing menus (with wine suggestions) based on local produce, from Cartmel Valley rabbit (with lardo, celery and borlotti beans) to Lakeland beef fillet (with Jacob's ladder, mushrooms and radish). Ingredients work effectively together to make appetising dishes. Ox tongue with an egg yolk, beetroot and watercress, for instance, may be followed by loin and cheek of Yorkshire pork with carrot 'ketchup', hazelnuts and chicory. Seafood is a strong suit too: witness seared scallops with seaweed, roast parsnips, walnuts and truffle, then wild sea bass fillet with shrimp butter, salt-baked celeriac and aubergine. There's a tasting menu as well as the carte, and puddings can be as inspired as pomegranate curd and sorbet with toasted rice and popcorn.

Chef Oli Martin **Seats** 32 **Times** 12-2/7-9, Closed L Mon-Fri **Prices** Prices not confirmed **Wines** 60 bottles over £30, 15 bottles under £30, 12 by glass **Parking** 20 **Notes** Sunday L, Children 12 yrs+

Pheasant Inn

Modern British

tel: 015242 71230 **Casterton LA6 2RX**
email: info@pheasantinn.co.uk **web:** www.pheasantinn.co.uk
dir: *M6 junct 36, A590 towards Kirby Lonsdale. At rdbt take 2nd exit A65 towards Skipton. At next rdbt take 2nd exit A65 to Skipton. Turn left onto A683 to Casterton, Barbon & Sedbergh*

Unpretentious dining in an old coaching inn

An 18th-century coaching inn with a proper bar complete with real ales and snug. Grab a table by the fire in the bar, or head on through to the slightly more refined restaurant – the menu is the same throughout. Expect dishes that reflect the easy-going pub setting but don't lack ambition. A starter of braised pig's cheek with Bury black pudding and caramelised apples is soft, sweet and tender in all the right places, or go for shallot tarte Tatin with glazed goats' cheese. Follow with lightly-battered king prawns with hand-cut chips, or a Med-inspired baked fillet of turbot, and finish with a spot-on crème brûlée.

Chef Duncan Wilson **Seats** 40 **Times** 12-2/6-9, Closed 25-26 Dec **Prices** Prices not confirmed **Wines** 7 bottles over £30, 26 bottles under £30, 8 by glass **Parking** 32 **Notes** Sunday L, Vegetarian available, Children welcome

KIRKBY STEPHEN — Map 18 NY70

The Inn at Brough

Modern British NEW

tel: 01768 341252 **Main St, Brough CA17 4AY**
email: enquiries@theinnatbrough.co.uk **web:** www.theinnatbrough.co.uk
dir: *M6 junct 38, A685 to Kirkby Stephen, then Brough. A66 exit to Brough & Kirkby Stephen*

Quality cooking in a stylish inn

A thorough makeover has added a chic, contemporary look to this 18th-century coaching inn on Brough high street, and the kitchen toes that up-to-date line with switched-on modern ideas. A penchant for local and regional supplies drives the menu, kicking off with an exemplary cheese and onion soufflé matched with cider and onion velouté, then more of those assertive flavours arrive in a main course of slow-cooked pork belly with black pudding bonbons, apple sauce, creamy mash and red wine jus. They do a fine soufflé here, so why not wind things up with a chocolate version paired with buttermilk ice cream and honeycomb?

Chef David Parker **Seats** 42, Pr/dining room 16 **Times** 12-2.30/6-9 **Prices** Fixed D 3 course £25, Starter £4.50-£6, Main £11-£24, Dessert £5.50-£6.50 **Wines** 14 bottles over £30, 20 bottles under £30, 10 by glass **Parking** 20, On street **Notes** Seasonal menu, Wed steak menu, Sunday L £10-£19, Vegetarian available, Children welcome

LUPTON — Map 18 SD58

Plough Inn

Modern British

tel: 015395 67700 **Cow Brow LA6 1PJ**
email: info@theploughatlupton.co.uk **web:** www.theploughatlupton.co.uk
dir: *M6 junct 36 onto A65 signed Kirkby Lonsdale*

Smart contemporary looks and savvy pub food

Enjoying a new lease of life since the team behind The Punchbowl Inn in Crosthwaite carried out a major makeover, the Plough sports a clean-lined contemporary look without sacrificing the best of its pubby character. It's a classy act with tasteful colours, leather sofas, and a Brathay slate-topped bar set against the cosiness of wooden floors, beams, real fires and the like. Home-made pork pies are a speciality here, served with piccalilli and salad, and you can follow that with two-day braised beef brisket with parsley mash, Savoy cabbage, crispy bone marrow and proper gravy. For dessert, vanilla pannacotta comes with damson compôte and Jammy Dodger shortbread.

Chef Matt Adamson **Seats** 120, Pr/dining room 8 **Times** 12-9, All-day dining **Prices** Prices not confirmed **Wines** 16 bottles over £30, 25 bottles under £30, 9 by glass **Parking** 40 **Notes** Sunday L, Vegetarian available, Children welcome

NEAR SAWREY — Map 18 SD39

Ees Wyke Country House

Modern, Traditional British

tel: 015394 36393 **LA22 0JZ**
email: mail@eeswyke.co.uk **web:** www.eeswyke.co.uk
dir: *On B5285 on W side of village*

Homely Lakeland cooking where Beatrix Potter took her hols

Beatrix Potter spent her holidays in this white Georgian house. These days, on a scale small enough to unite guests, a four-course dinner menu is served at a single start time. A pair of choices is offered at most stages, beginning perhaps with seared scallops and a balsamic-dressed salad of shoots and cress, before a fixed fish dish such as cayenne-peppered haddock. A main course could be beautifully fresh sea bass in the company of spring onions, chilli, garlic and ginger, or noisettes of local lamb in red wine jus. The sticky toffee pudding displays a lighter touch than is customary, but still comes with hot butterscotch sauce.

NEWBY BRIDGE — Map 18 SD38

Lakeside Hotel Lake Windermere

Modern British V

tel: 015395 30001 **Lakeside LA12 8AT**
email: sales@lakesidehotel.co.uk **web:** www.lakesidehotel.co.uk
dir: *M6 junct 36 follow A590 to Newby Bridge, straight over rdbt, right over bridge. Hotel within 1m*

Lakeside modern dining with a choice of restaurants

The Lakeside sits, as you might expect, on the southern shore of Lake Windermere, surrounded by wooded slopes. It began as a coaching inn in the 17th century, and is now a substantial building, with a lakeside terrace, spa and pool and a brasserie named after John Ruskin, as well as the Lakeview restaurant. Menu descriptions keep things simple for Lancashire soufflé and tomato jam, or ham hock terrine with brioche and pickles, among starters. Then comes Herdwick lamb shoulder with peas, mint and chilli, or whole lemon sole with watercress and lemon. Inspired desserts include passionfruit cheesecake with lime ice cream and goats' curd.

Chef Richard Booth **Seats** 70, Pr/dining room 30
Times 12.30-2.30/6.45-9.30, Closed 23 Dec-16 Jan **Prices** Fixed L 2 course £20-£25, Fixed D 3 course £39, Starter £8-£12, Main £19-£31, Dessert £7-£9 **Wines** 100 bottles over £30, 5 bottles under £30, 12 by glass **Parking** 200 **Notes** Fixed menu D 6 course £48, Children welcome

Whitewater Hotel

Modern, Traditional British V

tel: 015395 31133 **The Lakeland Village LA12 8PX**
email: enquiries@whitewater-hotel.co.uk **web:** www.whitewater-hotel.co.uk
dir: *M6 junct 36 follow signs for A590 Barrow, 1m through Newby Bridge. Right at sign for Lakeland Village, hotel on left*

Punchy modern British cooking by the River Leven

In a Victorian cotton mill beside the fast-flowing River Leven, the restaurant is a welcoming room with exposed stone walls. To start might be a warm salad of red mullet with Niçoise vegetables, tapenade and sardine vinaigrette, or flavour-packed oxtail and smoked ham hock terrine, served in a neat cylinder with pickled vegetables and horseradish dressing. Main courses are given an extra dimension by sauces: a glossy, rich red wine jus for pan-fried monkfish tail in a pleasingly piquant crust of chorizo and rosemary, and one of Madeira and summer truffle for fillet of beef with wild mushrooms and vegetables. For pudding, try prune and pistachio parfait.

Chef Pascal Tabard **Seats** 50, Pr/dining room 20 **Times** 7-9, Closed L all week **Prices** Fixed D 3 course fr £32.50 **Wines** 5 bottles over £30, 31 bottles under £30, 8 by glass **Parking** 30 **Notes** Children welcome

PENRITH — Map 18 NY53

Stoneybeck Inn

Modern British NEW V

tel: 01768 862369 **Bowscar CA11 8RP**
email: reception@stoneybeckinn.co.uk **web:** www.stoneybeckinn.co.uk
dir: *M6 junct 41, take A6 (Penrith) exit, continue for approx 1m. Left at rdbt onto A6, Stoneybeck on right*

Fell views and a locally-inspired menu

A traditional looking inn in a stunning location with views over the Cumbrian Fells, yet close to the M6, Stoneybeck has been much extended to include accommodation as well as wedding and conference facilities. It's opened up and contemporary on the inside, and well-turned-out staff do a good job of looking after proceedings. The kitchen turns out updated versions of classic dishes, so roast loin of Cumbrian lamb comes with mini shepherd's pie and lettuce sauce, or stick with beer-battered fish and chips. Local wood pigeon stars in a first course with smoked black pudding crumb, while, for dessert, 'Anyone for Pimm's' is a bit of modern summer fun.

Chef Steven Pott **Seats** 80, Pr/dining room 130 **Times** 12-9, All-day dining, Closed 26 Dec **Wines** 15 bottles over £30, 17 bottles under £30, 7 by glass **Parking** 70 **Notes** Sunday L £7-£11, Children welcome

RAVENGLASS Map 18 SD09

The Pennington Hotel

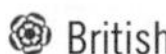 British

tel: 0845 450 6445 *(The only charge for this call will be your phone company's access charge)* **CA18 1SD**
email: info@penningtonhotels.com **web:** www.penningtonhotels.com
dir: *M6, junct 36 to A590 Barrow, right Greenodd A5092, joining A595 Muncaster/ Ravenglass. Hotel in village centre*

Fashionable dishes in a Tudor coaching inn

The venerable black and white hotel wears its age on its sleeve, having started out as a coaching inn in the Tudor era. Culinary modernism is the order of the day in the light, relaxing dining room, where choices might include salmon cured in beetroot and gin with horseradish crème fraîche and lime jelly, and main-course belly and fillet of pork with black pudding, buttered kale and apple soup. Seafood is imaginatively handled, as when halibut arrives with a crab beignet, asparagus and herbed gnocchi in lemon cream sauce, and it all concludes with desserts that score highly for novelty, such as Piña Colada cheesecake with pineapple compôte and coconut popcorn.

Chef Helen Todd **Seats** 36, Pr/dining room **Times** 12-2.30/7-9 **Prices** Fixed L 2 course £12.95-£19.95, Fixed D 3 course £24.50-£32.50, Starter £6.95-£10.95, Main £9.95-£22.95, Dessert £4.95-£8.95 **Wines** 14 bottles over £30, 16 bottles under £30, 8 by glass **Parking** 20 **Notes** Sunday L £9.95-£11.95, Vegetarian available, Children welcome

ROSTHWAITE Map 18 NY21

Scafell Hotel

Modern British

tel: 017687 77208 **CA12 5XB**
email: info@scafell.co.uk **web:** www.scafell.co.uk
dir: *M6 junct 40 to Keswick on A66. Take B5289 to Rosthwaite*

British dining with an international twist

Surrounded by peaks and the lush greenery of the Borrowdale Valley, the Scafell Hotel is ideal for those seeking time in the great outdoors. The Riverside Bar and lounge bar offer informal dining, with the main restaurant a more formal option. Salmon is cured in-house and matched with avocado and tomato salsa, while another starter sees flaked crab with linguine given a nicely judged hit of chilli. Main-course herb-crusted shoulder and noisette of lamb is partnered with Thai-style vegetables, and pan-roasted monkish comes in a Mediterranean-style combination of confit plum tomatoes, red peppers and red onions. Finish with a light and fluffy mousse of chocolate, Tia Maria and mocha.

Chef Paul Wilson **Seats** 65 **Times** 12-2.30/6.30-9, Closed L Mon-Sat **Prices** Prices not confirmed **Wines** 35 bottles over £30, 57 bottles under £30, 11 by glass **Parking** 100 **Notes** Sunday L, Vegetarian available, Children welcome

SEASCALE Map 18 NY00

Sella Park House Hotel

Traditional British

tel: 0845 450 6445 *(The only charge for this call will be your phone company's access charge)* & 01946 841601 **Calderbridge CA20 1DW**
email: info@penningtonhotels.com **web:** www.penningtonhotels.com
dir: *From A595 at Calderbridge, follow sign for North Gate. Hotel 0.5m on left*

Celebrating Cumbrian produce by the Calder

Six acres of lovely gardens running down to the River Calder make the historic 16th-century manor house a popular venue for tying the knot. The kitchen hauls in splendid seasonal Cumbrian produce: vegetables, fruit and herbs are picked fresh at nearby Muncaster Castle, and great care is taken in tracking down the best local meat and fish. The Priory restaurant makes a traditional setting for ideas that run the gamut from tried-and-tested potted shrimps and smoked salmon with mustard-dressed salad, to lamb chump with dauphinoise and braised red cabbage in redcurrant and rosemary jus. For dessert, toffee apple bread-and-butter pudding rounds things off nicely.

Chef Sara Westbrook **Seats** 34, Pr/dining room 40 **Times** 12-3/6-9 **Prices** Starter £6.95-£10.95, Main £10.95-£24.95, Dessert £6.95-£8.95 **Wines** 14 bottles over £30, 16 bottles under £30, 6 by glass **Parking** 30 **Notes** Sunday L, Vegetarian available, Children welcome

TEMPLE SOWERBY Map 18 NY62

Temple Sowerby House Hotel & Restaurant

Modern British

tel: 017683 61578 **CA10 1RZ**
email: stay@templesowerby.com **web:** www.templesowerby.com
dir: *7m from M6 junct 40, midway between Penrith & Appleby, in village centre*

Boldly modern cooking overlooking the garden in Eden

Temple Sowerby is a smart family-run country hotel where the kitchen specialises in a boldly modern style with plenty of European influence. To start, try the imaginative flavours of the soy and ginger-cured salmon with coconut and jasmine rice, avocado and coriander sorbet, pickled lime and sesame nori. Follow up with the flavoursome poached and seared breast of Cumbrian chicken, confit leg, bacon toastie, leek and potato velouté in a truffled chicken jelly reduction. Finish with a well-executed spiced Bramley apple and oat slice, real apple parfait, yogurt sorbet and burnt apple marshmallow or, depending on the time of year, a hot toddy winter dessert.

Chef Daniel Przekopowski **Seats** 24, Pr/dining room 24 **Times** 7-9, Closed 8 days Xmas, L all week **Prices** Fixed D 3 course £43 **Wines** 10 bottles over £30, 30 bottles under £30, 7 by glass **Parking** 20 **Notes** Vegetarian available, Children 12 yrs+

WATERMILLOCK **Map 18 NY42**

Macdonald Leeming House

 Modern British

tel: 01768 486674 **CA11 0JJ**
email: leeminghouse@macdonald-hotels.co.uk **web:** www.macdonald-hotels.co.uk
dir: *M6 junct 40, continue on A66 signed Keswick. At rdbt follow A592 towards Ullswater, at T-junct turn right, hotel 3m on left*

Ambitious country-house cooking on the shores of Ullswater

An impressive-looking property with direct access to Ullswater. For full-on Lakeland dining, head for the elegant Regency Restaurant, where floor-to-ceiling windows give views to the lake and fells. Pressed confit duck legs partnered by poached plums and red wine syrup, and smoked salmon terrine by herby lemon butter, pink peppercorns and fennel salad. Dishes are well executed and attractively presented, seen in main courses of flavoursome slices of roast loin of Highland lamb with rösti, carrot purée, crushed peas and rosemary jus, and baked plaice fillets with sauté potatoes, broccoli and béarnaise. End on an international note with lemongrass pannacotta with mango milkshake.

Rampsbeck Country House Hotel

 Modern British V

tel: 017684 86442 **CA11 0LP**
email: enquiries@rampsbeck.co.uk **web:** www.rampsbeck.co.uk
dir: *M6 junct 40, A592 to Ullswater, T-junct turn right at lake's edge. Hotel 1.25m, on lake side*

Smart modern cooking in elegant lakeside setting

Occupying a stunning Lakeland setting with views across Ullswater, this white-painted hillside villa is set within 18 acres of grounds. Old-world luxury combined with contemporary comforts create the full country-house experience. The dining room has all the period details, plus neatly laid tables and a menu with its roots in classical French cooking. Start, perhaps, with a pressing of Cumbrian ham hock, salad of peas and onions, macadamia and poached hen's egg. Roast loin of Herdwick hogget, with braised shoulder and anchoiade and thyme-infused sauce is a notable main course. Note: the restaurant will be closing for renovations between September 2016 and May 2017.

Chef Ben Wilkinson **Seats** 40, Pr/dining room 16 **Times** 12-1.45/7-9, Closed 12 Sep 2016-May 2017 **Prices** Fixed L 3 course £32, Fixed D 3 course £50.95 **Wines** 38 bottles over £30, 52 bottles under £30, 7 by glass **Parking** 30 **Notes** Fixed D 4/5 course £59.95/£68.95, Sunday L £32, Children 10 yrs+

WINDERMERE **Map 18 SD49**

Beech Hill Hotel & Spa

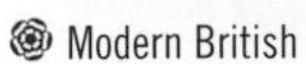 Modern British V

tel: 015394 42137 **Newby Bridge Rd LA23 3LR**
email: reservations@beechhillhotel.co.uk **web:** www.beechhillhotel.co.uk
dir: *M6 junct 36, A591 to Windermere. Left onto A592 towards Newby Bridge. Hotel 4m from Bowness-on-Windermere*

Appealing modern cooking on the shores of Windermere

After canapés and pre-dinner drinks you can soak up the dramatic views over Lake Windermere to the fells beyond from Burlington's Restaurant. The menu is altogether more wide-ranging than that usually found in such environments, embracing crab and langoustine aïoli with langoustine and saffron bisque, and poached turbot fillet with asparagus and oyster vichyssoise. The kitchen clearly has a grounding in the French repertory and adds its own spin on dishes. Cannon of lamb is accompanied by a haggis croquette, for instance, along with Jerusalem artichoke boulangère, mushy peas and mint purée. Puddings – and breads – are well up to snuff too, among them blueberry custard brûlée.

Chef Lukasz Zebryk **Seats** 130, Pr/dining room 90 **Times** 12-5/7-9, Closed D 25 Dec **Prices** Prices not confirmed **Wines** 25 bottles over £30, 25 bottles under £30, 13 by glass **Parking** 60 **Notes** Fixed D 5 course £39.95, Children welcome

Belsfield Restaurant

Modern British NEW

tel: 015394 42448 **Laura Ashley The Belsfield, Kendal Rd LA23 3EL**
email: belsfield@lauraashleyhotels.com **web:** www.lauraashleyhotels.com/thebelsfield
dir: *M6 junct 36, A591 Windermere, follow signs for Bowness. At mini rdbt bear left & take 1st left (Kendal Rd). Hotel 200yds on right*

Stunning lakeside setting for globally-influenced cooking

Just ten minutes' walk from Bowness, this lovingly restored Windermere hotel is set in six acres of landscaped gardens. As you might expect from a hotel owned by the Laura Ashley homewear brand, the restaurant is tastefully furnished. It forms an elegant lakeside setting for a menu that fuses traditional British dishes with inspiration from further afield. Butternut squash bhaji, red lentil soup and cumin crème fraîche is a well-balanced starter and might precede roast Cartmel venison haunch, haggis ravioli, Jerusalem artichoke purée and chanterelles. Leave room for plum bavarois, crumbled amaretti, spiced baked plum and brown sugar meringue.

Chef Gareth Owen **Seats** 70, Pr/dining room 60 **Times** 6.30-9, Closed L all week **Wines** 37 bottles over £30, 24 bottles under £30, 6 by glass **Parking** 60 **Notes** 5 course D £38-£48, Sunday L £24.95-£30.95, Vegetarian available, Children welcome

Briery Wood Country House Hotel

Modern British NEW

tel: 015394 33316 **Ambleside Rd, Ecclerigg LA23 1ES**
email: info@brierywood.co.uk **web:** www.lakedistrictcountryhotels.co.uk
dir: *M6 junct 36, A591 for 15m past Kendal and Windermere. Briery Wood signed on right*

Lakeland comfort and country-house cuisine

Set in seven acres of grounds, close to the shores of Lake Windermere, Briery Wood is a charming, white-painted property, dating to the late 19th century. It's a cosy, relaxing place with an informal atmosphere. In the dining room you'll find attentive staff serving modern country-house style cooking. Dishes might range from breast of wood pigeon with crisply fried smoked cheddar beignets and celeriac purée, to braised halibut with smooth, buttery creamed potato. A light, accurately cooked dessert of poached rhubarb with vanilla cream cheese, Grasmere gingerbread and lemon brings things to a close, and coffee comes with home-made petits fours.

Chef John Bell **Prices** Fixed D 3 course £30 **Wines** 16 bottles over £30, 41 bottles under £30 **Notes** Afternoon tea £19.90, Vegetarian menu on request, Sunday L £22.95

Gilpin Hotel & Lake House

WINDERMERE **Map 18 SD49**

Modern British V

tel: 015394 88818 **Crook Rd LA23 3NE**
email: hotel@thegilpin.co.uk **web:** www.thegilpin.co.uk
dir: *M6 junct 36 take A590/A591 to rdbt N of Kendal, then B5284 for 5m, Gilpin is on right*

Dynamic contemporary cooking in fabulous family-run hotel

Built as a modest enough country house at the outset of the Edwardian era, Gilpin has been in the Cunliffe family since just after the Great War. Its stunning location above Windermere may take a little finding among the winding lanes hereabouts, but persistence is amply rewarded, for it is now a luxurious Lakeland hotel in 22 acres, with fresh flowers and candlelight creating a refined atmosphere in all three dining rooms. Attentive, flawless service keeps things running smoothly out front, and the rest is up to Hrishikesh Desai, who comes with today's indispensable imprimatur of having won a TV cookery contest. His cooking is replete with technical skills, depth of flavour and clean, seductive presentation. Things take flight on the dinner menu, opening unexpectedly perhaps with a poached fillet of rose veal alongside its glazed sweetbreads, as well as smoked celeriac purée, tomato and pine nut salsa and an emulsion mustard dressing. Chilli-glazed poached lobster comes in a stunning composition with a fritter of the claw, avocado mousse, citrus and tobiko roe. Sticking with seafood, you might progress to expertly timed turbot with brown shrimps, hand-rolled macaroni and baby artichokes in an emulsified truffle dressing, but consider also roast Goosnargh duck, its leg meat in a spring roll, with an Indian-inflected chutney sauce of apple, ginger and sultanas. Everything makes a strong visual impression, and the matchless balancing of flavours speaks of ebullient confidence. The finishing flourish might be feather light almond and citrus cake with blood orange textures and bitter almond ice cream, or baked passionfruit cream with tarragon jelly, glazed raspberries and yogurt and black pepper sorbet. Canapés, appetisers and breads are all up to the mark, and there are some expertly chosen wines to conjure with.

Chef Hrishikesh Desai **Seats** 60, Pr/dining room 20 **Times** 12-9.30, All-day dining **Prices** Tasting menu £85, Starter £7-£10, Main £13-£18, Dessert £8-£12 **Wines** 181 bottles over £30, 6 bottles under £30, 15 by glass **Parking** 40 **Notes** Fixed D 4 course £65, Sunday L £35-£40, Children 7 yrs+

WINDERMERE *continued*

Cedar Manor Hotel & Restaurant

Modern British

tel: 015394 43192 **Ambleside Rd LA23 1AX**
email: info@cedarmanor.co.uk **web:** www.cedarmanor.co.uk
dir: *From A591 follow signs to Windermere. Hotel on left just beyond St Mary's Church at bottom of hill*

Peaceful small hotel with impressive seasonal cooking

Built of grey stone in 1854, the manor occupies a peaceful spot in attractive gardens, complete with eponymous cedar, on the outskirts of Windermere. It's a small hotel with an elegant restaurant and well-trained, unstuffy staff. Seasonality leads the kitchen, which turns out modern country-house dishes starting with smoked haddock mousseline with Morecambe Bay shrimps and curried cream saffron and mussel sauce. Main courses include rump of lamb roasted pink and served with spring pea salad, toasted almond espuma, tempura pea shoots and dauphinoise potatoes, while dessert matches dark chocolate torte with orange and lavender foam, and tonka bean and walnut ice cream.

Chef Roger Pergl-Wilson **Seats** 22, Pr/dining room 10 **Times** 6.30-8.30, Closed Xmas & 6-25 Jan, L all week **Prices** Fixed D 3 course £39.95 **Wines** 11 bottles over £30, 26 bottles under £30, 7 by glass **Parking** 12 **Notes** Vegetarian available, Children 12 yrs+

Gilpin Hotel & Lake House

– see page 101

Holbeck Ghyll Country House Hotel

Modern British V NOTABLE WINE LIST

tel: 015394 32375 **Holbeck Ln LA23 1LU**
email: stay@holbeckghyll.com **web:** www.holbeckghyll.com
dir: *3m N of Windermere on A591, right into Holbeck Lane (signed Troutbeck), hotel 0.5m on left*

Classical Lakeland cooking overlooking Windermere

Sitting proud above the shimmering expanse of Lake Windermere, Holbeck Ghyll enjoys panoramic views of the pikes and fells. Inside, the house is consummately stylish, it's art nouveau signature decor beautifully maintained, and an air of a peaceable retreat reigns supreme. Confident country-house cookery discreetly offset with a little French-inspired modernity is the deal here, opening with confit duck terrine with pear, green beans and brioche, while main course stars roasted wild turbot supported by creamed leeks, crisp ham and red wine sauce. A dessert of vanilla bavarois with blackcurrant and liquorice sorbet is given textural variety with the crunch of brandy snap, honeycomb and a shard of blackberry meringue.

Holbeck Ghyll Country House Hotel

Chef Darren Comish **Seats** 50, Pr/dining room 20 **Times** 12.30-2/7-9.30 **Prices** Fixed L 3 course £35, Fixed D 3 course £68, Tasting menu £88, Starter £19, Main £30, Dessert £19 **Wines** 270 bottles over £30, 29 bottles under £30, 13 by glass **Parking** 50 **Notes** Sunday L, Children 8 yrs+

See advert opposite

Lindeth Howe Country House Hotel & Restaurant

Modern British

tel: 015394 45759 **Lindeth Dr, Longtail Hill LA23 3JF**
email: hotel@lindeth-howe.co.uk **web:** www.lindeth-howe.co.uk
dir: *1m S of Bowness onto B5284, signed Kendal and Lancaster. Hotel 2nd driveway on right*

Imaginative modern cooking in enviable location

Beatrix Potter not only lived in this classic country house on a hillside overlooking Windermere and the mountains, but wrote some of her tales here. To be fair, the word 'hillside' undersells what are in fact six acres of sweeping gardens, worth exploring before eating in the handsome dining room. Here, a modern British menu of contemporary and creative dishes offers smoked Applewood twice-baked cheese soufflé with pickled pear and caramel hazelnuts, followed by pan-fried duck breast and confit leg, apricots, pak choi, spicy carrot purée and potato gratin. Finish with chocolate and orange tart, white chocolate cookies and Kendal mint cake sorbet from the mouth-watering dessert selection.

WINDERMERE *continued*

Linthwaite House Hotel & Restaurant

Modern British

tel: 015394 88600 **Crook Rd LA23 3JA**
email: stay@linthwaite.com **web:** www.linthwaite.com
dir: *A591 towards The Lakes for 8m to large rdbt, take 1st exit (B5284), 6m, hotel on left. 1m past Windermere golf club*

Adventurous contemporary cooking with captivating Lakeland views

The Rosette award for this establishment has been suspended due to a change of chef. Reassessment will take place in due course under the new chef. In a county hardly short of lovely country-house hotels, Linthwaite has plenty of distinctive appeal. This large white house sits on a rise overlooking Lake Windermere and has immaculate gardens and soothing views, while the interior is decorated in refined style. The dining room is neatly divided into three separate areas done in varying levels of formality, with brightly patterned seating and a light and airy feel. Confident and efficient staff deliver high-achieving contemporary dishes, which mix and match global influences in elegant presentations. First up might be an al dente egg yolk raviolo with truffled ceps, hazelnuts and rosemary, while earthy garnishes of pickled onion and walnuts add depth to a terrine of chicken and roasted garlic. At main, there could be an exotically aromatic way with crackled pork jowl, which arrives with vanilla mash and subtle notes of star anise and cinnamon. Indian-spiced halibut with sweet potato and red lentils is perfectly timed, gaining edge from its coconut, coriander and lime gel accompaniments. Desserts too are sensuously scented, as for lemon posset with Turkish Delight ice cream and Parma violet meringues, while the richness of caramel cheesecake and honeycomb is offset by the sharpening effect of banana and lime ice cream.

Seats 64, Pr/dining room 16 **Times** 12.30-2/7-9.30, Closed Xmas & New Year (ex residents) **Prices** Fixed L 2 course £17, Tasting menu £65-£70 **Wines** 70 bottles over £30, 34 bottles under £30, 11 by glass **Parking** 40 **Notes** Fixed D 4 course £55-£60, Sunday L £24.95, Vegetarian available, Children 7 yrs+ D

Macdonald Old England Hotel & Spa

Traditional British, European

tel: 015394 87890 **23 Church St, Bowness LA23 3DF**
email: sales.oldengland@macdonald-hotels.co.uk **web:** www.macdonaldhotels.co.uk
dir: *Through Windermere to Bowness, straight across at mini-rdbt. Hotel behind church on right*

Stylish modern dining and stunning lake views

Standing right on the shore of England's largest lake, this Windermere hotel and spa offers superb views across the water towards the fells, particularly through the restaurant's floor-to-ceiling windows and terrace. The menu has broad appeal, from steaks cooked on the grill, through to some gently contemporary dishes based on top-quality regional ingredients. You might, perhaps, start with hand-dived scallops served with cauliflower purée, while roast lamb rump, pea purée, potato gratin, Chantenay carrots and rosemary jus is a typical main course. For dessert, coconut pannacotta, pineapple, lime, rum and ginger beer sorbet provides a tropical end to a meal.

Chef Adam Crosbie **Seats** 170, Pr/dining room 60 **Times** 6.30-9.30, Closed L all week **Prices** Starter £6-£11, Main £12-£28, Dessert £4-£6 **Wines** 40 bottles over £30, 15 bottles under £30, 13 by glass **Parking** 100 **Notes** Vegetarian available, Children welcome

Merewood Country House Hotel

Modern British NEW

tel: 015394 46484 **Ambleside Rd, Ecclerigg LA23 1LH**
email: info@merewoodhotel.co.uk **web:** www.lakedistrictcountryhotels.co.uk
dir: *M6 junct 36, A591 for 15m past Kendal & Windermere. Merewood sign on right opposite National Park Visitor Centre*

Creative fine dining in classic Lakeland setting

Built in 1812 from stone quarried in the hotel's grounds, Merewood is perfectly positioned to make the best of the views over Lake Windermere. There are 20 acres of woodland and gardens, and this classic Lakeland country house is equally on the money on the inside, with period features including oak panelling in the two smart dining rooms. The local environment provides many of the ingredients for the table, with the kitchen bringing contemporary flair to the fine-dining format. Start with glazed chicken wings with consommé jelly and Jerusalem artichoke mousse before a main course of cod with a cheesy topping and red wine sauce.

Chef Carl Semple **Seats** 40, Pr/dining room 32 **Times** 7-9, Closed exclusive use days **Prices** Fixed D 3 course £39 **Wines** 24 bottles over £30, 50 bottles under £30, 7 by glass **Parking** 60 **Notes** Sunday L £26, Vegetarian available, Children welcome

Miller Howe Hotel

Modern British V NOTABLE WINE LIST

tel: 015394 42536 **Rayrigg Rd LA23 1EY**
email: info@millerhowe.com **web:** www.millerhowe.com
dir: *M6 junct 36. Follow A591 bypass for Kendal. Enter Windermere, continue to mini rdbt, take left onto A592. Miller Howe is 0.25m on right*

Romantic lakeside setting and polished country-house cooking

Miller Howe is the yardstick by which other country-house hotels are judged. 'Modern British with a twist' is the self-described cooking style, with home-grown and wild produce in evidence, while presentation is precise and colourful. Expect starters such as prawns in shellfish bisque with black pudding, mandarin purée and segments, coriander and crushed nuts, a tour de force of flavours and textures. No less impressive are main courses of pink-roast rump of lamb with glazed sweetbreads, courgette purée, tomatoes and sheep's curd milk or John Dory with asparagus, sorrel and brown butter hollandaise. Desserts include a textbook blackcurrant soufflé with hot chocolate sauce and a Parma Violets macaroon.

Chef Kieran Smith **Seats** 80, Pr/dining room 30 **Times** 12.30-1.45/6.45-8.45 **Prices** Fixed L 2 course £23, Fixed D 3 course £47.50 **Wines** 100 bottles over £30, 50 bottles under £30, 12 by glass **Parking** 40 **Notes** Fixed D 4 course £47.50, Sunday L £30, Children welcome

Porto

Modern British

tel: 015394 48242 **3 Ash St, Bowness LA23 3EB**
email: info@porto-restaurant.co.uk **web:** www.porto-restaurant.co.uk
dir: *Take A5074 from Windermere down hill into Bowness-on-Windermere*

Eclectic modern cookery in a stylish town-centre venue

In the heart of Bowness-on-Windermere, this low-roofed white-fronted old house has seating on two floors, a heated roof terrace and a summer garden, the main room done up in red and gold with mirrors, black napery and crystal light fixtures. The food is an eclectic mix of European and Asian influences amid more straightforward fare. First up, a classic twice-baked Cumbrian cheddar soufflé, offset by a white wine and chive sauce, cherry tomatoes and rocket. Mains include the 'pig plate': slow cooked belly, pulled pork bubble-and-squeak and pigs in blankets, garnished with apple purée and creamy mustard sauce. Finish with chocolate ganache cake, salted caramel, popcorn and richly flavoured vanilla ice cream.

Chef David Bewick **Seats** 68, Pr/dining room 50 **Times** 12-2/6-9, Closed 24-26 Dec, 2nd wk Jan-2nd wk Feb, Tue **Prices** Starter £6-£9, Main £14-£25 **Wines** 10 bottles over £30, 20 bottles under £30, 7 by glass **Parking** On street **Notes** Vegetarian available, Children welcome

The Ryebeck

Modern British

tel: 015394 88195 **Lyth Valley Rd LA23 3JP**
email: info@ryebeck.com **web:** www.ryebeck.com
dir: *Phone for directions*

Imaginative modern cooking by the shining expanse of Windermere

Formerly known as Fayrer Garden, The Rybeck is an appealingly isolated country house overlooking the shining expanse of Windermere. The informal conservatory dining room serves up a delicious view and a modern British menu that shows off the technical skills of the team in the kitchen. 'Tuna on a rock' reveals an understanding of Asian flavours with the shiitaki parfait matched with kombu, kimchi and wasabi, while another starter brings together the flavours of liquorice and mandarin to perk up a pan-roasted pigeon breast. Move on to turbot with more of that Asian influence, or Cumbrian pork belly with sticky cheek and rainbow chard.

Chef Dominic Clarke **Seats** 52 **Times** 12.30-2/6.30-9, Closed L Mon-Sat **Prices** Fixed D 3 course £45, Tasting menu £65 **Wines** 19 bottles over £30, 21 bottles under £30, 9 by glass **Parking** 30 **Notes** Tasting menu 7 course, Afternoon tea, Sunday L £24.50, Vegetarian available, Children 6 yrs+

The Samling

Modern British V NOTABLE WINE LIST

tel: 015394 31922 **Ambleside Rd LA23 1LR**
email: info@thesamlinghotel.co.uk **web:** www.thesamlinghotel.co.uk
dir: *M6 junct 36, A591 through Windermere towards Ambleside. 2m. 300yds past Low Wood Water Sports Centre, just after sharp bend turn right into hotel entrance*

Dynamic British cooking in a revamped Windermere retreat

The spectacular view over Lake Windermere is timeless, but time does not stand still at the Samling and 2016 has seen exciting developments and the arrival of a new chef. Nick Edgar arrived hotfoot from Le Manoir aux Quat' Saisons to a brand new restaurant, kitchen and chef's table in a stunning modern stone and glass extension. The charming old country house is getting a revamp, too, while the 67 acres of grounds includes a kitchen garden to ensure a steady supply of first-rate ingredients for much of the year. What is not home-grown comes from a close-knit community of suppliers listed on the menu. The fixed-price carte and tasting menu (including an imaginative veggie version) offer up creative combinations that reveal true balance on the plate. A first course pan-fried foie gras, for example, comes with pineapple purée and caramelised fruit, plus watercress purée and chorizo – a hugely successful partnership. Next up, loin of venison has perfect poise, with a silky jus enriched with chocolate, or go for sea bass with curried mussels and cauliflower. Everything looks pretty on the plate, not least a richly indulgent dessert of banana and caramel. The wine list is an impressive beast that covers the best of the world's regions.

Chef Nick Edgar **Seats** 22, Pr/dining room 8 **Times** 12-2/6.30-9.30 **Prices** Fixed L 3 course £30-£80, Fixed D 3 course £60, Tasting menu £80 **Wines** 198 bottles over £30, 26 bottles under £30, 22 by glass **Parking** 20 **Notes** Fixed L 4 course £30, ALC 5 course, Tasting menu 8 course, Sunday L, Children welcome

Storrs Hall Hotel

Modern British V

tel: 015394 47111 **Storrs Park LA23 3LG**
email: enquiries@storrshall.com **web:** www.storrshall.com
dir: *On A592 2m S of Bowness, on Newby Bridge road*

Ambitious Lakeland cooking with views over Windermere and the fells

The Rosette award for this establishment has been suspended due to a change of chef. Reassessment will take place in due course under the new chef. The setting is a grand Georgian mansion in 17 acres of pristine grounds with a National Trust-owned temple folly, and an elegant dining room looking through vast windows to inspirational Lakeland views, taking in sweeping gardens with giant stone urns and immaculate topiary, and onwards towards the shore of Lake Windermere and the brooding fells beyond. It's a pretty impressive backdrop then for some ingenious modern country-house cooking, delivered via a five-course dinner menu built from intricate, boldly flavoured dishes. A starter of poached rabbit loin seems to have it all, with accompaniments of Alsace bacon, maple peas, puréed parsnip and winter truffle, or there may be an eastern-influenced flamed and grilled mackerel dish seasoned with gomashio (Japanese sesame and salt), and matched with pickled cucumber and miso emulsion. Main course might showcase tenderly roasted halibut with smoked mussels and baked golden beetroot, or add rhubarb and spiced granola to duck breast and leg in jus gras. For veggies, it could be barbecued Jerusalem artichokes, sprout shells and celeriac crisps, with parsley oil dressing. Innovation is maintained through to a dessert of frozen lemon custard with yuzu crémeux, fennel pollen ice cream and green tea. Thoroughly professional formal service completes the picture.

Chef Steve Love **Seats** 82, Pr/dining room 40 **Times** 12.30-2.30/7-9, Closed L Mon-Sat **Wines** 71 bottles over £30, 7 bottles under £30, 12 by glass **Parking** 50 **Notes** D 5 course £52, Themed evenings, Afternooon tea, Sunday L £19.50-£26.50, Children welcome

WINDERMERE *continued*

The Wild Boar Inn, Grill & Smokehouse

Traditional British NEW

tel: 015394 45225 **Crook LA23 3NF**
email: thewildboar@englishlakes.co.uk **web:** www.thewildboarinn.co.uk
dir: *2.5m S of Windermere on B5284. From Crook 3.5m, on right*

Smart, rustic country inn with buzzy open kitchen

The white-painted Wild Boar is a classic inn with a host of stylish bedrooms, a smart bar, and a restaurant with an open kitchen at its heart. They even have their own on-site microbrewery. The dining area has oak beams and darkwood tables, which are lit by flickering candles in the evening. The menu includes local ingredients such as the full-flavoured sirloin steak, cooked just right and served with mashed potatoes and onion rings, or the game that finds its way into a raised pie. Their own-smoked products arrive on a deli board to share, and there's classic stuff like fish and chips too.

Chef Miroslav Likus **Seats** 100, Pr/dining room 30 **Times** 12-2.30/6.30-9 **Prices** Starter £4.50-£9, Main £13-£38, Dessert £3.50-£10 **Wines** 38 bottles over £30, 52 bottles under £30, 17 by glass **Parking** 30 **Notes** Sunday L £16.50-£21.50, Vegetarian available, Children welcome

DERBYSHIRE

BAKEWELL Map 16 SK26

Piedaniel's

Traditional French, European

tel: 01629 812687 **Bath St DE45 1BX**
dir: *From Bakewell rdbt in town centre take A6 Buxton exit. 1st right into Bath St (one-way)*

Bistro cooking done with personal warmth and charm

Piedaniel's is run with great personal warmth and charm by a husband-and-wife team who keep the town supplied with reliable bistro cooking. Starters encompass a simple salad of smoked chicken and roast cherry tomatoes dressed in white truffle oil, or perhaps a saffron-fragranced take on moules marinière. Main courses nail their colours to the mast of hearty prime cuts – confit duck leg, lamb shank, beef fillet topped with red onion marmalade in wild mushroom casserole – while fish gets a look-in in the form of cod crusted in lemon and parsley, sauced with white Burgundy. Finish with brioche-and-butter pudding in Grand Marnier custard, or proper crêpes Suzette.

BASLOW Map 16 SK27

Cavendish Hotel

Modern British V

tel: 01246 582311 **Church Ln DE45 1SP**
email: info@cavendish-hotel.net **web:** www.cavendish-hotel.net
dir: *M1 junct 29 follow signs for Chesterfield. From Chesterfield take A619 to Bakewell, Chatsworth & Baslow*

Classic and modern dishes à la Chatsworth

The Cavendish is a stone-built hotel acquired in 1830, where dining consists of a roll call of modern classics such as seared scallops with black pudding and pea purée, roast pigeon breast with couscous, and loin and haunch of venison with celeriac and beetroot in chocolate jus. But the beaten track is also profitably abandoned for the likes of tandoori monkfish cheek with pumpkin purée, butternut squash cake with wilted greens and spiced lentils, and pecan pie with blackberries and salted brown butter ice cream. If you're a stickler for tradition, the artisan English cheeses are of the gold standard, and there's apple crumble and vanilla ice cream too.

Chef Mike Thompson **Seats** 50, Pr/dining room 18 **Times** 12-2.30/6.30-10, Closed D 25 Dec **Prices** Fixed L 2 course £39.50, Fixed D 3 course £49.50 **Wines** 35 bottles over £30, 21 bottles under £30, 11 by glass **Parking** 40 **Notes** Kitchen table £85, Sunday L £27.50, Children welcome

Fischer's Baslow Hall

– *see opposite*

BEELEY Map 16 SK26

The Devonshire Arms at Beeley

Modern British NOTABLE WINE LIST

tel: 01629 733259 **Devonshire Square DE4 2NR**
email: enquiries@devonshirebeeley.co.uk **web:** www.devonshirebeeley.co.uk
dir: *6m N of Matlock & 5m E of Bakewell, located off B6012*

Classically-inspired dining on the Chatsworth estate

A night or two in one of the guest rooms would allow you to say you'd stayed at Chatsworth, sort of, as this stone-built village inn is situated in the heart of the estate. Expect cask-conditioned ales and a terrific wine list, and some contemporary pub food. Dishes combine diverse ingredients successfully, as when chicken, mushroom and pistachio arrive in a terrine with accompanying apple and ale chutney, plus some treacle bread. Next up, South Coast brill is served with smoked mackerel fricassée, while dark chocolate and hazelnut frangipane tart shows off the fine pastry skills among the kitchen team.

BRADWELL Map 16 SK18

The Samuel Fox Country Inn

Modern British

tel: 01433 621562 **Stretfield Rd S33 9JT**
email: enquiries@samuelfox.co.uk **web:** www.samuelfox.co.uk
dir: *M1 junct 29, A617 towards Chesterfield, onto A619 towards A623 Chapel-en-le-Frith. B6049 for Bradwell, restaurant on left on leaving Bradwell*

Hearty Peak District sustenance with a modern touch

A stone-built inn near the Pennine Way named after the Victorian steel magnate who invented the folding ribbed umbrella. Breads of the day, variously flavoured with treacle or with Henderson's relish and onion, make an encouraging prelude to starters such as pig's trotter and ham with a slow-cooked egg and crispy potato in anchovy sauce, or a sturdy broth composed of kohlrabi with brown shrimps and sea lettuce. Seasonal game is a winner, perhaps roast breast and braised leg of pheasant with cabbage in Madeira, or there may be poached lemon sole with cavolo nero and Jerusalem artichokes. Finish with chocolate parfait, served with coffee sorbet and a burnt clementine.

Chef James Duckett **Seats** 40 **Times** 12-2.30/6-9, Closed 2-27 Jan, Mon-Tue, L Wed-Thu, D 25 Dec **Prices** Fixed D 3 course £20-£26, Tasting menu £49, Starter £6-£9, Main £13-£20, Dessert £6.50-£7.50 **Wines** 10 bottles over £30, 30 bottles under £30, 12 by glass **Parking** 15 **Notes** Tasting menu 7 course, Early bird D 6-7pm Wed-Sat, Sunday L £21-£26, Vegetarian available, Children welcome

Fischer's Baslow Hall

BASLOW Map 16 SK27

Modern European V

tel: 01246 583259 **Calver Rd DE45 1RR**
email: reservations@fischers-baslowhall.co.uk
web: www.fischers-baslowhall.co.uk
dir: *From Baslow on A623 towards Calver. Hotel on right*

Razor-sharp modern country-house cooking

This fine Edwardian house, built in the style of a 17th-century manor with protruding wings and mullioned windows, is reached by a winding driveway lined with mature chestnut trees. It's a grand enough spot, but built on an intimate scale – more a restaurant with rooms than the full stately home schtick. With just six tables and the recent de rigueur addition of a chef's bench in the kitchen to tend, the formally-dressed service team bring polished attentiveness to the whole experience. Rupert Rowley is a formidably talented chef whose willingness to experiment without straying from core values of flag-waving sourcing of seasonal produce is paraded at dinner in his 'Classic Menu', and a 'Taste of Britain' tasting menu, and in a lunch offering that's rather easier on the wallet. The on-trend combinations and pin-sharp techniques seem to exist in a parallel universe to the genteel formality of the dining room, so things get off to a flying start with the vibrant canapés and fabulous breads (among them black treacle and stout, and hazelnut and raisin), before sous-vide cooking brings melt-in-the-mouth tenderness to a game starter of hay-baked partridge with pan-fried foie gras, celeriac and truffle dumplings and ceps. Otherwise, start with pan-fried scallops with an Asian-accented medley of toasted sesame purée, rice cracker and ponzu dressing. Mains showcase pedigree meats such as perfectly-cooked saddle of wild venison matched with roast pear, date purée, Brussels sprouts, trompette de mort and shimeji mushrooms and chocolate sauce. If you're in the mood for fish, it is equally-well handled: pan-fried John Dory might come with beetroot fondant, toasted almonds and thyme velouté. It all ends with a playfully-inventive dessert involving a chocolate tree trunk with sap-green lime sorbet and purée, spearmint 'moss' and chocolate sorbet.

Chef Rupert Rowley **Seats** 55, Pr/dining room 38
Times 12-1.30/7-8.30, Closed 25-26 & 31 Dec **Prices** Fixed L 2 course £20.16, Fixed D 3 course £72, Tasting menu £80-£128, Starter £20.50-£22, Main £30, Dessert fr £17 **Wines** 110 bottles over £30, 20 bottles under £30, 6 by glass **Parking** 20 **Notes** Taste of Britain L £60/£100, wknd L 2/3 course £32/£38, Sunday L £32-£38, Children 5/8yrs+ L/D

BUXTON Map 16 SK07

Best Western Lee Wood Hotel

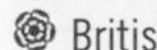 British

tel: 01298 23002 **The Park SK17 6TQ**
email: reservations@leewoodhotel.co.uk **web:** www.leewoodhotel.co.uk
dir: *M1 junct 24, A50 towards Ashbourne, A515 to Buxton. From Buxton town centre follow A5004 Long Hill to Whaley Bridge. Hotel approx 200mtrs beyond University of Derby campus*

Conservatory dining in the Peak District

Refurbished style exudes from every pore of Lee Wood, a Georgian grey-stone manor house in the Peak District. Dining goes on in an expansive conservatory room with fronds of hanging foliage overhead and refreshing views of the grounds all about. The young service team runs the show with admirable efficiency, delivering modern brasserie cooking that scores some hits. A meal might run from roast chicken and wild mushroom terrine with soused vegetables, potato salad and beetroot mayonnaise, to a main course of pork with black pudding purée and sautéed potatoes in cider oil dressing. The assiette of desserts may well be the high point of the show.

Chef Simon Gould **Seats** 150, Pr/dining room 10 **Times** 12-2/5.30-9.15 **Prices** Fixed L 2 course £17.95, Fixed D 3 course £30, Starter £6.25-£7.25, Main £14.50-£28.95, Dessert £6.50-£9.60 **Wines** 6 bottles over £30, 22 bottles under £30, 7 by glass **Parking** 40 **Notes** Pre-theatre menu, Sunday L £17.95-£24.95, Vegetarian available, Children welcome

CHESTERFIELD Map 16 SK37

Casa Hotel

Modern British, Mediterranean

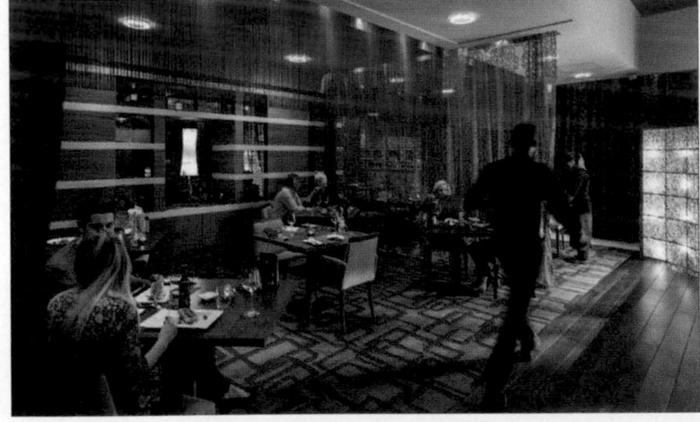

tel: 01246 245990 & 245999 **Lockoford Ln S41 7JB**
email: cocina@casahotels.co.uk **web:** www.casahotels.co.uk
dir: *M1 junct 29 to A617 Chesterfield/A61 Sheffield, 4th exit 1st rdbt A61, 1st exit 2nd rdbt, hotel on left*

Celebrate all things Spanish in a lopsided 'pomo' hotel

Casa's Cocina restaurant is an über-chic space with darkwood, white chairs and floor-to-ceiling windows. The menu has a selection of salads and tapas running from a board of Spanish charcuterie to a croquette of hake, cheese and chives with tartare dressing. Among successful starters are seared scallops with black pudding purée, truffle butter and apple jelly and crisps, and carpaccio with horseradish cream, red pepper coulis, watercress and pork crackling. The Josper grill comes into its own for steaks with a choice of sauces, and there might be paella, or venison hotpot with Savoy cabbage, swede purée and roasting juices. Puddings include retro rice pudding with home-made blueberry jam.

Chef Andrew Wilson **Seats** 100, Pr/dining room 200 **Times** 12-4/6-10, Closed 1 Jan, BH Mon, L Mon-Sat **Prices** Fixed L 2 course £14.50, Starter £5-£10, Main £14-£29, Dessert £5-£7.50 **Wines** 31 bottles over £30, 34 bottles under £30, 12 by glass **Parking** 200 **Notes** Early bird menu 6-7pm Mon-Fri, 5.30-6.30pm Sat, Sunday L £14.95-£23.95, Vegetarian available, Children welcome

Peak Edge Hotel at the Red Lion

Modern British V

tel: 01246 566142 **Darley Rd, Stone Edge S45 0LW**
email: sleep@peakedgehotel.co.uk **web:** www.peakedgehotel.co.uk
dir: *M1 junct 29, A617 to Chesterfield. At rdbt take 1st exit onto A61, at next rdbt 2nd exit onto Whitecotes Ln, continue onto Matlock Rd (A632) then Darley Rd (B5057)*

Inventive cooking in a Georgian inn next to a brand-new hotel

A new-build stone edifice on the border of the Peak District National Park, the family-owned hotel is handy for the historic houses of Chatsworth and Haddon Hall. Not all is pristine modernity, for next door is the Red Lion, a Georgian coaching inn that is home to the hotel's bar and bistro, where the stock-in-trade is inventive contemporary British cooking. First up might be pigeon breast with fig and ricotta tart, before main course brings nicely timed pollack with crab risotto in langoustine oil with apple and fennel salad. Proceedings conclude in like manner with banana-peanut bavarois and chocolate ale cake.

Chef Joseph Grayson **Seats** 80 **Times** 12-9.30, All-day dining **Prices** Prices not confirmed **Wines** 16 bottles over £30, 27 bottles under £30, 9 by glass **Notes** Afternoon tea, Sunday L, Children welcome

CLOWNE Map 16 SK47

Hotel Van Dyk

Modern British V

tel: 01246 810219 **Worksop Rd S43 4TD**
email: info@hotelvandyk.co.uk **web:** www.hotelvandyk.co.uk
dir: *M1 junct 30, towards Worksop, at rdbt 1st exit, next rdbt straight over. Through lights, hotel 100yds on right*

Sugar-white hotel with appealing modern British cooking

The white-fronted Van Dyk stands on the A619 not far from Chesterfield. Amid the surrounding ruggedness, it looks a little like a sugar-frosting confection, which only adds to its idiosyncratic character. Inside, it's geared up for weddings and business. There's a hint of old-school formality about the Bowden dining room, with swagged curtains, a trio of chandeliers, and a baby grand piano. Modern northern cooking is the bill of fare, with dishes founded on sound culinary logic. Open with duck liver and orange pâté with Madeira jelly and cranberry compôte, as a prelude to seared monkfish tails with roasted salsify and girolle mushrooms.

Chef Ben Richardson **Seats** 89, Pr/dining room 14 **Times** 12-9.30, All-day dining **Prices** Prices not confirmed **Wines** 7 bottles over £30, 28 bottles under £30, 13 by glass **Parking** 120 **Notes** Sun D last orders 7.30pm, Sunday L, Children welcome

DALBURY Map 10 SK23

The Black Cow

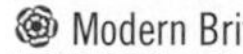 Modern British

tel: 01332 824297 **The Green, Dalbury Lees DE6 5BE**
email: enquiries@theblackcow.co.uk **web:** www.theblackcow.co.uk
dir: *From Derby A52 signed Ashbourne, Kirk Langley; turn into Church Lane, then Long Lane, follow signs to Dalbury Lees*

Real ales and pub favourites opposite the village green

Bedecked in pink and purple flower baskets, The Black Cow dominates the village green in Dalbury Lees. International pub favourites form the backbone of the kitchen's output, with reliable satisfaction to be had from Thai-style salmon fishcakes and chilli dip, or chicken Caesar, for beginners. Follow on with ale-battered cod with mushy peas, or velvety-tender braised lamb shank with red onion marmalade and creamy mash in rosemary and garlic jus. Head for sticky toffee or apple and blueberry crumble for dessert, while a plethora of real ales from breweries such as Jennings, Dancing Duck and Mr Grundy add class to the drinking options.

Chef Daniel Edwards **Seats** 30, Pr/dining room 25 **Times** 12-2/6-9, Closed D Sun **Prices** Prices not confirmed **Wines** 1 bottle over £30, 17 bottles under £30, 8 by glass **Parking** 12, On street **Notes** Sunday L, Vegetarian available, Children welcome

DARLEY ABBEY Map 11 SK33

Darleys Restaurant

Modern British V

tel: 01332 364987 **Haslams Ln DE22 1DZ**
email: info@darleys.com **web:** www.darleys.com
dir: *A6 N from Derby (Duffield road). Right in 1m into Mileash Ln, to Old Lane, right, over bridge. Restaurant on right*

Modern British cooking by the water's edge

This converted silk mill by the River Derwent is the setting for some bright, modern cooking making good use of regional produce. Nori-wrapped Loch Duart salmon is a thoroughly contemporary way to start a meal, with crispy squid, ginger and soy, while another first course has fun with goats' cheese and pineapple. Main course fillet of Derbyshire beef with layers of potato and mushrooms and a shallot purée shows respect for classical ways. Another main course combines sustainable Icelandic cod with smoked bacon polenta and clam sauce, and, when it comes to dessert, there's creativity on show in a mini lemon cake with Swiss meringue and red berry lollipop parfait.

Chef Jonathan Hobson, Mark Hadfield **Seats** 70 **Times** 12-2/7-9.30, Closed BHs, 1st 2 wks Jan, D Sun **Prices** Fixed L 2 course fr £19.95, Tasting menu £50, Starter £7.90-£9.50, Main £21.50-£24.50, Dessert £8.25 **Wines** 33 bottles over £30, 64 bottles under £30, 18 by glass **Parking** 9 **Notes** Sunday L £30, Children welcome

DERBY Map 11 SK33

Masa Restaurant

Modern European V

tel: 01332 203345 **The Old Chapel, Brook St DE1 3PF**
email: enquiries@masarestaurantwinebar.com
dir: *8m from M1 junct 25. Brook St off inner ring road near BBC Radio Derby*

Modern brasserie dishes in a converted chapel

This stylish contemporary restaurant occupies the gallery of an old chapel, with a lounge bar on the ground floor, and the lawned front garden and rear patio available for outdoor imbibing. The restaurant deals in brasserie-style dishes via a sensibly concise carte and terrific value set menu (lunchtime and mid-week evenings). Start with an attractively presented ham hock and guinea fowl ballotine, served with red onion marmalade and pickled girolles, and move on to pan-fried sea bass sitting on tagliatelle, or trio of pork in the fruity company of apple compôte, blackberries and glazed pear. Finish with lemon and lime crème brûlée or date sponge with tonka bean ice cream.

Chef Matt Gabbitas **Seats** 120 **Times** 12-2/6-9, Closed Tue **Prices** Fixed L 2 course fr £19.95, Fixed D 3 course fr £24.95, Starter £5-£11, Main £14-£25, Dessert £5-£7 **Wines** 12 bottles over £30, 34 bottles under £30, 11 by glass **Parking** On street (pay & display), Brook St car park **Notes** Tasting menu 7 course once per month, Sunday L fr £24, Children welcome

FROGGATT Map 16 SK27

The Chequers Inn

Modern British

tel: 01433 630231 **S32 3ZJ**
email: info@chequers-froggatt.com **web:** www.chequers-froggatt.com
dir: *On A625 between Sheffield & Bakewell, 0.75m from Calver*

Rustic Peak District inn with hearty modern dishes

The Tindalls' country inn in the Hope Valley charms, with a warm colour scheme, wooden pub-style furniture and a fireplace creating a relaxing atmosphere. The menu deftly steers between stalwarts and modern offerings. Open with roast pigeon breast, perfectly timed, with brown bread purée, pickled wild mushrooms, crisp brioche wafers and a rich jus, ahead of duck breast, the crisp skin rubbed with salt-and-pepper and sprinkled with caraway seeds, accompanied by salt-baked celeriac, Savoy cabbage, mash and an orange and red wine reduction. Standards continue into puddings such as orange and olive oil cake with orange curd and sorbet and walnut 'mayo'.

Chef Lindsey Divens **Seats** 90 **Times** 12-2.30/6-9, Closed 25 Dec **Prices** Starter £5.50-£9, Main £12-£20, Dessert £6-£7 **Wines** 3 bottles over £30, 34 bottles under £30, 10 by glass **Parking** 50 **Notes** Sunday L £13.95-£14.50, Vegetarian available, Children welcome

GRINDLEFORD Map 16 SK27

The Maynard

Modern British

tel: 01433 630321 **Main Rd S32 2HE**
email: info@themaynard.co.uk **web:** www.themaynard.co.uk
dir: *M1/A619 into Chesterfield, onto Baslow, A623 to Calver right into Grindleford*

Anglo-French magic à la Peak District

If Grindleford sounds like the made-up location of a Miss Marple mystery, The Maynard suits it to perfection, its stone-built majesty rising out of the Derwent Valley. Lightly sautéed breast of wood pigeon opens the show, served with braised baby leeks and puréed butter beans in a port reduction. This is followed by accurately timed sea bass dressed in lemon, with Jersey Royals and a summer salad of peas and rocket, or 'chicken cooked two ways' – confit leg and poached and roasted breast (so three ways, really) – with lemon spinach and colcannon in tarragon sauce. Finish with a multi-faceted coconut tasting, its chocolate mousse and sphere of sponge cake the highlights.

Chef Mark Vernon **Seats** 50, Pr/dining room 120 **Times** 12-3/6.30-9, Closed 25 Dec, 1 Jan, L Sat **Prices** Prices not confirmed **Wines** 7 by glass **Parking** 60 **Notes** Sunday L, Vegetarian available, Children welcome

HATHERSAGE Map 16 SK28

George Hotel

Modern British

tel: 01433 650436 **Main Rd S32 1BB**
email: info@george-hotel.net **web:** www.george-hotel.net
dir: *In village centre on junction of A625/B6001*

Novel ideas from a hard-working Peak District kitchen

The 500-year-old stone-built hotel looks like a little castle and its interiors maintain the impression of dignified venerability, the hefty stones of the walls offset by wooden floors and simple furniture in the smartly attired dining room. The hard-working kitchen makes many of the foundation elements of the menu in-house, while most of the rest is sourced from trusted Peak District suppliers. Start with scallops in the contemporary company of hay-smoked pigeon breast (plus chestnut purée and chocolate oil), move on to braised cod with chorizo and chicken wing, and finish in an equally creative modern manner with pumpkin pie brûlée.

The Plough Inn

Modern European

tel: 01433 650319 **Leadmill Bridge S32 1BA**
email: sales@theploughinn-hathersage.co.uk **web:** www.theploughinn-hathersage.co.uk
dir: *1m SE of Hathersage on B6001. Over bridge, 150yds beyond at Leadmill*

Sustaining modern dishes in a Tudor riverside inn

Set in nine acres of grounds that slope gently to the River Derwent, the stone-built 16th-century Plough is welcoming and friendly. The courtyard's the place to be in summer, and the dining room is always smartly turned out. The same might be said of the cooking. A starter might be seared foie gras on toast with home-made sweet pickle, and you could follow that with poached fillet of beef with fondant potato, butternut squash purée, buttered kale, and a horseradish and ginger cream. Vegetarians might opt for orzo with white beans, confit fennel, courgettes and goats' cheese.

Chef Robert Navarro **Seats** 40, Pr/dining room 24 **Times** 11.30-9.30, All-day dining, Closed 25 Dec **Prices** Fixed L 2 course £20-£25, Fixed D 3 course £26-£32.50, Starter £5-£12, Main £14-£27.50, Dessert £6-£7.50 **Wines** 22 bottles over £30, 23 bottles under £30, 20 by glass **Parking** 40 **Notes** Mon-Fri smaller portions fixed L 3 course £20, Sunday L £14-£26, Vegetarian available, Children welcome

HIGHAM Map 16 SK35

Santo's Higham Farm Hotel

Modern International

tel: 01773 833812 **Main Rd DE55 6EH**
email: reception@santoshighamfarm.co.uk **web:** www.santoshighamfarm.co.uk
dir: *M1 junct 28, A38 towards Derby, then A61 to Higham, left onto B6013*

Locally-sourced fare in a Derbyshire farmstead hotel

Santo Cusimano runs a highly individual rural retreat. With the rolling Amber Valley all about, it's in a prime slice of Derbyshire walking country, and has been fashioned from an old farmstead. The dining room is designed to soothe the senses, with an air of soft-focus pastel charm and smart table settings. Menus mobilise plenty of pedigree local produce and given the owner's provenance, Italian influences are never distant. Start with a pressing of corn-fed chicken with poached prunes, move on to roasted rack and slow-braised shoulder of spring lamb, and finish with a sugar hit from pecan pie with caramelised bananas and praline ice cream.

Chef Cameron Smith **Seats** 50, Pr/dining room 34 **Times** 12-3/7-9.30, Closed BHs, L Mon-Sat, D Sun **Prices** Starter £5-£7, Main £9.50-£25, Dessert £5.50-£9.50 **Wines** 13 bottles over £30, 37 bottles under £30, 6 by glass **Parking** 100 **Notes** Sunday L £9.95-£15.95, Vegetarian available, Children welcome

HOPE Map 16 SK18

Losehill House Hotel & Spa

@@ Modern British V

tel: 01433 621219 **Lose Hill Ln, Edale Rd S33 6AF**
email: info@losehillhouse.co.uk **web:** www.losehillhouse.co.uk
dir: *A6187 into Hope. Take turn opposite church into Edale Rd. 1m, left & follow signs*

Glorious Peak District views and interesting contemporary cooking

The Orangery Restaurant in this secluded spot in the Peak District National Park offers stunning views from a light-filled, comfortable room with a contemporary look. The kitchen has a modern, creative style, adding novel and intriguing elements to many dishes. Rolled lamb leg, for instance, is accompanied by leek ash, camomile gel and turnips, and fillet of mackerel by carrot ketchup, carrot purée and sultanas – and those are just starters. Confident techniques and good judgement result in a main course of local venison loin with pommes Anna, beetroot, leeks and cocoa nib crumb. Inventive desserts include orange cheesecake with a raspberry bubble, orange jelly and raspberry sorbet.

Chef Darren Goodwin **Seats** 50, Pr/dining room 30 **Times** 12-2.30/6.30-9 **Prices** Prices not confirmed **Wines** 36 bottles over £30, 12 bottles under £30, 6 by glass **Parking** 25 **Notes** Taste of Losehill 7 course, Sunday L, Children welcome

MATLOCK Map 16 SK35

Stones Restaurant

@@ Modern British V

tel: 01629 56061 **1c Dale Rd DE4 3LT**
email: info@stones-restaurant.co.uk
dir: *Phone for directions*

Modern Mediterranean-influenced dining with a riverside terrace

Stones may be an intimate basement venue, but it has the best of both worlds on fine days, thanks to a stylish conservatory and tiled sun terrace perched above the Derwent. The decor is a mix of subtle earthy tones, to match a Mediterranean-inflected menu of contemporary modern British dishes. Well-judged combinations get under way with roasted salt cod, confit chicken wing and puréed mushrooms. For main, there might be braised blade of beef with pearl barley risotto and charred broccoli, or venison loin with its own 'shepherd's pie', and the closer might be rhubarb and ginger rice pudding with cardamom ice cream.

Chef Kevin Stone **Seats** 44, Pr/dining room 16 **Times** 12-1.30/6.30-8.30, Closed 25 Dec-5 Jan, Sun (some), Mon, L Tue **Prices** Fixed L 2 course £22-£24, Fixed D 3 course £36-£43, Tasting menu £42-£48.50 **Wines** 12 bottles over £30, 27 bottles under £30, 9 by glass **Parking** Matlock train station **Notes** Sunday L £22-£25, Children welcome

MELBOURNE Map 11 SK32

The Bay Tree

@ Modern British, New World

tel: 01332 863358 **4 Potter St DE73 8HW**
email: enquiries@baytreerestaurant.com
dir: *From M1(N) junct 23a or junct 24 (S) take A453 to Isley Walton, turn right & follow signs to Melbourne town centre*

Riotously colourful dishes in a dashing room

The stone façade of what was once several shops on a hill prepare you for the different levels of the place inside, but the menus make dishes sound misleadingly straightforward. Beetroot salad is served carpaccio-style, with asparagus, walnuts, apple and Roquefort tossed in balsamic vinaigrette, a riot of colour. Even chicken liver parfait is vividly offset by bright red onion confit. Artichoke hearts with tomato centres flank a piece of artichoke-crusted baked sea bass with peas, while the pink lamb rack is all adazzle with tomato fondue and black olive jus. Chocolate ganache tart set with raspberries has a tart-matching coulis and whipped cream to hold the dish together.

Chef Rex Howell **Seats** 60 **Times** 10.30-3/6.30-9.30, Closed 1 Jan, BHs, Mon-Tue, D Sun **Prices** Fixed L 2 course £12.50-£25, Fixed D 3 course £32.50 **Wines** 6 by glass **Parking** On street, Free public car park **Notes** Champagne breakfast £24.50 Wed-Sat, Sunday L £26, Vegetarian available, Children welcome

Harpur's of Melbourne

@ Modern French NEW

tel: 01332 862134 & 01283 248178 **2 Derby Rd DE73 8FE**
email: info@harpursofmelbourne.co.uk **web:** www.harpursofmelbourne.co.uk
dir: *From A50 exit signed Melbourne/Swadlincote. Continue for 5m, in centre of Melbourne on left*

Modern dishes and pub classics in an inn with lots going on

The inn evolved in the 19th century from a pair of Georgian houses in this lovely market town. These days, it puts on all sort of special occasions, and there's plenty going on in the smart first-floor restaurant. Pub classics such as mussels in beer, burgers, and steaks with chunky chips are the backbone, but there are also modern dishes like duck liver parfait rolled in shiitaki mushrooms, served with cured breast and plum sauce, or rolled fillet of cod with mango and Asian spices and two purées, one of cauliflower, one of sweet potato. Exhilaratingly colourful desserts include passionfruit parfait and blood orange pannacotta with pineapple and coconut.

Chef Lee Emerson **Seats** 75 **Times** 12-2.30/6-9.30 **Prices** Fixed L 2 course £15.95, Fixed D 3 course £24.95, Starter £4.95-£6.95, Main £11.95-£19.95, Dessert £4.50-£7.95 **Wines** 6 bottles over £30, 26 bottles under £30, 11 by glass **Parking** 25 **Notes** Champagne breakfast, Sunday L £15.95-£19.95, Vegetarian available, Children welcome

The Peacock at Rowsley

ROWSLEY **Map 16 SK26**

Modern British V

tel: 01629 733518 **Bakewell Rd DE4 2EB**
email: reception@thepeacockatrowsley.com
web: www.thepeacockatrowsley.com
dir: *A6, 3m before Bakewell, 6m from Matlock towards Bakewell*

Winning modern combinations, Derbyshire-style

Under the same aristocratic ownership as nearby Haddon Hall, this 17th-century mansion built of Derbyshire stone comes in just the right dimensions to make for a classy boutique country-house hotel. The opulent interiors are deeply comfortable, from the relaxing lounge to a stone-walled bar hung with oil paintings that makes a very cosy retreat, and decadently damson-hued dining rooms. Head chef Dan Smith's stint in Tom Aikens' kitchen shows in his precise, technical dexterity, use of top-class produce, quirky spins of presentation and off-the-wall combinations here and there. A texturally lively starter of skate and mussels with cauliflower, seaweed, salty purslane, smoked butter sauce and puffed wild rice offers a perfectly thought-through array of flavours, otherwise you might get going with smoked venison tartare, red cabbage and goats' curd. At main course stage, lamb cutlet and braised and rolled neck with Ossau-Iraty sheep's cheese, kale, chive crème fraîche, caramelised shallot and pearl barley in parsley cream is a dish full of forthright, pitch-perfect notes, while traditionalists might head for a rib-eye steak with chips, home-cured salt-beef salad, onion rings and béarnaise sauce. Fish cookery is equally-well considered, perhaps serving up hake with cauliflower, heritage potatoes, coastal herbs, brown shrimps and chicken wings. To finish, a meringue dome surrounded with clock face-like dots of pear (candied, compôte and poached) lifts to reveal a filling of pear sorbet and hazelnut foam, or if you prefer to end on a more substantial note, try bread-and-butter pudding with brown bread ice cream and custard. Excellent home-made breads, nibbles and amuse-bouche (Jerusalem artichoke velouté with grated truffle, pork croquette with apple, say) are wrought with the same attention to detail.

Chef Daniel Smith **Seats** 40, Pr/dining room 20 **Times** 7-9, Closed D 24-26 Dec, Sun **Prices** Tasting menu £65, Starter £6.50-£13.25, Main £26-£34, Dessert £6.50-£10.50 **Wines** 41 bottles over £30, 9 bottles under £30, 16 by glass **Parking** 25 **Notes** Sunday L £26.50-£33, Children 10 yrs+

The Peacock at Rowsley

The Peacock at Rowsley is cosy, chic boutique hotel, originally a manor house in the heart of the Peak District National Park and very close to Haddon Hall and Chatsworth House. Perfect for a countryside break with comfortable bedrooms including four posters and one of the best hotel suites in the region. Our award winning restaurant serves a delicious fine dining menu, crafted by Head Chef Dan Smith. Dan worked with notable chefs such as Tom Aikens before joining *The Peacock*. The atmospheric bar with open fire is a very convivial place to meet for lunch, dinner or just for a drink – with its own menu of freshly cooked local food. Treat yourself to a drink from the extensive cocktail menu. Sunday lunch at *The Peacock* is a local favourite. The hotel is famed for its excellent fly fishing on the Derbyshire Wye and river Derwent.

The Peacock at Rowsley, Derbyshire DE4 2EB • **Tel:** 01629 733518 • **Fax:** 01629 732671
Website: www.thepeacockatrowsley.com • **Email:** reception@thepeacockatrowsley.com

MORLEY Map 11 SK34

The Morley Hayes Hotel

 Modern British

tel: 01332 780480 **Main Rd DE7 6DG**
email: enquiries@morleyhayes.com **web:** www.morleyhayes.com
dir: *4m N of Derby on A608*

Appealingly eclectic cooking on a converted farm estate

Morley Hayes has been a dynamic hotel since the 1980s, and with its golf complex, conference facilities and wedding venue, it has most bases covered. The kitchen offers a roster of unpretentious modern dishes, with influences from around the globe adding vibrancy and colour. Crispy pork terrine with black pudding and rhubarb purée may whet the appetite for roast loin of local lamb given a Moroccan spin with lamb kofta, couscous and smoked aubergine, or you might head east for five spice-roasted duck with sweet potato purée, pak choi and soy sauce dressing. Finish with ginger beer rum baba with rhubarb compôte and vanilla cream.

REPTON Map 10 SK32

The Boot Inn

Modern British NEW

tel: 01283 346047 **12 Boot Hill DE65 6FT**
email: info@thebootatrepton.co.uk **web:** www.thebootatrepton.co.uk
dir: *From Repton Cross into Brook End, The Boot on right*

Micro-brewed ales and creative cooking

Five miles from the National Brewery Centre, you would expect beer to be a strong draw, especially in a refurbished 17th-century coaching inn. A range of evocatively named ales from its microbrewery is a plank of The Boot's huge popularity. Good things happen with the food too, with a classics menu supplemented by a creative carte. Expect Jerusalem artichoke risotto with burnt cobnuts, or silky chicken and foie gras parfait with pickles, to start. Then try barbecued sea bass with a rolled oat and pancetta croquette and salt-baked beets, before a finale of chocolate, passionfruit and yogurt ices, precariously piled and sauced with sweet Japanese rice wine.

Chef Rob Taylor **Seats** 65 **Times** 12-3/6-9 **Prices** Fixed L 2 course £12.95-£14.95, Starter £4.95-£8, Main £11.95-£25, Dessert £5.50-£6.50 **Parking** 9, On street **Notes** Brunch, Pre-theatre, Special occasions menu available, Sunday L £10.95-£24.95, Vegetarian available, Children welcome

ROWSLEY Map 16 SK26

The Peacock at Rowsley

– see page 112 and advert on page 113

THORPE Map 16 SK15

The Izaak Walton Hotel

Modern, Traditional NEW

tel: 01335 350981 & 350555 **Dovedale DE6 2AY**
email: reception@izaakwaltonhotel.com **web:** www.izaakwaltonhotel.com
dir: *A515 onto B5054, to Thorpe, continue straight over cattle grid & 2 small bridges, 1st right & sharp left*

Modern country house cooking in a rural retreat

This creeper-clad country house where the author of *The Compleat Angler* used to stay when he fished in the River Dove (hence the name) has glorious views over the Dovedale Valley and the Derbyshire peaks. Decorated in rich hues of red and gold, the elegant Haddon Restaurant favours a traditional candlelight-and-linen look, contrasting with the up-to-date creative menu. Home-cured gravad lax with crab pâté and avocado purée opens the show, followed by a duo of rabbit loin and crispy croquette matched with garlic and rosemary-infused fondant potato, wilted spinach and pancetta jus. End with lime posset and macaroon with chocolate crackling and soil.

Chef Simon Harrison **Seats** 120, Pr/dining room 40 **Times** 6-10, Closed L Mon-Sat **Prices** Fixed L 2 course fr £18.95, Fixed D 3 course £35-£39 **Wines** 14 bottles over £30, 27 bottles under £30, 6 by glass **Parking** 50 **Notes** Sunday L £18.95-£21.95, Vegetarian available, Children welcome

DEVON

AXMINSTER Map 4 SY29

Fairwater Head Hotel

Modern British

tel: 01297 678349 **Hawkchurch EX13 5TX**
email: info@fairwaterheadhotel.co.uk **web:** www.fairwaterheadhotel.co.uk
dir: *A358 into Broom Lane at Tytherleigh, follow signs to Hawkchurch & hotel*

Modern classic dishes in a rural Devon retreat

Just five miles from the old carpet town of Axminster, Fairwater Head enjoys panoramic views over the Axe Valley and stands amidst three acres of manicured lawns. An appealing grey stone building covered in climbing foliage, attractive interiors contribute to the relaxed rural ambience, and the elegant Greenfields dining room boasts smart table linen and friendly, informal service. Flawless Devon produce is worked into an extensive choice of modern classic dishes. Expect a silky cream of cauliflower soup, followed by baked cod loin, lobster sauce, new potatoes and baby vegetables. Finish with sticky toffee pudding and clotted cream ice cream.

Chef Tony Golder **Seats** 60, Pr/dining room 18 **Times** 12-2/7-9, Closed Jan, L Mon-Tue, Thu-Fri **Prices** Starter £5.50-£6, Main £11.95-£27.95, Dessert £2.25-£6 **Wines** 6 bottles over £30, 62 bottles under £30, 12 by glass **Parking** 40 **Notes** Sunday L £11.95-£25, Vegetarian available, Children welcome

BAMPTON Map 3 SS92

The Swan

◎◎ Modern British

tel: 01398 332248 **Station Rd EX16 9NG**
email: info@theswan.co **web:** www.theswan.co
dir: *Phone for directions*

Stylish pub with contemporary cooking

The Swan is a smart country pub – warm colours, lots of oak, a few sofas, soft lighting – with a convivial atmosphere. The bar is very much the heart of the operation, but it's easy to see why the whole place can be full of diners. Good ingredients are cooked simply, with the end result offering integrity, flavour and value. Expect inventive dishes like goats' curd fritters with pickled beetroot and orange, then hake fillet with rarebit, tomato dressing, leeks and bacon jam. Steak-and-kidney suet pudding will please traditionalists, and to finish there may be classic vanilla pannacotta with strawberries and oats.

Chef Paul Berry **Seats** 60, Pr/dining room 20 **Times** 12-2/6-9.30, Closed 25 Dec, D 26 Dec **Prices** Starter £4.95-£8.95, Main £10.95-£22, Dessert £5.95 **Wines** 10 bottles over £30, 45 bottles under £30, 40 by glass **Parking** Opposite, 100 spaces **Notes** Sunday L £10.95-£11.95, Vegetarian available, Children welcome

BEESANDS Map 3 SX84

The Cricket Inn

◎ Modern British

tel: 01548 580215 **TQ7 2EN**
email: enquiries@thecricketinn.com **web:** www.thecricketinn.com
dir: *From Kingsbridge follow A379 towards Dartmouth, at Stokenham mini-rdbt turn right for Beesands*

Seafood specialities at historic inn

Smack on the seafront overlooking the shingle beach, with stunning views across Start Bay, The Cricket enjoys an unrivalled location and retains every ounce of its identity as a former fisherman's pub. Blackboard menus advertise what has been freshly drawn from the bay, backed up by stalwarts such as scallops and chorizo on saffron risotto, and whole lobsters done thermidor. A bowl of creamy crab soup is smooth and satisfying, and the unimpeachable freshness of the shellfish is celebrated in simple mains such as king prawn linguine with confit tomatoes, fennel, chilli, garlic and ginger. Baked Alaska is all the rage right now, and comes with orange meringue and mango.

Chef Scott Heath **Seats** 65, Pr/dining room 40 **Times** 12-2.30/6-8.30, Closed 25 Dec **Prices** Prices not confirmed **Wines** 2 bottles over £30, 26 bottles under £30, 12 by glass **Parking** 30 **Notes** Breakfast (May-Sep), Sunday L, Vegetarian available, Children welcome

BIGBURY-ON-SEA Map 3 SX64

Burgh Island Hotel

◎ Modern British NEW

tel: 01548 810514 **Burgh Island TQ7 4BG**
email: reception@burghisland.com
dir: *M5/A38 : follow signs to Bigbury on Sea/Burgh Island. Call for parking directions (do not drive over beach)*

British food and classy dining in iconic island hotel

Dine where Agatha Christie, Noël Coward and other pre-war luminaries once dined, in this classic art deco hotel off the South Devon coast. At low tide you can walk to it, at high tide you ride a tractor on stilts. Guests buy into the period atmosphere by dressing up to the nines in black tie and evening gowns for dinner in the all-original ballroom. Prepare to welcome back the 1930s. A frequently-changing menu typically offers poached Beesands lobster tail, lobster mousse, chickpea and red pepper salad; pan-fried halibut with cauliflower purée, gnocchi, brown shrimp, asparagus and Muscatel butter; and banana soufflé with crème caramel.

Chef Tim Hall **Times** 12-3/6.30-Close, Closed L Mon-Sat **Notes** D 4 course £75, Sunday L £62

BIGBURY-ON-SEA *continued*

The Oyster Shack

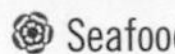 Seafood

tel: 01548 810876 & 810934 **Stakes Hill TQ7 4BE**
email: bigbury@oystershack.co.uk
dir: *A379 Modbury to Kingsbridge road, B3392 to Bigbury, left at St Anns Chapel, signed to Oyster Shack 1m on left*

Waterside spot for simple seafood dining

A warm-hearted place with a casual atmosphere, where a friendly greeting gets everything off on the right foot. Super-fresh seafood is the name of the game, and it's all the better if you sit outside under the sail-like awning. Giant blackboards reveal what's on offer from crabs and lobsters, to fishy plates such as whole roasted gurnard with anchovy butter. Start with oysters (grilled with blue cheese and smoked bacon, say), and follow with a fruits de mer or a staggeringly good fillet of hake with roasted pepper, chorizo and mussels. Finish with cherry and chocolate brownie, and drink beer, cider or something from the short (mostly white) wine list.

Chef Andy Richardson **Seats** 60 **Times** 12-3/6-9, Closed 25 Dec, 2-31 Jan, D Sun (Nov-24 Mar) **Prices** Fixed L 2 course fr £14, Fixed D 3 course fr £16, Starter £5.50-£8.50, Main £12.50-£23.50, Dessert £4.50-£8.75 **Wines** 7 bottles over £30, 12 bottles under £30, 7 by glass **Parking** 25 **Notes** All day dining 7 days/wk in summer, Sunday L, Vegetarian available, Children welcome

BRIXHAM Map 3 SX95

Quayside Hotel

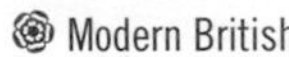 Modern British

tel: 01803 855751 **41-49 King St TQ5 9TJ**
email: reservations@quayside.co.uk **web:** www.quaysidehotel.co.uk
dir: *From Exeter take A380 towards Torquay, then A3022 to Brixham*

The freshest seafood by the harbour

The restaurant at the Quayside Hotel majors in seafood and what reaches the menu depends on the catch – skate, black bream, pollack, turbot and more, it's a piscine lottery. Judging by a beautiful piece of cod, cooked just right (baked with herb crust and served with tomato salsa), the kitchen knows how to treat this prime product with respect. There are non-seafood options too, such as minestrone soup, grilled sirloin steak, veggie risotto and banoffee iced parfait for dessert, but there's no bigger draw than the plateau de fruits de mer. It all takes place in a newly decorated, candlelit dining room with harbour views and a refreshing lack of pretence.

Chef Andy Sewell **Seats** 40, Pr/dining room 18 **Times** 6.30-9.30, Closed L all week **Prices** Prices not confirmed **Wines** 6 bottles over £30, 23 bottles under £30, 10 by glass **Parking** 30 **Notes** Vegetarian available, Children 5 yrs+

BURRINGTON Map 3 SS61

Northcote Manor

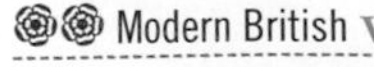 Modern British V

tel: 01769 560501 **EX37 9LZ**
email: rest@northcotemanor.co.uk **web:** www.northcotemanor.co.uk
dir: *M5 junct 27 towards Barnstaple. Left at rdbt to South Molton. Follow A377, right at T-junct to Barnstaple. Entrance after 3m, opposite Portsmouth Arms railway station and pub. (NB do not enter Burrington village)*

Tranquil country-house setting and well-sourced modern British food

The old stone manor is these days a classy country-house hotel with an impressive restaurant. The menu makes good use of seasonal ingredients and there's a good showing of West Country game and seafood. Start with a succulent terrine of ham hock matched with apple chutney and honey-roasted parsnip purée, followed by line-caught mullet and seared scallops, partnered by silky pommes purée and butternut squash, all finished with a fresh herb dressing. Meat fans might go for a tournedos of free-range Devon Red Ruby beef with dauphinoise potatoes, woodland mushrooms, carrots and Madeira gravy, and for pud there's apple tarte Tatin with blackberry crumble, clotted cream and butterscotch sauce.

Chef Richie Herkes **Seats** 34, Pr/dining room 50 **Times** 12-2/7-9 **Prices** Fixed D 3 course £45 **Wines** 22 bottles over £30, 34 bottles under £30, 9 by glass **Parking** 30 **Notes** Gourmet 3 course £90 selected dates, Sunday L, Children welcome

CHAGFORD Map 3 SX78

Gidleigh Park – *see opposite*

DARTMOUTH Map 3 SX85

The Dart Marina Hotel

Modern British V

tel: 01803 832580 **Sandquay Rd TQ6 9PH**
email: reception@dartmarinahotel.com **web:** www.dartmarina.com
dir: *A3122 from Totnes to Dartmouth. Follow road which becomes College Way, before Higher Ferry. Hotel sharp left in Sandquay Rd*

Confident modern cooking in contemporary riverside hotel

The hotel is a contemporary paradise with neutral colour tones, tasteful and trendy furniture and a swish spa, and it's also home to the River Restaurant. Views of the river are guaranteed through floor-to-ceiling windows, while the menu features regional produce. Local crab finds its way into tortellini, dressed with red pepper and crab foam, and seared pigeon breast arrives with fig Tatin and a port and hazelnut vinaigrette. Among main courses, sea bream is served with an Asian spin and braised beef is cooked bourguignon-style and partnered with horseradish pommes purée. Modern desserts include Alunga chocolate and hazelnut mousse with hazelnut gel and candied hazelnut.

Chef Peter Alcroft **Seats** 86 **Times** 12-2/6-9, Closed 23-26 & 30-31 Dec, L Mon-Sat **Prices** Fixed L 2 course £14.95-£19.95, Fixed D 3 course £30-£35, Starter £5-£15, Main £10-£29, Dessert £5-£12 **Wines** 38 bottles over £30, 26 bottles under £30, 20 by glass **Parking** 100 **Notes** Sunday L £10.95-£24.95, Children welcome

The Grill Room

British NEW

tel: 01803 833033 **Royal Castle Hotel, 11 The Quay TQ6 9PS**
email: enquiry@royalcastle.co.uk **web:** www.royalcastle.co.uk
dir: *Phone for directions*

Fine ingredients and River Dart views

With the River Dart in sight, it's refreshing to see an emphasis on locally caught, fresh fish in the first-floor dining room of this 17th-century quayside hotel, while die-hard carnivores will find no fault with the prime slabs of British beef and Devon lamb on offer. There is nothing here to challenge, just generous, satisfying dishes with all the right accents, whether it's organic, home-cured salmon with herb aïoli, cucumber jelly and shaved fennel, or perfectly-timed brill with lentils, olives, sun-dried tomatoes and potatoes. Local meat fans might find pan-seared loin of lamb with glazed sweetbreads, carrot and ginger purée and mashed potato.

Chef Ankur Biswas **Seats** 60, Pr/dining room 70 **Times** 12-2/6-10 **Prices** Tasting menu £25.95-£45, Starter £6.50-£8.95, Main £13.95-£21.95, Dessert £6.95-£7.95 **Wines** 7 bottles over £30, 21 bottles under £30, 13 by glass **Parking** On street **Notes** L separate menu 2 mains £19.50, Sunday L £13.95-£19.95, Vegetarian available, Children welcome

Gidleigh Park

CHAGFORD **Map 3 SX78**

Modern European V NOTABLE WINE LIST

tel: 01647 432367 **TQ13 8HH**
email: gidleighpark@gidleigh.co.uk **web:** www.gidleigh.com
dir: *From Chagford Sq turn right at Lloyds TSB into Mill St, after 150yds right fork, across x-rds into Holy St. Restaurant 1.5m*

Contemporary cooking in idyllic Dartmoor isolation

The Rosette award for this establishment has been suspended due to a change of chef. Reassessment will take place in due course under the new chef. When Gidleigh was built in 1928 for an Australian shipping entrepreneur with a taste for Elizabethan revivalism, nobody thought to install a hot tub on the roof. Still, time and fashion march on, and hotel guests can now rest assured that outdoor bathing is very much on the agenda. Despite its nostalgic architectural looks, the old place has always been au courant, as may be seen from a glance at the interiors, which are full of exquisite arts and crafts detailing, and a fair bit of quality reproduction 20s furniture. The views from the terrace over lush wooded grounds that descend to the River Teign, which ambles unassumingly through the estate, are the last word in luxuriant tranquillity, giving the lie to the notion that Dartmoor, in whose northern stretches Gidleigh lies, is a bleak and unforgiving place. In late 2015, it was announced that the long residency of chef Michael Caines here would be coming to an end, and that his successor was to be Michael Wignall (ex Pennyhill Park in Surrey). At the time of going to press, the kitchen team was still in development, but early indications were that there are going to be thrills aplenty under the new regime. Wignall combines a complex style with a light touch, so that neither the seven- nor ten-course tasting menus overwhelm. Proceedings work to an impressive rhythm, with one well-balanced dish succeeding another, the whole composition orchestrated to exciting effect. These may be early days, but there is already much to admire. Opening the seven-course deal, a serving of tender slow-cooked octopus comes with langoustine and lime, Mexican marigold, fennel and couscous for an array of fascinating flavours. Next is rabbit loin with assertive accompaniments of snails bolognaise, braised celery and chorizo porridge, and then a gentle interlude for some textured carrots, baked and smoked, unified by silky goats' curd. A strong seafood dish sees plump St Austell mussels bathed in smoked juices, along with barbecued hispi, salsify and burnt leek, while the main business is full-flavoured Norfolk quail, brilliantly accompanied by a rich ricotta dressing, as well as fermented garlic, ceps and crosnes. The first of two desserts is a tour de force combining a warm custard doughnut with toffee apple and cinnamon crumble, and the closing act is a novelty number, a crunchy, gooey signature take on the chocolate-and-peanut Snickers bar. Canapés and petits fours are as innovative as the rest, while a refreshingly simple approach is taken with bread, an appetising sourdough. Ensconced in oak-panelled majesty in one of the three dining rooms, you might feel like splashing out on some wine. An authoritative list of around 1,300 items awaits, furnished by a knowledgeable and enthusiastic sommelier.

Chef Michael Wignall **Seats** 52, Pr/dining room 22
Times 12-2/7-9.45 **Prices** Prices not confirmed **Wines** 1190 bottles over £30, 10 bottles under £30, 16 by glass **Parking** 45
Notes Signature menu 8 course £143, ALC 3 course £118, Children 8 yrs+ D

DARTMOUTH *continued*

The Seahorse

Mediterranean, Seafood

tel: 01803 835147 **5 South Embankment TQ6 9BH**
email: enquiries@seahorserestaurant.co.uk
dir: *Phone for directions*

Bountiful fresh seafood by the Dart estuary

Located in the bustling strip along the Dart waterfront, The Seahorse is an inviting evening venue, while big windows let in the Devon light on summer days. Mussels cultured in nearby Elberry Cove, summer crustacea and seasonal veg from the vicinity and from markets just across the Channel add lustre to menus that take in risotto of mixed seafood, bream fillet steamed in paper with garlic, rosemary and chilli, roast turbot fillet with chive butter and – for the seafood refuseniks – osso buco. Many dishes are cooked over an open charcoal fire, used for anything from monkfish to rump steak. To finish, lemon sorbet with elderflower fizz makes a distinguished finale.

DODDISCOMBSLEIGH Map 3 SX88

The Nobody Inn

Modern British

tel: 01647 252394 **EX6 7PS**
email: info@nobodyinn.co.uk **web:** www.nobodyinn.co.uk
dir: *From A38 turn off at top of Haldon Hill, follow signs to Doddiscombsleigh*

Satisfying dining in characterful country inn

This characterful 17th-century inn has a good local reputation, built upon many qualities including its stylish food, excellent local cheeses, hefty wine list and a 240-long list of whiskeys. Reached via winding lanes, inside it has blackened beams, mismatched tables, and walls adorned with plenty of visual interest. The seasonal menu has its feet on the ground, so there are fish, chips and burgers alongside fare such as a warm, crisply-coated chorizo Scotch egg paired nicely with piri piri mayonnaise. At mains, try well-timed pan-fried lamb's liver with bacon, peas, good mash and onion gravy, before a well-textured and flavoured sticky ginger pudding with clotted cream.

DREWSTEIGNTON Map 3 SX79

The Old Inn

Traditional International V

tel: 01647 281276 **EX6 6QR**
email: enquiries@old-inn.co.uk
dir: *A30 W, exit Cheriton Bishop, Drewsteignton, Castle Drogo, turn left at Crockenwell, follow signs to Drewsteignton. A38 to A382 Bovey Tracy, Mortonhampstead, turn right at Sandy Park, continue past Castle Drogo, follow signs to Drewsteignton*

Well-judged cooking in a Dartmoor village inn

In a charming village on the edge of Dartmoor, this former coaching inn houses Duncan Walker's small restaurant with three letting rooms and two dining rooms offering fewer than 20 covers. Calm, relaxing and informal are the buzz words here, with plain wooden furniture and subdued lighting in the dining rooms, one in sage green, the other claret, and a menu perfectly in keeping with the style of the place, offering just four choices per course at dinner. Walker's cooking is marked by a lack of sensationalism, judiciously combining top-drawer fresh ingredients so dishes are strong on flavours. Grilled loin of rabbit in Parma ham, moist and succulent, is accompanied by top-class gnocchi, lemon and sage as a starter, jostling for attention with sautéed lobster with pea and mint velouté. Main courses are intelligently composed too, with sauces and gravies adding depth; vanilla sauce for roast fillet of sea bass, of pinpoint accuracy, on a bed of spinach with scallops and asparagus, and Madeira jus for grilled loin of venison with black pudding and boulangère potatoes. Puddings elicit oohs and aahs, if passionfruit soufflé is anything to go by, the sauce poured in at table, accompanied by coconut ice cream.

Chef Duncan Walker **Seats** 17, Pr/dining room 10 **Times** 12-2/7-9, Closed 3 wks Jan, 1st wk Jun, Sun-Tue, L Wed-Thu **Prices** Fixed L 3 course fr £32, Fixed D 3 course fr £52 **Wines** 24 bottles over £30, 21 bottles under £30, 4 by glass **Parking** Village square **Notes** Service flexible, pre book, tables 6 or more by arrangement, Children 12 yrs+

ERMINGTON Map 3 SX65

Plantation House

Modern British V

tel: 01548 831100 **Totnes Rd PL21 9NS**
email: info@plantationhousehotel.co.uk **web:** www.plantationhousehotel.co.uk
dir: *Phone for directions*

Simple but convincing country cooking in the Erme valley

This elegant boutique hotel exudes character, with stunning garden views at the front, bucket chairs in twisted wicker at solid darkwood tables, and attractive soft furnishings in both dining rooms. After a swig of truffled wild garlic and nettle soup, it's on with a beautifully rendered dish of shellfish in a Thai broth of chilli, lime, ginger, lemongrass and coconut. Crackly-skinned duck makes a majestic main, served with well-seasoned dauphinoise in Merlot jus, while fish might be grilled turbot on a potato and chive cake in lime hollandaise. Dessert may be cardamom pannacotta with gingered rhubarb syrup and sorbet, or crème brûlée with blood orange and rosé wine jelly.

Chef Richard Hendey, John Raines **Seats** 28, Pr/dining room 16 **Times** 7-9, Closed L all week (ex parties) **Prices** Prices not confirmed **Wines** 27 bottles over £30, 25 bottles under £30, 6 by glass **Parking** 30 **Notes** 4/5 course D £36/£39.50, Children welcome

EXETER Map 3 SX99

ABode Exeter

Modern British, French

tel: 01392 319955 **Cathedral Yard EX1 1HD**
email: tables@abodeexeter.co.uk **web:** www.adobeexeter.co.uk
dir: *Town centre, opposite cathedral*

Classy cooking in charming hotel

This charming hotel occupies a prime spot at Cathedral Yard, a beautiful and historic open area in the city centre and is ideally located for local transport links. The venerable hotel comprises a buzzy tavern, café/grill, cocktail bar and the main event, the fine-dining restaurant set in a handsome room with original features and a smart contemporary finish. Carefully executed dishes might open with roast quail with a quail's egg and herb purée, followed by salt-cod loin in the lively company of smoked paprika, lemon purée, samphire, chorizo and dressed crab. Finish with dark chocolate fondant with pistachio ice cream.

Chef Alex Gibbs **Seats** 65, Pr/dining room 80 **Times** 12-2.30/6-9.30 **Prices** Prices not confirmed **Wines** 83 bottles over £30, 27 bottles under £30, 11 by glass **Parking** Car park Mary Arches St **Notes** Afternoon tea £15, Sunday L, Vegetarian available, Children welcome

Barton Cross Hotel & Restaurant

Traditional British, French V

tel: 01392 841245 & 841584 **Huxham, Stoke Canon EX5 4EJ**
email: bartonxhuxham@aol.com **web:** www.thebartoncrosshotel.co.uk
dir: *0.5m off A396 at Stoke Canon, 3m N of Exeter*

Reliably good, well-judged food in thatched hotel

Just a few miles from Exeter, this 17th-century thatched longhouse occupies a delightful rural spot. Low beams, inglenook fireplaces and cob walls abound, and while the minstrels' gallery looks like it could do service as a medieval banqueting hall, there's nothing archaic about what arrives on the plate in the restaurant. The kitchen deals in straightforward Anglo-European cooking, sending out a rustic, creamy chicken liver parfait with onion toast and orange chutney. Main course sees precisely-timed sea bass fillets teamed with a tomato and basil tart, while enterprising desserts include vanilla pannacotta, peach compôte and hazelnut wafers.

Chef Nicholas Beattie **Seats** 50, Pr/dining room 26
Times 12.30-2.30/6.30-11.30, Closed L Mon-Thu **Prices** Fixed D 3 course £29.50, Starter £6-£8, Main £12-£18, Dessert £6 **Wines** 30 bottles over £30, 60 bottles under £30, 10 by glass **Parking** 50 **Notes** Children welcome

The Olive Tree

British NEW

tel: 01392 272709 **Queens Court Hotel, 6-8 Bystock Terrance EX4 4HY**
email. enquiries@queenscourt-hotel.co.uk **web:** www.queenscourt-hotel.co.uk
dir: *Exit dual carriageway at junct 30 onto B5132 (Topsham Rd) towards city centre. Hotel 200yds from Central Station*

West Country ingredients and a romantic mood

The walls of this rather romantic hotel restaurant are decorated with Venetian masks, but don't expect an Italian menu – a pasta or risotto will no doubt be up for grabs (perhaps squid ink spaghetti with pan-fried squid, grey mullet and Nantua sauce)- the kitchen mostly deals in modern British food built on a bedrock of Devon's fine produce. Hand-dived Brixham scallops arrive in a tried-and-tested partnership with black pudding, while honey-glazed duck breast is pan-fried and served with couscous, celeriac purée and rosemary jus. Chiming with the season, dessert brings vanilla pannacotta with summer berries and raspberry sorbet.

Chef Gerald Bucur **Seats** Pr/dining room 28 **Times** 6.30-9, Closed L all week
Prices Tasting menu £45, Starter £4.25-£6.50, Main £12.15-£21.50, Dessert £5-£6
Wines 1 bottle over £30, 24 bottles under £30, 9 by glass **Notes** Tasting menu 6 course, Vegetarian available

Southernhay House

Modern British NEW

tel: 01392 439000 **36 Southernhay East EX1 1NX**
email: home@southernhayhouse.com **web:** www.southernhayhouse.com
dir: *M5 junct 30 (S), follow signs for city centre, at inner ring road rdbt (Vue Cinema), left to Western Way, 1st right & 1st left. A38 junct 30 (N) as above*

Georgian elegance and a great cocktail bar

Captain William 'The Orientalist' Kirkpatrick of the East India Company bought this fine Georgian detached villa in 1805. Between then and 2011, when it became a boutique hotel, its occupants included doctors, physicians and a chartered accountancy practice. Perhaps that helps to explain why the sensitively designed dining room, with its artful juxtaposition of period and contemporary artwork, feels like a private members' club. On the short menu, among the essentially British dishes are crispy ham hock with soft-boiled egg and apple; hake with purple sprouting broccoli and confit potato; fillet steak, fondant potatoes, wild mushrooms and cherry tomatoes; and banana parfait with coconut sorbet.

Chef John Kay **Seats** 30, Pr/dining room 16 **Times** 12-2.30/6-9.30 **Prices** Fixed L 3 course £34, Fixed D 3 course £34, Starter £6-£8, Main £14.40-£21.50, Dessert £7-£10 **Wines** 13 bottles over £30, 22 bottles under £30, 10 by glass **Parking** NCP, on street **Notes** Sunday L, Vegetarian available

EXMOUTH Map 3 SY08

Les Saveurs

Modern French, International

tel: 01395 269459 **9 Tower St EX8 1NT**
email: lessaveurs@yahoo.co.uk
dir: *A376 to Exmouth, left at rdbt. Right at next rdbt onto Rolle St. Tower St on right*

French fish cookery and more near the Exe estuary

On a sleepy pedestrianised street behind a beautiful church, the recently refurbished Les Saveurs ticks all the right neighbourhood-restaurant boxes – cosiness, informality, fine cooking. 'Saveurs' means 'flavours', which is clearly one of the chef's watchwords in a kitchen that celebrates seafood like Exmouth mussels with garlic shallots, white wine and parsley, and rich Mediterranean fish soup with rouille, grated emmental cheese and garlic croûtons. Flavours, of course, are also integral to meat dishes such as roasted marinated duck breast on gratin dauphinoise potatoes with pomegranate sauce. Reflecting the chef's French heritage is gâteau Breton with apple compôte and salted caramel sauce.

Chef Olivier Guyard-Mulkerrin **Seats** 30, Pr/dining room 30
Times 7-10.30, Closed Nov-Apr advance bookings only, Sun-Mon (ex by special arrangement), L all week **Prices** Fixed D 3 course £34-£43.95, Starter £8.50-£10, Main £18-£25, Dessert £7.50-£8.95 **Wines** 10 bottles over £30, 18 bottles under £30, 5 by glass **Parking** On street/council offices **Notes** Vegetarian dishes on request, Children 10 yrs+

HAYTOR VALE Map 3 SX77

Rock Inn

@@ Modern British, European

tel: 01364 661305 & 661556 **TQ13 9XP**
email: info@rock-inn.co.uk **web:** www.rock-inn.co.uk
dir: *From A38 at Drum Bridges, onto A382 to Bovey Tracey. In 2m take B3387 towards Haytor for 3.5m, follow brown signs*

Modern classic dishes at a Dartmoor inn

The rustic Rock Inn's pre-Victorian air, provides a welcoming backdrop to the modern European culinary style on show in its candlelit dining room. A crisp-coated duck Scotch egg with chilli jam and salad leaves is a well-executed starter or go for goats' cheese mousse with fig chutney, crostini and salad leaves. At main, there's plenty of satisfaction to be had from a flavoursome pan-fried stone bass with olive-crushed new potatoes, tomato fondue, caramelised fennel and chorizo. Finish with vanilla pannacotta, chocolate and brandy sorbet, plum purée and orange biscotti, or a platter of West Country cheeses and home-made chutney.

Chef Mark Tribble, Sean Newton, Josh Tolley **Seats** 75, Pr/dining room 20 **Times** 12-2.15/6.30-9, Closed 25-26 Dec **Prices** Fixed D 3 course £24.95, Starter £6.95-£8.95, Main £10.95-£19.95, Dessert £5.95-£7.95 **Wines** 20 bottles over £30, 50 bottles under £30, 16 by glass **Parking** 25 **Notes** Sunday L £10.95-£17.95, Vegetarian available, Children welcome

HONITON Map 4 ST10

The Deer Park Country House Hotel

@@ Modern British

tel: 01404 41266 **Weston EX14 3PG**
email: admin@deerparkcountryhotel.co.uk **web:** www.deerparkcountryhotel.co.uk
dir: *Phone for directions*

Modern cooking in boutique country house

This 18th-century Georgian mansion set in 80 acres of glorious grounds is a quintessentially English set-up brought into the 21st century with a sprinkle of boutique style and great food served in an elegant dining room to seal the deal. Begin with watercress soup, salt-cod beignet and aïoli, although the River Exe mussels with white wine and garlic cream is another diverting starter. Follow, perhaps, with roasted rump of grass-fed Devon lamb, smoked aubergine, wild garlic and sweetbread. Finish with a moreish dessert of dark chocolate brownie with hazelnut praline and salted caramel ice cream, or maybe pick from a selection of perfectly kept West Country cheeses.

Chef Andrew Storey **Seats** 45, Pr/dining room 30 **Times** 12-2.30/6.30-9.30 **Prices** Fixed D 3 course fr £35 **Wines** 17 bottles over £30, 29 bottles under £30, 7 by glass **Parking** 60 **Notes** Sunday L £24-£28.50, Vegetarian available, Children welcome

The Holt Bar & Restaurant

@@ Modern British

tel: 01404 47707 **178 High St EX14 1LA**
email: enquiries@theholt-honiton.com
dir: *At west end of High St*

Imaginative, impressive cooking in a local pub

The Holt's main dining area is upstairs: open-plan, with a wooden floor, simple decor, candlelight, and pleasant, efficient service. Food is a serious commitment here and standards are consistently high, with the menu a happy blend of the traditional and more à la mode. Salmon is smoked in-house for a traditional starter with rye toast, or there may be a tart of artichoke, olives and feta. Following on might be well-timed breast and confit leg of duck, served with ultra-crunchy roasties and Savoy cabbage, or smoked haddock rarebit conjured into a main course with champ, celeriac and leeks. Finish with chocolate cloud cake in fudge sauce with preserved berry meringues.

Chef Angus McCaig, Billy Emmett, Will Scott **Seats** 50 **Times** 12-2/6.30-10, Closed 25-26 Dec, Sun-Mon **Prices** Starter £6-£7.50, Main £14.50-£19, Dessert £6-£7.50 **Wines** 6 bottles over £30, 25 bottles under £30, 6 by glass **Parking** On street, car park 1 min walk **Notes** Bread, smoked & cured food classes, Vegetarian available, Children welcome

ILFRACOMBE Map 3 SS54

Hancock's Dining Room

@@ Modern British NEW

tel: 01271 863272 & 07931 551487 **The Habit Boutique Rooms, 46-48 Fore St EX34 9DN**
email: info@thehabitboutiquerooms.com **web:** www.thehabitboutiquerooms.com
dir: *M5 junct 27 take A361 to Barnstaple, follow signs to Ilfracome/Brauton. At Mullacott rdbt take 2nd exit to Ilfracombe. After 2m, 2nd exit at rdbt onto Church Rd/A361. Follow High St until road splits, take slight left down hill onto Fore St. 100 yds on left*

Creative modern dining in boutique hotel

The restaurant at the trendy Habit Boutique Hotel is on the money when it comes to its contemporary design aesthetic, with its retro touches and lack of stuffiness. The service is serious yet relaxed, and well-informed regarding the complexities of the menu, for this is thoroughly modern dining. First-class ingredients also underscore the menu. Begin with neatly trimmed quail – perfectly pink – with bone marrow, tortellini and a flavoursome broth, before moving onto Lundy cod in a dish with clams and samphire that truly evokes the sea. A tea and biscuit inspired dessert showcases the skills in the kitchen with its accompanying parfait, gel, mousse and dehydrated milk.

Chef Alex Fulluck **Seats** 28, Pr/dining room 20 **Times** 6-9.30, Closed Sun (Jul-Aug), L Mon-Sat **Prices** Prices not confirmed **Parking** Car park **Notes** Sunday L, Vegetarian available, Children welcome

The Olive Room

@@ Modern British

tel: 01271 867831 & 879005 **56 Fore St EX34 9DJ**
email: info@thomascarrchef.co.uk **web:** www.thomascarrchef.co.uk
dir: *A361 into Ilfracombe, through lights into High St. At end fork left into Fore St, continue straight down, pass no entry signs, on left hand side*

Clever modern cooking from a rising star

After honing his skills in the kitchens of Restaurant Nathan Outlaw and Michael Caines's Coach House at Kentisbury Grange, Thomas Carr's cooking is on a roll, and he has set up shop in the dining room of the Georgian Olive Branch Guest House. Spanking-fresh line-caught fish landed daily at the harbour appears in a starter of Lundy plaice served with a crispy oyster, brown shrimps, and an invigorating cucumber dressing, followed by well-timed lamb loin paired with a fritter of shoulder meat, plus bubble-and-squeak, charred broccoli, a fried egg, roast garlic and rosemary. For dessert try carrot cake cheesecake – with creamy orange curd and cinnamon ice cream.

Chef Thomas Carr, John Cairns **Seats** 18 **Times** 12-2/6-9, Closed Sun-Mon, L Tue **Prices** Fixed L 2 course £16, Tasting menu £40-£65, Starter £7-£10, Main £18-£24, Dessert £7.50-£8.50 **Wines** 3 bottles over £30, 16 bottles under £30, 9 by glass **Parking** NCP Fore St **Notes** Vegetarian available, Children welcome

The Quay Restaurant

Modern, Traditional British, European

tel: 01271 868090 **11 The Quay EX34 9EQ**
email: info@11thequay.co.uk
dir: *Follow signs for harbour and pier car park. Restaurant on left before car park*

Classic brasserie menu on the harbour front

Perched on the harbour front of this north Devon coastal town, the Quay has a strong sense of identity. Adorned with original artworks by Damien Hirst at his more docile, the Atlantic Room with its vaulted ceiling is a bright and breezy setting for internationally-inspired brasserie classics. Crab claws or crispy calamari in garlic mayonnaise, native oysters, or scallops in coriander, lime and chilli all make the most of the location, while for main, there are Exmoor steaks, cod and chorizo, or chicken breast with asparagus in tarragon cream. Finish with bread-and-butter pudding, or lemon curd cheesecake.

Chef Henry Sowden **Seats** 45, Pr/dining room 26 **Times** 12-2.30/6-9, Closed 25-26 Dec, 2 wks Jan **Prices** Starter £7.50-£12.50, Main £9.50-£25, Dessert £6-£7 **Wines** 29 bottles over £30, 17 bottles under £30, 10 by glass **Parking** Pier car park 100yds **Notes** Vegetarian available, Children welcome

Sandy Cove Hotel

Modern British

tel: 01271 882243 **Old Coast Rd, Combe Martin Bay, Berrynarbor EX34 9SR**
email: info@sandycove-hotel.co.uk **web:** www.sandycove-hotel.co.uk
dir: *A399 to Combe Martin, through village towards Ilfracombe for approx 1m. Turn right just over brow of hill marked Sandy Cove*

Simple cooking, local produce, views to die for

With stunning views of both the bay and the wild landscape of Exmoor, Sandy Cove Hotel offers the best of both worlds. Positioned to maximise the vista with large windows (and a terrace when the weather allows), the restaurant offers a hypnotic view. Like the decor, the menu keeps things gently modern, too, sticking to familiar and successful combinations. Start with a well-presented confit chicken terrine studded with pistachios, prunes and apricots, before moving on to sea bass, creamed beans, celeriac purée and red wine jus. For dessert, vanilla pannacotta with grappa strawberries makes for a full-flavoured finale.

Chef Neil Gilson **Seats** 150, Pr/dining room 30 **Times** 6.30-9, Closed L all week **Prices** Starter £5.95-£7.25, Main £12.95-£19.95, Dessert £5.25-£6.95 **Wines** 3 bottles over £30, 28 bottles under £30, 3 by glass **Parking** 50 **Notes** Vegetarian available, Children welcome

ILSINGTON Map 3 SX77

Ilsington Country House Hotel

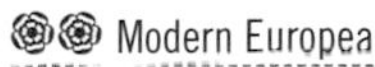 Modern European

tel: 01364 661452 **Ilsington Village TQ13 9RR**
email: hotel@ilsington.co.uk **web:** www.ilsington.co.uk
dir: *A38 to Plymouth, exit at Bovey Tracey. 3rd exit from rdbt to Ilsington, then 1st right, hotel on right in 3m*

Great Dartmoor views and confident cooking

A substantial white property, Ilsington's diverse menu includes some divertingly appealing dishes. Take a starter of seared mackerel fillets, accompanied by chilli and tomato couscous, a chorizo and pea pancake, leeks and Avruga oil, or duck breast, which is plated with hogs pudding, beetroot, roasted courgettes and blackberry gastrique. Accompaniments complement the main ingredients without swamping them, seen in main courses of roast chicken with a maple and mustard gel, pommes Anna, pea purée, mushrooms, confit tomato and smoked beetroot, and pavé of hake with sauce nero, chorizo and chickpea cassoulet and Bombay-style potatoes. Finish with cinnamon pannacotta with strawberry and elderflower jelly, a rice pudding fritter and honeycomb.

Chef Mike O'Donnell **Seats** 75, Pr/dining room 70 **Times** 12-2/6.30-9, Closed 3-13 Jan, L Mon-Sat **Prices** Fixed D 3 course fr £38, Tasting menu £55-£85 **Wines** 12 bottles over £30, 32 bottles under £30, 7 by glass **Parking** 60 **Notes** Sunday L £19-£22.50, Vegetarian available, Children welcome

KENTISBURY Map 3 SS64

Kentisbury Grange

Modern British V

tel: 01271 882295 **EX31 4NL**
email: reception@kentisburygrange.co.uk **web:** www.kentisburygrange.com
dir: *From Barnstaple take A3125. At rdbt take 2nd exit onto A39 to Burrington through Shirwell & Arlington. After Kentisbury Ford, follow signs for hotel for approx 0.75m*

Creative modern cooking in a stylish old coach house

The Coach House restaurant at the Grange was once just that – a 17th-century edifice a short scrunch across the gravel from the hotel – and is kitted out with rustic-chic oak tables, banquette seating and contemporary artworks. Ingredients are sourced from nearby, including crabs from Lundy and ducks from the farm next door. A first course of crisp-fried duck liver comes with balanced additions of rhubarb and raisins in five-spice dressing, as a prelude to seared sea bass with a roast langoustine and smoked pancetta in ginger-vanilla jus. The cheeseboard flies the flag for Devon, while desserts run to classic lemon tart with Cassis sorbet.

Chef Thomas Hine **Seats** 54, Pr/dining room 16 **Times** 12-2/6-9 **Prices** Fixed L 2 course £19.95, Fixed D 3 course £45, Tasting menu £65, Starter £10-£15, Main £25-£30, Dessert £10 **Wines** 34 bottles over £30, 41 bottles under £30, 12 by glass **Parking** 70 **Notes** Sunday L £19.95-£24.95, Children welcome

KINGSBRIDGE Map 3 SX74

Buckland-Tout-Saints

Modern British V

tel: 01548 853055 **Goveton TQ7 2DS**
email: enquiries@bucklandtoutsaints.co.uk **web:** www.tout-saints.co.uk
dir: *Turn off A381 to Goveton. Follow brown tourist signs to St Peter's Church. Hotel 2nd right after church*

Classic country-house dining with regional accent

Set in four acres of stunning grounds in the South Hams, this handsome William and Mary-era manor house provides a classy country-house package. The interior is packed with period details such as wood panelling and grand fireplaces, not least in the Queen Anne Restaurant, with its Russian pine and duck egg blue paintwork. The kitchen turns out modern British cooking with a good showing of regional ingredients. Pan-fried foie gras is teamed with pressed ham hock, roasted fig and port reduction, while pan-fried cod with chorizo and white bean bouillon and coriander is a typical main.

Chef Ted Ruewell **Seats** 40, Pr/dining room 40 **Times** 12-2/7-9 **Prices** Prices not confirmed **Wines** 30 bottles over £30, 30 bottles under £30, 10 by glass **Parking** 70 **Notes** Sunday L, Children welcome

KNOWSTONE Map 3 SS82

The Masons Arms

 Modern British

tel: 01398 341231 **EX36 4RY**
email: enqs@masonsarmsdevon.co.uk
dir: *Signed from A361, turn right once in Knowstone*

Strong contemporary cooking on the edge of Exmoor

In the idyllic village of Knowstone, this thatched 13th-century country inn is set deep in the lush, countryside on the Devon and Somerset border. Mark Dodson once cooked under Michel Roux at Bray, which might explain the flair and precision evident in the kitchen. A salad of smoked duck and duck liver parfait, rhubarb chutney and brioche toast shows a strong skills set. For main course, well-timed fillets of John Dory might turn up with crab risotto, bouillon and mange-tout tempura. Honey pannacotta, roasted pistachio and honeycomb and pistachio ice cream ends a meal with a flourish.

Chef Mark Dodson, Jess Thorne **Seats** 28 **Times** 12-2/7-9, Closed 1st wk Jan, Feb half term, 1 wk Aug BH, Mon, D Sun **Prices** Fixed L 2 course £20, Starter £8.50-£12.80, Main £19.80-£26.50, Dessert £8.75-£10.50 **Wines** 41 bottles over £30, 17 bottles under £30, 9 by glass **Parking** 10 **Notes** Sunday L £36.50, Vegetarian available, Children 5 yrs+ D

LIFTON Map 3 SX38

Arundell Arms

 Modern British V

tel: 01566 784666 **Fore St PL16 0AA**
email: reservations@arundellarms.com **web:** www.arundellarms.com
dir: *Just off A30 in Lifton, 3m E of Launceston*

Traditional Anglo-French cooking with contemporary detailing

What looks like a rural pub on the outside is an elevated country hotel within, with lavish traditional furnishings and a large dining room. The kitchen offers a traditionally-based Anglo-French repertoire founded on quality materials. First off could be a grilled John Dory fillet on creamed lentils with brown shrimps and a scallop fritter, the overture possibly to pork tenderloin with chicken mousseline in a sauce of Cornwall's Rattler cider. There's a gentle richness to the impact of dishes, seen in Aylesbury duck with dauphinoise and rhubarb in peppercorn sauce, and most temptingly of all in dark chocolate terrine with marinated orange and Amaretto ice cream.

Chef Steven Pidgeon **Seats** 70, Pr/dining room 24 **Times** 12-2.30/7-10, Closed D 24-26 Dec **Prices** Fixed L 2 course fr £19.50, Tasting menu £49.50, Starter £9.50-£11.50, Main £19.50-£25, Dessert £8.95 **Wines** 5 bottles over £30, 5 bottles under £30, 7 by glass **Parking** 70 **Notes** Sunday L £19.50-£25, Children welcome

LYNMOUTH Map 3 SS74

Rising Sun Hotel

 British, French

tel: 01598 753223 **Harbourside EX35 6EG**
email: reception@risingsunlynmouth.co.uk **web:** www.risingsunlynmouth.co.uk
dir: *M5 junct 23 (Minehead). Take A39 to Lynmouth. Opposite the harbour*

Modern British cooking in a convivial harbourside inn

The Rising Sun rocks with good vibrations with its proper bar plus an atmospheric oak-panelled dining room. The food strikes a balance between hearty generosity and contemporary combinations, with plenty of seafood dishes. Start with a modern classic seared king scallops with cauliflower cream and crisp pancetta – or an 'old favourite' such as chicken livers enriched with baby onions, pancetta and a balsamic and Madeira sauce (with brioche for the juices). Next up, a generous portion of wild sea bass with samphire and bouillabaisse sauce, or chargrilled rib-eye with field mushrooms and twice-cooked chips, and finish with a well-made crème brûlée.

PLYMOUTH Map 3 SX45

Artillery Tower Restaurant

Modern British

tel: 01752 257610 **Firestone Bay, Durnford St PL1 3QR**
dir: *1m from city centre & rail station*

Bistro food in a Tudor gunnery tower

A 16th-century circular gunnery tower on Plymouth waterfront, be sure to grip the handrail tight as you climb the spiral staircase. Arched windows that once served as gun emplacements in three-foot walls surround the dining space, where simple modern bistro food is the drill. Expect Mediterranean fish soup and harissa to start, or game terrine in cider sauce, as lead-ins to substantial main dishes of peppered venison loin with cranberry and orange compôte, duck breast and confit leg with quince, or roasted pollack with crab gratin and spinach, sauced in white wine. Finish with chocolate nemesis and chocolate sorbet, or wait 20 minutes for freshly baked cherry frangipane tart with Amaretto ice cream.

Chef Peter Constable **Seats** 26, Pr/dining room 16
Times 12-2.15/7-9.30, Closed Xmas, New Year, Sun-Mon, L Sat **Prices** Fixed D 3 course fr £40 **Wines** 5 bottles over £30, 20 bottles under £30, 6 by glass **Parking** 20, Evening only **Notes** Vegetarian available, Children welcome

Barbican Kitchen

 Modern

tel: 01752 604448 **Plymouth Gin Distillery, 60 Southside St PL1 2LQ**
email: info@barbicankitchen.com **web:** www.barbicankitchen.com
dir: *On Barbican, 5 mins walk from Bretonside bus station*

Convincing brasserie food from the Tanner brothers

The Plymouth Gin distillery is home to the Tanner brothers' vibrant restaurant, and entering past the huge vats gives a reminder of the esteemed history of the building. The Barbican Kitchen, recently completely refurbished, spreads over two floors and packs a visual punch with its bold colours and contemporary prints. The menu is a feel-good foray into contemporary tastes with a West Country flavour. There are burgers and steaks alongside the likes of seared calves' liver with horseradish mash and confit onion. Start with fried duck egg with crispy confit duck, and finish with crème brûlée with chocolate chip cookie.

Chef Martyn Compton, Christopher & James Tanner **Seats** 100, Pr/dining room 22 **Times** 12-2.30/6-9.30, Closed 25-26 & 31 Dec, Sun **Prices** Prices not confirmed **Wines** 5 bottles over £30, 23 bottles under £30, 29 by glass **Parking** Drakes Circus, Guildhall **Notes** Fixed 2/3 course L menu pre-theatre, Vegetarian available, Children welcome

Best Western Duke of Cornwall Hotel

Modern British, European

tel: 01752 275850 & 275855 **Millbay Rd PL1 3LG**
email: enquiries@thedukeofcornwall.co.uk **web:** www.thedukeofcornwall.co.uk
dir: *City centre, follow signs 'Pavilions', hotel road is opposite*

Modern cooking with West Country produce in a Victorian hotel

A Plymouth landmark for the past 150 years, you certainly can't miss the Duke of Cornwall hotel with its imposing Gothic exterior and Corinthian-style pillars. The recently refurbished restaurant is suitably elegant, with its domed ceiling, chandelier and clothed tables. The kitchen works a modern European repertoire with a decent showing of West Country ingredients. Chicken liver parfait, blueberries, pickled shallots and toasted focaccia is a well executed classic and it might precede a well-timed stone bass with brown shrimp, lemon and herb-crushed new potatoes. To finish, poached rhubarb is a harmonious partner to ginger ice cream.

Chef Kevin Scargill **Seats** 80, Pr/dining room 30 **Times** 7-10, Closed 26-31 Dec, L all week **Prices** Starter £6.50-£7.50, Main £17-£21, Dessert £5.50-£6.50 **Wines** 8 by glass **Parking** 40, Also on street (free 4pm-10am) **Notes** Vegetarian available, Children welcome

The Greedy Goose

Modern British

tel: 01752 252001 **Prysten House, Finewell St PL1 2AE**
email: enquiries@thegreedygoose.co.uk
dir: *Exit A38 Marsh Mills. Follow Embankment Rd onto Gdynia Way. At Cattedown rdbt, take Exeter St to Royal Parade. 2nd left at rdbt*

Contemporary cooking in a venerable Barbican house

Tucked away in the oldest part of Plymouth, ancient beams bear witness to this building's antiquity. The up-to-date cooking is built on seasonal West Country produce, so start with pan-fried scallops with crispy black pudding fritters and celeriac purée, or perhaps duck liver parfait, rillettes and crackling with pear pickle and brioche. Creedy Carver duck also stars in a main course, supported by red cabbage, caramelised parsnips, fondant potatoes and rich gravy, while local boats supply the goodies for a multi-layered dish comprising plaice fillets with sea spinach, crisp Exmouth mussels, seaweed gnocchi, citrus-pickled fennel and mussel bisque. To finish, nougat and white chocolate parfait comes with raspberry sorbet.

Chef Ben Palmer **Seats** 50, Pr/dining room 30 **Times** 12-2.30/5-close, Closed 25 Dec, Sun-Mon **Prices** Fixed L 2 course £10, Fixed D 3 course £12, Tasting menu £50-£58, Starter £6-£13, Main £13-£34, Dessert £6-£9 **Wines** 43 bottles over £30, 33 bottles under £30, 12 by glass **Parking** Pay & display next to restaurant **Notes** Tasting menu 6 course, Sun L menu 1st Sun of month only, Sunday L fr £13, Vegetarian available, Children 4 yrs+

Langdon Court Hotel & Restaurant

Traditional British, French V

tel: 01752 862358 **Adams Ln, Down Thomas PL9 0DY**
email: enquiries@langdoncourt.com **web:** www.langdoncourt.com
dir: *Signed from A379 at Elburton rdbt*

Impressive regional cooking at a Tudor manor house

A 16th-century manor house in the beautiful South Hams, Langdon Court has played host to royal personages and their consorts since the days of Henry VIII and Catherine Parr. A country-house hotel since 1960, local farms and Devon fishermen supply the kitchen, where the cooking continues on an impressive upward trajectory. Bream fillet with cockle, clam and chicken broth is one of the stand-out starters and might be followed by beef fillet, Jacob's Ladder, celeriac risotto, shallots and veal jus. A light and delicate tonka bean soufflé, coconut custard and pineapple sorbet is a hugely successful dessert.

Seats 36, Pr/dining room 92 **Times** 12-3/6.30-9.30 **Prices** Fixed L 2 course £16, Fixed D 3 course £35, Tasting menu £50-£65, Starter £7-£14, Main £18-£24, Dessert £7-£10 **Wines** 26 bottles over £30, 26 bottles under £30, 8 by glass **Parking** 60 **Notes** Breakfast £15, Sunday L £15.95-£20, Children welcome

Rock Salt Café and Brasserie

Modern British

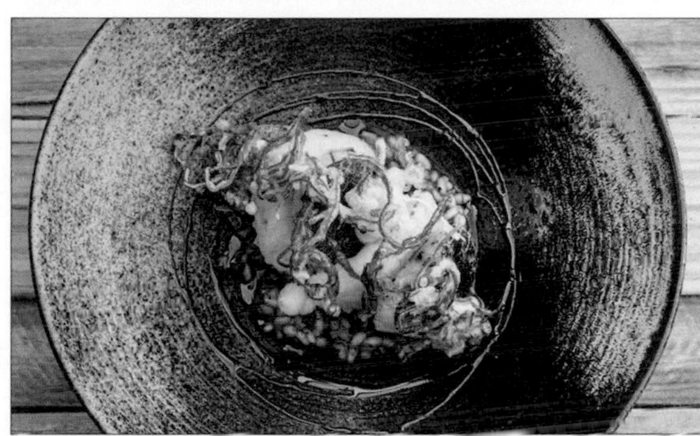

tel: 01752 225522 **31 Stonehouse St PL1 3PE**
email: info@rocksaltcafe.co.uk **web:** www.rocksaltcafe.co.uk
dir: *Between Brittany ferry port & Royal William Yard*

Informal all-day eatery with confident cooking

The sign outside this slate-tiled former pub says 'good, honest food' and that's certainly what this place is all about. Open all day, all week, the easy-going seaside vibe strikes a relaxed pose but takes the food seriously. There's attention to detail whether it's breakfast, lunch or dinner and the kitchen is flexible enough to send out a steak sandwich alongside a memorable main of butter-roasted monkfish, cauliflower, chickpeas, spiced seaweed and cashews. It might be preceded by pork, skate and peanut broth and followed by a tropical dessert of pandanus pannacotta, mango, passionfruit and honeycomb.

Chef David Jenkins, Joe Turner **Seats** 60, Pr/dining room 25 **Times** 10-3/5-10, Closed 24-26 Dec, 1-8 Jan **Prices** Fixed L 2 course £12, Tasting menu £50-£75, Starter £3.95-£8.95, Main £7.50-£19.95, Dessert £5.50-£7.50 **Wines** 6 bottles over £30, 24 bottles under £30, 6 by glass **Parking** On street **Notes** Pre theatre, Supper club, Pan Asian evenings, Sunday L £11.95-£14.95, Vegetarian available, Children welcome

PLYMOUTH *continued*

The Wildflower Restaurant

Traditional British NEW

tel: 01822 852245 **Moorland Garden Hotel, Yelverton PL20 6DA**
email: stay@moorlandgardenhotel.co.uk **web:** www.moorlandgardenhotel.co.uk
dir: *Phone for directions*

British flavours on the edge of Dartmoor

The Moorland Garden Hotel's colourful and smart restaurant has views over the pristine garden to wild Dartmoor beyond, with floor-to-ceiling windows and its own terrace to ensure the best is made of the setting. The kitchen focuses on British flavours and ensures a good deal of what is served is sourced from hereabouts. Start with brioche topped with Dawlish wild mushrooms and a fried quail's egg, with the aroma of white truffle oil to give it a further lift, followed by pavé of salmon with braised fennel, gremolata mash and brown shrimps, and, to finish, a touch of exoticism in the shape of iced mango parfait.

Chef Rob Murray **Seats** 70 **Times** 12-2/6.30-9.30 **Prices** Fixed L 2 course £15.95-£19.95, Fixed D 3 course £29.95, Starter £4.95-£9.75, Main £10.95-£18.95, Dessert £4.95-£5.95 **Wines** 4 bottles over £30, 24 bottles under £30, 9 by glass **Parking** 35 **Notes** Afternoon tea £15.95, Sunday L £19.95-£22.95, Vegetarian available, Children welcome

PLYMPTON Map 3 SX55

Treby Arms

Modern European

tel: 01752 837363 **Sparkwell PL7 5DD**
email: trebyarms@hotmail.co.uk
dir: *A38 Plympton turn off towards Langage & Dartmoor Zoological Park, signed Sparkwell*

Modern cooking of a high order from the 2012 *MasterChef* champ

Resident chef Anton Piotrowski has seen an upsurge in business since his triumph on a *MasterChef: The Professionals.* Stake your claim early and be rewarded with energetic modern cookery of a high order. First up might be a slab of meaty terrine composed of suckling pig and black pudding, garnished with mandarin, pickles and toasted brioche. Among main courses, a small fillet of John Dory appears alongside a courgette flower stuffed with scallop and shrimp mousse and a king prawn wrapped in a jacket of pork crackling. Herb-rolled venison loin with confit onion, red cabbage and carrots looks more the part. Elegant desserts include a meringue globe encasing lemon curd and matching sorbet.

Chef Anton Piotrowski **Seats** 60 **Times** 12-3/6-9.30, Closed 25-26 Dec, 1 Jan, Mon **Wines** 19 bottles over £30, 28 bottles under £30, 11 by glass **Parking** 14, Village hall opposite **Notes** Sunday L £16.95, Vegetarian available, Children welcome

ROCKBEARE Map 3 SY09

The Jack In The Green Inn

Modern British V

tel: 01404 822240 **EX5 2EE**
email: info@jackinthegreen.uk.com
dir: *3m E of M5 junct 29 on B3174*

A creative powerhouse in a Devon country pub

The Jack looks and feels like a pub, with no airs and graces, just a satisfying mix of old and new throughout its series of atmospheric rooms. There's a refined contemporary polish to the kitchen's output, and flavour is always king. A savoury 'crème brûlée' made with chicken liver and wild morel mushrooms with celeriac and truffle is a good way to start, followed by a well-thought-out main course of five spice-scented Creedy Carver duck breast pointed with the tart note of griottine cherries, plus sweet potato fondant and pak choi. To finish, there's a zingy confection of lemon posset, lime pannacotta, mint and tequila granita and salted lemon ice cream.

Chef Matthew Mason **Seats** 80, Pr/dining room 60 **Times** 12-2/6-9, Closed 25 Dec-5 Jan **Prices** Fixed L 2 course £21-£25.75, Fixed D 3 course £25, Tasting menu £42.50, Starter £5.50-£8.50, Main £18.50-£27.50, Dessert £6.50-£8.50 **Wines** 60 bottles over £30, 40 bottles under £30, 12 by glass **Parking** 120 **Notes** Sunday L £16.50-£25.75, Children welcome

SALCOMBE Map 3 SX73

The Jetty

British Seafood NEW

tel: 01548 844444 **Salcombe Harbour Hotel, Cliff Rd TQ8 8JH**
email: salcombe@harbourhotels.co.uk **web:** www.salcombe-harbour-hotel.co.uk
dir: *From A38 Exeter to Plymouth dual carriageway take A384 to Totnes then follow A381 to Kingsbridge & onto Salcombe. On entering Salcombe carry along Main Rd, do not take town signs. Follow this road down hill into Bennett Rd, after 0.25m hotel is on right*

Contemporary feel-good dining with views

There are fabulous views over the estuary from The Jetty's prime position within the Salcombe Harbour Hotel. The hotel's spa facilities, and even a private cinema, offer many distractions, but time is never better spent than when sitting in the smart, contemporary restaurant and choosing something off the menu created by regional foodie powerhouse Alex Aitken. Begin with top quality roast scallops, in the fashionable company of confit pork belly and apple purée, and follow on with a fine version of classic fish and chips, sea bass with beurre blanc, or West Country steaks. An outside table is a warm weather treat.

Chef Gary Pickles **Seats** 90 **Times** 12-2.30/6-9.30 **Prices** Fixed L 2 course £14.50, Fixed D 3 course £19.95, Starter £7.95-£15.50, Main £15.50-£28.50, Dessert £6.50-£12.50 **Wines** 63 bottles over £30, 25 bottles under £30, 16 by glass **Parking** On street **Notes** Crustacean menu, Sunday L £20-£27.50, Vegetarian available, Children welcome

Soar Mill Cove Hotel

Modern British

tel: 01548 561566 **Soar Mill Cove, Marlborough TQ7 3DS**
email: info@soarmillcove.co.uk **web:** www.soarmillcove.co.uk
dir: *A381 to Salcombe, through village follow signs to sea*

Top-notch West Country produce and fab sea views

This family-run hotel is in a lovely location, with the cove below and uninterrupted sea views. The kitchen has its roots in the classical techniques with a modern spin. Thus, sautéed scallops are partnered by melting crab thermidor and sautéed leeks. Presentation is a strength, seen in a main course of roast chicken breast wrapped in bacon with Madeira jus accompanied by earthy girolles, parsnip purée and a tartlet of caramelised shallots. A fish option might be roast monkfish in ham with wild mushrooms, spinach and red wine sauce. Breads are made in-house, and puddings may stretch to lemon and lime posset with vibrant raspberry coulis and home-made shortbread.

Chef I Macdonald **Seats** 60 **Times** 10.30-5/6-9, Closed Jan **Prices** Fixed L 2 course £18, Fixed D 3 course £39 **Wines** 21 bottles over £30, 25 bottles under £30, 6 by glass **Parking** 25 **Notes** Vegetarian available, Children welcome

SAUNTON Map 3 SS43

Saunton Sands Hotel

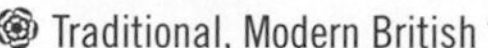

Traditional, Modern British V

tel: 01271 890212 & 892001 **EX33 1LQ**
email: reservations@sauntonsands.com **web:** www.sauntonsands.com
dir: *Exit A361 at Braunton, signed Croyde B3231, hotel 2m on left*

Imaginative and complex cooking beside a beach

The location alone is a draw at this long white art deco hotel overlooking a three-mile stretch of unspoiled sandy beach. Watch the sun set from the terrace or soak up the maritime views from the stylish restaurant with original 1930s chandeliers. The kitchen is impassioned about using only West Country produce and turns out some stimulating dishes in the contemporary mould. The daily-changing menu might open with a complex starter of liquorice cured salmon with pickled cockles and accompaniments of orange, carrot and ginger, and proceed to lamb loin with smoked mussels, kohlrabi and mint jelly. Puddings include pistachio olive oil cake with rhubarb sorbet.

Chef D Turland, Jamie Coleman **Seats** 200, Pr/dining room 60 **Times** 12-2/6.45-9.30 **Prices** Fixed L 2 course £17.90-£25.20, Fixed D 3 course £36 **Wines** 53 bottles over £30, 54 bottles under £30, 18 by glass **Parking** 140 **Notes** Sunday L £19.95, Children welcome

SHALDON Map 3 SX97

ODE dining

British

tel: 01626 873977 **21 Fore St TQ14 0DE**
email: contact@odetruefood.com
dir: *Cross bridge, 1st right into Shoreside, directly left into car park*

Top-quality local and organic produce in coastal village

Ethically-sourced and organic produce is the name of the game at this small restaurant, named after its postcode. Among the refined and ambitious dishes are starters like salted and slow-cooked cod with granola and bay leaf cream, or sugar-cured duck breast with a salad of pickled turnips and pears. Accuracy and a flair for successful combinations are apparent in main courses such as a winter offering of guinea fowl with squash, braised lentils and shiitaki mushrooms. End with artisan cheeses or one of the imaginative puddings: walnut and date tart with vanilla and Earl Grey cream, or burnt cream with apple jelly and a rosemary scone.

Chef Tim Bouget **Seats** 24 **Times** 7-9.30, Closed 25 Dec, BHs, Sun-Tue, L all week **Prices** Fixed D 3 course £35-£45, Tasting menu £45-£55 **Wines** 10 bottles over £30, 10 bottles under £30, 5 by glass **Parking** Car park 3 mins walk **Notes** Wed-Thu 2/3 course £25-£30/£30-£35, Vegetarian available, Children 8 yrs+

SIDMOUTH Map 3 SY18

Hotel Riviera

Modern British

tel: 01395 515201 **The Esplanade EX10 8AY**
email: enquiries@hotelriviera.co.uk **web:** www.hotelriviera.co.uk
dir: *From M5 junct 30 take A3052 to Sidmouth. In centre of The Esplanade*

Modern British dining in Regency Sidmouth

The name may suggest Cannes or Las Vegas, but Devon has its very own version of seaside grandeur, and the spotless bow-fronted Riviera is a prime example of it. Tables on an outdoor terrace make the most of the summer weather, and a menu of gently modernised British cooking has something to cater for most tastes. Kick off with warm lobster and crab mousse, or perhaps chicken liver parfait with sweet red onion marmalade. Mains encompass grilled Dover sole, Devonshire steaks cooked on the grill, and roast duck breast served with its braised leg and rösti potato. Finish off with the likes of raspberry parfait.

Chef Martin Osedo **Seats** 85, Pr/dining room 65 **Times** 12.30-2/7-9 **Prices** Fixed L 2 course £26, Fixed D 3 course £39, Starter £10.50-£14, Main £16-£32, Dessert £6.50-£10.50 **Wines** 45 bottles over £30, 31 bottles under £30, 13 by glass **Parking** 26 **Notes** Fixed L 4 course £29.50, D 5 course £43, Sunday L £26-£29.50, Vegetarian available, Children welcome

The Salty Monk

Modern British V

tel: 01395 513174 **Church St, Sidford EX10 9QP**
email: saltymonk@btconnect.com **web:** www.saltymonk.co.uk
dir: *From M5 junct 30 take A3052 to Sidmouth, or from Honiton take A375 to Sidmouth, 200yds on right opposite church in village*

Gentle modern British food in a former salt house

The name is not a reference to a seafaring friar, but rather the building's 16th-century role as a store for the salt the monks' traded at Exeter Cathedral. The Garden Room restaurant makes a smart yet understated backdrop for unpretentious cooking. To begin, Capricorn goats' cheese pannacotta is pointed up with apricot and lentil relish, or there might be braised pork cheek set in its own jelly with home-made piccalilli and melba toast. Main course imaginatively pairs confit duck tartlet with slow-roasted belly pork, champ potatoes and a light porky jus bringing it all together. To finish, a classic lemon tart comes hot from the oven with clotted cream.

Chef Annette & Andy Witheridge, Scott Horn **Seats** 45
Times 12-1.30/6.30-9, Closed 1 wk Nov & Jan, Mon, L Tue-Wed **Prices** Fixed L 2 course £25, Fixed D 3 course £45, Tasting menu £65, Starter £6.50-£9.50, Main £10-£29.50, Dessert £6-£8.75 **Wines** 22 bottles over £30, 47 bottles under £30, 14 by glass **Parking** 20 **Notes** Tasting menu 7 course, Sunday L £29.50-£35, Children welcome

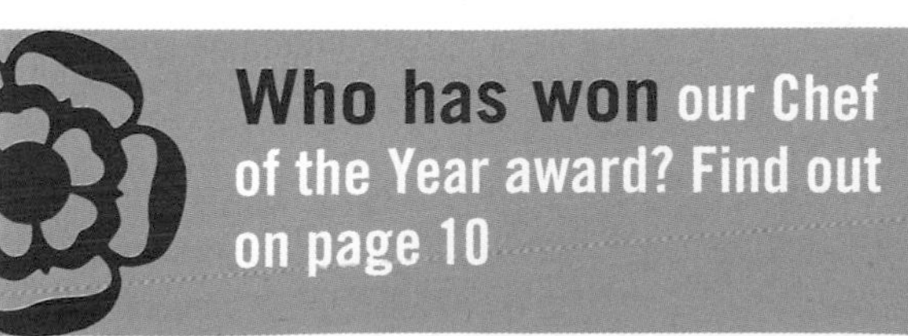

SIDMOUTH *continued*

The Victoria Hotel

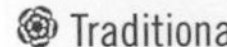 Traditional

tel: 01395 512651 **The Esplanade EX10 8RY**
email: reservations@victoriahotel.co.uk **web:** www.victoriahotel.co.uk
dir: *At western end of The Esplanade*

Timeless splendour beside the sea

The setting at the end of the town's impressive Georgian esplanade is alluring, with the expansive bay offered up in all its shimmering glory. Jacket and tie is still the dress code for gents dining in the Jubilee restaurant. From the doorman to the pianist tinkling the ivories, The Victoria oozes old-world charm and what appears on the plate is generally classically minded. Sautéed wild mushrooms, spinach and toasted brioche is one way to begin, followed by fillet of John Dory, braised baby gem lettuce and oyster mushrooms. Finish with pineapple upside down cake, rum and raisin ice cream.

STRETE Map 3 SX84

The Laughing Monk

Modern British

tel: 01803 770639 **Totnes Rd TQ6 0RN**
email: thelaughingmonk@btconnect.com
dir: *A38 & follow signs towards Dartmouth, 700yds past Dartmouth Golf Club take right turn to Strete. Restaurant on left just past church*

Resourceful and interesting cooking in the South Hams

The South West Coast Path runs practically outside the front door of this converted school, and both Slapton and Blackpool Sands are a mere mile off. Inside is a light-filled, airy space with an impressive inglenook and cheery atmosphere, and a kitchen making enviable use of Devon's resources in carefully-composed dishes with stimulating touches. Harissa-spiced red mullet turns up with crispy squid and sweet-sour peppers to start, prior to mains that also emphasise fish but don't scruple to take in lamb loin and faggot with rösti, cavolo nero and capers. Winter fruit sloe gin trifle with hazelnut cream is a good way to end.

Chef Ben Handley **Seats** 60 **Times** 6.30-9, Closed Xmas, Jan, Sun-Mon, L all week **Prices** Fixed D 3 course fr £28 **Wines** 6 bottles over £30, 23 bottles under £30, 5 by glass **Parking** 4, On street **Notes** Vegetarian available, Children welcome

TAVISTOCK Map 3 SX47

Bedford Hotel

 British

tel: 01822 613221 **1 Plymouth Rd PL19 8BB**
email: enquiries@bedford-hotel.co.uk **web:** www.bedford-hotel.co.uk
dir: *M5 junct 31, A30 (Launceston/Okehampton). Then A386 to Tavistock, follow town centre signs. Hotel opposite church*

Confident modern cooking in a Gothic hotel

Despite the castellated walls, this imposing Gothic building has always been about hospitality, and there is no lack of character or charm in the restaurant, with its moulded ceilings and panelled walls. The kitchen takes a more contemporary position, but a reassuringly gentle one. Chicken liver parfait, honey granola, toast and red onion marmalade is one way to begin, perhaps followed by Brixham hake, Cornish new potatoes, samphire, pak choi, chorizo and pickled mussels. Desserts such as Piña Colada, coconut parfait, pineapple salsa, rum granita show off good technical skills, and there is a strong showing of West Country cheeses.

Chef Mike Palmer **Seats** 55, Pr/dining room 30 **Times** 12-2.30/6-9, Closed 24-26 Dec **Prices** Fixed L 2 course £20, Fixed D 3 course £25-£35, Starter £3.50-£8.50, Main £11.50-£22, Dessert £5.50-£7.50 **Wines** 4 bottles over £30, 38 bottles under £30, 11 by glass **Parking** 48 **Notes** Breakfast, Sunday L, Vegetarian available, Children welcome

The Horn of Plenty

Modern British

tel: 01822 832528 **Gulworthy PL19 8JD**
email: enquiries@thehornofplenty.co.uk **web:** www.thehornofplenty.co.uk
dir: *From Tavistock take A390 W for 3m. Right at Gulworthy Cross. In 400yds turn left, hotel in 400yds on right*

Confident contemporary cooking and glorious valley views

The Rosette award for this establishment has been suspended due to a change of chef. Reassessment will take place in due course under the new chef. Built in 1866 for one James Richards, supervisor of the Duke of Bedford's mining interests, when copper and tin were the backbone of the Tamar Valley, the Horn sits on the Devon-Cornwall border, a stone-built manor house, now a picture of serenity glancing towards its past in the distant mine chimneys. It's a ravishing location and the place is run with reassuring warmth and confidence. Crab and prawns from the Exe estuary find their way into a salad aromatised with elements from much further east – curry, lime and cardamom – while the day's main fish is supplied from Brixham. Otherwise, there may be Hurdon Farm pork with hazelnuts, Jerusalem artichokes and truffle, or a sweetly tempting presentation of Hatherleigh Estate fallow deer with Crown Prince squash in Black Muscat jus. A veggie main course might look to north Africa for inspiration in pot-roast cauliflower with almonds, soft spices and preserved lemon. Apple and toffee cream with blackberries is an impeccable autumn finisher, or you might hop on the chocolate train with Valrhona delice, gâteau Opera and hazelnut ice cream. West Country cheeses come with pickles and jellies.

Seats 60, Pr/dining room 16 **Times** 12-2.15/7-9.45 **Prices** Fixed L 2 course £19.50, Fixed D 3 course £49.50, Tasting menu fr £65 **Wines** 38 bottles over £30, 23 bottles under £30, 10 by glass **Parking** 25, On street **Notes** Sunday L £19.50-£24.50, Vegetarian available, Children welcome

THURLESTONE Map 3 SX64

Thurlestone Hotel

British V

tel: 01548 560382 **TQ7 3NN**
email: enquiries@thurlestone.co.uk **web:** www.thurlestone.co.uk
dir: *A38 take A384 into Totnes, A381 towards Kingsbridge, onto A379 towards Churchstow, onto B3197 turn into lane signed to Thurlestone*

Stunning sea views and well-judged cooking using regional produce

The view across the golf course and sub-tropical gardens to the sea is a cracker (especially from the terrace), and with its proximity to Salcombe, the Thurlestone is a south Devon hotspot. The Margaret Amelia restaurant is a star attraction, with its formal table settings and glorious views through the floor-to-ceiling windows. The menu makes good use of the region's produce in dishes that have classical foundations. Ham hock terrine with black pudding crumb and quail's egg is a fashionable opener before slow-braised feather blade of West Country beef, or whole lemon sole with shrimps and samphire. Finish on vanilla pannacotta with textures of raspberries.

Chef Hugh Miller **Seats** 150, Pr/dining room 150 **Times** 12.30-2.30/7.30-9, Closed 2 wks Jan, L Mon-Sat **Prices** Fixed L 2 course £19.95, Fixed D 3 course £39.50 **Wines** 119 bottles over £30, 26 bottles under £30, 9 by glass **Parking** 120 **Notes** 4 course £39.50, Fish tasting menu, Sunday L £19.95-£22.95, Children welcome

TORQUAY Map 3 SX96

Corbyn Head Hotel

Modern, Traditional

tel: 01803 213611 **Torbay Rd, Sea Front TQ2 6RH**
email: info@corbynhead.com **web:** www.corbynhead.com
dir: *Follow signs to Torquay seafront, turn right on seafront. Hotel on right with green canopies*

Pretty seafront hotel with accomplished cooking

Bang on the seafront, with views over the bay, the white hotel with green awnings is a blaze of colourful flowers in summer. The Harbour View restaurant is a pretty room done out in shades of pink, where the kitchen sets itself high standards in turning out classically-inspired dishes. Among starters, there might be duck liver and foie gras terrine with leeks set in grain mustard jelly, while main courses are commendably restrained – perhaps grilled salmon with marinated roasted peppers in caper dressing. The finale could be pear poached in red wine with Kirsch-laced black cherry ice cream.

Chef Luke Hart **Seats** 80, Pr/dining room 20 **Times** 12-2.30/7-9 **Wines** 37 bottles over £30, 76 bottles under £30, 12 by glass **Parking** 40 **Notes** Fixed D 4 course £31, Sunday L £17.50, Vegetarian available, Children welcome

The Elephant Restaurant and Brasserie

Modern British

tel: 01803 200044 **3-4 Beacon Ter TQ1 2BH**
email: info@elephantrestaurant.co.uk
dir: *Follow signs for Living Coast, restaurant opposite*

Ambitious contemporary cooking from a Devon food hero

The Rosette award for this establishment has been suspended due to a change of concept. Reassessment will take place in due course. Overlooking Torquay's harbour, The Elephant is a two-tier operation, with a brasserie on the ground floor and a restaurant (limited opening) with a tasting menu – called The Room and sparkling with a modern vibe after refurbishment – upstairs. The whole place is run by chef-proprietor Simon Hulstone and his wife Katy, who also own a farm of 90 acres where they rear free-range pigs, sheep, hens and turkeys and grow seasonal fruit, herbs and vegetables, and what doesn't come from the farm is bought from local suppliers, all credited on the menu. Simon is an adventurous cook, his dishes combining ingredients in the modern style. Seared Brixham scallops are partnered by morcilla sausage and served with artichoke velouté, for instance, and another starter of crab is flavoured with dashi and accompanied by pea pannacotta and mango. Carnivores may prefer ham hock with grilled pineapple, a bantam egg and tarragon, then fillet and braised shin of aged beef with wild garlic and broccoli. Main course skrei cod fillet is fashionably partnered by chorizo and sauced with chicken jus and served with samphire and celeriac. Puddings are from the top drawer, judging by lemon and passionfruit tart with banana sorbet.

Chef Simon Hulstone **Seats** 75 **Times** 12-2/6.30-9, Closed 1st 2 wks Jan, Sun-Mon **Prices** Fixed L 2 course fr £14.50, Tasting menu fr £60, Starter £7-£11, Main £14.50-£24.50, Dessert £6.50-£9 **Wines** 24 bottles over £30, 30 bottles under £30, 8 by glass **Parking** Opposite restaurant **Notes** Vegetarian available, Children 12 yrs+

Grand Hotel

Modern European

tel: 01803 296677 **Torbay Rd TQ2 6NT**
email: reservations@grandtorquay.co.uk **web:** www.grandtorquay.co.uk
dir: *M5 junct 31, follow signs for Torquay. Follow signs for seafront*

Grand-hotel dining on the English Riviera

Occupying a prime position on Torquay's seafront, the Grand certainly has presence, built in Victorian times and expanding as the popularity of the English Riviera grew. The main dining option is the 1881 Restaurant, its genteel formality in keeping with its august past (Agatha Christie spent her honeymoon here). The menu sticks to traditional ideas with just enough contemporary thrust to satisfy both schools. Start with celeriac and apple soup, or dressed crab salad fired up with wasabi, and move onto pan-fried sea bass with king prawns and pearl barley. There are steaks cooked on the grill, and, for dessert, lemon posset comes with shortbread, candied lemons and berry compôte.

Chef Scott Harrison-Jones **Seats** 160, Pr/dining room 40 **Times** 12.30-3/6.30-9.30, Closed L Mon-Sat **Prices** Fixed D 3 course fr £30, Tasting menu fr £40 **Wines** 19 bottles over £30, 25 bottles under £30, 11 by glass **Parking** 30, Station car park opposite **Notes** Sunday L £15.95, Vegetarian available, Children welcome

The Headland Hotel

Modern, Traditional

tel: 01803 295666 **Daddyhole Rd TQ1 2EF**
email: info@headlandtorquay.com **web:** www.headlandtorquay.com
dir: *Phone for directions*

Confident cooking and a sea view

Overlooking the English Riviera, this Victorian villa was originally built for Russian royalty (the Romanovs, no less) and it occupies a prime spot with two acres of pretty gardens, a heated pool and an elegant restaurant named after those regal former residents. The grand dining room has a great sea view and a traditional finish. The kitchen turns out well-crafted dishes based on good quality-ingredients. Start with dill and cauliflower soup with rosemary oil, followed by grilled sea bream, samphire, roast tomatoes and onion coulis. Desserts can be as indulgent as an orange and chocolate truffle bar.

Chef Owen Isaacs **Seats** 140, Pr/dining room 20 **Times** 6.30-8.30 **Prices** Prices not confirmed **Wines** 6 bottles over £30, 24 bottles under £30, 9 by glass **Parking** 45 **Notes** Fixed D 6 course fr £24.95, Vegetarian available, Children welcome

TORQUAY *continued*

The Imperial Hotel

Modern British

tel: 01803 294301 **Park Hill Rd TQ1 2DG**
email: imperialtorquay@thehotelcollection.co.uk **web:** www.thehotelcollection.co.uk
dir: *M5 to Exeter, A380 then A3022 to Torquay. Park Hill Rd off Torwood St/Babbacombe Rd, just N of New Harbour*

Superb views and careful, unpretentious cooking

The Imperial's Victorian founders couldn't have chosen a better spot for their hotel, whose clifftop position has wide-ranging views over the bay and Channel. The kitchen chooses its ingredients diligently, making good use of fish and local produce, and turns out well-considered, carefully-timed dishes. It has a flair for presentation, too, without over-complicating what appears on the plate. Home-made Brixham fishcake is a well-executed starter, served with pea shoot salad, or go for a pressing of ham hock accompanied by a pear poached in red wine. Next up, rump of Highland lamb with spiced aubergine caviar and rosemary-flavoured potato fondant, and to finish, go for cherry pannacotta.

Chef Jacek Gorney **Seats** 170, Pr/dining room 350 **Times** 7-9.30, Closed L all week **Prices** Prices not confirmed **Wines** 15 bottles over £30, 47 bottles under £30, 18 by glass **Parking** 110, NCP town centre **Notes** Vegetarian available, Children welcome

Orestone Manor

Modern, European V

tel: 01803 328098 & 897511 **Rockhouse Ln, Maidencombe TQ1 4SX**
email: reception@orestonemanor.co.uk **web:** www.orestonemanor.com
dir: *A379 to Shaldon. Follow road through, hotel signed on left (beware sharp turn)*

Capable cooking in boutique manor house

This handsome Georgian manor house peeps occupies landscaped grounds over Lyme Bay. The main restaurant is a traditional space with wooden floors and linen-swathed tables – a suitable setting for the kitchen's ambitious à la carte menus. Classic French-accented technique delivers a refined starter of beetroot carpaccio with Vulscombe goats' cheese, red pepper jelly, pine nuts and apple and elderflower syrup. If the nearness of the briny puts you in the mood for fish, pan-fried brill fillet arrives with poached celery, wild mushrooms, smoked garlic mash, clams and ceps cream. For dessert, yogurt pannacotta pairs effectively with passionfruit coulis, mangosteen and hazelnuts, or go for artisan West Country cheeses.

Chef Neil & Catherine D'Allen, Nathen Hill **Seats** 55, Pr/dining room 22 **Times** 12-2.30/6.30-9.30, Closed 3-30 Jan **Prices** Fixed L 2 course £21, Fixed D 3 course £27, Tasting menu £47.50, Starter £6.50-£12.50, Main £16.50-£25, Dessert £6.50-£7.50 **Wines** 22 bottles over £30, 45 bottles under £30, 8 by glass **Parking** 38 **Notes** Tasting menu at wknds or by arrangement, Sunday L, Children welcome

TOTNES Map 3 SX86

The Riverford Field Kitchen

Modern British, Organic

tel: 01803 762074 **Riverford TQ11 0JU**
email: fieldkitchen@riverford.co.uk
dir: *From A38 Buckfastleigh, take A384 to Totnes. Left to Riverford Organics*

Vegetables take a starring role at this organic Devon farm

Wash Farm is the hub of the Riverford brand (they have farms around the country now), delivering organically grown fruit and veg across the land. Hunker down here at communal tables for hearty organic food, a fixed deal of whatever is on-the-money that day, always teeming with superlative vegetable and salad accompaniments. Start with roasted broccoli, shaved fennel and spiced cashews in blood-orange and ginger dressing, or griddled leeks with raisins and red onion – winning combinations both. Main course could be duck breast and leg with white beans and cavolo nero, with a cavalcade of veg accompaniments including baked swede, cheesy parsnips and balsamic onions.

Chef James Dodd **Seats** 72 **Times** 12.30-3/7-11.30, Closed 24-26 Dec, D Sun **Prices** Fixed L 3 course fr £23.50, Fixed D 3 course fr £27.50 **Wines** 2 bottles over £30, 16 bottles under £30, 7 by glass **Parking** 30 **Notes** Sunday L fr £23.50, Vegetarian available, Children welcome

The White Hart

Modern British NEW

tel: 01803 847150 & 847147 **Dartington Hall, The Darington Hall Trust TQ9 6EL**
email: reservations@dartingtonhall.com **web:** www.dartingtonhall.com
dir: *M5, A38 take Buckfastleigh junct A384 for 5m. Left at St Mary's church*

Local produce and medieval vibes

On the square at the heart of the 880-acre Dartington Hall Estate, the White Hart's stone floors and beamed ceilings are true to the medieval roots of the restored 14th-century building. Cheery, young staff add to the appeal, as does a menu that's an enticing mix of local produce, modern ideas and global accents. Mackerel escabèche arrives in a palate-tingling medley with wasabi crème fraîche, grapefruit, pickled vegetables and dill oil, followed by Denbury lamb rump with crisp polenta cubes, spinach, tomatoes and pea purée. Finish on a zingy high with lemon cream with shortbread, lemongrass jelly and lemon sorbet.

Chef Anuj Thakur **Seats** 68, Pr/dining room 48 **Times** 12-3/5.30-9 **Prices** Fixed L 2 course £15, Starter £4.95-£8.95, Main £12.95-£22.95, Dessert £5.95-£8.95 **Wines** 1 bottle over £30, 25 bottles under £30, 18 by glass **Parking** 200 **Notes** Sunday L £9.95, Vegetarian available, Children welcome

TWO BRIDGES Map 3 SX67

Two Bridges Hotel

Modern British

tel: 01822 892300 **PL20 6SW**
email: enquiries@twobridges.co.uk **web:** www.twobridges.co.uk
dir: *8m from Tavistock on B3357, hotel at junct with B3312*

Dartmoor coaching inn with modern British food

In a white-fronted building of obvious venerability, with a prettily appointed dining room named Tors, a gentle style of British modernism is practised, which might run to goats' cheese tortellini in tomato consommé, ahead of cheek, loin and belly of local pork in maple syrup with broccoli and walnuts. Chicken liver parfait has its richness offset by pickled veg, while a main-course seafood array provides hake, crayfish and little fishcakes with braised baby gem and mustard mash. Finish with crème brûlée and rhubarb sorbet, or boozed-up spotted dick with whisky custard and vanilla ice cream. West Country cheeses come with fig chutney.

WOOLACOMBE Map 3 SS44

Watersmeet Hotel

Traditional British, European

tel: 01271 870333 **Mortehoe EX34 7EB**
email: info@watersmeethotel.co.uk **web:** www.watersmeethotel.co.uk
dir: *M5 junct 27. Follow A361 to Woolacombe, right at beach car park, 300yds on right*

Punchy modern dishes and stunning sunsets

This sparkling-white meringue of a building stands above the bay at Mortehoe on the north Devon coast, with views across to Lundy. An enterprising fixed-price menu may lead you from smoked pigeon breast with a game sausage, Savoy cabbage purée and salt-baked beetroot to well-seasoned and carefully-timed plaice fillets in herb sauce with diced fried potatoes and bacon and hazelnut dressing, or perhaps a serving of Exmoor sirloin with a dinky steak-and-tongue pudding and truffled mash. Simple but boldly flavoured desserts encompass the likes of apple and vanilla delice with blackcurrant sorbet, or a pairing of pannacotta and zabaglione with plum compôte.

Chef John Prince **Seats** 56, Pr/dining room 18 **Times** 12-2/6.30-9 **Prices** Prices not confirmed **Parking** 40 **Notes** Sunday L, Vegetarian available, Children 8 yrs+

DORSET

BEAMINSTER Map 4 ST40

BridgeHouse

Modern European

tel: 01308 862200 **3 Prout Bridge DT8 3AY**
email: enquiries@bridge-house.co.uk **web:** www.bridge-house.co.uk
dir: *From A303 take A356 towards Dorchester. Turn right onto A3066, 200mtrs down hill from town centre*

Up-to-date cooking in a 13th-century building

Once home to a dozen priests, there is a tangible sense of the past within the thick stone walls of this 700-year-old house but a modern gloss prevents any feeling of stuffiness, particularly in the Beaminster Brasserie. The kitchen strikes a good balance between creativity and reassuringly classical thinking, with regional produce bringing a sense of place. Flavours hit the mark throughout, starting with crispy sea bream, pak choi, fennel, ginger, salt-and-pepper chilli squid and black bean sauce. A more traditional approach is evident in a seared duck breast, fondant potato, celeriac purée, Savoy cabbage and girolles.

Chef Geraldine Gay **Seats** 45, Pr/dining room 45 **Times** 12-2/7-9 **Prices** Fixed L 2 course £20, Starter £6.50-£10.95, Main £16.50-£23.50, Dessert £7.50-£11.50 **Wines** 21 bottles over £30, 28 bottles under £30, 11 by glass **Parking** 20 **Notes** Afternoon tea, Light bites fr £8.25, Fri steak & fish night, Sunday L £20-£25, Vegetarian available, Children welcome

BOURNEMOUTH Map 5 SZ09

Best Western The Connaught Hotel

Modern British

tel: 01202 298020 **30 West Hill Rd, West Cliff BH2 5PH**
email: reception@theconnaught.co.uk **web:** www.theconnaught.co.uk
dir: *Follow Town Centre West & BIC signs*

Traditionally-based British cooking in a grand seaside hotel

With sandy beaches stretching below, the grand old Connaught rules the roost on Bournemouth's West Cliff. The Blakes restaurant overlooks the hotel's own gardens, where candlelit outdoor tables are popular on balmy summer evenings. Inside, the lightly formal tone makes an agreeable ambience for traditionally-based British dishes. Accurately seared scallops make an early appearance in a starter alongside celeriac purée, salsa verde, micro fennel and pea shoots. That might be followed by rump of lamb, with pistachio, honey and mustard glaze, baby carrots, gnocchi, sweetbread fritter and Madeira jus. Chocolate and caramel tart with raspberry glaze is a typical dessert.

Best Western The Connaught Hotel

Chef Ben Nicol **Seats** 80, Pr/dining room 16 **Times** 6.30-9, Closed L all week (private lunches by arrangement) **Prices** Prices not confirmed **Wines** 30 bottles over £30, 25 bottles under £30, 13 by glass **Parking** 66 **Notes** Pre-theatre menu must pre-book, Vegetarian available, Children welcome

Bournemouth Highcliff Marriott Hotel

Modern British

tel: 01202 557702 **St Michael's Rd, West Cliff BH2 5DU**
email: reservations.bournemouth@marriotthotels.co.uk **web:** www.highcliffgrill.co.uk
dir: *Take A338 dual carriageway through Bournemouth, then follow signs for International Centre to West Cliff Rd, then 2nd right*

Up-to-date cooking in a colourful clifftop hotel restaurant

As the name suggests, this is a majestic seaside hotel in the grandest vein. The dining room has a stripped-down but colourful look of unclothed tables amid striped and spotted upholstery, while up-to-date ingredients and techniques distinguish the extensive menus. Smoked mutton 'bacon' with beer-pickled wild mushrooms and onions, jazzed up with horseradish, is an assertive opener. Brown crabmeat and quinoa makes an interesting accompaniment to fried hake, while local rose veal comes as roast loin and braised shin with salt-baked celeriac, curly kale and apple. Finish with a rhubarb and custard spin, the former poached and jellied, the latter set into a pannacotta garnished with honeycomb.

The Crab at Bournemouth

Seafood

tel: 01202 203601 **Exeter Rd BH2 5AJ**
email: info@crabatbournemouth.com **web:** www.crabatbournemouth.com
dir: *Follow signs to BIC, restaurant opposite*

Seafood specialist on the Bournemouth seafront

The epitome of a seafront venue, the Crab is part of the white-fronted Park Central Hotel, but functions as a restaurant in its own right, smartly done out in sandy hues against a background of darkwood. An array of fresh fish and shellfish is on the menu, starting with pan-fried scallops with black pudding mash, apple jus and crisp pancetta. For mains, you can't go wrong with a whole crab, thermidored, garlic-buttered, and served with gremolata potatoes, or herb-crusted cod with onion purée, wild mushrooms, Puy lentils and aubergine caviar. Finish with a trio of mango bavarois, vanilla cream and passionfruit sorbet.

Chef Nick Hope **Seats** 80 **Times** 12-2.30/5.30-10 **Prices** Prices not confirmed **Wines** 18 bottles over £30, 24 bottles under £30, 19 by glass **Parking** BIC **Notes** Pre-theatre 3 course 5.30-7pm £20.95, Sunday L, Vegetarian available, Children welcome

BOURNEMOUTH *continued*

The Green House

Modern British

tel: 01202 498900 **4 Grove Rd BH1 3AX**
email: info@thegreenhousehotel.com **web:** www.thegreenhousehotel.co.uk
dir: *Phone for directions*

Resourceful cooking built on eco-friendly produce

The Green House is a striking-looking, centrally-located property converted and run on sustainable principles. There are beehives on the roof, and the Arbor (Latin for 'tree' to further underline its green credentials) Restaurant deals in only organic, Fairtrade and farm-assured, mostly local produce. The seasonally-changing menu might open with south coast crab risotto served with an onion fritter, move on to venison loin with an accompanying suet pudding flavoured with juniper, or whole market fish of the day. For dessert, Indian-spiced doughnuts with condensed milk parfait and lime curd make for a creative finale.

Chef Andrew Hilton **Seats** 38, Pr/dining room 70 **Times** 12-2.30/5.30-9.30 **Prices** Prices not confirmed **Wines** 14 bottles over £30, 16 bottles under £30, 9 by glass **Parking** 30 **Notes** Pre-theatre 3 course £20, Sunday L, Vegetarian available, Children welcome

Hallmark Hotel Bournemouth Carlton

Modern, Traditional British

tel: 01202 552011 **East Overcliff BH1 3DN**
email: carlton@hallmarkhotels.co.uk **web:** www.hallmarkhotels.co.uk
dir: *M3/M27, follow A338 (Bournemouth). Follow signs to town centre & East Overcliff. Hotel is on seafront*

Traditional cooking in a grand old seaside hotel

Sitting proud on the East Cliff above Bournemouth's golden sands, the Carlton is an old smoothie of a seaside hotel. Frederick's restaurant, named after one of the former owners, suits the mood with its regal purple-red upholstery and swagged curtains. A discreet top layer of modern garnishing doesn't attempt to disguise the traditional British underlay to the menus, so expect smoked salmon and quail's eggs, or rich, well-seasoned crab and lobster bisque with Armagnac cream, to start. Main course brings on quality meats such as honey-glazed pork fillet wrapped in pancetta with walnut and pepper dressing, and the short dessert selection includes zesty lemon tart and clotted cream.

Hermitage Hotel

Traditional British V

tel: 01202 557363 **Exeter Rd BH2 5AH**
email: info@hermitage-hotel.co.uk **web:** www.hermitage-hotel.co.uk
dir: *Follow A338 (Ringwood-Bournemouth) & signs to pier, beach & BIC. Hotel directly opposite*

Seafront hotel with ambitious and thoughtful cooking

The restaurant at the Hermitage, opposite the beach and pier, is a large, traditionally-styled room (although plans are in the air to relocate it), with service on the correct side. The interesting menus offer variety aplenty, as they must with residents eating here perhaps every evening. Starters are along the lines of a terrine of pressed free-range chicken and wild mushrooms wrapped in Parma ham served with ale chutney and ciabatta, with main courses equally-well considered: perhaps hake fillet with asparagus, salad, new potatoes and hollandaise. Bring the curtain down with intense chocolate fondant with vanilla ice cream and chocolate sauce.

Chef Iain McBride **Seats** 120, Pr/dining room 50 **Times** 10-2/6.15-9 **Prices** Fixed D 3 course fr £23.25, Starter £7.95-£8.95, Main £17.95-£25.95, Dessert £6.25-£9.95 **Wines** 8 by glass **Parking** 60 **Notes** Sunday L, Children welcome

West Beach

Modern British, Seafood

tel: 01202 587785 **Pier Approach BH2 5AA**
email: enquiry@west-beach.co.uk **web:** www.west-beach.co.uk
dir: *100yds W of the pier*

Classy seafood dishes next to the beach

Virtually on the beach and with a sunny terrace almost within touching distance of the waves, you might be forgiven for thinking you were eating in a Spanish resort rather than a fish restaurant on the Jurassic Coast. Floor-to-ceiling picture windows make the most of the sea views and the Beachcomber-style interior is bright and contemporary with pastel shades and bleached wood. The freshest seafood simply cooked is the deal here and you might set out with a light and crisp tempura squid with a mixed radish salad. It could be followed by a spankingly fresh Weymouth wild sea bass fillet served with mixed shellfish cooked in a crab bisque.

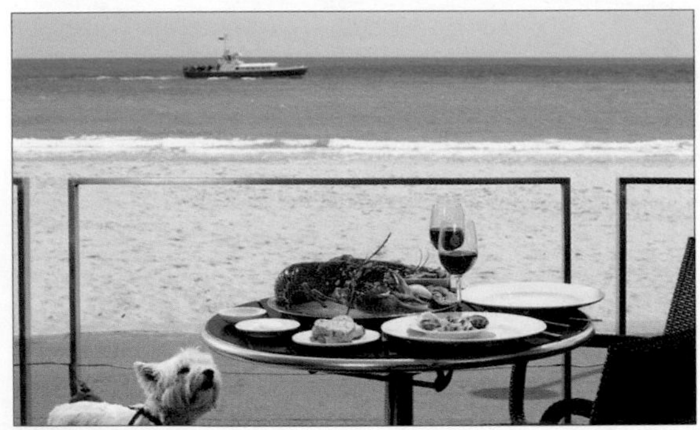

Chef Marcin Pacholarz **Seats** 75 **Times** 9-3.30/6-10, Closed 25 Dec, D Sun-Mon (winter) **Prices** Fixed L 3 course £30-£35, Fixed D 3 course £30-£35, Starter £5.50-£8.50, Main £16.50-£27, Dessert £5.50-£8.50 **Wines** 15 bottles over £30, 25 bottles under £30, 14 by glass **Parking** BIC car park **Notes** Vegetarian available, No children

BRIDPORT Map 4 SY49

Riverside Restaurant

Seafood, International

tel: 01308 422011 **West Bay DT6 4EZ**
email: neilriverside@hotmail.com **web:** www.riverside-restaurant.com
dir: *A35 Bridport ring road, turn to West Bay at Crown rdbt*

Long-standing harbourside fish restaurant

When the Watsons acquired this harbourside restaurant over 50 years ago, they were continuing a local tradition stretching back to Victorian days of serving pearly-fresh fish and seafood from the day's catch, with views over the sea. The cooking keeps things as simple as the prime materials require: Lyme Bay scallop and Portland crab chowder, deep-fried squid with aïoli and lemon, seafood platters, and oven-roasted hake with steamed tender stem broccoli. There are occasional forays into the modern cookbook. Not a fish fan? Then try braised lamb shanks with red wine reduction. Finish with Amaretto chocolate torte.

Chef A Shaw, E Webb, N Larcombe **Seats** 80, Pr/dining room 30 **Times** 12-2.30/6.30-9, Closed 30 Nov-12 Feb, Mon (ex BHs), D Sun **Prices** Fixed L 2 course £23, Starter £4.95-£11.50, Main £12.95-£25.50, Dessert £4.95-£8.50 **Wines** 14 bottles over £30, 45 bottles under £30, 15 by glass **Parking** Public car park 40 mtrs **Notes** Fixed L 1 course fr £6.95, Sunday L, Vegetarian available, Children welcome

CHRISTCHURCH Map 5 SZ19

Captain's Club Hotel & Spa

Modern European

tel: 01202 475111 **Wick Ferry, Wick Ln BH23 1HU**
email: enquiries@captainsclubhotel.com **web:** www.captainsclubhotel.com
dir: *Hotel just off Christchurch High St, towards Christchurch Quay*

Riverside brasserie dining of appealing simplicity

A glass-fronted boutique hotel by the River Stour, where the kitchen serves up modern brasserie fare, fully in keeping with the attractive surroundings. A slice of pig's cheek and apple terrine is big on flavour and comes with a sharp-shooting pea and radish salad, while classic seafood specialities such as moules marinière or whole dressed crab won't lack for subscribers. For the main course, opt for succulent lamb rump with beetrooted dauphinoise in red wine. Veggie possibilities include an Indian-spiced cauliflower risotto with coconut and coriander, and the dessert crowd-pleasers take in textbook crème brûlée with a chocolate chip cookie.

Chef Andrew Gault **Seats** 100, Pr/dining room 120 **Times** 11.30-10, All-day dining **Prices** Fixed L 3 course £30, Fixed D 3 course £30, Starter £7-£12, Main £13-£27, Dessert £6-£8 **Wines** 93 bottles over £30, 33 bottles under £30, 21 by glass **Parking** 41 **Notes** Sunday L £25, Vegetarian available, Children welcome

The Jetty

Modern British V NOTABLE WINE LIST

tel: 01202 400950 **95 Mudeford BH23 3NT**
email: dine@thejetty.co.uk
dir: *A35/A337 to Highcliffe. Right at rdbt, hotel & restaurant 1.5m on left*

Sleek venue with sharp, unfussy cooking

A dashing contemporary construction of glass and wood, The Jetty's culinary output is headed up by Alex Aitken. Provenance is everything here. In fine weather, grab a table on the terrace if you can, although floor-to-ceiling windows provide glorious views over Mudeford Quay. The kitchen turns out contemporary dishes taking inspiration from far and wide, so seared tuna gets a Japanese twist with avocado and wasabi ice cream (just the right punchiness), and there's a classical European approach to a fabulous fillet of sea bass with lemon butter sauce. There are meaty options such as calves' liver with truffle sausage, and desserts run to a summery New Forest strawberry creation

Chef Alex Aitken **Seats** 70 **Times** 12-2.30/6-10 **Prices** Fixed L 2 course fr £19.95, Fixed D 3 course fr £23.95, Tasting menu fr £59.50, Starter £7.95-£12.50, Main £19.95-£28.50, Dessert £7.50-£11.95 **Wines** 82 bottles over £30, 25 bottles under £30, 14 by glass **Parking** 40 **Notes** Mini gastro menu 4 course £25, Vegan menu, Sunday L £24.95-£29.95, Children welcome

The Lord Bute & Restaurant

British, Mediterranean

tel: 01425 278884 **179-181 Lymington Rd, Highcliffe on Sea BH23 4JS**
email: mail@lordbute.co.uk **web:** www.lordbute.co.uk
dir: *Follow A337 to Lymington, opposite St Mark's churchyard in Highcliffe*

Consistent cooking in a former castle entrance lodge

Once the entrance lodge to Highcliffe Castle, this eye-catching boutique hotel is superbly placed for access to the golden beaches and blustery clifftops of the Dorset coast. Modern within, the classical dining room boasts an orangery extension and well-drilled service to boot. The 20-year residency of chef Kevin Brown has ensured continuity in the cooking. A broad range of choices encompasses timeless offerings such as duck terrine served with spiced pear chutney and toasted brioche, followed by a fillet of hake wrapped in prosciutto ham, steamed samphire, crushed saffron-flavoured potatoes and clam, king prawn and mussel cream.

Chef Kevin Brown **Seats** 95 **Times** 12-2/7-9.30, Closed Mon, L Sat, D Sun **Prices** Fixed L 2 course £16.95 **Wines** 13 bottles over £30, 35 bottles under £30, 10 by glass **Parking** 50 **Notes** Sunday L £25.95, Vegetarian available, Children welcome

CHRISTCHURCH *continued*

Upper Deck Bar & Restaurant

Modern British V NOTABLE WINE LIST

tel: 01202 400954 & 483434 **95 Mudeford BH23 3NT**
email: upperdeck@harbourhotels.co.uk
web: www.christchurch-harbour-hotel.co.uk/upper-deck
dir: *A35/A337 to Highcliffe. Right at rdbt, hotel & restaurant 1.5m on left*

Chic waterside restaurant for local produce and stunning views

Whichever of the two restaurants at this classy hotel you choose, good views over the water are guaranteed, as is a fine showing of regional produce. Chef-patron Alex Aitken is the man behind it all. The Upper Deck is pretty swanky, featuring a sleek, contemporary bar and an upmarket seasidey vibe, or there's the recently extended terrace. The cooking takes a modern British route through contemporary tastes and, given the setting, plenty of locally-landed fish. Get going with cannelloni of smoked salmon, move on to a 'daily classic' such as confit duck leg (Tuesday), or sea bream with clam and shellfish butter sauce.

Chef Alex Aitken **Seats** 95, Pr/dining room 20 **Times** 12-2.30/6-9.45 **Prices** Fixed L 2 course £15.95, Fixed D 3 course fr £19.95, Tasting menu £45, Starter £7.50-£11.95, Main £19.50-£25, Dessert £6.95-£7.95 **Wines** 60 bottles over £30, 35 bottles under £30, 12 by glass **Parking** 100 **Notes** Brunch menu, Afternoon tea, Sunday L £21.50-£25, Children welcome

CORFE CASTLE Map 4 SY98

Mortons House Hotel

Modern British

tel: 01929 480988 **49 East St BH20 5EE**
email: stay@mortonshouse.co.uk **web:** www.mortonshouse.co.uk
dir: *In village centre on A351*

Clean-lined modern cooking with East Asian notes

Mortons is a beautifully-maintained Elizabethan manor of the 1590s on the Isle of Purbeck, within sight of Corfe Castle. An openness to East Asian tastes brings a teriyaki-sesame dressing to seared salmon seasoned with Dorset's own wasabi as an opener. This could be the prelude to fillet and braised cheek of pork with fondant celeriac and a rustic white bean cassoulet fragrant with rosemary, or sea bass with crab and tomato in a Thai-seasoned sauce of lemongrass and galangal. Sharp citric flavours illuminate Tuscan-style orange cake with lemon curd and mascarpone ice cream, and refreshment is also the keynote of chilled rice pudding served in cherry soup.

Chef Ed Firth **Seats** 60, Pr/dining room 22 **Times** 12-1.45/7-9 **Prices** Starter £6-£11, Main £15-£25, Dessert £7-£10 **Wines** 17 bottles over £30, 25 bottles under £30, 6 by glass **Parking** 40 **Notes** Sunday L £13-£24, Vegetarian available, Children 5 yrs+

DORCHESTER Map 4 SY69

The Wessex Royale Hotel

Modern European NEW

tel: 01305 262660 **High West St DT1 1UP**
email: info@wessexroyalehotel.co.uk **web:** www.wessexroyalehotel.co.uk
dir: *From A35 follow town centre signs. Straight on, hotel at top of hill on left*

Smart Georgian coaching-inn with elegantly simple cooking

This mid-18th-century coaching inn has classic Georgian good looks, and behind its neat black railings it boasts grand staircases and imposing fireplaces – although the white-walled dining room opts for an uncluttered style, with bare floor and tables, and an unpretentious service approach. Local supply lines furnish Lyme Bay scallops with crispy pork and apple, or a classic duo of ham hock terrine and piccalilli, while main courses pile on the panache for roast monkfish and squid with chorizo, spring onions and saffron potatoes. Desserts to tickle the fancy include a chocolate pairing (milk parfait and dark mousse) with honeycomb and raspberries.

Chef Nick Cherry **Seats** Pr/dining room **Times** 12-9.30, All-day dining, Closed L Sun **Prices** Starter £5.95-£7.50, Main £10.95-£18.50, Dessert £4.95-£6.25 **Wines** 4 bottles over £30, 23 bottles under £30, 12 by glass **Notes** Vegetarian available

EVERSHOT Map 4 ST50

The Acorn Inn

British

tel: 01935 83228 **28 Fore St DT2 0JW**
email: stay@acorn-inn.co.uk **web:** www.acorn-inn.co.uk
dir: *From A37 between Yeovil & Dorchester, follow Evershot & Holywell signs, 0.5m to inn*

Wessex country pub with a traditional approach

Plumb in the middle of Thomas Hardy's favourite stretch of England, the 16th-century coaching inn makes an appearance in *Tess of the d'Urbervilles* as the Sow and Acorn. To start, grilled local goats' cheese in orange dressing may be a safer bet than the more ambitious truffled gnocchi, but there's nothing wrong with correctly cooked plaice on the bone with triple-cooked chips and caper butter, and it's worth the wait for a slow-roasting of pork belly, served with appled mash in Madeira jus. The chocolate fondant is styled 'melt-in-the-middle' in supermarket fashion, but is a superior sponge with unctuous oozy filling, accompanied by brilliantly intense salted caramel ice cream.

Chef Guy Horley **Seats** 45, Pr/dining room 35 **Times** 12-2/7-9 **Prices** Starter £5-£8, Main £13-£23, Dessert £6-£12 **Wines** 16 bottles over £30, 26 bottles under £30, 39 by glass **Parking** 40 **Notes** Sunday L £14-£16, Vegetarian available, Children welcome

George Albert Hotel

Modern British

tel: 01935 483430 **Wardon Hill DT2 9PW**
email: enquiries@gahotel.co.uk **web:** www.georgealberthotel.co.uk
dir: *On A37 (between Yeovil & Dorchester). Adjacent to Southern Counties Shooting Ground*

Well-balanced modern dishes at a contemporary hotel

The George Albert opened its doors relatively recently, in 2010, but despite its newness, monogrammed carpets and starched table linen bring a traditional feel to Kings Restaurant. Seared scallops with leeks and mash in creamy mussel chowder is a beguiling opener, if you can resist the appeal of good old ham hock terrine and piccalilli. Main courses bring all their components together in well-balanced harmony, as in the quince purée, parsnip mash, fondant potato and baconed cabbage that come with duck breast in port jus, or grilled grey mullet with pak choi in lime butter. To finish, there may be sweet passionfruit pannacotta with mango sauce and pineapple.

Chef Andy Pike **Seats** 40, Pr/dining room **Times** 12-2.30/6.30-9 **Prices** Starter £5-£10, Main £7.50-£25, Dessert £5-£10 **Wines** 10 bottles over £30, 21 bottles under £30, 14 by glass **Parking** 200 **Notes** Sunday L £11.50-£25, Vegetarian available, Children welcome

Summer Lodge Country House Hotel, Restaurant & Spa

Modern British NOTABLE WINE LIST

tel: 01935 482000 & 482030 **Fore St DT2 0JR**
email: summerlodge@rchmail.com **web:** www.summerlodgehotel.com
dir: *1m W of A37 halfway between Dorchester & Yeovil*

Assured modern cooking in peaceful surroundings

Summer Lodge, within four acres of peaceful grounds, was built in 1798 as a dower house and enlarged in 1893 following plans drawn up by Thomas Hardy, a friend of the then owner and by profession an architect. The interior is plush and comfortable, while the restaurant is a pretty room, with floral fabrics covering banquettes, swagged curtains, a patterned carpet and an open fire. Staff are discreet, professional and friendly. Steven Titman's cooking is built on impeccable produce from the locality and whatever is grown in the hotel's garden, his style following British traditions with more modern and wide-ranging ideas in the mix. The dinner carte might open with beef tartare with summer truffle aïoli, an egg yolk and watercress, or more exotic tempura quail breast with confit leg, pickled kohlrabi, orange and soya and honey dressing. Dishes are imaginatively but sensibly composed, seen in main courses of Brixham cod fillet, timed to the second, with warm brandade, broccoli, roast chicken and sherry dressing, and in loin of Exmoor venison accompanied by shallots puréed in alc, roast chervil roots and a port reduction. An eye for presentation is evident, seen in puddings like rhubarb parfait with poached fruit, orange purée and vanilla sauce.

Chef Steven Titman **Seats** 60, Pr/dining room 20
Times 12-2.30/7-9.30, Closed 3-24 Jan **Prices** Fixed L 2 course £23, Fixed D 3 course £25-£45, Tasting menu £75-£165, Starter £13-£19, Main £22-£32, Dessert £11-£13 **Wines** 1450 bottles over £30, 15 bottles under £30, 25 by glass **Parking** 60 **Notes** Tasting menu 8 course, Surprise menu D 6 course £65/£120, Sunday L £39, Vegetarian available, Children welcome

FARNHAM Map 4 ST91

Museum Inn

Modern, Traditional British

tel: 01725 516261 **DT11 8DE**
email: enquiries@museuminn.co.uk **web:** www.museuminn.co.uk
dir: *Off A354 between Salisbury & Blandford Forum*

Ambitious cooking with a solid country-pub foundation

Victorian archaeologist General Augustus Pitt-Rivers was responsible for the Oxford museum collection that bears his name, and for extending the partly thatched Museum Inn. While there is a solid pub foundation to proceedings with ham hock terrine with red onion chutney and toast, there are also excursions over the Channel for pheasant Normandy-style, braised in local cider, or into Med territory for aubergine and feta schnitzel on red pepper coulis. Fish specials from the day-boats are chalked on the board, and a section of standards offers smoked haddock and salmon fish pie with gruyère-gratinated mash, or honey-mustard glazed ham and chips. Dessert might be rice pudding ritzed up with passionfruit.

Chef Neil Molyneux **Seats** 69, Pr/dining room 40 **Times** 12-2.30/6.30-9 **Prices** Starter £5.95-£7.95, Main £13.95-£22.95, Dessert £6.50-£9 **Wines** 35 bottles over £30, 22 bottles under £30, 18 by glass **Parking** 14 **Notes** Sunday L £15.50-£16.50, Vegetarian available, Children welcome

MAIDEN NEWTON Map 4 SY59

Le Petit Canard

Modern British, French

tel: 01300 320536 **Dorchester Rd DT2 0BE**
email: le-petit-canard2@btconnect.com **web:** www.le-petit-canard.co.uk
dir: *In centre of Maiden Newton, 8m W of Dorchester*

Honest, accomplished cooking in pretty village restaurant

A former coaching inn, this homely place has been run with passion and charm by Gerry and Cathy Craig for more than 15 years. The linen-covered tables are topped with flowers and candles, with wooden beams and exposed stonework adding to its appeal. Gerry's cooking does not try to reinvent the wheel, but neither is it stuck in the past. Confit duck leg with five spice has a good depth of flavour, while a main course fillet of trout comes with a herby butter, new potatoes and seasonal vegetables. Dessert might be warm lemon tart with lemon curd ice cream.

Chef Gerry Craig **Seats** 28 **Times** 12-2/7-9, Closed Mon, L all week (ex 1st & 3rd Sun in month), D Sun **Prices** Fixed D 3 course £34-£36.95 **Wines** 9 bottles over £30, 19 bottles under £30, 6 by glass **Parking** On street, village car park **Notes** Sunday L £26, Vegetarian available, Children 12 yrs+

POOLE Map 4 SZ09

Harbour Heights

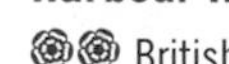 British, French

tel: 01202 707272 **73 Haven Rd, Sandbanks BH13 7LW**
email: reception@harbourheights.net **web:** www.fjbhotels.co.uk
dir: *From A338 follow signs to Sandbanks, restaurant on left past Canford Cliffs*

Spectacular views and modern bistro food

The teak-decked alfresco terrace of this 1920s art deco beauty offers views across Poole harbour but the glossy Harbar Bistro is an equally-inviting prospect. Check out the fresh fish counter, laden with the day's catch from Poole Quay, to steer you towards a main course starring a pavé of cod supported by butterbean, pea and chorizo fricassée and sherry emulsion. Otherwise, start with pan-fried pigeon breast with Puy lentils and sloe gin syrup, followed, perhaps, by venison loin with fondant potato, caramelised onion, wilted spinach, chestnut purée, and Vin Santo and hazelnut jus. Wrap things up with pear and almond tart with vanilla ice cream.

Chef Loic Gratadoux **Seats** 90, Pr/dining room 120 **Times** 12-2.15/7-9.15
Prices Fixed L 2 course £19.50-£28, Fixed D 3 course £29.50, Starter £7.50-£12, Main £16.50-£28, Dessert £7.50-£9.50 **Wines** 69 bottles over £30, 43 bottles under £30, 13 by glass **Parking** 50 **Notes** Sunday L £22.50-£29, Vegetarian available, Children welcome

POOLE *continued*

The Haven

 Modern British

tel: 01202 707333 **161 Banks Rd, Sandbanks BH13 7QL**
email: reservations@havenhotel.co.uk **web:** www.fjbhotels.co.uk/haven
dir: *Follow signs to Sandbanks Peninsula, hotel next to Swanage ferry departure point*

Delightful Poole Bay views and confident modern cooking

At the southern end of Sandbanks, this large white hotel dates from the 1880s. With its sea view, tiered tables and relaxed atmosphere, The Point brasserie is as close as you will get to dining on a cruise ship without leaving dry land. The kitchen buys the best regional produce but doesn't confine itself to the fruits of the sea. Start, for instance, with duck boudin, celeriac purée, plums, toasted hazelnuts and duck sauce. Dishes are seldom too elaborate: a hake fillet comes with Provençal grilled vegetables and salsa verde. Vanilla pannacotta and pineapple salad is one way to finish.

Chef Jason Hornbuckle **Seats** 80, Pr/dining room 156 **Times** 12-2/7-9 **Prices** Fixed L 2 course fr £26, Fixed D 3 course fr £34 **Wines** 32 bottles over £30, 31 bottles under £30, 13 by glass **Parking** 90 **Notes** Sunday L £26-£34, Vegetarian available, Children welcome

Hotel du Vin Poole

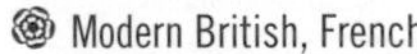 Modern British, French

tel: 01202 785578 **Mansion House, Thames St BH15 1JN**
web: www.hotelduvin.com
dir: *A350 into town centre follow signs to Channel Ferry/Poole Quay, left at bridge, 1st left is Thames St*

Bistro cooking in an elegant Georgian house

Hotel du Vin's Poole outpost is a bit of a landmark just off the quayside, a creeper-covered Georgian mansion. As expected, the kitchen deals in crowd-pleasing brasserie staples from over the Channel, all cooked just so. Start perhaps with crab toasts with sliced radish and black pepper mayonnaise, escargots in classic garlic and herb butter, or onion soup, and proceed to steak frites, pink-roast rump of lamb with broccoli and boulangère potatoes with chorizo, or sole meunière. Puddings are as Gallic as the rest of the package, among them Paris-Brest and tarte au citron, although bread-and-butter pudding flavoured with rum and banana may please patriots.

Chef Darren Rockett **Seats** 85, Pr/dining room 48 **Times** 12-2/5.30-10.30 **Prices** Fixed L 2 course £16.95, Fixed D 3 course £19.95, Starter £5.95-£11, Main £12.50-£29.50, Dessert £6.95-£9.95 **Wines** 10 by glass **Parking** 12, NCP (available until 11pm) **Notes** Sunday L £24.95, Vegetarian available, Children welcome

SHAFTESBURY Map 4 ST82

La Fleur de Lys Restaurant with Rooms

Modern French

tel: 01747 853717 **Bleke St SP7 8AW**
email: info@lafleurdelys.co.uk **web:** www.lafleurdelys.co.uk
dir: *Junct A350/A30*

West Country cooking in a former boarding school

Smartly linened-up tables are the order in the dining room of this creeper-covered restaurant with rooms. Lemon-yellow and exposed stone walls produce a relaxing atmosphere, and fixed-price menus, built on a core of modern French notions, offer a variety of choices. Start with smoked haddock soufflé on a bed of smoked salmon with coriander cream, or smoked chicken and chorizo salad with spicy apple relish. The main business arrives in the form of pan-fried fillet of veal topped with Parma ham served with mushrooms, pancetta and mustard sauce, or grilled lemon sole fillets with asparagus and lemony herb butter. Conclude with peach and ginger crème brûlée.

Chef D Shepherd, M Preston **Seats** 45, Pr/dining room 12 **Times** 12-2.30/7-10.30, Closed 3 wks Jan, L Mon-Tue, D Sun **Prices** Fixed D 3 course £36-£42 **Wines** 50 bottles over £30, 50 bottles under £30, 8 by glass **Parking** 10 **Notes** Sunday L, Vegetarian available, Children welcome

SHERBORNE Map 4 ST61

Eastbury Hotel

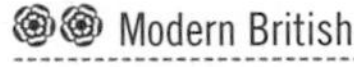 Modern British V

tel: 01935 813131 **Long St DT9 3BY**
email: enquiries@theeastburyhotel.com **web:** www.theeastburyhotel.co.uk
dir: *5m E of Yeovil, follow brown signs for Eastbury Hotel*

Cosmopolitan cooking in utterly English surroundings

The Eastbury offers a hint of country-estate living, with much of the kitchen's raw material coming from its garden and beehives. Despite the utterly English surroundings, the menu looks both eastwards for soy-glazed pig's cheek with aduki beans in yuzu dressing, or smoked salmon with lime and nori, and southwards for a main dish of Creedy Carver duck breast, accompanied by cassoulet of confit leg and sausage, slow-cooked gizzards, charred leeks and sweet onion. Skrei cod is seasoned with sumac, weighted with lardo, and dressed with coriander yogurt. Gird your loins for substantial desserts such as caramelised banana cake and peanut ice cream, or rhubarb mascarpone cheesecake with rhubarb sorbet.

Chef Matthew Street **Seats** 40, Pr/dining room 12 **Times** 12-2/6.30-9 **Prices** Tasting menu £55, Starter £8-£12, Main £12-£25, Dessert £7-£10 **Wines** 23 bottles over £30, 48 bottles under £30, 10 by glass **Parking** 20 **Notes** Tasting menu 7 course, Sunday L, Children welcome

The Green

Modern British, European

tel: 01935 813821 **3 The Green DT9 3HY**
email: info@greenrestaurant.co.uk
dir: *A30 towards Milborne Port, at top of Greenhill turn right at mini rdbt. Restaurant on left*

Creative modern dishes in picture-postcard property

The Green, in a Grade II listed building, sets its sights on locally and ethically sourced raw materials. Succulent chargrilled scallops come with a cylinder of black pudding and a dressing of leaves drizzled in sea buckthorn oil, toasted pine kernels adding some crunch. Quality ingredients are evident throughout: pink-roast rack of lamb, juicy and of super-meaty flavour, for instance, accompanied by an onion and potato cake and rich tarragon jus, and fillet of Cornish hake with roasted tomatoes and lemon butter. There are delicious desserts along the lines of ginger sticky toffee pudding, of clear toffee and ginger flavours, enhanced by lime leaf ice cream and Grand Marnier sauce.

Chef Alexander Matkevich **Seats** 40, Pr/dining room 24 **Times** 12-2.30/7-9.30, Closed Sun-Mon **Prices** Fixed L 3 course £20, Starter £6.95-£11.50, Main £16.50-£24, Dessert £6.95-£10.95 **Wines** 12 bottles over £30, 30 bottles under £30, 8 by glass **Parking** On street, car park **Notes** Vegetarian available, Children welcome

The Kings Arms

Modern British

tel: 01963 220281 **Charlton Herethorne DT9 4NL**
email: admin@thekingsarms.co.uk **web:** www.thekingsarms.co.uk
dir: *From A303 follow signs for Templecombe & Sherborne onto B3145 to Charlton Horethorne*

Hard-working kitchen in a modernised country inn

First licensed in the Regency era, Sarah and Tony Lethbridge have given this stone-built inn a thoroughly modern makeover, though not to the detriment of its original charm. Sarah heads up the kitchen, capitalising on West Country produce, as well as drying and curing meats in-house. The style of cooking looks beyond Britain, offering a Spanish-influenced starter of chargrilled asparagus, Serrano ham and poached duck egg, perhaps followed by pan-seared brill, warm salad of Jerusalem artichokes, fennel, broad beans, radish, salsa verde and new potatoes. Treacle tart is a dessert with Blighty stamped all over it.

Chef Sarah Lethbridge **Seats** 120, Pr/dining room 70
Times 12-2.30/7-9.30, Closed 25 Dec **Prices** Starter £5-£8, Main £10-£19, Dessert £6.50-£8 **Wines** 18 bottles over £30, 40 bottles under £30, 13 by glass **Parking** 30 **Notes** Sunday L £13, Vegetarian available, Children welcome

STUDLAND **Map 5 SZ08**

THE PIG on the Beach

Modern British V NOTABLE WINE LIST

tel: 01929 450288 **The Manor House, Manor Rd BH19 3AU**
email: info@thepigonthebeach.com **web:** www.thepighotel.com
dir: *A338 from Bournemouth, follow signs to Sandbanks ferry, cross on ferry, then 3m to Studland*

Garden-to-table cooking in a shabby-chic seaside manor

Part of a mini chain of quirky boutique hotels, this little piggy overlooks sandy Studland Bay. Fruit, veg and herbs are plucked from the walled kitchen garden, a coop of chickens and quails supplies eggs, and fish and seafood is locally landed. A main course of South Coast hake with plump Dorset cockles, foraged Alexanders, sea beets and Hampshire salami shows the style, as does local pork belly, smoked in-house and matched with olives, tomatoes and spring onions. Bookending this, an opener of grilled cuttlefish with braised veal tongue, rocket, roasted garlic and lemon crème fraîche, and for pudding, hazelnut and cocoa meringue with pressed pears and caramel sauce.

Chef Andy Wright **Seats** 70, Pr/dining room 12 **Times** 12-2.45/6.30-10 **Prices** Starter £6-£10.50, Main £14-£26, Dessert £7.50-£8.95 **Wines** 90 bottles over £30, 25 bottles under £30, 20 by glass **Parking** 30 **Notes** Sunday L, Children welcome

WEYMOUTH **Map 4 SY67**

Moonfleet Manor Hotel

Mediterranean NEW

tel: 01305 786948 **Fleet Rd DT3 4ED**
email: info@moonfleetmanorhotel.co.uk
dir: *Take Fleet Rd just off B1357 at Chickerell. Hotel at end of road*

Simple modern bistro cooking with literary associations

The village of Fleet played a central role in J. Meade Falkner's smuggling yarn, *Moonfleet* (1898), and the sparkling-white Georgian hotel, which gazes out over Chesil Beach, is the jewel in its crown. Inside is all squashy sofas and crackling fires, with bracing sea views from a pleasantly airy dining room. Simple modern bistro cooking is the deal, beginning perhaps with pressed smoked chicken terrine with Jerusalem artichoke purée and toasted walnuts, and moving on to roast hake accompanied by spicy chorizo cassoulet with a powdery brioche topping. End with today's favourite combination of chocolate and peanut – tart and ice cream, respectively – in passionfruit coulis.

Chef Stephen Wilson, Tony Smith **Seats** Pr/dining room 45 **Times** 12-2/5-close **Prices** Starter £7.25-£12.50, Main £8-£26, Dessert £5-£6 **Wines** 11 by glass **Notes** Sunday L, Children until 7.30

WIMBORNE MINSTER **Map 5 SZ09**

Les Bouviers Restaurant with Rooms

French

tel: 01202 889555 **Arrowsmith Rd, Canford Magna BH21 3BD**
email: info@lesbouviers.co.uk **web:** www.lesbouviers.co.uk
dir: *1.5m S of Wimborne on A349, turn left onto A341. In 1m turn right into Arrowsmith Rd. 300yds, 2nd property on right*

Francophile cooking in an elegant restaurant with rooms

A modern house in over five acres of land complete with stream and lake is the setting for this restaurant done out in shades of claret and gold, with contemporary artwork hanging on the walls. Cheese soufflé with watercress and horseradish sauce is a signature starter. Typical of the adventurous style is loin of veal with sautéed calves' sweetbreads, tomato confit, buttered spinach and a wild mushroom sauce, or brill on Puy lentils in saffron sauce with chorizo, courgettes and sunblush tomato. Innovative elements are introduced to puddings: chocolate and meringue ice cream for warm dark chocolate fondant, and crème brûlée flavoured with lemongrass, lemon and thyme.

Number 9

Modern British, Seafood

tel: 01202 887557 **West Borough BH21 1LT**
email: no9wimborne@aol.com
dir: *150 yds from The Square before Tivoli Theatre, on West Borough*

Modern menus perfect for pre-theatre diners

Handy for the nearby Tivoli Theatre, this 18th-century townhouse has become a stylish restaurant with uncluttered lines and unclothed tables flooded with daylight from the French windows. Greg Etheridge cooks to a modern template, with seafood and fish a notably strong suit. Fillet of Bradford Farm beef carpaccio with sweet onion purée, celeriac remoulade, rocket and balsamic salad is one successful starter. This might be followed by oven-baked skate wing, pan-fried potato gnocchi, pancetta, yellow courgette, cherry tomatoes, samphire and black olive tapenade. Finish with passionfruit crème brûlée, home-made ginger biscuits and lavender-sugared raspberries.

Chef Greg Etheridge **Seats** 50, Pr/dining room 30
Times 12-2.30/6-9.30, Closed Xmas, BH Mon, L Mon, D Sun **Prices** Fixed L 2 course £19.95, Fixed D 3 course £24.95, Starter £5.95-£9.95, Main £12.95-£24.95, Dessert £5.95-£8.50 **Wines** 3 bottles over £30, 18 bottles under £30, 9 by glass **Parking** On street or car park **Notes** Pre-theatre menu, Sunday L £12.95-£14.95, Vegetarian available, Children 6 yrs+

WYKE REGIS Map 4 SY67

Crab House Café

British, Seafood

tel: 01305 788867 **Ferrymans Way, Portland Rd DT4 9YU**
email: info@crabhousecafe.co.uk **web:** www.crabhousecafe.co.uk
dir: *A354 along Westwey once onto Portland Rd continue for just under a mile, at rdbt take 2nd exit for restaurant*

Fresh seafood in a laid-back beach hut

Situated in a spruced up wooden hut overlooking Chesil Beach, the Crab House Café has natural charms aplenty. Simplicity and freshness is the name of the game, with oysters coming from their own beds and everything sourced from within a 40-mile radius. Rustic benches outside are a treat in the warmer months, but it's all well and good if you've got to eat inside. Kick off with some oysters or home-smoked pollack mousse with a perky beetroot salsa, and follow up with whole John Dory flavoured with coriander and lime, but the fresh crabs are hard to ignore. Finish with milk chocolate and orange tart.

Chef Nigel Bloxham, Adam Foster **Seats** 40 **Times** 12-2/6-9, Closed mid Dec-Jan, Mon-Tue (ex 8 wks in summer), D Sun (Oct-Mar) **Prices** Prices not confirmed **Wines** 18 bottles over £30, 31 bottles under £30, 13 by glass **Parking** 40 **Notes** Sunday L, Vegetarian available, Children welcome

COUNTY DURHAM

BARNARD CASTLE Map 19 NZ01

The Morritt Country House Hotel & Spa

Modern French

tel: 01833 627232 **Greta Bridge DL12 9SE**
email: relax@themorritt.co.uk **web:** www.themorritt.co.uk
dir: *From A1 (east) exit at junct 57 onto A66 westbound. From M6 (west) exit at junct 40 onto A66 eastbound. Follow signs to Greta Bridge*

Full of character, a popular meeting place

The arrival of transport by mail coach in the 18th century saw this former farm develop into an overnight stop for travellers between London and Carlisle. Charles Dickens probably stayed here in 1839, hence the fine-dining restaurant is named after him. Following an amuse-bouche, two people might start by sharing wood pigeon with smoked yogurt, blueberry ketchup, spelt and sweet cicely, then continue in separate directions, one with pan-fried halibut, mussels, saffron potato, salsify and puréed kale, the other with Marley's beef rump cap with braised cheek, horseradish mayo, Jersey Royals and spinach purée. Among the desserts is rhubarb and custard anglaise with beurre noisette.

Chef Lee Stainthorpe **Seats** 60, Pr/dining room 50 **Times** 12-3/6-9, Closed Mon, L Tue-Sat **Prices** Prices not confirmed **Wines** 24 bottles over £30, 36 bottles under £30, 10 by glass **Parking** 30 **Notes** Sunday L, Vegetarian available, Children welcome

BILLINGHAM Map 19 NZ42

Wynyard Hall Hotel

Modern British

tel: 01740 644811 **Wynyard TS22 5NF**
email: reception@wynyandhall.co.uk **web:** www.wynyandhall.co.uk
dir: *A19 onto A1027 towards Stockton. At rdbt 3rd exit B1274 (Junction Rd). At next rdbt 3rd exit onto A177 (Durham Rd). Right onto Wynyard Rd signed Wolviston. Left into estate at gatehouse*

Accomplished cooking in a lavish country mansion setting

Built to impress, this vast Victorian pile sits in 150 acres of grounds with its own lake and a full complement of spa and wedding facilities. Inside, marble, mahogany and stained-glass combine in a display of jaw-dropping opulence, a style that continues in the Wellington Restaurant. To start, there's a terrine of ham hock with a crispy pork bonbon, apple purée and a sourdough crisp, while main course brings a duo of slow-cooked pork belly and cheek supported by broccoli and potato fondant. Elegance and comfort are key again in a finale of crème brûlée with Garibaldi biscuits and pistachio ice cream.

Chef Adam Heggarthy, Mehdi Amiri **Seats** 80, Pr/dining room 30 **Times** 12-3/7-9.30 **Prices** Fixed D 3 course £32, Tasting menu £50 **Wines** 51 bottles over £30, 30 bottles under £30, 10 by glass **Parking** 200 **Notes** Afternoon tea £21.50-£30, Sunday L £18-£25, Vegetarian available, Children welcome

DARLINGTON Map 19 NZ21

Headlam Hall

Modern British, French

tel: 01325 730238 **Headlam, Gainford DL2 3HA**
email: admin@headlamhall.co.uk **web:** www.headlamhall.co.uk
dir: *8m W of Darlington off A67*

Elegant country mansion with bright, modern cooking

Refurbished in early 2016, this handsome house dates from the beginning of the 17th century and retains plenty of period charm including its walled garden. The restaurant is a draw in its own right, offering diners a series of settings that take in an elegant panelled dining room and the more contemporary orangery. The kitchen delivers modern dishes based on classic combinations. Crisp lamb belly, minted pea purée, watercress and redcurrant jus is one enjoyable starter with plenty of textural contrast. It might be followed by spiced monkfish tail, Bombay potatoes, spinach and peas with a saffron cream.

Chef Derek Thomson **Seats** 70, Pr/dining room 30
Times 12-2.30/7-9.30, Closed 25-26 Dec **Wines** 20 bottles over £30, 38 bottles under £30, 10 by glass **Parking** 80 **Notes** Sunday L £25-£35, Vegetarian available, Children welcome

The Orangery

Modern British

tel: 01325 729999 **Rockliffe Hall, Rockliffe Park, Hurworth-on-Tees DL2 2DU**
email: enquiries@rockliffehall.com **web:** www.rockliffehall.com
dir: *A1(M) junct 57, A66(M), A66 towards Darlington, A167, through Hurworth-on-Tees. In Croft-on-Tees left into Hurworth Rd, follow signs*

Creative contemporary dishes in an ornate dining room

Conceived in the 18th century, Rockliffe began to take on a distinguished air at the onset of the Victorian era when the Surtees family, who were historians and landscape painters, acquired it. It lives up to its history by offering the full country-house deal, including state-of-the-art spa facilities and golf. The principal dining room, The Orangery, inhabits the original Old Hall, and is an eye-popping space replete with vaulted rafters and slender gilded pillars. Richard Allen strides into this glittering ambience with Vegetarian, Pescetarian, Tasting and Surprise menu options to the structured four-course carte. Somewhere along the way, you may encounter smoked fillet, parfait and tartare of sea trout with an oyster, roasted cucumber seeds and dill, or crab in Bloody Mary livery, colour-bombed with avocado and radish. Main courses look to offer variant cuts in the meat dishes – best end and casseroled leg of lamb, braised cheek and crispy belly of pork – or perhaps an eastern spin such as turbot with Asian shrimp risotto, cashews and kaffir lime. Then wander back through the annals of English domestic cookery for desserts like rhubarb with junket, milk sorbet and a doughnut, or down to the Med for pistachio and olive oil cake with chocolate and orange accompaniments.

Chef Richard Allen **Seats** 60, Pr/dining room 20 **Times** 6.30-9.30, Closed Sun-Mon, L Tue-Sat **Prices** Fixed D 3 course £45-£55, Tasting menu £75-£110, Starter £15, Main £25, Dessert £15 **Wines** 600 bottles over £30, 3 bottles under £30, 35 by glass **Parking** 300 **Notes** Vegetarian available, Children welcome

DURHAM Map 19 NZ24

Honest Lawyer Hotel

 Modern British

tel: 0191 378 3780 **Croxdale Bridge, Croxdale DH1 3SP**
email: enquiries@honestlawyerhotel.com **web:** www.honestlawyerhotel.com
dir: *A1 junct 61*

Something for everybody in a modern city hotel

A modern hotel with a bright and welcoming restaurant and a policy of sourcing produce from within 20 miles. Start with baked scallops with pancetta lardons and leeks in a creamy fish sauce, accompanied by a brioche topped with parmesan and herbs, or corned beef hash with black pudding, brown sauce and a fried egg. Main courses take in a trio of lamb (tender roast rump, cutlet and haggis spring roll), with honey and whisky sauce providing a good contrast, served with dauphinoise potatoes, as well as, say, grilled smoked cod loin on paella (prawns, chicken, chorizo and mussels). End with a familiar dessert like knickerbocker glory or sticky toffee pudding.

Chef Harry Bailie **Seats** 45, Pr/dining room 60 **Times** 12-9.30, All-day dining **Prices** Prices not confirmed **Wines** 2 bottles over £30, 27 bottles under £30, 7 by glass **Parking** 150 **Notes** Sunday L, Vegetarian available, Children welcome

Ramside Hall Hotel Golf & Spa

 International

tel: 0191 386 5282 **Carrville DH1 1TD**
email: mail@ramsidehallhotel.co.uk **web:** www.ramsidehallhotel.co.uk
dir: *A1(M) junct 62, A690 to Sunderland. Straight at lights. 200mtrs after bridge, right*

Carnivore heaven in golf-oriented hotel

Sprawling outwards from a largely Victorian house, 2015 saw the opening of a glossy spa and health club at Ramside. Culinary options run from straightforward carvery dishes to the menu in the brasserie-style Rib Room, a temple to slabs of locally reared 28-day aged beef. Just choose your cut (a peckish pair might go halves on a 30oz tomahawk rib-eye) which then arrives with roasted mushrooms, braised onions and a choice of classic sauces. Non-carnivores could go for grilled sea bass with braised fennel and herb velouté. Puddings include retro knickerbocker glory or baked Alaska.

HUTTON MAGNA Map 19 NZ11

The Oak Tree Inn

 Modern British

tel: 01833 627371 **DL11 7HH**
email: claireross67@hotmail.com
dir: *7m W on A66 from Scotch Corner*

Confident, creative cooking in a converted village inn

The Oak Tree is just the sort of unassuming village inn you'd like to come across when touring the Pennines. Main courses are clearly focused: top-class Scarborough cod is partnered with steamed Shetland mussels, parsnip purée and a hit of curry flavour, while best end of lamb might be supported by giant couscous, merguez sausage and cumin. Elsewhere, dishes are interesting without being overloaded with flavours, as seen in a warm salad of smoked duck and black pudding with a well-balanced honey and mustard dressing. Expect excellent home-baked breads, and the ice creams to accompany desserts, such as the salted caramel that comes with hot chocolate fondant, are also made on the premises.

Chef Alastair Ross **Seats** 20, Pr/dining room 20 **Times** 6.30-9.30, Closed 24-27 & 31 Dec, 1-2 Jan, Mon, L all week **Prices** Starter £5.80-£9.80, Main £19.50-£25, Dessert £6.95-£8.95 **Wines** 17 bottles over £30, 47 bottles under £30, 8 by glass **Parking** 3, On street **Notes** Vegetarian dishes & children's portions by prior arrangement, Children welcome

ROMALDKIRK Map 19 NY92

The Rose & Crown

Modern British, Continental

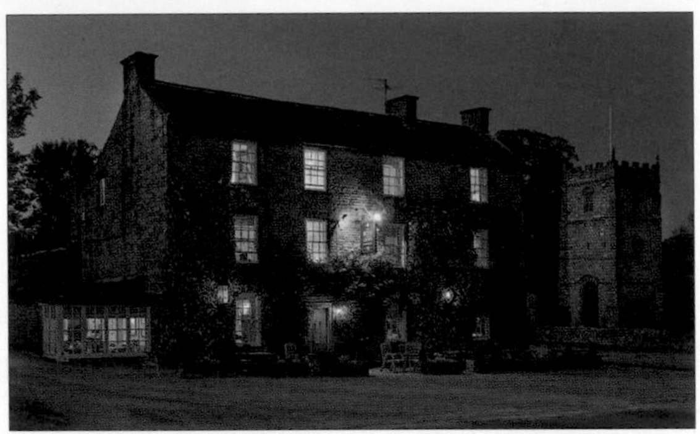

tel: 01833 650213 **DL12 9EB**
email: hotel@rose-and-crown.co.uk **web:** www.rose-and-crown.co.uk
dir: *6m NW of Barnard Castle on B6277*

Classically-based cuisine in a lovely old inn

In a tiny village with a Saxon church and the original stocks, this 18th-century inn is steeped in tradition. You're welcome to eat in the bar with its oak settles, antique chairs and crackling log fire, but at dinner many guests go for the candlelit oak-panelled dining room, where menus are built on local, seasonal produce. A starter of pan-fried pigeon breast with bacon and hazelnut crumble, pickled cabbage and rosemary sauce might be followed by a hearty main of pan-fried loin and braised shoulder of Hardwick mutton, peas, spinach, pan haggerty, turnip and mutton jus.

Chef Dave Hunter **Seats** 24 **Times** 12-2.30/6.30-9, Closed 23-27 Dec **Prices** Prices not confirmed **Wines** 22 bottles over £30, 34 bottles under £30, 10 by glass **Parking** 25 **Notes** Sunday L, Vegetarian available, Children 7 yrs+ D

SEAHAM Map 19 NZ44

The Ozone Restaurant

Asian Fusion

tel: 0191 516 1400 **Seaham Hall Hotel, Lord Byron's Walk SR7 7AG**
email: hotel@seaham-hall.com
dir: *From A19 take B1404 to Seaham. At lights straight over level crossing. Hotel approx 0.25m on right*

Asian flavours in a glamorous five-star hotel

In Seaham Hall's sleek Ozone Restaurant floor-to-ceiling windows and a wraparound outdoor terrace giving heavenly garden views act as a backdrop to the light and zingy fusion food sent from the open kitchen. Confit duck pancake with hoi sin sauce, crisp lettuce and cucumber makes a great starter, or crispy squid with coriander and sweet chilli might appeal, ahead of main courses such as Thai prawn curry or tempura cod with roast peanuts and Thai shallot and apple salad. For dessert, coconut pannacotta with roasted pineapple keeps things suitably oriental. Byron's Bar & Grill is the alternative spot for grill dining in sleek surroundings.

Chef Ross Stovold **Seats** 60 **Times** 11-5/6-9, Closed 25 Dec **Prices** Fixed L 2 course £19.50, Fixed D 3 course £26, Starter £6.50, Main £13, Dessert £6.50 **Wines** 10 bottles over £30, 8 bottles under £30, 11 by glass **Parking** 200 **Notes** Vegetarian available, Children welcome

Seaham Hall – Byron's Restaurant

Modern British NOTABLE WINE LIST

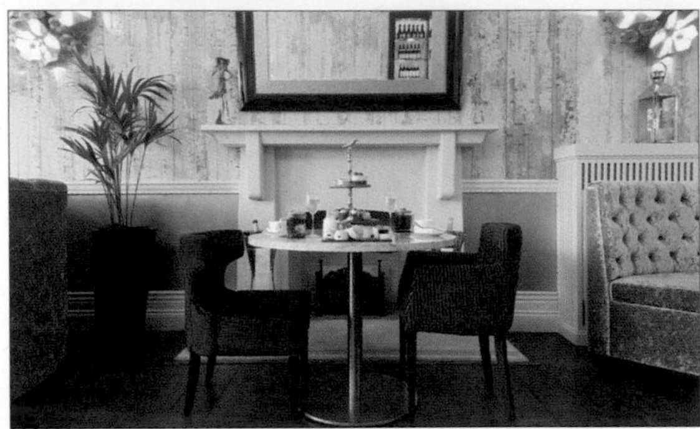

tel: 0191 516 1400 **Seaham Hall Hotel, Lord Byron's Walk SR7 7AG**
email: hotel@seaham-hall.co.uk **web:** www.seaham-hall.co.uk
dir: *From A19 take B1404 to Seaham. At lights straight over level crossing. Hotel approx 0.25m on right*

Modern grill dining in luxury hotel

These days a state-of-the-art spa hotel, the late-18th-century Seaham Hall also offers a brace of stimulating eating options. Byron's Restaurant is a swish contemporary space with a glossy sheen that offers a great meeting place. The kitchen delivers a crowd-pleasing menu aiming unashamedly at the hearts of carnivores, although well-sourced fish provides meat-free alternatives. Expect the likes of slow-cooked pork jowl and cheek with piccalilli, crisp toast and pork scratchings to start, followed by North East cod, spiced aubergines, borlotti beans and samphire. Lemon pannacotta, pistachio sponge and raspberry is one of the uncomplicated desserts.

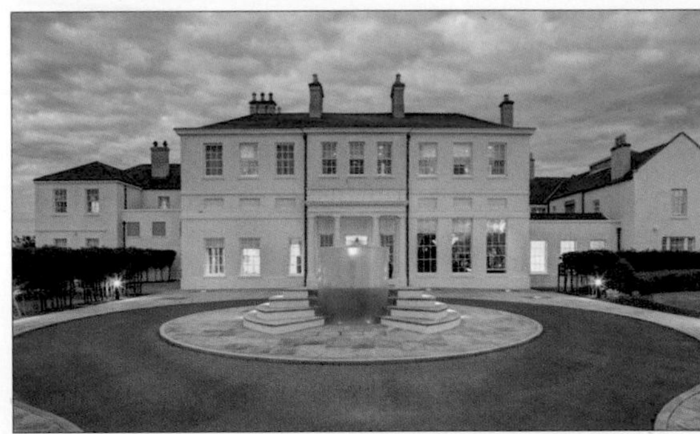

Chef Ross Stovold **Seats** 40, Pr/dining room 100 **Times** 12-2.30/6.30-9.30 **Prices** Fixed L 2 course fr £25, Starter £7-£16, Main £18-£30, Dessert £7-£9 **Wines** 148 bottles over £30, 20 bottles under £30, 24 by glass **Parking** 120 **Notes** Sunday L £25-£30, Vegetarian available, Children welcome

ESSEX

BRENTWOOD Map 6 TQ59

Marygreen Manor Hotel

Modern European V

tel: 01277 225252 **London Rd CM14 4NR**
email: info@marygreenmanor.co.uk **web:** www.marygreenmanor.co.uk
dir: *M25 junct 28, onto A1023 over 2 sets of lights, hotel on right*

Enterprising modern food in a Tudor mansion

Dating from the early 16th century, when it was built by a courtier of Catherine of Aragon, the manor is a perfect example of a half-timbered building, the restaurant an impressive room with a profusion of wall and ceiling timbers and carved stanchions. Classy ingredients are carefully handled and combined sympathetically to create some stimulating dishes. Start with a pairing of Orkney scallops and marinated salmon with nori and crème fraîche, before proceeding to the likes of venison with parsnips, girolles, pomegranate and blackberries. Vegetarians have a separate menu, and desserts include hazelnut praline crémeux with cocoa sponge and caramelised almond ice cream.

Chef Majid Bourote **Seats** 80, Pr/dining room 85
Times 12.30-2.30/7.15-10.15, Closed L Mon, D Sun, BHs **Prices** Fixed L 2 course £18, Fixed D 3 course £24, Tasting menu £48, Starter £7.50-£12, Main £23.50-£32, Dessert £7.50 **Wines** 72 bottles over £30, 51 bottles under £30, 12 by glass **Parking** 100 **Notes** Tasting menu 6 course, Sunday L, Children welcome

CHELMSFORD Map 6 TL70

County Hotel

 Modern European

tel: 01245 455700 **29 Rainsford Rd CM1 2PZ**
email: sales@countyhotelgroup.co.uk **web:** www.countyhotelgroup.co.uk
dir: *Off Chelmsford ring road close to town centre and A12 junct 18*

British and Mediterranean flavours in town-centre hotel

A short stroll from the railway station and town centre, the County Hotel has a cheery modern style, as typified in the County Kitchen restaurant, where oak floors and leather seats in summery pastel hues of mustard, mint and tangerine add colour to the neutral contemporary decor. Uncomplicated modern European cooking is the kitchen's stock-in-trade, starting with duck and ham hock terrine with pickled mushrooms, spiced apricot chutney and toasted walnut bread. Mains might bring lamb cutlets with Puy lentils, spinach and a zesty burst of gremolata. For dessert, there could be chocolate and Amaretto fondant with clotted cream ice cream.

Chef Roy Ortega **Seats** 64, Pr/dining room 135 **Times** 12-2.30/6-10, Closed L Sat **Prices** Fixed L 2 course £20-£25, Fixed D 3 course £30-£35, Starter £6-£10, Main £11-£22, Dessert £5-£8 **Wines** 18 bottles over £30, 22 bottles under £30, 6 by glass **Parking** 70 **Notes** Pre-theatre menu, Sunday L, Vegetarian available, Children welcome

COGGESHALL Map 7 TL82

Ranfield's Brasserie

French, European

tel: 01376 561453 **4-6 Stoneham St CO6 1TT**
email: food@ranfieldsbrasserie.co.uk **web:** www.ranfieldsbrasserie.co.uk
dir: *A12 from Chelmsford, exit at Kelvedon into Coggeshall. Restaurant in centre opposite clock tower*

Gutsy cooking in a buzzy brasserie

The brasserie has been a fixture of the local dining scene for almost 30 years. Its setting may be a 16th-century timbered house, but there's nothing old-style about the approach. The mood is laid-back and cosmopolitan and the one-off decor is akin to an eclectic art gallery done out with antique linen-clothed tables. Smart complex modern food is the deal, opening with a cake of blue crab, brown shrimps and lime, garnished with pickled sweetcorn and lotus root salad, before braised breast and seared saddle of excellent salt marsh lamb with houmous and sauce vièrge. Finish with Amarena cherry and almond tart and vanilla ice cream.

COLCHESTER Map 13 TL92

The North Hill Hotel

 Modern British

tel: 01206 574001 **51 North Hill CO1 1PY**
email: info@northhillhotel.com **web:** www.northhillhotel.com
dir: *Follow directions for town centre, down North Hill, hotel on left*

Traditional bistro fare plus coffee and cake

Unclothed lightwood tables lend a Nordic touch to the hotel's Green Room bistro, where the produce of East Anglia is celebrated with gusto, from Mersea oysters to Red Poll beef and extra virgin rapeseed oil for the dressings. The cooking is traditional bistro fare, beginning with seafood specialities such as dressed crab and citrus mayonnaise, or a salmon and crayfish fishcake in chervil dressing. Some days only sausages and mash in onion gravy will do, but if you're after something glitzier, look to lemon and garlic lamb with new potato crush and spinach in salsa verde. Coffee and cake is an all-day treat, the daily-changing specials including carrot and walnut.

COLCHESTER *continued*

Stoke by Nayland Hotel, Golf & Spa

Modern British

tel: 01206 262836 & 265843 **Keepers Ln, Leavenheath CO6 4PZ**
email: restaurant@stokebynayland.com **web:** www.stokebynayland.com
dir: *From A134, pass through the village of Nayland, ignoring signs to Stoke-by-Nayland. Continue on A134, shortly after Hare & Hounds turn right on to B1068 signed Stoke-by-Nayland Golf Club. Right in approx 1.5m*

Complex contemporary cooking overlooking the golf

This purpose-built hotel complex comes complete with spa, high-tech gym, two championship-level golf courses and The Lakes Restaurant, a bright and airy room with panoramic views. The enterprising kitchen sends out ambitious dishes such as hake fillet with pork crackling, white pudding, broccoli, potato mashed with bacon and mustard, and blood orange. Starters are equally eclectic, among them rum-cured salmon with lime purée, mint syrup ice, rum marshmallow and fizz, although there may also be more orthodox chicken liver parfait with apricot and sultana jam. For dessert, try a palate-challenging doughnut stuffed with sticky toffee bacon served with spiced coffee sugar, maple walnut ice cream and pancetta.

Chef Alan Paton **Seats** 100, Pr/dining room 60 **Times** 12.30-2.30/6.30-10 **Prices** Starter £6.95-£7.50, Main £13.25-£19.50, Dessert £5.50-£7.25 **Wines** 9 bottles over £30, 24 bottles under £30, 12 by glass **Parking** 350 **Notes** Sunday L £12.50-£19.50, Vegetarian available, Children welcome

DEDHAM Map 13 TM03

milsoms

Modern International

tel: 01206 322795 **Stratford Rd CO7 6HN**
email: milsoms@milsomhotels.com **web:** www.milsomhotels.com
dir: *7m N of Colchester, just off A12. Follow signs to Dedham then brown signs*

Global food in a fuss-free contemporary setting

This old creeper-covered house offers a little piece of boutique glamour in a pretty Essex village. The bar and brasserie strike a contemporary pose, the latter with its split-level dining room opening out onto a beautiful large terrace. The menu – which is available all day – sticks to the modern message and offers everything from posh lunchtime sandwiches to steaks and burgers cooked on the grill. An international flavour sees pumpkin samosa alongside Asian duck tacos among first courses, and mains such as slow-cooked lamb shank with elephant beans and feta, or a thick-cut Scottish hake number with chorizo, pepper and chickpea stew. Finish with spiced apple crumble cheesecake.

Chef Sarah Norman, Ben Rush **Seats** 80, Pr/dining room 30 **Times** 12-9.30, All-day dining **Prices** Starter £6-£9, Main £12.50-£29.50, Dessert £6.25-£6.95 **Wines** 26 bottles over £30, 38 bottles under £30, 20 by glass **Parking** 80 **Notes** Brunch, Sunday L, Vegetarian available, Children welcome

The Sun Inn

Rustic Italian, Modern British NOTABLE WINE LIST

tel: 01206 323351 **High St CO7 6DF**
email: office@thesuninndedham.com **web:** www.thesuninndedham.com
dir: *In village centre opposite church*

A taste of Italy in a village inn

The Sun is a 15th-century village inn with open fires, doughty timbers and panelling. Its culinary leanings are distinctly Mediterranean, with the kitchen turning fresh produce and quality Italian ingredients such as cured meats, cheeses and oils into uncomplicated, well-executed dishes. The menu opens with antipasti, with starters ranging from game terrine with date chutney and chicory and pomegranate salad, to crab crostini with pickled samphire, dill and crème fraîche. A pasta option may be orecchiette with duck ragù and ricotta salata. Main courses are along the lines of hake fillet with pancetta, spinach and girolles and puddings such as prosecco jelly with elderflower cream and raspberry granita.

Chef Jack Levine **Seats** 70 **Times** 12-2.30/6.30-9.30, Closed 25-26 Dec, 3-4 Jan **Prices** Starter £5-£7.50, Main £9.50-£22, Dessert £2-£7.50 **Wines** 44 bottles over £30, 46 bottles under £30, 20 by glass **Parking** 15 **Notes** Breakfast Fri-Sun, Afternoon tea, Sunday L £12-£16, Vegetarian available, Children welcome

Le Talbooth

Modern British, European V NOTABLE WINE LIST

tel: 01206 323150 **Stratford Rd CO7 6HN**
email: talbooth@milsomhotels.com **web:** www.milsomhotels.com/letalbooth
dir: *6m from Colchester follow signs from A12 to Stratford St Mary, restaurant on the left before village*

Classy creative cooking and lovely riverside setting

In a former toll house by the River Stour dating from Tudor times, the Milsom family have run this East Anglian stalwart for over half a century. Inside, the look is slick and contemporary, and the kitchen stays abreast of culinary trends. Pan-roasted skate wing served with razor clams, smoked shallots and lardo is a thoughtfully composed starter. Next up, pot-roast sea bass fillet is partnered with seared squid, saffron tagliatelle, spinach and pickled cockles, or you might try venison saddle with thyme-infused polenta, blackberries, kale and red wine jus. An inventive apple-themed dessert brings a classic tarte Tatin, sorbet, apple and sage doughnut and poached blackberries.

Chef Andrew Hirst, Ian Rhodes **Seats** 80, Pr/dining room 34 **Times** 12-2/6.30-9, Closed D Sun (Oct-Apr) **Prices** Fixed L 2 course £26, Starter £11.25-£18, Main £20-£33, Dessert £9-£12 **Wines** 250 bottles over £30, 46 bottles under £30, 19 by glass **Parking** 50 **Notes** Sunday L £38, Children welcome

GESTINGTHORPE **Map 13 TL83**

The Pheasant

 British

tel: 01787 465010 & 461196 **Audley End CO9 3AU**
web: www.thepheasant.net
dir: *Phone for directions*

Traditional country-pub cooking on the north Essex border

A spruced-up 500-year-old country inn on the road between Sudbury and Halstead, The Pheasant's trimly beamed ceilings are exactly what you expect to see, and dining goes on in a trio of interconnecting rooms adorned with plenty of greenery. Battered tiger prawns with garlic mayonnaise feature alongside grilled goats' cheese in sweet chilli dressing, before the main attraction arrives in the shape of local farm sausages with creamy mash and onion gravy, or duck breast with orange and fennel salad. Most things come with hand-cut chips, including the half-pound sirloins, and there are sticky toffee pudding in caramel sauce, or cider-laced apple crumble with real custard bringing up the rear.

Chef James Donoghue **Seats** 40, Pr/dining room 16 **Times** 12-3/6.30-9 **Prices** Starter fr £5.50, Main fr £12.50, Dessert fr £5.95 **Wines** 5 bottles over £30, 21 bottles under £30, 7 by glass **Parking** 25 **Notes** Sunday L, Vegetarian available, Children welcome

GREAT TOTHAM **Map 7 TL81**

The Bull & Willow Room at Great Totham

Modern, Traditional British

tel: 01621 893385 & 894020 **2 Maldon Rd CM9 8NH**
email: reservations@thewillowroom.co.uk **web:** www.thebullatgreattotham.co.uk
dir: *Exit A12 at Witham junct to Great Totham*

A 16th-century village inn with high-toned dining

This 16th-century village inn has an uncommonly posh eating area, the Willow Room, where the kitchen produces a repertoire of modernised pub classics and forays into the contemporary. Crisp-fried duck's egg with truffle-dressed Russian salad is an interesting starter, while mains might bring well-timed John Dory with warm potato and olive salad, pancetta and watercress, or breast of Barbary duck, the leg meat parcelled in tortellini, with pureed quince and creamed cabbage in blackberry jus. A typical dessert might be rich summer berry pannacotta with mint sorbet, or chocolate fondant with pistachio ice cream. A three-meat mixed roast with Yorkshire pudding is the star of the Sunday lunch offering.

Chef Luke Stevens **Seats** 75, Pr/dining room 20 **Times** 12-3/5-9.45 **Prices** Starter £4.95-£7.95, Main £10.95-£26.95, Dessert £3.50-£8.95 **Wines** 19 bottles over £30, 46 bottles under £30, 9 by glass **Parking** 80 **Notes** Fixed D Mon-Fri, Menus/prices change 8-10 wks, Sunday L, Vegetarian available, Children welcome

GREAT YELDHAM **Map 13 TL73**

The White Hart

 British, European

tel: 01787 237250 **Poole St CO9 4HJ**
email: mjwmason@yahoo.co.uk **web:** www.whitehartyeldham.com
dir: *On A1017, between Halstead & Haverhill*

Intricate modern British cooking in Tudor surroundings

Dating back to the early Tudor era, The White Hart is a classic timbered country inn set in extensive grounds. Crisp white napery and quality tableware confer distinctive class on the dining room, where a daring pairing of seared scallops and smoked duck breast, with shallot purée, pickled onion, grapefruit and radish, bursts with flavours, while citrus-cured trout comes with Cromer crab and a mousse of smoked salmon. At main, salt marsh lamb is stuffed with haggis alongside a pink noisette and a kidney, as well as rosemary polenta and wild mushrooms. In conclusion, go for strawberry cheesecake with matching jelly and sorbet and a white chocolate and Amaretto mousse.

HARWICH Map 13 TM23

The Pier at Harwich

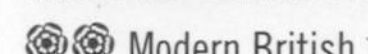

Modern British V

tel: 01255 241212 **The Quay CO12 3HH**
email: pier@milsomhotels.com **web:** www.milsomhotels.com
dir: *A12 to Colchester then A120 to Harwich Quay*

Spankingly fresh seafood and harbour views

Right on the quayside, the Pier provides super-fresh seafood and, following an extensive redevelopment, you can dine in the new first-floor brasserie and take the air in the outdoor balcony seating. Try tiger prawn ravioli with a punchy shellfish sauce, followed by pan-fried halibut, cooked simply and accurately and matched with spinach and hollandaise sauce. Chargrilled Dedham Vale steaks are an alternative to the fishy options (with skinny fries and traditional accompaniments), but Harwich crab, lobsters fresh out of the salt-water tanks and skate wing with capers and parsley butter make for stiff competition. Finish off with crème caramel with Turkish salad and a pistachio and sesame snap.

Seats 100, Pr/dining room 24 **Times** 12-2/6-9.30 **Prices** Prices not confirmed **Parking** 12, On street **Notes** Children welcome

HOCKLEY Map 7 TQ89

The Anchor Riverside Pub and Restaurant

Modern British

tel: 01702 230777 **Ferry Rd, Hullbridge SS5 6ND**
email: info@theanchorhullbridge.co.uk **web:** www.theanchorhullbridge.co.uk
dir: *Phone for directions*

Modern British food in an appealing waterside location

Shortly before the road ends at the River Crouch is this thoroughly modern gastropub where, if the weather's kind, you can sit outside in the extensive gardens with something grilled, a salad or just a sandwich. Otherwise, head for the restaurant, designed for lingering over a decent three-course meal. Try roasted hand-dived scallops with crispy suckling pig and apple purée, followed by tandoori-roast monkfish with masala potatoes and spinach, or duck cottage pie with wild mushrooms, pumpkin jam and chestnuts. Custard tart with grated nutmeg makes for a good dessert, but you might go for British cheeses with biscuits, pickled onions, grapes and piccalilli, or have both.

Chef Daniel Watkins **Seats** 160 **Times** 12-3/6-9.30, Closed 25 Dec **Prices** Prices not confirmed **Wines** 12 bottles over £30, 25 bottles under £30, 18 by glass **Notes** Sunday L, Vegetarian available, Children welcome

MANNINGTREE Map 13 TM13

The Mistley Thorn

Modern British, Seafood

tel: 01206 392821 **High St, Mistley CO11 1HE**
email: info@mistleythorn.co.uk
dir: *From A12 take A137 for Manningtree & Mistley*

Seafood-strong California cool on the Stour estuary

A gem of a place in an old coaching inn a short stroll from the harbour, the Georgian details remain in the bar and restaurant, and neutral colours keep it light, bright and contemporary. You might start with seared pigeon breast with roasted squash and move onto rib-eye of Red Poll beef. Look for the specials menu offering the catch of the day, grilled whole lemon sole with seaweed butter and hand-cut chips, maybe, or cider-cured sea trout with sea vegetables and shellfish sauce. Fans of oysters might kick off with half-dozen West Mersea rocks fried in a batter made with Aspall cider. Finish with lemon, almond and polenta cake.

Chef Sherri Singleton, Karl Burnside **Seats** 75, Pr/dining room 28 **Times** 12-2.30/6.30-9.30 **Prices** Fixed L 2 course fr £13.95, Fixed D 3 course £16.95, Starter £4.95-£6.95, Main £11.95-£21.95, Dessert £5.95-£7.50 **Wines** 4 bottles over £30, 34 bottles under £30, 17 by glass **Parking** 7 **Notes** Sunday L £16.95-£19.95, Vegetarian available, Children welcome

SOUTHEND-ON-SEA **Map 7 TQ88**

Holiday Inn Southend

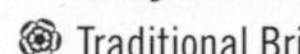

Traditional British

tel: 01702 543001 **77 Eastwoodbury Crescet SS2 6XG**
email: restaurantmgr@hisouthend.com **web:** www.1935rooftoprestaurant.com
dir: *Entrance to Southend Airport*

Slick modern dining with aeroplanes in the background

Calling all plane spotting foodies: both of your interests can be indulged in one fell swoop at the fifth-floor 1935 Restaurant overlooking the aviation action at Southend Airport. Naturally enough, soundproofing is of the highest order, and there's a real sense of occasion in the slick contemporary space when you look through the full-length glass windows and the runway lights put on a show in the evening. The kitchen deals in unpretentious classic and modern ideas, taking off with pork sliders or tempura king prawns, followed by dry-aged steaks cooked on the grill, traditional fish and chips, or wild mushroom risotto.

Chef Michael Walker **Seats** 82, Pr/dining room 14 **Times** 12-2.30/6-10 **Prices** Fixed L 2 course £16.95, Fixed D 3 course £25, Starter £4.95-£7.95, Main £9.50-£25.95, Dessert £4.50-£6.95 **Wines** 5 bottles over £30, 21 bottles under £30, 10 by glass **Parking** 226 **Notes** Afternoon tea £15.95/£21.95, Sunday L £12.95-£19.35, Vegetarian available, Children welcome

The Roslin Beach Hotel

British

tel: 01702 586375 **Thorpe Esplanade, Thorpe Bay SS1 3BG**
email: info@roslinhotel.com **web:** www.roslinhotel.com
dir: *On Thorpe Esplanade 2.5m past Southend Pier towards Shoeburyness*

Well-conceived dishes in a buzzy seaside setting

If you do like to be beside the seaside, The Roslin Beach Hotel has a sea-facing terrace, plus indoor space shielded by glass, so it is beach ready whatever the weather. The tables are dressed up in white linen and there's a buzzy ambience, plus a good showing of local seafood on the menu – a trendy retro prawn cocktail, perhaps. Mind you, some of the meat comes from the owners' farm in Hampshire, and steaks cooked on the grill are a big hit, while there is also herb-crusted rack of lamb with boulangère potatoes, green beans wrapped in Parma ham, and butternut squash velouté.

Chef Ross Caesar **Seats** 70, Pr/dining room 30 **Times** 12-2.45/6-9.30 **Prices** Fixed L 2 course £15, Fixed D 3 course £20 **Wines** 18 bottles over £30, 53 bottles under £30, 10 by glass **Parking** 57 **Notes** Afternoon tea £17.95, Sunday L £19.95-£25.95, Vegetarian available, Children welcome

STOCK **Map 6 TQ69**

The Hoop

Modern British

tel: 01277 841137 **High St CM4 9BD**
email: thehoopstock@yahoo.co.uk
dir: *A12 Billericay Galleywood junct, on B1007*

Assured modern cooking in an old pub

In the business of serving food and ale for 450 years, the weatherboarded Hoop has an atmospheric pub on the ground floor – acres of beams, draught ales at the bar – and an upstairs restaurant opened up to the rafters to create a more refined setting amid the exposed oak. The kitchen turns out modern food that wouldn't look out of place on the menu of a city brasserie: panko-crusted goats' cheese bonbons with caponata, for example, as a starter. Main courses might deliver venison and haggis Wellington with pickled and salt-baked beetroot and creamed potato. Finish with citrus bread pudding with home-made orange ice cream.

Chef Phil Utz **Seats** 40 **Times** 12-2.30/6-9, Closed Beer festival wk, 1st wk Jan, Mon, L Sat, D Sun **Prices** Prices not confirmed **Wines** 22 bottles over £30, 40 bottles under £30, 14 by glass **Parking** Village hall **Notes** Sunday L, Vegetarian available, Children welcome

TENDRING **Map 7 TM12**

The Fat Goose

Modern British

tel: 01255 870060 **Heath Rd CO16 0BX**
email: eat@fat-goose.co.uk
dir: *A120 to Horsley Cross, follow B1035 to Tendring/Thorpe-le-Soken. 1.5m on right*

Confident cooking in a charming former pub

The family-run Fat Goose is the kind of place where the kitchen bakes its own bread and local ingredients figure large on the menu. It's a restaurant, not a pub, but it still has an easy-going vibe and the interior blends old and new with aplomb, so expect slate floors, exposed beams and well-spaced wooden tables, and a warming wood-burning stove in the cooler months. The straight-talking menu kicks off with prawn and scallop ravioli, followed by Gressingham duck breast with passionfruit sauce. For dessert there's summer berry pudding with peach ice cream. There's a daily specials board, a deli and a kids' menu, too.

Chef Philip Hambrook-Moore **Seats** 80 **Times** 12-2.30/6.30-9.30, Closed Mon **Prices** Starter £4.75-£8.50, Main £11.50-£24, Dessert £3-£5.95 **Wines** 5 bottles over £30, 26 bottles under £30, 14 by glass **Parking** 50 **Notes** Sunday L £11.50-£18.50, Vegetarian available, Children welcome

GLOUCESTERSHIRE

ALMONDSBURY Map 4 ST68

Aztec Hotel & Spa

Modern British

tel: 01454 201090 **Aztec West BS32 4TS**
email: aztec-fb@shirehotels.com **web:** www.aztechotelbristol.com
dir: *M5 junct 16/A38 towards city centre, hotel 200mtrs on right*

Eclectic globally-inspired modern menu in a vibrant room

This restaurant occupies a contemporary space with a high-vaulted ceiling, rustic stone fireplace, polished wooden floors, leather seating and bold modern abstract art. The menu takes a broad sweep through global culinary culture, with British 28-day aged beef cooked on the chargrill a speciality. You might start with crispy duck with an accompanying coriander salad and pickled ginger, or home-made oxtail soup, the meat slow-cooked for five hours. Main courses take a similar international route, so tiger prawn linguine with chilli and garlic stands alongside Wainwright ale-battered haddock with thick-cut chips, mushy peas and lemon and tartare sauce. Desserts include warm chocolate brownie with raspberry ripple ice cream.

Chef Mike Riordan **Seats** 80, Pr/dining room 40 **Times** 12.30-2/6.30-9.30, Closed L Sat, D 25-26 Dec **Prices** Prices not confirmed **Wines** 12 by glass **Parking** 200 **Notes** Sunday L, Vegetarian available, Children welcome

ALVESTON Map 4 ST68

Alveston House Hotel

Modern European

tel: 01454 415050 **Davids Ln BS35 2LA**
email: info@alvestonhousehotel.co.uk **web:** www.alvestonhousehotel.co.uk
dir: *On A38, 3.5m N of M4/M5 interchange. M5 junct 16 N'bound or junct 14 S'bound*

Attractive Georgian hotel with traditionally-based menu

This Georgian hotel set within walled gardens with a restaurant to one side is well worth the short drive out from Bristol. Gardens with an ornamental lily pond are a pleasant drinking spot, and inside the place is done in calming pastel shades. Carriages, the dining room, offers a light lemon and cream backdrop to the modernised British and European dishes. A filo pastry tart of mushroom, fennel and red onion with goats' cheese dressing is the summer-season curtain-raiser to roast rack of lamb with Madeira jus, fondant potato and a salad of fennel, orange and watercress. Finish with champagne and elderflower pannacotta and fresh raspberries.

Chef Ben Halliday **Seats** 75, Pr/dining room 40 **Times** 12-1.45/7-9.30 **Prices** Fixed L 2 course £15, Starter £6-£8.50, Main £15.50-£24.75, Dessert £6-£7.25 **Wines** 6 bottles over £30, 27 bottles under £30, 6 by glass **Parking** 60 **Notes** Sunday L £19.50-£22.50, Vegetarian available, Children welcome

ARLINGHAM Map 4 SO71

The Old Passage Inn

Seafood, Modern British

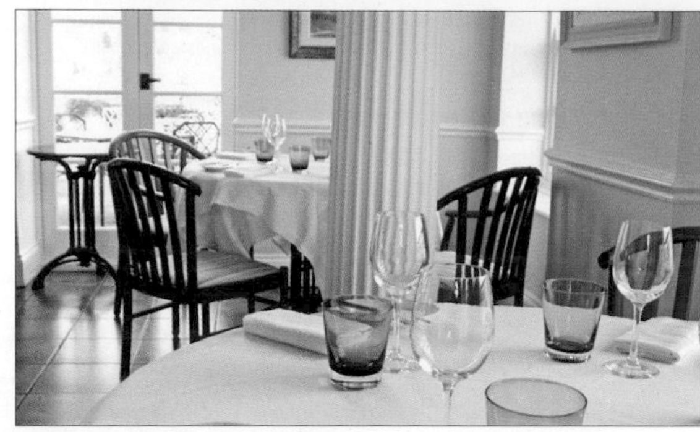

tel: 01452 740547 **Passage Rd GL2 7JR**
email: oldpassage@btconnect.com **web:** www.theoldpassage.com
dir: *M5 junct 13/A38 towards Bristol, 2nd right to Frampton-on-Severn, over canal, bear left, follow to river*

Seafood specialities overlooking a bend in the Severn

On the bank of the River Severn, The Old Passage is a white-painted restaurant with rooms. The kitchen's focus is on seafood, with choices like wild turbot fillet counterbalanced by oxtail, served with braised pak choi, celeriac purée and girolles or hake with saffron and tarragon butter, potato, fennel and tomato. Lobster comes natural, grilled or thermidor, and starters range from fish soup with the usual trimmings to seared scallops interestingly served with crispy pork terrine, apple purée and rum-soaked raisins. A meaty main might be roast breast and confit leg of pheasant with vegetables and puddings could be raspberry mousse with raspberry and champagne jelly and white chocolate sorbet.

Chef Mark Redwood, Jon Lane **Seats** 50, Pr/dining room 12 **Times** 12-2/7-9.30, Closed 25-26 Dec, Mon, D Sun, Tue-Wed (Jan-Feb) **Prices** Fixed L 2 course fr £16.50, Starter £8-£13.50, Main £19.50-£50 **Wines** 29 bottles over £30, 16 bottles under £30, 15 by glass **Parking** 40 **Notes** ALC menu only, Sunday L, Vegetarian available, Children L only

BARNSLEY Map 5 SP00

Barnsley House

◎◎ Modern European

tel: 01285 740000 **GL7 5EE**
email: info@barnsleyhouse.com **web:** www.barnsleyhouse.com
dir: *4m N of Cirencester on B4425 between Cirencester & Burford*

Uncomplicated country cooking overlooking the kitchen garden

The restaurant at 17th-century Barnsley House is named the Potager, after the ornamental and vegetable garden designed in the 1950s by Rosemary Verey, which it overlooks. Using fresh produce from the garden. Perfectly cooked lamb sweetbreads in a noteworthy jus are served with no more than morels and garden chard, or there might be smoked haddock and pea risotto. An Italian influence is evident in some dishes: a starter of Vincisgrassi, for instance, based on an 18th-century recipe for baked pasta with Parma ham, porcini mushrooms and truffles. End with a fruity pudding such as passionfruit tart with tangy lime syrup and mascarpone, or roasted figs with Venetian-style rice pudding.

Chef Francesco Volgo **Seats** 40, Pr/dining room 14 **Times** 12-2.30/7-9.30 **Prices** Fixed L 2 course £24, Starter £6-£13, Main £9-£31, Dessert £7 **Wines** 66 bottles over £30, 25 bottles under £30, 12 by glass **Parking** 25 **Notes** Sunday L, Vegetarian available, Children 12/14 L/D

BOURTON-ON-THE-WATER Map 10 SP12

The Dial House

◎◎◎ Classical French, Modern V

tel: 01451 822244 **High St GL54 2AN**
email: info@dialhousehotel.com **web:** www.dialhousehotel.com
dir: *Take A429 Cirencester Rd into Bourton. Dial House is set back from High St*

Amazingly fine food in a honeypot village

A mellow stone house dating from 1698 in a chocolate-box (and hyper-touristy) Cotswolds village may not be the most obvious place you'd come looking for top-drawer modern cooking, but prepare for a treat at the Dial House. There are large stone fireplaces as reminders of its antiquity, while the intimate dining room provides an elegant backdrop, and the staff deliver fine-tuned service with oodles of charm and personality. The kitchen takes its cue from France, yet also flies the flag for British ingredients, seeking out the best produce, much of it locally, and using it inspirationally. There are no duff ideas here, witness a starter of Portland white crab cannelloni rolled in apple jelly, which comes with brown crab emulsion, apple textures (diced, gel and sorbet) and sorrel. Techniques are spot on, and imaginative, confidently handled combinations extend to main courses – poached fillet of brill, of superb quality, with sautéed spinach, a deeply-flavoured oxtail raviolo, roasted salsify, cep purée and tempura samphire. Local meat fans might find poached and roast fillet of Cotswold beef with slow-braised short rib, shallot purée and potato gratin. To finish, a perfectly risen Valrhona chocolate soufflé married with pistachio ice cream and hot chocolate sauce is a match made in heaven.

Chef Paul Nicholson **Seats** 30, Pr/dining room 16 **Times** 12-2/7-9, Closed 1st wk Jan, Sun-Mon **Prices** Fixed D 3 course fr £59, Tasting menu fr £79 **Wines** 45 bottles over £30, 25 bottles under £30, 15 by glass **Parking** 15 **Notes** Tasting menu 5 course, Afternoon tea £22, Children 10 yrs+

BUCKLAND Map 10 SP03

Buckland Manor

◎◎◎ British NOTABLE WINE LIST

tel: 01386 852626 **WR12 7LY**
email: info@bucklandmanor.com **web:** www.bucklandmanor.co.uk
dir: *2m SW of Broadway. Take B4632 signed Cheltenham, then take turn for Buckland. Hotel through village on right*

Confident modern cooking in a grand country house

Built in the 13th century next to the village church and set in 10 acres of grounds, classic Cotswold country-house hotels don't come more impressive than Buckland Manor. The inside meets expectations, too, with wooden panels, mullioned windows, stone fireplaces and fine old furniture all present and correct. Formality is observed (jackets in the dining room please, gents) and the restaurant toes the style line, with its white-painted panels, portraits on the walls and elegantly dressed tables setting the tone. Headed-up by Will Guthrie, the kitchen strikes a more contemporary note, delivering pin-sharp modern British food that is creative and well judged without falling over itself to be cutting edge. Halibut is smoked on the premises and arrives in a first course with tomato and cumin bavarois, curry crackers, pickled mooli radish and coriander seed dressing. Next up, a visually striking main course delivers pan-fried hake partnered with black squid ink pappardelle, charred broccoli and caviar cream sauce, while meatier appetites might be assuaged by partridge breast and confit leg meat sausage with red onion and port purée and creamed leeks. For dessert, set chocolate cream is topped with praline for crunch, and matched with cherry sorbet, boozy griottine cherries and bubbly aerated chocolate.

Chef Will Guthrie **Seats** 40, Pr/dining room 14 **Times** 12.30-2/7-9 **Prices** Fixed L 2 course £24.50, Fixed D 3 course £67.50, Tasting menu £80 **Wines** 400 bottles over £30, 17 bottles under £30, 15 by glass **Parking** 20 **Notes** Tasting menu 7 course, Sunday L £32.50-£35, Vegetarian available, Children 8 yrs+

CHELTENHAM Map 10 SO92

The Beaufort Dining Room Ellenborough Park

Modern British V NOTABLE WINE LIST

tel: 01242 545454 **Southam Rd GL52 3NH**
email: info@ellenboroughpark.com **web:** www.ellenboroughpark.com
dir: *A46 right after 3m onto B4079, merges with A435, 4m, over 3 rdbts, left onto Southam Lane, right onto Old Road, right onto B4632, hotel on right*

High-gloss cooking in a luxurious Tudor mansion

Although the original house had been pottering along unexceptionably since the 1530s, Ellenborough really hit its stride when the first Earl of that ilk, erstwhile governor general of British India, moved himself and his wife into it 300 years later. The place itself is a sumptuous beauty in Cotswold honey, looking a little like an Oxford college, with a high-glitz panelled dining room, the Beaufort, at the centre of operations. Here, David Kelman explores the technical and expressive parameters of British modernism, in fixed-price menus of three, four or five courses. Opening with a salsify and artichoke salad with truffled lentils and crispy cabbage, proceedings roll on with a serving of Coln Valley smoked salmon sharply dressed in capers, gherkins and shallots, with puréed parsley and an egg yolk cooked sous-vide. At main course, there are high-grade meats such as Hereford Cross beef aged for 28 days, or Creedy Carver duck breast with gem lettuce and shimejis, the leg meat fashioned into a cottage pie with smoked potato. Desserts like a baked Alaska made with blood orange, vanilla and poppy seeds could be the harbinger of a final foray into the cheeseboard, accompanied by a jelly of celery, apple and thyme.

Chef David Kelman **Seats** 60, Pr/dining room 20 **Times** 7-10, Closed Mon, L Tue-Sat, D Sun **Prices** Fixed L 2 course fr £25, Fixed D 3 course fr £55, Tasting menu fr £75 **Wines** 510 bottles over £30, 25 bottles under £30, 12 by glass **Parking** 130 **Notes** Sunday L £25-£30, Children welcome

Le Champignon Sauvage

– see below

The Curry Corner

Bangladeshi, Indian

tel: 01242 528449 **133 Fairview Rd GL52 2EX**
email: info@thecurrycorner.com
dir: *From A40 turn right into Hewlett Rd, at mini-rdbt turn left*

Genuine Bangladeshi home cooking

This restaurant occupies a white Georgian townhouse on the edge of Cheltenham's main shopping area. It has a chic, contemporary look, featuring ruby-red wall coverings offset by carvings. Bangladeshi home cooking is the theme, with spices flown in from India, Morocco and Turkey, and fresh produce sourced locally. Dishes offer layers of flavours, from starters of strongly spiced Bengali-style crab samosas with potato and red onion to main courses such as monkfish strips and king prawns in saffron cream curry with screwpine, coconut, ginger and curry leaves. Breads, vegetables and chutneys are all good, as are attractively presented desserts like coconut sorbet with raspberry coulis.

Chef Shamsul & Monrusha Krori **Seats** 50 **Times** 5.30-10.30, Closed 25 Dec, Mon **Prices** Starter £4.95-£8.95, Main £10.95-£15.95, Dessert £6.95-£7.50 **Wines** 14 bottles over £30, 27 bottles under £30, 9 by glass **Notes** Vegetarian available, Children welcome

Le Champignon Sauvage

CHELTENHAM Map 10 SO92

Modern French
tel: 01242 573449 **24-28 Suffolk Rd GL50 2AQ**
email: mail@lechampignonsauvage.co.uk
dir: *S of town centre, on A40, near Cheltenham College*

Cooking from the heart in a civilised setting

It won't be long before we can count on the fingers of two hands the number of benchmark restaurants surviving from the first great post-war heyday of British dining in the 1980s. David and Helen Everitt-Matthias have been presiding here close on 30 years, and the place still feels as freshly minted as when it first emerged. The room is as quietly refined as ever, hung with striking modern artworks, its chatelaine Helen overseeing with gracious ease. David's cooking retains its cutting edge, marrying new techniques to classical French roots, coaxing soul-stirring depths of intensity out of often comparatively humble ingredients, and according the less humble their due dignity. It takes a particularly confident kind of ingenuity to think of stuffing a pig trotter with ox tongue and snails, and even more panache to bring it off, saucing it with roasted garlic cream for a bold, resonant opener. Butter-poached lobster is lured towards the land too with Jerusalem artichoke, pear and sorrel, and the same robustness is applied to main fish dishes that might take in halibut with cep cream, baby parsnips, chestnuts and black kale. Game is regally served, red-legged partridge attended by potato and fig terrine, Morteau sausage and kohlrabi choucroute. Then there are desserts designed to create memorable waves, as when rhubarb and hibiscus and their combined sorbet adorn a custard made with duck eggs, or bergamot parfait has its aromatic quotient boosted with liquorice cream and orange jelly.

Chef David Everitt-Matthias **Seats** 40 **Times** 12.30-1.15/7.30-8.30, Closed 10 days Xmas, 3 wks Jun, Sun-Mon **Prices** Fixed L 2 course fr £26, Fixed D 3 course fr £32 **Wines** 88 bottles over £30, 35 bottles under £30, 14 by glass **Parking** Public car park (Bath Rd) **Notes** Fixed D Mon-Fri only, ALC 2/3 course £50/£63, Children welcome

The Greenway Hotel & Spa

Modern British, French V NOTABLE WINE LIST

tel: 01242 862352 **Shurdington GL51 4UG**
email: info@thegreenway.co.uk **web:** www.thegreenwayhotelandspa.com
dir: *3m S of Cheltenham on A46 (Stroud) & through Shurdington*

Refined modern cooking in the Cotswolds

With glorious grounds and an abundance of original features, this impeccable Elizabethan manor has all the attributes needed to make a fine country-house hotel. Add to those contemporary embellishments of a swish spa, elegant bedrooms and elegant dining options, and the package is complete. The main fine-dining Garden Restaurant impresses with its take on refined, modern British cooking. Start with crab and apple cannelloni, apple textures and brown crab mayo, perhaps moving on to grilled fillet of sea bass, fennel, chicory, baby leeks and vanilla pomme purée. For dessert, try blueberries as both soufflé and milkshake with clotted cream ice cream.

Chef Marcus McGuinness **Seats** 60, Pr/dining room 22 **Times** 12-2.30/7-9.30 **Prices** Prices not confirmed **Wines** 200 bottles over £30, 40 bottles under £30, 11 by glass **Notes** ALC 3 course £49.50, Sunday L, Children welcome

Hotel du Vin Cheltenham

British, French, European

tel: 01242 588450 **Parabola Rd GL50 3AQ**
email: info.cheltenham@hotelduvin.com **web:** www.hotelduvin.com
dir: *M5 junct 11, follow signs for city centre. At rdbt opposite Morgan Estate Agents take 2nd left, 200mtrs to Parabola Rd*

Bistro dining in Cheltenham's restaurant quarter

The restaurant at the Cheltenham branch of this popular hotel chain follows the usual bistro look of wooden floor, unclothed tables, banquettes and a wine-related theme of empty bottles, prints and memorabilia. The menu goes along the expected bistro route, while the kitchen employs premium ingredients and produces carefully-cooked, compelling dishes. Kick off with chicken liver parfait with raisin chutney and sourdough toast before roast rump of lamb dressed with chorizo and pesto served with broccoli and boulangère potatoes. Finish in true French style with lemon tart and raspberry sorbet. Plenty of wines are available by the glass from the exceptional list.

AA RESTAURANT OF THE YEAR FOR ENGLAND 2016–17

Lumière

Modern British V 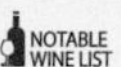

tel: 01242 222200 **Clarence Pde GL50 3PA**
email: info@lumiere.cc
dir: *Town centre, near bus station*

High-octane cooking from a hands-on chef

The discreet frontage is easy to miss on Clarence Parade, but look out for the restaurant's name etched onto the single window pane and a small awning over the door. Jon and Helen Howe's restaurant, with its gently contemporary interior and smart table settings, is one of the town's most alluring dining destinations, where everything from dynamic canapés (smoked eel and wasabi croquette, say) and breads (check out the amazing brown fig and raisin version) are made in-house. Jon runs the kitchen with verve, delivering a repertoire that reveals classical roots and an up-to-date approach. Every ingredient is on the plate for a reason, with every flavour and texture hitting home, and the food is very prettily arranged, too. A starter of diver-caught scallops, for example, arrives with a lovely glaze in the company of spiced pork belly and orange and star anise purée, while main-course Gigha halibut with oxtail croquette and chanterelles confirms the skilled hand at the stove. Cotswold fallow deer is a seasonal treat served up with heritage beetroots and a sauce enriched with chocolate, and a dessert of damson soufflé has local sloe gin poured into its heart at the table. Helen runs front-of-house with charm and confidence.

Chef Jon Howe **Seats** 25 **Times** 12-1.30/7-9, Closed 2 wks winter, 2 wks summer, Sun-Mon, L Tue-Thu **Prices** Fixed L 2 course £24, Fixed D 3 course £60, Tasting menu £65-£80 **Wines** 75 bottles over £30, 14 bottles under £30, 18 by glass **Parking** On street **Notes** Tasting menu 7/9 course, Children 8 yrs+

Monty's Brasserie

Modern British V

tel: 01242 227678 & 238811 **George Hotel, 41 St Georges Rd GL50 3DZ**
email: info@montysbraz.co.uk **web:** www.montysbraz.co.uk
dir: *M5 junct 11, follow signs to town centre. At lights (TGI Fridays) turn left onto Gloucester Rd. Straight on, at lights turn right onto St Georges Rd, Monty's 0.75m on left*

Smart seasonal brasserie cooking in stylish Grade II listed hotel

Situated in the heart of Cheltenham, this modern brasserie is part of the Grade II-listed George Hotel, built in the Georgian era. With bare-boarded floors, brown leather-look seats and unclothed tables, the friendly, uniformed staff add to the cheerful atmosphere. The kitchen takes sound seasonal ingredients, adding a degree of complication to dishes without pushing them too far. Seared Scottish scallops, for instance, come with crisp Parma ham, tomato and chorizo purée, sautéed courgettes and basil cress. A trio of Blythburgh pork might appear with apple and cider purée, and baby turnips. Finish with spiced apple tarte Tatin.

Chef Clemente Zamora **Seats** 40, Pr/dining room 32 **Times** 12-2/6-10, Closed 25-26 Dec **Prices** Fixed L 2 course £14.50, Fixed D 3 course £17, Starter £7-£10, Main £16-£26, Dessert £7-£8 **Wines** 17 bottles over £30, 25 bottles under £30, 7 by glass **Parking** 30 **Notes** Fixed D Sun-Thu 6-7pm, Sunday L £18-£22, Children welcome

CHIPPING CAMPDEN Map 10 SP13

The Kings

 Modern British V

tel: 01386 840256 **The Square, High St GL55 6AW**
email: info@kingscampden.co.uk **web:** www.kingscampden.co.uk
dir: *In centre of town square*

Uncomplicated British cooking on the square

A bow-windowed Georgian townhouse in Cotswold stone, The Kings stands proud on the town-centre square. British modernism is the kitchen's guidepost, so there might be wood pigeon breast with shallot cream, poached grapes and celery, or a creative salad of goats' curd with roast apple purée, walnuts and honey dressing. Main-course stone bass is timed spot-on and served with coco beans, brown shrimps, broccoli purée and lemon oil, while local meat fans might head for rump and crispy shoulder of Lighthorne lamb alongside celeriac, wild garlic, sheep's curd and hazelnut. In conclusion, bitter dark chocolate mousse and cocoa nib tuile are paired with the contrasting sharpness of blood orange sorbet.

Chef Ian Percival **Seats** 45, Pr/dining room 20 **Times** 12-2.30/6.30-9.30 **Prices** Fixed L 2 course £15.50-£17.50, Fixed D 3 course £32.50 **Wines** 25 bottles over £30, 22 bottles under £30, 10 by glass **Parking** 12 **Notes** Sunday L £16.50-£22.50, Children welcome

The Seagrave Arms

 Modern British

tel: 01386 840192 **Friday St GL55 6QH**
email: enquiries@theseagravearms.com **web:** www.seagravearms.com
dir: *A44 Oxford/Evesham, exit Broadway & follow B4632 towards Stratford-upon-Avon*

Cotswolds heartland village inn

Stone-built and four-square, the 400-year-old Seagrave is a Cotswolds inn of considerable character. Strong classic undertones are discernible beneath the modern British cooking style. An excellent line-up might be rabbit and Morteau sausage pie with cider gravy, well complemented by pickled mustard seeds, then slow-cooked, dry-aged beef rib with chips (the Seagrave's chips won a national award in 2015, by the way), carrots and smoked garlic purée, wrapping up with apple tart and vanilla ice cream. For a fish alternative, perhaps Cornish monkfish with beetroot, turnip, parsnip and pear cider sauce. A good selection of wines by the glass includes a sparkling white from Nyetimber's South Downs vineyard.

Three Ways House

Modern British

tel: 01386 438429 **Chapel Ln, Mickleton GL55 6SB**
email: reception@puddingclub.com **web:** www.threewayshousehotel.com
dir: *On B4632, in village centre*

More than just desserts at the home of the Pudding Club

This Cotswold-stone building dates back to 1870, but it was made world-famous in the 1980s with the formation of the Pudding Club. The Victorian hotel has oodles of period character, although the restaurant bucks the trend with a more contemporary look. The food is big-hearted British stuff, although the kitchen isn't afraid to look further afield for inspiration. Seared tuna, mango and chilli salsa is a typical starter, followed by roasted duck breast, bok choy and orange jus. Dessert has to be a steamed pud with custard or dark chocolate and hazelnut tart with vanilla ice cream.

Chef Tom Timms **Seats** 80, Pr/dining room 70 **Times** 12-2.30/7-9.30, Closed L Mon-Sat **Prices** Fixed L 2 course £15.50-£25, Fixed D 3 course £39 **Wines** 12 bottles over £30, 31 bottles under £30, 13 by glass **Parking** 37, On street **Notes** Pudding Club places £37, Sunday L £22.50-£26.75, Vegetarian available, Children welcome

CIRENCESTER Map 5 SP00

Jesse's Bistro

Modern British

tel: 01285 641497 & 07496 057266 **14 Blackjack St GL7 2AA**
email: info@jessesbistro.co.uk **web:** www.jessesbistro.co.uk
dir: *In town centre between the parish church & Roman Museum, behind Jesse Smith the Butchers*

Resourceful international cooking behind the butchers

Tucked into a brick-paved back alley in the town centre, the bistro has an old beamed interior and a British menu that makes excursions to the Mediterranean and East Asia. First up might be Serrano ham with salami, figs and pine nuts in sherry dressing, or perhaps a well-risen twice-baked cheese soufflé with poached pear and caramelised walnuts. Follow with a seafood main of Duart salmon and tiger prawns in soy and ginger broth, with crispy noodles, brown rice and bok choy, or there might be Gatcombe lamb rack and braised belly with bubble-and-squeak and baby turnips. Dark chocolate cheesecake with malted-milk Malteser ice cream makes a great finish.

Chef David Witnall **Seats** 55, Pr/dining room 12 **Times** 11.45-3/6.45-10, Closed D Sun-Mon **Prices** Fixed L 2 course £19.50, Starter £6-£13.50, Main £14.50-£28.50, Dessert £8 **Wines** 35 bottles over £30, 25 bottles under £30, 18 by glass **Parking** Old station car park **Notes** Sunday L, Vegetarian available, Children welcome

See advert opposite

CLEARWELL Map 4 SO50

Tudor Farmhouse Hotel & Restaurant

Modern British

tel: 01594 833046 **High St GL16 8JS**
email: info@tudorfarmhousehotel.co.uk **web:** www.tudorfarmhousehotel.co.uk
dir: *Off A4136 onto B4228, through Coleford, turn right into Clearwell, hotel on right just before War Memorial Cross*

Old and new ideas in the Forest of Dean

The name reveals all, although the charm-laden grey stone building looks a little more grand country cottage than former farmstead. Some old pub favourites turn up for starters such as corned beef hash with beans and brown sauce, or you might prefer honey-roast parsnip soufflé with blue cheese crumble and a sesame tuile. Mains look beyond British shores for Moroccan-spiced rump and braised shoulder of lamb with toasted couscous, preserved lemon, apricot and almonds, while the oxtail-and-fish modern classic is given an outing here with plaice, sprout tops and burnt cucumber in red wine. The signature dessert is rich chocolate cake with stout ale ice cream and malted honeycomb.

COLEFORD Map 4 SO51

The Miners Country Inn

Modern British, Traditional V

tel: 01594 836632 **Chepstow Rd, Sling GL16 8LH**
email: admin@theminerssling.co.uk **web:** www.theminerssling.co.uk
dir: *Phone for directions*

Top-quality ingredients in West Country orientated food pub

The Miners is a family-run dining pub in a tiny village in the Forest of Dean. Beamed ceilings and stone floors come as standard, while the restaurant is simply but tastefully decorated. A daily-changing menu selects from the best local produce available. Starters include a generous slab of flavour-packed chicken and wild mushroom terrine with mango and cumin compôte, and fishcakes with tomato and chilli jam. Among main courses, try roast belly pork, soft and tender, on mash with a slice of chorizo finished with creamy cider sauce, with beer-battered haddock with chips for traditionalists. Don't pass on desserts such as banana and toffee brioche pudding with banana ice cream.

Chef Steven Jenkins **Seats** 50 **Times** 12-3/5.30-11 **Prices** Fixed L 2 course £9.95, Starter £2.95-£8.50, Main £9.95-£19.95, Dessert £4.95-£7 **Wines** 2 bottles over £30, 10 bottles under £30 **Parking** 40 **Notes** Mon D pot luck half price menu, Sat D 2 steaks & wine £28.95, Sunday L £8.95-£9.95, Children welcome

CORSE LAWN Map 10 SO83

Corse Lawn House Hotel

 British, French V NOTABLE WINE LIST

tel: 01452 780771 **GL19 4LZ**
email: enquiries@corselawn.com **web:** www.corselawn.com
dir: *5m SW of Tewkesbury on B4211, in village centre*

Inspired menus in an appealing rural setting

The red brick house dates from the Queen Anne period and stands on the village green in front of a large pond where coaches and their horses were once scrubbed clean. Run by the Hine Cognac family since 1978, it's full of old-school charm. In the smart principal dining room, a classic modern British menu makes good use of trusted local supplies, adding Cornish scallops for a starter with black pudding, pancetta and pumpkin. The well-made wild duckling of strong flavour comes with braised red cabbage, crab apples and duck-fat potato fondant, while tonka pannacotta with poached plum and vividly intense damson sorbet makes an inspired finale.

Chef Martin Kinahan **Seats** 50, Pr/dining room 28 **Times** 12-2/7-9.30, Closed 24-26 Dec **Prices** Fixed L 2 course £22.50, Fixed D 3 course £33.50, Starter £6.95-£12.95, Main £17.95-£25.95, Dessert £6.95-£8.95 **Wines** 220 bottles over £30, 80 bottles under £30, 10 by glass **Parking** 60 **Notes** Sunday L £25.50, Children welcome

DAYLESFORD Map 10 SP22

Daylesford Farm Café

 Modern British

tel: 01608 731700 **GL56 0YG**
email: thefarm@daylesfordorganic.com
dir: *From Cheltenham take A40 & A436 through Stow-on-the Wold, follow signs to Daylesford farmshop*

Organic produce cooked with flair in converted barn

On the Gloucestershire farmland that spawned a mini-empire, the Daylesford Farmshop and Café occupies a smartly converted barn with a New England finish and an open-to-view kitchen. The food makes a virtue of simplicity, with quality ingredients allowed to shine. A first-course chicken liver parfait served in a Kilner jar has fabulous depth of flavour and comes with home-made ciabatta, or go for barley risotto with steamed celeriac, cavolo nero and pumpkin seed pesto. Venison pappardelle with woodland mushrooms and parmesan is a memorable pasta dish, and the finishing flourish could be deeply rich chocolate nemesis with vanilla ice cream.

EBRINGTON Map 10 SP14

The Ebrington Arms

 Modern British NOTABLE WINE LIST

tel: 01386 593223 **GL55 6NH**
email: reservations@ebringtonarms.co.uk **web:** www.theebringtonarms.co.uk
dir: *From Chipping Campden take B4035 towards Shipston-on-Stour, left to Ebrington*

Classic village inn with a modern menu

Still very much a pub, and right in the heart of the village by the green, the Ebrington has served its community for several hundred years, as is evident from its copious oak beams and flagged floors. The menu takes a contemporary line of original modern dishes, and there are daily specials and pub classics too. Start with torched fillet of mackerel in dashi broth, with avocado, green strawberries and borage, before seared steak and braised brisket with truffled macaroni cheese and roasted greens. On-trend ingredients keep things rocking through to tonka pannacotta with grapefruit jam, pistachio cake and blood orange ice cream.

Chef Ben Dulley **Seats** 50, Pr/dining room 30 **Times** 12-2.30/6-9.30, Closed 25 Dec **Prices** Starter £6-£8, Main £13-£22, Dessert £6-£8 **Wines** 22 bottles over £30, 40 bottles under £30, 10 by glass **Parking** 13 **Notes** Midwk L £8.50, Early bird Mon-Thu 6-7pm 2 course+wine £29, Sunday L £20-£25, Vegetarian available, Children welcome

GLOUCESTER Map 10 SO81

Hatton Court

 Classic British, French V

tel: 01452 617412 **Upton Hill, Upton St Leonards GL4 8DE**
email: res@hatton-court.co.uk **web:** www.hatton-court.co.uk
dir: *Phone for directions*

Modern British repertoire in creeper-covered country house

A country-house hotel not far from the M5, Hatton Court is smothered with climbing foliage, its little windows barely peeping through the green. The formal dining room is kitted out with linen-clad tables, wood panelling and full-drop windows at one end. Here, the modern British repertoire begins with a clutch of scallops in a light, coriandery curry emulsion with the requisite cauliflower purée and a scatter of raisins. Main course might be a pair of pork cuts, the loin and cheek, with some black pudding done up in a cabbage leaf. Desserts offer some fanciful ideas too, such as, perhaps, a tropical lattice with passionfruit and guava ice pops and passionfruit fool.

Chef Leon Rook **Seats** 75, Pr/dining room 50 **Times** 12-10, All-day dining **Prices** Fixed L 2 course fr £12, Fixed D 3 course £25-£40, Tasting menu £49 **Wines** 30 bottles over £30, 12 bottles under £30, 8 by glass **Parking** 100 **Notes** Afternoon tea fr £10, Sunday L, Children welcome

The Wharf House Restaurant with Rooms

 Contemporary British

tel: 01452 332900 **Over GL2 8DB**
email: enquiries@thewharfhouse.co.uk **web:** www.thewharfhouse.co.uk
dir: *From Over rdbt take A40 westbound to Ross-on-Wye, 1st right in 50 yds*

Appealing cooking in a former lock house by the Severn

The Wharf House overlooks a canal basin, and there are plenty of watery walks nearby. Eating out on the terrace might appeal, while the restaurant is an inviting prospect. 'We strive to work with the best of local suppliers,' declares the menu, and the produce benefits from modern treatments. Honey-roasted figs accompany air-cured ham and piccalilli, and chicken breast is stuffed with spinach, goats' cheese and sun-dried tomato and plated with roasted tomatoes, tomato chutney and smoked garlic potato purée. The fish of the day is always an option, and you could finish with exemplary rhubarb and ginger crumble with ginger ice cream.

Chef Stewart Brown, David Penny **Seats** 40 **Times** 12-close, All-day dining, Closed 22 Dec-8 Jan, Sun-Mon **Prices** Tasting menu £39.99, Starter £5.99-£8.99, Main £13.99-£22.99, Dessert £4.99-£6.50 **Wines** 24 bottles over £30, 25 bottles under £30, 7 by glass **Parking** 32 **Notes** Tasting menu 6 course, Vegetarian available, Children welcome

LOWER SLAUGHTER Map 10 SP12

The Slaughters Country Inn

◎◎ Modern British

tel: 01451 822143 **GL54 2HS**
email: info@theslaughtersinn.co.uk **web:** www.theslaughtersinn.co.uk
dir: *Exit A429 at 'The Slaughters' sign, between Stow-on-the-Wold & Bourton-on the-Water. In village centre*

Contemporary classic dishes in a fine-looking country hotel

This artfully-modernised, 17th-century Cotswold-stone inn makes good use of its riverside terrace in this peaceful village. In the 1920s the building was a crammer school for Eton College, thus it now has Eton's Restaurant, whose mullioned windows, bare polished-wood or pewter tables and stuffed fish give a country-house feel. Edging occasionally into pub grub territory – the modern British menu also covers the bar – there are seasonal soups of the day, roast plaice with green beans, capers, and brown shrimp and herb butter, and lemon cheesecake with pineapple and mint salad. And, no surprise, the casually dressed staff also serve Eton Mess.

Chef Chris Fryer **Seats** Pr/dining room 30 **Times** 12-3/6.30-9, Closed L Mon-Sat **Prices** Prices not confirmed **Wines** 15 bottles over £30, 10 bottles under £30, 8 by glass **Parking** 40 **Notes** Afternoon tea, Sunday L, Vegetarian available, Children welcome

The Slaughters Manor House

◎◎◎ Modern British V

tel: 01451 820456 **GL54 2HP**
email: info@slaughtersmanor.co.uk **web:** www.slaughtersmanor.co.uk
dir: *Off A429, signed 'The Slaughters'. 0.5m into village on right*

Contemporary cooking in an elegant Cotswolds hotel

Lower Slaughter Manor looks lovelier than ever since reopening in the spring of 2016 after a major refurb, and it even sports a new name. The new look has 500 years of history to live up to, and the shell of the place of course remains intact – an effortlessly charming Cotswold manor in a village unravaged by time. The dining room looks out on to the grounds through French windows, and now extends into part of the original chapel while retaining a large arched fireplace. The cooking keeps its contemporary edge, bringing prime materials together in fascinating counterpoint, and offering presentations of impeccable elegance. After lobster ravioli with rock melon, charred radicchio and basil, or curry-spiced marinated duck liver with apple and pickled mustard seeds, come truly eye-catching main-course meats – perhaps teriyaki Cotswold kid goat with fennel and pineapple. Technique is compelling throughout, as when sea bass arrives with intense oyster pannacotta, lime and cucumber. It all concludes in triumph with exotic flavours to the fore in lime yogurt mousse, scented with blood orange, rose and menthol, or whipped pistachio cream with matcha green tea, honey and bitter chocolate. The seven-course taster offers a dazzling circuit of the kitchen's abilities.

Chef Nik Chappell **Seats** 48, Pr/dining room 24 **Times** 12.30-2/6.30-9.30 **Prices** Fixed D 3 course £65, Tasting menu £80 **Wines** 180 bottles over £30, 19 bottles under £30, 9 by glass **Parking** 30 **Notes** Afternoon tea, Sunday L £28.50-£35.50, Children welcome

MORETON-IN-MARSH Map 10 SP23

Manor House Hotel

Modern British V

tel: 01608 650501 **High St GL56 0LJ**
email: info@manorhousehotel.info **web:** www.cotswold-inns-hotels.co.uk/manor
dir: *Off A429 at south end of town*

Classy modern cooking in a 16th-century gem

On the High Street of a tourist honeypot village, this Cotswold-stone hotel dates from the reign of Henry VIII. Careful renovation and updating have brought it squarely into the 21st century while retaining original features. The Mulberry Restaurant is a stylish room with generously spaced, dressed tables, comfortable dining chairs and on-the-ball staff. The kitchen demonstrates sound talent and produces appealing dishes without over-complicating things, with a full-on tasting menu up for grabs. Begin with terrine of duck with poached rhubarb, move on to rump of Lighthorne lamb served with its kidney and slow-cooked shoulder, and finish with a luxurious dark chocolate fondant.

Chef Nick Orr **Seats** 45, Pr/dining room 120 **Times** 12-2.30/7-9.30, Closed L Mon-Sat **Prices** Tasting menu £60 **Wines** 28 bottles over £30, 48 bottles under £30, 21 by glass **Parking** 32 **Notes** Tasting menu 8 course, Fixed D 4 course £42.50, Sunday L £19.95-£22.50, Children 8 yrs+

Redesdale Arms

Modern NEW V

tel: 01608 650308 **High St GL56 0AW**
email: info@redesdalearms.com **web:** www.redesdalearms.com
dir: *On A429, 0.5m from rail station*

Relaxed dining in historical Cotswold inn

Dating from the 17th century, this inn has been sympathetically updated to give it a more contemporary edge. There are two dining rooms, one in a rear conservatory, the other overlooking the high street. A glance at the menu shows a kitchen seaming the modern British vein. Ham hock terrine with a hint of cheese has a good depth of flavour, attractively presented on a slate with piccalilli and crisp breads, and may precede tail of Cornish monkfish, accurately timed and seasoned, vibrant anchovy salsa a good foil, served with dauphinoise potatoes. End with something like white chocolate and raspberry crème brûlée with crisp, light and flaky almond twists.

Chef James Hitchman **Times** 12-2.30/6.30-9 **Prices** Starter £5.95-£12.95, Main £11.95-£25.95, Dessert £5.95-£6.95 **Wines** 10 bottles over £30, 20 bottles under £30, 13 by glass **Notes** Bistro menu (ex Tue, market day menu), Sunday L £12.95-£14.95, Children welcome

White Hart Royal Hotel

Traditional British

tel: 01608 650731 **High St GL56 0BA**
email: whr@bulldogmail.co.uk **web:** www.whitehartroyal.co.uk
dir: *In town centre*

Modern cooking in a Cotswold coaching inn

There's no shortage of period features to remind visitors of the long heritage of this building. The Courtyard restaurant – outside tables are a fair-weather treat – is a linen-free zone, the darkwood tables and bold colours creating a smart-casual space that will do for a special occasion or for when no excuse is needed. The menu takes a modern, brasserie-style tack in starters such as barbecue pulled pork croquette with Cajun-spiced baby corn and chipotle purée, or pan-seared scallops with curried lentil salad. Move on to main-course confit chicken thighs with rösti potatoes and desserts such as pistachio crème brûlée.

NAILSWORTH Map 4 ST89

Wild Garlic Restaurant and Rooms

Modern British V

tel: 01453 832615 **3 Cossack Square GL6 0DB**
email: info@wild-garlic.co.uk **web:** www.wild-garlic.co.uk
dir: *M4 junct 18. A46 towards Stroud. Enter Nailsworth, turn left at rdbt and then an immediate left. Restaurant opposite Britannia Pub*

Bountifully-inventive modern cooking in garlic country

So prolific is wild garlic around these parts that the Beardshalls named their stylish restaurant with rooms after it. Cotswold tapas are one of the dining options, but it's on the main menus that the kitchen really shows its paces. Start with creamed goats' cheese and celeriac cannelloni in warm walnut dressing, or a grilled mackerel with smoked potato salad and shellfish sauce. Move on to shoulder of lamb with salt-baked parsnips, burnt onion and gremolata, or roasted brill with artichokes, wild mushrooms and spinach in red wine reduction. Local Woefuldane cheeses are enthusiastically supported if you don't fancy deep-fried rice pudding with poached Asian fruits in coconut sauce.

Chef Matthew Beardshall **Seats** 42 **Times** 12-2.30/7-9.30, Closed Mon-Tue, D Sun **Prices** Tasting menu £55-£80, Starter £7.95-£9.95, Main £15.50-£27.50, Dessert £4.95-£7.95 **Wines** 28 bottles over £30, 32 bottles under £30, 13 by glass **Parking** NCP, parking on street **Notes** Tasting menu 6 course, Brunch £3.95-£8.95, Sunday L £15.95, Children welcome

NETHER WESTCOTE Map 10 SP22

The Feathered Nest Country Inn

– see opposite

NEWENT Map 10 SO72

Three Choirs Vineyards

Modern British

tel: 01531 890223 **GL18 1LS**
email: ts@threechoirs.com **web:** www.three-choirs-vineyards.co.uk
dir: *2m N of Newent on B4215, follow brown tourist signs*

Up-to-the-minute cooking on a pedigree wine estate

Three Choirs estate also incorporates this hotel, where there are regular barbecues on the Vine Room terrace, and the up-to-the-minute cooking draws inspiration from other European wine-producing countries. Roast courgette and lemon risotto might precede a laden sharing platter of seafood, or something like black-eyed bean cassoulet with cumin mushrooms and pilaf. Top-gear meats are carefully sourced, as for cannon of lamb in salsa verde with roast garlic and pomme purée, while 21-day aged local beef fillet comes with all the expected trimmings, down to a peppercorned whisky sauce. Finish with white chocolate crème brûlée and raspberry shortbread, or the evergreen sticky toffee pudding and custard.

Chef Dan Tucker **Seats** 50, Pr/dining room 20 **Times** 12-2/7-9, Closed Xmas, 1st 2 wks Jan, L Mon **Prices** Fixed L 2 course £19.50, Starter £6.70-£12.95, Main £16.50-£28, Dessert £6.50-£8.50 **Wines** 10 bottles over £30, 24 bottles under £30, 14 by glass **Parking** 50 **Notes** Sunday L £24.50, Vegetarian available, Children welcome

The Feathered Nest Country Inn

NETHER WESTCOTE **Map 10 SP22**

Modern British

tel: 01993 833030 **OX7 6SD**
email: info@thefeatherednestinn.co.uk
web: www.thefeatherednestinn.co.uk
dir: *On A424 between Burford & Stow-on-the-Wold, signed*

A gem of a country pub in a beautiful Cotswold village

Originally an old malthouse in an Area of Outstanding Natural Beauty with wonderful views over the Evenlode Valley, the Feathered Nest has come a long way since Tony and Amanda Timmer took over a down-at-heel pub and treated it to a classy makeover. Nowadays, the Nest combines the functions of country pub, upmarket restaurant and hotel. The bar is a real feature, with saddles as bar stools, and elsewhere flagstone floors, beams and an inglenook add character, while the restaurant is on two levels. The sophisticated cooking really sets the place apart, as this kitchen produces vibrant, balanced and inventive dishes based on sound techniques and quality seasonal produce. Wild sea trout is served with elderflower gel and flowers, gooseberries, Avruga caviar and cucamelon (combining the flavours of cucumber and lime) to make a light, tasty and diverting summer starter, while winter may bring on consommé with game tortellini, buckwheat, Madeira and truffle. Main courses might take in rack of lamb, of stunning flavour, in a light crust with broad beans, watercress and pine nuts with exemplary sauces of black garlic and lamb jus, or you might look to the charcoal grill for a no-nonsense rib-eye steak with skinny chips, béarnaise sauce and bone marrow. Fish fans could opt for equally well-considered turbot fillet with brown shrimp tortellini, chanterelles, samphire and borage. Puddings make an impact too: consider half a coconut shell containing lime-infused coconut cream with tapioca and diced mango accompanied by mango ice cream, or an ethereally light morello cherry soufflé with Valrhona Manjari chocolate sauce. With over 240 bins covering the Old and New Worlds, the wine list is a pretty impressive piece of work too.

Chef Kuba Winkowski **Seats** 60, Pr/dining room 14
Times 12-2.30/6.30-9.30, Closed 25 Dec, Mon, D Sun **Prices** Fixed L 2 course £24, Starter £10-£18, Main £23-£33, Dessert £10-£12
Wines 215 bottles over £30, 29 bottles under £30, 19 by glass
Parking 45 **Notes** Sunday L £23-£33, Vegetarian available, Children welcome

STOW-ON-THE-WOLD Map 10 SP12

The Kings Head Inn

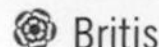 British

tel: 01608 658365 **The Green, Bledington OX7 6XQ**
email: info@kingsheadinn.net **web:** www.kingsheadinn.net
dir: *On B4450, 4m from Stow-on-the-Wold*

Refined pub fare in an atmospheric village inn

This mellow stone Cotswolds pub comes with a classic bar with wobbly floors, log fires, head-skimming beams and an unbuttoned dining room with solid oak tables on a flagstone floor. It's a textbook example of a switched-on village pub that is still the local boozer while the cooking is a definite notch or two up. A modern British menu showcases local free-range and organic materials, starting with devilled duck hearts on fried bread, then pan-fried pork belly with pig's cheek fritters, pickled carrots, spring cabbage and a cider reduction. Finish with warm carrot cake with sweet cream cheese, and carrot sorbet and sauce.

Old Stocks Inn

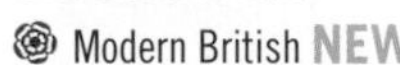 Modern British NEW

tel: 01451 830666 **The Square GL54 1AP**
email: info@oldstocksinn.com **web:** www.oldstocksinn.com
dir: *Phone for directions*

Vivid modern cooking in an updated Cotswolds inn

An appealing package of bright and funky modern decor, a fun ambience, an array of regionally-brewed craft beers and an inventive take on contemporary pub grub makes this revamped 17th-century Cotswolds inn worth checking out. Grilled and cured salmon with wasabi, orange purée and edible flowers is a lively opener. Move on to wild boar with a black pudding croquette, artichoke, crackling and apple, or you could look to the grill for a rib-eye steak with the hearty accompaniments of cep and truffle butter, bone marrow and potato rösti. Pudding delivers more deep comforts via a decadently rich chocolate torte with caramel cream.

Chef Wayne Sullivan **Seats** Pr/dining room **Times** 12-2.30/6.30-9 **Prices** Fixed L 2 course £16.95, Starter £6.50-£7, Main £14-£25, Dessert £6.50-£11.50 **Wines** 7 bottles over £30, 22 bottles under £30, 12 by glass **Notes** Afternoon tea Fri-Sat £18-£25, Vegetarian available

The Porch House

Modern British

tel: 01451 870048 **Digbeth St GL54 1BN**
email: book@porch-house.co.uk **web:** www.porch-house.co.uk
dir: *Phone for directions*

Historic inn with a classy modern menu

Claiming to be the oldest inn in England, the original building has been dated to AD 947, although a 21st-century refurbishment has matched its undoubted period charm. The bar is stocked with real ales, while the restaurant turns out some impressive modern British dishes. Twice-baked cheddar soufflé with leeks in grain mustard sauce packs a good flavour punch, followed by Cotswold lamb rump served with Jerusalem artichokes and green beans in a light lamb jus. Among desserts there might be rich chocolate mousse served warm with a sharp counterpoint of raspberry sorbet. There are sandwiches and sharing boards, too, alongside bar staples like grilled pork chops and sirloin steaks.

Chef Rob Chasteauneuf **Seats** 40, Pr/dining room 12
Times 12-2.30/6.30-9.30, Closed L Mon-Sat (Conservatory open), D Sun (Conservatory open) **Prices** Prices not confirmed **Wines** 13 bottles over £30, 26 bottles under £30, 11 by glass **Parking** 4 **Notes** Sunday L, Vegetarian available, Children welcome

Wyck Hill House Hotel & Spa

Modern British

tel: 01451 831936 **Burford Rd GL54 1HY**
email: info.wyckhillhouse@wyckhillhousehotel.co.uk **web:** www.wyckhillhousehotel.co.uk
dir: *A429 for Cirencester, pass through 2 sets of lights in Stow-on-the-Wold, at 3rd set of lights bear left signed Burford, then A424 signed Stow-on-the-Wold, hotel 7m on left*

Stylish contemporary cooking in smart Cotswolds hotel

With 100 acres of fabulous grounds, green-and-pleasant views over the Cotswold Hills and Windrush Valley, an oak-panelled bar and a glitzy spa, Wyck Hill House is a place to pamper yourself in. You might start with game terrine with fig chutney, black pudding biscotti and apple balsamic, and move on to main courses put together with fine-tuned precision, perhaps a full-bore partnership of Herefordshire beef with an ox cheek pithivier, dauphinoise potatoes, cep marmalade and Madeira jus. Rhubarb and custard might get a contemporary makeover for dessert.

Chef Mark Jane **Seats** 50, Pr/dining room 120 **Times** 12.30-2/7-9.30 **Wines** 21 bottles over £30, 26 bottles under £30, 11 by glass **Parking** 120 **Notes** Sunday L £15.95-£19.95, Vegetarian available, Children welcome

STROUD Map 4 SO80

The Bear of Rodborough

British, International

tel: 01453 878522 **Rodborough Common GL5 5DE**
email: info@bearofrodborough.info **web:** www.cotswold-inns-hotels.co.uk/index.aspx
dir: *M5 junct 13, A419 to Stroud. Follow signs to Rodborough. Up hill, left at top at T-junct. Hotel on right*

Thoroughgoing British modernism in a (sort of) library

This Cotswold hotel with its own vineyard is a handsome white-fronted beast. A stone-walled dining room enjoys ravishing countryside views and a menu of thoroughgoing British modernism. Successes include tandoori-spiced mackerel with a salad of tomato, red onion and fennel, and mains such as lamb rump and sausage in tomato fondue with aubergine and yogurt dressing, or roast cod with curly kale in celery cream sauce. Dessert might be pleasantly aromatic jasmine and green tea delice with pistachio sponge and passionfruit sorbet.

Chef Felix Prem **Seats** 70, Pr/dining room 50 **Times** 12-2.30/7-9.30, Closed L Mon & Sat **Prices** Fixed D 3 course £36 **Wines** 18 over £30, 36 bottles under £30, 8 by glass **Parking** 100 **Notes** Sunday L £21.95, Vegetarian available, Children welcome

Burleigh Court Hotel

British, Mediterranean

tel: 01453 883804 **Burleigh, Minchinhampton GL5 2PF**
email: burleighcourt@aol.com **web:** www.burleighcourthotel.co.uk
dir: *2.5m SE of Stroud, off A419*

Refined dining in family-run, Georgian hotel

Built of Cotswold stone early in the 19th-century, this imposing, ivy-clad manor house overlooks Golden Valley and the River Frome. Its Georgian-style interior incorporates an oak-panelled lounge and a dining room with comfortable, high-backed chairs, large windows revealing a beautiful three-acre garden, and decorated with scenes of the house's history. The menu might suggest starting with sautéed Cornish scallops and garden pea purée, smoked bacon and shallot dressing, then cep-marinated tenderloin of Gatcombe Estate pork (they're the Princess Royal's pigs) with braised red cabbage, swede purée and apple and cider jus. And, for dessert, iced apricot parfait, apricot confit and crushed almonds.

Chef Adrian Jarrad **Seats** 34, Pr/dining room **Times** 12-2/7-9, Closed Xmas **Prices** Fixed L 2 course £21, Starter £5.75-£10.95, Main £16.95-£24, Dessert £7.50-£9.75 **Wines** 8 bottles over £30, 8 bottles under £30, 8 by glass **Parking** 28 **Notes** Afternoon tea, Sunday L £27, Vegetarian available, Children welcome

TETBURY Map 4 ST89

Calcot Manor

Modern British

tel: 01666 890391 **Calcot GL8 8YJ**
email: reception@calcotmanor.co.uk **web:** www.calcotmanor.co.uk
dir: *M4 junct 18, A46 towards Stroud. At x-rds junct with A4135 turn right, then 1st left*

Charming 14th-century Cotswold retreat with vibrant modern cuisine

Calcot Manor is a boutique-style hotel of Cotswold stone with a health spa and a light-filled restaurant called The Conservatory. The kitchen works around a repertoire of imaginative modern dishes, and flavours have real punch. Starter options might be seared scallops with confit pork belly and cauliflower and truffle purée, or gazpacho with a ricotta-stuffed courgette flower, a seared langoustine and a quail's egg. Main courses range from honey roast duck breast with dauphinoise, carrot purée and chicory to herb-crusted rack of lamb with boulangère potatoes, garlicky creamed green beans and an intense gravy. End with impeccable praline soufflé with banana ice cream and hot toffee sauce.

Chef Michael Benjamin **Seats** 72, Pr/dining room 16 **Times** 12-2/7-9.30, Closed D 25 Dec **Prices** Starter £9-£14, Main £14-£38, Dessert £8 **Wines** 58 bottles over £30, 25 bottles under £30, 25 by glass **Parking** 150 **Notes** Sunday L £23-£28, Vegetarian available, Children welcome

The Close Hotel

Modern British

tel: 01666 502272 **8 Long St GL8 8AQ**
email: info@theclose-hotel.com **web:** www.theclose-hotel.com
dir: *From M4 junct 17 onto A429 to Malmesbury. From M5 junct 14 onto B4509*

Creative cooking in a 16th-century house

The Close Hotel is a handsome 16th-century pile, boasting period details and contemporary elegance. There are two dining options in the form of a brasserie and fine-dining restaurant. Any sense of old-school solidity is avoided by painting the panels in restful, fashionable shades and keeping the tables free of heavy linen (the Adam ceiling remains to impress traditionalists). The modern British menu strikes the right balance in this setting. Begin with a creative combination of butter-poached langoustine tails with wild rice, move on to duck breast paired with pear and gingerbread, and finish with white chocolate 'fondant' with a hit of vodka.

Chef Peter Lias **Seats** 54, Pr/dining room 26 **Times** 12-3/6.30-9.30 **Prices** Fixed L 2 course fr £14.50, Fixed D 3 course fr £42, Tasting menu fr £60, Starter £6.50-£8.50, Main £14.50-£23.50, Dessert £6.50-£8.50 **Wines** 11 bottles over £30, 20 bottles under £30, 6 by glass **Parking** 18 **Notes** Sunday L £21.95-£23.95, Vegetarian available, Children welcome

Hare & Hounds Hotel

Modern British

tel: 01666 881000 **Westonbirt GL8 8QL**
email: reception@hareandhoundshotel.com **web:** www.cotswold-inns-hotels.co.uk
dir: *2.5m SW of Tetbury on A433*

Charming Cotswold hotel with confident team in the kitchen

The Beaufort Restaurant is the culinary heart of this Cotswold-stone hotel just outside Tetbury. To start, you might choose Coquilles St. Jacques – 3 or 4 seared scallops with a topping of duchess potatoes in a baked cheese and bacon sauce. A main course sees pork two ways with a slow-cooked pork belly presented alongside a pork fillet and various apple textures and mini fondant potato. Ice rhubarb parfait may be your choice of dessert, the sharpness of the fruit well matched by the sweetness of mini meringues. There's an excellent selection of homemade breads (including a Guinness soda bread) to accompany the meal.

THORNBURY Map 4 ST69

Ronnie's of Thornbury

Modern European

tel: 01454 411137 **11 St Mary St BS35 2AB**
email: info@ronnies-restaurant.co.uk
dir: *Phone for directions*

Modern European cooking in a 17th-century schoolhouse

This 17th-century building wears its contemporary look well: stone walls, beamed ceilings, wooden floors and neutral hues are pointed up by paintings and photos by West Country artists. You can kick start the day with coffee and eggs Benedict at Ronnie's, or round it off with an excellent dinner. That might open with lasagne of braised ox cheek with wild mushrooms, before a main of pork tenderloin with mustard mash and Savoy cabbage in cider jus, or lightly spiced smoked haddock kedgeree. Tempting desserts include vanilla cheesecake with tropical fruit salad and passionfruit sorbet, or you could go for a savoury finish with the splendid array of English artisan cheeses.

Chef Ron Faulkner **Seats** 45 **Times** 12-3/6-10, Closed 25-26 Dec, 1-8 Jan, Mon, D Sun **Prices** Fixed L 2 course £15, Tasting menu £22-£55, Starter £8.50-£12, Main £17-£24, Dessert £6.50-£8.50 **Wines** 40 bottles over £30, 28 bottles under £30, 15 by glass **Parking** Car park **Notes** Daily menu 2/3 course £15/£20, Tasting menu L/D 5/6 course, Sunday L £21-£25, Vegetarian available, Children welcome

Thornbury Castle

Modern British, European

tel: 01454 281182 **Castle St BS35 1HH**
email: info@thornburycastle.co.uk **web:** www.thornburycastle.co.uk
dir: *M5 junct 16, N on A38. 4m to lights, turn left. Follow brown historic castle signs. Restaurant behind St Mary's church*

Heritage and modernity side by side in a Tudor castle

Step inside the oak doors and you'll find everything expected of a 500-year-old castle: log fires, panelling, stone staircases, suits of armour, tapestries – the lot. The menu in the hexagonal Tower restaurant, with its arrow slits, is in the modern British pastoral style, with invention and heritage running side by side. Duck terrine – leg, breast and liver studded with segments of potato – with rhubarb jelly and crème fraîche makes a stunning starter, and might be followed by beautifully cooked fillet of brill with morels, asparagus, violet potatoes and red wine dressing. Bring the curtain down with rhubarb parfait with sweet beetroot, white chocolate and elderflower.

UPPER SLAUGHTER Map 10 SP12

Lords of the Manor

@@@ British, French NOTABLE WINE LIST

tel: 01451 820243 **GL54 2JD**
email: reservations@lordsofthemanor.com **web:** www.lordsofthemanor.com
dir: *Follow signs towards The Slaughters 2m W of A429. Hotel on right in centre of Upper Slaughter*

Finely crafted French-inflected cooking in a magical Cotswold hotel

The Manor looks a treat whatever the time of day, its honeyed stone basking in the Cotswold sun, lights blazing in the mullioned windows at evening beckoning wanderers in the grounds to come in and join the party. Staff are expertly attuned to enhance the ambience with a wise mix of professionalism and relaxing warmth – the knowledgeable sommelier is a particular asset – and the dining room forgoes vibrant patterning in favour of a soft-focus neutral look with double-clothed tables and a few pictures on plain white walls. The menus showcase Richard Picard-Edwards' accomplished style of multi-layered modern cooking. Confident balancing of all elements is in evidence in an opener of port-marinated duck livers with peach, almonds and chamomile jelly in gingerbread sauce, its sweetly inviting flavours matched with an inclusive glass of dessert wine. Things take a more savoury turn in mains such as loin and haunch of Salisbury Plain venison with creamed celeriac, pickled red cabbage purée and blackberries in sloe gin sauce, or roast fillet of sea bass with smoked sausage and borlotti beans in a poultry jus. A well-risen soufflé of prunes, served with Earl Grey ice cream and chocolate and bergamot ganache, concludes proceedings.

Chef Richard Picard-Edwards **Seats** 50, Pr/dining room 30
Times 12-2.30/6.45-9.30, Closed L Mon-Fri **Prices** Fixed D 3 course £72.50, Tasting menu £85 **Wines** 400 bottles over £30, 95 bottles under £30, 15 by glass **Parking** 40 **Notes** Sat L fixed price 2/3 course £29.50/£37.50, Sunday L £37.50-£49.50, Vegetarian available, Children 7 yrs+

WINCHCOMBE Map 10 SP02

The Lion Inn

@ Contemporary British NEW

tel: 01242 603300 **37 North St GL54 5PS**
email: reception@thelionwinchcombe.co.uk **web:** www.thelionwinchcombe.co.uk
dir: *Phone for directions*

Period inn with a contemporary attitude

A 15th-century coaching inn in the centre of town, The Lion looks the part with its Cotswold-stone facade and abundance of original features. Alongside the period appeal is a more a contemporary attitude that sees the beams painted in fashionable grey and some well-chosen shabby-chic furniture. The dining room at the back is full of rustic charm and offers a modern repertoire including lobster tortellini and crab ravioli in a shellfish bisque, followed by duo of duck (breast and confit leg) or whole lemon sole with samphire and beurre noisette. Finish with a sizable chunk of sticky toffee pudding.

Chef Alex Dimitri **Times** 12-3/6-9 **Prices** Starter £5.50-£10.50, Main £15-£20

Wesley House

@@ Modern European

tel: 01242 602366 **High St GL54 5LJ**
email: enquiries@wesleyhouse.co.uk **web:** www.wesleyhouse.co.uk
dir: *In centre of Winchcombe*

Impressive modern cooking in a period house

Wesley House occupies a 15th-century half-timbered property built for a merchant. Good-quality produce is the key to the kitchen's success as it works around a modern European repertory. Cured sea trout is served atop well-gauged horseradish cream garnished with pickled beetroot, making a successful starter, or there might be carpaccio with piquillo peppers and rocket. A mastery of techniques is on show in crisp-skinned breast of corn-fed chicken with rich thyme sauce, peas, broad beans and sauté potatoes or roast sea bream with chorizo, cauliflower and paprika butter. Breads and canapés are spot on, and vanilla pannacotta with a meringue nest of summer berries rounds things off nicely.

Chef Cedrik Rullier **Seats** 70, Pr/dining room 24 **Times** 12-2/7-9, Closed Mon, D Sun **Prices** Fixed L 2 course £20, Fixed D 3 course fr £28, Tasting menu fr £35, Starter £7-£9, Main £14-£26, Dessert £7.50-£8.50 **Wines** 43 bottles over £30, 48 bottles under £30, 11 by glass **Parking** In the square **Notes** Sunday L, Vegetarian available, Children welcome

See advert opposite

GREATER MANCHESTER

ALTRINCHAM Map 15 SJ78

Earle by Simon Rimmer

Modern European

tel: 0161 929 8869 **4 Cecil Rd, Hale WA15 9PA**
email: info@earlerestaurant.co.uk
dir: *M56 junct 7 onto A556 towards Altrincham, follow signs to Hale*

Vibrant modern cooking in village brasserie

Telly chef Simon Rimmer's buzzy contemporary brasserie is an effortlessly stylish spot. Herringbone wood panelling and floors, bare-brick walls and unclothed wooden tables look the part, and you may see the man himself at the stoves in the open-to-view kitchen. Get going with confit treacle-cured salmon with spring onion and pickled ginger, and follow with an on-trend dish like pulled pork shoulder with spiced red cabbage and whipped potato, or roasted cod given a Middle Eastern spin with baba ganoush, saffron potatoes and tabbouleh salad. Finish with ginger sponge with salted caramel sauce and stem ginger ice cream, or local artisan cheeses with home-made biscuits and carrot chutney.

Chef Simon Rimmer **Seats** 65, Pr/dining room 14
Times 12-2/5.30-9.30, Closed 25-26 Dec, 1 Jan, L Mon **Prices** Fixed L 2 course £15, Fixed D 3 course £20, Tasting menu £50-£75, Starter £4.50-£8.50, Main £13.50-£24, Dessert £5.50-£6.50 **Wines** 17 bottles over £30, 20 bottles under £30, 8 by glass **Parking** Station car park **Notes** Sunday L £13-£19, Vegetarian available, Children welcome

BURY Map 15 SD81

Red Hall Hotel

Modern British

tel: 01706 822476 **Manchester Rd, Walmersley BL9 5NA**
email: contact@oscarsattheredhall.co.uk **web:** www.oscars.red-hall.co.uk
dir: *Phone for directions*

Crowd-pleasing food and countryside views

The hotel's conservatory-style restaurant goes by the name of Oscar's, and looks rather swish with its contemporary silver and grey tones and herringbone parquet floors. The modern British menu begins with an opener of cigar-like rolls of tuna sashimi filled with dressed white crab meat and pointed up with pickled shallots, tomato concasse and cucumber. Asian accents appear again at mains, when five spice and honey are used to flavour roast duck breast matched with a croquette of confit leg meat, fondant potato, braised leeks, pak choi and celeriac purée, and black cherry jus. At the end, caramelised lemon tart comes with almond macaroons and raspberries.

Chef Chris M Haddock **Seats** 45, Pr/dining room **Times** 12-2.30/5.30-9.30 **Prices** Fixed L 2 course £12.95-£13.95, Starter £7.50-£8.50, Main £12.95-£25, Dessert £6.95-£7.95 **Wines** 27 bottles over £30, 25 bottles under £30, 6 by glass **Parking** 60 **Notes** Fizzy Fri (sharing platter + prosecco £20), Sunday L £15.95-£19.95, Vegetarian available, Children welcome

DELPH Map 16 SD90

The Old Bell Inn

Modern British

tel: 01457 870130 **5 Huddersfield Rd OL3 5EG**
email: info@theoldbellinn.co.uk **web:** www.theoldbellinn.co.uk
dir: *From M62 junct 22, follow A672 to Denshaw junct signed Saddleworth. Left onto A6052 signed Delph. Through village left at x-rds, 150yds on left*

Up-to-date food with an imaginative edge

A traditional 18th-century coaching inn with a thoroughly contemporary attitude to dining, this pub holds a world record for its collection of 400 gins. In the modern restaurant, hearty, innovative food is created using an abundance of local raw materials. Pan-fried king scallops with ginger and coriander infused belly pork, smoked cauliflower purée, charred cauliflower and burnt apple purée is one impressive opener, followed perhaps by roast Goosnargh duck breast with cider fondant potatoes, five spice-glazed carrots and parsnips, creamed bacon sprouts and Cumberland sauce. Finish with white chocolate and yogurt pavé, gooseberry and elderflower ice cream.

Chef Mark Pemberton **Seats** 65 **Times** 12-9.30, All-day dining **Prices** Fixed D 3 course £30 **Wines** 5 bottles over £30, 24 bottles under £30, 10 by glass **Parking** 21 **Notes** Signature menu £25-£30, Pre-theatre menu, Sunday L, Vegetarian available, Children welcome

The Saddleworth Hotel

Modern European

tel: 01457 871888 **Huddersfield Rd OL3 5LX**
email: enquiries@thesaddleworthhotel.co.uk **web:** www.saddleworthhotel.co.uk
dir: *A62, located between A6052 & A670*

Contemporary cooking and moorland views

The Saddleworth feels like a real attempt to create a country inn for the modern era. Built of stone, with landscaped gardens, woodland, and sweeping views over the Lancashire moorland, it's not far from Oldham yet feels pleasingly remote from anywhere, and the location makes it a popular choice for weddings. The menu features modern European dishes, from well-made braised beef tortellini with Barolo wine and parmesan crisp, through perfectly-timed salmon with a Provençal crayfish sauce, samphire and crushed potatoes. Dessert could be the classic flavour combination of chocolate and raspberries in an excellent brownie, with pistachio parfait.

MANCHESTER Map 16 SJ89

ABode Manchester

Modern European V

tel: 0161 247 7744 **107 Piccadilly M1 2DB**
email: restaurantmanager@abodemanchester.co.uk **web:** www.abodemanchester.co.uk
dir: *In city centre, 2 mins walk from Piccadilly station*

Compelling modern cooking in stylish central hotel

The Manchester outpost of the glitzy hotel group is a former cotton warehouse built in 1898, evident in the original walnut staircase, tiling and wrought ironwork. Its restaurant is a two-tier room with a glossy contemporary look, and the cooking is excitingly innovative, while resting squarely on the classical repertoire. Openers take in wood pigeon and rhubarb with charred spring onion, garlic and shallots, and ambitions are amply met in main courses such as salmon and samphire, dressed in beurre noisette with a vivid carrot jus. Puddings alone are worth a visit here, among them an airy winter berry soufflé with cinnamon ice cream.

Chef Mariusz Dobies **Seats** 76, Pr/dining room 24 **Times** 12-2/6-10, Closed Sun, L Mon **Prices** Fixed L 2 course £25, Fixed D 2 course £25, Tasting menu £65-£80, Starter £9-£16, Main £15-£28, Dessert £8.95-£10 **Wines** 45 bottles over £30, 5 bottles under £30, 8 by glass **Parking** Dale St, Citi Park **Notes** Children welcome

The French by Simon Rogan

– see opposite

George's Dining Room & Bar

Modern British NEW

tel: 0161 794 5444 **17-21 Barton Rd, Worsley M28 2PD**
email: info@georgesworsley.co.uk
dir: *M60 junct 13, follow signs for Eccles, on B5211*

Sharp looks and switched-on food

The name of this posh gastropub pays homage to Victorian architect Sir George Gilbert Scott, but this place does not look backwards. The setting is stylish, with tan leather banquettes and neutral creamy hues, and the food is very much what you'd expect of a 21st-century kitchen. There's an inventive take on the burger theme, matching an aromatic prawn patty with Marie Rose sauce and olive oil soil, ahead of a trencherman's portion of suckling pig with duck fat potatoes and roasted carrots. The inventive streak shows through again in a dessert of Bramley apple pannacotta and sorbet with goji berry granola.

Chef Andrew Parker **Seats** 140, Pr/dining room 14 **Times** 12-10, All-day dining, Closed 1 Jan **Prices** Fixed L 2 course £12.95, Fixed D 3 course £25-£29, Starter £5.95-£10.50, Main £8.50-£29.50, Dessert £6.50 **Wines** 9 bottles over £30, 24 bottles under £30, 16 by glass **Parking** 17 **Notes** Brunch £1.50-£8.50, Sunday L £12.95-£20.95, Vegetarian available, Children welcome

Greens

Modern Vegetarian V

tel: 0161 434 4259 **43 Lapwing Ln, West Didsbury M20 2NT**
email: greensdidsbury@gmail.com
dir: *Between Burton Rd & Palatine Rd*

Veggie Mancunian star draws crowds for top flavours

TV chef Simon Rimmer's lively restaurant draws the crowds with exciting vegetarian cooking. Darkwood tables and chairs, with some banquettes, boarded and tiled floors, some funky wallpaper and spotlights dangling from the ceiling all create a positive impression. Precisely flavoured cooking is the hallmark of the kitchen, with ideas picked up from around the globe in a menu that bursts with bright and appealing dishes. Hits among starters include deep-fried oyster mushrooms with pancakes and plum sauce, followed by fennel and potato curry, or the house burger made with chickpeas and veggie black pudding. Finish with a well-made pineapple and coconut Bakewell tart.

Chef Simon Rimmer **Seats** 84 **Times** 12-2/5.30-10, Closed 25-26 Dec, 1 Jan, L Mon **Prices** Fixed L 2 course £12, Fixed D 2 course £12-£15, Starter £4.50-£7, Main £12.50-£13.50, Dessert £4.95-£6 **Wines** 7 bottles over £30, 25 bottles under £30, 7 by glass **Parking** On street **Notes** Sun all day menu, Sunday L £13-£15, Children welcome

Harvey Nichols Second Floor Brasserie

Modern European V NOTABLE WINE LIST

tel: 0161 828 8898 **21 New Cathedral St M1 1AD**
email: secondfloor.reservations@harveynichols.com
dir: *Just off Deansgate, town centre. 5 min walk from Victoria Station, on Exchange Sq*

Sleek setting for all-day dining with city views

Overlooking Exchange Square and the hustle and bustle of retail action in this central part of the city, the slick, contemporary second-floor brasserie provides a rather glamorous respite. An all-day menu increases its usefulness, so you can pop in for brunch, afternoon tea, or stick around to get the measure of the kitchen's brasserie-style output. Cocktails in the bar are a whole other kind of distraction. Start with duck liver parfait topped with hazelnuts, take in a 20th-century classic such as chicken Caesar salad, and follow with pan-fried stone bass with a rustic salsa verde, or a steak cooked in the Josper oven.

Chef Matthew Horsfield **Times** 10am-10pm, All-day dining, Closed 25-27 Dec, Etr Sun, D Sun-Mon **Prices** Fixed D 3 course £20-£25, Starter £5-£10, Main £11-£26, Dessert £5-£8 **Wines** 20 by glass **Parking** NCP under store opposite **Notes** Brunch, Sunday L, Children welcome

The French by Simon Rogan

MANCHESTER **Map 16 SJ89**

Modern British V NOTABLE WINE LIST

tel: 0161 236 3333 **Peter St M60 2DS**
email: info@the-french.co.uk **web:** www.qhotels.co.uk
dir: *M602 junct 3, follow Manchester Central Convention Complex signs, hotel opposite*

A cutting-edge revolution for The French

Manchester's foremost hotel is home to the city's principal dining opportunity, too, with the aforementioned Simon Rogan putting his name above the door and bringing his divertingly contemporary style to the great and the good of the northwest. The revamped French has stepped into the 21st century under the stewardship of one of the UK's most dynamic chefs, and its decor has evolved along with it, so the starchy formality has been replaced by a naturalistic look, with a luxe carpet that looks like floorboards and sleek 1960's-looking tables and chairs. There's lots of room between those tables, while the service remains as slick and professional as you'd hope for in this price bracket. The chef's farm up in Cumbria provides many of the ingredients that find their way onto the six- and ten-course tasting menus – there's a shorter (and cheaper) three-course option available during the day. Adam Reid heads up the kitchen and is charged with delivering the Rogan brand of dashingly contemporary food, where modern culinary techniques enhance rather than overpower the phenomenal ingredients. Expect some unusual native ingredients along the way, many of which have inexplicably fallen out of fashion. Barbecued asparagus is simple enough, simply perfect in fact, with crab and crispy chicken skin, and a punchy watercress purée, while a superb piece of hake gets star treatment in a dish with shrimps and sea herbs, and among sweet courses, you might not be expecting baked squash with caramel custard and barley malt biscuit, plus a little sorrel – truly inspired.

Chef Adam Reid, Simon Rogan **Seats** 55 **Times** 12-1.30/6.30-9, Closed Xmas, Sun-Mon, L Tue **Prices** Tasting menu £65-£85, Starter £11-£12, Main £18-£28, Dessert £9-£18 **Wines** 138 bottles over £30, 7 bottles under £30, 19 by glass **Parking** NCP behind hotel **Notes** Tasting menu 6/10 course L/D, Children 8 yrs+

MANCHESTER *continued*

Hotel Gotham

Modern European NEW

tel: 0161 413 0000 **100 King St M2 4WU**
email: honey@hotelgotham.co.uk **web:** www.hotelgotham.co.uk
dir: *NE on Portland St, left onto Charlotte St then continue onto Spring Gardens*

Inventive modern food and trendy retro looks

The sleek art deco lines of a vintage bank building make a good setting for this hip restaurant in a glossy boutique hotel. Parquet floors, metal-topped tables and semi-circular windows all feed into the retro styling, while the menus are all about vivid modern British combinations. Start with liquorice-cured trout with sticky burnt lemon jam, onion 'snow' and a goats' cheese macaroon, and follow up with poached chicken breast alongside ravioli filled with smoked leg meat, partnered by truffled white bean purée and crispy skin. Dessert cleverly pushes the right buttons with a malty mousse covered in caramelised white chocolate.

Chef Matthew Taylor **Times** 12-2.30/7-10 **Prices** Fixed D 3 course £24, Starter £6.50-£12.50, Main £16.50-£31.50, Dessert £7.50-£10.50 **Wines** 61 bottles over £30, 10 bottles under £30, 11 by glass **Notes** Afternoon tea £19.95, Pre-theatre 2/3 course £20/£24, Vegetarian available, Children welcome

Macdonald Manchester Hotel

Modern British, Scottish

tel: 0161 272 3200 **London Rd M1 2PG**
email: general.manchester@macdonald-hotels.co.uk
web: www.macdonaldhotels.co.uk/our-hotels/north-england/manchester/
dir: *Opposite Piccadilly Station*

City-centre temple to pedigree beef

The Macdonald is a modern hotel that looks like an office block until you get inside and find stylish comfort and a deep-windowed eating space with its kitchen on view. Prime slabs of pedigree beef from Scotland, the US and Argentina get star billing, aged for three weeks and treated to all the traditional trimmings, whether you want a melting fillet or a tastily spiced burger. Start with fishcakes in caper mayo, or Stornoway black pudding Scotch egg with home-made piccalilli. If it sounds like a vegetarian's nightmare, fear not; sweet potato, goats' cheese and red onion tart may help matters. Fill any remaining spaces with caramel peanut parfait.

Chef Mat Lloyd **Seats** 140 **Times** 5-10, Closed L all week **Prices** Fixed D 3 course £25, Starter £4.95-£9.95, Main £12.50-£27.95, Dessert £3-£8.50 **Wines** 24 bottles over £30, 17 bottles under £30, 13 by glass **Parking** 85, NCP **Notes** Vegetarian available, Children welcome

Malmaison Manchester

Modern British, International

tel: 0161 278 1000 **Piccadilly M1 3AQ**
email: manchester@malmaison.com **web:** www.malmaison.com
dir: *From M56 follow signs to Manchester, then to Piccadilly*

Modern comfort food in the city centre

This prime piece of heritage industrial architecture is plumb in the city centre. The interior is all boutiqued to the max, with eye-catching decorative flourishes in a soothing low-lit ambience, while cocktails and upscale brasserie food draw in the crowds. In the Smoak Bar Grill, the open-to-view kitchen produces surprising versions of modern comfort food, not least the range of steaks that are done on the Josper charcoal grill. Creamed brie with a wine-poached pear and candied pecans is an attractive opener, while mains run to confit duck with Puy lentils and garlic mash, or calves' liver and pancetta with roasted onions. Round things off with a vanilla-fragrant crème brûlée.

Manchester House Bar & Restaurant

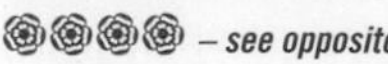 – *see opposite*

Mr Cooper's House and Garden by Simon Rogan

International

tel: 0161 932 4128 & 932 4198 **The Midland Hotel, Peter St M60 2DS**
email: info@mrcoopershouseandgarden.co.uk
dir: *From M6 junct 19 join M56. Follow signs city centre (A5103). Follow signs Manchester Central Convention Complex/Bridgewater Hall onto Medlock St. Through lights onto Lower Mosley St. Pass Bridgewater Hall on right, hotel facing you*

Cool and contemporary dining

The sister restaurant to the high-flying French is named after a coach-making family whose Victorian home this was. There is a 35-foot-high tree in the middle of the dining room – of course. This is the more casual dining option in the hotel, but seeing as this is Simon Rogan's version of casual dining, the culinary output is a cut above the norm. A first course full of sharp flavours brings together buttermilk-fried oysters with kimchee, pear and pickled fennel, before lamb rump turns up with spiced green lentils and minted courgettes in garlicky jus. Finish with pineapple Tatin served with peppered caramel and gingerbread ice cream.

Chef Sean McGinlay **Seats** 150 **Times** 12-2/5-10, Closed 25-26 Dec, 1 Jan **Prices** Fixed L 2 course £16, Fixed D 3 course £24, Starter £7-£12, Main £12-£23, Dessert £7-£8.50 **Wines** 31 bottles over £30, 19 bottles under £30, 12 by glass **Parking** NCP Manchester Central **Notes** Sunday L £16-£20, Vegetarian available, Children welcome

The Rose Garden

Modern British, European

tel: 0161 478 0747 **218 Burton Rd, West Didsbury M20 2LW**
email: info@therosegardendidsbury.com
dir: *Phone for directions*

European bistro food with urban boho credentials

The Rose Garden could be mistaken for a contemporary art space, its minimal gleaming-white ambience enlivened with punches of glaring colour. Pacey, on-point service contributes to an urban boho atmosphere, and the modern European bistro food does the rest. Softly braised octopus forms the centrepiece of a salad of heritage tomato, onion, fennel, croûtons and chilli, and might precede a juxtaposition of turbot fillet and snails with wilted baby gem in seaweed-salty spring vegetable nage. Squid salsa is inveigled into a main of pork belly and pineapple, and herbal fragrance lends character to desserts such as chocolate and rosemary delice with Italian meringue and a walnut tuile.

Chef William Mills **Seats** 58 **Times** 12-2/6-9.30, Closed 25-26 Dec, 1 Jan **Prices** Fixed L 2 course £15, Fixed D 3 course £21, Tasting menu £45-£75, Starter £7-£10, Main £14-£19, Dessert £6-£7.50 **Wines** 11 bottles over £30, 10 bottles under £30, 9 by glass **Parking** On street **Notes** Sunday L £15-£21, Vegetarian available, Children welcome

Sweet Mandarin

Chinese V

tel: 0161 832 8848 **19 Copperas St M4 1HS**
email: lisa@sweetmandarin.com
dir: *Top end of High Street opposite Old Smithfield Fish Market façade in Northern Quarter*

Wildly popular Chinese family restaurant run by honoured sisters

The Tse sisters, who run what has become one of the most popular Chinese restaurants for miles around, were awarded MBEs for their services to food in the 2014 New Year Honours list – quite a journey from when it first opened in 1950. It's a relaxed and comfortable glass-fronted venue, where, against a backdrop of red screens and lanterns, a mix of traditional and less familiar Chinese dishes is offered. Expect wonton soup, salt and chilli squid, and well-rendered main dishes like Emperor red chicken curry, or chillified Hunanese volcano beef. Veggie options include Mabel's claypot of tofu and Chinese mushrooms.

Chef Lisa Tse **Seats** 85 **Times** 5-11, Closed 25-26 Dec, Mon, L all week **Prices** Prices not confirmed **Wines** 1 bottle over £30, 13 bottles under £30, 7 by glass **Parking** Shudehill car park **Notes** Children welcome

MANCHESTER AIRPORT Map 15 SJ88

Best Western Plus Pinewood on Wilmslow

Modern, Traditional

tel: 01625 529211 **180 Wilmslow Rd SK9 3LF**
email: pinewood.res@pinewood-hotel.co.uk **web:** www.pinewood-hotel.co.uk
dir: *Phone for directions*

Contemporary setting for modern brasserie dining

This good-looking red-brick hotel is home to the thoroughly modern One Eighty restaurant, a sleek looking space with darkwood tables and fashionably muted tones. The menu maintains the brasserie attitude and reveals keen creativity in the kitchen. There's skill in the smoking of scallops which arrive with celeriac and apple purée, while duck liver pâté is served with warm brioche and spiced apple and pear chutney. Main courses include a glammed up burger (brioche bun, Applewood cheese, dry-cured bacon and onion marmalade) and a veggie open lasagne with wild mushrooms and spinach. There are sharing platter, steaks with triple-cooked chips, and desserts such as a retro banana split.

Chef Colin Starkey **Seats** 80 **Times** 12-4/6-9 **Prices** Prices not confirmed **Wines** 13 bottles over £30, 30 bottles under £30, 15 by glass **Notes** Seasonal menu £6.95-£19.95, Tasting menu 6 course, Sunday L, Vegetarian available, Children welcome

Manchester House Bar & Restaurant

MANCHESTER Map 16 SJ89

Modern British V

tel: 0161 835 2557 **Tower 12, 18-22 Bridge St M3 3BZ**
email: restaurant@manchesterhouse.uk.com
dir: *On Bridge St, on edge of Spinning Fields. Entrance in Tower 12 behind Waitrose*

Aiden Byrnes' see-and-be-seen venue for contemporary dining

Aiden Byrne's operation in Manchester House is a see-and-be-seen sort of spot, so if you'd like to kick-start the experience by slurping a cocktail and eyeballing the Mancunian beau monde, the lift whizzes you up to the 12th floor of Spinningfields' Tower 12 for a sharpener with cityscape views and DJs setting the mood. Then slide back down to the second floor, where Byrne's restaurant pays homage to Manchester's industrial heritage with its exposed girders, concrete and wrought-iron features. Diners rub shoulders with the chefs as they enter through the open kitchen, while the casually-dressed staff back up the laid-back vibe with impressive knowledge. If you're planning a Saturday evening visit, be aware that the only option is the 15-course tasting menu, but the rest of the time the carte leads the way, with the 8- and 15-course tasters available if the whole table is up for it, while veggies are sorted out with a dedicated meat-free carte and multi-course tasters. Dishes are imaginative and technically outstanding, kicking off with cured and baked mackerel with caviar, pickled radish and seaweed. Next up, an uber-posh and faultlessly constructed riff on the surf and turf theme involves a rich and unctuous braised beef cheek with Txogitxu tartare (that's gold-standard beef from the Basque heartlands), razor clam and fermented carrots, or there might be roasted monkfish with baby squid, goats' cheese and onion. For dessert, there's a pretty-as-a-picture assemblage of 'apples, Calvados and caramel' involving apple purée, terrine and cream with honeycomb, rich caramel, and Calvados ice cream.

Chef Aiden Byrne **Seats** 78, Pr/dining room 8 **Times** 12-2.30/7-9.30, Closed 1st 2 wks Jan, 2 wks summer, Sun-Mon **Prices** Fixed L 2 course £22.50, Tasting menu £60-£95, Starter £15, Main £35, Dessert £7.50 **Wines** 193 bottles over £30, 26 bottles under £30, 12 by glass **Parking** NCP King St West **Notes** Children welcome

OLDHAM Map 16 SD90

The White Hart Inn

@@ Modern British V NOTABLE WINE LIST

tel: 01457 872566 **51 Stockport Rd, Lydgate OL4 4JJ**
email: bookings@thewhitehart.co.uk **web:** www.thewhitehart.co.uk
dir: *M62 junct 20, A627, continue to end of bypass, then A669 to Saddleworth. Enter Lydgate turn right onto Stockport Rd. White Hart Inn 50yds on left*

Confident cooking in a moorland inn

Following a full refurbishment, the Dining Room restaurant is now the gastronomic centre of attention inside this rambling village inn that overlooks Manchester and the Cheshire plains. A seven-course tasting option showcases the kitchen's expertise, while the seasonal menu sets out heartily with pan-roasted cod with Puy lentils and Alsace bacon, followed by a main course displaying a keen eye for harmonious flavours and lively textural contrasts: lamb rump with goats' curd, raw courgette, braised and puréed shallots, onion ash and chilli oil. For pudding, a reworked old favourite sees rhubarb (poached and gel) matched with duck egg custard and a ginger biscuit.

Chef Mike Shaw **Seats** 50, Pr/dining room 32 **Times** 12-2.30/6-9.30, Closed 26 Dec, 1 Jan, Mon-Tue, L Wed-Sat, D Sun **Prices** Tasting menu £32-£50, Starter £6-£9.50, Main £14-£26.50, Dessert £7.50-£8.50 **Wines** 70 bottles over £30, 70 bottles under £30, 10 by glass **Parking** 75 **Notes** Tasting menu 7 course, Sunday L £25, No children

ROCHDALE Map 16 SD81

Nutters

 Modern British V NOTABLE WINE LIST

tel: 01706 650167 **Edenfield Rd, Norden OL12 7TT**
email: enquiries@nuttersrestaurant.com
dir: *From Rochdale take A680 signed Blackburn. Edenfield Rd on right on leaving Norden*

Personality-laden modern British food at a Gothic manor house

A television personality and larger-than-life character, Mr Nutter's restaurant is a family affair (mum and dad work here too), with the grand old house done out in a contemporary manner. The menu takes a modern British path, with plenty of flavours from Asia added to the mix, and regional ingredients providing a sense of place. Among starters, slow-roasted Dingley Dell pork belly is infused with Chinese flavours, while main courses might include pan-seared hake with ginger beer-battered scallop and tarragon hollandaise, or Goosnargh chicken served two ways (Parma ham-wrapped roulade and mini Kiev). Finish with dark and white chocolate cheesecake with Oreo crumb and honeycomb.

Chef Andrew Nutter **Seats** 143, Pr/dining room 100
Times 12-2/6.30-9.30, Closed 1-2 days after both Xmas & New Year, Mon
Prices Fixed L 2 course £13.95, Tasting menu £44, Starter £5.40-£9.80, Main £16.80-£24.50, Dessert £5.40-£7.80 **Wines** 126 bottles over £30, 88 bottles under £30, 10 by glass **Parking** 100 **Notes** Afternoon tea £15-£23.50, Business L £16.50-£19.50, Sunday L £25, Children welcome

The Peacock Room

@@ Modern British

tel: 01706 368591 **Crimble Hotel, Crimble Ln, Bamford OL11 4AD**
email: crimble@thedeckersgroup.com **web:** www.thedeckersgroup.com
dir: *M62 junct 20 follow signs for Blackburn, left onto B6222 (Bury road) contine for 1m Crimble Lane on left*

Art deco design and smart contemporary food

The Peacock Room is a fitting name for this flamboyantly decorated restaurant. Huge gold sculptures of the fowl on the door handles, a mirrored ceiling hung with chandeliers, cornicing picked out in gold, and plush seats on a busily patterned carpet all contribute to the exuberant style, while the birds parade the grounds. Dishes themselves are never over-elaborate, the kitchen delivering ham hock and chicken terrine with prunes and a pear purée infused with vanilla, followed by cod loin wrapped in prosciutto in the company of a pork belly fritter, and, to finish, a visually stunning cherry and almond cheesecake with almond ice cream.

Chef Robert Walker **Seats** 80 **Times** 12-2/6.30-9, Closed Mon-Tue, L Sat, D Sun **Prices** Fixed D 3 course £30-£33.95, Starter £5.50-£9.95, Main £16.95-£23.95, Dessert £4.50-£10 **Wines** 33 bottles over £30, 67 bottles under £30, 7 by glass **Parking** 120 **Notes** Afternoon tea £15.95, Sunday L £21.95-£25.90, Vegetarian available, Children welcome

STOCKPORT Map 16 SJ89

Damson Restaurant

 Modern European NEW v

tel: 0161 432 4666 **Heaton Moor SK4 4HY**
email: manager.hm@damsonrestaurant.co.uk
dir: *M60 junct 1, A5145, B5169 (Heaton Moor Road)*

Bright, modern cooking in buzzy local favourite

Among an unassuming row of shops is this gem of a restaurant with a damson paint job and a few pavement tables. Inside it reveals itself to be quite the looker with its fashionably warm colour scheme and sensuous fabrics. The menu has kerb appeal too, with a tasting menu, fixed-price option and excellent veggie choices in support of the à la carte. The kitchen's grasp of flavours and textures is revealed in a first-course duck rillettes with poached pears, toasted hazelnuts and orange purée. Move on to pan-roasted fillet of sea bass, or Middlewhite pork belly with a croustillante of braised cheek.

Chef Simon Stanley, Jake Buchan **Seats** 75, Pr/dining room 10 **Times** 12-2.30/5-9.30, Closed 26 Dec, 1 Jan, Mon & Sat, D Sun closes at 7.30 **Prices** Fixed L 2 course £20, Fixed D 3 course £25, Tasting menu £50, Starter £8.95-£11.95, Main £18.95-£27.95, Dessert £7.95-£14.95 **Wines** 40 bottles over £30, 45 bottles under £30, 170 by glass **Parking** On street **Notes** L special £10 Tue-Fri, Sunday L £15-£25, Children welcome

WIGAN Map 15 SD50

Wrightington Hotel & Country Club

Modern International

tel: 01257 425803 **Moss Ln, Wrightington WN6 9PB**
email: info@bennettsrestaurant.com **web:** www.bennettsrestaurant.com
dir: *M6 junct 27, 0.25m W, hotel on right after church*

Unfussy cooking and top-notch leisure facilities

This modern hotel is on the edge of Wigan within peaceful countryside. Bennett's Restaurant has a stylishly elegant look but a relaxed atmosphere and brisk young staff dispel any notion of formality. 'Lancashire Classics' puzzlingly includes a multinational main course of prawn tempura in panko breadcrumbs with Caesar salad topped with parmesan and olives, with a mix of the traditional and contemporary found elsewhere. A smoked salmon parcel enclosing mousseline of prawn, cod and salmon, served with lemon crème fraîche, could be followed by accurately seared duck breast with blackberry jus and cabbage sautéed with bacon. Desserts end positively with lemon parfait with lemon cream, or rhubarb and plum syllabub.

WORSLEY Map 15 SD70

Grenache

 Modern British, French

tel: 0161 7998181 **15 Bridgewater Rd, Walkden M28 3JE**
email: info@grenacherestaurant.co.uk
dir: *Off Bridgewater Road B5232*

Classy basement restaurant with French classical technique

Grenache's basement dining room, a stylish space done out in magenta and white with abstract artworks and hospitable staff. The cooking leans towards a French axis, with classical technique underlying the modern combinations. The unctuous smoothness of a pressed foie gras terrine gains texture from a salad of cobnuts, granola, greengages and grapes. Then it could be herb-crusted halibut with well-made scallop tortellini and cauliflower or perhaps roasted rump and braised shoulder of lamb with pesto mash and ratatouille in rosemary jus. A slice of gloriously rich treacle tart comes with clotted cream ice cream, with macerated raspberries to keep up the vitamin count.

Chef Mike Jennings **Seats** 40 **Times** 12.30-2.30/5.30-close, Closed Mon-Tue, L Wed, D Sun **Prices** Fixed L 2 course £16.95, Fixed D 3 course £23.95, Tasting menu £49.50, Starter £7.95-£11.95, Main £17.95-£25.95, Dessert £6.95-£19.95 **Wines** 32 bottles over £30, 32 bottles under £30, 17 by glass **Parking** On street **Notes** Sunday L £23.95, Vegetarian available, Children welcome

HAMPSHIRE

ALRESFORD Map 5 SU53

Pulpo Negro

 Modern

tel: 01962 732262 **28 Broad St SO24 9AQ**
email: info@pulponegro.co.uk
dir: *Phone for directions*

Spanish tapas in the English countryside

Alresford – famous for its watercress, steam railway and clear-running chalk streams – has rather improbably added a sunny slice of the Med to its quintessentially-English appeal with the arrival of Pulpo Negro. There's a smart-casual, modern feel-good vibe about the place, with its floorboards, café-style chairs, pews and wooden tables. The appealing tapas menu features succulent, full-flavoured secretto (shoulder) Ibèrica, slow-cooked Ibèricus tomatoes bursting with sweetness, spicy Alejandro chorizo teamed with local watercress, and individual piquillo pepper tortilla. The finish, go for crèma Catalana or Spanish cheeses, while well-selected Spanish wines (alongside a good showing of sherry and gin) send all home happy.

Chef Andres Alemany **Seats** 40 **Times** 12-3/6-11, Closed 25-26 Dec, 1 Jan, Sun-Mon (ex L BH) **Prices** Prices not confirmed **Wines** 17 bottles over £30, 23 bottles under £30, 25 by glass **Parking** On street **Notes** Tapas dishes £2-£12, Vegetarian available, Children 5 yrs+

ALTON Map 5 SU73

The Anchor Inn

 British

tel: 01420 23261 **Lower Froyle GU34 4NA**
email: info@anchorinnatlowerfroyle.co.uk **web:** www.anchorinnatlowerfroyle.co.uk
dir: *From A31, turn off to Bentley*

Impressive and wide-ranging cooking at a village inn

The 16th-century Anchor has all the elements of a traditional country inn down to its low beams, walls full of pictures and double-sided bar. It's a popular spot, attracting not just drinkers, but also takers for a wide-ranging menu displaying high levels of culinary skill and ingenuity. Pub stalwarts of fish and chips are there, but so too is excellent hogget done three ways, with imam bayaldi, apricot and pine nuts, a goats' cheese cigar and roast garlic purée. That might follow a simple sauté of wild mushrooms with a crisped egg and watercress. Inventive desserts include custard tart served with smoked brown sugar ice cream.

ANDOVER Map 5 SU34

Esseborne Manor

 Modern British V

tel: 01264 736444 **Hurstbourne Tarrant SP11 0ER**
email: info@esseborne-manor.co.uk **web:** www.esseborne-manor.co.uk
dir: *Halfway between Andover & Newbury on A343, just 1m N of Hurstbourne Tarrant*

Confident modern cooking in bucolic country house

In an Area of Outstanding Natural Beauty, Esseborne is a dignified Victorian country house where chef Dennis Janssen creates modern dishes that sparkle. It's not all whizz-bang, though, and there is evident classical thinking going on. Pigeon features in a first course with black pudding and cauliflower, with the zippy flavours of cumin and capers, or go for a combination of ham hock terrine with piccalilli and gingerbread. Main-course cod with ox cheek and salsify delivers satisfying flavours, or go for a classic wild mushroom risotto. There's a tasting menu, too, plus contemporary desserts such as an apple and toffee pressing with walnut cake and goats' cheese ice cream.

Chef Dennis Janssen **Seats** 35, Pr/dining room 80 **Times** 12-2/7-9.30 **Prices** Fixed L 2 course £17-£24, Starter £6-£8.50, Main £10.50-£24, Dessert £7-£7.50 **Wines** 37 bottles over £30, 50 bottles under £30, 15 by glass **Parking** 40 **Notes** Afternoon tea £15, Sunday L £25, Children welcome

The George and Dragon

British NEW

tel: 01264 736277 **The Square, Hurstbourne Tarrant SP11 0AA**
email: info@georgeanddragon.com **web:** www.georgeanddragon.com
dir: *N of Andover on A343, in middle of village*

From a standing start, already ticking the right boxes

Hurstbourne Tarrant now has its 16th-century coaching inn back, following its long and sympathetic renovation. Its light and airy, low-ceilinged spaces, bare tables and fires provide just the right setting for an essentially British menu of pub favourites and more innovative dishes. Look for tea-smoked duck breast, wilted spinach, shallots and Jerusalem artichoke purée as a starter. Try a main course of baked cod (fish arrives daily from Cornwall) with Old Winchester cheese rarebit, poached potatoes, mange-touts and dill white wine sauce. Follow with a dessert of chocolate brownie, white chocolate and wasabi ice cream. Wines are the head chef's special project, so try something a little different.

Chef Paul Day **Seats** 65, Pr/dining room 24 **Times** 12-3/6-9.30 **Prices** Fixed L 2 course £12.95, Starter £4.95-£7.95, Main £10.95-£21.95, Dessert £2-£6.75 **Wines** 13 bottles over £30, 22 bottles under £30, 12 by glass **Parking** 18 **Notes** Sunday L £13.50-£14.95, Vegetarian available, Children welcome

BARTON-ON-SEA Map 5 SZ29

Pebble Beach

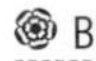 British, French, Mediterranean

tel: 01425 627777 **Marine Dr BH25 7DZ**
email: mail@pebblebeach-uk.com **web:** www.pebblebeach-uk.com
dir: *Follow A35 from Southampton onto A337 to New Milton, turn left onto Barton Court Av to clifftop*

Upbeat brasserie cooking with a clifftop sun terrace

A clifftop perch gives this modern bar-brasserie a sweeping vista across Christchurch Bay to the Needles and the Isle of Wight. Inside is a buzzy split-level venue where high stools at the oyster bar allow views of the open-plan kitchen. An alfresco terrace is irresistible when the weather behaves. Fish and seafood are strong suits, producing perhaps a main course of monkfish and squid braised in a spicy bisque of shellfish, tomato and brandy, served with broccoli and rice. That might be preceded by rabbit pâté with tapenade straws and rosé wine jelly, while dessert furnishes pistachio and almond nougat glacé with poached apricots.

Chef Pierre Chevillard **Seats** 90, Pr/dining room 8 **Times** 11-2.30/6-11, Closed D 25 Dec, 1 Jan **Prices** Starter £6.70-£17.40, Main £8.99-£38, Dessert £7.40-£11.50 **Wines** 25 bottles over £30, 25 bottles under £30, 16 by glass **Parking** 20 **Notes** Sunday L, Vegetarian available, Children welcome

BASINGSTOKE Map 5 SU65

Audleys Wood

 Modern British

tel: 01256 817555 & 0845 072 7405 *(Calls cost 7p per minute plus your phone company's access charge)* **Alton Rd RG25 2JT**
email: audleyswood@handpicked.co.uk
web: www.handpickedhotels.co.uk/thesimondsroom
dir: *M3 junct 6. From Basingstoke take A339 towards Alton, hotel on right*

Local ingredients cooked with classical flair in a grand setting

This striking Victorian property stands in seven acres of grounds and woodland and has all the trappings of a luxury country-house hotel. The main restaurant is the grand Simonds Room, its panelled walls hung with framed tapestries against ornate carved oak cornicing. A classical vein runs through the menu of otherwise modern British ideas. Beef fillet comes with roasted shallots and fondant potato, but also oxtail and beetroot cannelloni. Starters include an up-to-the-minute dish of Stilton brûlée with pear, frozen grapes and pecans. The same ingenious balance is seen in an elaboration of strawberries and cream, served with scarlet compôte, pink peppercorn ice cream and biscotti crumbs.

Chef Mark Burton **Seats** 20, Pr/dining room 40 **Times** 7-10, Closed Mon, L Tue-Sat **Prices** Fixed D 3 course £49, Tasting menu £65 **Wines** 70 bottles over £30, 9 bottles under £30, 18 by glass **Parking** 70 **Notes** Sunday L £18-£34, Vegetarian available, Children welcome

Oakley Hall Hotel

Modern British

tel: 01256 783350 **Rectory Rd, Oakley RG23 7EL**
email: enquiries@oakleyhall-park.com **web:** www.oakleyhall-park.com
dir: *M3 junct 7, follow Basingstoke signs. In 500yds before lights turn left onto A30 towards Oakley, immediately right onto unclass road towards Oakley. In 3m left at T-junct into Rectory Rd. Left onto B3400. Hotel signed 1st on left*

Classically-based cooking with Jane Austen connections

Jane Austen enthusiasts will find references to Oakley Hall in her work. As a young woman, she was a frequent visitor. The new Glasshouse restaurant is the setting for classically-based British menus that draw their raw materials from the kitchen garden. Thai-spiced butternut soup with coriander oil vies with rabbit and pheasant terrine and quince chutney for starters, before mains follow on with well-handled prime cuts such as duck breast with dauphinoise in redcurrant sauce, hake fillet with king prawns and samphire on crab velouté, and traditional sirloin with roast cherry tomatoes and wild mushroom sauce. Consider poached pear in red wine syrup with cinnamon ice cream to finish.

Chef Justin Mundy **Seats** 100, Pr/dining room 300 **Times** 12-2/6.30-9.30 **Prices** Prices not confirmed **Wines** 77 bottles over £30, 10 bottles under £30, 12 by glass **Parking** 100 **Notes** Afternoon tea £22.95, Sunday L, Vegetarian available, Children welcome

BAUGHURST Map 5 SU56

The Wellington Arms

Modern British

tel: 0118 982 0110 **Baughurst Rd RG26 5LP**
email: hello@thewellingtonarms.com **web:** www.thewellingtonarms.com
dir: *M4 junct 12 follow Newbury signs on A4. At rdbt left signed Aldermaston. Through Aldermaston. Up hill, at 2nd rdbt 2nd exit signed Baughurst, left at T junct, pub 1m on left*

Top pub food crafted from the most local of local produce

The Wellington Arms is a dining pub with a capital D. A good deal of what you eat will have found its way into the kitchen from the garden, and the rest won't have travelled very far. The old pub itself has scrubbed up very nicely indeed – crackling fires, tiled floor and wooden tables put it at the rustic-chic end of the spectrum. Pheasant, rabbit and pork terrine with spiced apple chutney and sourdough toast is a typically-forthright starter, followed by roast fillet of Brixham cod with preserved lemon crust, sautéed samphire and Puy lentils. To finish, perhaps orange marmalade sponge with proper custard.

Chef Jason King **Seats** 40, Pr/dining room 18 **Times** 12-3/6-9.30, Closed D Sun **Prices** Prices not confirmed **Wines** 45 bottles over £30, 21 bottles under £30, 9 by glass **Parking** 25 **Notes** Sunday L, Vegetarian available, Children welcome

BEAULIEU Map 5 SU30

Beaulieu Hotel

British

tel: 023 8029 3344 **Beaulieu Rd SO42 7YQ**
email: beaulieu@newforesthotels.co.uk **web:** www.newforesthotels.co.uk
dir: *On B3056 between Lyndhurst & Beaulieu. Near Beaulieu Road railway station*

Modern British cooking in the New Forest

The red-brick former coaching inn stands in landscaped grounds within open heathland on the edge of the village of the same name. Its traditionally-styled dining room with seating upholstered in spring green makes a soothing setting for gently refined modern British cooking of distinctive flair. An assured opener comes in the form of chicory tart with walnut and pear salad and deep-fried blue cheese, and may be followed by buttery-sauced seared salmon with crushed new potatoes, capers and kale, or venison in chocolate with figs and turnips. The sound execution is characterised by a classic crème brûlée, served with blackberry jam and a doughnut finger.

Chef Michael Mckell **Seats** 60, Pr/dining room 80 **Times** 5.30-9.30, Closed L all week **Prices** Starter £6.50-£8, Main £12.50-£21.50, Dessert £5.50-£7 **Wines** 8 bottles over £30, 30 bottles under £30, 8 by glass **Parking** 60 **Notes** Vegetarian available, Children welcome

The Master Builder's at Buckler's Hard

Modern British

tel: 01590 616253 **Buckler's Hard SO42 7XB**
email: enquiries@themasterbuilders.co.uk **web:** www.themasterbuilders.co.uk
dir: *From M27 junct 2 follow signs to Beaulieu. Turn left onto B3056, then 1st left, hotel in 2m*

Unpretentious modern cooking and river views

The master builder commemorated in the name of this cosily rustic 18th-century hotel once built ships for Nelson's fleet on the grassy areas running down to the River Beaulieu. With those tranquil watery views as a backdrop, you can expect sound modern British cooking based on well-sourced local ingredients – home-made linguine with Dorset crab, lemon and thyme oil as a starter, then a ballotine of local pheasant pointed up with tart blackberry jus and matched with roast root vegetables, buttery kale and mash. For dessert, there's a deconstructed take on Millionaire's shortbread, or you might go for a plate of impeccably local cheeses.

BEAULIEU *continued*

The Montagu Arms Hotel

Modern European NOTABLE WINE LIST

tel: 01590 612324 **Palace Ln SO42 7ZL**
email: reception@montaguarmshotel.co.uk **web:** www.montaguarmshotel.co.uk
dir: *From M27 junct 2 take A326 & B3054 for Beaulieu*

Refined country-house cooking with a modern touch

A brick-built ivy-clad 17th-century house in an enviable New Forest setting, this sumptuous hotel near the Beaulieu National Motor Museum offers all the right country-hotel comforts. Overlooking a charming sun-trap courtyard and well-manicured gardens, the wood-panelled Terrace Restaurant is the setting for Matthew Tomkinson's inspired classical cooking, which makes good use of organic produce grown in the hotel's well-maintained kitchen garden. Schooled in classic Anglo-French techniques, the kitchen (refurbished and extended in early 2016) isn't afraid to adopt contemporary British ideas. A starter of ravioli generously filled with Isle of Wight lobster and organic salmon shows considerable balance and restraint with a sauce vièrge and Lymington crab velouté as accompaniment. A main course escalope of South Coast turbot with sautéed wild mushrooms, braised pearl barley, caramelised endive and cep sauce displays perfect timing and the lightest of touches. A fine selection of artisanal English and French farmhouse cheeses arrive on the trolley as a possible conclusion to a meal, possibly after a dessert of warm salted caramel fondant served with a playful 'cider lolly' sorbet and crème fraîche. The interesting and diverse wine list includes many biodynamic examples and a good range is offered by the glass.

Chef Matthew Tomkinson **Seats** 60, Pr/dining room 32
Times 12-2/7-9, Closed Mon, L Tue **Prices** Fixed L 2 course £25, Tasting menu £90-£145, Starter £20, Main £35, Dessert £20 **Wines** 371 bottles over £30, 4 bottles under £30, 27 by glass **Parking** 50 **Notes** D 3 course ALC £70, Sunday L £37.50, Vegetarian available, Children 11 yrs+ D

Monty's Inn

Traditional British

tel: 01590 614986 & 612324 **Palace Ln SO42 7ZL**
email: reservations@montaguarmshotel.co.uk **web:** www.montaguarmshotel.co.uk
dir: *M27 junct 2, follow signs to Beaulieu*

Comforting English food in a 17th-century hotel

Specialising in hearty, unpretentious food that doesn't try to punch above its weight, Monty's Inn goes for a clubby look involving wood-panelled walls, wooden floors and unclothed tables – a posh country pub setting that opens with a home-made local pork Scotch egg with spiced apple sauce and dressed rocket. The coast isn't too far off, so fish is well represented by pan-roasted sea bass with lemon fondant potatoes, broccoli, shallot purée, crispy mussels and red wine jus, while meaty mains could offer ginger beer-glazed roast duck breast with a leg meat spring roll, bok choy and duck fat potatoes. For pudding, there's dark chocolate mousse with cherry sorbet.

Chef Robert McLean **Seats** 50 **Times** 12-2.30/6.30-9.30, Closed D 24-26 Dec, 1 Jan **Prices** Starter £5.95-£10.25, Main £12.25-£25.70, Dessert £1.75-£5.50 **Wines** 11 bottles over £30, 18 bottles under £30, 8 by glass **Parking** 40 **Notes** Sunday L fr £13.95, Vegetarian available, Children welcome

BRANSGORE Map 5 SZ19

The Three Tuns

British, European

tel: 01425 672232 **Ringwood Rd BH23 8JH**
email: threetunsinn@btconnect.com **web:** www.threetunsinn.com
dir: *On A35 at junct for Walkford/Highcliffe follow Bransgore signs, 1.5m, restaurant on left*

Appealing varied menu in a traditional thatched inn

The picture-postcard 17th-century thatched inn deep in the New Forest is a delight in summer, festooned with flowers, and cosy in winter as blazing log fires warm the low beamed bar and dining areas. The welcoming scene draws foodies and forest visitors for its charm and character, glorious sun-drenched garden, and an eclectic mix of pub classics and adventurous modern British dishes. The seasonal menu kicks off with snails and garlic butter with oxtail jus and bread for dipping, and might follow with fried halibut and gnocchi, garnished with cep purée, salted lemon and hazelnuts. To finish, orange and almond tart comes with brown butter ice cream.

BROCKENHURST Map 5 SU30

The Balmer Lawn Hotel

Modern British

tel: 01590 623116 & 625725 **Lyndhurst Rd SO42 7ZB**
email: info@balmerlawnhotel.com **web:** www.balmerlawnhotel.com
dir: *Take A337 towards Brockenhurst, hotel on left after 'Welcome to Brockenhurst' sign*

Fine dining at grand New Forest hotel

This imposing pavilion-style Victorian hunting lodge in a charming New Forest setting does good business as a friendly, family-run operation with excellent spa, sports and conference facilities. Expect modern cooking with a healthy showing of prime-quality, often local, materials – perhaps confit rabbit rillettes with plum ketchup and home-made pumpernickel bread, followed by roast saddle of lamb with beetroot mash, roasted butternut squash purée and curly kale, or 28-day matured Hampshire steaks from the grill with confit tomatoes, fat chips, mushrooms and watercress. Inventive endings run to 'textures of milk and honey' or classics like treacle tart with clotted cream.

Cambium

Modern British V NOTABLE WINE LIST

tel: 01590 623551 **Careys Manor Hotel & SenSpa, Lyndhurst Rd SO42 7RH**
email: zengarden@senspa.co.uk **web:** www.careysmanor.com/cambium
dir: *M27 junct 3, M271, A35 to Lyndhurst. A337 towards Brockenhurst. Hotel on left after Beaulieu sign*

Refined, contemporary dining in stylish spa hotel

The New Forest location inspired the interior designers of Careys Manor's classy contemporary restaurant, Cambium, and also informs the cooking of the dynamic team in the kitchen. There are three dining options in this handsome and much extended Victorian manor house with a luxe spa, but Cambium (named for the rings that indicate the age of a tree) is the pick of the bunch, a serene space with shades of gold and cream. Executive chef Paul Peters draws on the regional larder to create a modern menu combining classic flavour combinations with up-to-date techniques. There's a tasting menu, including an impressive veggie version, and an à la carte that gives the option of two or three courses. Full-of-flavour asparagus stars in a first course with crispy hen's egg and silky smooth velouté, before the arrival of gloriously tender loin and shoulder of lamb with goats' cheese bonbon, honey and wild garlic, or cod with an Asian spin. There's refinement all the way through, not least in a dessert that brings together the complementary flavours of vanilla pannacotta, various textures of rhubarb, and stem ginger ice cream. Alternatively, a deconstructed sticky toffee pudding also provides a great finish. The service is slick and informed.

Chef Paul Peters **Seats** 94, Pr/dining room 40 **Times** 7-9.30, Closed Sun, L all week **Prices** Fixed D 3 course £49.50, Tasting menu £65 **Wines** 43 bottles over £30, 13 bottles under £30, 12 by glass **Parking** 83 **Notes** Tasting menu 6 course, Children 8 yrs+

THE PIG

British V NOTABLE WINE LIST

tel: 01590 622354 **Beaulieu Rd SO42 7QL**
email: info@thepighotel.com **web:** www.thepighotel.com
dir: *M27 junct 2, follow A326 Lyndhurst, then A337 Brockenhurst onto B3055 Beaulieu Road. 1m on left up private road*

Home-grown and foraged food in a New Forest hotel

The Pig is a restaurant for our times, with cocktails served in old jam jars and a massage available in the old potting shed. Here in the wilds of the New Forest, the main passion is for home-grown and foraged ingredients. It's a buzzy place with a retro interior, the Victorian greenhouse dining room providing an informal setting for rustic, flavour-focused dishes. There's simple satisfaction in a starter of crab on toast with pickled fennel and mizuna. Follow with pork chop, parsnips and apple sauce, or suet-crusted pork pie and garlic mash, and end on treacle tart and lemon curd with Dorset mascarpone.

Chef James Golding **Seats** 95, Pr/dining room 14 **Times** 12-2.15/6.30-9.30 **Prices** Starter £5-£9, Main £10-£28, Dessert £7.50 **Wines** 159 bottles over £30, 44 bottles under £30, 20 by glass **Parking** 40 **Notes** Children welcome

Rhinefield House

Traditional British

tel: 01590 622922 & 0845 072 7516 *(Calls cost 7p per minute plus your phone company's access charge)* **Rhinefield Rd SO42 7QB**
email: rhinefieldhouse@handpicked.co.uk
web: www.handpickedhotels.co.uk/rhinefieldhouse
dir: *A35 towards Christchurch. 3m from Lyndhurst, turn left to Rhinefield, 1.5m to hotel*

Modern cooking in a stunning Victorian mansion

The present house sprang up in the late Victorian era. A Tudor-Gothic hybrid architecturally, the interiors are awash with finely crafted mouldings, copperwork, and beautiful examples of the lavatorialist's art, plus Grinling Gibbons carvings, ceilings by Fragonard, and a room modelled on the Alhambra. James Whitesmith supplies the culinary opulence to go with it. Seared scallops with chorizo and pea textures might set the pace, and be followed by sea bass with blowtorched chard and capers in clam dressing, or Parma-wrapped pork fillet with onion rösti in cider-laced mustard jus. Desserts might include buttermilk pannacotta with kiwi, mango and popping candy.

Chef James Whitesmith **Seats** 58, Pr/dining room 12 **Times** 12-5/7-10 **Prices** Fixed L 2 course fr £21.50, Fixed D 3 course fr £39, Starter £10.50-£12.50, Main £18.50-£28.50, Dessert £11-£15 **Wines** 151 bottles over £30, 14 bottles under £30, 18 by glass **Parking** 150 **Notes** Brunch menu, Sunday L £21.50-£26.50, Vegetarian available, Children welcome

BROCKENHURST *continued*

The Zen Garden Restaurant

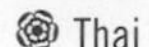 Thai V

tel: 01590 623219 & 623551 **The SenSpa, Careys Manor Hotel, Lyndhurst Rd SO42 7RH**
email: zengarden@senspa.co.uk
dir: *M27 junct 3, M271, A35 to Lyndhurst. A337 towards Brockenhurst. Hotel on left after Beaulieu sign*

Vibrant Thai cooking in a spa hotel

Within the SenSpa at Careys Manor Hotel in the New Forest is a smart Thai eatery with its gold columns, bamboo ceiling and darkwood tables and chairs. Classic tom yam soup kick-starts the palate with its sour, fiery and fragrant cocktail of tiger prawns, mushrooms, chilli, lemongrass, galangal and kaffir lime leaves, or you might get going with crispy fried soft-shelled crab with garlic and pink peppercorn sauce. Main-course wok-seared beef comes with red curry paste, beans, red cabbage, tumicuni ginger and chilli, and proceedings end with a sharp, cleansing dessert of pineapple carpaccio with agave syrup, fresh basil and coconut ice cream.

Chef Thosporn Wongsasube **Seats** 50, Pr/dining room 14 **Times** 12-2.30/7-9.30 **Prices** Prices not confirmed **Wines** 10 bottles over £30, 11 bottles under £30, 13 by glass **Parking** 130 **Notes** Sunday L, Children 14/16 D/L

BROOK Map 5 SU21

The Bell Inn

Modern British

tel: 023 8081 2214 **SO43 7HE**
email: bell@bramshaw.co.uk **web:** www.bellinnbramshaw.co.uk
dir: *M27 junct 1 onto B3079, hotel 1.5m on right*

Attractively presented modern cooking at a New Forest inn

In the ownership of the same family since George III was on the throne, The Bell is in a picturesque New Forest village not far from Lyndhurst, and is more than a simple country inn: it has a pair of golf courses. The interior looks the modernised rustic part, with blackboard menus and log fires in winter, and plenty of gracefully-presented local produce on offer. Confit quail and parsley pie with mushroom duxelle might kick things off, as the preamble to roast pheasant served with truffled dauphinoise potato and roasted root vegetables. Finish with a rib-sticking golden syrup sponge pudding with vanilla crème anglaise.

Chef James Burger **Seats** 60, Pr/dining room 40 **Times** 12-3/6.30-9.30 **Prices** Prices not confirmed **Wines** 21 bottles over £30, 22 bottles under £30, 13 by glass **Parking** 40 **Notes** Sunday L, Vegetarian available, Children welcome

BURLEY Map 5 SU20

Moorhill House Hotel

Modern, Traditional British

tel: 01425 403285 **BH24 4AG**
email: moorhill@newforesthotels.co.uk **web:** www.newforesthotels.co.uk
dir: *Exit A31 signed Burley Drive, through village, turn right opposite cricket pitch*

Well-executed British dishes at a New Forest hotel

Deep in the ancient woodland of the New Forest, near the pretty village of Burley, Moorhill's sits in its own handsome gardens. It's done out in light, attractive country-house style within, with log fires in winter. In the elegant dining room, straightforward but well-executed British dishes include devilled sardines on fennel-seed toast with cherry tomato and basil compôte. Move on to slow-roast pork belly with glazed apple and sautéed Savoy cabbage, sauced with the famous local Burley cider, or grilled haddock with chorizo and chickpea cassoulet. Cockle-warming puddings include a spiced rum parfait with ginger biscuits and coffee sauce, and black treacle and almond tart with orange ice cream.

CADNAM Map 5 SU21

Bartley Lodge Hotel

Traditional British

tel: 023 8081 2248 **Lyndhurst Rd SO40 2NR**
email: bartley@newforesthotels.co.uk **web:** www.newforesthotels.co.uk
dir: *M27 junct 1, A337, follow signs for Lyndhurst. Hotel on left*

Country-house cooking in elegant surroundings

In eight delightful Hampshire acres, the Grade II listed, 18th-century Bartley Lodge boasts many original features. A 'flexible dining' approach means the menu is available throughout the hotel, including in the Crystal Restaurant, with its elegant centrepiece chandelier and delicate blue and gold colour scheme. Start with goats' cheese pannacotta, pickled blackberries and malt-grain crisps. Then try pan-fried South Coast sea bass with crab risotto, confit tomatoes and pickled fennel, or something more traditional like 28-day matured rump steak with confit tomato, grilled flat-cut mushroom and chunky chips. Finish with an almond soufflé, passionfruit sorbet and mixed fruit jelly, or fig tart with pistachio ice cream.

Chef Stephen Sutton **Seats** 60, Pr/dining room 90 **Times** 5.30-9.30 **Prices** Prices not confirmed **Wines** 8 bottles over £30, 32 bottles under £30, 8 by glass **Parking** 90 **Notes** Sunday L, Vegetarian available, Children welcome

DOGMERSFIELD Map 5 SU75

Four Seasons Hotel Hampshire

 British

tel: 01252 853000 & 853100 **Dogmersfield Park, Chalky Ln RG27 8TD**
email: reservations.ham@fourseasons.com **web:** www.fourseasons.com/hampshire
dir: *M3 junct 5 onto A287 Farnham. After 1.5m take left to Dogmersfield, hotel 0.6m on left*

Fine-tuned contemporary cooking in a grand Georgian manor

Set within the expansive acreages of the Dogmersfield Estate, the Four Seasons' dining options include a bistro and café, but the main event is the Seasons restaurant, a light-filled space with French windows and an upscale, gently contemporary sheen. You might start with a soft-boiled duck's egg with girolles, glazed asparagus and a glossy duck emulsion, followed by roast beef tenderloin paired with oxtail-filled rigatoni, crispy potato, organic mushrooms and bordelaise sauce. Fishy mains could be pan-seared turbot with brown butter, spinach and basil purée and bouillabaisse jus. For a satisfying finish, go for something like crème brûlée infused with Hampshire lavender.

DROXFORD Map 5 SU61

Bakers Arms

 British, European

tel: 01489 877533 **High St SO32 3PA**
email: adam@thebakersarmsdroxford.com
dir: *Off A32*

Favourites and fancier in a homely Hampshire pub

The Bakers Arms is a whitewashed pub with a warmly welcoming atmosphere generated by hands-on young staff, an open fire and ceiling beams. The regularly-changing menu (with favourites like sausage and mash with onion gravy remaining constant) concentrates on great British traditions with forays further afield – pub grub this is not. Beautifully made smoked ham hock terrine is served with vibrant ale and onion chutney, to be followed by crisp-skinned pan-fried sea bass fillet, of melt-in-the-mouth consistency, on couscous with roast vegetables and coriander oil, or pan-fried kidneys with pancetta and horseradish mash. Desserts could include orange and lemon cake with clotted cream.

Chef Adam Cordery, Matt Hewitt, Kieron Rushworth **Seats** 45 **Times** 11.45-3/6-11, Closed D Sun **Prices** Fixed L 2 course £15, Fixed D 2 course £15, Starter £6-£7.50, Main £13-£20, Dessert £6.50 **Wines** 9 bottles over £30, 28 bottles under £30, 11 by glass **Parking** 30 **Notes** Sunday L £17.95-£18.95, Vegetarian available, Children welcome

EMSWORTH Map 5 SU70

Fat Olives

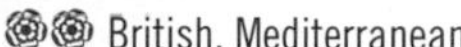 British, Mediterranean

tel: 01243 377914 **30 South St PO10 7EH**
email: info@fatolives.co.uk
dir: *In town centre, 1st right after Emsworth Square, 100yds towards the Quay. Restaurant on left with public car park opposite*

Locally-inspired inventive modern cooking near the quay

A 17th-century fishermen's cottage just a few steps from the quayside of pretty Emsworth harbour provides the setting for Lawrence and Julia Murphy's smart brasserie. The stripped-out interior of cream walls, wooden floors and unclothed tables is as unvarnished and honest as the food. Excellent raw materials do the talking and the menu is an appetising fusion of modern, well-thought-through ideas. It might take in salmon céviche with pickled cucumber and horseradish cream, then move on to roast duck breast with carrot houmous and orange in cumin jus. At the end, ginger parkin comes with plum compôte and matching sorbet.

Chef Lawrence Murphy **Seats** 25 **Times** 12-2.30/7-9.30, Closed 1 wk Xmas, 2 wks Jun, Sun-Mon **Prices** Fixed L 2 course £19.50-£19.90, Starter £6.95-£8.95, Main £15.95-£23.50, Dessert £6.95-£8.25 **Wines** 15 bottles over £30, 24 bottles under £30, 10 by glass **Parking** Opposite restaurant **Notes** Vegetarian available, Children 8 yrs+

36 on the Quay

Modern British, European

tel: 01243 375592 & 372257 **47 South St PO10 7EG**
email: info@36onthequay.co.uk **web:** www.36onthequay.co.uk
dir: *Last building on right in South St, which runs from square in centre of Emsworth*

Cooking of long-standing excellence on the harbourside

Ramon and Karen Farthing's chic restaurant with rooms in a quayside 17th-century house has established Emsworth as a foodie destination since it set up shop a generation ago. Harbour views are part of the attraction, and the restrained, modern dining room with tables dressed in their best whites attests to an operation that takes the business of fine dining and drinking with serious enthusiasm. Ramon's cooking is innovative stuff, backed with a sound, classical understanding of how flavours work together, and turbocharged with the excitement of modern technique. This is clear in a starter that makes a cannelloni of super-fresh crab encased in apple jelly to go with roasted and puréed artichoke, fresh apple and apple purée, puffed rice and foraged leaves. The watery setting brings fish to mind at main-course stage: poached cod is served with nut-brown butter sauce and herb crumb, accompanied with an elaborate assemblage of grilled langoustine, dehydrated cod skin with salt and vinegar jelly, roasted parsnips, and a pot of shellfish jelly, parsnip purée and parsley foam. Desserts continue the inventive ideas with a riff on tried-and-tested flavour combinations, taking in iced peanut parfait coated with crisp dark chocolate, coffee mousse topped with peanuts, and warm doughnuts with butterscotch sauce and orange jelly.

Chef Ramon Farthing, Gary Pearce **Seats** 45, Pr/dining room 12 **Times** 12-2/7-9.30, Closed 1st 2/3 wks Jan, 1 wk end May & Oct, 25-26 Dec, Sun-Mon **Prices** Fixed L 2 course fr £23.95, Fixed D 3 course fr £57.95, Tasting menu £29.95-£65 **Wines** 61 bottles over £30, 5 bottles under £30, 8 by glass **Parking** Car park nearby **Notes** Tasting menu L/D complete tables only, ALC menu £65, Vegetarian available, Children welcome

FAREHAM Map 5 SU50

Solent Hotel & Spa

Modern British, European

tel: 01489 880000 **Rookery Av, Whiteley PO15 7AJ**
email: solent@shirehotels.com **web:** www.shirehotels.com
dir: *M27 junct 9, hotel on Solent Business Park*

Sound brasserie cooking in a relaxed atmosphere

This contemporary spa hotel in Whiteley near Fareham is fine-tooled for relaxation, whether your preferred element be pool, massage table or dining room. The cooking takes a brasserie approach, with international classics, pasta dishes, steaks from the chargrill, and seasonal daily specials. Grainy-textured mushroom soup topped with fried mushrooms and pea shoots gets things off to a hearty start, or there may be tiger prawns and chilli dip, or smoked salmon with beetroot and horseradish crème fraîche. Crisp-skinned sea bass for main comes with a warm Niçoise salad, while sticky toffee pudding in hot treacle sauce with vanilla ice cream won't lack for takers at the finish.

Chef Peter Williams **Seats** 130, Pr/dining room 40 **Times** 12-9.30, All-day dining, Closed L Sat **Prices** Fixed L 2 course £21.95-£27.50, Fixed D 3 course £27.95-£35, Starter £3.50-£9.25, Main £12.75-£29.50, Dessert £3.95-£6.50 **Wines** 23 bottles over £30, 12 bottles under £30, 15 by glass **Parking** 200 **Notes** All day menu, Sunday L £21.95-£23.50, Vegetarian available, Children welcome

FARNBOROUGH Map 5 SU85

Aviator

 Modern European V

tel: 01252 555890 **Farnborough Rd GU14 6EL**
email: brasserie@aviatorbytag.com **web:** www.aviatorbytag.com
dir: *A325 to Aldershot, continue for 3m. Hotel on right*

Aviation-themed brasserie dining from the charcoal grill

The TAG timepiece manufacturer's aviation-themed hotel has landed on the Hampshire-Surrey border, in the vicinity of the celebrated air show at Farnborough. The uncomplicated modern brasserie food is centred on a repertoire of classic cuts of steak, done on the charcoal grill and served with béarnaise, bordelaise or peppercorn sauces. If your tastes extend to the very meaty, you might start with a portion of jugged hare and horseradish mash, but a gentler run-up is provided by shellfish in chickpea velouté, or goats' cheese and potato terrine with red onion purée and apple. A safe landing is achieved by means of blackberry mousse on cinnamon sponge with vanilla ice cream.

Chef Adam Fargin **Seats** 120, Pr/dining room 8 **Times** 12-2/6.30-10.30 **Prices** Fixed L 2 course fr £19, Fixed D 3 course fr £35, Tasting menu £65-£95, Starter £7.50-£13, Main £16-£32, Dessert £8-£9 **Wines** 44 bottles over £30, 18 bottles under £30, 16 by glass **Parking** 169 **Notes** Sunday L fr £29.50, Children welcome

HAMBLE-LE-RICE Map 5 SU40

The Bugle

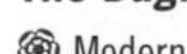 Modern British

tel: 023 8045 3000 **High St SO31 4HA**
email: manager@buglehamble.co.uk
dir: *M27 junct 8 to Hamble-Le-Rice. In village follow signs to foreshore*

Traditional and modern fare in an ancient riverside inn

The Bugle's carefully-restored interiors with their solid brickwork, bare floorboards, low ceilings and beams are exactly what a venerable country inn should look like, while the kitchen offers a clever mix of pub stalwarts and modern dishes. Fish and chips, Sunday roasts and sandwiches keep traditionalists happy, while the gastro brigade delight in the likes of pressed rabbit and prune terrine with pickled turnip to start, followed by bream fillet with potato salad, creamed leeks and kale. Extras include a tempting bubble-and-squeak cake, and finishers are rewarded with honey-spiced pear with pistachio ice cream and honeycomb, or dark chocolate terrine with boozy cherries and clotted cream.

HAYLING ISLAND Map 5 SU70

Langstone Hotel

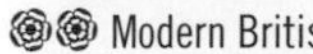 Modern British

tel: 023 9246 5011 **Northney Rd PO11 0NQ**
email: info@langstonehotel.co.uk **web:** www.langstonehotel.co.uk
dir: *From A27 signed Havant/Hayling Island follow A3023 across roadbridge onto Hayling Island & take sharp left on leaving bridge*

Creative spins on modern brasserie classics with views of the harbour

A contemporary hotel on the north shore of Hayling Island enjoying sweeping views towards Chichester Harbour. There is brasserie cooking of real flair here; witness goats' cheese and beetroot, the latter element appearing in salt-baked, sweet-pickled, grilled and raw guises, along with goats' cheese mousse and a distant waft of elderflower. Mains run to curried cod with pearl barley and grilled leeks, or a bravura take on duck and cherries, with succulent breast and rillettes of the leg-meat, as well as a slice of potato terrine. A speciality steak menu woos traditionalists, with fairground treats such as a dish of peanut parfait covered in popcorn and chocolate peanuts to finish.

Chef James Parsons **Seats** 120, Pr/dining room 120 **Times** 12.30-2/6.30-9.30 **Prices** Tasting menu £35-£40, Starter £6-£10, Main £14-£18, Dessert £6-£9 **Wines** 17 bottles over £30, 24 bottles under £30, 7 by glass **Parking** 220 **Notes** Sunday L £16.95-£18.95, Vegetarian available, Children welcome

HIGHCLERE Map 5 SU45

The Yew Tree

 Modern British

tel: 01635 253360 **Hollington Cross RG20 9SE**
email: info@theyewtree.co.uk **web:** www.theyewtree.co.uk
dir: *1m S of Highclere Village*

Modern British menus in a classic English pub

A classic English country inn in a ravishing setting near Highclere Castle. Traditional English cooking is the order of the day, overlaid with modern flourishes. Cod and salmon fishcakes are seasoned with chilli and dressed in mango mayonnaise, and local asparagus in season is topped with poached eggs and hollandaise. Roast lamb loin is spectacularly full of flavour, enhanced by chargrilled veg and a gutsy, garlicky salsa verde, while fish might be sparkling-fresh chalk-stream trout with new potatoes. A list of 'The Usual Suspects' keeps the fish and chips and burger brigade content. Cherry Bakewell is as good as it gets outside Derbyshire, matched with vanilla cream and cherry coulis.

HURSLEY Map 5 SU42

The King's Head

Classic British NEW

tel: 01962 775208 **Main Rd SO21 2JW**
email: enquiries@kingsheadhursley.co.uk **web:** www.kingsheadhursley.co.uk
dir: *M3 junct 11, follow signs to Winchester then Olivers Battery. At Badger Farm rdbt left onto A3090 to Romsey. In centre of village on left opposite church*

Sound regional cooking and skittles

An ivy-clad Georgian inn at the heart of a village community near Winchester, The King's Head has a lightly worn touch of refinement, with candlesticks on wooden tables, equestrian prints, tartan banquette, and a menu of sound, regionally-based cooking. Full-flavoured calves' liver terrine punctuated with green peppercorns, given edge with golden beetroot and orange, precedes a great piece of well-timed venison haunch with puréed squash, spiced onion rings and Jerusalem artichoke crisps, or sea bass and tiger prawns with smoked haddock fishcake in lemon-dill hollandaise. Sticky toffee pudding arrives as a slab of purest indulgence, with rich vanilla ice cream.

Chef Jenny Jones **Times** 12-3/6-9 **Prices** Starter £6.95-£7.95, Main £9.95-£23.95, Dessert £6.50 **Wines** 14 bottles over £30, 26 bottles under £30, 20 by glass **Notes** Afternoon tea, Sunday L

Hartnett Holder & Co

LYNDHURST **Map 5 SU30**

Italian V NOTABLE WINE LIST

tel: 023 8028 7167 & 8028 7177 **Lime Wood, Beaulieu Rd SO43 7FZ**
email: info@limewood.co.uk **web:** www.limewood.co.uk
dir: *A35 through Ashurst for 4m, then left in Lyndhurst signed Beaulieu, 1m to hotel*

Italian family cooking in a sophisticated New Forest hotel

If you go down to the woods today, the New Forest specifically, you could hardly do better than to find a beautifully-renovated Regency manor house built on the site of a 13th-century hunting lodge, imaginatively redesigned as a modern country hotel. Lime Wood's interiors have been created with great panache by in-demand designers David Collins and Martin Brudnizki, the expansive dining room all burgundy leather and parquet, the walls crowded with artworks, with seductive views over the grounds and water features. There are lodges tucked away in the forest, a classy spa, and attention to detail is evident from top to toe. The name represents the conjoined authority of Angela Hartnett (of Murano) and head chef Luke Holder, who between them devise and execute menus that spotlight regional produce including south coast seafood and the tempting output of the hotel's own smokehouse. Hartnett's Italian orientation is in evidence, producing a starter of flawless cavatelli pasta as a base for mussels and clams in parsley, garlic and chilli. Main course partners a pinkly roasted breast of duck with Jerusalem artichoke purée and anchovies, or sets red mullet in colourful sharp contrast with crab and pink grapefruit. If you've the capacity to do things the Italian way and fit in the full four courses, you might start with glorious antipasti such as game terrine with pumpkin jam, or creamy smoked cod's roe partnered with crackling, radish and rye crackers, and wrap things up with alluring desserts such as coffee pannacotta with mascarpone ice cream, or poached pear with saffron, goats' yogurt and lime. Bargain hunters should pop by for the unarguable value of the two-course set lunch menu.

Chef Angela Hartnett, Luke Holder **Seats** 70, Pr/dining room 16 **Times** 12-11, All-day dining **Prices** Fixed L 2 course fr £19.50, Starter £8.50-£15, Main £18-£30, Dessert £7-£16 **Wines** 550 bottles over £30, 15 bottles under £30, 20 by glass **Parking** 90 **Notes** Tavolo Della Cucina 5 course £65, Sharing menu, Sunday L £37.50, Children welcome

LYMINGTON Map 5 SZ39

The Elderflower Restaurant

Modern British, French

tel: 01590 676908 **4A Quay St SO41 3AS**
email: info@elderflowerrestaurant.co.uk
dir: *M27 junct for A337 Lyndhurst. At rdbt take 1st exit A31, follow A337 then B3054 Captains Row, left onto Nelson Pl then left onto Quay Rd*

Inspirational cooking full of bright ideas

A new dimension of classy Anglo-French dining arrived in Lymington with the opening of The Elderflower in 2014. Indian technique comes into play for a starter of curried mussels with smoked tapioca, spiced cauliflower purée and shallot bhajis, while a clump of samphire adds a salty hit. Next up might be Jurassic Coast veal – the loin, liver and panko-crumbed sweetbreads – which comes with a casserole of chanterelles and butter beans and fried kale in an ingenious crayfish bisque. Crème brûlée gets a twist with puréed chestnut worked into the custard, alongside sherry-soaked raisins, clove ice cream and ginger crumb.

Chef Andrew Du Bourg **Seats** 40 **Times** 12-2.30/6.30-9.30, Closed Mon, D Sun **Prices** Starter £7.50-£12.50, Main £19.50-£25.50, Dessert £7-£10 **Wines** 39 bottles over £30, 51 bottles under £30, 6 by glass **Parking** Quay car park **Notes** Sun champagne breakfast, Market tapas dishes £3.50-£8, Sunday L, Vegetarian available, Children welcome

Stanwell House Hotel

Modern European

tel: 01590 677123 **14-15 High St SO41 9AA**
email: enquiries@stanwellhouse.com **web:** www.stanwellhouse.com
dir: *M27 junct 1, follow signs to Lyndhurst into Lymington centre & High Street*

Modern seafood and bistro cookery at a historic address

After a spell as a ladies' finishing-school, Stanwell House became a hotel around the end of the last war. Start your culinary education with a crab and pink grapefruit cocktail, or mackerel on toast with elderflower, gooseberries and shallots. Move on to a majestic pairing of fried red mullet and braised chicken wing, with stir-fried noodles, Asian coleslaw and carrot and ginger purée. A secondary dining option, the Bistro, offers game consommé with crispy duck, and a main course of pork cuts, including a smoked potato and black pudding croquette, in Calvados jus. Finish with a spin on Pina Colada, comprising coconut parfait, Szechuan-spiced pineapple and a splash of rum.

LYNDHURST Map 5 SU30

The Glasshouse

Modern British

tel: 023 8028 6129 & 8028 3677 **Best Western Forest Lodge Hotel, Pikes Hill, Romsey Rd SO43 7AS**
email: enquiries@theglasshousedining.co.uk **web:** www.theglasshousedining.co.uk
dir: *M27 junct 1, A337 towards Lyndhurst. In village, with police station & courts on right, take 1st right into Pikes Hill*

Contemporary-style restaurant with well-judged cooking

On the outskirts of Lyndhurst, this hotel has had a thorough makeover, creating a hugely stylish environment. The menu covers a lot of ground, from burgers and light bites to a well-conceived starter of quail three ways (poached breast, confit leg and a mini Scotch egg) with a herb salad, creamed leeks and Albufera sauce. The kitchen generally mines the modern British vein, seen in seared veal tongue with spicy blackberry ketchup, sticky baby onions and watercress, and seared salmon fillet with a dressing of lime, basil and sour cream served with smoked haddock and potato brandade. Pudding might be rich double-layered chocolate pavé balanced by milk sorbet.

Hartnett Holder & Co

– see page 171 and advert opposite

MILFORD ON SEA Map 5 SZ29

Verveine Fishmarket Restaurant

Seafood

tel: 01590 642176 **98 High St, Lymington SO41 0QE**
email: info@verveine.co.uk
dir: *A337, B3058, Church Hill. Left onto High St, 200 mtrs on right*

Ultra-modern village seafood cookery

At the back of the fishmongers is the intimate, elegant dining room, reached by passing the kitchen, from which chef himself often emerges to bring your dish to table. A chunk of monkfish given the Madras treatment arrives with spiced carrot purée, plump raisins and sous-vide potato. Other possibilities are founded on East Asian seasonings, or go for slow-cooked pork cheek with burnt apple. Scallops with their corals to start come in a laverbread, oat and pancetta porridge, dressed in 50-year-old balsamic, while dessert might be a blueberry study incorporating pannacotta, sorbet, tuile, foam and fresh berries. Throw in creative canapés to complete a terrific meal.

Chef David Wykes **Seats** 32 **Times** 12-2/6.30-10, Closed 25 Dec-18 Jan, Sun-Mon **Prices** Fixed L 2 course fr £17, Tasting menu £45-£85, Starter £8.95-£15, Main £14-£27, Dessert £8.95-£12.50 **Wines** 24 bottles over £30, 27 bottles under £30, 6 by glass **Parking** On street, car park 200 mtrs **Notes** Fixed L 6 course £33, Tasting menu 4/6/8/10 course, Vegetarian available, Children welcome

NEW MILTON Map 5 SZ29

Chewton Glen Hotel & Spa

@@ Modern British V NOTABLE WINE LIST

tel: 01425 282212 **Christchurch Rd BH25 6QS**
email: reservations@chewtonglen.com **web:** www.chewtonglen.com
dir: *A35 (Lyndhurst) turn left through Walkford, 4th left into Chewton Farm Rd*

Classy cooking in luxury country-house hotel

Whether you are drawn by the desire to play golf on the nine-hole course, or prefer being pampered in the spa, Chewton Glen is a luxurious bolt-hole. The menu aims to satisfy with an output that deals in classic British and European combinations, while incorporating some global flavours. Start with monkfish cheeks in tempura batter, served with soba noodle salad, or ballotine of duck liver matched with roasted apple and vanilla purée, and move on to saddle of venison with pickled trompettes and chestnut purée, or Tuscan-style fish stew. For dessert, pear and blackberry clafoutis comes with lemon verbena ice cream.

Chef Luke Matthews **Seats** 164, Pr/dining room 70 **Times** 12-2/6-9.30 **Prices** Fixed L 3 course fr £26.50, Tasting menu £70-£115, Starter £9-£23, Main £21-£42, Dessert £7.50-£10 **Wines** 1800 bottles over £30, 80 by glass **Parking** 150 **Notes** Sunday L fr £39.50, Children welcome

See advert opposite

NORTHINGTON Map 5 SU53

The Woolpack Inn

@ Classic British

tel: 01962 734184 **Totford SO24 9TJ**
email: info@thewoolpackinn.co.uk **web:** www.thewoolpackinn.co.uk
dir: *From Basingstoke take A339 towards Alton. Under motorway, turn right (across dual carriageway) onto B3036 signed Candovers & Alresford. Pub between Brown Candover & Northington*

Pretty country inn with gently modernised food

In a tiny hamlet within the pretty Candover Valley, this Grade I listed flint-and-brick inn has retained its traditional country pub feel with open fires, flagstoned floors and real ales, although these days the emphasis is on food. A combination of traditional British pub dishes and European influences makes for an appealing menu that might kick off with cod and chorizo kebabs with tomato salsa and aïoli. Slow-cooked lamb, spiced chickpeas and mint yogurt looks to the Middle East for inspiration, with Pimm's jelly and vanilla cream making a summery finale. The pub also has an outdoor kitchen which comes into its own on the Sunday 'pizza night'.

Chef Matt Gisby **Seats** 50, Pr/dining room 14 **Times** 12-2.30/6.30-9, Closed D 25 Dec **Prices** Prices not confirmed **Wines** 25 bottles over £30, 22 bottles under £30, 12 by glass **Parking** 40 **Notes** Sunday L, Vegetarian available, Children welcome

OLD BURGHCLERE Map 5 SU45

The Dew Pond Restaurant

@ British, European

tel: 01635 278408 **RG20 9LH**
dir: *Newbury A34 South, exit Tothill. Follow signs for Highclere Castle, pass castle entrance on right, down hill & turn left signed Old Burghclere & Kingsclere, restaurant on right in approx 0.25m*

Classical cooking not far from the setting for *Downton Abbey*

The Dew Pond was once a pair of 16th-century drovers' cottages, now welded into a very chic, pastel-hued country restaurant, not far from Highclere Castle (aka *Downton Abbey* off the telly). The cooking is founded on classical principles with the sort of personal overlay that has won many local devotees. An exemplary souffle of Keen's cheddar with rocket and spring onion cream sauce is an accomplished opener, and might be followed by roasted sea bream with grilled tiger prawns, ratatouille and saffron potatoes. For dessert there may be that old standby, sticky toffee with praline ice cream.

OTTERBOURNE Map 5 SU42

The White Horse

@ Modern, Traditional British

tel: 01962 712830 **Main Rd SO21 2EQ**
email: manager@whitehorseotterbourne.co.uk
dir: *M3 junct 12/A335 1st exit at 1st rdbt & 2nd exit at next 2 rdbts, via Otterbourne Hill into Main Rd. Restaurant on left*

Modern pub grub done right

Descending from a hike along the spine of the South Downs, you couldn't ask for a more fortifying pitstop. This village hostelry looks every inch the modern dining pub with wooden and quarry-tiled floors, bare beams and mismatched vintage tables. The mood is unbuttoned and family-friendly, while the kitchen is driven by an enthusiasm for local ingredients, served up in a straightforward contemporary vein. This might translate as duck liver and pistachio terrine wrapped in smoked bacon with roasted pear purée, followed by trout fishcakes with ginger and lime-dressed summer slaw. Puddings take a similarly comfort-oriented route – perhaps chocolate brownie with salt caramel ice cream.

PETERSFIELD Map 5 SU72

JSW

 Modern British V 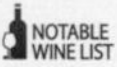

tel: 01730 262030 **20 Dragon St GU31 4JJ**
email: jsw.restaurant@btconnect.com
dir: *A3 to town centre, follow one-way system to College St which becomes Dragon St, restaurant on left*

Dynamic contemporary cooking in a made-over old inn

Jake Watkins' place is a Stuart coaching inn looking out on the centre of town, its connections rooted sufficiently deeply into Petersfield's past that it has three underground tunnels linking to other buildings, including one to what was the convent (maybe don't ask). The old cellar is now stuffed with the restaurant's authoritative wine stock, and the bedrooms have been comfortably kitted out for the stoppers. Watkins has been doing cutting-edge cookery here for a long while, but his inventiveness and enthusiasm are undimmed. Resisting the tendency to over-garnish, he presents witty takes on recognisable culinary currents, as when quail arrives sitting proud on an open raviolo with home-produced raisins and truffle. Suckling pig comes, with irresistible logic, 'with what it eats', before main courses usher on the likes of a spag bol makeover done with lamb, slow-cooked tomatoes and basil, or juxtapose sea bass delicately with lightly spiced mussels and lettuce. At dessert, there may be a fairgroundy spin on knickerbocker glory made with autumn fruits and cinnamon doughnuts, or a rice pudding cheesecake hybrid layered with tropical fruits. The multi-course tasters take you on a virtual mystery tour, with just the star ingredients credited – scallops, salmon, duck, lamb, and so intriguingly forth.

Chef Jake Watkins **Seats** 58, Pr/dining room 18 **Times** 12-1.30/7-9.30, Closed 2 wks Jan, May & summer, Mon-Tue, L Wed, D Sun **Prices** Fixed L 2 course £30, Fixed D 3 course £50, Tasting menu £45-£80 **Wines** 492 bottles over £30, 36 bottles under £30, 9 by glass **Parking** 19 **Notes** Tasting menu L/D 6/8 course, ALC 2/3 course £32.50/£49.50, Sunday L, Children 6 yrs+

Langrish House

 Traditional British

tel: 01730 266941 **Langrish GU32 1RN**
email: frontdesk@langrishhouse.co.uk **web:** www.langrishhouse.co.uk
dir: *A3 onto A272 towards Winchester. Hotel signed, 2.5m on left*

Vigorous modern British cooking at a South Downs house with a past

Langrish House has been home to the Talbot-Ponsonby family for seven generations, and when you see the gorgeous 17th-century mansion in 14 acres of undulating Hampshire, it's no surprise they've stayed. Frederick's restaurant immortalises an off-the-wall Victorian great-uncle and is a cosy, traditional spot, or you can dine in the low-lit intimacy of the old vaults below, dug by Royalist prisoners in the Civil War. Kick off with herb-coated salmon ballotine with fromage blanc, Avruga caviar and lime, before moving on to saddle of venison with its own biryani, rainbow chard and caramelised cauliflower. Winding up proceedings is blood orange soufflé with bay leaf ice cream.

Chef Nathan Marshall **Seats** 18, Pr/dining room 80 **Times** 12-2/7-9.30, Closed 27 Dec-10 Jan **Prices** Fixed L 2 course £18.95, Tasting menu £45, Starter £7.50-£13.50, Main £22-£16.50, Dessert £4.50-£6.50 **Wines** 26 bottles over £30, 19 bottles under £30, 11 by glass **Parking** 80 **Notes** Sunday L £18.95-£21.95, Vegetarian available, Children 7 yrs+

The Thomas Lord

 Modern British

tel: 01730 829244 **High St, West Meon GU32 1LN**
email: info@thethomaslord.co.uk
dir: *M3 junct 9, A272 towards Petersfield, right at x-rds onto A32, 1st left*

Inventive country pub cooking

A proper pub with fine local ales and a shabby-chic charm. On the food front, everything is made in-house, the garden supplies seasonal goodies, and the majority of materials come from small-scale local producers. The kitchen has some inventive ideas, starting with dressed Portland crab paired with brown crab custard, treacle bread and kohlrabi remoulade. Mains show off prime materials in the form of tender belly and fillet of pork, layered with black pudding and delivered with peas, broad beans, cauliflower purée, candied fennel, smoked apple purée and crackling. For afters, there's warm chocolate mousse in a chocolate tuile, aerated chocolate, brownie, salted caramel and buttermilk ice cream.

Chef Aaron Lawrence **Seats** 70 **Times** 12-2.30/6-9.30, Closed D 25-26 Dec, 1 Jan **Prices** Fixed L 2 course £18, Fixed D 3 course £23, Tasting menu £55, Starter £7-£10, Main £15-£22, Dessert £6.50-£8 **Wines** 13 bottles over £30, 26 bottles under £30, 14 by glass **Parking** 20 **Notes** Pre-theatre menu, Sunday L £12.50-£15.50, Vegetarian available, Children welcome

PORTSMOUTH & SOUTHSEA Map 5 SU60

Restaurant 27

 Modern European V

tel: 023 9287 6272 **27a South Pde PO5 2JF**
email: info@restaurant27.com
dir: *M27 junct 12, take M275 to A3, follow A288 South Parade, left Burgoyne Rd*

Vivid cooking based on thought-provoking combinations

The whitewashed building may look like a storage-shed, but inside is a smartly appointed, high-ceilinged dining room where chef-proprietor Kevin Bingham runs a fixed-price carte or six-course tasting menus that showcase the kitchen's abilities. Flavours are captivating, as when silky haddock and prawn velouté is garnished with a raviolo of orange and pine nuts, and marinated foie gras gains in intensity from its accompaniments of Granny Smith apple, honey and ginger. At main course, 'umami duck' is juxtaposed with Ibérico chorizo and feta, or there could be sea bass with smoked pancetta in scallop and clam chowder. To finish, crème brûlée is sharpened with blackcurrant and star anise.

Chef Kevin Bingham, Annie Smith **Seats** 34 **Times** 12-2.30/7-9.30, Closed Xmas, New Year, Mon-Tue, L Wed-Sat, D Sun **Prices** Fixed L 3 course £29, Fixed D 3 course £45, Tasting menu £42-£50 **Wines** 30 bottles over £30, 23 bottles under £30, 9 by glass **Parking** On street **Notes** Tasting menu 7 course Wed-Thu/8 course Fri-Sat, Sunday L, Children welcome

ROMSEY Map 5 SU32

The Three Tuns

Modern British

tel: 01794 512639 **58 Middlebridge St SO51 8HL**
email: manager@the3tunsromsey.co.uk
dir: *A27 bypass on A3030*

Classy pub cooking with lashings of period charm

Sympathetically remodelled, The Three Tuns retains its olden-times charm, with winter fires, exposed brickwork, and stuffed birds in glass cases. An extensive menu of pub classics aims to please all comers. Meaty things are dependably satisfying, as for ham hock terrine with piccalilli and pea shoots, or mains such as braised lamb shoulder in pan juices with fondant potato and puréed carrots. If it's fish you're after, there will be much rejoicing over devilled whitebait with aïoli, followed perhaps by grilled mackerel with courgettes and spring onions in salsa verde. Proceedings conclude with stickily glazed, citrussy treacle tart and vanilla ice cream, or chocolate marquise with salted caramel ice cream.

Chef Konrad Guza, Rob Price **Seats** 35 **Times** 12-2.30/6-9, Closed 25-26 Dec **Prices** Starter £5.95-£7.95, Main £11.95-£15.50, Dessert £6.50-£6.95 **Wines** 7 bottles over £30, 19 bottles under £30, 11 by glass **Parking** 14, On street **Notes** Sunday L fr £12.95, Vegetarian available, Children welcome

The White Horse Hotel & Brasserie

Modern British

tel: 01794 512431 **19 Market Place SO51 8ZJ**
web: www.thewhitehorseromsey.co.uk
dir: *M27 junct 3, follow signs for Romsey, right at Broadlands. In town centre*

Brasserie dining on a site noted for hospitality since the 12th century

At the heart of operations at the ancient White Horse is a brasserie-styled dining room, with a British-based roll call of dishes inflected with some European technique. Well-defined flavours shine forth from quality prime materials, and presentations are clean and appealing. A piece of finely timed salmon is partnered with seared foie gras and cumined lentils for an effective opener, while mains run to wild mushroom and leek lasagne with a fried duck egg, herb-crusted cod in butternut velouté, and chargrilled loin and braised neck of local lamb with a purée of haricots in balsamic jus. Go Spanish for dessert with soft-centred churros and toasted almonds, accompanied by raspberry sorbet.

The White Horse Hotel & Brasserie

Chef Nick O'Hallaran **Seats** 85, Pr/dining room 100 **Times** 12-3/6-10 **Prices** Starter £6.95-£12, Main £14-£32, Dessert £7 **Wines** 32 bottles over £30, 17 bottles under £30, 11 by glass **Parking** Car park nearby **Notes** Afternoon tea, Sunday L, Vegetarian available, Children welcome

See advert on page 177

ROTHERWICK Map 5 SU75

The Oak Room Restaurant

Traditional British V

tel: 01256 764881 **Tylney Hall Hotel, Ridge Ln RG27 9AZ**
email: sales@tylneyhall.com **web:** www.tylneyhall.co.uk
dir: *M3 junct 5, A287 to Basingstoke, over junct with A30, over rail bridge, towards Newnham. Right at Newnham Green. Hotel 1m on left*

Victorian house with Gertrude Jekyll gardens and a grand dining room

Tylney Hall is the place for classical country-house dining, and the Oak Room Restaurant delivers the goods in a setting involving oak panels, a domed ceiling and a tinkling grand piano. What arrives on the plate is a gently updated take on the classics, with splashes of modernity here and there. A seared fillet of sea bream is accompanied by fennel in coriander and ginger for a southeast Asian flourish, prior to venison loin with potato and pumpkin gratin and confit root veg in a sparse

continued across the page

but intense port reduction. Chocolate orange tart, its opulent filling offset by flaky pastry, orange purée and mascarpone ice cream, brings down the curtain.

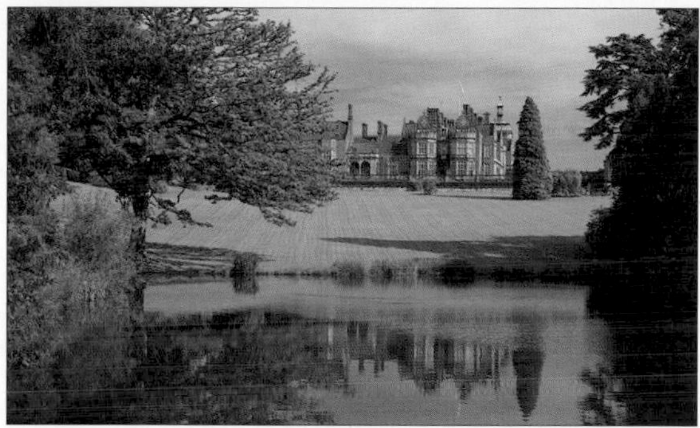

The Oak Room Restaurant

Chef Stephen Hine **Seats** 80, Pr/dining room 120 **Times** 12.30-2/7-10 **Prices** Prices not confirmed **Wines** 350 bottles over £30, 5 bottles under £30, 10 by glass **Parking** 150 **Notes** Sunday L, Children welcome

See advert below

ST MARY BOURNE **Map 5 SU45**

Bourne Valley Inn

British NEW

tel: 01264 738361 **SP11 6BT**
email: enquiries@bournevalleyinn.com **web:** www.bournevalleyinn.com
dir: *10 mins from A34 or A303. S of St Mary Bourne on B3048*

Appealing village pub with satisfying food

Known as BVI to its friends, this village pub has become a magnet for local foodies, with its main dining area in a converted barn with soaring beams and a contemporary, rustic-chic look. The menu presses the comfort button with an interesting mix of pub classics, down-to-earth cooking and an evangelical keenness for local produce. Warm ham hock is served with piccalilli running through, along with a crispy poached egg, home-made ketchup and salt-and-pepper crisps, then splendid local venison flavoured with honey and cumin comes with carrots, beetroot and balsamic jus. For pudding, there's treacle tart with pistachio ice cream.

Chef Ryan Stacey **Seats** 100, Pr/dining room 18 **Times** 12-3/6-9.30 **Prices** Starter £5.95-£8.50, Main £9.95-£17.50, Dessert £5.95 **Wines** 8 bottles over £30, 19 bottles under £30, 6 by glass **Notes** Afternoon tea (booking essential), Sunday L £11.50-£14.50, Vegetarian available, Children welcome

SOUTHAMPTON Map 5 SU41

Best Western Chilworth Manor

 Modern British

tel: 023 8076 7333 **Chilworth SO16 7PT**
email: sales@chilworth-manor.co.uk **web:** www.chilworth-manor.co.uk
dir: *1m from M3/M27 junct on A27 Romsey Rd N from Southampton. Pass Chilworth Arms on left, in 200mtrs turn left at Southampton Science Park sign. Hotel immediately right*

Brasserie-style cooking in a grand Edwardian hotel

A grand Edwardian pile in charming grounds, this classy hotel restaurant has plenty of period elegance, with oak panels and tables dressed in white linen cloths. Its upmarket brasserie-style fare contains regional ingredients and global influences. Start with pan-seared scallops with parsnip purée and a dressing combining apples and roasted hazelnuts, and follow on with Owtons of Hampshire saddle of venison with fondant potato and a fig and juniper berry sauce. There is a burger, too, and monkfish wrapped in nori. Finish with a fun dessert such as iced prosecco and rhubarb parfait with spiced ginger biscuits and a bag of delicious custard doughnuts.

Botleigh Grange Hotel

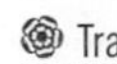 Traditional British

tel: 01489 787700 **Grange Rd, Hedge End SO30 2GA**
email: enquiries@botleighgrange.com **web:** www.botleighgrange.com
dir: *On A334, 1m from M27 junct 7*

Modern British classics in a stylish spa hotel

A gleaming white spa hotel not far from Southampton, Botleigh Grange has been around since the mid-17th century, yet the place looks pristinely maintained and box-fresh inside, with the Hampshire's dining room bathed in daylight from a glass-domed ceiling, and swagged curtains to frame the garden view. An expansive menu of modern British classics is on offer. Hampshire game terrine is one way to begin, or go for pan-seared scallops with butternut squash purée, before a main course roasted rump of lamb, or 10oz rib-eye steak with classic accoutrements. Mixed fruit crumble or sticky toffee pudding makes for a hearty finale.

Chef Aaron Furey **Seats** 100, Pr/dining room 350 **Times** 7-9.30, Closed L Mon-Sat **Prices** Starter £5.50-£7, Main £14.95-£22.50, Dessert £5.50-£6.50 **Wines** 16 bottles over £30, 29 bottles under £30, 10 by glass **Parking** 300 **Notes** Gourmet break 6 course, Sunday L £14.95-£17.95, Vegetarian available, Children welcome

Mercure Southampton Centre Dolphin Hotel

 Modern International

tel: 023 8038 6460 **34-35 High St SO14 2HN**
email: H7876@accor.com **web:** www.mercure.com
dir: *A33 follow signs for Docks & Old Town/IOW ferry, at ferry terminal turn right into High Street, hotel 400yds on left*

Historic hotel with crowd-pleasing menu

A 17th-century coaching inn boasting the likes of Jane Austen, Queen Victoria and Admiral Nelson among its former guests, several million pounds and a takeover from the Mercure chain later, it is a striking and characterful place to stay and to eat. In the Signature Restaurant, contemporary tones abound and it all looks suitably contemporary and unstuffy – darkwood tables, plenty of period character, and a menu that doesn't stray far from traditional, brasserie-style comforts. Baked ramekin of Hampshire pear with Stilton cream and watercress salad might precede steak and kidney pie, half a roast poussin with bubble-and-squeak and bread sauce, or a Casterbridge steak from the grill.

White Star Tavern, Dining and Rooms

 British

tel: 023 8082 1990 **28 Oxford St SO14 3DJ**
email: reservations@whitestartavern.co.uk **web:** www.whitestartavern.co.uk
dir: *M3 junct 14 onto A33, towards Ocean Village*

Confident modern dishes in a local hotspot

Bringing a touch of boutique style to Southampton, this place has a satisfying blend of period details and contemporary touches in the dining room, and an easy-going attitude. The kitchen produces some strident modern stuff such as starters of blow-torched smoked salmon with cucumber pickle and crumbed quail's egg, or seared scallops with cauliflower textures and black pudding. Among main courses, cod loin comes with a chestnut crust alongside artichoke purée and dauphinoise potatoes, and Wiltshire partridge with the leg meat in an accompanying raviolo, plus parsnip purée and sticky red cabbage. Finish with Bakewell tart with clotted cream ice cream and drunken cranberries.

STOCKBRIDGE Map 5 SU33

The Greyhound on the Test

 Modern British

tel: 01264 810833 **31 High St SO20 6EY**
email: info@thegreyhoundonthetest.co.uk **web:** www.thegreyhoundonthetest.co.uk
dir: *9m NW of Winchester, 8m S of Andover. Off A303*

Upmarket town inn with up-to-date food and local fishing rights

The Greyhound has no shortage of appeal, from upmarket, sumptuous bedrooms to a restaurant with that opened-up, country-chic vibe. The menu is a thoroughly up-to-date affair with regional produce at its heart; witness a starter of Broughton buffalo carpaccio with celeriac remoulade and pine nuts. At main course stage, super-fresh monkfish and scallops are served raw, céviche-style with finely shaved fennel, mooli radish and lime, or if you fancy something more visceral, the grill might supply best end of lamb, haggis and faggots with sweet-and-sour carrots and crushed olives. You're sure to go home happy after dark chocolate brownie with chocolate mousse, cherries and amaretti.

The Peat Spade Inn

Modern British

tel: 01264 810612 **Village St, Longstock SO20 6DR**
email: info@peatspadeinn.co.uk **web:** www.peatspadeinn.co.uk
dir: *M3 junct 8, A303 W approx 15m, then take A3057 Stockbridge/Andover*

Rustic cooking with a French feeling and fly-fishing in the vicinity

A stolid-looking red-brick country inn where close-set tables add to the dining-room buzz. Rustic cooking with more than a soupçon of French influence proves abidingly popular, seen here in the form of fried chicken livers on sourdough toast with charred sweetcorn in peppercorn sauce to start. Then come mains like accurately timed baked cod in a bouillabaisse of Portland shellfish with saffron gnocchi, fennel, samphire and aïoli that some may judge falls short of its garlicky duty, or venison loin with wild mushrooms, lentils and spiced bread purée. The modernist trail is then followed for desserts such as white chocolate pannacotta with raspberry sorbet and chocolate doughnuts in passionfruit coulis.

Chef Paul Dive **Seats** 53, Pr/dining room 16 **Times** 12-2.30/6.30-9.30, Closed D 26 Dec, 1 Jan **Prices** Prices not confirmed **Wines** 13 bottles over £30, 24 bottles under £30, 10 by glass **Parking** 19 **Notes** Pre-booking strongly recommended, Daily menu, Sunday L, Vegetarian available, Children welcome

The Three Cups Inn

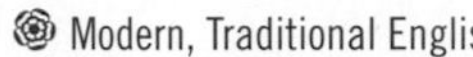

Modern, Traditional English

tel: 01264 810527 **High St SO20 6HB**
email: manager@the3cups.co.uk **web:** www.the3cups.co.uk
dir: *Phone for directions*

Old coaching inn with a modern menu

This 16th-century coaching inn is still very much a pub offering local ales, but it's also a dining destination with low-ceilinged dining room and an orangery extension opening up to the garden. There are en suite bedrooms, too. The kitchen makes good use of local foodstuffs, sending out the likes of beetroot-cured trout with horseradish pannacotta and smoked trout Scotch egg, while main course might see confit belly and braised shoulder of pork matched with potato, parsnip and apple purée, and mushroom and cider sauce. Bread is made on the premises and, for dessert, there's panettone bread-and-butter pudding with salted caramel ice cream.

Chef Ian Hamilton **Seats** 50, Pr/dining room 20
Times 12-2.30/6.30-9.30, Closed 25-26 Dec **Prices** Starter £5-£9, Main £11-£22, Dessert £5-£9 **Wines** 10 bottles over £30, 16 bottles under £30, 12 by glass **Parking** 15 **Notes** Sunday L £11-£18, Vegetarian available, Children welcome

WINCHESTER **Map 5 SU42**

Avenue Restaurant at Lainston House Hotel

Modern British V NOTABLE WINE LIST

tel: 01962 776088 **Woodman Ln, Sparsholt SO21 2LT**
email: enquiries@lainstonhouse.com **web:** www.lainstonhouse.com
dir: *2m NW off B3049 towards Stockbridge, junct with Woodman Ln*

Creative modern cooking in 17th-century country-house hotel

The restaurant at this 17th-century former hunting lodge in 63 bucolic acres outside of Winchester gets its name from an impressive mile-long avenue of lime trees in the grounds. The house itself is a delicious red-brick affair and its main dining room has plenty of period charm (and a view of that avenue of lime trees), with rich burgundy leather chairs and tables dressed up in pristine white linen. Four acres of the estate is given over to a kitchen garden to keep the Avenue Restaurant supplied with seasonal goodies, and chef Olly Rouse and his team turn first-class ingredients into creative modern plates of food while maintaining the integrity of the produce. Crab and herring are matched in a first course with the flavours of green tea and yuzu, while another puts textures of cauliflower with wood pigeon, puffed grains and pickled blackberries. Everything looks stunning on the plate. Next up, fresh-as-a-daisy turbot arrives with chicken wing in a fashionable combination, and glazed pork fillet, smoked bacon and black pudding gets counterpointed by a measured hit of pickled onion. There's a tasting menu with wine flight, and, among desserts, imaginative complementary flavours and textures ensure the occasion ends on a high (macadamia nuts, passionfruit, mango and milk ice cream, for example).

Chef Olly Rouse **Seats** 60, Pr/dining room 120 **Times** 12-2/7-9, Closed 25-26 Dec, L Sat, D 24 Dec **Prices** Fixed L 2 course £26, Fixed D 3 course £58, Tasting menu £78 **Wines** 120 bottles over £30, 30 bottles under £30, 9 by glass **Parking** 100 **Notes** ALC 2/3 course £48/£58, Afternoon tea £29.50, Sunday L £32-£39, Children welcome

The Black Rat

Modern British

tel: 01962 844465 & 841531 **88 Chesil St SO23 0HX**
email: reservations@theblackrat.co.uk
dir: *M3 junct 9/A31 towards Winchester & Bar End until T-junct. Turn right at lights, restaurant 600yds on left*

Culinary modernism with a traditional pub ambience

A white-fronted former pub on the edge of town, The Black Rat sets its sights firmly on culinary modernism. It's now most definitely a restaurant. At the moment, the kitchen's ambitious cooking is rather hit-and-miss, with oddball combinations of ingredients and techniques. When they hit, there's much to admire, as in a vibrantly colourful fish stew of bream, ling and gurnard with aïoli and saffron noodles, or grilled monkfish tail with cauliflower purée and grape couscous in verjus. Meat could be fine Elwy lamb with goats' curd and hay-baked turnips, and white chocolate cheesecake is an impressive finale, let down slightly by the accompanying chicory mousse and beetroot granola.

Chef Ollie Moore **Seats** 40, Pr/dining room 16 **Times** 12-2.15/7-9.30, Closed 2 wks Etr, 2 wks Oct/Nov, 2 wks Xmas & New Year, L Mon-Fri **Prices** Fixed L 2 course £25.95, Starter £9.75-£12.25, Main £19.75-£23.50, Dessert £8.95-£12.95 **Wines** 6 bottles over £30, 6 bottles under £30, 10 by glass **Parking** Car park opposite **Notes** Fixed L Sat-Sun only, Sunday L £25.95-£28.95, Vegetarian available, Children 12 yrs+ D

The Chesil Rectory

Modern British

tel: 01962 851555 **1 Chesil St SO23 0HU**
email: enquiries@chesilrectory.co.uk
dir: *S from King Alfred's statue at bottom of The Broadway, cross small bridge, turn right, restaurant on left, just off mini rdbt*

Modernised British dishes in a medieval house

A beautiful half-timbered building dating from 1450, The Chesil Rectory is the oldest house in Winchester. Enter through a low door to be greeted by a brilliantly preserved interior with low beams, charming inglenook fireplaces and exposed brickwork, and a quirky collection of taxidermy. The kitchen puts a gently modernised spin onto classic British dishes, bolstered by some that have nothing to do with the native repertoire, as in a starter of rosemary gnocchi with charred onions, artichokes and the crunch of hazelnuts. Among main courses, sticky glazed beef short rib and steamed sea bass with local mushrooms hit the spot.

Chef Damian Brown **Seats** 75, Pr/dining room 14
Times 12-2.20/6-9.30, Closed 25-26 Dec, 1 Jan **Prices** Fixed L 2 course £16.95, Fixed D 3 course £19.95, Starter £5.95-£10.95, Main £13.95-£20.50, Dessert £6.95 **Wines** 42 bottles over £30, 25 bottles under £30, 12 by glass **Parking** NCP Chesil St adjacent **Notes** Fixed menu Mon-Sat 12-2.20/6-7, Sun 6-9, Sunday L £21.95-£26.95, Vegetarian available, Children 12 yrs+ D

WINCHESTER *continued*

Holiday Inn Winchester

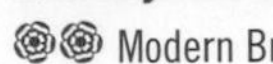 Modern British

tel: 01962 670700 **Telegraph Way, Morn Hill SO21 1HZ**
email: info@hiwinchester.co.uk **web:** www.hiwinchester.co.uk
dir: *M3 junct 9, A31 signed Alton, A272 & Petersfield. 1st exit at rdbt onto A31, 1.6m, take 1st exit into Alresford Rd, left into Telegraph Way*

Modern British cooking in the South Downs

On the edge of the South Downs National Park, the restaurant at this large purpose-built hotel goes to great lengths to source local produce. The high culinary standards elevate the cooking well above that normally seen in hotel chains and the modern cooking appeals to both leisure and corporate guests. A starter of pressed New Forest game terrine served with blood orange jam and toasted thyme brioche might lead on to a main of roasted guinea fowl supreme with red-legged partridge mousse, braised red cabbage, fondant potato and Puy lentils. Conclude with honeycomb parfait with lemon curd ice cream.

Chef Chris Keel **Seats** 128, Pr/dining room 200 **Times** 12-2/6.30-9.30 **Prices** Prices not confirmed **Wines** 17 bottles over £30, 34 bottles under £30, 10 by glass **Parking** 170 **Notes** Sunday L, Vegetarian available, Children welcome

Hotel du Vin Winchester

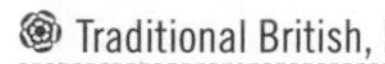 Traditional British, French

tel: 01962 841414 **14 Southgate St SO23 9EF**
email: info@winchester.hotelduvin.co.uk **web:** www.hotelduvin.com
dir: *M3 junct 11, follow signs to Winchester town centre, hotel on left*

Traditional British and French bistro fare in the first HdV

The first Hotel du Vin branch set the template for all the others – wooden floors, unclothed tables and cream walls hung with wine-related images – and the kitchen follows the familiar formula of traditional British and classic French dishes. A straightforward approach keeps flavours clear-cut: Shetland scallops with sauce vièrge, or steak tartare, followed by garlicky chicken schnitzel with salad, or sole meunière. Various salads and plats du jour extend the range – beer-battered haddock with chips on Fridays, for instance – and the impressively presented puddings include crêpe Suzette soufflé and tarte au citron with raspberry sorbet.

Marwell Hotel

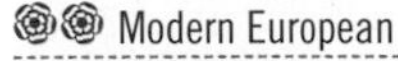 Modern European

tel: 01962 777681 **Thompsons Ln, Colden Common, Marwell SO21 1JY**
email: info@marwellhotel.co.uk **web:** www.marwellhotel.co.uk
dir: *B3354 through Twyford. 1st exit at rdbt (B3354), left onto B2177 signed Bishop Waltham. Left into Thompsons Ln after 250yds, hotel on left*

Contemporary-styled traditional dishes next door to the zoo

A pastoral retreat in the manner of an African safari lodge, Marwell is set in wooded grounds next door to a wildlife park, so the odd screech of a monkey is to be expected. Full-drop windows look out over the countryside, and the kitchen applies modern styling to mostly traditional dishes. Scallops with cauliflower purée come with balled apple and ink-dyed tempura for a well-balanced opening foray. All is present and correct in a main of minted lamb rump with a potato cake and celeriac purée. A chocolate fondant made with 70% gear is a stimulating finish, its fabulous riches offset with humble honeycomb and a faintly citric yogurt sorbet.

Chef Phil Yeomans **Seats** 60, Pr/dining room 120 **Times** 5.30-10, Closed 24-26 Dec **Prices** Fixed D 3 course £32, Tasting menu £49 **Wines** 10 bottles over £30, 10 bottles under £30 **Parking** 100, Marwell Zoo **Notes** Sunday L £22.50, Vegetarian available, Children welcome

Running Horse Inn

Modern International, British

tel: 01962 880218 **88 Main Rd, Littleton SO22 6QS**
email: info@runninghorseinn.co.uk **web:** www.runninghorseinn.co.uk
dir: *B3049 out of Winchester 1.5m, turn right into Littleton after 1m, Running Horse on right*

Innovative flavour-packed cooking in informal upgraded inn

The Running Horse is a revitalised village inn with a relaxed and informal dining environment: a wood-burning stove in a brick fireplace, some banquette seating, wooden tables and a mixture of artwork adorning the walls. The kitchen delivers stimulating full-flavoured dishes. Blow-torched scallops with mussels and samphire get things off to a great start – light and simple in concept, with clean flavours. Butter-poached chicken Kiev, with girolles, mash and kale, is food to make you smile: well-conceived, perfectly cooked and neatly presented. For dessert the vanilla rice pudding with ginger cake and cranberry gel is a real winner.

Chef Stewart Hellsten **Seats** 60 **Times** 12-2.30/6.30-9.30, Closed D 25 Dec **Prices** Prices not confirmed **Wines** 18 bottles over £30, 22 bottles under £30, 13 by glass **Parking** 40 **Notes** Sunday L, Vegetarian available, Children welcome

The Wykeham Arms

Modern British

tel: 01962 853834 **75 Kingsgate St SO23 9PE**
email: wykehamarms@fullers.co.uk **web:** www.wykehamarmswinchester.co.uk
dir: *S out of city along Southgate St. Take 3rd turning L into Canon St, inn on R at end*

Rustic, historic pub with contemporary tucker

A coaching inn since the mid-1700s, The Wykeham Arms is in the historic heart of the city. There are simple options listed as 'Home Comforts' on the menu – beer-battered South Coast haddock – but this is a kitchen that can turn out a starter as fashionable as boneless chicken wings with BBQ emulsion and blue cheese sauce. A bang-on piece of sea bream stars in a main course with a seared scallop, salt-baked celeriac and wild mushrooms, while another partners roasted venison loin with red cabbage ketchup and cocoa gnocchi (classic flavours delivered in a creative manner). Finish with peanut butter parfait with strawberry jelly and toast ice cream.

WOODLANDS Map 5 SU31

Woodlands Lodge Hotel

Modern British

tel: 023 8029 2257 **Bartley Rd, Woodlands SO40 7GN**
email: reception@woodlands-lodge.co.uk **web:** www.woodlands-lodge.co.uk
dir: *M27 junct 2, rdbt towards Fawley, 2nd rdbt right towards Cadnam. 1st left at White Horse Pub onto Woodlands Road, over cattle grid, hotel on left*

Kitchen garden produce at a New Forest hotel

When we say this hotel is 'in the New Forest', we mean it. The ancient woodland can be accessed directly from the Lodge's gardens, making it the perfect spot for a walking break. Hunters restaurant, where chairs and wall panels in delicate forest green match the view from the swagged windows, serves capably rendered modern British dishes with plenty of verve. Start with a smoked haddock croquette alongside a soft-poached egg, dressed in lemony hollandaise, and proceed to rosemary-marinated lamb rump with crisp lamb terrine, kale and pomme purée in minted port jus. Finish off with spiced crumble of rhubarb, apple and pecans, served with clotted cream.

Chef Andrew Smith **Seats** 30, Pr/dining room 35 **Times** 12-2.30/6.30-9 **Prices** Starter £5.50-£8, Main £15-£22, Dessert £5.50-£8 **Wines** 2 bottles over £30, 29 bottles under £30, 5 by glass **Parking** 80 **Notes** Sunday L, Vegetarian available, Children welcome

YATELEY Map 5 SU86

Casa Hotel & Marco Pierre White Restaurant

French, British

tel: 01252 873275 & 749142 **Handford Ln GU46 6BT**
email: info@wheelerscamberley.com **web:** www.wheelerscamberley.com
dir: *M3 junct 4a, follow signs for town centre. Hotel signed*

Comforting Anglo-French dining

The restaurant in this sprawling hotel occupies two areas with wooden beams and a real fire to bring a warm glow, and the tables wear white linen cloths for a little refinement. The menu is classic MPW: part French, part British, with plenty of things you want to eat. King scallops with cauliflower purée is a modern classic, the bivalves cooked just right. Move on to pan-roasted breast of guinea fowl with green beans, fondant potato and fine jus – a French brasserie dish of heart and soul – while Wheeler's venison pie with parsnip purée is a deeply satisfying option. Desserts include Cambridge burnt cream and sticky toffee pudding.

HEREFORDSHIRE

EWYAS HAROLD Map 9 SO32

The Temple Bar Inn

 Modern British

tel: 01981 240423 **HR2 OEU**
email: phillytemplebar@btinternet.com **web:** www.thetemplebarinn.co.uk
dir: *From Pontrilas (A465) take B4347 to Ewyas Harold. 1m left into village centre. Inn on right*

Renovated village pub with top-notch grub

Still a proper pub complete with a pool table, well-kept real ales, oak beams, flagstones and a blazing fire, this is an inviting spot with a friendly atmosphere and accomplished cooking. Tomato and basil vinaigrette is a vibrant foil to prawn and crab ravioli, while main-course duck breast is supported by a golden potato cake layered with pork fat and black pudding. Otherwise, you might take refuge in the robust comforts of fillet steak with rolled beef shin and suet pudding, creamed potato, kale and crispy bone marrow, and end with fig cake with a brandy snap and vanilla ice cream.

Chef Phillippa Jinman, Jo Pewsey **Seats** 30, Pr/dining room 45 **Times** 7-9, Closed 25 Dec, 1 wk Jan/Feb, 1 wk Nov, Sun-Tue, L all wk **Prices** Starter £4.50-£8, Main £12-£22, Dessert £5.95 **Wines** 5 bottles over £30, 14 bottles under £30, 5 by glass **Parking** 12 **Notes** Vegetarian available, Children welcome

HEREFORD Map 10 SO53

Castle House

Modern British

tel: 01432 356321 **Castle St HR1 2NW**
email: info@castlehse.co.uk **web:** www.castlehse.co.uk
dir: *City centre, follow brown signs to Castle House Hotel*

Culinary voyages into modern Britain within sight of Hereford Castle

The house began life as a pair of elegant villas during the Regency of George IV and is now owned by a local farmer whose produce features on the modern British menus. Start perhaps with grilled mackerel with horseradish gnocchi, beetroot and white chocolate adding a sweet element, followed perhaps by duck breast with sweet potato, green beans, pickled fennel and raspberry vinaigrette. Reversing the fish and meat order might produce braised neck of lamb and courgette lasagne sauced with salsa verde, then roast sea bass fillet with spiced lentils, vanilla-roasted butternut squash, langoustine and pear purée. Finish with white chocolate and dill parfait with pickled cucumber.

Chef Claire Nicholls **Seats** 40 **Times** 12-2/6.30-9.30 **Prices** Prices not confirmed **Wines** 57 bottles over £30, 41 bottles under £30, 9 by glass **Parking** 12 **Notes** Tasting menu 7 course, Sunday L, Vegetarian available, Children welcome

See advert on page 184

KINGTON Map 9 SO25

The Stagg Inn and Restaurant

Modern British V

tel: 01544 230221 **Titley HR5 3RL**
email: reservations@thestagg.co.uk
dir: *Between Kington & Presteigne on B4335*

Impeccable regional cooking in an old drovers' inn

Standing at the junction of two drovers' roads, The Stagg is a country inn on a medieval base with Victorian embellishments. It does everything country inns should, offering accommodation, local ales and good wines, and – the absolute essential these days – a menu of regionally-sourced, impeccably presented British food that works modern technique into deeply rooted traditional ideas. Herefordshire snails come with mushrooms, watercress and garlic butter, and locally-farmed meats are a joy – perhaps duck breast with pear, sumac and kale. Fish might be sea bass with fennel and samphire, while desserts offer the likes of treacle tart with yogurt sorbet.

Chef S Reynolds, M Handley **Seats** 70, Pr/dining room 30 **Times** 12-2/6.30-9, Closed 2 wks Jan-Feb, 1st wk Jun,1st 2 wks Nov, Mon-Tue **Prices** Starter £6.50-£9.90, Main £16.90-£24.90, Dessert £7-£8.90 **Wines** 28 bottles over £30, 48 bottles under £30, 8 by glass **Parking** 22 **Notes** Sunday L £21.50-£25.50, Children welcome

LEDBURY Map 10 SO73

Feathers Hotel

Modern British

tel: 01531 635266 **High St HR8 1DS**
email: mary@feathers-ledbury.co.uk **web:** www.feathers-ledbury.co.uk
dir: *M50 junct 2. Ledbury on A449/A438/A417. Hotel on main street*

Dynamic modern cooking in Tudor style

The heavily timbered Feathers is a wonderful slice of Tudor England, its oak-panelled venerability thrown into relief by a modern brasserie named after the hop variety Fuggles, and an upmarket dining room, Quills. Look for the likes of lamb kidneys in smoked paprika and sherry cream to start, or scallops with pork scratchings and apple, prior to well-rendered turbot on crab and spring onion risotto with courgette ribbons in shellfish sauce. Sirloins and fillets of local beef are a big draw, as are sweet things such as an ingenious bread-and-butter pudding made with pain au chocolat, served with salt caramel ice cream and chocolate sauce – an absolute treat.

Chef Susan Isaacs **Seats** 55, Pr/dining room 60 **Times** 12-2/6.30-9.30 **Prices** Starter £5.95-£7.75, Main £13.50-£26, Dessert £6.25-£6.75 **Wines** 47 bottles over £30, 81 bottles under £30, 12 by glass **Parking** 30 **Notes** Sunday L £16.50-£17.50, Vegetarian available, Children welcome

Verzon House

Modern British

tel: 01531 670381 **Trumpet HR8 2PZ**
email: info@verzonhouse.com **web:** www.verzonhouse.com
dir: *M50 junct 2, left at rdbt, follow A438 to Hereford, located on right*

Stylish and contemporary restaurant with rooms

A restaurant with rooms that strikes a good balance between rustic charm and contemporary style, Verzon House feels very much of our time. There is evident attention paid to the details, whether that's the quirky designer items dotted about the place or the careful sourcing of ingredients undertaken by the kitchen team. The Josper grill works its magic on Hereford beef – 28 day aged sirloin, say, served with triple-cooked chips – or a Middlewhite pork chop with a cider glaze. Start with summer vegetable gnocchi or a tartare of Cornish mackerel, and finish with tonka bean rice pudding. Afternoon tea and local ales add to the appeal of the place.

LEINTWARDINE **Map 9 SO47**

The Lion

Modern British

tel: 01547 540203 & 540747 **High St SY7 0JZ**
email: enquiries@thelionleintwardine.co.uk **web:** www.thelionleintwardine.co.uk
dir: *On A4113. At bottom of High Street by bridge*

Seasonal modern pub cooking on the Teme

Keen anglers will appreciate this village pub on the upper Teme, where trout and grayling are abundant. Others will just love the authentic air of a country inn, where old beams and inviting leather sofas play their homely part. Start with goats' cheese and spinach ravioli in truffled cream sauce with crispy leeks, as a possible overture to turbot with garlicky razor clams and chorizo-butter bean cassoulet, local beef fillet with dauphinoise, or a faithful rendering of hearty coq au vin. Pudding might be something sturdily British like a treacle and ginger suet sponge with custard. Light bites such as tomato and mozzarella bruschetta should satisfy the snackers.

Chef Paul Halmshaw **Seats** 50, Pr/dining room 20 **Times** 12-2.30/6-9.30, Closed 25 Dec **Prices** Starter £5-£9, Main £10-£24, Dessert £6-£9 **Wines** 10 bottles over £30, 28 bottles under £30, 11 by glass **Parking** 20 **Notes** Sunday L £14.95-£22.95, Vegetarian available, Children welcome

ROSS-ON-WYE **Map 10 SO52**

The Chase Hotel

British, Modern European

tel: 01989 763161 **Gloucester Rd HR9 5LH**
email: res@chasehotel.co.uk **web:** www.chasehotel.co.uk
dir: *M50 junct 4 onto A449. Take A40 towards Gloucester, turn right at rdbt into Ross-on-Wye. Hotel on left 0.25m*

Georgian country-house hotel with stylish restaurant

Every bit the contemporary dining room, Harry's Restaurant is named after the owner's grandson, not the iconic Venetian bar. Set in a large Georgian mansion with 11 acres of grounds, its modern shades of cream, tan and black, up-to-date furnishings and silk drapes blend with the original high ceilings and ornate plasterwork. The European comfort-oriented menu offers something for everyone, whether it's a roulade of king prawn and crab with ginger, chilli and mango salsa, or main-course roast pheasant breast with pheasant dumpling, fondant potato, braised red cabbage and bread sauce. Desserts follow the theme, pairing iced tiramisù with salted caramel doughnuts and toffee sauce.

Chef Richard Birchall **Seats** 70, Pr/dining room 300
Times 12-2/6-9.30, Closed 24-27 Dec **Prices** Fixed L 2 course £16, Starter £6-£9, Main £11-£23, Dessert £7-£10 **Wines** 12 bottles over £30, 33 bottles under £30, 13 by glass **Parking** 75 **Notes** Sunday L £16-£22.50, Vegetarian available, Children welcome

Glewstone Court Country House Hotel

Modern British, European

tel: 01989 770367 **Glewstone HR9 6AW**
email: info@glewstonecourt.com **web:** www.glewstonecourt.com
dir: *From Ross Market Place take A40/A49 (Monmouth/Hereford) over Wilton Bridge. At rdbt left onto A40 (Monmouth/S Wales), after 1m turn right for Glewstone. Hotel 0.5m on left*

West Country produce in an attractive Wye Valley Georgian hotel

This Georgian rural retreat is the model of a warmly welcoming country hotel. Delicately constructed mushroom ravioli made of sheer pasta are enhanced with chorizo and a salad of shredded chicken, lobster cocktails come with Bloody Mary gel, and salmon is cured in maple syrup and orange and served with a beetroot blini. Among main courses, things go Moroccan for the spiced lamb samosa, and apricot and pomegranate tabbouleh, that come with braised lamb rump, or there may be red snapper in sauce vierge. A signature take on banoffee produces cookie dough, caramel parfait and fudge, along with banana ice cream and chocolate shreds, for a triumphant finale.

Chef Vicky Lyons **Seats** 70, Pr/dining room 32 **Times** 12-2/7-9, Closed 26-29 Dec, 2-20 Jan, L Mon-Sat (ex residents & parties of 6+), D Sun (ex BHs & residents) **Prices** Starter £6-£9, Main £15-£24, Dessert £6.50-£8 **Wines** 20 bottles over £30, 24 bottles under £30, 13 by glass **Parking** 28 **Notes** Sunday L £17-£25, Vegetarian available, Children welcome

Wilton Court Restaurant with Rooms

Modern British

tel: 01989 562569 **Wilton Ln HR9 6AQ**
email: info@wiltoncourthotel.com **web:** www.wiltoncourthotel.com
dir: *M50 junct 4 onto A40 towards Monmouth at 3rd rdbt turn left signed Ross-on-Wye then take 1st right, hotel on right*

Intelligent modern cookery on the Wye riverside

A riverside setting on the Wye makes for much natural diversion at Wilton Court. The house itself partly dates back to around 1500 and was once the local magistrate's court. The Mulberry Restaurant delivers an intelligent modern British repertoire. Start, perhaps, with pan-seared scallops with black pudding and a carrot purée flavoured with cumin, before main courses such as slow-roasted Huntley pork belly matched with the flavours of celeriac, pear and sage, or beetroot risotto with goats' cheese salad. Regional cheeses get a listing of their own, or there are sweet indulgences like pain perdu with roasted plums flavoured with ginger and cinnamon.

Chef Rachael Williams **Seats** 40, Pr/dining room 12
Times 12-2.15/6.30-8.45, Closed 1st 2 wks Jan **Prices** Fixed L 2 course fr £16.95, Fixed D 3 course fr £32.50, Tasting menu fr £52.50, Starter £5.25-£9.25, Main £17.25-£24.50, Dessert £6.95-£7.50 **Wines** 8 bottles over £30, 37 bottles under £30, 9 by glass **Parking** 25 **Notes** Tasting menu 7 course (complete tables only), Sunday L £16.95-£19.95, Vegetarian available, Children welcome

HERTFORDSHIRE

ASHWELL Map 12 TL23

The Three Tuns

Modern British NEW

tel: 01462 743343 **6 High St SG7 5NL**
email: info@thethreetunsashwell.co.uk **web:** www.thethreetunsashwell.co.uk
dir: *A1(M) junct 10, after 1m signs for Ashwell*

Visually stunning British pub food

A red-brick inn with three guest rooms in a north Hertfordshire village, the Three Tuns has a refreshing informality, with bare tables on bare floors against blue and white walls, plus a garden terrace. Modern British pub food interspersed with old favourites is the order of the day. A trio of beetroot and goats' cheese croquettes arrives with pear and pomegranate salsa, balsamic gel and beetroot crisps, a visually stunning prelude to scarcely less dramatic sea bass with purple potatoes, vanilla-poached crayfish, smoked parsnip purée and passionfruit. To finish, there could be properly tangy lemon tart with raspberry sorbet, sprinkled with popping candy.

Chef John Beardsworth **Times** 12-2.30/6-9, Closed D Sun **Prices** Starter £5.95-£7.95, Main £11.95-£16.95, Dessert £4.95-£11.95 **Wines** 5 bottles over £30, 29 bottles under £30, 12 by glass **Notes** Sunday L, Children welcome

BERKHAMSTED Map 6 SP90

The Gatsby

Modern British

tel: 01442 870403 **97 High St HP4 2DG**
email: thegatsby@live.co.uk
dir: *M25 junct 20/A41 to Aylesbury, in 3m take left turn to Berkhamsted following town signs. Restaurant on left on entering High St*

Movies and brasserie cooking in a retooled art deco cinema

This stylish modern brasserie occupies a handsome art deco space with plenty of pictures of the golden age of British cinema. A starter of chargrilled artichoke and Swiss chard risotto, for example, might have caught Fellini's interest while the smoked fish kedgeree with soft boiled egg and Chiltern eye might have been down Hitchcock's street. Next up, fillet of halibut is served with a moules marinière sauce, lamb tagine is enriched with almonds and dates, and roast Barbary duck breast is dressed with a blackberry and anise sauce. Finish with treacle tart with candied pecans or a classic tarte Tatin with rum and raisin ice cream.

Chef Matthew Salt **Seats** 65 **Times** 12-2.30/5.30-10.30, Closed 25-26 Dec **Prices** Fixed L 2 course £14.95, Fixed D 3 course £20.90, Starter £7.95-£9.25, Main £14.95-£28.95, Dessert £7.95 **Wines** 25 bottles over £30, 27 bottles under £30, 16 by glass **Parking** 10 **Notes** Pre cinema menu Mon-Sat 12-2.30 & 5.30-6.30, Sunday L £15.95, Vegetarian available, Children welcome

BISHOP'S STORTFORD Map 6 TL42

Down Hall Country House Hotel

Modern British

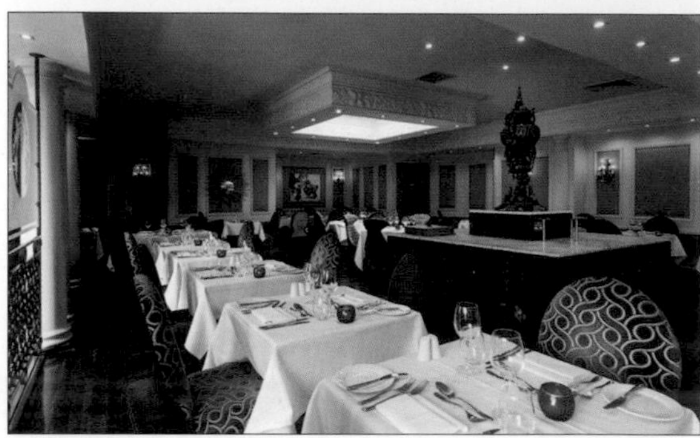

tel: 01279 731441 **Hatfield Heath CM22 7AS**
email: info@downhall.co.uk **web:** www.downhall.co.uk
dir: *Take A414 towards Harlow. At 4th rdbt follow B183 towards Hatfield Heath, keep left, follow hotel sign*

Brasserie-style menu in a grand house

The house originally dates from the 1300s, but its impressively grand Italianate exterior shows the mark of a Victorian makeover. The surrounding landscape – 110 acres all to itself – explains why this venue is such a hit with the wedding and conference brigade. With period details such as ornate cornices and white-painted columns, the dining room has a vibe reminiscent of an upmarket French brasserie. The kitchen delivers unruffled stuff such as Coln Valley smoked salmon with bacon and lentils, followed by corn-fed chicken breast with wild mushroom risotto or rib-eye steak with classic accompaniments. Finish with an equally classic lemon tart.

Chef Matt Hill **Seats** 60, Pr/dining room 200 **Times** 12.30-2/6.30-9.30, Closed 24 & 31 Dec, L Sat **Prices** Fixed L 2 course £25.95, Fixed D 3 course £32.50-£36.50 **Wines** 19 bottles over £30, 19 bottles under £30, 8 by glass **Parking** 120 **Notes** Sunday L £19.50-£24.50, Vegetarian available, Children welcome

Find out more about how we assess for Rosette awards on pages 8–9

CHANDLER'S CROSS Map 6 TQ09

Colette's at The Grove

 Modern European V NOTABLE WINE LIST

tel: 01923 807807 & 296015 **WD3 4TG**
email: info@thegrove.co.uk **web:** www.thegrove.co.uk
dir: *M25 junct 19, follow signs to Watford. At 1st large rdbt take 3rd exit. 0.5m, entrance on right*

Avante-garde cooking on a grand country estate

Once the little old place that the Earls of Clarendon called home, The Grove is these days a country-house hotel that seemingly has the lot, including an urban beach, which is quite a feat within the embrace of the M25. Winding elevated walkways uncoil through the estate, and in the great house itself, there are spa treatments, period architectural adornments, and a trio of dining options to keep you diverted, the acme being Colette's. In a gentle ambience of primrose walls and comfortable cream leather armchairs, Russell Bateman cooks up a storm, building a modern British repertoire on classical French foundations. First out of the blocks might be a precision-timed lobe of roasted duck foie gras with orange-laced butternut squash and mustard leaves, or perhaps scallop tartare with an oyster, celeriac and apple. All items are treated with respect, as in a translucently cooked fillet of cod with smoked roe and leeks in a buttery sauce dusted with powdered burnt leek, or loin and faggot of Wiltshire venison with pumpkin in a wintry mulled wine sauce. Desserts are immaculately turned out to look and taste their best, as when a pistachio cake comes crowned with Alunga chocolate mousse, alongside satsuma sorbet and pistachio ice cream.

Chef Russell Bateman **Seats** 44 **Times** 6.30-9.30, Closed Sun-Mon (ex BHs), L all week **Prices** Tasting menu £75-£85 **Wines** 8 bottles over £30, 4 bottles under £30, 24 by glass **Parking** 300 **Notes** ALC 3 course £65, Vegetarian tasting menu 7 course, Children 16 yrs+

The Stables Restaurant at The Grove

Modern British

tel: 01923 807807 & 296015 **WD3 4TG**
email: restaurants@thegrove.co.uk
dir: *M25 junct 19, A411 towards Watford. Hotel on right*

Creative modern cooking in George Stubbs' favourite stables

The original stable block of the Georgian mansion has been given a modern makeover under its rafters and is now the informal eatery at The Grove. The open-to-view kitchen is equipped with a wood-fired oven and chargrill, but the menu has a lot more going for it than pizzas and steaks. Imaginative starters run from chicken liver and foie gras brûlée to beetroot and goats' cheese tarte Tatin with truffled honey. Seafood gets a good airing, from aromatic crab cake to well-timed roast pollack with cockles, pancetta and Jerusalem artichoke purée. Dark chocolate tart and Baileys crème brûlée are popular finishers.

DATCHWORTH Map 6 TL21

The Tilbury

 Modern British

tel: 01438 815550 **Watton Rd SG3 6TB**
email: info@thetilbury.co.uk
dir: *A1(M) junct 7, A602 signed Ware & Hertford. At Bragbury End right into Bragbury Lane to Datchworth*

Village gastropub doing Datchworth proud

A good local watering hole and a place to eat seriously good food, The Tilbury's kitchen is driven by quality, starting with carefully sourced produce. A pub menu lists the likes of cottage pie or fish and chips with mushy peas and tartare sauce. Alternatively, move up a gear with a starter of chicken terrine with bacon jam and sweetcorn purée, followed by a robust plate of pork belly and loin with ham and squeak balls, bacon greens and apple sauce, or pan-fried turbot paired with girolles, baby onions, kale and mash. Pudding could be a cylinder of white chocolate parfait coated with pistachio crumbs and served with olive oil cake.

Chef Thomas Bainbridge **Seats** 70, Pr/dining room 36
Times 12-2.30/6-9.30, Closed some BHs, Mon, D Sun **Prices** Starter £6.50-£8.50, Main £12-£22.50, Dessert £6.50-£8 **Wines** 55 bottles over £30, 26 bottles under £30, 11 by glass **Parking** 40 **Notes** Sunday L £22, Vegetarian available, Children welcome

ELSTREE Map 6 TL19

Laura Ashley The Manor

 Modern British

tel: 020 8327 4700 **Barnet Ln WD6 3RE**
email: elstree@lauraashleyhotels.com **web:** www.lauraashleyhotels.com
dir: *From A1 take A411 from Stirling Corner. From M25 either junct 19 or 23*

Country-house dining and Laura Ashley styling

The Laura Ashley empire includes this 16th-century manor house restyled in plenty of contemporary beige. Setting off the mullioned windows in the Cavendish dining room, it makes for a cheering ambience in which to eat some well-considered country-house cooking. Purées abound, apple for the ham knuckle terrine, and the expected cauliflower for scallops in a lively currant and peppercorn dressing. Main courses explore the possibilities of gentle slow cooking for braised beef with glazed baby onions, mushrooms and creamy mash, or potato-crusted sea bass with Brussels sprouts and pea purée. Finish with the sensational trifle, a treat all the way from its crushed amaretti topping to its cherry compôte foundation.

Chef Stephanie Malvoisin **Seats** 40, Pr/dining room 40
Times 12.30-2/7-9.30, Closed L Sat **Prices** Fixed L 2 course £23, Fixed D 3 course £35, Tasting menu £49 **Wines** 33 bottles over £30, 11 bottles under £30, 12 by glass **Parking** 100 **Notes** Afternoon tea £24.95, Sunday L £24.95, Vegetarian available, Children welcome

FLAUNDEN Map 6 TL00

Bricklayers Arms

 British, French

tel: 01442 833322 & 831722 **Black Robin Ln, Hogpits Bottom HP3 0PH**
email: goodfood@bricklayersarms.com
dir: *M25 junct 20, A451 towards Chipperfield. Into Dunny Ln, 1st right into Flaunden Ln. 1m on single track*

Traditional country inn with well-crafted Anglo-French cooking

The Bricklayers is a cheery Georgian pub with a cosy atmosphere, rustic oak beams, log fire and brick bar, with tables in the garden and on the terrace. Food is a serious commitment, the kitchen sourcing locally and seasonally, supplementing the main menus with daily fish and vegetarian specials. 'English and French fusion' is the self-described style, so expect to find home-smoked fish with tomato chutney alongside tiger prawns and cockles flambéed in Pernod among starters. For main, there could be partridge breasts with lovage and courgettes in chestnut jus, and puddings may run to spiced rum cheesecake with caramelised orange.

Chef Claude Paillet, Alan Bell, Martin West **Seats** 95, Pr/dining room 50
Times 12-2.30/6.30-9.30, Closed 25 Dec **Prices** Fixed L 2 course £16.95, Fixed D 3 course £21.95, Starter £6.45-£10.95, Main £12.95-£25.95, Dessert £5.95-£7.45
Wines 96 bottles over £30, 34 bottles under £30, 16 by glass **Parking** 40
Notes Sunday L, Vegetarian available, Children welcome

HATFIELD Map 6 TL20

Beales Hotel

Modern British

tel: 01707 288500 & 288518 **Comet Way AL10 9NG**
email: outsidein@bealeshotels.co.uk **web:** www.bealeshotels.co.uk
dir: *On A1001 opposite Galleria Shopping Mall (follow signs for Galleria)*

Anglo-Med cooking in a striking modern hotel

The contemporary brasserie-style dining room at Beales looks surprisingly small for a hotel, but such intimacy creates an aura of exclusivity. Served by well-informed staff, the food is a mix of modern British classics and Mediterranean magic. A starter of Scottish salmon and tiger prawn ravioli served with a shellfish bisque shows the form from the outset. It might be followed by a precisely timed chargrilled lamb T-bone chop paired with crispy sweetbreads, baby courgettes, potato rösti and a deep-flavoured jus. Lemon meringue cheesecake with lemon sherbet and raspberry sorbet is one way to finish.

HEMEL HEMPSTEAD Map 6 TL00

Aubrey Park Hotel

Modern European NEW

tel: 01582 792105 **Hemel Hempstead Rd, Redbourn AL3 7AF**
email: reception@aubreypark.co.uk **web:** www.aubreypark.co.uk
dir: *M1 junct 9 follow Hemel Hempstead & St Albans signs for 3m, straight across 2 rdbts onto B487 signed Hemel Hempstead. Hotel on right*

Bistro classics in a quiet countryside location

It stands in nine acres of rolling countryside, dates back to 1287 and has an Iron Age hillfort in the grounds. Old in parts indeed, but Aubrey Park's interiors are contemporary, particularly the light, bright Brasserie, where friendly staff serve bistro classics of seared queen scallops with black pudding discs, crispy pancetta and pea and mint purée as a starter; corn-fed chicken supreme with pancetta, wild mushroom and leek cassoulet, followed by pan-fried sea bass with mussel, clam and sweetcorn chowder. For dessert, try warm chocolate fondant with hot berry compôte and vanilla ice cream.

Chef Lee Robinson **Seats** 56 **Times** 12.30-3/6-10, Closed L Mon-Sat **Prices** Starter £5.95-£10.95, Main £13.95-£22.50, Dessert £4.95-£7.95 **Wines** 4 bottles over £30, 17 bottles under £30, 11 by glass **Parking** 140 **Notes** Afternoon tea, Sunday L £18.95-£22.95, Vegetarian available, Children welcome

HITCHIN Map 12 TL12

The Radcliffe

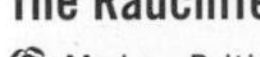

Modern British NEW

tel: 01462 456111 **31 Walsworth Rd SG4 9ST**
email: info@theradcliffe.co.uk
dir: *Midway between Hitchin Station & town on corner of Walsworth Rd & Verulam Rd*

Lively gastropub with please-all modern food

The Radcliffe is a lively gastropub operation designed to appeal to all comers. The transition from Victorian boozer to successful food pub, with the high-decibel ambience of the locals' bar still intact, has been helped along by the conservatory extension overlooking the garden, which provides a third dining venue on balmy days. A crowd-pleasing menu of modern British food is offered, setting out with smoked salmon and leek filo tart matched with lemon crème fraîche, followed by a hearty plate of venison haunch with poivrade sauce, creamy mash, roasted apple and blackberry sauce. For pudding there's elderflower pannacotta with gooseberries.

Chef Eric Huvelin **Seats** 60, Pr/dining room 35 **Times** 12-2.30/5.30-9.30, Closed 1 week Xmas, D Sun **Prices** Fixed L 2 course fr £17, Fixed D 3 course fr £28, Starter £6.70-£8, Main £16-£27, Dessert £4.50-£9 **Wines** 24 bottles over £30, 25 bottles under £30, 15 by glass **Parking** Queen Mother Theatre car park **Notes** Breakfast, Early evening menu 2/3 course £17/£21, Sunday L £12-£16, Vegetarian available, Children welcome

ST ALBANS Map 6 TL10

Chez Mumtaj

French, Asian

tel: 01727 800033 **Centurian House, 136-142 London Rd AL1 1PQ**
email: info@chezmumtaj.com **web:** www.chezmumtaj.com
dir: *Phone for directions*

Franco-Asian fusion food in opulent surroundings

Chez Mumtaj emanates class, with panelled walls and comfortable cream banquettes at correctly set clothed tables, and an open-to-view kitchen. As the name suggests, the style is a culinary hybrid: what the restaurant itself describes as 'haute cuisine in modern French-Asian dining', with classical techniques applied to tip-top produce. The long menu opens with mixed seafood platters, or duck samosa with ceps in filo, before rocking on with curried monkfish in Pondicherry bisque with nutmegged spinach, Kashmiri-style lamb shank and rösti, or black cod in lime and tomato curry with pickled samphire and coconut rice. Finish with chocolate fondant and vanilla ice cream.

Chef Chad Rahman **Seats** 100, Pr/dining room 16 **Times** 12-2.30/6-11, Closed 25 Dec, Mon **Prices** Fixed L 2 course £12.95-£15.95, Fixed D 3 course £18.95, Tasting menu £44.95, Starter £5.95-£12.95, Main £14.95-£24.95, Dessert £5.50-£6.95 **Wines** 27 bottles over £30, 22 bottles under £30, 14 by glass **Parking** On street & car park nearby **Notes** Early bird D menu, Sunday L, Vegetarian available, Children welcome

See advert opposite

St Michael's Manor

Modern British, European

tel: 01727 864444 **Fishpool St AL3 4RY**
email: reservations@stmichaelsmanor.com **web:** www.stmichaelsmanor.com
dir: *Off Hight St onto George St. Past Cathedral into Fishpool St. Hotel at bottom of Fishpool St*

Accomplished British cooking with lakeside views

A handsome Georgian mansion standing in five acres of landscaped gardens, St Michael's Manor provides the setting for food with top-class provenance delivered by an ambitious team. Choose from an uncomplicated brasserie-style menu, or trade up to the carte for a main course matching spiced tenderloin of pork and crispy pork cheek with mango and wilted pak choi. Fish might be steamed sea bass with Dorset crab crushed potatoes, sauce vièrge and herb salad. Before that, pan-fried scallops are pointed up with chorizo-flecked mayonnaise and cauliflower. For afters, try a vibrant combo of coconut pannacotta with mango and lime.

Chef Antony Schwarz **Seats** 130, Pr/dining room 22 **Times** 12-2/7-9.30, Closed L 31 Dec, D 25 Dec **Prices** Fixed L 2 course £19, Starter £8.50-£14.50, Main £15.50-£27, Dessert £8 **Wines** 36 bottles over £30, 43 bottles under £30, 12 by glass **Parking** 80 **Notes** Afternoon tea, Sunday L, Vegetarian available, Children welcome

Sopwell House

Modern British

tel: 01727 864477 **Cottonmill Ln, Sopwell AL1 2HQ**
email: enquiries@sopwellhouse.co.uk **web:** www.sopwellhouse.co.uk
dir: *M25 junct 22, A1081 St Albans. At lights left into Mile House Ln, over mini-rdbt into Cottonmill Ln*

Smart dining in Mountbatten's former country home

A splendid stately hotel, equipped with spa and wedding facilities, with dining divided among conservatory, brasserie and restaurant, depending on your preferred style. The last is a glamorous, high-ceilinged setting for modern cooking of great vigour. Crab tian with avocado, pink grapefruit and lemon purée brings new pizazz to an old classic, or there may be potted salt beef with a crisp-cooked quail's egg and horseradish crème fraîche. Main courses partner grilled trout with lobster linguini and seafood broth, while honey-roast duck comes with braised red cabbage and truffled chive mash. Desserts won't lack for takers when there's chocolate truffle and pistachio ice cream on offer.

Chef Gopi Chandran **Seats** 100, Pr/dining room 320 **Times** 12.30-2.30/7-9.30, Closed Mon-Tue, L Sat, D Sun **Prices** Fixed L 3 course £35, Starter £9.75-£12.75, Main £20-£28, Dessert £8.50-£9.50 **Wines** 32 bottles over £30, 20 bottles under £30, 14 by glass **Parking** 300 **Notes** L/D offer £55/£65 for 2 with wine, Sunday L £29, Vegetarian available, Children welcome

ST ALBANS *continued*

THOMPSON St Albans

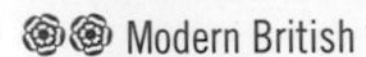
Modern British V

tel: 01727 730777 **2 Hatfield Rd AL1 3RP**
email: info@thompsonstalbans.co.uk **web:** www.thompsonstalbans.co.uk
dir: *M25 junct 22, A1081 London Rd to St Albans. At major x-rds right onto St Albans High St, 2nd right onto Hatfield Rd*

Classy contemporary cooking with interesting combinations

In a row of part-boarded cottages in the town centre, this is a smart, contemporary dining space. Previously at the nearby Auberge du Lac, Phil Thompson's menus show classical leanings and plenty of interesting combinations. There are set menus alongside the carte, as well as a six-course tasting menu. A starter of crisp pulled pork with beetroot, poached quince and cured pork neck is a confident starter, followed by roast saddle of Little Braxted lamb, with baked squash, mini jackets, anchovy butter and roast garlic. Finish with peanut butter custard, caramelised banana, sticky toffee pudding ice cream and salt caramel.

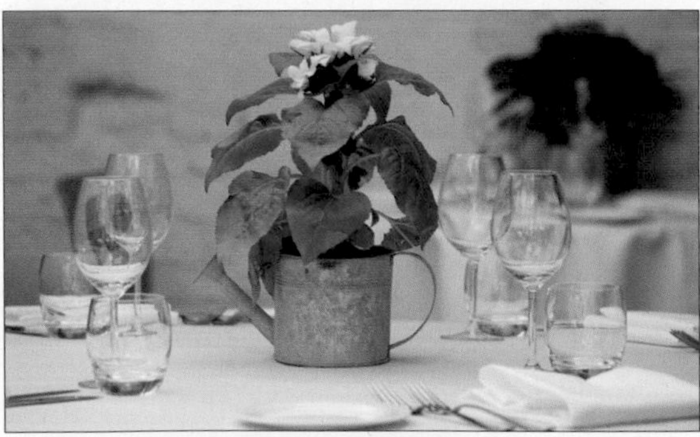

Chef Phil Thompson **Seats** 90, Pr/dining room 50 **Times** 12-2/6-9, Closed Mon, L Tue, D Sun **Prices** Fixed L 2 course £18.50, Fixed D 3 course £25, Tasting menu £59.50, Starter £11-£14.50, Main £21-£28, Dessert £4.50-£12.50 **Wines** 36 bottles over £30, 21 bottles under £30, 15 by glass **Parking** 0.25m away (signed) **Notes** Tasting menu 6 course, Sunday L £25-£29.50, Children welcome

TRING Map 6 SP91

Pendley Manor Hotel

Traditional British

tel: 01442 891891 **Cow Ln HP23 5QY**
email: sales@pendley-manor.co.uk **web:** www.pendley-manor.co.uk
dir: *M25 junct 20, A41 (Tring exit). At rdbt follow Berkhamsted/London signs. 1st left signed Tring Station & Pendley Manor*

Handsome manor house with modern cooking

The Victorian section at Pendley (there's also a modern annexe) offers period grandeur in spades, particularly in the Oak Restaurant where oak flooring, lofty ceilings, colourful patterned wallpaper, and swagged-back drapes at vast bay windows make an imposing setting. The cooking is totally 21st century: 'ham, eggs, chips, peas and ketchup' brings those components together in a refined version of the greasy spoon classic. At mains, butter-poached halibut fillet is teamed to good effect with chive mash, caramelised veal sweetbreads, gem lettuce, morels, green beans and a chicken stock lifted with sherry vinegar. Finally, peanut parfait arrives with dark chocolate mousse and caramel sauce.

Chef Martin White **Seats** 75, Pr/dining room 200 **Times** 12.30-2.30/7-9.30, Closed L Sat **Prices** Prices not confirmed **Wines** 13 bottles over £30, 33 bottles under £30, 7 by glass **Parking** 150 **Notes** Sunday L, Vegetarian available, Children welcome

WELWYN Map 6 TL21

Tewin Bury Farm Hotel

Modern British V

tel: 01438 717793 **Hertford Road (B1000) AL6 0JB**
email: restaurant@tewinbury.co.uk **web:** www.tewinbury.co.uk
dir: *A1(M) junct 6 (signed Welwyn Garden City), 1st exit A1000. 0.25m to B1000 Hertford Rd. Hotel on left*

Up-to-the-minute modern cookery on a working farm

A complex of barns on a working farm has been skilfully converted into this characterful modern hotel. The restaurant is a handsome room with a beamed ceiling above rafters, mustard-yellow banquettes, a boarded floor and bare-topped wooden tables. Many of the kitchen's raw materials are produced on-site, with the rest assiduously sourced. The menu is a slate of highly original, well-executed ideas, like black pudding Scotch egg with celeriac remoulade and tomato chutney, or cured and charred salmon with watercress and a parsley cake. Mains include turbot fillet with braised oxtail, beetroot and Russian salad, or chicken breast with braised leeks and artichoke purée.

Chef Grant Tomkins **Seats** 60, Pr/dining room 30 **Times** 12-2.30/6.30-9.30, Closed D 25 & 31 Dec **Prices** Fixed L 2 course £16.50, Starter £5.50-£6.50, Main £10.50-£17, Dessert £5.50-£6.50 **Wines** 13 bottles over £30, 19 bottles under £30, 12 by glass **Parking** 400 **Notes** All day dining on Sun 8am-8.30pm, Sunday L £19.95-£24.95, Children welcome

The Waggoners

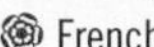 French

tel: 01707 324241 **Brickwall Close, Ayot Green AL6 9AA**
email: laurent@thewaggoners.co.uk
dir: *A1(M) junct 6 to B197, right into Ayot and 1st left Brickwall Close*

Contemporary French cooking in lovely village inn

With its venerable beams, inglenook fireplace and convivial ambience, the setting is that of a rather romantic, quintessentially English 17th-century inn, albeit with a nod to 21st-century tastes in the restaurant. There are seasonal influences drawn from the wider European cuisine, thus a summer meal opens with smoked duck salad with spiced apple chutney, watercress and radish and grain mustard dressing, or perhaps gazpacho with the added bonus of crayfish, avocado and grilled peppers. Following on, pan-fried sea bream is matched with saffron and fennel compôte and sauce vièrge, and things end on an impeccably summery note courtesy of a vanilla pannacotta with strawberry compôte and basil.

Chef Tom Burch **Seats** 65, Pr/dining room 35 **Times** 12-2.30/6.30-9, Closed D Sun **Prices** Fixed L 2 course £14.50, Tasting menu £26-£30, Starter £6-£14, Main £13-£24, Dessert £5-£14 **Wines** 40 bottles over £30, 60 bottles under £30, 22 by glass **Parking** 70 **Notes** Sunday L £18-£24, Vegetarian available, Children welcome

The Wellington

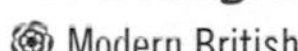 Modern British

tel: 01438 714036 **High St AL6 9LZ**
email: info@wellingtonatwelwyn.co.uk **web:** www.wellingtonatwelwyn.co.uk
dir: *A1(M) junct 6, on High Street in Welwyn village across from St Mary's Church*

Village inn with an appealing menu

The Wellington, on Welwyn's pretty high street, is an old coaching inn with rustic-chic exposed brick walls, real fires and a bar stocked with proper beers. The focus is firmly on the gastro side of the pub spectrum, with a simple, unpretentious menu. You might start with crispy duck and hoi sin dumpling, or go for one of the daily specials such as crab and tarragon bonbons with samphire, radish, cucumber and tarragon oil. Next up, a fillet burger, fish pie, or something a little more adventurous such as braised ox cheek with an oxtail lollipop.

WILLIAN Map 12 TL23

The Fox

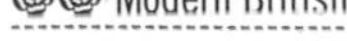 Modern British

tel: 01462 480233 **SG6 2AE**
email: reservations@foxatwillian.co.uk
dir: *A1(M) junct 9 towards Letchworth, 1st left to Willian, The Fox 0.5m on left*

Creative and accomplished cooking in a smart local pub

If you lived in a pretty village with just the one pub, you'd hope for it to be a stylish gastropub such as The Fox, its bar bristling with real ales, an open-plan dining room hung with artworks beneath a glazed ceiling, and a skilled kitchen whose ambition goes way beyond pub grub. Under the same ownership as The White Horse in Brancaster Staithe, supply lines to fish and seafood from the Norfolk coast are strong. Confit sea trout with pea mousse, fennel and tiger prawns opens the show, followed by pan-seared duck breast with potato rösti, spring greens, sweet potato purée and red wine jus.

Chef Sherwin Jacobs **Seats** 70 **Times** 12-2/6.30-9.15, Closed D Sun **Prices** Starter £4.95-£8.50, Main £10.95-£19.95, Dessert £4.95-£6.95 **Wines** 24 bottles over £30, 26 bottles under £30, 12 by glass **Parking** 40 **Notes** Sunday L £13.95-£15.95, Children welcome

ISLE OF WIGHT

NEWPORT Map 5 SZ48

Thompsons

Modern European NEW

tel: 01983 526118 **11 Town Ln PO30 1JU**
email: info@robertthompson.co.uk
dir: *From Coppins Bridge rdbt take Pyle Street exit, follow around to lights. Thompson's on left*

Well-crafted contemporary cooking from a local hero

Robert Thompson has long been an ambassador for the Isle of Wight and his eponymous restaurant has a genuine buzz to it. An open-plan kitchen ensures proper engagement with guests in the uncluttered dining room. The kitchen shows a serious commitment to island produce and dishes are eloquently executed. Big flavours abound in a tartine of chicken livers with caramelised celeriac, watercress and pickles. Baked hake, black cabbage, crown prince squash, pearl onions and confit potato is a well-orchestrated main, each element making an impact. Glazed lemon tart with yogurt sorbet is a fine way to round things off.

Chef Robert Thompson **Seats** 50 **Times** 12-3/6-10, Closed 10 days Nov, Xmas & Feb, Sun-Mon **Prices** Fixed L 2 course £17, Tasting menu £62, Starter £7-£15, Main £15-£28, Dessert £7-£11 **Wines** 31 bottles over £30, 18 bottles under £30, 10 by glass **Parking** Local car parks **Notes** Vegetarian available, Children welcome

SEAVIEW Map 5 SZ69

Seaview Hotel

British NEW

tel: 01983 612711 **High St PO34 5EX**
email: reception@seaviewhotel.co.uk **web:** www.seaviewhotel.co.uk
dir: *Take B3330 from Ryde to Seaview, left into Puckpool Hill, follow signs for hotel*

Seaside restaurant with the focus on fish

In the picturesque fishing village of Seaview, on the island's northeast coast, this long-established hotel is just 50 yards from the sea that supplies much of the fish on the menu. The cooking is refined with classic techniques letting tip-top ingredients speak for themselves. A late autumn starter of wood pigeon breast with parsnip purée, curly kale, chestnuts and truffled jus might be followed by line-caught sea bass, roast peppers, samphire, mussels and lemon thyme sautéed potatoes. Invention doesn't stop at desserts such as coconut and fennel pannacotta with chilli meringue, chervil and ginger syrup.

Chef Bruce Theobald **Seats** 50, Pr/dining room 25 **Times** 12-2.30/6-9, Closed Xmas, Mon (Nov-Feb), D Sun (Nov-Feb) **Prices** Fixed L 2 course £17, Fixed D 3 course £28 **Wines** 11 bottles over £30, 24 bottles under £30, 7 by glass **Parking** 10 **Notes** Sunday L £19.95, Vegetarian available, Children welcome

VENTNOR Map 5 SZ57

The Leconfield

 Traditional British V

tel: 01983 852196 **85 Leeson Rd, Upper Bonchurch PO38 1PU**
email: enquiries@leconfieldhotel.com **web:** www.leconfieldhotel.com
dir: *Upper Bonchurch on A3055, 1m from Ventnor, 2m from Shanklin opposite turning, Bonchurch Shute*

Homely cooking overlooking the Channel

On the south-facing side of the Isle of Wight, the picture-perfect Leconfield hotel is covered with climbing foliage. It sits above the village of Bonchurch looking out over the Channel, with inspiring views from the Seascape dining room and the conservatory. With service nicely pitched between formal and relaxed, and glass-topped tables on wicker supports, it's the setting for carefully wrought cooking that has a reassuring touch of the homely to it. A bowl of broccoli and Stilton soup delivers the right savoury, salty hit, or there may be mushrooms sautéed in smoked garlic and served on toasted brioche, followed by poached salmon in caper and lemon butter with puréed spinach, or slow-cooked leg of lamb on parsnip mash with redcurrant gravy. A rum-laced chocolate pot comes with matching ice cream and a sweet-and-sour berry compôte to make a satisfying array of flavours. Home-made breads add to the welcome sense of being looked after.

Chef Cheryl Judge **Seats** 26 **Times** 6.30-close, Closed 24-26 Dec, 3 wks Jan, L all week (ex by prior arrangement) **Prices** Fixed D 3 course £25-£37.95 **Wines** 1 bottle over £30, 15 bottles under £30, 3 by glass **Parking** 14 **Notes** Children 16 yrs+

The Royal Hotel

 Modern British V

tel: 01983 852186 **Belgrave Rd PO38 1JJ**
email: enquiries@royalhoteliow.co.uk **web:** www.royalhoteliow.co.uk
dir: *On A3055 (coast road) into Ventnor. Follow one-way system, left at lights into Church St. At top of hill left into Belgrave Rd, hotel on right*

Contemporary cooking in a charmingly old-fashioned setting

The Royal is a handsome slice of Regency grandeur on the Isle of Wight's southeastern coast. Inside, is a classic English tableau fully loaded with crystal chandeliers, parquet floors and decorative ironwork. The island's own Gallybagger cheese opens proceedings in a soaring soufflé, together with caramelised cauliflower purée, while main course teams poached and roasted chicken breast with crispy wings, baked onion, purée and florets of broccoli and chicken sauce. Fish is always a good bet here, perhaps brill fillet with hand-dived scallops, vanilla purée, foraged sea herbs and pickled raisins, while dessert could be baked almond ricotta cheesecake with rhubarb, and ginger baked Alaska with rhubarb consommé and compôte.

Chef Steven Harris **Seats** 120, Pr/dining room 40 **Times** 12-1.45/6.45-9, Closed 2 wks Jan or 2 wks Dec, L Mon-Sat **Prices** Fixed D 3 course £40-£53, Tasting menu £50-£75, Starter £9-£14, Main £22-£32, Dessert £9-£12 **Wines** 38 bottles over £30, 54 bottles under £30, 9 by glass **Parking** 50 **Notes** Sunday L £24-£30, Children 3 yrs+

YARMOUTH Map 5 SZ38

The George Hotel

Modern British, Mediterranean

tel: 01983 760331 **Quay St PO41 OPE**
email: info@thegeorge.co.uk **web:** www.thegeorge.co.uk
dir: *Between castle & pier, 2 mins walk from ferry terminal*

Modern British elegance looking over the sea

This elegant 17th-century townhouse turned boutique hotel has two dining venues – Isla's Restaurant and Conservatory. Both have commanding views over manicured lawns to the sea, with large abstract artworks against a neutral backdrop of taupe and beige. A meal in the elegant, stone-toned Isla's Restaurant ranges widely over the island larder, progressing perhaps from an amuse of asparagus, peas, almond granola and mushroom ketchup to a roast rack and braised shoulder of lamb, crushed minted peas, wild garlic, pea purée, purple sprouting broccoli and lamb jus. Finish with a superb poached rhubarb pannacotta with rhubarb and ginger jelly, rhubarb sorbet and a sumac and rhubarb essence.

Seats 70, Pr/dining room 18 **Times** 12-3/6-9.30, Closed last 2 wks Jan **Prices** Fixed L 2 course £18.50-£35, Fixed D 3 course £35-£55, Tasting menu £45-£77, Starter £5.95-£8.50, Main £12.95-£24, Dessert £6-£9.50 **Wines** 30 bottles over £30, 18 bottles under £30, 10 by glass **Parking** The Square, River Rd (long stay)
Notes Afternoon tea, Brunch selected dates, Sunday L £16.50-£35, Vegetarian available, Children welcome

KENT

ASHFORD Map 7 TR04

Eastwell Manor

British, European

tel: 01233 213000 **Eastwell Park, Boughton Lees TN25 4HR**
email: enquiries@eastwellmanor.co.uk **web:** www.eastwellmanor.co.uk
dir: *From M20 junct 9 take 1st left (Trinity Rd). Through 4 rdbts to lights. Left onto A251 signed Faversham. 0.5m to sign for Boughton Aluph, 200yds to hotel*

Broadly-based modern cooking in a grand manorial pile

With its vast grounds and immaculate gardens, Eastwell is very much the manorial pile, full of magnificent, well-appointed interiors. There is no automatic allegiance to traditional British ways in the cooking, however. So a sturdily constructed terrine of ham hock and foie gras, accompanied by pickled veg and truffled mayonnaise might be followed by a roasted fillet of stone bass that comes on vegetable stir-fry with pak choi and Thai-spiced purée or braised rump of Romney Marsh lamb with wild garlic, smoked yogurt and pine nuts in tapenade jus. A fixed-price menu offers

continued across the page

simpler dishes, while desserts aim to seduce with chocolate fondant with malted milk and brandy ice cream.

Eastwell Manor

Chef Neil Wiggins **Seats** 80, Pr/dining room 80 **Times** 12-2.30/7-10 **Prices** Fixed L 2 course £18.50, Fixed D 3 course £35, Tasting menu £60-£80, Starter £15.50 £18.50, Main £30-£38, Dessert £7.50-£15 **Wines** 163 bottles over £30, 123 bottles under £30, 14 by glass **Parking** 120 **Notes** Gourmet champagne evenings, Sunday L £22.50-£28.50, Vegetarian available, Children welcome

BIDDENDEN Map 7 TQ83

The West House

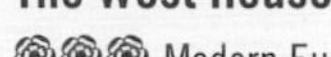 Modern European V

tel: 01580 291341 **28 High St TN27 8AH**
email: thewesthouse@btconnect.com
dir: *Junct of A262 & A274. 14m S of Maidstone*

Vanguard cooking in a charming Kentish village

The Garretts' restaurant with rooms on the high street of the wine village of Biddenden dates back to the 16th century, with its distinctive tiled apron and timbered frontage. Graham Garrett takes his inspiration from the fields, farms and coasts of Kent and melds pedigree ingredients into a style that owes a fair bit to sunny Mediterranean modes, with one foot firmly in the modernist camp. Pressed Ibérico pork with black pudding comes with a reimagined caponata of celeriac and apple, while sea bass fillet is robustly served by Jerusalem artichoke and lardo di Colonnata, among the main course options. They may be preceded by 'gravmax', Garrett's own coinage for cured mackerel with charcoaled beetroot, blackberries and horseradish, or perhaps a serving of crab in Mexican array with guacamole, lime and tortilla. Fresh garden produce is showcased on its own fixed-price menu, depending on what's just coming out of the ground or off the trees at various seasons. Turn to autumn bounty for desserts such as warm pumpkin cake with clementine, chestnuts and chocolate sorbet, or else maintain the Med theme with dulce de leche tart and sherry caramel. Neal's Yard cheeses come with an Eccles cake, and yes, there's a Kentish wine on the enterprising list.

Chef Graham Garrett, Tony Parkin **Seats** 32 **Times** 12-2/7-9.30, Closed 24-26 Dec & 1 Jan, Mon, L Sat, D Sun **Prices** Fixed L 3 course £25-£45, Fixed D 3 course £45, Tasting menu £60-£90 **Wines** 54 bottles over £30, 28 bottles under £30, 22 by glass **Parking** 7 **Notes** Tasting menu 6 course, Sunday L £38-£45, Children welcome

BOUGHTON MONCHELSEA Map 7 TQ75

The Mulberry Tree

Modern British

tel: 01622 749082 & 741058 **Hermitage Ln ME17 4DA**
email: info@themulberrytreekent.co.uk
dir: *B2163 turn into Wierton Rd straight over x-rds, 1st left East Hall Hill*

Precise modern cooking, full of the flavours of Kent

The Mulberry Tree's expansive dining area is done out in light contemporary style, with wooden floors, bare tables and patterned designer wallpaper. Diners come for well-tuned British cooking with European accents using local ingredients from a kitchen that tends its own garden, pigs and chickens. Skilfully woven flavours and precise timings are hallmarks. Start with smoked eel with leeks vinaigrette, Gentleman's Relish and dill and move on to roast pheasant breast with red cabbage, sprouts, pancetta jam, fondant potato and chestnut purée, or pan-fried hake fillet with ratatouille, mash and a white wine, thyme and mussel velouté. End on custard tart with cranberry jam.

Chef Robert Best **Seats** 70, Pr/dining room 16 **Times** 12-2/6.30-9.30, Closed 26 Dec, Mon, D Sun **Prices** Starter £6.50-£9.50, Main £14.50-£23.95, Dessert £6.95-£12.95 **Wines** 30 bottles over £30, 31 bottles under £30, 54 by glass **Parking** 60 **Notes** Sunday L £21.95-£24.95, Vegetarian available, Children welcome

CANTERBURY Map 7 TR15

ABode Canterbury

Modern European V

tel: 01227 766266 & 826678 **High St CT1 2RX**
email: reservations@abodecanterbury.co.uk **web:** www.abodecanterbury.co.uk
dir: *Phone for directions*

Modern European eating boutique-style

Not far from the cathedral, the Canterbury ABode is a half-timbered building that has been decoratively refashioned for the boutique crowd. A starter of wild mushroom risotto arrives with a parmesan crisp sticking out of it amid a ruffle of white wine foam. Dishes are also capable of striking the more robust note. Quail, cooked in a water bath and finished with a blow torch, is served with a hazelnut vinaigrette and truffled egg yolk, while a main course of pan-roasted monkfish is paired especially well with black quinoa and picked cockles. Options for dessert include a vanilla and goats' cheese cheesecake.

Chef Jauca Catalin **Seats** 76, Pr/dining room 12 **Times** 12-2.30/5.30-9.30, Closed L Mon-Thu **Prices** Fixed L 2 course £17, Fixed D 3 course £26.50, Tasting menu £65-£100, Starter £7.50-£13.95, Main £12.50-£23.95, Dessert £6.95-£9.95 **Wines** 41 bottles over £30, 9 bottles under £30, 21 by glass **Parking** 40 **Notes** Sunday L £20-£25, Children welcome

CANTERBURY *continued*

Best Western Abbots Barton Hotel

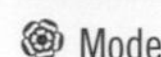 Modern British

tel: 01227 760341 **New Dover Rd CT1 3DU**
email: info@abbotsbartonhotel.com **web:** www.abbotsbartonhotel.com
dir: *A2 (N/S) A2050 (S) Canterbury city centre, A28 (E/W) A2 Dover. Hotel in New Dover Rd*

A ten-minute stroll from the cathedral and medieval city

Built in the mid-19th century as a large private house, this early Victorian Gothic pile has been a hotel since 1927. Although a second restaurant is mooted, diners currently eat in The Fountain Restaurant, whose modern British menu likes to declare Garden of England provenance in dishes such as duo of Romney Marsh lamb with dauphinoise potatoes, pea purée, and apple and mint relish, Alkham Valley Old Spot pork belly with soy and ginger marinade, and from an Orpington (which used to be in Kent) farm, seasonal vegetable platter dressed with extra-virgin Kentish rapeseed oil. The homemade breads are excellent. Finish with salted caramel and milk chocolate parfait.

Chef William Britton **Seats** 50, Pr/dining room 20 **Times** 7-9.30, Closed 25 & 31 Dec, L all week **Prices** Fixed D 3 course £24, Starter £6-£7.50, Main £22-£26, Dessert £6 **Wines** 14 bottles over £30, 42 bottles under £30, 13 by glass **Parking** 40 **Notes** Vegetarian available, Children welcome

The Dove Inn

 Modern British, Continental

tel: 01227 751360 **Plum Pudding Ln, Dargate ME13 9HB**
email: doveatdargate@hotmail.com
dir: *6m NW of Canterbury. A299 Thanet Way, turn off at Lychgate service station*

Attractive food-focused country pub

The Dove is a cosy and friendly village gastropub where the kitchen toes the contemporary British line. Seared scallops paired with black pudding and bacon chips, served with pea velouté, or chicken liver parfait with red onion jam are what to expect among starters, followed by roast hake fillet on potato purée with sautéed new potatoes, chorizo and wilted chard or, in season, roast leg of guinea fowl with black pudding mash, greens and a red wine jus. Gourmet wine dinners are run here, and the short menus may conclude with cherry Bakewell tart with berry compôte and cherry brandy ice cream.

The Goods Shed Restaurant

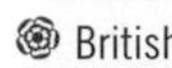 British

tel: 01227 459153 **Station Road West CT2 8AN**
email: restaurant@thegoodsshed.co.uk
dir: *Adjacent to Canterbury West train station*

Farmers' market menu at the railway station

This restaurant for the farmers' market next to Canterbury West station has chunky wood tables with views through majestic arched windows over the comings and goings below. It uses the market produce to the full, the selections changing with every service. Start with scallops thermidor, or a crab and tarragon 'risotto' of bulgar wheat, before main courses that go the distance with pedigree meats like 24-day aged rib-eye in Colston Bassett Stilton butter, or rack of lamb with prunes and pine nuts. Fish might be hake with curried mussels, and dessert a satisfyingly tart Bramley apple crème brûlée with cinnamon shortbread.

DARTFORD — Map 6 TQ57

Rowhill Grange Hotel & Utopia Spa

Modern European

tel: 01322 615136 **Wilmington DA2 7QH**
email: admin@rowhillgrange.com **web:** www.alexanderhotels.co.uk
dir: *M25 junct 3, take B2173 towards Swanley, then B258 towards Hextable. Straight on at 3 rdbts. Hotel 1.5m on left*

Soothing modernised dishes in Kentish rural tranquillity

A substantial 18th-century manor in acres of grounds that include a pond, Rowhill Grange is now an upmarket boutique hotel. RG's is the serious dining option, where roast hare (a welcome appearance) is served with textures of cauliflower and beer onions, for instance, and roast scallops with a scallop cracker, confit leek and leek ash mayonnaise. Main courses run to the full-blooded flavours of braised oxtail and kidney suet pudding with caramelised onion gravy. Fish, meanwhile, crops up as roast skate wing fashionably paired with pork belly and accompanied by red wine salsify and Swiss chard, with puddings along the lines of fluffy rhubarb soufflé with ginger ice cream.

DEAL — Map 7 TR35

Dunkerleys Hotel & Restaurant

Modern British

tel: 01304 375016 **19 Beach St CT14 7AH**
email: ddunkerley@btconnect.com **web:** www.dunkerleys.co.uk
dir: *Turn off A2 onto A258 to Deal, hotel 100yds before Deal Pier*

Seafood-based menu in a long-running seafront hotel

Run with down-to-earth friendliness by Ian and Linda Dunkerley, this relaxed and homely seafront hotel has a jauntily inviting air. Fuss-free dishes bring fresh local materials together in well-balanced combinations, and here in Deal seafood is the main deal, getting the show on the road with the likes of roast herring with horseradish slaw. The main event might star pan-fried turbot fillet on saffron velouté with kale and turned potatoes, or deep-fried local cod fillet with the usual accompaniments. If you need something meaty, there's confit pork belly with bacon, cabbage and champ, and, to finish, perhaps tarte Tatin with cinnamon ice cream.

Chef Ian Dunkerley, Josh Hackett **Seats** 50 **Times** 12-2.30/7-9.30, Closed Mon, D Sun **Prices** Fixed L 2 course fr £12.95, Tasting menu £36, Starter £7.95-£10.95, Main £12.95-£26.95, Dessert £5.95-£9.95 **Wines** 24 bottles over £30, 61 bottles under £30, 9 by glass **Parking** Public car park adjacent **Notes** Tasting menu 5 course, Sunday L £12.95-£16.95, Vegetarian available, Children welcome

DOVER — Map 7 TR34

The Marquis at Alkham

 Modern British

tel: 01304 873410 **Alkham Valley Rd, Alkham CT15 7DF**
email: reception@themarquisatalkham.co.uk **web:** www.themarquisatalkham.co.uk
dir: *M20 continue to A2. Take A260 exit & then onto Alkham Valley Rd*

Creative cooking and boutique chic deep in the Kent countryside

Modern art, stylish furnishings and boutique bedrooms make a fine impression at this restaurant with rooms where the smart restaurant offers a carte and two tasting menus (one offering the best of Kentish produce). Kick off with ham hock terrine partnered with tomato and apple chutney and toasted brioche. Among main courses, leg of guinea fowl is cooked slowly au vin, and arrives with dauphinoise potatoes, red cabbage and green beans. Desserts are a refined and comforting bunch, from lemon tart with chewy meringue and raspberry sorbet, to raspberry soufflé with white chocolate ice cream and crunchy pieces of honeycomb.

Chef Andrew King **Seats** 60, Pr/dining room 20 **Times** 12-2.30/6.30-9.30 **Prices** Fixed L 2 course £14.95, Tasting menu fr £65, Starter £7.50-£14.50, Main £16-£24, Dessert £8.50-£9.95 **Wines** 88 bottles over £30, 32 bottles under £30, 9 by glass **Parking** 26 **Notes** Fixed D 4 course £35, Sunday L £19.95-£22.95, Vegetarian available, Children 8 yrs+

Wallett's Court Country House Hotel & Spa

Modern British

tel: 01304 852424 **West Cliffe, St Margaret's-at-Cliffe CT15 6EW**
email: dine@wallettscourt.com **web:** www.wallettscourt.com
dir: *M2/A2 or M20/A20, follow signs for Deal (A258), 1st right for St-Margaret's-at-Cliffe. Restaurant 1m on right*

Modernist cooking in the Kent countryside

A straggling ruin when the Oakleys first looked it over in 1975, Wallett's is still theirs 40 years and buckets of TLC later. Cookery classes are now among the attractions. Fixed-price dinner menus kick off with smoked eel and fennel risotto with apple, radish and caviar, prior to aged fillet of beef with creamed leeks, foie gras and truffle, or sea bass with shrimps and capers in hollandaise. Meals end with Pina Colada parfait, or hot chocolate fondant. An enterprising eight-course tasting menu runs the rule from pork and apple arancini with aïoli and baguette to crème caramel with coconut granola.

Chef Michael Fowler **Seats** 60, Pr/dining room 40 **Times** 12-2.30/7-9 **Prices** Fixed L 2 course fr £16.95, Fixed D 3 course fr £45, Tasting menu fr £65 **Wines** 18 bottles over £30, 25 bottles under £30, 17 by glass **Parking** 50 **Notes** Tasting menu on request, Afternoon tea £10-£25, Sunday L £21-£45, Vegetarian available, Children welcome

EGERTON Map 7 TQ94

Frasers

 Modern British

tel: 01233 756122 **Coldharbour Farm TN27 9DD**
email: lisa@frasers-events.co.uk **web:** www.frasers-events.co.uk
dir: *Phone for directions*

Seasonal eating on an industrious Kentish farm

A hotel and cookery school are part of the set up here, along with a barn-style dining room with high ceilings and exposed timbers. Proceedings open with a smoked haddock Scotch egg with pickled cucumber and lemon mayonnaise, before moving on to pan-fried chicken suprême partnered by confit garlic-infused crushed potatoes, purple sprouting broccoli, wild garlic pesto and toasted pine nuts, or perhaps citrus and herb-crusted rack of Romney Marsh lamb with lyonnaise potatoes, carrots and leeks, and a red wine reduction. To finish, there are Kentish cheeses on hand for those determined to resist the allure of pear and frangipane tart with Amaretto ice cream.

Chef Alan Egan **Seats** 30, Pr/dining room 50 **Times** 12.30-3/6.30-9, Closed L subject to private functions, D subject to private functions **Prices** Starter £7.50-£9.50, Main £17.95-£26.95, Dessert £8.50 **Wines** 6 bottles over £30, 20 bottles under £30, 5 by glass **Parking** 30 **Notes** Brunch, Afternoon tea, Vegetarian available, Children welcome

FAVERSHAM Map 7 TR06

Faversham Creek & Red Sails Restaurant

Modern British NEW

tel: 01795 533535 **Conduit St ME13 7BH**
email: office@favershamcreekhotel.co.uk **web:** www.favershamcreekhotel.co.uk
dir: *M2 junct 6 onto A251. At T-junct left then right into The Mall. Pass railway station, continue on B2041. Left into Quay Ln*

Fine Kentish produce, confidently cooked

Once an 18th-century coaching inn, this hotel has had a modern makeover, with the Red Sails Restaurant sporting a suitably shipshape look involving bare brick walls and vibrant red stripy upholstery. The kitchen couldn't be in a better spot for hauling in Kent's rural and coastal bounty, which is used to good effect in a well-crafted main course of lamb loin and slow-cooked belly, with shallots, milk curd and pearl barley. Bookending that, a starter of foie gras parfait and confit duck leg is offset by tangy rhubarb chutney and gingerbread, while dessert brings lemon curd tart with meringue and iced tea and lime sorbet.

Chef Roger Heathcote, Scott Pendry **Seats** 36 **Times** 12-4.30/7-11, Closed Mon-Tue, D Sun **Prices** Fixed L 2 course £14.95-£20.95, Fixed D 3 course £17.95-£23.95, Tasting menu £45-£55, Starter £6.50-£8.50, Main £16-£22, Dessert £5.95-£10.95 **Wines** 18 bottles over £30, 22 bottles under £30, 14 by glass **Parking** 10 **Notes** Sunday L £17.95-£23.95, Vegetarian available, Children welcome

Read's Restaurant

Modern British NOTABLE WINE LIST

tel: 01795 535344 **Macknade Manor, Canterbury Rd ME13 8XE**
email: enquiries@reads.com
dir: *From M2 junct 6 follow A251 towards Faversham. At T-junct with A2 (Canterbury road) turn right. Hotel 0.5m on right*

Refined modern British cooking in an elegant Georgian manor

Chef-patron David Pitchford's Georgian manor house has long been a Kentish destination for those in the know. Set in lush grounds that provide much fresh produce for the kitchen, it feels like a country retreat, and is run with the friendly, grown-up affability we hope to find in such places. Read's was doing modern British before many others had cottoned on to it, the dishes carefully composed and based on sound culinary tradition. Citrus-marinated salmon is all tanged up with pickled cucumber and tangerine purée, followed by lamb loin and braised breast with cabbage and raisins, and then deep-filled lemon tart garnished with frosted blueberries.

Chef David Pitchford **Seats** 50, Pr/dining room 30 **Times** 12-2.30/7-10, Closed BHs, Sun-Mon **Prices** Fixed L 3 course £28, Fixed D 3 course £60, Tasting menu £65 **Wines** 100 bottles over £30, 45 bottles under £30, 18 by glass **Parking** 30 **Notes** Tasting menu 7 course, Vegetarian available, Children welcome

FAWKHAM GREEN Map 6 TQ56

Brandshatch Place Hotel & Spa

 Modern British

tel: 01474 875000 & 0845 072 7395 *(Calls cost 7p per minute plus your phone company's access charge)* **Brands Hatch Rd DA3 8NQ**
email: brandshatchplace@handpicked.co.uk
web: www.handpickedhotels.co.uk/brandshatchplace
dir: *M25 junct 3/A20 West Kingsdown. Left at paddock entrance/Fawkham Green sign. 3rd left signed Fawkham Rd. Hotel 500mtrs on right*

Witty modern brasserie cooking near Brands Hatch

Modern brasserie cooking of informality and wit is the theme in this handsome Georgian manor house – how about a 'Battenberg' of salmon and cod with caviar and cucumber dressing? – and dishes reflect attention to detail. The visual dazzle of poached mackerel in its setting of rhubarb jelly, radish and red-vein sorrel makes a bold opening statement, and there is much to enjoy in a main course pig medley encompassing earthy ham hock, well-trimmed belly and a croquette of the cheek, alongside puréed onion and rib-sticking mash in red wine. A red wine reduction also turns up with the must-have baked Alaska, offsetting the sweetness of its meringue shell.

Chef Carl Smith **Seats** 60, Pr/dining room 110 **Times** 12-2/7-9.30 **Prices** Fixed L 2 course £30, Fixed D 3 course £39, Starter £9.95-£12.50, Main £12.95-£26.95, Dessert £7.95-£8.50 **Wines** 92 bottles over £30, 8 bottles under £30, 18 by glass **Parking** 100 **Notes** Sunday L £23.50-£29.50, Vegetarian available, Children welcome

FOLKESTONE Map 7 TR23

Rocksalt Rooms

 Modern British

tel: 01303 212070 **2 Back St CT19 6NN**
email: info@rocksaltfolkestone.co.uk **web:** www.rocksaltfolkestone.co.uk
dir: *M20 junct 13, follow A259 Folkestone Harbour, then left to Fish Market*

Fabulous harbourside setting and a local flavour

Sitting on the harbour with a curving terrace cantilevered out over the water, a huge sliding glass wall to capitalise on the view and a classy, well-designed interior with oak floors, Rocksalt's menu has seafood at its heart, but there's also hay-baked rump of Romney Marsh lamb with anchovy potatoes or prime slabs of steak to keep carnivores happy. Start with smoked coley with creamy mash and a poached egg, and move on to poached cod fillet with samphire and celeriac and mussel broth, or roast thornback ray wing with hedgerow green garlic sauce. For dessert, there's baked egg custard tart with blackcurrant sorbet or buttermilk pudding with blood orange.

Chef Simon Oakley **Seats** 100, Pr/dining room 24 **Times** 12-3/6.30-10, Closed D Sun (winter) **Prices** Fixed L 2 course £21.50, Starter £3-£14.50, Main £12.50-£28, Dessert £6.50-£8.25 **Wines** 59 bottles over £30, 28 bottles under £30, 14 by glass **Parking** On street, pay & display car park **Notes** Seasonal offers, Sunday L £25-£30, Vegetarian available, Children welcome

GRAFTY GREEN Map 7 TQ84

Who'd A Thought It

Modern British V

tel: 01622 858951 **Headcorn Rd ME17 2AR**
email: joe@whodathoughtit.com **web:** www.whodathoughtit.com
dir: *M20 junct 8, A20 towards Lenham. 1m take Grafty Green turn, follow brown tourist signs for 4.5m*

Modern classic cooking in an unassuming Kentish village

A champagne and oyster bar with rooms in a Kentish village not far from the M20 designed with racy opulence. A menu of modern classics – scallops with cauliflower purée, beetroot and goats' cheese salad with candied walnuts and celery shoots, cider-braised pork belly with red cabbage, damsons and crackling – is brought off with persuasive aplomb, and prime ingredients are excellent. Witness a thyme-infused breast of corn-fed chicken with pearl barley and bacon risotto, served with charred baby onions and buttered cabbage. Shellfish platters and thermidor will please seafood purists, as will sticky toffee pudding with butterscotch sauce and salted caramel ice cream.

Chef Tobi Caira **Seats** 50 **Times** 11.30-9.30, All-day dining **Prices** Fixed L 2 course fr £19, Tasting menu £55-£85, Starter £6.50-£12, Main £18-£90, Dessert £6.50-£12 **Wines** 80 bottles over £30, 23 bottles under £30, 14 by glass **Parking** 45 **Notes** Sunday L £10-£13, Children welcome

HYTHE Map 7 TR13

Saltwood on the Green

Contemporary British NEW

tel: 01303 237800 **The Green, Saltwood CT21 4PS**
email: info@saltwoodrestaurant.co.uk
dir: *Phone for directions*

Appealing cooking in a restored 1900 building

This intimate restaurant occupies a restored general store that's been at the hub of local life since 1900. Framed photos sit alongside local artworks, and the decor has an unforced, mix-and-match look that sits well with the simple, unaffected culinary approach. The kitchen takes Kent's splendid produce, handles it with skill and respect and transforms it into a starter of duck hash with a poached egg and mustard aïoli, followed by locally landed ling with courgette fritters and cauliflower risotto. Puddings are pleasing too, with particular praise going to the impressive natural flavours in banana parfait topped with an airy banana espuma.

Chef Jeff Kipp **Times** 9-3/6-11, Closed Mon (Tue private parties only) **Prices** Fixed L 2 course £15, Starter £3-£9, Main £12-£21 **Wines** 9 bottles over £30, 12 bottles under £30, 16 by glass **Notes** Breakfast, Sun Brunch, Vegetarian available

LENHAM Map 7 TQ85

Chilston Park Hotel

 Modern British

tel: 01622 859803 & 0845 072 7426 *(Calls cost 7p per minute plus your phone company's access charge)* **Sandway ME17 2BE**
email: chilstonpark@handpicked.co.uk **web:** www.handpickedhotels.co.uk/chilstonpark
dir: *M20 junct 8*

Splendid Georgian mansion with elegant restaurant

Secluded in 22 acres of sublime landscaped gardens and parkland, Chilston Park brims with enough period authenticity, antiques and oil paintings that you might be inspired to dress as Jane Austen's Mr Darcy or Elizabeth Bennet for dinner in the unique, sunken Venetian-style Culpeper's restaurant. The kitchen deals in modern British cooking clearly rooted in the classics but with some inventive combinations. Goats' cheese mousse with butternut purée and toasted seeds might open the bidding, before a well-timed tranche of halibut arrives with saffron cocotte potatoes and marsh samphire in a citrus-spiked red wine emulsion. Proceedings conclude with a well-made apple and quince tart and milk sorbet.

Chef Rohan Nevins **Seats** 45, Pr/dining room 20 **Times** 7-9.30, Closed L Mon-Sat **Prices** Fixed D 3 course £39, Tasting menu £60, Starter £8.50-£10.50, Main £22-£36.50, Dessert £8.50-£12.50 **Wines** 60 bottles over £30, 15 bottles under £30, 18 by glass **Parking** 100 **Notes** Seasonal gourmet menu, Sunday L £25, Vegetarian available, Children welcome

LEYSDOWN-ON-SEA Map 7 TR07

The Ferry House Inn

British Gastro NEW

tel: 01795 510214 **Harty Ferry Rd ME12 4BQ**
email. info@theferryhouseinn.co.uk **web:** www.theferryhouseinn.co.uk
dir: *A249 over Sheppey Bridge, follow signs for Leysdown. Past Eastchurch, turn right before Leysdown onto Harty Ferry Rd*

Enterprising cooking in a 16th-century inn

The Ferry House, a country inn alongside the Swale Estuary, has put the Isle of Sheppey on the culinary map. It's possible to eat in the bar, but the majority of diners book into the raftered Barn Restaurant. The kitchen's style is modern British, so expect intelligently composed starters such as scallops with stout-braised lamb breast, pea purée and pickled kohlrabi, or pork terrine with sea buckthorn sauce. Then try confit duck leg with redcurrant jus, potato croquettes, greens and roast beetroot, or pan-fried salmon fillet on red pepper sauce with runner beans, chickpeas and tomatoes. End seasonally with vanilla crème brûlée with winter fruits.

Chef Vitalijs Kaneps **Seats** 40, Pr/dining room 20 **Times** 12-3/6-9, Closed 24-30 Dec, D Sun **Prices** Fixed L 2 course fr £11 **Wines** 1 bottle over £30, 23 bottles under £30, 24 by glass **Parking** 70 **Notes** Sunday L £12-£15, Vegetarian available, Children welcome

MAIDSTONE Map 7 TQ75

Fish on the Green

British, French

tel: 01622 738300 **Church Ln, Bearsted Green ME14 4EJ**
dir: *N of A20 on village green*

Refreshingly simple fish and seafood in a Kentish village

The pretty village green setting is quintessentially English and Fish on the Green has netted a strong local fan base with its fresh, unpretentious interior, clued-up staff, and the excellent fish and seafood on offer. Super-fresh materials are treated simply, setting out, perhaps, with pan-seared Scottish scallops with parsnip purée, crispy ham and shallot and honey dressing. Next up, try pan-roasted monkfish on wilted baby spinach with saffron and mussel velouté. If you don't fancy fish, there's always something like confit pork belly on black pudding mash with Savoy cabbage. Finish with apple, rhubarb and oat crumble with vanilla ice cream.

Chef Peter Baldwin **Seats** 50 **Times** 12-2.30/6.30-10, Closed Xmas, Mon (some), D Sun (some) **Prices** Fixed L 2 course £17.95, Starter £7-£11.75, Main £15-£28, Dessert £6.95 **Wines** 12 bottles over £30, 23 bottles under £30, 13 by glass **Parking** 50 **Notes** Vegetarian available, Children welcome

MARGATE Map 7 TR37

The Ambrette

Modern Indian

tel: 01843 231504 **44 King St CT9 1QE**
email: info@theambrette.co.uk
dir: *A299/A28, left into Hawley St B2055. Restaurant on right corner King St*

Modern Anglo-Indian food based on local prime produce

At both his Rye venue and here in Margate, Dev Biswal combines modern British and Indian flavours into an exciting fusion, amid decor that is more Anglo than Asian. The presentation of dishes is more akin to European food and there's bags of flavour and plenty of Kentish produce on show. A starter of crisped soft-shelled crab comes with smoked crab raita, samphire, and a crab and beetroot cake. Among mains, spice-rubbed sea bass is steamed in banana leaves and served with lentil kedgeree in coconut sauce, and there are hefty chocolate samosas in cardamom sauce with passionfruit and guava parfait to finish.

Chef Dev Biswal **Seats** 52 **Times** 11.30-2.30/5.30-9.30 **Prices** Fixed L 2 course £15.95, Tasting menu £44.95, Starter £5.20-£9.95, Main £11.95-£24.95, Dessert £6.95-£11.95 **Wines** 15 bottles over £30, 20 bottles under £30, 16 by glass **Parking** 10 **Notes** Pre-theatre menu until 6.30 & after 9pm, Sunday L, Vegetarian available, Children welcome

Sands Hotel

Modern European

tel: 01843 228228 & 07794 336063 **16 Marine Dr CT9 1DH**
email: info@sandshotelmargate.co.uk **web:** www.sandshotelmargate.co.uk
dir: *A28 to Marine Drive. B2051 in Margate*

Contemporary dining with a sea view

A breath of fresh air on the Margate seafront, Sands Hotel offers a contemporary experience with sweeping views of the sea. The team in the kitchen turn out impressive modern food based on first-class regional ingredients. There are classical foundations to many of the dishes, but there's no shortage of creativity either; salmon rillettes, for example, with crème fraîche jelly and pickled cucumber and fennel, or glazed duck breast with candied swede and charred chicory (dressed with a spiced honey jus). The sweet-toothed can end on a high with butterscotch pannacotta with glazed banana and chocolate sauce. Dining on the terrace is a fair-weather treat.

Chef Ryan Tasker **Seats** 64, Pr/dining room 56 **Times** 12-2/7-9 **Prices** Fixed L 2 course £15, Starter £6.50-£9, Main £13.50-£24, Dessert £6.50-£8 **Wines** 12 bottles over £30, 26 bottles under £30, 9 by glass **Parking** Car park 100 yds **Notes** Jazz & seasonal offers, Sunday L, Vegetarian available, Children welcome

ROCHESTER Map 6 TQ76

Topes Restaurant

◎◎ Modern British

tel: 01634 845270 **60 High St ME1 1JY**
email: julie.small@btconnect.com **web:** www.topesrestaurant.com
dir: *M2 junct 1, through Strood High St over Medway Bridge, turn right at Northgate onto High St*

An atmospheric gem in historic Rochester

On a corner of Rochester's high street, the castle and cathedral visible through side windows, Topes occupies a building spanning the 15th to 17th centuries, and could host a period drama with its wonky, sagging timbers. Inside is all linen fold panels and carved black beams, the patina of age relieved by light colours, uncluttered modern decor and a relaxing mood. Excellent Kentish produce underpins a starter of pigeon breast with parsnip purée, chanterelles and pickled blueberries, before main course brings on cod with charred baby gem and feta. A finale of apricot and walnut tart with maple pecan ice cream concludes things in style.

Chef Chris Small **Seats** 45, Pr/dining room 16 **Times** 12-2.30/6.30-9, Closed Mon, D Sun **Prices** Fixed L 2 course £19.50, Fixed D 3 course £25 **Wines** 19 bottles over £30, 35 bottles under £30, 10 by glass **Parking** Public car park **Notes** ALC 3 course £35, Afternoon tea £11.95, Sunday L £19.50-£25, Vegetarian available, Children welcome

SANDWICH Map 7 TR35

The Lodge at Prince's

◎◎ Modern British

tel: 01304 611118 **Prince's Dr, Sandwich Bay CT13 9QB**
email: j.george@princesgolfclub.co.uk **web:** www.princesgolfclub.co.uk
dir: *M2 onto A299 Thanet Way to Manston Airport, A256 to Sandwich, follow sign to golf course*

Golf-centric hotel with modern brasserie

The Lodge occupies a substantial purpose-built property of white walls and red roofs with a brasserie-style restaurant, a coolly elegant space in shades of pale blue/grey. Fashionable foams feature in some starters – one of bacon for seared scallops with belly pork, cauliflower and vanilla purée and shallots, for instance. Sea trout tartare is served with apple, fennel and gin and tonic sorbet, and could be followed by properly rested saddle of venison with chestnuts, figs, braised red cabbage and fondant potato, with a game faggot adding an extra dimension. Puddings do the trick, especially the light and delicate vanilla and coconut pannacotta with lime sorbet.

SITTINGBOURNE Map 7 TQ96

Hempstead House Country Hotel

◎ Traditional European

tel: 01795 428020 **London Rd, Bapchild ME9 9PP**
email: info@hempsteadhouse.co.uk **web:** www.hempsteadhouse.co.uk
dir: *1.5m from town centre on A2 towards Canterbury*

Modern and classical cooking in a Victorian hotel

Lakes Restaurant at this country-house hotel and spa gets its name from the family who built the original property in the mid-19th century. Elaborate swagged drapes hang at the large windows looking out to the grounds, chandeliers add a bit of glitter, and upholstered dining chairs are pulled up to formally set tables. The kitchen takes its cue from the contemporary British repertoire. Panko-coated venison and black pudding Scotch eggs is one way to start, followed by pan-fried fillet of cod with a bean and potato cassoulet, or roast guinea fowl breast served with a boudin and pickled beetroots.

Chef Paul Field, Peter Gilbey **Seats** 70, Pr/dining room 30 **Times** 12-2.30/7-10, Closed D Sun (non residents) **Prices** Fixed D 3 course £29.50, Starter £6.95-£9.50, Main £18-£24.50, Dessert £6.50-£7.50 **Wines** 16 bottles over £30, 53 bottles under £30, 4 by glass **Parking** 200 **Notes** Sunday L fr £19.95, Vegetarian available, Children welcome

STALISFIELD GREEN Map 7 TQ95

The Plough Inn

◎ British NEW

tel: 01795 890256 **ME13 0HY**
email: info@theploughinnstalisfield.co.uk
dir: *Phone for directions*

Oak-beamed wayside pub, strong on Kentish produce

High up on the North Downs, with far-reaching views, stands this 15th-century, timber-framed, Wealden hall house. Dining takes place in both a cosy pubby area, where an impressive list of past landlords is displayed, and a second space, more restaurant-like, yet still informal. Dishes are simply described and simply presented, as for example, smoked salmon pâté, brown crab mayo and guacamole; slow-cooked marinated pork belly, heritage carrots, beetroot and baked apple purée; and monkfish tails, baby vegetables, Anya potatoes and shellfish bisque. Cambridge burnt cream – Trinity College's own version of crème brûlée – with lemon curd and meringues rounds things off well.

Chef Richard Baker **Times** 12-2/6-9, Closed Mon, D Sun **Prices** Fixed L 2 course £13.95, Starter £6.95-£9, Main £10.50-£18.50, Dessert £6 **Wines** 6 bottles over £30, 23 bottles under £30, 12 by glass **Notes** Sunday L £13-£25.50, Vegetarian available, Children welcome

TENTERDEN Map 7 TQ83

The Swan Wine Kitchen

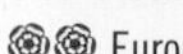 European

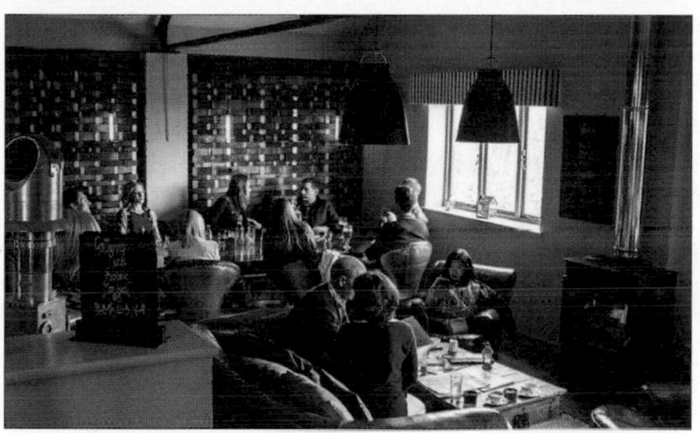

tel: 01580 761616 **Chapel Down Winery, Small Hythe Rd TN30 7NG**
email: booking@swanchapeldown.co.uk
dir: *B2082 between Tenterden and Rye*

In a vineyard, a restaurant with a difference

This striking, bare timber and galvanised steel building lies in the grounds of Chapel Down Winery, one of England's leading winemakers. Both bar and terrace offer countryside views, while from the open-plan kitchen comes a short but appealing choice of modern European dishes, such as a starter of octopus carpaccio, chorizo, puréed red pepper and smoked almonds. In similar vein are gilt head bream with cucumber consommé and herb gnocchi, and barbecued lamb rump served with wild garlic, morels and boulangère potatoes. Coconut pannacotta with kiwi sorbet and mango would be a fine way to finish. Why not tour the vineyard, before enjoying its wine?

Chef Tom Genty **Seats** 65, Pr/dining room 18 **Times** 12-3/6-9, Closed D Sun-Wed **Prices** Fixed L 2 course £19.50, Fixed D 3 course £21.50, Starter £6.50-£8, Main £13-£22, Dessert £6.50 **Wines** 16 bottles over £30, 8 bottles under £30, 7 by glass **Parking** 100 **Notes** Gathering menu 2/3 course Mon-Fri 12-3 advance booking req, Sunday L £24.50, Vegetarian available, Children welcome

TUNBRIDGE WELLS (ROYAL) Map 6 TQ53

Hotel du Vin Tunbridge Wells

 French, British

tel: 01892 526455 **Crescent Rd TN1 2LY**
email: reception.tunbridgewells@hotelduvin.com **web:** www.hotelduvin.com
dir: *Follow town centre to main junct of Mount Pleasant Rd & Crescent Rd/Church Rd. Hotel 150yds on right just past Phillips House*

French bistro food and a monster wine list

A Grade II listed Georgian mansion is home to HdV's operation in Tunbridge Wells and the enormous wine lists remain an integral part of the attraction of this hotel chain. The cooking continues on a solid French bistro basis, offering scallops in sauce vièrge, or chicken liver parfait on sourdough toast, to start, then sole meunière with brown shrimps, pedigree 28-day aged rib-eye with skinny chips and textbook béarnaise, or the more obviously Anglo comfort-food likes of 'shepherd's pie' made with duck. Vegetarian mains include parsnip and beetroot Tatin, or spelt risotto with chanterelles. To close, treacle tart is a moistly satisfying rendition, served with clotted-cream ice cream.

The Kentish Hare

Modern British V

tel: 01892 525709 **95 Bidborough Ridge, Bidborough TN3 0XB**
email: enquiries@thekentishhare.com
dir: *From A26 London Rd, take B2176 Bidborough Ridge. 0.9m to restaurant*

Dynamic modern cooking in a rejuvenated pub

Brothers Chris and James Tanner have transformed a closed-down pub into a dynamic, splendidly refurbished contemporary restaurant. Dishes that are squarely in the modern manner might include a starter of seared scallops, wafer-thin cauliflower slices, pine nuts and raisins in curry oil, which might presage a main course of deftly crackled pork belly accompanied by goats' cheese fondue and pickled mushrooms. An alternative route might be via chicken liver parfait with candied walnuts and pear jelly to smoked haddock risotto with leeks and a poached egg in grain mustard sauce. Finish with chocolate ganache with a liquid caramel centre (à la Rolo), served with salted popcorn and milk sorbet.

Chef C & J Tanner, Sam Spratt **Seats** 64 **Times** 12-2.30/6-9.30, Closed 1st wk Jan, Mon **Prices** Fixed L 2 course £18, Starter £5.95-£10.95, Main £13.50-£27.95, Dessert £5.95-£7.50 **Wines** 14 bottles over £30, 21 bottles under £30, 23 by glass **Parking** 24 **Notes** Sunday L £14.95-£15.95, Children welcome

The Spa Hotel

Modern, Traditional British

tel: 01892 520331 **Mount Ephraim TN4 8XJ**
email: reservations@spahotel.co.uk **web:** www.spahotel.co.uk
dir: *On A264 leaving Tunbridge Wells towards East Grinstead*

Country-house dining beneath crystal chandeliers

Tunbridge Wells has no shortage of buildings built in the 18th century to capitalise on the spa business. This hotel has a brasserie on site (Zagatos), while the main Chandelier Restaurant provides something rather more refined. Begin with a raviolo with a richly satisfying lobster filling and a foamy shellfish sauce on top, then perhaps try fillet of red mullet served with fregola pasta enriched with mussels, clams, scallops and squid. Among meat options, rump of Cornish lamb comes with risotto packed with wild garlic and broad beans. Among desserts, dark chocolate fondant is soft and yielding and partnered with a substantial chunk of honeycomb and tonka bean ice cream.

Chef Jarrod Cate **Seats** 80, Pr/dining room 200 **Times** 12.30-2/7-9.30, Closed L Sat **Prices** Fixed L 2 course £16, Fixed D 3 course £32 **Wines** 8 by glass **Parking** 150 **Notes** Sunday L, Vegetarian available, Children welcome

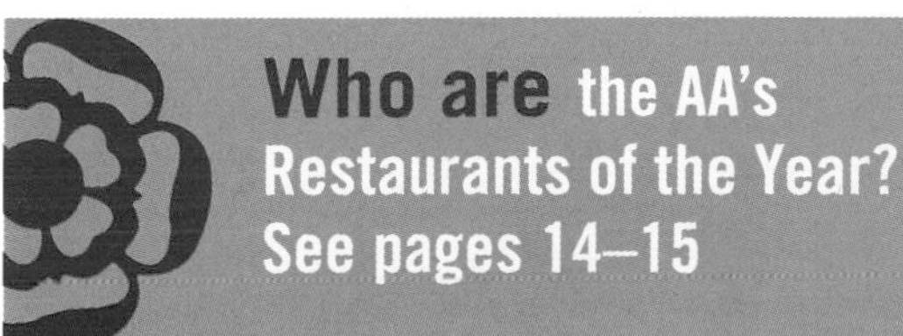

TUNBRIDGE WELLS (ROYAL) *continued*

Thackeray's

Modern European V

tel: 01892 511921 **85 London Rd TN1 1EA**
email: reservations@thackerays-restaurant.co.uk
dir: *A21/A26, towards Tunbridge Wells. On left 500yds after the Kent & Sussex Hospital*

Glossy modern European cooking at the novelist's home

This white weatherboarded house dates from the time of the Restoration, and was later home to William Makepeace Thackeray in 1860 when he wrote the essay 'Tunbridge Toys' about his childhood in the town. A sense of Victorian period elegance infuses the place, with smartly clothed tables and leafy wallpaper setting a refined tone. The core of Richard Phillips' modern European repertoire is Kentish produce, but there are forays to Cornwall and Orkney for immaculate seafood, Hereford for the beef, and Anjou for the famous squab pigeon, seen perhaps as a starter with foie gras, celeriac fondant and Savoy cabbage. Phillips can play delicate notes as well as the big cadenzas, so a serving of crab consommé with mackerel and pink grapefruit jelly could be followed by sirloin hung for 58 days, accompanied by saddle-fat roast potato and onion, chervil roots and puréed watercress in a deep red wine sauce. Kentish cobnuts go into the oil to dress a serving of sea bass with pearl barley risotto and confit lemon, and among the desserts, you could choose the bells and whistles of 'Tropical Forest' or the simpler white chocolate cheesecake with rhubarb jelly and sorbet.

Chef Richard Phillips, Shane Hughes **Seats** 70, Pr/dining room 16 **Times** 12-2.30/6.30-10.30, Closed Mon, D Sun **Prices** Prices not confirmed **Wines** 140 bottles over £30, 17 bottles under £30, 20 by glass **Parking** On street in evening, NCP **Notes** Sunday L, Children welcome

The Twenty Six

Modern British NEW

tel: 01892 544607 **15a Church Rd, Southborough TN4 0RX**
email: hello@thetwenty-six.co.uk **web:** www.thetwenty-six.co.uk
dir: *Phone for directions*

Creative seasonal cooking in an intimate setting

When it comes to the number of seats there are for diners in this cosy restaurant from Scott Goss, the clue is in the name. To keep things interesting for visitors and staff, the menu changes every day but dishes stick rigidly to the seasons. A summer meal might start with watercress mousse, burnt shallot and confit egg yolk and move on to rump of lamb with broad beans, pea purée and lamb gravy. Finish, perhaps, with lemon and raspberry posset served with pistachio granola. A carefully considered wine list showcases natural and biodynamic wines from small producers.

Chef Scott Goss **Seats** 26, Pr/dining room 22 **Times** 6-10, Closed Mon, L Tue-Sat **Prices** Fixed D 3 course fr £29.50 **Wines** 19 bottles over £30, 17 bottles under £30, 15 by glass **Notes** Sunday L, Vegetarian available, Children welcome

WEST MALLING Map 6 TQ65

The Swan

Modern British

tel: 01732 521910 **35 Swan St ME19 6JU**
email: info@theswanwestmalling.co.uk
dir: *M20 junct 4 follow signs for West Malling, left into Swan St. Approx 200yds on left*

Seasonal modern brasserie food in a stylish setting

Built as a coaching inn in the 15th century, The Swan underwent a stylish refurbishment in January 2015. Brasserie-style menus build on Kentish farm produce with influences from far and wide. Spiced chickpea fritters with spring onion and feta in tamarind dressing might be one way to start, the razor-sharp seasonings of sea bass céviche in fennel, orange and coriander an equally tempting one. Mains could be a roast rack of lamb for two, accompanied by mini shepherd's pies, while the grill produces steaks, or spatchcocked chicken with a salad of sweetcorn and cashews. An Anglo-Welsh cheese selection with truffle honey competes with the plentiful chocolate offerings to finish.

Chef Lee Edney **Seats** 90, Pr/dining room 28 **Times** 12-3.30/5.30-10, Closed 1 Jan, D Sun **Prices** Fixed L 2 course £16.50, Fixed D 3 course fr £20, Starter £6-£12.80, Main £13.20-£23.50, Dessert £7 **Wines** 72 bottles over £30, 32 bottles under £30, 17 by glass **Parking** Long-stay car park **Notes** All day fixed menu 2 course, Brunch £3-£8.50, Sunday L £13.20-£17.50, Vegetarian available, Children welcome

WHITSTABLE Map 7 TR16

The Sportsman

Modern British

tel: 01227 273370 **Faversham Rd, Seasalter CT5 4BP**
email: contact@thesportsmanseasalter.co.uk
dir: *On coast road between Whitstable & Faversham, 3.5m W of Whitstable*

Bracing freshness and absence of pretension in a Kentish pub

The Sportsman has a distinctly rustic, unpretentious look, with scuffed floorboards and plain walls hung with pictures above half-panelling. The kitchen makes everything in-house, including butter. Start with an appetiser of super-fresh oyster topped with warm chorizo before a first course of to-die-for soda bread smeared with soft cheese topped with home-smoked mackerel with apple jelly and a grating of horseradish, or pork terrine. Stunningly fresh braised brill fillet on tender leeks is topped with mussels and bacon and accompanied by creamy mash, and roast saddle of lamb arrives with seasonal vegetables. End with apple soufflé – well risen, light and airy – with salted caramel ice cream.

Chef Stephen Harris, Dan Flavell **Seats** 50 **Times** 12-2/7-9, Closed 25-26 Dec, 1 Jan, Mon, D Sun **Prices** Starter £7.95-£11.95, Main £19.95-£24.95, Dessert £7.95-£8.95 **Wines** 24 bottles over £30, 32 bottles under £30, 13 by glass **Parking** 20 **Notes** Sunday L, Vegetarian available, Children welcome

WROTHAM Map 6 TQ65

The Bull

Modern British

tel: 01732 789800 **Bull Ln TN15 7RF**
email: info@thebullhotel.com **web:** www.thebullhotel.com
dir: *Between M20 & M26 junct. In centre of village*

Contemporary cooking in old village inn

A 600-year-old country inn done out in shades of pink, with a mix of wooden and leather-look chairs at unclothed wooden tables. Seaweed pesto and goats' cheese cream add interesting elements to impressively braised lamb shoulder with minted Puy lentils, soused beetroot and peas, and another innovative main course might be seared cod fillet with fennel whitebait, truffled spinach, celeriac dauphinoise and almond-flavoured cauliflower purée. Starters include the likes of smoked salmon fishcakes with pea purée and a salad of citrus fruit, peas and mint – a well-conceived dish – and more mainstream chicken liver parfait with caramelised onions. For pudding try honey pannacotta with peach purée and apricots.

Chef James Hawkes **Seats** 60, Pr/dining room 12 **Times** 12-2.30/6-9 **Prices** Starter £7.50-£8.50, Main £15.95-£27.50, Dessert fr £7.50 **Wines** 28 bottles over £30, 29 bottles under £30, 17 by glass **Parking** 30 **Notes** Sunday L, Vegetarian available, Children welcome

LANCASHIRE

BLACKBURN Map 18 SD62

The Clog & Billycock

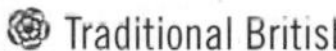

Traditional British

tel: 01254 201163 **Billinge End Rd, Pleasington BB2 6QB**
email: enquiries@theclogandbillycock.com
dir: *M6 junct 29/M65 junct 3. Follow signs to Pleasington*

Far more than just a village inn

Clogs and a billycock hat were the favourite attire of an early 20th-century landlord, when this was the Bay Horse Inn. Now one of top chef Nigel Haworth's Ribble Valley Inns, its plain facade gives way to a larger, more modern interior than you might expect, not least in the purple-upholstered dining areas. Pub classics sit alongside more inventive dishes, such as a starter of twice-baked Leagram's organic cheese soufflé is served with a cheese sauce and topped by a quenelle of beetroot relish. Mains include roast pan-fried hake fillet with Shetland mussel broth, scallions and samphire. End with simnel Bakewell tart with blood orange cream.

The Millstone at Mellor

Modern British

tel: 01254 813333 **Church Ln, Mellor BB2 7JR**
email: info@millstonehotel.co.uk **web:** www.millstonehotel.co.uk
dir: *4m from M6 junct 31 follow signs for Blackburn. Mellor is on right 1m after 1st set of lights*

Smart village inn with feel-good menu

Owned by Thwaites Brewery, whose ales are at the pumps, it's not all about beer at this old coaching inn. It also deals in feel-good menus that offer up pub classics, lunchtime sandwiches, locally sourced steaks cooked on the grill, and a few global flavours. Begin with a charcuterie board or go for duck spring rolls with plum sauce. Main courses can be as traditional as home-made burger or breaded chicken with garlic and herb butter. Those steaks are aged for 28 days – flat iron, maybe, or 8oz rib-eye – and come with flat-cap mushroom, baked tomato and thick-cut chips. Among desserts, sticky toffee pudding shows the style.

Chef Alan Holliday **Seats** 90, Pr/dining room 20 **Times** 12-9.30, All-day dining, Closed D 25-26 Dec, 1 Jan **Prices** Starter £4.95-£10.95, Main £9.95-£24.95, Dessert £5.95-£7.95 **Wines** 9 bottles over £30, 32 bottles under £30, 9 by glass **Parking** 45, On street **Notes** Sunday L, Vegetarian available, Children welcome

BURNLEY Map 18 SD83

White Swan at Fence

Modern British NEW

tel: 01282 611773 **300 Wheatley Lane Rd BB12 9QA**
email: info@whiteswanatfence.co.uk
dir: *Phone for directions*

Traditional pub with simply impressive food

Retaining all that makes the British pub such a national asset, while applying the highest standards in every department, the team at the White Swan create something special. It's a pub all right, with real fires and real ales and, but there's home-made damson vodka up for grabs, and a chef delivering powerful flavours on a fiercely seasonal menu. The fare changes daily and offers the likes of ceps with runny confit egg and shavings of autumn truffle, followed by Yorkshire grouse or wild sea bass with crayfish sauce. Finish with a sophisticated Valrhona chocolate pavé with ice cream flavoured with thyme and beer.

Chef Tom Parker **Seats** 40 **Times** 12-2/5.30-8.30, Closed Mon **Prices** Tasting menu £55-£65, Starter £5-£15, Main £16-£28, Dessert £6-£12 **Wines** 9 by glass **Parking** 20 **Notes** Sunday L £16-£22, Vegetarian available, Children welcome

BURROW Map 18 SD67

The Highwayman

Traditional British

tel: 01524 273338 **LA6 2RJ**
email: enquiries@highwaymaninn.co.uk
dir: *M6 junct 36 to A65 Kirkby Lonsdale, off A683*

Traditional British pub food with Lancashire emphasis

One of five Ribble Valley Inns, The Highwayman is built of pale local stone and stands just a field away from the River Lune. As well as the main restaurant and its smaller satellite rooms, there's seating outside for warmer days. Local place names pepper the menu, including Reggie's Goosnargh (a Lancashire village) chicken with Cumbrian ham-and-cabbage pressing and crispy chicken skin salad, and Flookburgh (on Morecambe Bay) shrimp porridge as starters. See also mains such as crispy black pudding with Kitridding (in deepest Cumbria) pig's cheek bacon, mashed potato, cabbage and pickled apples. The neighbouring county gets a name-check in lemon curd with Yorkshire rhubarb, rhubarb sorbet and meringue.

Chef Bruno Birkbeck **Seats** 120 **Times** 12-2/5.30-9 **Prices** Fixed L 2 course £13.50, Fixed D 3 course £16, Starter £5-£7.50, Main £10.50-£25, Dessert £3.50-£7 **Wines** 9 bottles over £30, 29 bottles under £30, 10 by glass **Parking** 45 **Notes** Fixed L/D Mon-Thu, Sunday L £5-£19.50, Vegetarian available, Children welcome

CLITHEROE Map 18 SD74

The Assheton Arms

 Contemporary Seafood

tel: 01200 441227 **Downham BB7 4BJ**
email: info@asshetonarms.com **web:** www.seafoodpubcompany.com/the-assheton-arms
dir: *A59 to Clitheroe then follow signs to Downham*

Outstandingly fresh seafood in an untouched conservation village

Although decidedly inland, this pub's ownership by Joycelyn Neve's Seafood Pub Company guarantees excellent Fleetwood-landed fish and seafood, although your dining choice extends way beyond what a trawler can net. Thus, while one possible starter is devilled crab, salmon and brown shrimp salad, another might be steamed Korean buns with crispy duck and spring onions. Mains too offer plenty of variety, such as hake fillet with udon noodles and crispy seaweed, Goan king prawn curry, toro pie filled with slow-cooked beef and chorizo, and Szechuan spiced chicken with egg-fried rice. For something light to follow, try passionfruit and blackberry mess with baby meringues.

Chef Antony Shirley **Seats** 90, Pr/dining room 12 **Times** 12-9, All-day dining **Wines** 24 bottles over £30, 30 bottles under £30, 13 by glass **Parking** 16 **Notes** Sunday L fr £12.50, Vegetarian available, Children welcome

GISBURN Map 18 SD84

Stirk House Hotel

 Modern, Traditional

tel: 01200 445581 **BB7 4LJ**
email: reservations@stirkhouse.co.uk **web:** www.stirkhouse.co.uk
dir: *M6 junct 32, W of village, on A59. Hotel 0.5m on left*

Modern Lancashire cooking in a Tudor manor

The majestic scenery of the Ribble Valley and the Forest of Bowland provide a wild Lancashire backdrop for the weathered stone walls of 16th-century Stirk House. Original plasterwork and an ornate fireplace add character to the restaurant, where friendly staff are well-briefed on the menu. The cooking relies on splendid Lancashire produce. Smooth chicken liver parfait comes with red pepper chutney and toasted sourdough bread, followed by herb-crusted baked cod with roasted cherry tomatoes, green beans and garlic oil, or there may be roast pork wrapped in prosciutto with wholegrain mustard mash and cider cream sauce. Rounding things off, there's apricot Bakewell tart with stem ginger ice cream.

Chef Chris Dobson **Seats** 60, Pr/dining room 50 **Times** 12-9, All-day dining, Closed Xmas **Prices** Starter £4.95-£8.50, Main £10-£20, Dessert £6-£9 **Wines** 9 bottles over £30, 23 bottles under £30, 9 by glass **Parking** 300 **Notes** Sunday L £13-£20, Vegetarian available, Children welcome

LANCASTER Map 18 SD46

Lancaster House

 Traditional British

tel: 01524 844822 **Green Ln, Ellel LA1 4GJ**
email: reception.lancaster@englishlakes.co.uk **web:** www.englishlakes.co.uk
dir: *3m from Lancaster city centre. From S: M6 junct 33, head towards Lancaster. Continue through Galgate village, turn left up Green Ln just before Lancaster University*

Regional brasserie cooking in a Lancashire event hotel

A little west of the M6, practically on the doorstep of the Lake District, Lancaster House is an events and leisure hotel on the university campus. Foodworks is the promising name of its restaurant, and a relaxed, hang-loose brasserie feel predominates, with unclothed tables, ornate light fittings and mural graphics of flat-capped folk going about their Lancashire business. It offers a seasonal menu of readily understandable brasserie fare such as duck liver pâté with spiced plum and apple chutney and toasted brioche, followed by the likes of sea bass and samphire in a dressing of lemon oil and balsamic. Finish with crème brûlée and shortbread.

LANGHO Map 18 SD73

Northcote

– see opposite and advert on page 204

LEYLAND Map 15 SD52

Best Western Premier Hallmark Hotel Preston Leyland

Modern British

tel: 01772 422922 **Leyland Way PR25 4JX**
email: leyland@hallmarkhotels.co.uk **web:** www.hallmarkhotels.co.uk
dir: *M6 junct 28, turn left, hotel 1st on left*

Modern hotel dining with a local flavour

A modern purpose-built hotel with a decor that treads a line between opulence and chintz. The Four Seasons dining room occupies a lavishly decorated octagonal space, with neo-classical sculptures, rich colours and well-spaced, well-dressed tables. The kitchen offers up classically inspired dishes with contemporary touches and a decent showing of regional produce. Confit pork belly, for example, comes with apple balsamic and deconstructed piccalilli to cut through its richness, with main courses serving up locally sourced steaks or cannon of lamb with buttered leeks and herby mash. Dessert include a classic crème brûlée with a cherry biscotti or a rhubarb crumble tart, and the cheeseboard stays true to Lancashire.

Chef Stuart McNorton **Seats** 80, Pr/dining room 20 **Times** 6.30-9.30, Closed Xmas, 31 Dec, L all week **Prices** Starter £5-£9, Main £16-£25, Dessert £6-£9 **Wines** 5 bottles over £30, 27 bottles under £30, 8 by glass **Parking** 100 **Notes** Vegetarian available, Children welcome

LYTHAM ST ANNES Map 18 SD32

Bedford Hotel

 Modern British

tel: 01253 724636 **307-313 Clifton Drive South FY8 1HN**
email: reservations@bedford-hotel.com **web:** www.bedford-hotel.com
dir: *From M55 follow signs for airport to last lights. Left through 2 sets of lights. Hotel 300yds on left*

Clearly focused cooking in seaside resort hotel

The Bedford is a welcoming, family-run Victorian hotel with lots going on. Its Cartland Restaurant has plenty of period charm, with decorative plasterwork, warm pastel tones, black-and-white prints of film stars and neatly laid tables. The cooking steers sensibly clear of left-field flavours. Venerable Lancashire cheesemaker Sandham's provides the wherewithal for an air-light soufflé, with caramelised red onion marmalade and a balsamic reduction providing the sweet-and-sour counterpoints. Next up, sea bass fillet is seared to perfection and matched with vine tomato and basil fondue, saffron potatoes and crisp leeks. The good ideas and careful execution continue at dessert stage with orange cheesecake topped with candied ginger.

Northcote

LANGHO **Map 18 SD73**

Modern British V NOTABLE WINE LIST

tel: 01254 240555 **Northcote Rd BB6 8BE**
email: reception@northcote.com **web:** www.northcote.com
dir: *M6 junct 31, 9m to Northcote. Follow Clitheroe (A59) signs. Hotel on left before rdbt*

Luxe Victorian manor with benchmark regional cooking

Northcote started life in the 1880s as a grand private manor house and still has that personal touch. Perched on the edge of the Ribble Valley near Blackburn amid views that are a verdant contradiction to those who think it's all grim up north, the old pile has steadily risen in the world thanks to the partnership of chef (now Chef Patron) Nigel Haworth and wine expert Craig Bancroft, who reinvented it as a country hotel many years ago. Now part of the swish Relais & Châteaux group, the place has a truly luxurious feel, with new guest rooms, a dedicated space for the cookery school and an updated restaurant that meets 21st-century expectations when it comes to interior design. Tables are smartly dressed and set with Riedel glassware, and staff maintain the engaging, friendly, helpful tone that makes a visit to Northcote so memorable. Lisa Goodwin-Allen's cooking has something to do with that too, as well as the commitment to Lancashire ingredients that was the foundation of Haworth's vision. Much of the produce comes from Northcote's extensive kitchen gardens, but regional game, seafood and the inimitable Lancashire cheese all play their part. Warm loin of Herdwick mutton, for example, with Jerusalem artichokes and honey and mint dressing is an opening salvo that makes the taste buds stand to attention. Main courses might star seared turbot in a picturesque medley with pickled lemon, seaweed, smoked crème fraîche and a novel take on 'chips', while meatier appetites are met by Goosnargh duckling with smoked duck ham and pulled leg meat, its richness leavened by spicy cabbage and blood orange. Dessert looks to the local terroir once more for an organic apple crumble soufflé partnered with Mrs Kirkham's Lancashire cheese ice cream. Superb cheeses come with home-made crackers and fruit and walnut loaf, and it's all supported by superb wines from a masterpiece of a wine list.

Chef Lisa Goodwin-Allen, Aled Williams, Nigel Haworth **Seats** 70, Pr/dining room 60 **Times** 12-2/7-9.30, Closed Food & Wine Festival **Prices** Fixed L 3 course £32, Tasting menu £88, Starter £12-£17, Main £28-£45, Dessert £12.50-£15 **Wines** 359 bottles over £30, 31 bottles under £30, 12 by glass **Parking** 60 **Notes** Fixed gourmet D 5 course £68, Seasonal L 3 course £32, Sunday L £42, Children welcome

Northcote

dedicated to perfection

Michelin-starred restaurant and country-house hotel Northcote has cemented its reputation as the go-to destination for luxury travel and dining in the UK.

Following extensive renovations and refurbishment in 2014 – which included a new-look restaurant, twelve new bedrooms, a cookery school, a chef's table and *The Louis Roederer Private Dining Rooms*, Northcote kicked off 2015 with the launch of the hughly anticipated *Garden Lodge*, an impressive new building of 7 bedrooms and a master suite, ideal for groups of up to 16 Gourmands.

The iconic Northcote is the country-house hotel of choice for discerning diners and seasoned travellers around the UK. An oasis of food and wine served with Northern hospitality from a highly talented team.

Northcote Road, Langho, Blackburn, Lancashire BB6 8BE
Tel: 01254 240555 • **Website:** www.northcote.com • **Email:** reception@northcote.com

LYTHAM ST ANNES *continued*

Best Western Glendower Hotel

Traditional British

tel: 01253 723241 **North Promenade FY8 2NQ**
email: info@glendowerhotel.co.uk **web:** www.glendowerhotel.co.uk
dir: *From M55 follow signs for Lytham St Annes then signs for Promenade*

Brasserie dining in a seafront hotel

A Victorian seafront hotel just along from the pier, the Glendower is home to Coast, a contemporary restaurant with a brasserie vibe. The kitchen turns out traditional British dishes with a twist on regional fare. Cottage pie, for example, arrives as a first course topped with truffle foam, or go for the more Euro-centric grilled sardine with tomato concasse and sautéed ratte potatoes. Calves' liver is served as a main course with textures of onion and a buttery champ, or try fillet of black bream with ratatouille and chorizo. Sirloin steak, chicken leg, gammon and salmon are cooked on the grill, and desserts include a modern interpretation of carrot cake.

Chef Pascal Parisee **Seats** 70, Pr/dining room 40 **Times** 6-9 **Wines** 5 bottles over £30, 18 bottles under £30, 8 by glass **Parking** 40 **Notes** Sunday L £9.95-£17.95, Vegetarian available, Children welcome

Clifton Arms Hotel

British

tel: 01253 739898 **West Beach, Lytham FY8 5QJ**
email: welcome@cliftonarms-lytham.com **web:** www.cliftonarms-lytham.com
dir: *On A584 along seafront*

Contemporary cooking in a genteel Lytham hotel

The present red-brick building dates from early Victorian times and is on the site of what was a small inn. Chic table settings with good napery and floral adornments look the part against the neutral hues of the main dining room, where bay windows give wide sea views. The kitchen delivers contemporary cooking that moves with the seasons. Scallops with carrot purée and pumpkin seeds scattered with pork crackling is an enjoyable starter, and might be followed by fillet of beef bourguignon with mashed potato, or mushroom and truffle risotto. Round off a meal with lemon and lime cheesecake with strawberry compôte.

Chef Paul Howard **Seats** 60, Pr/dining room 140 **Times** 12-2.30/6.30-9 **Prices** Starter fr £6, Main £15.50-£21.45, Dessert £5-£7 **Wines** 11 bottles over £30, 29 bottles under £30, 13 by glass **Parking** 50 **Notes** Brasserie menu at lunch, Sunday L fr £25, Vegetarian available, Children welcome

Greens Bistro

Modern British

tel: 01253 789990 **3-9 St Andrews Road South, St Annes-on-Sea FY8 1SX**
email: info@greensbistro.co.uk
dir: *Just off St Annes Sq*

Lancashire bistro cooking in a bright basement

For a basement bistro venue Greens looks bright and airy, with ornate high-backed chairs in light wood at smartly clothed tables, and deep green carpeting. The cooking is straightforward bistro fare based on pedigree Lancashire produce, including the county's famous cheese, which goes classically into a twice-baked soufflé, served with warm tomato salsa and rocket salad. Ribble sea bass is a treat for main, a thick tranche served with rösti and foraged samphire in saffron sauce. Meat might be lamb shoulder in rosemary-laced juices with a dollop of mashed maris pipers. Finish with apple crumble with rhubarb ripple ice cream when the orchard fruits come on stream.

Chef Paul Webster **Seats** 38 **Times** 6-10, Closed 25 Dec, BHs, 1 wk summer, Sun-Mon, L all week **Prices** Fixed D 3 course £19.70, Starter £5.25-£6.95, Main £14.50-£18.95, Dessert £5.25-£6 **Wines** 2 bottles over £30, 18 bottles under £30, 7 by glass **Parking** On street **Notes** Vegetarian available, Children welcome

MORECAMBE **Map 18 SD46**

The Midland

Modern British

tel: 01524 424000 **Marine Road West LA4 4BU**
email: themidland@englishlakes.co.uk **web:** www.englishlakes.co.uk/hotels/midland
dir: *A589 towards Morecambe, follow seafront signs, left on B5321 (Lancaster Rd) then Easton Rd, left into Central Drive. Right at rdbt on seafront. Left to hotel entrance*

Modern Lancashire cuisine in an art deco hotel

An art deco gem, The Midland was built by the London, Midland and Scottish Railway in 1933 in the 'streamline modern' style. There's a sharp modernity to the restaurant that suits the space, with a contemporary finish and neat white tablecloths to ensure everything is right and proper. Likewise, the menu meets contemporary expectations with its focus on regional ingredients and fashionable flavour combinations. Scallops are served with cauliflower purée, crispy bacon and pistachio crumb, and main courses are big on the feel-good factor. Try slow-cooked blade of beef, rib-eye steak, or poached plaice with ham fritter and red wine syrup. Finish with dark chocolate and rosewater cheesecake.

Chef Michael Wilson **Seats** 70, Pr/dining room 20
Times 12-1.30/6.30-9.30, Closed Xmas & New Year **Prices** Fixed L 2 course £19.95, Starter £5-£9.50, Main £14-£26.75, Dessert £6-£9 **Wines** 24 bottles over £30, 48 bottles under £30, 9 by glass **Parking** 60 **Notes** Vegan menu, Sunday L £17.95-£21.95, Vegetarian available, Children welcome

RILEY GREEN **Map 18 SD62**

The Royal Oak

Traditional British

tel: 01254 201445 **Blackburn Old Rd PR5 0SL**
email: royaloak@dininginns.co.uk
dir: *M65 junct 3 towards Walton le Dale, right at T-junct*

Unpretentious pub with confident cooking

Just a short distance from the Hoghton Tower in a beautiful part of Lancashire, this roadside inn has a proper pub atmosphere with traditional touches of open fires, stone walls and church pews. Whether you grab a table in the bar or the dining area, the modern British dishes are straightforward but cooked with confidence and flair. Hoi sin-glazed short rib beef with salt-and-pepper squid, pickled cucumber, chilli and coriander salad and wasabi mayonnaise is a typical starter, followed by pan-fried hake, cavolo nero, capers, tartare sauce and hand-cut chips. To end, chocolate brownie might be paired with caramelised banana, Chantilly and vanilla ice cream.

THORNTON Map 18 SD34

Twelve Restaurant and Lounge Bar

Modern British

tel: 01253 821212 **Marsh Mill Village, Marsh Mill-in-Wyre, Fleetwood Road North FY5 4JZ**
email: info@twelve-restaurant.co.uk **web:** www.twelve-restaurant.co.uk
dir: *A585 follow signs for Marsh Mill Complex. Turn right into Victoria Rd East, entrance 0.5m on left*

Stimulating modern cooking in contemporary setting

Virtually under the sails of an 18th-century windmill, Twelve has a stylish, urban interior and a kitchen that works with regional producers and suppliers to deliver an appealing contemporary menu. Kick off with Madras-cured salmon with charred spring onion and salad cream or woodland mushrooms with cep velouté and the whiff of truffles. Next up, hay-baked rack of lamb, barbecued Cumbrian pork chop, or loin of cod with caramelised chicory with a fruity hit of rhubarb. To finish, a fun banana butty arrives with salted popcorn, brûlée and shake. The Market menu is terrific value, and cracking Sunday roasts include roast topside of Bowland Forest beef.

Chef Graham Floyd **Seats** 106 **Times** 12-3/6.30-12, Closed 1st 2 wks Jan, Mon, L Tue-Sat **Prices** Fixed D 3 course £20, Starter £5.50-£7, Main £12-£23, Dessert £6-£8 **Wines** 33 bottles over £30, 35 bottles under £30, 12 by glass **Parking** 150 **Notes** Sunday L £15-£22, Vegetarian available, Children welcome

See advert opposite

WHALLEY Map 18 SD73

The Freemasons at Wiswell

Modern British NOTABLE WINE LIST

tel: 01254 822218 **8 Vicarage Fold, Wiswell BB7 9DF**
email: steve@freemasonswiswell.co.uk
dir: *A59, on edge of Whalley village near Clitheroe*

Exciting virtuoso cooking in a relaxed village inn

Ground-breaking cooking has put this small Riblle Valley village firmly on the map. Cobbled together from a trio of little cottages, it functions as both local pub and dining destination, with tables out front for summer evening drinkers, and a properly old-time feel inside, where rugs cover the floor and a stag's head peers down over proceedings. Lancashire lad Steven Smith combines delicacy of touch with true understanding of flavours in dishes that offer a seasonal tour in five or seven courses if you're in town for the taster. A soup of smoked haddock and charred leek comes with a fish finger 'hot dog' and umami mayo to set the thought-processes whirling, ahead of various preparations of Cévennes onion with foie gras and pear in a French expedition. Then it's back home for maple-glazed belly of suckling pig with its own sausage and Lancashire cheese potatoes in mead sauce, before the star of the show, truffled aged sirloin with hen-of-the-woods mushroom. Those intent on exploring the fish route might light on cod with squid risotto and chorizo in sauce nero, sharply spiked with yuzu. Finish with Amalfi lemon meringue pie garnished with tropical fruits and coconut ice cream.

Chef Steven Smith, Hywel Griffith **Seats** 70, Pr/dining room 14 **Times** 12-2.30/5.30-9, Closed 2 Jan for 2 wks, Mon-Tue **Prices** Fixed L 2 course £16-£25, Fixed D 3 course £20-£70, Tasting menu £55-£70, Starter £9.95-£17.95, Main £16.95-£35, Dessert £7.95-£11.95 **Wines** 108 bottles over £30, 56 bottles under £30, 30 by glass **Parking** In village **Notes** Fixed L/early D 3 course seasonal menu, Sunday L £25, Vegetarian available, Children welcome

The Three Fishes

British

tel: 01254 826888 **Mitton Rd, Mitton BB7 9PQ**
email: enquiries@thethreefishes.com
dir: *M6 junct 31, A59 to Clitheroe. Follow Whalley signs, B6246, 2m*

Village inn celebrating Lancashire food heroes

This, the flagship of the Ribble Valley Inns group, is dedicated to celebrating Lancashire's larder. It's a buzzing spot with a wide-ranging menu of modern pub ideas and old-favourites done right – fish and chips, for example, is line-caught haddock with dripping-cooked chips and marrowfat peas. Its head chef is making a fine job of delivering muscular regional flavours, thus Butler's Lancashire cheese supplies the oomph in a twice-baked soufflé with beetroot relish and cheese sauce, while North Sea cod stars in a main course with seaweed potatoes, brown shrimps and crispy mussels. At the end, a Bramley apple tart is served with vanilla ice cream and caramel.

Chef Ian Moss **Seats** 140 **Times** 12-2/5.30-9 **Prices** Fixed L 2 course £13.50, Fixed D 3 course £16, Starter £5-£8.50, Main £10.50-£25, Dessert £3.75-£6.50 **Wines** 9 bottles over £30, 29 bottles under £30, 10 by glass **Parking** 70 **Notes** Fixed L/D Mon-Thu, Sunday L £5-£19.50, Vegetarian available, Children welcome

WHITEWELL Map 18 SD64

The Inn at Whitewell

Modern British

tel: 01200 448222 **Forest of Bowland, Clitheroe BB7 3AT**
email: reception@innatwhitewell.com **web:** www.innatwhitewell.com
dir: *From S: M6 junct 31 Longridge follow Whitewell signs. From N: M6 junct 33 follow Trough of Bowland & Whitewell signs*

Traditional rural inn with wide-ranging feel-good food

This handsome 16th-century inn overlooking the River Hodder is a gem of stone floors and ancient beams, open fires, antique furniture and prints. You can eat in the bar areas or in the more formal restaurant. The kitchen has a confident touch, turning out a diverse menu including spicy fried squid in chilli lime and soy dressing with carrot and ginger salad, seared salmon fillet with smoked haddock, spinach, potato chowder and pea purée, or chargrilled beef sirloin with the usual trimmings. End with one of the traditional puddings or home-made ice cream.

Chef Jamie Cadman **Seats** 60, Pr/dining room 20 **Times** 12-2/7.30-9.30 **Prices** Prices not confirmed **Wines** 50 bottles over £30, 40 bottles under £30, 20 by glass **Parking** 70 **Notes** Sunday L, Vegetarian available, Children welcome

WREA GREEN Map 18 SD33

The Spa Hotel at Ribby Hall Village

Modern, Traditional

tel: 01772 674484 **Ribby Hall Village, Ribby Rd PR4 2PR**
email: brasserie@ribbyhall.co.uk **web:** www.ribbyhall.co.uk/spa-hotel
dir: *M55 junct 33 follow A585 towards Kirkham & brown tourist signs for Ribby Hall Village. Straight across 3 rdbts. Village 200yds on left*

Cooking with real flair in a smart spa hotel

As its name makes clear, there are some pretty swanky spa facilities at this classy adult-only retreat in 100 acres of Lancashire countryside. The Brasserie and its recently completed Orangery extension are another string to its bow, done out with orange and lime leather seats at unclothed tables. Start with barbecued salmon, served up with pickled white asparagus, samphire, caviar, and potato mousse. An impressive main course stars suckling pig in the form of roast loin and a croquette of braised shoulder with black pudding, salt-baked celeriac, apple textures and caramelised sprouts. For dessert, there's a faultless tarte Tatin of red wine-poached pears with vanilla ice cream.

Chef Michael Noonan **Seats** 46, Pr/dining room 30 **Times** 12-9, All-day dining **Prices** Tasting menu fr £57.50, Starter £7-£8.50, Main £16-£29, Dessert £8-£11 **Wines** 26 bottles over £30, 52 bottles under £30, 13 by glass **Parking** 100 **Notes** Booking advisable, Vegetarian available, No children

WREA GREEN *continued*

The Villa Country House Hotel

Classic British **NEW**

tel: 01772 804040 **Moss Side Ln PR4 2PE**
email: info@thevilla.co.uk **web:** www.thevilla.co.uk
dir: *M55 junct 3 follow signs to Kirkham, at Wrea Green follow signs to Lytham*

Modern British cooking in upscale country house hotel

Built as a 19th-century gentleman's residence, this three-storey, gabled mansion stands in rolling parkland at the end of a sweeping drive. Its striking, carefully restored interior incorporates a part-oak-panelled restaurant, with high-backed, salmon-coloured chairs, and bare tables waited upon by white-shirted staff. The carte offers confit chicken pressing with leek and artichoke, Lancashire goats' curd and wild garlic purée as a starter, followed by confit salmon fillet with salmon brandade, avocado, chorizo, red pepper and Kalamata olives. For a thrilling finish, try chocolate pot, salted caramel, passionfruit and hazelnut biscuits.

Chef Matthew Johnson **Times** 12-2/6-9.30 **Prices** Fixed D 3 course £22.95, Tasting menu £40-£65, Starter £4.50-£6.95, Main £11.95-£25, Dessert £5.25-£7.95 **Wines** 8 bottles over £30, 30 bottles under £30, 14 by glass **Notes** Fixed D Mon-Sat 6-7pm, Afternoon tea £11.95-£14.95, Sunday L £15.95-£19.95, Vegetarian available

WRIGHTINGTON **Map 15 SD51**

Corner House

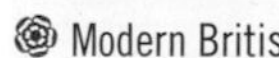
Modern British

tel: 01257 451400 **Wrightington Bar WN6 9SE**
email: info@cornerhousewrightington.co.uk
dir: *4m from Wigan. From M6 junct 27 towards Parbold, right after motorway exit, by BP garage into Mossy Lea Rd. On right after 2m*

Contemporary hostelry with pub classics and more

The Corner House dates from the 1830s and stands out on Wrightington Bar with its white and blue paint job and neatly trimmed creepers. The kitchen meets the expectations of those after traditional pub grub, while satisfying those seeking something more unusual. So you might start with an old classic (prawn cocktail) or a modern one (Goosnargh chicken liver parfait with onion marmalade and toasted brioche), and move on to fish and chips or tender braised ox cheek with a rich, glossy port jus. Steaks cooked on the grill arrive with mushrooms stuffed with brie, onion ring and chips, while, for dessert, crème brûlée comes with a homemade cookie.

Chef Ross Lawson **Seats** 60 **Times** 12-2.30/5-8.30, Closed 26 Dec **Prices** Fixed L 2 course £11.99, Fixed D 2 course fr £16.99, Starter £4.99-£9.99, Main £11.99-£26.99, Dessert £5.99-£7.99 **Wines** 9 bottles over £30, 26 bottles under £30, 8 by glass **Parking** 80 **Notes** Early bird Mon-Tue 5-6.30pm 2 course £14.99, Sunday L £17-£20, Vegetarian available, Children welcome

LEICESTERSHIRE

CASTLE DONINGTON

For restaurant details see East Midlands Airport

EAST MIDLANDS AIRPORT **Map 11 SK42**

Best Western Premier Yew Lodge Hotel & Spa

British

tel: 01509 672518 **Packington Hill DE74 2DF**
email: info@yewlodgehotel.co.uk **web:** www.yewlodgehotel.co.uk
dir: *M1 junct 24. Follow signs to Loughborough & Kegworth on A6. On entering village, 1st right, after 400yds hotel on right*

International cooking near East Midlands airport

At the heart of Yew Lodge is the original Georgian house with its views down Packington Hill. The Orchard restaurant is attractively traditional, with plenty of natural light. The menu takes a modern European approach, with occasional forays east for the likes of stir-fried noodles with Chinese greens and baby corn, or seared sea bass in Thai broth. Otherwise, expect grilled haloumi on a tart topped up with courgette, aubergine and peppers, before pulled pork with black pudding and apple-sultana salsa, or perhaps seared salmon with its own croquette in Caesar sauce. Desserts include carrot cake with crème fraîche sorbet, or summer berry Pavlova with ginger cream and lime granita.

KEGWORTH

For restaurant details see East Midlands Airport

LEICESTER **Map 11 SK50**

Hotel Maiyango

Modern International

tel: 0116 251 8898 **13-21 St Nicholas Place LE1 4LD**
email: reservations@maiyango.com **web:** www.maiyango.com
dir: *M1 junct 21, A5460 for 3.5m. Turn right onto A47 round St Nicholas Circle onto St Nicholas Place*

Fab decor and creative contemporary cooking

Bringing a dose of boutique razzle-dazzle to the centre of Leicester, Hotel Maiyango's restaurant sports a stylish North African/Middle Eastern look, with ornate lamps, contemporary chairs and rustic booths decorated with hanging fabrics. The menu has some interesting veggie options (maris piper and cumin whip with squash fritter, for example, followed by ricotta and parmesan ravioli with baby plum tomato stew). Main course steamed wild sea bass is served Asian-style with spiced coconut laksa and a chilli and mint relish, while Gressingham duck breast with confit leg fritter is a dish rooted in European tradition. Finish with a vegan green tea jelly with apple sorbet and chilli sugar.

Chef Salvatore Tassari **Seats** 55, Pr/dining room 80 **Times** 12-3/6.30-9.30, Closed 25 Dec, 1 Jan, L Sun-Mon **Prices** Fixed L 2 course £18.50, Fixed D 3 course £32, Tasting menu £25-£45 **Wines** 19 bottles over £30, 35 bottles under £30, 12 by glass **Parking** NCP **Notes** Brunch, Vegetarian tasting menu, Vegetarian available, Children welcome

LONG WHATTON — Map 11 SK42

The Royal Oak

Modern British

tel: 01509 843694 **26 The Green LE12 5DB**
email: enquiries@theroyaloaklongwhatton.co.uk **web:** www.theroyaloaklongwhatton.co.uk
dir: *M1 junct 24, A6 to Kegworth. Right into Whatton Road (becomes Kegworth Ln) to Long Whatton. From Loughborough, A6 towards Kegworth. Left onto B5324, right into Hathern Rd leading to The Green*

Skilful modern cooking in a smartly modernised village inn

The 21st-century incarnation of this thriving gastropub is seen in a smart interior, some natty bedrooms and a focus on food. That said, real ale is part of the plan, and a few pub classics, such as beer-battered cod and chips, remain on the menu. The kitchen turns out some lively stuff, such as goats' cheese soufflé with spiced apple and candied walnuts, or venison carpaccio with beetroot textures and parmesan to start. Impressive main courses may take in pork belly and black pudding roulade with crackling, Swiss chard, rösti and apple and celeriac velouté, or fish pie with green bean beignets. Finish with salted caramel pannacotta.

Chef James & Charles Upton **Seats** 45 **Times** 12-2.30/5.30-9.30 **Prices** Starter £5.25-£8.75, Main £11.50-£20.95, Dessert £5.95-£6.95 **Wines** 5 bottles over £30, 29 bottles under £30, 12 by glass **Parking** 30 **Notes** Early doors menu Mon-Fri 5.30-6.30, Sunday L £17.25-£21.50, Vegetarian available, Children welcome

MELTON MOWBRAY — Map 11 SK71

Stapleford Park

Modern International, British NOTABLE WINE LIST

tel: 01572 787000 & 787019 **Stapleford LE14 2EF**
email: reservations@stapleford.co.uk **web:** www.staplefordpark.com
dir: *A1 to Colsterworth onto B676, signed Melton Mowbray. In approx 9m turn left to Stapleford*

Aspirational cooking in a grand old Leicestershire house

Stapleford's lineage can be traced back to medieval times, the estate being owned by successive generations of the Earls of Harborough for nearly 500 years. Impeccable staff keep the elevated tone buoyant, and the cooking aims high too. Consider smoked mackerel pâté with celeriac remoulade and sourdough toast, or rabbit rillettes with soused carrots and sultanas to start, and then perhaps breast of corn-fed chicken with Toulouse sausage and cassoulet, the plate adorned with a swipe of vivid carrot purée. Finish with crisp-based almond and amaretti tart, served with Amaretto-laced coffee ice cream, or with fine British cheeses. Home-made breads arrive in four delicious flavoured versions.

Chef Luke Holland **Seats** 70, Pr/dining room 180
Times 12-2.30/6-9.30, Closed exclusive use days, L Mon-Sat **Prices** Prices not confirmed **Wines** 300 bottles over £30, 4 bottles under £30, 10 by glass **Parking** 120 **Notes** Sunday L, Vegetarian available, Children welcome

NORTH KILWORTH — Map 11 SP68

Kilworth House Hotel & Theatre

Modern British V

tel: 01858 880058 **Lutterworth Rd LE17 6JE**
email: info@kilworthhouse.co.uk **web:** www.kilworthhouse.co.uk
dir: *A4304 towards Market Harborough, after Walcote, hotel 1.5m on right*

Modern country-house cooking in a heritage hotel

A top-to-toe restoration overseen by the eagle eyes of English Heritage means period authenticity runs seamlessly through this Italianate 19th-century mansionThe Wordsworth Restaurant is the fine-dining option: a posh setting indeed, but the kitchen team rises to the occasion with a repertoire of classic country-house cooking brought gently up to date. Try pork belly with tomato red chard, tarragon and langoustine for starters, while main course partners sea trout with brown shrimps, samphire and sea herbs, or game season could see roast quail matched with creamed spelt, chanterelle mushrooms and walnuts. Desserts take in ideas like passionfruit mousse and sorbet with caramelised banana.

Chef Carl Dovey **Seats** 70, Pr/dining room 130 **Times** 12-2.30/7-9.30 **Prices** Fixed L 2 course £22.50, Tasting menu £49.50, Starter £6.95-£10.95, Main £13.95-£24.95, Dessert £7.50 **Wines** 44 bottles over £30, 35 bottles under £30, 10 by glass **Parking** 140 **Notes** Theatre menu in season 3 course £28, Tasting menu Wed-Sat, Sunday L £24.95-£28.95, Children welcome

QUORN — Map 11 SK51

Quorn Country Hotel

Modern British

tel: 01509 415050 **Charnwood House, 66 Leicester Rd LE12 8BB**
email: sales@quorncountryhotel.co.uk **web:** www.quorncountryhotel.co.uk
dir: *M1 junct 23/A6 towards Leicester, follow signs for Quorn*

Modern British flavours in a stylish country hotel

With manicured gardens and oak-panelled interiors, the Quorn Country Hotel near Loughborough has a 17th-century house at its heart. The restaurant, Shires, boasts formal table settings and professional service team, and the menu takes a modern British path. You might start with a ham hock terrine with piccalilli and parsnip purée, or seared scallops in the familiar company of cauliflower purée and bacon. Main-course salmon is partnered with a pea croquette, bubble-and-squeak cake and dressed with a prawn and lemon beurre blanc, or go for breast of Barbary duck with redcurrants and rosemary. Finish on lime cheesecake with lemon curd and a brandy snap filled with crème fraîche.

WYMESWOLD Map 11 SK62

Hammer & Pincers

 Modern European V

tel: 01509 880735 **5 East Rd LE12 6ST**
email: info@hammerandpincers.co.uk
dir: *Phone for directions*

Innovative modern global cooking with contemporary art

Having trained at The Savoy, this restaurant's owners know a thing or two about hospitality in the grand manner, but the mood here is decidedly more cutting edge. Begin with vigorously spiced curry-roast scallops with cumined cauliflower purée and Indian accoutrements, including a pakora, mango chutney and a scattering of poppadoms. That could be followed by pork fillet roasted in smoked paprika and garlic with chorizo and aïoli, or Moroccan-accented salmon chermoula wrapped in brik pastry on apricot and pistachio tabouleh. This is Stilton country, so Cropwell Bishop with quince paste might look as appealing as honey and rosemary rice pudding served with chunks of pear poached in red wine.

Chef Daniel Jimminson **Seats** 46 **Times** 12-2/6-9, Closed Mon, D Sun **Wines** 18 bottles over £30, 26 bottles under £30, 16 by glass **Parking** 40 **Notes** Sunday L £15-£23, Children welcome

LINCOLNSHIRE

GRANTHAM Map 11 SK93

Harry's Place

 Modern French

tel: 01476 561780 **17 High St, Great Gonerby NG31 8JS**
dir: *1.5m NW of Grantham on B1174*

Outstanding quality in a restaurant built for ten

The Hallams picked a formula when they opened here about 30 years ago, and they have quite rightly seen no reason to change it. In a converted farmhouse on the road through Great Gonerby near Grantham, the red-walled dining room is a pocket-sized haven of civilised hospitality, where Caroline sees that all is well out front and Harry struts his stuff in the kitchen. The menu format is as compact as the venue, a daily-changing rota of two choices at each stage, opening with a soup such as truffle-oiled mushroom, or something more artfully composed, perhaps smoked salmon cured in sloe gin, served with vodka crème fraîche, mango, avocado, lime and ginger, dobbed with caviar. Harry is a dab hand with alcohol-fuelled sauces and dressings, as may be seen again in mains, when white wine and Pernod light up a dish of sautéed brill with egg and capers, or red wine and Armagnac add richness to Lincoln Red beef fillet with tomato, onion and olive relish and horseradish mayonnaise. Expect to finish with prune and Armagnac ice cream garnished with passionfruit, or the famous cherry brandy jelly with yogurt and black pepper, or take up the option of a cheese extra, with finest English, Welsh and French specimens.

Chef Harry Hallam **Seats** 10 **Times** 12.30-3/7-9, Closed 2 wks from 25 Dec, 2 wks Aug, Sun-Mon **Prices** Starter £9.50-£22.50, Main £39.50, Dessert £8 **Wines** 19 bottles over £30, 2 bottles under £30, 4 by glass **Parking** 4 **Notes** Vegetarian meal on request at time of booking, Vegetarian available, Children 5 yrs+

GREAT LIMBER Map 17 TA10

The New Inn

Modern British, International NEW

tel: 01469 569998 **2 High St DN37 8JL**
email: enquiries@thenewinngreatlimber.co.uk **web:** www.thenewinngreatlimber.co.uk
dir: *M1 junct 31, M18, M180, 2m past Humberside airport on right*

Well-presented food in a stylish setting

In the heart of the Brocklesby Estate, this Grade II listed inn has been welcoming travellers and locals for almost 240 years. It's recently undergone a stylish refurbishment, and offers clean, modern lines and lots of period detail. The enthusiasm of the kitchen shows in the modern British dishes, vibrant presentation, and classical techniques. A starter of spiced Grimsby cod is accompanied by curried cauliflower purée and mango sauce. Guinea fowl with boudin blanc, Savoy cabbage and white onion purée comes with a rich red wine sauce, while lemon tart with marmalade ice cream makes a refreshingly zesty finale.

Chef Chris O'Halloran **Seats** 40, Pr/dining room 18 **Times** 12-2.30/6.30-9, Closed L Mon, D Sun **Prices** Tasting menu £55-£85, Starter £3-£9, Main £11-£27, Dessert £7-£8 **Wines** 32 bottles over £30, 22 bottles under £30, 12 by glass **Parking** 25 **Notes** Sunday L £15.50-£21.50, Vegetarian available, Children welcome

HORNCASTLE Map 17 TF26

Magpies Restaurant with Rooms

British, European

tel: 01507 527004 **73 East St LN9 6AA**
email: info@magpiesrestaurant.co.uk **web:** www.magpiesrestaurant.co.uk
dir: *A158 into Horncastle, continue at lights. On left opposite Trinity Centre*

Bright, contemporary cooking in the Lincolnshire Wolds

In a terrace of 200-year-old cottages, Magpies has decor of duck-egg blue, with mirrors, candlelight and drapes over the bay windows. Slow-roast pork belly might kick things off, spiced up with star anise accompanied by tortellini sauced with apple, garlic and Yarg, and crisp salt-and-pepper crackling. Roast loin of cod as a main goes Eastern, served in hoi sin sauce with a spicy vegetable spring roll, chilli-spiked Chinese leaves and rösti, or there may be fillet of venison stuffed with figs and macadamias served with sweet potato terrine, savoury Savoy cabbage and bread sauce. To finish, try a trio of desserts: chocolate mousse, espresso crème brûlée and dark chocolate fondant.

Chef Andrew Gilbert **Seats** 34 **Times** 12-2/7-9.30, Closed 26-30 Dec, 1-8 Jan, Mon-Tue, L 24 & 31 Dec, Sat **Prices** Fixed L 2 course £21, Fixed D 3 course £27-£48.50 **Wines** 72 bottles over £30, 72 bottles under £30, 13 by glass **Parking** On street **Notes** Wine evening £76.50, Sunday L £21-£26, Vegetarian available, Children welcome

HOUGH-ON-THE-HILL Map 11 SK94

The Brownlow Arms

British

tel: 01400 250234 **High Rd NG32 2AZ**
email: armsinn@yahoo.co.uk **web:** www.thebrownlowarms.com
dir: *Take A607 (Grantham to Sleaford road). Hough-on-the-Hill signed from Barkston*

Country-pub cooking in an elegant village inn

This Lincolnshire village inn has come up in the world, being as elegantly appointed as an interiors magazine country house, with tapestry-backed chairs and gilt-framed mirrors in a panelled dining room. Attentive, friendly service puts everyone at their ease, and the menu stays within the familiar territory of classic country-pub cooking. Braised ox tongue with celeriac remoulade, pickled shallots and piccalilli purée makes a robust opener, followed, perhaps, by a trio of lamb comprising pan-roasted cannon, seared liver and a shepherd's pie, served with carrots, spinach and rosemary jus. For dessert, there may be triple chocolate brownie with chocolate sauce and rocky road ice cream.

Chef Ruarardh Bealby **Seats** 80, Pr/dining room 26
Times 12-2.30/6.30-9, Closed 25-26 Dec, Mon, L Tue, D Sun **Prices** Starter £5.95-£12, Main £16.50-£28, Dessert £7.25 **Wines** 8 by glass **Parking** 26, On street **Notes** Sunday L £23.95-£26.95, Vegetarian available, Children 8 yrs+

LACEBY Map 17 TA20

Best Western Oaklands Hall Hotel

Modern British

tel: 01472 872248 **Barton St DN37 7LF**
email: reception@oaklandshallhotel.co.uk **web:** www.thecomfyduck.com
dir: *Phone for directions*

Eye-catching, inventive food in a Victorian mansion

The balustraded red-brick mansion, built in 1877, sits in five acres of landscaped parkland between the Wolds and the Humber and makes a pleasant spot for the full country-house experience. Dining takes place in the Comfy Duck Bistro, which goes for a modern brasserie look and delivers inventive modern British comfort food to match. Seared scallops are paired with roe salt, ham hock terrine, piccalilli purée and hazelnut crumb, ahead of a creative partnership of duck breast with home-made duck and orange sausage, roasted figs and caramelised butternut squash purée. Dessert brings passionfruit crème brûlée with blood orange sorbet, crushed pistachios and meringue sticks.

Chef Steven Bennett, Ant Cron **Seats** 80, Pr/dining room 25
Times 12-2.30/6-9.30, Closed 26 Dec, D 25 Dec **Prices** Starter £6.50-£7.95, Main £10.95-£25.95, Dessert £4.95-£6.50 **Wines** 5 bottles over £30, 36 bottles under £30, 14 by glass **Parking** 100 **Notes** Sun D special offer, Steak night Thu, Sunday L £11.95-£19.95, Vegetarian available, Children welcome

LINCOLN Map 17 SK97

Branston Hall Hotel

Modern British

tel: 01522 793305 **Branston Park, Branston LN4 1PD**
email: info@branstonhall.com **web:** www.branstonhall.com
dir: *On B1188, 3m S of Lincoln. In village, hotel drive opposite village hall*

Ambitious cooking with lake and parkland views

Branston Hall is a handsome old pile, with lofty decorative gables, pinnacle chimneys and interiors that evoke a more gentle pace of life. The Lakeside dining room follows the restful theme, with views over the park, and a culinary style which adds gently modernised twists to the classical country house repertoire – pulled pork, for example, in a composition with Orkney scallops, pease pudding, quail's egg and bacon. At main course stage, Gressingham duck breast is partnered by spiced pumpkin purée, fried kale, Agen prunes and a rich orange and pomegranate sauce. To finish, there's a millefeuille of peanut mousse and chocolate pannacotta with caramel sauce.

The Electric Bar & Restaurant

Modern British NEW

tel: 01522 565182 & 565180 **DoubleTree by Hilton Lincoln, Brayford Wharf North LN1 1YW**
email: info@electricbarandrestaurant.co.uk **web:** www.electricbarandrestaurant.co.uk
dir: *A1, A57 Lincoln Road, right onto Newland, follow signs for Brayford Road. Right onto Lucy Tower St, hotel at end*

A 21st-century restaurant with Norman cathedral views

This restaurant is on the site of Lincoln's old electricity works, so choosing its name was a no-brainer. It's on the fifth floor, and at night the lights are dimmed for clearer views of the neighbouring marina and surrounding city. Modern British food is typified from the start by smoked duck with pear purée, shaved pear, celery and roasted walnuts. Fillet of brill gets up-to-the-minute treatment with the enjoyable addition of caramelised ceps, pommes purées, lemon sprouting broccoli and roast chicken jus, while the contemporary approach is maintained to the end in banana and salted caramel tarte Tatin with whipped mascarpone and pecan brittle.

Chef Daryl Jackson **Seats** 70, Pr/dining room 30 **Times** 12-2/6-10 **Prices** Fixed L 2 course £16-£18, Fixed D 3 course £29-£40, Starter £5.95-£9.45, Main £12.95-£29.50, Dessert £6.95-£9.50 **Wines** 14 bottles over £30, 10 bottles under £30, 8 by glass **Parking** NCP 100yds from hotel **Notes** Dine with wine & Steak night offers, Sunday L, Vegetarian available, Children welcome

LINCOLN *continued*

The Old Bakery

 British, Italian

tel: 01522 576057 **26-28 Burton Rd LN1 3LB**
email: enquiries@theold-bakery.co.uk **web:** www.theold-bakery.co.uk
dir: *From A46 follow directions for Lincoln North then follow brown signs for The Historic Centre*

Restaurant with rooms in a converted bakery

Ivano and Tracey de Serio's restaurant with rooms is a homely place, with the feel of a farmhouse kitchen. Pork chine terrine, served with apples stewed in ginger beer, saffron piccalilli and pickled cucumber, is a beguiling mixture of messages to begin, while main courses are multi-layered, richly sauced affairs, running from, say, roast rack of lamb in a deeply flavoured tomato reduction with lovage-infused potatoes and roasted beetroot and aubergine to the market fish of the day. A five-course taster menu offers a comprehensive tour, and desserts include white chocolate and pistachio ganache with vanilla pannacotta and delicately flavoured star anise ice cream.

Chef Ivano de Serio **Seats** 65, Pr/dining room 15 **Times** 12-1.30/7-9, Closed 26 Dec, 1-16 Jan, 1st wk Aug, Mon, L Tue-Wed, D Sun **Prices** Fixed L 2 course £14.50-£19.95, Tasting menu £44-£68, Starter £6-£11.95, Main £16.50-£25.95, Dessert £5.50-£7.95 **Wines** 70 bottles over £30, 40 bottles under £30, 9 by glass **Parking** On street, public car park 20mtrs **Notes** Tasting menu 7/10 course, 5/8 course with wine £53-£65, Sunday L £19.95, Vegetarian available, Children welcome

Tower Hotel

 Modern

tel: 01522 529999 **38 Westgate LN1 3BD**
email: tower.hotel@btclick.com **web:** www.lincolntowerhotel.com
dir: *Next to Lincoln Castle*

Fashionable textures in the cathedral quarter

In the Bailgate district of the cathedral quarter, the Tower benefits from all the charm that medieval Lincoln has to offer. The backbone of its operation is finely detailed, up-to-date cooking, heralded by the arrival of a basket of home-made breads and flavoured butters. Gels, dusts and purées in profusion give evidence of an understanding of fashionable textural variety. The range might open with a smoked haddock 'Scotch egg' with pea coulis and lemon gel, proceed to pork belly braised for 36 hours, served with champ, sage custard and Bramley apple gel, and conclude triumphantly with shortbread-crumbed cinnamon brûlée with anise-roasted plum and clementine gel.

Chef Simon Walker **Seats** 48 **Times** 6-9.30, Closed 25-26 Dec, 1 Jan, L all week **Prices** Fixed D 3 course £26, Starter £4.50-£8.50, Main £10.50-£27.50, Dessert £6-£8 **Wines** 5 bottles over £30, 20 bottles under £30, 8 by glass **Parking** NCP opposite **Notes** Sunday L £11.95-£19.50, Vegetarian available, Children welcome

Washingborough Hall Hotel

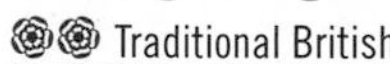 Traditional British

tel: 01522 790340 **Church Hill, Washingborough LN4 1BE**
email: enquiries@washingboroughhall.com **web:** www.washingboroughhall.com
dir: *B1190 into Washingborough. Right at rdbt, hotel 500yds on left*

Modern cooking in Georgian country house

Set in three acres of a sleepy Lincolnshire village, with a garden to provide herbs for the kitchen, Washingborough delivers all you would hope for in a Georgian manor turned country-house hotel. The smart Dining Room exudes quietly understated class with its restrained colours, unclothed tables, ornate marble fireplace and floor-to-ceiling windows overlooking the garden. Gently inventive contemporary ideas aim to soothe rather than challenge, starting with game terrine and ginger jam with sesame toast, followed by plaice roulade filled with smoked salmon mousse in beurre blanc. To finish, try old English nog tart (an egg-nogged version of custard tart) with poached pear.

Chef Dan Wallis **Seats** 50, Pr/dining room 110 **Times** 12-2/6.30-9, Closed L Mon-Sat **Prices** Starter £5.95-£7.95, Main £13.95-£26.50, Dessert £6.25-£8.50 **Wines** 17 bottles over £30, 37 bottles under £30, 12 by glass **Parking** 40 **Notes** Sunday L £18.50-£26.90, Vegetarian available, Children welcome

LOUTH — **Map 17 TF38**

Brackenborough Hotel

Modern British

tel: 01507 609169 **Cordeaux Corner, Brackenborough LN11 0SZ**
email: reception@brackenborough.co.uk **web:** www.oakridgehotels.co.uk
dir: *Hotel on main A16 Louth to Grimsby Rd*

Inventive bistro dining in a rural setting

Just outside the historical town of Louth, this small hotel is within beautifully maintained lawns and gardens and has lovely country views. The menu might be a crowd-pleaser, but the kitchen puts a great deal of effort and imagination into well-constructed, often unusual dishes. Start with chicken liver and Calvados parfait, rich and smooth, with quince and apple purée and toasted walnut bread, or wild mushroom béarnaise with a slow-cooked egg, and go on to roast chicken breast with celeriac and pea risotto with parmesan and truffle shavings, or grilled plaice fillets with beurre blanc, triple-cooked chips and mushy peas. Wind things up with treacle tart and ginger ice cream.

Chef Adam Harris **Seats** 78, Pr/dining room 120 **Times** 11.30-2.30/5-9.30 **Prices** Starter £4.25-£7.25, Main £9.95-£24.95, Dessert £5.45-£5.95 **Wines** 36 bottles over £30, 47 bottles under £30, 11 by glass **Parking** 80 **Notes** 2 people 2 course with wine £33, Sunday L £11.95, Vegetarian available, Children welcome

MARKET RASEN — **Map 17 TF18**

The Advocate Arms

Modern European, British

tel: 01673 842364 **2 Queen St LN8 3EH**
email: info@advocatearms.co.uk **web:** www.advocatearms.co.uk
dir: *Just off Market Place, High Street*

Confident cooking in a town-centre restaurant with rooms

The 18th-century restaurant with rooms in the centre of town has a contemporary finish and aims to impress with boutique styling and an open-plan interior. In the main restaurant, the output is broadly modern British, with some inventive combinations and plenty to satisfy traditionalists. Start with baked sea bass and braised fennel with prawn tortellini, and follow with slow-roast pork belly and butternut purée in cider reduction, or a panaché of fish with tomato and saffron salsa in champagne velouté. There are steaks too, served with trad accompaniments and a choice of sauces, and desserts such as raspberry and mint savarin with popping candy.

Chef Josh Kelly **Seats** 65, Pr/dining room 20 **Times** 7am-9.30pm, All-day dining, Closed D Sun (last orders 6.30) **Wines** 10 bottles over £30, 32 bottles under £30, 12 by glass **Parking** 6, Short walk **Notes** Sunday L £8.95-£10.95, Vegetarian available, Children welcome

SCOTTER Map 17 SE80

The White Swan

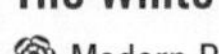 Modern British NEW

tel: 01724 763061 **9 The Green DN21 3UD**
email: info@whiteswanscotter.com **web:** www.whiteswanscotter.com
dir: *Phone for directions*

Welcoming spot for classic cooking

The whitewashed facade looks the very image of the coaching inn that The White Swan once was, but indoors the split-level restaurant conforms to contemporary expectations with neutral shades, pale wood and glass panels. The approach is decidedly unaffected, with hospitable service matched by appealing, well-executed food. Braised beef cheek is wrapped Tunisian-style in crispy filo pastry and served with buckwheat noodles and horseradish cream. To follow, you're in safe hands with herb-crusted rack of lamb with Jerusalem artichoke purée, rich lamby jus and fresh spring vegetables, and for afters, it's hard to pass on the classic delights of crème brûlée with home-made shortbread.

Chef Darren Taylor **Seats** 120, Pr/dining room 40 **Times** 12-9, All-day dining **Prices** Starter £4.50-£6.95, Main £10.95-£18.95, Dessert £4.95-£6.95 **Wines** 3 bottles over £30, 27 bottles under £30, 8 by glass **Parking** 25 **Notes** Afternoon tea, Sunday L £8.95-£10.95, Vegetarian available, Children welcome

SCUNTHORPE Map 17 SE81

Forest Pines Hotel & Golf Resort

Modern British

tel: 01652 650770 **Ermine St, Broughton DN20 0AQ**
email: forestpines@qhotels.co.uk **web:** www.qhotels.co.uk
dir: *M180 junct 4, towards Scunthorpe on A18. Continue straight over rdbt, hotel on left*

Sustainable seafood in a country-house hotel

The restaurant at this swish hotel is called Eighteen57 in honour of the year Grimsby's main fish dock opened. Its interior follows a piscine theme, with pictures, reliefs and murals celebrating the maritime world. The kitchen has an eye to sustainability, and fish and seafood feature prominently on an enticing modern repertoire, so a meaty main course of a duo of lamb – herb-crusted rack and confit belly – with garlic mash, sautéed spinach and a rich red wine sauce might follow tempura-battered king prawns with squid purée and green salad. Pudding may bring lemon tart with vanilla mascarpone and berry compôte.

Chef Paul Montgomery **Seats** 70 **Times** 6.30-10 **Prices** Prices not confirmed **Wines** 7 by glass **Parking** 400 **Notes** Vegetarian available, Children welcome

San Pietro Restaurant Rooms

Modern Mediterranean

tel: 01724 277774 **11 High Street East DN15 6UH**
email: info@sanpietro.uk.com **web:** www.sanpietro.uk.com
dir: *In Grade II listed Windmill at x-rds of Brigg Rd & Station Rd*

Stylish spot for creative cuisine

Pietro Catalano, who hails from Sicily, has created a restaurant with rooms in a former windmill that combines the best of Italian hospitality with a touch of boutique swagger. A first course dish of ballotine of rabbit and foie gras shows ambition, with its accompanying trio of pear (jelly, poached and velouté), plus some smoked loin and a pistachio biscuit. A fashionable partnership of turbot and crispy pork belly is up next, with tempura prawns and romanesco purée, or go for loin, daube and boudin of venison with sour cherry jus. For dessert, 'toast and marmalade' sponge is served with brown bread ice cream and orange crème anglaise.

Chef Pietro Catalano, Chris Grist **Seats** 80, Pr/dining room 14 **Times** 12-1.45/6-9.30, Closed 25-26 Dec, Sun, L Mon **Prices** Fixed L 2 course fr £14.95, Fixed D 3 course fr £27, Tasting menu fr £49.50 **Wines** 58 bottles over £30, 52 bottles under £30, 13 by glass **Parking** 22 **Notes** ALC 2/3 course £31.95/£38.50, Vegetarian available, Children welcome

SLEAFORD Map 12 TF04

The Bustard Inn & Restaurant

Modern British

tel: 01529 488250 **44 Main St, South Rauceby NG34 8QG**
email: info@thebustardinn.co.uk
dir: *A17 from Newark, turn right after B6403 to Ancaster. A153 from Grantham, after Wilsford, turn left for South Rauceby*

Sensitively refurbished old inn in peaceful village

The bar, with an open fireplace, flagstones and real ales, is the hub of this Grade II listed inn. A typical main might be two ways with beef (fillet and rillette), for instance, accompanied by Madeira sauce, a fricassée of greens, pommes Anna and wild mushrooms, and pan-fried sea bass fillet with crispy Parma ham, pesto mash and ratatouille. Starters tick all the right boxes too, taking in carefully grilled red mullet fillets with parmesan polenta and tomato fondue, and deep-fried squid with Thai noodles and sweet chilli dip, while puddings include apple crumble tart with blackberry ripple ice cream.

Chef Phil Lowe **Seats** 66, Pr/dining room 12 **Times** 12-2.30/6-9.30, Closed 1 Jan, Mon, D Sun **Prices** Fixed L 2 course £12.50, Starter £5.50-£9.50, Main £9.95-£28.50, Dessert £5.75-£6.95 **Wines** 15 bottles over £30, 28 bottles under £30, 11 by glass **Parking** 18, On street **Notes** Light L menu 2/3 course £12.50/£17, Sunday L £14.50-£24.50, Vegetarian available, Children welcome

STAMFORD Map 11 TF00

The Bull & Swan at Burghley

Traditional British

tel: 01780 766412 **High St, St Martins PE9 2LJ**
email: enquiries@thebullandswan.co.uk **web:** www.thebullandswan.co.uk
dir: *A1 onto Old Great North Rd, left onto B1081, follow Stamford signs*

Up-to-date cooking using regional produce in historic inn

The old stone inn used to be a staging post for coaches on the Great North Road and is nowadays an informal dining pub. Within are beams, stone walls, rugs on darkwood floors and caramel-coloured leather dining chairs. Regional produce is the backbone, with meat and vegetables from the nearby Burghley Estate, and the kitchen balances up-to-date ideas with the more traditional. Scorched ham hock with piccalilli, pea purée and toast has a nice balance of flavours. Main courses include seared halibut with red chard and sautéed greens in sauce Véronique , and proceedings conclude strongly with plum and pear Tatin and vanilla ice cream.

Chef Phil Kent **Seats** 40 **Times** 12-2.30/6-9 **Prices** Starter £3.50-£9.50, Main £12.95-£24.95, Dessert £7-£9.95 **Wines** 6 bottles over £30, 15 bottles under £30, 8 by glass **Parking** 7 **Notes** L/D offer £8/£25 pp for 2 mains & bottle of wine, Sunday L fr £14, Vegetarian available, Children welcome

STAMFORD *continued*

The George of Stamford

Traditional British V NOTABLE WINE LIST

tel: 01780 750750 **71 St Martins PE9 2LB**
email: reservations@georgehotelofstamford.com **web:** www.georgehotelofstamford.com
dir: *From A1 (N of Peterborough) onto B1081 signed Stamford and Burghley House. Follow road to 1st set of lights, hotel on left*

Historical institution treasured for its traditional values

History seeps from the pores of every mellow stone of this venerable coaching inn, which once fed and watered passengers on the Great North Road. The oak-panelled restaurant is a magnificent room with an old-world feel, and its menus are steadfastly traditional too: trolleys do the rounds to deliver the signature dish of roast sirloin of English beef, carved at the table. But it's not all heritage dining, for there are also king prawn tempura with lime and coriander salsa, followed by breadcrumbed rose veal cutlet in sage and lemon butter with avocado salad and potatoes forestière. Traditional sticky toffee is a good closing bet.

Chef Chris Pitman, Paul Reseigh **Seats** 90, Pr/dining room 40 **Times** 12.30-2.30/7.30-10.30 **Prices** Fixed L 2 course £27.45, Starter £8.35-£20.65, Main £17.45-£37.50, Dessert £8.25 **Wines** 121 bottles over £30, 29 bottles under £30, 21 by glass **Parking** 110 **Notes** Walk in L menu, Bistro menu, Sunday L, Children 10 yrs+

No.3 The Yard

British, European

tel: 01780 756080 **3 Ironmonger St PE9 1PL**
email: info@no3theyard.co.uk
dir: *Phone for directions*

Classic bistro cooking in a conservatory restaurant

It's well worth seeking out The Yard, tucked away behind buildings on Ironmonger Street in this charming old town. French windows in the ground-floor conservatory open on to a secluded courtyard and pretty garden, and there's more space upstairs, where monochrome photographs on brick walls show past times in Stamford. Creamy chicken liver parfait with grape and apple chutney and toasted brioche gets things off to a flier, before main course brings spicy pepper and prawn risotto as an accompaniment to chilli-glazed salmon fillet. Desserts are a class act too, among them a choc-fest trio of tart, mousse, and milk chocolate and honeycomb parfait.

Chef Tim Luff **Seats** 55, Pr/dining room 14 **Times** 11.30-2.30/6-9.30, Closed Mon, D Sun **Prices** Fixed L 2 course fr £15.95, Fixed D 3 course fr £22, Starter £7.50-£9, Main £13.50-£21.50, Dessert £4-£7 **Wines** 17 bottles over £30, 41 bottles under £30, 16 by glass **Parking** Broad St **Notes** Sunday L, Vegetarian available, Children welcome

Winteringham Fields

WINTERINGHAM Map 17 SE92

Modern British, European
tel: 01724 733096 **1 Silver St DN15 9ND**
email: reception@winteringhamfields.co.uk **web:** www.winteringhamfields.co.uk
dir: *Village centre, off A1077, 4m S of Humber Bridge*

Thrilling cooking on the Humber estuary

It's no surprise that Colin McGurran's first book puts Winteringham centre stage – *A Table at The Fields*, it's called – for this delectable restaurant with rooms has been his life for the last 10 years or so. Students of British restaurant history will know the address has long been a bright light in the culinary firmament, and under McGurran's tenure the place has grown to include its own farm from which the supply lines are always open. Produce is king here, and matched with the chef-patron's fervent imagination and creativity, lunch or dinner is a thrilling ride. The restaurant is richly done out with a mix of natural textures, quirky elements and luxurious touches, the overall impression both traditional and contemporary. Service is formal and professional. The evening offers up two 'Surprise' menus of seven or nine courses (lunch also offers a three- or four-course carte alongside the chance to be surprised). An opener might be virgin Bloody Mary jelly topped with plump prawns in a light sauce flavoured with the roe. Later on it's the turn of hand-dived scallops to steal the show, followed by a deeply indulgent lobster and truffle macaroni (including a boned chicken wing). Venison stars in a course with its tender loin partnering a wee venison pie and chestnut purée, while another gamey option might be salt-baked squab pigeon. Among sweet courses, the Pina Colada bomb is an opener fired up with lime and popping candy, before the main event, perhaps a pear, almond and white chocolate cheesecake. A well-chosen wine list has plenty to suit the creative style of the food.

Chef Colin McGurran **Seats** 60, Pr/dining room 12 **Times** 12-1.30/7-9, Closed 2 wks Xmas, last 2 wks Aug, Sun-Mon **Prices** Fixed L 3 course fr £39.95 **Wines** 20 by glass **Parking** 20 **Notes** L 4 course £45, D 7/9 course £75/£85, Vegetarian available, Children welcome

The William Cecil

Modern British

tel: 01780 750070 **High St, St Martins PE9 2LJ**
email: enquiries@thewilliamcecil.co.uk **web:** www.thewilliamcecil.co.uk
dir: *Exit A1 signed Stamford & Burghley Park. Continue & hotel 1st building on right on entering town*

Stylishly modernised Georgian hotel restaurant with creative menu

The hotel is an interesting amalgam of three Georgian houses built at different times, named after the Elizabethan statesman otherwise known as Lord Burghley. Just off the road to Stamford, it's a clever blend of old and new, the panelling done in lighter colours, with booth seating in the restaurant. The kitchen team sources locally and has plenty of creative flair at its disposal. That can be seen in a starter of smoked squab with pomegranate and dandelion, which might be followed by herb-crusted halibut with a sesame spring roll in vanilla sauce. Finish with baked rice pudding, chocolate sorbet and Earl Grey prunes.

Chef Phil Kent **Seats** 72, Pr/dining room 100 **Times** 12-3/6-9 **Prices** Starter £6.50-£9.50, Main £12-£24, Dessert £7-£8 **Wines** 25 bottles over £30, 23 bottles under £30, 11 by glass **Parking** 70 **Notes** Sunday L, Vegetarian available, Children welcome

WINTERINGHAM Map 17 SE92

Winteringham Fields

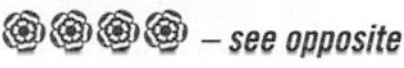 *– see opposite*

WOOLSTHORPE Map 11 SK83

Chequers Inn

Modern British

tel: 01476 870701 **Main St NG32 1LU**
email: justinnabar@yahoo.co.uk **web:** www.chequersinn.net
dir: *From A1 exit A607 towards Melton Mowbray, follow heritage signs for Belvoir Castle*

17th-century inn with impeccable modern regional cooking

A beautifully preserved 17th-century inn, the Chequers stands cheek-by-jowl with Belvoir Castle in a pastoral spot where Lincs meets Leics and Notts. Interiors match old and new, with brasserie-style tables and banquettes against imposing stone walls in the dining room, while the pub retains its rustic ambience with a big old fireplace and low ceilings to contain the happy babble. A menu of impeccably forward-thinking British food built from local supplies might start with grilled mackerel and olive and celery salsa, and rock on with blade of beef, served with caramelised onion mash, braised red cabbage and puréed celeriac. Conclude with orange pannacotta and meringue with orange confit.

Chef Andrew Lincoln **Seats** 70, Pr/dining room 20 **Times** 12-3/5.30-11, Closed D 25-26 Dec, 1 Jan **Prices** Starter £5.50-£10.50, Main £10.95-£23.50, Dessert £5-£7.50 **Wines** 35 bottles over £30, 41 bottles under £30, 33 by glass **Parking** 35 **Notes** Early dining offer all wk 6-7pm £7.77, Sunday L £13.95-£17.90, Vegetarian available, Children welcome

London

Index of London Restaurants

This index shows Rosetted restaurants in London in alphabetical order, followed by their postal district or location and plan/map references. Page numbers precede each entry.

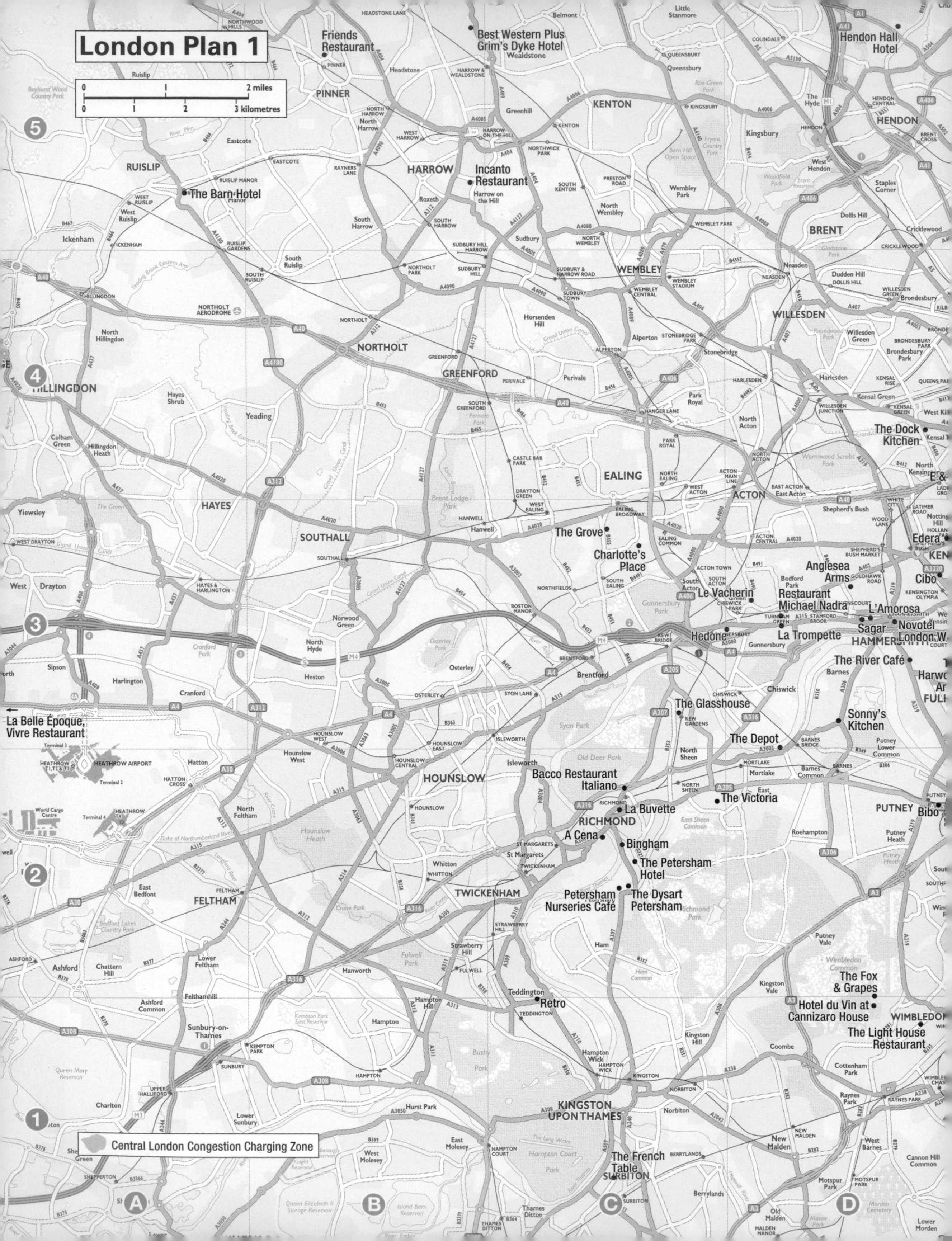

London Plan 1
0
1
2 miles
0
1
2
3 kilometres
Central London Congestion Charging Zone
5
4
3
2
1
A
B
C
D
Friends Restaurant
Best Western Plus Grim's Dyke Hotel
Hendon Hall Hotel
The Barn Hotel
Incanto Restaurant
The Dock Kitchen
The Grove
Charlotte's Place
Anglesea Arms
Restaurant Michael Nadra
L'Amorosa
Cibo
Le Vacherin
Sagar
Novotel London W
La Trompette
Hedone
The River Café
The Glasshouse
Sonny's Kitchen
The Depot
La Belle Époque, Vivre Restaurant
Bacco Restaurant Italiano
La Buvette
The Victoria
A Cena
Bingham
The Petersham Hotel
Petersham Nurseries Café
The Dysart Petersham
Retro
The Fox & Grapes
Hotel du Vin at Cannizaro House
The Light House Restaurant
The French Table
RUISLIP
PINNER
HARROW
KENTON
HENDON
BRENT
WEMBLEY
WILLESDEN
NORTHOLT
GREENFORD
HILLINGDON
HAYES
SOUTHALL
EALING
ACTON
HOUNSLOW
RICHMOND
TWICKENHAM
FELTHAM
PUTNEY
WIMBLEDON
KINGSTON UPON THAMES
SURBITON
HEATHROW AIRPORT

HARINGEY
TOTTENHAM
WALTHAM FOREST
WALTHAMSTOW
REDBRIDGE
ILFORD
HAMPSTEAD
CAMDEN
XO
Gilgamesh Restaurant Lounge
Manna
Odette's Restaurant
Michael Nadra Primrose Hill
La Collina
Grain Store
Trullo
Almeida Restaurant
The Drapers Arms
ISLINGTON
Frederick's Restaurant
Smokehouse
HACKNEY
Verden
The Empress
Typing Room
Mission
Verdi's Restaurant
TOWER HAMLETS
PLAN 6
NEWHAM
The Ledbury
SEE LONDON PLANS 2 - 5
CITY
WESTMINSTER
LAMBETH
CHELSEA
Marco Grill
The Painted Heron
Blue Elephant
London House
Craft London
WOOLWICH
GREENWICH
SOUTHWARK
Chapters All Day Dining
CLAPHAM
Tsunami
Trinity Restaurant
The Manor
The Dairy
Bistro Union
The Palmerston
Franklins
LEWISHAM
WANDSWORTH
Chez Bruce
Dabur
CATFORD
STREATHAM
MERTON
MITCHAM
BECKENHAM
BROMLEY
Chapter One
E
F
G
H

London Plan 2
0
250
500 metres
0
250
500 yards
A
B
C
D
E
6
5
4
3
2
1
St John's Wood
Maida Vale
Westbourne Green
PADDINGTON
Bayswater
Lisson Grove
Kensington Gardens
The Truscott Arms
Kurobuta
Salt and Honey
Angelus Restaurant
Nipa, Island Grill & Bar (Lancaster London)
Dinings
Clarke's
Lord's (Middlesex CCC & MCC)
Paddington Station
Paddington Recreation Ground
Whiteley's
Grand Union Canal
Regent's Canal
Little Venice
Westway
Marylebone Flyover
Bayswater Road
Edgware Road
Maida Vale
Westbourne Grove
Bishop's Bridge Road
Praed Street
Sussex Gardens
Wellington Road
Prince Albert Road
St John's Wood Road
Harrow Road
Chepstow Road
Pembridge Villas
Queensway
Eastbourne Terrace
Abbey Road Studios
BBC TV Studios
Peter Pan Statue
Speke's Monument
Physical Energy Statue
The Long Water
Italian Fountains
Embassy of Russia
Embassy of Lebanon
4
Congestion Charging Zone boundary
Restaurant
AA Restaurant of the Year

F
G
H
J
K
Regent's Park
The Hub
St John's Lodge
Capel Manor College
Open-air
Queen Mary's Gardens
The Holme
Boating Lake
London Business School
Regent's College
Tennis Centre
Park Square Gardens
Royal College of Physicians
Meliá White House
Euston Station
Margarete Centre
Maria Fidelis Convent Sch (Lower)
Netley Primary School
Schafer House
Language College
Police Station
HMRC
Wellcome Collection
UCL
University College London (UCL)
Sherlock Holmes
Lost Property Office
Madame Tussauds
Royal Academy of Music
Regent's Park
Royal National Orthopaedic
Fitzroy Square
YMCA
The Winter Garden (The Landmark)
Orrery
Iberica Marylebone
Fitzrovia
Villandry
Great Portland Street
Kitchen Table
Dabbous
Portland
Picture
Roka Charlotte Street
Salt Yard
Pied à Terre
The Ninth
Barnyard
Latium
Lima
The Riding House Café
Galvin Bistrot de Luxe
The Providores and Tapa Room
MARYLEBONE
Trishna
L'Autre Pied
Wallace Collection
Roux at The Landau (The Langham)
Hakkasan
Berners Tavern
The Mandeville Hotel
Levant
The Arch London
Piquet Restaurant
Ember Yard
The Montagu
Zoilo
Cocochan
Vasco & Piero's Pavilion Restaurant
The Lockhart
Locanda Locatelli
Blanchette
Arbutus Restaurant
Bo Drake
10 Greek Street
Texture Restaurant (Best Western Mostyn)
Roti Chai
Aqua Kyoto
Aqua Nueva
Social Eating House
Quo Vadis
The Red Fort
L'Escargot
Pollen Street Social
Assunta Madre
Sketch: The Gallery, The Parlour (Lecture Room & Library)
Antidote
Yauatcha
Barrafina
Frith Street
The Mayfair Chippy
The Beaumont
Little Social
Goodman
Andrew Edmunds
House of Ho
Gauthier Soho
La Petite Maison
Mews of Mayfair
Hibiscus
Polpo
Dehesa
Plum Valley
Roka Mayfair
Maze (London Marriott)
Bocca di Lupo
Fera at Claridge's
Wild Honey
NOPI
Mele e Pere
Sartoria
Palomar
J Sheekey
J Sheekey Oyster Bar
Le Gavroche Restaurant
Umu
Heddon Street Kitchen
HIX
DSTRKT
C London
Bellamy's
The Square
Alyn Williams at The Westbury
Veeraswamy Restaurant
Hakkasan Mayfair
Corrigan's Mayfair
Avista
Hélène Darroze at The Connaught
Cecconi's
The Keeper's House
Ten Room Restaurant
Sumosan Restaurant
The National Dining Rooms
JW Steakhouse (Grosvenor House)
Scott's Restaurant
Benares Restaurant
Peyote
Sexy Fish
HIX Mayfair
Bentley's Oyster Bar & Grill
Le Meridien Piccadilly
Estiatorio Milos
Quattro Passi
Babbo Restaurant
Kai Mayfair
Park Chinois
Nobu Berkeley ST
GYMKHANA
Al Duca
Mint Leaf Restaurant
The Chesterfield Mayfair
Cavendish London
Sofitel London St James
Alain Ducasse, China Tang & The Grill at The Dorchester
Novikov Asian / Italian Restaurant
The Wolseley
Quaglino's
The Greenhouse
Murano
The Ritz Restaurant
Cafe Murano
Le Caprice
CUT at 45 Park Lane
Tamarind
Seven Park Place by William Drabble
Sake No Hana
Podium, Galvin at Windows Restaurant & Bar
Kitty Fisher's
The Stafford London
Avenue
Chutney
Hyde Park
Marble Arch
Oxford Street
Speakers' Corner
Somers Town
St Pancras
Pullman London St Pancras
3
4

King's Cross
Pentonville
Searcys
St Pancras Grand
Somers Town
The Gilbert Scott
FINSBURY
St Pancras
Pullman London St Pancras
Moro
Clerkenwell
Otto's French Restaurant
The Modern Pantry
Le Café du Marché
Sosharu
St John
Malmaison Charterhouse Square
Bloomsbury
The Montague on the Gardens
Le Comptoir Gascon
Hix Oyster & Chop House
The Bleeding Heart
Holborn
Smiths of Smithfield Top Floor
Club Gascon
Rosewood London
Vanilla Black
The Chancery
The White Swan Pub & Dining Room
28-50 Wine Workshop & Kitchen
Hakkasan
St Giles
Great Queen Street
Bó Drake
10 Greek Street
Kopapa
Mon Plaisir
Barrafina Drury Lane
Cigalon
Lutyens Restaurant
Roka Aldwych
Arbutus Restaurant
Quo Vadis
L'Escargot
Barrafina Frith Street
L'Atelier de Joel Robuchon
The Delaunay
The Opera Tavern
Dicinnove, Chinese Cricket Club (Crowne Plaza London The City)
Gauthier Soho
The Ivy
Tredwells
Balthazar
Christopher's
Lima Floral
Clos Maggiore
Orso
Strand
J Sheekey & J Sheekey Oyster Bar
Spring
Kaspar's Seafood Bar & Grill, Savoy Grill
Les Deux Salons
The National Dining Rooms
Terroirs
Barrafina Adelaide Street
Estiatorio Milos
The Oxo Tower Restaurant
CITY OF LONDON
River Thames
Sofitel London St James
Massimo Restaurant & Bar
The Northall
RSJ, The Restaurant on the South Bank
The Royal Horseguards Hotel
Skylon
0 250 500 metres
0 250 500 yards

London Plan 3
Fifteen London - The Restaurant
The Clove Club
Saf
Merchants Tavern
Lyle's Tea Building
Brawn
Eyre Brothers
The Montcalm London City at The Brewery
HKK
L'Anima
L'Anima Café
Wright Brothers Spitalfields
St John Bread & Wine
Jago
Galvin HOP
Galvin La Chapelle
Taberna do Mercado
Canto Corvino
Upstairs at The Ten Bells
Boisdale of Bishopsgate
Super Tuscan
London Steakhouse Co - City
Eastway Brasserie
Duck & Waffle, SUSHISAMBA London
City Social
Manicomio City
Caravaggio
Barbecoa
Bread Street Kitchen
Coq d'Argent
Restaurant Sauterelle
Chamberlains Restaurant
Café Spice Namasté
Roast
Oblix
Shangri-La Hotel at the Shard
Congestion Charging Zone boundary
Restaurant
AA Restaurant of the Year

London Plan 4
2
Kensington Gardens
Round Pond
Sunken Gardens
Kensington Palace
Kensington Palace Green
Speke's Monument
'Time Flies' Clock Tower
Peter Pan Statue
The Long Water
Physical Energy Statue
Serpentine Gallery
Bandstand
St Govor's Well
Albert Memorial
The Flower Walk
Jenner Statue
Italian Fountains
Queen's Ice Rink
Lansdowne College
St Matthew's
Nursery
Police Station
Ranger's Lodge
Serpentine Bridge
Isis Statue
The Serpentine
The Lido
Diana Princess of Wales Memorial Fountain
Tennis Courts
Bowling Green
Embassy Slovak Republic
Embassy of Nepal
Embassy of Russia
Embassy of Lebanon
Romanian Embassy
Israel Embassy
Fire Station
Kensington Place
Notting Hill Gate
Clarke's
Hawkesdown House School
Min Jiang, Park Terrace Restaurant (Royal Garden)
Zaika of Kensington
KENSINGTON
The Milestone Hotel
Osteria 60
Babylon
High Street Kensington
Kensington & Chelsea Town Hall
St Mary Abbots
St Mary Abbots CE Primary School
Heythrop College
Thomas's Day School
Kitchen W8
Launceston Place
L'Etranger
Royal College of Art
Royal Albert Hall
Royal Geographical Society
Knightsbridge
Royal College of Music
Imperial College London
Science
Natural History
Darwin Centre
Victoria & Albert
The Oratory
Nozomi
Brompt
Police Station
Health Centre
Baden Powell House
Superstore
Millennium Bailey's Hotel London Kensington
Cromwell
Institute Français
Lycée Français
South Kensington
Gloucester Road
Bombay Brasserie
South Kensington
Our Lady of Victories RC Primary School
The Admiral Codrington
Bo Lang Restaurant
Bibendum Restaurant
Primary School
New Lotus Garden
EARL'S COURT STATION
Earl's Court
Cambio de Tercio
Capote y Toros
Brasserie Gustave
Tom's Kitchen
Royal Marsden
Le Colombier
Royal Brompton
St Luke's
Bousfield Primary School
St Cuthbert & St Matthias CE Primary School
Earls Court Exhibition Centre
CHELSEA
Gems Hampshire School
Register Office
Sports Centre
Fire Station
WEST BROMPTON STATION
West Brompton
St Luke's
Brompton Cemetery
Maze Grill Park Walk
Servite RC Primary School
Chelsea & Westminster
Eight Over Eight
Medlar Restaurant
Ambulance Station
Fulham Primary
Carlyle's House
0 250 500 metres
0 250 500 yards
KENSINGTON ROAD
HYDE PARK GATE
KENSINGTON GORE
CROMWELL ROAD
KENSINGTON HIGH STREET
KENSINGTON CHURCH STREET
NOTTING HILL GATE
EARL'S COURT ROAD
OLD BROMPTON ROAD
FULHAM ROAD
KING'S ROAD
BROMPTON ROAD
THURLOE PLACE
REDCLIFFE GARDENS
WARWICK ROAD
LILLIE ROAD
PEMBROKE ROAD
WEST CROMWELL ROAD
A315
A4
A3220
A3218
A308
A3217
6
5
4
3
2
1
A
B
C
D
E

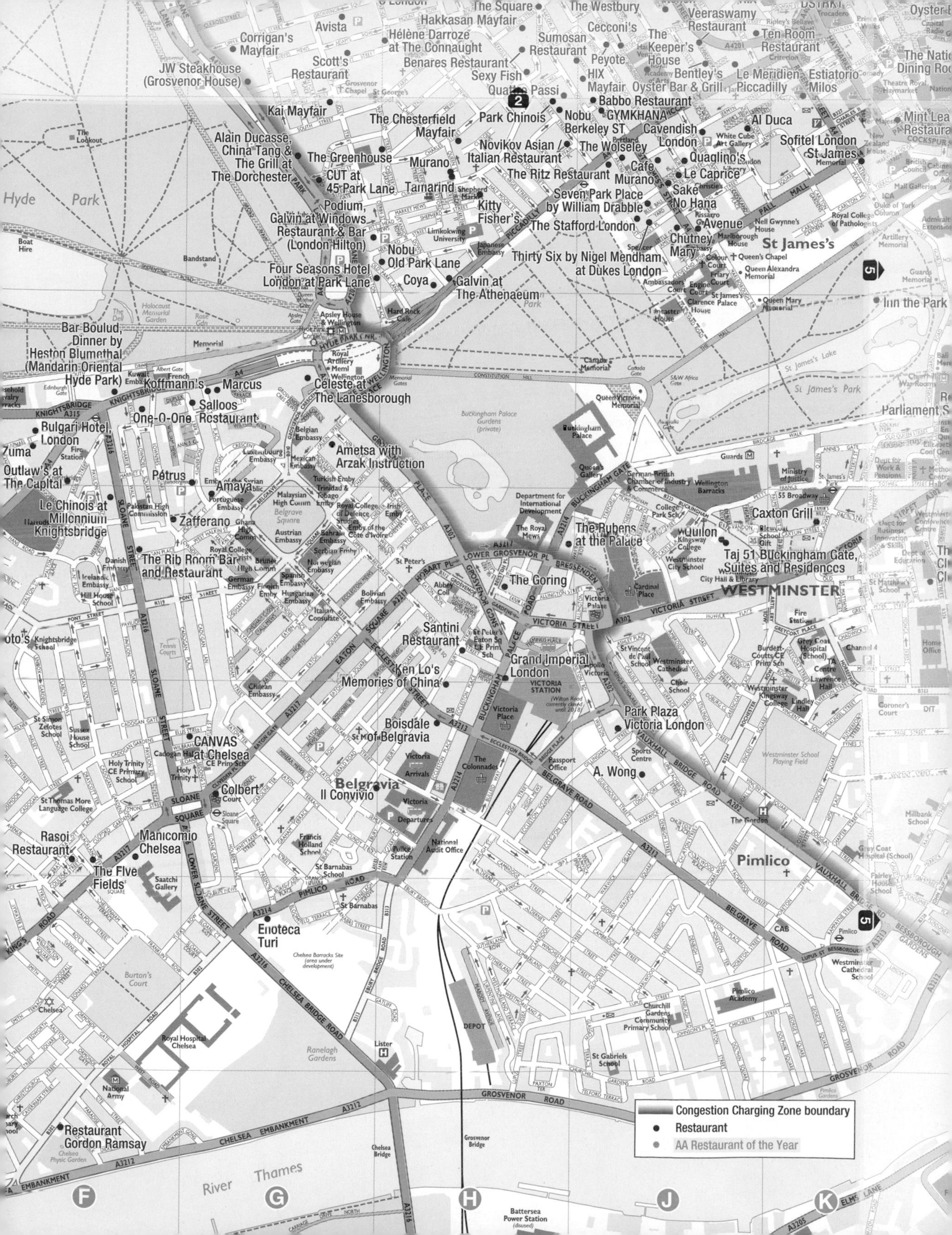

The Square
The Westbury
Veeraswamy Restaurant
Oyster Bar
Avista
Hakkasan Mayfair
Corrigan's Mayfair
Hélène Darroze at The Connaught
Cecconi's
The Keeper's House
Ten Room Restaurant
Sumosan Restaurant
Scott's Restaurant
Benares Restaurant
Peyote
The National Dining Rooms
JW Steakhouse (Grosvenor House)
Sexy Fish
HIX Mayfair
Bentley's Oyster Bar & Grill
Le Meridien Piccadilly
Estiatorio Milos
Quattro Passi
Babbo Restaurant
Kai Mayfair
The Chesterfield Mayfair
Park Chinois
Nobu Berkeley ST
GYMKHANA
Al Duca
Mint Leaf Restaurant
Alain Ducasse, China Tang & The Grill at The Dorchester
The Greenhouse
Novikov Asian / Italian Restaurant
The Wolseley
Cavendish London
Sofitel London St James
CUT at 45 Park Lane
Murano
Cafe Murano
Quaglino's
Le Caprice
Tamarind
The Ritz Restaurant
Sake No Hana
Podium, Galvin at Windows Restaurant & Bar (London Hilton)
Kitty Fisher's
Seven Park Place by William Drabble
The Stafford London
Avenue
Chutney Mary
Nobu Old Park Lane
Thirty Six by Nigel Mendham at Dukes London
St James's
Four Seasons Hotel London at Park Lane
Coya
Galvin at The Athenaeum
Inn the Park
Hyde Park
Bar Boulud, Dinner by Heston Blumenthal (Mandarin Oriental Hyde Park)
Koffmann's
Marcus
Céleste at The Lanesborough
Salloos
One-O-One Restaurant
Bulgari Hotel, London
Zuma
Outlaw's at The Capital
Ametsa with Arzak Instruction
Pétrus
Amaya
Le Chinois at Millennium Knightsbridge
Zafferano
The Rubens at the Palace
Caxton Grill
Quilon
Taj 51 Buckingham Gate, Suites and Residences
The Rib Room Bar and Restaurant
The Goring
WESTMINSTER
Santini Restaurant
Grand Imperial London
Ken Lo's Memories of China
Park Plaza Victoria London
Boisdale of Belgravia
CANVAS at Chelsea
A. Wong
Belgravia
Colbert
Il Convivio
Rasoi Restaurant
Manicomio Chelsea
The Five Fields
Pimlico
Enoteca Turi
Restaurant Gordon Ramsay
River Thames
Congestion Charging Zone boundary
Restaurant
AA Restaurant of the Year
F
G
H
J
K
2
5

Oyster Bar
Kaspar's Seafood Bar & Grill, Savoy Grill
Les Deux Salons
Terroirs
The National Dining Rooms
Barrafina Adelaide Street
Estiatorio Milos
The Oxo Tower Restaurant
Mint Leaf Restaurant & Bar
Sofitel London St James
Massimo Restaurant & Bar
The Northall
RSJ, The Restaurant on the South Bank
Skylon
The Royal Horseguards Hotel
Inn the Park
Union Street Cafe
The Anchor & Hope
Park Plaza County Hall London
Roux at Parliament Square
Park Plaza Westminster Bridge London
LAMBETH
H10 London Waterloo Hotel
The Cinnamon Club
Osteria Dell'Angolo
Chino Latino @ The Park Plaza Riverbank
Newington
Vauxhall
Kennington
River Thames
Waterloo Station
St James's Park
Tate Britain
Imperial War
The Kia Oval (Surrey CCC)
New Covent Garden Flower Market
0 250 500 metres
0 250 500 yards
A
B
C
D
E

London Plan 5
Congestion Charging Zone boundary
Restaurant
AA Restaurant of the Year
Roast
Oblix
Hutong
Shangri-La Hotel at the Shard
Magdalen
Brigade
Restaurant Story
Le Pont de la Tour
Pizarro
The Borough
Walworth
River Thames
Tower of London
Burgess Park
F
G
H
J
K
1
2
3
4
5
6

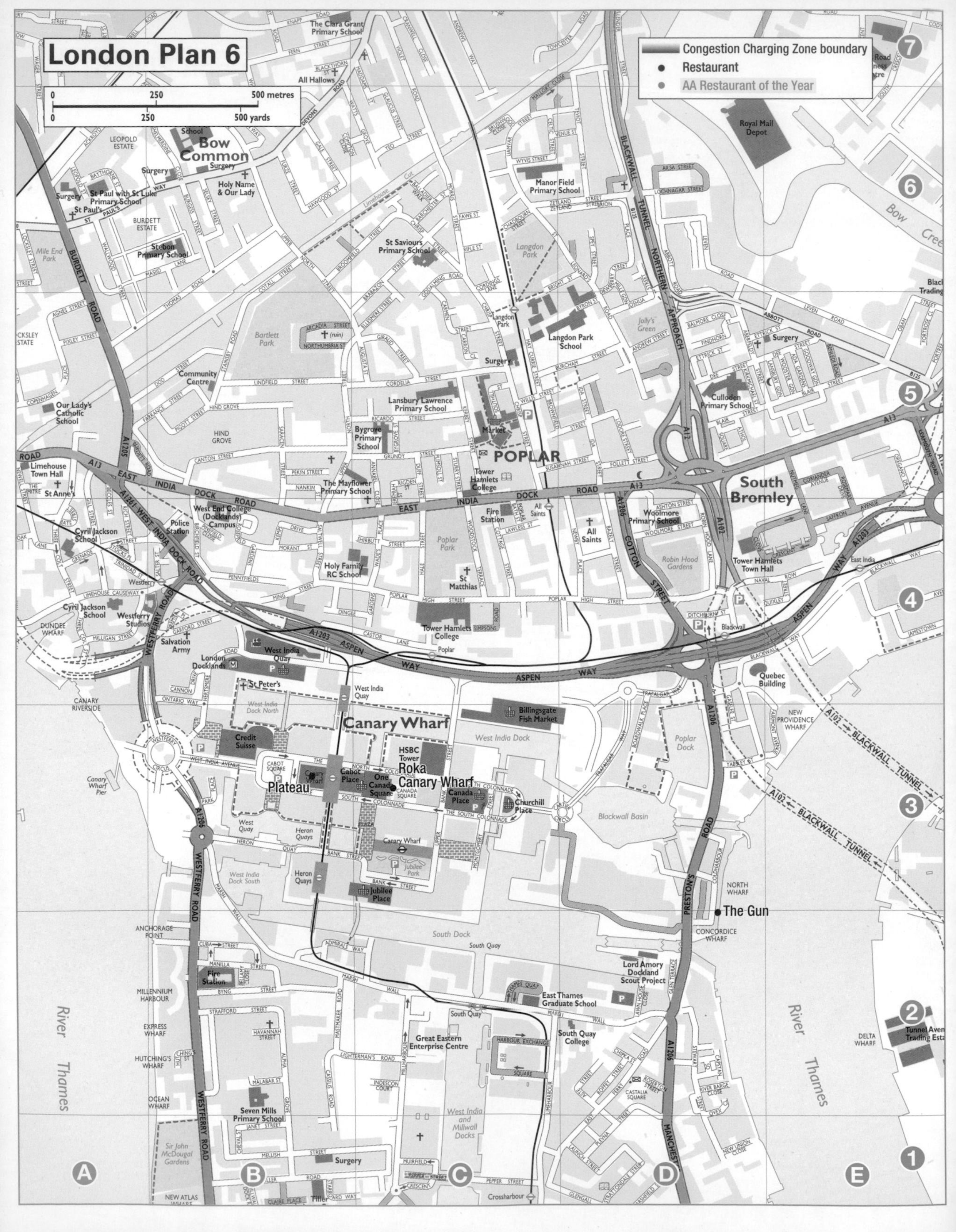
London Plan 6
0
250
500 metres
0
250
500 yards
Congestion Charging Zone boundary
Restaurant
AA Restaurant of the Year
Bow Common
LEOPOLD ESTATE
BURDETT ESTATE
The Clara Grant Primary School
All Hallows
Holy Name & Our Lady
St Paul with St Luke Primary School
St Paul's
Stebon Primary School
Mile End Park
Bartlett Park
Community Centre
Our Lady's Catholic School
HIND GROVE
Limehouse Town Hall
St Anne's
Cyril Jackson School
Westferry Studios
Salvation Army
Police Station
West End College (Docklands) Campus
St Saviours Primary School
Langdon Park
Langdon Park School
Jolly's Green
Lansbury Lawrence Primary School
Bygrove Primary School
Market
POPLAR
Tower Hamlets College
The Mayflower Primary School
Fire Station
All Saints
Poplar Park
St Matthias
Holy Family RC School
Manor Field Primary School
Royal Mail Depot
Bow Creek
Culloden Primary School
South Bromley
Woolmore Primary School
Robin Hood Gardens
Tower Hamlets Town Hall
Blackwall
Quebec Building
NEW PROVIDENCE WHARF
BLACKWALL TUNNEL
London Docklands
West India Quay
St Peter's
West India Dock North
Canary Wharf
Billingsgate Fish Market
West India Dock
Poplar Dock
Credit Suisse
HSBC Tower
Roka
Cabot Place
One Canada Square
Canary Wharf
Plateau
Canada Place
Churchill Place
Blackwall Basin
CANARY RIVERSIDE
Canary Wharf Pier
West Quay
Heron Quays
Jubilee Park
Jubilee Place
West India Dock South
NORTH WHARF
The Gun
CONCORDICE WHARF
South Dock
South Quay
ANCHORAGE POINT
Fire Station
MILLENNIUM HARBOUR
EXPRESS WHARF
HUTCHING'S WHARF
OCEAN WHARF
Lord Amory Dockland Scout Project
East Thames Graduate School
South Quay College
Great Eastern Enterprise Centre
West India and Millwall Docks
Seven Mills Primary School
Sir John McDougal Gardens
Surgery
Crossharbour
NEW ATLAS WHARF
Tiller
River Thames
DELTA WHARF
Tunnel Avenue Trading Esta
BURDETT ROAD
EAST INDIA DOCK ROAD
WESTFERRY ROAD
ASPEN WAY
COTTON STREET
PRESTON'S ROAD
MANCHESTER ROAD
BLACKWALL TUNNEL NORTHERN APPROACH
POPLAR HIGH STREET
A
B
C
D
E
1
2
3
4
5
6
7

LONDON

Restaurants are listed below in postal district order, commencing east, then north, south and west. Detailed plans 2-6 (pages 224–232) show the locations of restaurants with AA Rosette Awards within the Central London postal districts. If you do not know the postal district of the restaurant you want, please refer to the index preceding the street plans (pages 218–221) for the entry and map pages. The map plan reference for each restaurant also appears within its directory entry.

LONDON

LONDON E1

Café Spice Namasté

PLAN 3 J1

Indian

tel: 020 7488 9242 **16 Prescot St E1 8AZ**
email: binay@cafespice.co.uk
dir: *Nearest station: Tower Gateway (DLR), Aldgate, Tower Hill*

Vibrant modern Indian cooking in Whitechapel

Set in an imposing red-brick Victorian Gothic building, the interior of this vibrant Indian has brightly-painted walls and colourful fabrics that are matched by Cyrus Todiwala's refined, confidently spiced, inventive modern food, which draws on his Parsee roots and the best seasonal British ingredients. From menus with detailed notes, start with a fusion idea: a tart of Dorset snails cooked in a Goanese xacutti sauce and served with a tangy yogurt coleslaw. Move on to a rich, authentic pork vindaloo made with organic, rare-breed pork, or perhaps look to the tandoor for sea-fresh masala grilled halibut with garlic and red chilli risotto.

Chef Cyrus Todiwala **Seats** 120 **Times** 12-3/6.15-10.30, Closed Xmas, BHs, Sun, L Sat **Prices** Fixed L 3 course £35-£75, Fixed D 3 course £35-£75, Starter £5.75-£10.50, Main £14.50-£19.50, Dessert £5.25-£7.50 **Wines** 11 bottles over £30, 17 bottles under £30, 7 by glass **Parking** On street, NCP **Notes** Vegetarian available, Children welcome

Canto Corvino

PLAN 3 H3

Modern Italian NEW

tel: 020 7655 0390 **21 Artillery Ln E1 7HA**
email: info@cantocorvino.co.uk
dir: *Nearest station: Liverpool St*

Imaginative modern Italian cooking in Spitalfields

Canto Corvino ('song of the raven') brings modern Italian style to Spitalfields, with artwork on rough-hewn walls, comfortable chairs at well spaced tables, soft lighting and a lively atmosphere. The menu is as fashionable as the surroundings, divided into eight sections of modestly portioned dishes, all imaginatively assembled and well crafted. From stuzzichini comes crab with radish, chilli, cabbage and agretti salad, and from crudo comes black bream céviche with olives, blood orange and fennel. Well-made pasta includes duck tortelli with cime di rapa and Tuscan sausage, and the Josper grill comes into its own with monkfish, mussels, chilli, broccoli and fregola. End with the more familiar tiramisù.

Chef Tom Salt **Seats** 140, Pr/dining room 24 **Times** 12-3/6-10, Closed Xmas, New Year, D Sun **Prices** Prices not confirmed **Notes** Sunday L, Vegetarian available, Children welcome

Galvin La Chapelle

PLAN 3 H3

– see page 234

Galvin HOP

PLAN 3 H3

French, Italian

tel: 020 7299 0404 **35 Spital Square E1 6DY**
email: info@galvinrestaurants.com
dir: *Nearest station: Liverpool St*

The British pub reimagined by the Galvin brothers

The former Galvin Café à Vin is now Galvin HOP, a switch of allegiance of sorts, for it is now branded as a 'pub deluxe', with shiny copper tanks above the bar containing unpasteurised Czech lager. The menu could be described as modern pub or modern bistro, whatever floats your boat, with a repertoire that covers a lot of bases from deluxe hot dogs to Dorset snails cooked in the wood-fired oven. A starter of super-fresh Dorset crab mayonnaise on toast gets things off to a flyer, before a simply (and correctly) done Black Angus top sirloin, a luxe fish pie, or Kentish lamb Barnsley chop.

Chef Jack Boast, Jeff Galvin **Seats** 125, Pr/dining room 12 **Times** 11.30-10.30, All-day dining, Closed 25-26 Dec, 1 Jan, D 24 Dec **Prices** Fixed L 2 course fr £16.50, Fixed D 3 course fr £19.95, Starter £5-£10, Main £13-£19, Dessert £4-£6 **Wines** 14 bottles over £30, 10 bottles under £30, 14 by glass **Parking** On street, Spital Sq **Notes** Fixed D 6-7pm, Sunday L £16.50-£22.50, Vegetarian available, Children welcome

Jago

PLAN 3 J3

Mediterranean

tel: 020 3818 3241 **68-80 Hanbury St E1 5JL**
email: info@jagorestaurant.com
dir: *Nearest station: Liverpool St, Aldgate East*

Appealing modern cooking in E1

Jago occupies the ground floor of a former factory now housing creatives and IT entrepreneurs, many of whom use this light and informal restaurant as their staff canteen. The chef used to work for Ottolenghi, which explains the vibrant Middle Eastern-meets-Mediterranean cuisine on offer. Sticking rigidly to the seasons, a springtime meal might kick off with incredibly fresh sardines on toast accompanied by a mélange of marinated tomatoes, celery, parsley and lemon juice. A typical main course of rich, slow-cooked veal cheek goulash with orzo pasta and sour cream is big on flavour. It might be followed by a perfectly balanced vanilla pannacotta with poached rhubarb.

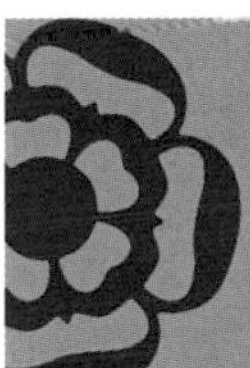

Read all about our Wine Award winners on pages 17–19

Galvin La Chapelle

LONDON E1 **PLAN 3 H3**

French NOTABLE WINE LIST

tel: 020 7299 0400
St Botolph's Hall, 35 Spital Square E1 6DY
email: info@galvinrestaurants.com
web: www.galvinrestaurants.com
dir: *Nearest station: Liverpool St*

Victorian school chapel with classic and modern French cooking

A sharp intake of breath is a quite understandable reaction as you enter the former chapel of St Botolph's girls' school, with its brown marble pillars soaring to the vaulted roof. The place has wow factor in spades thanks to its glamorous buzz, swagged curtains, plush brown leather seating and white linen tables, and the mezzanine level provides bird's-eye views of the action below. While towering magnificence is fine in the decor, it isn't necessarily what you want in the service approach, and fortunately an attentive and well-drilled team keeps La Chapelle purring along. The cooking conforms to the Galvin template: solidly grounded in modern and classic French ideas broadened to take in some distinctly contemporary British accents. The produce that underpins it all is second to none, if not always native – perhaps a starter of gold-standard seared Vendée foie gras with Medjool date purée and beef bouillon. Otherwise, begin with an intensely coloured and flavoured heritage beetroot risotto with whipped goats' cheese, pickled walnuts and balsamic. Razor-sharp technique and timing distinguish a main course of loin and faggot of venison with red cabbage, velvety celeriac purée and chanterelles, or big appetites might take on roast Chateaubriand of Cumbrian beef partnered with a millefeuille of rainbow chard and celery, and Hermitage sauce. Fish, too, is skilfully handled – perhaps grilled Cornish red mullet in a Mediterranean-accented composition with caponata, and sage and olive beignets. While classic desserts such as apple tarte Tatin with Normandy crème fraîche are hard to pass by, a trio of chocolate crémeux, pistachio sponge and blackberry sorbet proves a worthy alternative. French big guns lead the charge in a standout wine list.

Chef Jeff Galvin, Eric Jolibois **Seats** 115, Pr/dining room 27 **Times** 12-2.30/6-10.30, Closed 25-26 Dec, 1 Jan, D 24 Dec **Prices** Fixed L 2 course fr £24, Fixed D 3 course fr £29, Tasting menu £70-£150, Starter £15.50-£20.50, Main £25.50-£35.50, Dessert £9.50-£14.50 **Wines** 377 bottles over £30, 16 bottles under £30, 25 by glass **Parking** On street, NCP **Notes** Fixed price D 6-7pm, Tasting menu 7 course, Sunday L £27.50-£34.50, Vegetarian available, Children welcome

LONDON E1 *continued*

London Steakhouse Co – City

PLAN 3 H3

Modern European V

tel: 020 7247 5050 **East India House, 109-117 Middlesex St E1 7JF**
email: info@mpwsteakandalehouse.org
dir: *Nearest station: Liverpool St*

Quality City steakhouse in a bright basement setting

Part-owned by Marco Pierre White, this eatery offers a brasserie-style roster of timeless English dishes with French and Italian accents. As its name suggests, meat is the mainstay, running from Scottish steaks (take your pick from rib-eye, fillet or a 24oz Boston chop for two – with the usual choice of sauces) to the likes of calves' liver and dry-cured bacon, while non-carnivores could go for a rare tuna steak à la Sicilienne. Expect well-sourced steaks and unshowy cooking, but factor in side-order triple-cooked chips and veg, while desserts offer the thumb-sucking comforts of Bakewell tart or sticky toffee pudding. Throw in well-selected wines and good cocktails and all bases are covered.

Chef Richard Smith **Seats** 86, Pr/dining room 24
Times 12-3/5.30-10.30, Closed 25-26 Dec, 1 Jan **Prices** Fixed L 3 course £27.50, Fixed D 3 course £27.50 **Wines** 55 bottles over £30, 19 bottles under £30, 13 by glass **Parking** On street after 7pm **Notes** Afternoon tea, Sunday L, Children welcome

Lyle's Tea Building

PLAN 3 J4

Modern British V

tel: 020 3011 5911 **56 Shoreditch High St E1 6JJ**
email: reservations@lyleslondon.com
dir: *Nearest station: Liverpool St, Shoreditch High St*

Shoreditch hot-ticket for on-trend pared-back dining and vibe

Lyle's coolly casual warehouse good looks – think painted brick walls and pillars and low-hanging lights – have made it a 'must-go-to' outfit since it first opened. The food certainly delivers on the hype and expectation, via a daily roster that offers a selection of small and larger plates at lunch and a five-course, no-choice fixed-price menu at dinner. Prime produce and seasonality are key, including some lesser-used more gutsy cuts and innovative combinations. Take a pairing of warm beetroot, smoked eel and peppy horseradish, for instance, while lamb's hearts, broccoli leaves and anchovy has even more oomph. A stunningly light treacle tart comes with milk ice cream to cut through the sweetness

Chef James Lowe **Seats** 48 **Times** 12-2.30/6-10.30, Closed BHs, Xmas, New Year, Sun **Prices** Fixed L 3 course fr £35, Starter £6-£10, Main £14-£19, Dessert £5-£7.50 **Wines** 30 bottles over £30, 7 bottles under £30, 10 by glass **Notes** Fixed D 4 course £44, Children welcome

St John Bread & Wine

PLAN 3 J3

British

tel: 020 7251 0848 **94-96 Commercial St E1 6LZ**
email: reservations@stjohnbreadandwine.com
dir: *Nearest station: Liverpool St, Aldgate East*

Gutsy British cooking in Spitalfields

The name sums up the back-to-basics approach in this operation near Spitalfields Market, a canteen-like space with whitewashed walls, old wooden furniture and an open-to-view kitchen and bakery. Expect unfussy and robust dishes, driven by flavour and quality seasonal produce, including lesser-known cuts and ingredients such as pig's head stew, or blood cake and duck egg. There's no truck with three-course convention, just small and larger plates, so sharing is encouraged. Start with devilled duck hearts on home-made toast, or skate cheeks with tartare sauce, and proceed to pheasant and trotter pie. Breads are exceptional, and for pud, try Eccles cake and Lancashire cheese, or date loaf and butterscotch sauce.

Super Tuscan

PLAN 3 H3

Italian

tel: 020 7247 8717 **8a Artillery Passage E1 7LJ**
email: info@supertuscan.co.uk
dir: *Nearest station: Liverpool St*

Italian enoteca dining in a hang-loose atmosphere

The cheery Italian enoteca in Spitalfields is a hang-loose setting for inspired classic Italian home cooking. Antipasti sharing platters of salamis and/or cheeses are obvious ways to pique the appetite. Clipboard menus then offer the likes of arancini risotto balls made smoky with plenty of paprika, moreish broccoli heads fried in olive oil and anchovy batter, and heritage pasta dishes like mushroom tortelloni in cream sauce. Sturdier tastes are sated by meats such as roast kid pre-cooked in milk, the cooking liquor used to make a richly comforting sauce, or chargrilled veal chop with rosemary-spiked potatoes. Finish with melting chocolate and almond sponge cake, served with quality vanilla ice cream.

Chef Nick Grossi **Seats** 30 **Times** 12-2.30/5.30-10, Closed Xmas, New Year, Sun, L Sat **Prices** Starter £4-£11.95, Main £10.95-£20, Dessert £4.50-£9.95 **Wines** 36 bottles over £30, 25 bottles under £30, 15 by glass **Notes** Vegetarian available, Children welcome

Taberna do Mercado

PLAN 3 J3

Modern Mediterranean, Portuguese NEW

tel: 020 7375 0649 **Old Spitalfields Market, 107b Commercial St E1 6BG**
email: info@tabernamercado.co.uk
dir: *Nearest station: Liverpool St*

Portuguese-Inspired cooking in Old Spitalfields Market

'Market tavern' is appropriate, as this is within Old Spitalfields Market. It's a modest, even minimalist, place, spacious and bright, with wooden dining chairs at plain tables and painted brick walls. Small sharing plates of Portuguese-inspired food is the theme, built on specially sourced ingredients. Kick off with something from the 'snacks' section – perhaps prawn rissóis (a breaded pastry from the Lisbon region stuffed with shellfish) – and pick and mix from the rest of the menu, from imported cheeses and cured meats (perhaps smoked red wine sausage) to scallops with brown butter and walnuts, say, or cod tongue, and end with creamy egg sponge cake.

Chef Nuno Mendes, Antonio Galapito **Seats** 80 **Times** 12-10, All-day dining, Closed 24-28 Dec, L 1 Jan **Prices** Prices not confirmed **Wines** 13 by glass **Notes** Daily L special menu, Sunday L, Vegetarian available, Children welcome

LONDON E1 *continued*

Upstairs at The Ten Bells

PLAN 3 J3

 Seasonal Modern British

tel: 07530 492986 **First Floor, 84 Commercial St E1 6LY**
email: reservations@tenbells.com
dir: *Nearest station: Shoreditch High St*

Shabby-chic Spitalfields gaff for cool, inspired dining

Hip, pared-back and shabby-chic, this dining room is a trendy confection of mismatched furniture, scuffed floorboards, retro chandeliers and edgy contemporary art. The modern seasonal cooking is marked by flair and layers of flavour: take a 'wow' dessert of roast pineapple cleverly teamed with goats' milk rice pudding, yogurt crumb and madras sorbet. The compact yet appealing carte starts out with fashionable snacks such as buttermilk chicken and pine salt. Mains feature knockout combos like succulent rolled lamb breast and sweetbreads, accompanied by sweet sandy carrots, caraway and salted lemon. Relaxed and informed service fits the bill, as do the reasonable prices and excellent wines from France and Italy.

Verdi's Restaurant

PLAN 1 G4

 Traditional Italian

tel: 020 7702 7051 **237 Mile End Rd, Stepney Green E1 4AA**
email: info@gverdi.uk
dir: *Nearest station: Stepney Green*

Regional Italian home cooking in a converted Georgian pub

In a former pub dating back to the Georgian period, soft shades of green create a calming ambience and photos of family and local landmarks are dotted over the walls of the long, narrow room leading to the partially open kitchen. The simplicity of the room and decor is reflected by the no-frills home-cooking, which is mostly influenced by the Emilia-Romagna region of Italy; this is honest food with big flavours. A starter of risotto di seppia with calamari genuinely tastes of the sea and might precede a generous main course of braised rabbit with pine nuts, olives, raisins and rosemary. For pudding expect a traditional tiramisù.

Wright Brothers Spitalfields

PLAN 3 J3

Modern British Seafood

tel: 020 7377 8706 **8/9 Lamb St, Old Spitalfields Market E1 6EA**
email: spitz@thewrightbrothers.co.uk
dir: *Nearest station: Liverpool St*

The Wright stuff comes to Spitalfields

Sea-to-plate fish and seafood cookery in the bustling environs of Spitalfields Market. Start with a simple but effective dish of seared octopus, served in a fancy pan with chunks of chorizo and broad beans, or crab and scampi with curried mayonnaise and pickled pear. Continue, perhaps, with biting lemon and chilli with sea bass, or sweet grapes in classic lemon sole Véronique. There are meats too, such as duck with blood orange, and unashamedly populist desserts, such as caramel-centred chocolate pot, or green apple parfait with a cinnamon doughnut and crème fraîche ice cream. However, pairings of Scottish cheeses and malt whisky are a powerful distraction from the sweet stuff.

Chef Richard Kirkwood **Seats** Pr/dining room 40 **Times** 12-10.30, All-day dining, Closed BHs **Prices** Prices not confirmed **Wines** 52 bottles over £30, 9 bottles under £30, 21 by glass **Parking** On street **Notes** Express fixed menu, Sunday L, Vegetarian available, Children welcome

LONDON E2

Brawn

PLAN 3 K5

Traditional European NOTABLE WINE LIST

tel: 020 7729 5692 **49 Columbia Rd E2 7RG**
email: enquiries@brawn.co
dir: *Nearest station: Liverpool St, Bethnal Green, Hoxton*

Smart, honest cooking in trendy East London

Set among a run of artisanal shops, the corner-sited restaurant is a hard-edged, pared-back neighbourhood outfit. The trendy warehouse-like interior of whitewashed brickwork, high ceilings and dangling lamps now features a large open kitchen. Plain cafe tables and retro chairs foster the chilled look, and the European-focused daily-changing menu is driven by seasonality and provenance, following a simple path to deliver big-hearted flavours. Start with crab and celeriac remoulade, or Cornish mussels with leeks in cider and thyme, as curtain-raisers to skate and chanterelles, or lamb neck with fava beans, puntarelle and anchovies. There's tiramisù to finish.

Chef Ed Wilson **Seats** 70 **Times** 12-3/6-11, Closed Xmas, New Year, BHs, L Mon, D Sun **Prices** Fixed L 3 course £28, Starter £6.50-£16.50, Main £12.50-£22, Dessert £6-£7 **Wines** 98 bottles over £30, 25 bottles under £30, 14 by glass **Parking** On street **Notes** Sunday L £28, Vegetarian available, Children welcome

Typing Room

PLAN 1 G4

British, Modern European V

tel: 020 7871 0461 **Town Hall Hotel, Patriot Square E2 9NF**
email: reservations@typingroom.com
dir: *Nearest station: Bethnal Green*

Pizzazz and high-fashion cooking in Bethnal Green

The restaurant occupies what was the typing pool back when this boutique hotel was Bethnal Green's town hall. It's an attractive space with a decor of muted greys, a parquet floor, well-spaced marble-topped tables and an old fireplace. An open-to-view kitchen shows the chefs calmly working away. In charge is Lee Westcott, who's worked at some classy places over the years so isn't short of experience. Five- and seven-course no-choice tasting menus are the format, plus two- and three-course set-price lunches with a couple of options per course. Lee turns out some exciting stuff. A selection of snacks kicks off a meal, among them pig's head with smoked apple, before starters along the lines of mackerel fillet with kohlrabi, horseradish and tarragon, or celeriac, pear, fermented mushrooms and hazelnuts. Dishes are imaginatively conceived and successfully brought off. The richness of duck leg is offset by fermented cabbage, cavolo nero and turnips, and roast baby chicken is more conventionally served with garlic, asparagus and Jersey Royals. Fish might appear as lemon sole fillets in smoked butter with artichoke and walnuts, verjuice adding a sharper element, and puddings can be as experimental as pumpkin with coffee and orange, or beetroot with white chocolate and olives.

Chef Lee Westcott **Seats** 36 **Times** 12-2.15/6-10, Closed 24-26 Dec, 1 Jan, Sun-Mon, L Tue **Prices** Fixed L 2 course £24, Tasting menu £60-£75 **Wines** 85 bottles over £30, 8 bottles under £30, 13 by glass **Parking** Opposite (meter) **Notes** Children welcome

LONDON E5

Verden

PLAN 1 G4

Modern European

tel: 020 8986 4723 **181 Clarence Rd, Clapton E5 8EE**
email: info@verdenE5.com
dir: *Nearest station: Hackey Central, Hackney Downs, Clapham*

Corner pub turned smart wine bar and restaurant

As well as taking its wines very seriously, Verden bills itself as specialising in the 'world's best' salamis, smoked and cured meats, and hard, soft, goats', washed and blue cheeses, all offered in 40g mix-and-match portions for a tasting board. If it's dinner you're after, though, the small economically worded à la carte menu is changed weekly. Octopus carpaccio is a good place to start, thin slices blended with a heady sauce, coriander leaves and a delicate mayo. Follow with flavoursome stuffed saddle of rabbit with spring vegetables for textural contrast, with rich, well-balanced salted caramel chocolate pot to close proceedings. A 'feasting menu' is available for large parties.

Chef Joel Massey **Seats** 70, Pr/dining room 40 **Times** 12-3/6-late, Closed 24-26 Dec, 1 Jan, Mon, L Tue-Thu **Prices** Starter £5-£10, Main £10-£18, Dessert £1.50-£6 **Wines** 66 bottles over £30, 2 bottles under £30, 25 by glass **Parking** On street **Notes** Wknd brunch, Tue steak night, Sunday L £10-£16, Vegetarian available, Children welcome

LONDON E9

The Empress

PLAN 1 G4

Modern British

tel: 020 8533 5123 **130 Lauriston Rd, Victoria Park E9 7LH**
dir: *Nearest station: Cambridge Heath, Mile End*

Laid-back crowd-pleaser with simple, feisty dishes

This Victorian tavern fits right into its buzzy Victoria Park location. Red Chesterfields, fashionable retro lighting and bare-brick walls are suitably à la mode, and when it comes to food, the kitchen (headed-up by an ex L'Ortolan man) delivers honest stuff made with good quality ingredients. A starter of chargrilled octopus comes with sobrasada (a Spanish sausage) and olives, while another combines ricotta cheese and beetroot with sesame and seaweed. Move on to pork belly with its crispy skin and meltingly soft meat, served with spelt risotto and garlic purée, or cod with fregola and salsa verde. Among desserts, a suitably wobbly vanilla pannacotta arrives with rhubarb and candied almonds.

Chef Elliott Lidstone **Seats** 49 **Times** 12-3.30/6-10.15, Closed 25-26 Dec, L Mon (ex BHs) **Prices** Prices not confirmed **Wines** 24 bottles over £30, 42 bottles under £30, 16 by glass **Parking** On street **Notes** Brunch Sat-Sun, Sunday L, Vegetarian available, Children welcome

LONDON E14

The Gun

PLAN 6 D2

Modern British

tel: 020 7515 5222 **27 Coldharbour E14 9NS**
email: info@thegundocklands.com
dir: *Nearest station: South Quay DLR, Canary Wharf*

Gutsy British food in an historic waterside pub

Renovated a decade ago after a fire gutted the 250-year-old inn which once hosted Lord Nelson's trysts with Lady Emma Hamilton, this former dockers' boozer now wears the spruced-up look of a modern gastropub. There's a smart dining room in the main bar, cosy snugs at the back, and it's all decked out with wooden and slate floors and white linen on the tables. Set out with confit wild boar collar with celeriac remoulade and burnt apple purée ahead of roasted fillet of cod with lemon ricotta ravioli, samphire and caper beurre blanc. An indulgently rich dark chocolate mousse with confit oranges wraps things up in fine style.

Plateau

PLAN 6 B3

Modern French V NOTABLE WINE LIST

tel: 020 7715 7100 **4th Floor, Canada Place, Canada Square, Canary Wharf E14 5ER**
email: plateaureservations@danddlondon.com
dir: *Nearest station: Canary Wharf DLR*

Sophisticated, contemporary fine dining in futuristic landscape

Bag a window table to enjoy the incredible view over Canary Wharf from this fourth-floor restaurant with minimalist decor and an open plan kitchen. Marinated seared scallops, beautifully arranged on a glass dish, are served with cucumber marinated in squid ink, radish and amaranth, and make a popular starter. Innovative main courses include roast loin of rabbit in Parma ham stuffed with kidneys accompanied by a croquette of shoulder, braised baby gem lettuce and barigoule of artichokes, say, or roast monkfish with osso buco sauce, veal tongue and pipérade. A skilful pastry cook is behind a crisp pastry case for salted caramel and chocolate tart with raspberry coulis.

Chef Daniel McGarey **Seats** 120, Pr/dining room 30
Times 11.30-2.30/6-10.30, Closed 25 Dec, 1 Jan, Sun **Prices** Prices not confirmed
Wines 400 bottles over £30, 30 bottles under £30, 24 by glass **Parking** 500
Notes Tasting menu 6 course, Brasserie Sat L 2/3 course £32/£35, Children welcome

Roka Canary Wharf

PLAN 6 C3

Japanese NOTABLE WINE LIST

tel: 020 7636 5228 **1st Floor, 40 Canada Square E14 5FW**
email: infocanarywharf@rokarestaurant.com
dir: *Nearest station: Canary Wharf*

Top-flight Japanese cooking in Canary Wharf

A cool, ultra-modern interior of natural woods befits the setting in Canada Square. Contemporary Japanese robatayaki cuisine is the deal, based on the robata grill (diners sitting alongside can watch the chefs silently working), with first-class fresh produce the kitchen's stock-in-trade. From the grill come scallop skewers with wasabi and shiso, and beef fillet with chilli and spring onions. Seafood maki rolls (the likes of freshwater eel with avocado and cucumber) and sashimi (fatty tuna or squid) make good openers, while set-price brunches and a tasting menu are good ways in to the cuisine. Desserts might be dark chocolate and green tea pudding with crunchy Jivara dark chocolate and pear ice cream.

Chef Libor Dobis **Seats** 105, Pr/dining room 14 **Times** 11.45-3/5.30-11, Closed 25-26 Dec, 1 Jan **Prices** Prices not confirmed **Wines** 152 bottles over £30, 13 by glass **Parking** Canada Sq car parks **Notes** Sun brunch menu options £45/£55/£65, Vegetarian available, Children welcome

LONDON EC1

The Bleeding Heart
PLAN 3 D3

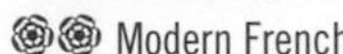 Modern French

tel: 020 7242 2056 **Bleeding Heart Yard, Off Greville St EC1N 8SJ**
email: bookings@bleedingheart.co.uk
dir: *Nearest station: Farringdon, Chancery Lane*

Discreet and romantic Hatton Garden favourite

Named after the courtyard where 17th-century 'It girl' Lady Elizabeth Hatton was killed by her jealous lover, this bastion of French cooking has atmosphere in spades. The cellar restaurant is popular for business lunches and romantic dinners. The kitchen deals in French fare built on sound British produce. Start with ballotine of confit duck and chicken with pistachio, saffron jelly and apple and raisin chutney, followed by an assiette comprising suckling pig and crackling with an apricot and sage faggot, a crispy pig's trotter cromesquis, fondant potato and Bramley apple sauce. To finish, the decadence of dark chocolate delice and caramel honeycomb is tempered by fresh mandarin and orange coulis.

Chef Julian Marshall **Seats** 110, Pr/dining room 40
Times 12-3/6-10.30, Closed Xmas & New Year (10 days), Sat-Sun (Bistro open Sat) **Prices** Prices not confirmed **Wines** 360 bottles over £30, 40 bottles under £30, 23 by glass **Parking** 20 evening only, NCP nearby **Notes** Vegetarian available, Children 7 yrs+

Le Café du Marché
PLAN 3 E3

 Traditional French

tel: 020 7608 1609 **Charterhouse Mews, Charterhouse Square EC1M 6AH**
dir: *Nearest station: Barbican*

Gallic cooking in a classically converted warehouse

This place drips classic cross-Channel country auberge style with its bare-brick walls, French posters, jazz pianist and candlelit tables set in a rustic-chic converted Victorian warehouse. The scene thus set, you can expect unreconstructed French provincial dishes on an uncomplicated two- or three-course fixed price menu – honest, peasant cooking built on fresh, well-sourced materials. Start with classic fish soup with croûtons, rouille and grated gruyère, and progress to pan-fried venison with cauliflower purée, apricot chutney and port sauce, or two might share a grilled leg of Pyrenean milk-fed lamb with flageolet beans and Madeira sauce. Finish with a chocolate and caramel bavarois, or the splendid selection of French cheeses.

Chef Simon Cottard **Seats** 120, Pr/dining room 65 **Times** 12-2.30/6-10, Closed Xmas, New Year, Etr, BHs, Sun, L Sat **Prices** Prices not confirmed **Parking** Next door (small charge) **Notes** Vegetarian available, Children welcome

The Clove Club
PLAN 3 H5

Modern British V

tel: 020 7729 6496 **Shoreditch Town Hall, 380 Old St EC1V 9LT**
email: hello@thecloveclub.com
dir: *Nearest station: Old St*

Magical culinary mystery tour in an old town hall

Shoreditch Town Hall was considered quite the showpiece when it opened back in the 1860s. As Shoreditch developed into a trendy hotspot in the 21st century, this grand dame of a building morphed into an arts and events venue, or, as they themselves put it, a 'non-traditional creative space'. The Clove Club is right at home in this setting with its casual vibe, chunky wooden floors and tables, and open-to-view kitchen pass which positively buzzes with activity. Note that making a reservation for dinner involves payment in advance via a pre-paid ticket system (lunch does not require such a commitment). At dinner, choose either the five-course or the 'extended dinner menu' – nine courses FYI – and expect an array of creative snacks to precede the officially declared courses. What arrives is blisteringly creative and contemporary, with unusual ingredients, imaginative combinations and inventive presentations. Slow-poached oyster with beef jelly and grilled cream is a compelling mix of flavours, flamed red mullet sashimi keeps good company with blood orange, wild fennel and garum (a fermented fish sauce that dates back to Roman times), and a thrilling meat course might be a little pancake of devilled Lincolnshire chicken. Among sweet courses, burnt clementine and buttermilk mousse is a hit. There's an inspired bar menu, too.

Chef Isaac McHale, Tim Spedding **Seats** 43 **Times** 12-4/6-12, Closed Xmas, New Year, Sun, L Mon **Prices** Tasting menu £95-£160, Starter fr £4.60, Main £32 **Wines** 85 bottles over £30, 2 bottles under £30, 18 by glass **Notes** Fixed price L/D 5 course £65/£115, Tasting menu 9 course, Children welcome

Club Gascon
PLAN 3 E3

French V NOTABLE WINE LIST

tel: 020 7600 6144 & 7600 1961 **57 West Smithfields EC1A 9DS**
email: info@clubgascon.com
dir: *Nearest station: Barbican, Farringdon, St Paul's*

Innovation and excitement from southwest France

Close to Smithfield Market and once a Lyons' teashop, this grand, oak-floored, marble-walled, high-ceilinged space, with blue banquettes at closely set tables, has been home to Pascal Aussignac's vibrant interpretation of the cooking of southwest France for almost 20 years. Knowledgeable staff are keen to help and include a sommelier offering 400-plus choices from the southern French wine list. The earthy dishes of Gascony and the southwest may be the root of Aussignac's inspiration, but you won't get peasant cooking here. The two-course set lunch is a bargain, but you can indulge yourself with the five-course seasonal market menu or a carte of tapas-sized dishes offered in five themed sections. The very best produce is selected and imported, ensuring that dishes, whether duck tartare, winkles, salted cod and aromatic artichokes or 'ultimate' foie gras, caviar d'Aquitaine and oceanic crisp, are of equally impressive quality. Glazed black cod is perfectly cooked and served on a sweet artichoke purée, with verjuice and deliciously crunchy grapes, while a scatter of pomegranate seeds adds sweetness, or you might try roast venison, cauliflower ribs, bone marrow and grand veneur sauce. Desserts are similarly notable – maybe rhubarb variation, hibiscus and blood orange rocks, or aromatic glazed pears, with frosted geranium, crumble and pickled gooseberries.

Chef Pascal Aussignac **Seats** 42 **Times** 12-2/6.30-10, Closed Xmas, New Year, BHs, Sun, L Sat **Prices** Fixed L 2 course £29, Fixed D 3 course £35, Tasting menu £68-£105, Starter £13.50-£16.50, Main £14-£27, Dessert £9-£14 **Wines** 400 bottles over £30, 30 bottles under £30, 15 by glass **Parking** NCP opposite restaurant **Notes** Tasting menu 5 course, Children welcome

Le Comptoir Gascon
PLAN 3 E3

Modern French

tel: 020 7608 0851 **61-63 Charterhouse St EC1M 6HJ**
email: info@comptoirgascon.com
dir: *Nearest station: Farringdon, Barbican, St Paul's*

Gutsy French dishes near Smithfield Market

Comptoir deals in the gutsy food of southwest France, delivering simple market-driven cooking with full-on flavours. Seared cod, baby gem and chorizo, wild garlic sauce is well executed, and desserts – like lemon tart or a classic chocolate fondant – keep things simple yet show acute technical ability in their making. The decor fits the bill with its modern-rustic vibe; exposed brickwork and ducting, dinky elbow-to-elbow wooden tables, small velour-covered chairs and wines tantalising from their shelves, while the miniscule deli counter – with displays of breads, conserves, pastries and the like – offers supplies to take away. Well-chosen wines are from southwest France... where else?

Chef Pascal Aussignac **Seats** 38 **Times** 12-2.15/6.30-10.15, Closed Xmas-31 Dec, BHs, Sun-Mon **Prices** Fixed L 3 course £26, Fixed D 3 course £26, Starter £6-£9.50, Main £9.50-£18.50, Dessert £4-£9 **Parking** NCP 50 mtrs **Notes** Vegetarian available, Children welcome

Hix Oyster & Chop House

PLAN 3 E3

Modern British V

tel: 020 7017 1930 **36-37 Greenhill Rents, Cowcross St EC1M 6BN**
email: reservations@hixoysterandchophouse.co.uk
dir: *Nearest station: Farringdon*

Accomplished ingredient-led Brit cooking in chilled-out Clerkenwell

Mark Hix's first outfit in a burgeoning portfolio perfectly embraces its Smithfield setting. Wooden floors, tiled walls and ceiling fans characterise the cool, pared-down space, pepped up by edgy artwork and a jazz soundtrack. The kitchen takes a direct approach, reflecting the Hix credo of quality seasonal ingredients treated with simplicity, respect and flair. Wild ingredients play their part, as do native and rock oysters, and fish such as whole Dover sole and béarnaise, though meats are a strong draw too – Barnsley lamb chop and grilled kidney come with bubble-and-squeak – Round off with home-spun desserts, such as spotted dick with butter and syrup.

Chef Jamie Guy **Seats** 65 **Times** 12-close, All-day dining, Closed 25-26 Dec, BHs, L Sat **Prices** Fixed L 2 course £19.50, Fixed D 3 course £22.50, Starter £6.50-£15.95, Main £12.95-£40, Dessert £3.50-£7.25 **Wines** 94 bottles over £30, 4 bottles under £30, 18 by glass **Parking** On street (meter) **Notes** D served from 5.30pm, Sunday L £23.95-£27.95, Children welcome

Malmaison Charterhouse Square

PLAN 3 E3

Modern French

tel: 020 3750 9402 **18-21 Charterhouse Square, Clerkenwell EC1M 6AH**
email: athwaites@malmaison.com **web:** www.malmaison.com
dir: *Nearest station: Barbican*

Modern French cooking in boutique surroundings

Like other hotels in the group, this branch is done out in best boutique fashion, with dramatic crimson and purple interiors, a sultrily lit bar and a brasserie in deep brown tones. The order of the day is lively modern French cooking with interesting variations. Starters include carpaccio with parmesan and truffle dressing, and tuna tartare with wasabi, pickled ginger, avocado and sesame and soy dressing. Main courses show the same range, from herb-crusted rack of lamb with Parmentier potatoes and minty salsa verde to Goan-style moules frites. There are steaks too, and, for dessert, puddings such as pineapple carpaccio with mint, lime, chilli and coconut sorbet.

Chef John Woodward **Seats** 70, Pr/dining room 14 **Times** 12-2.30/6-10.30, Closed L Sat **Prices** Fixed L 2 course £19.95, Fixed D 3 course £24.95, Starter £5.50-£14.50, Main £15-£55, Dessert £2-£6.50 **Wines** 24 bottles over £30, 14 bottles under £30, 30 by glass **Parking** 4, Charterhouse Sq **Notes** Sun brunch, Pre-theatre £19.95, Afternoon tea £17.50, Sunday L £21.95, Vegetarian available, Children welcome

The Modern Pantry

PLAN 3 E4

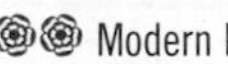 Modern Fusion

tel: 020 7553 9210 **47-48 St John's Square, Clerkenwell EC1V 4JJ**
email: clerkenwell@themodernpantry.co.uk
dir: *Nearest station: Farringdon, Barbican*

Creative fusion food in a trendy part of town

Set in two listed Georgian townhouses on St John's Square, this breezy all day eatery is an intimate, relaxed backdrop for a lively trek through the world of fusion cooking. Expect influences from around the globe, delivered in inspired combinations and stimulating contrasts of flavour and texture. Roam from seared diver-caught scallops with squid ink risotto, hijiki (an Asian sea vegetable), and a relish of beetroot and moromi, to roast cod with baked cauliflower, mustard and bacon sauce, mole rojo crumbs, and a pomegranate and fennel salad. For dessert, poached cranberries and gingerbread crumb add a novel spin to tonka bean pannacotta.

Chef Anna Hansen, Elizabeth Stables **Seats** 110, Pr/dining room 60 **Times** 12-10.30, All-day dining, Closed Xmas, New Year, Aug BH **Prices** Starter £6-£9.50, Main £17-£22, Dessert £2.80-£7.50 **Wines** 61 bottles over £30, 13 bottles under £30, 14 by glass **Parking** On street (meter) **Notes** Brunch menu Sat-Sun, Vegetarian available, Children welcome

The Montcalm London City at The Brewery

PLAN 3 G4

Traditional British

tel: 020 7614 0100 **52 Chiswell St EC1Y 4SB**
email: reservations@themontcalmlondoncity.co.uk
web: www.themontcalmlondoncity.co.uk
dir: *Nearest station: Liverpool St, Barbican, Moorgate*

Smart hotel with a taste of Britain on the menu

Samuel Whitbread built up one of the UK's foremost beer brands on this spot, and part of his one-time Georgian brewery has been converted into this swanky hotel. There are a couple of dining options in situ, all entirely in keeping with the Georgian setting. The all-day menu deals in modern classics such as a posh burger, while the main carte offers up a little more refinement in the form of celeriac velouté with pig's cheek, scrumpy mustard and choucroute, and a main course dish of pan-fried cod with confit chicken wings. Desserts are a sophisticated bunch including blood orange tart with heather honey and stem ginger ice cream.

Moro

PLAN 3 D4

Islamic, Mediterranean

tel: 020 7833 8336 **34-36 Exmouth Market EC1R 4QE**
email: info@moro.co.uk
dir: *Nearest station: Farringdon, Angel*

Lively Moorish and Spanish cuisine in a long-stayer

Sam and Samantha Clark's Moorish food takes its cue from Spain via North Africa to the eastern Mediterranean, a popular formula with regulars who spill out onto pavement tables in fine weather. You can perch at the bar washing down tapas with splendid sherries or sink into a harem-style bolster cushion at one of the closely-packed tables. Friendly staff keep it all together, while inventive menus deliver colourful dishes of big flavours. Try palourde clams in an invigorating herby broth of peas and salsa verde, then gold-standard Norwegian Skrei cod matched with tangy barberries, sweet herbs and chickpeas. Finish with a citrus blast of yogurt cake with pistachios and pomegranate.

Chef Samuel & Samantha Clark **Seats** 90 **Times** 12-2.30/6-10.30, Closed Xmas, New Year, BHs, D Sun **Prices** Prices not confirmed **Wines** 72 bottles over £30, 21 bottles under £30, 12 by glass **Parking** NCP Farringdon Rd **Notes** Sunday L, Vegetarian available, Children welcome

LONDON EC1 *continued*

St John

PLAN 3 E3

British

tel: 020 7251 0848 **26 St John St EC1M 4AY**
email: reservations@stjohnrestaurant.com
dir: *Nearest station: Farringdon*

Nose-to-tail eating at its best

St John has become something of a pilgrimage spot for anyone claiming foodie credentials. Set up in 1994 in a former Georgian smokehouse by Smithfield Market, the 'nose-to-tail' eating philosophy championing unglamorous, lesser-used cuts has turned on a generation of chefs to the robust, gutsy style. The long-running roast bone marrow with parsley salad is a surefire starter, followed by a rustic plate of braised rabbit with Savoy cabbage and green herb sauce. It's not all about the meat though – how about skate with monk's beard and capers? Desserts are equally comfort-spun, from the signature Eccles cake and Lancashire cheese, to buttermilk pudding with poached rhubarb.

Chef Jonathan Woolway **Seats** 110, Pr/dining room 18
Times 12-3/6-11, Closed Xmas, New Year, BHs, L Sat, D Sun **Prices** Starter £7-£15, Main £15-£28, Dessert £5-£9 **Wines** 85 bottles over £30, 18 bottles under £30, 17 by glass **Parking** On street (meter) **Notes** Feasting menu groups 10 or more, Vegetarian available, Children welcome

Smiths of Smithfield, Top Floor

PLAN 3 E3

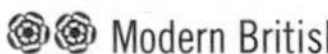
Modern British

tel: 020 7251 7950 **67-77 Charterhouse St EC1M 6HJ**
email: reservations@smithsofsmithfield.co.uk
dir: *Nearest station: Farringdon, Barbican, Chancery Lane*

Terrific views, buzzy City-suit vibe and spot-on ingredients

Smack opposite Smithfield Market, Top Floor offers rooftop views from its long, light-filled room through full-drop sliding glass doors and dream-ticket decked terrace. The kitchen produces light, modern, refined dishes of flair and flavour. Rare-breed beef steaks play a starring role (perhaps succulent 28-day dry-aged South Devon sirloin), though fish is also good – witness sparkling-fresh pan-fried halibut served with warm tartare sauce, vanilla mash and spinach. Finish with wobbly buttermilk pannacotta perfection, pepped up by honey-roast quince. White linen, funky dining chairs, semi-circular leather banquettes and unstuffy service are spot on, while wines are a serious bunch.

AA RESTAURANT OF THE YEAR FOR LONDON 2016–17

Sosharu

PLAN 3 E4

Japanese **NEW**

tel: 020 3805 2304 **64 Turnmill St EC1M 5RR**
email: reservations@sosharulondon.com
dir: *Nearest station: Farringdon*

Jason Atherton's inspirational foray into Japanese cuisine

Jason Atherton's restaurant portfolio expanded to seven London operations at the start of 2016 with the opening of this Japanese izakaya-style restaurant and bar (the name means 'social', in keeping with his other venues). The place has a glossy, suitably minimalist aesthetic inspired by traditional Japanese homes, and includes a downstairs cocktail bar and a 10-seat chef's table that goes by the name of Kisetsu. After years spent in stellar Japanese establishments, Alex Craciun is thoroughly immersed in Japanese culinary ways, and heads up the team of knife-wielding chefs who deliver exemplary sushi, sashimi and refined, highly-detailed dishes that offer plenty to entertain the eye and palate. Raw sea bream is rolled and filled with crispy potato shreds and pointed up with orange zest and wild garlic flowers, or you might set out with benchmark squid tempura with shredded papaya and spring onion. Main courses are defined by their look-at-me artistry, but every detail makes sense: pork belly comes in a bowl with udon noodles and king oyster mushrooms, all immersed in a punchy pork broth; sukiyaki hotpot of Wagyu beef layers flavours of glass noodles, leeks and shiitaki mushrooms. If you're prepared to pass on the impressive wine list, there are 50-plus sakes to explore.

Chef Alex Craciun, Jason Atherton **Seats** 74, Pr/dining room 6
Times 12-2.15/5.30-10, Closed Xmas, BHs, Sun **Prices** Starter £5-£15, Main £15-£25, Dessert £8 **Wines** 110 bottles over £30, 11 bottles under £30, 13 by glass **Parking** On street **Notes** L 6 dishes to share £29.50, Vegetarian available, Children welcome

LONDON EC2

L'Anima

PLAN 3 H4

Italian

tel: 020 7422 7000 **1 Snowden St, Broadgate West EC2A 2DQ**
email: info@lanima.co.uk
dir: *Nearest station: Liverpool St*

Southern Italian cooking with a sense of style

Classic southern Italian dishes are presented with contemporary flair at L'Anima. Home-made pasta is excellent, perhaps in the garganelli tubes that form the basis for a ragù of wild boar and pistachios, while fragrant saffron risotto is adorned with roast squab and Grana Padano. Mains might offer Sardinian shellfish stew or rabbit agrodolce, or there is cod marinated in liquorice and chilli, with burned baby gem and red onion purée. Bookending it all come sterling antipasti such as truffled pounded beef, or crab with apple, and unmissable dolci along the lines of monte bianco, a mountainous creation of meringue, chestnuts and vanilla cream in a sauce of mixed berries.

L'Anima Café

PLAN 3 H4

Italian

tel: 020 7422 7080 **10 Appold St EC2A 2AP**
email: info@lanimacafe.co.uk
dir: *Nearest station: Liverpool St*

Southern Italian soul food

A deli with imported produce and meals to go, a lively bar for all-day dining and an easy-going restaurant, this joint reflects the owner's passion for the flavours of Southern Italy. It's cool, casual and contemporary. Kick off with grilled calamari with a flavoursome pappa al pomodoro, or creamy Puglian burrata with roast peppers and anchovies. There's a wood-fired oven so the pizza is a good bet (the Aglio with smoked garlic and sun-dried tomatoes, say), or go for the wonderfully earthy flavours of rabbit stew. With top-notch pasta and desserts such as pannacotta with blueberries and grappa, plus regional Italian wines, L'Anima Café is one to know about.

Boisdale of Bishopsgate

PLAN 3 H3

Traditional British, French, Scottish

tel: 020 7283 1763 **Swedeland Court, 202 Bishopsgate EC2M 4NR**
email: manager@boisdale-city.co.uk
dir: *Nearest station: Liverpool St*

Cooking showcasing Scotland's best produce

Tucked away down a Dickensian alley near Liverpool Street station, Boisdale's City branch occupies an atmospheric vaulted basement. The cooking is simple, classic stuff founded on thoroughbred Scottish meats and seafood, so starters predictably include smoked salmon – perhaps with dressed crab, pickled vegetables and orange dressing – the range broadened by the likes of sautéed sweetbreads with maple-glazed bacon and mint hollandaise. Main courses tend to be safe bets: prime steaks with béarnaise, say, or guinea fowl with potato dumplings, wild garlic, morel mushrooms and parmesan and sage velouté. Finish with bread-and-butter pudding with orange marmalade and Glenfiddich custard.

City Social

PLAN 3 H2

Modern British, European

tel: 020 7877 7703 **Tower 42 EC2N 1HQ**
email: reservations@citysociallondon.com
dir: *Nearest station: Liverpool St*

High-flying cooking in a high-rise city tower

Located on the 24th floor of the old NatWest Tower, this sky-high restaurant offers panoramic London skyline views that befits one of the capital's most influential chef-patrons. Jason Atherton has enjoyed huge success with the likes of Pollen Street Social and Social Eating House and this City outpost delivers similarly top-drawer contemporary food. A sleek art deco look of golds and blacks, combined with jaw-dropping views from floor-to-ceiling windows adds a James Bond-style grandeur, as does the bar with its city slicker-friendly cocktails and hearty bar snacks. Executive Chef Paul Walsh extracts maximum flavour from humble ingredients and the well-presented, globally-influenced dishes have roots firmly planted in the classics. Try an opener of slow-cooked Tidenham duck with a harmonious match of amarena cherries, pistachio yogurt and hints of five spice and dried vinegar. Those searching for more international flavours can look to a main of Cornish line-caught cod and squid teamed with spicy ponzu, bok choy, miso aïoli and seaweed or Middle White pork loin and belly served with violet artichoke, shallots and black onion crackling. The technical prowess continues with a light and airy Kentish morello cherry soufflé with cherry jam and chocolate ice cream. The lively, interesting wine list offers plenty of diversity.

Chef Paul Walsh, Jason Atherton **Seats** 90, Pr/dining room 24 **Times** 12-2.45/6-10.30, Closed 25 Dec, 1 Jan, BHs, Sun, L Sat **Prices** Starter £12-£16, Main £24-£41, Dessert £9.50-£16 **Wines** 209 bottles over £30, 5 bottles under £30, 16 by glass **Parking** Finsbury Circus NCP **Notes** Tasting menu at Chef's table, Private dining menu fr £65, Vegetarian available, Children welcome

Coq d'Argent

PLAN 3 G2

French

tel: 020 7395 5000 **1 Poultry EC2R 8EJ**
email: coqdargent.co.uk
dir: *Nearest station: Bank*

French cuisine and rooftop terraces with Square Mile views

A stylish, modern, sharp-suit confection that comes properly dressed for the accomplished, big flavoured French cooking. Menus boast bags of luxury for City high rollers, from oysters, lobster or caviar to deep-wallet mains like fillet of beef Rossini teamed with pan-fried foie gras, sautéed mushrooms, a Madeira sauce and black truffle. Otherwise, for lighter options, check out the likes of roasted sea bream fillet served with an étuvée of artichoke, fennel and salsify in olive oil. Desserts, from classic vanilla crème brûlée to a warm gingerbread sponge slice (with stem ginger and cinnamon ice cream) likewise impress, while the wine list is a serious mover and service professional without being snooty.

Chef Damien Rigollet **Seats** 150 **Times** 11.30-4/5.30-11, Closed BHs, D Sun **Prices** Prices not confirmed **Wines** 600 bottles over £30, 60 bottles under £30, 30 by glass **Notes** Top table 3 course £25, Sunday L, Vegetarian available, Children welcome

Duck & Waffle

PLAN 3 H2

British, European

tel: 020 3640 7310 **110 Bishopsgate EC2N 4AY**
email: duckandwaffle@sushisamba.com
dir: *Nearest station: Liverpool St*

Mesmerising views 24/7

In a modern space open 24 hours a day, you can rock up first thing for a Belgian waffle known as the 'Full Elvis' (peanut butter and jelly) or a high-quality English breakfast, or anytime for the trademark duck & waffle (crispy leg confit, fried duck egg, mustard maple syrup). Small plates are the way to go (bigger plate options are available), with the likes of 'East End Eels' – excellent smoky fish with samphire and horseradish – and a luxe yellowfin tuna dish with foie gras. Desserts might include Spanish-style torrejas with cinnamon ice cream and orange posset with Aperol granité.

Chef Daniel Doherty **Seats** 260, Pr/dining room 18 **Times** 12-12, All-day dining **Prices** Prices not confirmed **Wines** 199 bottles over £30, 1 bottle under £30, 15 by glass **Notes** Breakfast, Wknd brunch, Late night menu, Sunday L, Vegetarian available, Children welcome

LONDON EC2 *continued*

Eastway Brasserie

PLAN 3 H3

British NEW

tel: 020 7618 7400 **ANdAZ Liverpool St, 40 Liverpool St EC2M 7QN**
email: londondining@andaz.com **web:** www.eastwaybrasserie.com
dir: *Nearest station: Liverpool St*

Comfort food all day long

There are seven restaurants and bars to choose from in the ANdAZ Liverpool Street London, to give it its full name, one of which is this take on a New York brasserie. It has its own entrance and with its open-to-view kitchen and massed ranks of tables it fulfils the brasserie brief. Open all day from breakfast to dinner, the carte offers up clam and mussel bisque to start, followed by pappardelle enriched with a rich ragout of slow-braised lamb. Steaks are cooked on the grill and served up with traditional sauces, burgers are de rigueur given the American USP, while a fishy main course might be roast stone bass with Thai green curry sauce with clams.

Chef Sam Dunleavy **Seats** 108 **Times** 12-11, All-day dining **Prices** Fixed L 2 course £21, Fixed D 3 course £25, Starter £7-£15, Main £12.50-£19, Dessert £6-£8 **Wines** 10 bottles over £30, 8 bottles under £30, 18 by glass **Notes** Wknd brunch, Vegetarian available

Eyre Brothers

PLAN 3 H4

Spanish, Portuguese

tel: 020 7613 5346 **70 Leonard St EC2A 4QX**
email: eyrebros@btconnect.com
dir: *Nearest station: Old St Exit 4*

Big, enticing Iberian flavours in Shoreditch

Darkwood floors, deep-brown banquettes and curvy wooden seats provide the setting for some impressive Iberian-based cooking, with the kitchen delivering full-on flavours from top-class produce treated with integrity and skill. An opener of boquerónes with walnuts, garlic and parsley evokes the flavours of the Mediterranean, or there might be morcilla with turnip greens and black-eyed beans in sherry vinegar and garlic. Follow with the authentic flavours of Portuguese-style pheasant braised in red wine with smoked tocino, chestnuts and mushrooms, or grilled dorada with aïoli and cauliflower sautéed with lemon and parsley. Sharing plates are other possibilities, and to end might be Galician almond tart.

Chef David Eyre, Joao Cleto **Seats** 85 **Times** 12-3/6.30-10.30, Closed Xmas-New Year, BHs, Sun, L Sat **Prices** Starter £6-£12, Main £12-£25, Dessert £2-£6 **Wines** 39 bottles over £30, 25 bottles under £30, 15 by glass **Parking** On street **Notes** Vegetarian available, Children welcome

HKK

PLAN 3 H4

Modern Chinese V

tel: 020 3535 1888 **Broadgate West, 88 Worship St EC2A 2BE**
email: reservations@hkklondon.com
dir: *Nearest station: Liverpool St, Shoreditch High St*

First-class Chinese cooking in revitalised City

Global restaurant group Hakkasan's City of London bridgehead stands in a street that exemplifies how rapidly the financial district is changing. Less than a working lifetime ago, it was a gastronomic desert round here; now this minimalist, clean-lined Chinese restaurant is typical of what defines dining in the capital's East Central district. An office-like entrance takes you into a dining area with a glass-walled kitchen, smart, lowish tables, chairs with plumped-up, slate-blue cushions, and comfortable banquettes. Even the pleasingly hard-yet-spongy flooring is attention seeking. Head chef Tong's creative take on modern Chinese cooking permits occasional European twists on a range of menus that include a multi-course tasting, with a vegetarian option. HKK is not for penny-pinchers, for this is the land of the fat annual bonus. Whether it offers value for money you can judge after a tasting menu dinner of, in part, chrysanthemum supreme seafood soup, wild sea bass with black truffle and balsamic vinegar, and grilled Japanese Wagyu beef with king sanpei sauce. On Saturday afternoons only, two people may opt for the Duck and Champagne menu featuring cherrywood-roasted whole Peking duck. Desserts pursue the fusion theme with ideas such as caramelised pineapple, kataifi and vanilla ice cream.

Chef Tong Chee Hwee **Seats** 63, Pr/dining room 14 **Times** 12-2.30/6-10, Closed BHs (some), Sun **Prices** Fixed L 3 course £29, Tasting menu £58-£88, Starter £7-£17.80, Main £12-£28.80, Dessert £8-£8.90 **Wines** 144 bottles over £30, 4 bottles under £30, 22 by glass **Parking** NCP, on street **Notes** Sat L duck & champagne menu 5 course £49, Children welcome

Manicomio City

PLAN 3 F2

Modern Italian

tel: 020 7726 5010 **Gutter Ln EC2V 8AS**
email: gutterlane@manicomio.co.uk
dir: *Nearest station: St Paul's*

Contemporary Italian with a cool City vibe

The city branch of Manicomio occupies a three-tiered, Sir Norman Foster-designed glass building with a buzzy ground-floor terrace and café-bar (open from breakfast) and a sleek first-floor restaurant dressed up with a decor as sober as the suited-and-booted city types at its black leather seats and white-linen-clad tables. Light and fresh contemporary Italian cooking that pays due respect to the provenance, seasonality and quality of its ingredients is the deal here, so start with rabbit tagliatelle with white wine, lemon, sage and capers, followed by line-caught hake with fregola, kohlrabi, tomato, wild fennel and Tropea onions, and finish with thyme and caramel pannacotta.

Merchants Tavern

PLAN 3 H4

@@@ Modern European

tel: 020 7060 5335 & 7033 1879 **36 Charlotte Rd EC2A 3PG**
email: booking@merchantstavern.co.uk
dir: *Nearest station: Liverpool St, Old St, Shoreditch High St*

Classy, flavour-packed cooking in a converted warehouse

This collaboration of Angela Hartnett, head chef Neil Borthwick and the founders of the Canteen group – high culinary credentials indeed – occupies a trendily converted Victorian warehouse, still to be seen with exposed brickwork, a huge skylight and a parquet floor. It's a large space, with comfortable semicircular banquettes and armed chairs at round dining tables, and a log-burner in the bar area. The carte is an enterprising slate of with-it ideas, running from small plates – perhaps crispy pork with Asian pickles, or oxtail croquettes – and plates for sharing, among them best end of veal with confit garlic, carrots and sautéed potatoes, to the full works, with the opportunity to sit at the kitchen counter and choose a bespoke menu. Starters include such beguiling combinations as duck raviolo with cabbage and mushroom consommé, and pickled mackerel with crème fraîche and potato salad. Main courses show the same approach to balance and vibrant flavours, bringing on ox cheek with smoked potato purée and black pepper, and roast chicken with roast onions, celeriac purée and Swiss chard. Piscine options may include accurately timed hake fillet in a brown butter crumb accompanied by salsify and lemon thyme, and puddings are compelling: try Yorkshire rhubarb with custard and pistachio meringue, or floating islands.

Chef Neil Borthwick **Seats** 85, Pr/dining room 22 **Times** 12-3/6-11, Closed 25-26 Dec, 1 Jan **Prices** Fixed L 2 course fr £18, Starter £7.50-£10, Main £16-£23, Dessert £7.50-£8.50 **Wines** 61 bottles over £30, 7 bottles under £30, 22 by glass **Parking** NCP Great Eastern St **Notes** Sunday L £20-£25, Vegetarian available, Children welcome

Miyako

PLAN 3 H3

@ Japanese V

tel: 020 7618 7100 **ANdAZ London, 40 Liverpool St EC2M 7QN**
email: london.restres@andaz.com **web:** www.andazdining.com/miyako
dir: *Nearest station: Liverpool St*

Traditional Japanese menu including takeaway boxes

Beside Liverpool Street station, Miyako is within the ANdAZ London hotel, although it has its own entrance where queues form at lunchtime for takeaway boxes. The restaurant itself has a cool, uncluttered look, thanks to large windows, walls veneered in pale wood and bamboo, and black-lacquered tables and chairs. A traditional Japanese menu takes in sushi such as octopus on hand-pressed rice, sashimi, and tempura prawns in thin, crisp batter, while among the specials may be wakame with udon noodles, or miso soup packed with salmon, scallops, sea bass, vegetables and tofu. Finish with yuzu macaroons with green tea ice cream and lemon crumble.

Chef Kosei Sakamoto **Seats** 30 **Times** 12-10.30, All-day dining, Closed Xmas, New Year, Sat-Sun **Prices** Prices not confirmed **Wines** 5 bottles over £30, 2 bottles under £30, 4 by glass **Parking** NCP London Wall **Notes** Children welcome

SUSHISAMBA London

PLAN 3 H2

@@ Japanese, Brazilian, Peruvian NOTABLE WINE LIST

tel: 020 3640 7330 **110 Bishopsgate EC2N 4AY**
email: reservationslondon@sushisamba.com
dir: *Nearest station: Liverpool St*

Trendy Japanese-meets-South American cuisine with capital views

Not the most famous of London's new skyscrapers, but Heron Tower is certainly up there in the culinary stakes. Japan, Brazil and Peru provide inspiration for a menu that deals in small grazing plates of Asian and South American fusion food. High-quality ingredients are a feature, not least the Kobe beef, which you can have cooked on a hot stone (ishiyaki) or sizzled on the robata grill. Flavours are spot on in options such as yellowtail tiradito with jalapeño and lemongrass, and the hot stuff is as equally on the money (lamb chop with red miso and lime, say). There's straight-up sushi, too, and desserts such as chocolate banana cake.

Chef Claudio Cardoso **Seats** 134, Pr/dining room 40 **Times** 11.30am-mdnt, All-day dining **Prices** Prices not confirmed **Wines** 189 bottles over £30, 1 bottle under £30, 13 by glass **Notes** Vegan & gluten free menus, Vegetarian available, Children welcome

LONDON EC3

Caravaggio

PLAN 3 H2

@ Modern Italian

tel: 020 7626 6206 **107-112 Leadenhall St EC3A 4AF**
email: caravaggio@etruscarestaurants.com **web:** www.caravaggiorestaurant.co.uk
dir: *Nearest station: Aldgate, Fenchurch St, Liverpool St*

Smart City Italian in former banking hall

There's a hint of 1930s ocean liner about this Square Mile Italian, the former banking hall with ornate lofty ceilings, splendid light fittings and an imposing staircase leading up to a mezzanine gallery. The pace is full-on at lunch when City suits turn up for the mix of traditional and contemporary regional Italian cooking, while evenings are more chilled. This is food of simplicity, generosity and flavour. Open with beetroot carpaccio and Langhe goat cheese, squeeze in Tuscan sausage penne, and then set about baked sea bass with black rice and Pernod sauce. Desserts fit the bill, including Piedmontese chocolate pudding with amaretti.

Chef Faliero Lenta **Seats** 150 **Times** 12-3/6.30-10, Closed Xmas, BHs, Sat-Sun **Prices** Fixed L 2 course £17.50, Fixed D 3 course £23, Starter £7-£13.90, Main £12.80-£22.50, Dessert £6.25-£7 **Wines** 120 bottles over £30, 30 bottles under £30, 17 by glass **Parking** On street **Notes** Vegetarian available, Children welcome

LONDON EC3 *continued*

Chamberlains Restaurant

PLAN 3 H2

Modern British, Seafood

tel: 020 7648 8690 **23-25 Leadenhall Market EC3V 1LR**
email: info@chamberlainsoflondon.com **web:** www.chamberlainsoflondon.com
dir: *Nearest station: Bank, Monument*

Super-fresh fish in the heart of the City

Spread over three floors amid the Victorian splendour of Leadenhall Market, Chamberlains buzzes with the power-lunch crowd from nearby offices. There's an all-weather terrace beneath the market's glass roof, while huge windows in the lively ground-floor dining room and more intimate mezzanine make for good people-watching. Sea-fresh seafood is what to expect in a menu that mixes classics (lobster bisque or skate wing with nut brown butter) with more modern thinking, setting out with silky butternut squash velouté with foie gras beignet, ahead of cod fillet with couscous, confit shallot, black cabbage and balsamic jus; meat options could run to roast grouse with turnips, crispy potatoes and rosehip jus.

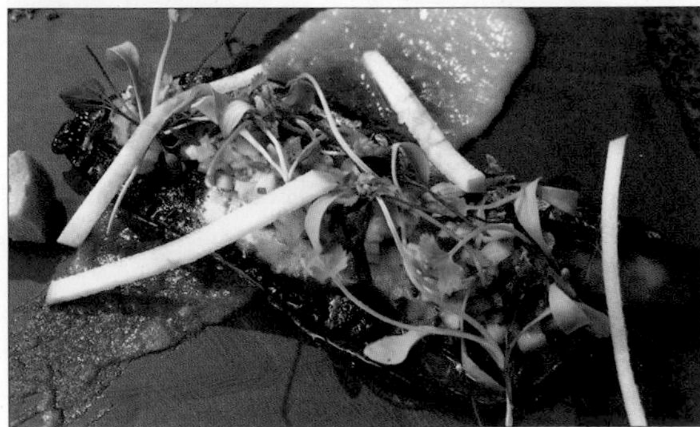

Chef Andrew Jones **Seats** 100, Pr/dining room 55
Times 12-2.30/5.30-9.30, Closed Xmas, New Year & BHs, Sat-Sun **Prices** Fixed L 2 course £19, Fixed D 3 course £29.50, Tasting menu £59, Starter £11.50-£16.50, Main £16.50-£46, Dessert £7-£10.50 **Wines** 76 bottles over £30, 18 bottles under £30, 13 by glass **Notes** Vegetarian available, Children welcome

Restaurant Sauterelle

PLAN 3 G2

Modern European, French

tel: 020 7618 2483 **The Royal Exchange EC3V 3LR**
email: pawelk@danddlondon.com
dir: *Nearest station: Bank*

Confident contemporary cooking in landmark building

Dining amid the Victorian pomp of the historic Royal Exchange certainly adds wow factor to proceedings at glossy Sauterelle, where a starter of seared Isle of Skye scallops with cauliflower mousseline, oyster leaves and toasted olives delivers a light, contemporary touch. Main courses bring medallions of fresh and well-timed monkfish on top of a bed of delicate Sicilian red prawn risotto, or a gamey combo of red-legged partridge with braised Savoy cabbage, crisp Ventrèche bacon and pomegranate that chimes perfectly with both the calendar and blue-blooded surroundings. At dessert, coffee and hazelnut combine decadently in a classic Opéra gâteau, offset by a dark chocolate ball filled with tart cherry coulis.

LONDON EC4

Barbecoa

PLAN 3 F2

Modern

tel: 020 3005 8555 **20 New Change Passage EC4M 9AG**
dir: *Nearest station: St Paul's*

Jamie Oliver's buzzing BBQ joint

Expect a backing track of lively chatter and music at this City temple to meat, flame and smoke. It's a cool glass-sided venue whose macho features – polished stone floor and brickwork – mix with low-slung leather banquettes, funky lighting and wine display cabinets. Cooking by fire, smoke and charcoal is the thing, using flashy bits of kit like robata grills, tandoor ovens, Texan pit smokers and wood-fired ovens. Tuck into signature dry-aged steaks, or try grilled lamb rack or pulled pork shoulder, perhaps with pukka duck-fat chips, while desserts might take in baked vanilla cheesecake with roasted peaches and star-turn Bellini sorbet. A posse of friendly staff keeps the party rolling.

Bread Street Kitchen

PLAN 3 F2

Modern British, European NOTABLE WINE LIST

tel: 020 3030 4050 **10 Bread St EC4M 9AJ**
email: info@breadstreetkitchen.com
dir: *Nearest station: Mansion House, St Pauls, Bank, Cannon St*

Vibrant, City-cool brasserie from the Gordon Ramsay stable

The name suggests a homely wholefood co-operative, but the reality is a cavernous, high-decibel, high-octane city-slicker operation, courtesy of Gordon Ramsay Holdings. Expect a soaring, warehouse-like space that mixes retro and modern looks with art deco references and the feel of a film set from Fritz Lang's *Metropolis*. Battalions of servers dressed in black ricochet to and fro, all friendly, engaging and on the ball, delivering quick-fire dishes from a lengthy all-day roster (including breakfast weekdays). Try potted salt-beef brisket or king crab and apple cocktail, then pork and fennel sausages with braised lentils, veggie cannelloni, or whole poussin cooked on the Josper grill.

Chef Erion Karaj, Paul Shearing **Seats** 250 **Times** 11.30-11, All-day dining, Closed 25-26 Dec, 1 Jan **Prices** Starter £7.50-£12.50, Main £12.50-£37, Dessert £6.50-£12 **Wines** 100+ bottles over £30, 23 bottles under £30, 56 by glass **Parking** Bread St, Watling St **Notes** Breakfast, Wknd brunch, Sunday L, Vegetarian available, Children welcome

The Chancery PLAN 3 D2

Modern European

tel: 020 7831 4000 **9 Cursitor St EC4A 1LL**
email: reservations@thechancery.co.uk
dir: *Nearest station: Chancery Lane*

Intimate, fine-tuned dining in legal land

This bijou restaurant draws in suited and booted professionals from the nearby worlds of law and finance. The kitchen team deliver immaculately presented, inventive modern European dishes, starting out strongly with an open ravioli of suckling pig shoulder with bacon and cider velouté. Next up is immaculately timed poached Cornish cod with lemon-infused prawns, roasted Jerusalem artichokes, fromage frais and wasabi, or you might go for roast guinea fowl with Morteau sausage roll, Savoy cabbage, parsley root and thyme jus gras. A richly indulgent chocolate fondant with walnut ice cream and 'crunchy stuff' hits the spot at dessert, and a well-chosen wine list rounds off a class act.

Chinese Cricket Club PLAN 3 E1

Chinese

tel: 020 7438 8051 **Crowne Plaza London – The City, 19 New Bridge St EC4V 6DB**
email: loncy.ccc@ihg.com
dir: *Nearest station: Temple, St Paul's, Blackfriars*

Classy Chinese in a modern City hotel

Named in honour of the original national Chinese cricket team, which played its first international match in 2009, CCC combines modern techniques with traditional and authentic Szechuan flavours. Prawn and pork sui mai, from the dim sum list, come as four light and fluffy dumplings packed with minced pork and prawn with a dipping sauce of chilli and tamarind. Follow on with tender beef tenderloin with black pepper and spring onions and a soy-based sauce with a serving of noodles, or fried sea bass with sweet-and-sour sauce, or scallops with black beans. Desserts are mainly Western, although a basil ice cream hinting of wasabi comes with dark chocolate tart.

Diciannove PLAN 3 E1

Italian

tel: 020 7438 8052 & 7438 8055 **Crowne Plaza London – The City, 19 New Bridge St EC4V 6DB**
email: loncy.refettorio@ihg.com **web:** www.refettorio.com
dir: *Nearest station: Blackfriars*

Slick Italian cookery in gleaming contemporary style

The slick Italian operation at the heart of the Crowne Plaza City branch looks like the upscale café of a smart contemporary art gallery, all gleaming uncovered surfaces, striped upholstery, and a bar lit in throbbing sunny yellow. A variously sized anything-and-everything platter, Il Supremo, may be the smart start, offering burrata, zucchini fritti, calamari, fennel salami, Tuscan prosciutto and more, much more. At main, rose veal is succulent and tender, and comes with rosemary fried potatoes, asparagus and gremolata, or there could be well-handled fish such as roast halibut on braised leeks and capers. Finish in sublime simplicity with a bowl of warm amarena cherries, ricotta and sweet pistachios.

Lutyens Restaurant PLAN 3 E2

Modern European NOTABLE WINE LIST

tel: 020 7583 8385 **85 Fleet St EC4Y 1AE**
email: info@lutyens-restaurant.com
dir: *Nearest station: Chancery Lane, St Paul's, Blackfriars*

Accomplished modern brasserie cooking in stylish setting

The elegant Lutyens-designed building now bears the Conran stamp, with its cool pastel tones, pale wood, and pixellated marble floors. Chef Henrik Ritzen's light-touch cooking is rooted in classic French technique but there are subtle hints of his Nordic roots. This is seen in an elegant starter of smoked eel with beetroot, Gourmande pear and bitter leaves based on superb raw materials, or a main-course involving haunch of venison teamed with pickled walnut purée, roasted celeriac and grey leg chanterelles. Fish is handled with equal skill – perhaps partnering poached monkfish with cockles, swede, lettuce and Jamón Ibérico de Bellota. Dessert brings spiced quince soufflé with stem ginger ice cream

Chef Henrik Ritzen **Seats** 120, Pr/dining room 26 **Times** 12-3/6-10, Closed Xmas & BHs, Sat-Sun **Prices** Prices not confirmed **Wines** 514 bottles over £30, 37 bottles under £30, 40 by glass **Parking** On street after 7pm, NCP **Notes** Vegetarian available, Children welcome

28-50 Wine Workshop & Kitchen PLAN 3 D2

Modern European

tel: 020 7242 8877 **140 Fetter Ln EC4A 1BT**
email: info@2850.co.uk
dir: *Nearest station: Chancery Lane*

Buzzy bistro in the heart of the City

This wine-centric basement dining room has petrol-blue walls, exposed brickwork and bare wooden tables. Sitting on a stool at the bar gives a view into the efficiently run kitchen, while smartly dressed staff provide sleek, unobtrusive service to the buzzing room. The menu is accessible bistro-style fare. A thick and punchy gazpacho with prawns and sweet morsels of pickled cucumber and olives is a delightful start; follow on with grilled rib-eye, or a perfectly-cooked sea trout with crushed new potatoes, samphire and caper beurre noisette. Apricot roasted with honey and lemon thyme and matched with Amaretto and apricot sorbet and almond palmiers is a pretty finish.

Chef Justin LeClair, Julian Baris **Seats** 60, Pr/dining room 12 **Times** 12-2.30/6-9.30, Closed Xmas, New Year, BHs, Sat-Sun **Prices** Fixed L 2 course £16.50, Starter £6.95-£9.75, Main £13.50-£16.95 **Wines** 65 bottles over £30, 15 bottles under £30, 30 by glass **Parking** NCP **Notes** Children welcome

LONDON EC4 *continued*

Vanilla Black

PLAN 3 D2

Modern Vegetarian V

tel: 020 7242 2622 **17-18 Tooks Court EC4A 1LB**
email: vanillablack@btconnect.com
dir: *Nearest station: Chancery Lane*

Classy vegetarian cookery in a hidden London location

Tucked down an alley off Chancery Lane, Andrew Dargue and Donna Conroy's slick restaurant is a million miles from the lentil bake school of vegetarianism. Muted contemporary colours blend with dark floorboards, antique framed photos and rustic pine tables, and what arrives on the plate lives up to the setting: innovative dishes combining quality ingredients with up-to-the-minute technique. Pumpkin and yeast terrine comes with cinder toffee and mulled pumpkin to start, before salted ash-baked celeriac and sea-beet with broccoli and yogurt curd, and the creativity is maintained with desserts like white chocolate and cep custard with tarragon cream cheese and toasted meringue.

Chef Andrew Dargue **Seats** 45 **Times** 12-2.30/6-10, Closed 2 wks Xmas & New Year, BH Mons, Sun **Prices** Fixed L 2 course £21.50, Fixed D 3 course £41.50 **Wines** 48 bottles over £30, 14 bottles under £30, 10 by glass **Parking** On street (meter) or NCP **Notes** Children welcome

The White Swan Pub & Dining Room

PLAN 3 D3

Modern British

tel: 020 7242 9696 **108 Fetter Ln EC4A 1ES**
email: info@thewhiteswanlondon.com
dir: *Nearest station: Chancery Lane*

City gastropub with classy first-floor restaurant

The panelled ground-floor bar and mezzanine balcony of this smart Holborn pub always heave with a boisterous crew of suited-and-booted drinkers unwinding after a hard day in the office. The top-floor dining room is much more soberly turned-out, however, with a kitchen that constantly produces up-to-date, well-flavoured dishes with an eye on seasonal produce. Thus, an autumnal dinner starts with artichoke and ceps velouté, poured at the table around a wild rabbit Scotch quail's egg, before Yorkshire red-legged partridge arrives in the company of chestnuts, chanterelles and game chips. To finish, there's damson soufflé with ginger and vanilla ice cream.

LONDON N1

Almeida Restaurant

PLAN 1 F4

French

tel: 020 7354 4777 **30 Almeida St, Islington N1 1AD**
email: almeida-reservations@danddlondon.com
dir: *Nearest station: Angel, Highbury & Islington*

French cooking opposite the theatre

A little walk from the hustle and bustle of Islington's busy centre rewards with good honest French food in a contemporary setting. The highly-regarded Almeida Theatre is opposite. In the airy room, dressed in fashionable contemporary neutrality, large windows look out onto the street. The food carries its French allegiances lightly, with some standout seasonal British ingredients taking centre stage. For first course, perhaps try the Orkney scallops with bacon and peas in a chive emulsion and follow up with roasted veal sweetbread in a cauliflower purée. Finish with a textbook crème brûlée à la vanille.

The Drapers Arms

PLAN 1 F4

British

tel: 020 7619 0348 **44 Barnsbury St N1 1ER**
email: info@thedrapersarms.com
dir: *Nearest station: Highbury & Islington, Angel*

Real gastropub serving no-nonsense modern British food

In the well-heeled backstreets of Islington, the Drapers Arms has a lived-in look featuring scuffed floorboards, mismatched chairs and bare tables around the central bar. There's an impressive range of real ales on tap, and a chalkboard list of gutsy bar food to go with it. But it's worth honing your appetite to tackle the menu of no-nonsense seasonal British cooking. A starter of grilled ox heart with green sauce and watercress pulls no punches, then duck breast with Muscat grapes and red cabbage follows in a similarly fuss-free vein. Pudding hits the comfort zone with a rib-sticking combo of gingerbread pudding accompanied by whipped cream and crunchy oats.

Chef Gina Hopkins **Seats** 80, Pr/dining room 55 **Times** 12-3.30/6-10, Closed 25-26 Dec **Prices** Starter £4-£8.50, Main £13.50-£18, Dessert £2.50-£6.50 **Wines** 50 bottles over £30, 33 bottles under £30, 13 by glass **Parking** On street **Notes** Sunday L £13.50-£18.50, Vegetarian available, Children welcome

Fifteen London – The Restaurant

PLAN 3 G5

Modern British

tel: 020 3375 1515 **15 Westland Place N1 7LP**
email: reservations@fifteen.net
dir: *Nearest station: Old St*

Vibrant seasonal cooking in north London

The original incarnation of Jamie Oliver's philanthropic restaurant enterprise continues to draw in the punters who come for the range of smaller and larger plates for sharing, all based on prime seasonal ingredients and delivering big, fresh flavours. You might start with Dorset crab with a spicy pork sausage and smoked crème fraîche, moving on to a short rib with a Roscoff onion, mash and Montgomery cheddar. The place still continues in its original purpose – to take in young unemployed people and prepare them for a career in the kitchen – so you can feel good about yourself as you enjoy a clementine pannacotta with ginger crumbs.

Frederick's Restaurant

PLAN 1 F4

Modern British

tel: 020 7359 2888 **106-110 Islington High St, Camden Passage, Islington N1 8EG**
email: dine@fredericks.co.uk
dir: *Nearest station: Angel*

Dining hotspot among Islington's antique quarter

A spacious modern interior, with smart cocktail bar upfront, lofty conservatory dining space and garden out back, proves a drawcard for the Islington set. Exposed or white-painted brick walls are hung with bold contemporary abstracts, while large planters, huge glass panels and natural tones bring the garden inside. The rock star pictures and leather panels of the Club Room ups the on-trend swagger. The the roster of light, modern Pan-European dishes is a real crowd pleaser. Take pistachio and herb-crusted tuna served with courgette and carrot spaghetti, given Asian spin with edamame beans and mirin dressing, and, for dessert, perhaps a vanilla pannacotta with rhubarb compôte.

Chef Adam Hilliard **Seats** 150, Pr/dining room 40
Times 12-2.30/5.45-11.30, Closed Xmas, New Year, BHs, Sun (ex functions)
Prices Prices not confirmed **Wines** 125 bottles over £30, 20 bottles under £30, 25 by glass **Parking** NCP Business Design Centre, on street **Notes** Sat brunch, Vegetarian available, Children welcome

Grain Store

PLAN 1 F4

Modern, European

tel: 020 7324 4466 **Granary Square, 1-3 Stable Square, King's Cross N1C 4AB**
email: eat@grainstore.com
dir: *Nearest station: King's Cross, St Pancras*

Classy globe-trotting fare in an industrial landscape

Renowned chef Bruno Loubet and the Zetter Group's Michael Benyan's Grain Store in newly trendy King's Cross blurs the boundary between kitchen and dining room in one massive industrial-looking space. There are ducts snaking across the high ceiling, chunky wooden tables, exposed brickwork and an all-round cool vibe. The kitchen combines classic French cooking with something altogether more globe-trotting. Vegetables get top billing (often listed first among ingredients) with miso aubergine and sprouting seeds and beans alongside crispy citrus chicken skin, and glazed pak choi, hot seaweed sushi and black garlic purée served with hake cooked a la plancha. Finish with King's Cross Eton Mess.

Chef Bruno Loubet **Seats** Pr/dining room **Times** 12-2.30/5.45-11.30, Closed 24-26 Dec, D Sun **Prices** Starter £6.50-£11, Main £13-£22, Dessert £3.50-£6.50 **Wines** 42 bottles over £30, 7 bottles under £30, 20 by glass **Notes** Vegetarian available, Children welcome

Smokehouse

PLAN 1 F4

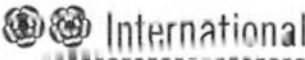 International

tel: 020 7354 1144 **63-69 Canonbury Rd, Islington N1 2DG**
email: info@smokehouseislington.co.uk
dir: *Nearest station: Highbury & Islington*

Meat meets fire in an Islington pub

One of a quartet of London pubs forming the Noble Inns group, this is an old Islington boozer that has seen new life as a temple to the simple, primeval principle of subjecting hunks of meat to fire and woodsmoke. In the yard are three giant smokers, fuelled by sustainable English oak, as is detailed on a blackboard above the open kitchen, and expect chunks of French classicism alongside East Asian sizzle. Kick off with chopped brisket roll flavoured with gochujang (a fermented Korean condiment), tuck into sticky pork belly, or short rib bourguignon, while veggies can enjoy vegetable fritto misto with burnt sweetcorn houmous.

Chef Neil Rankin **Seats** 50 **Times** 6-10, Closed 24-26 Dec, L Mon-Fri **Prices** Starter £7.50, Main £14-£18.50, Dessert £6.50-£7 **Wines** 18 bottles over £30, 21 bottles under £30, 11 by glass **Parking** On street **Notes** Sat brunch, Sunday L £16.50-£18, Vegetarian available, Children welcome

Trullo

PLAN 1 F4

Italian

tel: 020 7226 2733 **300-302 St Paul's Rd N1 2LH**
email: enquiries@trullorestaurant.com
dir: *Nearest station: Highbury & Islington*

Upbeat modern Italian cooking near Highbury Corner

Just off Highbury Corner, Trullo is a cracking little place, the setting for honest, ingredients-driven modern Italian cooking and a menu that changes with every sitting. Antipasti run to full-bore ideas such as ox tongue with agretti and anchovy, then follow with pasta – the signature pappardelle with beef shin ragù is a fine example of Italian comfort food done well. The charcoal grill adds a smoky edge to sea bass served with a lively salad of purple beetroot, lamb's lettuce and pistachios, or the oven might offer up rabbit leg braised with pancetta and shallots, and matched with baked cannellini beans. Finish with excellent almond tart and poached rhubarb.

Chef Conor Gadd, Tim Siadatan **Seats** 40, Pr/dining room 30 **Times** 12.30-2.45/6-10.15, Closed 25 Dec-3 Jan, some BHs, D Sun **Prices** Prices not confirmed **Wines** 40 bottles over £30, 11 bottles under £30, 11 by glass **Parking** On street **Notes** Large table menus £25-£45, Sunday L, Vegetarian available, Children welcome

LONDON NW1

La Collina

PLAN 1 E4

Modern Italian

tel: 020 7483 0192 **17 Princess Rd, Chalk Farm NW1 8JR**
email: info@lacollinarestaurant.co.uk
dir: *Nearest station: Chalk Farm, Camden Town*

Classy neighbourhood Italian for honest, simple cooking

La Collina is a relaxed neighbourhood Italian in Primrose Hill, its discreet black frontage slotted into an elegant terrace. Inside is simplicity itself: cream walls without adornment, dark pine floors, black leather seats, white tablecloths. A cast-iron spiral staircase leads to the basement, where you get a ringside seat before the tiny open kitchen. A starter of home-made pasta with Sardinian sausage, fennel seeds, tomato and chilli is just what Italian food is all about: simple, seasonal and fresh. Next up might be spanking-fresh baked sea bream with green beans, or cod with lentils, and to finish, the torta al cioccolato is heavenly.

Chef Diana Rinaldo **Seats** 40 **Times** 12-2.30/6-10.15, Closed Xmas wk, L Mon **Prices** Fixed L 2 course fr £15.50, Starter £7.50-£10.25, Main £13.50-£24, Dessert £6-£9 **Wines** 35 bottles over £30, 25 bottles under £30, 10 by glass **Parking** Free after 6pm & weekends **Notes** Vegetarian available, Children welcome

The Gilbert Scott

PLAN 3 B5

Modern British NOTABLE WINE LIST

tel: 020 7278 3888 **Renaissance St Pancras Hotel, Euston Rd NW1 2AR**
email: reservations@thegilbertscott.co.uk
dir: *Nearest station: St Pancras*

Versatile cooking in Gilbert Scott's majestic St Pancras hotel

Sir George Gilbert Scott was the architect responsible for the Midland Grand Hotel, built in 1873 and restored to its former Gothic Revival glory as the key travel hub to France arrived on its doorstep, it's now called the St Pancras Renaissance, which seems wholly appropriate. A ticket to ride is not required for lunch or dinner at the Marcus Wareing-run restaurant, but the gloriously revamped interior can certainly help you travel back in time – breathtakingly ornate and stylish, its glamorous cocktail bar and dining room have soaring ceilings and gilding galore. Open for breakfast, lunch, afternoon tea and dinner, the British-focused menu takes prime UK produce and a soupçon of French style to deliver a well-crafted, gently contemporary repertoire. Among first courses, pigeon and pistachio terrine keeps company with wonderfully sticky onion jam, followed by poached hake with tender squid and a punchy romesco sauce (a taste of the Med), Cumbrian pork neck with braised onion (bags of northern charm), or slow-cooked brisket with parmesan and radicchio (comfort food for the international traveller). To finish, prune and Armagnac tart is textbook stuff, but one glance at the cheese trolley and it's hard to resist. The wine list runs to 350 bins and includes big guns alongside small artisan producers.

Chef Dan Howes **Seats** 110, Pr/dining room 18 **Times** 12-3/5.30-11 **Prices** Fixed L 3 course £29, Fixed D 3 course £29, Tasting menu fr £45, Starter £7.50-£12.75, Main £16-£75, Dessert £3-£8.50 **Wines** 200 bottles over £30, 2 bottles under £30, 17 by glass **Parking** 12, NCP St Pancras **Notes** Afternoon tea, Sunday L, Vegetarian available, Children welcome

LONDON NW1 *continued*

Gilgamesh Restaurant Lounge PLAN 1 E4

 Pan-Asian

tel: 020 7428 5757 & 7428 4922 **The Stables Market, Chalk Farm Rd NW1 8AH**
email: reservations@gilgameshbar.com
dir: *Nearest station: Chalk Farm, Camden Town*

Pan-Asian dishes in a psychedelic re-creation of ancient Babylon

The exotic street food stalls of Camden's Stables Market are good preparation for a meal here, for Gilgamesh is no ordinary venue. Be prepared for a flamboyant, ancient Babylonian-themed interior – hand-carved wooden furniture, ornate walls of beaten bronze panels, palm trees, vast windows and nightclub-esque lighting. The menu delivers a Pan-Asian panoply of ideas: dim sum, sushi, Thai curries and more. Start with crispy squid with fiery Thai chillies and sweet-and-sour dipping sauce, and move onto green tea-infused smoked duck served with ginger, garlic and sesame-fried udon noodles. Dessert is a happy amalgam of burnt milk pannacotta, lime sorbet, pistachio sponge and yogurt.

Meliá White House PLAN 2 H4

Spanish, Mediterranean

tel: 020 7391 3000 **Albany St, Regent's Park NW1 3UP**
email: melia.white.house@melia.com **web:** www.melia-whitehouse.com
dir: *Nearest station: Great Portland St, Regent's Park, Warren St*

Inventive Spanish cooking in an art deco hotel

The Iberian-owned art deco hotel pays homage to its national cuisine in the elegant Spanish restaurant, L'Albufera. Serrano ham is carved from a trolley for traditionalists, otherwise grilled octopus with black olive chimichurri dressing and crunchy salsify, or spicy Spanish sausage cooked in cider with lavender are the sort of starters to expect. Paella comes in various forms – a black squid ink version with clams and monkfish, say – while mains could be slow-cooked suckling pig with paprika and garlic-mashed potatoes, mange-tout and thyme jus. For dessert, perhaps lemon posset topped with almond crumble and passionfruit foam, or finish instead with Spanish cheeses served with quince jelly.

Chef Juan Hely Pérez, David Aguado **Seats** 62, Pr/dining room 14 **Times** 7-10.30, Closed Sun, BHs, L all week **Prices** Prices not confirmed **Wines** 21 bottles over £30, 8 bottles under £30, 10 by glass **Parking** On street **Notes** Buffet L only in The Place, Vegetarian available, Children welcome

Michael Nadra Primrose Hill PLAN 1 E4

Modern European

tel: 020 7722 2800 **42 Gloucester Av NW1 8JD**
email: primrose@restaurant-michaelnadra.co.uk
dir: *Nearest station: Chalk Farm, Camden Town*

Global cuisine right by the canal

Nadra cooks on-the-money dishes of global cuisine, a reach that extends from tuna tartare and salmon céviche with chilli-pickled cucumber and salmon crackling, through Ibérico presa (shoulder steak) and belly, wild mushrooms and mash in Madeira jus, to an apple and pear version of kataifi, the Greek shredded pasta dish, accompanied by pistachio praline and ice cream and a dollop of wild thyme honey. Intriguing flavours pour forth from each dish, the fish options especially inspired – sea bass comes with siu mai-style prawn dumplings and bok choy in lemongrass-spiked crab bisque. The six-course tasting menu is excellent value, and includes a sorbet course served with a slug of Grey Goose vodka.

Chef Michael Nadra **Seats** 100, Pr/dining room 40 **Times** 12-2.30/6-10, Closed 24-26 Dec, 1 Jan **Prices** Fixed L 2 course £22-£27, Fixed D 3 course £38-£43, Tasting menu £48-£59 **Wines** 150 bottles over £30, 25 bottles under £30, 16 by glass **Parking** On street **Notes** Tasting menu 6 course, L 20% discount ALC menu, Sunday L, Vegetarian available, Children welcome

Odette's Restaurant PLAN 1 E4

Modern British V

tel: 020 7586 8569 **130 Regent's Park Rd NW1 8XL**
email: info@odettesprimrosehill.com
dir: *Nearest station: Chalk Farm*

Confident modern British cooking in a local favourite

Welsh celeb chef Bryn Williams took over this leafy Primrose Hill favourite back in 2008. The interior is a smart finish of cool pastel shades and exposed brick. Black banquettes and matching modern chairs, polished-wooden tables, parquet-style flooring and dangling globe lighting all fit with the stylish, urbane good looks without losing that intimate neighbourhood vibe. There's no less ambition about the kitchen's modern British output. Balanced, creative combinations, intelligent sourcing (including a sprinkling of Welsh ingredients, say, Carmarthen ham combining with sweet pear and mooli in a marinated scallop starter), pretty presentation and delicate, subtle flavours resonate in light modern dishes. The repertoire's delivered via fashionable tasting menu (including a veggie offering and a bespoke version if you're sat at the Kitchen Table downstairs), an amazing value weekday lunch, plus an intelligently compact carte that offers five options at each turn. Off the carte, expect mains like fabulous Goosnargh duck breast served with a tarte fine of smoked bacon and mushrooms, blood orange and crushed turnips, or perhaps melting Welsh lamb pepped up with spiced aubergine, artichokes and wild garlic. To close, pistachio cake, apple terrine and green apple sorbet, or the signature Odette's 'jaffa cake' with orange cream and marmalade that smacks of childhood memories.

Chef Bryn Williams, William Gordon **Seats** 70, Pr/dining room 10 **Times** 12-2.30/6-10, Closed 25-26 Dec, 1 Jan, Mon, L Tue **Prices** Fixed L 2 course fr £15, Tasting menu fr £47, Starter £7-£12, Main £16-£26, Dessert £7-£9 **Wines** 36 bottles over £30, 16 bottles under £30, 16 by glass **Parking** On street **Notes** Tasting/Vegetarian menu 6/10 course, L tasting menu £36, Sunday L, Children welcome

Pullman London St Pancras PLAN 3 A5

Modern European

tel: 020 7666 9000 & 7666 9038 **100-110 Euston Rd NW1 2AJ**
email: h5309@accor.com **web:** www.accorhotels.com/5309
dir: *Nearest station: King's Cross, Euston, St Pancras Int*

International menu in a contemporary railway hotel

This sleek hotel restaurant continues the cross-Channel link by refuelling Eurostar travellers at St Pancras International, just five minutes away. But that's as far as the belle epoque connection goes: this is a clean-cut 21st-century space constantly thrumming with activity. An open kitchen and Josper grill turn out an eclectic repertoire of uncomplicated modern European dishes such as Gloucester ham hock and leek terrine served with piccalilli and onion bloomer bread. Salt marsh lamb is sourced from Foulness Island and partnered with béarnaise sauce, tomato and basil salad and fine beans. To finish, salted caramel chocolate tart is nicely accompanied by vanilla custard ice cream.

Searcys St Pancras Grand PLAN 3 B6

Modern/Northern European

tel: 020 7870 9900 **Grand Ter, Upper Concourse, St Pancras International N1C 4QL**
email: stpg@searcys.co.uk
dir: *Nearest station: King's Cross, St Pancras*

French-inspired brasserie cooking at the Eurostar terminal

With Eurostar trains outside the window, it's fitting that this sleek art deco-esque brasserie offers a menu combining an entente cordiale of Pan-European flavours. Kick off with pan-fried scallops with chorizo, smoked cauliflower purée and samphire, or splash out on half-a-dozen oysters with a glass of fizz. Among main courses, the daily fish option brings pan-fried pollack with mussels, Jersey Royals and chive beurre blanc, or you might go for spatchcock poussin with chimichurri sauce. If you want to stay in Brit mode, there are posh burgers, steaks, and fish and chips. Dessert is velvety chocolate delice with orange sorbet.

The Winter Garden PLAN 2 F3

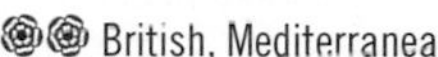

British, Mediterranean

tel: 020 7631 8000 & 7631 8230 **The Landmark London, 222 Marylebone Rd NW1 6JQ**
email: restaurants.reservation@thelandmark.co.uk **web:** www.wintergarden-london.com
dir: *Nearest station: Marylebone*

Classical cooking under a soaring glass roof

The Winter Garden is open all day, and the mood changes as does the hour (and the weather), for it is in the heart of the eight-storey atrium that forms the nucleus of the Landmark Hotel, a grand railway hotel of the old school. It makes an impressive spot to dine on classically minded modern food, starting with slow-cooked truffled beef ravioli in foie gras velouté. Norfolk Black free-range chicken might feature among main courses as breast and leg with cep purée and caramelised baby onions. Desserts are equally appealing, with sticky toffee pudding cranking up the comfort factor, served with salted caramel ganache.

Chef Gary Klaner **Seats** 90 **Times** 7am-10.30pm, All-day dining **Prices** Prices not confirmed **Wines** 25 by glass **Parking** 40, On street **Notes** Champagne brunch, Theatre/Opera D, Afternoon tea, Sunday L, Vegetarian available, Children welcome

LONDON NW3

Manna PLAN 1 E4

International Vegan

tel: 020 7722 8028 **4 Erskine Rd, Primrose Hill NW3 3AJ**
email: inquires@mannav.com
dir: *Nearest station: Chalk Farm*

Long-running neighbourhood vegetarian in leafy Primrose Hill

This long-time leader in gourmet vegetarian and vegan dining sits in a residential street in well-heeled Primrose Hill. Up-to-date decor with wooden floors and furniture gets a touch of class with designer wallpaper featuring silhouetted trees and birds and silver wreath-style light fittings. Carefully sourced produce is turned into vibrantly colourful dishes as the menu globetrots from Greek-style spanikopita tart with a salad of fennel, rocket, preserved lemon and dill salad, to a main course of wild mushroom ragù with chestnut polenta, seared kale, beetroot and horseradish slaw and parsnip crisps. For dessert, there's a light vegan take on sticky toffee pudding with vanilla ice cream and caramel sauce.

Seats 50 **Times** 12-3/6.30-11, Closed Xmas & New Year, Mon, L variable **Prices** Tasting menu £14-£22, Starter £7-£8, Main £14-£15, Dessert £7-£8 **Wines** 8 by glass **Parking** On street **Notes** Sunday L £14-£40, Children welcome

XO PLAN 1 E4

Pan-Asian

tel: 020 7433 0888 **29 Belsize Ln NW3 5AS**
email: xo@rickerrestaurants.com
dir: *Nearest station: Swiss Cottage, Belsize Park*

Asian variety act in well-heeled Belsize Park

A touch of big-city cool comes to the upscale 'village' of leafy Belsize Park in this slick space in shades of black, scarlet and lime green offering voguish Pan-Asian cuisine. The kitchen's repertoire is designed for sociable sharing and takes in everything from dim sum (prawn har gau dumplings or chilli-salt squid to get the taste buds standing to attention) to sashimi, sushi and tempura (such as black cod with yuzu aïoli). Among more substantial offerings, chicken is revved up with spicy sambal and a zingy, lime-dressed salad of coriander, bean sprouts, chopped peanuts and red chillies. Eye-catching cocktails, well-chosen wines and up-tempo music round off a polished package.

LONDON NW4

Hendon Hall Hotel PLAN 1 D5

Modern, Traditional British

tel: 020 8457 2200 & 0845 072 7448 *(Calls cost 7p per minute plus your phone company's access charge)* **Ashley Ln, Hendon NW4 1HF**
email: hendonhall@handpicked.co.uk **web:** www.handpickedhotels.co.uk/hendonhall
dir: *Nearest station: Hendon Central*

Historic North London mansion with contemporary cooking

Named after the 18th-century actor-manager David Garrick, who once lived here, the fine-dining restaurant at this impressive mansion works an upmarket modern look, with smart russet and gold high-backed chairs at formally-set tables. The kitchen scores hits with its up-to-date cooking, setting out with chicken liver parfait with apple chutney, or pea and ham soup with herb oil, ahead of pink and tender rib-eye steak complemented by peppercorn sauce with roast tomatoes and chips. Fish might appear on the concise menu as pan-fried bream fillet with minted crushed new potatoes and a creamy white wine sauce. Impressive desserts include lemon pannacotta with raspberry sorbet.

Chef Richard Walker **Seats** 60, Pr/dining room 18 **Times** 12.30-2.30/6.30-9.30 **Prices** Fixed D 3 course £32 **Wines** 60 bottles over £30, 6 bottles under £30, 17 by glass **Parking** 150 **Notes** Seasonal market menu 2/3 course £30-£37, Sunday L £14.95-£28.50, Vegetarian available, Children welcome

LONDON SE1

The Anchor & Hope PLAN 5 E5

British

tel: 020 7928 9898 **36 The Cut SE1 8LP**
email: anchorandhope@btconnect.com
dir: *Nearest station: Southwark, Waterloo*

Well-known gastropub with big-hearted cooking

Rock up at the bar of this rollicking Waterloo gastropub and try your luck for a table in the dining area (you can't book to eat, except for Sunday lunch). Every bit a proper no-frills boozer, the Anchor & Hope comes decked out in oxblood walls with well-worn wooden tables and mismatched hard chairs, while the scrum at the bar ups the decibels. The food fits the gritty mood, with big-hearted dishes on a menu that changes each session. Try warm snail and bacon salad, or a fish stew of halibut, gurnard, mussels and chickpeas. Pear and almond tart with clotted cream stays on theme.

LONDON SE1 *continued*

Brigade

PLAN 5 H6

British

tel: 0844 346 1225 *(Calls cost 7p per minute plus your phone company's access charge)* **The Fire Station, 139 Tooley St SE1 2HZ**
email: info@thebrigade.co.uk
dir: *Nearest station: London Bridge*

Turning up the heat in an old fire station

Brigade offers an upbeat, high-decibel vibe in an airy contemporary space helped along by the sounds, sights and smells of the central open kitchen (perch at the counter for a close-up view). Expect uncomplicated modern food driven by fresh, seasonal produce, much of it sourced from local suppliers and markets such as nearby Borough Market. Scotch egg with beetroot piccalilli and fennel and green apple slaw is a sound opening gambit, followed by a summery British take on seafood bouillabaisse with saffron and garlic rouille, or take the comfort route with a burger made from rump steak and shredded oxtail and finish with bitter chocolate tart with marmalade ice cream.

Chino Latino London

PLAN 5 C3

Modern Pan-Asian & Peruvian V

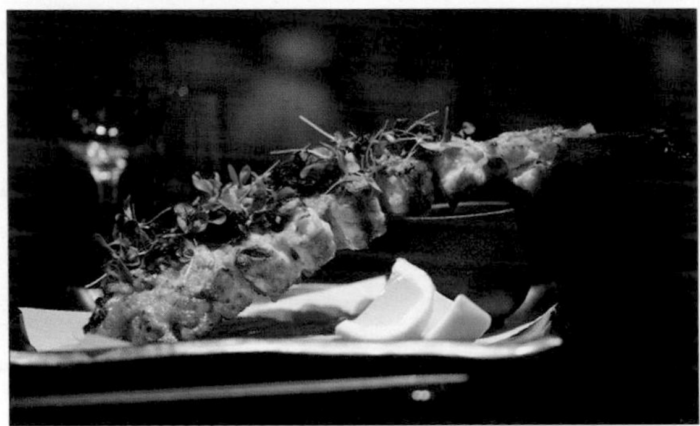

tel: 020 7769 2500 **Park Plaza Riverbank London, 18 Albert Embankment SE1 7SP**
email: london@chinolatino.co.uk **web:** www.chinolatino.eu/london
dir: *Nearest station: Vauxhall*

Asian and Latin American spice and fire on the South Bank

Pan-Asian food with Latin inflections is the approach at this rocking international chain that is resident at the Park Plaza hotel. Cocktail and sushi bars plus a sexy restaurant add up to a potently heady style mix. The kitchen delivers exquisitely presented dishes bursting with freshness, heat and umami. Two skewers of tender Wagyu beef come with aji panca sauce and gyozas and get a meal off to a flying start, to be followed perhaps by monkfish tail with yuzu jelly and pak choi flavoured with soya and sesame. Impressively wrought puddings include frozen cherry blossom 'air' with creamy iced rice and white chocolate sponge.

Chino Latino London

Chef Werner Seebach **Seats** 85 **Times** 12-2.30/6-10.30, Closed L Sat-Sun **Prices** Fixed D 3 course £48-£50, Tasting menu fr £49, Starter £4-£12, Main £10-£25, Dessert £6-£7.50 **Wines** 29 bottles over £30, 18 bottles under £30, 12 by glass **Parking** Q park Waterloo station **Notes** Children welcome

See advert opposite

H10 London Waterloo Hotel

PLAN 5 E5

European

tel: 020 7928 4062 **284-302 Waterloo Rd SE1 8RQ**
email: h10.london.waterloo@h10hotels.com **web:** www.hotelh10londonwaterloo.com
dir: *Nearest station: Lambeth North, Waterloo*

Spanish hotel cooking with views of Waterloo

The Waterloo H10's principal eating space is Three O Two, which looks like an airport café, with unclothed tables, plenty of daylight, and uplighters raking the white net curtains in the evenings. Expect classic tapas, as well as octopus and potato salad, rabbit and chicken paella, and ritzy main dishes like beef fillet with Menorcan Mahón cheese, garlic cream and a reduction sauce of Somontano wine. Pork cheeks with raisins and Parmentier potatoes, sauced in manzanilla sherry, are juicy and flavourful. Generously laden Catalan suquet seafood stews comprises salmon, squid, clams and mussels, and the dessert temptations take in variations on rice pudding, as well as nicely rich vanilla cheesecake.

Chef David Ovejo **Seats** 100, Pr/dining room 50 **Times** 6.30-10.30, Closed L all week (ex events) **Prices** Prices not confirmed **Wines** 9 bottles over £30, 37 bottles under £30, 16 by glass **Parking** NCP Library St or Elephant & Castle **Notes** Afternoon tea, Vegetarian available, Children welcome

Hutong

PLAN 5 G6

Northern Chinese

tel: 020 3011 1257 **Level 33, The Shard, 31 St Thomas St SE1 9RY**
email: hutongreservations@aqua-london.com
dir: *Nearest station: London Bridge*

Top-end Chinese dining on the 33rd floor

The view from the 33rd floor of The Shard is stunning, particularly at night with the shimmering lights below. The room is a bit of a looker itself, with red lanterns and an open-to-view wood-fired oven where ducks are cooking and drying, ready for the classic two-stage Peking-style presentation. The kitchen turns out some classy dim sum at lunchtime – succulent lamb and leek dumplings, say – while the carte pays homage to Northern Chinese cuisine, with fiery Szechuan dishes having their say too. Wunan-style cod fillet tossed with crispy soya beans and chilli is an impressive main course, and there are sweet black sesame dumplings for dessert.

LONDON SE1 *continued*

Magdalen

PLAN 5 H6

British, European

tel: 020 7403 1342 **152 Tooley St SE1 2TU**
email: info@magdalenrestaurant.co.uk
dir: *Nearest station: London Bridge*

Vibrantly flavoured and thoughtful cooking near London Bridge

With burgundy-coloured banquettes and walls, bentwood chairs at white-clothed tables covered with paper liners, and darkwood floors, Magdalen works a classy bistro look. Dishes are marked by their simplicity and combinations (backed by the kitchen's technical skill and careful choice of ingredients), so clear flavours speak for themselves. Saddleback pork terrine is helped along by preserved shiitaki mushrooms and tarragon, while main course fish stew is a vibrant bowl of hake, gilt head bream and clams in an intense stock pointed up with fennel and aïoli. Pastry skills are also exemplary, as witnessed in a preserved cherry and almond tart served with crème fraîche.

Chef James & Emma Faulks, David Abbott **Seats** 90, Pr/dining room 30 **Times** 12-2.30/6.30-10, Closed Xmas, BHs, Sun, L Sat **Prices** Fixed L 2 course fr £16.50, Starter £7.50-£12.50, Main £15.50-£26.50, Dessert £6-£7.50 **Wines** 58 bottles over £30, 15 bottles under £30, 12 by glass **Parking** On street **Notes** Vegetarian available, Children welcome

Oblix

PLAN 5 G6

American

tel: 020 7268 6700 **Level 32, The Shard, 31 St Thomas St SE1 9RY**
email: info@oblixrestaurant.com
dir: *Nearest station: London Bridge*

Steaks and more 32 floors up

Oblix occupies a seriously glamorous spot on the 32nd floor of The Shard with a slick, brasserie vibe, open kitchen, cool lounge bar, luxe cocktails and live music. The grill and Josper oven are the stars of the show, with veal chop and gremolata and Wagyu tenderloin providing a satisfying hit of protein. It's not all about the red stuff, though, for this kitchen turns out nifty starters such as grilled diver-caught scallops with lime and tamarind cream, and mains like as barbecue black cod with coriander salsa. Finish with a pecan nut and chocolate bar with bourbon ice cream, and then hit the bar.

The Oxo Tower Restaurant

PLAN 3 D1

Modern, Traditional British NOTABLE WINE LIST

tel: 020 7803 3888 **8th Floor, Oxo Tower Wharf, Barge House St SE1 9PH**
email: oxo.reservations@harveynichols.com **web:** www.oxotowerrestaurant.com
dir: *Nearest station: Blackfriars, Waterloo, Southwark*

Captivating views and modish food

On the eighth floor of the old Oxo building, this bar, brasserie and restaurant overlooks the river and St Paul's Cathedral, a world-class vista which never fails to impress. The cooking is modern British with a bit of globetrotting into Asian territory. Seared tuna with Granny Smith apple, radish and dandelion salad relies on deep-red, sashimi-grade tuna of exceptional quality for its impact, while main-course roast monkfish comes with a squid ink popadom, red pepper coulis and radishes, or there might be fillet of beef with girolles, parmesan gnocchi and spiced golden raisin purée. To finish, strawberry and champagne millefeuille with wild strawberry sorbet is a vibrant ode to summer.

Park Plaza County Hall London

PLAN 5 C5

Modern Italian

tel: 020 7021 1919 & 7021 1800 **1 Addington St SE1 7RY**
email: ppchres@pphe.com **web:** www.parkplazacountyhall.com
dir: *Nearest station: Waterloo, Westminster*

Italian favourites in Thames-side landmark building

Inside the snazzy modern hotel next to County Hall on the South Bank, L'Italiano restaurant is on a mezzanine level and has bags of style, including great views through the large glass wall. The heart of the culinary action is a wood-fired oven that, given the Italian focus of the place, means great pizzas (picante, perhaps, with salami, red onion and chill). Creamy burrata Pugliese comes with Taggiasca olives and marinated San Marzano tomatoes. Pasta and risotto options are available, while main could be duck breast with wild greens and Cremona mustard fruits. Desserts include latto fritto (fried milk, anyone?) with apple compôte and cinnamon ice cream.

Park Plaza Westminster Bridge London

PLAN 5 C5

Modern French

tel: 020 7620 7200 **SE1 7UT**
email: ppwlres@pphe.com **web:** www.parkplaza.com
dir: *Nearest station: Westminster, Waterloo*

Traditionally focused French brasserie dining near the Eye

Park Plaza's dining options centre on a French venue called Brasserie Joël, a monochrome space with a large tree in the middle and funky music filling the air. A mix of traditional and lightly modernised French dishes brings plenty of lustre to the brasserie-style menu. A starter of foie gras terrine comes with pain d'épices and delightfully sticky fig chutney, with perhaps rabbit in mustard cream and buttery mash, or Black Angus onglet and fries, to follow. Seafood is rendered with confident accuracy, as for grilled tiger prawns and scallops with butternut risotto and pea shoots, and proceedings end on a spectacular note with lemon tart and meringue flambée.

Chef Walter Ishizuka **Seats** 180, Pr/dining room 80 **Times** 12-2/5.30-10.30, Closed L Sat **Prices** Prices not confirmed **Wines** 53 bottles over £30, 19 bottles under £30, 14 by glass **Parking** NCP **Notes** Pre-theatre menu, Sunday L, Vegetarian available, Children welcome

Pizarro

PLAN 5 H4

Traditional Spanish

tel: 020 7378 9455 **194 Bermondsey St SE1 3TQ**
email: management@pizarrorestaurant.com
dir: *Nearest station: Bermondsey, Borough, London Bridge*

Spanish cooking at its best in foodie Bermondsey

A roomy, open-plan space that combines traditional Iberian touches – whole hams hanging at a Spanish tile-frieze bar, warm textures of wood – with a stripped back aesthetic that appeals to local hipsters. Don't expect the fiddly, molecular cooking that has made several Spanish chefs world famous: the kitchen deals in top-notch ingredients and simple, unfussy combinations. Tender grilled octopus matched with creamy, paprika-infused potato and egg caviar prepare the taste buds for a punchy main course of venison stew with chestnuts and earthy black trompette mushrooms, or there might be roast Segovian suckling pig with cranberry sauce. Finish with variations on chocolate – mousse, buñuelo, ice cream and truffle.

Restaurant Story

LONDON SE1 **PLAN 5 J5**

Modern British V NOTABLE WINE LIST

tel: 020 7183 2117 **199 Tooley St SE1 2UE**
email: dine@restaurantstory.co.uk **web:** www.restaurantstory.co.uk
dir: *Nearest station: London Bridge, Tower Hill*

White-hot opening from a global talent

In a starkly modern structure in what is essentially a traffic island at the Tower Bridge end of Tooley Street, Restaurant Story is one of London's most personal and compelling dining experiences. Tom Sellers has a CV including stints under Tom Aikens, Thomas Keller in New York and René Redzepi in Copenhagen, so expect a dining experience that reflects the new world order, where the waiters and chefs engage with you and generally make you feel more than a mere paying customer, with the meal very much a multi-sensorial experience. The whole event takes three to four hours – lunch or dinner – and follows a prescribed route from the 'snacks' to the excellent coffee, which arrives with a fabulous chocolate-covered tea cake. The room has a slick Scandinavian charm, deliberately egalitarian and free of intimidating formality, with floor-to-ceiling windows onto Tooley Street, cool designer chairs, blond wood tables, and an open-to-view kitchen which shows the kitchen team working with precision and unimaginable calm. Books line the shelves in meticulous colour co-ordinated order, and Tom invites you to bring a book to add to the collection (add your favourite story to the story of Restaurant Story). The menu arrives in an old book, appropriately enough, and the Full Story consists of chapter headings such as Sea, Childhood and The End. Things get going with the array of 'snacks' that arrive in quick succession, including a nasturtium flower filled with oyster emulsion and a wee terracotta flower pot filled with radishes, edible soil and wasabi yogurt. The imagination, technical skill, impressive flavours and sheer fun should win over even the most hardened cynic. The bread and dripping is a signature which should be on the menu for as long as its doors are open – a candle made of beef fat, fabulous sourdough bread, veal tongue and apple jelly, and a powerful beef jelly extract. Onions star in a dish with Old Tom gin, apple and a hit of lime, while fallow deer is a fine piece of meat, cooked to perfection, with yeast and dandelion in a captivating combination. The cheese course is like no other – Picnic, it's called – and it's very cool, arriving in a mini picnic basket with red gingham cloth (the cheese might be Hampshire's fabulous Tunworth). Among sweet courses, 'almond and dill' is an inspired combination of flavours, textures and temperatures (if it is white it is almond, if it is green it is dill). The passion for British ingredients and regionalism extends to fantastic cocktails, British beers, local gins, and there's advice on hand about what's best to drink with what.

Chef Tom Sellers **Seats** 40 **Times** 12-5/6.30-9.30, Closed 2 wks Aug, 2 wks Xmas, Sun, L Mon **Prices** Prices not confirmed **Wines** 147 bottles over £30, 4 bottles under £30, 11 by glass **Parking** On street, NCP **Notes** Fixed menu L 7 course £80, D 10 course £100, Children 4 yrs+

LONDON SE1 *continued*

Le Pont de la Tour PLAN 5 J6

Modern French

tel: 020 7403 8403 **The Butlers Wharf Building, 36d Shad Thames SE1 2YE**
email: lepontres@danddlondon.com
dir: *Nearest station: Tower Hill, London Bridge*

Great views and assured French cooking

The name translates as Tower Bridge, and that's what lies before you, a solid-gold view framed by the city skyscrapers. Expect well-executed food rooted in the French classics, where seafood is a strong suit (various types of oysters or a plateau de fruits de mer) and luxury ingredients come thick and fast. Start with roasted wood pigeon with confit leg tortellini, celeriac and pear, followed by pan-fried John Dory partnered by bone marrow, sauté squid and sauce bordelaise. Sticking with the Gallic theme, Valrhona milk chocolate mousse is served with salted caramel ice cream. If your wallet can stand it, the place is well known for its cracking wine list.

Restaurant Story PLAN 5 J5

– see page 253

Roast PLAN 5 G6

British V

tel: 020 300 6611 **The Floral Hall, Borough Market, Stoney St SE1 1TL**
email: info@roast-restaurant.com **web:** www.roast-restaurant.com
dir: *Nearest station: London Bridge*

Great British food in vibrant, historic South Bank market

A Southwark honeypot for a millennium, Borough Market is today a big tourist attraction. Roast occupies the ornate Floral Hall, transported from the old Covent Garden and, with views of the market, St Paul's Cathedral and The Shard, it's a splendid location. Taking nationwide inspiration, the menu kicks off with parsnip, potato and apple soup with Ticklemore goats' cheese and local Bermondsey Street honey. Next, a nicely rolled and stuffed, slow-roasted Wick's Manor (from Maldon, Essex) pork belly with crackling, mashed potato and Bramley apple sauce. For dessert, try soft-centred chocolate pudding with sea-salted caramel ice cream. In true market fashion, it's open for breakfast.

Chef Stuart Cauldwell **Seats** 120 **Times** 12-3.45/5.30-11, Closed 25-26 Dec, 1 Jan, D Sun **Prices** Fixed L 3 course £30-£37.50, Fixed D 3 course fr £30, Tasting menu £75-£110, Starter £8-£15, Main £24-£40, Dessert £7-£8 **Wines** 310 bottles over £30, 20 bottles under £30, 21 by glass **Parking** NCP Kipling St **Notes** Sunday L £37.50, Children welcome

RSJ, The Restaurant on the South Bank PLAN 5 D6

Modern European

tel: 020 7928 4554 **33 Coin St SE1 9NR**
email: tom.king@rsj.uk.com
dir: *Nearest station: Waterloo*

Pleasingly unfussy food and notable Loire wines

RSJ's long-standing appeal is down to its French and Italian-inspired menus that pack in the pre- and post-theatre and concert crowds, while the specialist Loire Valley wine list (hand-picked by the owner) is a show-stopper in itself. In the kitchen, unfussy food is elevated by intelligent flavour combinations and sound cooking – Cornish mackerel fillet with pickled red cabbage and watercress is a fresh and vibrant opener, followed by roasted hake with buttery crushed Jersey Royals lifted with lemon and chives, and a punchy sauce viérge. Pear and pine nut tart with home-made basil ice cream brings down the curtain.

Shangri-La Hotel at The Shard PLAN 5 G6

British, European V

tel: 020 7234 8008 & 7234 8000 **31 St Thomas St SE1 9QU**
email: ting.slln@shangri-la.com **web:** www.ting-shangri-la.com
dir: *Nearest station: London Bridge*

Asian influences and great city views

The Shangri-La occupies the 34th to 52nd floors of The Shard, so the full-drop windows in Ting, the restaurant on 35, pack quite a punch. The dining room is elegant, with a Chinoiserie feel, and the modern European menu has Asian influences. There's a chef's table, too, if you want to get close to the action. The five-course Market Menu might start with Dorset crab with apple, cauliflower and English caviar, and then take in chicken liver parfait and Cornish lobster risotto before a main of cured Ibérico pork, or Dover sole with wild garlic and yuzu butter glaze.

Chef Gareth Bowen, Marcus Klumb **Seats** 95 **Times** 12-2.30/6-11.15 **Prices** Tasting menu £65-£110 **Wines** 218 bottles over £30, 16 by glass **Parking** 15, NCP London Bridge **Notes** Market tasting menu 5 course, Children welcome

Skylon PLAN 5 C6

Modern British V

tel: 020 7654 7800 **Royal Festival Hall, Southbank Centre SE1 8XX**
email: skylonreservations@danddlondon.com
dir: *Nearest station: Waterloo Station*

Smart riverside dining at the Royal Festival Hall

Knock-out Thames-side views and its setting inside the Royal Festival Hall ensure that Skylon rocks. A real looker, the Southbank set up incorporates a hotspot centrepiece bar, swish grill and stellar restaurant, with chandelier-style lighting, soaring pillars, dramatic flower displays and low-slung contemporary seating. The kitchen speaks with a modern British accent, for example in an opener of melt-in-the-mouth smoked Lincolnshire eel teamed with crispy bacon potato cake and sweet sea kale salad. On the other hand, roasted wild sea bass is pepped up with Swiss chard and a lightly spiced mussel casserole, while a signature cherry crème brûlée tart with basil sorbet and cherry salad is the way to finish.

Chef Tom Cook **Seats** 100, Pr/dining room 33 **Times** 12-2.30/5.30-10.30, Closed 25 Dec, D Sun **Prices** Fixed L 2 course £25, Fixed D 3 course £32, Tasting menu £59, Starter £9.50-£17, Main £21.50-£39, Dessert £7.50-£13 **Wines** 362 bottles over £30, 21 bottles under £30, 22 by glass **Notes** Pre-theatre menu, Sunday L £25-£30, Children welcome

Union Street Café

PLAN 5 E6

Italian, Mediterranean

tel: 020 7592 7977 **47-51 Great Suffolk St SE1 0BS**
email: unionstreetcafe@gordonramsay.com
dir: *Nearest station: Southwark*

Ramsay's warehouse-styled urban-chic Italian

This café's casual, urban-chic warehouse sheen, with funky lighting, buffed concrete, striking artwork and an open kitchen, is a big hit, as is the cooking, driven by the best market produce. Skilled simplicity and a confident light modern touch keep the food high on flavour. Cotechino, with fonduta, lentils and truffle, delivers the authentic Italian goods, as does squid-ink gnocchi with clams, mussels and gurnard. Main courses run to full-on fallow deer with juniper, blackberries, celeriac and rainbow chard as well as Mediterranean-style octopus with lentil and mushroom purée. Finish with cannoli, the classic Sicilian pastry, with candied orange and pistachio ice cream.

Chef Davide Degiovanni **Seats** 125, Pr/dining room 20
Times 12-3/6-11, Closed 25-27 Dec, 1 Jan, D Sun **Prices** Fixed L 2 course £19, Starter £8-£13, Main £11-£26, Dessert £7-£9 **Wines** 165 bottles over £30, 18 bottles under £30, 15 by glass **Parking** NCP, Ewer St **Notes** Events menu 3/4 course £35/£45, Sunday L £19-£29, Vegetarian available, Children welcome

LONDON SE3

Chapters All Day Dining

PLAN 1 H3

Modern British

tel: 020 8333 2666 **43-45 Montpelier Vale, Blackheath Village SE3 0TJ**
email: info@chaptersblackheath.com **web:** www.chaptersrestaurants.com
dir: *Nearest station: Blackheath*

Blackheath Village eatery buzzing all day long

In a super spot overlooking the heath from its pavement tables or through floor-to-ceiling windows, Chapters covers all the bases from breakfast to modern brasserie classics at lunch and dinner. Top-quality ingredients provide the foundations for well-presented, clean-flavoured dishes, starting with deep-fried cod brandade with poached egg, gribiche sauce and pea shoots, then corn-fed chicken with pearl barley risotto, pancetta and stem broccoli. The Josper grill might supply Kentish double Barnsley lamb chop or a rib-eye steak, and to finish, there's Valrhona chocolate pudding. Add in stonking value fixed-price options, well-chosen wines (with plenty by glass or pichet) and you've got a dynamic neighbourhood winner.

Chapters All Day Dining

Chef Nick Simmons **Seats** 100 **Times** 8am-11pm, All-day dining, Closed 2-3 Jan **Prices** Fixed L 2 course fr £12.95, Fixed D 3 course fr £17.50, Starter £5.55-£10.50, Main £12.95-£14.95, Dessert £4.50-£7.50 **Wines** 24 bottles over £30, 40 bottles under £30, 17 by glass **Parking** Car park by station & on street **Notes** Fixed L Mon-Thu, Sunday L, Vegetarian available, Children welcome

LONDON SE10

Craft London

PLAN 1 H3

Modern British NEW

tel: 020 8465 5910 **Peninsula Square SE10 0SQ**
email: hello@craft-london.co.uk **web:** www.craft-london.co.uk
dir: *Nearest station: North Greenwich*

Trendy spot for creative British food

Café, bar, restaurant and shop, Craft London is a thriving enterprise in a modern construction of glass and steel next to the O2. The restaurant, on the first floor, has a striking contemporary finish with bold colours, cool lighting, floor-to-ceiling windows and an open-to-view kitchen. Mostly British ingredients are given 21st-century va-va-voom by a creative team who deliver inspiring plates that demand to be eaten. Smoked and grilled eel is a dish of poise and balance thanks to the clever use of treacle, gloriously fat scallops come with Scottish girolles and mead and anchovy sauce, while the clay-baked duck is something of a signature.

Chef Stevie Parle **Seats** 90 **Times** 12-3/5.30-10.30, Closed Xmas, Sun-Mon, L Tue-Fri **Prices** Fixed L 3 course £35, Fixed D 3 course fr £35, Starter £8-£12, Main £18-£29, Dessert £6-£8 **Wines** 50 bottles over £30, 7 bottles under £30, 12 by glass **Parking** O2 parking next door **Notes** Pre-show 4 course '60 minute' menu £35, Vegetarian available, Children welcome

LONDON SE22

Franklins

PLAN 1 F2

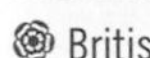

British

tel: 020 8299 9598 **157 Lordship Ln, East Dulwich SE22 8HX**
email: info@franklinsrestaurant.com
dir: *Nearest station: East Dulwich*

Hearty British cooking on East Dulwich high street

British produce is celebrated zealously at Franklins, an exemplary neighbourhood eatery that combines the virtues of a pubby bar and a buzzy bistro at the rear that's all exposed brick, bare floorboards, big Victorian mirrors, and paper-clothed tables with an open view into the kitchen. There are gutsy starters such as haslet – a meatloaf of chopped pork and offal – with home-made piccalilli, followed by straight-up platefuls of lamb's kidneys with Swiss chard and mustard, or hearty, no-frills ideas such as red-legged partridge with butternut squash and bacon. Caramelised apple and almond frangipane tart keeps pudding firmly in the comfort zone.

Chef Ralf Wittig **Seats** 42, Pr/dining room 24 **Times** 12-12, All-day dining, Closed 25-26 & 31 Dec, 1 Jan **Prices** Fixed D 3 course £16.95, Starter £7.50-£9.50, Main £14.50-£22.50, Dessert £6-£7.50 **Wines** 16 bottles over £30, 30 bottles under £30, 15 by glass **Parking** Bawdale Rd **Notes** Sat brunch, Sunday L £13.50, Vegetarian available, Children welcome

The Palmerston

PLAN 1 F2

Modern British, European

tel: 020 8693 1629 **91 Lordship Ln, East Dulwich SE22 8EP**
email: info@thepalmerston.co.uk
dir: *Nearest station: East Dulwich*

Modern cooking in a traditional East Dulwich pub

This classic Victorian corner pub in East Dulwich is an inviting prospect with its clubby wood panelling, racing-green leather banquettes and scrubbed-wood tables and chairs. A quick glance over the menu shows that this kitchen prizes seasonal British produce. Home-cured salt-cod fritters with spiced tomato sauce and aïoli make a straight-talking opener, or you might kick off with smoked eel with beetroot, damson jelly, horseradish and mustard cress. Next up, grilled rabbit leg comes with a punchy stew of braised ganxet beans, chorizo, kale and salt-baked celeriac, and for pud, an inventive take on the trifle theme brings terrific English pink winter rhubarb with Swiss roll, amaretti and sherry.

Chef Jamie Younger, Robert Willcox **Seats** 70, Pr/dining room 26 **Times** 12-2.30/7-12, Closed 25-26 Dec, 1 Jan **Prices** Fixed L 2 course £14.50, Starter £4.75-£11, Main £14.50-£24, Dessert £5-£8 **Wines** 40 bottles over £30, 20 bottles under £30, 30 by glass **Parking** On street **Notes** Light menu 3-6pm, Brunch menu Fri-Sun, Sunday L £12.50-£17.50, Vegetarian available, Children welcome

LONDON SE23

Babur

PLAN 1 G2

Modern Indian

tel: 020 8291 2400 **119 Brockley Rise, Forest Hill SE23 1JP**
email: mail@babur.info web: www.babur.info
dir: *Nearest station: Honor Oak Park*

Modern Indian cuisine in a cool brasserie-style setting

Babur is not hard to spot: just look for the life-size tiger prowling the roof. Inside the look is classy and modern with striking artworks and funky lighting. The cooking delivers an adventurous canter through the contemporary Indian idiom, while wines are spice-friendly, with recommendations included on the menu. Quality ingredients – many not common in Indian cooking – and judicious spicing are graced with well-dressed presentation. Chargrilled monkfish tikka in spiced coconut broth is a lively starter, followed by meltingly tender spice crusted shoulder of lamb with beetroot rice, or there might be rabbit, pot-roasted with mustard and ginger. Finish with an East-meets-West dessert of saffron and pistachio praline kulfi

Chef Jiwan Lal **Seats** 72 **Times** 12-2.30/6-11.30, Closed 26 Dec, L 27 Dec, 1 Jan, D 25 Dec **Prices** Tasting menu £32.95-£35.95, Starter £6.75-£8.50, Main £14.95-£18.95, Dessert £5.25-£6.95 **Wines** 11 bottles over £30, 32 bottles under £30, 13 by glass **Parking** 15, On street **Notes** Vegetarian tasting menu £29.95-£32.95, Sunday L £9.95-£14.95, Vegetarian available, Children welcome

See advert opposite

LONDON SW1

Al Duca

PLAN 4 J6

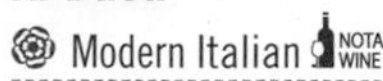

Modern Italian NOTABLE WINE LIST

tel: 020 7839 3090 **4-5 Duke of York St SW1Y 6LA**
email: alduca@btconnect.com
dir: *Nearest station: Green Park*

Buzzy, fairly priced Italian in St James's

This upmarket Italian is tucked away in a discreet St James's street behind Fortnum & Mason. With its buzzy ambience and sensible pricing it's clear why the place is perennially popular. A concertina glass frontage folds back for alfresco eating on fine days, while chatty and knowledgeable staff also play their part. The repertoire of gently modernised Italian dishes has stood the test of time. Start with risotto with clams and saffron, followed by pan-fried fillet of cod with chickpeas and fresh tomatoes, or pan-fried pork belly with celeriac mash, sautéed Savoy cabbage and raisins. Finish with a textbook tiramisù or chocolate and almond cake with pistachio ice cream

Amaya

PLAN 4 G4

Modern Indian NOTABLE WINE LIST

tel: 020 7823 1166 **Halkin Arcade, Motcomb St SW1X 8JT**
email: amaya@realindianfood.com
dir: *Nearest station: Knightsbridge, Hyde Park, Sloane Sq*

Fine Indian cuisine with plenty of kitchen theatre

Behind a grand façade on Halkin Arcade, Amaya has taken the traditional grilled food of the Indian sub-continent and glammed it up for the Knightsbridge postcode by injecting a bit of contemporary sophistication to proceedings. The room has a sleek modern finish, colourful artworks from Kerala and Bengal, and a centrepiece open kitchen where you can watch the action at the tandoor ovens. The tandoor takes centre stage as the primary cooking method alongside the tawa (flat griddle) and sigri (charcoal grill), and you can order large or small plates to suit your mood (sharing means you get to try more things). The food arrives in waves, as it is ready, so get ready for succulent chicken tikka fired up with black pepper, chargrilled sea bass served on a banana leaf, chilli lamb chops, and some interesting veggie options such as paneer tikka or griddled white sweet potato with tamarind and yogurt. Methi chicken biryani is an alternative to the grilled options, and the platters are a good bet if you're feeling indecisive. Finish with chocolate Rasmalai surprise – a pretty construction with a lime sponge at its centre – or grilled fruit kebab with saffron shrikhand.

Chef Karunesh Khanna **Seats** 99, Pr/dining room 14
Times 12.30-2.15/6.30-11.30, Closed D 25 Dec **Prices** Tasting menu £60-£85
Parking NCP **Notes** Fixed D 6 course £80-£115, Vegetarian tasting menu £40-£65, Sunday L, Vegetarian available, Children 3 yrs+

LONDON SW1 *continued*

Ametsa with Arzak Instruction

PLAN 4 G5

New Basque NOTABLE WINE LIST

tel: 020 7333 1234 **The Halkin by COMO, Halkin St, Belgravia SW1X 7DJ**
email: ametsa.thehalkin@comohotels.com
web: www.comohotels.com/thehalkin/dining/ametsa
dir: *Nearest station: Hyde Park Corner*

Earthy, modern Basque cooking in wealthy Belgravia

New Basque cuisine has a way to go in Britain before it's as ubiquitous as Indian or Chinese. But in London, at least, the opportunity to enjoy this northern Spanish region's earthy flavours awaits at The Halkin by COMO luxury hotel in Belgravia. Here top chef Elena Arzak, of San Sebastián's famous restaurant-owning dynasty, oversees the culinary output of this curiously but pragmatically named eating place. Just off the lobby is the Halkin Bar, where the 'Flights of Sherries and Brandies' menu includes tapas and Western classics. Star attraction in the restaurant – food apart, naturally – is the ceiling, from which hang myriad spice-filled glass tubes (7,000 if you must know!), a conversation piece that's enough initially to distract one from the menu. Start perhaps with foie corn cob, cocoa and vinaigrette dressing, then a tuna main course served under a glass dome with a seared, nay possibly even smoking, cinnamon stick and apple purée. For dessert, how about a rich and tasty orange French toast and spinach, rhubarb foam and tomato ice cream? Pairing dishes with wines proposed by Ametsa's sommelier, the tasting menu comes at a higher price.

Chef Sergio Sanz Blanco, Elena Arzack **Seats** 60, Pr/dining room 24
Times 12-2/6.30-10.30, Closed 24-26 Dec, 1 Jan, Sun, L Mon **Prices** Fixed L 2 course £27.50-£52, Fixed D 3 course fr £38, Tasting menu £105-£154, Starter £16.50-£28, Main £26-£39, Dessert £12.50 **Wines** 126 bottles over £30, 4 bottles under £30, 13 by glass **Parking** On street (after 6pm) **Notes** Fixed L 4 course £52, L Tasting menu £52-£68, Vegetarian available, Children welcome

Avenue

PLAN 4 J6

Modern British, American

tel: 020 7321 2111 **7-9 St James's St SW1A 1EE**
email: avenuereservations@danddlondon.com
dir: *Nearest station: Green Park*

Buzzy modern restaurant and bar with its heart in New York

Avenue is a stylish American-inspired gaff. The long bar sets a classy tone, while the restaurant spreads out around a 'wine-glass' chandelier and decanting bar. The big-city-cool look comes with semi-circular banquettes, low-back chairs and funky 'tilting' lamps. Expect modern American fare with a fresh, clean-flavoured touch characterised by a pinch of spice. Take signatures like clam chowder (served in hollowed-out sourdough with littleneck clams and paper bag 'crumbled' bay crackers) or desserts like 'donut holes' (with cinnamon sugar, raspberry jam and bourbon chocolate). In between, perhaps sea-fresh stone bass mains (with Old Bay spice pepping up a spring vegetable succotash), Black Angus hamburgers or grain-fed beef steaks.

A. Wong

PLAN 4 J3

Chinese

tel: 020 7828 8931 **70 Wilton Rd, Victoria SW1V 1DE**
email: info@awong.co.uk
dir: *Nearest station: Victoria*

Exploring China's vast culinary range

In an unassuming modern block down the road from Victoria station is one of London's most dynamic Chinese restaurants. Andrew Wong acknowledges the melting pot that is Chinese cuisine, a result of trade, migration and invasion, and helped by the fact the country has 14 national borders. Respect is shown for traditional ways, but this is modern dining too, so there are contemporary elements to many of the dishes. Take a seat at the bar counter or at one of the wooden tables, or secure the kitchen table if you fancy getting up close and personal. Dim sum such as the pork and prawn dumpling are fine versions indeed, served on a crisp piece of pork crackling in this case, or go for the inspired Yunnan mushroom, pork and truffle version with its earthy broth. In the evening, the 10-course tasting menu is hard to resist with its egg cooked in green tea at precisely 63 degrees, and Shaanxi pulled lamb 'burger'. Off the regular à la carte, there's plenty that catches the eye, from the Dung Po slow-braised Blythburgh pork belly to the razor clams that arrive with braised sea cucumber and wind-dried sausage. Creative desserts include chilli barbecued pineapple with Beijing street-style yogurt (made in-house and flavoured with lemongrass).

Chef Andrew Wong **Seats** 65, Pr/dining room 12
Times 12-2.30/5.30-10.30, Closed Xmas, Sun, L Mon **Prices** Prices not confirmed **Wines** 28 bottles over £30, 32 bottles under £30, 10 by glass **Parking** On street **Notes** 2 course with wine £14.95 until 6.30pm, Vegetarian available, Children welcome

Bar Boulud

PLAN 4 F5

French, American NOTABLE WINE LIST

tel: 020 7201 3899 **Mandarin Oriental Hyde Park, 66 Knightsbridge SW1X 7LA**
email: barboulud@mohg.com
dir: *Nearest station: Knightsbridge*

Very classy bistro cooking from superstar chef

Daniel Boulud's London restaurant bursts with contemporary glamour. The zinc-topped bar is a cool see-and-be-seen spot, staff whizz about, there's a contented hum in the dining rooms complete with open kitchen for cheffy action, while the menu speaks French with English translations. High-quality ingredients are prettily presented: rabbit terrine with asparagus and carrot is packed with flavour, while sea bass grilled a la plancha and served with ratatouille is a classy rustic-chic main course. For dessert, top-class pâtisserie skills bring a classy confection of hazelnut dacquoise, milk chocolate mousse, praline feuillantine, caramelised hazelnuts and chocolate sorbet. Burgundy and the Rhone are the stars of the stellar wine list.

Boisdale of Belgravia

PLAN 4 H3

Modern British

tel: 020 7730 6922 **15 Eccleston St SW1W 9LX**
email: info@boisdale.co.uk
dir: *Nearest station: Victoria*

Jazz and fine Scottish produce in a posh postcode

A combination of jazz venue, bar and restaurant, this warren of rooms in a Regency townhouse has a clubby decor and scarlet walls hung with jazz-related pictures. As at its Bishopsgate sibling, the cooking showcases fine Scottish produce, skilfully and accurately handled. A warm salad of roast wood pigeon with oyster mushrooms, Puy lentils and dandelion is a happy blend of flavours, followed by top-quality wild venison haunch fillet partnered with venison haggis, roast chervil root, blackberries, crispy oak moss and game gravy. The Highland theme continues to a finale of Valrhona hot chocolate and whisky fondant with honeycomb ice cream, and whisky and orange gel.

Chef Chris Zachwieja **Seats** 140, Pr/dining room 22
Times 12-3/6-11.15, Closed Xmas, New Year, Etr, BHs, Sun, L Sat **Prices** Fixed L 2 course £24.50, Starter £6.75-£19.50, Main £14.75-£35, Dessert £7.75-£10 **Wines** 176 bottles over £30, 20 bottles under £30, 28 by glass **Parking** On street, Eccleston St **Notes** Pre-theatre 2 course £11.95, Vegetarian available, Children welcome

Café Murano

PLAN 4 J6

 Northern Italian

tel: 020 3371 5559 **33 St James's St SW1A 1HD**
email: reception@cafemurano.co.uk
dir: *Nearest station: Green Park*

Celebrated chef Angela Hartnett's relaxed St James's Italian

Angela Hartnett's eatery is anything but a 'café', rather a sophisticated, albeit relaxed, take on a pop-in-every-day Italian. The slim room is a looker, from its marble-topped bar to wooden floors, brown banquettes and eye-catching lighting. The cooking is equally on cue, with a northern Italian menu of simple, rustic (if refined, well-executed and well-presented) lightly portioned dishes, from squid-ink linguine with crab, chilli and agretti, or a salad of burrata, peppers and anchovies, to zabaglione. In between might come braised ox cheek with polenta, carrots and baby onions, or a fish option of perhaps sea bream fillet with clams, mushrooms, samphire and potatoes.

Chef Sam Williams **Seats** 86, Pr/dining room 22
Times 12-2.45/5.30-10.45, Closed 25-26 Dec, D Sun, 24 & 31 Dec **Prices** Fixed L 2 course fr £19, Fixed D 3 course fr £23, Starter £8.50-£11, Main £16-£22, Dessert £6-£7 **Wines** 37 bottles over £30, 10 bottles under £30, 13 by glass **Notes** Fixed D 10-11pm, Sharing menu Sun £33 pp, Sun ALC menu, Sunday L, Vegetarian available, Children welcome

CANVAS at Chelsea

PLAN 4 G3

 Modern European

tel: 020 7823 4463 **1 Wilbraham Place, Belgravia SW1X 9AE**
email: info@canvasatchelsea.com
dir: *Nearest station: Sloan Sq*

Creative cooking just off Sloane Square

In a quiet street close to Sloane Square, subterranean Canvas boasts high ceilings, white columns, pastel tones and luxe red leather chairs softened by voile curtains. The chef's menu showcases light, refined, inventive modern European cooking. A fillet of wild sea bass is offset with large mussels and clams in a refined broth and saffron emulsion, while beef sirloin is accompanied by smoked bone marrow, braised short rib and watercress purée. Don't hold back on desserts like a stunningly light, warm pistachio cake bursting with nuttiness, topped-off with juicy baby roasted figs and saffron ice cream.

Le Caprice

PLAN 4 J6

Modern European V

tel: 020 7629 2239 & 7016 5220 **Arlington House, Arlington St SW1A 1RJ**
email: reservations@le-caprice.co.uk
dir: *Nearest station: Green Park*

Renowned Mayfair favourite

There's an ageless feeling to this iconic Mayfair favourite with smart linen-covered tables, crockery stamped with the restaurant's own logo, and David Bailey's monochrome photographs of young-looking celebs on the walls. Creamy risotto with butternut squash, finely chopped cobnuts and melted taleggio is a fine rendition, while main courses are often the highlight: perhaps neat slices of Glencoe venison, meltingly tender, with creamed Savoy cabbage and an attention-grabbing plum tarte Tatin. Some ideas are pulled in from the East – seen in monkfish and prawn tikka masala with saffron pilaf, for instance – and among puddings might be chocolate mousse with orange ice cream.

Chef Andy McLay **Seats** 86 **Times** 12-12, All-day dining, Closed 25-26 Dec, L 1 Jan, D 24 Dec **Prices** Prices not confirmed **Wines** 110 bottles over £30, 6 bottles under £30, 29 by glass **Parking** On street, NCP **Notes** Wknd brunch menu, Sunday L, Children welcome

Cavendish London

PLAN 4 J6

British

tel: 020 7930 2111 **81 Jermyn St SW1Y 6JF**
email: info@thecavendishlondon.com **web:** www.thecavendishlondon.com
dir: *Nearest station: Green Park, Piccadilly*

Lively cooking in a smart hotel behind Fortnum & Mason

Among the gentlemen's outfitters of Jermyn Street, the Cavendish is as chic as can be, adorned with a plethora of striking modern paintings. The first-floor dining room may look out on St James's, but conjures in its name – Petrichor – the scent of freshly moistened earth after the first rains. The kitchen draws on thoroughbred suppliers for materials such as Wicks Manor ham hock, served à la Benedict with hollandaise and spinach. After that, it may be sea bream with brown shrimps and curried cauliflower purée in capered lemon butter. Hold your nerve for a dessert billed as Chocolate Avalanche – ganache with honeycomb and hazelnut ice cream.

Chef Nitin Padwal **Seats** 80, Pr/dining room 70
Times 12-2.30/5.30-10.30, Closed 25-26 Dec, 1 Jan, L Sat-Sun & BH Mon
Prices Fixed L 2 course £24.50, Fixed D 3 course £29, Starter £8.50-£12.50, Main £17.50-£22, Dessert £6.50-£9.50 **Wines** 31 bottles over £30, 12 bottles under £30, 10 by glass **Parking** 60, Secure on-site valet parking **Notes** Pre-theatre menu Sun-Thu 5.30-6.30/Fri-Sat 5-6.30pm, Vegetarian available, Children welcome

Caxton Grill

PLAN 4 K4

Modern European, British NOTABLE WINE LIST

tel: 020 7222 7888 **St Ermin's Hotel, 2 Caxton St, St James Park, Westminster SW1H 0QW**
email: reservations@sterminshotel.co.uk **web:** www.caxtongrill.co.uk
dir: *Nearest station: Victoria, St James's Park*

Confident modern cooking in a luxury hotel

The Rosette award for this establishment has been suspended due to a change of chef. Reassessment will take place in due course under the new chef. Situated in the audaciously grand St Ermin's Hotel, this is a surprisingly modern venue with a soothing colour scheme, striking contemporary artworks, and designer furniture. Formerly the haunt of Adam Handling, who left in March 2016 to launch his own place, the restaurant at St Ermin's has a new turn of direction as the Caxton Grill with a modern European menu and premium steaks cooked on the Josper grill. A dedication to sustainability and sourcing local ingredients is most demonstrably shown by its interior green wall of seasonal herbs and plants as well as the honey made by its own bees on the hotel's roof. There's also an outdoor terrace overlooking the courtyard where champagne cocktails and European and Asian bento boxes are up for grabs, while the bar has a fine collection of whiskies.

Chef Sylvan Chevereau **Seats** 72, Pr/dining room 10
Times 12-2/6-10.30, Closed L Sat-Sun, 26 & 31 Dec, BHs **Prices** Fixed L 3 course £30-£49, Fixed D 3 course £30-£49, Tasting menu £95-£126, Starter £5-£10, Main £17-£43, Dessert £10 **Wines** 65 bottles over £30, 18 bottles under £30, 29 by glass **Parking** Valet parking **Notes** Vegetarian available, Children welcome

LONDON SW1 *continued*

Céleste at The Lanesborough

PLAN 4 G5

French, British V

tel: 020 7259 5599 **Hyde Park Corner SW1X 7TA**
email: info@lanesborough.com
web: www.lanesborough.com/eng/restaurant-bars/celeste
dir: *Nearest station: Hyde Park Corner*

Outstanding modern French cooking in ultra-luxe hotel

The Rosette award for this establishment has been suspended due to a change of chef. Reassessment will take place in due course under the new chef. The Lanesborough is pretty much at the beating heart of the capital as its porticoed and balustraded frontage faces Hyde Park from the famous Corner, with a pillared and pedimented elevation at the back. The place exudes five-star class from every pore, from the moment somebody opens your taxi door to the luxurious book-lined bar, which feels like somewhere you might work on your memoirs, to a dining room with dripping chandeliers and an array of cameos mounted on walls in robin's-egg blue. The cooking has taken on a gilded contemporary French ambience, complete with theatrical presentations – the truffle-powdered Landes foie gras and brioche come to table looking like a mossy bank on a wooden board, or there may be langoustine ravioli, the claw meat whisked into a velouté spiked with espelette pepper. Main courses pull out the stops for stunning venison smoked over juniper wood, presented before carving, lustrously coloured with beetroot and cabbage in imperial purple, in an intense red wine jus, or perhaps poached cod with Tokyo turnips in brown shrimp broth. At dessert, a dark chocolate cube filled with mint sorbet is like the greatest after-dinner mint ever, and comes garnished with a chocolate twig sprouting mint leaves.

Chef Florian Favario, Eric Frechon **Seats** 100, Pr/dining room 12
Times 12.30-2.30/7-10.30 **Prices** Fixed L 2 course £28, Tasting menu £75-£85, Starter £18-£28, Main £30-£48, Dessert £10-£14 **Wines** 550 bottles over £30, 20 by glass **Parking** 25 **Notes** Tasting menu 5/7 course, Vegetarian tasting menu 5 course, Children welcome

Le Chinois at Millennium Knightsbridge

PLAN 4 F4

tel: 020 7201 6330 **17 Sloane St, Knightsbridge SW1X 9NU**
email: lechinois@millenniumhotels.co.uk **web:** www.millenniumhotels.com/knightsbridge
dir: *Nearest station: Knightsbridge, Victoria*

Lengthy Chinese menu in a glam setting

The Millennium is a modern Sloaneland hotel aimed at the style-conscious. Darkwood and plum-coloured pillars, as well as a row of birdcage light fittings, make a bright backdrop to the refined Cantonese-based cooking on offer, which veers between textbook traditionalism and newer ideas. Open with a palate-priming bowl of Szechuan-style hot-and-sour lobster soup, or salt-and-pepper soft-shelled crab. Head-turning main dishes include sautéed prawns glazed in honey and lemon, steamed whole sea bass with preserved vegetables and shredded pork, and venison sizzling in ginger and spring onions on a hot stone plate. Chinese sweets such as red bean pancakes are a safe bet to finish on.

Chef Anthony Kong **Seats** 65 **Times** 12-10.30, All-day dining **Prices** Prices not confirmed **Wines** 30 bottles over £30, 8 bottles under £30, 14 by glass **Parking** 8, Chargeable, NCP Pavilion Rd **Notes** Sunday L, Vegetarian available, Children welcome

Chutney Mary

PLAN 4 J6

Modern Indian NEW NOTABLE WINE LIST

tel: 020 7629 6688 **73 St James's St SW1A 1PH**
email: chutneymary@realindianfood.com
dir: *Nearest station: Green Park*

Old favourite at a new address

The move from Chelsea to St James's has given Chutney Mary a new lease of life, not to mention a swanky cocktail bar and some smart private dining rooms. The restaurant has a suitably luxurious sheen with rich, colourful fabrics and designer chairs, but the closely-packed tables remain linen-free. The creative modern Indian cuisine runs to inspiring combinations such as tamarind-glazed duck in a top-drawer salad, or another starter of baked venison samosa. Follow on with kid goat biryani or red snapper tikka and expect well-judged spicing throughout. Finish with citrusy nimbu tart with rhubarb sorbet and verbena jelly. Look out for the global wines and creative cocktails.

Chef Manav Tuli, Uday Salunkhe **Seats** 112, Pr/dining room 32
Times 12-2.15/6-10.30, Closed Sun **Prices** Fixed L 2 course £26, Tasting menu £55-£80, Starter £8-£15, Main £16-£38 **Notes** Veg tasting menu £49, Gourmet menu £70-£99 complete tables, Vegetarian available

The Cinnamon Club

PLAN 5 A4

Modern Indian NOTABLE WINE LIST

tel: 020 7222 2555 **The Old Westminster Library, 30-32 Great Smith St SW1P 3BU**
email: info@cinnamonclub.com
dir: *Nearest station: Westminster, St James Park*

Inventive Indian food in a grand listed building

Former public buildings often make good venues, particularly those built with a bit of empire pomp, like the old Westminster Library with its handsome façade, book-lined galleries and high-end feel. Here, classy modern Indian cooking combines Asian and European techniques to deliver bang-on flavours. A starter of fenugreek-scented tandoori cod with curry leaf and lime crumble shows a fine balance of flavours. Ingredients are top quality, too, as in a main course roast saddle of Romney Marsh lamb with corn sauce, pickled root vegetables and masala cashew nut. Dessert is a fusion idea: dark chocolate and rasgulla (milk curds in syrup) tart with tangy calamansi and chilli sorbet.

Chef Vivek Singh, Rakesh Ravindran **Seats** 130, Pr/dining room 60
Times 12-2.45/6-10.45, Closed BHs (some), Sun, D 25 Dec **Prices** Fixed L 2 course £22, Tasting menu £85-£160, Starter £7.50-£24, Main £16-£34, Dessert £7.50-£10 **Wines** 308 bottles over £30, 15 bottles under £30, 37 by glass **Parking** Abingdon St **Notes** Tasting menu 8 course, Feast menu for 4+ £65pp, Vegetarian available, Children welcome

Colbert

PLAN 4 G3

tel: 020 7730 2804 **50-52 Sloane Square, Chelsea SW1W 8AX**
email: info@colbertchelsea.com
dir: *Nearest station: Sloane Sq*

Paris comes to Sloane Square

Inspired by the grand boulevard cafés of Paris, the Colbert sits smack on Sloane Square and bustles with a wonderful feel-good vibe from breakfast to late evening, with a lengthy all-day menu that doesn't talk three-course formality. Grab eggs Benedict or croquet-monsieur to top-dollar Beluga caviar, or steak tartare to sea-fresh lemon sole goujons with tartare, or crank up the ante with Chateaubriand for two – there's something for every occasion. The essence of the cooking is clean simplicity, defined by premium ingredients and flavour without cheffy grandstanding. Blackboard specials (bouillabaisse perhaps) bolster output, while the bar gets rammed and street-side alfresco tables are a hot ticket.

Chef Maarten Geschwindt **Seats** 140 **Times** 8am-11.30pm, All-day dining, Closed Xmas **Prices** Starter £6.75-£14.75, Main £9.95-£31.50, Dessert £4.25-£7.95 **Wines** 50 bottles over £30, 8 bottles under £30, 37 by glass **Notes** Cover charge £1.75 L/D in dining rooms, Sunday L £9.95-£31.50, Children welcome

Dinner by Heston Blumenthal

PLAN 4 F5

British NOTABLE WINE LIST

tel: 020 7201 3833 **Mandarin Oriental Hyde Park, 66 Knightsbridge SW1X 7LA**
email: molon-dinnerhb@mohg.com **web:** www.dinnerbyheston.com
dir: *Nearest station: Knightsbridge*

A gastronomic lesson in time travel from Heston

Heston Blumenthal may be best known for his cutting-edge molecular cooking, but his fascination with culinary history underpins the food served within the luxurious setting of the Mandarin Oriental Hotel. A time-travelling trip through half a millennium of British cooking is recreated by executive chef Ashley Palmer-Watts, who cooks dishes developed with his Fat Duck mentor. As befits a venue overlooking Hyde Park, the setting is grand yet understated, but a waspish sense of humour is evident in jelly mould light fittings. A floor-to-ceiling glass wall kitchen allows diners to observe the chefs at close quarters – watching pineapples turning on clockwork rotisseries, for example. The ideas may be centuries old, but the techniques are very much of the moment. A starter of Earl Grey tea-cured salmon with lemon salad, gentleman's relish, wood sorrel and smoked roe is evidence that the Georgians knew all about flavour combinations and a Victorian-era Hereford rib-eye with mushroom ketchup turns up with Blumenthal's equally timeless triple-cooked chips. Prepare to be transported to the Middle Ages for a dessert of 'Sambocade' (c.1390) comprising goats' milk cheesecake, elderflower and apple, perry-poached pear and smoked candied walnuts.

Chef Ashley Palmer-Watts **Seats** 149, Pr/dining room 12
Times 12-2.30/6.30-10.30 **Prices** Fixed L 3 course £38, Starter £17-£19.50, Main £28-£42, Dessert £13.50-£16 **Wines** 500 bottles over £30, 24 by glass
Parking Valet parking, NCP **Notes** Vegetarian available, Children 4 yrs+

Enoteca Turi

PLAN 1 D2

Italian

tel: 020 7730 6327 & 7730 3663 **87 Pimlico Rd SW1W 8PH**
email: info@enotecaturi.com
dir: *Nearest station: Sloane Square*

Regional Italian food in a buzzing venue

Run by the same family since 1990, Enoteca Turi has upped sticks and moved from Putney to Chelsea. The focus is on regional Italian flavours, with the menu highlighting the origins of each dish (Piedmont, Puglia, etc.). The whole place still buzzes with life and the menu presents high quality, seasonal ingredients. Among antipasti, braised cuttlefish might come with chickpea purée and deep-fried pasta, or grilled fillet of mackerel with fennel and blood orange salad and a citrus dressing. Next up, a duck dish with a punchy sauce flavoured with liver, served with polenta gnocchi and cavolo nero. The wine list, sorted by region, offers matches for every dish.

Chef Gonzalo Luzarraga **Seats** 75, Pr/dining room 25
Times 12-2.30/6-10.30, Closed 25-26 Dec, 1 Jan, Sun, L BH Mon **Prices** Fixed D 3 course fr £26.50, Starter £9.25-£14.50, Main £11.50-£27.75, Dessert £5.50-£10.75 **Wines** 16 bottles under £30, 13 by glass **Parking** On street **Notes** Pre-theatre menu, Vegetarian available, Children welcome

Estiatorio Milos

PLAN 2 K1

Greek, Mediterranean Seafood NEW

tel: 020 7839 2080 **1 Regent St, St James's SW1Y 4NR**
email: london@estiatoriomilos.com
dir: *Nearest station: Oxford Circus, Piccadilly Circus, Bond St*

Modern Greek seafood and meat dishes at a smart address

The august surroundings of deep windows with voile coverings, frosted glass globe lighting and white linen here make a handsome backdrop for its modern Greek food. The cooking is full of both sea-fresh savour and hearty meaty robustness. Expect starters of tender sashimi-style octopus on Santorini broad bean purée, with shallot and caper dressing, followed by crisp-skinned medium-rare salmon with broccoli and cauliflower, or grilled lamb chops and côte de (Angus) boeuf for two. The sides alone will have you dreaming of a holiday booking: Lefkada lentils; Prespes giant beans; almond skordalia; cooling tzatziki. Finish with karidopita, orange-scented spicy walnut cake, with vanilla ice cream.

Chef Costas Spiliadis **Times** 12-2.45/5.30-11 **Prices** Fixed L 3 course £29 **Wines** 16 by glass **Notes** Pre/post-theatre 3 course £49, Sun D 4 course £49, Vegetarian available

The Goring

PLAN 4 H4

Traditional British V NOTABLE WINE LIST

tel: 020 7396 9000 **Beeston Place SW1W 0JW**
email: diningroom@thegoring.com **web:** www.thegoring.com
dir: *Nearest station: Victoria*

A century-old family-run hotel with classical and modern cooking

Luxury hotels don't come much better than this Belgravia landmark, which opened its doors back in 1910. It emanates class and exquisite taste, with its fine period details, from coved ceilings to marble fireplaces, expensive furnishings and luxury fabrics. Start off with a glass of champagne or a cocktail in the warmly atmospheric bar before dining in the restaurant. Designed by Viscount Linley, with a relaxing decor of gold and white, ornate plasterwork, drapes at the windows and with impeccable service, it's full of light by day and lit by crystal chandeliers after dark. Tradition meets modernism on Shay Cooper's menus as he gives a creative tweak to the classical repertoire. Pressed rabbit terrine sounds a familiar enough starter, but it's served with pickled carrots, Welsh rarebit and mustard, while cured sea bream comes with pickled fennel, radish and lemon purée. Ingredients are of a top order, and techniques are unflinchingly spot on. Beef Wellington, lobster omelette with chips and lobster Caesar salad, and fallow deer with a glazed faggot, duxelle, quince and pine nuts are all up for grabs among main courses. Lunch brings on a rolling daily special – fish pie on Monday, for instance – and puddings and cheeses are wheeled round on a trolley.

Chef Shay Cooper **Seats** 70, Pr/dining room 50 **Times** 12-2.30/6-10, Closed L Sat **Prices** Fixed L 3 course fr £45, Fixed D 3 course fr £56.50 **Wines** 450 bottles over £30, 5 bottles under £30, 22 by glass **Parking** 7 **Notes** Pre-theatre 2 course £35, Sunday L fr £50, Children welcome

LONDON SW1 *continued*

Grand Imperial London

PLAN 4 H4

Cantonese, Chinese V

tel: 020 7821 8898 **The Grosvenor, 101 Buckingham Palace Rd SW1W 0SJ**
email: reservations@grandimperiallondon.com **web:** www.grandimperiallondon.com
dir: *Nearest station: Victoria*

Upscale Chinese dining amid Victorian grandeur

The oriental artefacts, artworks, calligraphy and black lacquered seats illustrate that classic and modern Cantonese cooking is the Grand Imperial's business these days. There's a dim sum menu at lunchtime, with intriguing options such as abalone and prawn dumpling, marinated jellyfish with wasabi, or steamed chicken claws in black bean sauce. Dim sum appear on the carte menu too, otherwise set out with salt-and-pepper soft-shelled crab, or soups such as hot-and-sour Szechuan soup with lobster, before mains of sautéed scallop, prawn and broccoli in XO sauce, braised whole turbot with turnip and spring onions, or classic Peking duck.

Chef Rand Cheung **Seats** 140, Pr/dining room 26 **Times** 12-10.45, All-day dining, Closed 25-26 Dec **Prices** Fixed L 2 course £13.50-£30, Fixed D 3 course £23-£48, Tasting menu £48, Starter £5-£16, Main £10-£49, Dessert £5-£8 **Wines** 60 bottles over £30, 10 bottles under £30, 12 by glass **Parking** NCP **Notes** Meal deals, Sunday L £13.50-£48, Children welcome

Il Convivio

PLAN 4 G3

Modern Italian

tel: 020 7730 4099 **143 Ebury St SW1W 9QN**
email: ilconvivio@etruscarestaurants.com **web:** www.ilconvivio.co.uk
dir: *Nearest station: Victoria, Sloane Sq*

Smart, friendly modish Italian in Belgravia

A family-owned Italian in a Georgian townhouse on swanky Ebury Street, Il Convivio is a favourite of the Belgravia set. The predominantly Italian wine list shows serious intent from the off, while the kitchen offers modern renditions of classic combinations underpinned by quality Italian and British seasonal produce. Witness home-made pasta, like limoncello tagliolini combined with palourde clams, broccoli, datterini tomato tartare and Sardinian bottarga, while, from the bank-manager-friendly fixed-price lunch menu, perhaps sparkling-fresh pan-fried sea trout served with crushed maris pipers, black olives and sun-dried tomatoes. Finish on a high, with an innovatively presented pistachio pannacotta with orange marmalade, open cannoli tuile and ricotta ice cream.

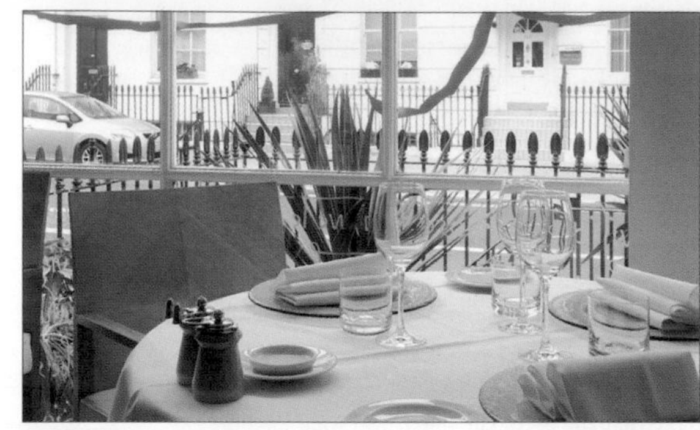

Il Convivio

Chef Cedric Neri **Seats** 65, Pr/dining room 14 **Times** 12-3/6-11, Closed Xmas, New Year, BHs, Sun **Prices** Fixed L 2 course £17.50, Fixed D 3 course £29, Starter £8.50-£17.50, Main £14-£25, Dessert £7-£7.75 **Wines** 142 bottles over £30, 28 bottles under £30, 14 by glass **Parking** On street **Notes** Vegetarian available, Children welcome

Inn the Park

PLAN 5 A5

British

tel: 020 7451 9999 **St James's Park SW1A 2BJ**
email: reservations@innthepark.com
dir: *Nearest station: St James's Park, Charing Cross, Piccadilly*

Seasonal British cooking in St James's Park

The curving wooden pavilion blends unobtrusively into St James's Park – an idyllic setting considering it's smack in the centre of London. Inside, it's a light-flooded space with a Scandinavian-feeling decor of tubular steel chairs, leather banquettes and apricot-topped tables. Sliding glass walls open onto a covered wooden terrace that is the trump card on a balmy day when you're in the market for fresh, impeccably seasonal British produce prepared without fuss. Start with smoked eel with horseradish and celeriac remoulade, followed by tender pink rump of lamb with kale, sautéed baby potatoes and salsa verde. For pud, try plum and apple hazelnut crumble with custard.

Ken Lo's Memories of China

PLAN 4 H3

Chinese

tel: 020 7730 7734 **65-69 Ebury St SW1W 0NZ**
email: moc@londonfinediningroup.com
dir: *Nearest station: Victoria*

Classy Chinese dishes at a long-standing Belgravia venue

This sumptuous restaurant was created by the late Kenneth Lo, one of modern Chinese gastronomy's early movers and shakers. Oriental screen dividers, clothed tables and a bottle store create a fine-dining ambience for classy Chinese cooking. The lengthy menu features crispy soft-shelled crab in excellent tempura, five spice spare ribs and soups such as lamb and cucumber. Move on to velvety slices of quick-fried lamb given a kick of ginger and spring onions, Cantonese-style sweet-and-sour prawns or crispy aromatic duck. Accompaniments such as fluffy fried rice studded with shrimps, chicken and peas are spot on, and there may be mango sorbet to finish.

Koffmann's

PLAN 4 G5

@@@ French NOTABLE WINE LIST

tel: 020 7235 1010 & 7107 8844 **The Berkeley, Wilton Place SW1X 7RL**
email: koffmanns@the-berkeley.co.uk
dir: *Nearest station: Knightsbridge, Hyde Park Corner*

Top-drawer regional French cooking from a virtuoso

The split-level brasserie space within Knightsbridge's Berkeley Hotel has played host to the sweeping winds of culinary fashion over the last couple of decades, but its present incarnation as Pierre Koffmann's Gascon foothold in well-heeled London is easily its classiest. Autumnal hues of green and brown against slate-grey compose a relaxed ambience, with a discreet glass-fronted kitchen affording views of the brigade at work in the pass. Fluent service from a French team inspires confidence, and Koffmann's refined interpretations of the cuisine of southwest France combine rusticity with presentational elegance. When did polenta get so sophisticated? Never more so than when Koffmann's rich creamy version turns up topped with sautéed girolles and an egg yolk in a rich chicken jus. Otherwise, luxe things up with a starter of hot foie gras and chicory in Sauternes sauce, before moving on to grilled lobster in herb butter, herb-crusted lamb rack with parsnip purée and petits pois, or the magisterial braised duck leg with beans and black olives. Excellent pastry work is assured for a mirabelle frangipane tart served with milky sorbet and a little crème anglaise, or else wait the 15 minutes or so for a perfectly risen pistachio soufflé with matching ice cream.

Chef Pierre Koffmann **Seats** 120, Pr/dining room 16 **Times** 12-2.30/6-10.30 **Prices** Fixed L 2 course fr £22.50, Tasting menu £80-£100, Starter £12-£16, Main £25-£40, Dessert £9-£15 **Wines** 260 bottles over £30, 6 bottles under £30, 22 by glass **Parking** Knightsbridge car park **Notes** Pre-theatre menu 2/3 course £24/£28, Sunday L £22.50-£26, Vegetarian available, Children welcome

Marcus

PLAN 4 G5

@@@@@ – *see page 264*

Mint Leaf Restaurant & Bar

PLAN 5 A6

@ Modern Indian

tel: 020 7930 9020 **Suffolk Place, Haymarket SW1Y 4HX**
email: reservations@mintleafrestaurant.com **web:** www.mintleafrestaurant.com
dir: *Nearest station: Piccadilly, Charing Cross*

Modern Indian food at an upbeat West End address

A contemporary Indian eaterie to grace the West End, the Mint Leaf is a buzzy, nightclubby venue with svelte and seductive looks, a dimly lit mood prevailing in the rather glam cocktail bar and the main restaurant, where spotlights and low-slung pendant lights enhance darkwood tables. The kitchen sends out a wide-ranging medley of classics and some original, contemporary fusion preparations. Lamb seekh kebab with coriander sauce is a time-honoured opener, otherwise salmon fillet with kasundi mustard, turmeric and ajwain seed might appeal. For main course, king fish and coconut stew is perked up with curry leaf, mustard and tamarind, or there might be pot-roasted rabbit fennel spiced with mustard, chilli and onion seed.

Mint Leaf Restaurant & Bar

Chef Rajinder Pandey **Seats** 144, Pr/dining room 66
Times 12-3/5.30-11, Closed 25-26 Dec, 1 Jan, L Sat-Sun **Prices** Prices not confirmed **Wines** 100 bottles over £30, 17 bottles under £30, 13 by glass **Parking** NCP, on street **Notes** Pre-theatre menu 5-7pm 2/3 course £13.95/£17.95, Vegetarian available, Children welcome

One-O-One

PLAN 4 F5

@@@ French NEW V

tel: 020 7235 8050 **The Park Tower Knightsbridge, 101 Knightsbridge SW1X 7RN**
email: oneoone@luxurycollection.com **web:** www.oneoonerestaurant.com
dir: *Nearest station: Knightsbridge*

Glamorous seafood cookery with a French flavour

The Park Tower is a soaring glass edifice overlooking Hyde Park, a glittering slice of 1970s futurama that still looks newly conceived. The pick of the dining options is Pascal Proyart's One-O-One, a landlocked London shrine to exemplary seafood cooking, a language in which Proyart has been fluent since his Breton boyhood. The room is restful rather than five-star flash, furnished with comfortable seating, the wood walls adorned with abstract images, and the best tables enjoy an aerial view of Knightsbridge. Seafood is the name of the game, though the contexts are often robust, as witness a starter of four caramelised scallops teamed with a lobe of duck foie gras, given earthy depth with wild mushrooms and spinach, dressed in jus gras and vermouth foam. Main course might support translucent, milky-white cod with a truffled cassoulet of Paimpol beans and a parsley version of béarnaise. There are meat options too, perhaps venison loin with parsnips, kumquat, cranberries and whole peppercorn poivrade, and dessert echoes the confident balance achieved throughout when lime parfait and ginger ice cream form the dual focus of a dish incorporating pain d'épices, salted caramel and meringue, or with a fruity little number combining lemon posset with orange sorbet, champagne jelly and blackberries.

Chef Pascal Proyart **Seats** 52, Pr/dining room 30
Times 12-2.30/6.30-10, Closed Sun-Mon **Prices** Fixed L 2 course £19.50, Fixed D 3 course £29.50, Tasting menu £75-£121, Starter £11-£38, Main £24-£52, Dessert £8-£16 **Wines** 82 bottles over £30, 1 bottle under £30, 11 by glass **Parking** UPark **Notes** Children welcome

Marcus

LONDON SW1 **PLAN 4 G5**

Modern European, British V 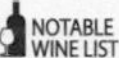

tel: 020 7235 1200 **Wilton Place, Knightsbridge SW1X 7RL**
email: reservations@marcuswareing.com
web: www.marcus-wareing.com
dir: *Nearest station: Knightsbridge, Hyde Park Corner*

Impeccable benchmark contemporary cooking

Recognition by first name alone must surely be considered a sign of success in the cheffing game. Marcus's national recognition is helped by appearances on the Beeb's *MasterChef: The Professionals*, which lays bare Mr Wareing's evident passion for his profession, not to mention his exacting standards and supreme technical ability. He's been a big-hitter on the London dining scene for a lot longer than he's been a 'face' on TV, and The Berkley remains the place to head for if you really want to get a measure of the man. Walk confidently past the limos outside, breeze through the lobby, proceed through the Caramel Room, and expect a sincere greeting from the team out front. The room itself has a sleek contemporary finish, nothing too stiff, with some vivid modern art to add splashes of colour. Mark Froydenlund is the man charged with delivering the Marcus Wareing style, which is rooted in classical good sense, with modern ideas introduced in a measured and assured way. Everything looks stunning on the plate, and, like every top chef, Wareing ensures the very best produce finds its way into his kitchen. The set lunch menu is a great value introduction to the place, while the tasting menu offers the opportunity to go the whole hog (an excellent vegetarian version is one of the most eye-catching in the capital). It all kicks off with dynamic little canapés such as red polenta topped with black olive crumb, and then there's fennel and polenta bread that lingers long in the memory. First course proper might be a crabby number that sees the crustacean shipped up from Dorset and served as crisp beignet, au naturel and added to a rich sauce, with chargrilled courgette, white peach and cobnuts completing a masterclass of complementary flavours and textures. Among main courses, pink and tender grouse stars in a dish with fontina cheese and a bang-on bread sauce, with little kicks of sweetness from the accompanying plump red grapes, while Herdwick lamb is enriched with anchovies, and sea bass gets a zesty hit from bergamot. There's plenty of showboating when it comes to dessert, with the kitchen pulling out the stops to deliver the likes of a combination of white chocolate, blackcurrant and coconut, or another that brings out the best of the classic combination of lemon and meringue with the additional flavour of iced tea. Save room for the stupendous cheeses, delivered via a trolley, but it's all too easy to blow the budget on something from the stellar wine list – over 1,000 bins – which includes the option to taste some of the rarer wines by the glass.

Chef Marcus Wareing, Mark Froydenlund **Seats** 90, Pr/dining room 16 **Times** 12-2.30/6-10.30, Closed 4-10 Jan, Sun **Prices** Prices not confirmed **Wines** 950 bottles over £30, 13 by glass **Parking** NCP, on street, valet **Notes** Children welcome at lunch only

LONDON SW1 *continued*

Osteria Dell'Angolo

PLAN 5 A4

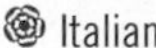 Italian

tel: 020 3268 1077 **47 Marsham St SW1P 3DR**
email: osteriadell_angolo@btconnect.com
dir: *Nearest station: St James's Park, Westminster*

Modern Italian classics in Westminster

The sunny orange awnings of this Westminster Italian bring a splash of Mediterranean colour to Marsham Street. Warm yellow and amber tones, terracotta-coloured leather seating and large windows fill the space with light. A semi-open kitchen offers a glimpse of the cheffy action as staff deliver regional classics and modern interpretations, with simplicity and flavour to the fore. Try home-made stracci pasta with spicy nduja salami and cherry tomato sauce accompanied by a topping of cacio ricotta, while, for seafood lovers, top-notch roasted fillet of wild sea bass comes with crispy skin set on a bed of iron-rich spinach in a light palourde clam broth.

Chef Massimiliano Vezzi **Seats** 80, Pr/dining room 22
Times 12-3/6-10.30, Closed Xmas, New Year, last 2 wks Aug, BHs, Sun, L Sat
Prices Fixed L 2 course £17.50, Starter £7.50-£11, Main £12-£25, Dessert £5.50-£9.50 **Wines** 200 bottles over £30, 8 bottles under £30, 12 by glass **Parking** 6
Notes Vegetarian available, Children welcome

Park Plaza Victoria London

PLAN 4 J3

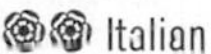 Italian

tel: 020 7769 9771 **239 Vauxhall Bridge Rd SW1V 1EQ**
email: reservations@tozirestaurant.co.uk **web:** www.tozirestaurant.co.uk
dir: *Nearest station: Victoria*

Venetian sharing plates in a contemporary space

Recently refurbished, this vibrant Italian restaurant and bar serves classic Venetian cicchetti dishes from the open kitchen. With its full-length windows and original Fiat 500 at the entrance, the room is sleek and modern with lots of natural wood and neutral colours. It's a classy and chilled-out setting to sip a Bellini as you choose from a menu that includes salads, pasta, soup, grilled meats and seafood, and dishes to share. A light and full-flavoured wood-fired pizzetta mozzarella with wild mushrooms and black truffle might be followed by a simple burrata with heritage tomatoes and basil.

Pétrus

PLAN 4 G5

Modern French V

tel: 020 7592 1609 **1 Kinnerton St, Knightsbridge SW1X 8EA**
email: petrus@gordonramsay.com
dir: *Nearest station: Knightsbridge, Hyde Park, Sloane Sq*

Immaculate modern cooking from the Ramsay stable

The Rosette award for this establishment has been suspended due to a change of chef. Reassessment will take place in due course under the new chef. Granted, Pétrus may be at the high-gloss end of the Gordon Ramsay empire, catering to the minted sharp suits, high heels and occasion diners, but it's so much more besides. The room looks comfortable, modern and bright without trying to be overly cool, with its reassuring leather chairs and white linen, the pastel tones jazzed up by splashes of thematic claret, and the centrepiece walk-in glass wine store does justice to the Pétrus name. An effortlessly luxe, sophisticated outfit then, but it's not just an exercise in pompous self-regard: the light modern cooking displays real panache, while service is spot-on without being too fussy. Begin with a flawless scallop, which has travelled from Orkney to be seared and served with bacon and braised kombu in egg sabayon, or with the sautéed foie gras, which comes fragrant with elderflower and enriched with mead, as though it were an old English tradition, albeit with puffed wild rice. Prime British materials are the main-course stars – Gigha halibut, Herdwick lamb, Hereford beef fillet – the last with Dorset snails, rainbow chard and puréed parsnip. Desserts sound straightforward but arrive as architectural marvels, conjured from citrus bavarois and blood orange, or milk chocolate delice with raspberry and rosemary ice cream.

Seats 55, Pr/dining room 8 **Times** 12-2.30/6.30-10.30, Closed 22-26 Dec, Sun
Prices Fixed L 3 course £37.50-£75, Fixed D 3 course £75, Tasting menu £95
Wines 428 bottles over £30, 2 bottles under £30, 27 by glass **Parking** On street (free after 6.30pm)/NCP Park Towers **Notes** Chef's menu 5 course, Children welcome

Quaglino's

PLAN 4 J6

European

tel: 020 7930 6767 **16 Bury St SW1Y 6AJ**
email: quaglinos@danddlondon.com
dir: *Nearest station: Green Park, Piccadilly Circus*

Glamorous brasserie dining on the cruise-ship scale

Once the favoured watering-hole Evelyn Waugh and the future Edward VIII, Quaglino's is a masterpiece of art deco style on the cruise-ship scale, complete with golden-lit staircase to tempt out your inner Gloria Swanson. Flavours shine from the plate: soused charred mackerel with mustard onion compôte and vodka dill pickle won't get forgotten in a hurry. Mains offer roast breast and croquetted leg of pheasant with cabbage and pear in truffled jus, or a whole sea bass for sharing, served on saffron pilaf and beurre blanc. A profiterole makeover sees a ball of cracked choux filled with salted caramel, but doused in chocolate sauce by the waiter as of old.

LONDON SW1 *continued*

Quilon

PLAN 4 J4

Indian NOTABLE WINE LIST

tel: 020 7821 1899 **41 Buckingham Gate SW1E 6AF**
email: dine@quilon.co.uk **web:** www.quilon.co.uk
dir: *Nearest station: St James's Park, Victoria*

Upmarket venue for southwest Indian cuisine

Set in the swish St James' Court hotel, Quilon offers a designer-led, ultra-modern interior, and cooking that showcases the cuisine of India's southwest, mixing traditional and more inventive ideas, with tip-top materials the backbone of the kitchen's output. Crab cakes are packed with juicy chunks of sweet claw meat, shredded curry leaves, ginger and green chillies, while main-course seafood moilee is an upmarket take on a classic south Indian fish stew, made with halibut and prawns in a creamy broth of coconut milk, turmeric, ginger and garlic. The kitchen pays the same care and attention to rice and breads, and the show closes with baked yogurt flavoured with confit orange, mango and lychee.

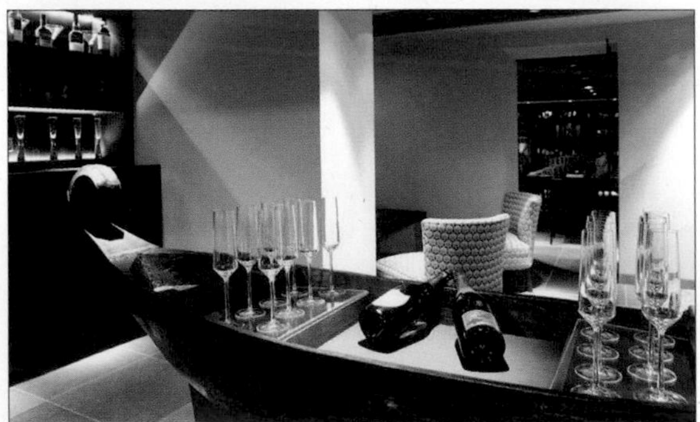

Chef Sriram Aylur **Seats** 90, Pr/dining room 16 **Times** 12-2.30/6-11, Closed 25 Dec **Prices** Fixed L 2 course £27, Tasting menu £60-£80, Starter £9-£16, Main £11-£41, Dessert £8-£10 **Wines** 130 bottles over £30, 4 bottles under £30, 16 by glass **Parking** On street, NCP **Notes** Sunday L £27-£36, Vegetarian available, Children welcome

The Rib Room Bar and Restaurant

PLAN 4 F4

Modern British

tel: 020 7858 7250 **Jumeirah Carlton Tower, Cadogan Place SW1X 9PY**
email: reservations@theribroom.co.uk **web:** www.theribroom.co.uk
dir: *Nearest station: Knightsbridge*

Old stalwarts and seasonal modernity in a Sloaneland hotel

On the ground floor of a luxury Knightsbridge hotel, The Rib Room has an air of affluence. It's a large restaurant, with flowers on clothed tables, button-back leather-look chairs, a square-patterned carpet and slatted blinds at the windows. There's even a cigar bar and terrace, which says something about the clientele it attracts. The reputation of the place rests on the beef and steaks, as it has done since it opened in 1961. It's a well-earned reputation too, with top-quality meat cooked comme il faut, ranging from onglet through sirloin to Wagyu fillet (at a price) with a choice of sauces, among them béarnaise and bone marrow. But there's much more to the menu than beef, and the kitchen moves with the times. As well as prawn cocktail with Marie Rose sauce, starters might run to lobster and roast tomato bisque floated with crab ravioli, or smoked chicken salad with walnuts and persillade. Dover sole meunière, lobster thermidor and rib of beef with the usual accompaniments are fixtures, or go for the more adventurous pork tenderloin with potato-wrapped black pudding, swede and purple mustard sauce, or seared plaice fillet with poached crayfish tails, broccoli and a seaweed and caper broth. End with traditional treacle tart with tangy lemon, thyme and vanilla ice cream.

Chef Ian Rudge **Seats** 120, Pr/dining room 20 **Times** 12-2.45/6.30-10.45 **Prices** Fixed L 2 course £19-£28, Fixed D 3 course £24.50-£38, Starter £14-£22, Main £27-£44, Dessert £8-£12 **Wines** 439 bottles over £30, 11 bottles under £30, 29 by glass **Parking** 78 **Notes** Sunday L £55, Vegetarian available, Children welcome

Roux at Parliament Square

PLAN 5 B5

Modern European V NOTABLE WINE LIST

tel: 020 7334 3737 **Parliament Square SW1P 3AD**
email: roux@rics.org
dir: *Nearest station: Westminster*

Modern French gastronomy with a touch of Roux grandeur

One always expects a touch of grandeur under the Roux imprimatur, and Michel Jnr's venue within heckling distance of the Palace of Westminster occupies a berth within the headquarters of the Royal Institution of Chartered Surveyors, itself the architectural work of Alfred Waterhouse, who also did Kensington's Natural History Museum. The dining rooms are predominantly white with crisp linen, fine glassware and shelf displays of de luxe Cognac and vintage Armagnac. Steve Groves offers a sensitively modernised take on classical French cuisine, the presentations all spare contemporary elegance, the flavours deep and booming. Roast langoustine with prawn tortellini and sea flora in a teak-brown shellfish consommé is a distinguished opener to slow-cooked belly of hogget, thick slices of earthy muttony profundity on a swatch of red cabbage purée, alongside a poached half-pear and parsnip crisps. Sauces tend to be served separately at first and main courses to enhance the aromatic impact as the dish is dressed with them. Dessert might be almost inelegantly hefty, as in the towering lump that is Valrhona Caramelia chocolate delice with liquid bitter chocolate poured in, on a crumbly base of malted biscuit with a scoop of stout ale ice cream. Look to the seasonal ices and sorbets for light relief.

Chef Steve Groves **Seats** 56, Pr/dining room 10
Times 12-2/6.30-10, Closed Xmas, New Year, BHs, Sat-Sun **Prices** Fixed L 3 course £35, Fixed D 3 course £59, Tasting menu £79 **Wines** 194 bottles over £30, 1 bottle under £30, 16 by glass **Parking** NCP Semley Place **Notes** ALC menu 3 course £59, Children welcome

The Royal Horseguards

PLAN 5 B6

@@ Modern British

tel: 020 7451 9333 & 7451 0390 **2 Whitehall Court SW1A 2EJ**
email: 1212royalhorseguards@guoman.co.uk **web:** www.guoman.co.uk
dir: *Nearest station: Embankment, Charing Cross*

Enterprising cooking near Whitehall

This grand old pile was home to the Secret Service in World War I, and now makes an upmarket base for London's attractions. Its posh restaurant comes kitted out with plush crimson banquettes and deals in appealing modern brasserie-style food with its roots in French classics. Expect starters such as Old Spots pork belly with braised pineapple, port jus and bitter cress and move on to venison loin with Lyonnaise potatoes, sprouts, chestnuts and English ham, or straightforward grills beef rib, perhaps with a choice of classic sauces. To finish, perhaps a pineapple variant of tarte Tatin jazzed up with caramel, spiced passionfruit sauce and coconut crunch ice cream.

Chef Graham Chatham **Seats** 100, Pr/dining room 24 **Times** 12-3/5.30-10 **Prices** Fixed L 2 course £22, Fixed D 3 course £25, Starter £7.50-£14, Main £12.50-£28, Dessert £7-£10 **Wines** 27 bottles over £30, 2 bottles under £30, 9 by glass **Parking** Q park Trafalgar Sq **Notes** Table d'hôte menu L/D 2/3 course £22/£25, Pre-theatre menu, Sunday L £25, Vegetarian available, Children welcome

The Rubens at the Palace

PLAN 4 H4

@@ Modern British

tel: 020 7834 6600 **39 Buckingham Palace Rd SW1W 0PS**
email: bookrb@rchmail.com **web:** www.redcarnationhotels.com
dir: *Nearest station: Victoria*

Traditionally styled hotel dining opposite the Palace

Occupying a prime spot opposite Buckingham Palace Mews, The Rubens has been a hotel since 1912, when it became the obvious choice for those attending functions at the Palace. The menu opens with a powerfully flavoured Arbroath smokie fishcake with a poached egg in chive butter, alongside the prawn and crayfish cocktails, Caesar salad, and smoked salmon. Buccleuch steaks form the centrepiece, perhaps Chateaubriand or a hefty rib-eye on the bone, matched with truffled macaroni cheese and creamed spinach in peppercorned Cognac sauce. By contrast, fried hake with salsify and sea beets is straight from the modern repertoire. Finish with banana profiteroles and chocolate sauce.

Chef Imtiaz Kader **Seats** 26, Pr/dining room 60 **Times** 7.30-10.30, Closed 24-27 Dec, L all week **Prices** Starter £10-£18, Main £17-£42, Dessert £9 **Wines** 93 bottles over £30, 17 bottles under £30, 16 by glass **Parking** NCP at Victoria Coach Station **Notes** Sunday L £24-£29, Vegetarian available, Children welcome

Sake No Hana

PLAN 4 J6

@@ Modern Japanese V NOTABLE WINE LIST

tel: 020 7925 8988 **23 Saint James's St SW1A 1HA**
email: reservations@sakenohana.com
dir: *Nearest station: Green Park, Piccadilly Circus*

Sophisticated Japanese cooking in a smart part of town

A striking L-shaped space with a lattice ceiling, bamboo columns and full-length windows hung with screens – it could only be a Japanese restaurant. There's a sushi counter, and a menu offering contemporary and traditional dishes made with top quality ingredients. Among smaller bites, octopus is cooked until meltingly tender and served with a sesame dressing, sea bass comes sashimi-style with a chilli ponzu dressing, while the charcoal grill chips in with teriyaki-glazed lamb cutlets or corn-fed chicken with a sauce rich with chilli, ginger and garlic. There are sushi rolls such as one filled with fatty tuna and avocado, or king crab, seared salmon and nashi pear.

Chef Hideki Hiwatashi **Seats** 100, Pr/dining room 32 **Times** 12-3/6-11, Closed 25 Dec, 1 Jan, Sun **Prices** Prices not confirmed **Wines** 8 by glass **Parking** NCP **Notes** L Bento fr £27, L4/D6 course fr £31/£41, Umai Sat £47, Children welcome

Salloos Restaurant

PLAN 4 G5

@ Pakistani

tel: 020 7235 4444 **62-64 Kinnerton St SW1X 8ER**
dir: *Nearest station: Knightsbridge*

Authentic Pakistani cooking in a discreet Knightsbridge mews

Salloos is a pukka, family-run outfit with an intimate first-floor dining room, done out in warm tones of chocolate brown and flame-orange, while the atmosphere is traditional and the service politely formal. Consistently sound Pakistani cooking is the kitchen's strength – the chef of 40 years assures confident spicing in well-tuned Mughlai cuisine. Salloos is renowned for its tandooris, so kick off with a top-class minced lamb seekh kebab, and follow with house specialities such as tandoori lamb chops or a Khyber region chicken karahi: de-boned chicken cooked in an iron wok with tomatoes, ginger, green chillies and fresh coriander.

Chef Abdul Aziz **Seats** 65 **Times** 12-11, All-day dining, Closed Xmas, Sun **Prices** Starter £7.50-£13, Main £19-£27, Dessert £7.50 **Wines** 37 bottles over £30, 11 bottles under £30, 2 by glass **Parking** Kinnerton St car park (meter) **Notes** Vegetarian available, Children 8 yrs+

Santini Restaurant

PLAN 4 H4

@ Traditional Italian

tel: 020 7730 4094 & 7730 8275 **29 Ebury St SW1W 0NZ**
email: santini@santinirestaurant.com **web:** www.santinirestaurant.com
dir: *Nearest station: Victoria*

Faithful Italian cooking in ritzy surroundings

The traditional values of a family-run Italian restaurant underpin this glossy Belgravia darling, and Latin style runs all the way from the recently refurbished interior to the waiters and the wine list. Impeccably sourced seasonal ingredients treated with a light touch are at the core, starting with the likes of tuna carpaccio with grapefruit, rocket and a caper vinaigrette. If you prefer to start with classic pasta, you can't get much more authentic than spaghetti alle vongole. Main courses take in zuppa di pesce, served with toasted sourdough, as well as classic grilled calves' liver with crispy pancetta and spinach, with zabaione to finish.

Chef Cristian Gardin **Seats** 65, Pr/dining room 30 **Times** 12-3/6-11, Closed Xmas, 1 Jan **Prices** Tasting menu £40-£65, Starter £8-£20, Main £13-£35, Dessert £8-£12 **Wines** 134 bottles over £30, 16 by glass **Parking** Meter (no charge after 6.30pm) **Notes** Pre-theatre menu, Sunday L, Vegetarian available, Children welcome

LONDON SW1 *continued*

Seven Park Place by William Drabble PLAN 4 J6

– *see below*

Sofitel London St James PLAN 4 K6

French, British

tel: 020 7968 2900 **6 Waterloo Place SW1Y 4AN**
email: thebalcon.london@sofitel.com **web:** www.sofitelstjames.com
dir: *Nearest station: Piccadilly Circus*

A touch of French style on Pall Mall

The Balcon restaurant at this imposing hotel is suitably capacious and stylish, done out in the grand Parisian manner with double-height ceiling, soaring columns, a duo of matching spiral staircases, plus a charcuterie and champagne bar. The menu ploughs a brasserie furrow with British and French influences along the way. Start with a fluffy twice-baked cheese soufflé with lobster and crème fraîche sauce, or garlicky snails, and go on to grilled lemon sole with sage-flavoured burnt butter and spinach. Meat-eaters may prefer roast suckling pig with fondant carrots, apples and cider jus, and all diners could finish with vanilla pannacotta with seasonal red fruits.

The Stafford London PLAN 4 J6

Modern, Traditional British, European

tel: 020 7518 1124 & 7493 0111 **16-18 St James's Place SW1A 1NJ**
email: info@thelyttelton.com **web:** www.thestaffordlondon.com
dir: *Nearest station: Green Park*

Luxurious hotel dining in exclusive location

Tucked away in a discreet street near Green Park, The Stafford is a luxurious St James's address that is worth tracking down. The kitchen takes top-notch British produce, subjects it to contemporary treatments and comes up with ambitious dishes glowing with Mediterranean colour. A quail millefeuille pointed up with summer truffle and sun-dried tomato makes a bright, attractive lead-in to a classy main course of perfectly-timed grilled brill with vegetable spaghetti and champagne and caviar beurre blanc. At the end, blueberries add a creative twist to Bakewell tart with ginger and almond ice cream. The wine list runs to over 600 bins with a sommelier to help navigate the way.

Chef Carlos Martinez **Seats** 52, Pr/dining room 44 **Times** 12-2.30/6-10, Closed D 25 Dec **Prices** Prices not confirmed **Wines** 340 bottles over £30, 5 bottles under £30, 11 by glass **Parking** NCP on Arlington Street **Notes** Pre-theatre menu 5.30-7pm 2/3 course £25/£35, Sunday L, Vegetarian available, Children welcome

Seven Park Place by William Drabble

LONDON SW1 **PLAN 4 J6**

Modern French NOTABLE WINE LIST

tel: 020 7316 1600 **St James's Hotel and Club, 7-8 Park Place SW1A 1LP**
email: info@stjameshotelandclub.com **web:** www.stjameshotelandclub.com
dir: *Nearest station: Green Park*

Assured French cooking in a riotously decorated club

Snugly ensconced within the St James Hotel and Club, William Drabble's restaurant emerged virtually a generation ago now from what was Aubergine. It's worth emphasising the visual impact of the decor, where gold-coloured seating meets chocolate-brown walls adorned with expansive art nouveau foliage. Sitting in the recess, you might feel you're in the dining car of a luxurious central European railway carriage. Polished service suits the tone, and Drabble's cooking defies its Chelsea address by sourcing produce from northern England and Scotland, fashioning it into dishes that look relatively simple, but are precisely defined. Take a first course of scallop carpaccio topped with sliced Jerusalem artichoke in a truffled emulsion dressing; what could err on the side of blandness in lesser hands has depths of resonant flavour. Alternatively, a griddled red mullet fillet is adorned with goats' cheese and puréed garlic in red wine sauce, while main-course fish might be beautifully seared sea bass with salt-baked celeriac and apple. The game season produces fantastic grouse, the breast roasted on the bone, the offals minced into a potato-topped cake, with plump blackberries adding sweetness and a big booming port jus the foundation. In a world given over to technical innovation, the old skills are all the more gladly appreciated, as when a proudly risen, intensely flavoured passionfruit soufflé is offset by rich dark chocolate sauce. Appetisers, pre-dessert and petits fours add class to the whole occasion, while breads are fairly straightforward. An excellent wine list is as opulent as the surroundings demand.

Chef William Drabble **Seats** 34, Pr/dining room 40 **Times** 12-2/7-10, Closed Sun-Mon **Prices** Fixed L 2 course fr £26.50, Fixed D 3 course fr £63, Tasting menu fr £75 **Wines** 421 bottles over £30, 3 bottles under £30, 20 by glass **Parking** On street and NCP **Notes** Fixed 6 course menu gourmand, Vegetarian available, Children welcome

Taj 51 Buckingham Gate, Suites and Residences PLAN 4 J4

Modern European

tel: 020 7769 7766 **SW1E 6AF**
email: kona.london@tajhotels.com **web:** www.taj51buckinghamgate.co.uk
dir: *Nearest station: St James Park, Victoria*

Southern European menu in opulent surroundings

At Kona, the stylishly smart decor – in soft greys and whites with well-dressed tables and good attention to detail – shows there's obviously no expense spared. The culinary inspiration is southern Europe. A bowl of velvety lobster bisque with a quenelle of white crabmeat and crème fraîche seems a suitably opulent starting point. At main course, there's Sussex lamb two ways, pinkly tender cannon and bolognaise, served with well-made polenta and pesto. Finish with a vibrant Mayer lemon and poppy streusel with added sweetness coming from the accompanying meringue. It is worth noting that all of this is more than matched by the switched-on service.

Chef David Tilly, Daniel Ayton **Seats** 44, Pr/dining room 12
Times 6-10.30, Closed Sun, L all week **Prices** Tasting menu £45, Starter £10, Main £18-£28, Dessert £8 **Wines** 75 bottles over £30, 19 bottles under £30, 16 by glass **Notes** Tasting menu 7 course, Afternoon tea £27.50-£40, Vegetarian available, Children welcome

Thirty Six by Nigel Mendham at Dukes London PLAN 4 J6

Modern British

tel: 020 7491 4840 **35 St James's Place SW1A 1NY**
email: thirtysix@dukeshotel.com **web:** www.dukeshotel.com
dir: *Nearest station: Green Park*

Precise and non-technological modern British cooking

Discreetly hidden away in a turning off St James's Street, Dukes is a luxury hotel of elegance and refinement. Fittings and furnishings are of the highest order, and guests are pampered by correct but relaxed and friendly staff. The Champagne Lounge is a popular place for a pre-dinner drink, while the restaurant is a relatively modestly sized room with the stylish, moneyed look expected in a hotel of this calibre. Nigel Mendham is no fan of high-tech culinary alchemy, preferring to focus on time-honoured techniques and the best British ingredients. That's not to say that he steers clear of contemporary innovation, adding his own personal stamp to his output. A well-rounded starter of artichoke hearts and purée gets a kick from winter truffle gel and a salt hit from duck ham, crowned by a confit duck egg. Main courses extend to turbot fillet in a herby hazelnut crust with the contrast of pancetta, accompanied by celeriac, mussels and sea parsley. A meaty alternative might be rump of lamb and spiced neck with curried cauliflower and couscous. Desserts are worth exploring too, among them perhaps a theme on apples: compressed fruit, sorbet and purée, goats' curd adding a degree of richness.

Chef Nigel Mendham **Seats** 36 **Times** 12-2.30/6-9.30, Closed L Mon, D Sun **Prices** Fixed L 2 course £25, Fixed D 3 course £29, Tasting menu £75, Starter £20, Main £20, Dessert £20 **Wines** 62 bottles over £30, 2 bottles under £30, 13 by glass **Parking** Holiday Inn, Britannia car park **Notes** Tasting menu 6 course, Early bird menu 3 course £31/£36, Sunday L £26-£29, Vegetarian available, Children welcome

Zafferano PLAN 4 F4

Modern Italian NOTABLE WINE LIST

tel: 020 7235 5800 **15 Lowndes St SW1X 9EY**
email: zafferano@londonfinedininggroup.com
dir: *Nearest station: Knightsbridge*

Refined but authentic Italian cooking in Knightsbridge

Zafferano has always held its head high among the upper echelons of the UK's contemporary Italians, ever since Giorgio Locatelli opened the place back in 1995. The kitchen gives classic dishes a sophisticated spin and superb ingredients remain at the heart of it all, starting with antipasti like cured bresaola beef with rocket and goats' cheese dressing. Pasta dishes here are something special – perhaps veal osso buco ravioli with gremolata, or paccheri tubes with aubergine, nduja sausage and salted ricotta. Secondi could be pot-roasted monkfish with sautéed chard and pine nuts and sultana sauce, or classic chicken paillard. To finish, honey pannacotta might be paired with white grape compôte.

Chef Daniele Camera **Seats** 140, Pr/dining room 26 **Times** 12-11, All-day dining, Closed 25 Dec **Prices** Fixed L 2 course fr £26.50, Starter £12-£29.50, Main £15-£44.50, Dessert £9-£16 **Wines** 600 bottles over £30, 5 bottles under £30, 6 by glass **Parking** NCP behind restaurant **Notes** Vegetarian available, Children welcome

LONDON SW3

The Admiral Codrington PLAN 4 E3

British NEW

tel: 020 7581 0005 **17 Mossop St SW3 2LY**
email: info@theadmiralcodrington.co.uk. **web:** www.theadmiralcodrington.co.uk
dir: *Nearest station: South Kensington*

Classy pub dining room with feel-good menu

The Cod is a proper pub with real ales at the pumps, red leather stools and a wee terrace for supping outside. It's also a dining address with cosy booths, pretty banquettes and fish-themed prints, plus private rooms upstairs. The menu offers globally-inspired stuff such as salt-and-pepper squid fired up with green chillies and sweet and salty nuoc cham dip, alongside leek and mushroom pie or a salad of heritage squash with whipped goats' cheese. Steaks are cooked on the grill – sirloin on the bone, for example – and come with traditional accompaniments, while desserts run to classic sticky toffee pudding.

Chef Orell Hoilett **Seats** 40, Pr/dining room 32 **Times** 11.30-11, All-day dining, Closed 24-26 Dec **Prices** Starter £6.50-£9.50, Main £10.50-£28, Dessert £4.50-£7 **Wines** 34 bottles over £30, 19 bottles under £30, 19 by glass **Parking** Pay & display Draycott Ave & Denyer St **Notes** Sunday L £14.50-£16.50, Vegetarian available, Children welcome

LONDON SW3 ***continued***

Bibendum Restaurant

PLAN 4 E3

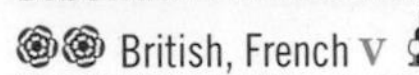
British, French V NOTABLE WINE LIST

tel: 020 7581 5817 **Michelin House, 81 Fulham Rd SW3 6RD**
email: reservations@bibendum.co.uk
dir: *Nearest station: South Kensington*

Modern classics at a Chelsea institution

The Michelin building merits a visit for the art nouveau wall friezes and mosaic floors of the ground-floor oyster bar. But the first-floor dining room has a special magic, particularly on bright days when the Michelin man stained-glass windows light up an amazingly luminous space. A new head chef took over the reins in April 2015, but traditional French dishes still mix with modern British ideas on the re-jigged menu. You might start with Burgundy snails – a fixture for 28 years – ahead of a tranche of turbot with béarnaise sauce, or two might share a roasted guinea fowl. To finish, perhaps an Armagnac baba with prunes and vanilla ice cream.

Chef Peter Robinson **Seats** 80 **Times** 12-2.30/6.30-10.30, Closed 24-26 Dec, 1 Jan **Prices** Fixed L 3 course £36, Starter £8-£25, Main £17.50-£38, Dessert £8-£12 **Wines** 786 bottles over £30, 12 bottles under £30, 22 by glass **Parking** On street **Notes** Sun D 3 course £36, Sunday L £36, Children welcome

Bo Lang Restaurant

PLAN 4 E3

Chinese

tel: 020 7823 7887 **100 Draycott Av SW3 3AD**
email: reservations@bolangrestaurant.co.uk
dir: *Nearest station: South Kensington*

Enterprising dim sum in Chelsea

This is the Chelsea hangout for lovers of dim sum, a dimly lit space with lanterns dangling from the ceiling, and grey leather sofas and charcoal velvet chairs contrasting with lots of wood. Start off with a mixed dim sum platter, among them prawn with chive, and saffron scallop with cod, all well executed with clear flavours. Main courses are no less accomplished: perhaps baked black cod with pak choi, or tender and succulent stir-fried beef in oyster and ginger sauce. Accompaniments – fried rice, say, or broccoli in light soya sauce – are of the same high standards, and you could end with frozen lemongrass yogurt.

Brasserie Gustave

PLAN 4 E2

French

tel: 020 7352 1712 & 7352 1800 **4 Sydney St SW3 6PP**
email: info@brasserie-gustave.com
dir: *Nearest station: South Kensington*

Classic French cuisine in an upmarket brasserie

With classic French posters on the bright yellow walls, rich red leather banquettes and French music playing over the sound system, this place could hardly be more Gallic. Roasted bone marrow comes with a teaspoon to make sure you get every last delicious smidgeon, plus parsley and gherkin salad and a powerful red wine sauce, while duck foie gras terrine is combined with ham hock and artichokes. Gilt head bream arrives with crispy skin and soft flesh in a main course with aubergine purée and confit tomatoes, or go for confit duck leg with home-made pickled white cabbage (choucroute). Finish with a tarte Tatin for two.

Chef Laurence Glayzer **Seats** 50, Pr/dining room 16 **Times** 12-3/6-10.30, Closed Xmas, Aug, L Mon-Fri **Prices** Fixed L 2 course fr £19.50, Fixed D 3 course fr £22.50, Tasting menu £39-£55, Starter £8-£16, Main £17-£39, Dessert £6.50-£16 **Wines** 102 bottles over £30, 7 bottles under £30, 11 by glass **Parking** On street **Notes** Sunday L £23.50-£28, Vegetarian available, Children welcome

Le Colombier

PLAN 4 D2

Traditional French

tel: 020 7351 1155 **145 Dovehouse St SW3 6LB**
email: lecolombier1998@aol.com
dir: *Nearest station: South Kensington*

Classic authentic French bistro in Chelsea

On a buzzy corner beside the Royal Marsden Hospital, long-running Le Colombier is the epitome of the neighbourhood French restaurant. The front conservatory – bathed in sunlight and leafy fronds – is a fine-weather hot ticket, while the main dining room is an equally sunny confection of cream and blues. Openers might be duck liver terrine, perhaps, served with fig jam, or mains like steak tartare with frites, fillet of beef with béarnaise, or wild sea bass fillet served with lemon-spiked olive oil, spinach and potatoes. Desserts are similarly vintage; from a decadent tarte Tatin to crêpe Suzette or crème brûlée, while the all-French wine list is the perfect accomplice.

Chef Philippe Tamet **Seats** 70, Pr/dining room 28 **Times** 12-3/6.30-10.30 **Prices** Fixed L 2 course £19.50-£23.50, Starter £6.90-£19.50, Main £19.20-£38, Dessert £7.90-£8.90 **Wines** 195 bottles over £30, 32 bottles under £30, 10 by glass **Parking** On street (meter) **Notes** Sunday L £23, Vegetarian available, Children 10 yrs+

Eight Over Eight

PLAN 4 D1

Pan-Asian

tel: 020 7349 9934 **392 King's Rd SW3 5UZ**
email: eightovereight@rickerrestaurants.com
dir: *Nearest station: Sloane Sq, South Kensington*

Pan-Asian cooking in a cool, buzzy Chelsea favourite

This King's Road branch of Will Ricker's oriental fusion trio (also E&O and XO) is a sleek, high-ceilinged space flooded with light from huge windows by day and a soft-focus glow from oriental-style lights by night. Paper-clothed tables, slick banquettes and black lacquered chairs complete the on-trend, up-tempo vibe. It's not all style over substance: a well-conceived roster of Pan-Asian dishes kicks off with tiger prawn and black cod sui mai dumplings, followed by roast sea bass with chilli and lime. There's also dim sum, sushi and sashimi, as well as curries and Asian salads, skilfully prepared and presented with plenty of style.

The Five Fields

PLAN 4 F3

– *see opposite*

The Five Fields

LONDON SW3 **PLAN 4 F3**

Modern British V NOTABLE WINE LIST

tel: 020 7838 1082 **8-9 Blacklands Ter SW3 2SP**
email: info@fivefieldsrestaurant.com
dir: *Nearest station: Sloane Sq*

Stunning ingredients and creative flair

It's over two hundred years since this area was mapped by John Rocque and the pastoral name of Five Fields was transcribed into history. Chef-patron Taylor Bonnyman has revived the name for his dashing townhouse restaurant which has taken to this part of the city like a duck to water. With experience at some top addresses in New York, London and Paris, Bonnyman and his team – including head chef Marguerite Keogh – deliver intelligent, thrilling and sometimes playful contemporary food that is based on outstanding ingredients, some grown in their own kitchen garden in East Sussex. The dining room is a soothingly elegant space with neutral, natural colours, and plush designer leather chairs, looking the part for this exclusive postcode. There's a swanky private dining room on the first floor, too. Whether you go for the eight-course tasting menu or à la carte, expect stunning looking plates and clearly defined flavours. Foie gras parfait arrives covered in beetroot jelly, with soft goats' cheese, pistachio and raspberry combining to create a memorable course, while Orkney scallops is another winner, superbly fresh and arriving atop pumpkin purée with radicchio and sea buckthorn. A superb chicken consommé is the star of a main course with chanterelles and Jerusalem artichokes, and among desserts, a chocolate moelleux is served with apricot jelly and sake lees, a by-product of the production of sake, flavours an accompanying ice cream. All the little nibbles you might expect at this level are present and correct, for example crab tartlet with golden beetroot, and a pre-dessert of cherry soda with lemon ice cream.

Chef Taylor Bonnyman, Marguerite Keogh **Seats** 40, Pr/dining room 10 **Times** 6.30-10, Closed Xmas, 2 wks Jan, Sat-Sun **Prices** Fixed D 3 course fr £60, Tasting menu fr £80 **Wines** 435 bottles over £30, 15 bottles under £30, 17 by glass **Parking** On street, NCP 150 yds **Notes** No child menu, Children 6 yrs+

LONDON SW3 *continued*

Manicomio Chelsea

PLAN 4 F3

® Modern Italian

tel: 020 7730 3366 **85 Duke of York Square, Chelsea SW3 4LY**
email: info@manicomio.co.uk
dir: *Nearest station: Sloane Sq*

Bustling modern Italian just off Sloane Square

Originally built as the military asylum of the Duke of York barracks, Manicomio presents a cool, calming image, with its planked floor, wall banquettes and vivid artwork. Contemporary Italian cooking sees many ingredients imported from the Motherland: perhaps speck d'Aosta in a starter with mozzarella and baby artichokes, and lentils from Umbria to accompany roast hake fillet, parsley pesto and spinach. The menu is evenly divided between fish and meat, the latter extending to chargrilled quail skewered with chicken livers on polenta with vin cotto sauce, followed by a main of grilled sirloin with bone marrow, braised ox cheek and roast squash. Finish with tiramisù or treacle and lemon tart.

Chef Tom Salt **Seats** 70, Pr/dining room 30 **Times** 12-3/6.30-10.30, Closed Xmas & New Year, D Sun (Jan-Feb) **Prices** Fixed L 2 course £19.75, Starter £8.75-£10.75, Main £16.50-£26.50, Dessert £6.75-£7 **Wines** 78 bottles over £30, 23 bottles under £30, 18 by glass **Parking** On street **Notes** Pre-theatre menu, Sunday L, Vegetarian available, Children welcome

Nozomi

PLAN 4 E4

®® Contemporary Japanese

tel: 020 7838 1500 & 7838 0181 **14-15 Beauchamp Place, Knightsbridge SW3 1NQ**
email: enquiries@nozomi.co.uk
dir: *Nearest station: Knightsbridge*

Contemporary Japanese cooking in slick setting

This place has had a makeover and now sports silver-grey metallic walls and textured banquettes, subdued lighting, and a trendy soundtrack to create an upbeat, modern space. The deal is authentic contemporary Japanese cuisine. A selection of sushi is a good way to start – perhaps black cod tempura maki, or chicken gyoza dumplings with lemon ponzu sauce, or grilled king crab with asparagus and miso aïoli. Not surprisingly in this postcode, luxuries are strewn around, among them tempura lobster with chilli ponzu and kimchi mayo, or the lobe of seared foie gras that accompanies duck breast served with spicy miso, baby carrots and leeks.

Outlaw's at The Capital

PLAN 4 F5

®®® British, Seafood V NOTABLE WINE LIST

tel: 020 7591 1202 **Basil St, Knightsbridge SW3 1AT**
email: outlaws@capitalhotel.co.uk **web:** www.capitalhotel.co.uk
dir: *Nearest station: Knightsbridge*

The best of Cornish seafood in London

If Nathan Outlaw's Cornish flagship is too far-flung for a visit, his London set-up in The Capital, a splendid boutique townhouse hotel just around the corner from Harrods, might offer easier access to the stellar seafood cooking. The restaurant occupies an understated art deco-esque space with blond wood panelling, paintings of seahorses, wall mirrors and unclothed tables, and the clued-up service team takes a more unbuttoned approach than is often the case in London restaurants at this rarefied level. Obviously Outlaw can't be regularly at the stoves here, so Tom Brown (formerly at Outlaw's St Enodoc restaurant), heads up the kitchen, ensuring that the emphasis remains to let top-class Cornish materials speak eloquently for themselves, helped along with pin-sharp technique. Seafood and saffron soup sounds simple enough, but here it rises to another plane, with impeccably-handled lobster and octopus delivering bursts of clearly-defined flavours, plus a breaded oyster, red pepper, fennel and dill all having their part to play. Next up, succulent monkfish is wrapped in bacon and helped along by cabbage and clams, and it's all offset with a trenchant red wine tartare dressing. To finish, passionfruit tart comes hot from the oven with toasted coconut and yogurt sorbet. The set lunch deal offers remarkable value.

Chef Nathan Outlaw, Tom Brown **Seats** 35, Pr/dining room 24
Times 12-2/6.30-10, Closed Sun **Prices** Prices not confirmed **Wines** 37 by glass **Parking** 8 **Notes** Tasting menu 5 course, BYO wine Thu, Children welcome

Rasoi Restaurant

PLAN 4 F3

®®® Modern Indian V NOTABLE WINE LIST

tel: 020 7225 1881 **10 Lincoln St SW3 2TS**
email: info@rasoirestaurant.co.uk
dir: *Nearest station: Sloane Sq*

Chelsea townhouse with ground-breaking Indian cooking

Ring the bell at Vineet Bhatia's restaurant in a swish Chelsea townhouse, and you enter a chic space, with silk wall hangings, designer wallpapers, Indian artefacts and antiques, and the heady aroma of eastern spices in the air. The new wave style of cooking is delivered via menus structured in the western three-course format (helpful staff will decode the often baffling descriptions), with seven-course prestige and vegetarian taster deals on offer. Expect palate-tingling dishes that fizz with originality: chilli and garlic add va-va-voom to seared scallops, partnered in an inventive opening salvo with Mumbai street food-inspired Chowpatty bhaji, a vibrant dish of tomato, veg, potato and spices, or there might be Mughlai lamb seekh kebab with cashews and a samosa filled with pickled achari vegetables. Next up, sea bass fillets are spiked with South Indian sambar sauce, and served with black and white coconut rice, a quenelle of coconut khichdi, a trenchant lime foam and plantain chips. Otherwise, go for Kashmiri lamb shank with rajma pulao (spicy rice and kidney beans) and spinach kofta, or equally precise and refined veggie creations – perhaps aubergine 'steak' with raspberry and fennel crumble, Burani yogurt raita and basil cress. Intriguing desserts include the signature chocolate samosa with rose petal and vanilla ice cream.

Chef Vineet Bhatia **Seats** 35, Pr/dining room 14
Times 12-2.30/6-10.30, Closed Xmas, New Year, BHs, Mon, L Tue-Sat
Prices Fixed L 2 course £24-£30, Fixed D 3 course £66-£70, Tasting menu £79-£169, Starter £21-£26, Main £33-£51, Dessert £12-£16 **Wines** 300 bottles over £30, 10 bottles under £30, 10 by glass **Parking** On street **Notes** Tasting menu 7 course, Sunday L £24-£36, Children welcome

Restaurant Gordon Ramsay

PLAN 4 F1

French, European V 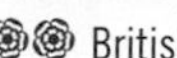

tel: 020 7352 4441 **68 Royal Hospital Rd SW3 4HP**
email: reservations@gordonramsay.com
dir: *Nearest station: Sloane Sq*

The mothership of the Gordon Ramsay empire

The Rosette award for this establishment has been suspended due to a change of chef. Reassessment will take place in due course under the new chef. It's hard to keep track, but at the last count the Gordon Ramsay brand extended to 30 or so venues around the globe, taking in 14 addresses in London, a brace apiece for France and Italy, a sprinkling of locations across Asia and the Middle East, and venues across the pond from Las Vegas to Atlantic City. This venue remains the flagship, first opening its doors in 1998. The dining room is surprisingly intimate – just 45 or so seats – with clean-lined, art deco-influenced looks and plush, pastel-hued tones giving a sophisticated sheen to the space. The service, led by Jean-Claude Breton, has long been a stand-out feature of a visit, and it remains gracious and extremely proficient, with his charming manner making every guest feel like a regular visitor. The fixed-price lunch menu represents remarkable value, making it the entry point for anyone looking to sample the RGR experience on a budget (relatively speaking...), while the Prestige and Seasonal Inspiration menus offer the opportunity to go for the high-rolling end of the spectrum. The wallet-denting wine list is a serious piece of work with the world's best producers vying for your attention, and sommelier Jan Konetzki and his team to steer the way.

Chef Gordon Ramsay, Matt Abé **Seats** 45 **Times** 12-2.15/6.30-10.15, Closed 1 wk Xmas, Sat-Sun **Prices** Fixed L 3 course £65-£110, Fixed D 3 course fr £110, Tasting menu £145-£195 **Wines** 1300 bottles over £30, 5 bottles under £30, 22 by glass **Notes** Tasting menu 7 course, Children welcome

Tom's Kitchen

PLAN 4 E2

British, French

tel: 020 7349 0202 **27 Cale St, South Kensington SW3 3QP**
email: info@tomskitchen.co.uk
dir: *Nearest station: South Kensington, Sloane Sq*

First-class brasserie food from top-class chef

With its utilitarian good looks, Tom's Kitchen fizzes with life and bonhomie and it is the all-day, ground-floor brasserie where most of the action takes place at tightly packed wooden tables. Spicy crab cake, perked up with a cucumber and chilli salsa and packed with a goodly amount of crab, shows the way, or go for something along the lines of roast Yorkshire pigeon. Slow-cooked pork belly or roast monkfish tail are among the options for main while desserts might be apple and blackberry crumble with toasted almond ice cream. There's another branch in Somerset House in the West End.

Chef James Verity, Tom Aikens **Seats** 75, Pr/dining room 62
Times 12-3.30/6-10.30, Closed 25-26 Dec, D 24 Dec **Prices** Starter £6-£11, Main £16-£50, Dessert fr £6.50 **Wines** 50 bottles over £30, 18 bottles under £30, 13 by glass **Parking** On street **Notes** Sunday L, Vegetarian available, Children welcome

LONDON SW4

Bistro Union

PLAN 1 E2

British

tel: 020 7042 6400 **40 Abbeville Rd, Clapham SW4 9NG**
email: eat@bistrounion.co.uk
dir: *Nearest station: Clapham South*

True-Brit food in neighbourhood bistro

This is exactly the sort of easy-going neighbourhood eatery we'd all like on our patch. You can perch on wooden bar stools with your cutlery and menu in individual drawers under the counter, choosing something like pickled quail's eggs or salt-cod fritters with aioli from a menu of on-trend nibbles hand-written onto a roll of brown paper. What leaves the kitchen is creative, fun, and built with British-led ingredients – ox tongue is smoked in house and comes in the vibrant company of beetroot, horseradish and pickled walnuts. Mains could bring roast mallard with lentils, roast squash and black mustard. Hearty puds include ginger parkin with salted caramel sauce.

Chef Adam Byatt **Seats** 40 **Times** 12-4/5-10, Closed 24-27 & 31 Dec **Prices** Starter £6-£10, Main £11-£22, Dessert £1.50-£12 **Wines** 24 bottles over £30, 16 bottles under £30, 13 by glass **Parking** On street **Notes** Brunch, Sun Supper 5.30-8.30pm £26 child under 10 free, Sunday L, Vegetarian available, Children welcome

The Dairy

PLAN 1 E2

Modern British V

tel: 020 7622 4165 **15 The Pavement, Clapham SW4 0HY**
email: bookings@the-dairy.co.uk
dir: *Nearest station: Clapham Common*

Relaxed bar-bistro serving innovative modern food

This buzzy operation has a dinky bar and a bistro behind with a pared-back look and flag-stoned floors. The open kitchen produces well-crafted dishes with clean flavours and modern presentation. Kick off with sourdough bread with home-made smoked bone marrow butter, then graze through a selection of small plates. Smoked eel brandade with green olive and piquillo pepper perks the taste buds up before the big flavours of Kentish corn, white polenta and barbecued duck heart. Next comes sea-fresh monkfish with heritage tomatoes and West Coast lemon sole. For dessert, fresh apricot and apricot sorbet with apricot kernel pannacotta and green almond brings a clever interplay of summery flavours.

Chef Robin Gill **Seats** 40 **Times** 12-11, All-day dining, Closed Xmas, Mon, L Tue, D Sun **Prices** Prices not confirmed **Wines** 48 bottles over £30, 12 bottles under £30, 8 by glass **Notes** Brunch Sat-Sun, Children welcome

LONDON SW4 *continued*

The Manor

PLAN 1 F2

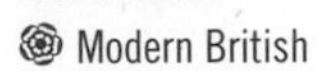 Modern British V

tel: 020 7720 4662 **148 Clapham Manor St SW4 6BX**
email: reservations@themanorclapham.co.uk
dir: *Nearest station: Clapham North, Clapham Common*

Inventive cooking in side-street bistro

Converted in 2014 from a long-established tapas bar, the decor at The Manor is simple (loos excepted), which makes it easy to concentrate instead on the far more important job of studying the part-seasonal, part-daily changing menu. And well thought out they are, too, with hardly a dish that could be described as familiar. For example, try a starter of 'Mavie' skate and smoked roe, followed by barbecued lamb ribs, heart and sweetbreads, and dessert of salted almond mousse with Guinness bread parfait, banana and chocolate. Equally interesting alternatives feature Galician octopus, honey-smoked asparagus with mead, and suckling pig belly, although not, of course, on the same plate.

Chef Dean Parker **Seats** 55 **Times** 12-3/6-10, Closed 21-29 Dec, 1 Jan, Mon, L Tue, D Sun **Prices** Tasting menu £45, Starter £5.50-£7.50, Main £9.50-£12, Dessert £7 **Wines** 30 bottles over £30, 4 bottles under £30, 13 by glass **Parking** On street **Notes** L menu 4 course £25, Tasting menu 7 course, Children welcome

Trinity Restaurant

PLAN 1 E2

 British, European

tel: 020 7622 1199 **4 The Polygon, Clapham SW4 0JG**
email: dine@trinityrestaurant.co.uk
dir: *Nearest station: Clapham Common*

Dynamic modern cooking in Clapham

You might have seen Adam Byatt on the *Great British Menu* – his restaurant certainly brings some modern-day verve to Clapham Old Town. There is no need for the lucky locals to head north in search of culinary thrills with this gem on their doorstep, and non-locals need only jump on the Northern Line. The contemporary dining room is watched over by a slick service team who maintain a confident air throughout proceedings. There's a tasting menu and carte available lunch and dinner, plus a good-value lunch, while the weekend lunch menu includes 45-day aged beef rump cap with Yorkshire pudding. The kitchen combines classic and modern ideas in dishes that impress with their invention and satisfy with their relative simplicity. Seared salmon cured in blood orange alongside beetroot, barigoule and dill might make an impressive lunch opener. A main course might feature a pot-roast Bresse pigeon with salt-baked celeriac and creamed spinach, or another option might be roast fillet of cod, parsley soup and charred squid. The adroit technical skills in this kitchen are on show again at dessert stage, with an Amadei chocolate cremosa delivering precisely balanced flavours, or in a cheesecake with poire granité and pear sorbet.

Chef Adam Byatt **Seats** 50 **Times** 12.30-2.30/6.30-10, Closed 24-27 Dec, 1-2 Jan **Prices** Fixed L 2 course fr £25, Starter £8-£14, Main £26-£32, Dessert £6-£9 **Wines** 280 bottles over £30, 22 bottles under £30, 16 by glass **Parking** On street **Notes** Sunday L fr £25, Vegetarian available, Children welcome

Tsunami

PLAN 1 F2

Japanese

tel: 020 7978 1610 **5-7 Voltaire Rd SW4 6DQ**
email: clapham@tsunamirestaurant.co.uk
dir: *Nearest station: Clapham North, Clapham High St*

Cool looks and on-trend Japanese fusion food

This original branch of the two Tsunami outlets (the other is on Charlotte Street in the West End) appeals to crowds of thirty-somethings eager for first-class sushi and sashimi and slick modern Japanese fusion food. Okay, the open-planned space may be hard-edged and high-decibel, but it's really sociable, with the kitchen delivering fresh, skilful, smart-looking classic-meets-contemporary dishes designed for sharing and grazing. Witness unagi (freshwater eel) and foie gras nigiri and seafood tempura, or mains like top-dollar grilled black cod in sweet miso, or truffle rib-eye. Crossover desserts could feature a lemongrass and lime pannacotta.

Chef Ken Sam **Seats** 75 **Times** 12.30-3.30/5.30-11, Closed 24-26 Dec, 1 Jan, L Mon-Fri **Prices** Prices not confirmed **Wines** 22 bottles over £30, 8 bottles under £30, 13 by glass **Parking** On street **Notes** Fixed D 5 course £37/£42, Sunday L, Vegetarian available, Children welcome

LONDON SW5

Cambio de Tercio

PLAN 4 C2

 Spanish

tel: 020 7244 8970 **163 Old Brompton Rd SW5 0LJ**
email: cambiodeterciogroup@btconnect.com
dir: *Nearest station: Gloucester Rd*

Vibrant modern Spanish cooking in a setting to match

Folding full-length glass windows open Tercio up to the street, while inside it has a dark, intimate, Spanish feel – black slate floors, mustard yellow and fuchsia pink walls hung with striking modern artworks. The food is equally colourful and good looking, ranging from traditional tapas to innovative dishes such as oxtail caramelised in red wine matched with apple and lemon-thyme air. More substantial mains run to Basque-style hake casserole with parsley sauce, razor clams, mussels and cockles, or grilled skate with crunchy pig's trotters, Burgos morcilla terrine and orange vinaigrette. Desserts keep the creativity on stream with the likes of crispy Cuban mojito in a caramel ball.

Capote y Toros

PLAN 4 C2

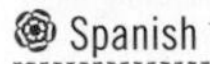 Spanish V

tel: 020 7373 0567 **157 Old Brompton Rd SW5 0LJ**
email: cambiodeterciogroup@btconnect.com
dir: *Nearest station: South Kensington, Gloucester Rd*

Authentic tapas plus interesting specialities

A few doors away from sibling Cambio de Tercio, Capote y Toros describes itself as a tapas, ham and sherry bar. It has vivid decor with photographs of matadors and hams hanging from the ceiling above the bar. Live flamenco music and a friendly team providing attentive levels of service add to the laid-back sense of fun; more than 100 sherries and a patriotic wine list play a part too. Dive into the likes of roasted bone marrow with veal jus and salsa brava toast, chorizo cooked in fino sherry, plates of top-notch charcutería, and Galician-style octopus. Desserts are equally true to the motherland.

Chef Luis Navacerrada Lanzadera **Seats** 25 **Times** 6-11.30, Closed Xmas, Sun-Mon, L all week **Prices** Fixed D 3 course £16-£60, Starter £5.25-£29.75, Dessert £6.50-£6.90 **Wines** 110 bottles over £30, 35 bottles under £30, 6 by glass **Parking** On street **Notes** Children welcome

New Lotus Garden

PLAN 4 B3

Chinese

tel: 020 7244 8984 **15 Kenway Rd SW5 0RP**
email: jiang.hubert@gmail.com
dir: *Nearest station: Earl's Court*

Neighbourhood Chinese that really hits the spot

Down a residential street in Earl's Court, the white-painted New Lotus Garden is a powerhouse of Pekinese and Cantonese cooking. The long menu doesn't really stand out from the crowd, but execution is good and the flavours sing out. Start with salt-and-pepper asparagus, or succulent barbecue spare ribs, or mussels in black bean sauce. Among main courses, twice-cooked belly of pork with preserved vegetables hits the spot, or try the spicy crispy shredded beef. Vegetarians get a decent choice with things like aubergines braised in black bean sauce, and there is a good range of noodle dishes.

LONDON SW6

Blue Elephant

PLAN 1 E3

Thai V

tel: 020 7751 3111 **The Boulevard, Imperial Wharf, Townmead Rd SW6 2UB**
email: london@blueelephant.com
dir: *Nearest station: Imperial Wharf*

Lavish riverside setting for upmarket Thai dining

With its mini rainforest of luxuriant foliage, orchids on darkwood tables and a gilded bar modelled on the Royal Barge of Thailand, Blue Elephant's decor is over the top, but enjoyably so. The lengthy menu is divided into Thai cooking of 'the past', 'today' and 'tomorrow', plus a couple of tasting options and a vegetarian section. Start in the present with 'paper prawns' – tiger prawns wrapped in rice-paper stuffed with minced chicken and crushed peanuts, with a plum dipping sauce – followed by steamed whole sea bass with organic lemongrass, fresh lime juice, Thai pickled garlic and crushed chillies. Service is charming and there's a riverside alfresco terrace.

Chef Nooror Somany **Seats** 150, Pr/dining room 8
Times 12-2.30/7-10.30, Closed 25-28 Dec, 1 Jan, Mon, L Tue-Sat **Prices** Tasting menu £45-£55, Starter £9-£15, Main £18-£28, Dessert £6.50-£9 **Wines** 100 bottles over £30, 5 bottles under £30, 13 by glass **Parking** Car park next to Imperial Wharf tube station **Notes** Sun brunch, Sunday L fr £35, Children welcome

The Harwood Arms

PLAN 1 E3

British

tel: 020 7386 1847 **27 Walham Grove, Fulham SW6 1QR**
email: admin@harwoodarms.com
dir: *Nearest station: Fulham Broadway*

Supplier-led British cooking in smart gastropub

On an unassuming backstreet in trendy Fulham, the stylish Harwood Arms is one of Britain's top gastropubs. Inside you could almost forget you're in London, with photos of outdoor country pursuits hung on grey and cream walls, and rustic wooden tables. On the menu, first class, carefully-sourced English produce is cooked with confidence; Berkshire rabbit faggots, for example, with split peas, smoked bacon and pickled mushrooms is a robust way to start, before moving on to a fish course of wild sea bass with cauliflower, oat-crusted mussels and preserved lemon. Baked stem ginger custard with honeycomb ice cream is an unerringly satisfying finale.

Marco Grill

PLAN 1 E3

British Grill

tel: 020 7915 2929 **M&C Hotels at Chelsea FC, Stamford Bridge, Fulham Rd SW6 1HS**
email: info@marcogrill.com
dir: *Nearest station: Fulham Broadway*

Steakhouse and brasserie-style dishes at Stamford Bridge

Yes, it's that Marco who's behind this glossy steakhouse in Chelsea football ground, which is how you know that this is a world away from normal footie fan fare. Melt-in-the-mouth tuna carpaccio is matched with the punchy flavours of coriander shoots and ginger, then as top-class 35-day aged steaks are the main culinary thrust here, a rib-eye is seared to perfection and delivered with triple-cooked chips and a textbook béarnaise. Otherwise go for a Gallic brasserie classic – perhaps roast rack of lamb with Mediterranean vegetables, gratin dauphinoise and sauce paloise. Puddings are a strong suit, as in a chocolate mousse duo in a dark chocolate dome with raspberry sauce.

Chef Roger Pizey **Seats** 70 **Times** 6-10.30, Closed 2 wks Jul-Aug, Sun-Mon, L all week **Prices** Starter £7-£10.50, Main £15.50-£26, Dessert £6.50 **Wines** 20 bottles over £30, 7 bottles under £30, 8 by glass **Parking** 10 **Notes** Steak club Thu, Vegetarian available, Children welcome

LONDON SW7

Bombay Brasserie

PLAN 4 C3

Indian

tel: 020 7370 4040 **Courtfield Close, Courtfield Rd SW7 4QH**
email: dine@bombayb.co.uk
dir: *Nearest station: Gloucester Rd*

Stylish address with modern Indian cooking

This South Ken institution blends culinary influences from all India – Parsi, Bengali, Goan, Gujerati, Mughal, even Portuguese. There are two sumptuously-styled dining rooms, one with deep-pile banquettes under impressive chandeliers, the other a lighter, conservatory-roofed space with well-spaced tables. The food uses kitchen-ground, lightly toasted spices to impart maximum flavour. Start with patrani macchi – lemon sole steamed in a banana leaf with coriander, chilli and coconut. Follow with kadipatta chicken tikka from the clay oven, Kerala halibut curry with coconut, red chillies and tamarind, or the vegetarian adraki gobi: cauliflower florets, onion, tomatoes and garlic. For dessert, try the traditional Indian ice cream, malai kulfi.

Chef Prahlad Hegde **Seats** 185, Pr/dining room 16
Times 12-2.30/6.30-11.30, Closed 25 Dec, L Mon **Prices** Fixed L 3 course £25, Fixed D 3 course £46-£115, Tasting menu £53-£58, Starter £9-£11, Main £9-£25, Dessert £8-£11 **Wines** 97 bottles over £30, 7 bottles under £30, 18 by glass
Parking Millennium Gloucester Hotel next door **Notes** Sat-Sun buffet L £31, Sunday L £31, Vegetarian available, Children welcome

LONDON SW7 *continued*

Bulgari Hotel, London

PLAN 4 F5

Modern French, Italian Riviera NOTABLE WINE LIST

tel: 020 7151 1025 & 7151 1010 **171 Knightsbridge SW7 1DW**
email: reservations@rivealondon.com **web:** www.rivealondon.com
dir: *Nearest station: Knightsbridge*

Franco-Italian cooking in relaxed and stylish surroundings

Alain Ducasse has spread his culinary wings far and wide over an illustrious career, both geographically and stylistically. So although London boasts his most formal style of haute cuisine at the Dorchester, there is also the option of his take on the simple sunny fare of that southern European cusp where Provence meets Italy. This too is a hotel restaurant, ensconced within the confines of the glittering Bulgari, but the mood is much more hang-loose, despite the grand entry down a sweeping staircase. Polished floorboards and art deco-style mirrors in curved booths set a lovely retro theme, the sort of Riviera touch where you might long to spot Audrey Hepburn, and the menus follow suit with an array of small plates of undemanding, but stylishly realised Mediterranean food. Octopus and confit potato salad in spring onion pesto, or chestnut velouté with roasted butternut, might fire the starting-gun, and be followed by glisteningly fresh sea bass in beefy daube sauce with chicory, veal fillet with heritage carrots, shallots and capers, or perhaps a spelt 'pasta' dish with broccoletti dressed in aged parmesan. Finish with the likes of lemon sablé and limoncello sorbet, or pear and chestnut ice cream coupe.

Chef Alexandre Nicolas **Seats** 82, Pr/dining room 24 **Times** 12-2.30/6.30-10.30 **Prices** Fixed L 2 course £26, Starter £7-£12, Main £24-£36, Dessert £6-£7 **Wines** 400 bottles over £30, 4 bottles under £30, 12 by glass **Parking** NCP Pavillion Rd **Notes** Sunday L £26-£32, Vegetarian available, Children welcome

L'Etranger

PLAN 4 C4

French, Japanese NOTABLE WINE LIST

tel: 020 7584 1118 & 7823 9291 **36 Gloucester Rd SW7 4QT**
email: etranger@etranger.co.uk
dir: *Nearest station: Gloucester Rd*

A Franco-Japanese handshake in chic South Ken surroundings

L'Etranger has a tenacious local following among the well-heeled of South Kensington. It's dressed to impress, as befits a marriage of French chic and Japanese precision. Marinated mackerel with mooli and Granny Smith is a bracing way to begin, or there may be truffled miso quail with mustard ice cream, or traditional sashimi platters. Main courses add yuzu foam to sea bass and shiitaki mushrooms with raisin purée, or add a vivid splash of parsley chlorophyll to Grade 9 wagyu sirloin. Lunch is simpler – perhaps foie gras terrine with port jelly and pain d'épices, then cod and squid with chorizo. Finish with a light cheesecake with fig compôte.

Chef Chris Siomadis **Seats** 64, Pr/dining room 20 **Times** 12-3/5.30-11, Closed 26-27 Dec **Prices** Prices not confirmed **Wines** 1400 bottles over £30, 60 bottles under £30, 12 by glass **Parking** NCP **Notes** Degustation 6 course £75, Pre/post-theatre 3 course menu, Sunday L, Vegetarian available, Children welcome

Millennium Bailey's Hotel London Kensington

PLAN 4 C3

Italian

tel: 020 7331 6308 & 7331 6301 **140 Gloucester Rd SW7 4QH**
email: olives.baileys@millenniumhotels.com **web:** www.olivesrestaurant.co.uk
dir: *Nearest station: Gloucester Rd*

Uncomplicated Italian food in South Ken

The elegantly restored Victorian townhouse hotel in upmarket South Kensington is handy for the museums as well as some serious shopping. The main dining room, Olives, a long narrow room with unclothed tables and pastel-shaded upholstery, goes for a pared-down look, the better to offset the uncomplicated Italian cooking on offer. The classically structured menu takes in antipasti such as porchetta with fennel and chilli relish, intermediates such as pumpkin gnocchi with balsamic beef and shaved parmesan, and mains like breast and confit leg of duck with beetroot salad and mash. Finish with the utter simplicity of coffee-flavoured crème caramel, or pineapple carpaccio infused with vanilla.

Osteria 60

PLAN 4 C5

Modern Italian

tel: 020 7368 5700 **Baglioni Hotel London, 60 Hyde Park Gate, Kensington Rd, Kensington SW7 5BB**
email: brunello.london@baglionihotels.com **web:** www.baglionihotels.com
dir: *Nearest station: High St Kensington*

Modern and classic Italian cooking in Kensington

With a view facing Kensington Gardens for terrace diners, the main area of this stylish Italian restaurant takes its cue from Milan's trattorias of the 1950s and was created in association with a Milanese design company. The food looks to marry the 'best of British' seasonal ingredients with Italian staples and incorporates many classic Italian dishes alongside more contemporary interpretations. Typical dishes might include carpaccio of wild sea bass with sea urchins, scialatielli pasta with salt cod and amatriciana sauce or perhaps risotto with San Marzano tomatoes and smoked provolone. For dessert, try tiramisù croccante or Amalfi lemon tart with sorrel sorbet.

Chef Ivan Simeoli **Seats** 70, Pr/dining room 60 **Times** 12.30-3/5.30-11 **Prices** Prices not confirmed **Wines** 4 bottles under £30, 8 by glass **Parking** 2, On street Kensington Rd/De Vere Gardens **Notes** Pre-theatre menu 5.30-7pm all wk £25-£29, Sunday L, Vegetarian available, Children welcome

Zuma

PLAN 4 F5

Modern Japanese

tel: 020 7584 1010 **5 Raphael St, Knightsbridge SW7 1DL**
email: info@zumarestaurant.com
dir: *Nearest station: Knightsbridge*

Buzzy modern Japanese in fashionable Knightsbridge

An effortlessly cool playground of the beau monde, Zuma appeals to lovers of contemporary Japanese food and slick design. The vibe is high octane, buoyed by the buzzing front bar-lounge offering 40 different sakes. A lengthy roster of in-vogue sharing plates offers crispy fried squid pepped up by green chilli and lime, or, from the robata, succulent pork skewers (stickily glazed) with lively mustard miso, while classics like vegetable tempura and signatures like marinated black cod (wrapped in hoba leaf) find their place too. Desserts, such as yuzu cheesecake with raspberry granité and black sesame, bridge the East-West divide, while sushi is exemplary.

Chef Bjoern Weissgerber, Ben Orpwood **Seats** 175, Pr/dining room 14 **Times** 12-3/6-11, Closed 25 Dec **Prices** Prices not confirmed **Wines** 13 by glass **Parking** On street **Notes** Sunday L, Vegetarian available, Children welcome

LONDON SW10

Maze Grill Park Walk

PLAN 4 C1

Modern American NEW

tel: 020 7255 9299 **11 Park Walk SW10 0AJ**
email: mazegrillparkwalk@gordonramsay.com
dir: *Nearest station: South Kensington, Fulham Broadway*

Prime steaks, and more, in Chelsea

On one side of the room at Maze Grill Park Walk is a neat line of tables at lime green banquettes, on the other is a long bar. The intention is to replicate the grill rooms of Manhattan, with a menu almost solely of prime steaks, all cooked exactly as requested on the Montague grill. Choose from six-ounce fillet to triple-seared Wagyu, sold by the weight, select a sauce – bone marrow with shallots, say – and decide on a side order of vegetables from a list of eight. Starters concentrate on sushi, and you could end with chocolate cake.

Chef Owen Sullivan **Seats** 60 **Times** 12-11, All day dining **Prices** Starter £4-£16, Main £14-£45, Dessert £6-£8 **Wines** 73 bottles over £30, 6 bottles under £30, 13 by glass **Parking** On street **Notes** Sunday L £25-£35, Vegetarian available, Children welcome

Medlar Restaurant

PLAN 4 D1

Modern European NOTABLE WINE LIST

tel: 020 7349 1900 **438 King's Rd, Chelsea SW10 0LJ**
email: info@medlarrestaurant.co.uk
dir: *Nearest station: Sloane Sq, Earl's Court, Fulham Broadway*

Fashionable Chelsea spot for cooking of gutsy potency

One of Chelsea's more talked-about dining spots, Medlar looks box-fresh, with Lincoln-green banquette seating against mirror panels in one section, leading to a back room done in crisp white with a foliate pattern in thin green tracery on the walls. There's a fresh-feeling atmosphere, which might lead you to expect an ethereal approach to the food, but Joe Mercer Nairne's food has gutsy, earthy substance. He specialises in taking often humble ingredients and less common cuts and subjecting them to treatments that bring out all their intrinsic flavour, in dishes that are easy to understand but still full of commanding potency. Take a starter such as crab raviolo with brown shrimps and samphire on leek fondue in a rich bisque, and then perhaps move on to a winning braised beef cheek with smoked parsley root purée, pickled onions and bacon crumb. Other meats such as duck breast and venison loin have all their innate intensity conjured forth, the latter perhaps paired with rissole, choucroute, beetroot and braised shallot. The dessert list might include pear beignet with warm dipping chocolate and Chantilly cream or a buttermilk pannacotta with poached English rhubarb and pistachios.

Chef Joe Mercer Nairne **Seats** 85, Pr/dining room 28
Times 12-3/6.30-10.30, Closed Xmas, 1 Jan **Prices** Fixed L 2 course £22.50, Fixed D 3 course £46 **Wines** 384 bottles over £30, 19 bottles under £30, 13 by glass **Parking** On street (may be difficult during lunch) **Notes** Prix fixe menu, Sat L 2/3 course £25/£30, Sunday L £30-£35, Vegetarian available, Children welcome

The Painted Heron

PLAN 1 E3

Modern Indian

tel: 020 7351 5232 **112 Cheyne Walk SW10 0DJ**
email: info@thepaintedheron.com
dir: *Nearest station: South Kensington*

First-rate modern Indian near the river

This upscale Chelsea Indian is a thoroughly modern affair with an understated, clean-lined interior. The cooking is smart and seasonal: in game season there's partridge with spicy minced lamb sauce, or perhaps mallard with root vegetable mash and curry sauce. Starters could be home-smoked monkfish tikka with carom seeds or perhaps chargrilled lamb chops with nutmeg flowers, while main courses cater to traditionalists with a mutton curry. Otherwise try duck tikka with mint, followed by the South Indian-inspired spice-crusted sea bass fillets with coconut rice and Malabari curry. The dessert list offers sticky gulab jamun with passionfruit mousse or pistachio and pear cup cake with chai cream and mango samosa.

Chef Yogesh Datta **Seats** 70 **Times** 11.30-3.30/6-11, Closed L 1 Jan, D 24 Dec **Prices** Fixed L 2 course £14.95-£25, Starter £7.50-£9.50, Main £12.50-£19.50, Dessert £4-£5 **Wines** 40 bottles over £30, 19 bottles under £30, 10 by glass **Parking** On street **Notes** 5 course £38 (with unlimited prosecco or Cobra beer £55), Sunday L, Vegetarian available, Children welcome

LONDON SW11

London House

PLAN 1 E3

Modern European

tel: 020 7592 8545 & 7592 7952 **7-9 Battersea Square, Battersea Village SW11 3RA**
email: londonhouse@gordonramsay.com
dir: *Nearest station: Clapham Junction*

Modern comfort food and cocktails too

The Rosette award for this establishment has been suspended due to a change of concept and chef. Reassessment will take place in due course under the new chef. After a recent revamp, London House is a family-friendly address that also happens to have a cracking array of cocktails and whiskies. The fabulous old Georgian building was built for the business of hospitality and has seen a good few oysters shucked over the years. It's now part of the Gordon Ramsay empire, and oysters are no longer part of the package, but what is up for grabs is a roster of feel-good British and French inspired dishes that runs from brunch to dinner. Begin with mussels cooked in garlic butter, served with sourdough bread, or crispy pig's head croquette with sauce gribiche. Among main courses, the grill turns out steaks and half a chicken, while the carte extends to monkfish with mussels in a laksa sauce, or roast lamb with grelot onions and artichokes. Children get their own menu. The dessert menu deals in comforting stuff such as rhubarb and custard doughnuts or sticky toffee pudding. Cocktails include the claret cobbler with red wine, fresh raspberries, lemon and orange.

Chef George Lyon **Seats** 63 **Times** 12-11, All-day dining **Prices** Fixed L 2 course £15, Starter £8-£11.50, Main £16.50-£24, Dessert £7.50-£9.50 **Wines** 38 bottles over £30, 10 bottles under £30, 12 by glass **Parking** On street **Notes** Wknd brunch, Vegetarian available, Children welcome

LONDON SW13

Sonny's Kitchen

PLAN 1 D3

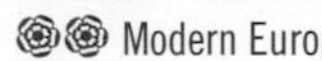
Modern European

tel: 020 8748 0393 & 8741 8451 **94 Church Rd, Barnes SW13 0DQ**
email: manager@sonnyskitchen.co.uk
dir: *Nearest station: Barnes*

Popular and highly regarded neighbourhood restaurant

Part restaurant, part food store, Sonny's is buzzing towards its third decade. A neutral designer-chic decor involves textures of wood, leather, ceramic tiles, glass bricks and white walls hung with art. Precise flavours and textures are delivered in a starter of chargrilled spatchcock quail with quinoa, pomegranate, pistachio and raisins. Main course brings an exemplary slab of roast cod matched with pea purée and potato and ham galette, while meatier offerings run to slow-cooked veal cheek with hand-made strozzapreti pasta, girolles and smashed peas. It all ends on a satisfying note with a warm chocolate fondant with milk ice cream and a squidgy-centred pistachio macaroon.

Chef Elliot Luscombe **Seats** 100, Pr/dining room 18 **Times** 12-2.30/6.30-10.30, Closed Xmas, New Year, BHs **Prices** Fixed L 2 course £17.95, Fixed D 3 course £22.50, Starter £6-£9, Main £14-£33, Dessert £6-£8 **Wines** 36 bottles over £30, 24 bottles under £30, 20 by glass **Parking** On street **Notes** Brunch Sat-Sun £4.50-£9.50, Sunday L £21-£25, Vegetarian available, Children welcome

LONDON SW14

The Depot

PLAN 1 D3

Modern European, British

tel: 020 8878 9462 **Tideway Yard, 125 Mortlake High St, Barnes SW14 8SN**
email: info@depotbrasserie.co.uk
dir: *Nearest station: Barnes Bridge*

Popular, relaxed, neighbourhood brasserie by the river

The Depot pulls in the crowds with its knockout riverside views and crowd-pleasing European brasserie-style food. It's a good-looking venue with a skeleton rowing boat hanging above herringbone parquet floors and mustard and coffee-coloured walls. Foie gras and ham hock terrine with dandelion, walnut and shallot salad and toasted brioche starts things off, followed by roast brill fillet with lemon butter, baby artichoke, samphire, potato and pea fricassée, or you might keep it classic with a chargrilled bavette with chips and garlic béarnaise. It all finishes comfortingly with a pot of Venezuelan chocolate with salted caramel mousse and shortbread. Fixed-price options, bar and children's menus help keep the locals returning.

Chef Gary Knowles **Seats** 120, Pr/dining room 60 **Times** 12-3.30/6-10 **Prices** Fixed L 2 course £14.50, Fixed D 3 course £18.50, Starter £5-£12.50, Main £11.95-£22.50, Dessert £6 **Wines** 13 bottles over £30, 33 bottles under £30, 20 by glass **Parking** On site after 6.30pm & wknds, on street **Notes** Sunday L £14.95-£16.95, Vegetarian available, Children welcome

The Victoria

PLAN 1 C2

Modern British

tel: 020 8876 4238 **10 West Temple Sheen SW14 7RT**
email: bookings@thevictoria.net **web:** www.thevictoria.net
dir: *Nearest station: Mortlake*

Great all-rounder by the park

A short stroll from Richmond Park, The Victoria is co-owned by TV chef Paul Merrett and the kitchen's modern British output impresses with its ambition and execution. A first course Loch Duart salmon sashimi is spot on, topped with shallot and chilli crunch and served with ketjapmanis (an Indonesian sauce) and pickled cucumbers. Among main course options, chargrilled leg of lamb comes with Middle Eastern accompaniments, South Devon rib-eye steak arrives with béarnaise sauce and 'thrice cooked' chips, and pan-roasted rainbow trout is partnered with cockles, bacon and monk's beard. Finish with dark chocolate shortbread with milk chocolate mousse and nut brownie ice cream.

LONDON SW15

Bibo

PLAN 1 D2

Modern Italian

tel: 020 8780 0592 **146 Upper Richmond, Putney SW15 2SW**
email: info@biborestaurant.com
dir: *Nearest station: East Putney*

High-energy East Putney Italian with bags of pedigree

Rebecca Mascarenhas, London restaurateur with the Midas touch when it comes to neighbourhood outfits, launched this cracking local Italian in March 2014 and it hit the ground running. Classic Italian style with a strong regional accent, using simple seasonal combinations that allow prime ingredients to shine, is what it's about. Pasta is a forte, perhaps spot-on pappardelle with slow-cooked pork ragù, while mains, like spanking-fresh sea bass with fennel and Swiss chard in vincotto, or veal shin with creamy polenta, deliver plenty of flavour. Desserts such as cannoli with kumquats and pistachios, in-house breads, all-Italian wines and sunny service maintain stellar form.

Chef Tomasz Zadlo **Seats** 70 **Times** 12-2.30/6-10.30, Closed 24-26 Dec, BHs, L Good Fri, D Etr Sun **Prices** Fixed L 2 course £16.50, Fixed D 3 course £22.50, Starter £6.50-£9.50, Main £13-£18, Dessert £5.50-£7.50 **Wines** 62 bottles over £30, 16 bottles under £30, 12 by glass **Parking** On street **Notes** Brunch menu Sat-Sun, Sunday L, Vegetarian available, Children welcome

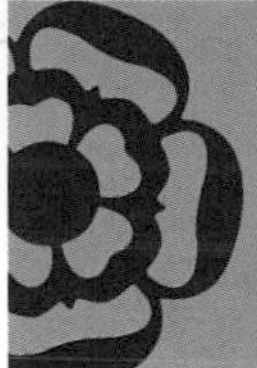

Who has won our Food Service Award? See page 13

LONDON SW17

Chez Bruce

PLAN 1 E2

Modern British 

tel: 020 8672 0114 **2 Bellevue Rd, Wandsworth Common SW17 7EG**
email: enquiries@chezbruce.co.uk
dir: *Nearest station: Wandsworth Common, Balham*

Supremely accomplished cooking in a neighbourhood stalwart

Bruce Poole has been an influential presence on the London restaurant scene over the last 20 years, branching out with The Glasshouse in Kew and La Trompette in Chiswick, and even finding the time to write a signature cookbook. The Wandsworth mothership shows a studied disregard for the whims of fashion: a purple frontage opens into a white-walled room hung with tasteful art and furnished with linen-clad tables on herringbone parquet floors, and staff demonstrate unflappable aplomb. The setting suits Poole's unfussy but highly classy cooking to perfection, and the menu is rooted in the sunny flavours of southern France and the wider Mediterranean. Foie gras and chicken liver parfait is a typically forthright opener, or there may be cod brandade with mussel Kievs, monk's beard, basil oil and garlic. Ingredients all taste supremely of themselves, as in a main course of Shetland salmon with crème fraîche, brown shrimps, samphire, pickled cucumber and sorrel, or you might stick with the heritage cookbook for a serving of côte de boeuf with chips and béarnaise. To finish, pedigree chocolate forms the backbone of a hot pudding, served with praline parfait. Otherwise, bow out on a savoury note with an array of immaculately ripened cheeses from the board.

Chef Bruce Poole, Matt Christmas **Seats** 75, Pr/dining room 16 **Times** 12-2.30/6.30-10, Closed 24-26 Dec, 1 Jan **Prices** Fixed L 3 course fr £29.50, Fixed D 3 course £49.50 **Wines** 750 bottles over £30, 30 bottles under £30, 15 by glass **Parking** On street, station car park **Notes** L menu 3 course Dec, wknds & BHs £35, Sunday L, Vegetarian available, Children L only

LONDON SW19

The Fox & Grapes

PLAN 1 D2

Traditional British

tel: 020 8619 1300 **9 Camp Rd, Wimbledon SW19 4UN**
email: reservations@foxandgrapeswimbledon.co.uk
dir: *Nearest station: Wimbledon*

Country pub charm by the Common

On the edge of Wimbledon Common, this place has the feel of an upscale inn with a menu offering a slick take on some old favourites. Avocado prawn cocktail is a starter with bags of retro appeal, but there's also the more contemporary cured salmon with pickled kohlrabi and horseradish yogurt. Among main courses, a fashionably pimped-up burger is present and correct (topped with Ogleshield cheese), and there's a Middle Eastern spin to partridge flavoured with ras el hanout and served with chickpeas and preserved lemons. The Butcher's Board lists the various cuts of steak on offer, and, to finish, there might be treacle tart with stem ginger ice cream.

Hotel du Vin at Cannizaro House

PLAN 1 D1

Modern British, European

tel: 020 8879 1464 **West Side, Wimbledon Common SW19 4UE**
email: info@cannizarohouse.com **web:** www.cannizarohouse.com
dir: *Nearest station: Wimbledon*

British modernism in a lavish Wimbledon mansion

The acquisition of Cannizaro House is something of a key-change for the Hotel du Vin group. Its hotels are always highly individual buildings with personality to spare, but not as eye-poppingly posh as this late-Georgian mansion. Seared tuna with an egg yolk and Shetland black potato makes a bold opening statement. European traditions are creatively tweaked, as when whipped duck rillettes with Agen prunes are given a pain d'épices dressing, or fermented truffle lights up a main-course risotto enriched with mascarpone as well as parmesan. Meals conclude either with Neal's Yard cheeses, or an ingeniously constructed dessert such as spiced morello cherry crumble with walnut snow.

The Light House Restaurant

PLAN 1 D1

Modern International

tel: 020 8944 6338 **75-77 Ridgway, Wimbledon SW19 4ST**
email: info@lighthousewimbledon.com
dir: *Nearest station: Wimbledon*

Cheerful neighbourhood restaurant with appealing cooking

The Light House is a beacon of fresh seasonal cooking just a short stroll from Wimbledon Common. Appealing menus of fresh, modern-bistro style dishes are on offer, with plenty of sunny, Mediterranean flavours cooked up in the open kitchen. Chicken liver and tarragon pâté with apricot chutney and toast gets things off to a flying start, or there could be harissa mackerel with aubergine and tahini dip and piquillo peppers. Next out, steamed hake with Jersey Royals, peas, spinach and champagne butter sauce is a delightful light, fresh and seasonal summery dish. And who could fail to be won over by puddings like vanilla yogurt pannacotta with cherry compôte.

Chef Chris Casey **Seats** 80, Pr/dining room 12 **Times** 12-2.45/6-10.30, Closed 24-26 Dec, 1 Jan, D Sun **Prices** Fixed L 2 course £15.95 **Wines** 61 bottles over £30, 24 bottles under £30, 19 by glass **Notes** Fixed D 2/3 course Mon-Thu 6-7.30pm £18.95/£23.95, Sunday L, Vegetarian available, Children welcome

LONDON W1

Alain Ducasse at The Dorchester

PLAN 4 G6

– *see page 280*

Alyn Williams at The Westbury

PLAN 2 H1

– *see page 280*

Andrew Edmunds

PLAN 2 J1

Modern European

tel: 020 7437 5708 **46 Lexington St, Soho W1F 0LW**
dir: *Nearest station: Oxford Circus, Piccadilly Circus*

Evergreen, rustic, Soho favourite

The tiny ground-floor dining room of this bistro stalwart is one of the West End's most intimate and romantic venues. With its simple rustic decor – wood floors and church pews, elbow-to-elbow tables with paper tablecloths, all low-lit by candles in wine bottles – it has an old Soho feel of a Dickensian tavern. The kitchen takes an equally uncomplicated and honest approach, producing seasonal, ingredients-driven dishes on a daily-changing handwritten menu that might take you from half a woodcock with braised lentils, via whole Cornish mackerel with fennel, blood orange and beetroot, or ox cheek ragù with pappardelle, to bergamot and pistachio cheesecake.

Chef Bob Cairns **Seats** 63 **Times** 12-3.30/5.30-10.45, Closed Xmas, Etr **Prices** Prices not confirmed **Wines** 154 bottles over £30, 42 bottles under £30, 7 by glass **Notes** Sunday L, Vegetarian available, Children welcome

Alain Ducasse at The Dorchester

LONDON W1 **PLAN 4 G6**

Contemporary, Modern French V NOTABLE WINE LIST

tel: 020 7629 8866 **The Dorchester, 53 Park Ln W1K 1QA**
email: alainducassereservations@alainducasse-dorchester.com
dir: *Nearest station: Hyde Park Corner, Marble Arch*

Unashamedly classical French haute cuisine

Alain Ducasse has two-dozen restaurants around the world in such glitzy locations as Monaco and Las Vegas, varying from simply stylish bistros to luxurious bastions of contemporary French cuisine. The Dorchester is firmly in the latter category. The dining room positively shimmers, which his mostly down to the 4,500 fibre optic lights that create the Table Lumière, a glamorous cocoon in the centre of the room in which sits a private table. The view over park Lane is through one-way glass to ensure a sense of privacy and exclusivity, while the service is world class – impeccably dressed, knowledgeable and smooth. The attention to detail is evident from the get-go, with perfect bread and an amuse-bouche that combines tender coco beans and confit chicken leg in a light broth with black truffle. Next up, soft-baked egg with chicken liver and lobster is another show stopper: an ingenious combination of first-class ingredients and technical virtuosity, dressed with a rich, decadent and velvety chicken jus. Roasted fillet of brill is a more traditional dish in its concept and execution, but no less thrilling, with textbook boulangère potatoes, and confit lemon and anchovy to elevate the plate to exalted status. Rib and saddle of venison is a meaty main course of refinement and earthy richness (keeping company with a glossy grand veneur sauce), and, to finish, 'Apple delight' is a harmonious textural and visual experience. The French-focused wine list covers a lot of ground and offers succour to the most ardent grape fan, and when it comes to the spend, the sky is the limit.

Chef Jean Philippe Blondet, Angelo Ercolano, Alberto Gobbo **Seats** 82, Pr/dining room 30 **Times** 12-1.30/6.30-9.30, Closed 1st wk Jan, Etr wknd, 3 wks Aug, 26-30 Dec, Sun-Mon, L Sat, 31 Dec **Prices** Fixed L 3 course £60, Fixed D 3 course £95, Tasting menu £135 **Wines** 18 by glass **Parking** 20 **Notes** Seasonal £180, Menu Jardin £110, Black Truffle menu £240, Children 10 yrs+

Alyn Williams at The Westbury

LONDON W1 **PLAN 2 H1**

French, European V NOTABLE WINE LIST

tel: 020 7183 6426 **37 Conduit St W1S 2YF**
email: alynwilliams@westburymayfair.com **web:** www.alynwilliams.com
dir: *Nearest station: Oxford Circus, Piccadilly Circus, Green Park*

Innovation, top-flight skills and heaps of glamour

The Westbury hails from a time when first impressions were not considered to be important. From the outside, it could be an office-block, but inside all is sedate, five-star style. A little way along the ground floor is Alyn Williams' preserve, a serenely relaxing room done in varnished darkwood surfaces with a scintillating carpet and illuminated wine store at one end. The tone of service is both impeccably correct and voluble in its welcome, and it all makes a confidence-inspiring backdrop for the culinary fireworks to come. Williams has trained with the best, but explores his own territory here with a highly personal take on modern European cuisine, using unusual ingredients and techniques for a performance best experienced in the form of the tasting menu that is the only option on weekend evenings, as dishes are taken up from the carte and others make their debut. Evenly caramelised scallops of stunning freshness are dressed with thinly shaved truffle on a flawless spring onion risotto, which might be followed on the carte by tender sirloin of Devon ruby beef with accompanying tartare, potatoes cooked in the dripping, baby turnips and fragrant elderflower gel. For the tasting menu, foraged ingredients such as gutweed and beach greens lend character to the fish dishes, perhaps hake with clams, and marinated quail turns up with violet mustard and a confit egg yolk. Aerated chocolate desserts are a particularly successful party trick, here partnered with mandarin and gingerbread ice cream, while a technically unimpeachable vanilla pannacotta is offset by the bracing sharpnesses of blackberry and limoncello.

Chef Alyn Williams **Seats** 65, Pr/dining room 20 **Times** 12-2.30/6-10.30, Closed 1-17 Jan, 18 Aug-4 Sep, Sun-Mon **Prices** Fixed L 3 course fr £65, Tasting menu £80-£140, Starter fr £20, Main fr £35, Dessert fr £10 **Wines** 450 bottles over £30, 10 bottles under £30, 15 by glass **Parking** 20 **Notes** Fixed ALC 3 course £65, Tasting menu 7 course (with wine), Children welcome

Antidote

PLAN 2 J2

Modern European

tel: 020 7287 8488 **12a Newburgh St W1F 7RR**
email: contact@antidotewinebar.com
dir: *Nearest station: Oxford Circus*

Trendy spot with creative menu

Trendily tucked away in a cobbled, 'off-the-radar' lane behind Carnaby Street, Antidote offers the perfect fix for organic/biodynamic wine lovers and foodies alike. Upstairs, above its bustling wine bar, the dining room is a relaxed oasis, with a fashionable pared-back look of grey walls, floorboards, funky silver bistro chairs, and dangling Edison-style light bulbs. The kitchen delivers imaginative modern stuff such as sake-cured mackerel with walnut milk, apple and çalcot (a type of Spanish onion), or an equally creative Brussels sprout number with almonds and Montgomery cheddar. Move on to tender roe deer with fermented cabbage, and finish with clementine and goats' curd tart.

Chef Michael Hazlewood **Seats** 45 **Times** 12-2.30/6-10.30, Closed Xmas, BHs, Sun **Prices** Tasting menu fr £40 **Wines** 260 bottles over £30, 10 bottles under £30, 20 by glass **Parking** On street **Notes** Tasting menu 4 course, Vegetarian available, Children welcome

Aqua Kyoto

PLAN 2 J2

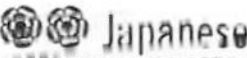 Japanese

tel: 020 7478 0540 **240 Regent St W1B 3BR**
email: reservation@aqua-london.com
dir: *Nearest station: Oxford St*

Classy Japanese food in super-cool rooftop setting

This modern Japanese outfit is on the top floor of the former Dickins & Jones building, so there are great rooftop views from the terrace. Kyoto's ultra-designed dining room shimmers with contemporary style. Moody black, red and gold complement the theatre of a sunken centrepiece sushi bar, charcoal grill and jaw-dropping lantern-style light fitting. Visually striking, well-constructed dishes and top-drawer ingredients are the thing: take king crab tempura with crab miso, or perhaps twice-cooked crispy pork belly with langoustine and yuzu pepper to high-rolling Wagyu beef with garlic ponzu and grape icicles. Otherwise there's cracking sushi and sashimi, fashionable wines and super cocktails.

Aqua Nueva

PLAN 2 J2

 Spanish

tel: 020 7478 0540 **5th Floor, 240 Regent St W1B 3BR**
email: reservation@aqua-london.com
dir: *Nearest station: Oxford Circus*

Fashionable restaurant for Spanish wines and top-notch tapas

A lift whizzes you up from ground-floor street life to jet-set high life at this slick fifth floor restaurant. It's the sort of place where people come to see and be seen as much as for the contemporary renditions of tapas based on top-end Spanish ingredients, so take your pick from a bilingual menu full of good-sounding ideas. Old favourites abound, from salt-cod croquettes to morcilla blood sausage with roasted peppers, or lamb shoulder confit. Otherwise, a three-course format might start with ox cheek cannelloni with tomato confit, potato purée and guacamole, then continue with black cuttlefish rice with aïoli, and conclude with coffee sponge with Amaretto jelly.

Arbutus Restaurant

PLAN 2 K2

Modern French

tel: 020 7734 4545 **63-64 Frith St W1D 3JW**
email: info@arbutusrestaurant.co.uk
dir: *Nearest station: Tottenham Court Rd*

Adventurous French bistro cooking off Soho Square

When Arbutus opened a decade ago, its aim was to bring contemporary bistro food to a style-hungry Soho crowd that didn't want to pay the earth for it. The result has been a resounding success, as the busy nature of the place indicates. Small café tables out front, with battleship-grey banquettes further in to match the frontage, are the decorative order, while the big photographic print of New York seems a little irrelevant. Lively French-inspired bistro dishes are absolutely to the point, however, and deliver plenty of earthy, positive impact. Smoked eel and kohlrabi in a dill emulsion vies with pork brawn terrine, burnt apple purée and gribiche among starters, before the main business centres on substantial proteins such as rabbit saddle and shoulder croquettes with broad beans and black garlic, or an early summer serving of sea trout with Jersey Royals and asparagus in watercress hollandaise. Homely British-style finishers encompass custard tart, or a simple serving of arbutus honey ice cream, or you can pile on the Euro-style via Manjari chocolate delice with dulce de leche and salted peanuts. An enlightened approach to wine sees all listings offered by the 250ml carafe, so you can go on matching solids and liquids throughout.

Chef Anthony Demetre, Luke Finegan **Seats** 55
Times 12-2.30/5-11.30, Closed 25-26 Dec, 1 Jan, Sun **Prices** Fixed L 2 course £23-£26, Fixed D 3 course £26-£40, Starter £7-£10, Main £15-£22, Dessert £6-£8 **Wines** 40 bottles over £30, 10 bottles under £30, 50 by glass **Notes** Pre-theatre D 5-6.30pm 3 course £19.95/£20.95, Vegetarian available, Children welcome

The Arch London

PLAN 2 F2

Modern British

tel: 020 7725 4825 **50 Great Cumberland Place W1H 7FD**
email: hunter486@thearchlondon.com **web:** www.thearchlondon.com
dir: *Nearest station: Marble Arch*

Vibrant cooking near Marble Arch

Just a short stroll from Marble Arch, The Arch is a charming hotel spread over seven Georgian townhouses. A stone oven comes into its own with some main courses, from game pie to whole sea bass with orange and rosemary butter; a steak from the grill is another option, with a handful of other options, among them fish stew with saffron aïoli, and breaded veal escalope on a bed of spinach topped with a well-timed fried egg, anchovies and caper butter. Starters include carpaccio with tapenade, parmesan and rocket, while among the enjoyable puddings are cappuccino pannacotta with coffee crumble, chocolate ice cream and banana foam.

Chef Gary Durrant **Seats** 72, Pr/dining room 40 **Times** 12-10.30, All-day dining **Prices** Fixed L 2 course £19, Fixed D 3 course £23, Starter £7.50-£12.50, Main £15-£24, Dessert £6.50 **Wines** 30 bottles over £30, 10 bottles under £30, 9 by glass **Parking** NCP 2 mins **Notes** Express menu (L & pre-theatre), Afternoon tea, Breakfast, Sunday L £22.50, Vegetarian available, Children welcome

LONDON W1 *continued*

Assunta Madre

PLAN 2 H2

Italian Seafood

tel: 020 3230 3032 **9-10 Blenheim St W1S 1LJ**
email: info@assuntamadre.com
dir: *Nearest station: New Bond St*

Authentic Italian seafood dishes in the West End

This popular Italian is named after a fishing boat owned by proprietor Giovanni Micalusi, himself an ex-fisherman. Not surprisingly, the freshest seafood and fish, much of it flown in from Italy every day, is the deal here and there's even a fish tank near the board displaying photos of Micalusi with visiting film stars. The time-honoured combination of exposed brick walls and beams provides a classic trattoria backdrop to a meal that might begin with vermicelli alle vongole veraci – a pasta dish packed with clams – followed by pescespade in guazzetto comprising slices of swordfish in a light tomato and olive sauce. A simple cherry tart is a typical dessert.

L'Autre Pied

PLAN 2 G3

Modern European V

tel: 020 7486 9696 **5-7 Blandford St, Marylebone Village W1U 3DB**
email: info@lautrepied.co.uk
dir: *Nearest station: Bond St, Baker St*

Exciting contemporary cooking off Marylebone High Street

The Rosette award for this establishment has been suspended due to a change of chef. Reassessment will take place in due course under the new chef. The Other Foot is the younger sibling of the Foot on the Ground, the celebrated Pied-à-Terre a few blocks away. Just off voguish Marylebone High Street in this well-heeled central London 'village', L'Autre Pied offers a bright and contemporary place to dine, whether you're seeking respite from the ambiguous joys of nearby Oxford Street or, more likely, just fancy eating somewhere exceptionally good. It makes judicious use of its space with rosewood tables, leather chairs and booths with cherry-red banquettes. Menus are all things to all comers, whether your business is pre-theatre, plat du jour, or bring-it-on multi-course taster. There's a carte too, and it all features considered modern Anglo-French cooking that makes exuberant sense. Cornish crab is dressed in Riesling and comes with bisque-flavoured pannacotta, as well as avocado, cucumber and English wasabi, as a possible intro to mains such as new season's Manx lamb with a potato croquette ritzed up with Riseley, a washed-rind Berkshire sheep's cheese, as well as spring greens and rosemary. You may be surprised to find passionfruit in the baked Alaska, and positively astonished to find it anointed with Lapsang Souchong.

Chef Graham Long **Seats** 53, Pr/dining room 16 **Times** 12-2.30/6-10.45, Closed 4 days Xmas, 1 Jan, D Sun **Prices** Fixed L 2 course fr £24, Tasting menu £72-£79, Starter £12-£17.50, Main £25-£29.50, Dessert £10-£14 **Wines** 200 bottles over £30, 6 bottles under £30, 10 by glass **Notes** Sunday L £39.50, Children welcome

Avista

PLAN 2 G1

Italian

tel: 020 7596 3399 & 7629 9400 **Millennium London Mayfair, Grosvenor Square W1K 2HP**
email: reservations@avistarestaurant.com **web:** www.avistarestaurant.com
dir: *Nearest station: Bond St*

Classic Italian flavours and creative flair

The Millennium Hotel Mayfair with its Georgian frontage and grand neo-classical Doric columns is an imposing presence on Grosvenor Square, while its Avista restaurant, with its own separate entrance, is one of the most inspiring modern Italian restaurants in the capital. The dining room is suitably attired for the Mayfair postcode, with a contemporary finish including modern artworks and even some exposed brickwork. Executive chef Arturo Granato's bilingual menus deliver classic combinations in a modern manner, but the 21st-century cooking techniques enhance the first-rate produce rather than obscure them. Start, perhaps, with hand-picked Cornish crab cleverly matched with pickled shallots, a light Granny Smith apple foam and coconut snow, or beef tartare with Caesar dressing and some fresh truffle. Pasta options might include red cabbage tagliolini in a venison ragù enriched with Barolo, while a fishy secondi might be lemon sole in a wonderfully light batter partnered with trompette mushrooms, candied onion and Jerusalem artichoke soup. There's plenty of finesse at dessert stage, too, judging by a dark Valrhona chocolate number with the flavours of pistachio and mandarin, or the house's version of a classic tiramisù with the addition of hazelnut crumble to raise it up a level or two.

Chef Arturo Granato **Seats** 75, Pr/dining room 12 **Times** 12-2.30/6-10.30, Closed 1 Jan, Sun, L Sat **Prices** Fixed L 2 course £23, Fixed D 3 course £29, Tasting menu £75, Starter £11.50-£19.50, Main £19-£29, Dessert £7.50-£11.50 **Wines** 73 bottles over £30, 4 bottles under £30, 11 by glass **Parking** On street, NCP **Notes** Vegetarian available, Children welcome

Babbo Restaurant

PLAN 4 J6

Modern Mediterranean

tel: 020 3205 1099 **39-40 Albemarle St W1S 4JQ**
email: reservations@babborestaurant.co.uk **web:** www.babborestaurant.co.uk
dir: *Nearest station: Green Park*

Italian family hospitality in Mayfair

Located in the heart of Mayfair, Babbo's recent stylishly contemporary refurbishment has retained that special feel of a family-run business. The exciting menu is a fusion of Mediterranean dishes that use top drawer fine-aged ingredients from around the world. A main course might feature grilled sea bream with vanilla parsnip purée or perhaps the beef cheek and truffle potato, before moving on to mouth-watering desserts, all home-made, including ice cream, sorbets and tiramisù. This is all accompanied by a wine list that aims to excite rather than challenge and vibrant cocktails that complement the chef's tasting menu.

Chef Carlo Scotto **Seats** 56, Pr/dining room 14 **Times** 12-3/6-11, Closed 25-26 Dec, 1 Jan, L Sat-Sun **Prices** Fixed L 2 course £25, Tasting menu £120, Starter £9-£12.50, Main £16.50-£35, Dessert £8.50-£12.50 **Wines** 162 bottles over £30, 1 bottle under £30, 13 by glass **Notes** Vegetarian available, Children welcome

Barnyard

PLAN 2 K3

Farmhouse

tel: 020 7580 3842 **18 Charlotte St W1T 2LZ**
email: info@barnyard-london.com
dir: *Nearest station: Goodge St*

Country cool with plenty of flavour on Charlotte Street

It may feel a bit 'themed', with a rustic feel, chunky wood and corrugated walls, but this brainchild of Ollie Dabbous has plenty of substance as well as style. It's laid back and comfortable, and you'll find full-flavoured, hearty dishes with broad appeal on the brown paper menu. Graze on warm cornbread or smoked butter and mushroom croquettes, and then move on to potted shrimp on a toasted pikelet with samphire and parsley, wild boar toad-in-the-hole, or beef on toast with watercress, pickles and warm garlic buttermilk. Finish with apple and cloudberry crumble.

Chef Ollie Dabbous **Seats** 40 **Times** 12-3/5-10.30, Closed 25-26 Dec, 1 Jan, Etr BH **Prices** Starter £7-£15, Dessert £6 **Wines** 7 bottles over £30, 6 bottles under £30, 9 by glass **Parking** On street **Notes** Brunch, Fixed L £18.50, Pre-theatre until 5.30pm, Vegetarian available, Children welcome

Barrafina Frith Street

PLAN 2 K2

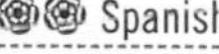 Spanish

tel: 020 7813 8016 **54 Frith St W1D 4SL**
email: jose@barrafina.co.uk
dir: *Nearest station: Tottenham Court Rd*

Classic Spanish tapas at a marble counter in Soho

When there is no time to linger over dining, tapas is often the answer, and while the term nowadays covers anything that comes in pocket-sized portions, the original Spanish article remains the bedrock. Barrafina is a prime exponent of the genre. A long marble counter facing an open kitchen is the setting for gorgeous mouthfuls of strong savoury satisfaction – ham and cheese croquettes, Iberian pork ribs, pan-fried skate with tapenade and capers, herb-crusted rabbit shoulder. It's served efficiently, though the no-bookings policy means you may have to wait your turn – but what better opportunity to kick back with a glass of manzanilla?

The Beaumont

PLAN 2 G1

British, American

tel: 020 7499 9499 & 7499 1001 **8 Balderton St, Mayfair W1K 6TF**
email: info@colonygrillroom.com **web:** www.colonygrillroom.com
dir: *Nearest station: Bond St*

Appealing old-fashioned brasserie dining in art deco style

On the south side of Oxford Street, not far from Selfridges, The Beaumont is a burnished slice of Mayfair elegance where bow-tied waiters bring brasserie food such as potted Morecambe Bay shrimps with brown bread and butter, omelette Arnold Bennett, and servings of caviar. You can unblushingly dine on gammon and pineapple once again in London, or there may be neatly manicured lamb cutlets with béarnaise and a side order of rosemary-roasted pumpkin. Who remembers steak Diane? Veal Pojarski? Here they are, alongside more voguish touches such as fried chicken in buttermilk with spiced remoulade. Sumptuously layered trifle crammed with fruit and lashed with amontillado sherry makes a satisfying finish.

Bellamy's

PLAN 2 H1

French

tel: 020 7491 2727 **18-18a Bruton Place W1J 6LY**
email: gavin@bellamysrestaurant.co.uk
dir: *Nearest station: Green Park, Bond St*

Classy brasserie just off Berkeley Square

With its setting just off Berkeley Square, effortlessly classy good looks and slickly professional service, Bellamy's epitomises the chic, timeless French brasserie genre. Leather banquettes, pale yellow walls (lined with tasteful French posters and mirrors), white linen and staff in bow ties and waistcoats add to the authentic look. The kitchen excels in simple, ungimmicky, clear flavoured dishes, so start with rich duck rillettes, followed by red mullet fillets casseroled in a tomato, cumin and tamarind sauce, and finish with a classic crème brûlée. Fabulous all-French wines and an interconnecting afternoon oyster bar and a chic evening cocktail bar complete the experience.

Chef Stephane Pacoud **Seats** 70 **Times** 12-2.30/7-10.30, Closed Xmas, New Year, BHs, Sun, L Sat **Prices** Fixed L 2 course £21.50, Fixed D 3 course £26.50, Starter £6.50-£19, Main £16.50-£29, Dessert £7.50 **Wines** 63 bottles over £30, 5 bottles under £30, 19 by glass **Parking** On street, NCP **Notes** Vegetarian available, Children welcome

Benares Restaurant

PLAN 2 H1

Modern Indian V

tel: 020 7629 8886 & 7514 2805 **12a Berkeley Square W1J 6BS**
email: reservations@benaresrestaurant.co.uk
dir: *Nearest station: Bond St, Green Park*

Innovative new-wave Indian on Berkeley Square

Atul Kochhar's high-rolling Mayfair thoroughbred purrs with the sheen of a glitzy nightclub. Well-drilled staff take a serious approach, and Kochhar's crossover Anglo-Indian cooking always excites with its groundbreaking ideas, sharp technique and gorgeous presentation. Start with a lamb shami kebab and tandoori cutlet with mint and tamarind relish and baby radish for a palate-priming overture. Move on to South Indian seafood kofta balls in tomato and ginger sauce with poriyal vermicelli, or tandoori-spiced quail supreme with wild mushroom biryani, quail's egg and pineapple raita. The East-meets-West style concludes with a cheesecake-style rasmalai with chocolate ice cream, crunchy chocolate balls and ground pistachios.

Chef Atul Kochhar **Seats** 120, Pr/dining room 36
Times 12-2.30/5.30-11, Closed 25-26 Dec, 1 Jan, Sun **Prices** Fixed L 2 course fr £29, Fixed D 3 course fr £35, Starter £14-£27, Main £28-£37, Dessert £9.50-£12
Wines 300 bottles over £30, 10 bottles under £30, 17 by glass **Parking** On street
Notes Fixed menu until 6.30pm, Children before 7pm

LONDON W1 *continued*

Bentley's Oyster Bar & Grill

PLAN 2 J1

British, Irish NOTABLE WINE LIST

tel: 020 7734 4756 **11-15 Swallow St W1B 4DG**
email: reservations@bentleys.org **web:** www.bentleys.org
dir: *Nearest station: Piccadilly Circus*

Lovingly restored seafood bar and restaurant in Piccadilly

Celebrating its 100th birthday in 2016, the illustrious oyster bar is a highly popular, feel-good rendezvous, while upstairs, the Grill restaurant takes a more formal, sophisticated approach. Start with a light seafood céviche with avocado, peppy lime and scallions if opting out of the oyster route, and perhaps continue with pan-fried turbot served with grilled calçots and sweet and tangy caper-raisin sauce. Portioning is light and prices lean toward West End grabby, but ingredients are excellent, service slick and wines a superb bunch. Desserts range from classics to the more modern chilli and ginger pineapple with coconut parfait. A few meat options from the wood-fired grill keep carnivores onside.

Chef Richard Corrigan, Michael Lynch **Seats** 70, Pr/dining room 60 **Times** 12-3/5.30-11, Closed 25 Dec, 1 Jan, L Sat (Grill only) **Prices** Fixed L 2 course £25, Starter £10-£22.50, Main £18.50-£80, Dessert £7-£9 **Wines** 100 bottles over £30, 5 bottles under £30, 24 by glass **Notes** Pre-theatre menu 2/3 course £26/£29, Sunday L, Vegetarian available, Children welcome

Berners Tavern

PLAN 2 J2

Contemporary British 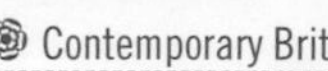

tel: 020 7908 7979 **The London Edition, 10 Berners St W1T 3NP**
email: bernerstavern@editionhotels.com **web:** www.bernerstavern.com
dir: *Nearest station: Oxford Circus*

Modern brasserie dining in a room of untavern-like opulence

This palatial space with a magnificent plaster ceiling, chandelier, and walls crowded with pictures, is nothing like a tavern. Jason Atherton oversees the cooking, which is in his contemporary brasserie style. Restyled classics such as lobster and prawn cocktail, or a starter of chicken liver and foie gras parfait with a jointed quail in sherry caramel, get things going. Main dishes might be gruyère-crusted cod with braised clams and leeks, gnocchetti and sprouting broccoli, or try almost homely roast chicken breast with bacon and mash in coq au vin sauce with smoked garlic salsa verde. Rhubarb trifle and lemon thyme ice cream, topped with crumbled meringue, arrives in a jar.

Chef Phil Carmichael, Jason Atherton **Seats** 114, Pr/dining room 14 **Times** 12-10.30, All-day dining **Prices** Fixed L 2 course fr £24.50 **Wines** 330 bottles over £30, 25 bottles under £30, 19 by glass **Parking** On street, NCP & car park **Notes** All-day menu, Fixed L menu, Sunday L, Vegetarian available, Children welcome

Blanchette

PLAN 2 J2

Modern, Traditional French Tapas V

tel: 020 7439 8100 **9 D'Arblay St, Soho W1F 8DR**
email: info@blanchettesoho.co.uk
dir: *Nearest station: Oxford Circus*

Hip French bistro dining in the hinterland of Soho

Opened by three brothers from across the Channel, Blanchette delivers imaginative bistro-style French cuisine served as sharing plates. The charcuterie and cheese selections show what this place is all about – salami-style Rosette de Lyon and truffled saucisson from the Rhône region, plus ewes-milk Tomme de Corse and Fourme d'Ambert among the fromages. The kitchen comes up with some good things in support – a plate of trompette mushroom-crusted monkfish with roasted pumpkin, truffle and sun-dried tomato sauce, or another dish that combines braised lamb shoulder with anchovy, rosemary and soubise sauce. Veggie options take in tarte fine of leek and Bleu de Basque, while puddings include chocolate and hazelnut dacquoise with crème fraîche ice cream.

Chef Tam Storrar **Seats** 54, Pr/dining room 14 **Times** 12-3/5.30-11 **Prices** Fixed L 2 course fr £20, Fixed D 3 course fr £40, Starter £3.50-£10, Main £6.50-£10, Dessert £6.25 **Wines** 17 bottles over £30, 7 bottles under £30, 15 by glass **Parking** Car park, Poland St **Notes** Charcuterie & cheese platters when kitchen closed, Sunday L, Children welcome

Bocca di Lupo

PLAN 2 K1

Italian NOTABLE WINE LIST

tel: 020 7734 2223 & 7734 7128 **12 Archer St W1D 7BB**
email: info@boccadilupo.com
dir: *Nearest station: Piccadilly Circus*

Regional Italian sharing plates in the heart of Soho

High-energy, high-octane and great fun, Bocca di Lupo rocks. Grab a stool at the long marble bar's 'chef's counter' to enjoy the culinary theatre, or head into the restaurant area proper, with its polished wood tables and feature lighting. The lengthy, daily-changing menu offers small or large plates, while everything is regionally name-checked, likewise the corking Italian wines. Expect pukka tagliolini with squid ragù or home-made lamb sausage and earthy lentils, and don't overlook salads like a headlining radish, celeriac, pomegranate, pecorino and truffle dressing assemble. Desserts, like gelato – from their own ice cream parlour, Gelupo opposite – or perhaps a pear and hazelnut tart all hit the spot.

Chef Jacob Kenedy **Seats** 75, Pr/dining room 32
Times 12.15-3.45/5.15-10.45, Closed 25 Dec, 1 Jan **Prices** Starter £5-£20, Main £7-£28.50, Dessert £6-£10 **Wines** 140 bottles over £30, 15 bottles under £30, 20 by glass **Parking** NCP Brewer St **Notes** Sunday L, Vegetarian available, Children welcome

Bó Drake

PLAN 3 A2

Korean, Modern Asian

tel: 020 7439 9989 **6 Greek St W1D 4DE**
email: contact@bodrake.co.uk
dir: *Nearest station: Tottenham Court Road, Leicester Sq*

Bustling on-trend Soho Korean-Mexican outfit

Tucked away at the top-end of Greek Street, Bó Drake is made for Soho; a no reservation, modern Asian-European outfit delivering slow-cooked and smoky barbeque street-food flavours at wallet-friendly prices. Try brisket bao (melting 12-hour smoked beef brisket with peppy mustard barbecue relish served in a bao, (a soft rice-flour bun), its flavours cut through with the crunch and freshness of cucumber and fried lotus root. Otherwise, go for Bo ssäm (succulent pulled pork, smoky and with spicy attitude), accompanied by dipping sauces of spring onion oil, ssamjiang (fiery Korean soy sauce) and kimchi (fermented vegetables) that you lettuce-wrap together to offer a taste sensation that dances on the palate.

Chef Matteo Frugone **Seats** 55 **Times** 12-2.30/5.30-11, Closed Xmas, New Year **Prices** Starter £8-£10, Main £10-£22, Dessert £4-£8 **Wines** 8 bottles under £30 **Parking** On street **Notes** Express L Bento menu, Sunday L £25-£40, Vegetarian available, Children welcome

Cecconi's

PLAN 2 J1

Traditional Italian

tel: 020 7434 1500 **5a Burlington Gardens W1S 1EP**
dir: *Nearest station: Piccadilly Circus, Oxford Circus*

Swanky Mayfair address for top-class seasonal Italian cooking

Cecconi's is a classic all the way from the glamorous Mayfair crew slurping cocktails and cicchetti at the island bar down to the black-and-white humbug-striped marble floors, green leather upholstery and slick Italian staff. Dedication to top-class seasonal produce is clear, and it's simply prepared to deliver full-on flavours. Kickstart the taste buds with superb grilled octopus with sautéed potatoes, sun-dried tomatoes, sweet red peppers and broccoli, then move on to splendid pasta such as crab ravioli. Main course brings an outstanding slab of halibut with clams and mussels and capers, or you might go meaty with a classic chicken paillard with rocket and parmesan.

The Chesterfield Mayfair

PLAN 4 H6

Traditional British

tel: 020 7491 2622 **35 Charles St, Mayfair W1J 5EB**
email: bookch@rchmail.com **web:** www.chesterfieldmayfair.com
dir: *Nearest station: Green Park*

Cosseting luxury, Mayfair style

A fine Georgian property jam-packed with antiques and run with a touch of old-school charm. A first-course suckling pig's cheek croquette looks pretty on the plate, joined by a sliver of black pudding and sweetcorn purée, while another puts Orkney king scallops in the fashionable company of chicken wings (plus girolles, pea purée and cobnuts). Move on to a spiced-up line-caught sea bass with curried mussels and finish with an English strawberry tart topped with a scoop of powerful peppermint crisp ice cream. There's a pre-theatre menu if you're in a hurry to catch a show (or simply after a good deal) and afternoon tea is served in the conservatory.

China Tang at The Dorchester

PLAN 4 G6

Classic Cantonese

tel: 020 7629 9988 **53 Park Ln W1K 1QA**
email: reservations@chinatanglondon.co.uk
dir: *Nearest station: Hyde Park Corner*

Classic Cantonese cooking in five-star Park Lane surroundings

The basement of The Dorchester is home to this opulent homage to 1930s Shanghai with a glam cocktail bar and a restaurant replete with refined Chinoiserie and art deco mirrored columns. The cooking is classic Cantonese, although the quality of the produce takes the menu of familiar dishes and all-day dim sum to a higher plane. Luxuries are liberally sprinkled around but you don't have to break the bank; exemplary seafood dumplings show a kitchen that doesn't waste time with unnecessary embellishments, likewise the spicy Szechuan prawns. Elsewhere, there's classic Peking duck or humble braised pork belly cooked in a clay pot with preserved vegetables.

C London

PLAN 2 H1

Italian

tel: 020 7399 0500 **23-25 Davies St W1K 3DE**
email: london@crestaurant.co.uk
dir: *Nearest station: Bond St*

Venetian elegance and celeb spotting in Mayfair

C London is sibling to Venice's famous Harry's Bar and is a haunt of the international glitterati. The high-gloss dining room looks sleek with its art deco styling and mirror-sheen, panelled walls and white-jacketed, slickly professional staff. It's certainly not all style over substance – the classic Italian cooking is founded on top-class produce and doesn't disappoint. Take ultra-fresh tuna tartare with intense tonnato sauce, then textbook risotto with artichoke hearts and scampi. Breads are fabulous, a Bellini aperitif is almost a requisite, and for dessert, there's a fine tiramisù. Factor in a buzzing atmosphere, 15% service and prices set with the celebrity in mind.

LONDON W1 *continued*

Cocochan

PLAN 2 G2

Pan-Asian

tel: 020 7486 1000 **38-40 James St, Marylebone W1U 1EU**
email: info@cocochan.co.uk **web:** www.cocochan.co.uk
dir: *Nearest station: Bond St*

Pan-Asian fusion cooking in vibrant West End setting

If you hanker after the cuisines of Thailand, Vietnam, China, Japan and Korea, head over to this address near Oxford Street. The menu offers a Pan-Asian panoply that includes creative dim sum such as chicken croquettes with yuzu mayo and crispy aromatic duck rolls, alongside classic sushi and sashimi (spicy tuna and spring onion ura maki, say, or salmon sashimi). There are small snacks and salads along the lines of chicken thigh teriyaki skewers and confit duck salad with watermelon, and full-on main courses that run to stir-fried tiger prawn sambal and red duck curry with pineapple and bamboo shoots. Desserts include the exotic sounding yuzu cheesecake with kumquat compôte.

Chef Sherif Hassan **Seats** 80, Pr/dining room 35 **Times** 12-12, All-day dining, Closed 25 Dec **Prices** Fixed L 2 course £15.50, Fixed D 3 course £40-£50, Starter £4-£4.50, Main £17-£28, Dessert £4.50-£7 **Wines** 40 bottles over £30, 15 bottles under £30, 15 by glass **Parking** On street **Notes** Bento box L min £15.50, Sunday L £16-£18, Vegetarian available, Children welcome

Corrigan's Mayfair

PLAN 2 G1

– see opposite and advert below

Coya

PLAN 4 H6

Modern Peruvian

tel: 020 7042 7118 **118 Piccadilly, Mayfair W1J 7NW**
email: info@coyarestaurant.com
dir: *Nearest station: Hyde Park Corner*

Peruvian cooking and bags of style

With three open kitchens, a céviche counter, an open charcoal grill, and a pisco bar, Coya is a hive of Peruvian-inspired activity. The kitchen delivers classy plates of food that are rich with South American flavours and a contemporary swagger. Ingredients are spot-on throughout, such as a plate of octopus cooked on the Josper grill and partnered with Peruvian olives. The meat cookery is also impressive; corn-fed baby chicken, for example, with aji panca (a dark red pepper) and coriander. The signature dessert is the corn sundae, consisting of sweetcorn ice cream and popcorn, or go for the salted caramel ganache with blood orange and pisco.

Corrigan's Mayfair

LONDON W1 PLAN 2 G1

British, Irish V NOTABLE WINE LIST

tel: 020 7499 9943 **28 Upper Grosvenor St W1K 7EH**
email: reservations@corrigansmayfair.com
web: www.corrigansmayfair.com
dir: *Nearest station: Marble Arch*

Finely crafted gutsy cuisine and top service in Mayfair

Richard Corrigan's high-gloss flagship restaurant, in sight of Park Lane, is as big-hearted, warm and generous as the celebrity chef himself. As befits the snazzy Mayfair postcode, the art deco-style hunting-themed room resonates with a modern, casually clubby luxury, jazzed up with playful touches. Think ostrich feather lampshades, shimmering copper wall panels or witty artworks, while swanky leather seating and white linen add the traditional comforts. A marble-topped entrance bar (with baby grand piano) is the place for cocktails, while the front of house team are as friendly and polished as everything else. The cooking shuns cheffy pretension in favour of bold, comforting, uncluttered dishes that reflect the seasons. There's flair and high technique too, as well as a distinctly Asian strand winding its way through, but flavour, simplicity and precision reign. There is a tasting menu if you want chef to take charge, but choosing from the à la carte, it's evident that meat and game are the star turn, and keen carnivores will head straight for the likes of roast Goosnargh duck with Thai red curry and fresh lychees, or roast saddle of rabbit with spinach and wild leeks. But sustainable fish has its say too, for example in whole Dover sole, simply accompanied by a classic brown shrimp meunière, or line-caught cod with Jersey Royals and wild garlic. Both express Corrigan's unadulterated style. For dessert, perhaps Yorkshire crumble soufflé with vanilla cream, or chocolate mousse jazzed up with candied popcorn and peanuts. Prices reflect the deep-wallet postcode, and you'll also need to factor in the necessary side dishes, but the fixed-price seasonal lunch menu offers the glam without a call to the financial advisor. A galaxy of stars populates the serious wine list.

Chef Richard Corrigan, Alan Barrins **Seats** 85, Pr/dining room 30 **Times** 12-3/6-10, Closed Xmas, BHs, L Sat, D Sun **Prices** Fixed L 2 course £25, Tasting menu £75, Starter £9.25-£24, Main £15.75-£38.50, Dessert £7.50-£11 **Wines** 18 by glass **Parking** On street **Notes** Tasting menu 6 course, Seasonal market menu L, Sunday L, Children welcome

LONDON W1 *continued*

CUT at 45 Park Lane

PLAN 4 G6

Modern American

tel: 020 7319 7467 & 7493 4545 **45 Park Ln W1K 1BJ**
email: cut.45L@dorchestercollection.com **web:** www.dorchestercollection.com
dir: *Nearest station: Hyde Park Corner, Green Park*

High-gloss temple of beef Dorchester-style

Among the many and varied gastronomic offerings within the Dorchester group, there's sure to be something to inspire, and those who fancy a steak should make a beeline for CUT. This is the London offshoot of a Beverly Hills original, and while it also trades in prime beef's best friend, prime lobster (in salads, club sandwiches, and with crab in a tomato- and horseradish-laced cocktail), real beef is the principal focus. Australian and Japanese Wagyu, Black Angus burgers, South Devon filet mignon, USDA rib-eye minute steak with fries: they're all here, aged wet or dry, sold by weight, and timed to the second on the grill, with eight sauces to choose from. The menu offers other fare, perhaps prawn and asparagus risotto with parmesan, followed by Label Rouge black chicken with morels in thyme jus, but there's no mistaking why most punters have pitched up here. If you feel you deserve a pudding after all that, finish with banana brûlée cream pie, gâteau Opéra with espresso ice, or sticky toffee date cake with apricot jam. The cheeses come with nut bread, quince paste, candied walnuts and honeycomb. And then, after a period of tranquil digestion, a run in Hyde Park might appeal.

Chef David McIntyre **Seats** 70, Pr/dining room 14 **Times** 12-2.30/6-10.30 **Prices** Fixed L 2 course £32, Tasting menu £150, Starter £12-£26, Main £28-£140, Dessert £12 **Wines** 597 bottles over £30, 22 by glass **Parking** Valley parking **Notes** Brunch, Vegetarian available, Children welcome

Dabbous

PLAN 2 J3

Modern British

tel: 020 7323 1544 **39 Whitfield St, Fitzrovia W1T 2SF**
email: info@dabbous.co.uk
dir: *Nearest station: Goodge St*

Ingenious modern dining under bare lightbulbs

On a corner in Fitzrovia, not a million miles from Oxford Street, Ollie Dabbous' restaurant reflects current trends in both interior design and culinary thinking. Ollie's world is free of chintz and heavy sauces. The stark interior shows the bones of the building with exposed ducts, bare light bulbs, concrete and metal, while the cool 60s-style chairs look the business. When it comes to the menu, expect unusual foraged ingredients, creative presentation, and exciting flavours. The set dinner and tasting menu offer no choice, so settle down and go with the flow. The set lunch requires a couple of decisions and is fabulous value for money given the level of cooking. An opening salvo might be sea trout tartare with candy beetroot and marigold shoots, the flavours and textures hitting the mark, followed by duck egg mayonnaise on toast with spring truffles and white asparagus. There's clarity of flavour throughout and the apparent simplicity belies the skill and technical proficiency in the kitchen. A meat course might be barbecued pork jowl flavoured with juniper and caraway, and, to finish, a cherry blossom teacake is served with Tahitian vanilla ice cream. Head down into the equally hip Oskar's Bar in the basement for cocktails incorporating home-made syrups and infusions.

Chef Ollie Dabbous **Seats** 36 **Times** 12-2.15/6.30-9.30, Closed 1 wk Etr, 1 wk Xmas, Sun **Prices** Fixed L 3 course £28, Tasting menu £69 **Wines** 110 bottles over £30, 10 bottles under £30, 16 by glass **Notes** Fixed L/D 4 course £35/£59, Children welcome

Dehesa

PLAN 2 J1

Spanish, Italian

tel: 020 7494 4170 **25 Ganton St W1F 9BP**
email: info@dehesa.co.uk
dir: *Nearest station: Oxford Circus*

First-rate tapas in Soho

Dehesa comes from the same stable as Salt Yard and Opera Tavern and, like them, is a charcuterie and tapas bar dedicated to the cuisines of Spain and Italy. It's a small place and it's easy to see why it gets so busy: quality ingredients are handled professionally, following authentic recipes, to bring the flavours of those two countries to life in London. Bar snacks of house-cured duck breast, or jamón Ibérico, with a glass of fino make pleasing partners, or select from the full list of unfussy hot and cold dishes. Venetian-style sardines with sautéed onions, sultanas and pine nuts, and piquant salt-cod croquettes with sauce romesco are among the fish options, with tender confit pork belly with rosemary-scented cannellini beans, and fried lamb cutlet with broad beans, chilli and mint among the meat. You might not need extra vegetables like patatas fritas, but leave room for tempting puddings like chocolate cake with cappuccino ice cream.

Dinings

PLAN 2 E3

Japanese, European

tel: 020 7723 0666 **22 Harcourt St W1H 4HH**
dir: *Nearest station: Edgware Rd, Marylebone*

Pint-sized basement room doing dazzling Japanese tapas

There's scarcely room to swing a chopstick here, but exquisitely-crafted Japanese tapas are the draw. The creative kitchen fuses Japanese and modern European dishes, so check out the blackboard specials, then tackle the lengthy menu by sharing a bunch of small dishes. Seared Cornish squid sushi with yuzu kosho does a tap dance on your taste buds. Then try tar-tar chips (home-made potato crisps) filled with seafood, meat, vegetables and sauces. It's all a delight, from crispy pork belly with apple salsa and Korean chogochujang sauce, to double-cooked Scottish salmon with truffle teriyaki sauce, and fusion desserts like kokuto brown sugar-flavoured crème brûlée with green tea ice cream.

DSTRKT

PLAN 2 K1

Modern American

tel: 020 7317 9120 **9 Rupert St W1D 6DG**
email: reservations@dstrkt.co.uk
dir: *Nearest station: Piccadilly Circus*

Nightclub-style dining at the cutting edge

This restaurant/nightclub hybrid occupies a cavernous, high-decibel witches' grotto in black and gold, where continental cuisines and Pan-Asian modes meld into a gigantic global fusion. Starters are sized for pick'n'mixing: flash-fried cubes of tuna are topped with soy foam and supported by avocado purée, and a single tentacle of grilled octopus comes with earthy caramelised chickpea purée, fresh peas and preserved orange. For mains, ostrich skewers come with a mustard and Guinness dipping sauce, and grilled lamb cutlets arrive with lamb pancetta, smoky aubergine purée and piquillo pepper coulis. Finish with caramelised apple frangipane tart with apple purée and ice cream and Cognac cream.

Ember Yard

PLAN 2 J2

Spanish, Italian NOTABLE WINE LIST

tel: 020 7439 8057 **60-61 Berwick St W1F 8SU**
email: info@emberyard.co.uk
dir: *Nearest station: Oxford Circus*

Hot spot for chargrilled and smoked Italian and Spanish tapas

Ember Yard is the latest in the chain of uptempo tapas outfits that have been trending in the capital in recent years. The food comes inspired by Spain (the Basque country in particular) and Italy, and is smoked or cooked simply on a Basque-style wood and charcoal grill. Sharing platters of classy charcuterie and cheeses are sourced from peerless suppliers like everything else, otherwise start with chargrilled cuttlefish with a sweet hit from honey-roasted butternut squash and citrus-packed gremolata, and don't miss the melt-in-the-mouth chargrilled Ibérica presa (shoulder), served with whipped jamón butter. Finish in style with moist vanilla and almond cake, ricotta and juicy loquats.

Chef Jacques Fourie **Seats** 120, Pr/dining room 18 **Times** 12-12, All-day dining, Closed 25-26 Dec **Prices** Prices not confirmed **Notes** Vegetarian available, Children welcome

L'Escargot

PLAN 3 A2

French, Mediterranean

tel: 020 7439 7474 & 7494 1318 **48 Greek St W1D 4EF**
email: bc@lescargotrestaurant.co.uk **web:** www.lescargotrestaurant.co.uk
dir: *Nearest station: Tottenham Court Rd, Leicester Sq*

French cuisine through and through

Open almost any book on Soho and this near-century-old institution probably gets several paragraphs. Occupying a fine Georgian townhouse once home to the Duke of Portland, its black-painted frontage is surmounted by a giant snail above which fly the French Tricolor and the Union Flag. The menu is based on bourgeois French cuisine, although not all is recognisably so, as the grilled pork cutlet with papaya testifies. Expect a warming celeriac and truffle soup starter, then a main of duck confit, rainbow chard, chilli and ginger, or lobster thermidor. Oh yes, and snails. For dessert, try pear-based tarte Bourdaloue.

L'Escargot

Chef James Tyrrel **Seats** 80, Pr/dining room 60 **Times** 11-4/5-11.30, Closed 25-26 Dec, 1 Jan, D Sun **Prices** Fixed L 2 course fr £15, Fixed D 3 course fr £17.50, Starter £4-£14, Main £16-£32, Dessert £6-£12 **Wines** 80 bottles over £30, 12 bottles under £30, 12 by glass **Parking** NCP Chinatown, on street parking **Notes** Fixed L & D 2/3 course pre/post-theatre, Sunday L £17.50, Vegetarian available, Children 10 yrs+

Fera at Claridge's

PLAN 2 H1

– see page 290

Four Seasons Hotel London at Park Lane

PLAN 4 G6

Italian V

tel: 020 7319 5206 **Hamilton Place, Park Ln W1J 7DR**
email: amaranto.lon@fourseasons.com **web:** www.fourseasons.com/london/dining
dir: *Nearest station: Green Park, Hyde Park Corner*

Carefully crafted Italian grand-hotel dining

The Four Seasons stands in modern grandeur at Hyde Park Corner, a distinctly plutocratic node of central London. In the restaurant, carefully-crafted Italian dishes embrace the simplicity that everyone seeks in Italian food. Open with inspired antipasti such as culatello and melon, or burrata with broad beans and raw artichoke. Silky pasta encases finely textured rabbit for a ravioli dish with a counter-intuitive garnish of langoustines and a scattering of fragrant tarragon. Next is a deftly executed dish of fried calamari on tomato and rocket salad dressed with pesto, or grilled veal chop with sauté potatoes. A retooled tiramisù is garnished with a salted tuile set with cocoa nibs.

Chef Eliano Crespi **Seats** 58, Pr/dining room 10 **Times** 12-2.30/6.30-10.30 **Prices** Prices not confirmed **Wines** 200 bottles over £30, 10 bottles under £30, 200 by glass **Parking** 10 **Notes** Fixed L 2/3 course, Brunch, Afternoon tea, Sunday L, Children welcome

LONDON W1 *continued*

Galvin at The Athenaeum

PLAN 4 H6

Modern British

tel: 020 7640 3557 **116 Piccadilly W1J 7BJ**
email: info@athenaeumhotel.com **web:** www.athenaeumhotel.com
dir: *Nearest station: Hyde Park Corner, Green Park*

The Galvin brothers' latest adventure

Dating from the mid-19th century, the art deco Athenaeum occupies a prime Mayfair spot overlooking Green Park. A vertical garden on the outside is a feature, while the restaurant pours on the style with an extensive refurbishment taking place in the first half of 2016, which will see the restaurant reopen as part of the Galvin brothers' empire, although this is the first time they've taken on all the food operations of an entire hotel – room service included if you're planning a stay and want to get a taste of their offering. Expect very smart modern British-style cooking and inventive cuisine – one to watch for the future.

Chef William Lloyd Baker **Seats** 90, Pr/dining room 70 **Times** 12-2.30/6-10.30 **Prices** Fixed L 2 course £17.50-£19.50, Fixed D 3 course £23.50-£25.50, Starter £6.50-£15, Main £10.50-£35, Dessert £5-£8.50 **Wines** 94 bottles over £30, 12 bottles under £30, 22 by glass **Parking** Brick St car park **Notes** Afternoon tea, Pre-theatre, Sunday L £18.50-£29.50, Vegetarian available, Children welcome

Galvin at Windows Restaurant & Bar

PLAN 4 G6

Modern French

tel: 020 7208 4021 **London Hilton on Park Ln, 22 Park Ln W1K 1BE**
email: reservations@galvinatwindows.com
dir: *Nearest station: Green Park, Hyde Park Corner*

Modern European cooking in the sky

As London grows increasingly full of very tall buildings, restaurants in the sky become more common. Here at the Park Lane Hilton you'll find one of the earliest to boast 360-degree views of the capital, the 28th-floor Windows. And who could ever tire of the view? Battersea Power Station, Buckingham Palace, The London Eye, the Houses of Parliament, Hyde Park and the distant arch of Wembley Stadium – it's certainly worth trying for a window table. The modern French cooking is infinitely stylish, with echoes of the very smart bistro style associated with the Galvin brothers clearly audible, although head chef Joo Won also looks a little further afield. Get things rolling with seared yellowfin tuna, caviar Baeri d'Aquitaine, confit grapefruit and sweet soy, or cured Loch Fyne salmon with Dorset crab, beetroot, horseradish and dill. Move on to fillet of stone bass with stir-fried pork, artichoke barigoule and coriander, or roasted loin and ragoût of South Downs venison, red cabbage, salsify and dark chocolate. Desserts are equally inspiring – maybe the Valrhona chocolate sphere with milk foam, hazelnut cremeaux and blood orange, or lemon posset, poached rhubarb, candied ginger and almond crumble.

Chef Joo Won, Chris Galvin **Seats** 130 **Times** 12-2.30/6-10.30, Closed BHs, 26 Dec, 9 Apr, 7 May, L Sat, D Sun, 25 Dec **Prices** Prices not confirmed **Wines** 248 bottles over £30, 36 bottles under £30, 31 by glass **Parking** NCP **Notes** Tasting menu 6 course, Dégustation menu, Sunday L, Vegetarian available, Children welcome

Fera at Claridge's

LONDON W1 **PLAN 2 H1**

Modern British V

tel: 020 7107 8888 **Brook St W1K 4HR**
email: reservations@feraatclaridges.co.uk **web:** www.feraatclaridges.co.uk
dir: *Nearest station: Bond St, Green Park*

Dynamic modern cooking courtesy of Simon Rogan

Simon Rogan's restaurant ticks all the boxes for inspirational culinary creativity while keeping the special-occasion sheen you expect at Claridge's. If your Latin is rusty, 'Fera' means wild, reflecting Rogan's passion for nature's natural bounty. The decor elegantly evokes the natural world in the slate-grey and mossy-green palette, burnished walnut tables, and bleached, skeletal branches soaring up to a stained glass ceiling. With a stack of AA rosettes under his belt at the mothership, L'Enclume in Cumbria, and The French in Manchester's Midland Hotel, Mr Rogan is one of the UK's premier chefs, his inspiration and creativity backed by prodigious technical ability, as is apparent with a series of delightful little nibbles such as rabbit suspended in pea espuma, or beetroot macaroon with pumpkin seeds. A first course of sea-fresh lobster arrives with the textural contrast of crispy chicken wings, helped by black garlic sauce, anise and hyssop, while Portland crab delivers stunningly clear, simple flavours alongside pickled red dulse and oyster and fennel juice. There's plenty of 'wow' in a main course of 55-day, dry-aged pork – the fillet and belly meat melting in the mouth – with grilled and puréed baby carrots, grilled lettuce, blewit mushrooms, and the subtle pepperiness of nasturtium flowers. Another matches halibut with pine oil, hen of the woods mushrooms, parsnip and chestnuts. For dessert, the acidity of cherries – macerated and sorbet – is tempered by pungent goats' cheese, apricot and pumpernickel. Choose from the carte, a seven-course tasting menu, or the stonking value set lunch, and the experience will linger long in the memory. And wine? The scintillating list has all bases covered with some fascinating bottles.

Chef Simon Rogan, Dan Cox **Seats** 94, Pr/dining room 12 **Times** 12-2/6.30-10, Closed D 25 Dec **Prices** Fixed L 3 course £39, Tasting menu £75-£110, Starter £19-£24, Main £24-£38, Dessert £12-£15 **Wines** 500 bottles over £30, 7 bottles under £30, 17 by glass **Parking** On street, NCP **Notes** Children 5 yrs+

Galvin Bistrot de Luxe

PLAN 2 G3

French NOTABLE WINE LIST

tel: 020 7935 4007 **66 Baker St W1U 7DJ**
email: info@galvinrestaurants.com **web:** www.galvinrestaurants.com
dir: *Nearest station: Baker St*

Well-crafted French cooking in stylish bistro

Authentic decor and slick staff make this place feel so Parisian it almost makes a trip on Eurostar redundant. The seasonally-inspired menus (including a great value lunch and early evening prix-fixe) deliver well-executed French bistro classics with a modern touch. Witness a punchy ballotine of rabbit, boudin noir and pistachios, its richness cut by tangy spiced apricot chutney, or a splendid slab of poached Peterhead cod supported by sautéed wild mushrooms and mushroom purée, roasted salsify and fish velouté. Desserts include a masterful strawberry soufflé and sorbet, and the signature tarte Tatin is as good as it gets, while the wine list is a Francophile's dream.

Chef Chris Galvin, Tom Duffill **Seats** 110, Pr/dining room 22
Times 12-2.30/6-10.30, Closed 25-26 Dec, 1 Jan, D 24 Dec **Prices** Fixed L 3 course fr £21.50, Fixed D 3 course fr £23.50, Starter £6.50-£15, Main £17-£29, Dessert £6-£12 **Wines** 159 bottles over £30, 12 bottles under £30, 17 by glass **Parking** On street, Portman Sq car park **Notes** Prix fixe L Mon-Sat & D 6-7pm, Sunday L £18.50-£28.50, Vegetarian available, Children welcome

Gauthier Soho

PLAN 3 A1

French V NOTABLE WINE LIST

tel: 020 7494 3111 & 7851 9382 **21 Romilly St W1D 5AF**
email: info@gauthiersoho.co.uk
dir: *Nearest station: Leicester Sq*

Outstanding modern French cooking in the heart of Soho

There's nothing quite like having to buzz for admittance to give your meal that exclusive feeling, making you feel you're in on a secret known only to the honoured few. Once inside the shiny black front door of Alexis Gauthier's intimate Soho restaurant you'll find bright white walls and tablecloths, mirrors, fresh flowers and art, all adding to a welcoming and cheerful atmosphere. It's the perfect setting for the complex modern French cooking. There are various set menu choices, as well as tasting options – including a vegetarian one. Gauthier is a confidently instinctive cook and everything is sourced with incredible care, resulting in technically impressive and perfectly balanced dishes. A winter lunch might begin with ballotine of quail with toasted walnuts, followed by sea trout with root vegetables, yuzu, soy sauce and honey, or pork fillet stuffed with dates and accompanied by sumac, leeks and pommes noisettes. The tasting menus offer a stunning exploration of flavour and texture, maybe black truffle risotto, or shoulder and loin of Welsh lamb – the latter pink roasted and the former thyme braised – with herb and parmesan celeriac. Yorkshire rhubarb comes with grenadine and crumble, and the selection of unpasteurised French cheeses is well worth exploring.

Chef Gerard Virolle, Alexis Gauthier **Seats** 60, Pr/dining room 32
Times 12-2.30/6.30-10.30, Closed Xmas, BHs, Sun, L Mon **Prices** Fixed L 2 course fr £18, Fixed D 3 course fr £45 **Wines** 150 bottles over £30, 30 bottles under £30, 20 by glass **Parking** On street, NCP Chinatown **Notes** Fixed D 4/5 course £55/£65, Deluxe L 3 course with wine £40, Children welcome

Le Gavroche Restaurant

PLAN 2 G1

– see page 292

Goodman

PLAN 2 J1

British, American NOTABLE WINE LIST

tel: 020 7499 3776 **26 Maddox St W1S 1QH**
email: reservations@goodmanrestaurants.com
dir: *Nearest station: Oxford Circus*

American-style Mayfair steakhouse serving prime cuts

Dark banquettes and booth seating, photographs hanging on the walls and a wooden floor create a clubby, intimate atmosphere at this upmarket steakhouse based on the New York prototypes. Select from the various cuts on the menu, from fillet, through bone-in sirloin to porterhouse, the last priced per 100 grammes, and it will be cooked as requested and served with béarnaise, pepper or Stilton sauces. Wide-ranging starters take in Caesar salad and the luxury of lobster cocktail or pan-fried foie gras with roasted figs, oyster mushrooms and truffled honey. Puddings are no afterthought: consider honeycomb parfait with banana sorbet, or cookie sundae with chocolate and caramel sauce.

The Greenhouse

PLAN 4 H6

– see page 292

The Grill at The Dorchester

PLAN 4 G6

Modern British NOTABLE WINE LIST

tel: 020 7317 6531 **Park Ln W1K 1QA**
email: thegrill.TDL@dorchestercollection.com
web: www.dorchestercollection/london/the-dorchester
dir: *Nearest station: Hyde Park Corner, Marble Arch*

Top quality eating at a world-class hotel

There's a been a Grill room at the Dorchester since 1931 and today's new look version is a shimmering and elegant room. Come here for a strikingly good veal chop, perfectly rested, that comes with a creamy mushroom sauce, or go for peppered organic Aberdeen Angus prime rib, or Scottish salmon steak with béarnaise. The grill works its magic on some first-course scallops, too, served with an autumn salad and rich truffle dressing, with other options including chicken Caesar salad or duck foie gras with red onion chutney. Finish with a zesty lemon tart, or try one of the soufflés (Sicilian pistachio, for example, with salted caramel).

Chef Christophe Marleix **Seats** 65 **Times** 12-2.30/5.30-10.30 **Prices** Fixed L 2 course £29, Starter £10-£38, Main £22-£49, Dessert £13-£14 **Wines** 12 by glass **Parking** 20 **Notes** Pre-theatre menu 3 course £39, Sunday L £48-£68, Vegetarian available, Children welcome

Le Gavroche Restaurant

LONDON W1 **PLAN 2 G1**

French V

tel: 020 7408 0881 **43 Upper Brook St W1K 7QR**
email: bookings@le-gavroche.com
dir: *Nearest station: Marble Arch*

Unwavering commitment to classical French gastronomy

When Le Gavroche opened its doors just short of a half-century ago, French gastronomy was still imperfectly grasped on these shores, even among London cognoscenti, and if that picture was transformed, it is in large measure because Albert Roux and, later, his son Michel, never wavered in their commitment to international cooking's ancien régime. It's true there are a few more new-fangled dishes now, but if there were no solid gold tradition, nobody else would know what they were rebelling against. The setting is a serene basement room, run with the kind of punctilious courtesy that is virtually a dead language in London now, and the bill of fare an extended homage to the most rigorous training in excellence. Start with roast scallops in coral crumb with carrots, sauced with yellow Chartreuse, if you're after new directions, and if you're not, look to the old and flawless standbys – the artichoke stuffed with truffled foie gras mousse, the lobster mousseline and caviar in champagne butter. Extraordinary quality in the prime materials is the hallmark of principal dishes like Pyrenean milk-fed lamb with piquillos in minted jus, and roasted T-bone of turbot in chive butter. A Menu Exceptionnel in this context had better do as it promises, and undoubtedly does, all the way to its little pistachio-chocolate gâteau, garnished with bitter chocolate sorbet and dried fruits doused in rum. French and British artisanal cheeses are the best, served with authoritative knowledge, as is the compendious wine list, which will make you kick yourself for not buying a EuroMillions ticket.

Chef Michel Roux Jnr **Seats** 60, Pr/dining room 6 **Times** 12-2/6-10, Closed Xmas, New Year, BHs, Sun-Mon, L Sat **Prices** Fixed L 3 course £56, Tasting menu £126-£210, Starter £19.80-£62.60, Main £28.40-£60.80, Dessert £16.80-£40.60 **Wines** 2500 bottles over £30, 25 bottles under £30, 25 by glass **Parking** NCP Park Lane **Notes** Tasting menu 8 course, Fixed L menu, Children welcome

The Greenhouse

LONDON W1 **PLAN 4 H6**

Modern French V NOTABLE WINE LIST

tel: 020 7499 3331 **27a Hay's Mews, Mayfair W1J 5NY**
email: reservations@greenhouserestaurant.co.uk
dir: *Nearest station: Green Park, Bond St*

Gastronomic delights in a discreet Mayfair location

The Greenhouse has been a top destination restaurant for years. Tucked away in a wide Mayfair mews, its decked pathway leads to a serenely stylish space, where super-slick service helps to create an oasis of calm and refinement. Restful shades of beige and ivory are offset by modern darkwood floors, avocado-coloured leather banquettes and chairs, tables immaculate in their finest white linen, and a feature wall with a filigree display of tree branches. A succession of high-flying chefs have run the show at the Greenhouse, and today's incumbent is Arnaud Bignon, an instinctive chef who uses the best ingredients as his starting point and combines techniques old and new to produce dishes with clean, precise flavours that look beautiful on the plate. Spectacular canapés (fennel and aniseed macaroon, tuna and melon wrapped in nori, perhaps) get the taste buds standing to attention from the start. Menus tantalise with brief descriptions that give no clue as to the craft and technical know-how on display: Orkney scallops and sea urchin might get a lift from fennel and clementine – a delightful opener that's light, fresh, beautifully balanced and full of textural contrasts. Next up, a splendid piece of monkfish, served with onion, banana, kaffir lime and Egyptian dukkah spices, or organic Rhug Estate lamb, roasted to perfection, matched inventively with aubergine, fiery harissa and soya. Desserts thrill with their pin-sharp execution – perhaps a sesame praline soufflé supported by pear, ginger, and Williamine pear liqueur. The cheese trolley comes loaded with pedigree, perfectly ripened items, and a knowledgeable sommelier is at hand to navigate a phenomenal wine list.

Chef Arnaud Bignon **Seats** 60, Pr/dining room 12
Times 12-2.30/6.30-11, Closed Xmas, BHs, Sun, L Sat **Prices** Fixed L 2 course fr £35, Fixed D 3 course fr £95, Tasting menu £110-£125 **Wines** 3300 bottles over £30, 22 bottles under £30, 27 by glass **Parking** On street **Notes** Children welcome

LONDON W1 *continued*

GYMKHANA

PLAN 4 J6

Contemporary Indian V

tel: 020 3011 5900 **42 Albermarle St W1S 4JH**
email: info@gymkhanalondon.com
dir: *Nearest station: Green Park*

Exciting modern Indian food in a Raj-era club setting

It may be designed to look like a colonial-era Indian gentlemen's club, but there's nothing retro about this restaurant's inventive new-wave Indian cooking. Soft-shelled crab Jhalmuri is deep-fried in crunchy spiced batter and matched with puffed rice, samphire and coriander, while an expertly spiced kid goat methi keema is rich, comforting and fragrant with fenugreek leaves. Elsewhere, wild boar vindaloo, or wild muntjac biryani with pomegranate and mint raita catch the eye, while game lovers might go for quail seekh kebab with chutney. Dessert is a perfect fusion of Anglo-Indian ideas: zingy rhubarb chutney atop a sweet ras malai cheese dumpling soaked in cardamon-infused milk with crushed pistachios and almonds.

Chef Rohit Ghai, Karam Sethi **Seats** 90, Pr/dining room 14
Times 12-2.30/5.30-10.30, Closed Xmas, 1 Jan, Sun **Prices** Fixed L 2 course £25, Tasting menu £70-£120, Starter £4-£14, Main £9-£38, Dessert £6-£9 **Wines** 169 bottles over £30, 14 bottles under £30, 14 by glass **Parking** Albemarle St
Notes Fixed L/D 4 course £35 (£65 inc wine), Tasting menu 7 course, Children until 7pm

Hakkasan

PLAN 2 K2

Modern Chinese

tel: 020 7927 7000 **8 Hanway Place W1T 1HD**
email: reservation@hakkasan.com
dir: *Nearest station: Tottenham Court Rd*

New wave Chinese cooking in a see-and-be-seen setting

Escape the Oxford Street crowds in this chic basement and you're immediately captivated by its modern Chinoiserie design, super-cool cocktail bar, open kitchen and uptempo, nightclubby vibe. Innovative new-wave and classic Cantonese dishes cover all bases, and luxury ingredients abound. Start with exemplary salt-and-pepper squid, or jasmine tea-smoked organic pork ribs, before moving on to crispy-skinned pipa duck in plum sauce, or perhaps roasted silver cod with champagne and honey. Desserts stick to Western themes: witness a Jivara milk chocolate bomb with hazelnut praline and Rice Krispies. A heavyweight wine list and an exciting cocktail selection completes the picture.

Chef Tong Chee Hwee **Seats** 210, Pr/dining room 20
Times 12-3.15/5.30-11.15, Closed 25 Dec **Prices** Prices not confirmed **Wines** 400 bottles over £30, 2 bottles under £30, 10 by glass **Parking** NCP Great Russell St
Notes Sunday L, Vegetarian available, Children welcome

Hakkasan Mayfair

PLAN 2 H1

Chinese NOTABLE WINE LIST

tel: 020 7907 1888 & 7355 7701 **17 Bruton St W1J 6QB**
email: mayfairreservation@hakkasan.com
dir: *Nearest station: Green Park*

Inspirational Chinese cooking in luxury surroundings

It's fair to say that since Hakkasan set up shop in its original Hanway Place venue in 2001, it has changed the way we regard Chinese food. The Mayfair branch sets a suitably high tone with a doorman at the entrance, and a slinky look of burnished wood, marble and leather combining with moody lighting to give a feeling of high-rolling luxury. Anyone familiar with the lexicon of Chinese menus will find familiar-sounding dishes, but this food is a cut above in terms of quality of produce (the menu is dripping with top-end ingredients and luxuries), inspiration and execution. Staff are slick, friendly and on the ball – they need to be, given the number of covers spread over its two perpetually heaving floors. Foie gras adds an upmarket note to the centre of sesame seed-coated prawn balls, which explode with distinct flavours of garlic, ginger and chives, and come with deep-fried seaweed and tempura-battered enoki mushrooms for textural variation. A well-conceived main course of spicy stir-fried venison with eryngii mushrooms, baby leeks and dried chillies is distinguished by accurate timing, spicing and seasoning. Desserts take their inspiration from the Western repertoire, such as apple and vanilla crème brûleé served with Calvados, crème fraîche and crystallised fennel.

Chef Tong Chee Hwee, Tan Tee Wei **Seats** 220, Pr/dining room 14
Times 12-3.15/6-11.15, Closed 24-25 Dec, L 26 Dec, 1 Jan **Prices** Prices not confirmed **Wines** 400 bottles over £30, 10 bottles under £30, 9 by glass **Parking** NCP **Notes** Afternoon menu 3.15-5pm, Vegetarian available, Children welcome

Heddon Street Kitchen

PLAN 2 J1

European, International

tel: 020 7592 1212 **3-9 Heddon St, Regent Street Food Quarter W1B 4BD**
email: heddonstreetkitchen@gordonramsay.com
dir: *Nearest station: Green Park, Oxford Circus*

Buzzy brasserie in the heart of the West End

Part of Gordon Ramsay's impressive London empire, this sleek brasserie just off Regent Street has brought an unmistakable slice of New York to the edge of Mayfair. Set across two floors, it's loud, buzzy and lively – a fun place aimed at the younger crowd, more than those looking for a quiet business meal. A simple starter of rigatoni with tomatoes, aubergines, buffalo mozzarella and pecorino might precede a main course of roasted cod, crushed potatoes, artichoke, salted capers, red wine and lemon sauce. An oozing chocolate fondant with salted caramel and Amaretto ice cream is a typical dessert. There's a cracking cocktail list too.

Hélène Darroze at The Connaught

PLAN 2 H1

– *see page 294*

Hibiscus

PLAN 2 J1

– *see page 295*

HIX

PLAN 2 J1

British

tel: 020 7292 3518 **66-70 Brewer St W1F 9UP**
email: reservations@hixsoho.co.uk
dir: *Nearest station: Piccadilly Circus*

A celebration of British ingredients

The mothership of Mark Hix's restaurant empire pays homage to Brit Art with an eclectic collection of artworks by celebrated artists like Damien Hirst and Tracey Emin. Hix's patriotic brasserie fare supports seasonality and regional produce, including some lesser-used ingredients such as alexanders maybe partnering fabulous steamed fillets of St Mary's Bay red mullet and knockout Morecambe Bay shrimps. The cooking focuses on the simple treatment of prime produce, as in the wonderfully tart Yorkshire rhubarb with creamy saffron custard to finish. Though carte prices are high, the fixed-price option is easier on the wallet. The bustling, clubby Mark's Bar downstairs is the place for cocktails.

Hélène Darroze at The Connaught

LONDON W1 **PLAN 2 H1**

French V NOTABLE WINE LIST

tel: 020 3147 7200 & 3147 7108 **Carlos Place W1K 2AL**
email: helenedarroze@the-connaught.co.uk
web: www.the-connaught.co.uk
dir: *Nearest station: Bond St, Green Park*

Complex cooking from a French star in a British hotel institution

Hélène Darroze arrived at this blue-blooded true-Brit bastion back in 2008, and has gone on to secure its place as a world-class dining destination that bears her own stamp. A protégée of French super-chef Alain Ducasse, who encouraged her to swap the business suit for chef's whites, Hélène Darroze established her presence on the Parisian gastronomic scene with her eponymous Left Bank restaurant before crossing the Channel to re-orient the Connaught kitchen's compass on a more southerly bearing. The principal dining room received a touch of va-va-voom at the same time. The classy makeover by Paris-based designer India Mahdavi ushered in a more curvy, swirly, feminine touch – riotously patterned silver and lime upholstery and colourful abstract artworks – to lighten the Connaught's clubby Edwardian panelling, and it makes a fine setting for Darroze's exuberant creations. This woman has cooking in her DNA: Darroze hails from the Landes region of southwest France and is a fourth-generation chef, brought up with an ingrained respect for quality produce (her family produces its own Armagnac), and here are all the luxurious ingredients anyone could reasonably ask for. Dishes headlined with 'caviar', 'foie gras' and 'Wagyu beef', for example, are marshalled in intelligent contemporary ideas. There's even a bit of fun in the proceedings, when diners' choose five, seven or nine courses from principal ingredients presented on balls on a solitaire board. Each element of every dish has been carefully thought through, as is evident in the bowl of three tortellini filled with sweet onion purée, topped with slivers of lardo di Colonnata and onion leaves, on to which is poured a dashi broth infused with toasted barley. Flavours linger powerfully, as when the heat of a tandoori-spiced scallop is offset by sweet heritage carrots and a sauce of lemongrass and spring onions, or when cod arrives in a picturesque medley with shavings of white asparagus, nettle sauce and a dusting of golden bottarga. The fusion elements also work to potent effect in mains such as pinkly seared veal with its sweetbreads, served with pea beignets, wild leeks and capers in parmesan cream, or turbot with coco beans, seaweed and clams. East Asian seasonings resurface when pineapple is seasoned with lemongrass, black pepper and coconut foam. A delicately constructed chocolate sphere has windows let into it allowing views of the yellow yuzu jelly inside, the whole supported by a layer of salted caramel with cashews mixed in. The service team sing from the same song sheet, and the whole experience is beautifully orchestrated from start to finish. The 1,000-bin wine list, like everything else here, is a class act, with prices that reach some fairly dizzying heights.

Chef Hélène Darroze **Seats** 60, Pr/dining room 20
Times 12-2/6.30-10, **Prices** Fixed L 2 course £30 **Wines** 735 bottles over £30, 25 by glass **Parking** South Audley car park **Notes** L 4 course £45, Tasting 9 course, Wknd menu £95 for 2, Sunday L £45-£155, Children welcome

Hibiscus

LONDON W1 **PLAN 2 J1**

Modern French NOTABLE WINE LIST

tel: 020 7629 2999 **29 Maddox St, Mayfair W1S 2PA**
email: enquiries@hibiscusrestaurant.co.uk
dir: *Nearest station: Oxford Circus, Marble Arch*

Top-class modern French cooking from a master of his art

A decade has passed since Claude Bosi uprooted his lauded Ludlow restaurant and relocated to London. At the time, the move raised eyebrows: a chef of Bosi's standing could have set up shop in a fancy hotel, but always one to plough his own furrow, he opted instead for a discreet place – in swanky Mayfair, admittedly, but nothing too flash, somewhere rather dignified. A makeover in 2013 gave the place a more contemporary face, with muted tones and modern artworks, pale oak floors, tables turned out in their best white linen, and a magnificent floral display in the centre of the room. Bosi has a thorough grounding in French culinary traditions thanks to a childhood spent at his parents' restaurant in Lyon (France's food 'capital') followed by a stint with super-chef Alain Ducasse. The result is a passionate chef who puts his all into sourcing the best ingredients, mostly from around the UK, and turning them into stunning compositions on the plate. At the bargain end, the three-course lunchtime menu (with half a bottle of wine, coffee and petits fours thrown in) is terrific value for food of this level, otherwise there's a seven-course 'classics' menu, which is a great introduction to Bosi's modern take on the cuisine of his homeland, or those who are happy to embrace the unknown can opt for the surprise menu, and put themselves in the very safe hands of a chef at the peak of his powers – after all, you're unlikely to encounter anything that is less than stunningly successful. Expect to be served artfully constructed dishes that are swooningly pretty but never lack punch. You might open with salsify and smoked hay velouté with black garlic and a huge umami hit of three-year-aged parmesan, or be guided by the dictum that says good things come in small parcels, as when delicate ravioli are filled with Herefordshire snails and partnered with white ham and parsley liquor in a clever take on that classic Gallic idea. Mains bring together combinations that meld together as a whole while maintaining the integrity of each individual element – an immaculately handled piece of Dorset skate wing, for example, served à la grenobloise with brown butter, capers, parsley and lemon. Or try meltingly tender braised ox cheek alongside heritage carrots and blood orange. It's not unusual to see vegetables cropping up in desserts, but a sweet potato cheesecake really works, especially when it's offset with blood orange and meringue, or there could be a powerful chocolate mousse served with basil ice cream and star anise brittle. Matching wine to such adventurous flavours is quite a challenge, so consider splashing out on wine flights, or let the sommelier guide you through the eclectic list.

Chef Claude Bosi **Seats** 48, Pr/dining room 18
Times 12-2.30/6.30-10.30, Closed 24-26 Dec, 1 Jan, Sun-Mon, L Tue-Wed **Prices** Fixed L 3 course £49.50, Tasting menu £135, Starter £12.50-£34, Main £19-£42, Dessert £8.50-£18 **Wines** 345 bottles over £30, 4 bottles under £30, 22 by glass **Parking** On street **Notes** Tasting menu 7 course, ALC menu L only, Vegetarian available, Children welcome

LONDON W1 *continued*

HIX Mayfair

PLAN 2 J1

Traditional British V NOTABLE WINE LIST

tel: 020 7518 4004 **Brown's Hotel, Albemarle St, Mayfair W1S 4BP**
email: hixmayfair@roccofortehotels.com **web:** www.roccofortehotels.com
dir: *Nearest station: Green Park*

Modern cooking, traditional ingredients, contemporary art

The Brown's Hotel dining room has undergone many manifestations, but the present one, under Mark Hix, is one of the most inspired. Against a backdrop of work by contemporary British artists, including Tracey Emin and Bridget Riley, Hix's menus receive dazzling execution. Thoroughbred British produce and foraged foods pour forth on menus that encompass crispy duck salad with pickled cherries and wild herbs, and seared scallops with wild boar bacon and chanterelles. Fine prime ingredients such as seasonal game are treated with respect, not muddled into a crowd of supporting characters, so everything makes perfect sense. As does treacle tart served with Neal's Yard crème fraîche.

Chef Mark Hix, Lee Kebble **Seats** 80, Pr/dining room 70 **Times** 12-3/5.30-11 **Prices** Fixed L 2 course fr £27.50, Fixed D 3 course fr £32.50, Starter £8.50-£19.50, Main £22.50-£42.50, Dessert £6.50-£8 **Wines** 235 bottles over £30, 14 by glass **Parking** Valet/Burlington St **Notes** Pre-theatre 5.30-7.30pm Mon-Sat, Sunday L fr £37.50, Children welcome

House of Ho

PLAN 2 K1

Modern Vietnamese

tel: 020 7287 0770 **55-59 Old Compton St, Soho W1D 6HR**
email: info@houseofho.co.uk
dir: *Nearest station: Piccadilly Circus*

Buzzy Vietnamese joint with a fusion flavour

Bobby Chinn is quite the star in Asia with TV shows, books and a restaurant in Hanoi to his name, and he's in Old Compton Street with this lively, buzzy place. Tables are close together, cocktails rule, and the food is a mix of traditional and contemporary Vietnamese. From the 'Light & Raw' section comes duck 'a la banana' blossom salad or spicy salmon tartare, while 'Hot & Grilled' delivers barbecue baby back ribs with a light Asian slaw. Sharing is the way to go, with apple-smoked pork belly with braised cabbage and chicken potato curry coming in generous portions. Finish with lemon-scented crème brûlée.

Ibérica Marylebone

PLAN 2 H4

Modern Spanish

tel: 020 7148 1615 **195 Great Portland St W1W 5PS**
email: reservations@ibericarestaurants.com **web:** www.ibericarestaurants.com
dir: *Nearest station: Great Portland St, Regent's Park*

An authentic taste of Spain in the heart of Marylebone

Ibérica occupies a sizable corner plot and there's a decidedly Ibérian feel to the interior, with a marble-topped bar in the double-height space, plus tiles, huge lanterns and a deli section with hanging hams. A mezzanine level adds even more tables. Tapas and pinchos are the name of the game, and the focus is on the Asturias region of northern Spain. There are all the anticipated cured meats, plus artisan cheeses, fried squid with aïoli, twice-cooked lamb with marinated cherry tomatoes and peppers, and seasonal game such as Asturian hare and bean stew. Spanish wines and sherries help you on your way.

Chef Nacho Manzano, Luis Contreras, César Garcia **Seats** 100, Pr/dining room 30 **Times** 11.30-11, All-day dining, Closed 25-26 Dec & BHs, D Sun **Prices** Fixed L 3 course £12, Tasting menu £28-£35, Starter £4-£18, Main £9-£195, Dessert £4-£7 **Wines** 65 bottles over £30, 16 bottles under £30, 35 by glass **Notes** Vegetarian available, Children welcome

JW Steakhouse

PLAN 2 G1

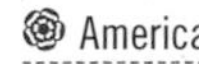

American

tel: 020 7399 8460 & 7399 8400 **Grosvenor House Hotel, Park Ln W1K 7TN**
email: info@jwsteakhouse.co.uk **web:** www.jwsteakhouse.co.uk
dir: *Nearest station: Marble Arch*

Prime steaks and cocktails on Park Lane

The expansive JW brings American-style steakhouse dining to the Grosvenor House in an ambience of black and white ceramic floor tiles and parquet, dressers and a menu offering variations of cuts and sauces. The beef is either thoroughbred USDA-approved or grass-fed Aberdeen Angus, the former taking in bone-in Kansas City strip, the latter rib-eye. Choose your meat and a sauce (red wine, say) or a topping (perhaps blue cheese) plus a side order of vegetables. Alternatives include grilled sea bream with chilli and coriander, and calves' liver and bacon, with starters such as shrimp and avocado cocktail, or carpaccio, and puddings like apple pie.

Chef Simon Conboy **Seats** 120, Pr/dining room 12 **Times** 12-2.30/6-10.30 **Prices** Starter £8-£25, Main £16-£52, Dessert £7-£14 **Wines** 15 by glass **Parking** 90 **Notes** Sunday L £24-£28, Vegetarian available, Children welcome

Kai Mayfair

PLAN 4 G6

Modern Chinese V NOTABLE WINE LIST

tel: 020 7493 8988 **65 South Audley St W1K 2QU**
email: reservations@kaimayfair.co.uk
dir: *Nearest station: Marble Arch*

Vibrant Chinese cooking in opulent Mayfair setting

This swanky Chinese restaurant is decorated in rich hues, with arty photographs on the walls. The cooking shows accurate timing, judicious use of spicing and seasoning, and subtle combinations of flavours and textures. Try a decadent fusion idea pairing pan-fried foie gras with caramelised cashews, white pepper, spring onions, its richness cut with grapes and passionfruit dressing. Next up, top-class Ibérico pork loin comes with bean and shrimp crumble, Washington apple compôte and Granny Smith jelly. The menu opens unusually with a page of desserts, showing how seriously they are taken here, and Amadei chocolate fondant with pistachio ice cream, crumbs and powder demonstrates the creative approach.

Chef Alex Chow **Seats** 85, Pr/dining room 12
Times 12-2.15/6.30-10.45, Closed 25-26 Dec, 1 Jan **Prices** Starter £14-£85, Main £18-£95, Dessert £11 **Wines** 342 bottles over £30, 14 by glass **Parking** Directly outside **Notes** Sunday L £85, Children welcome

The Keeper's House

PLAN 2 J1

Modern British

tel: 020 7300 5881 **Royal Academy of Arts, Burlington House, Piccadilly W1J 0BD**
email: keepershouse@peytonandbyrne.co.uk
dir: *Nearest station: Piccadilly Circus*

Appealing contemporary cooking in the Royal Academy

The Keeper's House was installed in the 19th century as a grace-and favour apartment for the steward of the Royal Academy collections. A strikingly attractive restaurant has been fashioned here, the recessed rooms imitating those of the galleries upstairs. As well as inspiring cocktails and English wines, there's a menu of spruce modern British and European cooking. Start with a flavoursome caramelised shallot and mushroom tart and then consider a perfectly cooked cod with sea purslane and leek and watercress purée, and, to finish, a simple, but excellent Yorkshire rhubarb syllabub. It's members only until 4pm, and then all are welcome.

Chef Chris Dines **Seats** 65, Pr/dining room 45 **Times** 12-3/5.30-10, Closed Sun
Prices Fixed L 2 course £20.50, Starter £7.50-£10, Main £14-£21, Dessert £7.50
Wines 46 bottles over £30, 12 bottles under £30, 15 by glass **Parking** On street
Notes Pre-theatre menu 5.30-7pm 2/3 course £20.50/£25.50, Vegetarian available, Children welcome

Kitchen Table

PLAN 2 J3

Modern British V

tel: 020 7637 7770 **70 Charlotte St W1T 4QG**
email: kitchentable@bubbledogs.co.uk
dir: *Nearest station: Goodge St*

Sitting at the counter, chatting with the chefs

It is just possible, of course, that you might want to book a restaurant table somewhere to thrash out the details of a contract, or catch up with an old friend. This isn't it. Kitchen Table is much more the kind of place you come not just to concentrate intensely on what you're eating, but to chat to the chefs about it while they're getting it ready. Nineteen inquisitive souls are berthed around two sides of the culinary action in a gently lit, almost after-hours kind of ambience. Around a dozen or more daily-changing dishes – really, who's counting? – will come your way, labelled by their main ingredients, which have themselves come the way of the kitchen according to what trusted suppliers have told them is good that day. Guest chefs happen in for one night only. It's an open-ended kind of a thing, a poster-child for new London dining. A menu might go something like this: Oyster; Chicken; Scallop; Monkfish; Sole; Truffle; Asparagus; Duck; Goat; Rhubarb; Orange; Caramel. And that's pretty much all you need to know in advance of the arrival of each explosively creative dish. One or two items are stalwarts of the repertoire, such as the crispy chicken skin with rosemary mascarpone and bacon jam, while others come and go. Roe deer on a bed of shredded onion simmered in yogurt with slivered raw chestnuts and elderberries, burrata with damson purée, the curiously intense pear sponge with svelte liquorice ice cream are all deeply memorable morsels. Occasionally, the slight air of the science laboratory creates expectations that aren't quite fulfilled on the palate, but overall the aim is true, and the scattergun approach means there's always something new to talk about.

Chef James Knappett **Seats** 19 **Times** 6-11, Closed Sun-Mon, L all week
Prices Tasting menu £88 **Wines** 50 bottles over £30, 8 by glass **Parking** On street
Notes No children

Kitty Fisher's

PLAN 4 H6

Modern British

tel: 020 3302 1661 **10 Shepherd Market W1J 7QF**
dir: *Nearest station: Green Park*

Robust British cooking in stylish surroundings

Closely packed tables and stools at the bar offer diners two options in this low-lit, atmospheric, Bohemian-style restaurant with red velvet banquettes, retro light fittings and candles. The modern British food is driven by what's available at the market on the day, with the wood-fired grill being the workhorse of the kitchen. Dishes are deceptively simple, as demonstrated in a starter of breaded Cornish mussels with wild garlic mayonnaise followed by precisely cooked, well-rested lamb cutlets served with a punchy and well-balanced sauce of anchovy, mint and parsley. An intense chocolate mousse accompanied by poached rhubarb, crème fraîche and a sprinkling of toasted hazelnuts is one satisfying way to finish.

Chef Tomos Parry **Seats** 36 **Times** 12-2.30/6.30-9.30, Closed Sun, L Sat
Prices Starter £5-£12.50, Main £18-£30, Dessert £6-£8 **Wines** 19 bottles over £30, 4 bottles under £30, 11 by glass **Parking** On street, NCP Shepherd St
Notes Vegetarian on request, Galician Steak min 2 share £80, Vegetarian available, Children welcome

Latium

PLAN 2 J3

Italian NOTABLE WINE LIST

tel: 020 7323 9123 **21 Berners St W1T 3LP**
email: info@latiumrestaurant.com
dir: *Nearest station: Goodge St, Oxford Circus, Tottenham Court Rd*

Regional Italian cooking with ravioli a speciality

This smart Fitzrovia restaurant features stone mosaics and arty Italian photography to liven up a sober backdrop of black leather banquettes set against neutral walls. Ravioli fans will be pleased to find a menu devoted to the medium, offering pasta parcels stuffed with oxtail in celery sauce, or a selection of fish ravioli with sea bass bottarga. Elsewhere, the kitchen delivers the goods with comforting chicken tortellini in chicken broth, followed by roast monkfish with a silky chickpea and rosemary sauce, Swiss chard and fried celeriac. To finish, there's a creative winter season take on pannacotta, flavoured with chestnut and matched with pear poached in red wine.

Chef Stefano Motto **Seats** 50 **Times** 12-3/5.30-10.30, Closed 24-26 Dec, 1 Jan
Prices Fixed L 2 course £16, Fixed D 3 course £21, Starter £7.50-£16.50, Main £16-£24.50, Dessert £4-£11 **Wines** 100 bottles over £30, 25 bottles under £30, 14 by glass **Parking** On street, NCP **Notes** Pre-theatre menu 2/3 course £16/£21, Sunday L £6.50-£19.50, Vegetarian available, Children welcome

LONDON W1 *continued*

Levant

PLAN 2 G2

Lebanese, Middle Eastern

tel: 020 7224 1111 **Jason Court, 76 Wigmore St W1U 2SJ**
email: reservations@levant.co.uk
dir: *Nearest station: Bond St*

The scents and flavours of the Middle East

Levant brings the authentic flavours of the Middle East to Wigmore Street, along with an exotic decor of rich fabrics, carved wood, candlelight and lamps. Choose a succession of grazing-sized plates to share, starting perhaps with soujok (spicy Armenian sausage with tomatoes, parsley and garlic), or deep-fried squid with sumac. Freshly cooked meat dishes are succulent and full of flavour, from a skewer of grilled minced lamb with herbs, onions and spices to a pastry case of chicken, onions and pine nuts. Vegetarians get a good deal, with tabouleh and grilled haloumi, served with tomatoes, green olives and mint, among the options. Finish with Baklava, fresh fruit and Turkish delight.

Lima

PLAN 2 K3

Modern Peruvian

tel: 020 3002 2640 **31 Rathbone Place, Fitzrovia W1T 1JH**
email: enquiry@limalondon.com
dir: *Nearest station: Goodge St, Tottenham Court Rd*

Buzzy, contemporary setting for a genuine taste of Peru

This glass-fronted restaurant, named after Peru's capital, brings that country's contemporary cuisine to the West End. Excellent Peruvian ingredients are the backbone, all handled confidently and skilfully. Start with slices of raw scallops with velvety yellow pepper purée and fresh-tasting ground and dried muña mint corn, or perhaps a simple salad of radishes, red potato, avocado and passionfruit. Tender and juicy duck breast escabèche may follow, with roast Andean potatoes and cylinders of red and purple mash, or warm salmon céviche with plantain majado, aji limo pepper and ginger. Palate-bursting flavours are also evident in puddings like cactus mousse with crisp wafers of rocoto peppers, meringue and coconut.

Little Social

PLAN 2 H2

French, Modern European NOTABLE WINE LIST

tel: 020 7870 3730 **5 Pollen St W1S 1NE**
email: reservations@littlesocial.co.uk
dir: *Nearest station: Oxford Circus*

Backstreet Parisian bistro chic chez Atherton

The chilled-out yet unmistakeably classy baby brother of Pollen Street Social smack opposite, Jason Atherton's Little Social (part of his expanding restaurant portfolio), takes a decidedly modern look at the neighbourhood Parisian bistro. Hidden behind its discreet black frontage, the interior looks every part 'little' at first sight, but then it seems to roll on forever from its entrance dining-bar. The relaxed, buzzy soundtrack is spot-on too, likewise the switched-on front of-house team. Oxblood-leather banquettes and booths, unclothed tables and café-style chairs provide the comforts, while globe lighting, mirrors and atmospheric Parisian-lifestyle photographs, posters and wall-mounted Michelin maps add authenticity without cliché. The well-honed cooking is equally impressive, putting quality above cheffy showiness, applying a light modern spin to top-drawer ingredients delivered with classy presentation and smack-in-your-mouth flavour. The roster is basically London-meets-Paris (and beyond): witness warm subtly smoked eel with earthy beetroot, peppy horseradish cream and watercress, while roasted Cornish line-caught cod comes teamed up with perky Asian-spiced cauliflower and a show-stopping aromatic duck broth. Dishes to share might include four-day aged Buccleuch Estate rib-eye, served with roasted bone marrow, béarnaise and peppercorn sauces and beef-dripping chips. Desserts have a classic leaning, perhaps an apple tarte Tatin to share, while the maple-glazed doughnuts are something of a house favourite.

Chef Cary Docherty **Seats** 55, Pr/dining room 8
Times 12-2.30/6-10.30, Closed 25-26 Dec, 1-2 Jan, BHs, Sun **Prices** Fixed L 2 course fr £21, Fixed D 3 course fr £25, Starter £10-£16.50, Main £15-£79, Dessert £4.50-£16 **Wines** 60 bottles over £30, 3 bottles under £30, 23 by glass **Parking** Burlington car park, Cavendish Sq **Notes** Exclusive hire, Prix-fixe menu, Vegetarian available, Children welcome

Locanda Locatelli

PLAN 2 G2

Italian NOTABLE WINE LIST

tel: 020 7935 9088 **8 Seymour St W1H 7JZ**
email: info@locandalocatelli.com **web:** www.locandalocatelli.com
dir: *Nearest station: Marble Arch*

Fabulous top-class Italian cooking of daring simplicity

The Locanda is a class act, suiting its location in this well-heeled neighbourhood. Comfortable ivory bucket seats, a parquet floor, textured wooden walls, diaphanous drapes and booths divided by etched-glass screens combine to make a fashion statement. It can be difficult to book a table, not because Giorgio Locatelli is a celebrity chef but because people clamour to sample his innovative take on Italian cuisine. The menu, in Italian with English subtitles, is laid out conventionally enough, from antipasti to dolci, but there's nothing conventional about the cooking. A salad of burrata cheese, blood orange, black olives, fennel and bread crisps impresses for its bursts of clear-cut flavours, as does another starter of pork sausage with Savoy cabbage, butter foam and saffron rice. Pasta dishes are the real deal, among them pappardelle with hare ragù spiked with cocoa, and contorni are worth exploring: perhaps sautéed cavolo nero with cured pork belly. Main courses, of top-end ingredients, show a kitchen firing on all cylinders: pan-fried cod fillet, perfectly timed, served simply with lentils and parsley sauce, say, or the full-bodied flavours of roast breast of guinea fowl with liver crostino, black truffle and glazed carrots. Don't pass on puddings when there's chocolate and orange fondant with coconut crumble and orange sorbet up for grabs.

Chef Giorgio Locatelli **Seats** 70, Pr/dining room 50
Times 12-3/6-11, Closed 24-26 Dec, 1 Jan **Prices** Starter £9.50-£17, Main £24.50-£31.50, Dessert £6.50-£13.50 **Wines** 576 bottles over £30, 30 bottles under £30, 18 by glass **Parking** NCP adjacent (meter) **Notes** Sunday L, Vegetarian available, Children welcome

The Lockhart

PLAN 2 F2

American

tel: 020 3011 5400 **22-24 Seymour Place W1H 7NL**
email: info@lockhartlondon.com
dir: *Nearest station: Marble Arch*

America's Deep South off Edgware Road

A boarded floor, simple wooden tables and chairs, old railway benches and walls of exposed whitewashed brick give this restaurant an unassuming look. The cuisine of the southern states of the USA is the theme, which translates into homely cooking high on flavour. Try catfish gumbo – tender rice with okra, pork sausage and bright white flakes of fish – or wedge salad with bacon, chopped egg and buttermilk ranch dressing. Move on to ribs in a BBQ reduction with tomato and cucumber salad, or skate wing in a lightly spiced crab dressing with charred broccoli. Equally authentic are puddings such as the chocolate chess or lemon icebox pies.

Chef Brad McDonald, Nathaniel Hancock **Seats** 35, Pr/dining room 30 **Times** 12-3/6-10, Closed 24-25 Dec, D Sun **Prices** Fixed D 3 course £22, Starter £6-£9.50, Main £15-£23, Dessert £7 **Wines** 30+ bottles over £30, 5 bottles under £30, 10 by glass **Parking** On street **Notes** Sun brunch, Vegetarian available, Children welcome

The Mandeville Hotel

PLAN 2 G2

Modern British

tel: 020 7935 5599 **Mandeville Place W1U 2BE**
email: info@mandeville.co.uk **web:** www.mandeville.co.uk
dir: *Nearest station: Bond St, Baker St*

Brasserie food in a stylish boutique hotel

Understated contemporary decor and a calming ambience are the hallmarks of this stylish boutique hotel, while unclothed tables and bottle-green banquettes set the tone in the restaurant. Starters include chicken liver pâté with red onion marmalade, and crispy squid with lemon and garlic mayonnaise. The Josper grill is to the fore among main courses, from rib-eye steak, pink and succulent, with mushrooms and chips to an unusual cod and shrimp burger with tartare sauce. Elsewhere are a few salads, some sharing platters and classics like fish and chips with mushy peas. Familiar-sounding lemon posset and sticky toffee pudding are among desserts.

The Mayfair Chippy

PLAN 2 G1

British

tel: 020 7741 2233 & 7843 9090 **North Audley St W1K 6WE**
email: reservations@eatbrit.com
dir: *Nearest station: Bond St, Marble Arch*

A fish and chip restaurant fit for Mayfair

As a pairing, Mayfair and Chippy breaks new ground, and so it should. This wealthy quarter of W1 has as much right to a quintessentially British fish and chip restaurant as anywhere else. It certainly looks the part – all black and white chequerboard tiled floors, marble-topped tables, mirrored walls and fish-themed prints. And it serves crispy Cornish squid, roast garlic and mayo; Devon cod loin with parsley crust, mussels and samphire; and other much-loved British fare like shepherd's pie, and warm chocolate pudding with salted caramel ice cream and cinder toffee. For Mayfair, the small wine selection is attractively priced.

Chef Pete Taylor, Desiree Inezhaley **Seats** 45, Pr/dining room 14 **Times** 12-10, All-day dining, Closed Xmas, New Year, D Sun, 24 Dec **Prices** Fixed L 2 course £15.75-£50, Starter £6-£30, Main £9.75-£20, Dessert £5-£7 **Wines** 5 bottles over £30, 10 bottles under £30, 11 by glass **Parking** On street **Notes** Sunday L, Vegetarian available, Children welcome

Maze

PLAN 2 G1

French, Asian V

tel: 020 7107 0000 & 7592 1350 **London Marriott Hotel, 10-13 Grosvenor Square W1K 6JP**
email: maze@gordonramsay.com **web:** www.gordonramsay.com/maze
dir: *Nearest station: Bond St*

Global Mayfair modernism near the US embassy

The Rosette award for this establishment has been suspended due to a change of chef. Reassessment will take place in due course under the new chef. Set on Mayfair's exclusive Grosvenor Square, within hallooing distance of the United States embassy, Maze is enveloped within the London Marriott Hotel and is quite the vision of cool modernity. Beyond a swish busy bar, the restaurant is a light-filled, split-level affair punctuated by tall windows, bold colour, and cream leather seating. Service is professional, unstuffy and smack in tune with its modern backing track, and the wine list is viewed via laptop computer, which should save a few trees. Maze pioneered the now commonplace small-plate format of a succession of disparate, randomly ordered dishes, but has now undergone an evolution in the direction of a traditional carte – with a seven-course chef's taster menu to boot. Under the new kitchen team, the cooking retains its innovative edge, matching and mixing British, European and East Asian modernist modes for sushi platters, or beef tataki with smoked ponzu and pickled mooli, followed by roast turbot with orzo and mussels in saffron sauce, or breast and crisped leg of poulet de Bresse for two, served with salt-baked beetroot and wild garlic. Vegetarian dishes are full of creative energy too, and the finale might be white chocolate cheesecake garnished with tarocco (this season's happening blood orange variety) and ginger beer.

Chef Luke Armstrong **Seats** 94, Pr/dining room 90 **Times** 12-3/5.30-11 **Prices** Tasting menu fr £92, Starter £16-£19, Main £28-£32, Dessert £9.50-£13 **Wines** 600 bottles over £30, 10 bottles under £30, 23 by glass **Parking** On street **Notes** Fixed L/D 4/5/6 course £35/£42/£50, Children welcome

Mele e Pere

PLAN 2 J1

Italian

tel: 020 7096 2096 **46 Brewer St, Soho W1F 9TF**
email: info@meleepere.co.uk
dir: *Nearest station: Piccadilly Circus*

Dynamic Italian basement venue

'Apples and Pears' looks a riot of colour and conviviality on its Soho corner. At ground-floor level is a café area, but the main dining goes on downstairs in a dynamic, russet walled basement room. Italian sharing plates are the principal draw to start, with San Daniele ham and gnocchi, deep fried squid and smoked aïoli, or beef carpaccio with pecorino among the offerings. Then it's braised veal shin with wild mushrooms and polenta, with perhaps an intermediate pasta dish or risotto to bridge the gap. To finish, how about a maraschino cherry sundae with blackcurrant and vanilla ice creams, or mascarpone cheesecake with white chocolate and wild berries.

Chef A Mantovani **Seats** 90 **Times** 12-11, All-day dining, Closed 25-26 Dec, 1 Jan **Prices** Fixed L 2 course £16.50, Fixed D 3 course £19.50, Starter £5-£7.50, Main £15-£29, Dessert £6-£6.50 **Wines** 51 bottles over £30, 25 bottles under £30, 16 by glass **Parking** NCP **Notes** Pre-theatre menu until 7pm £16.50-£19.50, Vegetarian available, Children welcome

Le Meridien Piccadilly

PLAN 2 J1

Modern British V

tel: 020 7734 8000 & 7851 3085 **21 Piccadilly W1J 0BH**
email: piccadilly.terrace@lemeridien.com **web:** www.lemeridienpiccadilly.com
dir: *Nearest station: Piccadilly Circus*

Grills and a lot more at a top-end hotel

Within Le Meridien is a series of vast public rooms, including the impressive Terrace and Baran atrium-style space with a curved glass ceiling, columns and darkwood tables. The menu features grills from Red Poll rib-eye to lamb cutlets, but there's plenty more of interest. Among starters, a ballotine consists of wood pigeon, duck liver and pancetta, served with quince and radish purée, and scallops are glazed with Welsh rarebit and accompanied by dried ham and celeriac purée. Main courses run from fish pie to treacle-blackened duck breast with confit leg, pea purée and pommes Anna, and bringing up the rear could be lemon syllabub.

Chef Daniel Ayton **Seats** 80 **Times** 12-2.30/5.30-10.30 **Prices** Fixed D 3 course fr £25 **Wines** 38 bottles over £30, 4 bottles under £30, 8 by glass **Notes** Chef's table 5 course £99 (max 10 people), Wknd brunch £56, Children welcome

LONDON W1 *continued*

Mews of Mayfair

PLAN 2 H1

tel: 020 7518 9388 **10-11 Lancashire Court, New Bond St, Mayfair W1S 1EY**
email: info@mewsofmayfair.com
dir: *Nearest station: Bond St*

Fashionable setting for modern brasserie cooking

The Mayfair set converge on this stylish bar and restaurant, hidden from the Bond Street crowds on a narrow cobbled alleyway. With its terrace tables and roll-back doors, on a warm day it feels more Mediterranean than West End. The street-level cocktail bar and basement lounge make a glam statement, while the first-floor brasserie has a relaxed vibe. The kitchen delivers a please-all roster of seasonal dishes driven by prime, responsibly sourced produce. There are feel-good options such as the Mews burger and fish and chips alongside the likes of confit pork belly with Orkney Isle scallops, or Hereford rib-eye cooked on the Josper grill.

Chef Michael Lecouteur **Seats** 70, Pr/dining room 28
Times 12-3.30/6-11.30, Closed 25 Dec, D Sun **Prices** Starter £3-£13, Main £15-£57, Dessert £6-£8 **Wines** 40 bottles over £30, 5 bottles under £30, 12 by glass **Parking** On street, NCP **Notes** Sunday L £20-£40, Vegetarian available, Children welcome

The Montagu

PLAN 2 F2

@@ Modern British

tel: 020 7299 2037 **Hyatt Regency London, The Churchill, 30 Portman Square W1H 7BH**
email: montagu.hrlondon@hyatt.com
dir: *Nearest station: Marble Arch*

Modern comfort food in smart West End venue

The swanky five-star hotel has many riches, not least Locanda Locatelli, with a separate entrance and a life of its own. The hotel's Montagu restaurant has plenty to offer, too, with a menu of smart, modern British ideas and views over Portland Square. There are liveried doormen out front and elegant proportions within. An open kitchen ensures a buzz in the room and the food takes an upbeat brasserie approach. You might start with braised oxtail tortellini topped with truffle foam, and move on to seared fillet of sea bass in a spot-on lobster and corn bisque, and finish with an updated Black Forest gâteau.

Chef Felix Luecke **Seats** 60 **Times** 12-10.45, All-day dining **Prices** Fixed L 2 course £25, Fixed D 3 course £30, Starter £8-£21, Main £16.50-£40, Dessert £7.50-£12 **Wines** 41 bottles over £30, 3 bottles under £30, 16 by glass **Parking** 12 **Notes** Chef's table 5/7 course £75/£95, Wknd brunch £49/£70, Sunday L £70, Vegetarian available, Children welcome

Murano

PLAN 4 H6

@@@@ – *see below*

Murano

LONDON W1 **PLAN 4 H6**

Modern European, Italian influence
tel: 020 7495 1127 **20-22 Queen St W1J 5PP**
email: muranorestaurant@angela-hartnett.com
dir: *Nearest station: Green Park*

Classy showcase for Italian-led contemporary cooking

Angela Harnett's early culinary inspiration came from her Italian grandmother and aunties, while it was her time in Gordon Ramsay's empire during its heyday where she developed her professional skills. These days she's one of the UK's foremost chefs. At this Mayfair address, Hartnett's style of Italian-inspired food is up for grabs, and female chef Pip Lacey heads up the brigade. It's a luxurious space, but subtle and refined, with the namesake Murano glass making an appearance in arty, modern chandeliers. This kitchen delivers an impressive crab ravioli with crystal clear tomato water, peas and broad beans, plus similarly remarkable more Pan-European dishes such as scallops with parsnip purée and scallop velouté. The ingredients are out of the top drawer. There's plenty of creativity on show, too, such as the praline yogurt that accompanies crispy pork belly with white coco beans and plums. When it comes to pasta, they really hit the mark: macaroni with chestnuts, brown shrimps and clams, for example, is a stunning combination. Among fishy options, hake arrives with octopus carpaccio and paprika butter, and turbot in luxe partnership with langoustines. For dessert, the caramelised Amalfi lemon tart is an exemplary version of a classic, or go for a sexed up chocolate brownie with mandarin sorbet, candied kumquats and salted caramel ice cream. The wine list focuses on Italy while not disregarding the rest of the world, and has particularly interesting organic and biodynamic options.

Chef Angela Hartnett, Pip Lacey **Seats** 46, Pr/dining room 12
Times 12-3/6.30-11, Closed Xmas, Sun **Prices** Fixed L 2 course £28, Fixed D 3 course £65, Starter £15, Main £35, Dessert £15 **Wines** 745 bottles over £30, 7 bottles under £30, 21 by glass **Parking** Carrington St NCP **Notes** Fixed D ALC menu 4/5/6 course £75/£85/£95, Vegetarian available, Children welcome

The Ninth

PLAN 2 K3

Modern French, Mediterranean NEW

tel: 020 3019 0880 **22 Charlotte St W1T 2NB**
email: bookings@theninthlondon.com
dir: *Nearest station: Goodge St, Tottenham Court Rd, Oxford Circus*

Cool, chilled-out outfit underpinned by pure pedigree

The Ninth is NYC-born chef and TV regular Jun Tanaka's first solo venture since leaving the Pearl in Holborn, and so-called as it's the ninth place he's worked in. Tanaka shuns past fine-dining ostentation for a relaxed, cool look and modern menu of sharing dishes. The decor is a pared-back look from exposed brick walls, decorated concrete, floorboards and mirrors, dotted with eye-catching statement pieces like dangling glass lighting or metal wine cages and wine glass racks. The entrance slate-tiled bar comes with high stools, while leather banquettes and café-style chairs provide the comforts alongside mahogany or white marble-topped tables. A light Mediterranean menu is underpinned by a classic French influence and bursts with seasonality and flavour, taking an on-trend sharing approach. Dividing into nine categories (there's that number again), the roster's focus treats vegetable dishes with the same importance as everything else. In-vogue snacks like big-hit oxtail croquettes or barbajuans pep up the interest factor, while smoked duck breast might come with caramelised chicory and walnuts, or a delightful cavolo nero vegetarian dish with hazelnut pesto. Desserts are classics, such as an absolute perfection pain perdu teamed with honeycomb and vanilla ice cream. Service is relaxed but spot-on, while the wine list is inspired.

Chef Jun Tanaka **Seats** Pr/dining room 22 **Times** 12-10.30, All-day dining, Closed BHs, Sun **Prices** Fixed L 2 course £17, Starter £2-£10, Main £14-£23, Dessert £6.50-£12 **Wines** 48 bottles over £30, 7 bottles under £30, 18 by glass

Nobu Berkeley ST

PLAN 4 H6

Japanese, Peruvian V 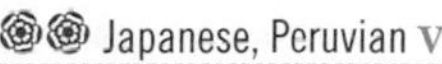

tel: 020 7290 9222 **15 Berkeley St W1J 8DY**
email: berkeleyst@noburestaurants.com
dir: *Nearest station: Green Park*

Super-cool Mayfair hot-spot for great Japanese food

Nobu's glossy Berkeley Street outpost still draws in the Mayfair fashionistas who come for the see-and-be-seen buzz of the ground-floor bar, before winding up the spiral staircase to the cool minimalist David Collins-designed restaurant. Traditionalists can head straight for the sushi bar, or for a bit of fun DIY dining with chefs supervising your efforts around a sunken hibachi grill. Whichever path you take, expect first-rate ingredients, exquisite presentation, and the cleanness and precision of Japanese cooking. Open with soft-shelled crab kara-age with ponzu, or a hybrid whitefish sashimi with aji amarillo (yellow chilli) salsa, then move on to the signature black cod with miso or rib-eye anticucho skewers.

Chef Mark Edwards, Rhys Cattermoul **Seats** 180 **Times** 12-2.30/6-1am, Closed 25 Dec, L Sun (ex Mother's & Father's Day), D 24 Dec **Prices** Tasting menu £85-£95 **Wines** 200 bottles over £30, 10 by glass **Parking** Mayfair NCP **Notes** Tasting menu 6 course, Bento box L £39.50-£49.50, Children welcome

Nobu Old Park Lane

PLAN 4 H6

Japanese, Peruvian

tel: 020 7447 4747 **Metropolitan London, Old Park Ln W1K 1LB**
email: london@noburestaurants.com **web:** www.noburestaurants.com
dir: *Nearest station: Hyde Park Corner, Green Park*

Top-end Japanese dining with views over Hyde Park

Londoners met Nobu Matsuhisa's brand of Japanese precision and South American spice back in 1977. It remains a fashionable and super-cool restaurant, and quality remains high. Seafood sparkles, from sea bass sashimi with dried red miso and yuzu sauce to salmon tartare with wasabi. South America is the inspiration for dishes such as lobster céviche with quinoa, and sea bass with red jalapeño miso. Otherwise there are Japanese staples of sushi and sashimi along with less familiar sea urchin tempura, say, and Wagyu rump tataki with wasabi salsa and tozazu. Desserts are no afterthought, among them a chocolate bento box with green tea ice cream.

Chef Mark Edwards **Seats** 160, Pr/dining room 40 **Times** 12-2.15/6-10.15, Closed 25 Dec, 1 Jan, L 24 Dec **Prices** Fixed L 3 course £29-£33.50, Starter £6.25-£29.50, Main £15.50-£42.50, Dessert £11.50-£12.50 **Wines** All bottles over £30, 22 by glass **Parking** Car park nearby **Notes** L 5 course £70-£80, D 7 course £85-£100, Bento box £39.50, Sunday L, Vegetarian available, Children welcome

NOPI

PLAN 2 J1

Mediterranean

tel: 020 7494 9584 **21-22 Warwick St W1B 5NE**
email: contact@nopi-restaurant.com
dir: *Nearest station: Oxford Circus, Piccadilly Circus*

Ottolenghi's inventive take on zingy Middle Eastern flavours

Inspired by the sun-drenched cuisines of the Middle East, North Africa and the Mediterranean, owner Yotam Ottolenghi's cooking is creative stuff, bursting with punchy flavours and delivered in dishes made for sharing in an all-white brasserie-style space, or in the basement at two large communal tables with ringside seats for the open-to-view kitchen. Whichever you choose, the vibe is a chatty hubbub of people tucking into the forthright flavours of twice-cooked baby chicken with lemon myrtle salt and chilli sauce, then sea bass with spring greens and Calabrese peppers, and rich chocolate mousse with orange oil and crème fraîche to finish.

Chef Yotam Ottolenghi, Ramael Scully **Seats** 100 **Times** 12-2.45/5.30-10.15, Closed 25-26 Dec, 1 Jan, D Sun, BHs **Prices** Starter £8.90-£13.90, Main £19.90-£24.90, Dessert £4.90-£9 **Wines** 55 bottles over £30, 3 bottles under £30, 36 by glass **Parking** On street **Notes** Pre-theatre menu £24.50, Sunday L, Vegetarian available, Children welcome

Novikov Asian Restaurant

PLAN 4 H6

Chinese, Pan-Asian

tel: 020 7399 4330 **50a Berkeley St W1J 8HA**
dir: *Nearest station: Charing Cross, Green Park*

Style-conscious Pan-Asian dining in Mayfair

The Asian Room of Russian restaurateur Arkady Novikov's see-and-be-seen Mayfair food palace offers a palate-tingling mix of Japanese, Chinese, Thai and Malaysian dishes. A seat in the slick brasserie-style space means you can watch the busy team of chefs behind a glass wall among mounds of super-fresh produce resembling an Asian street market. They send out skilfully-made prawn 'money bag' dumplings and crispy salt-and-pepper squid to get the taste buds standing to attention. Elsewhere, there's grilled baby chicken with miso or steamed sea bass with ginger and soy, while an East-meets-West fusion of mango tiramisù keeps things lively at dessert stage. There's also an Italian venue downstairs.

LONDON W1 *continued*

Novikov Italian Restaurant

PLAN 4 H6

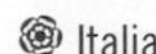 Italian

tel: 020 7399 4330 **50a Berkeley St W1J 8HA**
email: reservations@novikovrestaurant.co.uk
dir: *Nearest station: Green Park*

Plutocratic Italian cooking and dazzling displays

The Novikov complex, fronted by street-level security guards, includes an Italian room with striped walls in the vast basement, where cornucopian displays dazzle on arrival. Chefs beaver away behind a glass screen producing creditable renditions of uncontroversial Italian food including fritto misto and excellent cured meats, including venison and Sardinian wild boar prosciutto. Unimpeachably fresh sea bream has come all the way from the Med, and is dressed in Capezzana olive oil, and there are wood-fired oven and Josper grill offerings such as lamb cutlets in mint sauce. Pannacotta with mixed berries in syrup is the real creamy deal, or forsake Italy altogether for green tea brûlée with guava sorbet.

Orrery

PLAN 2 G3

Modern French V

tel: 020 7616 8000 **55-57 Marylebone High St W1U 5RB**
email: orreryreservations@danddlondon.com
dir: *Nearest station: Baker St, Regent's Park*

Stylish, elegant restaurant above designer store

This Marylebone hotspot cuts a contemporary swagger with classy good looks, polished service and skilful, contemporary French cuisine. On the first floor above the Conran store, the long, narrow room is fashionably clean-lined in the classic Terence Conran style and filled with light from its striking arched windows and room-length ceiling skylight. Pale blue banquettes and chairs blend with blond wood, mirrors and white linen, while a glass wine cellar signals that the grape is taken seriously here. Menus are driven by prime ingredients and seasonality, and come dotted with luxuries (attracting the odd supplement here and there), with dishes showing a lightness of touch, matched by eye-catching presentation and flavours to savour. Classical roots are clear in an opener starring foie gras parfait with apple chutney and Poilâne toast, while to follow, a sea-fresh pavé of salmon is served with wilted spinach and tomatoes, and complemented by a fabulous sauce vièrge. Meat dishes also deliver strongly, perhaps a duo of Black Leg chicken and pork belly matched with peas and champagne velouté. There's no let up at dessert stage either: witness Manjari chocolate pannacotta with crunchy chocolate crumble and raspberry sorbet. An intimate bar, summer roof terrace and street-level épicerie add further appeal.

Chef Igor Tymchyshyn **Seats** 110, Pr/dining room 12
Times 12-2.30/6.30-10, Closed 26 Dec, L 31 Dec **Prices** Fixed L 2 course £26.50, Fixed D 3 course fr £29.50, Tasting menu £75-£220, Starter £8-£23.50, Main £15-£39, Dessert £6.50-£11 **Wines** 400 bottles over £30, 33 bottles under £30, 14 by glass **Parking** NCP, 170 Marylebone Rd **Notes** ALC menu, Gourmand menu £65, Potager menu £65, Sunday L £32.50, Children welcome

Palomar

PLAN 2 K1

 Middle Eastern

tel: 020 7439 8777 **34 Rupert St W1D 6DN**
email: info@thepalomar.co.uk
dir: *Nearest station: Piccadilly Circus, Leicester Sq*

Authentic Middle Eastern cuisine in Soho

In the throbbing heart of theatreland, this bijou restaurant has picked up glowing reviews from food critics since opening. The cooking looks to the Levant, North Africa and southern Spain for inspiration and the sunny flavours have broad appeal. A quirkily named and beautifully presented 'Octo-houmous' sees octopus cooked over charcoal served with chickpea masabacha and cherry tomato confit. Main courses deliver the likes of corn-fed chicken cooked in buttermilk with Jerusalem spices and teamed with rainbow chard and freekeh (roasted wheat grain). Desserts are equally diverting – perhaps a rose-scented malabi (a Middle Eastern classic) with raspberry coulis and coconut meringue with pistachio crunch.

Chef Tomer Amedi **Seats** 50 **Times** 12-2.30/5.30-11, Closed 25-26 Dec **Prices** Starter £6-£9.50, Main £9.50-£25, Dessert £5-£7 **Wines** 36 bottles over £30, 5 bottles under £30, 14 by glass **Parking** Q park Chinatown **Notes** Sunday L £9.50-£18, Vegetarian available, Children welcome

Park Chinois

PLAN 4 H6

Chinese 

tel: 020 3327 8888 **17 Berkeley St, Mayfair W1J 8EA**
email: reservations@parkchinois.com
dir: *Nearest station: Green Park, Piccadilly Circus, Oxford Circus*

An opulent Chinese restaurant and jazz venue in Mayfair

In the dining room, a piano, drums and microphone await the next jazz turn. White linen dresses the tables, red banquettes one side, floral-patterned tub seats the other. The dinner menu starts with Duck de Chine: roasted duck with one of five caviars, accompanied by pancake, Thai cucumber, spring onion and duck sauce. Then, respectively, from Commence, First and Second sections: soft-shell crab, coconut, curry leaf and dried red pepper chilli; rice soup, scampi and Australian abalone; and Welsh lamb, air-dried rib-eye beef, Chinese chive, dried shrimp and red chilli. Lunch starts with a dim sum course. Entry level for wines is north of £40.

Chef Lee Che Liang **Times** 12-3.30/6-2am **Prices** Starter £8-£85, Main £10.50-£48, Dessert £10.50-£12 **Notes** Vegetarian available

La Petite Maison

PLAN 2 H1

French, Mediterranean

tel: 020 7495 4774 **54 Brooks Mews W1K 4EG**
email: info@lpmlondon.co.uk
dir: *Nearest station: Bond St*

The flavours of the Midi in Mayfair

Modelled on its sister restaurant in Nice, the open-plan room exudes a breezily Mediterranean vibe transposed to an ultra-posh postcode. The sun-drenched flavours of the Côte d'Azur and its Italian neighbours turn up in a starter of salt-cod croquettes with oven-roasted pepper relish, or the likes of pissaladière tart of onions and anchovies. Main course delivers turbot with a rich barigoule stew of artichokes, chorizo, white wine and olive oil, or you might go for pasta – home-made tagliolini with clams, say – while two could share a whole roasted Black Leg chicken with foie gras. The Gallic focus runs through to a finale of exemplary vanilla crème brûlée.

Peyote

PLAN 2 J1

Mexican

tel: 020 7409 1300 **13 Cork St, Mayfair W1S 3NS**
email: info@peyoterestaurant.com
dir: *Nearest station: Green Park*

Modern Mexican food good for sharing in Mayfair

That it's named after a Chihuahuan desert cactus is a pointer to the Mexican theme, and indeed some of that country's finest chefs have come here to give modern interpretations of its cuisine. It's been given a modern makeover, over two levels, which sees closely set wooden tables and artistic skulls making a bold design statement. Well-informed staff are on hand to offer guidance through the menu of plates ideal for sharing; octopus tiradito, for example, with lemon salsa, or céviche of prawn, tomatillo and lime salsa. Lamb chops arrive with tomato and mint habanero salsa. To finish, cheesecake is served with hibiscus granité.

Chef Stamatios Loumousiotis **Seats** 110, Pr/dining room 12
Times 12-3/6-1, Closed Xmas, New Year, Sun, L Sat **Prices** Fixed L 3 course fr £24, Fixed D 3 course £60-£90, Starter £7-£13, Main £14-£38, Dessert £7.50 **Wines** 88 bottles over £30, 7 bottles under £30, 11 by glass **Notes** Fixed L 4 course £29, Vegetarian available, Children welcome

Picture

PLAN 2 H3

Modern European V

tel: 020 7637 7892 **110 Great Portland St W1W 6PQ**
email: info@picturerestaurant.co.uk
dir: *Nearest station: Oxford Circus*

Top-call for small-plate dining with a touch of pedigree

Set up by three talented deserters from the acclaimed Arbutus/Wild Honey stable (a manager and two chefs), this switched-on outfit presses all the on-trend buttons. It has grey-washed walls, floorboards, retro furnishings and food that's more cheffy than the trendy brown-paper menus, tea-towel napkins, accessible pricing, or casually dressed staff might suggest. The kitchen deals in fresh, prettily dressed, fashionable 'small plates' spiked with flavour and flair. Open with caramelised onion with cavolo nero and parmesan, while lamb neck gets the 'Picture' treatment teamed with butternut squash, toasted farro and hispi cabbage. Desserts might feature chocolate mousse with Williams pear, milk jam and amaranth popcorn.

Chef Alan Christie, Colin Kelly **Seats** 55 **Times** 12-2.30/6-10.30, Closed Xmas, BHs, Sun **Prices** Tasting menu £39-£43, Starter £8, Main £12, Dessert £6 **Wines** 12 bottles over £30, 14 bottles under £30, 21 by glass **Parking** On street **Notes** Tasting menu 6 course, Food menu all dishes £8-£12, Children welcome

Pied à Terre

PLAN 2 J3

Modern French, European V NOTABLE WINE LIST

tel: 020 7636 1178 **34 Charlotte St W1T 2NH**
email: reservations@pied-a-terre.co.uk
dir: *Nearest station: Goodge St*

Art on a plate in one of Charlotte Street's finest

The discreet narrow-fronted premises has always somehow belied one of the premier addresses on multi-restauranted Charlotte Street, and the feeling of stepping into somewhere very exclusive, secretive, even members-only, is part of the thrill. A small smart bar leads into the narrow dining room, where mirrors deceptively extend the space and the head-turning artwork takes its inspiration from used kitchen paraphernalia. Andy McFadden arrives from L'Autre Pied, which continues to act as a nursery kitchen for the big brother, but the finely detailed style of inventive modern cooking remains. Beautifully caramelised duck foie gras with an oat crust is punctuated by sharp notes of pomegranate, with spinach and a verjus sauce adding subtle acidity. That may be followed by crisply rendered suckling pig belly with braised loin, strongly seasoned with sage, the richness intensified with chorizo and creamily puréed butternut squash. Fish could be halibut, delightfully paired with brown shrimps in beurre noisette, with some cavolo nero and lemon. Boost your nutrient intake with a carrot cake dessert, its cream cheese appearing in little truffle-like balls, the health kick delivered by a 'multivitamin' sorbet made from a plethora of fruit juices. It all comes with one of the most comprehensive (and dangerously seductive) wine lists in the district.

Chef Andy McFadden **Seats** 40, Pr/dining room 14
Times 12.15-2.30/6-11, Closed 2 wks Xmas & New Year, Sun, L Sat **Prices** Fixed L 2 course fr £29.50, Fixed D 3 course fr £80, Tasting menu £105-£145 **Wines** 750 bottles over £30, 20 bottles under £30, 25 by glass **Parking** Cleveland St **Notes** ALC 2/3 course £65/£80, Tasting menu 10 course, Children welcome

Piquet Restaurant

PLAN 2 K2

Contemporary British, French NEW

tel: 020 3826 4500 **92 94 Newman St W1T 3EZ**
email: enquiries@piquet-restaurant.co.uk
dir: *Nearest station: Tottenham Court Rd, Oxford Circus, Goodge St*

Classy Anglo-French joint off Oxford Street

In the hinterland where Fitzrovia meets the bedlam of Oxford Street, Piquet is a civilised oasis offering a menu inspired by the best of English and French traditions. The good-looking room has an understated glamour, with a fashionably retro appeal and a European sheen, plus a view into the kitchen. The kitchen turns put classy stuff such as Pithiviers of Littlebourne snails with Madeira jus to start, or crab raviolo with samphire and shellfish dressing, followed by a lusty casserole of monkfish and chorizo, or lamb cutlets served up with confit shoulder, artichokes and carrot purée. Find a friend and you can finish with pear and red wine Tatin.

Chef Allan Pickett **Times** 12-3/5.30-11, Closed D Sun **Prices** Fixed L 2 course £16.50, Fixed D 3 course £19.50, Tasting menu £45-£95, Starter £8-£13.50, Main £15-£27, Dessert £6-£14 **Wines** 33 bottles over £30, 8 bottles under £30, 17 by glass **Notes** Tasting menu 5/7 course, Fixed D 5.30-6.45pm only, Sunday L £19.50

Plum Valley

PLAN 2 K1

Chinese

tel: 020 7494 4366 **20 Gerrard St W1D 6JQ**
dir: *Nearest station: Leicester Sq*

Contemporary Cantonese cooking and cool decor in Chinatown

Plum Valley stands out on Gerrard Street with its sleek black frontage and inside it has a dark, contemporary finish. Service is brisk. The mainstay of the menu is classic Cantonese stuff, with plenty of familiar dishes and some perky modern stuff, too. Vietnamese vegetable spring rolls are as crisp and golden as you might hope, while veggies might opt for spicy tofu in a light batter. There's a dim sum platter and main courses such as braised lobster with ginger and spring onion (at the pricier end of the spectrum), or braised pork belly with rice wine and sweet vinegar, or even pan-fried ostrich.

LONDON W1 *continued*

Podium
PLAN 4 G6

Modern European NEW

tel: 020 7208 4022 **London Hilton on Park Ln, 22 Park Ln W1K 1BE**
email: info@podiumrestaurant.com **web:** www.podiumrestaurant.com
dir: *Nearest station: Hyde Park Corner*

Please-all hotel eatery on Park Lane

This swish all-day eatery in the Park Lane Hilton fits the bill when you're tootling around Mayfair and fancy a relaxed pit-stop with an eclectic, comfort-oriented menu. Dishes show minimum posturing and can be as simple as burgers, steaks or beer-battered cod and chips, while a starter of seared scallops with apple salad and sauce, and walnut purée ups the ante, ahead of roast corn-fed chicken with sweet pea and corn ragù and baby gem hearts. For pudding, there's a deconstructed take on a Black Forest theme: chocolate mousse with a liquid cherry centre, fresh cherries and cream.

Chef Anthony Marshall **Seats** 80 **Times** 12-11, All-day dining **Prices** Fixed L 2 course £23, Fixed D 3 course £27-£40, Starter £7-£16, Main £17-£39, Dessert £7-£10 **Wines** 10 bottles over £30, 5 bottles under £30, 7 by glass **Parking** 140 **Notes** Afternoon tea £36-£46, Sunday L £27, Vegetarian available, Children welcome

Pollen Street Social
PLAN 2 H2

– see opposite

Polpo
PLAN 2 J1

Italian

tel: 020 7734 4479 & 7287 1152 **41 Beak St W1F 9SB**
dir: *Nearest station: Piccadilly Circus*

Bustling Venetian-style bacaro in the heart of Soho

This pint-sized space is constantly rammed, and you can't book in the evenings, so expect to queue beside the bar with its high stools for dining. The decor is pared-back, all elbow-to-elbow tables, exposed brick and floorboards. Food-wise, the deal is affordably priced, Italian-style small plates sent out quick-fire. It's simple, boldly-flavoured stuff: expect crispy seafood fritto misto, roast belly pork with braised apple, or lamb and mint meatballs. Italian wines come by glass, carafe and bottle, while a bijou basement Campari bar gets going at 5.30pm. There are five sibling Polpos in central London, as well as branches in Brighton, and Harvey Nichols Knightsbridge and Leeds.

Portland
PLAN 2 H3

Modern British NEW

tel: 020 7436 3261 **113 Great Portland St W1W 6QQ**
email: info@portlandrestaurant.co.uk
dir: *Nearest station: Oxford Circus*

Compact, seasonal menu of big-hitting flavours

Just up the road from the BBC, new-kid-on-the-block Portland has been making headlines of its own with its on-cue vision of new-Brit cuisine, scoring high with precision cooking, unstuffy, spot-on service and understated good looks. On first impression, Portland feels more neighbourhood gaff than city-slicker, with its small pared-back interior of wooden tables and chairs, plain white walls, dangling retro-like Edison lighting, and a fast tempo backing track. Upfront, the in-vogue counter and high stalls look out streetwise, while at the back, the must-have open kitchen fires up the culinary action. The concise menu brims with innovation and a genuine sense of seasonality. Vibrant small snack plates are a fantastic prelude and might include the lightest, flavour-packed mini white truffle and gruyere macaroons, or fabulously succulent big-mouthed barbecue smoked eel pared with refreshing radish and cultured Guernsey cream. There's modern gloss to the presentation, with skilled balance to dishes alongside texture and colour interest, as in a starter of perfectly timed salsify doused in 'kicking' Comté shavings and 'crispy' air-dried Mangalitsa pig. At mains, Denham Estate deer might come dotted with 'sweet' elderberry to balance salt-baked celeriac and 'crisp' buckwheat. The equally stimulating wine list delivers a top choice by glass, including all of its 'Special' wines.

Chef Merlin Labron-Johnson **Seats** 36, Pr/dining room 17 **Times** 12-2.30/6-10, Closed 23 Dec-3 Jan, Sun **Prices** Starter £8-£11, Main £14-£28, Dessert £6-£9 **Wines** 20 bottles over £30, 8 bottles under £30 **Parking** NCP Portland Place **Notes** Vegetarian available, Children welcome

The Providores and Tapa Room
PLAN 2 G3

International Fusion NOTABLE WINE LIST

tel: 020 7935 6175 **109 Marylebone High St W1U 4RX**
email: anyone@theprovidores.co.uk
dir: *Nearest station: Bond St, Baker St, Regent's Park*

Twin-faceted venue for inventive fusion cooking

To experience New Zealander Peter Gordon's cooking – some of the most exciting and innovative fusion food in the capital – head upstairs to Providores. How about a lively starter of seared yellowfin tuna with papaya, carrots, cucumber salad, lime chilli dressing, toasted nori sauce, peanuts and sesame? Main courses seem a tad calmer in comparison. Beef pesto is a signature dish – tender fillet with pesto and a salad of chard, courgettes and beetroot with olives – and there might be crispy pork belly with dashi-braised sprouts, Puy lentils, apple and peanut butter flavoured with lemongrass. End with what the menu calls 'pumpkin pie – sort of', if you dare.

Chef Peter Gordon **Seats** 38, Pr/dining room 40 **Times** 12-2.30/6-10.30, Closed 25-26 Dec, L Sat-Sun **Prices** Prices not confirmed **Wines** 158 bottles over £30, 7 bottles under £30, 20 by glass **Parking** On street **Notes** Fixed D 2-5 course £33-£63, Sat-Sun Brunch menu, Vegetarian available, Children welcome

Quattro Passi
PLAN 2 H1

Italian, Mediterranean

tel: 020 3096 1444 **34 Dover St W1S 4NG**
email: info@quattropassi.co.uk
dir: *Nearest station: Green Park*

Classy Italian in the heart of Mayfair

Antonio Mellino captures the essence of Southern Italy in his sleek Mayfair establishment where top-notch ingredients (many imported from Italy), home-made pasta and solid technical skills are the foundations of the kitchen. Super-fresh piscine produce is treated with respect in no-frills dishes such as a starter of chargrilled octopus served on a warm bed of grilled fennel and courgette arrives with a rich celeriac cream. For main course, a well-judged and precisely cooked dish of scialatielli pasta with pumpkin, cuttlefish, prawns and mint is a harmonious combination. Desserts are no less impressive: for example the pastiera Napoletana is as rich as it is elaborate.

Chef Antonio Mellino **Seats** 80, Pr/dining room 45 **Times** 12-3/6.30-10.30, Closed Sun **Prices** Prices not confirmed **Wines** 300 bottles over £30, 6 bottles under £30, 20 by glass **Parking** Berkeley Sq **Notes** Vegetarian available, Children welcome

Pollen Street Social

LONDON W1 **PLAN 2 H2**

Modern British V
tel: 020 7290 7600 **8-10 Pollen St W1S 1NQ**
email: reservations@pollenstreetsocial.com
dir: *Nearest station: Oxford Circus*

Sophisticated cooking in Atherton's sleek flagship

Jason Atherton has certainly clocked up a few air miles as he now appears on four continents. With the opening in 2016 of his foray into Japanese cuisine at Sosharu, he's now up to seven restaurants in London alone, but this sleek Mayfair venue is the jewel in the crown. With its high-chair bar seating under globe lights, clothed tables on a wooden floor, glassed-in kitchen views and a dessert bar that maybe one of the capital's foremost guilty pleasures, the place boasts a dynamic buzz. Dining here most definitely fits into the 'fine' category, but the vibe is the polar opposite of what that tag can imply: hushed tones and hovering waiters are out, and fun is definitely allowed. Every last ounce of energy is devoted to the pursuit of ingenuity in food and drink, but before you begin, note the menu credits for the provenance of many of the main items, together with their mileages. For example, that langoustine from Gairloch has travelled 636 miles. The five- and eight-course tasting menus will lure many, and non-carnivores will be thrilled that they are amply sorted out with vegetarian and vegan options, but you can also stick to time-honoured convention and cherry pick your way through the carte. Of course, Atherton himself has an empire to run, so the day-to-day cooking is down to head chef Dale Bainbridge, who interprets the boss's complex, highly-detailed dishes with pin-sharp precision. Start with a bowl of smoked eel, pickled apple, buttermilk foam and green apple purée, all brought together by a beetroot broth poured at the table, or sea-fresh crab served in a vibrant salad with apple, coriander, black garlic and sourdough crisps, alongside brown crab meat foam on toast, all offset by an astringent lemon purée. Next up, roasted John Dory of unimpeachable quality arrives in a faultlessly seasonal partnership with English asparagus, Jersey Royals and wild mushrooms – this delightful Spring dish is a masterclass in treating top-quality produce with care, restraint and respect. As for meatier ideas, roasted squab pigeon (its leg wrapped in potato) comes with cabbage, Alsace bacon and a head-spinningly intense cottage pie topped with potato purée, with further flavours and textural interest provided by pickled walnuts, Périgord truffle and morels. Assuming you haven't cut to the chase and gone straight for the dessert bar in the first place, finish with a highly technical take on the theme of blackcurrant Eton Mess, or the zippy sweet-and-sour delights of marmalade cake with pain d'épice and sea buckthorn sorbet. The thrilling wine list travels the globe to seek out lesser-known artisan bottles alongside blue-blooded French vintages, and the Coravin wine system allows big-spenders to splash out top-class stuff by the glass.

Chef Jason Atherton, Dale Bainbridge **Seats** 52, Pr/dining room 12 **Times** 12-2.45/6-10.45, Closed BHs, Sun **Prices** Fixed L 2 course £32, Starter £16.50-£18.50, Main £33.50-£38, Dessert £11.50-£13 **Wines** 800 bottles over £30, 8 bottles under £30, 20 by glass **Parking** On street, car park Mayfair, Park Lane **Notes** Tasting menu 5/8 course, Children welcome

LONDON W1 *continued*

Quo Vadis

PLAN 2 K2

Modern British

tel: 020 7437 9585 **26-29 Dean St W1D 3LL**
email: reception@quovadissoho.co.uk
dir: *Nearest station: Tottenham Court Rd, Leicester Sq*

Smart British cooking at a Soho institution

Tan banquettes, modern art and mirrors on the walls and stained-glass windows provide the backdrop for accomplished cooking at this Soho stalwart, with the kitchen favouring the modern British style. The daily-changing menu might open with game and pistachio terrine with pickles or less familiar razor clams with fennel and monk's beard. Combinations are well considered so dishes maintain interest without over-elaboration: a comforting main course of ox cheeks comes with carrots and pickled walnuts, and cod fillet with sea vegetables and aïoli. The daily pie might be chicken, served with mashed potato, and desserts hit the mark: perhaps buttermilk pudding with lemon curd and rhubarb.

Chef Jeremy Lee **Seats** 72, Pr/dining room 32 **Times** 12-3/5.30-11, Closed BHs (ex Good Fri), 25 Dec, 1 Jan, Sun **Prices** Prices not confirmed **Wines** 108 bottles over £30, 4 bottles under £30, 11 by glass **Parking** On street or NCP **Notes** Theatre fixed menu 2/3 course £19.50/£22.50, Vegetarian available, Children welcome

The Red Fort

PLAN 2 K2

 Indian

tel: 020 7437 2525 & 7437 2115 **77 Dean St, Soho W1D 3SH**
email: info@redfort.co.uk
dir: *Nearest station: Leicester Sq, Tottenham Court Rd*

Authentic modern Indian in the heart of Soho

This sleek, red-fronted Indian cuts a dash with its white linen, smart staff, leather seating and walls of inlaid sandstone and Mogul arch motif. It turns out classic Mogul cooking and more up-to-date dishes, combining fine British produce with authentic sub-continental flavours, at fairly hefty prices. A traditional Hyderabadi bhuna gosht delivers chunks of Herdwick lamb with rich, aromatic spicing, tempered with a cooling cucumber raita. For seafood lovers, there's grilled stone bass fillet with mustard, coconut milk and curry leaf sauce. In the basement, the vaulted Zenna Bar is a hot spot for after-work cocktails and lighter bites.

Chef Vijay Singh Panwar **Seats** 84 **Times** 12-2.30/5.30-11.15, Closed Sun, L Sat **Prices** Fixed L 2 course £15-£25, Fixed D 3 course £18-£59, Tasting menu £39-£59, Starter £7-£15, Main £17-£42, Dessert £7-£16 **Wines** 170 bottles over £30, 24 bottles under £30, 13 by glass **Parking** NCP Brewer St **Notes** Pre-theatre menu 2/3 course £15/ £18, Vegetarian available, Children 3 yrs+

The Riding House Café

PLAN 2 J3

Modern European

tel: 020 7927 0840 **43-51 Great Titchfield St W1W 7PQ**
email: info@ridinghousecafe.co.uk
dir: *Nearest station: Oxford Circus*

Buzzy all-day brasserie near Oxford Street

Handy for the Oxford Street shops. The Riding House Café is a big, high-decibel, all-day operation with an urban brasserie vibe. Head for a swivel seat at the white-tiled island bar overlooking the open kitchen, park at the long refectory table, or there are classic marble topped tables and a separate space with panelled walls and more intimate mood. A flexible menu of small plate options and modern brasserie dishes is the deal at lunch and dinner (don't forget to factor in the necessity for side orders), so start with Moorish lamb with smoked aubergine, then follow with yogurt-marinated spatchcock poussin with salt-baked celeriac and pomegranate, and wind things up with cinnamon doughnuts with chocolate sauce.

Chef Paul Daniel **Seats** 115, Pr/dining room 14 **Times** 12-10.30, All-day dining, Closed 25-26 Dec, 1 Jan, D 24 Dec **Prices** Prices not confirmed **Wines** 15 bottles over £30, 15 bottles under £30, 20 by glass **Parking** On street **Notes** Sunday L, Vegetarian available, Children welcome

The Ritz Restaurant

PLAN 4 J6

British, French V NOTABLE WINE LIST

tel: 020 7300 2370 **150 Piccadilly W1J 9BR**
email: dining@theritzlondon.com **web:** www.theritzlondon.com
dir: *Nearest station: Green Park*

Arresting dining in sumptuous formal restaurant

The Ritz Restaurant is a truly beautiful dining room, with its Louis XVI-inspired decor of murals, frescoed ceiling, gilded statues, opulent drapes at floor-to-ceiling windows and chandeliers reflected in mirrored walls. Formal and knowledgeable service comes from an army of warmly hospitable uniformed staff. Dining here is quite an occasion, with trolleys and cloches much in evidence. The culinary heritage was established by Auguste Escoffier, so the kitchen has quite a lot to live up to. It succeeds. The style might be based on the classical French repertoire, but John Williams MBE tweaks and modernises dishes so compositions are more suitable for today's expectations. 'Langoustine, celery and lovage' is the bald description of one starter of lovely plump shellfish, beautifully timed, with delicate lovage gel, cauliflower purée and bisque, some celery adding a crisp element. Or try foie gras terrine cut by spicy pineapple. Ingredients are of the highest order, and standards never falter. A main course of venison, pink and tender, comes with red cabbage, silky celeriac purée, pomme soufflés, some chestnuts and sliced apples, with a glossy sauce sweetened with blackcurrant poured at the table, and another, of sea bass fillets, is accompanied by no more than pumpkin and shellfish sauce. Desserts can be highlights, among them caramelised apple millefeuille with Calvados ice cream.

Chef John T Williams MBE **Seats** 90, Pr/dining room 60 **Times** 12.30-2/5.30-9.30 **Prices** Fixed L 3 course £49, Fixed D 3 course £95, Starter £18-£35, Main £40-£49, Dessert £14-£19 **Wines** 450 bottles over £30, 48 by glass **Parking** 10, NCP **Notes** Menu surprise 6 course £95, 'Live at the Ritz' menu £95, Sunday L £49, Children welcome

Roka Charlotte Street

PLAN 2 J3

Japanese

tel: 020 7580 6464 **37 Charlotte St W1T 1RR**
email: infocharlottestreet@rokarestaurant.com
dir: *Nearest station: Goodge St, Tottenham Court Rd*

Stylish robata cookery full of freshness and umami

There could scarcely be a more fitting image of London media land than the clusters of contented diners sitting behind a row of potted plants on Charlotte Street eating modern Japanese food. This branch of the Roka group reliably packs them in, and if you venture beyond the potted plants, there's a huge room filled with daylight from full-height windows, and equipped with chunky furniture in natural woods. Pride of place is the robata counter, where close-up views of the kitchen action are mesmeric. The menu's fusion temptations include maki rolls filled with piri-piri-spiced yellowfin tuna and cucumber, or tempura-battered soft-shelled crab in a dressing of roasted chilli. Meat options have all the pedigree one expects, whether for Korean-spiced lamb cutlets, smoked duck breast with barley miso and kumquats, or the legendary Wagyu beef with pickled mushrooms. Baby back ribs are coated over and over at the grill before you, before being garnished with a line of slivered cashews and spring onion. Technical skills are given free rein in desserts such as a pasta tube made to resemble bamboo, filled with apple mousse, accompanying banana ice cream and salted cocoa crumble.

Chef Hamish Brown **Seats** 350, Pr/dining room 20
Times 12-3.30/5.30-11, Closed Xmas **Prices** Prices not confirmed **Wines** 200 bottles over £30, 10 bottles under £30, 20 by glass **Notes** Vegetarian available, Children welcome

Roka Mayfair

PLAN 2 G1

Modern Japanese

tel: 020 7305 5644 **30 North Audley St W1K 6ZF**
email: infomayfair@rokarestaurant.com
dir: *Nearest station: Bond St, Marble Arch*

Dazzling robata grill cuisine in Mayfair

One of four Roka's across the capital, the Mayfair outfit is as pulsating and downright cool as all the others. Just a short distance from Oxford Street, it's a stylish contemporary space of natural wood, steel, concrete and acres of glass, with a Japanese robatayaki charcoal grill at the heart of everything (grab a seat at the counter to feel the full force). Wherever you sit, the eager service team run the show with charm and bags of energy. A tasting menu takes away the need to make a decision. Top-notch sushi and sashimi (California maki, say, with crab and avocado) shouldn't be missed, classic tempura include a tiger prawn version, black cod, crab and crayfish are packed into tasty fried dumplings, and be aware that plates arrive as when they're ready and the idea is that you share stuff with your dining companion. From the robata grill comes spiced chicken wings, or black cod marinated in yuzu miso, and there's no lack of luxury ingredients such as foie gras, Wagyu beef and caviar. Desserts show both Asian and European sensibilities, such as an almond cake that is served with cherry ripple ice cream and crispy lotus, or dark chocolate and green tea pudding.

Chef Luca Spiga **Seats** 113 **Times** 12-3.30/5.30-11.30, Closed 25 Dec
Prices Prices not confirmed **Wines** 100 bottles over £30, 3 bottles under £30, 13 by glass **Notes** Wknd all day dining, Sunday L, Vegetarian available, Children welcome

Roti Chai

PLAN 2 G2

Modern Indian

tel: 020 7408 0101 **3 Portman Mews South W1H 6AY**
email: infowala@rotichai.com
dir: *Nearest station: Bond St, Marble Arch*

Vibrant Indian street food close to Oxford Street

Here is a restaurant of two halves taking its inspiration from the street stalls and railway cafés of the Indian sub-continent. The ground-floor, canteen-style Street Kitchen serves homely 'street food', while the basement Dining Room offers more refined nouveau Indian cooking. The look is part-industrial, mixed with darkwood floors and railway carriage references in wall-mounted luggage racks and brass-framed mirrors. Expect a modern take on Indian flavours. Tikki wala mini-burgers filled with chilli chicken and green slaw get things started in the Street Kitchen, followed by macher jhol – Bengali fish curry with kasundi mustard. For dessert, there's dark chocolate tart with cinnamon cream as well as kulfi.

Roux at The Landau

PLAN 2 H3

Modern European, French V NOTABLE WINE LIST

tel: 020 7636 1000 **The Langham, London, Portland Place W1B 1JA**
email: reservations@thelandau.com **web:** www.rouxatthelandau.com
dir: *Nearest station: Oxford Circus*

Highly polished modern cuisine à la Roux

The Roux dining room at the elegant Langham Hotel opposite the BBC building is a haven of traditional values. If things have gone dressed-down and laid-back elsewhere, here the elevated tone of the panelled oval room does justice to the highly polished cooking of the Roux ethos, now in the hands of a former *MasterChef* finalist. The main carte may open with seared scallops with creamed coco beans and chanterelles, prior to Ibérico pork chop with trotter and lentil fondue, smoked bacon and hispi cabbage. At the close, pear Tatin bestows comfort in the company of walnut crumble and brandy ice cream.

Chef Oliver Boon **Seats** 100, Pr/dining room 18 **Times** 12-2.30/5.30-10.30, Closed 2 wks Jan, L Sat, D Sun **Prices** Fixed L 3 course £37-£45, Fixed D 3 course £37-£45, Tasting menu £70-£120, Starter £11-£25, Main £20-£42, Dessert £8.50-£12
Wines 250 bottles over £30, 17 by glass **Parking** On street, NCP **Notes** Sun brunch £45, Children welcome

Salt Yard

PLAN 2 J3

Italian, Spanish

tel: 020 7637 0657 **54 Goodge St W1T 4NA**
email: info@saltyard.co.uk
dir: *Nearest station: Goodge St*

Top-notch tapas just off Tottenham Court Road

This buzzy restaurant in fashionable Fitzrovia deals in small-but-perfectly formed plates of vibrant food with a Spain-meets-Italy theme. The ground floor bar is the place for a glass of prosecco or cava with a plate of cured meats or cheese. For something more substantial, take a seat and graze, tapas-style, through a mix of the familiar and creative. Courgette flowers stuffed with goats' cheese and drizzled with honey will perk up the palate, and there are good technical skills on show. Lamb cutlets are perfectly cooked and served with fennel, caponata and saffron aïoli, or go for roast hake with ajo blanco, sautéed baby artichokes and olive crumble.

Chef Benjamin Tish, Dan Sherlock **Seats** 60 **Times** 12-3/5.30-11, Closed 25 Dec, 1 Jan **Prices** Prices not confirmed **Wines** 17 by glass **Parking** NCP Cleveland St, Goodge Place (meter) **Notes** Tapas menu £5-£10.50, Vegetarian available, Children welcome

LONDON W1 *continued*

Sartoria

PLAN 2 J1

Italian V

tel: 020 7534 7000 & 3195 9794 **20 Savile Row W1S 3PR**
email: sartoriareservations@danddlondon.com
dir: *Nearest station: Oxford Circus, Green Park, Piccadilly Circus*

Smart setting for modern Italian cooking

Taking its name from the Italian for tailor's shop, Sartoria is an impeccably well-dressed operation. Switched-on, polished service comes courtesy of staff dressed to look the part. The menu straddles classic and contemporary Italian cooking. Cappelletti ('little hat') pasta stuffed with goats' cheese bob around in a rich, piping hot chicken broth with spinach and parmesan, ahead of sea bream with white beans, semi-dried tomatoes and fresh mint. Meaty offerings might run to fillet of lamb with artichoke, pine nuts and wild plums, while the dolci department comes up with traditional Napoli cake for dessert.

Chef Francesco Mazzei **Seats** 100, Pr/dining room 50
Times 12-3/5.30-12, Closed 25-26 Dec, 1 Jan, Etr Mon, Sun (open for private parties only) **Prices** Prices not confirmed **Wines** 119 bottles over £30, 23 bottles under £30, 13 by glass **Parking** On street **Notes** Children welcome

Scott's Restaurant

PLAN 2 G1

Seafood V NOTABLE WINE LIST

tel: 020 7495 7309 **20 Mount St W1K 2HE**
dir: *Nearest station: Bond St, Green Park*

Bags of style and first-rate seafood

Glamour fills this place, from its charming service to the eye-catching mountain of seafood on ice in the swanky champagne bar. Apart from 'spot the celebrity', there are mosaics, huge mirrors, oak-panelled walls, leather seats, and modern British artworks to catch the eye, plus a menu brimming with top-notch seafood. Classics pepper the roster alongside more contemporary dishes; how about potted shrimps or tempura fried squid with peppy wasabi mayo and lime? Follow on with, Dover sole roasted cod with mixed beans, chorizo and padrón pepper? Desserts follow suit including wobbly mango pannacotta perfection with coconut and yuzu granita.

Chef Dave McCarthy **Seats** 140, Pr/dining room 40 **Times** 12-10.30, All-day dining, Closed 25-26 Dec, D 24 Dec **Prices** Starter £8.75-£16.25, Main £18.75-£30, Dessert £8.75-£10 **Wines** 195 bottles over £30, 3 bottles under £30, 25 by glass **Parking** On street **Notes** Sunday L, Children welcome

Sexy Fish

PLAN 2 H1

Asian Seafood NEW

tel: 020 3764 2000 **Berkeley Square House, Berkeley Square W1J 6BR**
email: press@caprice-holdings.co.uk
dir: *Nearest station: Green Park*

Glam and bling at Mayfairs star-struck new opening

This lavish new outfit reputedly cost a cool £15m, and the interiors are simply jaw dropping, from acres of onyx to aquatic-themed artworks by big names, and a water wall cascading behind the bar. The feel is glittering art deco with bags of bling and glam. The menu offers a lengthy sharing-plate roster of Asian-inspired fish and seafood. Think sashimi yellowtail, Californian maki rolls, prawn gyoza or lobster tempura to modern-day classics like miso-glazed Chilean sea bass from the robata. A few meaty options, like sticky pork ribs or doshville Wagyu beef steaks keep carnivores onside, while, Japanese whisky, cocktails and champagne add fizz.

Chef Ben Orpwood **Seats** Pr/dining room 48 **Times** 12-11, All-day dining **Prices** Main £5.75-£110, Dessert £2.75-£9.50 **Wines** 134 bottles over £30, 2 bottles under £30, 27 by glass

Sketch (The Gallery)

PLAN 2 J1

– see opposite

Sketch (Lecture Room & Library)

PLAN 2 J1

– see page 310

Sketch (The Parlour)

PLAN 2 J1

Modern European

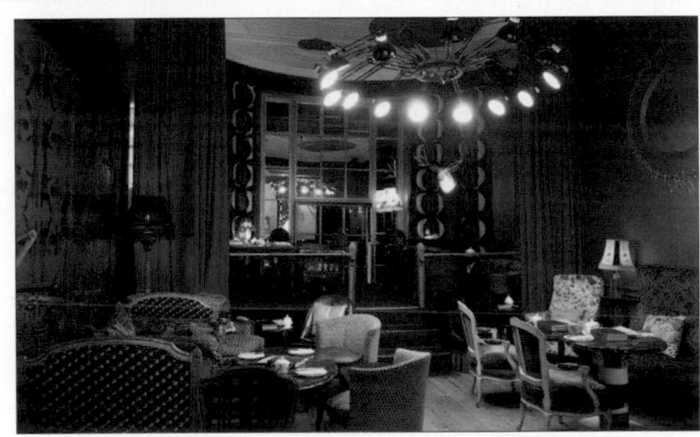

tel: 020 7659 4500 **9 Conduit St W1S 2XG**
email: info@sketch.london **web:** www.sketch.london
dir: *Nearest station: Oxford Circus, Green Park, Bond St*

Eccentric, arty setting for casual dining and drinking

French super-chef Pierre Gagnaire's Sketch spans various eating and drinking spaces (see also Lecture Room & Library and The Gallery), with The Parlour being the entry-level option. It's a funky, theatrical and glamorous boudoir-style take on an all-day café serving breakfast, afternoon tea and informal European comfort food (from noon) before morphing into a lively evening cocktail bar. Smoked haddock soufflé with curried leek fondue is an impressive opener, before larger plates – chicken fricassée with ceps and Stilton mash, or Galician beef and foie gras burger. As for cakes, ooh la la: try the chocolate and caramel gâteau for a paragon of top-drawer French pâtisserie.

Chef Pierre Gagnaire, Herve Deville **Seats** 50 **Times** noon-1am, All-day dining, Closed Xmas, 1 Jan **Prices** Starter £9.50-£25, Main £12-£24, Dessert £1.50-£5.50 **Wines** 30 bottles over £30, 2 bottles under £30, 17 by glass **Parking** NCP Soho **Notes** Sunday L £14, Vegetarian available, Children welcome

Sketch (The Gallery)

LONDON W1 **PLAN 2 J1**

Modern European NOTABLE WINE LIST

tel: 020 7659 4500 **9 Conduit St W1S 2XG**
email: info@sketch.uk.com **web:** www.sketch.london
dir: *Nearest station: Oxford Circus, Green Park, Bond St*

Virtuoso cooking in artist-designed restaurant

The brasserie option at the super-cool Sketch (where art meets culinary pizzazz) is like no other brasserie. Witty, playful cartoons (courtesy of celebrated Brit artist David Shrigley) fill the walls alongside a touch of designer glam from India Mahdavi. It's a striking open space, with a dusty pink hue, low-slung funky barrel chairs and banquettes and clever lighting. The crockery is designed by Shrigley too, so expect a few additional wry messages on the white ceramics to greet last mouthfuls. As always, service remains a highlight, with charming, informed staff positively brimming with enthusiasm like it was the opening night. To match the glossy, happening vibe, beautiful people and art, über-chef Pierre Gagnaire's food doesn't hold back on creativity either, with vibrancy, sheer skill and a sense of fun evident throughout. The man's a 'flavoursmith'; take an opener that teams crabmeat, tête de veau and squid with jellied cucumber, a golden creamy brandade gougère and green apple, all beautifully crafted, executed and presented. Likewise, a tranche of salt marsh Yorkshire lamb comes with a balanced oregano-scented zing and a touch of the Med with its accompaniment of black olive aubergine caviar, baby padrón peppers and mange-tout, matched by a knockout jus. Show-stopping desserts are an absolute must here; witness a light, almost fly-away bitter almond pannacotta, teamed with salted caramel parfait, poached pears and blue milk foam, while the wine list (and sommelier advice) prove a corker too. It's not cheap, but the menu does contain a few options that won't make a financial advisor blush.

Chef Pierre Gagnaire, Herve Deville **Seats** 150
Times 12-4.30/6.30pm-2am, Closed Xmas, New Year, BHs, L all week **Prices** Starter £13-£25, Main £20-£30, Dessert £9-£11
Wines 85 bottles over £30, 9 bottles under £30, 15 by glass
Parking On street, NCP **Notes** Afternoon tea £45, Vegetarian available, Children welcome

Sketch (Lecture Room & Library)

LONDON W1 PLAN 2 J1

WINNER OF THE AA WINE AWARD FOR ENGLAND AND OVERALL WINE AWARD WINNER 2016–17

Modern European V NOTABLE WINE LIST

tel: 020 7659 4500 **9 Conduit St W1S 2XG**
email: info@sketch.london **web:** www.sketch.london
dir: *Nearest station: Oxford Circus, Green Park, Bond St*

Multiform dishes of exhaustive complexity

Once inside this classical-looking Grade II listed building, it is evident that Sketch shakes up the world order with a riot of creativity and colour. The vision of Mourad Mazouz in partnership with French super-chef Pierre Gagnaire, Sketch has stayed at the vanguard of culinary ambition since it opened over a dozen years ago. The main culinary adventures take place in the first-floor Lecture Room & Library where you enter into a riot of vibrant pinks, orange and gold, huge vases and dangling chandeliers (one of which was recently bought by a punter). Tables are formally dressed and the plush armchairs make for a cosselting experience, further enhanced by the passionate service – professional, polished and pleasantly relaxed. The menu consists of gourmet rapide lunch, à la carte and tasting option. Whichever you choose, expect modern cuisine that surprises and exhilarates. The rapide is a good bet for mere mortals, for Sketch is pricey... seriously so. The complex layering of flavours and textures, multiple elements to each dish, and boundless innovation make dining here a memorable experience (the team will advise the order in which you should consume various parts of a course to maximise the intended impact). To start, a Lake District zander soufflé with white summer truffle is as light as can be while a stuffed courgette flowers and baby squid evokes the Med, and crayfish salad is the final part of an intoxicating equation. Sea bass stars in a main course with foie gras, the various parts resulting in a triumphant dish, while among sweet courses meringue tarta is built upwards from a base of Muscat jelly, with Australian black truffle and gold leaf adding a sense of luxury to this Pavlova-inspired finale. Everything from the amuse-bouche such as arancini with their own 'sketchup' (beetroot jam) and vodka martini jelly shows a sense of fun and an attention to detail.

Chef Pierre Gagnaire, Johannes Nuding **Seats** 50, Pr/dining room 24 **Times** 12-2.30/6.30-11, Closed 18-29 Aug, 23-30 Dec, 1 Jan, BHs, Sun-Mon, L Sat **Prices** Fixed L 2 course £35, Starter £42-£49, Main £49-£80, Dessert £17-£28 **Wines** 773 bottles over £30, 11 bottles under £30, 43 by glass **Parking** NCP Soho, Cavendish Sq
Notes Tasting & vegetarian tasting menu 6 course, Children 6 yrs+

LONDON W1 *continued*

Social Eating House

PLAN 2 J2

Modern British V NOTABLE WINE LIST

tel: 020 7993 3251 **58-59 Poland St W1F 7NS**
email: reservations@socialeatinghouse.com
dir: *Nearest station: Oxford Circus*

Vintage chic and classy cooking with flavours galore

Looking good with its exposed brick walls, whitewashed copper ceiling, weathered leather banquettes and restored furniture, this ground-floor restaurant also has a counter overlooking the kitchen where people can watch the chefs at work or enjoy a nine-course tasting menu. Chef-patron Paul Hood works closely with co-owner Jason Atherton (of Pollen Street Social) to create a range of highly individual, inventive dishes. Jars to share ('while drinking', says the menu) are a good way into the style, one being confit duck leg rillette with mango and coriander. Nifty ideas are tried and tested and these dishes burst with flavours, often in unusual combinations. Confit spring rabbit, for instance is served as a starter with a chicken and young leek terrine, celeriac, almond, truffle and spinach. A perfectly timed roasted Cornish hake with vadouvan spice comes with alliums and brassicas, while the chargrilled rump steak with béarnaise, chips and salad is simply perfection. The kitchen puts its back into puddings too: consider banana Tatin with a hazelnut and banana financier and fromage frais sorbet, or coconut panacotta with blood orange, black olive caramel and a blood orange sorbet

Chef Paul Hood **Seats** 75, Pr/dining room 8 **Times** 12-2.30/6-10.30, Closed 25-26 Dec, BHs, Sun **Prices** Fixed L 2 course £21, Tasting menu £62, Starter £12.50-£15.50, Main £18-£79, Dessert £8.50-£9.50 **Wines** 151 bottles over £30, 9 bottles under £30, 25 by glass **Parking** Q park, Poland St **Notes** Chef's experience £110, Children welcome

The Square

PLAN 2 H1

– see below

Sumosan Restaurant

PLAN 2 H1

Japanese Fusion

tel: 020 7495 5999 **26b Albermarle St, Mayfair W1S 4HY**
email: info@sumosan.com
dir: *Nearest station: Green Park*

Contemporary Japanese cooking in a glossy setting

Sumosan's up-to-date Japanese cooking is a magnet for crowds of international jet-setters and well-heeled denizens of Mayfair. The vibe is always on the boil and luxury abounds in immaculately-presented dishes built on top-class ingredients. To get things rolling, there's deep-fried spicy squid with red and green chillies, or excellent sushi – T&T (tuna and truffle) roll, or sea urchin wrapped in grilled toro ponzu – prepared by chefs at an open marble-topped counter, as well as sashimi dishes and teppan grilling. Fusion ideas bring forth such as lamb chops furikaki in a salty, nutty, crunchy coating of sesame seeds, almonds, and spices.

The Square

LONDON W1 **PLAN 2 H1**

Modern French V

tel: 020 7495 7100 **6-10 Bruton St, Mayfair W1J 6PU**
email: reception@squarerestaurant.com
dir: *Nearest station: Bond St, Green Park, Oxford Circus*

World-class cooking from a long-running Mayfair star

The Rosette award for this establishment has been suspended due to a change of chef. Reassessment will take place in due course under the new chef. In March 2016, an era ended and a new one began as former owner and driving culinary force Philip Howard announced the sale of the Square to Marlon Abela, a man who knows a thing or two about the restaurant business, being at the helm of a high-end transatlantic portfolio. We await developments under a reconstituted kitchen team, but major changes of direction can, thankfully, be ruled out. The past quarter-century has seen a formidable reputation built here for refined modern French-oriented cuisine that utilises a wealth of thoroughbred British produce, in a style that is undeniably glossy and sophisticated, but doesn't wear its technical resourcefulness on its sleeve. The old red phone box still marks the spot a few yards from Berkeley Square, and behind the half-frosted glass is a civilised room with space to manoeuvre between smartly clothed tables, large abstract artworks, and a service brigade that is a model of courteous vigilance. Dishes unashamedly mix high and humble, as for the roast foie gras that comes with Yorkshire rhubarb and walnut granola, and the sense of flavours firing on all cylinders is strong and true in another opener of sautéed langoustines with parmesan gnocchi in truffled potato emulsion. Delving deep into the French tradition, mains might produce roast guinea hen with a smoked sausage of its leg, creamed morels and white asparagus, or precision-timed Cornish cod and white sprouting broccoli in smoked anchovy and red wine. A plate of gariguette strawberries, sheep's yogurt and basil is a gently satisfying finisher.

Seats 75, Pr/dining room 18 **Times** 12-2.30/6.30-10.30, Closed 24-26 Dec, 1 Jan, L Sun, BHs **Prices** Prices not confirmed **Wines** 14 by glass **Parking** NCP on Grosvenor Hill **Notes** ALC 3 course £95, Tasting menu with matching wine £190, Children welcome

LONDON W1 *continued*

Tamarind

PLAN 4 H6

 Indian

tel: 020 7629 3561 **20 Queen St, Mayfair W1J 5PR**
email: manager@tamarindrestaurant.com
dir: *Nearest station: Green Park*

Classy, contemporary Indian cooking with a European touch

Tamarind was in the vanguard of design-led new-wave Indians when it opened in 1995. The expansive basement still works a glamorous contemporary chic with linen-clad tables tended by formally dressed, charming staff. The cooking takes its cue from the rich Mogul dishes of the Indian northwest, which makes ample use of the tandoor, but the kitchen likes to experiment with modern European ideas too. Start with grilled scallops topped with roasted peppers, move on to Awadhi murgh – chicken with melon seeds and yogurt – or lamb biryani, and make sure you give due attention to the kebab section. A six-course tasting menu features signature dishes from Tamarind's repertoire.

Chef Peter Joseph **Seats** 90 **Times** 12-2.45/5.30-11, Closed 25-26 Dec, 1 Jan **Prices** Fixed L 2 course fr £21.50, Fixed D 3 course £35-£72, Tasting menu fr £75 **Wines** 162 bottles over £30, 3 bottles under £30, 16 by glass **Parking** NCP **Notes** Pre-theatre D £35 5.30-6.45pm & 10-10.45pm, Sunday L fr £32, Vegetarian available, Children 5 yrs+

10 Greek Street

PLAN 3 A2

Modern British, European

tel: 020 7734 4677 **W1D 4DH**
email: info@10greekstreet.com
dir: *Nearest station: Charing Cross, Tottenham Court Rd*

Modern-day Soho bistro with flexible approach

A Soho bistro reinvented for the present age, the lively modern cooking at number 10 has plenty to say for itself. Fish dishes in two sizes, such as gurnard with Jerusalem artichokes and black pudding, or mackerel chermoula with pomegranate and pistachio, indicate a flexible approach. Starters might be octopus carpaccio with chicory, fennel and blood orange, and meat mains perhaps venison with sprout tops and a parsnip and juniper pancake, or Middlewhite pork with romanesco, pine-nuts and puréed raisins. Finish with affogato, or pecan pie with maple and stout ice cream. All-day tapas such as crumbed goats' cheese and honey or mussel fritters are great snacking options.

Chef Cameron Emirali **Seats** 30, Pr/dining room 12 **Times** 12-2.30/5.30-10.45, Closed Xmas, Sun **Prices** Starter £7-£10, Main £14-£22, Dessert £5-£8 **Wines** 15 bottles over £30, 16 bottles under £30, 20 by glass **Parking** China Town, NCP Upper St Martins Lane **Notes** Vegetarian available, Children welcome

Ten Room Restaurant

PLAN 2 J1

Modern European NEW

tel: 020 7406 3333 **Hotel Café Royal, 68 Regent St W1B 4DY**
email: restaurants@hotelcaferoyal.com **web:** www.hotelcaferoyal.com
dir: *Nearest station: Piccadilly Circus*

Modern cooking in the gilt-edged Café Royal

This swanky all-day dining room has a weight of expectations to live up to with its five-star location in the historic Café Royal, but fear not, the striking contemporary setting is unlikely to disappoint. Grounded in the French classics, the menu spreads its wings into modern European territory, opening the show with a lush terrine of confit duck and foie gras wrapped in smoked duck ham, followed by seared scallops with roasted artichoke and spiced mussels. Don't skip pudding, especially when it's mandarin delice with pistachio and chocolate. The Ten Room accommodates all comers, from breakfast through lunch to cream tea, pre- and post-theatre menus and dinner.

Chef Armand Sablon **Seats** 65 **Times** 12-2.30/5.30-10.30 **Prices** Fixed L 2 course fr £28, Fixed D 3 course fr £35, Starter £8-£95, Main £25-£45, Dessert £8-£14 **Wines** 70 bottles over £30, 11 bottles under £30, 21 by glass **Parking** NCP **Notes** Vegetarian available, Children welcome

Texture Restaurant

PLAN 2 F2

– see opposite

Trishna

PLAN 2 G3

Indian V

tel: 020 7935 5624 **15-17 Blandford St W1U 3DG**
email: info@trishnalondon.com
dir: *Nearest station: Bond St, Baker St*

The distinctive flavours of southwest India brought to Marylebone

Trishna takes a minimalist decorative line in two dining rooms done out with oak floors and tables, painted brickwork, mirrored walls, and hues of cream and duck-egg blue. The kitchen celebrates the coastal cuisine of southwest India in fresh, flavour-packed contemporary dishes, with equal attention to meat and vegetarian ideas. Baby squid with onions, coconut and lemongrass makes a cracking starter, followed by cod fillet with mustard oil and potatoes, or crab distinctively flavoured with chilli and garlic. Carnivores could go for Keralan-style partridge, then guinea fowl biriyani with basmati rice. Desserts end creatively with bread-and-butter pudding flavoured with fennel, poppy seeds and black pepper.

Chef Karam Sethi, Rohit Ghai **Seats** 65, Pr/dining room 12 **Times** 12-2.30/6-10.30, Closed 24-27 Dec, 1-3 Jan **Prices** Fixed L 2 course £20-£36, Fixed D 3 course £28-£52, Tasting menu £60-£100, Starter £8.50-£12, Main £10-£24, Dessert £7.50-£9 **Wines** 150 bottles over £30, 15 bottles under £30, 14 by glass **Parking** On street, NCP **Notes** L bites 2-5 course £18.50-£33.50, Tasting menu 5/7 course, Sunday L £20-£70, Children welcome

Umu

PLAN 2 H1

– see page 314

Vasco & Piero's Pavilion Restaurant

PLAN 2 J2

Modern Italian

tel: 020 7437 8774 **15 Poland St W1F 8QE**
email: eat@vascosfood.com
dir: *Nearest station: Oxford Circus*

Seasonal Umbrian cooking in hospitable Soho favourite

This stalwart of the Soho dining scene has been plying its trade since 1989. Warm colours and subtle lighting add to the authentic Mediterranean ambience. The handwritten menu changes after each serving, so you can take seasonality for granted. Rustic, home-style cooking delivers clear flavours in a starter of spaghettini with calamari, garlic and black ink sauce, followed by a fillet of sea bass served with a herb dressing, steamed vegetables and new potatoes. Among meatier fare, there might be roast shoulder of pork with cannellini beans and crispy kale, or calves' liver and onions with sautéed cabbage, and to finish, there's a textbook tiramisù.

Chef Vasco Matteucci **Seats** 50, Pr/dining room 36 **Times** 12-3/5.30-10, Closed BHs, Sun, L Sat **Prices** Fixed L 2 course £17.50, Fixed D 2 course £17.50, Starter £5-£11.75, Main £16.50-£26.50, Dessert £5-£8 **Wines** 35 bottles over £30, 19 bottles under £30, 12 by glass **Parking** NCP car park opposite **Notes** Tasting menu on request, Vegetarian available, Children 5 yrs+

Veeraswamy Restaurant

PLAN 2 J1

 Indian

tel: 020 7734 1401 **Mezzanine Floor, Victory House, 99 Regent St W1B 4RS**
email: info@realindianfood.com
dir: *Nearest station: Piccadilly Circus*

Stylish sub-continental cooking in Britain's oldest Indian restaurant

This lavishly elegant first-floor venue has served London stylishly since 1926, and the cooking pays homage to the regional classics of the sub-continent and keeps step with trendy new-wave ideas influenced by street snacks. Vivid spicing is a hallmark of time-honoured chicken tikka, or try a contemporary idea such as crab cakes vibrant with ginger, lime and chilli. Kashmiri rogan josh is a tried-and-true classic, the soft shank meat enhanced with crimson cockscomb flowers and saffron, or go for a luxuriant Malabar lobster curry with coconut and green mango. To finish, coconut and lemongrass put an exotic spin on pannacotta, or there's an exemplary gulab jamun.

Veeraswamy Restaurant

Chef Uday Salunkhe **Seats** 114, Pr/dining room 24
Times 12-2.30/5.30-11.30, Closed D 25 Dec **Prices** Fixed L 2 course fr £27.50, Starter £7.50-£18, Main £21-£41, Dessert £7-£9.50 **Wines** 18 by glass **Parking** On street after 8pm/wknds, NCP **Notes** Business L 2 course, ALC D only, Pre-theatre 2/3 course, Sunday L £30, Vegetarian available, Children 3+ yrs+

See advert on page 315

Texture Restaurant

LONDON W1 **PLAN 2 F2**

Modern European V
tel: 020 7224 0028 **4 Bryanston St W1H 7BY**
email: info@texture-restaurant.co.uk **web:** www.texture-restaurant.co.uk
dir: *Nearest station: Marble Arch, Bond St*

Creative and dynamic cooking with Icelandic soul

Agnar Sverrisson has been wowing diners with his pin-sharp Scandi-accented modern European cooking for a decade and the venue, next to a smart Georgian hotel just off Oxford Street, indeed has a breezy Scandinavian feel. Whether you go for the à la carte or tasting menus (there are versions available lunch and dinner, and dedicated fish and vegetarian options), or the cracking value of the set lunch menu, expect sharply executed cooking and Sverrisson's trademark lightness of touch. This is down to his avoidance of cream or butter among the savoury courses, and minimal use of sugar in the sweet stuff, plus creativity and talent at balancing flavours and, yes, textures. Nordic influences are clearly at work, notably in the shape of Icelandic cod, lamb and yogurt-like skyr, but the modern European side of things is to the fore, as typified in a starter of Norwegian king crab and black Périgord truffles matched with celeriac and walnuts, or a dish of chargrilled Anjou pigeon with the deftly-judged accompanying flavours of sweetcorn, shallot, bacon popcorn and red wine essence. High-flying technical skill ensures flavours hit the mark in ideas such as Cornish turbot and shellfish with shaved and puréed fennel. For dessert, white chocolate mousse and ice cream appears in an inventive dish with dill and cucumber. This superlative food is backed by a splendid wine list that clearly has a love affair with Burgundies and Rieslings, with expert advice on hand.

Chef Agnar Sverrisson **Seats** 52, Pr/dining room 16
Times 12-2.30/6-10.30, Closed 2 wks Xmas, 2 wks Aug, 1 wk Etr, Sun-Mon, L Tue
Prices Fixed L 3 course £36.90, Tasting menu fr £85, Starter £15.90-£40, Main £29.90-£41.50, Dessert £13.50 **Wines** 600 bottles over £30, 6 bottles under £30, 30 by glass **Parking** NCP Bryanston St **Notes** Scandinavian fish tasting menu, Children welcome

Umu

LONDON W1 **PLAN 2 H1**

Japanese NOTABLE WINE LIST

tel: 020 7499 8881 **14-16 Bruton Place W1J 6LX**
email: reception@umurestaurant.com
web: www.umurestaurant.com
dir: *Nearest station: Green Park, Bond St*

Kaiseki dining in low-lit high style

The exterior is anonymous and discreet, with entry gained by pressing the buzzer of the sliding door. Once inside, a greeting is called out in the best tradition of Japanese hospitality, the wood-toned interiors imitating an upmarket Kyoto kaiseki place, with multi-ethnic waiting staff swishing slickly about the dimly-lit space. Chef Yoshinori Ishii has a pedigree at the top end of this style of modern Japanese cooking and no stone is left unturned in the search for super-fresh materials – the ingredients come from all over the world, but Britain's prime produce has a good showing. Naturally, a smart Mayfair address such as Umu is unlikely to lack for Japanese business custom, so the food is not cheap, but it is seriously good. Bento-box lunches remove the need to agonise over the extensive main menu, and the kaiseki set menu is a good way to go if you're on unfamiliar territory, as long as the whole table is game for it. Its many courses include the likes of mukouzuke (saké-steamed Normandy red clam, scallops, Japanese cucumber, plum sake sauce and a sea water shot) and yakimono (chargrilled rabbit loin and a croquette of diced leg meat supported by morel purée and wasabi watercress oroshi). The carte is a cornucopia of sea-fresh fish and seafood and gold-standard meats, perhaps smoked Irish wild eel with plum shiso sauce, or chargrilled Wagyu beef with vegetables and sesame ponzu sauce. At the end, there may be a Japanese take on tiramisù incorporating matcha green tea, sparkling saké and raspberry. There are no fewer than 160 sakés to choose from or, if none of those suit your taste, 800 or so pedigree wines.

Chef Yoshinori Ishii **Seats** 64, Pr/dining room 10
Times 12-2.30/6-11, Closed Xmas, New Year, BHs, Sun, L Sat
Prices Starter £21-£75, Main £28-£95, Dessert £8-£20 **Wines** 860 bottles over £30, 25 by glass **Parking** On street, NCP Hanover Hill
Notes Kaiseki menu £155, Vegetarian available, Children welcome

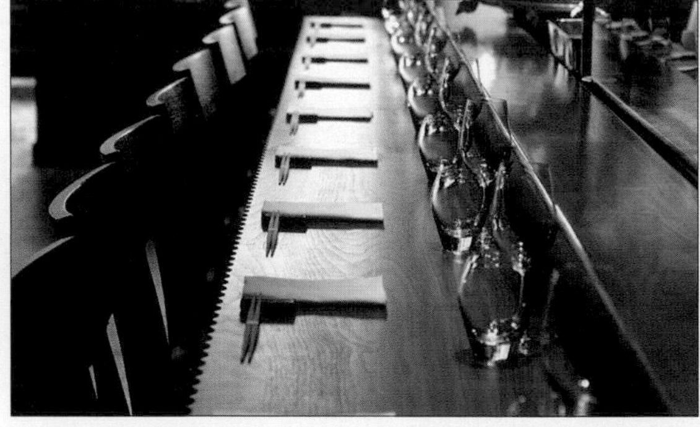

LONDON W1 *continued*

Villandry Great Portland Street PLAN 2 H3

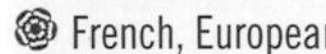 French, European

tel: 020 7631 3131 **170 Great Portland St W1W 5QB**
email: greatportlandstreet@villandry.com
dir: *Nearest station: Great Portland St, Oxford Circus*

Mediterranean all-dayer in media-land

Embracing the all-day-dining concept with aplomb, the Great Portland Street Villandry offers something for everyone. Amble through to the casual café/bar with its fabulously eye-catching lampshades, or take a seat in the more formal restaurant. It's bright and airy throughout and the food reflects this with a light Mediterranean vibe and reliance on seasonal ingredients. Tender chilli squid might give way to king scallops in a flavourful lobster bisque with chorizo. Raspberry meringue kisses end the meal on a high. If you don't have time for the full three courses, stay for a hot sandwich, stone-baked pizza or a meze platter.

Wild Honey PLAN 2 H1

Modern European

tel: 020 7758 9160 **12 Saint George St W1S 2FB**
email: info@wildhoneyrestaurant.co.uk
dir: *Nearest station: Oxford Circus, Bond St*

Refined and relaxed brasserie cooking in Mayfair

The sister restaurant to Soho's Arbutus may be opposite the magnificent St George's Church in the heart of Mayfair, but it is refreshingly free from pretension or stuffiness. Run by experienced practitioners Anthony Demetre and Will Smith, this French-style, wood-panelled bistrot deluxe delivers the same brand of refined modern brasserie cooking set against an elegant backdrop of crimson banquettes and mustard-yellow chairs. For even more informal Gallic dining, grab a stool at the onyx-topped front bar, perhaps with a plate of hand-chopped Scottish beef tartare and oyster mayo, and a 250ml carafe of wine. Luxury ingredients work happily alongside humbler cuts of meat in the kitchen, which is grounded in classic technique but not afraid to show a more contemporary hand. Devon crab is accompanied by apple, celeriac and sea herbs, while crisp pig's head turns up with silky potato purée and pickled radish. At main course, a classic Marseille-influenced bouillabaisse with grilled fish and all the proper accompaniments rubs shoulders with venison teamed with crushed Delica pumpkin and Armagnac sauce. For something sweet, try poached pear, chocolate sorbet, coffee cream and warm madeleine cake or choose from a selection of carefully considered British and French artisanal cheeses.

Chef Anthony Demetre **Seats** 65 **Times** 12-2.30/6-10.30, Closed 25-26 Dec, 1 Jan, Sun **Prices** Fixed D 3 course £35 **Wines** 45 bottles over £30, 6 bottles under £30, 50 by glass **Parking** On street **Notes** Early supper menu 3 course £35, Tasting menu on request, Vegetarian available, Children welcome

The Wolseley PLAN 4 J6

Traditional European V

tel: 020 7499 6996 **160 Piccadilly W1J 9EB**
email: reservations@thewolseley.com
dir: *Nearest station: Green Park*

Bustling landmark brasserie stylishly serving all day

The Wolseley fizzes with energy. Staff rush about, customers chatter, and that's the case all day long, from breakfast, brunch, lunch and afternoon tea, through to evening meals. Start with a timeless brasserie classic such as avocado vinaigrette, or a coarse terrine of venison and pigeon (served with a beetroot chutney and toast), followed by lemon sole St Germain with tartare sauce, a simple steak, or schnitzel. Desserts carry on in the same classic vein with baked vanilla cheesecake and banana split. Breakfast is anything from full English to grilled kipper with mustard butter, and the all-day concept fits the bill whether you're after savoury satisfaction or a sweet treat.

Chef Maarten Geschwindt **Seats** 150, Pr/dining room 12 **Times** 7am-mdnt, All-day dining **Prices** Starter £7.50-£24.75, Main £12.75-£38, Dessert £4.75-£8 **Wines** 50 bottles over £30, 4 bottles under £30, 38 by glass **Parking** NCP Arlington St **Notes** Afternoon tea, Sunday L, Children welcome

Yauatcha PLAN 2 J2

Modern Chinese

tel: 020 7494 8888 **15 Broadwick St W1F 0DL**
email: reservations@yauatcha.com
dir: *Nearest station: Tottenham Court Rd, Piccadilly, Oxford Circus*

New-wave Chinese cooking in a cool Soho address

A colourful array of pâtisserie opens the show in Yauatcha's ground-floor 'tea house', but in the basement dining room things are lively and loud. The menu impresses with its exciting blend of traditional Cantonese favourites and more intriguing contemporary compositions. Venison puffs are Wellington-style flaky pastry dim sum with notes of hoi sin, chilli and sesame, while traditionalists might stick with prawn and chicken siu mai dumplings. Larger plates also deliver exhilarating flavours, as seen in a dish of stir-fried scallops with lotus root or hakka-style pork belly with cloud ear mushrooms. Not normally a high point of the oriental repertoire, the creative fusion-style desserts here are a real treat.

Zoilo PLAN 2 G2

Argentine

tel: 020 7486 9699 **9 Duke St W1U 3EG**
email: info@zoilo.co.uk
dir: *Nearest station: Bond St*

Authentic flavours of Argentina and an easy-going atmosphere

South American food is all the rage these days, and the full-on version at Zoilo is inspired by Argentina's regions, from Patagonia to Mendoza. Covering two floors on classy Duke Street, it features exposed brick walls and darkwood tables, plus basement counter seats in front of the open kitchen. Sharing is the name of the game, encompassing satisfying items such as lamb empanada stuffed with carrot, garlic and mint, or crab on toast with humita and pickled turnips. Grilled sweetbreads for main come with sweet peanuts in blood orange and criolla sauce. To finish, try dulce de leche crème brûlée with banana ice cream.

Chef Diego Jacquet **Seats** 48, Pr/dining room 10
Times 12-2.30/5.30-10, Closed Xmas, BHs, Sun **Prices** Fixed L 2 course £9.95, Tasting menu £39.95-£42.95, Main £2.95-£27.95, Dessert £6.95-£8.45 **Wines** 47 bottles over £30, 8 bottles under £30, 27 by glass **Parking** On street
Notes Vegetarian available, Children welcome

LONDON W2

Angelus Restaurant
PLAN 2 D1

Modern French NOTABLE WINE LIST

tel: 020 7402 0083 **4 Bathurst St W2 2SD**
email: info@angelusrestaurant.co.uk
dir: *Nearest station: Lancaster Gate, Paddington Station*

Classy French brasserie with vibrant cooking

A former pub which was transformed into a classy Parisian-style brasserie by renowned sommelier, Thierry Tomasin, Angelus Restaurant continues to impress with its luxe, art nouveau-inspired finish and ambitious, modern French cooking. It looks smart with its panelling and red leather banquettes, and the wine list offers some seriously good drinking, so this is a place worth knowing about. The kitchen turns out ambitious stuff, rooted in French tradition with modern ideas on show – wild rabbit and smoked gammon terrine, say, with dehydrated trompette mushrooms. Follow up with a deconstructed lamb navarin, or poached turbot in a shellfish and sea vegetable nage.

Chef Pierre Needham **Seats** 40, Pr/dining room 22 **Times** 10am-11pm, All-day dining, Closed 24-25 Dec **Prices** Fixed L 2 course £22, Starter £9-£16, Main £19-£25, Dessert £9-£22 **Wines** 600 bottles over £30, 20 bottles under £30, 4 by glass **Parking** On street **Notes** All day brunch menu £3.50-£60, Sunday L £22-£27, Vegetarian available, Children welcome

Island Grill & Bar
PLAN 2 D1

Modern European

tel: 020 7551 6070 & 7551 6000 **Lancaster London, Lancaster Ter W2 2TY**
email: eat@islandrestaurant.co.uk **web:** www.islandrestaurant.co.uk
dir: *Nearest station: Lancaster Gate*

Polished brasserie-style cooking with Hyde Park views

Island Grill & Bar is on the ground floor of the hotel with views over the busy road to Hyde Park opposite. Settle on something from the grill – perhaps a steak with béarnaise or pork cutlets – or go for fillet of salmon in a saffron-infused consommé with spinach, potato and brown shrimps, or roast spring chicken, moist and tasty, in a rich jus with cavolo nero and classic Sarladaise potatoes. Starters might be dressed crab and avocado with a salad of cucumber and mint or Chinese-style pork belly with noodles and melon and cucumber salad with chilli, lime and coriander. For pudding, who could resist honeycomb pannacotta?

Chef Adam Woolven **Seats** 68 **Times** 7.30am-10.30pm, All-day dining **Prices** Fixed L 2 course fr £15.50, Fixed D 3 course fr £35, Starter £6-£8, Main £14-£24, Dessert £5-£7 **Wines** 10 bottles over £30, 12 bottles under £30, 20 by glass **Parking** Hotel or on street **Notes** Fixed D served until 7pm, Sunday L, Vegetarian available, Children welcome

Kurobuta
PLAN 2 E2

Japanese

tel: 020 7920 6444 **17-20 Kendal St, Marble Arch W2 2AW**
email: info@kurobuta-london.com
dir: *Nearest station: Marble Arch, Edgeware Rd*

On-trend Japanese fusion cooking

With its plain white walls and wooden benches, the stripped-down look and hip musical policy makes Kurobuta a popular, buzzy place. Inspired by Japan's izakaya taverns, the man at the reins of this Japanese fusion operation is Scott Hallsworth, former head chef at Nobu. This impressive culinary CV shows in a lively opener of baby shrimp tempura with kimchee mayo and spicy shiso dressing. Clear, well-paired flavours continue in mains of miso grilled baby chicken with spicy lemon garlic sauce and inventive desserts include a warm chocolate mousse with cherry sorbet, marinated cherries and pistachio macaroon.

Chef Scott Hallsworth **Seats** 100 **Times** 12-10.30pm, All-day dining **Prices** Prices not confirmed **Wines** 17 bottles over £30, 4 bottles under £30, 8 by glass **Parking** On street, NCP nearby **Notes** Average spend per head £40-£50, Brunch £35, Sunday L, Vegetarian available, Children welcome

Nipa
PLAN 2 D1

Traditional Thai

tel: 020 7551 6039 **Lancaster London Hotel, Lancaster Ter W2 2TY**
email: nipa@lancasterlondon.com
dir: *Nearest station: Lancaster Gate*

Precise Thai cooking in an authentic setting overlooking Hyde Park

There's a cracking view over Hyde Park from this refined Thai restaurant with its wood panels and tables topped with Thai orchids. Begin with a classic appetiser (chargrilled chicken with peanut sauce and cucumber relish), or go for a selection, and move on to a soup such as a sterling version of tom yum koong, fired up with chilli, lemongrass and lime. Among main courses, crisp-fried salmon with minced prawn shows excellent balance of flavours, or go for a spicy green coconut curry filled with chicken and Thai aubergines. Set menus prevent the need to make difficult decisions, and, for dessert, mango sticky rice with coconut cream is spot on.

Chef Sanguan Parr **Seats** 55 **Times** 5-10.30, Closed L all week **Prices** Fixed D 3 course £35-£42, Tasting menu £53-£72, Starter £11-£12, Main £16-£22, Dessert fr £9 **Wines** 21 bottles over £30, 10 bottles under £30, 13 by glass **Parking** Paddington **Notes** Khantok menu 5-7pm £25, Vegetarian available, Children welcome

Salt and Honey
PLAN 2 D1

Modern European NEW

tel: 020 7706 7900 **28 Sussex Place W2 2TH**
email: bookings@saltandhoneybistro.com
dir: *Nearest station: Paddington, Lancaster Gate*

Seasonal dining in a relaxed bistro setting

A neighbourhood bistro in the hinterland between Paddington and Hyde Park, Salt and Honey indicates little allegiance to any cuisine in particular, preferring to concentrate on delivering good quality seasonal UK produce, plus some stuff shipped over from mainland Europe, in appealing seasonal combinations. If you're looking for a box, it probably shows more Italian influence than anything else. In a mellow, simply decorated room with tree-themed paintings and a few retro touches, expect salmon cured in lemongrass and Manuka honey to precede sea bream with a mash enriched with truffle, plus clams and parsley pesto. Finish with a set lemon crème with granola praline and meringue.

Chef Scott Dennis **Seats** 45, Pr/dining room 10 **Times** 12-3/5.30-10, Closed Mon **Prices** Starter £5.95-£9.50, Main £12.95-£23.95, Dessert £4.50-£9 **Wines** 10 bottles over £30, 15 bottles under £30, 20 by glass **Parking** On street **Notes** Wknd brunch, Sunday L £5.95-£23.95, Vegetarian available, Children welcome

LONDON W4

Hedone

PLAN 1 D3

Modern European

tel: 020 8747 0377 **301-303 Chiswick High Rd W4 4HH**
email: reservations@hedonerestaurant.com
dir: *Nearest station: Chiswick Park, Gunnnersbury*

Chiswick temple to superb produce cooked with flair

Central London does not hold all the aces when it comes to dining in the capital, for Chiswick High Road in little old W4 is home to one of the country's most idiosyncratic and thrilling restaurants. This is the realm of Mikael Jonsson, a Swede whose passion for ingredients is matched only by his insatiably curious mind. The space has plenty of fashionable Scandinavian naturalness and neutrality, with exposed brick walls, striking artworks, blond wood, natty designer chairs, and, yes, an open-to-view kitchen. Choose one of the tasting menus and go with the flow, including the wine flight so that your drinks suit the food. Such is the creativity in the kitchen that dishes change during service, so you might not be eating exactly the same things as the person on the next table. Things start with the exceptional sourdough bread and move onto an array of beautiful looking plates that pack a punch. Cornish rock oysters are matched with a delicate apple foam, a hand-dived scallop is cooked in its own juices and matched with dried seaweed powder. Roasted breast and leg of squab comes with smoked potatoes, blackcurrant purée, rocket and lemongrass purée and a foie gras sauce. Among sweet courses, fresh English blueberries arrive with blueberry syrup, topped with a tiny crisp meringue and lemon and rosemary sorbet.

Chef Mikael Jonsson **Seats** Pr/dining room 16
Times 12-2.30/6.30-9.30, Closed Sun-Mon, L Tue-Thu **Prices** Tasting menu fr £85 **Notes** Fixed L £45

Restaurant Michael Nadra

PLAN 1 D3

Modern European

tel: 020 8742 0766 **6/8 Elliott Rd, Chiswick W4 1PE**
email: chiswick@restaurant-michaelnadra.co.uk
dir: *Nearest station: Turnham Green*

Classy modern cooking in Chiswick

A stalwart of the Chiswick dining scene, this classy restaurant's Pan-European fixed-price repertoire offers bags of interest. Melting sautéed foie gras is combined with the balanced sharpness of poached Yorkshire rhubarb, nasturtium leaves and a warm mini brioche loaf to accompany, showing a light modern touch and looking pretty on the plate. Witness also classy mains, perhaps with a Mediterranean lilt like top-drawer slow-roasted Ibérico presa teamed with wonderfully tender suckling pig belly, crisp crackling, braised chicory, fennel salad and pickled grapes that deliver sweet explosions on the palate. Desserts, like pineapple carpaccio with lime, chilli, ginger crumble and coconut ice cream, hold up form too.

Chef Michael Nadra **Seats** 55 **Times** 12-2.30/6-10, Closed Xmas, 1 Jan, D Sun **Prices** Fixed L 2 course £22-£32, Fixed D 3 course £38-£48, Tasting menu £48-£59 **Wines** 130 bottles over £30, 15 bottles under £30, 16 by glass **Parking** On street **Notes** Tasting menu 6 course, Sunday L £22-£29, Vegetarian available, Children welcome

La Trompette

PLAN 1 D3

 Modern European NOTABLE WINE LIST

tel: 020 8747 1836 **5-7 Devonshire Rd, Chiswick W4 2EU**
email: reception@latrompette.co.uk
dir: *Nearest station: Turnham Green*

Relaxing, uptempo, Chiswick favourite for modern cooking

La Trompette rocks...this neighbourhood restaurant par excellence has been playing to packed houses since 2001. The mood is relaxed, with a broad glass frontage opening onto a narrow street-side terrace, while inside white linen and a beige colour palette meet bright abstract artworks. Spot-on service is a high point, likewise a cracking wine list, while the switched-on kitchen's light, creative and pretty modern European output comes underpinned by classical foundations. Take sea-fresh roast cod served with buttermilk barley, fat Fowey mussels, cider and grilled cabbage, while a light crème fraîche tarte comes dressed-up with Medjool date and clementine coulis.

Chef Rob Weston **Seats** 88, Pr/dining room 16
Times 12-2.30/6.30-10.30, Closed 24-26 Dec, 1 Jan **Prices** Fixed L 2 course £24.50-£27.50, Fixed D 3 course £49.50, Tasting menu £75 **Wines** 500 bottles over £30, 25 bottles under £30, 19 by glass **Parking** On street **Notes** Sunday L £32.50, Vegetarian available, Children L only

Le Vacherin

PLAN 1 D3

 French

tel: 020 8742 2121 **76-77 South Pde W4 5LF**
email: info@levacherin.com
dir: *Nearest station: Chiswick Park*

French classics in smart, relaxed neighbourhood bistro

This neighbourhood bistro certainly conjures the mood and looks of cross-Channel dining, so the classic French cooking comes as no surprise. You might find beignets of frogs' legs with sauce gribiche alongside grilled red mullet paired with peas, broad beans and saffron aïoli, while a main-course roast rump of Hereford beef is partnered by bone marrow, watercress, pommes allumettes and bordelaise sauce. If you are after a real hit of rustic authenticity, how about an assiette of duck, comprising magret, leg, gizzards and foie gras with Puy lentils? For dessert, try pear and almond tart with raspberry ripple ice cream. The prix-fixe menu is particularly good value in any language.

Chef Malcolm John **Seats** 72, Pr/dining room 36 **Times** 12-2.30/6-11, Closed BHs, L Mon **Prices** Fixed L 2 course £19.50-£28, Fixed D 3 course £24.50-£28, Starter £8.50-£15, Main £12.50-£29, Dessert £6.50-£9 **Wines** 200 bottles over £30, 15 bottles under £30, 12 by glass **Parking** On street (meter) **Notes** Fixed price menu until 7pm, Steak & wine £9.95 before 8pm, Sunday L £19.50-£28, Vegetarian available, Children welcome

LONDON W5

Charlotte's Place
PLAN 1 C3

Modern European, British

tel: 020 8567 7541 **16 St Matthews Rd, Ealing Common W5 3JT**
email: restaurant@charlottes.co.uk
dir: *Nearest station: Ealing Common, Ealing Broadway*

Splendid seasonal food in a neighbourhood gem

This sparkling neighbourhood bistro has impeccable ethical credentials, sourcing its materials from like minded local suppliers and working in tune with the seasons to ensure there's always something to catch the interest on its breezy modern menus. The setting suits the food: an unpretentious yet stylish blend of black leather seats at unclothed darkwood tables on well-trodden wooden floors. Starter might be a roasted butternut squash with truffle curd and a cep mushroom pickle, while the main course offers slow-cooked lamb rump with salsify and roast garlic and anchovy. Delicious dessert options include a plum and almond tart with mulled wine ice cream.

Chef Lee Cadden **Seats** 54, Pr/dining room 30 **Times** 12-3/6-9.30, Closed 26 Dec, 1 Jan, D 25 Dec **Prices** Prices not confirmed **Wines** 133 bottles over £30, 29 bottles under £30, 11 by glass **Parking** On street **Notes** Early D 6-7pm 3 course with aperitif £30, Vegetarian available, Children welcome

The Grove
PLAN 1 C3

Classic British, French

tel: 020 8567 2439 **The Green, Ealing W5 5QX**
email: info@thegrovew5.co.uk **web:** www.thegrovew5.co.uk
dir: *Nearest station: Ealing Broadway*

European brasserie dishes opposite the Ealing film studios

A brick-built block of an old pub, The Grove is permanently abubble with convivial atmosphere, its bustling kitchen on view from the dining room. European brasserie cooking done with care and flair includes the likes of fried lamb's sweetbreads with minted pea purée and wild garlic, Spanish charcuterie and manchego boards with olives and home-baked bread, and robust main dishes such as roasted hake on crushed new potatoes in caper beurre noisette. Sticklers for tradition will welcome garlicky pork sausages with mash in thyme gravy, beer-battered haddock and mushy peas, or the 28-day aged Angus rib-eye with green peppercorn sauce. Finish with a properly bracing lemon tart and raspberry sorbet.

Chef Marek Ciskal **Seats** 80 **Times** 12-4/6-10 **Prices** Starter £5.50-£8.50, Main £12.50-£19.50, Dessert £5-£6.50 **Wines** 13 bottles over £30, 32 bottles under £30, 19 by glass **Parking** On street, shopping centre multi-story **Notes** Questors pre/post-theatre & Mon supper 20% food discount, Sunday L £13.50-£19, Vegetarian available, Children welcome

LONDON W6

L'Amorosa
PLAN 1 D3

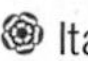 Italian

tel: 020 8563 0300 **278 King St, Ravenscourt Park W6 0SP**
email: bookings@lamorosa.co.uk
dir: *Nearest station: Ravenscourt Park*

Local Italian with plenty to tempt

This neighbourhood restaurant on Hammersmith's main drag has a man with pedigree at the stoves in the shape of ex-Zafferano head chef Andy Needham. The setting is smart-casual – darkwood floors, classy polished wood tables, buttoned brown leather banquettes and cream-painted walls hung with modern art. A starter plate of pumpkin ravioli delivers pitch-perfect pasta with rich gorgonzola sauce and crispy deep-fried sage, followed by sea-fresh roast cod with chickpeas, samphire and salsa verde, while meaty mains could see a classic osso buco braised veal shin partnered by tangy gremolata and saffron risotto. Pear and almond tart with mascarpone cream or timeless tiramisù make a fine finale.

Chef Andy Needham **Seats** 40 **Times** 12-2.30/6-10, Closed Xmas 1 wk, BHs, Sun-Mon **Prices** Fixed L 2 course £16.50, Fixed D 3 course £19-£30, Starter £7-£8, Main £12-£19, Dessert £6-£9 **Parking** Free parking after 5pm & wknds **Notes** Vegetarian available, Children welcome

Anglesea Arms
PLAN 1 D3

Modern British

tel: 020 8749 1291 **35 Wingate Rd, Ravenscourt Park W6 0UR**
dir: *Nearest station: Ravenscourt Park, Goldhawk Rd, Hammersmith*

Superior cooking in a pioneering gastropub

The Anglesea Arms was one of the pioneering London gastropubs, and after a relaunch in June 2014, it's as popular today as it ever has been. A seared mackerel fillet with a cod and truffle fritter and beetroot and watercress salad with lemon dressing is a perfect summery opener, followed by the porcine pleasure of Gloucestershire Old Spots pork belly, pointed up inventively with roast peach, spinach and lentils; if you're in the mood for fish, there might be hake with girolle mushrooms, samphire, radishes and broad beans. Finish with almond milk pannacotta with cherry sorbet and compôte, or warm chocolate and ale cake with ale caramel sauce and cereal milk ice cream.

Chef Philip Harrison **Seats** 37 **Times** 12.30-3/6-10, Closed 24-26 Dec, L Mon-Thu (excl BH) **Prices** Starter £6-£9, Main £14.50-£18, Dessert £6-£7 **Wines** 23 bottles over £30, 25 bottles under £30, 16 by glass **Parking** On street, pay & display (free at wknds) **Notes** Sunday L, Vegetarian available, Children welcome

Novotel London West
PLAN 1 D3

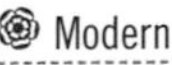 Modern British

tel: 020 8741 1555 **1 Shortlands W6 8DR**
email: H0737@accor.com **web:** www.novotellondonwest.co.uk
dir: *Nearest station: Hammersmith*

Modern comfort food in a contemporary hotel

This hotel is a 24/7 kind of place, with the Artisan Grill restaurant being the hub of the culinary output. The modern space with a glass façade offers views of the hotel's comings and goings, and the menu does its best to cover most bases. The eponymous grill turns out steaks in familiar formats, and there's also all the comfort of traditional steak and kidney pie in a rich gravy with colcannon, or mussels marinière with chips. Desserts continue to raise the comfort factor with, perhaps, chocolate fondant, which has a light sponge and oozing liquid centre.

LONDON W6 *continued*

The River Café PLAN 1 D3

 Italian

tel: 020 7386 4200 **Thames Wharf Studios, Rainville Rd W6 9HA**
email: info@rivercafe.co.uk
dir: *Nearest station: Hammersmith*

Outstanding Italian cooking from a riverside legend

Once more unto the café, the Hammersmith waterside bolt-hole that helped inaugurate the turn to Mediterranean simplicity in late 1980s London. A long steel-topped bar runs along one side, a wall of deep windows overlooks a narrow stretch of green and then the Thames on the other. At one end of the room is a wood burner, alongside a bank of ranges where the rest of the cooking is done, and the whole place is presided over by immensely friendly waiting staff, whose knowledge of the authentic Italian menus and extensive matching wine list are hard to fault. The kitchen has resisted all temptation to gild the lily, allowing beacons of simple tradition such as fritto misto of red mullet, cuttlefish and violet artichoke, with a wedge of unwaxed Amalfi lemon, to shine. Fish is always stunning, as witness the wood-roasted whole Dover sole fragrantly dressed in oregano, marjoram and lemon, which comes with cime di rapa and slow-cooked Pugliese tomatoes. Meat could be veal shin with its marrow, simmered in Nebbiolo wine, alongside tomato bruschetta and cavolo nero. If you've room for a primo pasta dish, the crab linguine remains a reference point, as does the wonderfully gooey pear frangipane tart, served with softly whipped cream.

Chef Joseph Trivelli, Ruth Rogers, Sian Owen **Seats** 120, Pr/dining room 18 **Times** 12.30-3/7-11, Closed 24 Dec-1 Jan, BHs, D Sun **Prices** Prices not confirmed **Wines** 230 bottles over £30, 14 by glass **Parking** 29, Valet parking evening & wknds, pay & display **Notes** Sunday L, Vegetarian available, Children welcome

Sagar PLAN 1 D3

Indian Vegetarian V

tel: 020 8741 8563 **157 King St, Hammersmith W6 9JT**
email: info@sagarveg.co.uk
dir: *Nearest station: Hammersmith, Ravenscourt Park*

Cracking-value South Indian vegetarian dining

Behind Sagar's glass frontage, this Indian restaurant has an almost Scandinavian feel with pale wood floors, chairs, tables and walls. Expect well-crafted dishes, smartly attired service and wallet-friendly prices. The roster focuses on South Indian staples such as crisp paper-thin dosas (rice and lentil pancakes with various fillings) and uthappams (lentil 'pizzas'), while a starter of Kancheepuram idli delivers fluffy rice and lentil steamed dumplings with fresh coconut chutney. The lengthy output takes in Bombay chowpati (street snacks) like crispy puri, plus all-inclusive thali platters and simple curries such as brinjal bhaji – aubergine and green pepper cooked in fresh tomato with South Indian spices.

Chef S Sharmielan **Seats** 60 **Times** 12-3/5.30-10.45, Closed 25-26 Dec **Prices** Prices not confirmed **Wines** 911 bottles under £30, 8 by glass **Parking** On street **Notes** Children welcome

LONDON W8

Babylon PLAN 4 B5

 Modern British

tel: 020 7368 3993 **The Roof Gardens, 99 Kensington High St W8 5SA**
email: babylon@roofgardens.virgin.com **web:** www.roofgardens.virgin.com
dir: *Nearest station: High St Kensington*

Richard Branson's showpiece brasserie

The seventh floor heated terrace here is one of the ever-growing number of places to enjoy London's changing skyline. The contemporary British menu shows considerable originality as in a starter of roasted scallops with Aura heritage potato sauce, chorizo, fried capers, chives and black olives. For a main, consider hearty roasted breast and leg of Norfolk Black chicken with beer-braised shallots, mustard king cabbage, beer- and treacle-cured bacon and crushed Mayan Gold potatoes. Desserts show plenty of thought too, judging by Earl Grey tea, burnt honey tart, toasted meringue and bergamot curd and poppy seed ice cream.

Chef Ian Howard **Seats** 100, Pr/dining room 12 **Times** 12-2.30/6.30-10.30, Closed 24-26 Dec, 1 Jan, D Sun **Prices** Fixed L 2 course £24, Fixed D 3 course £52, Starter £8.50-£14, Main £18-£33, Dessert £8-£10.95 **Wines** 80 bottles over £30, 13 bottles under £30, 20 by glass **Parking** NCP Young St **Notes** Sunday L £32-£35, Vegetarian available, Children welcome

See advert opposite

LONDON W8 *continued*

Belvedere

PLAN 1 E3

British, French

tel: 020 7602 1238 **Abbotsbury Rd, Holland House, Holland Park W8 6LU**
email: sales@belvedererestaurant.co.uk **web:** www.belvedererestaurant.co.uk
dir: *Nearest station: Holland Park*

Modern brasserie-style dishes in upscale Holland Park

Belvedere was once the summer ballroom of Holland House, so expect high ceilings and bags of art deco glitz with giant shell-like lampshades, bevelled mirrors and parquet flooring, while white linen and modern leather seating provide the comforts. A marble staircase sweeps up to a mezzanine and a terrace, but it's not all about the surrounds: accomplished Anglo-French brasserie cooking produces starters like seared scallops with shallot purée and smoked bacon dressing. Mains could bring roast Goosnargh duck breast with colcannon, and plum and port jus. A top-value daily menu delivers the goods at lunch and early evening without gold card pricing.

Chef Gary O'Sullivan **Seats** 90 **Times** 12-2.30/6-10.30, Closed 26 Dec, 1 Jan, D Sun **Prices** Prices not confirmed **Wines** 120 bottles over £30, 12 bottles under £30, 12 by glass **Parking** Council car park **Notes** Wknds L menu 3 course £27.50/£29.50 (summer), Sunday L, Vegetarian available, Children welcome

Clarke's

PLAN 4 A6

Modern British, Italian

tel: 020 7221 9225 **124 Kensington Church St W8 4BH**
email: restaurant@sallyclarke.com
dir: *Nearest station: Notting Hill Gate*

Full-on flavours chez Sally

Sally Clarke's eponymous restaurant is on two levels: a light-filled ground-floor room and a larger basement with an open-to-view kitchen. Her cooking is founded on the best, freshest produce available in the markets each day, which means the menu changes at each session. Vegetables, herbs and salad leaves are often brought from Sally's own garden. The modern British output shows Italian leanings, so Scottish squid salad comes with puntarelle and agretti, and Cornish red mullet fillets with Sardinian fregola and roasted purple artichokes. Chargrilled rib of beef is designed for sharing, and, to finish, yogurt and orange pannacotta is served with a ginger florentine.

Chef Sally Clarke, Michele Lombardi **Seats** 90, Pr/dining room 30 **Times** 12.30-2.30/6.30-10, Closed 8 days Xmas & New Year, 2 wks Aug, Sun **Prices** Prices not confirmed **Wines** 80 bottles over £30, 10 bottles under £30, 8 by glass **Parking** On street **Notes** Breakfast Mon-Sat, Sun L menu some wknds, Vegetarian available, Children welcome

Kensington Place

PLAN 4 A6

 British

tel: 020 7727 3184 **201-209 Kensington Church St W8 7LX**
email: kensingtonplace@danddlondon.com **web:** www.kensingtonplace-restaurant.com
dir: *Nearest station: Notting Hill Gate*

Bustling seafood brasserie next door to the fishmonger's

The glass-fronted brasserie championed a new brisk informality in high-end dining when it opened in 1987. In an atmosphere of infectious buzz, with a large communal table for the sociably inclined, the fish and seafood catches of the day receive due credit. Kick things off with a textbook fish soup, served with rouille, croùtons and gruyère, and happiness is assured. Main dishes take in roast hake with a smoked haddock fishcake and garlic sausage or braised suckling pig with black pudding and a pasty of smoked ham hock for meatheads. All are reunited for populist desserts like sponge-topped dark chocolate mousse with peanut praline and milk ice cream.

Chef Tim Peirson **Seats** 110, Pr/dining room 36 **Times** 12-3/6.30-10.30, Closed 24-25 Dec, 1 Jan, BHs, L Mon, D Sun **Prices** Fixed L 2 course £20, Fixed D 3 course £25, Starter £7.50-£13.50, Main £14.50-£28.50, Dessert £6.25-£7 **Wines** 61 bottles over £30, 8 bottles under £30, 17 by glass **Parking** On street **Notes** Sunday L £20-£25, Vegetarian available, Children welcome

Kitchen W8

PLAN 4 A4

Modern British NOTABLE WINE LIST

tel: 020 7937 0120 **11-13 Abingdon Rd, Kensington W8 6AH**
email: info@kitchenw8.com
dir: *Nearest station: High St Kensington*

Exciting modern cooking in a neighbourhood star

Pale walls hung with colourful artwork, neat upholstered dining chairs at floor-length-clothed tables and gentle lighting all confirm that this is a class act, generating a feeling of well-being among diners. The proprietors (she of Sonny's in Barnes, he is ex of The Square in Mayfair) know what they're doing, and the cooking here of the first order. Top-rate ingredients are the bedrock of the operation, and the seasonally-changing menus are a roll call of sharp contemporary culinary ideas, with enough choice to intrigue all comers. A strong streak of innovation is apparent in some dishes, seen in multi-flavoured starters of Orkney scallops with charred celeriac, chanterelles, chicken skin and truffle pesto, and in tartare of fallow deer with pickled walnuts, Ibérico lardo, beetroot and nasturtiums. Main courses have enough complexity to maintain interest without going over the top and illustrate the kitchen's attention to detail. Cod fillet, for instance, is poached with seaweed and served with ras el hanout, cauliflower, sea beets and veal sweetbreads, and Ibérico pork loin comes with smoked celeriac, charred pears, bacon dauphine and a sherry reduction. Puddings make an impact too, among them chocolate pavé with peanut ice cream, salt caramel, praline and lime, and intriguing quince sorbet with beetroot and orange.

Chef Mark Kempson **Seats** 75 **Times** 12-2.30/6-10, Closed 25-26 Dec, BHs **Prices** Fixed L 2 course £22, Fixed D 3 course £28, Tasting menu £60, Starter £8.95-£16.95, Main £19.95-£29.95, Dessert £5.95-£8 **Wines** 110 bottles over £30, 10 bottles under £30, 14 by glass **Parking** On street, NCP High St **Notes** Fixed D early bird menu 6-7pm, Sunday L £30-£35, Vegetarian available, Children welcome

Min Jiang

LONDON W8 **PLAN 4 B5**

Chinese

tel: 020 7361 1988 **Royal Garden Hotel, 2-24 Kensington High St W8 4PT**
email: reservations@minjiang.co.uk **web:** www.minjiang.co.uk
dir: *Nearest station: High St Kensington*

Stylish and authentic Chinese cuisine overlooking Hyde Park

The glass and stone tower that is the Royal Garden Hotel celebrated its half-century in 2015, although it still looks as though it could have gone up a couple of years ago. It's a landmark building, overlooking Kensington Gardens and Hyde Park, city vistas that come into their own from a table in the tenth-floor Min Jiang Chinese restaurant. Upscale Chinese cuisine in five-star hotels can be hit-and-miss (the risk is that you find yourself eating sweet-and-sour pork at about ten times what it would cost in Chinatown), Min Jiang delivers an emphatic riposte to the doubters. A strikingly stylish design job features a collection of Chinese porcelain against a contemporary interpretation of red lacquered walls, tables are laid up with stiff white linen, and the service is proficient and helpful, with unpatronising explanations of dishes for anybody still getting their bearings. Authenticity is a watchword here, and the extensive menus of dim sum and the appearance of global classics of the Chinese repertoire such as Beijing duck, crisp-fried squid in salt and pepper, and spring rolls, substantiate that claim. Yet the precision of the cooking raises the place above much of what goes on in Chinatown, and is particularly impressive in the fast-cooked dishes. Xiao long bao dumplings made with blue swimmer crab, or steamed scallop in XO sauce, are stimulating appetisers, preparing the way for tenderly seared beef rib on a bed of shredded onion in rich Mongolian sauce, or chilli-hot gong bao made with corn-fed chicken. Desserts are not the strongest suit, but white chocolate and chilli cheesecake with sweet-and-sour strawberries may yet become a modern classic.

Chef Weng Han Wong, Steve Munkley **Seats** 80, Pr/dining room 20 **Times** 12-3/6-10.30 **Prices** Starter £7-£8, Main £12-£62.50, Dessert £6.50-£14.50 **Wines** 229 bottles over £30, 3 bottles under £30, 15 by glass **Parking** 200 **Notes** Dim Sum menu, Vegetarian available, Children welcome

LONDON W8 *continued*

Launceston Place

PLAN 4 C4

Modern European NOTABLE WINE LIST

tel: 020 7937 6912 **1a Launceston Place W8 5RL**
email: launcestonplace@danddlondon.com
dir: *Nearest station: Gloucester Rd, High St Kensington*

Modern dining in a genteel Kensington mews

Consisting of four Victorian houses on the corner of an upmarket mews, Launceston Place could be mistaken for a smart neighbourhood joint. But cross the threshold and the first-class service team swings into action while the interior design (a series of spaces in shades of grey with modern artworks on the walls) catches the eye. The kitchen's output is rooted in French classical ways and incorporates contemporary techniques to good effect. Start with a dish that combines a hen's egg, bacon and baked celeriac, topped with lardo and yeast foam, followed by a spot-on slow-cooked cod with clam pesto, and finish with a dressed up dark chocolate nemesis.

Chef Raphael Francois **Seats** 50, Pr/dining room 12
Times 12-2.30/6-10, Closed Xmas, Etr, Mon, L Tue **Prices** Fixed L 2 course £28.50, Fixed D 3 course £35, Tasting menu £70, Starter fr £21, Main fr £30, Dessert fr £12 **Wines** 352 bottles over £30, 4 bottles under £30, 15 by glass **Parking** On street, car park off Kensington High St **Notes** ALC prices for L only, Market menu 3 course £55, Sunday L £40, Vegetarian available, Children welcome

The Milestone Hotel

PLAN 4 B5

Modern British NOTABLE WINE LIST

tel: 020 7917 1000 **1 Kensington Court W8 5DL**
email: bookms@rchmail.com **web:** www.milestonehotel.com
dir: *Nearest station: High St Kensington*

Unreconstructed haute cuisine in patterned luxury

A stolid red-brick corner edifice in affluent Kensington, formal service in the lead-windowed Cheneston dining room extends to a commis chef on hand to carve from the roast-of-the-day trolley. A prawn and crayfish cocktail with brown bread and lemon is spanking-fresh and richly dressed, and might precede fried tenderloin and slow-roasted belly of Dingley Dell pork, which has perfect crackling, well-seasoned potato galette and a fortifying jus. Finish with a chocolate study that combines a smooth dark parfait, deeply rich mini brownies, a crisp tuile and butterscotch sauce. Incidentals offer a nod to modernism with foaming appetisers and pre-desserts, the latter perhaps lemon curd mousse under yogurt froth.

Chef Alexandras Diamantis **Seats** 30, Pr/dining room 8 **Times** 12-2.30/5.30-10.30 **Prices** Fixed L 2 course fr £26, Fixed D 3 course fr £29, Starter £12-£28, Main £17-£42, Dessert £9-£16 **Wines** 200 bottles over £30, 10 bottles under £30, 12 by glass **Parking** NCP Young St off Kensington High St **Notes** Pre-theatre 2/3 course £26/£29, Vegetarian available, Children welcome

Min Jiang

PLAN 4 B5

– see page 323 and advert opposite

Park Terrace Restaurant

PLAN 4 B5

Modern Seasonal

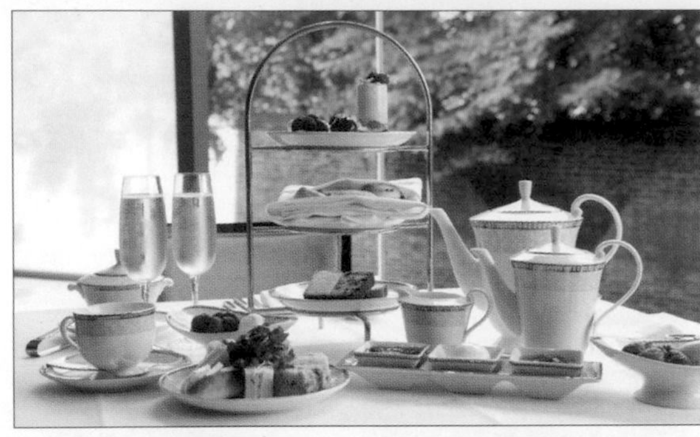

tel: 020 7361 0602 **Royal Garden Hotel, 2-24 Kensington High St W8 4PT**
email: reservations@parkterracerestaurant.co.uk **web:** www.parkterracerestaurant.co.uk
dir: *Nearest station: High St Kensington*

Sophisticated modern British cuisine overlooking Kensington Gardens

With its leafy views over Kensington Gardens, the upscale Royal Garden Hotel's location takes some beating. The contemporary decor in the restaurant reflects the park-life theme, with a natural colour palate, wood veneer and large black-and-white images of trees. Steve Munkley's modern British cooking is light, clear-flavoured and uncomplicated, and shows commitment to local British suppliers and seasonality. Seared sesame-crusted tuna is matched with a palate-sharpening Bloody Mary sorbet, followed by chargrilled T-bone of halibut, crispy cod's cheek, Lyonnaise potatoes, asparagus and tartare sauce, and to finish, there's prune and Cognac double-baked soufflé with brandy cream. Service is clued-up and friendly, while the value lunch keeps the Kensington locals on-side.

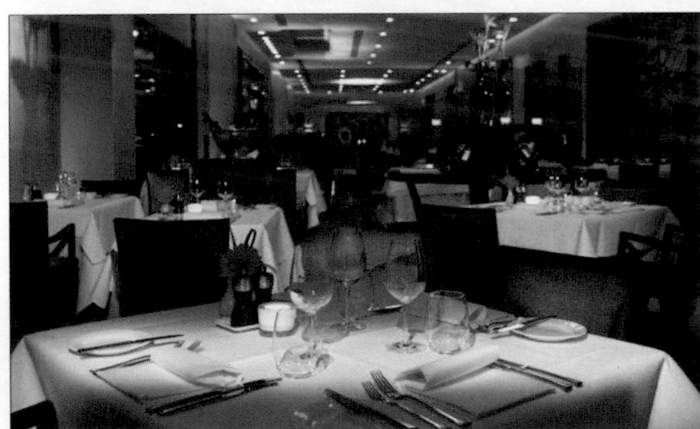

Chef Steve Munkley **Seats** 90, Pr/dining room 40 **Times** 12-10.30, All-day dining **Prices** Fixed L 2 course fr £16.50, Fixed D 3 course fr £37.50, Starter £6.95-£11, Main £8.50-£28.50, Dessert £6.25-£8 **Wines** 90 bottles over £30, 9 bottles under £30, 14 by glass **Parking** 200 **Notes** Pre-theatre menu, Afternoon tea, Lounge menu, Sunday L £21-£26, Vegetarian available, Children welcome

See advert on page 326

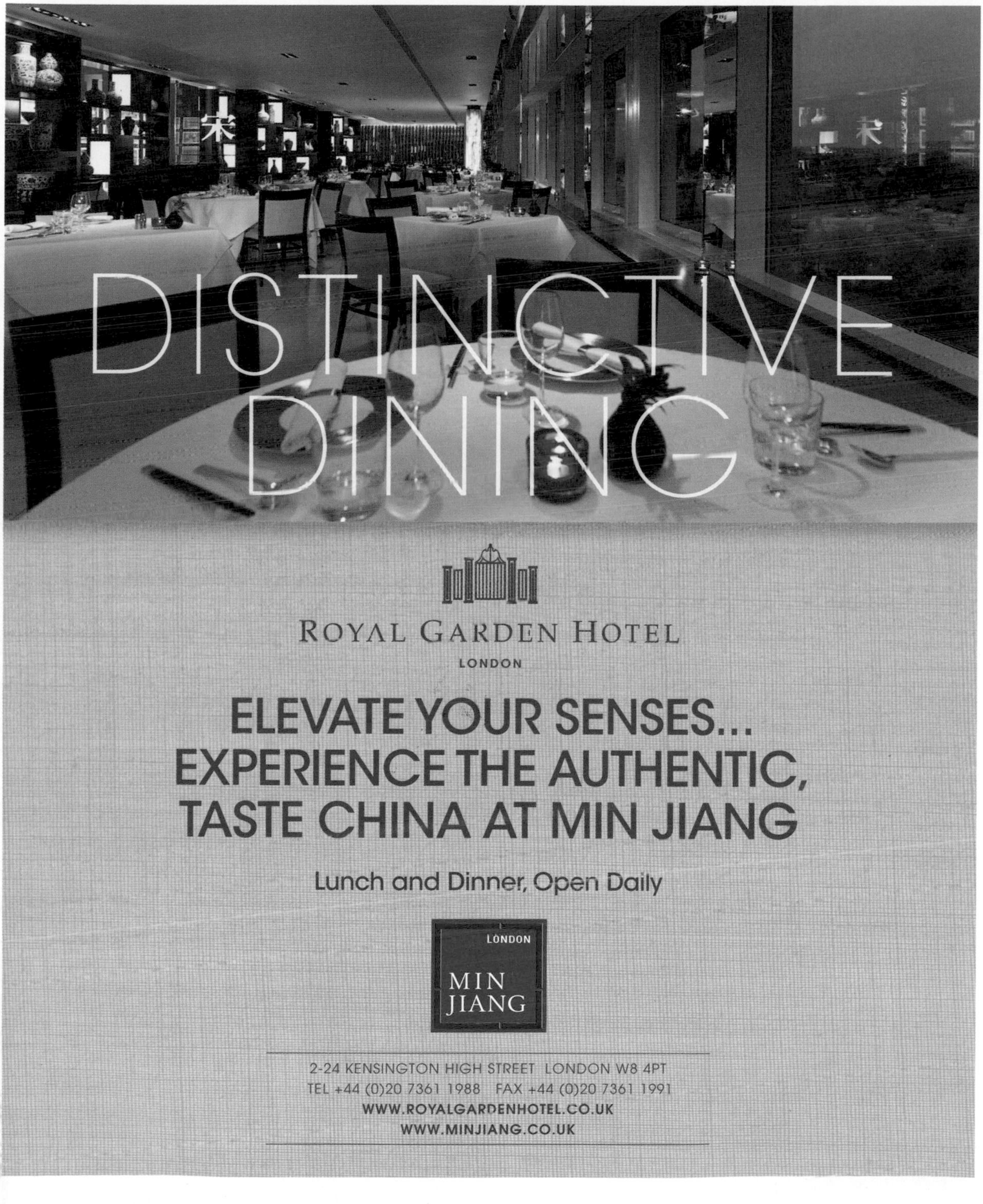
DISTINCTIVE
DINING
ROYAL GARDEN HOTEL
LONDON
ELEVATE YOUR SENSES...
EXPERIENCE THE AUTHENTIC,
TASTE CHINA AT MIN JIANG
Lunch and Dinner, Open Daily
LONDON
MIN
JIANG
2-24 KENSINGTON HIGH STREET LONDON W8 4PT
TEL +44 (0)20 7361 1988 FAX +44 (0)20 7361 1991
WWW.ROYALGARDENHOTEL.CO.UK
WWW.MINJIANG.CO.UK

LONDON W8 *continued*

Zaika of Kensington

PLAN 4 B5

 Indian NEW V

tel: 020 7795 6533 **1 Kensington High St W8 5NP**
email: Zaikareservations@Zaika-restaurant.co.uk
dir: *Nearest station: High St Kensington*

High-calibre modern Indian cuisine

With its high ceilings, oak panels and colonial pictures, the grand former bank building has the feel of a Raj-era gentlemen's club, which is a perfect fit for this posh Indian. Taking classic, Moghul-inspired North Indian dishes as its starting point, the kitchen throws creative touches into the mix to conjure scintillating, palate-tingling flavours. Leading the charge are the likes of ajwaini macchi – monkfish marinated with ginger, yogurt, carom seeds and turmeric – followed by a consummate version of Allepey fish curry, delivering perfectly-timed kingfish in creamy coconut and ginger sauce, or a feisty chicken tikka in smoked tomato and garlic sauce.

Chef Shoeb Haider **Seats** Pr/dining room 18 **Prices** Fixed L 3 course £21.50, Starter £7.50-£16.50, Main £7.50-£38, Dessert £6-£12 **Notes** Fixed D 4 course £55, Pre/post-theatre 3 course £26.50

LONDON W9

The Truscott Arms

PLAN 2 B4

Modern British NOTABLE WINE LIST

tel: 020 7266 9198 **55 Shirland Rd, Maida Vale W9 2JD**
email: joinus@thetruscottarms.com **web:** www.thetruscottarms.com
dir: *Nearest station: Warwick Ave*

Classy made-over pub with contemporary flavour

A five-storey Victorian property that operates as a proper pub, with the main restaurant upstairs, and an outside terrace with funky coloured tables and chairs. Genuine effort is made to give the menu a regional flavour. Start with veal sweetbreads flavoured with lavender honey or some Wye Valley asparagus with morels, almonds and bergamot. Among main courses, South Downs lamb (neck and tongue) are partnered with a host of fresh British vegetables, and halibut gets a lovely smoky flavour from its accompanying smoked clams. Finish with an egg with Bartlett (or Williams) pear and perry sorbet, or a wild strawberry number with meringues and black pepper crumble.

Chef Aidan McGee **Seats** 52, Pr/dining room 34 **Times** 12-4/6-11, Closed Mon-Tue **Wines** 151 bottles over £30, 79 bottles under £30, 32 by glass **Parking** On street **Notes** Sunday L £18, Vegetarian available, Children welcome

LONDON W10

The Dock Kitchen

PLAN 1 D4

Modern International

tel: 020 8962 1610 **Portobello Docks, 342/344 Ladbroke Grove W10 5BU**
email: reception@dockkitchen.co.uk
dir: *Nearest station: Ladbroke Grove, Kensal Rise, Kensal Green*

Appealingly eclectic cooking by the canal

A one-time pop-up outfit at Tom Dixon's furniture design gallery, the long, narrow dining space has a chilled-out warehouse vibe with central open kitchen. Stevie Parle's kitchen showcases global flavours and ingredients inspired by his travels, with influences as far and wide as the Med, Middle East or South America. Take a spicy attitude Mexican birria (stew) of top-drawer monkfish, cod and octopus served with a Mexican winter salad and corn tortillas, or perhaps Chinese pork knuckle (for two) teamed with grilled leeks, cucumber pickle, ground peanuts and jasmine. Finish with a moist, textbook pistachio and nutmeg cake and saffron yogurt or Amalfi lemon tart.

LONDON W11

E&O

PLAN 1 D4

Pan-Asian

tel: 020 7229 5454 **14 Blenheim Crescent, Notting Hill W11 1NN**
email: eando@rickerrestaurants.com
dir: *Nearest station: Notting Hill Gate, Ladbroke Grove*

East Asian grazing plates for the Notting Hill cognoscenti

E&O is trend-central with the Notting Hill hangers-out and fashionistas. The decor may be a bit scuffed these days, but the high-octane vibe (ramped-up by a lively front bar) puts the experience-factor in overdrive. The chocolate brown and cream colour palette is on trend, with leather seating, louvered screening, oversized oriental-style lighting and paper-clothed tables. The young-at-heart pack the place for the fashionable, well-conceived Pan-Asian cuisine alongside some great cocktails. All the classics are here; sushi and sashimi (perhaps a spicy tuna roll) or tempura (avocado and sweet potato), while top-dollar back cod with sweet miso cranks up the ante, and a lychee and mango green curry the spice attitude.

Edera

PLAN 1 D3

Modern Italian

tel: 020 7221 6090 **148 Holland Park Av W11 4UE**
email: roberto@edera.co.uk
dir: *Nearest station: Holland Park*

Well-liked neighbourhood Italian in leafy Holland Park

Decked out on tiered levels, with light walls hung with big mirrors and linen-dressed tables, this minimally-styled Holland Park eatery pulls in a well-heeled crowd for its fashionable Sardinian-accented Italian cooking. The kitchen certainly knows its stuff, keeping things simple and straightforward, allowing the excellent ingredients to speak for themselves. There is much that is familiar from the Italian mainland, bolstered by a daily specials list featuring the likes of chargrilled sea bream with courgettes and basil oil, and baked salted sea bass with potato salad, but the chef is Sardinian, so there might be spaghetti with grey mullet roe, plus Sicilian cannoli for pudding.

Chef Carlo Usai **Seats** 70, Pr/dining room 20 **Times** 12-11, All-day dining, Closed 24 Dec-1 Jan **Prices** Prices not confirmed **Wines** 13 by glass **Parking** On street parking **Notes** Black truffle menu all year, White truffle menu in season, Vegetarian available, Children welcome

The Ledbury

PLAN 1 E4

– see below

The Ledbury

LONDON W11 PLAN 1 E4

Modern British V NOTABLE WINE LIST

tel: 020 7792 9090 **127 Ledbury Rd W11 2AQ**
email: info@theledbury.com
dir: *Nearest station: Westbourne Park, Notting Hill Gate*

Imaginative cooking from a supremely talented chef

Since opening its doors in 2005, The Ledbury, under Australian chef Brett Graham, has evolved into one of London's very best restaurants. The Notting Hill setting sets it physically apart from the high-flying gaffs in the centre of town, but the kitchen's output is entirely in tune with current trends – powerful flavours from ingredients that are enhanced by the cooking techniques, never overpowered. There's a small terrace out front, behind an army of planters, while the interior is understated, stylish and contemporary. The staff are thoroughly professional, but also rather fun to be around. From the fixed-price four-course carte, set lunch and tasting menus (including a mightily impressive veggie version) come simply stunning looking, creative dishes that eat as well as they look. Start with white beetroot baked in clay, flavoured with caviar salt and served with smoked and dried eel, or a delightful artichoke number with Muscat grapes and walnuts. To follow, grilled cuttlefish keeps company with new season's garlic and cracked wheat, and Cornish turbot is the heart and soul of a course with oyster cream and brown bread. The quality of the ingredients is truly impressive, and they get the respect they deserve from a kitchen team who display outstanding ability, evident in a glorious piece of Ibérico pork partnered with purple carrots cooked in hay. The creativity doesn't stop at dessert stage – how about pear cooked in brown butter with Jerusalem artichoke ice cream and malt cake? Outstanding. The excellent wine list favours France while embracing the entire world, and also includes a range of sake and non-alcoholic cocktails.

Chef Brett Graham **Seats** 55 **Times** 12-2/6.30-9.45, Closed 25-26 Dec, Aug BH, L Mon-Tue **Prices** Fixed L 3 course £50, Tasting menu fr £115 **Wines** 819 bottles over £30, 10 bottles under £30, 16 by glass **Parking** Talbot St **Notes** 4 course L £85, 4 course D Mon-Thu £95, Children 12 yrs+

LONDON W14

Cibo

PLAN 1 D3

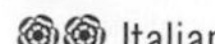 Italian

tel: 020 7371 2085 & 7371 6271 **3 Russell Gardens W14 8EZ**
email: reservations@ciborestaurant.net
dir: *Nearest station: Olympia, Shepherd's Bush*

W14's friendly and highly individual Italian flagship

The epitome of the authentic neighbourhood Italian, long-serving Cibo is still a big hit with savvy Holland Park-ers. Breads – from carta di musica to focaccia – and nibbles like olives and mini pizzas raise expectation from the off. Pasta is the real deal too – perhaps ravioli filled with duck in a wild mushroom sauce, while starters like marinated roast peppers, courgettes and aubergines, teamed with creamy mozzarella shout of the Mediterranean too. This is skilful Italian cooking showing respect of prime ingredients, flavour and precision. Mains like grilled swordfish simply served alongside baby tomatoes, olives and capers, and desserts (classics such as pannacotta and tiramisù) are equally convincing.

Chef Piero Borrell **Seats** 50, Pr/dining room 14
Times 12.15-3/6.15-10.30, Closed Xmas, Etr BHs, Sun, L Sat **Prices** Fixed L 2 course £24.50, Starter £9-£13.50, Main £14.50-£28, Dessert £5-£7.50 **Wines** 26 bottles under £30, 4 by glass **Parking** On street **Notes** Vegetarian available, Children welcome

LONDON WC1

The Montague on the Gardens

PLAN 3 B3

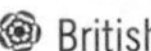 British

tel: 020 7612 8416 & 7612 8412 **15 Montague St, Bloomsbury WC1B 5BJ**
email: aarapi@rchmail.com **web:** www.montaguehotel.com
dir: *Nearest station: Russell Sq, Holborn, Tottenham Court Rd*

Stylish hotel bistro with modern comfort classics

The bowler-hatted doorman at the entrance is a clue that this is a classy boutique hotel, on a quiet street near the British Museum. Its Blue Door Bistro is a welcoming and informal dining room, decorated with a frieze depicting London in around 1850. There's mahogany panelling, with contemporary wall lights and good use of mirrored glass and flowers on clothed dining tables. Simplicity is the kitchen's byword, producing starters such as crab cakes with celeriac remoulade or a classic Caesar salad, before main courses such as sea bass in a champagne sauce or prawn Stroganoff. Finish with rice pudding with salted caramel.

Chef Martin Halls **Seats** 40, Pr/dining room 100 **Times** 12.30-2.30/5.30-10.30
Prices Fixed L 2 course £19-£24, Fixed D 3 course £24-£28, Starter £6-£12, Main £14-£38, Dessert £7-£10 **Wines** 65 bottles over £30, 2 bottles under £30, 17 by glass **Parking** On street, Bloomsbury Sq **Notes** Pre-theatre 2/3 course £19/£24, Sunday L, Vegetarian available, Children welcome

Otto's French Restaurant

PLAN 3 C4

Classic French

tel: 020 7713 0107 **182 Gray's Inn Rd WC1X 8EW**
email: enquiries@ottos-restaurant.com
dir: *Nearest station: Chancery Lane*

Classic French cooking with old school service

Small, intimate and owner-run, this old-school French restaurant feels like it has been here for decades. As befits a traditional French restaurant, the wine list is hefty in both range and price and the food displays confident cooking skills, high-quality ingredients and the type of heavy saucing you rarely encounter this side of the Channel. Fresh ravioli of snails marinated in Chablis served with bordelaise red wine sauce with bone marrow, Bayonne ham and mushrooms makes for a rich start to a meal, particularly if followed by the showstopping canard de Rouen à la pressé, finished off at the table. Leave room for classic tarte Tatin and crème anglaise.

Chef Thierry Lakermance **Seats** 45, Pr/dining room 30
Times 12-3/6-10, Closed Xmas, BHs, Sun, L Sat **Prices** Fixed L 2 course £24, Starter £9.50-£16.50, Main £19.50-£34.50, Dessert £6.50-£14.50 **Wines** 200 bottles over £30, 20 bottles under £30, 10 by glass **Parking** On street **Notes** Children 8 yrs+

Rosewood London

PLAN 3 C3

Modern European

tel: 020 3747 8620 & 3747 8621 **252 High Holborn WC1V 7EN**
email: mirrorroom@rosewoodhotels.com **web:** www.rosewoodhotels.com/london
dir: *Nearest station: Holborn*

British heritage cookery in a magnificently restored building

This magnificent building on High Holborn is a fine setting, and the old East Banking Hall with its soaring marble pillars is now a modishly grand restaurant. A brasserie menu of traditional British dishes brought into the present day offers the likes of Marie Rose shellfish cocktail with avocado, or fried squid with Gentleman's Relish to start. Majestic follow-ups include roast beef rib, served with a fine, deeply flavoured gravy and crisp onion rings, or perfectly timed, garlic-buttered grilled lobster with sea vegetables and chips. Desserts include baked rice pudding with a blob of blackcurrant jam, sherried-up trifle, or banana with custard.

Chef Amandine Chaignot **Seats** 70, Pr/dining room 20 **Times** 12-2.30/6-10
Prices Fixed L 2 course fr £28, Fixed D 3 course £35, Starter £15-£22, Main £19-£33, Dessert £12 **Wines** 350 bottles over £30, 4 bottles under £30, 16 by glass
Parking 12 **Notes** Afternoon tea, Sunday L £40, Vegetarian available, Children welcome

LONDON WC2

L'Atelier de Joël Robuchon

PLAN 3 A2

Modern French V

tel: 020 7010 8600 **13-15 West St WC2H 9NE**
email: info@joelrobuchon.co.uk
dir: *Nearest station: Leicester Sq, Covent Gdn, Tottenham Court Rd*

Innovative dining from a French master-chef in a glam setting

Tucked away on a quiet side-street on the fringes of Covent Garden, Robuchon's central London bolt-hole offers three storeys of urban elegance, with a brace of restaurants, a glamorous bar and a rooftop terrace for spying on the theatre crowds. The ground floor room has a view of the chefs busily prepping and plating, but upstairs is a more classical dining room format, in a dark design setting relieved by splashes of colour in the paper place mats. Xavier Boyer oversees a conscientious interpretation of Robuchon's globally disseminated modern French cuisine, which retains a foot in the bistro ethos. Foie gras terrine with toasted pain de campagne and fig jelly, or tuna salad with crunchy vegetables, prepare the way for robust main courses such as mildly spiced roast venison with poached baby pears, or the stunning stuffed quail with heavenly mash, this element being one of the recipes that helped make Robuchon's name. Imaginative desserts take in an impressive clear sugar column filled with passionfruit and banana cream topped with rum granité and coconut foam and moated with passionfruit sauce.

Chef Xavier Boyer **Seats** 43, Pr/dining room 12 **Times** 12-3/5.30-11, Closed Aug BH, 25 Dec, 1 Jan **Prices** Fixed L 2 course £35-£50, Tasting menu £95-£214, Starter £16-£49, Main £25-£80, Dessert £11-£15 **Wines** 250 bottles over £30, 4 bottles under £30, 16 by glass **Parking** Valet parking service **Notes** Pre-theatre 3/4 course (with wine), Sunday L £55-£80, Children 10 yrs+

Balthazar

PLAN 3 B1

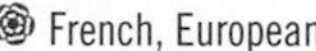 French, European

tel: 020 3301 1155 **4-6 Russell St WC2B 5HZ**
email: info@balthazarlondon.com
dir: *Nearest station: Covent Garden*

All-day French brasserie fare and a high-energy atmosphere

The London offshoot of the legendary New York brasserie has played to packed houses since opening in 2013. It's a real looker, a large, high-ceilinged room decked out with mosaic floors, darkwood panelling, art deco lighting, red-leather banquettes and antique mirrors. The places buzzes from breakfast through to lunch, afternoon tea and dinner with menus delivering a line-up of classic French brasserie fare, from snails with garlic butter to salad Niçoise and moules frites, as well as a more up-to-date roasted stone bass with artichoke purée, smoked aubergine, baby fennel, and tomato, basil and olive dressing. Desserts are exemplary renditions of comfort classics like crème brûlée or apple tarte Tatin.

Barrafina Adelaide Street

PLAN 3 B1

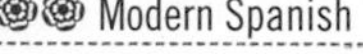 Modern Spanish

10 Adelaide St WC2N 4HZ
email: info@barrafina.co.uk **web:** www.barrafina.co.uk
dir: *Nearest station: Charing Cross, Leicester Sq, Embankment*

Vibrant spot for stunning tapas

Tapas is the name of the game here and the place is cool and packed to the rafters. The no booking policy means queues are likely and, once in, you sit at the marble counter and tuck into small plates full of flavour. There are daily specials galore, superb cured meats and lots of things you've maybe not tried before. The crab croquetas should not be missed, there's milk-fed lamb's brains, fabulously fresh hake cooked on the plancha, deeply satisfying arroz de marisco, classic tortilla – the cooking is spot-on, the produce first class. Sweet courses offer no less satisfaction, and to drink there are excellent sherries and Spanish wines.

Chef Nieves Barragán Mohacho **Seats** 29, Pr/dining room 32
Times 12-3/5-11, Closed Xmas, New Yr, BHs **Prices** Prices not confirmed **Wines** 17 bottles over £30, 11 bottles under £30, 21 by glass **Notes** Vegetarian available, Children welcome

Barrafina Drury Lane

PLAN 3 B2

Spanish tapas NEW

43 Drury Ln WC2B 5AJ
email: info@barrafina.co.uk
dir: *Nearest station: Covent Garden, Holborn*

Buzzy spot for switched-on Spanish tapas

The Barrafina brand is clearly on a roll with its lively repertoire of classic and modern tapas dishes, opening its third branch in theatreland. It's the perfect spot for diners who want to grab and graze through a few little plates of big flavours in the pre- and post-theatre slots. The Spanglish menu (cheery staff are happy to translate) offers ideas as traditional as plates of cold meats – coppa Ibérica, say – or classic tortilla. Elsewhere, there could be pork belly with mojo verde sauce or milk-fed lamb's sweetbreads. The place operates a no-bookings policy and takes groups of up to four people.

Chef Nieves Barragán Mohacho, Diego Garcia Fernandez **Seats** 23, Pr/dining room 24 **Times** 12-3/5-11, Closed 25-26 Dec, 1 Jan, BHs **Prices** Prices not confirmed **Wines** 22 bottles over £30, 7 bottles under £30, 22 by glass **Notes** No high chairs available, Vegetarian available

Christopher's

PLAN 3 C1

Contemporary American

tel: 020 7240 4222 **18 Wellington St, Covent Garden WC2E 7DD**
email: reservations@christophersgrill.com
dir: *Nearest station: Embankment, Covent Garden*

Lively Stateside eating in an elegant Covent Garden room

This elegant eatery on the fringes of Covent Garden features a grand staircase, winding up from the uptempo street-level Martini Bar, while corniced high ceilings tower over the airy dining room, where chairs and banquettes in grey and lemon deliver bags of contemporary swagger. The kitchen's repertoire of Stateside cooking comes equally well dressed, with prime steaks of USDA beef and Maine lobster taking top billing. Otherwise smoky BBQ lamb fillet is teamed with samphire and rocket salsa verde and blackened salmon with jambalaya risotto, cress salad and tomato jam, catches the eye. Favourites, like New York vanilla cheesecake or Key Lime tart wink at the finish, while cracking wines give the Americas top billing.

Chef Francis Agyepong **Seats** 110, Pr/dining room 40
Times 12-3/5-11.30, Closed Xmas, 1 Jan **Prices** Fixed L 2 course fr £20, Fixed D 3 course fr £24, Starter £6-£14, Main £16-£45, Dessert £7 **Wines** 100+ bottles over £30, 5 bottles under £30, 12 by glass **Notes** Fixed D theatre Mon-Sat 5-6.15 & 10-11.30, Sun supper menu, Vegetarian available, Children welcome

Cigalon

PLAN 3 D2

Mediterranean

tel: 020 7242 8373 **115 Chancery Ln WC2A 1PP**
email: bookings@cigalon.co.uk
dir: *Nearest station: Chancery Lane, Temple, Covent Garden, Holborn*

Provençal-style cooking in legal land

A former auction house focusing on the cuisine of Southern France and Corsica in a surprisingly sunny setting. The chefs in the open-to-view kitchen make good use of the grill to create Provençal-inspired dishes such as grilled lamb saddle with smoked anchovies and Swiss chard, or loin of venison with sage gnocchi and wild mushrooms. It's simple, full-flavoured stuff. A starter of chicken liver terrine comes with pickled veg to cut through the richness, while another sees cannelloni filled with beef from the Camargue (enriched with a red wine and bone marrow sauce). For dessert, tuck into dark chocolate tart with orange blossom ice cream. Baranis is their basement bar.

Chef Julien Carlon **Seats** 60, Pr/dining room 8 **Times** 12-2.15/5.45-10, Closed Xmas, New Year, BHs, Sat-Sun **Prices** Fixed L 2 course fr £21.50, Fixed D 3 course fr £34.50, Starter £8-£13, Main £14-£22, Dessert £7-£8.50 **Wines** 40 bottles over £30, 5 bottles under £30, 11 by glass **Parking** On street **Notes** Vegetarian available, Children welcome

LONDON WC2 *continued*

Clos Maggiore

PLAN 3 B1

3 Rosettes – *see opposite*

The Delaunay

PLAN 3 C2

1 Rosette European

tel: 020 7499 8558 **55 Aldwych WC2B 4BB**
email: reservations@thedelaunay.com
dir: *Nearest station: Holborn, Covent Garden*

Brasserie dining in the grand European tradition

The Delaunay, like its ever-popular Piccadilly sibling, The Wolseley, was conceived in the style of the grand café-restaurants of central Europe, making a vibrant, glamorous spot, great for people watching, with slick, service and an all-day dining repertoire. Start with sautéed pierogi dumplings with cottage cheese, sage, onion and paprika butter, then sea trout with summer vegetables and sorrel beurre blanc. If you're up for something more substantial, go for Hungarian Goulash or Wiener schnitzel, and don't think of skipping dessert when there's apple and gooseberry strudel or white and dark Bavarian chocolate cream up for grabs. The Counter – with a separate entrance – offers a fabulous takeaway service.

Les Deux Salons

PLAN 3 B1

2 Rosettes French

tel: 020 7420 2050 **40-42 William IV St WC2N 4DD**
email: info@lesdeuxsalons.co.uk
dir: *Nearest station: Charing Cross, Leicester Sq*

Authentic French brasserie menu in the heart of theatreland

The French-focused repertoire at Les Deux Salons extends to entrées such as a simple plate of first-rate charcuterie, an artisanal black pudding served with a fried egg, and snail and bacon pie. Next up, the Josper oven provides the prime protein in the shape of bavette steak and frites and 300 grams of côtes de veau with truffle honey, or alternatively go for a lighter option such as lemon sole meunière. A sharing option might be rack of Welsh lamb with fondant potato, confit garlic and rosemary jus. Finish in classic brasserie style with ile flottante or the tart of the day. The prix-fixe menu is extremely good value.

Great Queen Street

PLAN 3 B2

1 Rosette British, European

tel: 020 7242 0622 **32 Great Queen St WC2B 5AA**
email: greatqueenstreet@googlemail.com
dir: *Nearest station: Covent Garden, Holborn*

Best of British in a bustling eatery

A long pub-like room with an open kitchen at the back, this is a busy, high-decibel place with an easy-going, friendly and completely unpretentious vibe. The twice-daily-changing menu deals in quality produce where seasonality, sourcing and provenance are king. Intelligently simple, unfussy Brit fare with gutsy, big flavours is the kitchen's preference. There's no three-course formality, with dishes laid out in ascending price order, so mix-and-match with small plates – cured, marinated sardines and panzanella, say – and larger dishes like lamb neck fillet with bobby beans, mint and tomatoes, or shin of beef with peas, and finish with buttermilk pudding with stewed apple and salty caramel.

Chef Tom Norrington-Davies, Sam Hutchins **Seats** 70
Times 12-2.30/6-10.30, Closed BHs, D Sun **Prices** Fixed L 2 course £18, Starter £4.80-£10.80, Main £13.80-£30, Dessert £3-£7.80 **Wines** 50 bottles over £30, 12 bottles under £30, 11 by glass **Notes** Sunday L, Vegetarian available, Children welcome

The Ivy

PLAN 3 A1

1 Rosette British, International V

tel: 020 7836 4751 **1-5 West St, Covent Garden WC2H 9NQ**
dir: *Nearest station: Leicester Sq*

High standards all round underpin a worldwide reputation

A new central dining bar was part of Martin Brudnizki's 2015 redesign of this celebrated theatreland dining institution, but he wisely left untouched the original harlequin stained-glass windows, green leather banquettes, mirrors and specially commissioned British art. Tables remain a tad neighbourly, but will that matter if a 'celeb' sits within earshot? The classic British and international food remains appealing, typified by a starter of sautéed ceps with creamed polenta and pangritata, and main dishes such as miso-blackened salmon with shellfish broth and pickled kohlrabi, or classic shepherd's pie. To finish, there could be spiced maple and pecan pear tart with vanilla ice cream.

Chef Gary Lee **Seats** 100, Pr/dining room 60 **Times** 12-11.30, All-day dining, Closed 25-26 Dec, 1 Jan **Prices** Starter £8-£15.75, Main £14.75-£37.50, Dessert £6.75-£9.25 **Wines** 109 bottles over £30, 5 bottles under £30, 18 by glass **Parking** Valet service **Notes** Post-theatre menu, Sunday L, Children welcome

J. Sheekey & J. Sheekey Oyster Bar

PLAN 3 B1

1 Rosette Seafood V

tel: 020 7240 2565 **32-34 St Martin's Court WC2N 4AL**
dir: *Nearest station: Leicester Sq*

Renowned theatreland fish restaurant

Very much a London legend, this enduring and much-loved seafood restaurant in the heart of theatreland began life as a seafood stall in the 19th century. J Sheekey expanded the business into adjoining properties and it has been a haunt of the great and the good ever since. Inside is a warren of snug wood-panelled dining rooms, plus a seafood and oyster bar, and a menu listing relatively straightforward fish and shellfish dishes prepared from superb quality raw ingredients. Start with blackened mackerel salad, or a choice of oysters, followed by whole Devon cock crab, or pan-fried slip soles with seaweed and caper butter.

Chef Andy McLay **Seats** 114 **Times** 12-3/5.30-12, Closed 25-26 Dec, 1 Jan, D 24 Dec **Prices** Fixed L 2 course fr £23.75, Starter £9.75-£15.75, Main £15.75-£42, Dessert £7.50-£9.50 **Wines** 83 bottles over £30, 3 bottles under £30, 30 by glass **Parking** On street, NCP **Notes** Sunday L, Children welcome

Kaspar's Seafood Bar & Grill

PLAN 3 C1

1 Rosette British, Japanese Seafood V

tel: 020 7836 4343 **The Savoy, Strand WC2R OEU**
email: savoy@fairmont.com **web:** www.kaspars.co.uk
dir: *Nearest station: Embankment, Covent Garden, Charing Cross*

Seafood dining in dazzling art deco surroundings

The centrepiece of Kaspar's striking, art deco-inspired dining room is the seafood and oyster bar. You won't meet Kaspar there, but if you are part of a table of 13, this sculpted cat can make numbers up to 14, maintaining an old Savoy tradition (ask your stripey-trousered and waistcoated waiter to elaborate). At bar or table, a robust lobster bisque makes an excellent starter, followed by perfectly grilled Atlantic halibut and lemon hollandaise sauce, a fruits de mer platter, smoked or cured fish, or a grill, and exotic guava and passionfruit salad for dessert. A good range of wines is offered by the glass and carafe.

Chef Holger Jackisch **Seats** 114, Pr/dining room 14 **Times** 12-11.30, All-day dining **Prices** Fixed L 2 course £25, Fixed D 3 course £39-£69, Starter £10-£21, Main £19-£39, Dessert £9 **Wines** 60 bottles over £30, 60 by glass **Parking** 20 **Notes** Fixed L 12-3pm, Pre-theatre 5-6.30pm, Post-theatre 10-11pm, Children welcome

Clos Maggiore

LONDON WC2 **PLAN 3 B1**

Modern French, Mediterranean V NOTABLE WINE LIST

tel: 020 7379 9696 **33 King St, Covent Garden WC2E 8JD**
email: enquiries@closmaggiore.com **web:** www.closmaggiore.com
dir: *Nearest station: Covent Garden, Leicester Sq*

An intimate French oasis in the heart of Covent Garden

Plumb in the heart of Covent Garden theatreland, Clos Maggiore does a very good job of seeming to be both indoors and out. There's a woodland charm to the interior, with privet hedging forming part of the wall decor, and the small intimate room at the back with flowering plants arching overhead comes with a retractable glass roof, so that on summer nights you can dine under the neon-lit London night sky. Linen-skirted tables and discreet jazz furnish the place with a finishing touch of plush. It makes a romantic backdrop for Marcellin Marc's refined French modernism, which acknowledges the Italian name of the place as far as constructing a tortellino of lobster, scallop and king prawn for starter, before depositing it in a rich bisque sauce with wilted gem lettuce and a langoustine, while the chef's French heritage may shine through in a reworked classic involving shoulder of Loire Valley rabbit with sweet-and-sour black radish and wholegrain mustard mousseline. Two nationalities of pig make it into a main course of loin and confit cheek of Ibérico pork with Alsace bacon and a slew of petits pois, or there may be Scottish halibut (including a name check for the boat that landed it) with brandade and squid, before the Tricolor is hoisted high for a dessert of cylindrical Valrhona milk chocolate mousse with salted hazelnut feuillantine and Armagnac jelly, accompanied by burnt honey ice cream. Given the location, there's not surprisingly a prix-fixe, pre-theatre menu, with suggested pre-dinner cocktails, plus a tasting menu backing up the sizable à la carte menu. A wine list of serious scope and class is a good excuse to linger in one of the capital's most romantic destinations.

Chef Marcellin Marc **Seats** 70, Pr/dining room 23
Times 12-2.30/5-11, Closed 24-25 Dec **Prices** Fixed L 2 course £19.50, Fixed D 3 course £29.50, Tasting menu £45-£55, Starter £8.90-£16.50, Main £18.90-£39.50, Dessert £7.50-£9.50
Wines 1900 bottles over £30, 10 bottles under £30, 21 by glass
Parking On street, NCP **Notes** Post-theatre menu Mon-Thu 10-11pm £24.50-£29.50, Sunday L £29.50-£34.50, Children L only

LONDON WC2 *continued*

Kopapa

PLAN 3 B2

@@ Fusion

tel: 020 7240 6076 **32-34 Monmouth St, Seven Dials, Covent Garden WC2H 9HA**
email: information@kopapa.co.uk
dir: *Nearest station: Covent Garden*

Culinary Covent Garden alchemy from a master of fusion cuisine

With elbow-to-elbow tables, big Kiwi artworks, fashionable seating and a bar for dining and cocktails, Kopapa is the complete ticket, its globetrotting fusion food just right for sharing, and delivered all day. Witness a not-to-be-missed crispy tempura 'pocket' filled with high-kicking spiced dhal inari that comes counterbalanced by caramelised coconut and cooling pickled green papaya 'spaghetti', or perhaps try pan-fried scallops with sweet chilli sauce and crème fraîche. Elsewhere, larger offerings might feature succulent lamb rump satay with a taro root rösti, pak choi, rosemary, miso and peanut sauce. Desserts (like coffees) are top drawer too: perhaps a tropical-esque Alphonso mango and coconut pannacotta served in a sublime kiwi gazpacho.

Chef Peter Gordon **Seats** 66 **Times** 12-11, All-day dining, Closed 25-26 Dec, D 24 Dec **Prices** Prices not confirmed **Wines** 22 bottles over £30, 8 bottles under £30, 18 by glass **Parking** On street **Notes** Pre-theatre menu until 7pm Mon-Sat (9.30pm Sun), Vegetarian available, Children welcome

Lima Floral

PLAN 3 B1

@@ Modern Peruvian

tel: 020 7240 5778 **14 Garrick St WC2E 9BJ**
email: enquiry@limafloral.com
dir: *Nearest station: Leicester Sq*

A blast of Peruvian sunshine in theatreland

A blast of South American vivacity in Covent Garden. Tiger's milk is a zesty citrus marinade for producing sea bream céviche, which comes with thick avocado purée, crisp-dried onions and toasted puffed cancha corn. More corn, whizzed up this time, comes with chicken chalaca for main, served with gentle aji panca chilli sauce, and given texture with purple potato 'paper' and slivers of raw asparagus. Peru pretty much invented the potato, so expect lots of it, as well as a similar tuber, olluquito, which comes here with suckling pig. To finish, fine Palo Blanco chocolate is turned into a rich mousse, topped with oats and garnished with honeycomb and nasturtiums.

Chef Virgilio Martinez, Robert Ortiz **Seats** 60, Pr/dining room 12
Times 12.30-2.30/5.30-10.30, Closed Xmas, New Year, L Mon, D Sun **Prices** Fixed L 2 course £17-£42, Fixed D 3 course £24-£50, Starter £7-£14, Main £10-£28, Dessert £7-£8 **Wines** 27 bottles over £30, 8 bottles under £30, 13 by glass
Parking On street **Notes** Brunch, Sunday L £18-£30, Vegetarian available, Children welcome

Massimo Restaurant & Bar

PLAN 5 B6

@ Modern, Traditional Italian

tel: 020 7998 0555 **Corinthia Hotel London, 10 Northumberland Av WC2N 5AE**
email: tables@massimo-restaurant.co.uk
dir: *Nearest station: Embankment, Charing Cross*

Grand Roman style in the West End

Set in the glitzy Corinthia Hotel (though with its own street entrance), Massimo's low-lit dining room is a flambouyant show-stopper. Though eponymous chef Massimo Riccioli no longer presides over proceedings, you'll still find bold-flavoured, authentic regional Italian cooking, albeit with premium ingredients for an international jet-setter audience. The menu covers all the bases in traditional Italian format. Try home-made cacao pasta teamed with wild boar ragù, or a well-balanced assemble of slow-cooked cod with escarole (endive-esque), zingy capers and black olives, while a flourless chocolate cake with Amaretto ice cream might feature in the finale. Wines are a cracking Italian-dominated bunch, and the hotel-style service is switched on and friendly.

Mon Plaisir

PLAN 3 B2

@ Traditional French

tel: 020 7836 7243 **19-21 Monmouth St WC2H 9DD**
email: monplaisirrestaurant@googlemail.com **web:** www.monplaisir.co.uk
dir: *Nearest station: Covent Garden, Leicester Sq*

A Francophile's delight in theatreland

Impervious to fads and fashion and about as French as they come, the original front dining room has changed little since the 1940s (unapologetically Parisian bistro), while beyond there's a series of lighter, cosy rooms including a mezzanine-style loft. The menu mixes the times, too; country terrine is jazzed up with artichoke chutney, before heading to the Med for a main course of sea bass fillet with potato, olive and basil cake and sauce vièrge. Elsewhere there are timeless classics such as snails with garlic and parsley butter, or coq au vin. Close-set tables, resolutely French service and regional wines and cheeses add to the authenticity and upbeat vibe.

Chef Francois Jobard **Seats** 100, Pr/dining room 25
Times 12-2.30/5.45-11.15, Closed Xmas, New Year, BHs, Sun **Prices** Fixed L 2 course £15.95, Fixed D 3 course £17.95-£27.95, Starter £6.95-£13.95, Main £15.95-£28, Dessert £6.50-£9.95 **Wines** 50 bottles over £30, 21 bottles under £30, 20 by glass
Notes Fixed D pre-theatre 2/3 course, Menu du Mois 2/3 course, Vegetarian available, Children welcome

The National Dining Rooms

PLAN 3 A1

@ British

tel: 020 7747 2525 **Sainsbury Wing, The National Gallery, Trafalgar Square WC2N 5DN**
email: ndr.reservations@peytonandbyrne.co.uk
dir: *Nearest station: Charing Cross*

Simple, seasonal cooking in a prime spot

This sleek all-day operation stands in a dream location overlooking Trafalgar Square from the National Gallery. The unfussy modern British repertoire shows a keen eye on the seasons, starting with a Cornish crab salad with Jersey Royals, gem leaves, wild herbs and cocktail sauce that shouts 'springtime'. Main course could be a superior take on an old friend – slow-cooked gammon with peppered pineapple, chips, a quail's egg with crisp pancetta and home-made brown sauce – or John Dory with lentils, salsify, horseradish and Savoy cabbage. It all ends with a fun 'broken' lemon pie with crisp pastry atop the lemon curd filling and peaks of soft meringue all around.

The Northall

PLAN 5 B6

British

tel: 020 7321 3100 **Corinthia Hotel London, 10a Northumberland Av WC2N 5AE**
email: restaurants.london@corinthia.com web: www.thenorthall.co.uk
dir: *Nearest station: Charing Cross, Embankment*

Celebrating British produce in five-star style

The Northall is dedicated to all things British, with the produce of artisan growers and breeders showcased in the modern national culinary style. Cumbrian beef tartare is finely shredded, bound with well-seasoned mayonnaise, surrounded by wasabi, pickled girolles and breadsticks and topped with an egg yolk. Impeccable seafood cookery produces a main course of seared sea bass with confit octopus and razor clams, an ingenious 'risotto' made of riced saffron potato, and assertive garlic velouté. Lamb is the aristocratic Herdwick, served with caramelised shallot purée in minted jus. Savoury notes in desserts, often a minefield, are mobilised well for rosemary parfait with fig carpaccio, lemon verbena curd and honeycomb.

Chef Garry Hollihead **Seats** Pr/dining room 30 **Times** 12-3/5.30-11 **Prices** Fixed L 2 course fr £25, Fixed D 3 course fr £28, Tasting menu £55-£90, Starter £10-£18, Main £15-£28, Dessert fr £9 **Wines** 200 bottles over £30, 2 bottles under £30, 22 by glass **Parking** On street **Notes** Theatre menu 2/3 course £24/28, Sunday L, Vegetarian available, Children welcome

The Opera Tavern

PLAN 3 C1

Spanish, Italian

tel: 020 7836 3680 **23 Catherine St, Covent Garden WC2B 5JS**
email: info@operatavern.co.uk
dir: *Nearest station: Covent Garden*

High-impact tapas dishes in operaland

The Tavern is a classic old London pub, repurposed as an upscale, two-storeyed tapas joint. You could go three-course if you're an old stickler, but little dishes are the principal bill of fare. They pack quite a punch: a truffle-buttered, panko-crumbed scallop with braised peas and prosciutto has a lot going for it, as does impeccably Spanish roasted salt hake with saffron-almond sauce and beans. Superb meats are treated with respect, as for Ibérico loin with morcilla and a purée of pickled apricots, or beef shin with girolles, smoked anchovies and salsa verde. Pink prosecco jelly with raspberries and meringue ice cream is a light way to conclude.

Chef Jamie Thickett, Ben Tish **Seats** 45 **Times** 12-3/5-11.30, Closed 25 Dec, 1 Jan **Wines** 24 by glass **Notes** Fixed tapas menus 3 course over 8 people £37.50-£42.50, Sunday L fr £15, Vegetarian available, Children welcome

Orso

PLAN 3 C1

Modern Italian

tel: 020 7240 5269 & 7845 6474 **27 Wellington St WC2E 7DA**
email: info@orsorestaurant.co.uk
dir: *Nearest station: Covent Garden*

Regional Italian food in a lively basement

The long-running all-day Italian eaterie is tucked away in an expansive Covent Garden basement that was once an orchid warehouse. Now it's all white-tiled columns and framed photos of Milan in the 1950s, and the place fairly buzzes with chatter, clinking glasses and unstuffy quick-fire service, with a crowd-pleasing menu showcasing regional Italian cooking. Expect platters of classic antipasti, crab linguine with lime and chilli, roast chicken in spicy nduja dressing with rosemary and garlic potatoes and rocket, and then torta di cioccolato with clotted cream to finish. A fixed-price pre-theatre option and all-Italian wine list add to the timeless appeal.

Chef Moruff Abiuse **Seats** 90 **Times** 12-12, All-day dining, Closed 25 Dec **Prices** Fixed L 2 course £16.75-£19.50, Fixed D 3 course fr £19.50, Starter £4.95-£9.95, Main £11.95-£22.50, Dessert £5.95-£8.55 **Wines** 20 bottles over £30, 16 bottles under £30, 16 by glass **Notes** Pre/post-theatre 2/3 course £16.75/£19.50, Sunday L £16.75-£19.50, Vegetarian available, Children welcome

Roka Aldwych

PLAN 3 C2

 Contemporary Japanese

tel: 020 7294 7636 **71 Aldwych WC2B 4HN**
email: infoaldwych@rokarestaurant.com
dir: *Nearest station: Temple, Holborn*

Impressive robatayaki specialities – and more

Roka is characterised by top-drawer ingredients, with the freshest of seafood, to-the-second timings and artful presentation. The speciality is robatayaki: contemporary-style Japanese barbecued food. Examples are skewers of chicken with spring onions and tender smoked duck breast, charred on the outside, pink inside, with barley, miso and sticky, intense kumquat paste, or black cod marinated in yuzu miso with home-made hajikami. Sushi are good bets too, such as Wagyu gunkan (beef sushi with Oscietra caviar, spring onions and ginger), as are hotpots like lamb with crab and wasabi tobiko. Puddings include Japanese pancakes with banana, toffee and black sugar syrup, and cherry blossom ice cream accompanying almond crème brûlée.

Chef Hamish Brown **Times** 12-3.30/5.30-11.30, Closed 25 Dec **Prices** Prices not confirmed **Notes** L menu £27, Vegetarian available, Children welcome

Savoy Grill

PLAN 3 C1

British, French V

tel: 020 7592 1600 **1 Savoy Hill, Strand WC2R 0EU**
email: savoygrill@gordonramsay.com
dir: *Nearest station: Charing Cross*

Classically inspired cooking at a Premier League address

The Savoy's iconic Grill has always been the place to see and be seen. The handsome, low-lit art deco room inspires with its walnut panelling, mirrors and plush banquettes. The cooking is international, with classic foundations – there's even a roster of Escoffier signature dishes, from which a glazed omelette Arnold Bennett makes a comforting starter. The fish and shellfish section might offer lobster thermidor or Dover sole, while a 40-day aged rump steak with marrowbone and shallot sauce fits the bill for main course. Elsewhere, there are 'roasts, braises and pies'. Dessert brings pineapple tarte Tatin with coconut ice cream, and a heavyweight wine list raises the bill skywards.

Chef Kim Woodward **Seats** 98, Pr/dining room 40 **Times** 12-3/5.30-11 **Prices** Fixed L 2 course £26-£38.95, Fixed D 3 course £28-£40.95, Tasting menu £39, Starter £9-£16, Main £22-£43, Dessert £85-£12 **Wines** 300 bottles over £30, 20 by glass **Notes** Pre-theatre 2/3 course, Escoffier signature 4 course, Sunday L £42-£46, Children welcome

Spring

PLAN 3 C1

@@ European

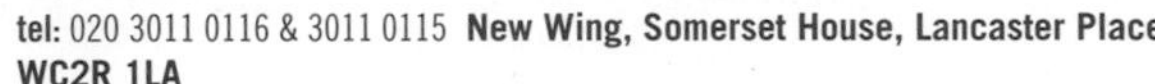

tel: 020 3011 0116 & 3011 0115 **New Wing, Somerset House, Lancaster Place WC2R 1LA**
email: reservations@springrestaurant.co.uk
dir: *Nearest station: Temple, Covent Garden, Charing Cross*

Classy cooking in a light and elegant dining room

After winning much acclaim at the rustic glasshouse restaurant of Petersham Nurseries, Skye Gyngell has brought her trademark style to the grander stage of Somerset House. The regularly-changing Mediterranean menu delivers good-looking plates of seasonal fair with flavours that shine. A knockout starter of squid with chilli oil and mashed broad beans shows a kitchen that knows what works with what, while generous mains triumph with a pairing of grilled lamb and asparagus, boosted by a clear-flavoured lovage salsa verde. The lightest black treacle cake is cleverly teamed with citrus curd, warming candied ginger and zesty clementine. Though prices are high, a fixed-price lunch option eases the bottom line.

Chef Skye Gyngell **Seats** 100, Pr/dining room 35
Times 12-2.30/5.30-10.30, Closed 25-29 Dec, D Sun **Prices** Fixed L 2 course fr £27.50, Fixed D 3 course fr £31.50, Starter £14-£21, Main £18-£35, Dessert £9-£12 **Wines** 73 bottles over £30, 5 bottles under £30, 11 by glass **Parking** On street, NCP **Notes** Pre-theatre menu 5.30-6.30pm, Sunday L, Vegetarian available, Children welcome

Terroirs

PLAN 3 B1

@@ Mediterranean, European

tel: 020 7036 0660 **5 William IV St, Covent Garden WC2N 4DW**
email: enquiries@terroirswinebar.com
dir: *Nearest station: Covent Garden, Charing Cross*

Big-hearted French cooking with flavours to the fore

Terroirs is a buzzy, split-level affair: you enter on the ground floor, the downstairs space is dominated by a big zinc-topped bar, and you can eat where you like. The style is provincial French cooking with a nod towards the Mediterranean. Kick off with snails on toast with silky garlic and parsley sauce and bacon. Dishes are never over-complicated or ostentatiously novel, and flavours are big and hearty, as in a main course of Lanarkshire lamb shoulder served in lamb broth with turnips, carrots, leeks, pearl barley and mint. As a finale, a textbook jiggly pannacotta with tangy pink forced rhubarb is hard to beat.

Chef Michal Chacinski **Seats** 120, Pr/dining room 40 **Times** 12-11, All-day dining, Closed Xmas, New Year, Etr, BHs, Sun **Prices** Starter £7.50-£9.75, Main £17.50-£19.75, Dessert £6.50-£7.50 **Wines** 200 bottles over £30, 30 bottles under £30, 18 by glass **Notes** Fixed 1 course L £10, Vegetarian available, Children welcome

Tredwell's

PLAN 3 B1

@@ Modern British

tel: 020 3764 0840 **4a Upper St Martin's Ln, Covent Garden WC2H 9NY**
email: hello@tredwells7dials.com
dir: *Nearest station: Leicester Sq*

Contemporary comfort food, Marcus Wareing-style

Tredwell's spreads over three floors with a basement cocktail bar and two airy, retro-looking dining rooms lit by large windows. The menu describes itself as 'modern London cooking' which translates as good-quality Brit ingredients sexed up with globetrotting flavours. A starter of light and creamy chicken liver mousse is served in a Kilner jar with a layer of bacon jam, while main-course sea bass arrives with silky carrot purée and earthy lentils. Meaty ideas take in the likes of braised lamb belly with aubergine and tomato curry or pork chops with baked celeriac, while pain perdu with maple ice cream and crispy bacon provides a sweet and salty conclusion.

Chef Chantelle Nicholson **Seats** 120, Pr/dining room 60
Times 12-3/5-11, Closed 25-26 Dec, 1 Jan, D Sun **Prices** Fixed L 2 course £21-£29, Starter £6.50-£10.50, Main £14-£35, Dessert £5-£10 **Wines** 50 bottles over £30, 1 bottle under £30, 15 by glass **Parking** Townsave Shelton St **Notes** Pre-theatre 2/3 course £21/£25, Sunday L £27-£30, Vegetarian available, Children welcome

GREATER LONDON

BARNET Map 6 TQ29

Savoro Restaurant with Rooms

Modern European, British

tel: 020 8449 9888 **206 High St EN5 5SZ**
email: savoro@savoro.co.uk **web:** www.savoro.co.uk
dir: *M25 junct 23 to A1081, continue to St Albans Rd, at lights turn left to A1000*

Contemporary good looks and well-judged menus

Behind a rather quaint-looking shop front, the restaurant has a cool, contemporary interior. 'Simple execution of good technique' is the kitchen's mantra, with everything made in house. A terrine of foie gras and duck confit is partnered by pickled apricots, apple and chervil and pain d'épice, and seared scallops by pea purée and macadamia nuts. Menus encompass the familiar as well as the more adventurous: grilled rib-eye with béarnaise, say, whole sea bass stuffed with herbs, or chicken danoise with rhubarb compôte, pickled cucumber, Parisienne potatoes and chicken jus. Puddings are no afterthought when among them might be lemon crème brûlée with raspberries and ginger shortbread.

Chef Pritesh Bangera **Seats** 100, Pr/dining room 50 **Times** 12-3/6-11, Closed 1 Jan, 1 wk New Year, D Sun **Prices** Fixed L 2 course £14.95-£17.95, Fixed D 3 course fr £29.95, Starter £7-£10, Main £17-£24, Dessert fr £6 **Wines** 30 bottles over £30, 30 bottles under £30, 12 by glass **Parking** 6, On street **Notes** Early eve menu Mon-Thu 2 course £14.95, Sunday L, Vegetarian available, Children welcome

BROMLEY

Chapter One PLAN 1 H1

– see page 336

CROYDON Map 6 TQ36

Albert's Table

Modern British NEW

tel: 020 8680 2010 **49c Southend CR0 1BF**
email: reservations@albertstable.co.uk
dir: *Phone for directions*

Neighbourhood outfit sporting fine pedigree

Chef-patron Joby Wells has brought culinary prowess to South Croydon. Its unobtrusive setting and dark frontage conceal a high quality act: Joby has worked in some of the capital's big names. Calming beiges, browns and soft whites hit the spot, with walls lined by mirrors, wallpapered panels and artwork, while service is friendly but with professional clout. The generous, big-flavoured and well-presented modern cooking hits the spot. Try a seafaring-inspired dish of Atlantic cod paired with mussels, samphire and a scallop velouté, or perhaps English veal (roast and braised) served with peas, smoked bacon, wild garlic and grilled new potatoes. In-house breads are a triumph, and wines a well-selected bunch.

Chef Joby Wells, Jesse Anderton **Seats** 60, Pr/dining room 30 **Times** 12-2.30/6.30-10.30, Closed Mon, D Sun **Prices** Starter £5-£14, Main £14-£25, Dessert £5-£9 **Wines** 37 bottles over £30, 17 bottles under £30, 8 by glass **Parking** Restaurant Quarter car park behind, on street **Notes** Sunday L £14

ENFIELD Map 6 TQ39

Chace Brasserie

Modern British

tel: 020 8884 8181 **Royal Chace Hotel, 162 The Ridgeway EN2 8AR**
email: reservations@royalchacehotel.co.uk **web:** www.royal-chace.com
dir: *3m from M25 junct 24, 1.5m to Enfield*

Imaginative cooking in a classy setting with rural views

Enfield Chase ('chace' in medieval times) was once a royal deer park. The Royal Chace Hotel stands in pretty grounds and is a popular place, not least for weddings. Much admired too is the elegant, first-floor Brasserie (with no lift access) offering linen-clothed tables with candles and fresh flowers, and modern British cooking. Start with seared scallops, sweetcorn purée, crispy pancetta, tempura tiger prawn and lemon-scented samphire, follow with grilled chicken breast on carrot with ginger, Madeira cream sauce and sweet potato crisps. You may well want to end with vanilla crème brûlée and fruit compôte.

HADLEY WOOD Map 6 TQ29

West Lodge Park Hotel

Modern British

tel: 020 8216 3900 **Cockfosters Rd EN4 0PY**
email: westlodgepark@bealeshotels.co.uk **web:** www.bealeshotels.co.uk
dir: *On A111, 1m S of M25 junct 24*

Polished cooking in a parkland setting

The restaurant at this imposing white mansion is named after the portraitist Mary Beale, whose works hang on the walls. It is a stylish room, with well-spaced tables and huge windows looking over the surrounding parkland, and the kitchen team cooks in confident, unfussy style. Salt beef croquettes with pea purée and pea shoots is an impressive starter, followed by pan-fried plaice glazed in honey and served with a salad of pickled cucumber, rocket, tomatoes and Jersey Royals or venison haunch steak with bubble-and-squeak, crushed swede and cherry jus. To finish, try the trio of blueberry frangipane tart, raspberry cheesecake and blackberry pannacotta.

Chef Wayne Turner **Seats** 92, Pr/dining room 110 **Times** 12.30-2/7-9.30 **Prices** Fixed L 2 course £23-£33, Fixed D 3 course fr £29.50, Tasting menu fr £69, Starter £6.50-£12.50, Main £16.50-£26.50, Dessert £6.50-£10.50 **Wines** 57 bottles over £30, 44 bottles under £30, 14 by glass **Parking** 75 **Notes** Sunday L, Vegetarian available, Children welcome

Chapter One

BROMLEY **PLAN 1 H1**

Modern European V

tel: 01689 854848 **Farnborough Common, Locksbottom BR6 8NF**
email: info@chaptersrestaurants.com
web: www.chaptersrestaurants.com
dir: *On A21, 3m from Bromley. From M25 junct 4 onto A21 for 5m*

Strikingly refined cooking in an out-of-town hotspot

Locksbottom's finest is to be found at the busy intersection of two A-roads a few miles from junction 4 of the M25. If that sounds a bit hurly-burly, rest assured that the accessibility of the place works greatly in its favour. The tone is stylish, refined, with dark floorboards and smartly dressed tables, a feature wall upholstered in red silk and prints of food pictures in abundance. Andrew McLeish has always pitched his menus democratically, both for pricing and with a sense of what people want to eat. There is a strong classical base to what he does, reaching back to established standards of culinary excellence in flavour and presentation, and incorporating modern ideas to fit those foundations. Seafood cookery is exemplary, both in a starter of mussel, squid and chorizo risotto with parmesan and crème fraîche, tending to the richer end of the spectrum, and in main course roast hake, its white flesh shining translucently, with gnocchi, girolles and samphire, gently deepened with a purée of smoked celeriac. Prime meats might encompass haunch of sika venison, or Josper-grilled American rib-eye, but also a poached and roasted breast of guinea fowl with truffled gnocchi and leeks in an expressive gamey jus. Copiously detailed desserts might produce caramelised lemon tart amid an array of blackberry sorbet, orange sherbet, lemon and blackberry gel and candied lemon, or hot Valrhona fondant with chocolate soil, orange gel and cardamom ice cream. The Brasserie offers simpler but equally well-executed dishes such as apple, blue cheese and walnut salad, lamb tagine with rose-petal harissa, and crème brûlée.

Chef Andrew McLeish **Seats** 120, Pr/dining room 55 **Times** 12-2.30/6.30-10.30, Closed 2-4 Jan **Prices** Fixed L 3 course £19.95, Tasting menu £55-£77, Starter fr £9.70, Main fr £22, Dessert fr £8.25 **Wines** 20 bottles over £30, 20 bottles under £30, 13 by glass **Parking** 90 **Notes** Brasserie menu light L Mon-Sat 12-3pm, Sunday L fr £24.95, Children welcome

HARROW ON THE HILL

Incanto Restaurant

PLAN 1 B5

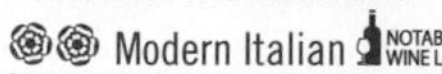

Modern Italian NOTABLE WINE LIST

tel: 020 8426 6767 **The Old Post Office, 41 High St HA1 3HT**
email: info@incanto.co.uk **web:** www.incanto.co.uk
dir: *M4 junct 3 at Target rdbt, follow signs A312 Harrow. Continue through South Harrow, turn right at Roxeth Hill, turn left at top of hill*

Contemporary European cooking in a modern setting

The one-time Victorian post office is delivering an altogether more sybaritic package to the local community these days in the shape of Incanto, a deli, café and restaurant with a modern European spin. The deli-café is to the front, but the main culinary action takes place in the split-level restaurant at the rear. The tasting menu allows for a full-on examination of the kitchen team's talents, while the veggie version is a treat too. Expect feel-good starters such a risotto rich with crab and lobster, before a main course dry-aged beef with truffle and oxtail. Finish with passionfruit cheesecake or a classic tiramisù.

Chef Ciprian Marginean **Seats** 64, Pr/dining room 30
Times 12-2.30/6.30-9.30, Closed 24-26 Dec, 1 Jan, Etr Sun, Mon, D Sun **Prices** Fixed L 2 course £17.50, Fixed D 3 course £22, Tasting menu £42-£55, Starter £6.50-£9.50, Main £16.50-£23, Dessert £7-£8 **Wines** 39 bottles over £30, 20 bottles under £30, 9 by glass **Parking** On street **Notes** Sunday L £6.50-£23, Vegetarian available, Children welcome

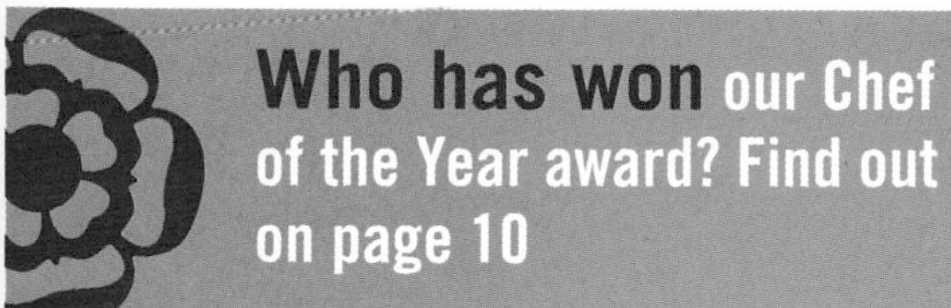

HARROW WEALD

Best Western Plus Grim's Dyke Hotel

PLAN 1 B5

British, European

tel: 020 8385 3100 **Old Redding HA3 6SH**
email: reservations@grimsdyke.com **web:** www.grimsdyke.com
dir: *3m from M1 between Harrow & Watford*

Modern British cooking in a country setting

The former home of Sir William Gilbert (Sullivan's dramatic mate), Grim's Dyke is a grand house in 40 acres of well-tended gardens and natural woodland. Gilbert's Restaurant occupies what was once the billiard room. Traditional decor remains in keeping, the formal tone maintained by uniformed staff. The kitchen displays affection for English classics such as fish and chips and beef stew with dumplings, but there's a lot more going on here, expanding into a broader repertoire of classic European influences. Beetroot-cured gravad lax with smoked salmon mousse and root slaw might precede venison au poivre with dauphinoise, with desserts such as pistachio and griottine brûlée.

Chef Daren Mason **Seats** 60, Pr/dining room 88 **Times** 12.30-2/7-9.30, Closed 24 Dec, 1 Jan, L Sat, D 25-26 Dec **Prices** Fixed L 2 course fr £12.95, Fixed D 3 course fr £21, Starter £5.50-£8.50, Main £12.95-£14, Dessert £5.50-£6.50 **Wines** 65 bottles over £30, 35 bottles under £30, 12 by glass **Parking** 100 **Notes** Supplement charges apply fixed D, Sunday L £26.50, Vegetarian available, Children welcome

HEATHROW AIRPORT (LONDON)

La Belle Époque

PLAN 1 A3

French

tel: 020 8757 7777 **Sofitel London Heathrow, Terminal 5, Wentworth Dr, London Heathrow Airport TW6 2GD**
email: labelleepoque@sofitelheathrow.com **web:** www.sofitel.com
dir: *M25 junct 14, follow signs to Terminal 5*

Airport hotel dining of inventiveness and complexity

Reached by a covered walkway from Terminal 5, the Sofitel hotel group has created something so special at this Heathrow property that it is a destination in its own right. The building is a remarkable piece of modernist styling and it seems fitting that the newest Heathrow terminal should boast a cutting-edge venue such as La Belle Époque. The contemporary dishes have an Anglo-French influence but the kitchen isn't afraid to add Asian twists, as when a moist, perfectly seasoned piece of Irish trout is poached with tamarind, pearl barley and miso broth for an arresting first course. Sticking with the Asian theme, a main course Barbary duck breast is marinated in honey and ginger and roasted to pink perfection alongside a confit leg of the same bird and an earthy accompaniment of potato Sarladaise, root vegetable purée and a rich duck liver jus with plenty of backbone. There is a lot going on here, yet the kitchen keeps its eye firmly on the ball. A vibrant dessert of Gariguette strawberry terrine semi-fredo is teamed with crunchy granola, silky smooth tonka bean custard and fennel pollen. Excellent home-made breads and an extensive, carefully constructed wine list offering plenty by the glass complete the package.

Chef Mayur Nagarale **Seats** 88, Pr/dining room 20
Times 12-2.30/6-10, Closed Xmas, BHs, Sun, L Sat **Prices** Prices not confirmed
Wines 236 bottles over £30, 6 bottles under £30, 16 by glass **Parking** 400
Notes Vegetarian available, Children welcome

HEATHROW AIRPORT (LONDON) *continued*

Vivre Restaurant

PLAN 1 A3

 International

tel: 020 8757 5027 & 8757 7777 **Sofitel London Heathrow, Terminal 5, Wentworth Dr, London Heathrow Airport TW6 2GD**
email: vivre@sofitelheathrow.com
dir: *M25 junct 14, follow signs to Terminal 5*

Assured international cooking from an open-to-view kitchen

The Sofitel at Heathrow Terminal 5 boasts more decent eating than many airport hotels. As an alternative to the fine French goings-on in La Belle Époque, Vivre offers informal dining in an open-plan room of colourful contemporary design. The kitchen team are on view at their wokking and pizza-throwing, and service puts everyone at their ease. The large menu changes seasonally, but is built around a core of stalwarts. Among notable offerings are crab millefeuille served on a hot slate with radish and cucumber, pinkly moist lamb cutlets with matching spring roll, aubergine purée and couscous, and classic lemon meringue pie with vibrant raspberry sorbet.

Chef Anthony Roy **Seats** 235 **Times** 6-10.30, Closed L all week **Prices** Starter £6.95-£9.50, Main £14.50-£58, Dessert £5.50-£8 **Wines** 27 bottles over £30, 6 bottles under £30, 26 by glass **Notes** Vegetarian available, Children welcome

KESTON Map 6 TQ46

Herbert's

British, International

tel: 01689 855501 **6 Commonside BR2 6BP**
email: info@thisisherberts.co.uk
dir: *M25 junct 4, follow A21 Bromley*

Contemporary flavours where London meets the country

Herbert's overlooks some of the 55 hectares of Keston Common and its oak floors, oval-backed chairs and wooden-topped tables create a warm, relaxing atmosphere. The food is modern with a global spin, as in interesting starters like half a roasted quail with orange and walnut crumble or beetroot and haloumi croquettes with pesto aïoli. Main course might be home-made squid-ink pasta with mussels, squid, tiger prawn and sauce vièrge, and there is a choice of sauces to accompany steaks – and a number of appealing vegetarian dishes. Finish with dulce de leche cheesecake and cream. There's a wide range of bar snacks, too.

Chef Angela Herbert-Bell **Seats** 52, Pr/dining room 32
Times 12-3/6.30-10, Closed Mon **Prices** Starter £4.50-£8.50, Main £10-£26, Dessert £5.50-£10.95 **Wines** 12 bottles over £30, 12 bottles under £30, 21 by glass **Parking** Free car park 1min walk away **Notes** Breakfast, Wknd brunch, Sunday L £19.95-£22.95, Vegetarian available, Children welcome

KEW

The Glasshouse

PLAN 1 C3

– see opposite

PINNER

Friends Restaurant

PLAN 1 B5

Modern British

tel: 020 8866 0286 **11 High St HA5 5PJ**
email: info@friendsrestaurant.co.uk **web:** www.friendsrestaurant.co.uk
dir: *M25 junct 17 then via Northwood to Pinner. 2 mins walk from Pinner tube station*

Heartwarming French bistro fare in an old timbered house

Occupying a 400-year-old timbered building in Betjeman's suburban Metro-Land, the decor is intimate and rather romantic, with a low-beamed ceiling and contemporary black leather seats at white linen tables. After more than two decades in business, local supply lines are strong, while top-grade meat and fish comes from Smithfield and Billingsgate markets. Open the show with wood pigeon accompanied by cauliflower purée, pancetta lardons and balsamic, moving on to Shetland sea trout helped by the kick of lemongrass and ginger with fondant potato and samphire. At the end, the tang of orange sauce transforms bread-and-butter pudding.

Chef Terry Farr, James Allan **Seats** 40, Pr/dining room 30
Times 12-3/6.30-10, Closed 25-26 Dec, 1 Jan, BHs, Mon, D Sun **Prices** Fixed L 2 course £13.75, Fixed D 3 course £22.50, Starter £4.50-£10, Main £16.50-£23.50, Dessert £6.50-£8.50 **Wines** 31 bottles over £30, 28 bottles under £30, 12 by glass **Parking** Nearby car parks **Notes** Sunday L £24-£29.50, Vegetarian available, Children welcome

KEW

The Glasshouse

PLAN 1 C3

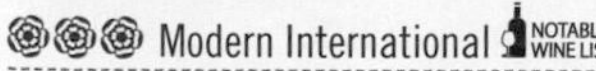

tel: 020 8940 6777 **14 Station Pde TW9 3PZ**
email: info@glasshouserestaurant.co.uk
dir: *Just outside Kew Gardens underground station*

French-based cooking of exemplary consistency

The Glasshouse has hit on a winning formula that keeps this classy neighbourhood eatery perennially rammed with lucky Kew residents. First and foremost, of course, there's the food: what's not to like about seasonally driven modern European cooking built upon the solid foundations of classical French cuisine bourgeoise that makes its impact without any need to resort to culinary flimflam? Then there's the setting, a light-flooded, unbuttoned and slickly neutral contemporary space with full-drop plate glass windows that stand out in the parade of shops near Kew Gardens tube station. Conscientious and clued-up staff are the icing on the cake, with Berwyn Davies leading the kitchen brigade's efforts in producing simple and sumptuous openers such as Orkney scallop céviche with toasted hazlenuts, shaved fennel and orange dressing. Main courses bring a similarly accomplished layering of flavours and textures in dishes that might include red-legged partridge with a white sausage, braised puy lentils and roasted baby beetroot or baked polenta with wild mushrooms, baby onions, turnip tops and mustard cream. Desserts also achieve a level of refinement that only comes with top-level technical ability – perhaps dark chocolate mousse with caramelised hazelnut, cremino and a pear sorbet.

Chef Berwyn Davies **Seats** 60 **Times** 12-2.30/6.30-10.30, Closed 24-26 Dec, 1 Jan **Prices** Fixed L 2 course £24.50, Fixed D 3 course £49.50 **Wines** 479 bottles over £30, 5 bottles under £30, 13 by glass **Parking** On street (meter) **Notes** Sunday L £30-£35, Vegetarian available, Children L only

RICHMOND UPON THAMES

Bacco Restaurant Italiano

PLAN 1 C2

Italian

tel: 020 8332 0348 **39-41 Kew Rd TW9 2NQ**
email: bookings@bacco-restaurant.co.uk
dir: *A316 towards Richmond Station or town centre, 2 min walk from tube*

Family hospitality and traditional Italian cooking

This smart independent Italian next to the Orange Tree Theatre has built a loyal local fan base, who come for its lively vibe and straight-talking contemporary cooking. There's a decked terrace out on the pavement, and inside it's all bare floorboards, colourful artwork, and convivial elbow-to-elbow tables. Among starters, you might encounter king prawns with sautéed Sardinian fregola and sun-dried tomatoes, and pasta is freshly made in-house every day, appearing as twisted tubes of casarecce with slow-cooked wild boar ragù. Mains deliver basil and lemon-roasted cod with caponata, or perhaps calves' liver in sage butter. Tiramisù is always a good way to finish, or there's vanilla pannacotta with mango coulis.

Chef Valerio Cariotti **Seats** 50, Pr/dining room 27
Times 12-2.30/5.45-11, Closed Xmas, New Year, BHs, D Sun **Prices** Prices not confirmed **Wines** 20 bottles over £30, 30 bottles under £30, 16 by glass
Notes Sunday L, Vegetarian available, Children welcome

Bingham

PLAN 1 C2

Modern British V NOTABLE WINE LIST

tel: 020 8940 0902 & 8940 8009 **61-63 Petersham Rd TW10 6UT**
email: info@thebingham.co.uk **web:** www.thebingham.co.uk
dir: *On A307, near Richmond Bridge*

Peerless produce cooked with intelligent simplicity

The riverside setting near Richmond Bridge is the first ace in the Bingham's hand. It's a delight on summer days, and could scarcely be handier for those with big event tickets at Wimbledon or Twickenham, depending on the time of year. Inside the refined Georgian house, all is calm civility, with a measured service tone in the chandeliered and mirrored dining room. Gently conceived modern British creations are the order of the day, opening with wasabi-fired pickled mackerel, seared cucumber and frozen crème fraîche, or quail and tamarind with hazelnut crumbs and nasturtiums. Main courses tack to a more traditionally founded repertoire, but score highly for quality and precision when beef tenderloin arrives with beer-pickled onions and thyme mash, or salmon is partnered with grilled gem lettuce, baby veg and beetroot. Desserts too offer ingenious tweaks on classical ideas: lemon tart with white chocolate sorbet, hot chocolate fondant with orange and rosemary ice cream, yogurt parfait with an oat granola of rhubarb and pistachios and bergamot curd. Little Binghamists have their own menu to peruse, while you get stuck into the magisterial wine list. A Market Lunch menu offers excellent value, built around mains such as braised ox cheek and cabbage with celeriac and horseradish purée.

Chef Andrew Cole **Seats** 40, Pr/dining room 90
Times 12-2.30/6.30-10.30, Closed D Sun **Prices** Fixed L 2 course £17, Starter £6-£14, Main £11-£26, Dessert £5-£12.50 **Wines** 201 bottles over £30, 18 bottles under £30, 14 by glass **Parking** 20, Town centre **Notes** Tasting menu, Sunday L £38, Children welcome

La Buvette

PLAN 1 C2

French, Mediterranean V

tel: 020 8940 6264 **6 Church Walk TW9 1SN**
email: info@labuvette.co.uk
dir: *3 mins from train station, opposite St Mary Magdalene Church, off main High St on corner of Tesco Metro*

Cheery bistro serving French classics and more

If the sun is shining on Richmond, La Buvette's courtyard tables come into their own, but this place is a winner all year round when it comes to classic bistro dining. It's down a leafy walkway off the main high street, with closely packed tables and a menu of familiar dishes backed up by daily specials. Kick off with a starter of marinated mackerel with beetroot salad and horseradish cream. Main-course roast venison comes with wild mushroom pithivier, parsnip purée and hispi, and there's steak, too, in the form of chargrilled onglet. Dessert delivers old favourites such as apple tarte fine with vanilla ice cream.

Chef Buck Carter **Seats** 50 **Times** 12-3/5.45-10, Closed 25-26 Dec, 1 Jan, Good Fri, Etr Sun **Prices** Fixed L 2 course £18.50, Fixed D 3 course £18.50, Starter £5.75-£9.50, Main £13.75-£19, Dessert £5.25-£9.50 **Wines** 19 bottles over £30, 14 bottles under £30, 16 by glass **Parking** NCP Paradise Rd **Notes** Sunday L fr £18.50, Children welcome

RICHMOND UPON THAMES *continued*

The Dysart Petersham

PLAN 1 C2

Modern British V

tel: 020 8940 8005 **135 Petersham Rd, Petersham TW10 7AA**
email: enquiries@thedysartpetersham.co.uk **web:** www.thedysartpetersham.co.uk
dir: *By pedestrian gate to Richmond Park in centre of Petersham*

Fantastic ingredients used creatively in an Arts and Crafts setting

The Dysart occupies a 1904 Arts and Crafts building with original leaded windows and wooden window frames facing south over Richmond Park. Sunshine streams in on bright days, and a low-key jazz soundtrack floats around the elegant room. To start, how about roast quail, with dehydrated Petersham nettles, fermented chilli and fresh peas? Mains made with top-class ingredients might offer a three-way serving of Middlewhite pork (loin, belly and nut-crusted gammon) partnered with velvety Cévennes onion purée, radicchio, and black truffle mustard, or perhaps wild sea bass with lemon celeriac, and a spiced kaffir lime and green chilli sauce. It ends strongly with a burnt honey custard with Chablis apple.

Chef Kenneth Culhane **Seats** 50, Pr/dining room 40
Times 11.30-3/5.30-9.30, Closed 25 Dec, Mon (ex BHs & Dec), D Sun **Prices** Fixed L 2 course fr £25, Fixed D 3 course fr £29.50, Tasting menu fr £72.50, Starter £8.50-£25, Main £17.95-£30, Dessert £7-£10.50 **Wines** 163 bottles over £30, 39 bottles under £30, 15 by glass **Parking** 30 **Notes** Wknd fixed L 3 course £35, Fixed D Tue-Thu only, Sunday L, Children until 8pm

The Petersham Hotel

PLAN 1 C2

British, European V

tel: 020 8939 1084 & 8940 7471 **Nightingale Ln TW10 6UZ**
email: restaurant@petershamhotel.co.uk **web:** www.petershamhotel.co.uk
dir: *From Richmond Bridge rdbt A316 follow Ham & Petersham signs. Hotel in Nightingale Ln on left off Petersham Rd*

Classic cookery overlooking a bend of the Thames

Built on the side of Richmond Hill in 1865, The Petersham's dining room has river views, comfortable banquette seating and smartly dressed tables. On the great value set menu you'll find chicken liver parfait with a range of heritage beetroots and pink onions, followed by Dingley Dell pork loin with creamed potatoes, pancetta and Agen prunes. Trade up to the carte and the opener might be roast poussin with pearl barley, celeriac and artichokes, followed by a tranche of wild sea bass with smoked shrimps, baked pasta, braised leeks and sea purslane. Desserts include rice pudding beignets with chocolate sauce, or classic tarte Tatin with caramel ice cream.

Chef Adebola Adeshina **Seats** 70, Pr/dining room 30
Times 12.15-2.15/7-9.45, Closed 25-26 Dec, 1 Jan, D 24 Dec **Prices** Fixed L 2 course £22.95, Fixed D 3 course £26.95, Starter £8-£16, Main £16-£34, Dessert £8
Wines 93 bottles over £30, 34 bottles under £30, 8 by glass **Parking** 45
Notes Degustation menu 5 course £95, Sunday L £34.50, Children welcome

Petersham Nurseries Café

PLAN 1 C2

Modern British, Italian NOTABLE WINE LIST

tel: 020 8940 5230 **Church Ln, Petersham Rd TW10 7AB**
email: info@petershamnurseries.com
dir: *Adjacent to Richmond Park & Petersham Meadows. Best accessed on foot or bicycle along the river*

Fresh, vibrant Italian-inspired cooking from garden to plate

This busy one-off restaurant is a romantically quirky, shabby-chic place, with its dirt floor and mismatched tables and chairs, but that's all part of the fun. The kitchen sends out a weekly-changing menu of modern Italian-accented ideas inspired by the seasons and the bounty of fresh produce plucked from the garden (including edible flowers and herbs straight from the walled potager). Marinated spatchcock quail with rosemary, romesco and rocket is a light and vibrant opener, followed by monkfish with steamed clams, chilli, garlic, spring leeks, fennel and sea aster. Finish with vanilla pannacotta with thyme and poached cherries.

Chef Damian Clisby **Seats** 120, Pr/dining room 20 **Times** 12-3, Closed Etr Sun, 25 Dec, Mon (ex BHs), D all week **Prices** Starter £5-£14, Main £17-£28, Dessert £4.50-£7 **Wines** 110 bottles over £30, 6 bottles under £30, 9 by glass **Parking** Local car park **Notes** Supper Club 15 evenings/yr £75, Vegetarian available, Children welcome

RUISLIP

The Barn Hotel

PLAN 1 A5

Modern French

tel: 01895 636057 **West End Rd HA4 6JB**
email: info@thebarnhotel.co.uk **web:** www.thebarnhotel.co.uk
dir: *A40 onto A4180 (Polish War Memorial) exit to Ruislip. 2m to hotel entrance at mini-rdbt before Ruislip tube station*

Assertive modern cooking at a Middlesex boutique hotel

An expansive modern boutique hotel handy for inward-bound travellers at Heathrow, The Barn might sound rather agricultural, but stands in fact in three acres of attractive landscaped gardens. A Jacobean effect has been created in the dark-panelled dining room, Hawtrey's, and the scene is set with chandeliers, oil paintings, and painstaking descriptions of the dishes as they're delivered. The bright, modern cooking sees scallops in the fashionable company of glazed pork belly, plus a spiced carrot mousse, and lemon sole poached in coconut milk and partnered with crab, herb gnocchi and a sauce flavoured with grapes and almonds. Finish with Sambuca custard tart.

SURBITON

The French Table

PLAN 1 C1

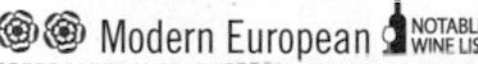

Modern European NOTABLE WINE LIST

tel: 020 8399 2365 **85 Maple Rd KT6 4AW**
email: enquiries@thefrenchtable.co.uk
dir: *5 min walk from Surbiton station, 1m from Kingston*

Modern cooking in a twinned restaurant and bakery

In a leafy quarter of Surbiton, The French Table is the sort of smart neighbourhood eatery we'd all like on our patch. Well-conceived modern French cooking is delivered via three-course, prix-fixe lunch and evening menus, supplemented by a five-course taster. Cromesquis of ham hock and red onion with Puy lentil and truffle salad, caramelised confit garlic and truffle vinaigrette opens the show, ahead of loin and shoulder of lamb with aubergine purée, ratatouille, spiced barley couscous and almonds, and lavender jus. Pastry skills are top drawer here – as you'd hope with its sibling boulangerie/patisserie, The French Tarte, next door – as seen in baked chocolate tart with macerated orange, mandarin coulis and Seville orange ice cream.

Chef Eric Guignard **Seats** 48, Pr/dining room 32
Times 12-2.30/7-10.30, Closed 25-26 Dec, 1-3 Jan, Sun-Mon **Prices** Fixed L 2 course £19.50, Fixed D 3 course £42, Tasting menu £28-£48 **Wines** 62 bottles over £30, 35 bottles under £30, 10 by glass **Parking** On street **Notes** Vegetarian available, Children welcome

TEDDINGTON

Retro

PLAN 1 C1

French V

tel: 020 8977 2239 **114-116 High St TW11 8JB**
email: retrobistrot@aim.com
dir: *A313 Teddington High St*

Le retro-cooking véritable de la France

The core of Retro's menu is classic French bistro cookery, tracing a lineage from foie gras terrine, apple chutney and brioche to vanilla-rich crème brûlée, via the likes of guinea fowl with carrots Vichy and potato fondant in red wine. Discreet modernisation of the repertoire can be productive too, as when a clutch of scallops turns up on grainy sweetcorn purée with crisped bacon, followed perhaps by confit pork belly with spiced apple and pickled white cabbage, or a roasting of halibut with baby spinach in mussel cream. Chocomaniacs will go gaga for the glorious soufflé with its matching double-choc ice cream and sauce, while others enjoy a quintet of cheeses.

Chef François Fayd'Herbe de Maudave **Seats** 110, Pr/dining room 50
Times 12-3.30/6.30-11, Closed Xmas, 1 Jan, BHs, D Sun **Prices** Fixed L 2 course fr £10.50, Fixed D 3 course £22.50-£29.50, Starter £7-£18, Main £13.50-£28.50, Dessert £7-£12.50 **Wines** 56 bottles over £30, 30 bottles under £30, 26 by glass **Parking** On street **Notes** Fixed D 2/3 course min price applies Mon-Thu, max Fri-Sat, Sunday L £22.50-£29.50, Children welcome

TWICKENHAM

A Cena

PLAN 1 C2

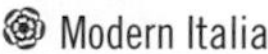

Modern Italian

tel: 020 8288 0108 **418 Richmond Rd TW1 2EB**
email: acenarichmond@gmail.com
dir: *100yds from Richmond Bridge*

Reliable Italian cooking near Richmond Bridge

An informal neighbourhood bistro-style Italian dishing up comforting, authentic cooking. Open with a stimulating partnership of pan-fried Cornish mackerel fillet with grilled cucumber salad and move on to pan-roasted lamb rump matched with a vibrantly minty salsa verde, braised tomato with onions and buttery smashed cannellini beans. There's pasta too, of course – perhaps fusilli with a cacciatore sauce of rabbit braised with vegetables, tomato, white wine and herbs. For pudding, torta di Verona is a moresome, tiramisù-like confection of light sponge soaked in bitter-sweet Amaretto liqueur and Marsala, layered with gooey mascarpone and served with blueberries and roasted almonds. Cheeses and wines all speak with an Italian accent.

Chef Nicola Parsons **Seats** 55 **Times** 12-2/7-10, Closed Xmas & BHs, L Mon, D Sun **Prices** Starter £6.50-£10.50, Main £8.50-£23.50, Dessert £5-£6 **Wines** 60 bottles over £30, 13 bottles under £30, 16 by glass **Parking** On street **Notes** Fixed L 3 course pre-rugby £50, Express L Tue-Sat £10, Sunday L £21-£25, Vegetarian available, Children welcome

MERSEYSIDE

FRANKBY

Map 15 SJ28

Riviera at Hillbark

French, Mediterranean NOTABLE WINE LIST

tel: 0151 625 2400 **Hillbark Hotel & Spa, Royden Park CH48 1NP**
email: enquiries@hillbarkhotel.co.uk **web:** www.hillbarkhotel.co.uk
dir: *M53 junct 3, A552 (Upton), right onto A551 (Arrowe Park Rd). 0.6m at lights left into Arrowe Brook Rd. 0.5m on left*

Sunny Mediterranean food in a half-timbered spa hotel

This all-mod-cons spa hotel features a light-filled Riviera dining room, which embraces a sweeping Mediterranean arc from Nice to Liguria, presented in the grazing format of little and large dishes, courtesy of super-cool modern brasserie service. The smaller offerings include carpaccios of yellowfin tuna or venison, Niçoise salad, and tomatoes dressed in PX vinegar, while their bigger counterparts may be straightforward hunks of protein – orange-glazed duck legs, Goosnargh chicken breast, sea bass – or the likes of truffle risotto or puttanesca pasta. Finish on a refreshing note with citrus posset and pistachio granita, or with lemon sorbet doused in iced vodka.

Chef Ellie Fletcher **Seats** 44, Pr/dining room 16 **Times** 12-2.30/6-10 **Prices** Starter £4.50-£13, Main £12-£20, Dessert £4.50-£8 **Wines** 419 bottles over £30, 64 bottles under £30 **Parking** 160 **Notes** Afternoon tea £25 (with champagne £33), Sunday L, Vegetarian available, Children welcome

HESWALL Map 15 SJ28

Burnt Truffle

Modern British NEW

tel: 0151 342 1111 **106 Telegraph Rd, Heswall CH60 0AQ**
email: burnttrufflerestaurant@gmail.com **web:** www.burnttruffle.net
dir: *Take A540 into Heswall. On right*

Big, bold flavours in an informal modern bistro

The sibling of the Sticky Walnut in Chester, Burnt Truffle follows a similar contemporary bistro vibe with its roster of intelligently updated classics, and good-looking decor featuring natural textures of wood, stone and slate. Expect inventive, well-executed dishes of bold flavours. Beef tartare comes with pickled mooli radish, puffed rice, crispy shallots and smoked radish, followed by a pleasingly visceral cut from the budget section of the cow – Jacobs ladder – braised and glazed short rib of beef with watercress, truffle and parmesan chips and onion purée. For dessert, there's lemon curd with meringue, blackberry jelly, coconut biscuit and marshmallow.

Chef Michael Wong **Seats** 53 **Times** 12-2.30/6-10, Closed 25-27 Dec **Prices** Starter £5-£8.50, Main £14-£23, Dessert £5.50-£6 **Wines** 13 bottles over £30, 28 bottles under £30, 11 by glass **Parking** 10 **Notes** Sunday L £18-£22, Vegetarian available, Children welcome

LIVERPOOL Map 15 SJ39

The Art School Restaurant, Liverpool

Modern International V

tel: 0151 230 8600 **1 Sugnall St L7 7EB**
email: eat@theartschoolrestaurant.co.uk **web:** www.theartschoolrestaurant.co.uk
dir: *Up Leece St then Hope St, follow A5039 around to back of Liverpool Philharmonic, taking 1st road on right. Restaurant on this road, and is only door on Sugnall St*

Confident modernist cooking in a new city-centre venue

Local food hero Paul Askew has brought thoroughgoing British culinary modernism to Liverpool. Dishes are carefully composed, full of imaginative juxtapositions, and confidently rendered. A fat butter-seared scallop sits regally amid smoked pork loin, caramelised celeriac purée and a slew of golden raisins in Sauternes and garlic vinaigrette. These are just a prelude to properly trimmed red-legged partridge with a mini Cox's apple tart, a parmesaned cabbage parcel and quince paste for a fine autumnal main course. Fish could be a hake fillet robustly supported by morcilla and Brussels sprouts. A well-executed pear and apricot frangipane tart makes a fitting served with white chocolate mascarpone and limoncello syrup.

The Art School Restaurant, Liverpool

Chef Paul Askew **Seats** 50 **Times** 12-2.30/5-9.30, Closed 25-26 Dec, 1 Jan, Sun-Mon **Prices** Fixed L 2 course £23.50, Fixed D 3 course £69, Tasting menu £89 **Wines** 248 bottles over £30, 22 bottles under £30, 13 by glass **Parking** On street **Notes** Pre-theatre menu, Children welcome

The London Carriage Works

Modern British NOTABLE WINE LIST

tel: 0151 705 2222 & 709 3000 **Hope Street Hotel, 40 Hope St L1 9DA**
email: eat@hopestreethotel.co.uk **web:** www.thelondoncarriageworks.co.uk
dir: *Follow cathedral & university signs on entering city, at centre of Hope St between two cathedrals*

Regionally focused menu in a trendy hotel conversion

The stripped-back interior of the old workshop is a very modern setting with large windows to give a view of the street action. The menu makes much of provenance and there's a satisfying regional flavour to the food. Things might kick off with torched Sykes Fell ewes cheese, served with roasted figs, golden beetroot, hibiscus and ruby port syrup, moving on to a pan-roasted north Atlantic halibut fillet, baby turnips, cocotte potatoes, crispy Cumbrian air dried ham and leek, and finishing off with mille feuille of dark and milk chocolate with hazelnut cream, marinated blackberry, Earl Grey ice cream and poppy tuile.

Chef David Critchley **Seats** 100, Pr/dining room 50 **Times** 12-3/5-10, Closed D 25 Dec **Prices** Fixed L 2 course £19.50, Fixed D 3 course £25, Starter £5.50-£14, Main £14-£29, Dessert £7-£12 **Wines** 125 bottles over £30, 45 bottles under £30, 21 by glass **Parking** On street, car park opposite **Notes** Breakfast, Afternoon tea, Pre-theatre menu, Sunday L £19.50-£25, Vegetarian available, Children welcome

Malmaison Liverpool

Modern British

tel: 0151 229 5000 **7 William Jessop Way, Princes Dock L3 1QZ**
email: liverpool@malmaison.com **web:** www.malmaison.com
dir: *On Princes Dock near the Liver Building*

Modern brasserie on the waterfront

On the landward side of Princes Dock, Malmaison's first purpose-built hotel is a new landmark for the maritime city. Echoing the city's industrial heritage, the exposed bricks, lighting gantries and air ducts of the double-height brasserie, are balanced by the warm, plush, purple and black furnishings. For modern brasserie dishes, start with ahi tuna tartare, avocado, wasabi, pickled ginger, black sesame and soy dressing. Follow with herb-crusted West Country lamb, Parmentier potatoes and mint salsa verde, or roast Atlantic cod with shellfish vinaigrette and samphire. Finish with pineapple carpaccio with mint, lime and coconut sorbet, or Valrhona dark and milk chocolate torte with crème Chantilly.

Mowgli

Indian NEW V

tel: 0151 708 9356 **69 Bold St L1 4EZ**
email: info@mowglistreetfood.com **web:** www.mowglistreetfood.com
dir: *Phone for directions*

Reworked Indian street food in rough-edged surroundings

Restaurateur Nisha Katona brings Indian street and domestic food to Liverpool, in a space with rough-edged Stateside appeal. High-concept recreations of popular subcontinental dishes begin with chat bombs, crisp potato shells with chickpeas, spices and yogurt garnished with pomegranate, and sublime bhel puri, a crunchy blend of split lentils, nuts and vermicelli in sweet-sour tamarind sauce. Main dishes like the slowly simmered house lamb curry showcase melting meat, marrowbone, anise, plums, coriander and chilli, garnished with threads of fresh ginger. The gulab jamun might just become your favourite version, the doughnuts drenched in syrup, accompanied by an excellent vanilla ice cream. There's a vegan menu too.

Chef Gavin Barker **Seats** 64 **Times** 12-10, All-day dining, Closed 25-26 Dec, 1 Jan **Prices** Prices not confirmed **Wines** 8 bottles under £30, 5 by glass **Parking** On street **Notes** Children welcome

Panoramic 34

Modern European NEW

tel: 0151 236 5534 **34th Floor, West Tower, Brook St L3 9PJ**
email: info@panoramic34.com
dir: *From A565 in Liverpool, into Old Hall St then left into Brook St*

Contemporary dining with stunning views

If you want the lowdown on the local geography, Panoramic 34 offers it up on a plate: stunning views from the 34th floor of a residential tower block cover the city, the Mersey flowing out to sea, and the mountains of North Wales. The lift takes you to a sleek, modern dining room with floor-to-ceiling windows and plush table settings. Sole Veronique is a contemporary take on a classic dish, or start with scallops with cauliflower purée and charred chicory. Move on to fillet of beef with pearl barley, Scottish girolles and parsley purée, then a striking looking dessert based around blackberries, honey and G&T.

Chef Phil Daley **Seats** 80, Pr/dining room 16 **Times** 12-3/6-9.30, Closed 25-26 Dec, 1 Jan, Mon **Prices** Fixed L 2 course £22, Tasting menu £65-£95, Starter £8-£13.50, Main £19.50-£27, Dessert £8 **Wines** 78 bottles over £30, 28 bottles under £30, 10 by glass **Parking** Q Park Capital, The Strand **Notes** Afternoon tea £20-£31.50, Sunday L £22-£26.50, Vegetarian available, Children welcome

Fraiche

OXTON Map 15 SJ28

Modern French, European V
tel: 0151 652 2914 **11 Rose Mount CH43 5SG**
email: contact@restaurantfraiche.com
dir: *M53 junct 3 towards Prenton. In 2m left towards Oxton. Fraiche on right*

Cutting-edge cooking on the Wirral peninsula

Chef-patron Marc Wilkinson's idiosyncratic Wirral restaurant in the leafy conservation village of Oxton is a congenial home for his tireless researches and discoveries. With just five tables (and a chef's table in a glass room), he can give full rein to his extraordinary culinary creativity. Every detail is thought through, from the understated decor of the room itself to the sculptures, artworks, soundtrack and images projected onto the walls. Well-drilled, attentive and knowledgeable staff brief you on the intricacies of the six-courses – menu descriptions are minimal. Classical French foundations underpin ingredients and techniques, although produce is often transmuted into visually beguiling presentations involving the alchemy of dusts, powders, gels and foams. Small-but-perfectly-formed appetisers pave the way for the meal proper, which might kick off by matching almond gazpacho with cherry and asparagus. Main courses bring scallops partnered with smoked lime butter and wild rice, while charcoal-grilled rib-eye of beef is boosted by textures of salsify and celeriac. Sweet courses bring a final flourish of techno wizardry displayed in ideas including lemongrass pannacotta with sour cherry foam, fizzy grapes with mint, lemon sponge filled with lemon curd, sorrel and candied lemon zest, and an enigmatic ending described simply as 'salt or sugar'. Lunch is a shorter four-course affair, but no less arresting in its creativity, perhaps built around monkfish cheeks with olives and orange, before pork belly with sherry-poached salsify and rocket. There's a 300-bin list, and you might as well go for broke and fork out for wine flights since huge effort goes into pairing unusual, revelatory choices to each dish.

Chef Marc Wilkinson **Seats** 12, Pr/dining room 12 **Times** 12-1.30/7-close, Closed 25 Dec, 1 Jan, 2 wks Aug, Mon-Tue, L Wed-Thu **Prices** **Wines** 260 bottles over £30, 30 bottles under £30, 8 by glass **Parking** On street **Notes** Tasting menu L £45/D £85, Sunday L £45, Children 8 yrs+

LIVERPOOL *continued*

60 Hope Street Restaurant

Modern British V

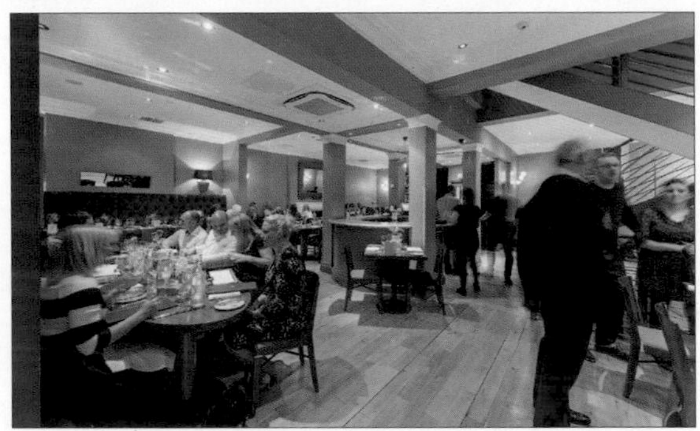

tel: 0151 707 6060 **60 Hope St L1 9BZ**
email: info@60hopestreet.com **web:** www.60hopestreet.com
dir: *From M62 follow city centre signs, then brown tourist signs for cathedral. Hope St near cathedral*

Confident modern cooking near the cathedrals

In a handy spot, close to the Philharmonic Hall and the two cathedrals, this popular Georgian townhouse restaurant still pulls in the crowds 15 years down the line. Simple, seasonal British food with a Mediterranean glow is the deal, starting with the comfort and fun of crisply-fried ham hock terrine with egg, chips and béarnaise sauce, followed by pan-fried salmon with a cassoulet of Spanish white beans and chorizo. Otherwise, go for something like roast rump of Cumbrian lamb with duck fat potatoes, parsnips and carrots and mint jus, and finish with pear and almond tart with dulce de leche ice cream.

Chef Neil Devereux **Seats** 90, Pr/dining room 40 **Times** 12-2.30/5-10.30, Closed 26 Dec, 1 Jan **Prices** Fixed L 2 course £19.95, Fixed D 3 course £24.95, Starter £6.95-£11.50, Main £22-£32, Dessert £7.95-£8.75 **Wines** 40 bottles over £30, 25 bottles under £30, 9 by glass **Parking** On street **Notes** Pre-theatre 5-7pm, Sunday L £15-£25, Children welcome

OXTON Map 15 SJ28

Fraiche

– *see page 343*

PORT SUNLIGHT Map 15 SJ38

Riviera at Leverhulme

French, Mediterranean

tel: 0151 644 6655 & 644 5555 **Leverhulme Hotel, Central Rd CH62 5EZ**
email: enquiries@leverhulmehotel.co.uk **web:** www.leverhulmehotel.co.uk
dir: *From Chester: M53 junct 5, A41 (Birkenhead) in approx 4m left into Bolton Rd, on at rdbt, 0.1m right into Church Drive. 0.2m hotel on right. From Liverpool: A41 (Chester), 2.7m, 3rd exit at 3rd rdbt into Bolton Rd (follow directions as above)*

Locally sourced natural flavours amid art deco philanthropy

The whiter-than-white interiors of the Leverhulme are fitting for a building that has its origins in cleanliness. One of the Edwardian era's great philanthropists, Lord Leverhulme, opened the place in 1907 as a cottage hospital for soap works employees at his Port Sunlight garden village, and who wouldn't find their health restored amid such exquisite art deco surroundings? The French-Mediterranean menu is now an experimental mix of small and large plates that come to table as they're finished. Expect thin-sliced octopus in lemon oil, Brillat-Savarin in pesto, then orange-glazed confit duck legs, or even a whole sea-bream for two, before closing with white chocolate and vanilla risotto.

Chef Ellie Fletcher **Seats** 60, Pr/dining room 20 **Times** 12-2.30/6-10 **Prices** Starter £4.50-£13, Main £12-£20, Dessert £4.50-£8 **Wines** 85 bottles over £30, 43 bottles under £30, 126 by glass **Parking** 70 **Notes** Afternoon tea £20-£28, Sunday L, Vegetarian available, Children welcome

SOUTHPORT Map 15 SD31

Bistrot Vérité

French

tel: 01704 564199 **7 Liverpool Rd, Birkdale PR8 4AR**
dir: *Phone for directions*

Traditional French cooking in Birkdale village

Marc and Michaela Vérité's place is the essence of a neighbourhood bistro. The tables are closely packed, the staff are clued-up, and the place generates a contented buzz. Start perhaps with a daily special such as baked crab thermidor jazzed up with some crispy samphire and croûtes. Next up, roast haunch of red deer is a modern number with a tasting of pear and fois gras cromesquis, finished with a deeply flavoursome red wine jus, or go for Scottish mussels in marinière mode. 'Le steaks' include rib-eye, fillet and Chateaubriand for two (served with frites, salad and choice of classic sauce). Finish with tarte Tatin or rhubarb and custard millefeuille.

Chef Marc Vérité, Daniel Simpson **Seats** 45 **Times** 12-1.30/5.30-late, Closed 1 wk Feb & 1 wk Aug, Sun-Mon, L Tue **Prices** Fixed L 2 course £15 **Wines** 12 bottles over £30, 29 bottles under £30 **Parking** Birkdale station **Notes** Vegetarian available, Children welcome

Gusto Trattoria

Modern Italian

tel: 01704 544255 **58-62 Lord St PR8 1QB**
email: info@gustotrattoria.co.uk
dir: *In centre of Southport*

A taste of Italy in Southport

Gusto is a trattoria with a nice line in cheerful bonhomie and some good and proper Italian cooking. The two rooms are looked over by the charming service team and the open kitchen adds to the buzz of the place. The food does not attempt to reinvent the wheel, just to do things properly. The pizzas are very good – the 'ortolana', for example, topped with grilled vegetables – while octopus salad is a first course filled with the flavours of the Med. Pasta is made in-house and desserts such as pannacotta with raspberries and caramel sauce hit the spot.

Chef Giorgio Lamola **Seats** 38 **Times** 12-3/5-10, Closed Mon (excl BH) **Prices** Starter £3.95-£7.95, Main £6.50-£9.45, Dessert £3.95-£5.45 **Parking** On street **Notes** Open all day Sat-Sun 12-10, Vegetarian available, Children welcome

Vincent Hotel

® British, European, Japanese

tel: 01704 883800 **98 Lord St PR8 1JR**
email: manager@thevincenthotel.com **web:** www.thevincenthotel.com
dir: *M58 junct 3, follow signs to Ormskirk & Southport*

Skilful cooking in a stylish hotel

The V Café and Sushi Bar at this stylish contemporary hotel is the place to be in the evening, with lights dimmed and candles lit. Tables are closely packed and floor-to-ceiling windows look onto bustling Lord Street (alfresco dining is an option). The menu roams around Britain and Europe before arriving in Japan with some platters of authentic sushi and sashimi, with a section of 'gringo sushi for non-fish-lovers' – sausage and bacon tempura, for example. Choosing from the European side of the fence, you might start with seared scallops with glazed pork belly, and move on to classic fish and chips or duck shepherd's pie.

Chef Andrew Carter **Seats** 85, Pr/dining room 12 **Times** 7.30am-9.30pm, All-day dining **Prices** Starter £4.50-£9.95, Main £12.95-£28.95, Dessert £6.50-£14.95 **Wines** 12 bottles over £30, 19 bottles under £30, 5 by glass **Parking** 50, Valet parking **Notes** Fixed D 3 course Sun-Thu, Sunday L £13.95, Vegetarian available, Children welcome

THORNTON HOUGH **Map 16 SJ38**

The Lawns Restaurant at Thornton Hall

®®® Modern European V

tel: 0151 336 3938 **Neston Rd CH63 1JF**
email: reservations@thorntonhallhotel.com **web:** www.lawnsrestaurant.com
dir: *M53 junct 4 onto B5151 & B5136, follow brown tourist signs (approx 2.5m) to Thornton Hall Hotel*

Imaginative menus in an all-action hotel

On the southern side of the picturesque Wirral village of Thornton Hough, this classy hotel and spa is a big hit on the wedding circuit. At its heart is The Lawns Restaurant, a dining destination occupying a grand room with windows onto the garden (hence the name), with a pleasing mix of old and new in the form of wooden panels and stylish contemporary furniture. Begin with a sharpener in the smart lounge before heading into the restaurant. The kitchen, under the direction of Head Chef Ben Mounsey, delivers a creative modern menu with minimalist descriptions. 'Tagliatelle' turns out to be a clever idea – sous-vide squid cut into ribbons, served with razor clams and a beurre blanc flavoured with yuzu. Next up, 'tongue n cheek' is a playful introduction to a tasty number of sticky and tender cheek and crispy tongue alongside caramelised fennel and a punchy green sauce, or go for tuna with the flavours of celeriac, dashi and capers. There's no less invention at dessert stage judging by winning combination of chocolate, beetroot and sour cherries – a rich mousse, delicious ice cream and superbly light mousse respectively. The six-course gourmet menu resolves all indecision as does the nine-course tasting menu.

Chef Ben Mounsey **Seats** 45, Pr/dining room 24 **Times** 12-2.30/6-9.30 **Prices** Fixed L 2 course £18, Tasting menu £80 **Wines** 100 bottles over £30, 27 bottles under £30, 18 by glass **Parking** 250 **Notes** ALC 2/3 course £34/£39, Gourmet L/D 5/6 course £40/60, Sunday L £22.50, Children welcome

WALLASEY **Map 15 SJ29**

Canteen

® Modern British, European

tel: 0151 6383633 **45 Wallasey Rd CH45 4NN**
email: bookings@canteenrestaurant.co.uk
dir: *Liscard town centre, approx 1.5m from Wallasey/Liverpool tunnel. 100 mtrs from Boot public house*

Competitively priced brasserie-style food

From the street the premises look rather unassuming but don't be deterred. The long, simply styled room you'll enter is decorated in black, grey and silver, with a small bar near the entrance and a young, friendly serving team. Well-balanced flavours are brought out in starters of home-made chicken liver parfait with red onion marmalade, and sticky chipolatas with honey and wholegrain mustard. Turning to the mains, choices include slow-roasted, home-cured pork belly with Chinese five spice, Asian slaw and sweet chilli, and marinated smoked fish kedgeree risotto with a free-range egg. For vegetarians, there's gnocchi with pumpkin, feta and pine nuts.

Chef Alan Wycherley **Seats** 25 **Times** 5-9, Closed BHs, 26 Dec, 1 Jan, Sun-Mon, L all week **Prices** Prices not confirmed **Wines** 2 bottles over £30, 16 bottles under £30, 5 by glass **Parking** On street, car park in adjacent street **Notes** Vegetarian available, Children welcome

NORFOLK

BAWBURGH **Map 13 TG10**

The Kings Head Bawburgh

®® Modern British NEW

tel: 01603 744977 **Harts Ln NR9 3LS**
email: kingsheadbawburgh@hotmail.com **web:** www.kingsheadbawburgh.co.uk
dir: *Exit A47 signed university & hospital onto B1108 (Whatton). 500yds right into Stocks Hill. Into centre of Bawburgh, opposite river*

Confident cooking in charming dining pub

The pub itself – with six charming bedrooms – may well date from the early 17th century, but the king in question is Edward VII (born 1841), chosen for his reputation as a bon viveur. There are real ales and the likes of fish and chips up for grabs, plus low oak beams, real fires and plenty of character. Its reputation as a dining pub is confirmed by its well-judged output such as the nicely caramelised scallops that arrive with cauliflower purée and black pudding, a subtle flavour of cumin running through the dish, and the precision and thrilling simplicity of roasted rump of lamb with celeriac purée, charred leeks and Chantenay carrots.

Chef Dan Savage **Seats** 62, Pr/dining room 20 **Times** 12-2/5.30-9, Closed D 25-26 Dec, 1 Jan **Prices** Fixed L 2 course £16-£33, Fixed D 3 course £22-£41, Starter £6-£7, Main £11-£26, Dessert £5-£8 **Wines** 5 bottles over £30, 31 bottles under £30, 12 by glass **Parking** 30 **Notes** Breakfast, Sunday L, Vegetarian available, Children welcome

BLAKENEY Map 13 TG04

The Blakeney Hotel

 Modern British

tel: 01263 740797 **The Quay NR25 7NE**
email: reception@blakeneyhotel.co.uk **web:** www.blakeneyhotel.co.uk
dir: *From A148 between Fakenham & Holt, take B1156 to Langham & Blakeney*

Accomplished modern cooking in a quayside hotel

Those who like to be by the sea need look no further: this hotel is in a perfect spot on the quay, with magnificent views over the estuary to Blakeney Point Area of Outstanding Natural Beauty. Well-sourced raw materials underpin the operation in the sea-facing restaurant. Start with a traditional French-style fish soup made from local seafood, or home-cured gravad lax, and move on to halibut with an Asian spin, or roasted fillet of Angus beef with fondant potato, girolles and spring greens. To finish, try vanilla pannacotta with summer berry jelly.

Morston Hall

 Modern British V NOTABLE WINE LIST

tel: 01263 741041 **Morston, Holt NR25 7AA**
email: reception@morstonhall.com **web:** www.morstonhall.com
dir: *On A149 (coast road) between Blakeney & Stiffkey*

Seven-course dinner menu on the alluring north Norfolk coast

Standing at the edge of the Blakeney National Nature Reserve in coastal north Norfolk, Morston is a 17th-century country seat with commanding views of the briny. Inside, all is heightened elegance, the conservatory dining room done in delicate vernal green with fresh flowers abounding. Polished service ensures the evening drill runs like a well-oiled engine. Guests gather at sevenish for drinks, then take their seats for the eight o'clock show that is the seven-course tasting menu. Following an appetiser, a soup appears, perhaps silky potato velouté enriched with parmesan, black truffle and basil oil, before a miso-glazed chicken wing arrives with a confit egg yolk. A vegetable course might offer roasted cauliflower in onion broth, ahead of a fish – monkfish roasted on the bone in ras el hanout and raspberry vinegar – and the main meat, maybe guinea-fowl with smoked potato mousse, baby leeks and trompettes. A pre-dessert, yogurt sorbet with green tea and lime mousse, heralds the final flourish, perhaps glazed passionfruit tart and mango sorbet. Wonderful home-made breads and a trolley of fine cheeses add authority to the occasion, and the pre-selected wine flight is worth signing up for, with imaginative pairings of unlikely stars from Croatia and Tasmania.

Chef Galton Blackiston, Greg Anderson **Seats** 50 **Times** 12.15-close/7.15-close, Closed Xmas 3 days, Jan, L Mon-Sat **Prices** Tasting menu fr £68 **Wines** 140 bottles over £30, 10 bottles under £30, 15 by glass **Parking** 50 **Notes** Afternoon tea (ex Sun), Sunday L fr £38, Children welcome

BRANCASTER STAITHE Map 13 TF74

The White Horse

 Modern British

tel: 01485 210262 **PE31 8BY**
email: reception@whitehorsebrancaster.co.uk **web:** www.whitehorsebrancaster.co.uk
dir: *On A149 (coast road) midway between Hunstanton & Wells-next-the-Sea*

Seafood-led cooking on the Norfolk coastal marshes

Here, the big skies of north Norfolk can be viewed over platefuls of fantastic regional produce, a sight made even better following an extensive refurbishment. In a location such as this, diners are bound to have fish and seafood in mind. Brancaster's finest mussels turn up in the company of garlic, parsley, white wine and cream, while mains can be as timeless as fish and chips with minted mushy peas, or as contemporary as pan-roasted sea bass with squid ink risotto, parsley root and on-trend crispy chicken skin. Local meat fans might find roast venison loin with game hotpot, parsnips, Savoy cabbage and cocoa nib jus.

Chef Fran Hartshorne **Seats** 100 **Times** 12-2/6.15-9 **Prices** Starter £5.95-£8, Main £13-£21.95, Dessert £6-£8 **Wines** 22 bottles over £30, 26 bottles under £30, 14 by glass **Parking** 30 **Notes** Sunday L £12.95-£16.50, Vegetarian available, Children welcome

COLTISHALL Map 13 TG21

Norfolk Mead Hotel

 Modern British

tel: 01603 737531 **Church Ln NR12 7DN**
email: info@norfolkmead.co.uk **web:** www.norfolkmead.co.uk
dir: *From Norwich take B1150 to Coltishall village, right with petrol station on left, 200 yds church on right, go down driveway*

Bright, modern cooking in a charming small country-house hotel

This handsome old house in the heart of the Norfolk Broads is looking dapper with its contemporary, country-chic finish. The smart restaurant follows the theme, seamlessly blending period features with an uncluttered style – white walls, abstract artworks, and simple flower arrangements. Windows look out over pretty gardens. On the food front, the kitchen hauls in fine local ingredients and offers a vibrant modern British menu. Start with scallops fired up with Cajun spicing, and move on to a fillet of beef with crisp pommes Anna, onion purée, tomato jam, Shropshire blue fritter, savoy cabbage and peppercorn sauce. Finish with a chocolate fondant, milk chocolate ice cream and hazelnut lollipop.

Chef Anna Duttson, Damien Woollard **Seats** 40, Pr/dining room 22 **Times** 12-2.30/6.30-9, Closed L Mon-Sat **Prices** Fixed D 3 course fr £35 **Wines** 22 bottles over £30, 31 bottles under £30, 8 by glass **Parking** 45 **Notes** Afternoon tea £15, Sunday L, Vegetarian available, Children welcome

CROMER Map 13 TG24

The Grove Cromer

Modern British

tel: 01263 512412 **95 Overstrand Rd NR27 0DJ**
email: enquiries@thegrovecromer.co.uk **web:** www.thegrovecromer.co.uk
dir: *Into Cromer on A149, right at 1st mini rdbt into Cromwell Rd. At double mini rdbt straight over into Overstrand Rd, 200mtrs on left*

Polished and passionate cooking on the coast

A private path leads through woodland to the beach from this north Norfolk hotel, a substantial white Georgian house partly covered in creepers. In the restaurant, it's all about clear, fresh flavours. Scallops are given a novel accompaniment of a paprika-spiked risotto of parsnips, peas and lime, while local quail comes with wilted kale (from the garden) and poached pears. Main courses are also carefully considered: seasonal roast pheasant with fondant potatoes and blackberry jus, for instance, and pan-seared sea bass fillet with prawn and mussel velouté and chive mash. Five Norfolk cheeses with quince jelly are an alternative to desserts along the lines of chocolate and marmalade bread-and-butter pudding.

Chef Michael West **Seats** 48, Pr/dining room 30 **Times** 12-2/6-9, Closed Jan (phone to check), L Mon-Sat (winter) **Prices** Starter £6-£10, Main £13-£22, Dessert £7-£8 **Wines** 30 bottles over £30, 9 bottles under £30, 10 by glass **Parking** 15 **Notes** Breakfast £12.95, Sunday L, Vegetarian available, Children welcome

Sea Marge Hotel

Modern British

tel: 01263 579579 **16 High St, Overstrand NR27 0AB**
email: seamarge@mackenziehotels.com **web:** www.mackenziehotels.com
dir: *A140 to Cromer, B1159 to Overstrand, 2nd left past Overstrand Church*

Haute cuisine in a seaside village hotel

The Sea Marge is a family-run Edwardian hotel of great charm with terraced lawns sitting just above the coastal path, and glorious marine views from the panelled dining room. First up might be a pairing of seared scallops with crab and langoustine ravioli, garnished with saffron-scented baby veg, in creamy shellfish broth. A main course of beetroot-marinated salmon with potato cake in salsa verde might appeal next, but there could also be smoked chicken breast with a little chicken cottage pie and a ball of cabbage and bacon in a sauce of café au lait. Chocolate and ginger terrine with salted caramel ice cream makes a good finish.

Chef Rene Ilupar **Seats** 80, Pr/dining room 40 **Times** 12-2/6.30-9.30 **Prices** Fixed D 3 course £21, Starter £6.50-£7.25, Main £11.25-£21, Dessert £6-£8 **Wines** 4 bottles over £30, 24 bottles under £30, 7 by glass **Parking** 50 **Notes** Afternoon tea, Sunday L, Vegetarian available, Children welcome

The White Horse Overstrand

Modern European, British

tel: 01263 579237 **34 High St, Overstrand NR27 0AB**
email: enquiries@whitehorseoverstrand.co.uk **web:** www.whitehorseoverstrand.co.uk
dir: *From A140, before Cromer, turn right onto Mill Rd. At bottom turn right onto Station Rd. After 2m, bear left onto High St, White Horse Overstrand on left*

Great Norfolk produce cooked with flair

In a pretty village a short walk to the sea, this Victorian inn's restaurant occupies a converted barn, given a sleek modern look within flint walls and oak ceiling trusses. The kitchen's a hive of industry, making everything on the premises, from excellent breads to ice creams. Confit pork belly with sweet potato mousse, baked beans and apple and cider purée is a nicely balanced starter, while smoked ham hock rillettes and beetroot jam add depth to a main course of pavé of cod with roast ratte potatoes and mushrooms. Puddings seem to consist of trios, among them maybe vanilla pannacotta with apple fritters and white chocolate buttons.

Chef Nathan Boon **Seats** 80, Pr/dining room 40 **Times** 12-3/6-9.30 **Prices** Prices not confirmed **Wines** 3 bottles over £30, 20 bottles under £30, 8 by glass **Parking** 6, On street **Notes** Sunday L, Vegetarian available, Children welcome

GREAT BIRCHAM Map 13 TF73

The Kings Head Hotel

Modern British

tel: 01485 578265 **PE31 6RJ**
email: info@thekingsheadhotel.co.uk **web:** www.the-kings-head-bircham.co.uk
dir: *A148 to Hillington through village, 1st left Bircham*

Classic and modern food in an revamped old inn

The Kings Head is an old inn that has had an injection of boutique styling. You can pop into the bar for posh scampi and chips or head into the restaurant with its gently contemporary decor and tuck into something a little more creative. The kitchen makes good use of Norfolk's plentiful larder, so there might be a starter of smoked Norfolk ham (served with honey-mustard dressing and pickled veg) followed by roast loin of local pork, or go for a fishy main such as grilled fillet of bream with Med-style accompaniments. Everything looks good on the plate, including a fashionable dessert of salted caramel and chocolate tart.

Chef Nicholas Parker **Seats** 80, Pr/dining room 30 **Times** 12-2/6-9 **Prices** Prices not confirmed **Wines** 8 bottles over £30, 46 bottles under £30, 14 by glass **Parking** 25 **Notes** Sunday L, Vegetarian available, Children welcome

GREAT YARMOUTH Map 13 TG50

Andover House

Modern British

tel: 01493 843490 **28-30 Camperdown NR30 3JB**
email: info@andoverhouse.co.uk **web:** www.andoverhouse.co.uk
dir: *Opposite Wellington Pier, turn onto Shadingfield Close, right onto Kimberley Terrace, follow onto Camperdown. Hotel on left*

Breezily contemporary cooking in townhouse

A touch of boutique styling has been sprinkled over this white-painted Victorian terrace, and these days it's a rather cool hotel, restaurant and bar, with a spruce look of fashionable muted pastel tones and a distinct lack of chintz. The restaurant is filled with blond wood with nary a tablecloth in sight and is a bright and breezy environment for the cooking, which fits the bill to a T. The cooking treads a contemporary path offering up lemon tiger prawn cocktail with butter crumb and Bloody Mary sauce, followed by slow-cooked ox cheek with salt-baked carrot and bourguignon sauce, and glazed lemon tart to finish.

Chef Dave Nash **Seats** 37, Pr/dining room 18 **Times** 6-9.30, Closed 24-25 Dec, Sun, L all week **Prices** Starter £5.50-£7.75, Main £13-£19, Dessert £5.25-£8 **Wines** 3 bottles over £30, 19 bottles under £30, 8 by glass **Parking** On street **Notes** Vegetarian available, Children 13 yrs+

Imperial Hotel

Modern British

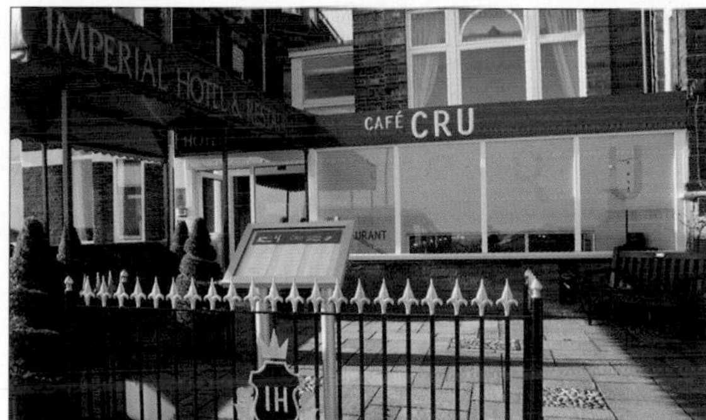

tel: 01493 842000 **North Dr NR30 1EQ**
email: reception@imperialhotel.co.uk **web:** www.imperialhotel.co.uk
dir: *Follow signs to seafront, turn left. Hotel opposite waterways*

Modern brasserie classics in a grand old seaside hotel

Generations of the Mobbs family have run the Imperial since the 1930s, when one of its attractions was that guests were seated at separate tables. Its physiognomy has changed with the addition of a glassed-in terrace for watching the tide roll in, and the Café Cru restaurant, where frosted glass panels divide the booths to demonstrate that separate tables are still the elevated norm. Classic dishes from the present-day brasserie repertoire are the stock-in-trade, opening perhaps with seared scallops and butternut purée in pea vinaigrette, and pressing on with salmon and mussels in white wine and cider sauce, then dark rum pannacotta and raspberries.

Chef Simon Wainwright **Seats** 60, Pr/dining room 140 **Times** 12-2/6.30-10, Closed 24-28 & 31 Dec, L Sat, Mon, D Sun **Prices** Starter £5.50-£9, Main £12-£20, Dessert £6.95-£9 **Wines** 10 bottles over £30, 30 bottles under £30, 12 by glass **Parking** 45 **Notes** Afternoon tea, Sunday L £18-£22.50, Vegetarian available, Children welcome

GREAT YARMOUTH *continued*

The Prom Hotel

Contemporary British NEW V

tel: 01493 842308 **77 Marine Pde NR30 2DH**
email: info@promhotel.co.uk **web:** www.promhotel.co.uk
dir: *Phone for directions*

Holiday-resort hotel specialising in modern British food

Overlooking the seafront, the Prom is also close to the bright lights and attractions of Marine Parade, the town's famous Golden Mile. Strollers is its newly extended, attractively furnished restaurant, with a small bar, perfectly positioned for pre-meal drinks. Yarmouth's trawler fleet has all but disappeared, but fish and seafood still have their place on the modern British menu. Start with seared king scallops and black pudding, and continue with baked cod loin, cannellini bean and cherry tomato stew, and roasted Mediterranean vegetables. Alternatively, perhaps roast chicken supreme, lemon, thyme and garlic, Lyonnaise potatoes, roasted carrots and sprouting broccoli. Pub-style meals are served in the separate Mermaid bar.

Chef Chris Hall, Leigh Schofield **Seats** 40 **Times** 12-2.30/6-10, Closed L Mon-Sat **Prices** Starter £5.50-£9.50, Main £12.50-£24.50, Dessert £5.25-£8.50 **Wines** 15 bottles over £30, 19 bottles under £30, 9 by glass **Parking** 30 **Notes** Sunday L £22, Children welcome

GRIMSTON — Map 12 TF72

Congham Hall Country House Hotel

Modern British, European V

tel: 01485 600250 **Lynn Rd PE32 1AH**
email: info@conghamhallhotel.co.uk **web:** www.conghamhallhotel.co.uk
dir: *6m NE of King's Lynn on A148, turn right towards Grimston. Hotel 2.5m on left (do not go to Congham)*

Creative contemporary cooking in charming Georgian house

The Georgian house was built in the 1780s by a wealthy King's Lynn merchant and has gorgeous gardens, a swish spa and a restaurant full of genuine period charm. A herb garden in the grounds produces an astonishing 400 varieties. French windows look onto the garden from the dining room, where the cooking that arrives at pristine linen-clad tables is gently modern in outlook, producing a starter of seared scallops and pork in artichoke velouté with capers, apple and yuzu, and for main course, lamb rump with pea purée, wild mushrooms and salsa verde, concluding with blackberry parfait and oat crumble.

Chef Nick Claxton Webb **Seats** 50, Pr/dining room 18 **Times** 12-2/7-9 **Prices** Starter £6.95-£9.95, Main £14.95-£26.95, Dessert £6.50-£9.50 **Wines** 78 bottles over £30, 38 bottles under £30, 16 by glass **Parking** 50 **Notes** Sunday L £27.50, Children welcome

HEACHAM — Map 12 TF63

Heacham Manor Hotel

Mediterranean, European

tel: 01485 536030 & 579800 **Hunstanton Rd PE31 7JX**
email: info@heacham-manor.co.uk **web:** www.heacham-manor.co.uk
dir: *On A149 between Heacham & Hunstanton. Near Hunstanton rdbt with water tower*

Fine local produce by the Norfolk coast

The wide-open skies of Norfolk's fabulous coast make Heacham Manor an attractive prospect, and the place even comes with its own coastal golf course. Originally built as an Elizabethan manor, the hotel has been brought smartly up-to-date and its airy conservatory-style Mulberry Restaurant has been extended and modernised. The kitchen's output is simple, contemporary and makes good use of local ingredients. Kick off with pan-seared scallops with confit pork belly and apple purée, follow up with chargrilled rib-eye with roasted shallots and wild mushrooms, or crab and green pea risotto enriched with lemon mascarpone. Finish with rum baba or a pretty-looking Baileys pannacotta.

Chef Mark Tomeo **Seats** 65, Pr/dining room 16 **Times** 12-2.30/6.30-9 **Prices** Prices not confirmed **Parking** 30 **Notes** Afternoon tea, Sunday L, Vegetarian available, Children welcome

HETHERSETT — Map 13 TG10

Park Farm Hotel

Modern British

tel: 01603 810264 **NR9 3DL**
email: enq@parkfarm-hotel.co.uk **web:** www.parkfarm-hotel.co.uk
dir: *6m S of Norwich on B1172*

Unfussy modern cooking in a spa hotel

This hotel and its spa and conference facilities are surrounded by 200 acres of countryside. The contemporary, open-plan restaurant looks out over the gardens while uniformed staff deliver the kitchen's well-presented and well-timed modern British fare. This includes a starter of home-made tortellini with sweet, roasted squash, wild mushrooms, sage crisps for added texture, and sage dressing. Next up, an aromatic main of pan-fried seabass fillet is served on soft, silky confit leek purée with crab gnocchi, fondant potato and beurre blanc sauce. Finish on a high with tangy, light lemon Pavlova roulade with raspberry coulis.

HOLT — Map 13 TG03

The Lawns

Modern European

tel: 01263 713390 **26 Station Rd NR25 6BS**
email: info@lawnshoteltholt.co.uk **web:** www.lawnshotelholt.co.uk
dir: *A148 (Cromer road). 0.25m from Holt rdbt, turn left, 400yds along Station Rd*

Populist cooking in a Georgian townhouse

A small hotel dating from Georgian times, The Lawns offers a number of dining options: bar, conservatory, restaurant and south-facing garden. It's a warm and friendly place, reflected in a menu of largely comfortingly reassuring dishes pinned on East Anglian produce – local asparagus with hollandaise, for example, or duck liver terrine with quince purée and toasted brioche to get things off the mark, then mains of slow-cooked belly pork with stuffed baked apple and spring onion mash, or perhaps sea bass fillet with coriander crushed new potatoes and tomato salsa. To finish, there's a no-nonsense chocolate and almond torte with vanilla ice cream.

Chef Leon Brookes, Adam Kobialka **Seats** 60 **Times** 12-2/6-9, Closed D 25 Dec **Prices** Prices not confirmed **Wines** 2 bottles over £30, 32 bottles under £30, 12 by glass **Parking** 18 **Notes** Breakfast, Sunday L, Vegetarian available, Children welcome

The Pheasant Hotel & Restaurant

Modern, Traditional

tel: 01263 588382 **Coast Rd, Kelling NR25 7EG**
email: enquiries@pheasanthotelnorfolk.co.uk **web:** www.pheasanthotelnorfolk.co.uk
dir: *On A149 coast road, mid-way between Sheringham & Blakeney*

Modern British coastal cooking and afternoon tea

With the stretching beaches and marshland of the north Norfolk coast on hand, The Pheasant is plumb in one of the country's most fashionable resort areas. The cooking is modern British, with seafood a strong suit. Expect a smokehouse platter to start, laden with salmon, prawns and mackerel, pickled veg and tartare, or classic scallops with local black pudding, before pork belly with clapshot and burnt orange purée, or sea trout on leek velouté with charred chicory. The finisher might be banana loaf with a matching fritter and malt ice cream. Afternoon teas, with scones and crustless sandwiches piled on cake stands, are an abiding part of The Pheasant's appeal.

Chef Giles Copley **Seats** 78, Pr/dining room 30 **Times** 12-2/6-9 **Prices** Starter £6.25-£8.50, Main £13.50-£26.50, Dessert £6-£8.70 **Wines** 12 bottles over £30, 34 bottles under £30, 22 by glass **Parking** 50 **Notes** Sunday L £20-£26.95, Vegetarian available, Children welcome

HUNSTANTON Map 12 TF64

Caley Hall Hotel

Modern British V

tel: 01485 533486 **Old Hunstanton Rd PE36 6HH**
email: mail@caleyhallhotel.co.uk **web:** www.caleyhallhotel.co.uk
dir: *On A149, Old Hunstanton*

Well-judged menus on the Norfolk coast

Built around a manor dating from 1648, Caley Hall is a short walk to the wide beaches on The Wash, a twitcher's paradise. Its restaurant, in a former stable block, is a relaxing-looking room with a tartan carpet and high-backed leather-look seats at well-spaced tables. It's a popular place offering precisely cooked, quality East Anglian produce. The short menu has some contemporary touches without rocking any boats; start with grilled fillet of Norfolk mackerel, say, with a trendy slaw and apple gel, followed by braised pig's cheek and roasted loin with celeriac and truffle purée and a jus of local Aspall's cider.

Chef Shayne Wood **Seats** 80 **Times** 12-9, All-day dining, Closed 19-27 Dec, 8-20 Jan **Prices** Starter £6.50-£7.95, Main £12.95-£21.95, Dessert £5.50-£8 **Wines** 1 bottle over £30, 23 bottles under £30, 8 by glass **Parking** 50 **Notes** Sunday L £10.95-£20.95, Children welcome

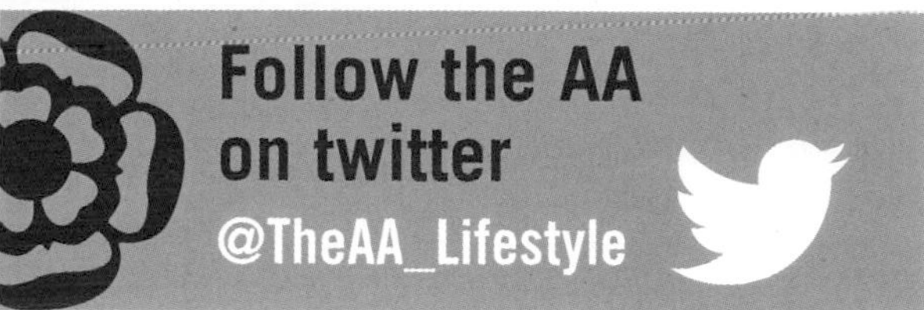

The Neptune Restaurant with Rooms

Modern European V

tel: 01485 532122 **85 Old Hunstanton Rd, Old Hunstanton PE36 6HZ**
email: reservations@theneptune.co.uk **web:** www.theneptune.co.uk
dir: *On A149*

Precision-tuned cooking in a smartly converted Norfolk inn

A short hop from the beach at Old Hunstanton, this Georgian coaching inn has been gently boutiqued into the 21st century by Kevin and Jacki Mangeolles. Few are immune to the charm of the north Norfolk coast these days, and the small restaurant here plays its part in the scene with a display of local artwork, real fires and a light relaxing colour scheme. Clean presentations and clarity of flavour, along with rarefied technical ability, are the hallmarks of Mangeolles' style. Fish and seafood are from just up the coast, and the regional game is among the best in England. That last might be roast quail, tenderly succulent and complemented intelligently with the freshness of a leafy green bean salad, sweetly rich aubergine purée and shallot dressing. For the riches of the sea, look to accurately timed sea bass with artichoke, a sweet potato dumpling and wild garlic, while an earthier route might be via a duo of pork belly and veal sweetbread with salt-baked leek, shiitakes and creamed celeriac. Poached savarin sponge is the centrepiece of a delectable dessert that also builds in sweet local strawberries with a matching sorbet, as well as an acidic hit from concentrated lemon curd.

Chef Kevin Mangeolles **Seats** 24 **Times** 12-1.30/7-9, Closed Jan, 2 wks Nov, 26 Dec, Mon, L Tue-Sat (ex by arrangement) **Prices** Fixed D 3 course £55, Tasting menu £72 **Wines** 80 bottles over £30, 20 bottles under £30, 18 by glass **Parking** 6, On street **Notes** Sunday L £29.50-£35, Children 10 yrs+

KING'S LYNN Map 12 TF62

Bank House

Modern British

tel: 01553 660492 **King's Staithe Square PE30 1RD**
email: info@thebankhouse.co.uk **web:** www.thebankhouse.co.uk
dir: *Follow signs to Old Town and onto quayside, through floodgate, hotel on right opposite Custom House*

Gently modernised British cooking on the quayside

This Georgian townhouse hotel on the quayside in the town's cultural district was once a bank. Inside, a trio of smart dining rooms have polished tables, candlelight and music, and trade in modernised traditional British fare. Start with a slab of Parma-wrapped pork belly terrine and sticky carrot chutney, or double-baked goats' cheese soufflé with Puy lentils, before pressing on to fried ray in cockle butter with crispy seaweed and saffron potatoes, or a 9oz steak in peppercorn sauce. Desserts do their best to look the part and are a little over-zealous in their garnishing, but the principal offerings, perhaps lemon tart and raspberry sorbet, are good enough to stand alone.

Chef Stuart Deuchars **Seats** 100, Pr/dining room 40 **Times** 12-9.30, All-day dining **Prices** Starter £5.25-£8.50, Main £11-£20.50, Dessert £3.50-£7.25 **Wines** 15 bottles over £30, 30 bottles under £30, 22 by glass **Parking** On quayside or Baker Lane car park **Notes** Pre-theatre 2 course £15, Fresh fish Friday, Afternoon tea, Sunday L fr £12.50, Vegetarian available, Children welcome

KING'S LYNN *continued*

The Duke's Head Hotel

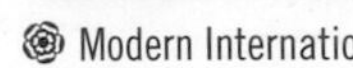

Modern International

tel: 01553 774996 **5-6 Tuesday Market Place PE30 1JS**
email: reception@dukesheadhotel.com **web:** www.legacy-hotels.co.uk
dir: *From A10/A47/A17 enter King's Lynn via South Gates rdbt. Hotel opposite Corn Exchange.*

Period charm and seasonal menus

The hotel occupies a prime spot on the town's main square, its sky blue frontage and period features making a fine first impression. There's a contemporary bistro-style restaurant called Gryffens and a fine-dining option, Turners Restaurant. The latter is an elegant space with well-dressed tables and a feeling of old meeting new. The kitchen brings classical and modern ideas to the table, with the fixed-price seasonal menu offering up a mini Greek salad or potted crayfish with pickled cucumber among first courses. Move on to pan-fried duck breast (cooked just right) with boulangère potatoes and a punchy blackcurrant sauce, and finish with lemon and thyme pannacotta.

LODDON **Map 13 TM39**

The Loddon Swan

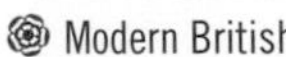

Modern British

tel: 01508 528039 **23 Church Plain NR14 6LX**
email: info@theloddonswan.co.uk **web:** www.theloddonswan.co.uk
dir: *Phone for directions*

Quality cooking in a revamped country inn

Close to the stunning River Chet, this former 18th-century coaching inn reopened in 2012 after a comprehensive refurbishment that retained its traditional charm while bringing it into the 21st century. While much is made of local sourcing of ingredients, the menu mixes modern British dishes with Mediterranean classics, offering chargrilled steaks alongside slow-roasted tomato ragout, gnocchi, olives, crispy chickpeas and pesto-dressed leaves. Equally impressive dishes range from a starter of pressed lamb shoulder, with peas, mint, broad bean and radishes to a main course of slow-braised Heckingham beef cheek, fondant potato, roasted shallot and red wine jus. To finish, try lemon curd tart, basil meringues and raspberry gel.

Chef Jason Wright **Seats** 70, Pr/dining room 30 **Times** 12-2.30/6.30-9, Closed 26 Dec, D Sun (Jan-Apr) **Prices** Fixed L 2 course £12.50-£15.95, Starter £5.95-£8.25, Main £10.95-£18.95, Dessert £5.25-£6.95 **Wines** 10 bottles over £30, 26 bottles under £30, 6 by glass **Parking** 15, Car park opposite **Notes** Sunday L £9.95-£11.95, Vegetarian available, Children welcome

NORTH WALSHAM **Map 13 TG23**

Beechwood Hotel

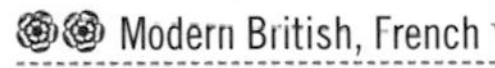

Modern British, French V

tel: 01692 403231 **20 Cromer Rd NR28 0HD**
email: info@beechwood-hotel.co.uk **web:** www.beechwood-hotel.co.uk
dir: *From Norwich on B1150, 13m to N Walsham. Left at lights, next right. Hotel 150mtrs on left*

Charming hotel with good local ingredients on the menu

Hospitality is top of the agenda at this charming country house hotel, with hands-on owners and plenty of staff ensuring that guests are well looked after. There's a small bar, a cosy lounge with sofas to sink into and a traditional restaurant. The kitchen sources most ingredients from within 10 miles of the hotel and sends out contemporary British ideas, opening with Cromer crab and herb tart with thermidor ice cream and a Walsingham cheese tuile, followed by cannon of lamb partnered by parsnip purée and crisps, dauphinoise potatoes, roast garlic and rosemary jus. Finish with chocolate delice with orange cream and amaretti biscuit.

Chef Steven Norgate **Seats** 60 **Times** 12-2/6.45-8.45, Closed L Mon-Tue **Prices** Fixed L 2 course £16.50, Fixed D 3 course £40 **Wines** 30 bottles over £30, 30 bottles under £30, 8 by glass **Parking** 20 **Notes** Sunday L £18-£24, Children welcome

NORWICH **Map 13 TG20**

Benedicts

Modern British V

tel: 01603 926080 **9 St Benedicts St NR2 4PE**
email: info@restaurantbenedicts.com
dir: *Just off inner ring road. Turn right by Toys-R-Us, 2nd right into St Benedicts St. Restaurant on left by pedestrian crossing*

Revelatory cooking in the heart of Norwich

Richard Bainbridge took over the reins in spring 2015 and subsequently won the 2015 Great British Menu serving starter and dessert to the WI, so diners can be assured of exciting 21st-century food that's brimful of revelations, courtesy of stimulating combinations of excellent materials. A starter of suckling pig is served in its own broth with broad beans, scorched Baby Gem lettuce, quark cheese, green beans and mushrooms, ahead of a summery main course matching locally caught wild sea trout with turnip, passionfruit, yogurt, lemon and Jersey Royals. To finish, there's a vibrant pudding of hay-baked pannacotta with raspberries, elderflower, honeycomb and dill granité.

Chef Richard Bainbridge **Seats** 40, Pr/dining room 16 **Times** 12-2/6-10, Closed 3-11 Apr, 7-22 Aug, 25 Dec-7 Jan, Sun-Mon **Prices** Fixed L 2 course £16, Tasting menu £54 **Wines** 16 bottles over £30, 7 bottles under £30, 24 by glass **Parking** On street, car parks nearby **Notes** ALC L/D 2/3 course £29/£36, Children welcome

Best Western Annesley House Hotel

Modern

tel: 01603 624553 **6 Newmarket Rd NR2 2LA**
email: annesleyhouse@bestwestern.co.uk **web:** www.bw-annesleyhouse.co.uk
dir: *On A11, close to city centre*

Easy-going modern British cooking outside the city walls

Standing just outside the old city walls, Annesley's landscaped gardens impart a country-house feel, and an old vine supplies sweet red grapes to garnish the cheese plates. A pair of scallops comes with curried apple, capers and sultanas and the requisite purée of celeriac, while more traditional smoked salmon is served warm with a quail's egg and fennel salad. Mains might be roast guinea fowl with confit garlic and braised baby gem or seared tenderloin and crisped belly of pork with a little portion of ham hock lasagne in grain mustard sauce. Today's favourite dessert components of chocolate, salted caramel and nuts are piled on to a tart for afters.

Chef Steven Watkin **Seats** 30 **Times** 12-2/6-9, Closed Xmas & New Year, L Sun **Prices** Fixed D 3 course £34.75, Starter £7.50, Main £22, Dessert £7.75 **Wines** 2 bottles over £30, 17 bottles under £30, 7 by glass **Parking** 29 **Notes** Pre-theatre menu from 6pm by arrangement, Vegetarian available, Children welcome

Brasteds

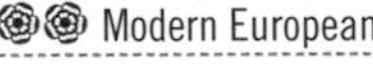

Modern European

tel: 01508 491112 **Manor Farm Barns, Fox Rd, Framingham Pigot NR14 7PZ**
email: enquiries@brasteds.co.uk **web:** www.brasteds.co.uk
dir: *A11 onto A47 towards Great Yarmouth, then A146. After 0.5m turn right onto Fox Rd, 0.5m on left*

Exciting skilful cooking in a stylish barn conversion

In the village of Framingham Pigot, Brasteds occupies a converted barn, a charming room of raftered ceiling, oak floor and brick walls. Sure-footed experience brings the complex food together. Starters might be poached ray wing with grape gel, steamed clams and a chorizo and truffle cream. For mains, classic bouillabaisse might make an appearance, or accurately sautéed sea bass plated with creamed potato, artichoke purée spiked with chervil, sticky red cabbage and lemon butter sauce, while lamb fillet gets the Wellington treatment, accompanied by confit of shoulder, minted pea and potato crumble and a rich jus. Cherries feature in cooked, sorbet and caramelised form in Bakewell tart.

The Maids Head Hotel

 Modern British

tel: 01603 209955 **Tombland NR3 1LB**
email: winepress@maidsheadhotel.co.uk **web:** www.maidsheadhotel.co.uk
dir: *A147 to N of city. At rdbt for A1151, signed Wroxham, follow signs for Cathedral & Law Courts along Whitefriars. Hotel approx 400mtrs on right along Palace St*

Simple modern cooking in Britain's oldest hotel

The brick-built hotel in the city centre lays claim to being the UK's oldest, having been feeding and watering East Anglian travellers for 800 years. Dining goes on in a glassed-in courtyard with a quarry-tiled floor and simple wooden tables. Expect to start with the likes of Cromer crab mousse with tomato gel, seaweed salad and avocado oil, before progressing to a Parma-wrapped breast of corn-fed chicken with bubble-and-squeak, roasted beetroot and a jus of cider and thyme, or seared sea bass on mussel and courgette risotto with buttered leeks in white wine sauce. Dessert might be a verrine of strawberries and Greek yogurt, accompanied by strawberry ice cream.

Chef Magic Pomierny **Seats** 100, Pr/dining room 130 **Times** 12-2/6.30-9.30 **Prices** Fixed L 2 course £20, Fixed D 3 course £25, Tasting menu £49, Starter £7-£8, Main £14-£24, Dessert £7-£9 **Wines** 15 bottles over £30, 38 bottles under £30, 39 by glass **Parking** 60 **Notes** Fixed D 5 course with wine £49, Sunday L £12.95-£17.95, Vegetarian available, Children welcome

The Old Rectory

 Modern British

tel: 01603 700772 **103 Yarmouth Rd, Thorpe St Andrew NR7 0HF**
email: enquiries@oldrectorynorwich.com **web:** www.oldrectorynorwich.com
dir: *From A47 southern bypass onto A1042 towards Norwich N & E. Left at mini rdbt onto A1242. After 0.3m through lights. Hotel 100mtrs on right*

Georgian rectory hotel with a local flavour

Creepers cover the large Georgian house, giving the impression the garden is attempting to reclaim the land – but this red-brick former rectory is here to stay. The daily-changing menu has a good showing of regional produce. Starters of partridge, pork and prune terrine or lime-marinated organic salmon fillet with grapefruit, pickled vegetables and orange dressing are typical of the output. Among main courses, baked fillet of cod is served with saffron mash, leeks, peas and roasted tomato dressing, and Gressingham duck might feature as leg confit served with baked Jersey Royals, roast Puy lentils and a selection of vegetables. Puddings may bring white chocolate and vanilla tart with rhubarb.

Chef James Perry **Seats** 18 **Times** 7-9, Closed Xmas, New Year, Sun-Mon, L all week **Prices** Fixed D 3 course £27-£35 **Wines** 6 bottles over £30, 16 bottles under £30, 5 by glass **Parking** 16 **Notes** Vegetarian available, Children welcome

Roger Hickman's Restaurant

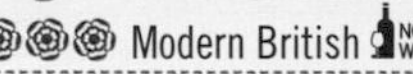 Modern British NOTABLE WINE LIST

tel: 01603 633522 **79 Upper St Giles St NR2 1AB**
email: info@rogerhickmansrestaurant.com
dir: *In city centre, from A147 at rdbt into Cleveland Rd, 1st left into Upper St Giles St*

A haven of high-achieving British food with French underpinnings

Embedded in its little cul-de-sac in the St Giles quarter, a short hop from the cathedral, Roger Hickman's welcoming venue is done in clean, simple but elegant style. The floor is bare, but the tables are dressed in two layers, and there are a few small pictures on the plain white walls. Staff are a real asset, being attentive and discreet, announcing the composition of each dish as it turns up, and forthcoming with recommendations if needed. Hickman's small team produces refined modern Anglo-French cooking with the emphasis on intensity of flavour and seasoning, opening a menu with roe deer tartare spiked with fennel and capers, or a classic pairing of scallops with ham hock, black pudding and apple purée, garnished with puffed pork skin. Main items are timed with sensitivity and combined with flair, as when pinkly seared charred rib-eye arrives with Parmentier potatoes, puréed carrot and ceps in a mealy jus, or when delicately poached humble lemon sole is teamed grandly with lobster, as well as peas and crushed Jersey Royals. Desserts are full of contrasting textures: chocolate mousse and hazelnut sponge come with clementine segments and sorbet, chocolate crunch and a swipe of creamy praline.

Chef Roger Hickman **Seats** 40 **Times** 12-2.30/7-10, Closed 2 wks Jan, Sun-Mon **Prices** Fixed L 2 course fr £20, Fixed D 3 course fr £45, Tasting menu £60-£100 **Wines** 95 bottles over £30, 14 bottles under £30, 12 by glass **Parking** On street, St Giles multi-storey **Notes** Pre-theatre £20/£25 Tue-Thu, L tasting menu £40/£70, Vegetarian available, Children welcome

St Giles House Hotel

Modern British

tel: 01603 275180 **41-45 St Giles St NR2 1JR**
email: reception@stgileshousehotel.com **web:** www.stgileshousehotel.com
dir: *A11 into central Norwich. Left at rdbt signed Chapelfield Shopping Centre. 3rd exit at next rdbt. Left onto St Giles St. Hotel on left*

Classic and modern dishes in an architectural gem

Beyond the hotel's magnificent pillared façade is a palatial interior of marble floors, oak panelling and elaborate plaster ceilings, all sharpened with a stylish contemporary makeover. The SGH Bistro is the setting for the kitchen's appealing repertoire of uncomplicated, up-to-date cooking. Clearly defined flavours leap out from every skilfully rendered dish, be it roast pigeon served with foie gras, shallot and a tart cherry sauce, or a main course of lightly-spiced roast monkfish delivered in a mussel and herb broth with spiced butter, a crispy potato cake and bok choy. To finish, it's worth the wait for a freshly-cooked apple tarte Tatin with cinnamon ice cream.

Chef Ellery Powell **Seats** 50, Pr/dining room 48 **Times** 11-10, All-day dining **Prices** Fixed L 2 course £27.50, Fixed D 3 course £32.50, Starter £6.50-£8, Main £16-£22, Dessert £6.50-£8 **Wines** 23 bottles over £30, 37 bottles under £30, 19 by glass **Parking** 30 **Notes** Afternoon tea £13.50, Sunday L £17.50-£21.50, Vegetarian available, Children welcome

NORWICH *continued*

Stower Grange

 Modern British

tel: 01603 860210 **40 School Rd, Drayton NR8 6EF**
email: enquiries@stowergrange.co.uk **web:** www.stowergrange.co.uk
dir: *Norwich ring road N to ASDA supermarket. Take A1067 (Fakenham road) at Drayton, right at lights into School Rd. Hotel 150yds on right*

Country-house dining with simplicity and style

The ivy-covered country house in its own wooded grounds a few miles out of Norwich is a charming family-run hotel where contemporary cooking based on quality ingredients aims to satisfy rather than startle. Begin with a grilled mackerel, simply adorned with peas, lemon and cucumber, or a voguish pigeon breast starter with a salad of pomegranate, hazelnuts and watercress. Fish continues to show well at main-course stage, in the form of crisp-skinned sea bass with wild mushrooms, beetroot and puréed onions, while the game season brings on roast pheasant with orange-spiked cabbage. Finish with apple and pecan pie and clotted cream ice cream, or white chocolate and raspberry cheesecake.

Chef Lee Parrette **Seats** 25, Pr/dining room 100
Times 12-2.30/6.30-9.30, Closed 26-30 Dec, D Sun **Prices** Starter £6-£7.95, Main £12.50-£21.50, Dessert £6.50 **Wines** 6 bottles over £30, 37 bottles under £30, 8 by glass **Parking** 40 **Notes** Light bite menu £5.50-£9.50, Sunday L fr £27, Vegetarian available, Children welcome

Thailand Restaurant

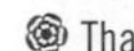 Thai V

tel: 01603 700444 **9 Ring Rd, Thorpe St Andrew NR7 0XJ**
email: siamkidd@aol.com
dir: *From Southern bypass, follow airport signs. At top of hill past Sainsbury's*

True flavours of Thailand in busy out-of-town restaurant

Plants and hanging baskets add dash to the exterior of this well-established restaurant. Inside, the decor is as busy as the bamboo-framed upholstered seats are busy with customers: drapes over the windows, statues in niches, friezes on beams and lots of greenery. The kitchen demonstrates accurate spicing and seasoning plus spot-on timing to replicate Thailand's cuisine here in the suburbs of Norwich. Try namoo (deep-fried minced pork within a bread base served with plum and chilli sauce) or beef musaman – braised steak stewed with red curry paste, roasted peanuts and new potatoes. Finish with a refreshing sorbet or tuck in to bananas in creamy coconut milk sauce.

Chef Anan Sirphas, Sampoin Jukjan **Seats** 55 **Times** 12-3/6-10, Closed 25 Dec, L Sat-Sun **Prices** Prices not confirmed **Wines** 20 bottles over £30, 20 bottles under £30, 7 by glass **Parking** 25 **Notes** Children 5 yrs+

SHERINGHAM — Map 13 TG14

Dales Country House Hotel

British, European

tel: 01263 824555 **Lodge Hill, Upper Sheringham NR26 8TJ**
email: dales@mackenziehotels.com **web:** www.mackenziehotels.com
dir: *On B1157, 1m S of Sheringham. From A148 Cromer to Holt road, take turn at entrance to Sheringham Park. Hotel 0.5m on left*

Smart modern cooking in rural Norfolk

This step-gabled Victorian mansion has period charm in spades, although the cooking in Upchers restaurant takes a rather more contemporary European view of things. Lamb kofta with spiced aubergine caviar, cucumber and mint raita and Madras foam might open the show. With the briny so near, a fillet of sea bass with herby crushed potatoes, wilted greens, fennel purée and caper and tomato sauce is a good bet. Local meat often appears in two-way servings such as roast smoked breast and poached leg of guinea fowl served with fondant potato, mushroom purée and smoked pancetta jus. To finish, maybe cappuccino crème brûlée with chocolate truffle bonbons or Norfolk cheeses.

Chef Rene Ilupar **Seats** 70, Pr/dining room 40 **Times** 12-2/7-9.30 **Prices** Fixed D 2 course fr £21.95, Starter £6-£7.25, Main £14.95-£20.50, Dessert £5.50-£8.50 **Wines** 6 bottles over £30, 26 bottles under £30, 7 by glass **Parking** 50 **Notes** Fixed L £14 per couple, Afternoon tea, Sunday L, Vegetarian available, Children welcome

SNETTISHAM — Map 12 TF63

The Rose & Crown

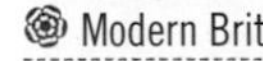 Modern British

tel: 01485 541382 **Old Church Rd PE31 7LX**
email: info@roseandcrownsnettisham.co.uk **web:** www.roseandcrownsnettisham.co.uk
dir: *From King's Lynn take A149 N towards Hunstanton. After 10m into Snettisham to village centre, then into Old Church Rd towards church. Hotel 100yds on left*

Consistently popular village inn with hearty cooking

The interior of this country inn is all twisty passageways, low beams and flagged floors, with real ales in the busy bar. It isn't unknown for locals to dine here three or four times a week, returning for seared scallops with cauliflower and tonka bean purée, or venison and black pudding Scotch egg with parsnip and apple remoulade. Main courses are equally innovative, among them baked cod fillet with Puy lentil, turnip and pancetta stew, cavolo nero and honey-roast parsnips, or taleggio-stuffed chicken breast with polenta and sage, roast figs and pesto. Don't overlook the house classics or puddings like cherry cheesecake with popcorn sauce.

Chef Jamie Clarke **Seats** 160, Pr/dining room 30 **Times** 12-9, All-day dining **Prices** Starter £5.50-£8.50, Main £7.50-£22, Dessert £3.95-£8 **Wines** 9 bottles over £30, 30 bottles under £30, 14 by glass **Parking** 70 **Notes** Non resident breakfast £10.50, Sunday L £14.50, Vegetarian available, Children welcome

STALHAM Map 13 TG32

The Ingham Swan

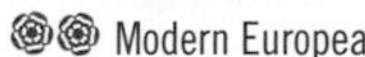

Modern European

tel: 01692 581099 **Sea Palling Rd, Ingham NR12 9AB**
email: info@theinghamswan.co.uk **web:** www.theinghamswan.co.uk
dir: *A419 follow signs for Ingham. Next to church*

14th-century thatched foodie inn with daily-changing menu

Originally part of Ingham priory, the 14th-century Swan presents the timeless face of a thatched chocolate box inn to the 21st-century world. If you fancy a pint, there's a cosy bar, but the driving force is the stylish rustic restaurant where Norfolk flint walls, oak parquet floors, beams and an inglenook are overlaid with modern art. Daily-changing menus might open with belly pork and pulled pork fritter with apple boudin and purée, followed by pan-roasted sea trout with crispy Cromer crab cakes, buttered samphire and asparagus, and sauce vièrge. End with a zesty trio of lemon posset, drizzle cake and ice cream.

Chef Daniel Smith **Seats** 55 **Times** 12-2/6-9, Closed 25-26 Dec **Prices** Fixed L 2 course £16.50, Fixed D 3 course £28, Tasting menu £55, Starter £7-£11, Main £16-£30, Dessert £7-£8 **Wines** 27 bottles over £30, 21 bottles under £30, 9 by glass **Parking** 12, On street **Notes** Sunday L £31, Vegetarian available, Children welcome

THETFORD Map 13 TL88

Elveden Courtyard Restaurant

Traditional British

tel: 01842 898068 **London Rd, Elveden IP24 3TQ**
email: lucy.wright@elveden.com
dir: *On A11 between Newmarket & Thetford, 100mtrs from junct with B1106*

Fresh seasonal cooking in a busy farm shop

The 10,000 acres of the Guinness estate in Norfolk are the base for a modern agricultural enterprise supplying a formidable annual tonnage of fresh produce, with a raftered farm shop at its heart. The all-day restaurant it incorporates is a bright, open space with granite tables and a weekly-changing lunch menu of sensitively cooked seasonal dishes. Goats' cheese and caramelised onion tart is a straight-talking opener, followed by haddock and chips with crushed peas and chunky home-made tartare sauce, or perhaps pheasant au vin from the estate with beef dripping roasted potatoes and seasonal veg. Finish with a chocolate and Guinness layered torte.

Chef Scott Taylor **Seats** 80 **Times** 9.30-5, Closed 25-26 Dec, D all week **Prices** Prices not confirmed **Wines** 6 bottles under £30, 6 by glass **Parking** 200 **Notes** Sunday L, Vegetarian available, Children welcome

THURSFORD Map 13 TF93

The Old Forge Seafood Restaurant

Seafood

tel: 01328 878345 **Fakenham Rd NR21 0BD**
email: sarah.goldspink@btconnect.com **web:** www.seafoodnorthnorfolk.co.uk
dir: *On A148*

Rustic seafood cooking in a historic former forge

The whitewashed former coaching station and forge used to be a resting place for pilgrims heading to Walsingham. A sympathetic refurbishment means beams, York stone floor and the original iron hooks where the horses were shod are in evidence in the cosy, buzzy restaurant. It's all about the seafood here: expect good, honest, rustic cooking, often with Spanish influences and using herbs grown in The Old Forge's garden. There might be smoked eel with horseradish, dressed Cromer crab, Sicilian-style swordfish, fruit de mer platters, and the classic Spanish zarzuela. Steak and lamb shank provide meaty alternatives, and, for dessert, there might be lemon meringue pie.

Chef Colin Bowett **Seats** 28 **Times** 6.30-10, Closed Mon, L all week **Prices** Prices not confirmed **Wines** 1 bottle over £30, 12 bottles under £30, 5 by glass **Parking** 12 **Notes** Opening times vary (phone to check), no late bkgs Jan-Feb, Vegetarian available, Children 5 yrs+

TITCHWELL Map 13 TF74

Titchwell Manor Hotel

Modern European

tel: 01485 210221 **PE31 8BB**
email: margaret@titchwellmanor.com **web:** www.titchwellmanor.com
dir: *On A149 (coast road) between Brancaster & Thornham*

Exciting modern cooking at a family-run coastal hotel

This delightful boutique hotel occupies a classic Norfolk setting with views towards the coast over the RSPB reserve of Titchwell Marsh. Run by the Snaith family since 1988, this converted Victorian farmhouse runs with genuinely warm-hearted efficiency, and the region's produce, particularly excellent seafood, gets star billing on chef Eric Snaith's menus. The light-filled conservatory restaurant overlooks an abundant walled garden that supplies the kitchen with vegetables and herbs. It's a notably laid-back setting for the vibrant contemporary cooking. A knack of combining unusual flavours and textures produces a first course of Jerusalem artichoke soup with truffle bread-and-butter pudding and confit yolk, or there may be a more traditional starter of Brancaster mussels, shallot and white wine. At main, there are first-class locally reared and-landed meats and fish, the latter perhaps displayed in a precisely cooked plaice on the bone with root vegetables and red wine sauce. If meat is your thing, loin and belly of venison make an appearance with roast pumpkin, chocolate and salsify. Sound technique and intelligent flavour combinations are in consistent evidence right through to a finale of bread pudding with marmalade and currant ice cream or a rich chocolate delice with rum and raisin.

Chef Eric Snaith **Seats** 80 **Times** 12-5.30/6.30-9.30 **Prices** Fixed L 2 course £15, Tasting menu £45-£65, Starter £5-£12, Main £9-£28, Dessert £5-£10 **Wines** 54 bottles over £30, 40 bottles under £30, 9 by glass **Parking** 50 **Notes** Tasting menu D 5/8 course, Sunday L £14-£30, Vegetarian available, Children welcome

WIVETON Map 13 TG04

Wiveton Bell

British, European

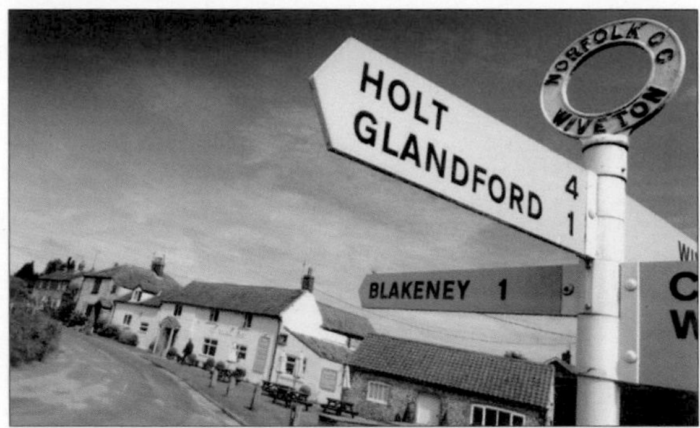

tel: 01263 740101 **The Green, Blakeney Rd NR25 7TL**
email: wivetonbell@me.com **web:** www.wivetonbell.co.uk
dir: *1m S of Blakeney on the Holt road*

Flying the regional flag in a north Norfolk country inn

An authentic Georgian country pub on the village green, the Bell is near Blakeney and the salt marshes of north Norfolk and is done up in light and airy modern fashion. The cooking has a pleasingly traditional air about it, so you might have smoked haddock and horseradish fishcake with a poached egg, then pork belly slow-cooked for 12 hours, served with cider-braised apple, fennel fritters and champ. There are also precisely cooked classics such as beer-battered fish and chips, or puff-pastried partridge pie with roasted roots. Finish on Eton Mess made with winter fruits, or orange and star anise blancmange with candied orange.

WYMONDHAM Map 13 TG10

Kindreds Restaurant

Modern French, British NEW

tel: 01953 601872 **2 Bridewell St NR18 0AR**
dir: *Phone for directions*

Contemporary dining in a former pub

This former pub has maintained much of its original character in the shape of exposed beams and real fireplaces, and there's a genuine charm to the place. Even though a bar remains in situ, this is very much a restaurant, and one with fine dining in mind. The kitchen's modern and creative output includes the addition of a gin and tonic jelly and warm salmon fritter to elevate oak-smoked salmon to a higher level. Main courses might include a well-executed dish of Dingley Dell pork (belly and fillet) with apple purée and black pudding, or grilled wing of skate with King's Lynn brown shrimps.

Chef Mark Dixon **Times** 12-2/6-9 **Prices** Fixed L 2 course £17, Starter £6.50-£9.50, Main fr £12.95, Dessert fr £6.95 **Wines** 40+ bottles over £30, 3 bottles under £30, 9 by glass **Parking** Car park nearby **Notes** Sunday L, Vegetarian available

Number Twenty Four Restaurant

Modern British

tel: 01953 607750 **24 Middleton St NR18 0AD**
web: www.number24.co.uk
dir: *Town centre opposite war memorial*

Comfortable, homely venue with appealing cooking

Hewn out of a row of Georgian cottages, the Griffins' comfortably furnished restaurant has a smart but homely feel. To start there are appealing offerings as mild goats' cheese and cauliflower tart on rocket and pine nut salad, followed by seared sirloin with grain mustard mash, flat mushrooms and kale in rumbustious ale gravy, or grilled halibut with more mash in a sauce of white wine, capers and crayfish. The veggie main course could be roasted squash cannelloni with mascarpone and sage in amontillado cream. A stonkingly rich, soft-textured chocolate mousse cake served warm with maple and walnut ice cream and chocolate sauce is a grand finale.

Chef Jonathan Griffin **Seats** 60, Pr/dining room 55 **Times** 12-2/7-9, Closed 26 Dec, 1 Jan, Mon, L Tue, D Sun **Prices** Fixed L 2 course £16.95-£21.45, Fixed D 3 course £27.50-£33.45 **Wines** 3 bottles over £30, 30 bottles under £30, 7 by glass **Parking** On street opposite, town centre car park **Notes** Sunday L £16.95-£18.95, Vegetarian available, Children welcome

NORTHAMPTONSHIRE

DAVENTRY Map 11 SP56

Fawsley Hall

Modern British

tel: 01327 892000 **Fawsley NN11 3BA**
email: info@fawsleyhall.com **web:** www.fawsleyhall.com
dir: *A361 S of Daventry, between Badby & Charwelton, hotel signed (single track lane)*

Assertive modern British cooking in a grand setting

Plantagenets, Tudors and Georgians all had a go at creating the beguiling architectural mishmash we see today, and it screams 'grand' with its oak panels, stone arches and the fabulous Cedar Restaurant, where a beamed ceiling, huge inglenook and flickering candlelight create a sense of occasion. That said, a proper feeling of intimacy pervades the place, and the kitchen deals in imaginative 21st-century ideas. Among first courses, roasted scallops arrive in the fashionable company of pork belly and pickled cauliflower, rump of English lamb stars among main courses and to finish toffee pannacotta is partnered with coffee soil and honeycomb.

KETTERING Map 11 SP87

Kettering Park Hotel & Spa

Modern British

tel: 01536 416666 **Kettering Parkway NN15 6XT**
email: kpark.reservations@shirehotels.com **web:** www.ketteringparkhotel.com
dir: *Off A14 junct 9 (M1 to A1 link road), hotel in Kettering Venture Park*

International classics in a characterful hotel restaurant

A member of the Shire spa hotels group, Kettering Park belies its location in a business park by having a degree of charming personality about it. The menu deals in the international stalwarts of today, but turned out with proficiency and style, and there is a buffet featuring a selection of local produce, from Melton Mowbray pies to Leicestershire cheeses. Kick start the taste buds with a salad of winter greens, goats' cheese, beetroot, roasted hazelnuts and pomegranate, before a comforting main course of pan-roasted chicken breast with parsnip mash, crispy bacon, shallots in red wine and mushrooms. Finish with warm treacle tart with clotted cream and a sherry reduction.

Chef Jamie Mason **Seats** 90, Pr/dining room 40 **Times** 7-9.30, Closed Xmas, New Year (ex residents & pre-booked), L all week **Prices** Fixed D 3 course £33.50-£52.50, Starter £5-£10.50, Main £12.75-£29.50, Dessert £6.50-£7.95 **Wines** 27 bottles over £30, 49 bottles under £30, 16 by glass **Parking** 200 **Notes** Vegetarian available, Children welcome

Rushton Hall Hotel and Spa

@@@ Modern British

tel: 01536 713001 **Rushton NN14 1RR**
email: enquiries@rushtonhall.com **web:** www.rushtonhall.com
dir: *A14 junct 7, A43 to Corby then A6003 to Rushton, turn after bridge*

Flavour-driven modern cookery in stately surroundings

The grandiose 16th-century Rushton Hall is resonant with some of English history's greatest hits – or misses, as the case may be. The Tresham family who once lived here got mixed up in the damp squib that was the Gunpowder Plot. At the more illustrious end of things, the Hall received guests from a cast of famous characters that included Charles Dickens. Dinner guests still gather for aperitifs in the Great Hall, before a stately progression to the handsome dining room, where service from silver trays is the norm and classical music plays. Adrian Coulthard's modern British dishes are very much flavour-driven, with simple presentations of contemporary classic ideas. An Indian spin is given to a first course of seared scallops that comes with little cauliflower beignets, crisply puffed rice and raisins, while the loin, scrag and sweetbread of local lamb, the neck meat encased in a potato tube, make a distinguished ensemble for a main that also features aubergine, tenderstem broccoli, spring onions and anchovy. Fish might be seared turbot with smoked salmon tortellini in cockle broth. At dessert, a lemon study delivers plenty of penetrating tang in the various forms of mousse, meringue and curd, accompanied by a fragrant basil sorbet.

Chef Adrian Coulthard **Seats** 40, Pr/dining room 60 **Times** 12-2/7-9, Closed L Mon-Sat **Prices** Fixed D 3 course £55 **Wines** 57 bottles over £30, 24 bottles under £30, 19 by glass **Parking** 140 **Notes** Afternoon tea £25, Sunday L £30, Vegetarian available, Children 10 yrs+ D

NASSINGTON Map 12 TL09

The Queens Head Inn

@ Modern British

tel: 01780 784006 **54 Station Rd PE8 6QB**
email: info@queensheadnassington.co.uk **web:** www.queensheadnassington.co.uk
dir: *A1(M) N exit Wansford, follow signs to Yarwell & Nassington*

Inviting riverside inn with treats from the grill

Standing on the banks of the River Nene, The Queens Head is a delightful mellow stone inn with a relaxed vibe and a solid line in muscular modern cooking built on locally sourced ingredients. The 200-year-old hostelry still functions as a pub if you fancy a jar, but food drives the action these days, with a charcoal-fired Josper grill taking pride of place in the kitchen. If you're up for some serious meat action, the steaks are impeccably sourced, and even extend to a rib-eye of Wagyu beef. Otherwise, you might take on potted smoked mackerel followed by sea bass with ginger, chilli and soy.

Chef Craig Lemmon **Seats** 40, Pr/dining room 70 **Times** 12-2.30/6-9 **Wines** 6 bottles over £30, 23 bottles under £30, 14 by glass **Parking** 45 **Notes** Sunday L £10-£21, Vegetarian available, Children welcome

NORTHAMPTON Map 11 SP76

The Hopping Hare

@ Modern British V

tel: 01604 580090 **18 Hopping Hill Gardens, Duston NN5 6PF**
email: info@hoppinghare.com **web:** www.hoppinghare.com
dir: *Take A428 from Northampton towards West Haddon. Left onto Hopping Hill Gardens, follow signs*

Ambitious cooking in a contemporary setting

The Hopping Hare is a 21st-century venue: the bar offers a stylish place to meet, while the restaurant is informal and atmospheric. The culinary output includes impressive grazing boards filled with cheeses, salmon, pastrami and such like, and extends to ambitious British dishes like a starter of pan-fried pigeon breast with Jerusalem artichoke purée, sticky honey-glazed chestnuts and black pudding crumb. There are French classical influences in dishes like a main course pan-fried Gressingham duck breast with confit leg, sautéed Savoy cabbage and Earl Grey jus, and a dessert of pineapple and star anise tarte Tatin or lavender and honey pannacotta with vanilla-poached pink rhubarb and ginger beer sorbet.

Chef Jennie Bowmaker **Seats** 80 **Times** 12-10, All-day dining **Prices** Fixed L 2 course £16.95, Starter £5.50-£5.95, Main £12.95-£23.95, Dessert £4.95-£5.75 **Wines** 10 bottles over £30, 25 bottles under £30, 9 by glass **Parking** 40, On street **Notes** Sunday L £16.95-£19.95, Children welcome

OUNDLE Map 11 TL08

The Talbot Hotel

@ British

tel: 01832 273621 **New St PE8 4EA**
email: talbot@bulldogmail.co.uk **web:** www.thetalbot-oundle.com
dir: *A605 Northampton/Oundle at rdbt exit Oundle A427 Station Road, turn onto New Street*

Classic and modern comfort food in an ancient hostelry

If The Talbot looks ancient, that's maybe because its stone façades, mullioned windows and grand timber staircase were recycled from Fotheringhay Castle in the 17th century. Nowadays it does a brisk trade as a hotel, coffee house and eatery, aka the restaurant, where bare tables and classy cutlery work well in the modern, minimalist-yet-comfy space. Start with crab linguine ramped up with dill, lemon, chilli crème fraîche and shaved truffle, followed by a home-baked, shortcrust pastry-topped steak, ale and mushroom pie with thick-cut chips. Otherwise, go for more up-to-date roast lamb rump with Moroccan-spiced couscous and chickpea salsa and finish with fig and almond tart sauced with honey ice cream.

Chef David Simms **Seats** 48, Pr/dining room 64 **Times** 12-2.30/6.30-9.30 **Prices** Prices not confirmed **Wines** 9 bottles over £30, 30 bottles under £30, 16 by glass **Parking** 30 **Notes** Sunday L, Vegetarian available, Children welcome

WEEDON Map 11 SP65

Narrow Boat at Weedon

Modern, Traditional British

tel: 01327 340333 **Stowe Hill, A5 Watling St NN7 4RZ**
email: info@narrowboatatweedon.co.uk **web:** www.narrowboatatweedon.co.uk
dir: *M1 junct 16 follow signs to Flore. At A5 junct S towards Towcester. On Grand Union Canal*

Waterside inn has all bases covered

Nope, it's not actually on the water, but plenty of boats moor by this popular gastropub. It's easy to find on the A5, offers watery rural views, and serves food in both the bar and the (more formal) restaurant. The kitchen offers everything from pub classics, stone-baked pizzas, and more up-to-date ideas in the restaurant. Launch the meal with seared scallops, burnt apple purée, celeriac and apple remoulade, pancetta. Cruise on to lamb rump with dauphinoise potatoes, pea purée (given a lift with mint gel and confit cherry tomato), lamb neck ballotine, baby vegetables, red wine jus. End decadently with peanut butter parfait.

WHITTLEBURY Map 11 SP64

Whittlebury Hall

Modern British, European

tel: 01327 857857 & 0845 400 0002 *(Calls cost 7p per minute plus your phone company's access charge)* **NN12 8QH**
email: reservations@whittleburyhall.co.uk **web:** www.whittleburyhall.co.uk
dir: *A43/A413 towards Buckingham, through Whittlebury, turn for hotel on right (signed)*

Contemporary and creative fine dining and motor racing

This plush neo-Georgian hotel with a Rolls Royce of a spa and a sophisticated restaurant is just a Ferrari's roar away from Silverstone. While the slick front-of-house team help diners relax in the slow lane, the kitchen hits top gear with modern British cooking underpinned by finely tuned classical techniques. A starter called 'ham, egg and chips' delivers ham hock and Serrano ham with truffled scrambled egg and golden raisin jus. Main courses include sea bass with garlic, sauce basquaise, mussels and grapes, or veal sirloin with lentils, celeriac root, pied bleu mushrooms and baby turnips. For pudding, a take on millefeuille is served with raspberries and champagne and lemon sorbet.

NORTHUMBERLAND

BAMBURGH Map 21 NU13

Waren House Hotel

Modern, Traditional British

tel: 01668 214581 **Waren Mill NE70 7EE**
email: enquiries@warenhousehotel.co.uk **web:** www.warenhousehotel.co.uk
dir: *Exit A1 on B1342, follow signs to Bamburgh. Hotel close to Budle Bay, approx 2m from A1*

Local supplies for country-house cooking

Tradition is the watchword in the kitchen of this classic country-house hotel, starting with diligent sourcing of the region's finest ingredients, which are brought together in a broadly modern British style. Pan-seared scallops are matched with creamed cauliflower, pea shoots, raisins and a mildly curry-spiced dressing, followed by a well-conceived main course partnering cumin-braised pork belly with cabbage and apple, cider jelly, puffed crackling, and a honeyed apple sauce. Fish cookery is handled with equal aplomb. Dark chocolate fondant with a richly oozing centre is a good way to finish, particularly as it comes with white chocolate sorbet, crème fraîche, and chocolate streusel.

Chef Steven Owens **Seats** 30 **Times** 6-8.45, Closed L all week **Prices** Starter £8.45-£9.95, Main £17.95-£24, Dessert £6.50-£9.95 **Wines** 65 bottles over £30, 120 bottles under £30, 8 by glass **Parking** 15 **Notes** Vegetarian available, Children 14 yrs+

BERWICK-UPON-TWEED Map 21 NT95

Magna

 Indian

tel: 01289 302736 & 306229 **39 Bridge St TD15 1ES**
email: oliul.khan@gmail.co.uk
dir: *A1 Berwick next to the old bridge*

Traditional Indian cooking by the Tweed

Close to the bridge over the Tweed at the lower end of the walled town, Magna has earned a reputation for top-notch Indian cooking since it opened in 1982. Occupying a grand Victorian building, bright red chairs and marble-topped tables add a cheery glow to the place. The menu offers plenty of familiar curry-house staples, but what sets it apart is the use of local meats and locally-grown vegetables. Start with tandoori barbecued venison, or a bowl of Mulligatawny soup. For main courses, go for the chef's special massala or king prawn green Bengal.

Chef Oliul Khan, Suman Ahmed **Seats** 85, Pr/dining room 40 **Times** 12-2/5-11.30 **Prices** Fixed L 2 course £6.50-£12.95, Fixed D 3 course £20.70-£37.95, Starter £2.95-£6.95, Main £5.50-£12.95, Dessert £2.95-£4.95 **Wines** 2 bottles over £30, 16 bottles under £30, 6 by glass **Parking** 60 **Notes** Sunday L £6.50-£12.95, Vegetarian available, Children welcome

BLANCHLAND Map 18 NY95

The Lord Crewe Arms Blanchland

Traditional British

tel: 01434 675469 **The Square DH8 9SP**
email: enquiries@lordcrewearmsblanchland.co.uk
web: www.lordcrewearmsblanchland.co.uk
dir: *Phone for directions*

Age-old hospitality 21st-century style

Built for the residents of Blanchland Abbey in the 1100s, this wonderfully historic inn has served everyone from monks to lead miners. It seems unlikely that the latter, after a long, hard day underground, would have been much interested in the inn's architecture, not even the vaulted stone crypt, now an atmospheric bar. Upstairs is the Bishop's Dining Room, which clearly intends to make a regular customer of you by offering such appealing dishes as potted crab on toast with brown crab mayonnaise, Boccadon Farm veal rump, roasted Loch Duart salmon, and chargrilled flat-iron steak. Finish with Alnwick rum and nut tart, or rhubarb fumble.

Chef Simon Hicks **Seats** 40, Pr/dining room 14 **Times** 12-2.30/6-9 **Prices** Prices not confirmed **Wines** 26 bottles over £30, 25 bottles under £30, 11 by glass **Parking** 30 **Notes** Sunday L, Vegetarian available, Children welcome

CHATHILL Map 21 NU12

Doxford Hall Hotel & Spa

Modern British V

tel: 01665 589700 **NE67 5DN**
email: info@doxfordhall.com **web:** www.doxfordhall.com
dir: *8m N of Alnwick just off A1, signed Christon Bank & Seahouses. B6347 then follow signs for Doxford*

Modern treatments of local supplies

Doxford Hall's restaurant has chandeliers in ornate ceilings, a stone fireplace, deep-red walls and menus reflecting 21st-century dining expectations. Seared scallops with two croquettes of slowly cooked pig's cheek and celeriac remoulade is a starter of intense, distinct flavours, as is rabbit and Parma ham rillette with beetroot and truffled mayonnaise. Mains might be roast loin of lamb with a copper pan of braised meat topped with a cobbler along with a spoonful of pea and onion fricassée and a glossy sauce, or curried fish pie and a soft-boiled duck's egg accompanying roast fillet of hake. Pudding could be moist lemon cake with matching iced parfait and lemony caramel sauce.

Chef Michael Thorpe **Seats** 60, Pr/dining room 200 **Times** 12-2/6.30-9.30 **Prices** Fixed L 2 course £25, Starter £7.95-£9.50, Main £18.50-£27.50, Dessert £6.50-£8.50 **Wines** 25 bottles over £30, 47 bottles under £30, 15 by glass **Parking** 100 **Notes** Afternoon tea, Sunday L, Children welcome

CORNHILL-ON-TWEED Map 21 NT83

Tillmouth Park Country House Hotel

Modern British

tel: 01890 882255 **TD12 4UU**
email: reception@tillmouthpark.force9.co.uk **web:** www.tillmouthpark.co.uk
dir: *A698, 3m E from Cornhill-on-Tweed*

Seasonal cooking in a splendid mansion

Close to the Scottish border, this splendid Victorian mansion is surrounded by 15 acres of landscaped grounds. Entry to the elevated Library Dining Room – with candlelit tables and views over the grounds – is via a beautiful wooden staircase around the edge of the tower. The kitchen turns out classically based modern British food with menus driven by the best of local produce. Goats' cheese pannacotta with semi-dried cherry tomatoes and basil compôte starts things off, followed by a well-made risotto of Eyemouth smoked haddock turbocharged with fresh chilli and lemon. Hot chocolate fondant with vanilla ice cream is another classic done well to bring things to a close.

Chef Piotr Dziedzic **Seats** 40, Pr/dining room 20 **Times** 7-9, Closed 26-28 Dec, Jan-Mar, L all week **Prices** Starter £4.95-£9.50, Main £13.50-£19.95, Dessert £5.95-£8 **Wines** 28 bottles over £30, 34 bottles under £30, 5 by glass **Parking** 50 **Notes** Vegetarian available, Children welcome

HEXHAM Map 21 NY96

Barrasford Arms

Modern, Traditional British

tel: 01434 681237 **NE48 4AA**
email: contact@barrasfordarms.co.uk **web:** www.barrasfordarms.co.uk
dir: *A69 at Acomb onto A6079 towards Chollerton. Left at church, follow signs to Barrasford*

Confident cooking in an authentic country inn

In the peaceful village of Barrasford, close to Hadrian's Wall, this ivy-clad country inn is surrounded by the undulating grandeur of the Northumberland hills. The three dining rooms are kitted out with rustic furniture, the walls hung with pictures of the place in bygone days. Tony Binks works to a modern English template, the emphasis firmly placed on produce from local estates and punchy flavours. Twice-baked Cheddar cheese soufflé is a characteristically robust start, followed by roast pork tenderloin with spring onion clapshot, tenderstem broccoli and cider sauce. Finish with apple, hazelnut and polenta crumble and vanilla custard.

Chef Tony Binks **Seats** 60, Pr/dining room 10 **Times** 12-2/6.30-9, Closed 25-26 Dec, BHs, Mon, D Sun **Prices** Fixed L 2 course £15, Starter £5.95-£7, Main £14-£18.50, Dessert £6.50-£7 **Wines** 1 bottle over £30, 19 bottles under £30, 7 by glass **Parking** 30 **Notes** Sunday L £17-£19.50, Vegetarian available, Children welcome

HEXHAM *continued*

Langley Castle Hotel

@@ Modern British

tel: 01434 688888 **Langley NE47 5LU**
email: manager@langleycastle.com **web:** www.langleycastle.com
dir: *From A69 S on A686 for 2m. Hotel on right*

Thrilling modern food in a genuine castle

A traditional restaurant with a creative and modern output. Via a table d'hôte and tasting menu, expect dishes rooted in classical good sense and made with high quality ingredients, but also some cutting edge techniques and bold ideas. Start, perhaps, with the playfully named 'liver, bacon and onion', which is in fact foie gras ganache with jamón Ibérico and various textures of onion. Main courses deliver the same level of refinement: Cartmel Valley venison, say, with sauerkraut, pulses and chocolate, or a fine piece of Isle of Gigha halibut with English samphire, razor clams and chorizo. Finish with 'a taste of chocolate' (tart, powder and crisp) served with iced parsnip.

LONGHORSLEY **Map 21 NZ19**

Macdonald Linden Hall, Golf & Country Club

@@ Modern British

tel: 01670 500000 **NE65 8XF**
email: lindenhall@macdonald-hotels.co.uk **web:** www.macdonaldhotels.co.uk/lindenhall
dir: *7m NW of Morpeth on A697 off A1*

Appealing mainstream cooking in a grand Georgian manor

This late-Georgian manor house sits in 450 acres amid views of the Cheviots and wild Northumberland landscapes. Naturally, a hotel of this standing comes with a championship golf course and full complement of spa and health and fitness facilities. The upscale Dobson Restaurant – warm autumnal tones of russet and brick-red, linen-clothed tables and relaxed, professional service – makes a refined setting for well-conceived dishes. Ham hock terrine is accompanied by mustard mayonnaise, then main course brings roasted corn-fed chicken breast stuffed with sun-blushed tomato mousse and matched with sweet potato fondant, braised red cabbage and red wine jus. To finish, there's a classic lemon meringue pie with raspberry sorbet.

MATFEN **Map 21 NZ07**

Matfen Hall

 Modern British

tel: 01661 886500 **NE20 0RH**
email: info@matfenhall.com **web:** www.matfenhall.com
dir: *A69 signed Hexham, leave at Heddon-on-the-Wall. Then B6318, through Rudchester & Harlow Hill. Follow signs on right for Matfen*

Dinner in the library at an ancestral home

Matfen Hall, a creation of the Victorian era, within 300 acres of parkland, today offers all modern amenities from spa treatments to golf. The panelled library, replete with shelves of old volumes, does duty as the dining room. The contemporary menus make a neat counterpoint to the surroundings, offering chicken and mussel paella with rabbit tempura and a sautéed prawn to start, then roast sea trout with seafood chowder highlighted by Toulouse sausage and pancetta, or spatchcock chicken with boulangère potatoes, summer vegetables and truffle sauce. Coconut pannacotta with pineapple and strawberry salsa and pineapple jelly makes a fine finish.

MORPETH **Map 21 NZ18**

Eshott Hall

@@ British, European

tel: 01670 787454 **Eshott NE65 9EN**
email: info@eshotthall.co.uk **web:** www.eshotthall.co.uk
dir: *Eshott signed from A1. N of Morpeth*

Ambitious cooking of Northumbrian produce

Between Morpeth and Alnwick, Eshott Hall is a compact boutique hotel in a handsome Georgian property – a perfect base from which to explore the Northumberland National Park and end the day with dinner in the elegant restaurant, with its moulded plasterwork on the walls, a soothing gold colour scheme and a fire in cooler weather. Pigeon breast with beetroot, blackberry and dark chocolate is the sort of lively starter to expect. Main courses maintain the style, perhaps venison loin with kohlrabi, black cherries, baby leeks and bubble and squeak fritters. End with something like blueberry Bakewell tart with cinnamon ice cream.

Chef Andrew Blakey, Ross Oram **Seats** 30, Pr/dining room 30 **Times** 12-2.30/6-8.30, Closed private functions **Prices** Fixed L 3 course £29, Fixed D 3 course £42 **Wines** 25 bottles over £30, 21 bottles under £30, 7 by glass **Parking** 60 **Notes** Sunday L £29, Vegetarian available, Children 6 yrs+

NOTTINGHAMSHIRE

BARNBY MOOR **Map 16 SK68**

Restaurant Bar 1650

@ Modern European NEW

tel: 01777 705121 **Ye Olde Bell Hotel DN22 8QS**
email: enquiries@yeoldebell-hotel.co.uk **web:** www.yeoldebell-hotel.co.uk
dir: *A1(M) south near junct 34, exit Barnby Moor or A1(M) north exit A620 Retford. Hotel on A638 between Retford & Bawtry*

Roadside hotel with stylish restaurant

This roadside hotel and restaurant just off the A1 has business bases covered, beauty therapies aplenty, and lots of room for functions. When it comes to dining, there's a bistro in the St Leger bar, but the main event is the oak-panelled Restaurant Bar 1650, with its own art deco-style bar area and modern chandeliers to add a touch of glamour. Start with potted pork with beetroot textures and an apple lolly, or an indulgent truffle brûlée with goats' cheese vol-au-vent. Move on to rainbow trout with sweet and sour fennel, or steak cooked on the grill, and finish with deconstructed blueberry cheesecake.

Chef Richard Allen **Seats** 40, Pr/dining room 200 **Times** 12-2.30/5.30-9.30, Closed L Sun **Prices** Prices not confirmed **Wines** 23 bottles over £30, 29 bottles under £30, 17 by glass **Parking** 200 **Notes** Vegetarian available, Children welcome

FARNDON Map 17 SK75

Farndon Boathouse

Modern British, European, International

tel: 01636 676578 **Off Wyke Rd NG24 3SX**
email: info@farndonboathouse.co.uk
dir: *From A46 rdbt (SW of Newark-on-Trent) take Fosse Way signed Farndon. Turn right into Main St signed Farndon. At T-junct turn right into Wyke Lane, follow Boathouse signs*

Up-to-date brasserie cooking in a riverside setting

The leafy banks of the River Trent make an interesting contrast to the contemporary exposed ducting, industrial-style lighting, stone floors and glazed frontage of the stylish Boathouse. The kitchen sources locally and seasonally and uses modern cooking techniques such as sous-vide to squeeze every molecule of flavour from the ingredients. Contemporary brasserie dishes run from pan-fried scallops with belly pork flavoured with honey and soy accompanied by Japanese vegetables and wasabi, to main courses of roast pheasant breast with potato terrine, carrot purée, balsamic fig and roast roots, or beer-battered haddock fillet. Finish with plum frangipane tart with limoncello sorbet and vanilla meringues.

GUNTHORPE Map 11 SK64

Tom Browns Brasserie

Modern International

tel: 0115 966 3642 **The Old School House, Trentside NG14 7FB**
email: info@tombrowns.co.uk **web:** www.tombrowns.co.uk
dir: *A6097, Gunthorpe Bridge*

From Victorian learning to modern brasserie cooking

The homage to Thomas Hughes' plucky Victorian schoolboy denotes the fact that this large riverside building was a place of education in the 19th century. A compendious first-course gathering of seared Shetland scallops, Ibérico chorizo, sweet potato and butter bean purée is intriguingly garnished with a strip of dried sweet potato dusted with icing sugar. The follow-up could be superb pork belly accompanied by Savoy cabbage, apple and vanilla purée, and potato and sage terrine in mustard jus, or perhaps fillets of sea bass with an array of artichokes, beetroot, gnocchi and salsa verde. A triumphant finale may be light-pastried chocolate and orange millefeuille with a flavoursome blood orange sorbet.

Chef Peter Kirk **Seats** 100, Pr/dining room 20 **Times** 12-2.30/6-9.30, Closed D 25-26 Dec **Prices** Fixed L 2 course fr £16.95, Fixed D 3 course £19.95-£35, Starter £5.50-£12.95, Main £11.95-£26.95, Dessert £6.50-£8.50 **Wines** 19 bottles over £30, 39 bottles under £30, 19 by glass **Parking** 28, On street **Notes** Fixed D 6-7pm, Sunday L £10.95-£13.95, Vegetarian available, Children welcome

NOTTINGHAM Map 11 SK53

Hart's Restaurant

Modern British

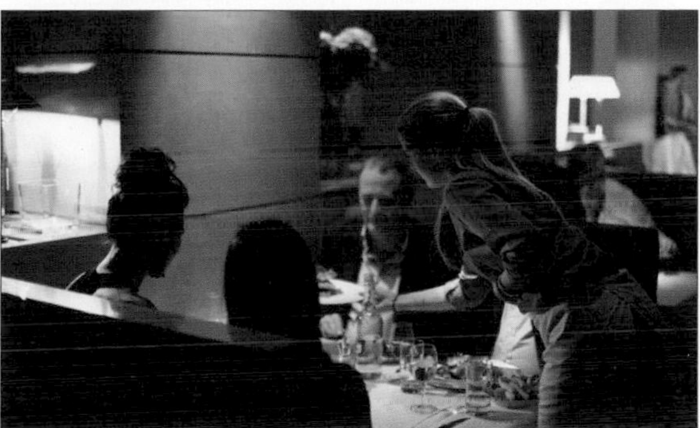

tel: 0115 988 1900 & 911 0666 **Standard Hill, Park Row NG1 6GN**
email: ask@hartsnottingham.co.uk **web:** www.hartsnottingham.co.uk
dir: *At junct of Park Row & Ropewalk, close to city centre*

Smart contemporary cooking from a skilled team

With its contemporary good looks, booth seating and recently extended bar, Hart's is a welcoming restaurant with an approachable, daily-changing menu. Main courses might be corn-fed chicken breast poached in chicken and mushroom stock and served with spelt and chicken risotto enriched with Madeira, cream, parmesan and lemon, or there might be roast cod with spiced lentils, orange-glazed salsify, curly kale and lemon and hazelnut dressing. Bookending them is a starter of pan-fried sea bass with tart escabèche-style fennel and carrot counterpointing a creamy parsley purée, and to finish, poached Yorkshire rhubarb matched with kaffir lime-flavoured pannacotta and pistachio brittle. There's an interesting wine list arranged by style.

Chef Daniel Burridge **Seats** 80, Pr/dining room 100 **Times** 7am-10.30pm, All-day dining, Closed 1 Jan, L 31 Dec, D 25-26 Dec **Prices** Starter £7.50-£8.50, Main £15.50-£29.95, Dessert £6.25-£8.50 **Wines** 7 by glass **Parking** 15, Mount Street NCP (discounted), on street **Notes** Plat du jour £13.95, Afternoon tea £21.95, Sunday L £23, Vegetarian available, Children welcome

NOTTINGHAM *continued*

MemSaab Restaurant

@@ Indian

tel: 0115 957 0009 **12-14 Maid Marian Way NG1 6HS**
email: contact@mem-saab.co.uk
dir: *5 mins walk from Nottingham Castle. Opposite Park Plaza Hotel*

Vibrant northern Indian cooking in a big city-centre venue

A gigantic venue of 200 covers, there's a real vibrancy about this place. Tender salmon tikka are redolent of fenugreek and marinated in yogurt lit up with garam masala. A signature starter comes in the form of tandoori ostrich, roasted in garlic and red chilli. Meats benefit from the tenderising influence of slow cooking, as when lamb shank falls obligingly from its bone into cardamom-laced sauce, accompanied by spinach-topped masala mash, while king prawns are marinated in onion-seeded yogurt and chargrilled with peppers. There's a taster trio of desserts, comprised of sticky gulab jamun, bread-and-butter pudding, and a shot glass of phirni, a saffron milk pudding garnished with pistachios.

MemSaab Restaurant

Chef Majid Ashraf **Seats** 200, Pr/dining room 60 **Times** 5.30-10.30, Closed 25 Dec, L all week **Prices** Starter £4.95-£9.95, Main £8.95-£21.95, Dessert £4.95-£6.50 **Wines** 11 bottles over £30, 34 bottles under £30, 12 by glass **Parking** NCP Mount St, NCP St James St **Notes** Early D menu 2 course, Vegetarian available, Children welcome

See advert below

Restaurant Sat Bains with Rooms

NOTTINGHAM **Map 11 SK53**

Modern British V 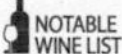 NOTABLE WINE LIST

tel: 0115 986 6566 **Lenton Ln, Trentside NG7 2SA**
email: info@restaurantsatbains.net
web: www.restaurantsatbains.com
dir: *M1 junct 24, A453 for approx 8m. Through Clifton, road divides into 3, take middle lane signed 'Lenton Lane Industrial Estate', then 1st left, left again. Follow brown Restaurant Sat Bains sign*

Analytical dining from a quicksilver creative intellect

The setting, on the edge of an out-of-town industrial estate and near a flyover is not what you'd expect when you're fizzing with anticipation at the prospect of having finally bagged a table at one of the UK's top foodie addresses. But that's soon forgotten once you're ensconced in the converted Victorian farmhouse, where all is soothing neutrality and cossetting professionalism, the main restaurant dominated by statement artworks on a grand scale. What follows is a quite breath-taking journey through cutting-edge cooking that is more than anything driven by taste. We've probably all suppressed an inner groan at some point when confronted by a menu with a 'concept', but the menu concept here at Sat Bains goes straight to the heart of what food is all about, deploying a colour-coded approach to guide the way, the idea being to reveal the balance of flavours in each dish via an analytical approach to the building blocks of food, based on the five taste categories – sweet, sour, salt, bitter and umami. If you're the sort of customer who likes to get into the thick of the action, make a reservation for the Chef's Table or Kitchen Bench. What is on offer has been prepared with precision and unerring skill, with every taste, texture and temperature put under the microscope in the development kitchen before it passes muster and arrives in front of you, ready to take your palate to places you don't usually go when seated at a dining table. Choose between the seven- and ten-course tasting menus. Dish descriptions are minimalist, the dishes themselves are anything but; duck egg, peas and mint sounds like a happy partnership, and indeed it is, spectacular even, a vivid green ice cream of tantalising sweetness arriving with a perfectly poached egg and a thin shard of bread. Follow that with a scallop creation which combines seared and raw bivalves, each beautiful specimens, with variations in texture provided by nuts and seeds and cauliflower and vanilla purée, and then a crab 'satay' which is full of surprises and outstanding flavours. There's a 'crossover' dish that arrives after the savoury courses to ease you into desserts such as a seemingly simple construction of chocolate, coffee and olive oil that delivers a perfect chocolate mousse, intense coffee gel and whizzy olive oil jelly. If you feel inspired by your visit, book an early return via a place on the Kitchen Workshop, where you can pick up some tricks of the trade. Gourmet vegetarians should be knocking down the door for their bespoke dishes that have undergone the same vigorous R&D process as the main menu. The exceptional wine list has a colour-coding system all of its own, highlighting acidity, fruit, mineral, oak and non-fruit, with lots of things to drink that you've quite possibly never come across before.

Chef Sat Bains **Seats** 40, Pr/dining room 14
Times 12-1/6-9.45, Closed 2 wks Jan, 1 wk May, 2 wks Aug, Sun-Tue **Prices** Prices not confirmed **Wines** 30 by glass **Parking** 22
Notes L 7 course £85, D 7/10 course £85/£95, Chef's table £125, Children 8 yrs+

Park Plaza Nottingham

 Pan-Asian

tel: 0115 947 7444 & 947 7200 **41 Maid Marian Way NG1 6GD**
email: nottingham@chinolatino.co.uk **web:** www.chinolatino.eu
dir: *A6200 (Derby Rd) into Wollaton St. 2nd exit into Maid Marian Way. Hotel on left*

East Asian food gets the Latin treatment

Latin America meets the Far East in this Nottingham branch of the Park Plaza. Set across two levels, this buzzy restaurant and bar fuses pan-Asian cooking with international cuisine on the globe-trotting menu. A starter of grilled scallops with yuzu aïoli and wasabi peas brings a distinctive Japanese flavour to proceedings, with a truly Latino edge to a main course of sea bass, smoked chipotle miso and tenderstem broccoli. Thai and Korean currents join the flow too, the latter incorporating lamb cutlets marinated in Korean hot pepper paste. Finish with hot chocolate fondant, white chocolate sauce and ginger ice cream.

Chef Paul Thacker **Seats** 70, Pr/dining room **Times** 12-10.30, All-day dining, Closed Xmas, Sun **Prices** Prices not confirmed **Wines** 28 bottles over £30, 7 bottles under £30, 11 by glass **Parking** 30, Hotel chargeable. On street, NCP **Notes** 4 course L £10.95, Vegetarian available, Children welcome

Restaurant Sat Bains with Rooms

@@@@@ *– see page 361*

World Service

@@ Modern British

tel: 0115 847 5587 **Newdigate House, Castle Gate NG1 6AF**
email: info@worldservicerestaurant.com **web:** www.worldservicerestaurant.com
dir: *200mtrs from city centre, 50mtrs from Nottingham Castle*

Sharp cooking amid idiosyncratic surroundings

Renaissance-styled Newdigate House was built in 1675. Its idiosyncratic interior mines a colonial vein, the warm orange and copper hues of the main dining room offset with oriental artefacts: Buddha heads, Indian statuary and objets d'art in vitrines. If the restaurant's name isn't enough of a hint, the cooking has a gentle East-meets-West theme. A duo of beef rib and octopus is hotted up with wasabi and cooled by seaweed salad, before sea bream arrives with smoked salmon, mussels and creamed leeks in shellfish bisque. At the end, sticky carrot cake with figs and ginger ice cream keeps the good ideas coming.

Chef James Nicholas **Seats** 80, Pr/dining room 34 **Times** 12-2.15/7-10, Closed 26 Dec, 1-7 Jan, D Sun (ex Dec & BH Sun) **Prices** Fixed L 2 course £14.95, Fixed D 3 course £24.95, Starter £5-£14.95, Main £14.95-£26.50, Dessert £5.50-£8.50 **Wines** 113 bottles over £30, 58 bottles under £30, 17 by glass **Parking** NCP **Notes** No fixed D Sat, Sunday L £14.95-£19.95, Vegetarian available, Children 12 yrs+ D

OLLERTON **Map 16 SK66**

Thoresby Hall Hotel

@@ British, International

tel: 01623 821000 & 821008 **Thoresby Park NG22 9WH**
email: thoresbyhall@bourne-leisure.co.uk **web:** www.warnerleisurehotels.co.uk
dir: *Phone for directions*

Classic grill menu overlooking Humphry Repton's gardens

The principal restaurant at Thoresby has undergone a restyling. Now known as the Blue Grill, it has an informal feel, with a grill menu that embraces Wagyu, USDA and local beef. Steamed lobsters are on hand for the surf-and-turf platters. Inventive touches accompany the hunks of protein, with Asian-spiced cauliflower and pak choi accompanying the braised pig's cheek, or perhaps a main-course salad of roast pigeon with parsnip purée, scorched spring onions and hazelnuts. Extensive sides and sauces make for happy mixing and matching, and by the sweet stage you may be ready for sharing platters of fairground treats – candyfloss, marshmallows, ice cream cones, doughnuts and toffee apples.

RETFORD **Map 17 SK78**

Blacksmiths

@@ Modern British NEW

tel: 01777 818171 **Town St, Clayworth DN22 9AD**
email: will@blacksmithsclayworth.com **web:** www.blacksmithsclayworth.com
dir: *From A1 Blyth junct take A614 to Bawtry. Right on to A361, after Everton turn right to Clayworth*

Bright, contemporary cooking in a stylish inn

A beautifully revamped inn in a village dating back to the 12th century, Blacksmiths is still a local pub, but with three attractively furnished bedrooms and a restaurant serving divertingly modern food, it's also a destination worth crossing county lines to visit. The interior is rustic and stylish. The pub side is covered by real ales and classy bar food such as rabbit and chorizo pie, but the main menu really impresses with contemporary stuff such as pan-fried scallops with trotter bonbon and burnt apple purée, followed by perfectly pink local venison loin, or wild sea bass with squid ink linguine. A class act.

Chef Liam Philbin **Seats** 70, Pr/dining room 30 **Times** 12-2.30/6-9.15, Closed 1st week Jan, Mon, D Sun **Parking** 20 **Notes** Sunday L £19.95-£24.95, Vegetarian available, Children welcome

OXFORDSHIRE

BANBURY **Map 11 SP44**

Best Western Plus Wroxton House Hotel

Modern British

tel: 01295 730777 **Wroxton St Mary OX15 6QB**
email: reservations@wroxtonhousehotel.com **web:** www.wroxtonhousehotel.com
dir: *From M40 junct 11 follow A422 (signed Banbury, then Wroxton). After 3m, hotel on right*

Modern brasserie dishes in a thatched hotel restaurant

Wroxton House is a honey-stone beauty in a photogenic thatched village near Banbury. Its restaurant occupies what was a terraced row of cottages, and is all oak beams and columns with an inglenook fireplace. Table settings are smart and the kitchen team turns out thoughtfully composed modern brasserie dishes founded on classic combinations. Start with seafood salad with Marie Rose sauce, or a terrine packed with chicken, leek and bacon, move on to chargrilled rib-eye or sea bass matched with a risotto enriched with crab and crayfish. To finish, bread-and-butter pudding is made with panettone, and artisan cheeses come with home-made chutney.

Chef Marc Ward **Seats** 60, Pr/dining room 80 **Times** 7-9, Closed L Mon-Sat **Prices** Fixed D 3 course fr £33 **Wines** 7 bottles over £30, 35 bottles under £30, 10 by glass **Parking** 70 **Notes** Sunday L £21-£23.50, Vegetarian available, Children welcome

The Three Pigeons Inn

Contemporary British

tel: 01295 275220 **3 Southam Rd OX16 2ED**
email: manager@thethreepigeons.com **web:** www.thethreepigeons.com
dir: *M40 junct 11, left A422, left A361. Inn on left at lights on corner of Southam Rd & Castle St*

Charming town inn with modern rustic cooking

This old red-brick inn has been servicing the needs of the community since the 17th century. Today's incumbents took over in 2011 and brought the place back to life. There's a light-filled dining room extension (the Winter Garden), panelled bar, cosy bedrooms and a smart courtyard garden. The menu offers modern British dishes such as a pretty tian of oak-smoked salmon, crayfish and avocado, followed by a hearty but refined main course combining venison haunch with black pudding, plus rosemary and thyme dauphinoise, blueberry coulis and a cauliflower and almond purée. For dessert, apple crumble with crème anglaise competes with a pear poached in hot chocolate.

The White Horse

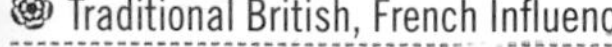
Traditional British, French Influence

tel: 01295 812440 **2 The Square, Kings Sutton OX17 3RF**
email: julie@whitehorseks.co.uk
dir: *Phone for directions*

Award-winning cooking in appealing village pub

This old pub has been given a makeover that, while creating a clean, modern look, still ensures that you are reminded of its past. Clearly popular, it has received regional food accolades for its British and European cooking. Typical is a starter of crispy pig's head with pancetta, black pudding, rhubarb and pistachio, breast and leg of Loomswood duck with carrot, cumin and lentil dhal as a main, and lemon cheesecake with stem-ginger ice cream to finish. Fillet of sea bream is one of several fish options, and for vegetarians there's pea, broad bean and barley risotto. A good choice of wines includes both the Old and New Worlds.

Chef Hendrik Dutson **Seats** 40, Pr/dining room 7 **Times** 12-2.30/6-9, Closed Mon (ex BHs), D Sun **Prices** Fixed L 2 course £11, Tasting menu £39.95-£59.95, Starter £5.70-£7.10, Main £11.50-£24, Dessert £4.50-£6.95 **Wines** 3 bottles over £30, 29 bottles under £30, 21 by glass **Parking** 14, On street **Notes** Steak night Tue fr £14.95, Sunday L £12-£20, Vegetarian available, Children welcome

BURFORD **Map 5 SP21**

The Angel at Burford

Modern British

tel: 01993 822714 **14 Witney St OX18 4SN**
email: enquiries@theangelatburford.co.uk **web:** www.theangelatburford.co.uk
dir: *Phone for directions*

Contemporary cooking in traditional Cotswold inn

Just off the main street in pretty Burford, this welcoming, traditional and recently refurbished Cotswold stone inn oozes character. Perfectly kept pints of Hook Norton ales lure drinkers to the cosy and bustling bar, with the all-day bar menu offering sandwiches, burgers and a charcuterie board alongside the main carte. Try the smooth chicken liver pâté on toasted ciabatta with pineapple and pepper chutney, perhaps followed by Parma ham-wrapped monkfish medallions with pea and mint risotto. Salted caramel pannacotta with granola and lemon crème fraîche is one choice for those with a sweet tooth. Look out for the summer beer festival.

Chef Mike Burkert **Seats** 36, Pr/dining room 14 **Times** 12-9.30, All-day dining **Prices** Starter £5.50-£9.25, Main £12.50-£22.50, Dessert £6.95-£10.50 **Wines** 4 bottles over £30, 32 bottles under £30, 6 by glass **Parking** On street, car park **Notes** Sunday L £14.95, Vegetarian available, Children welcome

The Bay Tree Hotel

Modern British

tel: 01993 822791 **Sheep St OX18 4LW**
email: info@baytreehotel.info **web:** www.cotswold-inns-hotels.co.uk/baytree
dir: *A40 or A361 to Burford. From High St turn into Sheep St, next to old market square. Hotel on right*

Elizabethan inn with modern classic menu

Built in Cotswold stone, this is a stylishly appointed place with a dining room that was fully refurbished in 2015, and a menu of modern-classic English food. That can only mean scallops on cauliflower purée, and it's a reliable version, with light caramelisation bringing out the sweetness of the shellfish. Mains range from roasted trout and samphire in crab bisque and lemon beurre blanc to capably handled rack of suckling pig with creamed leeks and cider-apple gel. A loosely textured chocolate and blood orange tart with candied peel makes up in flavour what it lacks in structural integrity, or try banana bread millefeuille with salted caramel and banana sorbet.

Chef Shawn Lovegrave **Seats** 70, Pr/dining room 24 **Times** 12-2/7-9.30 **Prices** Fixed L 2 course fr £14.50, Fixed D 3 course fr £36 **Wines** 44 bottles over £30, 51 bottles under £30, 27 by glass **Parking** 55 **Notes** Breakfast £11.50-£13, Sunday L £19.95-£21.95, Vegetarian available, Children welcome

BURFORD *continued*

The Bull at Burford

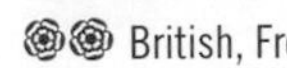 British, French

tel: 01993 822220 **105 High St OX18 4RG**
email: info@bullatburford.co.uk **web:** www.bullatburford.co.uk
dir: *On A40 between Cheltenham & Oxford, in town centre*

Confident cooking in a former coaching inn

The High Street of Burford is rich with historic buildings, including The Bull, which first opened its doors in 1610 as a coaching inn. The facade maintains the period character, of course, but inside there's a little more leeway to bring in a contemporary touch or two. The kitchen turns out bright, contemporary stuff, inflected with modern European ideas. Among starters, wild boar terrine arrives in the company of fig relish, and confit pork belly with black pudding bonbons and cider apple chutney. Move on to traditional fish and chips or medallions of venison and hare in a rich red wine sauce.

Chef Peter Juszkiewicz **Seats** 40 **Times** 12-2/7-9 **Prices** Starter £5.95-£9.75, Main £12.95-£19.95, Dessert £6.50-£7.25 **Wines** 36 bottles over £30, 39 bottles under £30, 12 by glass **Parking** 6, On street **Notes** Sunday L, Vegetarian available, Children welcome

The Lamb Inn

Modern British V

tel: 01993 823155 **Sheep St OX18 4LR**
email: info@lambinn-burford.co.uk **web:** www.cotswold-inns-hotels.co.uk/lamb
dir: *Exit A40 into Burford, down hill, take 1st left into Sheep St, hotel last on right*

Intricate contemporary cooking in old weavers cottages

Despite its humble beginnings as a row of weavers' cottages, The Lamb, just off Burford's historic main street, has plenty of charm and character, and its wisteria covered Cotswold stone walls make a pretty first impression. Once over the threshold, any thoughts of humble weavers disappear in a set of stylishly furnished public rooms, warmed by log fires in the cooler months, with an abundance of original features to ensure a sense of place. The characterful bar with stone-flagged floor is a welcoming spot, but the main dining goes on in the smart restaurant overlooking the garden and courtyard, where the country-chic decor fashions a gently contemporary setting. The skilful team in the kitchen deliver complex modern British constructions via a fixed-price carte and tasting menu. Start with a terrine of guinea fowl and ham hock, an attractive plate with texture and flavour to the fore, followed perhaps by pan-fried halibut – fresh as a daisy – with razor clams and a brace of purées, or duck breast with chicory jam and quince purée. Among desserts, 'apples' is another good-looking plate with pannacotta the starring element, or go for 'chocolate and orange' with its pistachio and dark chocolate brownie, kumquat jam and blood orange sorbet.

Chef Peter Galeski **Seats** 40, Pr/dining room 20 **Times** 12-2.30/7-9.30 **Prices** Fixed L 2 course fr £25, Fixed D 3 course fr £45, Tasting menu fr £55 **Wines** 60 bottles over £30, 40 bottles under £30, 12 by glass **Parking** Care of The Bay Tree Hotel **Notes** Tasting menu 8 course with dégustation wines, Sunday L £23-£27, Children welcome

CHECKENDON Map 5 SU68

The Highwayman

Modern, Traditional British

tel: 01491 682020 **Exlade St RG8 0UA**
dir: *Exlade St signed off A4074 (Reading/Wallingford road), 0.4m*

Nice mix of menus in a welcoming country local

Tucked away in a secluded hamlet, this rambling 16th-century inn is all brickwork, beams and wood-burner in a huge inglenook. Fine ales are on tap in the pubby bar, and all bases are covered in the food department by steaks from the grill, home-made pies – wild boar with sage and apple, perhaps – and a carte with plenty of seasonal focus. Game pâté with pickled vegetables is a great way to start, followed by roast pork belly with black pudding faggot, barley, turnips, apple jelly and mustard jus. Round off with treacle tart with ginger and honey ice cream or a rhubarb duo of Pavlova and coulis.

Chef Paul Burrows **Seats** 55, Pr/dining room 40 **Times** 12-2.30/6-10, Closed 25 Dec, 1 Jan, Mon, D Sun **Prices** Prices not confirmed **Wines** 5 by glass **Parking** 30 **Notes** Sunday L, Vegetarian available, Children welcome

CHINNOR Map 5 SP70

The Sir Charles Napier

Modern British, European V NOTABLE WINE LIST

tel: 01494 483011 **Sprigg's Alley OX39 4BX**
email: info@sircharlesnapier.co.uk
dir: *M40 junct 6, B4009 to Chinnor. Right at rdbt to Sprigg's Alley*

Resourceful blend of old and new in a beautiful country inn

On a hill amid beech woods, this red-brick inn is surrounded by beautifully maintained gardens full of oversized sculptures. There's also a courtyard under a trellis for alfresco dining. The interior is instantly appealing, with a beamed bar, log fires, squishy sofas and unclothed wooden tables interspersed with distinctive modern sculptures. Relaxed, good-natured and discreet service ensures there's no hint of pretension. Anthony Skeats's kitchen turns out intelligently balanced dishes that team up familiar and often esoteric ingredients, so there's much to enjoy at every turn. Seared scallops with chicken wings are sauced with Asian broth and accompanied by pak choi, and might be followed by venison loin with a faggot, pearl barley, confit turnip and grue de cacao. Raw materials are of exceptional quality, and seasonality is to the fore: samphire is seen in summer accompanying sea trout along with beetroot, fennel and orange, while new season's lamb appears earlier in the year, served pink, with tomatoes, capers and a mint jus. Timings are spot on: roast ribs of beef are served rare, and stone bass is roasted to the second and served with linguine, mussels and samphire. Puddings end on a high note, among them perhaps coconut rice pudding with mango and lemongrass ice cream.

Chef Anthony Skeats **Seats** 75, Pr/dining room 45 **Times** 12-3.30/6.30-10, Closed 25-27 Dec, Mon, D Sun **Prices** Fixed L 2 course £16.50-£19.50, Fixed D 2 course £16.50-£19.50, Tasting menu fr £65, Starter £10.50-£15.50, Dessert £8.50-£10.50 **Wines** 192 bottles over £30, 59 bottles under £30, 10 by glass **Parking** 60 **Notes** Fixed L Tue-Fri, Fixed D Tue-Thu, Sunday L £40-£50, Children welcome

CHIPPING NORTON Map 10 SP32

The Chequers

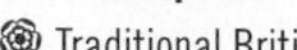 Traditional British

tel: 01608 659393 **Church Rd, Churchill OX7 6NJ**
email: reservations@thechequerschurchill.com
dir: *Phone for directions*

Modern pub grub done right

A village pub with a focus on food, The Chequers has been done up with a bit of individuality and doesn't look the same as everywhere else. There's nothing fussy about the culinary output, but time has been taken to seek out good quality ingredients such as British charcuterie and oysters from the south coast. Snails and mushrooms arrive on toast, rich with parsley and garlic, while main courses include steaks such as flat iron and rib eye served with chips cooked in duck fat. Alternatively go for breaded lemon sole with fennel slaw and brown shrimps. To finish, rhubarb Mess and banoffee pot are modern takes on classic puds.

Chef Jono Grey **Seats** 40, Pr/dining room 12 **Times** 12-3/6-9.30, Closed D Sun **Prices** Fixed L 2 course £12.50, Starter £6-£10, Main £9-£18, Dessert £2-£6 **Wines** 31 bottles over £30, 10 bottles under £30, 10 by glass **Parking** 15 **Notes** Sunday L, Vegetarian available, Children welcome

Wild Thyme Restaurant with Rooms

Modern British

tel: 01608 645060 **10 New St OX7 5LJ**
email: enquiries@wildthymerestaurant.co.uk **web:** www.wildthymerestaurant.co.uk
dir: *A44 Evesham, through Market Place. On left opposite Sainsbury's car park*

Contemporary style and a regional flavour

Grade II listed and 400 years old, this smart little restaurant with rooms (35 covers and three bedrooms) has original features on show, but the place feels bright and contemporary just the same. That's down to the easy-going look of exposed stone walls, modern artworks and white-painted woodwork, with the wooden tables left unclothed. Chef-patron Nick Pullen seeks out top-notch seasonal regional produce and cooks smart, contemporary British food that deals in intelligent flavour combinations. Try salt-cured local venison to start, followed by wild rabbit (confit leg and the loin served en croute with smoked bacon), or risotto of Jerusalem artichokes and spring onion.

Chef Nicholas Pullen **Seats** 35, Pr/dining room 14 **Times** 12-2/7-9, Closed Sun-Mon, L Tue-Wed **Prices** Fixed L 2 course £20-£30, Fixed D 3 course £25-£37.50 **Wines** 21 bottles over £30, 19 bottles under £30, 10 by glass **Parking** Public car park 3 min walk **Notes** Vegetarian available, Children welcome

DEDDINGTON Map 11 SP43

The Unicorn Inn

Modern British

tel: 01869 338838 **Market Place OX15 0SE**
email: info@unicorndeddington.co.uk **web:** www.unicorndeddington.co.uk
dir: *Phone for directions*

Robust flavours in traditional village pub setting

In the heart of the village, this refurbished 17th-century former coaching inn has a cosy bar warmed by a real fire to please discerning drinkers and a relaxed restaurant with its exposed stone walls and open kitchen. Chef-patron Johnny Parke's modern British cooking is prepared with good technique and plenty of flair. A well-presented starter of chicken and duck liver parfait, pistachio, poached rhubarb and toast could be followed by roast fillet of stone bass, buttered potato, Swiss chard, artichoke and Ibérico ham. Round things off with the home-made raspberry Bakewell tart and salted caramel ice cream. When the sun shines, tables on the attractive rear terrace are highly prized.

Chef Johnny Parke **Seats** 60, Pr/dining room 16 **Times** 12-2.30/6.30-9.30, Closed 1 Jan, D 25 Dec **Prices** Fixed L 2 course £12, Starter £5-£10, Main £12-£17, Dessert £6-£8 **Wines** 12 bottles over £30, 23 bottles under £30, 12 by glass **Parking** Market car park **Notes** Fixed L Mon-Fri only, Sunday L, Vegetarian available, Children welcome

FARINGDON Map 5 SU29

The Eagle

 Modern European

tel: 01367 241879 **Little Coxwell SN7 7LW**
email: eaglelittlecoxwell@gmail.com **web:** www.eagletavern.co.uk
dir: *A420, follow signs for 1m to Little Coxwell village*

Modern pub food with continental influences

The Eagle is a rather grand architectural affair for a village local but an air of warmth and tranquillity prevails, and the menu is strong on continental influences. First off might be a dish of potted rabbit adorned with pickled carrot, mustard seeds and prune chutney, or there could be a savoury take on crème brûlée made from Oxford Blue cheese with rhubarb sorbet. At main cod is pan-roasted and served in creamy shellfish bisque with buttery leeks and saffron potatoes, while local lamb comes with asparagus and minted sheep's yogurt. Grape strudel with raspberry sorbet and crème anglaise is a successful new spin on an old favourite.

Restaurant 56

Modern British V

tel: 01367 245389 & 241272 **Sudbury House, 56 London St SN7 7AA**
email: restaurant56@sudburyhouse.co.uk **web:** www.restaurant56.co.uk
dir: *M40 junct 9, A34 Swindon, follow A420 towards Swindon/Oxford*

Imaginative cooking with a sense of fun

The handsome Georgian house was once owned by music critic and BBC Controller of Music, Sir William Glock, and, now much extended, it is a useful bolt hole on the edge of the Cotswolds for business events, weddings, and anyone who has got wise to the exciting contemporary cooking of Andrew Scott. Surrounded by nine acres of its own lush green grounds, the original house has plenty of character. When it comes to dining, there's the choice of the modern Magnolia Brasserie or the elegant, refined fine-dining Restaurant 56. Here chef Scott delivers his three tasting menus ('Introduction', 'Prime' and 'Progressive'), and you can expect complex and creative courses based on first-class ingredients. A game terrine is pointed up by burnt orange and quince in an opening course on the shortest of the tasting menus, followed perhaps by cod ravioli in a roasted cod broth. Menu descriptions are brief and often enigmatic, particularly on the 'Progressive' menu – S&S minestrone, say, followed by pigeon 2012 – with top-notch ingredients to the fore and acute technical skills in evidence. Among sweet courses, rhubarb 'n' custard is an imaginative take on an old favourite, and mandarin parfait with granola and crème fraîche is a harmonious combination of flavours and textures.

Chef Andrew Scott **Seats** 24, Pr/dining room 12 **Times** 6-9, Closed Sun-Mon, L all week (ex for private bkgs of 8+) **Prices** Tasting menu £45-£85 **Wines** 87 bottles over £30, 14 bottles under £30, 18 by glass **Parking** 70 **Notes** Afternoon tea £28, Children 12 yrs+

FARINGDON *continued*

The Trout Inn

Modern British NEW

tel: 01367 870382 **Buckland Marsh SN7 8RF**
email: info@troutinn.co.uk **web:** www.troutinn.co.uk
dir: *A415 from Abingdon signed Marcham, through Frilford to Kingston Bagpuize. Left onto A420. 5m, right signed Tadpole Bridge. Or M4 (E'bound) junct 15, A419 towards Cirencester. 4m, onto A420 towards Oxford. 10m, left signed Tadpole Bridge*

Fine Cotswold ingredients by the Thames

A number of moorings are available on the River Thames, but even those who come by more regular means can enjoy the location as the lawn rolls down to the water's edge. This charming old inn has a smart country finish, with flagstone floors, beams, log burners, and country prints. The kitchen uses the region's best produce to deliver sharp, modern fare such as sweet-and-sour mackerel with beetroot and crème fraîche, or citrus-cured trout with coral mayonnaise. Next up, loin of venison is full of flavour, served with Puy lentils, and steaks, pork chop and trout are cooked on the grill.

Times 12-2.30/6.30-8.30 **Prices** Starter £6-£7.50, Main £6.95-£25, Dessert £1.50-£7.50 **Wines** 19 bottles over £30, 30 bottles under £30, 15 by glass **Notes** Sunday L, Vegetarian available, Children welcome

FYFIELD **Map 5 SU49**

The White Hart

Modern British

tel: 01865 390585 **Main Rd OX13 5LW**
email: info@whitehart-fyfield.com **web:** www.whitehart-fyfield.com
dir: *A420 Oxford-Swindon, 7m S of Oxford A34*

Traditionally based British food with a minstrels' gallery

Built as a chantry house at the tail-end of the Plantagenet era, The White Hart offers traditionally-based British food with contemporary flourishes. Pink-cooked pigeon turns up with caramelised onions and toasted pine kernels on puff pastry for an impressive beginner, while mains run to well-timed fish such as salmon, served with fish fingers or a copper pan of fish pie, and meats such as pheasant with boxty potato cake and winter veg. Steaks are top-drawer: 28-day aged rib-eyes in béarnaise with proper chips. Sharing boards of fish, meze or antipasti are another option. Dessert could be a study in cherry, with purée, tuile, sorbet and Kirsch-soaked fruit accompanying pistachio cake.

The White Hart

Chef Mark Chandler **Seats** 45, Pr/dining room 32
Times 12-2.30/6.45-9.30, Closed Mon (ex BHs), D Sun **Prices** Fixed L 2 course fr £17, Starter £6.50-£11, Main £12-£25, Dessert £6.50-£7.50 **Wines** 28 bottles over £30, 26 bottles under £30, 11 by glass **Parking** 60 **Notes** Tasting menu on request, D 2/3 course £25/£31.50 for 8+, Sunday L £26-£29, Vegetarian available, Children welcome

GORING **Map 5 SU68**

The Leatherne Bottel

British, French

tel: 01491 872667 **Bridle Way RG8 0HS**
email: leathernebottel@aol.com
dir: *M4 junct 12 or M40 junct 6, signed from B4009 towards Wallingford*

Anglo-French cooking by the Thames

The Bottel floats serenely on the Thames with the Chilterns as a backdrop. It's a lovely spot, and the place is a dining destination of long repute, weathering the vicissitudes of culinary fashion without getting stuck in any ruts. The accent is Anglo-French, perfectly seen in a meal that follows a petit Crottin goats' cheese, roast fig and chestnut purée with beef Wellington complete with a porty reduction. Lighter fish dishes might include seared turbot with shallot gratin in smoked haddock chowder, and meals come to a satisfying conclusion with something like a pear poached in Pinot Noir served with clotted cream and toasted almonds.

Belmond Le Manoir aux Quat'Saisons

GREAT MILTON **Map 5 SP60**

Modern French V 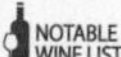

tel: 01844 278881 **Church Rd OX44 7PD**
email: manoir.mqs@belmond.com
web: www.belmond.com/lemanoir
dir: *M40 junct 7 follow A329 towards Wallingford. After 1m turn right, signed Great Milton and Le Manoir aux Quat' Saisons*

Benchmark French cooking of rare excellence

Raymond Blanc has eased comfortably into his fourth decade at the Manoir, one of the great surviving testaments to the sea-change wrought in British gastronomy in the 1980s. Youthful untutored exuberance has ceded to honeyed maturity over the years, as though to match the surroundings, the sympathetic persona burnished with a regular TV presence. The old place is partly corporate-owned these days, but not so as you'd notice. Its singular charm and personal ways are intact. Even those just popping in for lunch should allow time for a shuftic around the grounds, where the glasshouses and vegetables patches pour forth their provender, and a space for the taking of tea in the Japanese fashion is among the amenities. Inside, refurbishments have been afoot in the main dining room, which of course retains its gentling view of the gardens, and the service ethos remains at a rarefied pitch of consideration. Does this read a little like a mea culpa for past practices? 'I have realised that constant interruptions by the restaurant team can reduce the enjoyment of your meal and, as such, I have decided to place [i.e. leave] a copy of the menu on the table for you to see what each course is, without lengthy explanations.' At least these issues are at the forefront of policy making here. It's hardly as though the dishes are not worthy of lengthy explanations. Gary Jones, Benoit Blin and the team raise the bar skywards in the interpretation of Blanc's seasonally oriented, intricately composed dishes, presented on monthly-changing menus that are noticeably more classical in outlook nowadays than they once were. March brings on a dazzlingly colourful terrine of garden beetroot with horseradish sorbet, or adds rhubarb and a cloud of ginger to seared duck liver. At main course, there may be delicately braised brill fillet, its oyster and cucumber accompaniments spiked with the smouldering note of wasabi, or perhaps a generous serving of Aberdeen Angus, the fillet roasted, the Jacob's ladder braised, in a gloriously intense red wine jus. Every single element in each dish is as carefully considered as every other, down to the garden chard and cauliflower that come with a VIP double-act of sea bass and scallops in subtle red wine essence. The various prix-fixe deals offer scenic routes through the repertoire, and there are more modernist goings-on on the Découverte option – steamed sole with langoustines in ginger consommé, duck breast with caramelised chicory in clementine, yuzu and jasmine. At the finishing-line, there could be roast pineapple with its partnering sorbet alongside rum baba, or something as bewitching as milk chocolate and Earl Grey crumble with banana and passionfruit sorbet. Wines will add to the outlay, naturellement, but what wines!

Chef Raymond Blanc, Gary Jones **Seats** 100, Pr/dining room 50 **Times** 12-2.30/7-10, Closed **Prices** Starter £46, Main £52-£54 **Wines** 650 bottles over £30, 40 by glass **Parking** 60 **Notes** Fixed 5/7 course L £82/£127 D £138/£159, Sunday L, Children welcome

GREAT MILTON *continued*

The Miller of Mansfield

British V

tel: 01491 872829 & 07702 853413 **High St RG8 9AW**
email: reservations@millerofmansfield.com **web:** www.millerofmansfield.com
dir: *M40 junct 7, S on A329 towards Benson, A4074 towards Reading, B4009 towards Goring. Or M4 junct 12, S on A4 towards Newbury. 3rd rdbt onto A340 to Pangbourne. A329 to Streatley, right at lights onto B4009 into Goring*

Stylish country inn with contemporary menus

An 18th-century coaching inn made over to chime with our times, The Miller offers sharp modern British output. Flickering candles on smart oak tables set the mood. A starter of warm salmon bradan rost comes with hot and creamy horseradish mayonnaise and a sweet and sticky syrup of mirin and soy, while another might be a refined button mushroom soup with black truffle and pickled mushrooms. Gigha halibut arrives slow cooked in a main course with charred leeks, Jerusalem artichoke purée and a red wine sauce enriched with smoked bacon. Finish with tonka bean pannacotta with pistachio cake and blackberries (fresh, gel and meringue).

Chef Nick Galer **Seats** 60, Pr/dining room 12 **Times** 12-2.30/6-9 **Prices** Fixed L 2 course £16, Starter £6.50-£8, Main £14.25-£23.50, Dessert £6-£7.50 **Wines** 26 bottles over £30, 13 bottles under £30, 17 by glass **Parking** 2 **Notes** Sun supper club 1 course £12.50 6-8pm, Sunday L, Children welcome

GREAT MILTON Map 5 SP60

Belmond Le Manoir aux Quat'Saisons

– see page 367

HAILEY Map 11 SP31

The Lamb Inn

 Traditional British

tel: 01993 708792 **Steep Hill, Crawley OX29 9TW**
email: lambcrawley@yahoo.co.uk **web:** www.lambcrawley.co.uk
dir: *Phone for directions*

Smartly presented contemporary food in a convivial atmosphere

At this whitewashed Georgian inn at the heart of a peaceful Cotswold village the cooking is presented with much flair and thought, homemade breads arriving swaddled in a little cloth bag. Hot-smoked salmon cut chunkily and served warm with beetroot cubes and apple purée might almost be an old-fashioned pub dish, but then main course brings loin and faggot of venison with braised red cabbage and parsnip-vanilla purée in a sweetly viscous chocolate gravy, or perhaps lemon sole roasted on the bone with brown shrimps, sprouting broccoli and cep sauce. Dessert comes in a Mason jar containing blood orange posset, citrus meringue and orange sorbet in tart blood orange soup.

Orwells

HENLEY-ON-THAMES Map 5 SU78

Modern British

tel: 0118 940 3673 **Shiplake Row, Binfield Heath RG9 4DP**
email: eat@orwellsatshiplake.co.uk
dir: *A4155 to Binfield Heath, take Plough Lane to Shiplake Row, restaurant on left*

Creative contemporary dining in a Georgian country pub

The whitewashed 18th-century property in a village near the Oxfordshire-Berkshire border may look like a rustic old country pub, but the interior tells another story. Granted, the ancient beams and floorboards are still in evidence, but the truth is Orwells is a thrusting contemporary restaurant and its decor fits the mood of our times with mellow duck-egg blue walls, quirky pictures and high-quality tableware. Chef-patrons Liam Trotman and Ryan Simpson have a wealth of experience and have created a little foodie oasis in the green countryside of South Oxfordshire. Their own smallholding just down the road produces around 75 per cent of the fruit and veg used in the kitchen, and what isn't home-grown is sourced with due diligence. This fiercely seasonal approach combined with phenomenal technical skill results in beautifully crafted dishes and relatively complex constructions that seldom fail to impress. A superb piece of seared mackerel is partnered with smoked eel, lardons, tart apple and puréed beetroot, and then, in a paradoxical piece of whimsy, a red-hot kick from silky-smooth horseradish ice cream. Next up, a dish of Herefordshire beef is a perfect celebration of the beast, while a tranche of cod arrives with oysters and leeks in a buttery sauce, and a shard of crispy chicken skin. A dessert of apple and salted caramel is a ball (literally and metaphorically), while a cheesecake brings the winning pairing of rhubarb and custard. Brilliant home-made breads (Wessex brown and sourdough, say), and a very clever amuse bouche inspired by a Lincolnshire Poacher ploughman's, show Orwells' class runs from top to bottom.

Chef Ryan Simpson, Liam Trotman **Seats** 40, Pr/dining room 20 **Times** 11.30-3/6.30-9.30, Closed 2 wks beg Jan, 1 wk Jun, 2 wks beg Sep, Mon-Tue, D Sun **Prices** Fixed L 2 course £15, Fixed D 3 course £25, Tasting menu £70, Starter £9-£14, Main £22-£30, Dessert £9 **Wines** 125 bottles over £30, 29 bottles under £30, 37 by glass **Parking** 30 **Notes** Tasting menu with/without wines, Sunday L £30-£35, Vegetarian available, Children welcome

HENLEY-ON-THAMES Map 5 SU78

The Baskerville

Modern British V

tel: 0118 940 3332 **Station Rd, Lower Shiplake RG9 3NY**
email: enquiries@thebaskerville.com **web:** www.thebaskerville.com
dir: *2m S of Henley in Lower Shiplake. Exit A4155 into Station Rd, inn signed*

Red-brick pub with the focus on food

This Baskerville is a handsome beast, a contemporary kind of inn that offers beer and bar snacks, comfortable rooms, and a restaurant that produces serious modern British grub. The kitchen's ambitious output extends to starters of crispy fried salt-and-pepper squid or pan-seared wood pigeon with sloe gin jelly and pickled wild mushrooms. There are lots of sound combinations among main courses, too: an oriental-inspired slow-cooked pork belly dish, say, or Gressingham duck breast with a marmalade glaze (served with truffled mash and blackberry jus). Pub classics like steak, ale and mushroom pie and Sunday roasts play to the gallery, with comforting desserts such as plum and finger crumble.

Chef Jamie Herridge **Seats** 58, Pr/dining room 12 **Times** 12-9.30, All-day dining, Closed 1 Jan, D Sun **Prices** Fixed L 2 course £21.50-£35, Fixed D 3 course £28-£42, Starter £5-£11.50, Main £14-£23.50, Dessert £6.50-£7 **Wines** 27 bottles over £30, 32 bottles under £30, 17 by glass **Parking** 15, Also at Shiplake Station **Notes** Sunday L £29-£33, Children welcome

The Cherry Tree Inn

Modern British, European

tel: 01491 680430 **Main St, Stoke Row RG9 5QA**
email: enquiries@thecherrytreeinn.co.uk **web:** www.thecherrytreeinn.co.uk
dir: *On A4155 from Henley-on-Thames exit B481 to Sonning Common. Follow Stoke Row signs, turn right for inn*

Popular old inn serving good, honest food

This old brick and flint inn is the sort of pub every village should have, not just for its ales and atmosphere but for the quality of its modern British cooking. Perfectly roast local pigeon comes with a salad of beetroot, pine nuts and rocket enhanced by raspberry dressing to make a particularly effective starter. Sauces and gravies never fail to impress among main courses: one of star anise jus for confit duck leg with fondant potato and red cabbage, a rich red wine reduction for tender organic roast chicken breast with root vegetable mash, roast parsnips and kale. An excellent pudding choice might be caramel pannacotta with berry compôte.

Chef Chris & George **Seats** 65, Pr/dining room 12 **Times** 12-3/6.30-9.30 **Prices** Starter £4.95-£7.25, Main £11.50-£19.95, Dessert £5.95 **Wines** 12 bottles over £30, 12 bottles under £30, 8 by glass **Parking** 30 **Notes** Breakfast, Sunday L £4.50-£14.95, Vegetarian available, Children welcome

Hotel du Vin Henley-on-Thames

European

tel: 01491 848400 **New St RG9 2BP**
email: info.henley@hotelduvin.com **web:** www.hotelduvin.com
dir: *M4 junct 8/9 signed High Wycombe, take 2nd exit and onto A404 in 2m. A4130 into Henley, over bridge, through lights, up Hart St, right onto Bell St, right onto New St, hotel on right*

French bistro specials in a Georgian brewery

Hotel du Vin always chooses impressive buildings, and the Henley branch is no exception: a Thames-side Georgian property that was the HQ of Brakspears brewery. Bistro classics plus a few less standard dishes are what to expect, as at the other branches, all cooked just as they should be. Perfectly steamed moules marinière or chicken liver parfait with raisin chutney and sourdough bread get things off to a promising start before steak frites, sole meunière with caper and brown shrimp beurre noisette or Toulouse sausage and mash. Treacle tart may not be particularly French but it makes a good conclusion, and there's always perennial crème brûlée.

Orwells

– see opposite

Shaun Dickens at The Boathouse

Modern British NEW V

tel: 01491 577937 **Station Rd RG9 1AZ**
email: enquiries@shaundickens.co.uk
dir: *Phone for directions*

Thames-side vistas and detailed, fine-tuned cooking

The boathouse name, in a town famous for its regatta, gives a good indication of the fabulous setting mere feet from the Thames: think decked terrace out front and floor-to-ceiling glass windows to display the watery vista. There's real pedigree aboard here, for chef Shaun Dickens has worked at the likes of Belmond Le Manoir aux Quat' Saisons, Thomas Keller's Per Se in New York and L'Ortolan near Reading. His light, modern, highly detailed and precise cooking shows panache and passion, with interesting textures, colours and flavours and beguiling presentation. Start, perhaps, with the delicious spot-on flavours of chicken, walnut, chicory, pickled onion, and then maybe move on to a perfectly cooked cod with braised chard, orange and a red wine reduction. A great way to end the meal is with a financier with green apple sorbet, sage and a chamomile infusion. Other desserts like 'Orange' (with tagette, chocolate streusel and star anise) keep the bar high. The dining room suits the food; light and contemporary, with unclothed tables, cream leather chairs and splashes of colour from abstract artworks. Service led by wife Gemma is cheerily friendly, knowledgeable and professional, while a bar at the rear adds further kudos to a class act.

Chef Shaun Dickens **Times** 12-2.30/7-9.30, Closed Mon-Tue **Prices** Fixed L 2 course £25.95, Tasting menu £52-£121, Starter £11-£14, Main £20-£26, Dessert £10 **Wines** 51 bottles over £30, 10 bottles under £30, 10 by glass **Notes** Tasting menu 7/8 course, Children welcome

KINGHAM Map 10 SP22

The Kingham Plough

Modern British

tel: 01608 658327 **The Green OX7 6YD**
email: book@thekinghamplough.co.uk **web:** www.thekinghamplough.co.uk
dir: *B4450 from Chipping Norton to Churchill, 2nd right to Kingham. Left at T-junct, Plough on right*

Modernised country food in a family-friendly inn

There are no airs and graces at this old stone pub in a pretty Cotswolds village. The atmosphere is warm and welcoming, with sofas and roaring fires in the bar, and a rustic-looking restaurant with bare stone walls, a beamed ceiling and plain wooden tables and chairs. Emily Watkins is an inspired chef, with her own modernised, exciting take on classic British cooking. She's evangelical about sourcing the best local produce and making everything on site, including ketchup and ice cream (also on sale to take away). The bar menu takes in everything from Scotch quail's egg to chicken and ham hock pie with greens, while the restaurant fare is altogether more ambitious. Starters include partridge terrine with a parsnip and apple croquette, parsnip crisps and burnt apple purée, and garlicky parsley soup floated with Hereford snails and wood blewits. The same imaginative and labour-intensive approach goes into main courses, with combinations intelligently considered. Pork belly is partnered by a pheasant sausage, sauced with pork and pheasant consommé and served with caramelised onions and haricot beans. Dover sole is roasted with lemon and rosemary, accompanied by potato dumplings, spinach and brown butter. The finale might be chocolate and orange delice with orange curd ice cream and honeycomb.

Chef Emily Watkins, Ben Dulley **Seats** 54, Pr/dining room 20 **Times** 12-2/6.30-9, Closed 25 Dec, D Sun **Prices** Starter £9-£12, Main £16-£25, Dessert £7-£8 **Wines** 42 bottles over £30, 14 bottles under £30, 7 by glass **Parking** 30 **Notes** Sunday L £18-£20, Vegetarian available, Children welcome

The Wild Rabbit

Modern British

tel: 01608 658389 **Church St OX7 6YA**
email: theteam@thewildrabbit.co.uk **web:** www.thewildrabbit.co.uk
dir: *Phone for directions*

Eclectic contemporary cooking in a super-posh pub

A 'reinvention of the British inn', say Daylesford Organic, the owners. You can decide for yourself when you visit this rather upmarket, 18th-century Cotswolds pub, with its stripped-back walls, open fires and simple, hand-crafted furniture. Food is available from the rustic-chic bar – Lancashire hot pot with cucumber and red onion slaw and smashed fresh mint, for example – as well as the expansive restaurant, where a spanking-new open kitchen makes an eye-catching feature set against all the exposed stone and timbers. Britain, France and the Mediterranean all have their say in an eclectic menu, beginning with a two-way serving of mackerel involving a seared fillet with mint-infused pickled cucumber and rhubarb purée, and tartare with horseradish cream. Next up, sirloin and glazed rib of organic beef appear alongside slow-roasted bacon, onion purée, mushrooms infused with Chardonnay vinegar, and red wine sauce in a full-throttle dish that hangs together convincingly. For dessert, the palate-cleansing effect of a well-risen passionfruit soufflé is boosted further by passionfruit sauce poured in at the table, and offset by silky iced coconut. Or you might leave the final word to the cheese board and try Daylesford's tangy organic cheddar, aged for at least eight months. French wines hold sway, including a selection from Daylesford's own vineyard.

Chef Tim Allen **Seats** 50, Pr/dining room 16 **Times** 12-2.30/7-9.30 **Prices** Starter £12-£15, Main £20-£30, Dessert £7-£9 **Wines** 36 bottles over £30, 22 bottles under £30, 15 by glass **Parking** 20 **Notes** Breakfast, Sunday L, Vegetarian available, Children welcome

MILTON COMMON Map 5 SP60

The Oxfordshire

 Modern British

tel: 01844 278300 **Rycote Ln OX9 2PU**
email: info@theoxfordshire.com **web:** www.theoxfordshire.com
dir: *From S M40 junct 7 onto A370 towards Thame. Hotel on right in 2m*

Modern British cooking in golfing hotel

Whether you're at this new-build hotel in the Chilterns for golf or pampering, the Sakura restaurant has sweeping views of the course and countryside from its picture windows as a backdrop to a broad-ranging menu of modern dishes spiked with global influences. Kick off with monkfish nuggets with saffron aïoli, then roasted sea bass with lemon, fennel, basil and roasted red pepper butter, or rump of lamb with ratatouille, sweet potato fondant and minty salsa verde. Unreconstructed carnivores are sorted out with straight-up grilled steaks served with a choice of classic sauces, grilled tomatoes, watercress and triple-cooked chips. How about spotted dick with vanilla custard to finish?

Chef Craig Heaseley **Seats** 50, Pr/dining room 40 **Times** 6.30-9.30, Closed Xmas, New Year **Prices** Fixed L 2 course £19.95-£23, Fixed D 3 course £28-£32, Starter £4.95-£8.95, Main £14.95-£24.95, Dessert £5.95-£9.10 **Wines** 10 bottles over £30, 20 bottles under £30, 10 by glass **Notes** Vegetarian available, Children welcome

MURCOTT Map 11 SP51

The Nut Tree Inn

 Modern European V 

tel: 01865 331253 **Main St OX5 2RE**
dir: *M40 junct 9. A34 towards Oxford, take 2nd exit for Islip. At Red Lion pub turn left, then 3rd right signed Murcott*

Confident cooking in a pretty village inn

Refurbished in spring 2015, the place has retained its structure of stone walls and gnarled beams, a venerable backdrop for contemporary dishes that are designed to tease maximum flavour from exemplary ingredients. A salad of the Nut Tree's own garden roots in balsamic vinaigrette with vegetable crisps is an appealing simple opener. Follow with wild mushroom fricassée with parmesan and rosemary croquette, roast saddle and faggot of lamb in sauce vièrge, with an array of provençale veg, including puréed aubergine, or an Indian-spiced treatment of cod garnished with almonds and raisins. Bringing up the rear could be warm chocolate fondant with orange ice cream, or a plate of artisan cheeses.

Chef Michael & Mary North **Seats** 70, Pr/dining room 36 **Times** 12-2.30/7-9, Closed 2 wks from 27 Dec, Mon-Tue, D Sun **Prices** Tasting menu £60-£108, Starter £8-£15, Main £12-£35, Dessert £7.50-£12 **Wines** 101 bottles over £30, 23 bottles under £30, 15 by glass **Parking** 30 **Notes** Tasting menu 8 course, Sunday L, Children welcome

OXFORD Map 5 SP50

Bear & Ragged Staff

British, European

tel: 01865 862329 **Appleton Rd, Cumnor OX2 9QH**
email: enquiries@bearandraggedstaff.com
dir: *A420 to Cumnor, left at mini rdbt towards Appleton*

Trend-conscious cooking and contemporary design

The Bear offers an appealing mixture of traditional atmosphere and contemporary design. Masses of artwork on cool green walls in the dining room, offset the roughcast stone, and forward-thinking menus offer trend-conscious British food. Grilled mackerel with mussels, potato salad, puréed spinach and spring onion dressing gets things off to a fine start, perhaps followed by braised pig's cheek and belly with celeriac fondant in apple jus. A more traditional French note is sounded in fried lamb's kidneys with pancetta in sherry dressing, or in classic coq au vin. Stay on the French track for dark chocolate and orange soufflé with Grand Marnier Chantilly.

Chef Joseph Woods **Seats** 90, Pr/dining room 15 **Times** 12-9.30, All-day dining **Prices** Starter £5-£10, Main £12-£25, Dessert £5-£7 **Wines** 15 bottles over £30, 30 bottles under £30, 20 by glass **Parking** 30 **Notes** Breakfast, Sunday L £12-£30, Vegetarian available, Children welcome

Cotswold Lodge Hotel

British, European

tel: 01865 512121 **66a Banbury Rd OX2 6JP**
email: info@cotswoldlodgehotel.co.uk **web:** www.cotswoldlodgehotel.co.uk
dir: *A40 Oxford ring rd onto A4165 Banbury Rd signed city centre/Summertown. Hotel 2m on left*

Straight-talking modern food in a Victorian mansion

This stately Victorian villa is replete with period style, all high ceilings, sweeping staircases and expansive bay windows, but given a modern facelift. The kitchen deals in contemporary food with clear European accents, turning out a pressed game terrine of guinea fowl, duck, rabbit, pistachios and leeks, countered by a lively quince chutney, among starters. For mains, pan-fried lamb might come with samphire, turnips, Parmentier potatoes, apricots and rosemary jus, while fish dishes could see seared gurnard partnered with kohlrabi, pak choi, and tomato butter sauce. End with rhubarb and stem ginger pannacotta with pineapple carpaccio and orange sorbet, or bow out with a plate of Oxfordshire cheeses.

Gee's Restaurant

Mediterranean

tel: 01865 553540 **61 Banbury Rd OX2 6PE**
email: info@gees-restaurant.co.uk
dir: *N off A4165, from city centre right onto Banbury Rd, located just past Bevington Rd*

Med-influenced brasserie cooking in a glasshouse

Gee's continues to delight townies and gownies on the northern edge of the city centre. The glasshouse setting sees potted olive trees and lightweight café-style furniture in a room flooded with natural light, and the style is Med-influenced modern brasserie cooking. A wood-fired oven turns out pizzetti and sharing ribs of beef, while a charcoal grill cooks steaks, burgers and chops of lamb, pork or venison, served with creamed spinach. Crab mayonnaise or artichoke fritters are good starters, while fish lovers may enjoy whole sea bass simply dressed in lemon and parsley. Finish with blood orange tart, or a serving of prune ice cream glooped with treacly Pedro Ximenez sherry.

Macdonald Randolph Hotel

Traditional British

tel: 01865 256400 **Beaumont St OX1 2LN**
email: acanthus.randolph@macdonald-hotels.co.uk
web: www.macdonaldhotels.co.uk
dir: *M40 junct 8, A40 towards Oxford, follow city centre signs, leads to St Giles, hotel on right*

All-day bistro cookery in grand city-centre hotel

The Rosette award for this establishment has been suspended due to a change of chef. Reassessment will take place in due course under the new chef. The Randolph is a honey-stoned magnificence on a corner of St Giles overlooking the Ashmolean Museum, its Gothic-arched windows and flags in Oxford dark blue making it a true landmark of the university city. The interiors retain a feel of olden times, with grandfather clocks, misty landscapes in oils, and stone fireplaces adorning the public rooms. Following a fire, the dining room reopened as Acanthus in April 2016, and has now taken on a more informal aspect, although there are still some fine still-lifes on the deep green walls. Unclothed tables and banquette seating are the setting for a kitchen production that has jettisoned the old fine-dining tag in favour of a less stuffy, all-day modern bistro approach. Sandwiches, savouries, burgers and croques are available in the daylight hours, while dinner offers the likes of deep-fried cod cheeks with samphire in sauce ravigote to kick off, before loin, neck and kidney of Scottish lamb with artichokes in truffled jus, or else seared halibut with pickled shiitakes and spinach, sauced in port. Fig tart served with pistachio ice cream makes for a sumptuous finale, and even the sultanas that garnish a crème caramel have been considerately soaked in Sauternes.

Seats 90 **Times** 7am-10pm, All-day dining **Prices** Starter £5-£12, Main £10-£22, Dessert £5-£12 **Wines** 120 bottles over £30, 20 bottles under £30, 15 by glass **Parking** 35, Chargeable (pre-booking essential) **Notes** Pre-theatre menu 2 course with wine £23.95, Sunday L, Vegetarian available, Children welcome

Malmaison Oxford

Modern British, French

tel: 01865 268400 **Oxford Castle, 3 New Rd OX1 1AY**
email: oxford@malmaison.com **web:** www.malmaison.com
dir: *M40 junct 9 (signed Oxford/A34). Follow A34 S to Botley Interchange, then A420 to city centre*

Crowd-pleasing food in the old prison canteen

Oxford's old slammer is now leading a reformed life as a classy hotel, with seductive bedrooms in the cells and a moodily-lit brasserie in the former basement canteen. The cooking is a little bit French, a little bit British, and a little bit global. The feel-good results are starters like ahi (yellowfin) tuna tartare with avocado, pickled ginger, soy and lime dressing and wasabi, alongside chicken liver parfait and classic prawn cocktail. Moules marinière will sort out the Francophiles, while steaks and burgers seared on the grill, or pan-fried sea bass with chorizo, black olives, new potatoes and mussel vinaigrette please everyone. And for dessert, perhaps a Valrhona chocolate soufflé.

The Oxford Kitchen

Modern British V

tel: 01865 511149 **215 Banbury Rd, Summertown OX2 7HQ**
email: hello@theoxfordkitchen.co.uk **web:** www.theoxfordkitchen.co.uk
dir: *Centre of Summertown. 5 min from A40 on Banbury Road. 1.5m from Oxford city centre*

Seriously good cooking and contemporary verve

Rubbing shoulders with high-end boutiques and stylish delis along busy Banbury Road, The Oxford Kitchen is establishing itself as a foodie landmark. Start with an impressive Creedy Carver duck composition involving smoked breast, confit and parfait, with hazelnuts and poached quince to leaven the richness. A perfectly tuned main of Cornish stone bass with roasted cauliflower, golden raisins, almonds and curry displays commendable lightness of touch, or a more robust duo of beef fillet and braised ox cheek with potato purée, watercress, black truffle, and red wine essence might appeal. Harmonious flavour combinations continue at dessert, with an on-trend trifle with poached figs, almond sponge and Amaretto cream.

Chef John Footman **Seats** 80, Pr/dining room 50 **Times** 12-2.30/6-9.30, Closed 1st 2 wks Jan, Mon, D Sun **Prices** Fixed L 2 course £18, Fixed D 3 course £22.50, Starter £7-£15.50, Main £15.50-£28, Dessert £7.50-£9.50 **Wines** 22 bottles over £30, 24 bottles under £30, 11 by glass **Parking** NCP opposite **Notes** Sunday L £7-£24, Children welcome

OXFORD *continued*

Oxford Thames Four Pillars Hotel

Modern International

tel: 01865 334444 **Henley Rd, Sandford-on-Thames OX4 4GX**
email: thames@four-pillars.co.uk **web:** www.oxfordthameshotel.co.uk
dir: *Exit A4074 signed Sandford-on-Thames. Right at T-junct/mini rdbt. Hotel 0.5m on left on Henley Road*

Straightforward dining in a stylish spot with river views

In 30 acres of parkland running down to the river, this smart hotel makes a tranquil base a short drive from the centre. Its contemporary River Room restaurant takes care of the gastronomic side of the equation with a please-all menu that has its share of classic dishes – from carpaccio with parmesan shavings to rib-eye steak with peppercorn sauce – with some modern ideas too. Ham hock, foie gras and parsley roulade with piccalilli makes a sound starter, followed by rump of lamb with sweetbreads in a rich jus accompanied by minted peas, carrots and asparagus. To finish, there may be chilli-spiked chocolate pot with biscotti.

Chef Claudio Costea **Seats** 150, Pr/dining room 50 **Times** 7-9.30, Closed 25 & 31 Dec, L Mon-Sat **Prices** Fixed D 3 course £29.95-£40.95, Tasting menu £49, Starter £7.95, Main £17.95-£25.95, Dessert £7.95-£10.95 **Wines** 14 bottles over £30, 18 bottles under £30, 11 by glass **Parking** 150 **Notes** Sunday L £16.95-£17.95, Vegetarian available, Children welcome

STADHAMPTON **Map 5 SU69**

The Crazy Bear

Modern British

tel: 01865 890714 **Bear Ln OX44 7UR**
email: enquiries@crazybear-stadhampton.co.uk **web:** www.crazybeargroup.co.uk
dir: *M40 junct 7, A329. In 4m left after petrol station, left into Bear Lane*

Rebooted Tudor inn with comforting brasserie classics

We often comment on Tudor inns carefully converted to preserve their original character, but the epithet 'crazy' is the clue that a different approach, to put it mildly, has been adopted here. Pink cushioned walls, a leopard-print carpet, big steel mirrors and a kind of herringbone overhead wine store set the scene for what's on offer in the English arm of the operation. The substantial list of contemporary brasserie food majors in comfort-oriented classics, such as scallops and black pudding with pea purée, followed by beef, ale and mushroom pie with champ potatoes. End with apple tart Tatin with vanilla ice cream.

Chef Martin Picken **Seats** 40, Pr/dining room 140 **Times** 12-10, All-day dining **Prices** Prices not confirmed **Wines** 235 bottles over £30, 21 bottles under £30, 20 by glass **Parking** 100 **Notes** Sunday L, Vegetarian available, Children welcome

Thai Thai at The Crazy Bear

Modern Thai

tel: 01865 890714 **Bear Ln OX44 7UR**
email: enquiries@crazybear-stadhampton.co.uk
dir: *M40 junct 7, A329. In 4m left after petrol station, left into Bear Lane*

Southeast Asian cooking in a Tudor village inn

Crazy Bear's first outfit occupies a Tudor inn in an Oxfordshire village. As well as a modern British dining room, it boasts a Thai restaurant with crimson velvet beams, scatter cushions and tables that resemble brass platters balanced on boxes. There are forays beyond Thailand, for Peking duck rolls dipped in hoi sin, or grilled black cod in miso and sake, but the core of the repertoire is palate-tingling Thai classics, from pork satay to scallops and tiger prawns in red curry to steamed squid in a firestorm of chillies, lemongrass, lime leaves and coriander. Finish with homely treacle tart with milk ice cream.

SWINBROOK **Map 10 SP21**

The Swan Inn

Modern British

tel: 01993 823339 **OX18 4DY**
email: info@theswanswinbrook.co.uk **web:** www.theswanswinbrook.co.uk
dir: *A40 towards Cheltenham, turn left to Swinbrook*

Historic village inn with locally sourced ingredients

The wisteria-clad 16th-century Swan is the quintessential village pub, with an apple orchard to the rear and the Windrush River running by. The kitchen sources seasonal ingredients with care (traceability is a big deal here), and knows how to turn it into some skilfully rendered dishes – pork and game terrine with celeriac remoulade and toast, for example, followed by a whole local partridge with glazed parsnips, braised red cabbage and thyme and chestnut gravy, or a tried-and-tested pub favourite such as braised faggots with swede mash, red onion and ale and sage gravy.

TOOT BALDON **Map 5 SP50**

The Mole Inn

Modern European

tel: 01865 340001 **OX44 9NG**
email: info@themoleinn.com
dir: *5m S of Oxford, restaurant 15 mins from M40 junct 7*

Country pub with globally inspired cooking

In a quiet village on the outskirts of Oxford, The Mole Inn is everything a country inn should be, adorned with framed mirrors and run by a casual but professional team. A starter of devilled lamb's kidneys with chargrilled ciabatta might be followed by rump of lamb, pea and mint mash, grain mustard cabbage and roast garlic. More globally influenced dishes could include grilled natural smoked haddock, curry creamed leeks, curly kale and coriander mash, and Café de Paris butter. To finish, what could be better than chocolate and orange cheesecake, walnut ice cream and raspberry sip? A small conservatory to one side makes a pleasant summer retreat.

Chef Gary Witchalls **Seats** 70 **Times** 12-2.30/7-9.30, Closed 25 Dec **Wines** 7 bottles over £30, 24 bottles under £30, 8 by glass **Parking** 40 **Notes** Sunday L £14-£15.95, Vegetarian available, Children welcome

WANTAGE **Map 5 SU38**

The Star Inn

Modern British

tel: 01235 751873 **Watery Ln, Sparsholt OX12 9PL**
email: info@thestarsparsholt.co.uk **web:** www.thestarsparsholt.co.uk
dir: *From B4507, 4m W of Wantage, turn right to Sparsholt. The Star Inn signed*

Reinvented inn with accomplished food

Inside this solid 300-year-old inn in the quintessentially English village of Sparsholt, all is decluttered and open plan with chunky wooden furniture and plain white walls, and the food has a suitably modern accent. An impressive starter balances the richness of foie gras and duck liver parfait with pear chutney and granola, and comes with a buttery home-made brioche bun. Mains partner pan-fried halibut with sweet millet, purple sprouting broccoli, samphire, and a buttermilk cream sauce laden with squid, mussels and cockles. Dessert takes mango as a theme to play with, served in an iced parfait with nougat, and as a purée, powder and frozen carpaccio with rose sorbet.

Chef Matt Williams **Seats** 45, Pr/dining room 40 **Times** 12-2.30/6.30-9.30 **Prices** Starter £5.50-£7.50, Main £16.50-£29.50, Dessert £5.95-£7.50 **Wines** 20 bottles over £30, 21 bottles under £30, 12 by glass **Parking** 20 **Notes** Sunday L, Vegetarian available, Children welcome

WATLINGTON Map 5 SU69

The Fat Fox Inn

British, French

tel: 01491 613040 **13 Shirburn St OX49 5BU**
email: info@thefatfoxinn.co.uk **web:** www.thefatfoxinn.co.uk
dir: *M40 junct 6 onto B4009 S for 2.5m. On right in village*

Rustic, unfussy country-pub food

The Fat Fox lurks in a small market town on the edge of the Chilterns, and is a proper old country inn with an inglenook fireplace and wood-burning stove. The menu offers hearty portions of rustic, unfussy food with just the right amount of modern tweaking – so expect venison in the Scotch egg. Pub favourites such as mussels in Thai green curry, or chicken liver parfait with sharp chutney, pique the appetite for robust main dishes like a mash-topped trad fish pie made with haddock, salmon and king prawns, served with seasonal greens, venison stew with mashed swede, or a real steak-and-kidney suet pudding, with fig frangipane to finish.

Chef Mark Gambles **Seats** 26, Pr/dining room **Times** 12-3/6.30-10, Closed L 25 Dec, 1 Jan **Prices** Fixed L 2 course £12-£22, Fixed D 3 course £20-£36, Starter £4-£8, Main £10-£22, Dessert £6 **Wines** 2 bottles over £30, 21 bottles under £30, 12 by glass **Parking** 20 **Notes** Breakfast £10.50, Sunday L £10-£15, Vegetarian available, Children welcome

WESTON-ON-THE-GREEN Map 11 SP51

The Manor Restaurant

Modern European

tel: 01869 350621 **Northampton Rd OX25 3QL**
email: house@themanorweston.co.uk **web:** www.westonmanor.co.uk
dir: *M40 junct 9, exit A34 to Oxford then 1st exit on left signed Weston-on-the-Green/ Middleton Stony B4030. Right at mini rdbt, hotel 400yds on left*

Grand period room and modern cooking

Dating back some 900 years, The Manor is a grand pile in glorious gardens, now a swish hotel with a restaurant in the 11th-century Baron's Hall – a rather special room with a 30-foot-high ceiling, acres of panels and a giant chandelier. The kitchen turns out bright, modern food via tasting or carte menus. A fashionable surf 'n' turf combo turns up amongst the starters – Native lobster cooked a la plancha, with chicken wing, leek purée and a truffle-flavoured sauce – while main course brings spiced Herdwick mutton with pickled grapes and ratte potatoes. Flavours hit the mark in a dessert of Yorkshire rhubarb sorbet with fromage blanc and almonds.

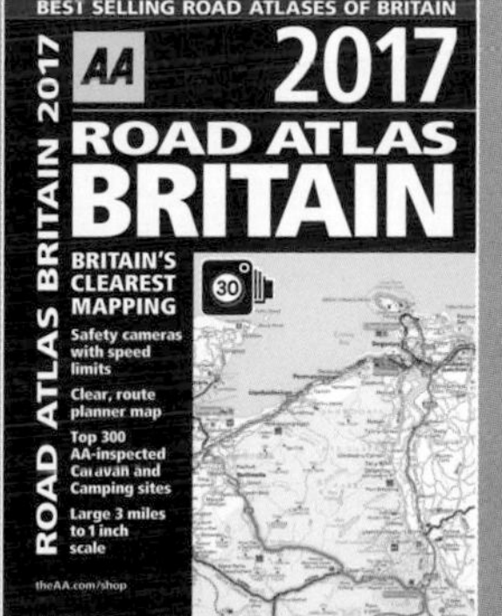

WITNEY Map 5 SP31

Hollybush Witney

British NEW

tel: 01993 708073 **35 Corn St OX28 6BT**
email: info@hollybushwitney.com
dir: *In town centre*

Up-to-date comfort food and a buzzy ambience

The Hollybush is a buzzy gastropub run by a youthful team that successfully delivers the gastronomy part without neglecting that essential pub side of the equation. There are real ales at the hand pumps and a menu that comes up with pub classics such as local sausages with mash and onion gravy alongside more modern British fare like duck liver parfait with orange and star anise jelly. A main course of brined and roasted chicken breast with celeriac fondant, roasted salsify, toasted hazelnuts and thyme jus shows ambition and creativity, while puddings head straight for the comfort zone with good old lemon meringue tart.

Chef Liam Whittle **Seats** Pr/dining room 35 **Times** 12-9.30, All-day dining **Prices** Starter £5.50-£8, Main £12.50-£19.50, Dessert £6.50-£8 **Wines** 14 bottles over £30, 17 bottles under £30, 10 by glass **Parking** On street & town centre free parking **Notes** Sunday L, Vegetarian available, Children welcome

Old Swan & Minster Mill

 Traditional British

tel: 01993 774441 **Old Minster OX29 0RN**
email: reception@oldswanandminstermill.com **web:** www.oldswanandminstermill.com
dir: *Exit A40 signed Minster Lovell, through village right T-junct, 2nd left*

Charming country pub by the River Windrush

The quintessentially Cotswolds village of Minster Lovell makes the perfect history-steeped setting for the Old Swan, a smart country inn with rooms next door in the more contemporary surrounds of Minster Mill. There's a local flavour to the menu (including produce grown in the kitchen garden) which sees daily specials sitting alongside pub classics. A fishcake of salmon, wholegrain mustard and spring onion makes a diverting opener, teamed with citrus crème fraîche, while cannon of new season lamb comes with almond stuffing, button mushrooms, and wild garlic and rosemary jus. For pudding, blackcurrant sorbet makes a well-judged counterpoint to an intense dark chocolate torte. The riverside garden is a treat.

The Restaurant at Witney Lakes Resort

Modern British

tel: 01993 893012 & 893000 **Downs Rd OX29 0SY**
email: restaurant@witney-lakes.co.uk
dir: *2m W of Witney town centre, off B4047 Witney to Burford road*

Popular brasserie cooking in a resort hotel

The sprawling modern resort in west Oxfordshire caters for iron-pumpers, niblick-swingers and the nuptial trade, as well as offering contemporary brasserie cooking in a destination restaurant that has acquired a dedicated local following. Tables on a lakeside terrace embrace the sunnier months, and the core attraction is a menu of dependable modern classic dishes. Opening with beetroot- and gin-cured salmon dressed in horseradish crème fraîche, you might go on to Gressingham duck breast with honey-roast plums, or sirloin on the bone, its chips done in garlic, rosemary and parmesan. For afters, there's lemon posset and blueberry compôte, or sticky toffee with mascarpone ice cream.

Chef Sean Parker, Ryan Priddey **Seats** 75 **Times** 12-3/6.30-9, Closed 25 & 31 Dec, 1 Jan, L Sat, D Sun-Mon **Prices** Fixed L 2 course fr £15, Starter £5-£7.50, Main £12.50-£21, Dessert £5-£7 **Wines** 6 bottles over £30, 25 bottles under £30, 7 by glass **Parking** 400 **Notes** Sunday L, Vegetarian available, Children welcome

WOODCOTE Map 5 SU68

Woody Nook at Woodcote

 Modern British V

tel: 01491 680775 **Goring Rd RG8 OSD**
email: info@woodynookatwoodcote.co.uk
dir: *Opposite village green*

International flavours and top-notch Australian wines

Opposite the village green and cricket pitch, creeper-hung Woody Nook couldn't look more English with its leaded windows and beams. The menu has an international slant, with an ingenious kitchen turning out starters such as arancini stuffed with sun-dried tomatoes and mozzarella in puttanesca sauce and crab flavoured with ginger, citrus, coriander and chilli and sauced with rouille. Mains sound more familiar to 21st-century ears: ham-wrapped monkfish tail, say, with fettuccine sauced with tomato and basil, and chargrilled beef fillet with peppercorn sauce, fondant potato, mushrooms and tomatoes. End with exotic pineapple carpaccio with coconut ice cream and rum and ginger sauce or the admirable selection of cheese.

Chef Stuart Shepherd **Seats** 50 **Times** 12-2.30/7-9.30, Closed Xmas, Mon-Tue, D Sun **Prices** Fixed L 2 course £15.95, Fixed D 3 course £22.90, Starter £5.95-£8.95, Main £15.95-£23.95, Dessert £6.95 **Wines** 8 by glass **Parking** 25 **Notes** Sunday L £17.95-£24.90, Children welcome

WOODSTOCK Map 11 SP41

The Feathers Hotel

 Modern British

tel: 01993 812291 **Market St OX20 1SX**
email: enquiries@feathers.co.uk **web:** www.feathers.co.uk
dir: *From A44 (Oxford to Woodstock), 1st left after lights. Hotel on left*

Modern British cooking in a colourfully boutiqued hotel

A brick-built inn in a handsome Cotswold market town, The Feathers has long been a local fixture. There can be no doubt about its having been coaxed into the boutique hotel era when you get inside, including the dining room with its raspberry-red banquettes and bold artworks. A copiously stocked gin bar is in the record-books for having the most varieties on offer. Thoroughly modern British cooking is the order of the day. Start with duck confit and fennel risotto, move on to saddle of venison with forced rhubarb and red wine sauce, and finish with dark chocolate tart with coffee parfait.

Chef Ian Matfin **Seats** 40, Pr/dining room 24 **Times** 12-2.30/6.30-9, Closed Mon, L Tue-Fri, D Sun **Prices** Fixed L 2 course £37.50-£42.50, Fixed D 3 course £45-£56, Tasting menu £55-£61.50 **Wines** 80 bottles over £30, 10 bottles under £30, 16 by glass **Parking** On street **Notes** Sunday L £14.95-£29.50, Vegetarian available, Children welcome

Macdonald Bear Hotel

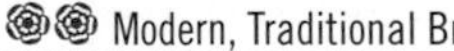 Modern, Traditional British

tel: 01993 811124 **Park St OX20 1SZ**
email: general.bear@macdonald-hotels.co.uk **web:** www.macdonaldhotels.co.uk/bear
dir: *M40 junct 9 follow signs for Oxford & Blenheim Palace. A44 to town centre, hotel on left*

Accomplished modern cooking in medieval hotel

This former coaching inn has its origins in the Middle Ages, although the kitchen clearly has its fingers on the pulse of today's tastes. Plump, lightly caramelised scallops are offset by buttery chorizo salsa and charred leeks, to be followed perhaps by seared loin of Highland venison with figs, celeriac, smoked Jerusalem artichoke and port jus. Fish gets a decent airing among main courses: for instance, accurately timed pan-seared fillet of wild brill accompanied by baby squid, sweetcorn and creamed potato. The kitchen's attention to detail extends to canapés, and puddings can be a visual delight: deeply flavoured dark chocolate tart, say, with cherry salsa and noteworthy pistachio ice cream.

Chef Paul Bell **Seats** 65, Pr/dining room 26 **Times** 12.30-2.30/7-9.30 **Prices** Fixed L 2 course fr £22.50, Starter £5-£9.50, Main £15-£26, Dessert £4-£7.50 **Wines** 30 bottles over £30, 20 bottles under £30, 16 by glass **Parking** 50 **Notes** Sunday L £23.50-£29.50, Vegetarian available, Children welcome

WOOTTON Map 11 SP41

The Killingworth Castle

 Modern British

tel: 01993 811401 & 01386 593223 **Glympton Rd OX20 1EJ**
email: reservations@thekillingworthcastle.com **web:** www.thekillingworthcastle.com
dir: *M40 junct 9, 2m outside Woodstock on Glympton Road, on edge of Wootton*

Unfussy cooking in a restored 17th-century inn

The inn has been an integral part of its community since the 1630s. When the Alexanders (who also run the Ebrington Arms near Chipping Campden) took over in 2012, the old place received the investment it needed, while retaining all its earthy charm and period character. It's the kitchen's output that makes the place stand out – imaginative cooking that isn't unduly fussy. Mackerel on tapenaded toast comes topped with salami and dressed in parsley oil to start, ahead of stone bass with creamed leeks in chicken jus, or rose veal with girolles and white bean purée. End on a high with chocolate mousse and peanut parfait.

Chef Dan Watkins **Seats** 68, Pr/dining room 20 **Times** 12-2.30/6-9, Closed 25 Dec **Prices** Starter £6-£8, Main fr £13, Dessert £6-£8 **Wines** 22 bottles over £30, 40 bottles under £30, 10 by glass **Parking** 40 **Notes** Early bird for 2 Mon-Thu 6-7pm, Monthly food night, Sunday L, Vegetarian available, Children welcome

RUTLAND

CLIPSHAM Map 11 SK91

The Olive Branch

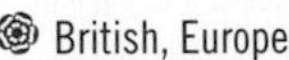 British, European V

tel: 01780 410355 **Beech House, Main St LE15 7SH**
email: info@theolivebranchpub.com **web:** www.theolivebranchpub.com
dir: *2m from A1 at Stretton junct, 5m N of Stamford*

Charming village dining inn firing on all cylinders

The Olive Branch serves a fine pint of local ale as well as home-made mulled wine, sloe gin and fruity cocktails flavoured with foraged berries and herbs. It's clear that this is a kitchen with a passion for seasonal, local stuff and food that is big on flavour and with the easy-going atmosphere of the great British pub. Daily-changing menus and blackboards offer everything from classic fish and chips to pan-seared scallops with black pudding and quince, and a main-course haunch of venison with juniper fondant potato, braised red cabbage and roast parsnips that brims with rich flavours and hearty intentions. Finish with lemon verbena meringue pie with raspberry sorbet.

Chef Sean Hope **Seats** 45, Pr/dining room 20 **Times** 12-2/6.30-9.30, Closed D 25 Dec, 1 Jan **Prices** Fixed L 2 course £18.50, Starter £6.50-£12.50 **Wines** 60 bottles over £30, 20 bottles under £30, 16 by glass **Parking** 15 **Notes** D 5 course £31.50, Sunday L £16.50-£27.50, Children welcome

Hambleton Hall

OAKHAM **Map 11 SK80**

British V NOTABLE WINE LIST

tel: 01572 756991 **Hambleton LE15 8TH**
email: hotel@hambletonhall.com **web:** www.hambletonhall.com
dir: *8m W of A1 Stamford junct (A606), 3m E of Oakham*

Superb fine dining in majestic country-house hotel

Back in the 1880s, fox hunting was an aspirational pursuit, and one wealthy Victorian brewer built Hambleton as his hunting season holiday home, as any chap of substance would. A water feature, otherwise known as Rutland Water reservoir (now a nature reserve) arrived on the hall's doorstep in 1970 to enhance the splendour of the setting, and Tim and Stefa Hart added the icing on the cake when they bought the place in 1979 and created a country-house hotel of distinction. It is a handsome place that delivers grandeur on a human scale and was always meant for entertainment and pleasurable pursuits, a laudable aim which continues today with elegant bedrooms, chic public rooms and a fabulous restaurant to complete the sybaritic picture. Chandeliers, oil paintings and linen-swathed tables provide reassuring formality, and the service throughout is charming, professional and engaging. Aaron Patterson has headed the kitchen team since 1992, and his food is refined, creative, and firmly rooted in sound culinary thinking. They have their own bakery, so the bread is a cut above, and everything from the canapés to the petits fours is beautifully made and delivered via tasting and à la carte menus. Among starters, champagne foam and shellfish cappuccino might add suitably luxurious notes to a lasagne of Dorset crab, while main course could see roast fillet of brill in a full-throttle partnership with braised pig's trotter, smoked ham hock, Colfiorito lentils and parsley, or go for glazed and smoked venison faggot with slow-roasted loin, parsley root purée, pickled walnuts and king cabbage. Everything looks picture-perfect on the plate and the balance of flavours and technically spot-on cooking continues through to dessert: a light-as-air almond and Amaretto soufflé with quince and honey ice cream, perhaps, or pear and blackberry terrine with caramel ice cream. The wine list brims with interesting things from producers large and small.

Chef Aaron Patterson **Seats** 60, Pr/dining room 20
Times 12-2/7-9.30, **Prices** Fixed L 2 course fr £26.50, Fixed D 3 course fr £68, Tasting menu fr £85 **Wines** 20 bottles under £30, 10 by glass **Parking** 40 **Notes** ALC 3 course £68, Sunday L fr £55, Children 5 yrs+

LYDDINGTON Map 11 SP89

The Marquess of Exeter

 Modern European

tel: 01572 822477 **52 Main St LE15 9LT**
email: info@marquessexeter.co.uk **web:** www.marquessexeter.co.uk
dir: *M1 junct 19, A14 to Kettering, then A6003 to Caldecott. Right into Lyddington Rd, 2m to village*

Welcoming village inn with appealing menus

The Marquess of Exeter has plenty of character and charm. The bedrooms are smart and contemporary, the bar has a roaring fire and exposed stone walls, while the restaurant is an equally unpretentious and attractive space. Salt-and-chilli cuttlefish with Thai salad show globe-trotting tendencies, but equally you might go for black pudding fritters with home-made piccalilli. It's all good honest stuff with broad appeal. Herb-crusted rack of lamb is cooked just right, served with dauphinoise potatoes and marinated shallots, and fish and chips plays to the gallery. There are sharing dishes such as rib of Derbyshire beef, and, for dessert, vanilla pannacotta shows sharp technical skills.

OAKHAM Map 11 SK80

Barnsdale Lodge Hotel

Modern British

tel: 01572 724678 **The Avenue, Rutland Water, North Shore LE15 8AH**
email: enquiries@barnsdalelodge.co.uk **web:** www.barnsdalelodge.co.uk
dir: *Turn off A1 at Stamford onto A606 to Oakham. Hotel 5m on right (2m E of Oakham)*

Simple British cooking at an ancestral family seat

The Noel family have lived at Barnsdale since the accession of George III. To one side of the Earl of Gainsborough's Exton estate, it's a handsome country seat on the north shore of Rutland Water, with an idiosyncratically decorated main dining room, garden room and alfresco courtyard. Surveying the patio gardens, it's festooned with parasols and animal objets d'art, and plays host to simple modern British menus featuring produce from the vegetable garden. A meal might follow an inspired and satisfying course from artichoke and wild mushroom tart to teriyaki duck breast with pak choi and fine noodles, or sea bass with bubble-and-squeak and crayfish sauce.

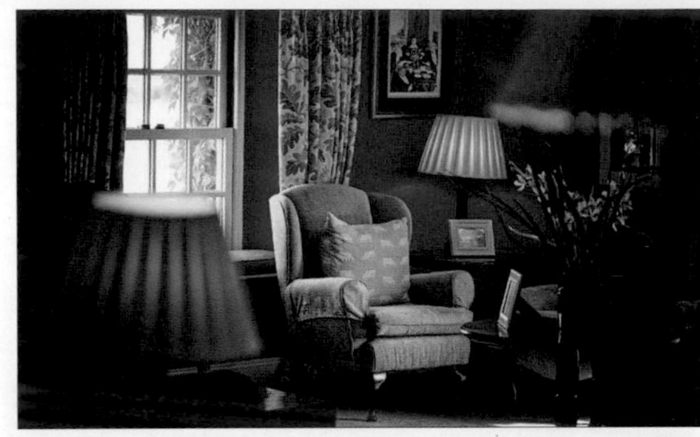

Barnsdale Lodge Hotel

Chef James Butterfill **Seats** 120, Pr/dining room 200 **Times** 12-2/6.30-9.30 **Prices** Fixed L 2 course £13.50-£18.50, Fixed D 3 course fr £30, Starter £6.50-£9.50, Main £14.50-£24.95, Dessert £5.50-£6.50 **Wines** 31 bottles over £30, 58 bottles under £30, 17 by glass **Parking** 250 **Notes** Sunday L, Vegetarian available, Children welcome

Hambleton Hall

– see page 375

UPPINGHAM Map 11 SP89

The Lake Isle

British, French

tel: 01572 822951 **16 High St East LE15 9PZ**
email: info@lakeisle.co.uk **web:** www.lakeisle.co.uk
dir: *M1 junct 19 to A14 Kettering, at rdbt take A43 signed Corby then A6003 to Rockingham/Uppingham. Continue to pedestrian lights Uppingham, right onto High St, Lake Isle on right after the square*

Georgian townhouse hotel with confident cooking

An 18th-century property is the setting for this restaurant with rooms in the market town of Uppingham. Crispy panko-crumbed scallops are served with pork belly, curry crème, butternut squash, peanuts and herbs in a starter of multiple flavours and textures, following suit with a main course of pan-fried duck breast with balsamic-infused baby beets, cippolini onions, chicory and polenta studded with feta and walnuts. Oriental influences are apparent in grilled fillet of sea bass with Japanese mushrooms, toasted cucumber, prawn and sesame fishcakes and wasabi. Puddings return to base in the shape of pot au chocolat with mini doughnuts, or sticky plum, port and ginger compôte with rice pudding parfait.

WING Map 11 SK80

Kings Arms Inn & Restaurant

Modern British

tel: 01572 737634 **13 Top St LE15 8SE**
email: info@thekingsarms-wing.co.uk **web:** www.thekingsarms-wing.co.uk
dir: *1m off A6003, between Oakham & Uppingham*

Enterprising supplier-led cooking in a traditional inn

Stone walls, beams and flagstones are reminders that this village inn dates from the 17th century. Real ales are dispensed in the bar, and there's an informal dining room. Everything is sourced from within 30 miles, and the place's own smokery contributes to a satisfying starter of smoked pigeon breast and black pudding with game chips, and quince and morello cherry chutney. Main courses are equally forthright, perhaps loin of hare with beetroot and chocolate purée, rissolé potatoes, root veg and kale. Afters such as sticky toffee and Rutland ale pudding with butterscotch sauce and Grainstore Ale ice cream are not to be missed.

Chef James Goss **Seats** 32 **Times** 12-2.30/6.30-9, Closed L Mon, D Sun **Prices** Starter £7.50-£12.50, Main £14-£32, Dessert £7-£28 **Wines** 30 bottles over £30, 20 bottles under £30, 33 by glass **Parking** 20 **Notes** Sunday L £12-£18, Vegetarian available, Children welcome

SHROPSHIRE

GRINSHILL Map 15 SJ52

The Inn at Grinshill

Modern British, European

tel: 01939 220410 **The High St SY4 3BL**
email: sales@theinnatgrinshill.co.uk **web:** www.theinnatgrinshill.co.uk
dir: *7m N of Shrewsbury towards Whitchurch on A49, signed 0.5m in centre of village on left*

Remote destination for contemporary pub cooking with show-kitchen

A gleaming-white decor with pictures printed high on the ceiling beams is the setting for friendly, efficient service and confident modernised pub cooking. Scotch egg is made here with salt cod and a deliciously runny centre, dressed with a swoosh of saffron aïoli, or go for pine-smoked duck with caramelised orange in a chicory and pine nut salad. A hunk of pork fillet is wrapped in pancetta, and the accompaniments all do their bit; potato fondant done in red wine, puréed celeriac, kale with bite, apple gel, Calvados sauce. A wine- and cinnamon-poached pear with mincemeat ice cream is well worth trying. A well-chosen wine list accompanies.

Chef Joshua Huxtable, Brett Waslin **Seats** 35, Pr/dining room 40 **Times** 6.30-9.30, Closed Mon-Tue, L Mon-Sat (ex by prior arrangement), D Sun, BHs **Wines** 13 bottles over £30, 26 bottles under £30, 10 by glass **Parking** 35 **Notes** Sunday L £14-£23.50, Vegetarian available, Children welcome

IRONBRIDGE Map 10 SJ60

Restaurant Severn

 British, French

tel: 01952 432233 **33 High St TF8 7AG**
dir: *Travelling along High St pass Restaurant Severn on right, to mini rbdt, take 3rd exit onto Waterloo St, continue 50mtrs to car park on left*

Sound cooking beside the Ironbridge gorge

Eric and Beb Bruce's small restaurant blends in with the terrace of souvenir and tea shops facing Abraham Darby's World Heritage cast iron bridge. Inside, however, sunny yellow walls, bare wooden floors, unclothed tables and high-backed toffee leather chairs give an intimate brasserie look. Full advantage is taken of the local larder, supplemented by home-grown organic seasonal materials. Classical French influences are evident in starters such as a wild mushroom soufflé with crispy leeks and Madeira sauce, while mains partner fillets of sole and sea bass with vermouth and sorrel sauce. Puddings are Beb Bruce's domain – perhaps glazed lemon tart with passionfruit sorbet.

Chef Eric & Beb Bruce **Seats** 30 **Times** 12-2/6.30-8.30, Closed BHs, Mon-Tue, L Wed-Sat, D Sun **Prices** Fixed D 3 course £27.95-£29.95 **Wines** 15 bottles over £30, 30 bottles under £30, 6 by glass **Parking** On street & car park opposite **Notes** Sun L once mthly, Gourmet evenings mthly 4 course £29.95, Sunday L £17.95-£19.95, Vegetarian available, Children Sun L only

LUDLOW Map 10 SO57

The Charlton Arms

Modern British

tel: 01584 872813 **Ludford Bridge SY8 1PJ**
email: reservations@thecharltonarms.co.uk **web:** www.thecharltonarms.co.uk
dir: *A49, turn onto B4361, Charlton Arms 1.9m on left just before bridge*

Classic food by the river

On Ludford Bridge and a short walk from historic Ludlow Castle, this smart, modernised stone-built pub has a lovely tiered terrace overlooking the River Teme. Inside, the airy dining area is relaxed and informal with scrubbed wooden floorboards and mismatched chairs. The menu focuses on classy renditions of British pub classics with a Gallic twist, perhaps starting with wild boar terrine and pickled vegetables or Cornish crab and gruyère quiche with caramelised chicory. It might be followed by whole sea bream with white beans and bacon or chicken Kiev, skinny fries and caramelised onion ketchup. Comforting desserts include sticky toffee pudding and salted caramel and lime sorbet.

Chef Lee Barnett **Seats** 40 **Times** 12-3/6-9.30, Closed D 25-26 Dec, 1 Jan **Prices** Starter £5.50-£8, Main £10.50-£19, Dessert £4.50-£6.50 **Wines** 6 bottles over £30, 18 bottles under £30, 14 by glass **Parking** 30 **Notes** Sunday L £10.50-£14.50, Vegetarian available, Children welcome

LUDLOW *continued*

The Clive Bar & Restaurant with Rooms

Modern British

tel: 01584 856565 & 856665 **Bromfield SY8 2JR**
email: info@theclive.co.uk **web:** www.theclive.co.uk
dir: *2m N of Ludlow on A49, near Ludlow Golf Club, racecourse & adjacent to Ludlow Food Centre*

Assured regional cooking in Clive of India's former residence

Once the home of Clive of India, then a pub, this brick-built Georgian house has been imaginatively refurbished to form a restaurant with rooms. Seasonality dictates the modern British menu, which may feature pickled wild mushrooms as an accompaniment for chicken liver parfait with toasted sourdough bread. That might be succeeded by rack and rump of lamb, with a separate pan of kidney hotpot, served with minted peas, broad beans and croquette potatoes, or seared sea bass fillet with summery-sounding pea risotto, samphire and salsa verde. To finish comes a pretty textbook rendering of crème brûlée scattered with raspberries, a shortbread biscuit on the side.

Chef Alan Cartwright **Seats** 90 **Times** 12-3/6-10, Closed 26 Dec **Prices** Starter £4.50-£9.50, Main £8.95-£23.50, Dessert £5-£8.50 **Wines** 19 bottles over £30, 36 bottles under £30, 9 by glass **Parking** 80 **Notes** Sunday L £11.50-£14, Vegetarian available, Children welcome

Dinham Hall Hotel

Modern British

tel: 01584 876464 **By The Castle SY8 1EJ**
email: info@dinhamhall.com **web:** www.dinhamhall.com
dir: *Town centre, off Market Place, opposite Ludlow Castle*

Ambitious modern British cooking opposite the castle

The three-storey Georgian house in the town centre opposite the castle features a pretty terrace for summer dining, while the restaurant is in two sections, one under a large skylight, the other in the original building. The kitchen constructs its output on a solid bedrock of local supplies, producing starters such as chicken and leek terrine with mushrooms, white beans and pear jelly. Moving on, you may come across tender monkfish masala with butternut squash and sauté potatoes in chicken jus, or venison fillet with braised red cabbage in thyme-scented red wine sauce, and finish with pistachio and black treacle frangipane tart with treacle ice cream.

Chef Tom Jacks **Seats** 36, Pr/dining room 60 **Times** 12.30-2.30/6.30-9.30, Closed L Mon **Prices** Fixed D 3 course £34.95 **Wines** 20 bottles over £30, 50 bottles under £30, 8 by glass **Parking** 16, On street **Notes** Sunday L, Vegetarian available, Children 7 yrs+

The Feathers Hotel

British, European

tel: 01584 875261 **The Bull Ring SY8 1AA**
email: enquiries@feathersatludlow.co.uk **web:** www.feathersatludlow.co.uk
dir: *From A49 follow town centre signs to centre. Hotel on left*

Gentle modern British cooking in a venerable timbered inn

The timber-framed property, converted to an inn in around 1670, has been sensitively decorated to retain its history, as witness the dining room, where dark brown upholstery and crisp white linen blend in with stone walls, beams and an inglenook. The kitchen goes for a gentle take on the modern British idiom, partnering ham hock terrine with piccalilli and a crispy quail's egg, ahead of roast rack of lamb with smoked bacon, dauphinoise, peas, broad beans and braised baby gem, or herb-crusted roast hake fillet with mussels, tartare sauce and mini chips. Close with the likes of vanilla pannacotta with rhubarb and ginger ice cream.

Chef Stuart Forman **Seats** 50, Pr/dining room 30 **Times** 7-9, Closed L all week **Prices** Fixed D 3 course £39.95-£42 **Wines** 14 bottles over £30, 23 bottles under £30, 10 by glass **Parking** 36 **Notes** Vegetarian available, Children welcome

Fishmore Hall

Modern European V

tel: 01584 875148 **Fishmore Rd SY8 3DP**
email: reception@fishmorehall.co.uk **web:** www.fishmorehall.co.uk
dir: *A49 from Shrewsbury, follow Ludlow & Bridgnorth signs. 1st left towards Bridgnorth, at next rdbt left onto Fishmore Rd. Hotel 0.5m on right after golf course*

Renovated country house with high-impact, thoughtful cooking

Virtually derelict as recently as 2007, Fishmore has been restored to the dignity it deserves. A Georgian country pile just off the A49 outside Ludlow, it's as sparkling white as royal-iced wedding cake, with a portico entrance and orangery extension, where Forelles restaurant enjoys views of rolling Shropshire. Andrew Birch offers a modern take on classic country-house cuisine, with multi-course tasters leading the charge and local ingredients in abundance. The seafood will have made the longest journey of course, but is of exemplary freshness, with Cornish crab set amid pink grapefruit, sweetcorn and crème fraîche, or silky main course cod appearing with shrimps, courgettes and basil. Otherwise, proceedings might open with an ambrosial treatment of asparagus soup, adorned with smoked salmon, caviar and a slow-cooked egg. Rose veal fillet and its sweetbread make a distinguished main, the former timed to accurate pink, the latter crisped on the surface, yielding and velvety within, alongside pressed potato, morels, beans and peas, the whole thing aromatised with wild garlic and lemon. Rhubarb turns up at dessert stage, in the various forms of poached, sorbet and a limpid jelly layer topping richly creamy white chocolate cheesecake. Copious incidentals, including exemplary breads, show the unwavering attention to detail.

Chef Andrew Birch **Seats** 60, Pr/dining room 20
Times 12.30-2.30/7-9.30, Closed Mon, L Tue, D Sun **Prices** Fixed L 2 course fr £24, Fixed D 3 course fr £49, Tasting menu £65-£80 **Wines** 40 bottles over £30, 20 bottles under £30, 10 by glass **Parking** 30 **Notes** Sunday L £24-£29.50, Children welcome

Old Downton Lodge

Modern British V

tel: 01568 771826 & 770175 **Downton on the Rock SY8 2HU**
email: bookings@olddowntonlodge.com **web:** www.olddowntonlodge.com
dir: *From Ludlow take A49 to Shrewsbury. Left to Knighton A4113, left to Downton. Old Downton Lodge after 3m*

Impressively creative cooking in a fascinating historic setting

Proving that Ludlow is still worth a visit for the gastronomically inclined, this charming restaurant with rooms, set in beautiful countryside just six miles from the town, is a comfortable hodge-podge of architectural styles – Georgian, warm red-brick, half-timbered, medieval – set around a flower-filled courtyard. The sitting room was once the stable, and the restaurant, in one of the oldest parts, has all the atmosphere of a medieval great hall, with stone walls, tapestry and chandelier. Head chef Karl Martin makes the most of the fantastic home-grown and local produce available in his daily-changing menus, a set-price choice of five, seven or nine courses that explore texture and flavour in original and inspiring ways. Everything looks beautiful and you can be sure that nothing arrives on the plate without due consideration. Menu descriptions are simple – for example 'salmon, mussels, buttermilk, garlic, monks bread', or 'duck, carrot, chicory, pineapple, pine', giving just a hint of what to expect. Fruit appears in unexpected places – pomegranate with cod, perhaps, creating unusual combinations that are endlessly fascinating and very successful. Desserts are equally thoughtful and interesting – rice pudding might come with artichoke and beetroot, and barbecued pear with gingerbread and crème fraiche.

Chef Karl Martin **Seats** 25, Pr/dining room 45 **Times** 6-9, Closed Xmas, Feb, Sun-Mon, L all week **Prices** Tasting menu £45-£75 **Wines** 32 bottles over £30, 12 bottles under £30, 11 by glass **Parking** 20 **Notes** Tasting menu 5/7/9 course, Children 13 yrs+

Overton Grange Hotel and Restaurant

Modern British

tel: 01584 873500 **Old Hereford Rd SY8 4AD**
email: info@overtongrangehotel.com **web:** www.overtongrangehotel.com
dir: *M5 junct 5. On B4361 approx 1.5m from Ludlow towards Leominster*

Edwardian country house with modern British dishes

The white and red-brick-faced Edwardian country house is classic in style both outside and in, where panelled walls and squashy sofas in front of log fires make a thoroughly inviting impression. A thoroughgoing excursion into modern British territory is mounted by the kitchen. After a starter perhaps of game ravioli in girolle velouté, crisp-skinned sea bass with clams, earthy mushrooms, fondant potato and asparagus is impressively well-timed, and glazed lemon tart with raspberry sorbet and crunchy meringue garnish ends things on a high. The show-stopping main course on the tasting menu might be roast organic guinea fowl done three ways, including a confit of the leg.

Chef Wayne Smith, Alex Marston **Seats** 40, Pr/dining room 24 **Times** 12-2.30/7-9.30 **Prices** Fixed L 3 course £32.95, Fixed D 3 course £39.95 **Wines** 30+ bottles over £30, 30+ bottles under £30, 12 by glass **Parking** 50 **Notes** Sunday L £26.95, Vegetarian available, Children 6 yrs+

MARKET DRAYTON **Map 15 SJ63**

Goldstone Hall

Modern British

tel: 01630 661202 **Goldstone Rd TF9 2NA**
email: enquiries@goldstonehall.com **web:** www.goldstonehall.com
dir: *4m S of Market Drayton off A529 signed Goldstone Hall Hotel. 4m N of Newport signed from A41*

Modern British ideas in a manor-house hotel

The two stand-out elements to Goldstone Hall are its magnificent gardens and ambitious restaurant. The kitchen garden is a major part of the operation, providing fresh, seasonal produce for the table, and the kitchen turns out bright, modern dishes while avoiding jumping on the bandwagon of every contemporary fashion. Excellent amuse-bouche gets things off to a flying start, as do the home-made breads. Then try crab and ginger salad, say, with confit fennel and lemon, followed by slow-cooked beef with bubble-and-squeak, Shropshire Blue bonbon and confit cabbage. Finish with a simple and well-executed lemon tart with raspberry sorbet.

Chef Chris Weatherstone **Seats** 60, Pr/dining room 14 **Times** 11-3/7-10 **Prices** Fixed L 2 course fr £24, Fixed D 3 course £45-£50 **Wines** 50 bottles over £30, 47 bottles under £30, 16 by glass **Parking** 70 **Notes** Afternoon tea, Sunday L fr £32, Vegetarian available, Children welcome

MUCH WENLOCK Map 10 SO69

Raven Hotel

 Modern British

tel: 01952 727251 **30 Barrow St TF13 6EN**
email: enquiry@ravenhotel.com **web:** www.ravenhotel.com
dir: *M54 junct 4 or 5, take A442 S, then A4169 to Much Wenlock. In town centre*

Ambitious cooking in a 17th-century coaching inn

This former coaching inn has period charm, with venerable beams, log fires and hand-pulled ales available in the bar. On the dining front, though, things are positively 21st-century, for the kitchen turns out smart, modern European constructions. A typically ambitious starter is slow-roasted celeriac soup topped with chorizo beignet and parmesan emulsion. Main course might bring forth a surf and turf number, pairing roast fillet of Mortimer Forest venison with lobster, plus haricot blanc, pancetta and lobster espuma. There's a tasting menu, too, serving up 68°C loin of cod. Desserts run to Granny Smith pannacotta with warm apple cake and apple ice cream, and the cheese selection is first class.

Chef Jason Hodnett **Seats** 40, Pr/dining room 14 **Times** 12-2.30/6.45-9.30, Closed 25-26 Dec **Prices** Fixed D 3 course £39, Tasting menu £45-£59 **Wines** 10 bottles over £30, 41 bottles under £30, 12 by glass **Parking** 30 **Notes** Sunday L £18.99-£21.99, Vegetarian available, Children welcome

MUNSLOW Map 10 SO58

Crown Country Inn

 Modern British

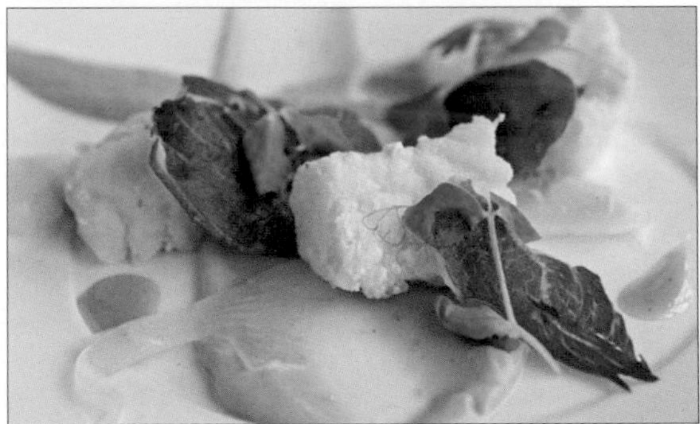

tel: 01584 841205 **SY7 9ET**
email: info@crowncountryinn.co.uk **web:** www.crowncountryinn.co.uk
dir: *On B4368 between Craven Arms & Much Wenlock*

Classy modern cooking in old village inn

In an Area of Outstanding Natural Beauty, the Crown dates from Tudor times and was first licensed in 1790. The kitchen has a 'Local to Ludlow' policy that might take in a reworking of breakfast for black pudding croquettes with Boston beans, bacon and 'fried bread', or involve adding pea pesto, prosciutto and pickled fennel to scallops, for starters. Inspired mains include tapenade-crusted salmon with olive oil mash and creamed leeks in beurre rouge and braised Bridgnorth brisket with butter bean fricassée, roast roots, pickled walnuts and polenta fritters. For afters, orange crème brûlée with cranberry ice cream rubs shoulders with banana parfait and caramel popcorn in toffee sauce.

Crown Country Inn

Chef Richard Arnold **Seats** 65, Pr/dining room 42 **Times** 12-2/6.45-8.45, Closed some days during Xmas, Mon, D Sun **Prices** Fixed L 2 course £21, Starter £6-£8, Main £16-£22, Dessert £5-£7.50 **Wines** 5 bottles over £30, 22 bottles under £30, 6 by glass **Parking** 20 **Notes** Sunday L £17-£24, Vegetarian available, Children welcome

NORTON Map 10 SJ70

The Hundred House

 British, French

tel: 01952 580240 **Bridgnorth Rd TF11 9EE**
email: reservations@hundredhouse.co.uk **web:** www.hundredhouse.co.uk
dir: *Midway between Telford & Bridgnorth on A442. In village of Norton*

Quirky charm meets skilled modern cuisine

Run by the Phillips family since the mid-1980s, The Hundred House is brimful of character and personality. The rather handsome Georgian coaching inn has stylish bedrooms that fall into the boutique end of the spectrum by contemporary classifications, a bar serving some pretty nifty pub grub, and a brasserie and restaurant producing classy dishes based on tip-top regional ingredients. Expect the likes of sweet-spiced scallops with minted houmous and thyme roasted courgettes, followed by rack of lamb alongside a mini moussaka and harissa sauce, or go for local sirloin steak with chips. Damson bavarois makes a fine finale.

Chef Stuart Phillips **Seats** 80, Pr/dining room 34 **Times** 12-2.30/6-9.30, Closed D 25-26 Dec **Prices** Starter £5.95-£12.95, Main £17.95-£24.95, Dessert £6.95-£7.95 **Wines** 9 bottles over £30, 36 bottles under £30, 12 by glass **Parking** 60 **Notes** Gourmet evenings, Sunday L £12-£21.95, Vegetarian available, Children welcome

OSWESTRY Map 15 SJ22

Pen-y-Dyffryn Country Hotel

Modern British

tel: 01691 653700 **Rhydycroesau SY10 7JD**
email: stay@peny.co.uk **web:** www.peny.co.uk
dir: *3m W of Oswestry on B4580*

Locally based cooking on the frontiers of England and Wales

A construction company built the rectory, church and village school here in 1840. Nowadays, the church is on the Welsh side of the border and the rectory, now a country hotel, is in England. With sweeping views over the valley, it's a relaxing place, traditionally furnished in country-house style, with striking abstract paintings of the local landscape. The modern Anglo-Welsh cooking uses organic materials in dishes such as guinea fowl, apricot and pistachio terrine with sticky date chutney and toasted brioche, followed by Welsh lamb rump with ratatouille, Parmentier potatoes and rich lamby jus. The finale might be good old treacle tart with custard and poached pear.

Chef Richard Jones **Seats** 25 **Times** 6.45-11, Closed 20 Dec-21 Jan, L all week **Prices** Fixed D 3 course £33-£41 **Wines** 40 bottles over £30, 40 bottles under £30, 6 by glass **Parking** 18 **Notes** Vegetarian available, Children 3 yrs+

Sebastians

International, French

tel: 01691 655444 **45 Willow St SY11 1AQ**
email: sebastians.rest@virgin.net **web:** www.sebastians-hotel.co.uk
dir: *From town centre turn into Willow St signed Selattyn. Hotel on left in 400yds*

Skilled French cooking in boutique venue

In a 16th-century inn, full of cossetting beamed character, but not stuck in the past, monthly-changing set-price dinner menus take you through three courses of well-crafted, Gallic-influenced ideas, with an appetiser to set the ball rolling, and a sorbet before mains, or for tighter budgets there's a great value mid-week market menu. Start with well-made game terrine served with brioche and Cumberland sauce, followed by roasted leg and loin of lamb matched with wild mushroom pearl barley risotto and roast garlic purée, or a rich bouillabaisse of fish, shellfish and potatoes poached in saffron and fennel. Desserts might revert to British comfort mode with steamed marmalade pudding with Drambuie custard.

Chef Mark Fisher **Seats** 45 **Times** 6.30-9.30, Closed 25-26 Dec, 1 Jan, Etr Mon, Sun-Mon, L all week **Prices** Prices not confirmed **Wines** 18 bottles over £30, 31 bottles under £30, 8 by glass **Parking** 6, On street **Notes** 5 course D £44.50, Vegetarian available, Children 12 yrs+

Wynnstay Hotel

British

tel: 01691 655261 **Church St SY11 2SZ**
email: info@wynnstayhotel.com **web:** www.wynnstayhotel.com
dir: *In town centre, opposite church*

Modern classics in a Georgian setting complete with bowling-green

The Wynnstay's Four Seasons restaurant has upped its game since a new head chef took the helm in 2015, producing modern British cooking based on reinvented versions of dishes taken from the Wynnstay's 1960s' menus. Ham hock terrine with a soft poached egg, asparagus and pea shoots is helped along by a piquant wholegrain mustard dressing, or you might start with a classic French onion soup with a gruyère croûte. Main-course sea bass is matched with sautéed potatoes, peas and chorizo, or if you're in the mood for meat, there could be the retro delights of pan-seared Gressingham duck breast à l'orange. Dessert brings a textbook crème brûlée with shortbread.

SHIFNAL Map 10 SJ70

Park House Hotel

 Modern European

tel: 01952 460128 **Park St TF11 9BA**
email: reception02@parkhousehotel.net **web:** www.parkhousehotel.net
dir: *From M54 junct 4 take A464 through Shifnal; hotel 200yds after railway bridge*

Modern cooking in singular market town hotel

Two 17th-century country houses – one red brick, one white stucco – have been pasted together to make Park House, an upmarket venue in a pleasant Shropshire market town. The kitchen focuses on quality local produce in a repertoire of comfort classics – sirloin steak with blue cheese or peppercorn sauces, fish pie, or beer-battered haddock and proper chips – and straightforward modern European ideas. Spiced lamb terrine with flatbread and pear chutney leads the way, followed by a piggy plate of pork loin and a pulled pork bonbon with fondant potato and smoky red wine jus. At the end, coconut pannacotta is offset with astringent poached blackberries and crunchy honeycomb.

SHREWSBURY Map 15 SJ41

Albright Hussey Manor Hotel & Restaurant

Modern British

tel: 01939 290571 **Ellesmere Rd, Broad Oak SY4 3AF**
email: info@albrighthussey.co.uk **web:** www.albrighthussey.co.uk
dir: *2.5m N of Shrewsbury on A528, follow signs for Ellesmere*

Confident modern cooking in a fascinating Tudor house

This Tudor hotel with strangely unmatched wings (built only 35 years apart) is stocked with fascinating antiques, both martial and domestic. Confident contemporary food is served up in a beamed room with mullioned windows and a pleasing coral-pink colour scheme. Start with gently spiced ham hock terrine dressed with raisin relish and baby gem and apple salad, or home-cured salmon with beetroot. Mains include crisply seared sea bass with scallops and vegetable 'spaghetti' in a rich beurre blanc containing sorrel, or medallion of local beef with oxtail ravioli, fondant potatoes and spinach. Finish with Amaretto soufflé laced with honey, accompanied by matching ice cream, or else a fine local cheese.

Drapers Hall

 Modern, Traditional

tel: 01743 344679 **10 Saint Mary's Place SY1 1DZ**
email: goodfood@drapershallrestaurant.co.uk **web:** www.drapershallrestaurant.co.uk
dir: *From A5191 (St Mary's St) on one-way system into St Mary's Place*

Updated classic cooking in a medieval dining room

Dating back to 1485, Draper's Hall may be one of the oldest buildings in Shrewsbury but it's all overlaid with a funky modern edge, with beige tartan wool chairs at white-clothed tables and music playing softly in the background. When it comes to the menu, tried-and-tested combinations benefit from some gently updated touches. Crispy-skinned sea bass is served with saffron potatoes, green beans, and spinach wilted in wine adding a sharp edge to cut through a rich bisque-like bouillabaisse sauce. Bookending this, there's chicken liver parfait with caramelised orange, onion marmalade and sourdough toast to start, and to wrap things up, a well-crafted dessert of lemon tart with basil ice cream.

SHREWSBURY *continued*

Henry Tudor House Restaurant and Bar

Modern British

tel: 01743 361666 **Henry Tudor House, Barracks Passage SY1 1XA**
email: hello@henrytudorhouse.com
dir: *Phone for directions*

Modern British food in medieval building

Among the town's oldest half-timbered buildings, HTH's whimsical interior boasts a Parisian-style zinc bar-top bathed in ever-changing coloured light while elegant chandeliers in the blue-tiled conservatory shine out through delicate iron birdcages. Whether you want a hearty stew, a delicate soufflé or something between the two, there will be something to suit from the all-day menu's range of classics, or from the more elaborate evening selection. Begin maybe with cured mackerel, rhubarb, radish and ginger ponzu dressing, move on to a tasty rabbit pie with lardo, peas and carrots, or baked red mullet with Mediterranean vegetables, then what better than peaches and cream with vanilla pannacotta, charred peaches and champagne?

Chef Chris Conde **Seats** 32, Pr/dining room 18 **Times** 12-9.30, All-day dining, Closed 25-26 Dec, 1 Jan **Prices** Fixed L 2 course fr £16, Fixed D 3 course fr £25, Tasting menu £35-£65 **Wines** 14 bottles over £30, 20 bottles under £30, 12 by glass **Parking** On street, NCP **Notes** Tasting menu 5/7/9 course, Sunday L, Vegetarian available, Children welcome

Lion & Pheasant Hotel

British

tel: 01743 770345 **49-50 Wyle Cop SY1 1XJ**
email: info@lionandpheasant.co.uk **web:** www.lionandpheasant.co.uk
dir: *From S & E: pass abbey, cross river on English Bridge to Wyle Cop, hotel on left. From N & W: follow Town Centre signs on one-way system to Wyle Cop. Hotel at bottom of hill on right*

Classic modern brasserie cooking in a townhouse hotel

This coaching inn has stood since the 16th century just before the street called Wyle Cop becomes a bridge over the River Severn. Its period facade gives way to a contemporary New England-style interior, with neutral tones and tongue-and-groove-panelling combining harmoniously with the old brickwork and beams. There's a rather cool bar with a real fire, and a smart but relaxed restaurant that focuses on modern British meals such as pea and watercress soup with pig's head croquette, followed by pan-fried lemon sole, creamed potatoes, summer greens and clams in white wine sauce. End on apple pannacotta, nougat, apple and Calvados sorbet with raspberry butter.

Porter House SY1

Modern British, International, American V

tel: 01743 358870 **15 St Mary's St SY1 1EQ**
email: info@porterhousesy1.co.uk **web:** www.porterhousesy1.co.uk
dir: *In Shrewsbury town centre, on the one-way system, almost opposite St Mary's Church*

Trendy brasserie food with upscale burgers a speciality

A recent makeover gave this place a 21st-century monochrome look, all white walls and charcoal-grey furniture. Local sourcing is a given, with Shropshire beef a particularly proud boast. It turns up, along with a little Wagyu for luxury, in the form of upscale burgers and 28-day aged steaks cooked on the grill, while the rest of the menu offers trendy preparations such as New Orleans fish pie, pulled pork burrito and fajitas. It creates a mid-Atlantic feel in unassuming Shrewsbury, through to desserts like triple chocolate brownie. Brunchers, start your taste buds with one of the Bloody something hangover cocktails, before moving on to a steak sandwich with slaw.

Chef Daniel Smith, Nigel Titley **Seats** 60, Pr/dining room 45 **Times** 10-10, All-day dining, Closed 25-26 Dec **Prices** Prices not confirmed **Wines** 10 bottles over £30, 31 bottles under £30, 22 by glass **Parking** Town centre **Notes** Brunch, Children welcome

TELFORD — Map 10 SJ60

Chez Maw Restaurant

Modern British V

tel: 01952 432247 **Ironbridge TF8 7DW**
email: info@thevalleyhotel.co.uk **web:** www.chezmawrestaurant.co.uk
dir: *M6/M54 from junct 6 take A5223 to Ironbridge for 4m. At mini island right, hotel 80yds on left*

Modern British cooking in a hotel near the Iron Bridge

On the bank of the Severn in Ironbridge, and barely a rivet's throw from the famous river-spanning construction, the Valley Hotel was once owned by Arthur Maw and his family, suppliers of ceramic tiles, hence the name of its restaurant, which looks rather spiffy after a recent makeover. Its contemporary offerings range widely, so a starter might be venison, pigeon and pheasant terrine with home-made pickle, quail's egg, and caper and raisin purée. Next up, pulled shoulder of Welsh lamb with potato rösti, plus turnip, carrot, leek and pearl barley in lamb broth. Finish with sticky toffee pudding with caramelised banana and caramel sauce.

Chef Barry Workman **Seats** 50, Pr/dining room 30 **Times** 12-2/7-9.30, Closed 26 Dec-2 Jan, L Sat-Sun **Prices** Starter £5.25-£8.50, Main £13.95-£22, Dessert £6.50-£8.50 **Wines** 2 bottles over £30, 37 bottles under £30, 7 by glass **Parking** 100 **Notes** Children welcome

Hadley Park House

Modern British

tel: 01952 677269 **Hadley Park TF1 6QJ**
email: info@hadleypark.co.uk **web:** www.hadleypark.co.uk
dir: *M54 junct 5, A5 (Rampart Way), at rdbt take A442 towards Hortonwood, over double rdbt, next rbdt take 2nd exit, hotel at end of lane*

Locally based cooking at a well-maintained Georgian manor

The origins of Hadley Park remain shrouded in mystery, but it seems likely to have been built in the mid-Georgian era, the 1770s perhaps. An august red-brick manor house in a couple of acres of lovely gardens, it's a popular venue for summertime country weddings. The conservatory extension dining room in the form of Dorrells is dedicated to the elegant pursuit of regionally sourced modern British cooking. Begin with pan-seared scallops with salt-baked cod bonbons, or warm duck confit salad with soft-boiled egg, then move on to whole plaice with caper and parsley butter, or the house burger.

Chef Kevin Fellows **Seats** 80, Pr/dining room 16 **Times** 12-2/6.30-9.30, Closed 26 Dec **Prices** Fixed L 2 course fr £15.95, Starter £5.25-£9.25, Main £10.95-£21.95, Dessert £4.95-£5.50 **Wines** 6 bottles over £30, 26 bottles under £30, 12 by glass **Notes** Early bird menu 15% discount until 7.30pm, Sunday L, Vegetarian available, Children welcome

UPTON MAGNA Map 10 SJ51

The Haughmond

 Modern British V

tel: 01743 709918 **Pelham Rd SY4 4TZ**
email: contact@thehaughmond.co.uk **web:** www.thehaughmond.co.uk
dir: *Phone for directions*

Multi-component dishes in a country inn

A total refurbishment completed at the end of 2015 has brought a bright, contemporary feel to this traditional roadside village inn. Family-run, it retains a pubby atmosphere, while drawing diners from afar. Classics of steak and oxtail pie and burgers can be enjoyed in the bar, while the new Basil's restaurant offers a more fine-dining experience. A simple but delicious haggis Scotch egg with spiced raspberry purée might lead on to beef Wellington with château potatoes, green beans and rich gravy. For dessert, try a comforting egg custard tart with poached rhubarb and clotted cream ice cream.

Chef Martin Board **Seats** 48, Pr/dining room 20 **Times** 12-3/6-9 **Prices** Fixed L 2 course £11-£14, Tasting menu £40-£60, Starter £6-£9, Main £11-£19, Dessert £6-£9 **Parking** 30 **Notes** Sunday L £11-£18, Children welcome

SOMERSET

AXBRIDGE Map 4 ST45

The Oak House

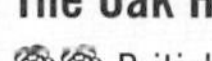 British, International

tel: 01934 732444 **The Square BS26 2AP**
email: info@theoakhousesomerset.com **web:** www.theoakhousesomerset.com
dir: *M5 junct 22 onto A38 north, turn right to Axbridge, signed*

Adventurous combinations in a stylish restaurant with rooms

Parts of the Oak House date from the 11th century. Inside, a stylish mix of old and new places it at the boutique end of the design spectrum. Steaks are cooked on the grill – 10oz rib-eye, say – and arrive with triple-cooked chips, field mushroom and tomato, plus a choice of sauces. Starters include a seafood cocktail (crab, crayfish and prawns) or a tasting of pork which includes a pulled pork bonbon and Bramley apple purée. Spiced monkish is an alternative to the red meat, accompanied by onion bhaji and textures of beetroot and sweet potato. For dessert, 'chocolate orange' combines chocolate soil, honeycomb and orange powder.

Chef James Stephens **Seats** 40 **Times** 12-3/6-9 **Prices** Starter £4.50-£8.95, Main £16.95-£26.95, Dessert £4.75-£8.95 **Wines** 6 bottles over £30, 22 bottles under £30, 15 by glass **Parking** 100mtrs **Notes** Sunday L £17.95-£20.95, Vegetarian available, Children welcome

BATH Map 4 ST76

Allium Restaurant at The Abbey Hotel

 Modern British

tel: 01225 461603 **1 North Pde BA1 1LF**
email: reservations@abbeyhotelbath.co.uk **web:** www.abbeyhotelbath.co.uk
dir: *M4 junct 18/A46 for approx 8m. At rdbt right onto A4 for 2m. Once past Morrisons stay in left lane & turn left at lights. Over bridge & right at lights. Over rdbt & right at lights. Hotel at end of road*

Stunning modern brasserie cooking in a Georgian hotel

The Abbey's facade is the epitome of Bath's elegant Georgian style, but beyond the pedimented portico entrance is a contemporary boutique-style interior. At every turn are lots of eye-catching artworks (including one of Warhol's Marilyns in the Artbar) and aesthetic flourishes, not least in the Allium, with its bare darkwood tables, wooden floor, drapes and a relaxed and unbuttoned atmosphere. This is the showcase for Chris Staines's expressive and often experimental cooking, which borrows from a number of cuisines to create his own unique style. How about pan-fried fillet of salmon with cauliflower quinoa, charred cauliflower, balsamic shallots and a mussel beignet, or pan-fried duck breast with miso-braised turnips, mushroom purée, figs and chicory? Such combinations work because Staines handles his ingredients confidently and intelligently. More familiar may be roast venison with red cabbage, sprouts, mushrooms and a sloe gin consommé, while starters can be of the order of Japanese-style salmon tartare with avocado, grapefruit, pickled Thai shallots and squid ink crisp, and as comforting as ham hock terrine with remoulade and piccalilli. Desserts can range from straightforward affogato to vanilla crème brûlée with cinnamon ice cream and caramel apple compôte and crumble, all elements combining to make an effective whole.

Chef Chris Staines **Seats** 60, Pr/dining room 14 **Times** 12-3/5.30-9 **Prices** Fixed L 2 course £19.50, Fixed D 3 course £25, Starter £7.50-£10, Main £15-£24.50, Dessert £5-£9 **Wines** 32 bottles over £30, 26 bottles under £30, 20 by glass **Parking** Manvers St, Southgate Centre (charge made) **Notes** Fixed D 5.30-7, Afternoon tea, Sunday L £24-£28, Vegetarian available, Children welcome

Bailbrook House Hotel

 Modern British V

tel: 01225 855100 **Eveleigh Av, London Road West BA1 7JD**
email: sales.bailbrook@handpicked.co.uk **web:** www.bailbrookhouse.co.uk
dir: *M4 junct 18/A46, at bottom of long hill take slip road to city centre. At rdbt take 1st exit, London Rd. Hotel 200mtrs on left*

Satisfying cooking in a boutique country house

Set in 20 acres of parkland, Bailbrook is a handsome Georgian country mansion done out in classy contemporary boutique style. Its Cloisters Restaurant is the fine-dining option, an intimate split-level space where you might start with wood pigeon breast with pickled shiitake mushrooms and smoked bacon lardons, set off with a walnut vinaigrette. Main-course cannon of lamb gets a pine nut and herb crust, and is partnered with a potato pressing, caramelised shallots, carrots and a glossy rosemary jus. Flavours counterpoint well in fish dishes such as halibut fillet with pea and bacon fricassée, Jersey Royals and girolles, and dessert might be a rich chocolate fondant with pistachio ice cream.

Chef Jonathan Machin **Seats** 64, Pr/dining room 14 **Times** 12.30-2/7-9.30, Closed L Mon-Sat **Prices** Fixed D 3 course £39, Starter £9-£14, Main £19-£35, Dessert £9-£14 **Wines** 78 bottles over £30, 17 bottles under £30, 16 by glass **Parking** 100 **Notes** Afternoon tea £21.95, Sunday L £19-£27.95, Children welcome

BATH *continued*

The Bath Priory Hotel, Restaurant & Spa

Modern European, British V NOTABLE WINE LIST

tel: 01225 331922 **Weston Rd BA1 2XT**
email: info@thebathpriory.co.uk **web:** www.thebathpriory.co.uk
dir: *Adjacent to Victoria Park*

Impeccable modern cooking in a gorgeously decorated house

Standing in four pretty acres of grounds within a short stroll of the city centre shops and historic sites, the gloriously Gothic Bath Priory provides a luxurious country-house experience, including a swanky spa and top-notch eaterie. The restaurant has a suitably refined demeanour and views out over the manicured garden. Head chef Sam Moody's gently contemporary cooking sits well in this setting, with the kitchen garden providing its seasonal bounty. Crispy Cornish monkfish is a feel-good opener, served with spiced tomato compôte and curry mayonnaise, or go for an intriguing Wiltshire partridge escabèche with truffle, ham hock and pea purée. Among main courses, truffle butter enriches poached turbot, while a plate of local pork includes its shoulder, cheek and belly matched with burnt apple and paprika jus. There's no less craft and skill on show at dessert stage, where a hot Bramley apple soufflé is partnered with salted toffee ice cream. A tasting menu showcases the kitchen's talents, a set lunch option is a good introduction, and afternoon tea is a genuine treat. The impressive wine list has a good showing by the glass.

Chef Sam Moody **Seats** 50, Pr/dining room 72 **Times** 12-2.30/6.30-9.30 **Prices** Fixed L 2 course £24.50, Fixed D 3 course £80, Tasting menu £95 **Wines** 453 bottles over £30, 20 bottles under £30, 11 by glass **Parking** 40 **Notes** Tasting menu D 7 course, Menu surprise 11 course, Sunday L, Children 12 yrs+

The Chequers

Modern British

tel: 01225 360017 **50 Rivers St BA1 2QA**
email: info@thechequersbath.com **web:** www.thechequersbath.com
dir: *City centre near The Royal Crescent and The Circus*

Thrilling cooking in a Georgian gastropub

The Chequers has been providing drink and victuals since 1776. Food is the core of the operation, with all ingredients sourced locally and everything made from scratch. Start with that old stager, salt-and-pepper squid with garlic aïoli, if you like, but why not step outside the box with something like seared scallops with smoked pork belly, cauliflower, candied lime and cumin velouté? For main course try super-fresh lemon sole partnered with a crab bonbon and bisque, fennel, samphire, saffron potatoes and marinated tomato, or perhaps venison haunch with smoked garlic dauphinoise, red cabbage and blackberries. End on a high with burnt custard flavoured with mango, passionfruit and coconut.

Chef Tony Casey **Seats** 60, Pr/dining room 20 **Times** 12-2.30/6-9.30, Closed 25 Dec, L Mon-Fri **Prices** Starter £6.95-£11.50, Main £14.95-£24.95, Dessert £7.50-£8.95 **Wines** 23 bottles over £30, 41 bottles under £30, 26 by glass **Parking** On street **Notes** Sunday L £13.95-£16.50, Vegetarian available, Children welcome

The Circus Café and Restaurant

Modern European

tel: 01225 466020 **34 Brock St BA1 2LN**
email: ali@allgolden.co.uk
dir: *From West side of The Circus turn into Brock St, 2nd building on right heading towards the Royal Crescent*

Impressive upmarket cooking near the Royal Crescent

In a prime location between The Circus and Royal Crescent stands this upmarket all-day eatery where the monthly-changing menu is based on fine West Country produce. Start with a Med-inspired octopus dish with roasted peppers, and a caraway and coriander sauce, or a zesty undyed smoked haddock carpaccio. Among main courses, loin of venison is cooked as requested and arrives with parsnip purée and a red wine sauce enriched with Venezuelan chocolate, and calves' liver is served pink with a piquant sherry and grain mustard gravy. There's always a fish option, and among puddings might be warm rice pudding with honey-coated figs and cardamom, or a sorbet flavoured with Campari.

Chef Alison Golden, Máté Andrasko **Seats** 50, Pr/dining room 32 **Times** 10am-mdnt, All-day dining, Closed 3 wks from 24 Dec, Sun **Prices** Starter £6.30-£7.10, Main £17.10-£20, Dessert £4.70-£6.70 **Wines** 11 bottles over £30, 20 bottles under £30, 7 by glass **Parking** On street, NCP Charlotte St **Notes** ALC D, Vegetarian available, Children 10 yrs+

The Dower House Restaurant

Modern British V

tel: 01225 823333 **The Royal Crescent Hotel & Spa, 16 Royal Crescent BA1 2LS**
email: info@royalcrescent.co.uk **web:** www.royalcrescent.co.uk
dir: *From A4, right at lights. 2nd left onto Bennett St. Continue into The Circus, 2nd exit onto Brock St*

An elegant dining solution in an elegant city

The Dower House stands in secluded gardens behind the luxury Royal Crescent Hotel, right in the middle of John Wood the Younger's famous Georgian architectural masterpiece. Refinement, elegance and comfort are guaranteed, with carpeted floors, petrol-blue and gold soft furnishings and rich silk drapes, flowers on well-spaced tables laid with crisp white linen and tea lights, and French windows opening on to the gardens. Friendly uniformed staff know their way round both the modern British-with-French-roots menus and the excellent wine list, although a sommelier is also on hand. The unpretentious but top-quality fare from head chef David Campbell is exemplified by a vibrant starter of tea-cured organic salmon, avocado wasabi, Japanese radish in shiso and oyster yogurt soup. Among the handful of main courses, expect a perfectly cooked and subtly spiced brill with Moroccan quinoa, cauliflower, orange and coriander; roast squash pigeon with parsnip, apple boudin noir and lentils; and loin and neck of salt marsh lamb with carrot, ginger, cumin and lemon. Perhaps rhubarb with a thick and creamy custard featuring gingerbread cubes for that extra flavour might suit for dessert? Fine extras include an amuse of ginger pannacotta-style mousse to cleanse the palate and a delicious brown treacle bread.

Chef David Campbell **Seats** 60, Pr/dining room 20 **Times** 7-9, Closed L all week **Prices** Tasting menu £72, Starter £12.95-£16.50, Main £27.50-£29.95, Dessert £12.50-£13.50 **Wines** 200 bottles over £30, 18 bottles under £30, 10 by glass **Parking** 17, Charlotte St (charge for on site parking) **Notes** Afternoon tea, Children welcome

The Hare & Hounds

Modern British

tel: 01225 482682 **Lansdown Rd BA1 5TJ**
email: info@hareandhoundsbath.com **web:** www.hareandhoundsbath.com
dir: *M4 to A46 Bath for 4m, right A420 Bristol. After 0.8m take left to Bath Racecourse for 1.5m, then left towards Bath. Hare & Hounds on left in 2.5m*

Impressive committed cooking with glorious views

A mile and a half north of Bath, The Hare & Hounds is an enticing bolt hole with glorious views from its hilltop location. Huge leaded windows look over the terrace and allow light into the neat interior where wood proliferates: tables, chairs, panelling and floor. It's relaxed and informal, but the kitchen has a serious commitment to food and draws on top-grade produce. Starters might include pan-fried scallops with black pudding, cauliflower purée and hazelnut butter, while main course could bring venison shepherd's pie with spiced red cabbage and parsnip crisps. Desserts are another strong suit: try rice pudding with mulled pears and winter fruits.

Chef Ashley Woodland **Seats** 70, Pr/dining room 14 **Times** 12-3/5.30-9 **Prices** Starter £5-£9.50, Main £11-£22, Dessert £3-£6.50 **Wines** 15 bottles over £30, 42 bottles under £30, 28 by glass **Parking** 30 **Notes** Sunday L £13-£16, Vegetarian available, Children welcome

BATH *continued*

Jamie's Italian

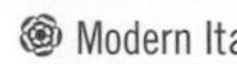 Modern Italian

tel: 01225 432340 **10 Milsom Place BA1 1BZ**
email: bath.office@jamiesitalian.com
dir: *From A4 follow signs to city centre. Opposite Jolly's department store*

Jamie's winning way with real Italian food

The formula is simple: find a nice building, fit it out with a trendy rustic look and run it with a wholesome lack of formality. The format clearly works, judging by the queues that build at busy times (bookings are taken for large groups only). Fresh, rustic Italian dishes are what the kitchen deals in, built on well-sourced raw materials. Sharing planks of excellent cured meats, Italian cheeses, pickles and vegetables make a popular opener. Then it's on to pasta, which is made fresh each day – porcini fettuccini, say, or a main course of chicken milanese. End on Arctic Swiss roll with a chocolate mascarpone centre and butterscotch sauce.

Macdonald Bath Spa

 Modern British V

tel: 01225 444424 **Sydney Rd BA2 6JF**
email: sales.bathspa@macdonald-hotels.co.uk
web: www.macdonald-hotels.co.uk/bathspa
dir: *From A4 follow city centre signs for 1m. At lights left signed A36. Turn right after pedestrian crossing, left into Sydney Place. Hotel 200yds on right*

Well-judged menu in grand Georgian hotel

The city of Bath has been about spa treatments and self-indulgence since Roman times, and the Bath Spa hotel keeps the pampering tradition alive. Its majestic Georgian facade sets a grand tone, running through to the classy Vellore Restaurant in the original ballroom, where pillars and a high-domed ceiling add to a stately air, and engaging staff and a helpful sommelier keep things on track. The kitchen delivers unfussy dishes along the lines of ham hock and chicken terrine with soused vegetables, ahead of slow-cooked Highland lamb shank with colcannon potatoes and red wine jus. To finish, rum baba might come with plum trifle.

Chef Andrew Britton **Seats** 80, Pr/dining room 120 **Times** 7-10, Closed L all week **Prices** Fixed D 3 course fr £45 **Wines** 140 bottles over £30, 20 bottles under £30, 12 by glass **Parking** 160 **Notes** Children welcome

Marlborough Tavern

 Modern British

tel: 01225 423731 **35 Marlborough Buildings BA1 2LY**
email: info@marlborough-tavern.com **web:** www.marlborough-tavern.com
dir: *200mtrs from W end of Royal Crescent, on corner of Marlborough Buildings*

Seasonal cooking and proper beer

This straight-talking foodie pub has a pleasingly unstuffy vibe and local ales and ciders on tap. Fare could be as simple as home-made burgers or fish and chips, or at the more gastro end, a five-course tasting menu with matching wines. The latter sets out with beetroot matched with goats' cheese pannacotta, poached fig and toasted walnut, progressing via scallops with confit pork belly, celeriac purée and hazelnut butter. Next comes a main course of tarragon and mustard-crusted Red Ruby beef fillet with creamy smoked garlic mash, wild mushrooms, crispy shallot rings and port and thyme jus. Finish with toffee apple cake with salted caramel and cider brandy ice cream.

Chef Daniel Edwards **Seats** 60 **Times** 12-2.30/6-10 **Prices** Fixed L 2 course £13, Starter £6.25-£8, Main £13-£24.50, Dessert £6.50-£8.50 **Wines** 23 bottles over £30, 42 bottles under £30, 26 by glass **Parking** On street opposite **Notes** Sunday L £13-£15.50, Vegetarian available, Children welcome

Menu Gordon Jones

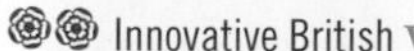

Innovative British V

tel: 01225 480871 **2 Wellsway BA2 3AQ**
email: info@menugordonjones.co.uk **web:** www.menugordonjones.co.uk
dir: *5 mins from city centre up Wells Rd (A367), restaurant in corner of road opposite local shops*

Avante-garde cooking from a rising star

Gordon Jones has form in Bath, having run the kitchen in the Royal Crescent Hotel. Now he's doing his own thing in an unassuming little spot with foodies beating down the door. A starter of 'mushroom cappuccino' (cep mousse, smoked milk foam and parmesan madeleine) might be followed by a carnival of flavours and textures, perhaps cured sea trout with popcorn, marmalade purée, cucumber, cauliflower couscous, oca de Peru tubers, capers and mayonnaise. Then squab pigeon may arrive with wheat berries, spinach, mushroom, onion, crispy 'brick' bread and chervil root. Desserts follow the multi-layered approach, perhaps teaming toffee apple mousse with a cinnamon doughnut, white chocolate shards and blackcurrant sorbet.

Chef Gordon Jones **Seats** 22 **Times** 12.30-2/7-9, Closed 35 days a year (variable), Sun-Mon **Prices** Prices not confirmed **Wines** 22 bottles over £30, 10 bottles under £30, 6 by glass **Parking** On street **Notes** Tasting menu L 5 course £45, D 6 course £55, Children 12 yrs+

The Olive Tree at the Queensberry Hotel

Modern British V NOTABLE WINE LIST

tel: 01225 447928 **Russell St BA1 2QF**
email: reservations@thequeensberry.co.uk **web:** www.olivetreebath.co.uk
dir: *100mtrs from the Assembly Rooms*

Accomplished cooking in chic boutique Georgian townhouse hotel

It may have been original owner the 8th Marquess of Queensbury who had this splendid row of townhouses built in 1771, but Laurence and Helen Beere have worked tirelessly to develop it into a top-ranking boutique hotel. Built from Bath stone, this remains one of the most impressive addresses in the spa city. The owners' passion for hospitality have created a winning blend of traditional meets contemporary, resulting in civilised spaces that seem almost timeless. A major revamp in 2015 saw a refurbishment of the kitchen and dining room in The Olive Tree restaurant downstairs. The dynamic cooking and sharp technical skills of head chef Chris Cleghorn is showcased via a choice of seasonal tasting menus, including an impressive one for vegetarians. Whichever route you take, the classically inspired modern British dishes show an impressive commitment to local produce. Flavour combinations are well considered and intelligently executed – pan-fried scallops, for example, with shellfish bisque, pak choi and grapefruit, followed by a main course of slow-cooked brill with creamed and charred leek, shimeji mushrooms, black truffle and Noilly Prat sauce. Blackberry parfait with 72% Valrhona chocolate, stem ginger and blackberry sorbet brings things to a close.

Chef Chris Cleghorn **Seats** 60, Pr/dining room 30 **Times** 12-2/7-10, Closed L Mon-Thu **Prices** Fixed D 3 course fr £30, Tasting menu £60-£75, Starter £9.50-£14, Main £19-£26.95, Dessert £8 **Wines** 320 bottles over £30, 17 bottles under £30, 18 by glass **Parking** On street (meter) **Notes** Sunday L £24-£30, Children welcome

BATH *continued*

Woods Restaurant

Modern British, French

tel: 01225 314812 & 422493 **9-13 Alfred St BA1 2QX**
email: woodsinbath@gmail.com
dir: *Phone for directions*

Contemporary bistro cooking in a Georgian setting

Woods stands in a very 'Bath' setting, occupying the ground floor of five Georgian townhouses, and its comfortable bistro look is pretty much timeless. The cooking is broadly European, with French and Italy to the fore, and a British flavour here and there. A first course dish of grilled White Lake goats' curd with red pepper confit, crushed hazelnuts and vanilla honey is a vibrant construction. Confit of chicken leg with peas, Dijon mustard and herby cream sauce is a bistro classic, or there might be Brixham crab linguine with a red Thai curry sauce and baby coriander. Finish with New York-style cheesecake with raspberry sauce.

CASTLE CARY **Map 4 ST63**

The Pilgrims

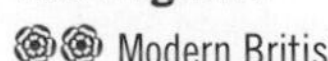

tel: 01963 240597 **Lovington BA7 7PT**
email: jools@thepilgrimsatlovington.co.uk **web:** www.thepilgrimsatlovington.co.uk
dir: *On B3153, 1.5m E of lights on A37 at Lydford*

Impeccable West Country produce in a stone-built village inn

The name honours those who passed this way on their quest to find King Arthur's tomb. The stone-built inn is now a restaurant with rooms, run with cheerful bonhomie by the Mitchisons – Sally presiding over front of house and Jools running the kitchen with the sound ethos that the most important quality in a chef is restraint. The place showcases local suppliers, thus Lyme Bay scallops might be supported by local black pudding and sweet potato purée, while roast pheasant breast wrapped in thigh meat with pork, pistachios and bacon is matched with braised Savoy cabbage. Dessert is a simple but effective cider-cooked Somerset apple crumble.

Chef Julian Mitchison **Seats** 25 **Times** 12-3/7-11, Closed Sun-Mon (ex BHs & L last Sun of month), L Tue-Thu **Prices** Starter £6-£9, Main £18-£25, Dessert £6-£9 **Wines** 7 bottles over £30, 21 bottles under £30, 15 by glass **Parking** 40 **Notes** Sunday L £15-£18, Children welcome

CHEW MAGNA **Map 4 ST56**

The Pony & Trap

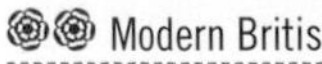

tel: 01275 332627 **Knowle Hill BS40 8TQ**
email: info@theponyandtrap.co.uk
dir: *Take A37 S from Bristol. After Pensford turn right at rdbt onto A368 towards Weston-Super-Mare. In 1.5m right signed Chew Magna & Winford. Pub 1m on right*

Stonking modern pub food in a country cottage inn

Chef Josh Eggleton is becoming quite a household name these days after his storming 2014 telly performance on the Great British Menu. Away from the limelight, he is to be found at the stoves in The Pony & Trap, a revitalised 200-year-old country cottage pub in lush Chew Valley countryside. A summer's lunch kicks off with chilled courgette soup poured around crab mayonnaise and pointed up with wild chive oil and wood sorrel. Next, a piggy plateful of rare breed pork chop, pulled pork shoulder, home-made 'hodge podge' black pudding, crackling and cauliflower purée hits the spot. For pudding, there's a refreshing key lime pie with lemongrass sorbet.

CORTON DENHAM **Map 4 ST62**

The Queens Arms

Modern British

tel: 01963 220317 **DT9 4LR**
email: relax@thequeensarms.com **web:** www.thequeensarms.com
dir: *A303 exit Chapel Cross signed South Cadbury & Corton Denham. Follow signs to South Cadbury. Through village, after 0.25m turn left up hill signed Sherborne & Corton Denham. Left at top of hill, pub at end of village on right*

Enterprising West Country cooking in a charming country pub

This mellow, stone 18th-century inn is set amid buxom hills on the Somerset-Dorset border where a glance at the menu shows a clear love for local produce and a creative mind. A typical starter might be pan-roasted scallops with tempura soft-shelled crab, salsa rossa and Serrano ham. Main course loin and braised haunch of locally shot venison goes down a treat with shallot and garlic purée, salsify, pommes Anna, chargrilled broccoli and a rich, sweet date jus. Or there could be pan-fried John Dory with chicken and smoked bacon mousse, oyster and Pernod velouté, brown shrimps and spinach gnocchi. For dessert, lemon meringue tart is allied with cherry sorbet.

Chef Ben Abercombie **Seats** 78, Pr/dining room 45 **Times** 12-3/6-10 **Prices** Starter £7.25-£9.50, Main £13.95-£22.95, Dessert £6.25-£9.95 **Wines** 19 bottles over £30, 25 bottles under £30, 21 by glass **Parking** 20 **Notes** Meal deal film offer £12.50, Sunday L £11.95-£16.95, Vegetarian available, Children welcome

DULVERTON **Map 3 SS92**

Tarr Farm Inn

Modern British

tel: 01643 851507 **Tarr Steps, Liscombe TA22 9PY**
email: enquiries@tarrfarm.co.uk **web:** www.tarrfarm.co.uk
dir: *6m NW of Dulverton. Off B3223 signed Tarr Steps, signs to Tarr Farm Inn*

Gently tweaked country cooking on the River Barle

In the heart of Exmoor, Tarr Farm is a Tudor inn immediately above the Tarr Steps bridge. There's a palpable sense that each dish knows what it's about, as when glazed spatchcocked quail comes with potato salad for a full-flavoured opener, or when a bounty of shellfish – clams and prawns as well as mussels – go into classic marinière. Fish shows up well at main too, for grilled John Dory and crayfish bonne femme with orange-soaked raisins, while rump of moorland lamb arrives with dauphinoise, shallots and confit garlic in Madeira jus. A perfectly creamy pannacotta offset with the sharpness of stewed blueberries makes a great finish.

Chef Steve Cox **Seats** 50, Pr/dining room 20 **Times** 12-3/6.30-9.30, Closed 1-10 Feb **Prices** Starter £4.95-£7.95, Main £11.95-£24.95, Dessert £6.50-£8.50 **Wines** 58 bottles over £30, 42 bottles under £30, 12 by glass **Parking** 40 **Notes** Sunday L, Vegetarian available, Children 10 yrs+

Woods Bar & Dining Room

Modern British, French

tel: 01398 324007 **4 Banks Square TA22 9BU**
email: woodsdulverton@hotmail.com
dir: *From Tiverton take A396 N. At Machine Cross take B3222 to Dulverton. Establishment adjacent to church*

Locally sourced cooking in a rural Somerset inn

On the edge of Exmoor, Woods is a pub cunningly disguised on the outside to look like a café. The interior scene is cheered with a log fire in winter, and wooden partitions roughly divide the place between the drinking of local ales and the eating of locally-sourced food. The kitchen offers intricately worked modern British cooking. Start with a tart of seasonal woodcock, garnished with prosciutto and puréed dates in Madeira sauce, ahead of roast ling fillet with mussels, clams, almonds, bacon and broccoli. At meal's end, there's a choice from home-made ice cream and sorbet flavours such as liquorice, white peach, and apple and star anise.

EXFORD Map 3 SS83

Crown Hotel

Modern British

tel: 01643 831554 **Park St TA24 7PP**
email: info@crownhotelexmoor.co.uk **web:** www.crownhotelexmoor.co.uk
dir: *From Taunton take A38 to A358. Turn left at B3224 & follow signs to Exford*

Good full-flavoured cooking in a handsome coaching inn

The 17th-century Crown sits at the heart of pretty Exford Village, in three acres of grounds surrounded by countryside and moorland – huntin', shootin' and fishin' territory. Naturally, then, this is a dog- and horse-friendly establishment, where the bar (complete with stag's head) is an appealingly rustic spot for pub classics. The elegant dining room cranks things up a notch or two. First out is twice-baked cheese soufflé with red onion jam and a splash of balsamic, followed by a steak cooked on the grill or whole grilled plaice. Creamy rice pudding with salted caramel brings it all to a satisfying close.

Chef Raza Muhammad **Seats** 45, Pr/dining room 20 **Times** 6.45-9.15, Closed L all week **Prices** Starter £4.95-£10.95, Main £10.95-£23.95, Dessert £6.50-£10.50 **Wines** 20 bottles over £30, 12 bottles under £30, 19 by glass **Parking** 30 **Notes** Vegetarian available, Children welcome

FIVEHEAD Map 4 ST32

Langford Fivehead

Modern British NEW V

tel: 01460 282020 **Lower Swell TA3 6PH**
email: rebecca@thelangford.co.uk **web:** www.langfordfivehead.co.uk
dir: *Phone for directions*

Elegant farm-to-plate cooking

The Tudor manor house at Lower Swell stands in seven acres of mature grounds, full of cedars, box and yew. A contemporary dining room with modern artworks has a relaxed feel, and elegantly simple farm-to-plate eating is the order of the day. Concise menus offer three choices at each stage. Spring might offer smooth scallop mousse and white crabmeat layered between pasta sheets in chive beurre blanc, then superbly flavourful loin and shoulder of new season's lamb with spring onions, swede, baby carrots and pomme dauphine in a richly sticky jus. A towering crumble-topped rhubarb soufflé with ginger ice cream is the headline closing act.

Chef Olly Jackson **Seats** 22, Pr/dining room 12 **Times** 12.15-2.15/7-9.30, Closed 2 Jan for 2 wks, 24 Jul for 2 wks, Sun-Mon, L Tue, Sat **Prices** Fixed L 2 course fr £27.50, Fixed D 3 course fr £37.50 **Wines** 36 bottles over £30, 16 bottles under £30, 16 by glass **Parking** 8 **Notes** Children 8 yrs+

HINTON CHARTERHOUSE Map 4 ST75

Homewood Park Hotel & Spa

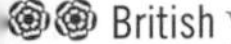

British V

tel: 01225 723731 **Abbey Ln BA2 7TB**
email: info@homewoodpark.co.uk **web:** www.homewoodpark.co.uk
dir: *6m SE of Bath on A36, turn left at 2nd sign for Freshford*

Impressive culinary artistry in ten acres of parkland

Homewood came to prominence during the first wave of the country-hotel movement in the 1980s. The chef takes the modern British bull by the horns for dishes such as glazed pig's cheek with cheddar pommes purée and chard, a finely judged dish that is halfway to a main. When the main course itself arrives, it could be crisp-skinned sea bream, briefly seared and served with baby squid and samphire in lemongrass foam, or maybe rack and braised shank of lamb with minted pea purée and shallots. Abandon all obligation to choose at dessert stage with an assiette comprising blackberry parfait, white chocolate mousse, almond marshmallow and various froths and berries.

Chef Simon Addison **Seats** 70, Pr/dining room 40 **Times** 12-2.30/6.30-9.30 **Prices** Fixed L 2 course £19.50, Tasting menu £65, Starter £7.50-£10, Main £21-£27, Dessert £8.50-£9.50 **Wines** 50 bottles over £30, 10 bottles under £30, 10 by glass **Parking** 40 **Notes** Afternoon tea, Sunday L £22-£26.50, Children welcome

HOLCOMBE Map 4 ST64

The Holcombe Inn

British, International, French V

tel: 01761 232478 **Stratton Rd BA3 5EB**
email: bookings@holcombeinn.co.uk **web:** www.holcombeinn.co.uk
dir: *From Bath or Shepton Mallet take A367 (Fosse Way) to Stratton. Follow inn signs*

Welcoming country inn with classic and modern menu

The Holcombe is a textbook country inn with winter fires, local ales and amicable staff. Regional ingredients, including the produce of its own garden, supply the menus of mostly traditional fare. Scallops with cauliflower and spiced aubergine, or salt-and-pepper squid with salad and aïoli, are well-turned-out starters, while the main business might extend to noisette and braised neck of lamb with vegetable tagine and quinoa. Stick with fish for main, and you could be in for herb-crusted cod alongside dauphinoise and sprouting broccoli in a dressing of tomato and basil. Desserts get creative with a raspberry and nougat parfait choc ice to accompany Valrhona brownie and candied hazelnuts.

Chef Dan Kings **Seats** 65 **Times** 12-2.30/6.30-9, Closed D 25-26 Dec **Prices** Fixed L 2 course £19.95-£25, Fixed D 3 course £26-£30, Starter £6.25-£10.95, Main £12.95-£19.95, Dessert £5.95 **Wines** 9 bottles over £30, 30 bottles under £30, 16 by glass **Parking** 30 **Notes** Breakfast on booking, All day dining Fri-Sun, Sunday L £12.95-£19.95, Children welcome

HUNSTRETE Map 4 ST66

THE PIG near Bath

Modern British NOTABLE WINE LIST

tel: 01761 490490 **Hunstrete House, Pensford BS39 4NS**
email: info@thepignearbath.com **web:** www.thepighotel.com
dir: *On A368, 8m from Bath*

Hyper-local food in a switched-on country house

At first sight, The Pig is the archetypal English country-house hotel. Inside, however, the style is shabby-chic instead of chintz, the mood is chilled and hip and the whole operation has food at its heart, much of it brought in from The Pig's gardens or foraged from fields and woods. There's nothing fancy going on here, just great combinations, as in a starter of monkfish cheek and scallops with spinach and peas, or a classic main-course trio of chargrilled 35-day aged rib-eye with well-made béarnaise and triple-cooked chips. Desserts continue to toe the local, seasonal line, offering forced rhubarb – poached and in a fluffy mousse – with buttermilk sorbet.

Chef Kamil Oseka **Seats** 90, Pr/dining room 22 **Times** 12-2.30/6.30-9.30, Closed D 25 Dec **Prices** Starter £3.95-£8, Main £15-£23, Dessert £4.25-£7.50 **Wines** 198 bottles over £30, 41 bottles under £30, 34 by glass **Parking** 50 **Notes** Sunday L £16-£19, Vegetarian available, Children welcome

LOWER VOBSTER Map 4 ST74

The Vobster Inn

 British, European

tel: 01373 812920 **BA3 5RJ**
email: rdavila@btinternet.com **web:** www.vobsterinn.co.uk
dir: *4m W of Frome, between Wells & Leigh upon Mendip*

Traditional pub food with a Spanish, Italian and French twist

Surrounded by the rolling hills of greenest Somerset is this friendly pub with rooms. The chef-proprietor's Spanish heritage is reflected in the tapas and main courses such as pork belly with fabada asturiana, but things segue into Italian with crab and chilli linguine, or smoked haddock risotto topped with a poached egg. Try a starter such as fried Loire goats' cheese dressed with the inn's own honey, or French onion soup served with red pepper bruschetta before exploring a solid vein of traditional British pubbery, from rollmops with tracklements to steak and chips, and plaice with brown shrimps. Desserts include apple and plum crumble with double cream.

Chef Rafael F Davila **Seats** 40, Pr/dining room 40 **Times** 12-3/6.30-11, Closed 25 Dec, Mon (check at BHs), D Sun **Wines** 12 by glass **Parking** 60 **Notes** Sunday L £11.50, Vegetarian available, Children welcome

MIDSOMER NORTON Map 4 ST65

Best Western Plus Centurion Hotel

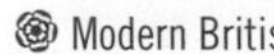 Modern British

tel: 01761 417711 & 412214 **Charlton Ln BA3 4BD**
email: enquiries@centurionhotel.co.uk **web:** www.centurionhotel.co.uk
dir: *Phone for directions*

Golfing hotel with careful, confident cooking

The restaurant in this modern family-run hotel is an inviting space, with a bright conservatory extension and menus full of appealing options. A platter of cured meats with mozzarella and sun-dried tomatoes is one way to begin, or go for seared scallops fashionably partnered by bacon with avocado. Traditionalists could follow on with a steak from the grill and a choice of sauces. Moroccan-style lamb with rice is another possibility for meat-eaters, with something like wild mushroom and squash ravioli for vegetarians. Finish with one of the choose-me puddings such as an assiette of Yorkshire rhubarb, or caramelised pear rice pudding.

Chef Sean Horwood **Seats** 60, Pr/dining room 120 **Times** 12-2/6-9.30, Closed 25-26 Dec, D Sun **Prices** Fixed L 3 course £20-£27, Tasting menu £25-£33, Starter £6-£7, Main £12-£24, Dessert £6-£11 **Wines** 9 bottles over £30, 19 bottles under £30, 7 by glass **Parking** 100 **Notes** Sunday L £11-£15, Vegetarian available, Children welcome

MILVERTON Map 3 ST12

The Globe

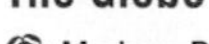 Modern British

tel: 01823 400534 **Fore St TA4 1JX**
email: adele@theglobemilverton.co.uk **web:** www.theglobemilverton.co.uk
dir: *M5 junct 26 onto A38, then B3187 to Milverton*

Hearty country-pub cooking

The Globe is still very much a pub, but it's a strong food destination too. The food is up-to-date country-pub fare, from fried chicken livers in sherry cream sauce, or cheddar and chive soufflé with walnut salad, to start. Move on to hearty main dishes such as enticingly gamey roast pheasant with smoked bacon and parsnip purée in a redcurrant sauce that stops usefully short of being too sweet. Sundays bring on traditionally garnished roasts – beef topside, lamb leg, pork – with roasties and Yorkshire puddings, while Somerset apple cake with matching compôte and cream takes care of the pudding business.

Chef Mark Tarry **Seats** 50 **Times** 12-3/6-11.30, Closed L Mon, D Sun **Prices** Starter £4.95-£7.95, Main £9.95-£18.95, Dessert £5.95-£6.95 **Wines** 2 bottles over £30, 25 bottles under £30, 10 by glass **Parking** 3 **Notes** Sunday L £10.95-£15.95, Vegetarian available, Children welcome

MONKSILVER Map 3 ST03

The Notley Arms Inn

 Classic British

tel: 01984 656095 **Front St TA4 4JB**
email: notleyarmsinn@hotmail.com **web:** www.notleyarmsinn.co.uk
dir: *From A358 at Bishop's Lydeard onto B3224. After 5m turn right onto B3188 to Monksilver*

Stimulating well-flavoured cooking in village inn

Chesterfields at an open fire, a mix of dining chairs and pew-style seating, and attentive staff add to the enjoyable experience of a visit to this whitewashed village inn. The kitchen turns out eloquently flavoured, well-executed dishes, among them a starter of foie gras brûlée with onion marmalade and brioche, then duck breast and foie gras mousse with red wine sauce, parsnip purée, vanilla mash and carrots, and smoked salmon linguine with toasted nuts and a creamy lemon sauce. Pub stalwarts like fish and chips may also appear, and to finish there may be tastes of cherry and chocolate – a play on Black Forest gâteau.

NORTH WOOTTON Map 4 ST54

Crossways

 Modern British

tel: 01749 899000 **Stocks Ln BA4 4EU**
email: enquiries@thecrossways.co.uk **web:** www.thecrossways.co.uk
dir: *Exit M5 junct 22 towards Shepton Mallet, 0.2m from Pilton*

Classy country inn with local ingredients and a Mediterranean twist

A thoroughly contemporary kind of inn these days, the 18th-century Crossways looks much the same as it always has from the outside, but a 21st-century makeover has opened-up the place, bringing soothing neutrally-toned modernity. It's the kind of place where you can eat what you want where you want, and there's a children's menu, too. The chef makes a big play for local and regional ingredients, with Somerset's finest on show, but there's a Mediterranean spin to proceedings. Confit duck and orange terrine with grape chutney and skin crumb gets the ball rolling, before herb-crusted rack of lamb or loin of cod infused with dill.

Chef Barney Everett **Seats** 100, Pr/dining room 86 **Times** 12-3/6-9, Closed L Sun **Prices** Fixed L 2 course £12, Starter £5-£10.50, Main £13.75-£29.75, Dessert £6-£8.50 **Wines** 8 bottles over £30, 24 bottles under £30, 7 by glass **Parking** 120 **Notes** Vegetarian available, Children welcome

OAKHILL Map 4 ST64

The Oakhill Inn

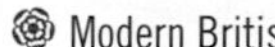 Modern British

tel: 01749 840442 **Fosse Rd BA3 5HU**
email: info@theoakhillinn.com **web:** www.theoakhillinn.com
dir: *On A367 between Stratton-on-the-Fosse & Shepton Mallet*

Modernised British cooking in an old stone inn

An ancient stone-built inn with hanging baskets is many people's idea of old England, and The Oakhill looks the part. The food itself edges more firmly into modern British territory than hitherto, although devotees of pub classics such as bubble-and-squeak topped with a poached egg, or fish and chips with mushy peas, have not been abandoned. Otherwise, look to ox cheek terrine with red onion compôte in balsamic, and then roast cod with leeks, mussels and new potatoes in fish soup. Sides include the nowadays indispensable dauphinoise, and a satisfying conclusion is reached with desserts that major on chocolate and toffee, but also find room for tarte Tatin.

Chef Neil Creese **Seats** 60 **Times** 12-3/6-9, Closed 25-26 Dec, D 1 Jan **Prices** Fixed L 2 course fr £13.50, Starter £5.95-£6.95, Main £11.95-£20.95, Dessert £4.50-£5.95 **Wines** 7 bottles over £30, 24 bottles under £30, 10 by glass **Parking** 12 **Notes** All day dining on Sun 12-9pm, Sunday L £9.95-£18.95, Vegetarian available, Children welcome

PORLOCK Map 3 SS84

The Oaks Hotel

Traditional British

tel: 01643 862265 **TA24 8ES**
email: info@oakshotel.co.uk **web:** www.oakshotel.co.uk
dir: *From E of A39, enter village (road narrows to single track) then follow hotel sign. From W: down Porlock Hill, through village, hotel sign on right*

Traditional cooking in the Exmoor National Park

On the edge of the village, this small hotel occupies an imposing Edwardian property with glorious views of Porlock Bay from the reception rooms and restaurant. The daily-changing four-course menu might open with a tartlet, its pastry soft and crumbly, of cherry tomatoes, goats' cheese and pine nuts before a fish course: perhaps hot smoked haddock mousse. Sauces are a strong suit: one of cheesy fennel for sea-fresh fillet of John Dory, port and redcurrant for roast fillet of Exmoor venison, accompanied by garden-fresh vegetables. Puddings include an excellent passionfruit custard tart, and lemon and raspberry roulade.

SHEPTON MALLET Map 4 ST64

Charlton House Spa Hotel

 Modern British

tel: 01749 342008 & 0844 248 3830 *(Calls cost 7p per minute plus your phone company's access charge)* **Charlton Rd BA4 4PR**
email: enquiries.charltonhousehotel@bannatyne.co.uk **web:** www.bannatyne.co.uk
dir: *On A361 towards Frome, 1m from town centre*

Contemporary cooking in a smart country house

A grand stone manor on the edge of Shepton Mallet, Charlton House combines period charm and contemporary style. A menu of modern British dishes includes flavours from beyond the European borders, so steamed tiger prawn with a coconut and green curry foam sits alongside carpaccio of scallop with raspberry and black pepper jelly among main courses. Next up, quail is wrapped in pancetta and roasted, and arrives in the company of thyme mash and roast swede, while fish options might include roast cod with pickled kohlrabi. For dessert try rhubarb trifle with Chantilly or more Asian flavours in the form of rice pudding with chilli and lychee sorbet.

Chef Stephen Yates **Seats** 60, Pr/dining room 80 **Times** 12.30-2.15/7-9.15 **Prices** Fixed L 2 course £15, Fixed D 3 course £39 **Wines** 22 bottles over £30, 25 bottles under £30, 9 by glass **Parking** 70 **Notes** Sunday L £25, Vegetarian available, Children welcome

SOMERTON Map 4 ST42

The Devonshire Arms

 Modern British

tel: 01458 241271 **Long Sutton TA10 9LP**
email: mail@thedevonshirearms.com **web:** www.thedevonshirearms.com
dir: *Off A303 onto A372 at Pudimore rdbt. After 4m, left onto B3165, signed Martock and Long Sutton*

Good honest cooking by the village green

This Georgian former hunting lodge turned restaurant with rooms is a convivial hub where people pop in for a jar of ale or cider in the bar, or for a full meal in the restaurant, while on a fine day, alfresco dining is on the cards in the courtyard and walled garden. Expect big-hearted cooking that seeks to comfort rather than challenge, with well-considered combinations – crab and tomato tartlet, followed by guinea fowl breast with truffle mousse, local pancetta, mash spring greens and herb jus, and for pudding, perhaps treacle tart with lemon curd and home-made buttermilk ice cream.

STON EASTON Map 4 ST65

Ston Easton Park Hotel

 Modern British V

tel: 01761 241631 **BA3 4DF**
email: reception@stoneaston.co.uk **web:** www.stoneaston.co.uk
dir: *A39 from Bath for approx 8m. Onto A37 (Shepton Mallet). Hotel in next village*

Properly memorable cooking at a Palladian manor

A grand Palladian mansion with sumptuous antique-packed interiors in 36 acres of grounds landscaped by Humphry Repton – including a Victorian walled kitchen garden that provides seasonal organic fruit, veg, herbs and edible flowers – Ston Easton is a delight. The team in the elegant Sorrel Restaurant deliver light and confident modern country house-style cooking, bursting with luxurious ingredients, intense flavours and pin-sharp presentations. How about cauliflower velouté, scallop céviche and caviar to start things off, followed perhaps by a cutlet and loin of lamb with celeriac and apple champ. Save room for dessert – maybe caramelised pear brûlée with lavender shortbread.

Chef Martin Baker **Seats** 40, Pr/dining room 80 **Times** 12-2/6.30-9.30 **Prices** Tasting menu £26.50-£49.50, Starter £7-£8, Main £16.50-£28.50, Dessert £6-£9 **Wines** 80 bottles over £30, 20 bottles under £30, 12 by glass **Parking** 60 **Notes** Afternoon tea £22.50, Sunday L fr £26, Children 8 yrs+ D

TAUNTON Map 4 ST22

Augustus

 European V

tel: 01823 324354 **3 The Courtyard, St James St TA1 1JR**
email: info@augustustaunton.co.uk
dir: *M5 junct 25. Town centre, next to cricket ground*

Refined simplicity in a Taunton courtyard

The repeated shrilling of the phone serves notice of the popularity of Richard Guest's courtyard restaurant in the town centre where the pared-down contemporary look complements the modern brasserie style food. A warm salad of solferino-balled vegetables accompanies beautifully caramelised scallops to begin, or there could traditional gnocchi with taleggio and rosemary cream. For main, straightforward fish dishes such as turbot with greens in mustard sauce, or John Dory with courgettes and tomato, allow their star performers to shine, while a bowl of rabbit saddle and roasted roots rustic satisfaction. Finish with crisp-shelled treacle tart with ginger ice cream or lemon posset with summer fruit compôte.

Chef Richard Guest **Seats** 28 **Times** 10-3/6-9.30, Closed 25 Dec, 1 Jan, Sun-Mon **Prices** Starter £5-£9.95, Main £10.95-£22, Dessert £5-£6.95 **Wines** 74 bottles over £30, 36 bottles under £30, 14 by glass **Parking** On street **Notes** Daily specials 3 of each course, Children welcome

The Mount Somerset Hotel & Spa

 British V

tel: 01823 442500 **Lower Henlade TA3 5NB**
email: info@mountsomersethotel.co.uk **web:** www.mountsomersethotel.co.uk
dir: *M5 junct 25, A358 towards Chard/Ilminster, right in Henlade (Stoke St Mary), left at T-junct. Hotel 400yds on right*

Soundly conceived British modernism with peacocks

A pristine white Regency manor house in four acres, The Mount fairly piles on the style. West Country produce finds its way on to menus of soundly conceived British modernism. Cauliflower purée be gone, as the scallops arrive with goats' cheese, pineapple and avocado aïoli, while venison, red cabbage and parsnips are resized into an appetising starter. Beef reared on Exmoor is aged for 28 days before the fillet is roasted and served with pink fir apple potatoes braised in duck fat. Fish might be Cornish turbot in vivid saffron nage with a crab and ginger raviolo. To finish, try the pear and almond cream tart with an ice cream of Somerset cider brandy.

Chef Mark Potts **Seats** 60, Pr/dining room 50 **Times** 12-2/7-9.30 **Prices** Prices not confirmed **Wines** 56 bottles over £30, 30 bottles under £30, 10 by glass **Parking** 100 **Notes** Sunday L, Children welcome

The Willow Tree Restaurant

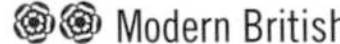 Modern British

tel: 01823 352835 **3 Tower Ln, Off Tower St TA1 4AR**
email: willowtreefood@hotmail.co.uk
dir: *200yds from Taunton bus station*

Pin-sharp cooking in a 17th-century townhouse

Chef-patron Darren Sherlock's intimate restaurant occupies a beamed 17th-century house in the heart of town. Locally reared meats and fish from Newlyn's day boats produce starters such as smoked haddock and leek tartlet with a slow-cooked truffled egg yolk and parsley dressing before mains that give those pedigree meats and fish star billing, whether it's pan-fried monkfish and scallops with 'linguine' of carrot and celeriac, home-made tarragon pasta and creamy lobster sauce, or roast rump of lamb with pommes Anna, ratatouille-style vegetables and black olive jus. Baking skills are evident in excellent home-made breads, and thought and workmanship are behind even straightforward-sounding desserts like bread-and-butter pudding with vanilla ice cream.

Chef Darren Sherlock **Seats** 25 **Times** 6.30-9, Closed Jan, Aug, Sun-Mon, Thu, L all week **Prices** Fixed D 3 course £27.95-£32.95 **Wines** 20 bottles over £30, 27 bottles under £30, 6 by glass **Parking** 20 yds, 300 spaces **Notes** Vegetarian available, Children 10 yrs+

TINTINHULL Map 4 ST41

Crown & Victoria

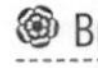 British

tel: 01935 823341 **Farm St BA22 8PZ**
email: info@thecrownandvictoria.co.uk **web:** www.thecrownandvictoria.co.uk
dir: *Westbound off A303 follow signs for Tintinhull*

Good honest cooking in a lovely village pub

This is the kind of country pub that spurs urbanites to up sticks and move to a rural idyll. It's a proper pub, with a changing rota of ales and a serious approach to food. The kitchen keeps things local, seeking out organic and free-range ingredients to treat with simplicity and integrity. A bowl of celeriac and Bramley apple soup is just the ticket, simple and well-made, enriched with toasted walnuts and Blue Vinney cheese. Main course might be well-timed roast cod in lemongrass velouté, with creamy, garlicky dauphinoise and a side-dish of veg, and the conclusion could be hot chocolate fondant with salt caramel centre and pistachio ice cream.

Chef Jenni Watson, Adrian McCavish, Alice Reddington **Seats** 100, Pr/dining room 45 **Times** 12-2.30/6.30-9.30, Closed D Sun **Wines** 8 bottles over £30, 18 bottles under £30, 8 by glass **Parking** 50 **Notes** Sunday L £11.50-£15.95, Vegetarian available, Children welcome

WELLS Map 4 ST54

Ancient Gate House Hotel

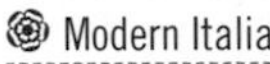 Modern Italian

tel: 01749 672029 **20 Sadler St BA5 2SE**
email: info@ancientgatehouse.co.uk **web:** www.ancientgatehouse.co.uk
dir: *1st hotel on left on cathedral green*

Italian home cooking by the old West Gate

The hotel incorporates nothing less than the Great West Gate that once formed part of the little city's medieval fortifications. Housed within it for the past 40 years has been Rugantino's, flying the flag for Italian home cooking. The lengthy menus deal in numerous favourites, from well-wrought pasta dishes such as linguine carbonara, and spaghetti del mare generously teeming with scallops, prawns, clams and crab, to main-course showstoppers like chicken breast stuffed with salsiccia and pine nuts with truffled mushroom cream sauce. Simple fish preparations are a good bet, for example sea bass with fennel and puréed red pepper. To finish, there are treats such as pannacotta and berry compôte.

Chef Jamie Cundill **Seats** 40, Pr/dining room 20 **Times** 12-2.30/6-10, Closed 25-29 Dec **Prices** Fixed L 2 course £10.90-£13.90, Fixed D 3 course £25-£30, Starter £3.25-£8.50, Main £9.50-£21.50, Dessert £5.50-£6.50 **Wines** 6 bottles over £30, 27 bottles under £30, 9 by glass **Parking** On street **Notes** Tasting menu, Pre/post cathedral concert menu, Sunday L, Vegetarian available, Children welcome

Best Western Plus Swan Hotel

Modern British

tel: 01749 836300 **Sadler St BA5 2RX**
email: info@swanhotelwells.co.uk **web:** www.swanhotelwells.co.uk
dir: *A39, A371, on entering Wells follow signs for Hotels & Deliveries. Hotel on right opposite cathedral*

An ancient inn with creative full-flavoured contemporary cooking

Once a coaching inn, The Swan is in the heart of Wells, close to the cathedral. The panelled restaurant is smart and comfortable, with a short but ingenious menu. Japanese cure mackerel comes with shiso salad and a ginger and carrot dressing, or there might be wood pigeon bruschetta with wilted radicchio chives and balsamic vinegar. Main courses might include roast south coast hake with olive oil mash, fennel 'two ways' and sauce vièrge, or whole roasted red-legged partridge with potato fondant and Savoy cabbage with bacon and walnuts. Check out the warm honey and stout tart for dessert.

Chef Adam Kennington **Seats** 50, Pr/dining room 90 **Times** 12-2/7-9.30 **Prices** Fixed D 3 course £27 **Wines** 14 bottles over £30, 21 bottles under £30, 7 by glass **Parking** 30 **Notes** Sunday L £17.95-£19.95, Vegetarian available, Children welcome

Goodfellows

Mediterranean, European

tel: 01749 673866 **5 Sadler St BA5 2RR**
email: goodfellowseat@gmail.com **web:** www.goodfellowswells.co.uk
dir: *Town centre near Market Place*

Creative fish restaurant with a café attached

Look for the plum-coloured facade in the town centre, and you can't go wrong. If it's first thing, breakfast is on hand in the café, or you might have a Danish and cappuccino for elevenses. Otherwise, sign up for some distinguished seafood-led cookery in the adjoining restaurant, where fish is handled confidently by a small, intensely focused brigade in the central open kitchen. A parcel of smoked salmon and crab with horseradish crème fraîche could precede pollock with black pudding and apple, caramelised chicory and crispy vine leaves. Don't skip dessert from the on-site pâtisserie, perhaps dark chocolate tart with candied orange zest and mandarin sorbet.

Goodfellows

Chef Adam Fellows **Seats** 35, Pr/dining room 20 **Times** 12-3.30/6-9.30, Closed 25-27 Dec, 1 Jan, D Sun-Tue **Prices** Fixed L 2 course fr £21, Tasting menu fr £48, Starter £7-£13, Main £13-£23, Dessert £6.50-£8 **Wines** 19 bottles over £30, 24 bottles under £30, 6 by glass **Notes** Tasting menu 5 course, Seafood menu, Sunday L £12-£14, Vegetarian available, Children welcome

WESTON-SUPER-MARE **Map 4 ST36**

The Cove

Modern British

tel: 01934 418217 **Marine Lake, Birnbeck Rd BS23 2BX**
email: info@the-cove.co.uk
dir: *From Grand Pier on Royal Parade N onto Knightstone Rd. Left into Birnbeck Rd. Restaurant on left*

Cool seaside brasserie with Mediterranean influence

Bucket-and-spade Weston-super-Mare is trading up these days, and this smartly revamped bistro-style restaurant on the seafront near Birnbeck Pier fits in admirably. The terrace perched above the water is the place to be on a balmy day, while full-length windows ensure a great view all year. Inside, its pared-back contemporary look wouldn't look out of place in a big city. The unpretentious, Mediterranean-accented menu kicks off with the likes of an Asian-inspired spiced pork belly, followed by whole baked sea bass en papillote, or fritto misto to share. Finish with chocolate brownie sundae or go for one of their home-made ice creams.

Chef Richard Tudor, Gemma Stacey **Seats** 65 **Times** 12-9, All-day dining, Closed 25 Dec, D Mon-Wed **Prices** Fixed L 3 course £14.50, Fixed D 3 course £19.95, Starter £3.95-£8, Main £10.95-£17.95, Dessert £3.95-£6.50 **Wines** 2 bottles over £30, 30 bottles under £30, 6 by glass **Parking** On street/car park **Notes** Sunday L £10.95, Vegetarian available, Children welcome

WINCANTON Map 4 ST72

Holbrook House

 Modern British

tel: 01963 824466 **Holbrook BA9 8BS**
email: enquiries@holbrookhouse.co.uk **web:** www.holbrookhouse.co.uk
dir: *From A303 at Wincanton, turn left on A371 towards Castle Cary & Shepton Mallet*

Diverting modern cooking in a house with a history

Holbrook is a handsome Georgian manor house on an estate that can trace its history back to the 13th century. There are many different spots for pre-dinner drinks, so don't rush, but take in the consummate professionalism of a place where staff are knowledgeable about the menus and there's a serious wine list to contemplate. Start with a finely-wrought wild mushroom risotto with Jerusalem artichoke velouté and crisps, followed by precise flavours all working together in mains of line-caught wild sea bass with crab tortellini, carrot and tarragon gratin and vermouth and chive broth. At dessert, an ethereal caramel soufflé comes with chocolate sauce and vanilla ice cream.

Chef Paul Hudson **Seats** 70, Pr/dining room 140 **Times** 12.30-2/7-9, Closed L Mon-Thu, D Sun **Prices** Fixed L 2 course £15, Starter £5.95-£7.95, Main £16.50-£28.50, Dessert £7-£9.50 **Wines** 10 by glass **Parking** 100 **Notes** Sunday L £19.50-£24.50, Vegetarian available, Children welcome

YEOVIL Map 4 ST51

Little Barwick House

 Modern British NOTABLE WINE LIST

tel: 01935 423902 **Barwick Village BA22 9TD**
email: reservations@barwick7.fsnet.co.uk **web:** www.littlebarwickhouse.co.uk
dir: *Turn off A371 Yeovil to Dorchester opposite Red House rdbt, 0.25m on left*

Simple but powerful dishes in an atmosphere of perfect hospitality

Tim and Emma Ford have quite the knack of making visitors feel instantly at home in their white-fronted country house, where modesty of scale translates into finely detailed hospitality. In a relaxing room looking out on the garden, with clothed tables and seating in windowpane check, diners exchange pleasantries with each other at conversational level instead of whispers, staff are attentive without pestering, and the focus is on the food. Younger son Olly and his dad make a formidable kitchen double act, with cooking that is soundly based on excellent fundamentals, rather than following fashion up a blind alley. Everything looks and tastes of itself, so there's no need to refer back to the menu for a reminder, from an opening pairing of grilled Cornish mackerel and fresh crab with carrot and orange escabèche to a mightily effective dessert plate of tropical fruits adorned with coconut pannacotta, banana bavarois and mango sorbet. In between might come softly roasted, deeply flavoured veal sweetbreads in Madeira with punchy wild mushroom risotto, or perhaps red mullet with crushed and basilled new potatoes in saffron sauce. A splendid wine list bears all the hallmarks of genuine enthusiasm for the subject and adds to the overall enjoyment.

Chef Timothy Ford **Seats** 40 **Times** 12-2/7-9, Closed New Year, 2 wks Jan, Sun-Mon, L Tue **Prices** Fixed L 2 course £25.95, Fixed D 3 course £49.95 **Wines** 143 bottles over £30, 23 bottles under £30, 29 by glass **Parking** 25 **Notes** D 2 course Tue-Thu, Vegetarian available, Children 5 yrs+

The Yeovil Court Hotel & Restaurant

 Modern European

tel: 01935 863746 **West Coker Rd BA20 2HE**
email: unwind@yeovilhotel.com **web:** www.yeovilhotel.com
dir: *2.5m W of town centre on A30*

Modern hotel with stimulating brasserie cooking

The entire ground floor of this low-slung white hotel on the outskirts of town is dedicated to eating, drinking and relaxing. It's a popular place, attracting guests with its interesting menus and skilful cooking. Seared scallops are partnered by pancetta and served with pea purée and shellfish oil, and may be followed by slices of roast pheasant with no more than lardons, spinach and potatoes. Various cultures are raided to extend variety: gnocchi with spinach and walnuts in creamy blue cheese sauce, for instance, then red snapper with couscous, peppers, spicy tomatoes, olives and rocket. Puddings might extend to pineapple jelly with mango sorbet and coconut and lime syrup.

STAFFORDSHIRE

LEEK Map 16 SJ95

Three Horseshoes Country Inn & Spa

@@ Modern International

tel: 01538 300296 **Buxton Rd, Blackshaw Moor ST13 8TW**
email: enquiries@threeshoesinn.co.uk **web:** www.threeshoesinn.co.uk
dir: *M6 junct 15 or 16 onto A500. Exit A53 towards Leek. 2m from town centre*

Grills and much more in a Peak District country inn

The stone-built inn overlooked by lowering gritstone outcrops in the southern stretches of the Peak District covers many bases. It's a country pub, a smart rural hotel and a chic brasserie and grill all in the one package. Original oak beams are offset by contemporary styling, with an open-to-view kitchen augmenting the dynamic atmosphere. The modern international cooking takes in scallops and chicken ballotine with celeriac and caramelised apple to start, followed by roast pheasant with a pastilla of the leg-meat, quince terrine and gingerbread, or sea bass with crab cannelloni in saffron sauce. Finish with passionfruit soufflé and matching sorbet.

Chef Mark & Stephen Kirk **Seats** 50, Pr/dining room 150 **Times** 6.30-9, Closed 24-26 Dec, L Mon-Sat **Prices** Fixed L 3 course £19.95, Tasting menu £22.50-£45, Starter £7.95-£10.25, Main £19.25-£24, Dessert £6.75-£8.50 **Wines** 47 bottles over £30, 67 bottles under £30, 10 by glass **Parking** 100 **Notes** Tasting menu 8 course, Sunday L, Vegetarian available, Children welcome

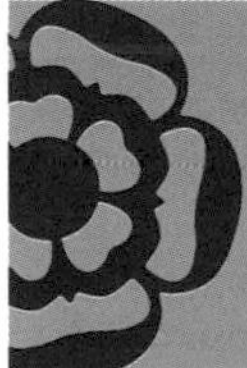

Find out more about how we assess for Rosette awards on pages 8–9

LICHFIELD Map 10 SK10

Netherstowe House

Modern British V

tel: 01543 254270 **Netherstowe Ln WS13 6AY**
email: reception@netherstowehouse.com **web:** www.netherstowehouse.com
dir: *A38 onto A5192, 0.3m on right into Netherstowe Ln. 1st left, 1st right down private drive*

Local produce presented well in a boutique setting

Genteel and refined, Netherstowe is a characterful house with origins dating back to the 12th century and there are period features throughout. In the elegant dining room with its white linen table cloths and silver candle holders, the food displays a passion for provenance and local producers. Attractively presented and contemporary, the cooking is underpinned by classic technique. Start with seared Brixham scallops, chicken, chorizo and smoked cauliflower and move on to a main course suckling pig rack, pork tenderloin, onion purée and broccoli. Finish with white chocolate 'choc ice' filled with passion fruit syrup and served with mango sorbet.

Chef Stephen Garland **Seats** 30, Pr/dining room 14 **Times** 12-2.30/6-9, Closed 1 Jan, D Sun **Prices** Fixed D 3 course £35-£40 **Wines** 75 bottles over £30, 27 bottles under £30, 9 by glass **Parking** 50 **Notes** Brunch, Afternoon tea, Sunday L, Children 12 yrs+

Swinfen Hall Hotel

Modern British NEW V

tel: 01543 481494 **Swinfen WS14 9RE**
email: info@swinfenhallhotel.co.uk **web:** www.swinfenhallhotel.co.uk
dir: *2m S of Lichfield on A38 between Weeford rdbt & Swinfen rdbt*

Classy modern country-house cooking in a Georgian mansion

The sika deer and rare-breed sheep roaming the 100 acres of parkland and woods around the impressive Georgian country house are not just there to look nice; they also turn up on the plate in the Four Seasons dining room. A half-acre Victorian walled garden plays its part in stocking the larder too, and what isn't home-grown is sourced with unimpeachable quality in mind. The restaurant is a formal affair with oak panelling, a hand-painted ceiling, opulent swagged drapes at sash windows, and linen-clad tables set with burnished silver, Wedgwood china and crystal glassware. The food fits the bill with classic combinations, attention to detail and well-judged elements of modernity, perhaps opening with a classy take on liver and onions – a seared lobe and parfait of foie gras with assertive onion velouté, bacon and Riesling. Following on might be butter-roasted cod with its new best friend, a chicken wing, alongside salsify and puréed ceps, the whole fragranced with lemon thyme, or perhaps pinkly succulent Cornish lamb noisettes with chargrilled cauliflower, romanesco and golden raisins in rich rosemary jus. A treat is in store at dessert in the shape of Valrhona chocolate ganache with roasted peanuts and salted caramel, served with delicately scented bay leaf ice cream.

Chef Ryan Shilton **Seats** 45, Pr/dining room 20
Times 12.30-2.30/7.30-9.30, Closed 26 Dec, 1 Jan, Mon, D Sun **Prices** Fixed D 3 course £52, Tasting menu £75 **Wines** 97 bottles over £30, 38 bottles under £30, 10 by glass **Parking** 80 **Notes** ALC L 2/3 course £29.5/£38, Vegetarian tasting menu £70, Sunday L £29.50-£38, Children welcome

STAFFORD Map 10 SJ92

The Moat House

Modern British

tel: 01785 712217 **Lower Penkridge Rd, Acton Trussell ST17 0RJ**
email: info@moathouse.co.uk **web:** www.moathouse.co.uk
dir: *M6 junct 13 towards Stafford, 1st right to Acton Trussell, hotel by church*

Confident, creative cooking by a canal

The Moat House is indeed moated, a part-timbered manor dating from the 14th century. Its seasonally changing carte might open with lobster and crab ravioli with chervil tuber purée, fennel choucroute and sauce armoricaine, or more straightforward asparagus velouté with duck yolk and mushroom brioche soldiers. Main courses can be complex too but equally satisfying: attractively presented pork tenderloin with peanut-crusted belly, an oriental-style sauce, king prawn, carrot and star anise purée and pak choi, or lemon sole not just given the meunière treatment but served with scallops, parsley root and chard. End with an inventive pudding such as Turkish delight cheesecake with rose water gel and chocolate sorbet.

Chef Matthew Davies, James Cracknell **Seats** 120, Pr/dining room 150
Times 12-2/6.30-9.30, Closed 25 Dec **Prices** Fixed L 2 course fr £18, Fixed D 3 course fr £30, Tasting menu fr £60, Starter £8-£12, Main £16-£28, Dessert £8-£9 **Wines** 77 bottles over £30, 74 bottles under £30, 19 by glass **Parking** 200 **Notes** Early doors menu, Gourmet menu, Afternoon tea, Sunday L £26, Vegetarian available, Children welcome

SUFFOLK

ALDEBURGH Map 13 TM45

Brudenell Hotel

Modern British, European

tel: 01728 452071 **The Parade IP15 5BU**
email: info@brudenellhotel.co.uk **web:** www.brudenellhotel.co.uk
dir: *A12/A1094, on reaching town, turn right at junct into High St. Hotel on seafront adjoining Fort Green car park*

Sunny brasserie cooking in a beachfront hotel

This privately owned hotel is virtually on Aldeburgh's beach so, naturally enough, seafood tops the bill, freshly delivered along with free-range meat each morning. Whole dressed crab with salad, new potatoes and lemon mayonnaise, lobster with tarragon mayonnaise and potato salad, and perfectly cooked plaice fillets with chunky tartare sauce, petits pois and fries are all possibilities. Or break the mould and opt for asparagus and goats' cheese tart, its pastry crisp and light, with pesto, or potted duck and pork with cornichons and toast, before pink saddle of lamb with wild rice, kale, shallots and a tomato and basil jus. Finish with a perfect sherry trifle or rhubarb fool.

ALDEBURGH *continued*

Regatta Restaurant

Modern British

tel: 01728 452011 **171 High St IP15 5AN**
email: rob.mabey@btinternet.com
dir: *Middle of High St, town centre*

Buzzy bistro, local seafood the stars

A nautical-themed mural and piscine prints leave no doubt that fresh local seafood, often landed on the beach, is the main thrust of the Mabeys' restaurant on the High Street. It's a cheery, relaxed place, with brown leather-look banquettes and upholstered dining chairs at plain wooden tables, and a blackboard of daily specials supporting the carte. Wild boar and beetroot arancini – a daily special – gets things off to a flying start, followed perhaps by pan-fried sea bass with chorizo, peppers and artichokes, or whole smoked prawns from their smoker out back. Round things off with rice pudding and a Kilner jar of 'almost plum jam'.

Chef Robert Mabey **Seats** 90, Pr/dining room 30 **Times** 12-2/6-late, Closed 24-26 & 31 Dec, 1 Jan **Prices** Fixed L 2 course fr £15, Fixed D 3 course fr £18, Starter £4.50-£8.50, Main £12-£22, Dessert £4.50-£8.50 **Wines** 6 bottles over £30, 30 bottles under £30, 12 by glass **Parking** On street **Notes** Gourmet evenings, Sunday L £13.50-£17.50, Vegetarian available, Children welcome

Wentworth Hotel

Traditional British V

tel: 01728 452312 **Wentworth Rd IP15 5BD**
email: stay@wentworth-aldeburgh.com **web:** www.wentworth-aldeburgh.com
dir: *From A12 take A1094 to Aldeburgh. In Aldeburgh straight on at mini rdbt, turn left at x-rds into Wentworth Rd. Hotel on right*

Family-run hotel with impeccable traditional cooking

Owned by the same family since 1920, the Wentworth has the deeply traditional feel of a smart country-house hotel with the bonus of splendid sea views from its peaceful spot on Aldeburgh's beachfront. Kitchen techniques are sound and seek to comfort rather than to challenge, starting, perhaps, with home-made fishcakes with sweet chilli dressing, while main courses run the gamut from slow-cooked pork belly with butternut squash purée, Savoy cabbage, mashed potato and apple sauce, to grilled hake fillet with pesto mash, roast Mediterranean vegetables and tomato coulis. Among desserts, try red wine-poached pear with cinnamon ice cream and gingerbread or the comfort of bread-and-butter pudding with custard.

Chef Jason Shaw **Seats** 100, Pr/dining room 28 **Times** 12-2.30/6-9 **Prices** Fixed L 2 course fr £14, Fixed D 3 course fr £26.50 **Wines** 21 bottles over £30, 53 bottles under £30 **Parking** 35 **Notes** Sunday L fr £23, Children welcome

The White Lion Hotel

British, French

tel: 01728 452720 **Market Cross Place IP15 5BJ**
email: info@whitelion.co.uk **web:** www.whitelion.co.uk
dir: *M25 junct 28 to A12 onto A1094, follow signs to Aldeburgh at junct on left. Hotel on right*

Modern brasserie dining on the seafront

Sitting in beachfront splendour by the shingle banks of Aldeburgh's strand, The White Lion deals in unpretentious brasserie dining, built on fine Suffolk ingredients – in fact, sourcing doesn't get more local than the fish landed a few steps away on the beach. If you can resist the temptations of haddock in Adnams beer-batter with chips and chunky tartare sauce, Cajun-spiced chicken breast with celeriac remoulade and sun-dried tomatoes is a fine main course. Bookending this are tempura king prawns with guacamole, mango and chilli dressing to start, and a moresome finale of flourless dark chocolate torte with popcorn praline and honeycomb ice cream.

Chef Ben Hegarty **Seats** 80 **Times** 12-3/5.30-9.30 **Prices** Fixed L 2 course £12.50, Fixed D 3 course £15.50, Starter £6.50-£9, Main £11.50-£21.50, Dessert £6.50-£8.50 **Wines** 10 bottles over £30, 20 bottles under £30, 20 by glass **Parking** 10, On street **Notes** Afternoon tea, Sunday L £14-£25, Vegetarian available, Children welcome

BROME **Map 13 TM17**

Best Western Brome Grange Hotel

Traditional British

tel: 01379 870456 **Norwich Rd, Nr Diss IP23 8AP**
email: info@bromegrangehotel.co.uk **web:** www.bromegrangehotel.co.uk
dir: *2m S of Diss on A140 between Ipswich & Norwich*

Former coaching inn with carefully presented classic cooking

It's easy to imagine horse-drawn carriages sweeping into the central courtyard of this 16th-century former coaching inn, with plenty of period details remaining inside and out. The Courtyard Restaurant, however, is a light and contemporary affair with vivid colours and well-spaced darkwood tables. The service team are a cheerful bunch. The menu takes a broadly classical approach with some sound thinking going on and an eye for presentation. Start with game terrine with pickled walnuts and Bramley apple jelly, and move on to an old favourite such as scampi and hand-cut chips, or the more modern pan-fried pheasant breast with Guinness and cumin jus.

Chef Matthew Cooke **Seats** 60, Pr/dining room 28 **Times** 12-2/6.30-9, Closed D 25 Dec **Prices** Starter £4.65-£7.50, Main £10.95-£14.95, Dessert £4.95-£6.95 **Wines** 2 bottles over £30, 23 bottles under £30, 9 by glass **Parking** 120 **Notes** Sunday L, Vegetarian available, Children welcome

BURY ST EDMUNDS **Map 13 TL86**

The Angel Hotel

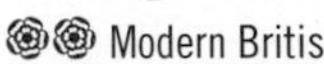

Modern British

tel: 01284 714000 **Angel Hill IP33 1LT**
email: staying@theangel.co.uk **web:** www.theangel.co.uk
dir: *From A134, left at rdbt into Northgate St. Continue to lights, right into Mustow St, left into Angel Hill. Hotel on right*

Med-influenced brasserie dining in creeper-covered hotel

Overlooking the cathedral and abbey walls, The Angel is celebrating 50 years under the same ownership and is a quintessential Georgian coaching inn. Its facade is suitably handsome and curtained with creepers, and inside, the generous spaces have been overlaid with a contemporary boutique look. The Eaterie's kitchen shows equally 21st-century sensibilities in its repertoire of upbeat brasserie food. Start with a Cromer crab and Granny Smith apple number, with verjus and crème fraîche, then follow with 32-day aged steak with hand-cut chips or fillet of cod dressed with a cockle sauce. For dessert, honey and lemon cheesecake is topped with an oatmeal crumb.

Chef Arron Jackson **Seats** 85, Pr/dining room 16 **Times** 12-9.45, All-day dining **Prices** Prices not confirmed **Wines** 41 bottles over £30, 18 bottles under £30, 33 by glass **Parking** On street **Notes** Sunday L, Vegetarian available, Children welcome

Best Western Priory Hotel

◎ Modern British, International

tel: 01284 766181 **Mildenhall Rd IP32 6EH**
email: reservations@prioryhotel.co.uk **web:** www.prioryhotel.co.uk
dir: *From A14 junct 43 take Bury St Edmunds W slip road. Follow signs to Brandon. At mini-rdbt turn right. Hotel 0.5m on left*

A peaceful setting for cooking with the surprise factor

A peaceful atmosphere reigns throughout the Priory, including in the Garden Room restaurant, which offers soft lighting and a comforting feeling of being looked after by endlessly helpful staff. The kitchen produces dishes that pull in inspiration from all over the known world, starting with spicy rabbit rissole dressed in Marsala. That might be the forerunner of duck breast in an east Asian mood, marinated in soy, mirin and yuzu, and bedded on soba noodles with pak choi in coriander and chilli broth. A dessert composition involving popcorn crumbs and caramel gel has a rather over-set tonka-bean pannacotta: try orange and almond tart with clotted cream instead.

Chef Matthew Cook **Seats** 72, Pr/dining room 28 **Times** 12-2/6-9.30 **Prices** Prices not confirmed **Wines** 22 bottles under £30, 9 by glass **Parking** 60, On street **Notes** Sunday L, Vegetarian available, Children welcome

Clarice House

◎ Modern European

tel: 01284 705550 **Horringer Court, Horringer Rd IP29 5PH**
email: bury@claricehouse.co.uk **web:** www.claricehouse .co.uk
dir: *From Bury St Edmunds on A143 towards Horringer and Haverhill, hotel 1m from town centre on right*

Well crafted, contemporary cooking at a spa retreat

Health and fitness are top of the agenda at this impressive neo-Jacobean mansion with a spa, swimming pool, gym and health and beauty salon. So there's no excuse for not shedding the calories gained in the restaurant. The menus steer a broadly European course, with starters ranging from a warm salad of pigeon breast with carrot purée and parsnip crisps to smoked salmon Welsh rarebit. Main courses are a mixed bag, taking in burger with fries as well as the healthier option of steamed snapper fillet with steamed vegetables, prawns and ginger and soy sauce. Devil-may-care diners could end with sticky toffee pudding with caramel sauce and vanilla ice cream.

The Grange Hotel

◎ Modern British

tel: 01359 231260 **Barton Rd, Thurston IP31 3PQ**
email: info@grangecountryhousehotel.com **web:** www.grangecountryhousehotel.com
dir: *A14 junct 45 towards Gt Barton, right at T-junct. At x-rds left into Barton Rd to Thurston. At rdbt, left after 0.5m, hotel on right*

Modern British classics in Tudor-style country house

The Grange did its bit in the last war, acting as a makeshift army hospital. It retains its period appeal, with an oak-panelled dining room setting the stage for informal modern British food. That latter-day classic, ham hock terrine with piccalilli shows up well, with delicately judged sea bass to follow, accompanied by Lyonnaise potatoes and braised fennel in caper butter. Seared cod is tenderly swaddled in Parma ham and served with chorizo and wilted greens in tomato velouté, before the voice of sweet temptation calls out in the tones of dark chocolate tart with white chocolate crème brûlée and pistachio ice cream.

Chef Darren Marchant **Seats** 32, Pr/dining room 40 **Times** 12-2/7-9, Closed 1 Jan **Prices** Starter £5.95-£6.95, Main £13.95-£19.95, Dessert £6.50-£9.95 **Wines** 20 bottles over £30, 22 bottles under £30, 12 by glass **Parking** 60 **Notes** Classic afternoon tea £14.65, Sparkling cream tea £18.95, Sunday L £18.95-£24.95, Vegetarian available, Children welcome

The Leaping Hare Restaurant & Country Store

◎◎ Modern British

tel: 01359 250287 **Wyken Vineyards, Stanton IP31 2DW**
email: restaurant@wykenvineyards.co.uk
dir: *8m NE of Bury St Edmunds, 1m off A143. Follow brown signs at Ixworth to Wyken Vineyards*

Vineyard restaurant with accomplished modern cooking

Set on a 1,200-acre farm complete with Shetland sheep and Red Poll cattle, plus a vineyard, The Leaping Hare occupies a splendid 400-year-old barn with a high raftered ceiling. What the farm doesn't provide is locally sourced, with fish landed at Lowestoft. The kitchen follows a straightforward route along classical lines, so expect starters of guinea fowl and ham hock terrine with caper and raisin purée, followed by a hearty dish of vine-smoked pheasant breast with celeriac and red cabbage. Fish might include roast cod with seasonal vegetables and mussel chowder – and things end on an upbeat note with dark chocolate and Cointreau Arctic roll.

Chef Simon Woodrow **Seats** 55 **Times** 12-2.30/7-9, Closed 2 wks Xmas, D Sun-Thu **Prices** Fixed L 2 course fr £18.95, Starter £6.95-£9.95, Main £14.95-£18.95, Dessert £6.95 **Wines** 6 bottles over £30, 11 bottles under £30, 13 by glass **Parking** 50 **Notes** Fri D 3 course £27.95, Sunday L, Vegetarian available, Children welcome

Maison Bleue

◎◎ Modern French

tel: 01284 760623 **30-31 Churchgate St IP33 1RG**
email: info@maisonbleue.co.uk
dir: *A14 junct 43 (Sugar Beet, Central exit) to town centre. Follow signs to the Abbey Gdns, Churchgate St is opposite cathedral*

Traditional and modern French seafood dishes

The Maison flies the tricolour for proudly French seafood cuisine in the bustling heart of Bury St Edmunds. The place is teemingly popular, indicating that the taste for unreconstructed Gallic cooking never went away. Start with a quenelle of poached chicken and blue cheese mousse accompanying a caramelised scallop garnished with truffle, or perhaps marinated langoustines with baby carrots and sprout leaves. The main deal arrives in the shape of sea bass with smoked onions in pumpkin velouté, or poached halibut with creamed mooli in Japanese dressing. There are meat dishes too – the beef featherblade is a cut above – and a study in chocolate and cherry to finish.

Chef Pascal Canevet **Seats** 60, Pr/dining room 35 **Times** 12-2/7-9, Closed Jan, 2 wks summer, Sun-Mon **Prices** Fixed L 2 course £19.50, Fixed D 3 course £35, Starter £7.95-£13.95, Main £19.95-£28.50, Dessert £7.95-£10.95 **Wines** 28 by glass **Parking** On street **Notes** Vegetarian available, Children welcome

BURY ST EDMUNDS *continued*

1921 Angel Hill

British NEW

tel: 01284 704870 **IP33 1UZ**
email: info@nineteen-twentyone.co.uk
dir: *A14 junct 43 (Sugar Beet, Central exit), 1921 at bottom of Northgate St on Angel Hill*

Simply refined cooking in historic centre

In a gloriously wonky period building that reflects the historical legacy of this ancient town, this decidedly up-to-date address is turning out inspired modern British food with seasonal and local ingredients to the fore. It all takes place in a room with a slick contemporary finish – nothing flash mind you, just smart and gently refined, with a keen and knowledgeable service team setting the tone. Sweet Mersea crab arrives in a prettily presented first course with tempura squid, fiery pickled mooli and avocado purée, followed by slow-cooked sirloin of beef with braised shin, salsify cannelloni and parsley purée. Finish with a celebration of summer in the form of strawberry consommé and lavender pannacotta. One to watch.

Chef Zack Deakins **Seats** 50, Pr/dining room 12 **Times** 12-2.15/6-9.15, Closed 23-30 Dec, Sun **Prices** Fixed L 2 course fr £15, Starter £6-£12, Main £16-£21, Dessert £6-£10 **Wines** 34 bottles over £30, 35 bottles under £30, 10 by glass **Parking** Ram Meadow or Angel Hill car parks **Notes** Vegetarian available, Children welcome

Pea Porridge

 Modern Bistro

tel: 01284 700200 **28-29 Cannon St IP33 1JR**
email: enquiries@peaporridge.co.uk
dir: *Off A14 towards town, in Northgate St turn left into Cadney Lane. Restaurant opposite Old Cannon Brewery*

Technically accomplished cooking of upbeat modern ideas

Two cottages dating from 1820 have been converted into this unpretentious restaurant where 'Simplicity' is key, although plenty of expertise goes into the cooking. Snails with bone marrow, bacon, parsley, capers and garlic is an alternative to something like lightly curried lamb's sweetbreads with kohlrabi and baby spinach. Main courses can be masterpieces of contrasting flavours: loin of muntjac deer, lightly cooked and rare, as requested, with butternut squash purée, beetroot, fondant potato and raisins spiked with harissa, or fillet of sea bream with spicy aubergine and tomato stew, brown shrimps and salsa verde. Puddings make just as much impact when there's champagne pannacotta with rhubarb, say, or tarte Tatin.

Chef Justin Sharp **Seats** 46, Pr/dining room 20 **Times** 12-2.30/6.30-10, Closed 2 wks Sep, 2 wks Xmas, Sun-Mon, L Tue **Prices** Fixed L 2 course £14.95, Fixed D 3 course £18.95, Starter £6.95-£9.75, Main £12.95-£21.95, Dessert £6.50-£8.50 **Wines** 15 bottles over £30, 25 bottles under £30, 9 by glass **Parking** On street **Notes** Vegetarian available, Children welcome

The White Horse

 Modern British

tel: 01284 735760 & 07778 996666 **Rede Rd, Whepstead IP29 4SS**
dir: *5m from Bury St Edmunds, 2m off A143 Bury/Haverhill*

Well-crafted, unfussy cooking in country gastropub

This stylishly made over, mustard-yellow village inn sits comfortably at the gastropub end of the spectrum, but without losing any of the features one hopes for – smart and cosy rooms with a copper-sheathed bar serving Suffolk ales, plus exposed beams, a huge inglenook and country-style tables. The kitchen here appreciates the value of top-class local ingredients, follows the seasons keenly, and cuts no corners, making everything from scratch (including their own bangers – how about pork, apple and sage?). From the blackboard menu, tuck into smoked haddock chowder, followed by the house steak burger or slow-cooked Suffolk ham hock with parsley sauce.

Chef Gareth Carter **Seats** 50, Pr/dining room 25 **Times** 12-2/7-9.30, Closed 25-26 Dec, D Sun **Prices** Prices not confirmed **Wines** 7 bottles over £30, 18 bottles under £30, 8 by glass **Parking** 30 **Notes** Sunday L, Vegetarian available, Children welcome

CAVENDISH **Map 13 TL84**

The George

Modern British

tel: 01787 280248 **The Green CO10 8BA**
email: thegeorgecavendish@gmail.com **web:** www.thecavendishgeorge.co.uk
dir: *A1092 into Cavendish, The George next to village green*

Med-inflected cooking in characterful inn

The handsome timbered George dates from the 16th century and is rooted into the fabric of its ancient Suffolk village. There are beams and bare-brick walls, but the understated Farrow & Ball neutral shades and classy cream seats combine in a tasteful, modern interior. The kitchen deals in no-nonsense modern comfort food with big, bold Mediterranean-inflected flavours that keep a keen eye on the seasons. You might start with ballotine of quail partnered with foie gras parfait, poached grapes and truffled mushroom toast, and follow with turbot fillet with saffron and spinach risotto, crab mousse and squid ink. Pudding could be a deliciously summery elderflower pannacotta with wild rose jelly.

DUNWICH **Map 13 TM47**

The Ship at Dunwich

Modern British

tel: 01728 648219 **St James St IP17 3DT**
email: info@shipatdunwich.co.uk **web:** www.shipatdunwich.co.uk
dir: *From N: A12, exit at Blythburgh onto B1125, then left to village. Inn at end of road. From S: A12, turn right to Westleton. Follow signs for Dunwich*

Locally based cooking in an ideally located coastal pub

Climbing foliage in the form of a trident adorns this red-brick pub in a coastal village. Surrounded by wild heathland and nature reserves, with a beach on hand and Southwold nearby, it's got the lot, including a garden with an ancient fig tree and a courtyard for outdoor dining. The menu takes in pork, pistachio and cherry terrine with onion marmalade to start, then slow-cooked pork belly with leek gratin, Lyonnaise potatoes, apple and date purée and red wine gravy to follow. At the end, try rich chocolate and beetroot cake with crème fraîche and boozy cherries, or fine East Anglian cheeses and home-made chutney.

Chef Sam Hanison **Seats** 70, Pr/dining room 35 **Times** 12-3/6-9 **Prices** Prices not confirmed **Wines** 3 bottles over £30, 19 bottles under £30, 8 by glass **Parking** 20 **Notes** Open all day for food Jul-Aug, Sunday L, Vegetarian available, Children welcome

FRESSINGFIELD Map 13 TM27

Fox & Goose Inn

Modern British

tel: 01379 586247 **Church Rd IP21 5PB**
email: foxandgoose@uk2.net
dir: *A140 & B1116 (Stradbroke) left after 6m, in village centre by church*

Village restaurant and bar with modern cooking

Fressingfield's timber-framed Tudor guild hall serves as the village inn, but if you want something more ambitious than well-crafted pub classics, head upstairs to the beamed restaurant for creative modern cooking driven by Suffolk's abundant larder. An opener of smoked salmon confit with apple and lemongrass consommé, coriander cress and coconut shows a kitchen aiming higher than the average pub offering. Mains include beef fillet with dauphinoise foam, roasted cauliflower, kale, sauté potatoes and red wine sauce, or slow-cooked hake with oyster mushrooms, potato gnocchi, shaved fennel, mushroom ketchup and lobster sauce. Finish with warm treacle and hazelnut tart with marinated prunes and vanilla ice cream.

Chef P Yaxley, M Wyatt **Seats** 70, Pr/dining room 35 **Times** 12-2/7-8.30, Closed 25-30 Dec, 2nd wk Jan for 2 wks, Mon **Prices** Fixed L 2 course £15.95-£20, Fixed D 3 course £34, Tasting menu £50-£75 **Wines** 14 bottles over £30, 38 bottles under £30, 11 by glass **Parking** 15 **Notes** Tasting menu 8 course, Sunday L £20-£25, Vegetarian available, Children 9 yrs+ D

HINTLESHAM Map 13 TM04

Hintlesham Hall Hotel

Modern European V

tel: 01473 652334 **George St IP8 3NS**
email: reservations@hintleshamhall.com **web:** www.hintleshamhall.com
dir: *4m W of Ipswich on A1071*

Polished cooking in top-ranking country-house hotel

Hintlesham Hall is a beautifully proportioned building of three wings, the façade a 1720 addition to the 16th-century core. The kitchen displays originality not commonly seen in such surroundings. Pan-fried scallops are served with butternut squash purée, a salted sesame tuile and tarragon dressing, and venison haunch carpaccio could come with onion and goats' cheese croquettes, watercress essence and a port reduction. Main courses allow clearly defined flavouring: seared medallions of monkfish are accompanied by tiger prawns and a shellfish reduction, and slow-cooked pork belly, tenderloin and cheeks are helped along by star anise sauce. Dessert might bring pear and green tea sorbet with melon and passionfruit sauce.

Hintlesham Hall Hotel

Chef Alan Ford **Seats** 80, Pr/dining room 80 **Times** 12-2/7-9.30 **Prices** Fixed L 2 course £18, Fixed D 3 course £33, Starter £12, Main £25, Dessert £9 **Wines** 100 bottles over £30, 64 bottles under £30, 9 by glass **Parking** 80 **Notes** Sunday L £19.50-£25.50, Children 12 yrs+ D

HORRINGER Map 13 TL86

The Ickworth

Modern Mediterranean NEW V

tel: 01284 735350 **IP29 5QE**
email: info@ickworthhotel.co.uk
dir: *A14 junct 42, follow brown signs for Ickworth*

National Trust dining with a difference

When Frederick Hervey, 4th Earl of Bristol, lived here in the early 18th century, he commissioned the impressive Rotunda to house his treasures. Frederick's, the restaurant named after him, is not without its delights either, not least its traditional style, crisp white linen, floor-to-ceiling windows and highly professional service. Maybe that it's a child-free zone is another. From the modern European menu consider seared king scallops, crushed peapods, home-cured ham and lemon; glazed rump, slow-cooked belly and cheek of Blythburgh pork, black pudding hash, smoked onions and baby leeks; and chocolate brownie with Jaffa cake ice cream. The long wine list takes a well-considered global approach.

Chef Lee Cooper **Seats** 78, Pr/dining room 34 **Times** 12-2.30/6-9.30 **Prices** Fixed L 2 course £30, Fixed D 3 course £40, Starter £7.50-£12, Main £11-£27, Dessert £7.50-£9.50 **Wines** 53 bottles over £30, 19 bottles under £30, 13 by glass **Parking** 50 **Notes** Sunday L £17.50-£21, Children welcome

INGHAM Map 13 TL87

The Cadogan Arms

Traditional British

tel: 01284 728443 **The Street IP31 1NG**
email: info@thecadogan.co.uk **web:** www.thecadogan.co.uk
dir: *A134, 4m from Bury St Edmunds*

Well-executed dishes in stylish gastropub

Flexibility is key in this smartly revamped former coaching inn, whether you just want a jar of real ale in the bar, a grazing board to snack on, or a full-blown meal. The decor is stylish with subdued lighting, upholstered sofas and chairs, and the kitchen cooks with an eye to the seasons and local producers. The menu includes pub classics such as fish and chips, burgers and steaks and if you fancy something more ambitious, you might start with Cromer crab and smoked salmon doughnuts with saffron mayonnaise, followed by Blythburgh pork fillet with apple, celery, walnuts and gnocchi. Pudding could be apple and cinnamon brioche ravioli.

Chef Michael Bell **Seats** 72 **Times** 12-2.30/6-9.30, Closed 25-26 Dec **Prices** Starter £4.50-£7, Main £8.50-£18.50, Dessert £2-£6 **Wines** 8 bottles over £30, 37 bottles under £30, 18 by glass **Parking** 39 **Notes** Sunday L £4.50-£15.50, Vegetarian available, Children welcome

IPSWICH Map 13 TM14

Best Western Claydon Country House Hotel

Modern British V

tel: 01473 830382 **16-18 Ipswich Rd, Claydon IP6 0AR**
email: enquiries@hotelsipswich.com **web:** www.hotelsipswich.com
dir: *A14, junct 52 Claydon exit from rdbt, 300yds on left*

Modern British cooking close to Ipswich

Two old village houses were joined seamlessly together to form this friendly, small-scale hotel. The Victorian-style restaurant, with its darkwood tables and high-backed chairs, overlooks the gardens through a conservatory extension. The kitchen draws on locally-sourced produce as the bedrock of its unfussy European-accented modern British dishes, with some ideas from further afield. Expect starters along the lines of Thai-style fishcakes with lime and chilli dip and mains such as roast chicken breast with dauphinoise and white wine sauce, or seared sea bass fillet with tomato and basil sauce and Mediterranean vegetables. End with jam sponge pudding with custard, or lemon tart with mango sorbet.

Chef Frankie Manners **Seats** 40, Pr/dining room 85 **Times** 12-2/7-9.30 **Prices** Fixed L 3 course £18.95, Fixed D 3 course £26.95 **Wines** 5 by glass **Parking** 80 **Notes** Sunday L £9.95-£16.95, Children welcome

Mariners

French, Mediterranean

tel: 01473 289748 **Neptune Quay IP4 1AX**
email: info@marinersipswich.co.uk
dir: *Accessed via Key St. Follow brown tourist signs to waterfront*

Classic brasserie cooking on an ex-gunboat

Mariners has quite a history: built as a gunboat in Bruges in 1899, it was sunk in 1940, became a hospital ship in the 1950s and was an Italian restaurant in Ipswich before becoming a French brasserie in 1994, moored on Neptune Quay in the marina. The decor features polished brass, burnished wood, chandeliers, muted blue upholstery and crisp tablecloths. Start with boneless brill fillet, curried salmon mousse and baby spinach millefeuille with butternut squash emulsion. Progress to pan-fried fillet of Scottish salmon, creamy wild mushroom Carnaroli risotto, soft-poached egg, and finish on iced pistachio and almond nougat with red fruit coulis.

Milsoms Kesgrave Hall

Modern International V

tel: 01473 333741 **Hall Rd, Kesgrave IP5 2PU**
email: reception@kesgravehall.com **web:** www.milsomhotels.com
dir: *A12 N of Ipswich/Woodbridge, rdbt onto B1214*

Boutique global modernism in the Suffolk woods

Hiding in woodland near Ipswich, this sparkling-white boutique hotel has verandah seating out front. Once inside the Brasserie dining room with its open kitchen and plain wooden tables, you write down your food order and take it to the bar for service. An extensive menu of global modernism kicks off with the likes of Wagyu carpaccio with pickled kohlrabi and truffled crème fraîche. Spot-on timing elevates a main course of wild salmon with samphire, asparagus and broad beans into the big league, or there may be guinea fowl in tomato consommé with Savoy cabbage and pancetta crisps. Go trad for afters with apple and sultana crumble and vanilla ice cream.

Chef Aarron Skerritt, Stuart Oliver **Seats** 80, Pr/dining room 24 **Times** 12-9.30, All-day dining **Prices** Starter £6.50-£12.50, Main £12.50-£26.50, Dessert £6.50-£7 **Wines** 38 bottles over £30, 43 bottles under £30, 18 by glass **Parking** 150 **Notes** Breakfast, Brunch, Afternoon tea, Sunday L, Children welcome

Salthouse Harbour Hotel

Modern British

tel: 01473 226789 **No 1 Neptune Quay IP4 1AX**
email: reservations@salthouseharbour.co.uk **web:** www.salthouseharbour.co.uk
dir: *A14 junct 53, A1156 to town centre & harbour, off Key St*

On-song brasserie flavours on the harbourside

A harbourside warehouse makeover in red brick with eye-popping interior collisions of lime-green and violet, the Salthouse deals in brasserie food with look-at-me flavours. Cured trout with fennel and pickled beetroot, or a sauté of wild mushrooms with parmesan and truffle on sourdough toast, are precursors to duck breast, pork belly and cod, the last appearing in Spanish guise with butter beans, spinach and chorizo. A gin and tonic arrives a little later than is conventional, in a dessert of apple and Hendrick's jelly, with cucumber sorbet and lime granita, while the braised pineapple is alive with chilli. Old-school reassurance is on hand in the form of sticky toffee pudding.

Chef Chris McQuitty **Seats** 70 **Times** 12-10, All-day dining **Prices** Fixed L 2 course £14, Fixed D 2 course £17.95, Starter £6.50-£11, Main £13-£23, Dessert £6-£8 **Wines** 42 bottles over £30, 23 bottles under £30, 31 by glass **Parking** Fore St, Duke St, along waterfront **Notes** Breakfast £14, Afternoon tea £17.50, Sunday L £20-£25, Vegetarian available, Children welcome

IXWORTH Map 13 TL97

Theobalds Restaurant

Modern British

tel: 01359 231707 **68 High St IP31 2HJ**
dir: *7m from Bury St Edmunds on A143 (Bury to Diss road)*

Seasonal modern British food in a beamed Tudor room

Theobald's Restaurant was converted from a whitewashed Tudor inn in 1981 and the place still pulls in diners with its consistency and attention to detail. Ancient beams abound and tables are dressed in pristine white. There's a monthly-changing carte, so February's offerings might bring the warmth and comfort of a twice-baked cheddar cheese soufflé with a crisp cheesy top, followed by roast breast and braised leg of Gressingham duck with caramelised apples, golden sultanas and port wine sauce. Locally reared meats and East Anglian fish are the mainstays, and the quality of raw materials is indisputable. Dessert could be a brioche bread-and-butter pudding with prune and Armagnac ice cream.

Chef Simon Theobald **Seats** 42, Pr/dining room 16 **Times** 12.15-1.30/7-9, Closed 10 days in spring/summer, Mon, L Tue-Thu, Sat, D Sun **Prices** Fixed D 3 course £29.50-£32.50, Tasting menu £33.50-£37.50 **Wines** 16 bottles over £30, 34 bottles under £30, 7 by glass **Parking** On street **Notes** Fixed L Fri, Fixed D Tue-Sat, Sunday L, Vegetarian available, Children 8 yrs+ D

LAVENHAM Map 13 TL94

Lavenham Great House 'Restaurant with Rooms'

Modern French

tel: 01787 247431 **Market Place CO10 9QZ**
email: info@greathouse.co.uk **web:** www.greathouse.co.uk
dir: *In Market Place (turn onto Market Lane from High Street)*

Modern French cooking in a medieval building

Lavenham is a beautiful market town with some truly fabulous and historic buildings, and the Great House is certainly one of them. Concealed behind the fine Georgian facade is a much older structure, dating to the 14th and 15th centuries. It's been a successful part of the local dining scene for the blink of an eye in comparison, but you can't argue with chef-patron Regis Crepy's 30-odd years at the top. There are period details throughout, but the dining room is a soothingly contemporary space, with pale panelled walls, comfortable seating, ancient oak floorboards and brick inglenooks. It may seem utterly English, but the techniques that underpin the cooking are entirely French. The smart front-of-house team serve an elegantly creative menu that might begin with Scottish beef tartare, capers, shallots, roasted bone marrow and toast, or baked Manx queenies with Jerusalem artichoke espuma, crunchy red beetroot, Tahitian vanilla pod and lime butter sauce. Follow with Suffolk pheasant breast, seared glazed salsify and sautéed wild chanterelles, or pan-fried fillet of halibut, carrot and cumin mash, and orange and coriander butter sauce. Finish with the 10-hours slow-cooked Braeburn apple with cider and Calvados, salted butter caramel and cinnamon ice cream.

Chef Regis Crepy **Seats** 40, Pr/dining room 15 **Times** 12-2.30/7-9.30, Closed Jan & 2 wks summer, Mon, L Tue, D Sun **Prices** Fixed L 2 course £19.95, Fixed D 3 course £36.50, Starter £11.95-£14.95, Main £19.95-£29.95, Dessert £7.95-£10 **Wines** 65 bottles over £30, 75 bottles under £30, 11 by glass **Parking** Market Place **Notes** Sunday L £36.50, Vegetarian available, Children welcome

The Swan at Lavenham Hotel and Spa

Modern, Traditional British NOTABLE WINE LIST

tel: 01787 247477 **High St CO10 9QA**
email: info@theswanatlavenham.co.uk **web:** www.theswanatlavenham.co.uk
dir: *From Bury St Edmunds take A134 (S) for 6m then take A1141 to Lavenham*

Modernist cooking beneath a medieval minstrels' gallery

Dating back to the 15th century, this characterful, asymmetrical timbered building is full of beams and period charm. The main restaurant is the Gallery, named for the medieval minstrels' balcony that can still be seen. The setting might be historic but the food is distinctly modern, and the menu might begin with salt-baked beetroot, caramelised walnuts, port-soaked blue cheese and berries, while mains could take in a trio of Suffolk pork with winter vegetables, or seared halibut with white fish cannelloni, braised turnips, shrimps and razor clams. Vanilla parfait with elderflower jelly and textures of raspberry shows the style at dessert.

Chef Justin Kett **Seats** 90, Pr/dining room 32 **Times** 12-2.30/7-9.30 **Prices** Fixed D 3 course £29.50, Starter £12.50, Main £23, Dessert £9-£12 **Wines** 111 bottles over £30, 32 bottles under £30, 11 by glass **Parking** 50 **Notes** Breakfast fr £13.95, High tea Mon-Sat, Sunday L £27.95, Vegetarian available, Children 5 yrs+

LONG MELFORD Map 13 TL84

Long Melford Swan

Modern, Contemporary British V

tel: 01787 464545 **Hall St CO10 9JQ**
email: info@longmelfordswan.co.uk **web:** www.longmelfordswan.co.uk
dir: *Phone for directions*

Confident modern cooking in stylish village restaurant

Slap bang in the middle of the high street, this elegant restaurant with rooms has undergone a complete refurbishment. In the kitchen, the ambitious young team conjure innovative combinations from tip-top ingredients. Global creativity is demonstrated in a flavour-packed starter of duck consommé, pork and prawn dumplings, chilli, ginger and pak choi. The flair and dexterity of the kitchen is equally evident in a main course of free-range pork loin teamed with chargrilled monkfish cheek, oyster mushroom, cider and mustard velouté and Ibérico ham. For those with more conservative palates, classic moules marinère is served in two sizes and simply grilled steaks and fish. Banana parfait makes a satisfying conclusion.

Chef Oliver Macmillan, Tom Bushell **Seats** 50, Pr/dining room 8 **Times** 12-2.30/6-9 **Prices** Fixed L 2 course fr £15.95, Starter £6.50-£12.50, Main £14-£23, Dessert £3.50-£7.50 **Wines** 30 bottles over £30, 35 bottles under £30, 20 by glass **Parking** On street **Notes** Brunch, Sunday L, Children welcome

LOWESTOFT Map 13 TM59

The Crooked Barn Restaurant

Modern British

tel: 01502 501353 **Ivy House Country Hotel, Ivy Lane, Beccles Rd, Oulton Broad NR33 8HY**
email: aa@ivyhousecountryhotel.co.uk **web:** www.ivyhousecountryhotel.co.uk
dir: *A146 into Ivy Lane*

Locally based cooking in a thatched barn

A 16th-century barn, its ceiling exposed to the rafters, is the destination eatery of Ivy House Country Hotel, set in 20 acres of grounds on Oulton Broad. The kitchen makes excellent use of the region's produce in some eclectic dishes. Start with a modern combo such as pan-fried scallops partnered by chorizo with split pea purée and chilli jam. Main-course fillet of beef is served in classical style with béarnaise, Lyonnaise potatoes, carrots and mange-tout, while fillet of lemon sole comes in rolls atop a herby potato cake alongside buttery brown shrimps, asparagus and peas. End with coffee mousse with oranges soaked in Tia Maria.

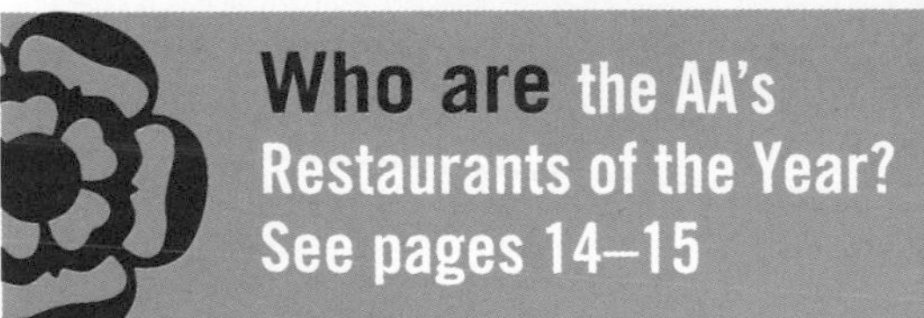

MILDENHALL Map 12 TL77

The Bull Inn

Modern British

tel: 01638 711001 **The Street, Barton Mills IP28 6AA**
email: reception@bullinn-bartonmills.com **web:** www.bullinn-bartonmills.com
dir: *Off A11 between Newmarket & Mildenhall, signed Barton Mills. Inn by Five Ways rdbt*

Funkiness in abundance in a multi-purpose pub

The Bull was the AA's Funkiest B&B of the Year last season, an attribute that is unmistakable from one glance at the menu. Brie fritters in berry coulis, smoked salmon Caesar, or ham and leek terrine with a beetroot-pickled egg make assertive openers to the main event, which might be a burger with optional garlic prawn skewer, or perhaps halibut with a backing trio of scallops in apple and vanilla Madeira jus. If you forsake the 500-year-old dining rooms for the bar or the great outdoors, the repertoire extends to pub classics such as chicken curry or sausages and mash. Finish with Baileys' and Amaretto cheesecake with coffee ice cream.

Chef Cheryl Hickman, Shaun Jennings **Seats** 60, Pr/dining room 30 **Times** 12-9, All-day dining, Closed 25-26 Dec **Prices** Prices not confirmed **Wines** 16 bottles over £30, 24 bottles under £30, 11 by glass **Parking** 60 **Notes** Sunday L, Vegetarian available, Children welcome

See advert opposite

NEWMARKET Map 12 TL66

Bedford Lodge Hotel

Modern International

tel: 01638 663175 **Bury Rd CB8 7BX**
email: info@bedfordlodgehotel.co.uk **web:** www.bedfordlodgehotel.co.uk
dir: *From town centre take A1304 towards Bury St Edmunds, hotel 0.5m on left*

Classy and inventive dishes near the famous racecourse

This extended one-time Georgian hunting lodge has a prime position near the racecourse and enough top-end facilities to satisfy a modern epicure. Start with corn-fed chicken and ham hock with pickled mushrooms, cauliflower purée, caper berries and shallot crisps, or perhaps honey-glazed duck with fondant potato, sprouting broccoli, cherries and almond praline. A busy main course showcasing red mullet comes with fresh herbs and lemon, a crab bonbon, Jerusalem artichoke, beetroot, crayfish velouté and white radish. Finish with a fun 'sweet shop' dessert comprising strawberry and bubble gum pannacotta, banana marshmallow, candyfloss, orange sherbet and macaroons, all exploding with colour, texture and sound effects.

Chef James Fairchild **Seats** 60, Pr/dining room 150 **Times** 12-9.30, All-day dining, Closed L Sat **Prices** Prices not confirmed **Wines** 93 bottles over £30, 30 bottles under £30, 16 by glass **Parking** 150 **Notes** Sunday L, Vegetarian available, Children welcome

The Packhorse Inn

Modern British

tel: 01638 751818 **Bridge St, Moulton CB8 8SP**
email: info@thepackhorseinn.com **web:** www.thepackhorseinn.com
dir: *A14 junct 39 onto B1506. After 1.5m turn left at x-rds onto B1085 (Moulton Rd). In Moulton, left into Bridge St*

Classy modern pub food in a stylishly reinvented country inn

The Rosette award for this establishment has been suspended due to a change of chef. Reassessment will take place in due course under the new chef. What was a traditional country pub in a village not far from the racing at Newmarket has been glossily boutiqued into a stylish eight-bedroom inn, although the bar at its heart still manages to do sterling service as Moulton's watering-hole. It all looks a sight for sore eyes, particularly when lit up at night. In the kitchen, meanwhile, they're avid for Suffolk produce from land and sea, which gets turned into elegant, vividly colourful dishes that exert a strong appeal to modern tastes. The brasserie-format menu has many populist touches, from the pork scratchings or croque monsieur appetisers to the platter of 'retro desserts' made for sharing. Elsewhere, today's earthy, gutsy preferences are celebrated in a salad of truffled goats' cheese, beetroot, pear and hazelnuts, and mains such as stone bass with razor clams, chicory and carrots, or local venison loin with blackberries and boulangère potatoes, are equally well-considered. A separate section of house favourites naturally takes in salmon fishcakes, rib-eye steaks and burgers, but also chicken breast with pancetta, white beans and mushrooms. If the retro desserts aren't your bag, look to dark chocolate torte with clementine sorbet, or start on the mini-nibbles – variously flavoured fruit pastilles or custard doughnuts.

Seats 65, Pr/dining room 32 **Times** 12-2.30/7-9.30, Closed D 25 Dec, 1 Jan **Prices** Prices not confirmed **Wines** 74 bottles over £30, 36 bottles under £30, 18 by glass **Parking** 30 **Notes** Sunday L, Vegetarian available, Children welcome

NEWMARKET *continued*

Tuddenham Mill

Modern British V NOTABLE WINE LIST

tel: 01638 713552 **High St, Tuddenham St Mary IP28 6SQ**
email: info@tuddenhammill.co.uk **web:** www.tuddenhammill.co.uk
dir: *M11 junct 9 towards Newmarket, then A14 exit junct 38 in direction of Norwich. Turn right at Herringswell road*

Imaginative cooking of unusual ingredients in a converted watermill

The mill still looks as if it could put in a hard day's work, but it's had a makeover. The riverside setting is positively serene and the contemporary decor within matches those views with original features and a clean, modern look. The bright, contemporary-style cooking features local and regional produce in creative dishes that utilise lots of modern culinary techniques. From the carte, for example, Worlington hen's egg enriches parsley soup among first courses, while North Sea hake arrives with mussel St Jacques and a sauce made of Debenham cider. Finish with lemon thyme rice pudding matched with Yorkshire rhubarb.

Chef Lee Bye **Seats** 54, Pr/dining room 18 **Times** 12-2.15/6.30-9.15 **Prices** Fixed L 2 course £15.50, Fixed D 3 course £19.50, Tasting menu £49.50, Starter £8-£9.50, Main £18-£26.50, Dessert £7.50-£11.50 **Wines** 138 bottles over £30, 33 bottles under £30, 13 by glass **Parking** 40 **Notes** Sunday L £19.50-£24.50, Children welcome

ORFORD **Map 13 TM45**

The Crown & Castle

Italian, British V NOTABLE WINE LIST

tel: 01394 450205 **IP12 2LJ**
email: info@crownandcastle.co.uk **web:** www.crownandcastle.co.uk
dir: *Off A12, on B1084, 9m E of Woodbridge*

Very good eating in a chic old Suffolk inn

There has been a hostelry on this site for 800 years, and today's incarnation, co-owned by Ruth Watson (she's also executive chef), one-time TV's Hotel Inspector, has an appealing combination of stylish bedrooms and an easy-going, rustic-chic restaurant. There's genuine character to the spaces within, where beams, unclothed wooden tables and comfortable cushioned chairs and benches help create a relaxed vibe. The daily-changing menu has an Italian accent these days, featuring the fashionable Venetian small plates, cicchetti, alongside flavour-driven dishes that showcase the region's excellent ingredients. Kick off with beef carpaccio with Harry's Bar dressing, then move on to chargrilled veal chop with sage butter, or pancetta-wrapped monkfish.

Chef Ruth Watson, Charlene Gavazzi **Seats** 60, Pr/dining room 10 **Times** 12.15-2.45/6.30-9.45 **Prices** Prices not confirmed **Wines** 73 bottles over £30, 57 bottles under £30, 14 by glass **Parking** 17, Market Sq, on street **Notes** Pre-concert supper (prior booking essential), Sunday L, Children 8 yrs+ D

SIBTON **Map 13 TM36**

Sibton White Horse Inn

Modern British

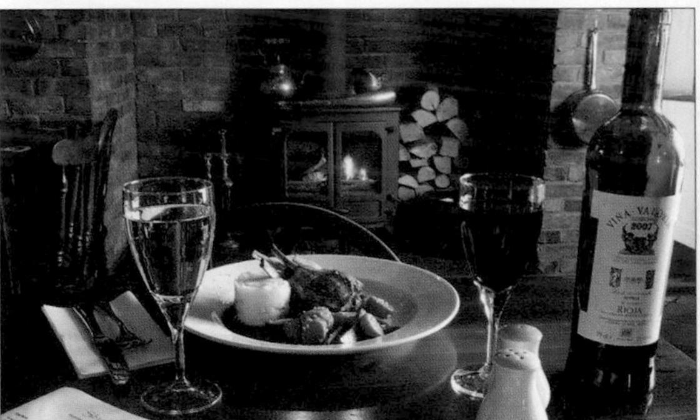

tel: 01728 660337 **Halesworth Rd IP17 2JJ**
email: info@sibtonwhitehorseinn.co.uk **web:** www.sibtonwhitehorseinn.co.uk
dir: *From A12 in Yoxford take A1120 signed Sibton & Peasenhall. 3m, in Peasenhall right opposite butcher's shop. White Horse 600mtrs*

Rustic 16th-century pub with modern global cooking

This fascinating pub's Tudor origins – low ceilings, mighty ships' timbers, quarry tiles – are impossible to miss. The bar has a raised gallery, an elegant dining room and a secluded courtyard. The kitchen produces globally influenced modern cooking that has won a heap of awards. So, how about confit of Gressingham duck roulade, duck liver parfait, roast celeriac and rhubarb chutney? Or you might prefer Blythburgh pork loin wrapped in Parma ham and braised belly, fondant potato, cavolo nero, chantenay carrots, black pudding fritter and grain mustard sauce. And let's not overlook lemon and pine nut parfait with confit orange, orange jelly and meringue for dessert.

Chef Gill Mason, Gareth Knights, Matt Lee **Seats** 40, Pr/dining room 18 **Times** 12-2/6.30-9, Closed 25-26 Dec, L Mon **Prices** Starter £6-£7.50, Main £12-£19.50, Dessert £6-£7.50 **Wines** 3 bottles over £30, 29 bottles under £30, 7 by glass **Parking** 50 **Notes** Sunday L £11.75-£15, Vegetarian available, Children 6 yrs+ D

SOUTHWOLD Map 13 TM57

Sutherland House

Modern British, Seafood

tel: 01502 724544 **56 High St IP18 6DN**
email: enquiries@sutherlandhouse.co.uk **web:** www.sutherlandhouse.co.uk
dir: *A1095 into Southwold, on High St on left after Victoria St*

Neighbourhood fish restaurant with diligent sourcing

A period property of genuine charm, Sutherland House has wooden beams, ornate ceilings, coving and real fireplaces, with fixtures and fittings creating a chic finish. Likewise, the cooking impresses with its modern ambitions, passion for seafood and loyalty to local ingredients. Start with the multiple flavours of treacle-cured salmon with ginger and lemongrass purée, radish, spring onions, pickled beetroot and dill crackers and move on to roast halibut fillet with bouillabaisse sauce and herby new potatoes. A meaty option might be slowly braised belly pork with black pudding, mash, apple fondant and cabbage, and dessert might deliver espresso pannacotta, with local cheeses a savoury alternative.

Chef Carl Slaymaker **Seats** 50, Pr/dining room 60 **Times** 12-2.30/7-9, Closed 25 Dec, 2 wks Jan, Mon **Prices** Prices not confirmed **Wines** 10 bottles over £30, 20 bottles under £30, 10 by glass **Parking** 1, On street **Notes** Sunday L, Vegetarian available, Children welcome

Swan Hotel

Modern British V

tel: 01502 722186 **High St, Market Place IP18 6EG**
email: swan.hotel@adnams.co.uk **web:** www.adnamshotels.co.uk
dir: *A1095 to Southwold. Hotel in town centre. Parking via archway to left of building*

Smart British cooking at Adnams' flagship hotel

Just in front of the Sole Bay brewery, the epicentre of the Adnams' empire's Southwold operations, is the Swan – a handsome bay-fronted hotel whose flagship restaurant has well-established supply lines to prime local materials, deployed in confident, full-flavoured cooking. Pumpkin and walnut tart is matched with a poached duck egg and grain mustard sabayon, or you might start with that time-honoured duo of seared scallops and home-made black pudding, partnered with celeriac purée, apple and walnuts. Main course brings a big-hearted dish of venison loin with herb mash, root vegetables and fig purée, sauced with port and orange. For pudding, there's big flavour in a fig and almond sponge.

Chef Rory Whelan **Seats** 65, Pr/dining room 36 **Times** 12-2.30/7-9 **Prices** Fixed L 2 course £15, Fixed D 3 course £35-£41.95, Starter £6-£9, Main £11-£22, Dessert £7-£8 **Wines** 8 by glass **Parking** 32 **Notes** Pre-theatre (summer only), Sunday L, Children welcome

Read all about our Wine Award winners on pages 17–19

STOKE-BY-NAYLAND Map 13 TL93

The Angel Inn

Modern British

tel: 01206 263245 & 07748 484619 **Polstead St CO6 4SA**
email: info@angelinnsuffolk.co.uk **web:** www.angelinnsuffolk.co.uk
dir: *From A134 onto Bear St (B1087), 2m on right in Stoke-by-Nayland*

A timbered Tudor pub goes modern British

A charming hostelry with quarry-tiled floors, exposed red-brick walls and a double-height ceiling in the dining area with oak beams and the original well. Fish dishes are nicely considered and well timed, from a slate-plated starter of seared scallops and tempura squid with chorizo dressing, to mains such as sea bass with saffron potatoes in seaweed butter. There are quality meats too, like saddle and confit leg of rabbit with smoked pancetta and butter bean ragout. Veggies might opt for chickpea and bean curry on saffron pilaf, while kids get their own menu. At close of business, the vanilla pannacotta is properly fragile and comes with lime-poached strawberries.

Chef Mark Allen **Seats** 60, Pr/dining room 10 **Times** 12-2.30/6-9.30 **Prices** Prices not confirmed **Wines** 12 bottles over £30, 14 bottles under £30, 10 by glass **Parking** 20 **Notes** Fish & Fizz Fri, Sunday L, Vegetarian available, Children welcome

The Crown

Modern British NOTABLE WINE LIST

tel: 01206 262001 **CO6 4SE**
email: info@crowninn.net **web:** www.crowninn.net
dir: *Stoke-by-Nayland signed from A12 & A134. Hotel in village off B1068 towards Higham*

Boutique hotel and village inn serving modern British food

Perfectly placed for exploring Constable country, the 16th-century Crown has morphed into a classy boutique inn with 11 swish bedrooms. The rambling beamed bar and dining areas sport a smart contemporary look with cockle-warming log fires. Monthly-changing modern British menus, supplemented by daily fish dishes on the chalkboard, reflect the seasons and show flair and imagination. Dinner might start with warm beetroot salad with chargrilled spring onions, Roquefort and focaccia croûtons, then continue with braised goat shoulder with roast garlic mash and purple sprouting broccoli. For pudding, lemon tart comes with lemon curd ice cream and raspberry beignets.

Chef Dan Hibble **Seats** 125, Pr/dining room 14 **Times** 12-2.30/6-9.30, Closed 25-26 Dec **Prices** Prices not confirmed **Wines** 244 bottles over £30, 76 bottles under £30, 32 by glass **Parking** 49 **Notes** Sunday L, Vegetarian available, Children welcome

SUDBURY Map 13 TL84

The Case Restaurant with Rooms

Modern British

tel: 01787 210483 **Further St, Assington CO10 5LD**
email: restaurant@thecaserestaurantwithrooms.co.uk
web: www.thecaserestaurantwithrooms.co.uk
dir: *On A134 between Sudbury & Colchester. 0.5m past Newton Golf Club*

Characterful Suffolk inn with brasserie-style menu

This charming country inn has a cosy little restaurant with a wood-burning stove, darkwood tables and ceiling beams. Host-led hospitality is the key to its success as well as the quality of the cooking. Start with one of the appealing first courses: perhaps a king prawn version of Caesar salad, or duck, orange and Grand Marnier pâté with caper berries. Mains might be poached fillet of plaice stuffed with salmon mousse accompanied by baby vegetables and new potatoes and roast shoulder of lamb on a bed of red cabbage and apple with redcurrant jus and mint-crushed potato. Puddings hit the mark in the shape of French apple tart with custard.

Chef Barry & Antony Kappes **Seats** 40 **Times** 8am-9pm, All-day dining, Closed L Mon, D Sun **Prices** Prices not confirmed **Wines** 7 bottles over £30, 19 bottles under £30, 14 by glass **Parking** 30 **Notes** Sunday L, Vegetarian available, Children welcome

THORPENESS Map 13 TM45

Thorpeness Golf Club & Hotel

Modern British

tel: 01728 452176 **Lakeside Av IP16 4NH**
email: info@thorpeness.co.uk **web:** www.thorpeness.co.uk
dir: *A1094 towards Aldeburgh, take coast road N for 2m*

Simple but sound cookery next to golf course

The heathland golf course adjacent to the sea was opened in 1922 and there are views over the third tee from the traditional and roomy restaurant (there's also a wood-panelled bar and a terrace with a watery vista). The daily-changing menu keeps things relatively simple, so you might start with tender ham hock with home-made remoulade and granary toast, or lemon and dill fishcake with chunky tartare sauce. Move on to pan-fried rib-eye with hand-cut chips and classic trimmings, or Thorpeness fish pie with cheesy mash and greens. Among desserts, chocolate profiteroles come filled with white chocolate cream and tangy lemon tart is served with lemon sorbet and raspberry coulis.

Chef Adam Thompson **Seats** 80, Pr/dining room 30 **Times** 12.30-3/7-9.30, Closed L Mon-Sat **Prices** Starter £5.50-£6.50, Main £13.50-£18.50, Dessert £5.50-£6.95 **Wines** 8 bottles over £30, 20 bottles under £30, 12 by glass **Parking** 80 **Notes** Sunday L £9.95-£17.95, Vegetarian available, Children welcome

WESTLETON Map 13 TM46

The Westleton Crown

 Modern British V 

tel: 01728 648777 **The Street IP17 3AD**
email: info@westletoncrown.co.uk **web:** www.westletoncrown.co.uk
dir: *A12 N, turn right for Westleton just after Yoxford. Hotel opposite on entering village*

Vibrant modern cooking in an ancient inn

This hotel, restaurant and pub, between Aldeburgh and Southwold, has its roots in the 12th century. 'Hearty yet sophisticated' cooking is the kitchen's aim, with the former apparent in chicken, leek and black pudding terrine with mustard dressing, then sirloin steak with all the trimmings. Asparagus with crispy bacon shavings, a herb-crumbed duck egg and aïoli is a starter with distinct, deep flavours, and might be followed by a nicely balanced main course of crisp-skinned fried sea trout fillet with asparagus, crushed potato and hollandaise. Ambition doesn't falter among puddings: expect chocolate and pistachio cake with chocolate sorbet and cherries.

Chef James Finch **Seats** 85, Pr/dining room 50 **Times** 12-2.30/6.30-9.30 **Wines** 23 bottles over £30, 21 bottles under £30, 9 by glass **Parking** 50 **Notes** Afternoon tea, Sunday L £19.95-£24.95, Children welcome

WOODBRIDGE Map 13 TM24

The Crown at Woodbridge

Modern European

tel: 01394 384242 **2 Thoroughfare IP12 1AD**
email: info@thecrownatwoodbridge.co.uk **web:** www.thecrownatwoodbridge.co.uk
dir: *A12 follow signs for Woodbridge onto B1438, after 1.25m from rdbt turn left into Quay Street & hotel on right, approx 100 yds from junct*

Intelligent contemporary cooking with East Anglia's fine produce

An expensive facelift relaunched The Crown as a stylish 21st-century inn back in 2009. The look is decidedly boutique, combining 16th-century features with a fresh, contemporary design ethos. The kitchen raids the Suffolk larder for its unfussy, big-hearted modern cooking. Local fish and seafood make a good showing on a wide-ranging menu, firstly in a duo of seared scallops with crispy pig's cheek jazzed up with jalapeño pepper-spiked gribiche and sauced with cider and caramel, followed by grilled skate wing with sautéed new potatoes, purple sprouting broccoli, and cockle and caper butter. Desserts get creative with rhubarb and blood orange jelly with ginger pannacotta, rhubarb and ginger sorbet and gingerbread.

Chef Daniel Perjési **Seats** 60, Pr/dining room 20 **Times** 12-2.30/6-9, Closed D 25 Dec (available for residents only) **Prices** Fixed L 2 course £15, Fixed D 3 course £20-£35, Starter £7-£8.50, Main £14-£24, Dessert £6.50-£9 **Wines** 58 bottles over £30, 31 bottles under £30, 26 by glass **Parking** 30 **Notes** Afternoon tea, Brunch, Sunday L £20-£25, Vegetarian available, Children welcome

Seckford Hall Hotel

Modern European, British

tel: 01394 385678 **IP13 6NU**
email: reception@seckford.co.uk **web:** www.seckford.co.uk
dir: *Hotel signed on A12 (Woodbridge bypass). Do not follow signs for town centre*

Modern country house cooking in a Tudor mansion

Approached by a sweeping drive through well-preened grounds, this blue-blooded Tudor pile impresses with its creeper-curtained brick façade, soaring chimneys and carved-oak front door. Culinary style is classical country house with a contemporary sensibility, offering starters like ham hock and parsley terrine with a crispy quail's egg and pickles, followed by roast pork tenderloin with fondant potato, Savoy cabbage, and a dried ham and cider sauce, or pan-roasted cod with wild garlic, pommes Anna, purple sprouting broccoli, shallots and red wine jus. Desserts might bring the old-school comforts of lemon meringue, or seek inspiration from the continent for a vanilla pannacotta with cherries, and an Amaretto and almond tuile.

Chef Ben Varszegi **Seats** 85, Pr/dining room 150 **Times** 12.30-2.30/7-9.30 **Prices** Fixed L 2 course fr £17.50, Fixed D 3 course fr £35, Tasting menu fr £45, Starter £6.70-£12.50, Main £18.95-£26.50, Dessert £6.95-£8.50 **Wines** 11 by glass **Parking** 100 **Notes** Sunday L fr £23, Vegetarian available, Children welcome

YAXLEY Map 13 TM17

The Auberge

Traditional, International

tel: 01379 783604 **Ipswich Rd IP23 8BZ**
email: aubmail@the-auberge.co.uk **web:** www.the-auberge.co.uk
dir: *5m S of Diss on A140*

Well-crafted dishes in a medieval Suffolk inn

Ancient beams, panelling and exposed brickwork dating back to medieval times are clear evidence that this was an inn for many centuries, but the name describes today's modern restaurant with rooms. The room is darkly intimate; tables are crisply laid with linen and lit by candles, and as the name would suggest, French influences underpin modern, skilfully rendered food that makes a virtue of simplicity. Start perhaps with Binham Blue cheese beignets with onion salad, before moving to braised ox cheek and seared beef fillet with marrowbone. Desserts go unashamedly for the populist vote, via plum pudding served with mulled wine sabayon.

Chef John Stenhouse, Mark Bond **Seats** 60, Pr/dining room 20 **Times** 12-2/7-9.30, Closed Sun, L Mon, Sat **Prices** Fixed L 2 course fr £18, Fixed D 3 course fr £26.50, Starter £5.50-£9.30, Main £15-£30, Dessert £6.95 **Wines** 22 bottles over £30, 28 bottles under £30, 13 by glass **Parking** 25 **Notes** Vegetarian available, Children welcome

SURREY

BAGSHOT Map 6 SU96

The Brasserie at Pennyhill Park

Modern British

tel: 01276 471774 & 478569 **Pennyhill Park Hotel & The Spa, London Rd GU19 5EU**
email: enquiries@pennyhillpark.co.uk
dir: *M3 junct 3, through Bagshot, left onto A30. 0.5m on right*

A contemporary take on the brasserie theme

The Brasserie is an informal and relaxed alternative to Pennyhill Park's high-flying Latymer. A colourful, stone-walled room, with bright banquettes and lots of windows, overlooks the pool and the huge spa complex. It's a swish setting for lively modern cooking offering a fresh spin on the brasserie repertoire, pairing rabbit terrine with confit leek, date purée, apple and pickled shimeji mushroom. Main courses deliver punchy, tightly-defined flavours, whether you go for classic grilled steaks, or a more enterprising dish of lamb rump roasted in parmesan crust, alongside peperonata, aubergine caviar, garlic purée with lamb sweetbreads and violet potato. Finish with a textbook crème brûlée and lemon madeleine.

Matt Worswick at The Latymer

Modern British V NOTABLE WINE LIST

tel: 01276 471774 & 486156 **Pennyhill Park Hotel & The Spa, London Rd GU19 5EU**
email: enquiries@pennyhillpark.co.uk **web:** www.exclusivehotels.co.uk
dir: *M3 junct 3, through Bagshot, left onto A30. 0.5m on right*

Stunningly crafted contemporary cooking in a luxurious hotel

Pennyhill Park seems to be an ever-expanding enterprise, with corporate jollies, spa aficionados, golfers and the England rugby union team, who use it as a training base, passing regularly through its doors. Fortunately, the Victorian estate has 120 acres to wander, and is naturally equipped with a fine dining venue, now under the aegis of Liverpool-born Matt Worswick, who has cooked his way around some of our most Rosette-laden kitchens. His tasting menus are among the more eye-catching, opening with sesame-dressed octopus and peanut purée to get the taste buds racing ahead of grilled red mullet, timed to the second and served with baby squid and brown crab foam. A veg dish comes next, perhaps salt-baked celeriac with truffle ice cream, and then loin and delicious crispy tongue of hogget with gremolata, asparagus and morels. The dessert composition is designed to end things on a fragrant note with caramelised lemon cream, lemon sorrel granita, buckwheat shortbread and meringue. Incidentals are clearly intended to win friends and influence people too, when appetisers run to smoked baba ganoush with cardamom yogurt in a savoury cornet topped with Bombay mix, and breads, which are also top-notch, come with both unsalted butter and whipped beef dripping dusted with onion powder.

Chef Matt Worswick **Seats** 40, Pr/dining room 8 **Times** 12.30-2/7-9, Closed 1st 2 wks in Jan, Mon-Tue, L Wed, Sat-Sun **Prices** Prices not confirmed **Wines** 300 bottles over £30, 20 by glass **Parking** 500 **Notes** No children

CAMBERLEY Map 6 SU86

Macdonald Frimley Hall Hotel & Spa

British, European

tel: 01276 413100 **Lime Av GU15 2BG**
email: general.frimleyhall@macdonald-hotels.co.uk
web: www.macdonaldhotels.co.uk/frimleyhall
dir: *M3 junct 3, A321 follow Bagshot signs. Through lights, left onto A30 signed Camberley & Basingstoke. To rdbt, 2nd exit onto A325, take 5th right*

Gentle modernist cooking at the home of Coal Tar Soap

The handsome mansion not far off the M3 was once home to William Valentine Wright, the man who gave Britain Coal Tar Soap. Its Linden restaurant has an intimate candlelit ambience in the evenings. A modern menu juxtaposes pressed corn-fed chicken terrine with rhubarb three ways and gingerbread, before main-course choices that take in fried hake fillet with truffled potato crush in lemon butter, or baked guinea fowl with a croquette of rosemary polenta in wild mushroom jus. Thoroughbred Scottish steaks are a popular feature, as are the intriguing desserts, which include chocolate and cherry cheesecake with popping chocolate soil, and 'torn' lemon sponge with crème fraîche sorbet.

CHOBHAM — Map 6 SU96

Stovell's

@@@@ – see opposite

DORKING — Map 6 TQ14

Emlyn at the Mercure Burford Bridge

@ Modern British

tel: 01306 884561 **Burford Bridge, Box Hill RH5 6BX**
email: emlyn@accor.com **web:** www.mercure.com
dir: *M25 junct 9, A245 towards Dorking. Hotel within 5m on A24*

Stylish take on classic flavours

A new chef has arrived, joined by a brand-new kitchen team here at the Mercure Burford Bridge, and they plan to shake things up with a new concept for the restaurant, blending classic flavours with modern techniques. The Emlyn is a white-walled room with curved banquettes in lilac, and you can expect a similarly fresh and stylish approach to the food. Begin with truffle risotto with duck egg yolk and pecorino, perhaps, and then move on to sea bass with Chinese broccoli, prawn dumpling dashi and soba noodles, or polenta with butternut squash, hazelnuts, Lancashire Bomb cheese and spinach.

Chef Nick Sinclair **Seats** 60, Pr/dining room 200 **Times** 12-2.30/7-9.30, Closed 1st wk Jan, L Mon, D Sun **Prices** Fixed L 2 course £19.95, Fixed D 3 course fr £23.95, Tasting menu £55-£90, Starter £8-£12, Main £17-£29, Dessert £6-£11 **Wines** 23 bottles over £30, 11 bottles under £30, 17 by glass **Parking** 140 **Notes** Vegetarian tasting menu, Sunday L £24.50-£29.50, Vegetarian available, Children welcome

Two To Four

@@ Modern European V

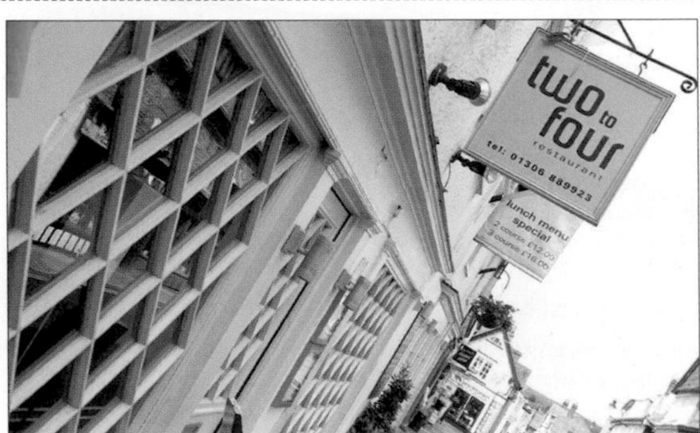

tel: 01306 889923 **2-4 West St RH4 1BL**
email: two_to_four@hotmail.co.uk **web:** www.2to4.co.uk
dir: *M25, exit at Leatherhead junct, follow signs to town centre*

Modern cooking in a thriving neighbourhood venue

Occupying a period building in the town centre, this is the sort of friendly restaurant we would all like on our manor. First-class ingredients are the name of the game in a repertoire of uncomplicated modern European-style dishes, all realised with technical verve. Mussels with chorizo and saffron and coriander cream is one starter, or more complex confit pig's cheek with truffled parsnip purée, pistachio powder, Parma ham and thyme jus. Main courses take in monkfish fillet with a grilled langoustine, shrimp bisque and courgettes, or beef fillet with marrowbone, bavarois sauce and asparagus. For dessert, try banana brûlée, glace and cromesquis with caramel popcorn.

Chef Rob Gathercole **Seats** 70, Pr/dining room 12 **Times** 12-2/6.30-10, Closed Xmas, Mon (subject to change) **Prices** Fixed L 2 course £12, Fixed D 2 course £19, Tasting menu £65, Starter £7.50-£9.95, Main £14-£24.95, Dessert £2.50-£8.50 **Wines** 21 bottles over £30, 19 bottles under £30, 8 by glass **Parking** West St car park **Notes** Children welcome

EGHAM — Map 6 TQ07

The Estate Grill at Great Fosters

@@ Modern British

tel: 01784 433822 **Stroude Rd TW20 9UR**
email: reception@greatfosters.co.uk
dir: *A30 (Bagshot to Staines) right at lights by Wheatsheaf pub into Christchurch Rd. Straight on at rdbt (pass 2 shop parades on right). Left at lights into Stroude Rd. Hotel 0.75m on right*

Ingredient-led and confident modern cooking

The Estate Grill chefs use Old Spots pigs reared in the grounds and honey from the apiary, as well as Cumbrian fell-bred lamb. The brasserie menu kicks off with excellent smoked pork with langoustines, apple and turnip, or beef tartare with a duck egg and potato mousse. Then try whole plaice with capers and parsley or 28-day aged rib-eye steak with béarnaise, creamy mash and truffle shavings for main. Sharing platters are possibilities – charcuterie to start and a selection of estate-reared pork for main – and meals end with winning puddings like ginger-flavoured rhubarb mousse with ice cream and parkin, and treacle tart with pear and chamomile sorbet.

Chef Marc Hardiman **Seats** 44, Pr/dining room 20 **Times** 12.30-2.30/5.30-9.30 **Prices** Starter £8-£18, Main £21-£34, Dessert £9 **Wines** 80 bottles over £30, 14 bottles under £30, 15 by glass **Parking** 200 **Notes** Sunday L £28-£35, Vegetarian available, Children welcome

Stovell's

CHOBHAM **Map 6 SU96**

Modern European, Contemporary

tel: 01276 858000 **125 Windsor Rd GU24 8QS**
email: enquiries@stovells.com **web:** www.stovells.com
dir: *M25 junct 11. Join A317 then take A320 towards Chobham, A319 turn right Windsor Road*

Exhilarating modern food in a Tudor farmhouse

Located in a renovated 500-year-old Tudor farmhouse in Surrey since 2012, Fernando Stovell's restaurant has gathered plaudits from day one. The whole operation is driven by a passionate enthusiasm for food and drink – they even distil their own organic gin. Inside, the place presents a gnarled picture attesting to its venerable age, all head-skimming ceilings and whitewashed brick walls punctuated by contorted black beams, complemented by contemporary-styled pictures of mushrooms. The pairing of unusual flavours and textures is clearly a passion, requiring an arsenal of skills to prepare and there's serious technical ability in the kitchen, supported by the proper kit, including a wood-fired oven, so the flavours ring true on the plate. Exhilarating virtuoso starters include warm aromatic foie gras with burnt grelot onions, toasted cobnuts, hay tea dressing and pennywort, or caramelised hand-dived scallops with kohlrabi and pine nut purée. Next up, splendid North Sea halibut receives exotic treatment, steamed in miso butter and partnered with bok choy and langoustine dim sum, or rib of beef for two chargrilled over vine cuttings, or guinea fowl served with guanciale, charred squash and cavolo nero. Impressive desserts include fig tarte Tatin with brown butter ice cream and grilled orange syrup, or you could finish on a savoury note with perfectly ripened artisan cheeses. Service is by a young, knowledgeable team and a first-rate sommelier, who create a welcoming atmosphere.

Chef Fernando Stovell **Seats** 60, Pr/dining room 14
Times 12-3.30/6-10.30, Closed Mon, L Sat, D Sun **Prices** Fixed L 2 course £16.50, Fixed D 3 course £42, Tasting menu £65-£70
Wines 87 bottles over £30, 16 bottles under £30, 14 by glass
Parking 20 **Notes** Tasting menu with wine £100, Sunday L, Vegetarian available, Children welcome

EGHAM *continued*

the runnymede-on-thames

British NEW

tel: 01784 220600 **Windsor Rd TW20 0AG**
email: info@therunnymede.co.uk **web:** www.therunnymedehotel.com
dir: *M25 junct 3, on A308 Windsor road*

Breezy brasserie food at the riverside

The scene could hardly be more Wind in the Willows, with the Thames burbling by, and outdoor tables and parasols set out by Bell Weir lock that lends its name to the kitchen and bar. The parquet-floored brasserie room has a light, breezy ambience. Start with a modern classic rendition of scallops, perfectly seared top and bottom, on artichoke purée with grated apple, and sail on to herb-crusted rack of lamb of eloquent flavour, or perhaps halibut with braised leeks and spinach, sauced with cider. At the end, consider a chunk of buttery Bramley apple pie with cinnamon ice cream, or hot treacle sponge pud with butterscotch sauce.

Chef Adesh Bissonauth **Times** 12-3/6-9.30, Closed L Mon, Sat **Prices** Starter £6.50-£16, Main £13-£24, Dessert £6.50 **Wines** 12 bottles over £30, 15 bottles under £30, 11 by glass **Notes** Afternoon Tea, Sunday L £18.95, Vegetarian available, Children welcome

The Tudor Room

Modern European V

tel: 01784 433822 **Great Fosters, Stroude Rd TW20 9UR**
email: reception@greatfosters.co.uk **web:** www.greatfosters.co.uk
dir: *A30 (Bagshot to Staines) right at lights by Wheatsheaf pub into Christchurch Rd. Straight on at rdbt (pass 2 shop parades on right). Left at lights into Stroude Rd. Hotel 0.75m on right*

Creative cooking in a grand manor house

If first impressions count, Great Fosters is off to a flying start to winning your heart for the stately-looking property is positively magnificent – copious gables, soaring chimneys, Saxon moat, glorious landscaped gardens and all. With 50 acres to explore including a tennis court, croquet lawn and a heated outdoor pool, the place is achingly English and formal, and it's no surprise to hear it's a big hit on the wedding circuit. When it comes to dining, the intimate Tudor Room is all you might expect in this setting – richly decorated, plush and stylish, with a 17th-century tapestry as a striking feature. Head chef Douglas Balish can call on the estate to provide fresh fruit, vegetables and herbs, and what doesn't come from the grounds is bought with quality in mind. His menus combine a classical sensibility and respect for the ingredients alongside modern cooking techniques and well-measured creativity. Perfectly seared scallops arrive with broccoli purée, crunchy hazelnut and truffle shavings in a well-crafted first course, followed perhaps by 28-day aged beef with a fine sauce, or line-caught sea bass matched with tender chicken and fermented garlic. Among desserts, a dish of chocolate and mango shows technical accomplishment and a touch of showmanship.

Chef Douglas Balish **Seats** 24, Pr/dining room 20 **Times** 12.30-2/7-9.15, Closed 2 wks Jan, 2 wks Aug, Sun-Tue, L Wed-Thu, Sat **Prices** Prices not confirmed **Wines** 245 bottles over £30, 12 by glass **Parking** 200 **Notes** L 4 course £38, D 6 course £58, with wine £65, Children welcome

GUILDFORD Map 6 SU94

The Grantley Arms

Modern British NEW

tel: 01483 893351 **The Street, Wonersh GU5 0PE**
email: hello@thegrantleyarms.co.uk
dir: *Phone for directions*

The best of gastropub cooking in smart surroundings

With its profusion of beams and stripped-back modern look – chunky wooden tables, wood floors and heritage-grey paintwork – the Grantley Arms is the very image of a thriving gastropub. The bar menu deals in straight-talking crowd pleasers – venison sausage rolls, charcoal-grilled steaks and the like – but in the restaurant the kitchen delivers classy modern British cooking. Butter-poached langoustines with radish, sea herbs, cucumber and oyster mayonnaise is a vibrant starter, followed by cannon and braised belly of Herdwick lamb partnered with truffled potato and three-cornered garlic. Finish on a high note with Valrhona Opalys white chocolate crémeux with blackberry sorbet, pistachio and anise.

Chef Matthew Edmonds **Seats** Pr/dining room 20 **Times** 6-9, Closed L all week, D Sun-Mon **Prices** Fixed D 3 course £35 **Notes** Vegetarian available, Children welcome

The Mandolay Hotel

Modern European

tel: 01483 303030 **36-40 London Rd GU1 2AE**
email: info@guildford.com **web:** www.guildford.com
dir: *M25 junct 10, follow A3 (S) for 7m. At rdbt 3rd exit onto London Rd for 1m*

Inventive European-accented cooking in a smart setting

The restaurant of this smart hotel certainly looks swish, and the kitchen delivers a menu suffused with creativity, from a very good roast partridge with boudin (very well made and delicious), parsley root and bergamot to start to a thoroughly well-timed main course of turbot and sea vegetables, which features blossom petals that pair well with the excellent consommé. Other mains include duck with Jerusalem artichoke, turnips and wild mushrooms or squab pigeon with a beetroot carpaccio and clementine. The meal could be rounded off with a spot-on dessert of chocolate fondant with pistachio ice cream

Chef Mark Lawton **Seats** 60, Pr/dining room 300 **Times** 12-10, All-day dining **Prices** Starter £7-£15, Main £18-£31, Dessert £7-£15 **Wines** 32 bottles over £30, 36 bottles under £30, 28 by glass **Parking** 25, G Live car park **Notes** Pre-theatre menu, Afternoon tea, Sunday L £15-£30, Vegetarian available, Children welcome

HASLEMERE Map 6 SU93

Lythe Hill Hotel & Spa

Modern British, French

tel: 01428 651251 **Petworth Rd GU27 3BQ**
email: lythe@lythehill.co.uk **web:** www.lythehill.co.uk
dir: *1m E of Haslemere on B2131*

Inspired British modernism in a 15th-century farmhouse

The listed ancient farmhouse dates back to 1475, and some of the guest rooms retain architectural features from those times. In the kitchen, the style is innovative modern British dishes interlaced with populist classics. Charred mackerel is served with tartare sauce, mandarin gel, black olives and fennel. Main course stars seared beef fillet with black truffle-flavoured Anna potatoes, bone marrow bonbons, turnip, cep soil and bordelaise sauce; if you're in the mood for fish, there could be seared salmon with olive crushed potatoes with fine beans, tomato coulis and sauce vièrge. For dessert, there's a well-conceived and executed trio of chocolate ganache caramelised banana and peanut mousse.

HORLEY

For restaurant details see Gatwick Airport (London), (Sussex, West)

OTTERSHAW Map 6 TQ06

Foxhills

Modern, Traditional British

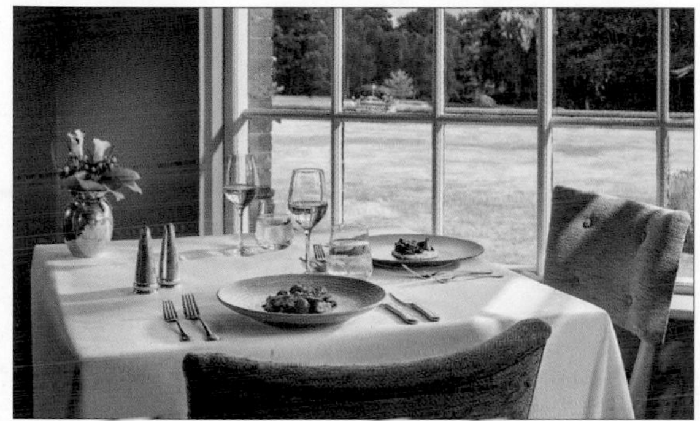

tel: 01932 704471 **Stonehill Rd KT16 0EL**
web: www.foxhills.co.uk
dir: *From M25 junct 11 take A320 to Woking. At 2nd rdbt take last exit Cobham Rd, right into Foxhills Rd, follow until T-junct, left into Stonehill Rd*

Contemporary cooking of vaulting ambition

This late-Georgian manor house was built by George Basevi, architect of London's Belgrave Square. With views over the balustraded lawns, the prospect is set fair for contemporary, ingredient-led cooking. A pasta starter combines the open lasagne and cannelloni principles for a richly earthy oxtail formula with baby leeks and beetroot, while langoustine could be chaperoned by pickled watermelon, carrot and pork crackling. Stone bass is also crisp-skinned, and comes with wafer-thin cauliflower and vine fruit, and there is further intrigue in a preparation of quail with truffled macaroni, pear, burnt leek and mushroom ketchup. Rhubarb crumble arrives in a tumbler, its crumb top covering layers of jelly and pannacotta.

Chef Luke Davis **Seats** 100 **Times** 12-2.30/6.30-9 **Prices** Fixed L 2 course £28-£36 **Wines** 96 bottles over £30, 25 bottles under £30, 17 by glass **Parking** 200 **Notes** ALC menu £60, Fixed D £36 Afternoon tea £22.50, Sunday L £32, Vegetarian available, Children welcome

REDHILL Map 6 TQ25

Nutfield Priory Hotel & Spa

Modern British

tel: 01737 824400 **Nutfield RH1 4EL**
email: nutfieldpriory@handpicked.co.uk **web:** www.handpickedhotels.co.uk/nutfieldpriory
dir: *On A25, 1m E of Redhill, off M25 junct 8 or M25 junct 6, follow A25 through Godstone*

New classic dishes in a Victorian Gothic house

Standing in 12 acres on Nutfield Ridge, the Priory is classic Victorian neo-Gothic, dating from the 1870s. The Cloisters has mullioned windows offering expansive views over the grounds and lake, and makes an appropriate backdrop for a refined, modern take on country-house cooking. You might start with lobster bisque with cannelloni of celeriac and lobster, then move on to a three-bone rack of lamb with pressed leek and potato gratin, red cabbage braised with plums, and garlic and rosemary crisps. Keen interest is maintained through to the many-layered desserts, which may include green banana parfait with salted sesame brittle and parsley ice cream.

Chef Alec Mackins **Seats** 60, Pr/dining room 60 **Times** 12.30-2/7-9.30 **Prices** Prices not confirmed **Wines** 84 bottles over £30, 11 bottles under £30, 26 by glass **Parking** 100 **Notes** Sunday L, Vegetarian available, Children welcome

REIGATE Map 6 TQ25

The Dining Room

Modern British

tel: 01737 226650 **59a High St RH2 9AE**
dir: *M25 junct 8/A217 follow one way system into High St. Restaurant on left*

Stimulating cooking on the High Street

Tony Tobin is well known to armchair chefs from his TV appearances and his restaurant has been a hit with foodies since 1993. Celeriac and apple risotto with smoked quail's breast and a poached quail's egg might appear among starters. Mains are all about pedigree materials: pan-roasted fillet of turbot, say, in a punchy surf-and-turf duo with braised oxtail, potato fondant, baby gem lettuce and a complementary kick from lemon oil, or beef fillet matched with cauliflower and potato dauphinoise, spinach, and truffle dressing. The inventive approach extends to puddings such as tonka bean and white chocolate mousse with chocolate soil, wattle seed ice cream and coffee jelly.

RIPLEY Map 6 TQ05

The Anchor

Modern British

tel: 01483 211866 **High St GU23 6AE**
email: info@ripleyanchor.co.uk **web:** www.ripleyanchor.co.uk
dir: *M25 junct 10 onto A3 towards Guildford, exit at junct for Ripley*

Relaxed dining pub with a side order of pedigree

The Anchor is a friendly gastropub in the modern idiom with a dusting of pedigree, with dark-wood furniture, slate floors and armchairs by a log-burner. The kitchen delivers simple dining-pub fare with creativity and panache. Dishes cover all the bases with a contemporary touch, for example starters of pressed ham hock and chorizo with squid and pineapple relish, and black pudding with a poached pear and pea purée. Sound technique is seen in braised ox cheek with roast sweet potato and mushroom spelt, and in pan-fried gurnard fillet with parsley sauce, grapes, celeriac and chard. To finish, try ginger rice pudding with roast plums.

Chef Michael Wall-Palmer **Seats** 46, Pr/dining room 8
Times 12-2.30/6-9.30, Closed Mon **Prices** Fixed L 2 course fr £15, Starter £6-£8, Main £12-£22, Dessert £6-£7 **Wines** 26 bottles over £30, 20 bottles under £30, 14 by glass **Parking** 14 **Notes** Supper menu 6-7pm, Sunday L £18-£19, Vegetarian available, Children welcome

Drake's Restaurant

Modern British NOTABLE WINE LIST

tel: 01483 224777 **The Clock House, High St GU23 6AQ**
email: info@drakesrestaurant.co.uk
dir: *M25 junct 10, A3 towards Guildford. Follow Ripley signs. Restaurant in village centre*

Modern cookery in a landmark Georgian house

The Rosette award for this establishment has been suspended due to a change of chef. Reassessment will take place in due course under the new chef. This is not a hard place to track down among the timbered houses in this well-heeled Surrey village – just look for the Georgian red-brick house with its landmark clock and gorgeous walled garden. The place has a light, understated feel offset by the rustic wood of doors and window frames. The kitchen presents an eclectic offering, driven first and foremost by considerations of flavour. There are some unusual juxtapositions at play here – but confidence, technical wizardry and good judgement mean that they work well together and each leaves a clear impression on the palate. Choose between two to four courses on the carte, otherwise 'Discovery' and 'Journey' are the two whole-table taster options, the latter opening intriguingly with cauliflower, hazelnut and caper berry, before Jerusalem artichoke alongside veal sweetbreads, watercress and cep biscuit. After a fish course such as brill with cucumber ketchup, lemon thyme and kohlrabi, it might be pheasant with apple cannelloni, celeriac and Wiltshire truffle. A pre-dessert, perhaps of rhubarb and custard, prepares the way for the grand finale uniting pear, cinnamon and hibiscus.

STOKE D'ABERNON Map 6 TQ15

Woodlands Park Hotel

Modern British

tel: 01372 843933 **Woodlands Ln KT11 3QB**
email: woodlandspark@handpicked.co.uk
web: www.handpickedhotels.co.uk/woodlandspark
dir: *A3 exit at Cobham. Through town centre & Stoke D'Abernon, left at garden centre into Woodlands Lane, hotel 0.5m on right*

Formal dining in a grand Victorian country house

Money was clearly no object for William Bryant, son of one of the founders of the match company, when he built this magnificent pile in 1885. It's set in landscaped grounds and gardens, and the squishy sofas of the Great Hall are great for people watching. Start with duck liver ballotine, its richness cut by sweet wine jelly, or leek and potato velouté with luxurious black truffle shavings. Main courses might be fillet and braised shoulder of lamb with goats' curd, roasted aubergine and caramelised cippolini onions, say, or pan-fried monkfish with spicy Puy lentils and tomato ragout. End with a textbook cherry clafoutis with clotted cream ice cream.

Chef Andrew Mackenzie **Seats** 35, Pr/dining room 150
Times 12-2.30/7-9.30, Closed L Mon-Sat **Prices** Prices not confirmed **Wines** 15 by glass **Parking** 150 **Notes** Sunday L, Vegetarian available, Children welcome

WARLINGHAM Map 6 TQ35

India Dining

 Modern Indian

tel: 01883 625905 **6 The Green CR6 9NA**
email: info@indiadining.co.uk
dir: *From M25 junct 6 follow signs Caterham then Warlingham*

Contemporary Indian cuisine in a cool setting

India Dining features a stylish cocktail bar, black leatherette banquettes, polished-wood tables and highly contemporary artworks. The authentic Pan-Indian cooking takes an equally creative, modern and upmarket approach. Take monkfish tikka to open, cooked in the tandoor, its peppy spicing not overwhelming the sparkling-fresh fish and cooled by a cucumber riata. Mains – like Bengali sea bass jhol – follow suit, accompanied by tangy-sweet lemon rice, while peripherals such as puppadoms, chutneys and breads are equally good. For meat lovers there's a Hyderabadi lamb biriyani and even sirloin chilli, while to finish, perhaps a passionfruit brûlée or chocolate fondant await.

Chef Asad Khan, Habibul Rahaman **Seats** 69 **Times** 12-2.30/5.30-11, Closed 1 Jan **Prices** Fixed L 2 course £19.95-£29.95, Fixed D 3 course £25-£60, Tasting menu fr £39.95, Starter £5.95-£11.95, Main £10.95-£26.95, Dessert £5.95-£9.95 **Wines** 20 bottles over £30, 32 bottles under £30, 12 by glass **Parking** On street, car park nearby **Notes** 2 dine 2 course with wine £29.95, Sunday L, Vegetarian available, Children welcome

WEYBRIDGE Map 6 TQ06

Brooklands Hotel

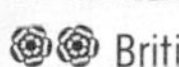 British, European

tel: 01932 335700 **Brooklands Dr KT13 0SL**
email: brasserie@brooklandshotelsurrey.com **web:** www.brooklandshotelsurrey.com
dir: *Phone for directions*

Striking modern hotel where British motor-racing began

This thrillingly modern structure overlooks the first purpose-built car-racing circuit in the world, opening back in 1907. There's a creative modern brasserie feel to the food, with the kitchen team keenly producing dishes that arrive dressed to thrill. Pan-fried scallops come with glazed pork belly, cauliflower purée and golden raisins, followed by pink and tender rump of lamb with Israeli couscous, smoked aubergine purée, and pomegranate seeds adding little tart explosions, or you might look to the grill for a straight-up steak – 28-day aged rib-eye, say, with the usual accompaniments. End on a tiramisù theme with a contrasting bitter chocolate sorbet.

Chef Adam Potten **Seats** 120, Pr/dining room 150 **Times** 12.30-2.30/6.30-10 **Prices** Fixed L 3 course £19.07, Starter £6.50-£10.95, Main £12.50-£34, Dessert £7-£9.50 **Wines** 76 bottles over £30, 18 bottles under £30, 14 by glass **Parking** 120 **Notes** Sunday L, Vegetarian available, Children welcome

EAST SUSSEX

ALFRISTON Map 6 TQ50

Deans Place

Modern British V

tel: 01323 870248 **Seaford Rd BN26 5TW**
email: mail@deansplacehotel.co.uk **web:** www.deansplacehotel.co.uk
dir: *Off A27, signed Alfriston & Drusillas Zoo Park. Continue south through village*

Modern country cooking on the edge of the South Downs

Once part of an extensive farming estate, Deans Place has been a hotel for a century, and its elegant modern decor makes a refreshing backdrop to the Victorian gardens and charming riverside location, while the stylish Dining Room offers the full-dress experience of fine table linen and glassware. The kitchen's contemporary output might see seared scallops paired with coriander purée and mango chilli salsa, followed by whole roasted partridge or pan-fried hake with herb gnocchi and crab dressing. Weekday lunches off the Terrace & Bar menu include the likes of burgers, fish and chips and steaks.

Chef Stuart Dunley **Seats** 74, Pr/dining room 50 **Times** 12.30-3/6.30-9.30 **Prices** Prices not confirmed **Wines** 25 bottles over £30, 47 bottles under £30, 10 by glass **Parking** 100 **Notes** Sunday L, Children welcome

BATTLE Map 7 TQ71

The Powder Mills Hotel

 Modern British V

tel: 01424 775511 **Powdermill Ln TN33 OSP**
email: jcowpland@thepowermills.com **web:** www.powdermillshotel.com
dir: *M25 junct 5, A21 towards Hastings. At St Johns Cross take A2100 to Battle. Pass abbey on right, 1st right into Powdermills Ln. 1m, hotel on right*

Appealing modern cooking near the 1066 battlefield

Powder Mills was once the site of a major gunpowder-making operation that helped defeat Napoleon. The pretty Georgian house stands in 150 acres of lush parkland and woods with a seven-acre fishing lake. It's the kind of place where the owner's Springer Spaniels sometimes welcome arrivals and dining takes place in the Orangery Restaurant, with a bright decor of wicker chairs, linen-clad tables and marble floors. The kitchen turns out creative contemporary dishes, including artichoke soup with a truffle beignet. Main course might partner halibut fillet with spiced mussel and clam broth and apple salad. Finish with rhubarb soufflé with quince and hibiscus sorbet.

Chef Callum O'Doherty **Seats** 90, Pr/dining room 16 **Times** 12-2/7-9 **Wines** 16 bottles over £30, 40 bottles under £30, 4 by glass **Parking** 100 **Notes** Library & conservatory menus, Sunday L £24.95-£26.95, Children 10 yrs+

BODIAM Map 7 TQ72

The Curlew Restaurant

 Modern British V NOTABLE WINE LIST

tel: 01580 861394 & 861202 **Junction Rd TN32 5UY**
email: enquiries@thecurlewrestaurant.co.uk
dir: *A21 south turn left at Hurst Green signed Bodiam. Restaurant on left at end of road*

Modern country-inn fare near the Castle

The white-faced Curlew is perched on what was the old coaching-route from Hastings to London. A relaxed countrified atmosphere prevails, with a roaring log-burner and a fresh, open look to the decor. Mackerel comes both scorched and in céviche, rootily dressed with beet and horseradish, while duck liver and foie gras parfait has both gingerbread and salted pineapple for sweet and savoury company. They could be followed by pinkish pine-smoked venison with spiced red cabbage, blackberries, and light clumps of sesame-scented granola, or a double act of cinnamon and anise chicken with monkfish. Clementine mousse with spiced fruit cake and egg nog is the truly thought-provoking way to finish.

Chef Michael Mealey **Seats** 64 **Times** 12-2.30/6.30-9.30, Closed Mon **Prices** Fixed L 2 course £20, Fixed D 3 course £25, Tasting menu £65, Starter £7.50-£10.50, Main £19.50-£26.50, Dessert £8-£9 **Wines** 64 bottles over £30, 16 bottles under £30, 23 by glass **Parking** 16 **Notes** Sunday L £19, Children welcome

BRIGHTON & HOVE Map 6 TQ30

Chilli Pickle

Regional Indian

tel: 01273 900383 **17 Jubilee St BN1 1GE**
email: bookings@thechillipickle.com **web:** www.thechillipickle.com
dir: *From the Steine (A23) right into Church Lane & right into Jubilee St. Next to myhotel Brighton, opposite Library*

Vibrant Indian flavours in buzzy venue

The Chilli Pickle's interior works a contemporary rustic look, with chunky tables, blond-wood floors and vivid splashes of colour while full-length glass walls create the impression of dining alfresco. The menu gives subcontinental clichés a swerve, dealing at lunchtime in smartly reworked thalis, dosai and street-food-inspired dishes – chickpea and tapioca fritters, for instance, ahead of Punjabi lamb curry with chillies, fenugreek and garam masala. At dinner, the kitchen cranks things up with duck dumplings with orange and chilli chutney, followed by tandoor-baked half guinea fowl with korma gravy and biryani rice, or sea bass fillet with clams, mussels and prawns in coconut curry and coconut rice.

Chef Alun Sperring **Seats** 115 **Times** 12-3/6-10.30, Closed 25-26 Dec **Prices** Fixed D 3 course £27.95, Starter £4.50-£7.50, Main £7.50-£18.50 **Wines** 6 bottles over £30, 18 bottles under £30, 12 by glass **Parking** NCP Church St **Notes** King Thali menu £13.50, Mon £10, Pre-theatre menu £13.50, Sunday L, Vegetarian available, Children welcome

GB1 Restaurant

@@ Modern British, Seafood

tel: 01273 224300 **The Grand Brighton, 97-99 King's Rd BN1 2FW**
email: reservations@grandbrighton.co.uk
dir: *On A259 (seafront road between piers) adjacent to Brighton Centre*

Seafood specialities in the stylishly remodelled Grand

Turn your back on the stunning Italianate Victorian design at this seafront landmark and enter the cool, clean lines of the GB1 restaurant. Seafood is the thing here, with a menu as bright and contemporary as the surroundings. If platters of oysters, crab or prawns, herby fish soup or fish fingers (actually panko-coated whitebait) in a bap with fries don't appeal, go for more exotic scallops marinated in sashimi with asparagus, vanilla and chervil. Meat-eaters can choose from a selection of grills, and desserts are as well handled: perhaps multi-flavoured lime pannacotta with chocolate frangipane cake, a pistachio cone and a dollop of mascarpone, all as pretty as a picture.

Chef Alan White **Seats** 90, Pr/dining room **Times** 12.30-4/5-10 **Prices** Fixed L 2 course £14.95, Tasting menu £45, Starter £6.75-£12.50, Main £14-£45, Dessert fr £6 **Wines** 48 bottles over £30, 13 bottles under £30, 14 by glass **Parking** Behind hotel **Notes** Midwk menu 2 course with wine £45, Sunday L £17.95, Vegetarian available, Children welcome

The Ginger Dog

@ Modern British

tel: 01273 620990 **12-13 College Place BN2 1HN**
email: gingerdog@gingermanrestaurants.com
dir: *College Place Eastbound, turn right opposite Brighton College*

Robust pub cooking à la McKellar

A once run-down corner pub in Kemp Town village has been given a makeover, with clean white walls and bright pink banquettes in the main dining area. Begin with a pairing of seared squid and breadcrumbed pig's trotter in smoked paprika pesto to get the taste buds fired up, or perhaps a bowl of velvety celeriac soup with truffled croûtons and a splash of Muscat vinegar. Main courses are earthy and filling, so expect a chickpea and aubergine stew under roast hake, or roast lamb rump with a sugared pastilla, rainbow chard, giant couscous and pomegranate. To finish, go for cherry clafoutis with almond cream and cherry sorbet, scented with meadowsweet.

Chef Nick Cain **Seats** 45, Pr/dining room 22 **Times** 12-2.30/6-10, Closed 25 Dec **Prices** Fixed L 2 course £15-£30, Fixed D 3 course £18-£35, Starter £6.50-£9.50, Main £12-£21.50, Dessert £6.50-£9 **Wines** 27 bottles over £30, 23 bottles under £30, 26 by glass **Parking** On street **Notes** 2 course 12-2pm & 6-7pm £12.50, Sunday L £12-£15.50, Vegetarian available, Children welcome

The Gingerman Restaurant

@@ Modern British

tel: 01273 326688 **21a Norfolk Square BN1 2PD**
email: gingerman@gingermanrestaurants.com
dir: *A23 to Palace Pier rdbt. Turn right onto Kings Rd. At art-deco style Embassy building turn right into Norfolk Sq*

Dynamic modern British cooking near the seafront

The Gingerman is committed to dynamic modern British cooking with an inventive slant, notably incorporating touches of the Maghreb tradition. Maple-glazed pigeon breast with pine nuts and dates vies for first-course attention with salmon 'pastrami' served with caramelised parsnip and labneh, as well as an egg yolk. Mains push the envelope further for vegetarian duck egg curry with a dosa, lemon pickle and green chutney, or there may be an anatomist's approach to beef – tongue and cheek as well as fillet – garnished with charred onion and parsley root in hearty braising juices. A soufflé for two is a pleasure, perhaps rhubarb with rhubarb and custard ice cream.

Chef Ben McKellar, Mark Charker **Seats** 32 **Times** 12.30-2/7-10, Closed 2 wks from New Year's eve, Mon **Prices** Fixed L 2 course £17, Fixed D 3 course £37 **Wines** 14 bottles over £30, 23 bottles under £30, 14 by glass **Parking** Regency Sq NCP **Notes** Sunday L, Vegetarian available, Children welcome

Hotel du Vin Brighton

@ Traditional British, French

tel: 01273 718588 **2-6 Ship St BN1 1AD**
email: info@brighton.hotelduvin.com **web:** www.hotelduvin.com
dir: *A23 to seafront, at rdbt right, then right onto Middle St, bear right into Ship St, hotel at sea end on right*

Upmarket bistro cooking off the seafront

The Brighton branch of the chain has all the expected Francophile touches, its walls adorned with posters and risqué pictures, leather-look banquettes running back to back down the centre and small wooden tables. A glance at the menu reveals more than your average bistro fare, with steak tartare with capers, gherkins and shallots followed by braised rabbit in rich cider sauce. The kitchen buys great-quality ingredients and treats them with respect. Chicken liver parfait with raisin chutney and sourdough toast might precede sole meunière, or daube of beef bourguignon with potato purée. Tarte au citron with raspberry sorbet is a good way to finish.

The Little Fish Market

@@@ Modern Fish

tel: 01273 722213 **10 Upper Market St BN3 1AS**
email: thelittlefishmarket@gmail.com
dir: *Just off Western Rd Upper Market St past Co-op. Restaurant on right*

Simply stunning seafood with a creative edge

There aren't many places around like The Little Fish Market, where a chef works alone in the kitchen and a solo server manages front of house, and especially not that turn out food of this standard. Chef-patron Duncan Ray has worked at The Fat Duck and Pennyhill Park, so knows a thing or two about top-end dining, and he offers – just off Hove's busy Western Road – stunning sustainable seafood cooked with attention to detail, accuracy and a thoughtful creative edge. The venue is simply done out with seafood-themed prints, wooden tables and a soothing neutrality, and it is comfortable and atmospheric in the evening. The fixed-price menu offers no choice and depends on what's been landed that day. Start with lemon sole topped with a thin layer of seaweed – simple and elegant – before 'rock pool', a crystal-clear dashi broth poured over white crabmeat, sweet brown shrimps and plump baked oyster. Next up, salt-cod brandade with sweet roasted red pepper and sauce gribiche, then a stunning piece of monkfish with carrot purée flavoured with star anise, squid, wilted gem lettuce and peanuts. Valrhona chocolate delice is a fine finish, matched with salted caramel ice cream.

Chef Duncan Ray **Seats** 22 **Times** 12-2/7-9.30, Closed 1 wk Mar, 2 wks Sep, Xmas, Sun-Mon, L Tue-Fri **Prices** Fixed L 2 course £20, Tasting menu £50 **Wines** 9 bottles over £30, 6 bottles under £30, 9 by glass **Parking** On street **Notes** Vegetarian available, Children 12 yrs+

BRIGHTON & HOVE *continued*

64 Degrees

Modern British NEW

tel: 01273 770115 **53 Meeting House Ln BN1 1HB**
email: info@64degrees.co.uk
dir: *In the southern end of The Lanes of Brighton*

Very affordable, daily-changing tasty small plates

In Brighton's famous Lanes, this bijou restaurant is big on small plates, the idea being tapas-style sharing. The menu's economically worded fish, veg and meat options – four of each – reveal nothing of how beautifully the open-kitchen team prepares them, thus 'Scallop, turnip, parsnip, miso' arrives as far more than the sum of its parts, the scallops glazed, turnips crisped wafer thin, parsnips cubed. Another succinct listing masks cuttlefish filled with its own tentacles, crispy pancetta and celeriac, served with gomasio mayo. And there's a lot more to 'Lamb leg, asparagus, broad bean, oyster' and 'Artichoke barigoule, red pepper, olives' than meets the eye.

Chef Samuel Lambert **Seats** 22 **Times** 12-3/6-9.45, Closed 25 Dec, 1 Jan **Prices** Prices not confirmed **Wines** 16 bottles over £30, 7 bottles under £30, 15 by glass **Parking** Black Lion St car park **Notes** Small plate menu £6-£27.50, Vegetarian available, Children welcome

Terre à Terre

Modern Vegetarian V

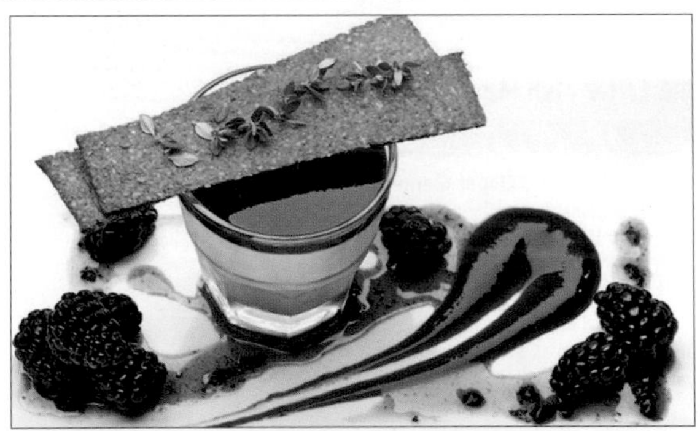

tel: 01273 729051 **71 East St BN1 1HQ**
email: mail@terreaterre.co.uk **web:** www.terreaterre.co.uk
dir: *Town centre, close to Brighton Pier & The Lanes*

Pioneering cooking from a quirky Brighton stalwart

Terre à Terre is a trendsetting restaurant serving creative, classy veggie-vegan food. It's just back from the seafront, and the pared-back dining area stretches back to a small terrace. The cheerful service team are happy to help with the eccentric menu's lengthy, sometimes baffling, descriptions. Inspiration comes from around the globe, majoring in Asian notes in steamed buns stuffed with Szechuan marinated halloumi, served with kimchi and miso chilli sauce, Main course mixes cheddar gnocchi, baked pumpkin and salsify noisette among its multifarious delights. Puds are good too: truffle brownie with blackberry and damson sauce and crème fraîche mint ice cream.

Chef A Powley, P Taylor, Matt Bowling **Seats** 110 **Times** 12-10.30, All-day dining, Closed 25-26 Dec **Prices** Fixed L 2 course fr £22, Fixed D 3 course fr £32, Starter £7-£14.50, Main £14.98-£15.95, Dessert £4.50-£9.30 **Wines** 12 bottles over £30, 34 bottles under £30, 12 by glass **Parking** NCP, on street **Notes** Terre à Verre menu (tapas, chips & wine carafe £22), Children welcome

Twenty Four St Georges

Modern European

tel: 01273 626060 **24-25 St Georges Rd, Kemp Town Village BN2 1ED**
email: reservations@24stgeorges.co.uk **web:** www.24stgeorges.co.uk
dir: *A23 Brighton, left onto Edward St to Eastern Rd, right onto College Place, left onto St George's Rd*

Creative cooking in relaxed neighbourhood venue

Tucked away in Kemp Town village, chef-proprietor Jamie Everton-Jones is established on the local foodie scene. The dining room is a relaxed and unshouty space, and the culinary deal includes well-executed dishes using the bounty of the Sussex coast and South Downs. A starter of lobster cannelloni with Sussex Blue cheese, tarragon, lemon gel and apple sets the tone, before a main course starring free-range chicken – breast and ballotine with chorizo stuffing – with a truffled croquette, oyster mushrooms, spring greens and Rioja jus. Desserts brings chocolate and orange sponge with crunchy honeycomb, and the tang of mango bavarois and sorbet.

Chef Alex Boudot **Seats** 52, Pr/dining room 12 **Times** 5.30-9.30, Closed 25-26 Dec, 1 Jan, Sun-Mon, L Tue-Fri **Prices** Fixed L 2 course £21.95, Fixed D 3 course £37, Tasting menu £59, Starter £6.95-£9.95, Main £12.95-£23.95, Dessert £7.95-£8.95 **Wines** 29 bottles over £30, 21 bottles under £30, 8 by glass **Parking** On street voucher **Notes** Vegetarian available, Children welcome

CAMBER — Map 7 TV91

The Gallivant

Modern British V NOTABLE WINE LIST

tel: 01797 225057 **New Lydd Rd TN31 7RB**
email: mark@thegallivanthotel.co.uk **web:** www.thegallivanthotel.co.uk
dir: *M20 junct 10 to A2070, left before Rye to Camber. Hotel on left opposite Beach exit D*

Local meats and seafood with New England style

Overlooking the Camber shoreline near Rye, The Gallivant has its heart in New England, where that laid-back eastern seaboard style translates as oceans of space, light wood, café furniture and a feeling that you might have stepped accidentally onto a small cruise-liner. Sourcing from within a 10-mile radius is an especially good idea when the radius takes in such impeccable stuff. The kitchen's contemporary output runs to wild sea bass escabèche and smoked chicken ballotine among first courses, followed by braised Winchelsea beef cannelloni or a classic bouillabaisse with saffron potatoes. To finish, dark chocolate torte arrives with frangelico jelly and roasted hazelnuts.

Chef Oliver Joyce **Seats** 45, Pr/dining room 100 **Times** 12-2.30/6-9.30 **Prices** Fixed L 2 course £16, Tasting menu £55, Starter £7-£11, Main £17-£24, Dessert £7-£9 **Wines** 109 bottles over £30, 24 bottles under £30, 23 by glass **Parking** 24 **Notes** Sunday L £30, Children welcome

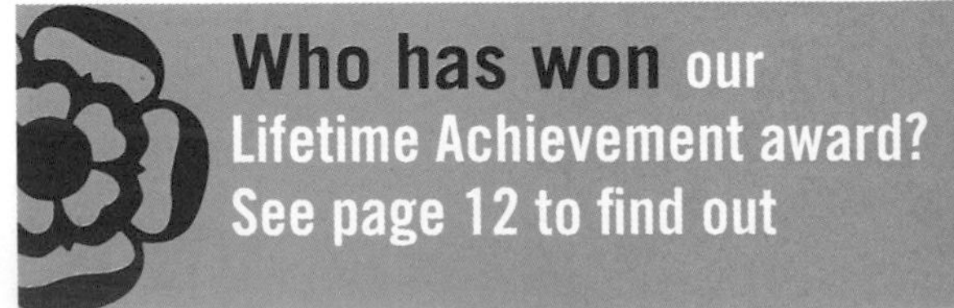

DITCHLING Map 6 TQ31

The Bull

Modern British NEW

tel: 01273 843147 **2 High St BN6 8TA**
email: info@thebullditchling.com **web:** www.thebullditchling.com
dir: *Exit A23 signed Pyecombe, left onto A273 signed Hassocks. Up hill, pass Pyecombe Golf Club on right, 2nd right into New Rd (B2112) to Ditchling. Right at mini rdbt, next left into car park*

Historic inn with culinary ambition

One of the oldest buildings in the village, The Bull has been central to this community for hundreds of years. Real fires, gnarled old beams: it's got the lot, and outdoors there's a garden with some raised beds to fuel the kitchen. Expect local ales at the pumps and plenty of regional ingredients on the menu of updated old favourites alongside more refined options. Ham hock terrine with piccalilli shows technical nous, followed perhaps by roasted duck breast with rösti potato and griottine cherry sauce, or fillet of wild sea trout with orzo pasta. Finish with poached rhubarb, orange curd and coconut sorbet.

Chef Dion Scott **Seats** 75, Pr/dining room 12 **Times** 12-2.30/6-9.30 **Prices** Starter £5-£8, Main £12-£22, Dessert £4.50-£8 **Wines** 22 bottles over £30, 14 bottles under £30, 19 by glass **Parking** 40 **Notes** Sunday L £21-£25, Vegetarian available, Children welcome

See advert on page 417

EASTBOURNE Map 6 TV69

Langham Hotel

– see opposite

The Mirabelle Restaurant

Modern, Classic NOTABLE WINE LIST

tel: 01323 412345 **The Grand Hotel, King Edwards Pde BN21 4EQ**
email: reservations@grandeastbourne.com **web:** www.grandeastbourne.com
dir: *Western end of seafront, 1m from Eastbourne station*

Grand seafront hotel with confident modern cooking

The Grand Hotel embodies glorious Victorian Empire pomp like few other seaside hotels. The Mirabelle restaurant makes an appropriately ritzy old-school setting, with cloches, trolleys and attentive and professional service. But there's nothing passé about the kitchen's contemporary take on flavour combinations and textures, with dishes revealing modern European thinking and fine-tuned techniques as in pike mousseline soufflé plated with salt-baked beetroot and truffled mayonnaise. Rump of Marsh lamb in a tapenade crust is served with sherry jus and a rosemary-flecked potato tortilla, and roast fillet of sea bass comes with potted shrimps, leeks and truffle. End in style with chocolate fondant with plum compôte.

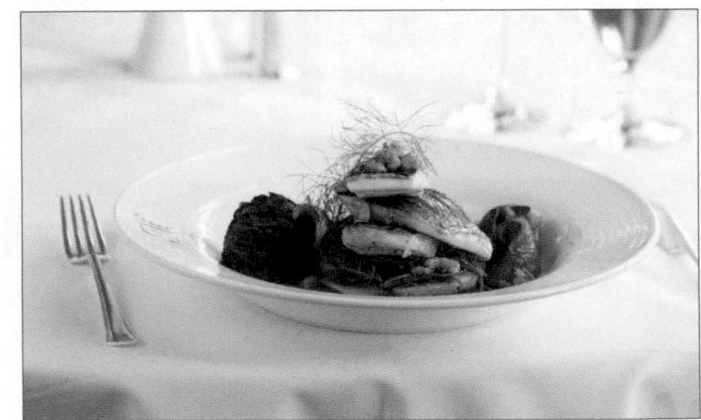

Chef Keith Mitchell, Gerald Roser **Seats** 50 **Times** 12.30-2/7-10, Closed 2-16 Jan, Sun-Mon **Prices** Fixed L 2 course fr £22, Fixed D 3 course fr £43.50, Tasting menu £63-£97, Starter £5.95-£8.50, Main £7.95-£16.95, Dessert £3.25-£4.20 **Wines** 221 bottles over £30, 24 bottles under £30, 11 by glass **Parking** 70 **Notes** Fixed L/D supplements added to price, Tasting menu 5 course, Sunday L, Vegetarian available, Children 12 yrs+

See advert on page 420

Langham Hotel

Modern British

tel: 01323 731451 **43-49 Royal Pde BN22 7AH**
email: neil@langhamhotel.co.uk **web:** www.langhamhotel.co.uk
dir: *A22 follow signs for seafront Sovereign Centre, take 3rd exit onto Royal Pde. Hotel on corner Royal Pde & Cambridge Rd*

Old-fashioned courtesies and a versatile menu

The bracing seafront of dear old Eastbourne fits this sparkling-white hotel like a glove, the marine views a treat from the conservatory dining room. While old-fashioned courtesies abound, the kitchen doesn't just stick to heritage Englishry, although you can go from potato and herb soup to sirloin and chips, with syrup sponge and custard to finish, if you've a mind. In between, though, there are wood pigeon salad with pickled mushrooms and roasted beetroot, nori-wrapped monkfish with spiced mussels, and cinnamon-infused fruity lamb tagine with orange, prunes and apricots. Things end on an upbeat with good pastry work in a pear frangipane tart, served with honey and ginger ice cream.

Chef Michael Titherington **Seats** 24 **Times** 12-2.30/6-9.30 **Prices** Fixed L 2 course £16.50, Fixed D 3 course £20.50, Starter £8-£10, Main £15-£20, Dessert £8-£10 **Wines** 1 bottle over £30, 29 bottles under £30, 15 by glass **Parking** On street **Notes** Sunday L £20.50-£22.50, Vegetarian available, Children welcome

FOREST ROW Map 6 TQ43

The Anderida Restaurant

Modern British NOTABLE WINE LIST

tel: 01342 824988 **Ashdown Park Hotel, Wych Cross RH18 5JR**
email: reservations@ashdownpark.com **web:** www.ashdownpark.com
dir: *A264 to East Grinstead, then A22 to Eastbourne. 2m S of Forest Row at Wych Cross lights. Left to Hartfield, hotel on right 0.75m*

Grand-hotel dining in an upmarket country house

Ashdown Park is a magnificent Victorian pile in acres of grounds, where the Anderida Restaurant's cooking is both classical and contemporary. Scallops are roasted and served atop cauliflower risotto with ceps purée and vichyssoise crumb to make an enjoyable starter. Main courses may seem a tad complex, but flavours work well together: beef fillet, for instance, served pink, comes with mozzarella quiche, broad beans, pork texture, artichoke purée and truffled mushrooms. Whole Dover sole meunière with new potatoes and buttered greens will appeal to those who prefer plainer food, while desserts follow the multi-flavoured route of tonka bean pannacotta with orange sponge, honey and saffron cream, pistachios, banana confit and lime meringue.

The Anderida Restaurant

Chef Andrew Wilson **Seats** 120, Pr/dining room 160 **Times** 12-2/7-9.30 **Prices** Fixed L 2 course fr £18.50, Fixed D 3 course fr £42.50, Tasting menu fr £74, Starter £9.50-£17.50, Main £19-£36.50, Dessert fr £10.50 **Wines** 250 bottles over £30, 16 bottles under £30, 12 by glass **Parking** 120 **Notes** Sunday L £29, Vegetarian available, Children welcome

See advert on page 420

HASTINGS & ST LEONARDS Map 7 TQ80

Bannatyne Spa Hotel Hastings

Modern British

tel: 0844 248 3836 *(Calls cost 5p per minute plus your phone company's access charge)* & 0344 248 3836 **Battle Rd TN38 8EA**
email: enquiries.hastingshotel@bannatyne.co.uk **web:** www.bannatyne.co.uk
dir: *M25 junct 5, A21 (Hastings). At 5th rdbt 2nd exit (Hastings/Filmwell). After 2 rdbts right (Folkestone/A259/Battle/A2100). Left at A2100/The Ridge Way. At 2nd rdbt right to hotel*

Imaginative cooking in a conservatory restaurant

Cooking is a serious business in this large and solid-looking hotel with extensive spa facilities. Begin with a properly made roulade of duck confit and foie gras, with classic celeriac remoulade and the sweet contrast of caramelised plums, or that hallowed trio of seared scallops with black pudding and cauliflower purée. Move on to a triple helping of lamb – pink loin, confit shoulder and sautéed sweetbreads with a selection of vegetables and red wine sauce. A fish offering might be pan-fried salmon fillet on peas à la France with saffron potato and mange-tout – and desserts are a strength, among them passionfruit pannacotta with mango, lemongrass and ginger soup.

Chef Chris Mouyiassi **Seats** 60, Pr/dining room 18 **Times** 12.30-2.30/6.30-9.30 **Prices** Fixed D 3 course fr £32 **Wines** 22 bottles over £30, 22 bottles under £30, 14 by glass **Parking** 150 **Notes** Sunday L, Vegetarian available, Children welcome

The Grand Hotel
EASTBOURNE
★★★★★

THE MIRABELLE RESTAURANT HAS A REPUTATION FOR SERVING DELIGHTFULLY CREATIVE DISHES
THE GARDEN RESTAURANT SERVES FINE FOOD IN AN INVITING AMBIENCE

The Grand Hotel, King Edwards Parade, Eastbourne, East Sussex, BN21 4EQ
01323 412345 www.grandeastbourne.com

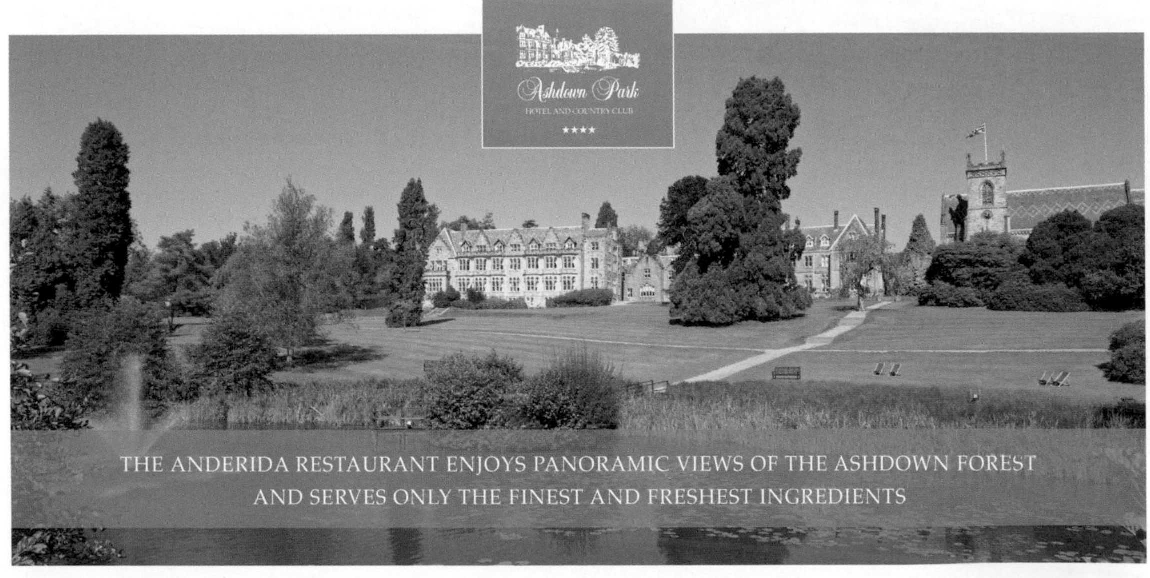

Ashdown Park Hotel & Country Club, nr Forest Row, East Sussex, RH18 5JR
01342 824988 www.ashdownpark.co.uk

LEWES Map 6 TQ41

Jolly Sportsman

Modern British, European

tel: 01273 890400 **Chapel Ln, East Chiltington BN7 3BA**
email: info@thejollysportsman.com
dir: *From Lewes A275, East Grinstead road, left onto the B2116 Offham, 2nd right into Novington Lane. In approx 1m first left Chapel Lane*

Rustic-chic inn serving up true Sussex flavour

Chef-patron Bruce Wass's weatherboarded country inn is well worth hunting down. There's a cosy bar area with casks on trestles and a rustic-chic restaurant with sage-green walls, colourful works from local artists, dark oak flooring and rough-hewn oak slab tables. The kitchen delivers punchy, contemporary cooking built on the freshest, local and seasonal produce. Foie gras comes pan-fried and as a velvety parfait with celeriac, Madeira jus and toasted brioche in a full-throttle opener, while Kentish lamb rump arrives with morcilla-stuffed piquillo peppers, fondant potato, peas and broad beans. End with chocolate, coffee and cardamom truffle cake with salt caramel ice cream.

RYE Map 7 TQ92

Mermaid Inn

British, Traditional French V

tel: 01797 223065 **Mermaid St TN31 7EY**
email: info@mermaidinn.com **web:** www.mermaidinn.com
dir: *A259, follow signs to town centre, then into Mermaid St*

Atmospheric medieval inn with classic and modern menu

In a town filled with spellbinding period buildings, this 600-year-old inn has bags of historic charm and atmosphere. The food in the restaurant, with its linen-fold panelling, takes an Anglo-French path, and there are appealingly contemporary dishes on the menu. Start with lobster and chilled tomato consommé, or multi-flavoured sautéed scallops on bacon vinaigrette with potato risotto and broccoli. Main courses may serve up cod fillet, landed in the bay, with rosemary polenta, sun-dried tomatoes, artichokes and olives, or Winchelsea beef fillet with roast shallots, beetroot, broccoli and horseradish crème fraîche. End with a show-stopping dessert like coconut pannacotta with ginger, lime and pineapple.

Mermaid Inn

Chef Benjamin Fisher **Seats** 64, Pr/dining room 14 **Times** 12-2.30/7-9.30 **Prices** Fixed L 2 course £21, Fixed D 3 course £38.50 **Wines** 15 bottles over £30, 22 bottles under £30, 15 by glass **Parking** 26 **Notes** Sunday L £22-£26, Children welcome

Webbe's at The Fish Café

Modern British

tel: 01797 222226 **17 Tower St TN31 7AT**
email: info@thefishcafe.com
dir: *100mtrs before Landgate Arch*

Local seafood in an informal converted warehouse

A brick-built warehouse constructed in 1907 houses this modern seafood restaurant. Exposed brickwork, high ceilings and fish-related artwork all feed in to the buzz of the ground-floor dining room where the chefs work their magic in the open-plan kitchen. Pan-fried cuttlefish with chorizo, sautéed potatoes and rocket and parsley salad is a vibrant starter, ahead of pan-fried wild sea bass fillets with suitably seasonal wild garlic, asparagus, new potatoes and mussel and chive sauce. Meat eaters won't feel left out with the likes of ox cheek with garlic and herb mash, caramelised onions and red wine jus. Finish with fennel seed pannacotta with orange compôte and sorbet.

Chef Paul Webbe, Matthew Drinkwater **Seats** 52, Pr/dining room 60 **Times** 11.30-2.30/6-9.30, Closed 24 Dec-10 Jan **Prices** Prices not confirmed **Wines** 10 by glass **Parking** Cinque Port St **Notes** Sunday L, Vegetarian available, Children welcome

TICEHURST Map 6 TQ63

Dale Hill Hotel & Golf Club

Modern European

tel: 01580 200112 **TN5 7DQ**
email: info@dalehill.co.uk **web:** www.dalehill.co.uk
dir: *M25 junct 5/A21. 5m after Lamberhurst turn right at lights onto B2087 to Flimwell. Hotel 1m on left*

Imaginative modern European menu in a golfing hotel

With its pair of 18-hole courses, golf may be top of the agenda at this hotel and country club but hill views, an indoor pool and gym, and a pair of restaurants are reasons enough for non-players to visit. The fine-dining Wealden View restaurant is the star attraction; modern European cooking is par for this particular course. You might tee off with ham hock with piccalilli vegetables and speck, and follow with curried sea bass fillet with spring onion pommes purée, mussel chowder and crisp pancetta, or sirloin steak with peppercorn sauce and the usual accompaniments. End with clementine posset with bourbon ice cream.

Chef Romain Escoffier **Seats** 60, Pr/dining room 24 **Times** 12-2.30/6.30-9, Closed L Mon-Sat, D 25 Dec **Prices** Fixed D 3 course fr £29 **Wines** 8 bottles over £30, 29 bottles under £30, 7 by glass **Parking** 220 **Notes** Sunday L £15-£19.50, Vegetarian available, Children welcome

UCKFIELD Map 6 TQ42

Buxted Park Hotel

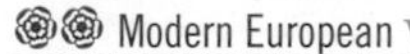

Modern European V

tel: 01825 733333 & 0845 072 7412 *(Calls cost 7p per minute plus your phone company's access charge)* **Buxted TN22 4AY**
email: buxtedpark@handpicked.co.uk **web:** www.handpickedhotels.co.uk/buxtedpark
dir: *From A26 (Uckfield bypass) take A272 signed Buxted. Through lights, hotel 1m on right*

Creative modern cooking in a Palladian mansion

A white mansion in immaculate gardens, Buxted Park was built in early Georgian times and nowadays offers the full country-house package. The restaurant features a mixture of table and booth seating, with curved lilac-upholstered banquettes against a white background. The kitchen produces an entertaining and carefully composed version of the modern European style. Foie gras three ways (brûlée, terrine and seared), with apple sorbet and port-infused cherries, makes a stunning starter, opening the way for perhaps another trio: of pork (crispy belly, roast loin and black pudding) with cider apple jus, pears in mustard and pressed greens. Conclude with lemon tart with strawberry ice cream.

Chef Mark Carter **Seats** 40, Pr/dining room 120 **Times** 12-2/7-9.30 **Prices** Fixed L 2 course £17.50, Fixed D 3 course £39, Starter £12.50-£16, Main £22-£32, Dessert £7.50-£9.50 **Wines** 95 bottles over £30, 5 bottles under £30, 18 by glass **Parking** 100 **Notes** Sunday L £25.95, Children welcome

East Sussex National Golf Resort & Spa

Modern British

tel: 01825 880088 **Little Horsted TN22 5ES**
email: dgm@eastsussexnational.co.uk **web:** www.eastsussexnational.co.uk
dir: *M25 junct 6, A22 signed East Grinstead & Eastbourne. Straight on at rdbt junct of A22 & A26 (Little Horsted). At next rdbt right to hotel*

Well-executed modern cooking and golf

Overlooking the greens and the South Downs, the vast Pavilion Restaurant offers a concise menu with plenty of choice. Start, perhaps, with the earthy flavours of rabbit and leek terrine with pistachios, carrot and sourdough bread. Dishes bring out upfront flavours without being gimmicky or ostentatious: pink and tender venison loin complemented by juniper sauce served with salsify, red cabbage, broccoli and violet potatoes, for instance, or brill fillet on a red wine jus with cockles, spinach and curried parsnip purée. Puddings are the real deal too, among them smooth chocolate tart, its pastry crumbly, with salted caramel ice cream and lime, or fig and almond cake with toffee sauce.

Chef Matthew Gardner **Seats** 90 **Times** 12-2.30/7-9.30, Closed L Sun **Prices** Fixed L 2 course £22.50, Fixed D 3 course £30, Starter £7.50-£11, Main £17-£26, Dessert £8-£13 **Wines** 12 bottles over £30, 23 bottles under £30, 9 by glass **Parking** 500 **Notes** Sunday L £16.95-£18.95, Vegetarian available, Children welcome

Horsted Place

Modern British

tel: 01825 750581 **Little Horsted TN22 5TS**
email: hotel@horstedplace.co.uk **web:** www.horstedplace.co.uk
dir: *From Uckfield 2m S on A26 towards Lewes*

Unpretentious country-house cooking in Victorian Gothic splendour

In 1850, Gothic Revivalist architect Augustus Pugin was commissioned to work his wonders here, hard on the heels of his design for the interior of the new Palace of Westminster. Outside are 1,100 acres of verdant Sussex countryside. Inside is a rich green dining room with well-spaced tables draped in floor-length white linen, and pictures of landscapes and horses. A meal from the modern British menu might comprise medallions of monkfish, Jerusalem artichoke purée and truffle oil, followed by moist and tender roasted saddle of fallow venison, braised red cabbage and vanilla-roasted pear, with ricotta fritters, compôte of blueberries and Greek yogurt to finish.

Chef Allan Garth **Seats** 40, Pr/dining room 80 **Times** 12-2/7-9.30, Closed 1st wk Jan, L Sat **Prices** Fixed L 2 course £19.95, Starter £9.50, Main £22, Dessert £9 **Wines** 74 bottles over £30, 24 bottles under £30, 9 by glass **Parking** 50 **Notes** Breakfast, Afternoon tea £19.50, Sunday L £28.50, Vegetarian available, Children 7 yrs+

WESTFIELD Map 7 TQ81

The Wild Mushroom Restaurant

Modern British

tel: 01424 751137 **Woodgate House, Westfield Ln TN35 4SB**
email: info@wildmushroom.co.uk
dir: *From A21 towards Hastings, left onto A28 to Westfield. Restaurant 1.5m on left*

Modern British cooking in a charming converted farmhouse

A converted 19th-century farmhouse surrounded by countryside just outside Hastings, Paul and Rebecca Webbe's restaurant is part of a local mini-empire. Original features like flagged floors and low beams impart a smart country feel to the ground-floor restaurant, helped along by friendly service. Sharp, contemporary cooking is the name of the game, delivered via set lunch, à la carte and tasting menus. Expect starters like chicken liver parfait with cobnut toast and balsamic pear purée, then perhaps roast rack and slow-cooked breast of lamb with apricot stuffing, dauphinoise potato and Kalamata olive purée a hit among main courses.

Chef Paul Webbe, Christopher Weddle **Seats** 40 **Times** 12-2.30/7-10, Closed 25 Dec, 2 wks at New Year, Mon-Tue, D Sun **Prices** Fixed L 2 course £18.95, Tasting menu £36, Starter £6.95-£9, Main £14.50-£22.50, Dessert £7.50-£9 **Wines** 33 bottles over £30, 38 bottles under £30, 10 by glass **Parking** 20 **Notes** Tasting menu 6 course, Sunday L £26, Vegetarian available, Children welcome

WILMINGTON Map 6 TQ50

Crossways

 Modern British

tel: 01323 482455 **Lewes Rd BN26 5SG**
email: stay@crosswayshotel.co.uk **web:** www.crosswayshotel.co.uk
dir: *On A27, 2m W of Polegate*

Country-house dining in relaxed restaurant with rooms

Crossways' appeal lies in the standard of the cooking and in the interesting monthly-changing four-course menu. Mango salsa is a good foil for duck terrine wrapped in pancetta, or start with a seafood pancake. Soup normally follows before the main course, where a straightforward approach brings out the flavours of quality ingredients: perhaps five lamb cutlets, roasted to pink, with a copybook version of port, redcurrant and rosemary sauce and seasonal vegetables, or, in season, roast breast of local pheasant with a shallot, bacon and chestnut sauce. There's always a fish dish of the day, and puddings include Swiss roll with raspberries and cream.

Chef David Stott **Seats** 24 **Times** 7.30-8.30, Closed 24 Dec-24 Jan, Sun-Mon, L all week **Prices** Prices not confirmed **Wines** 11 bottles over £30, 28 bottles under £30, 10 by glass **Parking** 20 **Notes** 4 course D £43, Vegetarian available, Children 12 yrs+

WEST SUSSEX

ALBOURNE Map 6 TQ21

The Ginger Fox

Modern British, European

tel. 01273 857888 **Muddleswood Rd BN6 9EA**
email: gingerfox@gingermanrestaurants.com
dir: *On A281 at junct with B2117*

English and Euro cooking on the South Downs

The Brighton-based Ginger group of restaurants and refashioned pubs has given its country bolt-hole a stripped-down look with slate floors, chunky tables and wood-burners plus a beer-garden and raised beds where the Fox's own vegetables are grown. The menu mixes English staples with modern European thinking, producing a rabbit Scotch egg with a delicious warm and runny quail egg to start. For main, a perfectly cooked breast of guinea fowl with a light and fluffy boudin will certainly appeal as might the poached rhubarb with white chocolate, fennel ice cream and meringue and rhubarb macaroons to boot.

Chef Ben McKellar, James Dearden **Seats** 62, Pr/dining room 22
Times 12-2/6-10, Closed 25 Dec **Prices** Fixed L 2 course £15, Starter £7-£9.50, Main £14-£22.50, Dessert £5.50-£8.50 **Wines** 18 bottles over £30, 25 bottles under £30, 20 by glass **Parking** 40 **Notes** Fixed L 2 course Mon-Fri until 7pm, Sunday L £12.50-£16.50, Vegetarian available, Children welcome

AMBERLEY Map 6 TQ01

Amberley Castle

@@@ Modern British V 

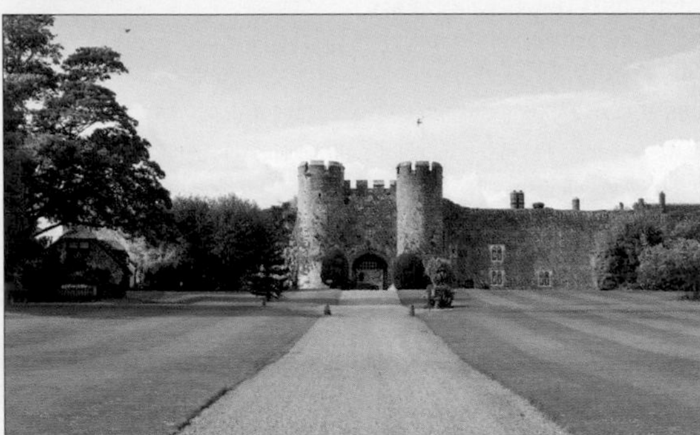

tel: 01798 831992 **BN18 9LT**
email: info@amberleycastle.co.uk **web:** www.amberleycastle.co.uk
dir: *Off B2139 between Storrington & Houghton*

Refined, contemporary cooking in a historical setting

There are quite a few hotels in the UK with 'castle' in their names, but few can compete with Amberley when it comes to living up to expectations – it's a 900-year-old Norman fortress with twin-towered gatehouse and portcullis, and battlements built to rebuff invaders sweeping over the South Downs. Goodness, it's impressive. Within its hefty stone walls, the public rooms have kept to the spirit of the antiquity of the place, while adding a sense of contemporary luxury. Its main dining room, the Queen's Room, has a 12th-century barrel-vaulted ceiling, open fireplace, murals, muskets and tapestries, and tables laid for the business of fine dining. The kitchen meets 21st-century expectations, blending modern techniques and European tradition to produce striking, harmonious dishes. First up could be clam and poached loin of rabbit with langoustine, Alsace bacon and violet artichoke and then comes either another fish in the shape of pave of halibut, fennel, clams with garganelli pasta, or the more outré Himalayan-style salt-aged lamb with a parcel of the neck meat in wild garlic and anchovy dressing. To finish, a banana parfait, chocolate namelaka and popcorn. The wine list lives up to the setting, with a knowledgeable sommelier on hand to advise.

Chef Conor Tomey **Seats** 56, Pr/dining room 12 **Times** 12-2/7-9.30 **Prices** Fixed L 3 course £34.50, Fixed D 3 course £67.50, Tasting menu £85 **Wines** 171 bottles over £30, 11 bottles under £30, 15 by glass **Parking** 40 **Notes** Sunday L £34.50, Children 8 yrs+

ARUNDEL Map 6 TQ00

The Town House

@@ Modern V

tel: 01903 883847 **65 High St BN18 9AJ**
email: enquiries@thetownhouse.co.uk **web:** www.thetownhouse.co.uk
dir: *Follow A27 to Arundel, onto High Street, establishment on left at top of hill*

Classy bistro cooking facing Arundel Castle

This smart restaurant with rooms is a place of enormous charm, its intimate dining room brought into the 21st century with high-backed black chairs, wooden floors and mirrors with funky striped frames. The kitchen takes the best of Sussex produce as the foundation for a menu of simple bistro dishes. Seared pigeon breast with pearl barley and wild garlic risotto is a faultlessly-executed starter, followed by roasted venison fillet with spinach, button mushrooms, baby onions, crisp roast potatoes and bacon jus. It's all presented with aplomb, and a dessert of pannacotta with poached rhubarb and a sablé biscuit brings the curtain down on a high note.

Chef Lee Williams **Seats** 24 **Times** 12-2.30/7-9.30, Closed 2 wks Etr, 2 wks Oct, Xmas, Sun-Mon **Prices** Fixed L 2 course fr £17.50, Fixed D 3 course fr £29.50 **Wines** 57 bottles over £30, 29 bottles under £30, 8 by glass **Parking** On street or nearby car park **Notes** Children welcome

BOSHAM Map 5 SU80

The Millstream Hotel & Restaurant

@@ Modern British

tel: 01243 573234 **Bosham Ln PO18 8HL**
email: info@millstreamhotel.com **web:** www.millstreamhotel.com
dir: *4m W of Chichester on A259, left at Bosham rdbt. After 0.5m right at T-junct signed to church & quay. Hotel 0.5m on right*

Stylish inventive cooking in a charming quiet setting

Built of red brick and flint, this charming hotel was originally three 17th-century workmen's cottages. On a balmy evening, the lawned gardens with ducks quacking along the millstream make an idyllic spot for drinks. The kitchen stays abreast of modern trends while keeping traditionalists happy. Starters can be as classic as home-smoked salmon with celeriac remoulade, or twice-baked cheese soufflé with cheddar and spring onion sauce. Combinations are intelligently considered, so pork fillet and belly are served with pickled apple and potato croquettes, and hake fillet with mussel and smoked bacon chowder. Puddings are worth exploring: try pistachio cake with cashew ice cream and almond cream.

Chef Neil Hiskey **Seats** 60, Pr/dining room 40 **Times** 12.30-2/6.30-9 **Prices** Starter £6.50-£11, Main £11.50-£26.50, Dessert £6-£8 **Wines** 28 bottles over £30, 34 bottles under £30, 13 by glass **Parking** 40 **Notes** Tasting menu 6 course with wine, Pre-theatre menu, Sunday L £27.50, Vegetarian available, Children welcome

CHICHESTER Map 5 SU80

Chichester Harbour Hotel

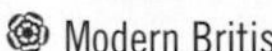 Modern British

tel: 01243 778000 **57 North St PO19 1NH**
email: enquiries@theshiphotel.net web: www.theshiphotel.net
dir: *From A27 follow signs for town centre and Chichester Festival Theatre. Restaurant signed from Northgate rdbt*

Modern brasserie cooking in a boutique city-centre hotel

In the heart of Chichester, this hotel presents a sober, red-brick Georgian exterior, but inside the designers have unleashed a riot of boutique style. Murray's Restaurant is a split-level dining room that works a classy colonial look with palm trees, touchy-feely fabrics, exposed floorboards and unclothed dark wood tables. Brasserie-style menus tick the right boxes, opening with confit duck and wood pigeon terrine with onion purée and toasted sourdough bread, and to follow, there are straight-up slabs of beef from the grill, or pan-seared cod with chorizo cassoulet and braised fennel. Classic French apple tart with cinnamon ice cream provides a simple but effective finisher.

Crouchers Country Hotel & Restaurant

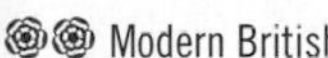 Modern British

tel: 01243 784995 & 07887 744570 **Birdham Rd PO20 7EH**
email: crouchers@btconnect.com web: www.croucherscountryhotel.com
dir: *From A27 Chichester bypass onto A286 towards West Wittering, 2m, hotel on left between Chichester Marina & Dell Quay*

Imaginative cooking in stylish hotel

During two decades as a stalwart of the Chichester dining scene, Crouchers has traded upwards from a simple B&B to a smart modern hotel near Dell Quay and the marina. A typical starter of lobster and salmon ravioli served with lobster bisque and parmesan snow might precede skilfully handled duck breast, served pink with crispy skin, together with a spring roll stuffed with confit duck and red onion marmalade, partnered by pak choi and a yuzu and wasabi dressing. Desserts maintain the high standards, as shown by the well-balanced flavours and textures of tonka bean cassonade with cocoa jelly, milk foam, amaretti crumbs and almond ice cream.

Earl of March

 Modern British

tel: 01243 533993 & 783991 **Lavant Rd PO18 0BQ**
email: info@theearlofmarch.com
dir: *On A286, 2m N of Chichester towards Midhurst, on the corner of Goodwood Estate*

Classy cooking in revamped old pub

Just a short drive out of Chichester, this 18th-century coaching inn looks out over the South Downs. There's a small patio garden, but most of the action takes place inside, in the large dining area or the snug bar area with a real fire and sofas. The menu includes old favourites such as beer-battered haddock with hand-cut chips alongside brasserie staples such as sole meunière, while starters might include a richly flavoured wild mushroom soup or seared scallops with black pudding and watercress emulsion. Desserts are a feel-good lot such as sticky toffee pudding with bourbon ice cream, or a crumble of pear, blackberry and almond.

Chef Giles Thompson, Adam Howden **Seats** 60, Pr/dining room 16
Times 12-2.30/5.30-9.30, Closed 25 Dec, Mon (Jan-Feb & Nov) **Prices** Fixed L 2 course £21.50, Fixed D 3 course £24.50, Starter £6.50-£9.50, Main £15.50-£21.50, Dessert £6.50-£7.50 **Wines** 42 bottles over £30, 33 bottles under £30, 24 by glass **Parking** 30 **Notes** Pre-theatre/Early bird menu 2/3 course, Sunday L £16.50-£25, Vegetarian available, Children welcome

Halliday's

 Modern British

tel: 01243 575331 **Watery Ln, Funtington PO18 9LF**
email: hallidaysdinners@aol.com
dir: *4m W of Chichester, on B2146*

Quality local produce cooked with flair

Halliday's occupies three flint-fronted thatched cottages dating from the 13th century, where chef Andy Stephenson sources first-rate produce from the local area. His seasonal summer menu begins with sautéed squid with chorizo, red wine, rocket and griddled ciabatta, or a croustade of roasted tomato, red onion and mozzarella with wild marjoram. Among meaty main courses, local rump of lamb teamed with baked aubergine, tomato, and basil oil is a bit of a treat, while fish might include wild black bream with shaved fennel, pink peppercorns and blood oranges. To finish, try an exemplary vanilla crème brûlée, whose richness is matched with a vibrant passionfruit sorbet and buttery shortbread.

Chef Andrew Stephenson **Seats** 26, Pr/dining room 12
Times 12-2.15/7-10.15, Closed 1 wk Mar, 2 wks Aug, Mon-Tue, L Sat, D Sun **Prices** Fixed L 2 course fr £17.50, Fixed D 3 course fr £28, Starter £7.25-£10.50, Main £18-£22, Dessert £7-£8.50 **Wines** 26 bottles over £30, 36 bottles under £30, 8 by glass **Parking** 12 **Notes** Sunday L £24, Vegetarian available, Children welcome

Richmond Arms

Eclectic

tel: 01243 572046 **Mill Rd, West Ashling PO18 8EA**
email: richmondarms@gmail.com
dir: *Phone for directions*

Inspired global cooking at the foot of the Downs

The whitewashed Richmond is one of the glories of West Ashling, a peaceful village at the foot of the South Downs, only five minutes from Chichester. Daily specials are written up on the blackboard, and there's a wood fired oven for traditional pizzas. Indeed, the extensive menus look far and wide for inspiration, from wood-roast aubergine with goats' curd, poppadoms and 'tandoori honey', to mains such as braised fallow venison shank in sweet Persian spices with nutty couscous, and grilled sea bass with a sweetcorn fritter and gingered squash in coconut and macadamia sambal. A dessert featuring Kahlúa brûlée, Baileys ice cream and Grand Marnier froth, certainly packs a punch.

Chef William Jack **Seats** 36, Pr/dining room 60 **Times** 12-3/6-11, Closed Mon-Tue, D Sun **Prices** Starter £2.99-£10.95, Main £14.95-£26.95, Dessert £6.95 **Wines** 22 bottles over £30, 25 bottles under £30 **Parking** 9, On street **Notes** Sunday L £15.95-£26.95, Vegetarian available, Children welcome

CHICHESTER *continued*

The Royal Oak Inn

Modern British, European

tel: 01243 527434 **Pook Ln, East Lavant PO18 0AX**
email: info@royaloakeastlavant.co.uk **web:** www.royaloakeastlavant.co.uk
dir: *From Chichester take A286 towards Midhurst, 2m to mini rdbt, turn right signed East Lavant. Inn on left*

Imaginative modern menu in a charming village inn

This 200-year-old pub serves real ale but puts food reassuringly high on the agenda. It's all served up in a rustic interior with exposed brick walls, beams, leather-look chairs and wooden tables. A starter of pork and apricot ballotine with spiced apricot compôte and toasted sourdough raises the bar well above pub grub level, and main courses are just as intelligently put together. Succulent roast breast of guinea fowl comes with crisp potato rösti, wilted greens with pancetta and a punchy wild mushroom jus, and a trio of pork comprising belly, tenderloin and black pudding bonbons is matched with carrot and anise purée, purple sprouting broccoli and red wine jus.

The Royal Oak Inn

Chef Fran Joyce **Seats** 55 **Times** 10-3/6-10.30 **Prices** Starter £5.95-£8.95, Main £13.50-£27.90, Dessert £4.95-£7.95 **Wines** 54 bottles over £30, 26 bottles under £30, 20 by glass **Parking** 25 **Notes** Pre-theatre menu from 5.30pm, Sunday L, Vegetarian available, Children welcome

See advert below

CHILGROVE Map 5 SU81

The White House

British, European

tel: 01243 519444 **High St PO18 9HX**
email: info@thewhitehorse.co.uk **web:** www.thewhitehorse.co.uk
dir: *From London, A3 to Portsmouth. Take A272 to Petersfield then right towards Pulens Ln B2199. At end turn left. After 3m, right onto B2146. Take B2141 into Chilgrove. On left. From Chichester, take road to Lavant, follow signs Chilgrove. On right*

Quirky pub restaurant with plenty of ambition

This stylish pub boasts plenty of quirky touches, right down to sheepskin throws on the high-backed benches and deer skulls, some of which sport sunglasses and scarves. A meal here showcases some modern British cooking of considerable poise and confidence, with pub classics sitting shoulder to shoulder with more fine-dining dishes. Start with goats' cheese and honey mousse with pistachio crumb, red pepper coulis and herb oil, before a generously proportioned warm salad of roasted guinea fowl with wild mushrooms, Parma ham and new potatoes. Impressive pastry skills are evident in a white chocolate and raspberry crème brûlée. Service from relaxed and friendly staff is informal and personable.

GATWICK AIRPORT (LONDON) Map 6 TQ24

Arora Hotel Gatwick

Modern British

tel: 01293 597701 & 530000 **Southgate Av, Southgate RH10 6LW**
email: gatwick@arorahotels.com **web:** www.arorahotels.com
dir: *M23 junct 10 then A2011 to Crawley. At 1st rdbt take 2nd exit towards town centre. At 2nd rdbt take 1st exit towards County Mall. Straight over at both sets of lights & County Mall should be on right. Under railway bridge, hotel on right*

Sharp cooking in a smart hotel eatery

Despite its name, this smart modern hotel is in Crawley town centre and its Grill restaurant is worth a visit in its own right. It's an airy open-plan room with clean-lined contemporary looks and diligently sourced British produce. Parma ham and saffron risotto give an Italian spin to slow-cooked pork cheeks, while a slab of seared cod from the nearby south coast is matched with peas, fondant new potatoes and red wine jus. Straight-up steaks or a two-way serving of pork belly with crackling and caramelised onion purée keep the carnivores happy, and for pudding, baked vanilla cheesecake is partnered by sherry-glazed fig, glazed Victoria plums and blackberry sorbet.

Chef Tony Staples **Seats** 70, Pr/dining room 15 **Times** 12-2.30/6-10, Closed L Sat-Sun **Prices** Prices not confirmed **Wines** 6 bottles over £30, 17 bottles under £30, 8 by glass **Parking** 210 **Notes** Vegetarian available, Children welcome

Langshott Manor

Modern European V

tel: 01293 786680 **Langshott Ln RH6 9LN**
email: admin@langshottmanor.com **web:** www.langshottmanor.com
dir: *From A23 take Ladbroke Rd, off Chequers rdbt to Langshott, after 0.75m hotel on right*

Dynamic contemporary cooking at an Elizabethan manor

An extended Elizabethan manor, Langshott has an authenticity that means it looks and feels more like the grand family home it once was as opposed to a stately home preserved in aspic. It's impressive enough though – there's a moat for a start – and the formal garden is anything but domestic. The period bones of the building bring atmosphere to the interior spaces and the designers have elevated the place to modern standards with well-chosen furniture and just the right amount of luxury. The Mulberry Restaurant is a sophisticated setting for some vibrant contemporary cooking from Phil Dixon and his team. The hotel's kitchen garden does its bit, too. Sensible combination show an understanding of what goes with what, and fashionable ideas are handled with a deft touch. Pan-seared monkish cheeks arrive in the company of tender duck confit, Puy lentils and a light sherry jus, which might be followed by braised fillet of wild halibut with leek and potato burek (a filled pastry) and a smattering of black truffle, or slow-cooked breasts of wood pigeon. A tasting menu supports the carte. Finish with an inspiring lemon soufflé with treacle tart and clotted cream, or some artisan cheeses with pear and tomato chutney.

Chef Phil Dixon **Seats** 55, Pr/dining room 60 **Times** 12-2.30/7-9.30, Closed L Mon-Sat **Prices** Fixed D 3 course fr £49.50, Tasting menu fr £70 **Wines** 62 bottles over £30, 7 bottles under £30, 11 by glass **Parking** 25 **Notes** Sunday L £29.50, Children welcome

Sofitel London Gatwick

British, French

tel: 01293 567070 & 555000 **North Terminal RH6 0PH**
email: h6204-re@accor.com **web:** www.sofitel.com
dir: *M23 junct 9, follow to 2nd rdbt. Hotel straight ahead*

Smart brasserie cooking by the North Terminal

An impressive central atrium makes a massive impact at this smart hotel close to Gatwick's North Terminal. The menu at La Brasserie, with its neatly laid tables and contemporary artworks, takes a modern British path, with a French accent; there are lots of original ideas and a sure hand at the stove. Start with seared scallops partnered by crisp chicken wings with teriyaki gel, or duck and veal terrine with plums, pickled girolles and ginger wine jelly. Next up might be rump of lamb roasted with thyme with squash, green beans, mushrooms and Madeira jus, or cod fillet with clams, lobster bisque, sea vegetables and spätzle.

Chef David Woods **Seats** 70, Pr/dining room 40 **Times** 6.30-10.30, Closed L all week **Prices** Fixed D 3 course £36.95-£45.95 **Wines** 34 bottles over £30, 11 bottles under £30, 18 by glass **Parking** 565 **Notes** Vegetarian available, Children welcome

GOODWOOD Map 6 SU80

The Goodwood Hotel

Modern British

tel: 01243 775537 **PO18 0QB**
email: reservations@goodwood.com **web:** www.goodwood.com
dir: *Off A285, 3m NE of Chichester*

Ambitious cooking on the Goodwood Estate

The luxury hotel is at the heart of the 12,000-acre Goodwood Estate, with the organic home farm providing the kitchens of its various restaurants with pork, lamb and beef. Seared scallops come in a fashionable pairing with crispy chicken wing, charred spring onions, sweet and savoury bacon jam, and wild garlic buds. Main course serves up that splendid Goodwood lamb with hay-baked beetroot and carrots, sorrel leaf, and charred asparagus, or there could be estate-reared Saddleback pork with aubergine, olive and baby vegetables. Fish options may include roast fillet of halibut with crayfish, sumac gnocchi, grapefruit, burnt cauliflower and sea herbs. At the finishing line try a dessert of peanut parfait and brittle with cherry sorbet.

Chef Mark Forman **Seats** 82, Pr/dining room 40
Times 12.30-2.30/6.30-9.30, Closed L Mon-Sat **Prices** Starter £6.50-£8, Main £15-£26 **Wines** 50 bottles over £30, 14 bottles under £30, 16 by glass **Parking** 200 **Notes** Vegetarian available, Children welcome

HAYWARDS HEATH Map 6 TQ32

Jeremy's at Borde Hill

Modern European, Mediterranean

tel: 01444 441102 **Balcombe Rd RH16 1XP**
email: reservations@jeremysrestaurant.com **web:** www.jeremysrestaurant.com
dir: *1.5m N of Haywards Heath, 10mins from Gatwick Airport. From M23 junct 10a take A23 through Balcombe*

Confident flavoursome cooking in idyllic garden setting

It is hard to imagine a more idyllic setting for summer dining than this contemporary restaurant in the quintessentially English Borde Hill Gardens. Jeremy's occupies a stylishly converted stable block overlooking the Victorian walled garden (which comes up trumps with fresh herbs and seasonal produce) and a dreamy south-facing terrace. Indoors, it's a wide open, bright space with modern art on the walls. Chef-patron Jeremy Ashpool calls upon a well-established network of small local producers and delivers big, bold flavours and colourful platefuls of modern, vibrant, Mediterranean-inflected food. Mont d'Or and chestnut ravioli, say, followed by Balcombe Estate venison, or line-caught brill with Selsey crab and sea beets.

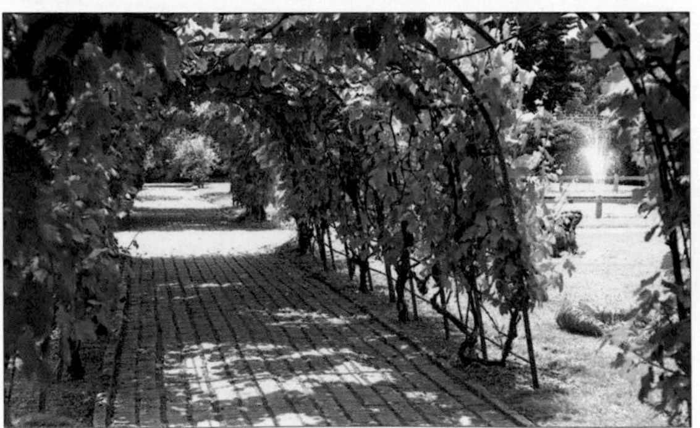

Chef Jimmy Gray, Jeremy Ashpool **Seats** 55 **Times** 12-3/7-9.30, Closed after New Year for 7 days, Mon, D Sun **Prices** Fixed L 2 course £18.50-£20, Fixed D 3 course fr £25, Tasting menu £40-£70, Starter £8.50-£11, Main £15-£25, Dessert £8-£9 **Wines** 19 bottles over £30, 16 bottles under £30, 18 by glass **Parking** 15, Overspill car park **Notes** Tasting menu 6 course, Fixed D midwk, Sunday L £30-£35, Vegetarian available, Children welcome

HORSHAM Map 6 TQ13

Restaurant Tristan

Modern British, French 

tel: 01403 255688 **3 Stan's Way, East St RH12 1HU**
email: info@restauranttristan.co.uk
dir: *Phone for directions*

Clever, creative cooking in historic surroundings

The 16th-century building in a pedestrianised street in the heart of old Horsham looks pretty historic, but chef-patron Tristan Mason's food is certainly of-the-moment stuff. Within, the setting blends ancient and modern elements with great effect: a striking beamed vaulted ceiling, wall timbers and bare floorboards sit alongside a contemporary décor. As is often the way with this kind of innovative, creative, technically skilful cooking, menus dispense with any description other than listing the components of each composition, but whether you go for three, four, six or eight courses, you can be sure that the full gamut of taste categories, textural contrasts and temperatures will be brought into play. Clever stuff, then, but this isn't just about techno flim-flam: having trained with Marco Pierre White, Mason's ideas are solidly grounded in classic French technique. An impressive, highly-detailed starter might see scallop paired with beef daube, parsley root and truffle. Fish and meat combinations are favoured, beautifully cooked and might explore the textures and flavours of lamb, kid and goat, while partridge could arrive alongside quince and bacon. Things are brought to a close with tour de force desserts involving, perhaps, a coconut soufflé helped along by passionfruit, lemongrass and Thai basil.

Chef Tristan Mason **Seats** 40 **Times** 12-2.30/6.30-9.30, Closed Sun-Mon **Prices** Prices not confirmed **Wines** 30 bottles over £30, 16 bottles under £30, 20 by glass **Notes** L 3/4 course £25/£30, D 4 course £45, Tasting 6/8 course, Vegetarian available, Children 10 yrs+

Wabi

Modern Japanese

tel: 01403 788140 **38 East St RH12 1HL**
email: reservations@wabi.co.uk
dir: *Corner Denne Rd & East St*

Trendy venue for top-class Japanese in Horsham's restaurant quarter

This former street-corner boozer is now stylish to the hilt, the ground floor is a trendy, upbeat cocktail bar with a raftered roof and a waterfall curtain. The first-floor restaurant has a more minimal, cool and calming Zen garden vibe, with tatami-screened booths above spotlit beds of white pebbles, and darkwood everywhere. Japanese flavours are the kitchen's inspiration, but modern European ideas also have their say. Get going with chicken karaage with kimchi coleslaw, or venison buns with spicy pine nut soy. For a knockout dish of head-spinning flavours, try tea-smoked lamb chops with smoky Japanese aubergine and spicy Korean red miso sauce.

Chef Cordelia Friday **Seats** 62, Pr/dining room 14
Times 12-2.30/6-10.30, Closed 25-26 Dec, BHs, Mon **Prices** Fixed D 3 course £15-£22.50, Tasting menu £55-£85, Dessert £2.50-£6.50 **Wines** 11 bottles over £30, 16 bottles under £30, 11 by glass **Parking** Car park **Notes** Vegetarian available, Children welcome

LICKFOLD Map 6 SU92

The Lickfold Inn

British V

tel: 01789 532535 **GU28 9EY**
email: dine@thelickfoldinn.co.uk
dir: *Signed from A272, 6m E of Midhurst. From A285, 6m S of Haslemere, follow signs for 'Lurgashall Winery', continue to Lickfold*

Thrilling, innovative cooking in a resurrected country inn

With its black timbers and beautiful herringbone brick, it's hard to believe this splendid Sussex inn was once declared 'permanently closed'. Thank goodness for Tom Sellers, who while busy with the success of Restaurant Story in London was not too busy to rescue the Lickfold. His background includes some of the world's best kitchens – the legendary Noma in Copenhagen, plus time spent with Tom Aikens and at Per Se in New York – which means you can expect exciting and unusual dishes. It's still a pub, though, so you can enjoy traditional pleasures like a pint and fancy bar snacks (a fish finger sandwich, maybe, or seasonal root crisps), but upstairs in the restaurant you'll find out what chef Graham Squire is up to in that state-of-the-art kitchen. There is no unnecessary description on the menu, where starters might include scallop, crab, sea herbs and buckthorn, or chicken and leek terrine with warm potato bread. Main courses take in beef, oyster and salt-baked celeriac as well as goose with sprout tops and potato purée, and you'll need to save room for the elegant desserts – bitter chocolate and blood orange, say, or rhubarb soufflé with burnt custard ice cream.

Chef Tom Sellers, Graham Squire **Seats** 40 **Times** 12-3/6-9, Closed 25-26 Dec, Mon-Tue, D Sun **Prices** Fixed L 2 course £19, Starter £8-£12, Main £18-£30, Dessert £7-£13 **Wines** 109 bottles over £30, 11 bottles under £30, 10 by glass **Parking** 20 **Notes** Sunday L £22-£28, Children welcome

LODSWORTH Map 6 SU92

The Halfway Bridge Inn

Modern British

tel: 01798 861281 **Halfway Bridge GU28 9BP**
email: enquiries@halfwaybridge.co.uk **web:** www.halfwaybridge.co.uk
dir: *From Petworth on A272 towards Midhurst, 3m on right*

Classic and modern pub fare in renovated old inn

This classy 18th-century roadside inn makes an inviting pitstop after a hike on the South Downs Way or a leisurely perusal of Petworth's antique emporia. The ambience is friendly and unbuttoned, while the kitchen deals in pub classics given a contemporary tweak, and with emphasis on local, seasonal materials. Kick off with potted game terrine with a classic duo of Cumberland sauce and melba toast, and follow with another rib-sticking idea – twice-cooked pork belly, rolled and stuffed with garlic and herbs, alongside bubble-and-squeak, and pear and cider sauce. To finish, cherry and almond frangipane tart comes with excellent vanilla and tonka bean ice cream.

Chef Clyde Hollett **Seats** 55, Pr/dining room 16 **Times** 12-2.30/6-10 **Prices** Starter £7.40-£8.20, Main £13.90-£29, Dessert £6.50-£8.50 **Wines** 10 bottles over £30, 27 bottles under £30, 24 by glass **Parking** 30 **Notes** All day dining Sat-Sun 12-9pm, Sunday L £16.50-£18.50, Vegetarian available, Children welcome

The Pass Restaurant

LOWER BEEDING Map 6 TQ22

Modern British V NOTABLE WINE LIST

tel: 01403 891711 **South Lodge Hotel, Brighton Rd RH13 6PS**
email: enquiries@southlodgehotel.co.uk **web:** www.southlodgehotel.co.uk
dir: *From A23 turn left onto B2110 & then right through Handcross to A281 junct. Turn left, hotel on right*

Ringside seats for a culinary firework display

The Rosette award for this establishment has been suspended due to a change of chef. Reassessment will take place in due course under the new chef. Just 28 or so lucky people at each sitting can grab a pew (or rather a leather banquette or high stool) at this restaurant in the swanky South Lodge Hotel. The kitchen is integral to the experience, with a view of the chefs in action and plasma screens to ensure you don't miss a trick. The waiting staff do an admirable job, but the chefs steal the show, bringing the food to the tables and describing each dish with passion and enthusiasm. New head chef Ian Swainson's six-course lunch menu includes braised razor clams with oyster emulsion, sauce nero and shrimp vinaigrette; onion consommé, porridge, onion foam and thyme oil; pink, black and green cured and barbecue salmon in teriyaki-style marinade and sesame dressing; roasted loin of pork with girolles, grelot onion and truffle sauce; finished off with a cheeseboard, grapes and crackers, a poached rhubarb and purée with rapeseed oil vinaigrette and balsamic meringue and a raspberry and beetroot mousse with textures of chocolate. The eight-course dinner menu features monkfish rolled in squid ink and a potato mousse with confit quail's egg among other creations.

Chef Ian Swainson **Seats** 28 **Times** 12-2/7-9, Closed 1st 2 wks Jan, Mon-Tue, L Wed **Prices** Tasting menu £29.50-£90 **Wines** 146 bottles over £30, 20 bottles under £30, 9 by glass **Parking** 200 **Notes** Fixed L 4/6/8 course £29.50-£59.50, D 6/8/10 course £70-£90, Sunday L £39.50-£59.50, Children 12 yrs+

LOWER BEEDING Map 6 TQ22

The Camellia Restaurant at South Lodge, an Exclusive Hotel

 British V NOTABLE WINE LIST

tel: 01403 891711 **Brighton Rd RH13 6PS**
email: enquiries@southlodgehotel.co.uk **web:** www.southlodgehotel.co.uk
dir: *On A23 left onto B2110. Turn right through Handcross to A281 junct. Turn left, hotel on right*

Vigorously original cooking in South Lodge's traditional dining room

A handsome Victorian mansion hotel in the Sussex countryside where a starter of crabmeat comes with roasted beetroot, clementine and watercress, while main courses offer some offbeat accompaniments to their central components. Loin and breast of lamb are partnered by salsify and spiced lentils in a striking passionfruit sauce, while stone bass arrives on a fatty jus gras with celeriac, romanesco and a carrot and coconut purée. Things settle a little for desserts such as plum Bakewell with marzipan ice cream, or classic Tatin for two, but cheese comes as a 'creation', perhaps served as a portion of Tunworth in a gougère with beetroot, manuka honey and fennel.

Chef Richard Mann **Seats** 100, Pr/dining room 140 **Times** 12.30-1.45/7-9.30 **Prices** Fixed L 2 course £19.50, Fixed D 3 course £37.50, Starter £9-£22, Main £19.50-£30, Dessert £9-£12 **Wines** 141 bottles over £30, 26 bottles under £30, 16 by glass **Parking** 200 **Notes** Sunday L £32.50, Children welcome

The Pass Restaurant – *see page 429*

PETWORTH Map 6 SU92

The Leconfield

Modern British

tel: 01798 345111 **New St GU28 0AS**
email: reservations@theleconfield.co.uk **web:** www.theleconfield.co.uk
dir: *Phone for directions*

Creative energy in a lively and popular restaurant

Petworth may be known for antiques but this red-brick former pub is firmly rooted in the 21st-century. All sorts of ideas find their way on to the menus, from a starter of fennel gravad lax paired with salmon rillettes, quail's egg, and apple and endive salad, to a main course starring a spanking-fresh fillet of grey mullet with saffron potato, leek chowder, fish soup, and wild garlic croûtons; local meat fans might go for a fillet mignon of Storrington pork with grapes and Pommery mustard, pommes boulangère, asparagus and black pudding crumble. To finish, there's a spot-on vanilla pannacotta with a compôte of seasonal berries and a crunchy almond tuile.

The Leconfield

Chef Paul Welburn **Seats** 80, Pr/dining room 30 **Times** 12-3/6-9, Closed Mon, L Tue, D Sun **Prices** Fixed L 2 course £23, Fixed D 3 course £30, Starter £8-£11, Main £15-£28, Dessert £7-£10 **Wines** 27 bottles over £30, 24 bottles under £30, 11 by glass **Parking** On street, car park **Notes** Sunday L £25-£30, Vegetarian available, Children welcome

ROWHOOK Map 6 TQ13

The Chequers Inn

British

tel: 01403 790480 **RH12 3PY**
email: thechequersrowhook@googlemail.com
dir: *From Horsham A281 towards Guildford. At rdbt take A29 signed London. In 200mtrs left, follow Rowhook signs*

Confident cooking in characterful village inn

A proper village local with flagstones, oak beams, chunky wooden tables, welcoming open fires and a battery of well-kept real ales on hand pump, The Chequers has been around since the 15th century, but it is in tune with modern tastes. When it comes to the kitchen, there are no pretensions or gimmicks, just bang-on-the-money modern ideas, from risotto of butternut squash and sage with Parmesan and olive oil, to pan-fried crispy bream fillet with merguez sausage cassoulet and buttered spinach. You could end with lemon and thyme pannacotta, meringue, blackcurrant and brandy snap.

Chef Craig Goldsmith **Seats** 40 **Times** 12-2/7-9, Closed 25 Dec, D Sun **Prices** Starter £5.50-£9.95, Main £14.95-£23.50, Dessert £4.95-£6.25 **Wines** 7 bottles over £30, 26 bottles under £30, 8 by glass **Parking** 40 **Notes** Sunday L £5.50-£23.50, Vegetarian available, Children welcome

RUSPER Map 6 TQ23

Ghyll Manor

Traditional British

tel: 0330 123 0371 & 01293 871571 **High St RH12 4PX**
email: reception@ghyllmanor.co.uk **web:** www.ghyllmanor.co.uk
dir: *M23 junct 11, A264 signed Horsham. Continue 3rd rdbt, 3rd exit Faygate, follow signs for Rusper, 2m to village*

Country-house cooking amid 40 acres of prime Sussex countryside

A timbered manor house in 40 acres of picture-perfect Sussex countryside, Ghyll Manor is an obvious candidate for a retreat from the city. Inside, an appealing mixture of period features and modern styling creates a harmonious impression, and there's a terrace overlooking the gardens for summer aperitifs. The kitchen team maintains a steady hand at the tiller for assured country-house cooking. Crayfish and avocado cocktail with a tempura-battered king prawn might be the curtain-raiser to confit chicken leg with white bean cassoulet, chorizo and kale. Finish with a poached pear in red wine and cinnamon syrup and vanilla ice cream.

Chef Matt Hancock **Seats** 48, Pr/dining room 40 **Times** 12-2/6.30-9.30 **Wines** 9 by glass **Parking** 50 **Notes** Sunday L fr £19.95, Vegetarian available, Children welcome

SIDLESHAM — **Map 5 SZ89**

The Crab & Lobster

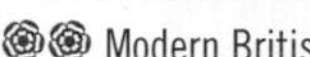 Modern British

tel: 01243 641233 **Mill Ln PO20 7NB**
email: enquiries@crab-lobster.co.uk **web:** www.crab-lobster.co.uk
dir: *A27 S onto B2145 towards Selsey. At Sidlesham turn left onto Rookery Ln, continue for 0.75m*

Switched-on modern menu in a waterside restaurant with rooms

The whitewashed 17th-century pub has become an upscale restaurant with rooms, and is looking spruce from top to bottom. On the edge of the Pagham Harbour nature reserve, it offers a stylish restaurant that aims to impress with ambitious, upscale modern British food that looks good on the plate and delivers bang-on flavours. Poached and deep-fried duck egg with black pudding and pea purée is a classy opener. Main courses run to well-timed, crisp-skinned halibut with braised salsify, button onions, girolles and pancetta in an intense red wine fish jus. Finish with gingery treacle tart and clotted cream ice cream.

Chef Sam Bakose, Clyde Hollett **Seats** 54 **Times** 12-2.30/6-10 **Prices** Fixed L 2 course £22.50, Starter £8-£13.75, Main £16.50-£29, Dessert £6.95-£8.95 **Wines** 30 bottles over £30, 24 bottles under £30, 25 by glass **Parking** 12 **Notes** Fixed L 2/3 course Mon-Fri, All day dining Sat-Sun, Sunday L £16.50-£18.50, Vegetarian available, Children welcome

TANGMERE — **Map 6 SU90**

Cassons Restaurant

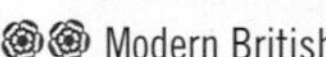 Modern British

tel: 01243 773294 **Arundel Rd PO18 0DU**
email: cassonsresto@aol.com
dir: *On Westbound carriageway of A27, 400mtrs from Tangmere rdbt*

Good eating near Goodwood

Chef-patronne Viv Casson ran a successful restaurant in France, so you can expect Gallic culinary influences to her work. Inside, the place gains character from the huge inglenook and low-beamed ceilings, while the modern menu takes in classically influenced ideas. Super-fresh crab from nearby Selsey appears with sweetcorn mousse, lime mayonnaise, lemon gel and potato 'glass' to start, ahead of more of that excellent locally-caught seafood – fillets of bass and turbot teamed with samphire, sautéed potatoes and sauce vièrge. Things get quite avante-garde at dessert, with a composition involving tangy lemon curd ice cream wrapped in vibrant rhubarb sorbet, with milk chocolate 'aero', rhubarb compôte and crumble.

Chef Viv Casson **Seats** 36, Pr/dining room 14 **Times** 12-2/7-10, Closed between Xmas & New Year, Mon, L Tue, D Sun **Prices** Fixed L 2 course £17, Starter £8-£11, Main £23, Dessert £8-£11 **Wines** 41 bottles over £30, 33 bottles under £30, 6 by glass **Parking** 30 **Notes** Gourmet & special events, Pre-theatre menu, Sunday L £22.50-£28, Vegetarian available, Children welcome

TILLINGTON — **Map 6 SU92**

The Horse Guards Inn

 Traditional British

tel: 01798 342332 **Upperton Rd GU28 9AF**
email: info@thehorseguardsinn.co.uk **web:** www.thehorseguardsinn.co.uk
dir: *On A272, 1m west of Petworth, take road signed Tillington. Restaurant 500mtrs opposite church*

Enterprising pub cooking near Petworth House

On the edge of Petworth Park, opposite the parish church, The Horse Guards is a relaxed and friendly pub dating back 350 years, with open fires, plain wooden tables and seats, beams and a boarded floor. It's a foodie destination with a daily changing menu showcasing what's been bought or foraged locally or dug up from the garden. Straightforward ideas kick off with pheasant and pork rillettes, offset with the contrasting tang of pickled courgette, while bold and hearty flavours ring out from a main course of slow-cooked lamb with buttery mash and salsa verde. To finish, there's a comforting sticky ginger parkin with vanilla ice cream.

Chef Mark Robinson **Seats** 55, Pr/dining room 18
Times 12-2.30/6.30-9, Closed 25-26 Dec **Prices** Starter £5.50-£8, Main £12-£22, Dessert £5.50-£8 **Wines** 33 bottles over £30, 15 bottles under £30, 14 by glass **Parking** On street **Notes** Sunday L £14-£19, Vegetarian available, Children welcome

TURNERS HILL — **Map 6 TQ33**

AG's Restaurant at Alexander House Hotel

British, French V

tel: 01342 714914 **East St RH10 4QD**
email: admin@alexanderhouse.co.uk **web:** www.alexanderhouse.co.uk
dir: *6m from M23 junct 10, on B2110 between Turners Hill & East Grinstead*

Inspired modern British cooking in boutique surroundings

The Rosette award for this establishment has been suspended due to a change of chef. Reassessment will take place in due course under the new chef. The Alexander House stands in a sprawling 120 acres of Sussex-Surrey borderland, an architectural mash-up featuring a castellated pseudo-medieval turret as well as soaring factory-style chimneys. Inside, its design job mobilises splotches of shouty colour in the bar and lounge, but sensibly opts for a more sober palate of royal-blue upholstery and white linen in AG's, the principal dining room. Innovative technique and pyrotechnical presentations are the hallmarks of dishes that have some rooting in the classical repertoire. First off might be seared foie gras with smoked eel and rhubarb in gin, a dish that mixes French and English modes to dynamic effect, or perhaps crab and avocado dressed in white balsamic with sourdough bread. At main, a pairing of lamb with its grown-up relative, mutton, comes with spring peas and Sussex Slipcote, a sharp ewes'-milk cheese, or there may be an in-vogue pairing of fish and meat – brill and ox cheek – with turnips and golden sultanas. French and British cheeses await those whose taste for the new hasn't quite yet run to kalamansi posset with confit pine nuts, honey, and rosemary-scented carrot sorbet. It all comes with a compendious wine list that offers a good choice by the glass.

Chef Darrel Wilde **Seats** 30, Pr/dining room 18 **Times** 12-2.30/7-9.30, Closed L Mon-Sat **Prices** Prices not confirmed **Wines** 140 bottles over £30, 10 bottles under £30, 15 by glass **Parking** 100 **Notes** Tasting menu with wine 8 course, Sunday L, Children 7 yrs+

Gravetye Manor Hotel

WEST HOATHLY **Map 6 TQ33**

Modern British V NOTABLE WINE LIST

tel: 01342 810567 **Vowels Ln RH19 4LJ**
email: info@gravetyemanor.co.uk **web:** www.gravetyemanor.co.uk
dir: *From M23 junct 10 take A264 towards East Grinstead. After 2m take B2028 to Haywards Heath. 1m after Turners Hill fork left towards Sharpthorne, immediate 1st left into Vowels Lane*

Modernist cooking, an Elizabethan mansion and heritage gardens

The gardens alone make this premier-league Elizabethan mansion worth a visit. The great Victorian landscaper William Robinson set up home here in 1884 and laid out its acres of grounds in the style we still see today, including a one-acre kitchen garden to supply the chefs with a cornucopia of freshly plucked, seasonal fruit and veg. As for the hotel, Gravetye delivers the upscale country house experience in spades, and as you'd hope in an operation of this standing, the restaurant keeps in step with the times, with the exceptionally talented George Blogg leading the kitchen team. A modernist style rules the roost, exploring novel combinations and textural contrasts, delivered via the seasonally changing carte, a seven-course tasting option and, at the entry level, an accessibly priced daily lunch menu. Proceedings kick off with a pressing of Rougié foie gras with Madeira jelly and almond brioche, with further flavour hits from dried capers and caramelised orange. Or there might be further luxury on offer in the shape of Sussex wagyu beef tartare with cow's curd, parsley yogurt and English wasabi. Mains show a sound grasp of how flavours work together, witness a precise and inspired dish of poached brill fillet with cuttlefish, its ink used in dramatic black macaroni, along with earthy celery hearts and charred lettuce. Local South Downs hogget could star in a three-way presentation, the loin, shoulder and sweetbread served with cabbage, lamb jus and mint jellies. To finish, hardened chocoholics will get their fix from a Guanaja chocolate pavé paired enterprisingly with roasted chicory root ice cream and cocoa nib crisps, or you might end on a savoury note by exploring a trolley laden with expertly ripened British artisan cheeses.

Chef George Blogg **Seats** 40, Pr/dining room 20
Times 12-2/6.30-9.30 **Prices** Fixed L 3 course £30, Tasting menu £40 **Wines** 350 bottles over £30, 18 by glass **Parking** 25 **Notes** All day menu 10am-10pm, Afternoon tea, ALC 3 course £65, Sunday L £40, Children 7 yrs+

TURNERS HILL *continued*

Reflections at Alexander House

Modern British V

tel: 01342 714914 **Alexander House Hotel, East St RH10 4QD**
email: admin@alexanderhouse.co.uk **web:** www.alexanderhouse.co.uk
dir: *6m from M23 junct 10, on B2110 between Turners Hill & East Grinstead*

Modern brasserie cooking in an elegant spa hotel

The handsome 17th-century mansion has moved into boutique territory after a thoroughly modern makeover, with pampering facilities to delight spa enthusiasts and a buzzy brasserie – Reflections – to lift the spirits still further (the fine-dining option is AG's Restaurant). Expect sleek chocolate-coloured leather banquettes, slate floors and subtle grey and peach tones on the walls, plus there's a champagne bar and tables in the courtyard for eating outdoors. Start with grilled, soy-and-lime-glazed mackerel fillet with fennel salad, moving on to a classic coq au vin, or red wine, radicchio and Gorgonzola risotto. Chocolate and hazelnut mousse with caramel sauce makes for a richly indulgent pud.

Chef Darrel Wilde **Seats** 70, Pr/dining room 12 **Times** 12-3/6.30-10 **Prices** Prices not confirmed **Wines** 25 bottles over £30, 5 bottles under £30, 12 by glass **Parking** 100 **Notes** Children welcome

WEST HOATHLY Map 6 TQ33

Gravetye Manor Hotel

– *see opposite*

TYNE & WEAR

GATESHEAD Map 21 NZ26

Eslington Villa Hotel

Modern British

tel: 0191 487 6017 **8 Station Rd, Low Fell NE9 6DR**
email: home@eslingtonvilla.co.uk **web:** www.eslingtonvilla.co.uk
dir: *Off A1(M) exit for Team Valley Trading Estate. Right at 2nd rdbt along Eastern Av. Left at car show room, hotel 100yds on left*

Reliable modern cooking in a Victorian villa

Originally built for a Victorian industrialist, today's hotel retains bags of period features, allied with contemporary verve and character. Dining goes on mainly in a conservatory extension with tiled floor and commanding views over the lawns, as well as in the interior room behind it. Start with an imaginative composition of blue cheese pannacotta with beetroot purée, apple and toasted peanuts, then move on to a well-executed main course pairing of pork fillet and shoulder with black pudding and potato bake and red cabbage. At the end, a purée of roast apple works well as a counterpoint to baked cheesecake with cinnamon ice cream and mini doughnuts.

Chef Jamie Walsh **Seats** 80, Pr/dining room 30 **Times** 12-2/5.30-9.45, Closed 25-26 Dec, 1 Jan, BHs **Prices** Fixed L 2 course £14.95-£16.95, Fixed D 3 course £28.50-£32.50 **Wines** 9 bottles over £30, 36 bottles under £30, 8 by glass **Parking** 30 **Notes** Early bird D 2/3 course £14.95/£17.95 from 5.30-6.45pm, Sunday L £17.95-£20.95, Vegetarian available, Children welcome

NEWCASTLE UPON TYNE Map 21 NZ26

artisan

Modern British

tel: 0191 260 5411 **The Biscuit Factory, 16 Stoddart St, Shieldfield NE2 1AN**
email: info@artisannewcastle.com
dir: *Phone for directions*

Contemporary dining in a stylish commercial art gallery

The Biscuit Factory is the UK's largest art, craft and design gallery, and there's craft of the culinary kind on show in the venue's artisan restaurant. The menu instils a sense of place with it regional bias, but there's certainly no lack of refinement on show in contemporary-minded dishes that look good on the plate. Start with warm salad of smoked haddock, with Puy lentils and horseradish cream, and follow on with rib-eye with 'thrice' cooked chips and a classic sauce, or fillet of North Sea cod in the company of a posh truffled mash. There's an early-evening menu, too, and desserts run to hot chocolate fondant with passionfruit sorbet.

Chef Andrew Wilkinson **Seats** 70, Pr/dining room 24
Times 12-2.30/5.30-9.30, Closed 25-26 Dec & 1 Jan, Mon, D Sun **Prices** Fixed L 2 course £15-£20, Fixed D 2 course £20-£24, Tasting menu £45-£80, Starter £6.50-£8.50, Main £14-£24, Dessert £7-£8.50 **Wines** 10 bottles over £30, 20 bottles under £30, 8 by glass **Parking** 20, On street **Notes** Sunday L £15.95-£18.95, Vegetarian available, Children welcome

NEWCASTLE UPON TYNE *continued*

Blackfriars Restaurant

Modern, Traditional British

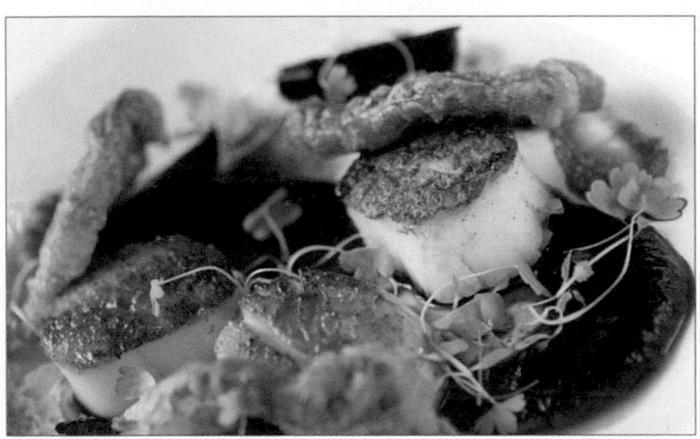

tel: 0191 261 5945 **Friars St NE1 4XN**
email: info@blackfriarsrestaurant.co.uk **web:** www.blackfriarsrestaurant.co.uk
dir: *Take only small cobbled road off Stowell St (China Town). Blackfriars 100yds on left*

Modern brasserie cooking in the old Dominican refectory

People have eaten well on this historic site since the 13th century, when it was the refectory for monks at the Dominican friary in the heart of medieval Newcastle. The kitchen deals in gutsy modern and classic brasserie dishes made from local ingredients. Buttered lobster and crab with home-made pasta, tomato and oyster leaf kicks things off, followed by seared venison with butternut squash purée, red cabbage and chocolate sauce. North Sea fish gets a good outing, in the shape, perhaps, of pan-fried cod with chorizo and white bean stew and tomato and dill dressing, while crowd-pleasing desserts include sticky toffee pudding with banana ice cream and salted butter caramel.

Chef Christopher Wardale **Seats** 80, Pr/dining room 50
Times 12-2.30/5.30-10, Closed Good Fri & BHs, D Sun **Prices** Fixed L 2 course £12-£18, Fixed D 3 course £36-£54, Starter £5-£12, Main £12-£25, Dessert £5-£9 **Wines** 14 bottles over £30, 31 bottles under £30, 8 by glass **Parking** Car park next to restaurant **Notes** Fixed menu 5.30-7pm, Sunday L £15-£21, Vegetarian available, Children welcome

Hotel du Vin Newcastle

British, French

tel: 0191 229 2200 **Allan House, City Rd NE1 2BE**
email: reception.newcastle@hotelduvin.com **web:** www.hotelduvin.com
dir: *A1 junct 65 slip road to A184 Gateshead/Newcastle, Quayside to City Rd*

French brasserie fare in designer hotel with superb wine list

The converted red-brick Edwardian warehouse of the Tyne Tees Steam Shipping Company enjoys commanding views of the city's many bridges, while, as might be expected from this well-established chain, the restaurant has the look of a French bistro, with darkwood floors and wooden-topped tables; patio doors open on to a courtyard for alfresco eating and drinking. You'll find the HdV trademark French brasserie fare, prepared from fresh seasonal produce, with starters like chicken liver parfait and classic mains such as a hearty cassoulet, or roast rump of lamb. What better to end with than apple tarte Tatin with crème Normande.

Chef Phil Hase **Seats** 86, Pr/dining room 22 **Times** 12-2.30/5.30-10 **Wines** 350 bottles over £30, 15 bottles under £30, 18 by glass **Parking** 15, On street (pay & display) **Notes** Sun brunch 4 course, Sunday L fr £22.95, Vegetarian available, Children welcome

House of Tides

– see opposite

Jesmond Dene House

Modern British, European NOTABLE WINE LIST

tel: 0191 212 3000 **Jesmond Dene Rd NE2 2EY**
email: info@jesmonddenehouse.co.uk **web:** www.jesmonddenehouse.co.uk
dir: *From city centre follow A167 to junct with A184. Turn right towards Matthew Bank. Turn right into Jesmond Dene Rd*

Imaginative modern cooking in an Arts and Crafts stately home

Jesmond Dene is an unexpected wooded valley just 10 minutes from Newcastle city centre. Built as a country house, this splendid building was designed by John Dobson, who was also responsible for much of the grandeur of the city's central streets. Updated in the 1870s, it's now an Arts and Crafts beauty with a welcoming atmosphere. There's a terrace for when the weather is good, and two dining rooms. Staff are friendly and efficient, and head chef Michael Penaluna's refined cooking makes the very best of high-quality local and seasonal produce. Everything is precisely conceived, from appetisers to pre-dessert, and the set menus at lunch and dinner offer five choices per course. There's also a carte, and an impressive 10-course tasting menu to boot. You could start with local wood pigeon, north country beetroot, pear, walnut and watercress, or ham knuckle terrine with pease pudding, apple and fennel, before a main of spelt barley risotto, perhaps, with baked Jerusalem artichoke, trompette mushrooms and truffle, or braised ox cheek with heritage vegetables and creamed potatoes. For dessert, the chocolate and blood orange cake comes with blood orange sorbet, while yogurt pannacotta is accompanied by roast plum and Szechuan pepper.

Chef Michael Penaluna **Seats** 80, Pr/dining room 24 **Times** 12-9, All-day dining **Prices** Fixed L 2 course £18.50, Fixed D 3 course £23.50, Tasting menu £95, Starter £7-£12.50, Main £14.50-£35, Dessert £7.50-£9.50 **Wines** 120 bottles over £30, 25 bottles under £30, 18 by glass **Parking** 64 **Notes** Tasting menu 10 course, Fixed D menu 5-7pm, Sunday L £22-£26, Vegetarian available, Children welcome

House of Tides

NEWCASTLE UPON TYNE **Map 21 NZ26**

Modern British V

tel: 0191 230 3720 **28-30 The Close NE1 3RF**
email: info@houseoftides.co.uk
dir: *Phone for directions*

Dynamic innovation on the Newcastle quayside

The Tyne Bridge is a near neighbour of the House of Tides, an iconic backdrop for a restaurant run by high-flying local lad Kenny Atkinson. Having made a name for himself in a number of top restaurants around the country, and got a TV career off the ground with appearances on Great British Menu and such like, Kenny (and wife Abbie) bagged a fantastic 16th-century former merchant's house on the quayside and have transformed it into one of the region's top dining addresses. The two floors have been restored with a keen eye for preservation – it is Grade I listed after all. The ground floor has original flagged floors and hefty cast-iron pillars, while the main dining room upstairs has copious characterful beams and a smart, contemporary finish. The whole place is stylish and unpretentious, a modern and informal setting for some dynamic cooking. The fixed-price menu offers four- or six-course options at lunch and dinner, with the longer tasting menu the only choice on Saturdays. Things get going with a series of 'snacks' including Highland haggis with spiced brown sauce before moving on to the first of the courses, cured salmon, say, with crab and Jersey royals. Expect thrilling contemporary cooking with cutting-edge ideas and impressive presentation, and with intelligently layered flavours. Smoked goose and liver terrine is matched with textures of apple, celeriac and hazelnuts, plus the aroma of fresh truffles, while another course sees top-drawer Herdwick lamb partnered with asparagus, wild garlic and morels. Among sweet courses, Amalfi lemons star in one thrilling dessert, while another sees crème brûlée flavoured with meadowsweet and served with gariguette strawberries. The wine list is arranged by style and opens with an inspired selection by the glass.

Chef Kenny Atkinson **Seats** 50, Pr/dining room 22
Times 12-2/6-10, Closed 2 wks Xmas New Year, Sun-Mon
Prices Fixed L 2 course £25, Fixed D 3 course £50, Tasting menu £55-£70 **Wines** 89 bottles over £30, 21 bottles under £30, 19 by glass **Parking** 70, £1.20/hr (free after 6pm) **Notes** Children 9 yrs+

NEWCASTLE UPON TYNE *continued*

Malmaison Newcastle

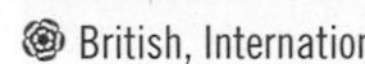

British, International

tel: 0191 245 5000 & 0844 693 0658 *(Calls cost 7p per minute plus your phone company's access charge)* **104 Quayside NE1 3DX**
email: newcastle@malmaison.com **web:** www.malmaison.com
dir: *A1 junct 65 to A184 signed Gateshead/Newcastle. Follow signs for city centre, then for Quayside/Law Courts. Hotel 100yds past Law Courts*

Stylish brasserie dining by the quay

The urban-cool boutique chain has taken a quayside warehouse as the starting point for its Newcastle outpost. The classy Chez Mal brasserie serves up a view over the Gateshead Millennium Bridge as well as a feel-good menu of globetrotting contemporary fare. Tuck into a classic prawn cocktail or Goan mussels in a coconutty curry sauce, before a Black Angus steak cooked on the grill, served with slow-roasted onion and soubise purée and a home-made steak sauce, the Mal burger with Ayrshire bacon and gruyère cheese, or seared tuna mignon with a Japanese spin. End in the comfort zone with Valrhona dark and milk chocolate torte.

Chef Sandeep Singh **Seats** 68, Pr/dining room 20 **Times** 12-2.30/6-11, Closed D 25 Dec **Prices** Fixed L 2 course £19.95, Fixed D 3 course £24.95, Tasting menu £55-£75, Starter £5-£12.50, Main £14-£49, Dessert £6.50-£12 **Wines** 60 bottles over £30, 22 bottles under £30, 30 by glass **Parking** 60, Sandgate (chargeable) **Notes** Brunch, Sunday L £19.95-£29.95, Vegetarian available, Children welcome

Peace and Loaf

Modern British NEW

tel: 0191 281 5222 **217 Jesmond Rd, Jesmond NE2 1LA**
email: bookings@peaceandloaf.co.uk
dir: *From A167(M) head N. A1058 (Tynemouth) junct. Left onto Osborne Ave then immediate left onto Jesmond Rd*

Avant-garde brasserie cooking for the Jesmond set

In the fashionable Jesmond district of Newcastle, this is a thoroughly 21st-century place, with bare-wood floor and brick walls offset by kooky decorative touches. Bag a table on the mezzanine floor for views of the kitchen pass and the folks below. The menus deal in avant-garde brasserie food with a rumbustious edge. Try pulled braised lamb shoulder with turnip 'spaghetti' and salsa verde, a preamble to a main dish of chicken pie and halibut fillet, sharing the same plate alongside variously treated mushrooms and some satiny mash. High-octane dark chocolate tart is lifted out of the ordinary by its accompaniments of cinder toffee, popcorn and linseed cream.

Chef David Coulson **Seats** 53 **Times** 12-2.30/5.30-9.30, Closed 25 Dec, 1 Jan, D Sun **Prices** Fixed D 3 course £19.95-£24.95, Tasting menu £70-£125, Starter £8-£12, Main £16-£25, Dessert £8-£15 **Wines** 13 bottles over £30, 19 bottles under £30, 10 by glass **Parking** On street **Notes** Sunday L, Vegetarian available, Children welcome

21 Newcastle

Modern British V

tel: 0191 222 0755 **Trinity Gardens, Quayside NE1 2HH**
email: office@21newcastle.co.uk
dir: *From Grey's Monument, S to Grey St & Dean St towards Quayside, left along the Quayside, 3rd left into Broad Chare. 1st right then 1st left into Trinity Gdns, restaurant on right*

Brasserie buzz on the Newcastle quayside

The spacious, glass-fronted brasserie, with its polished wooden floor, leather banquettes and neatly clothed tables, remains as buzzy as ever, with slick and smooth service ensuring that all is as it should be, and the appealing modern brasserie-style dishes playing a big part in the attraction. Terrine of Northumbrian game, hazelnuts and pistachios with quince chutney is one way in, then main course could offer pot roast pheasant with chestnut stuffing, grapes and Sauternes, or a straight-up rib-eye of Himalayan salt-aged beef with red wine sauce. Puddings can be a highlight, among them warm sticky ginger sponge with toffee apples and Calvados cream.

Chef Chris Dobson **Seats** 130, Pr/dining room 44 **Times** 12-2.30/5.30-10.30, Closed 25-26 Dec, 1 Jan, Etr Mon, D 24 Dec **Prices** Fixed L 2 course £17.50, Fixed D 3 course £22, Starter £6.80-£16.60, Main £16-£29.80, Dessert £6.20-£9.20 **Wines** 81 bottles over £30, 24 bottles under £30, 24 by glass **Parking** NCP/Council **Notes** Fixed L/D 2/3 course Mon-Sat D 5.30-7pm, Sunday L £18.50-£22, Children welcome

Vujon

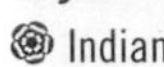

Indian

tel: 0191 221 0601 **29 Queen St, Quayside NE1 3UG**
email: mahtab@vujon.com
dir: *Phone for directions*

Fine-dining Indian style on the quayside

Set in the fashionable quayside area, Vujon has long been the smart place to go for new-wave Indian cuisine. A stylish contemporary-looking dining room and switched-on service are the backdrop to a creative mix of classic and up-to-date Indian dishes. Spicing is expert and can be delicate, particularly in a main course of seven-spiced Barbary duck breast marinated overnight in a clove-scented oven, served with sweet-sour apricot chutney, while the starter might be grilled scallops with peppercorns, fennel seed and star anise alongside orange and grape salad. Super-sweet gulab jamun dumplings soaked in saffron syrup, served with vanilla ice cream and dark chocolate sauce, make an interesting finale.

TYNEMOUTH Map 21 NZ36

Buddha Lounge

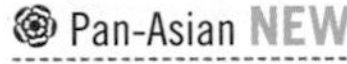

Pan-Asian NEW

tel: 0191 270 8990 **76 Front St NE30 4BP**
email: hello@buddhatynemouth.co.uk **web:** www.buddhatynemouth.co.uk
dir: *From Tynemouth Metro Station towards coast, venue on right at start of Front St in converted church hall*

Asian fusion cooking in a converted church

Fans of pan-Asian fusion cooking will enjoy this lively eatery. The setting is memorable: a converted church where a huge Buddha statue surveys a galleried upper floor beneath the soaring timber roof. Local ingredients and seafood from day boats shine through, appearing in vibrant ideas that take their cue from Indian, Japanese, Thai and Chinese cuisines. Start with prawn and avocado futomaki rolls pointed up with wasabi and pickled beetroot, followed by Thai red curry mussels singing with the flavours of fresh chillies and coriander, or punchy teriyaki beef skewers with straw noodles. To finish, there's a properly wobbly passionfruit pannacotta with mango and passionfruit purée.

Chef Carlo Giacomini **Seats** 92 **Times** 12-10, All-day dining, Closed 25 Dec, L 26 Dec **Prices** Fixed L 2 course £10, Starter £4-£16, Main £7-£26, Dessert £4-£6 **Wines** 7 bottles over £30, 13 bottles under £30, 8 by glass **Parking** On street **Notes** 'Two Share' eve offer 4 dishes Mon-Fri 4-7, Vegetarian available, Children welcome

WARWICKSHIRE

ALCESTER Map 10 SP05

Number 50

Modern British

tel: 01789 762764 **50 Birmingham Rd B49 5EP**
email: info@numberfifty.co.uk
dir: *From town centre towards Birmingham & M42. Restaurant is opposite Alcester Grammar School*

Unfussy cooking in a friendly modern bistro

A 17th-century cottage on the outside, Number 50 's interior has a contemporary style that mixes up ancient oak beams with cream-washed walls hung with modern art, and leather chairs at darkwood tables and slate placemats. The kitchen serves unpretentious modern British dishes that are big on flavour, cooked accurately and without fuss. Set-price menus offer great value, setting out with seared scallops with green pea pannacotta, pea purée and crispy pancetta, before roasted duck breast gets the spicy Szechuan treatment and is matched with potato terrine and liquorice jus. To finish, a simple classic is given a novel spin: rhubarb crumble soufflé comes with custard ice cream.

ALDERMINSTER Map 10 SP24

The Bell at Alderminster

British NEW

tel: 01789 450414 **Shipston Rd CV37 8NY**
email: info@thebellald.co.uk **web:** www.thebellald.co.uk
dir: *M40 junct 15, follow signs to Stratford-upon-Avon, then A3400 (Shipston on Stour) to Alderminster for approx 4m*

Smart gastropub with confident cooking

Part of the Alscot Estate, The Bell is a free house with classy bedrooms and a bar stocked with the estate's own ales, and a restaurant that successfully brings contemporary elements into the traditional space. Service is upbeat and effective. The menu deals in simple ideas with a modern touch. Warm ham hock salad is properly dressed, while baby squid, flavoured with lime and coriander and served with sweet pickled vegetables and egg noodles, brings an Asian flavour to proceedings. Main-course grilled mackerel comes with a saffron-infused risotto, or go for tender slow-cooked pork belly. Finish with a pretty dark chocolate and hazelnut torte.

Chef Stuart Hiorns **Seats** 85, Pr/dining room 20 **Times** 12-2.30/6.30-9 **Prices** Fixed L 2 course £13.50, Fixed D 3 course £16.50, Starter £4.75-£9.75, Main £13.50-£20.50, Dessert £3.35-£5.95 **Wines** 13 bottles over £30, 27 bottles under £30, 14 by glass **Parking** 30 **Notes** Sunday L £12.95-£16.95, Vegetarian available, Children welcome

Ettington Park Hotel

Modern, Traditional British

tel: 01789 450123 & 0845 072 7454 *(Calls cost 7p per minute plus your phone company's access charge)* **CV37 8BU**
email: ettingtonpark@handpicked.co.uk **web:** www.handpickedhotels.co.uk/ettingtonpark
dir: *M40 junct 15/A46 towards Stratford-upon-Avon, then A439 into town centre onto A3400 5m to Shipston. Hotel 0.5m on left*

Confident contemporary cooking in a Gothic mansion

A magnificent example of mid-Victorian Gothic architecture, Ettington Park stands in 40 acres of grounds in the Stour Valley. The interior bursts with antiques and walls hung with paintings, plus several friezes. Staff are friendly as they serve up some modern contemporary cooking. A deconstructed club sandwich is a successful amalgam of flavours consisting of chicken tortellini, tomato confit and aïoli, bacon foam, quail's eggs, little gem and breadcrumbs. A main course of seared scallops wrapped in smoked bacon comes with apple and fennel coleslaw, deep-fried brie and cranberry sauce. Puddings continue the labour-intensive approach, among them an attractive assiette of chocolate (millefeuille, cannelloni and lime-flavoured ganache).

ANSTY Map 11 SP48

Macdonald Ansty Hall

British

tel: 024 7661 2888 **Main Rd CV7 9HZ**
email: ansty@macdonald-hotels.co.uk **web:** www.macdonald-hotels.co.uk/anstyhall
dir: *M6/M69 junct 2 through Ansty village, approx 1.5m*

Tried-and-tested modern dishes not far from Stratford

Ansty Hall is a handsome, red-brick 17th-century mansion house set in eight acres of landscaped grounds amid the rolling farmland of Warwickshire. Within, all is elegantly furnished, not least in the classy Shilton dining room, where lavishly-draped sash windows offer views of the landscape. The emphasis is on British food wrought from good-quality seasonal produce, cooked without pretension and served without undue fanfare and fuss. Ham hock and leek terrine with chilled pease pudding gets things off the mark, followed by braised ox cheeks with toasted root vegetables and mash. Warm hazelnut and walnut sponge with home-made Muscovado ice cream and sweet pickled plums makes a great finale.

Chef Paul Kitchener **Seats** 60, Pr/dining room 40
Times 12.30-2.30/6.30-9.30, Closed D 25 Dec **Prices** Prices not confirmed **Wines** 12 by glass **Parking** 100 **Notes** Sunday L, Vegetarian available, Children welcome

ARMSCOTE Map 10 SP24

The Fuzzy Duck

Seasonal Modern British

tel: 01608 682635 **Ilmington Rd CV37 8DD**
email: info@fuzzyduckarmscote.com **web:** www.fuzzyduckarmscote.com
dir: *M40 junct 15*

Creative modern food in a swish gastropub

This upmarket gastropub with boutique bedrooms is looking pretty swanky these days after a makeover that made the most of the original character of the place (it's been doing the business as a coaching inn since the 18th century) and injected a bit of contemporary style. There's a serious approach to food and a pleasing lack of pretension to the modern British output. Kick off with home-cured salmon with bitter orange purée, before moving on to 'quack and mash' (slow-roasted duck leg) or ale-battered fish and chips, and desserts such as treacle tart with orange butterscotch, or dark chocolate fondant with stem ginger ice cream.

Chef Ben Tynan **Seats** 60, Pr/dining room 20 **Times** 12-2.30/6.30-9, Closed Mon, D Sun **Wines** 22 bottles over £30, 21 bottles under £30, 11 by glass **Parking** 15, On street **Notes** Sunday L fr £16, Vegetarian available, Children welcome

BRANDON Map 11 SP47

Mercure Coventry Brandon Hall Hotel & Spa

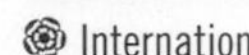

---

tel: 024 7654 6000 **Main St CV8 3FW**
email: h6625@accor.com **web:** www.mercure.com
dir: *A45 towards Coventry S. After Peugeot-Citroen garage on left, at island take 5th exit to M1 South/London (back onto A45). After 200yds, immediately after Texaco garage, left into Brandon Ln, hotel after 2.5m*

Feel-good dining in a smart manor-house hotel

Set in 17 acres of green-and-pleasant Warwickshire countryside, Brandon Hall is a smartly revamped 19th-century manor that has something for everyone. Tones of chocolate and green dominate in the smart, contemporary-styled Clarendon restaurant, while service is as keen as mustard and the kitchen follows the seasons. Whipped goats' cheese might star in a first course with gingerbread and golden and purple beetroots, while main courses run to rib-eye steak with Jenga chips and onion rings, or cod fillet with Dorset crab risotto and lobster sauce. Among desserts, a retro-style rhubarb and custard trifle comes in a glass jar with some mini doughnuts.

EDGEHILL Map 11 SP34

Castle at Edgehill

---

tel: 01295 670255 **Main St OX15 6DJ**
email: enquiries@castleatedgehill.co.uk **web:** www.castleatedgehill.co.uk
dir: *4m from M40 junct 10 or 7m from M40 junct 11*

Bright contemporary cooking in a Georgian castle

Built in 1742 to mark the centenary of the battle of Edgehill (the first major battle of the English Civil War), the Castle was converted to a pub in 1822. Expect creative modern cooking from a kitchen team that show their mettle with the likes of spot-on scallops with saffron-flavoured fennel, celeriac purée and spicy chorizo, or another starter that combines venison carpaccio with candied beetroot and honeyed parsnips. There might be venison among the main courses, too, pink and tender loin, served with feisty pieces of jerky, while a fishy main course is fillet of Cornish turbot with parsley root remoulade and trumpet mushrooms. Finish with baked Brillat-Savarin cheesecake.

HENLEY-IN-ARDEN Map 10 SP16

The Bluebell

---

tel: 01564 793049 **93 High St B95 5AT**
email: info@bluebellhenley.co.uk
dir: *M40 junct 4, A3400 (Stratford Rd) to Henley-in-Arden*

Modern cooking in a Tudor coaching inn

The Bluebell occupies a half-timbered coaching inn on Henley's uncommercialised High Street. Within are uneven flagged floors, beamed ceilings, draught beers in the bar and an enterprising restaurant menu that pulls in the punters. Expect starters along the lines of braised pig's cheek with lobster bisque, apple and bacon, followed by well-thought-out mains – perhaps cod with Welsh rarebit, chive potato cake and pea sauce, or a more orthodox rib-eye of 28-day-aged Herefordshire beef with pepper sauce and proper chips. Desserts are well regarded: perhaps orange and mascarpone cheesecake with milk ice cream and honeycomb, or chocolate mousse cake with raspberry sorbet.

Chef Andrew Taylor **Seats** 46 **Times** 8.30am-9.30pm, All-day dining **Prices** Prices not confirmed **Wines** 8 bottles over £30, 14 bottles under £30, 13 by glass **Parking** 20 **Notes** Sunday L, Vegetarian available, Children welcome

ILMINGTON Map 10 SP24

The Howard Arms

British NEW

---

tel: 01608 682226 **Lower Green CV36 4LT**
email: info@howardarms.com **web:** www.howardarms.com
dir: *M40 junct 15, A46 to Stratford-upon-Avon, A3400 to Oxford for 4m, then turn right signed Wimpstone & Ilmington*

Modern country pub dishes overlooking the village green

History seeps from every stone of the Howard, a 400-year-old inn on a Warwickshire village green to the south of Stratford. A big old stone fireplace, weathered armchairs and unclothed tables make for a relaxing ambience, and the cooking is in the modern country-pub mould. A backbone of ploughman's platters and beer-battered haddock and chips throws into relief the more new-fangled offerings. These might comprise seared scallops with black pudding crumble, carrot purée and cauliflower fritters, lamb rump with toasted almonds, sweet potato purée and roast shallots, and puddings such as toffee and banana in butterscotch, or cherry baked Alaska.

Chef Gareth Rufus **Seats** 45 **Times** 12-3/6-9.30 **Prices** Starter £6-£6.50, Main £10.50-£21, Dessert £6-£6.50 **Wines** 4 bottles over £30, 20 bottles under £30, 13 by glass **Notes** Some starters available as larger portion main meal option, Sunday L, Vegetarian available

KENILWORTH Map 10 SP27

The Cross at Kenilworth

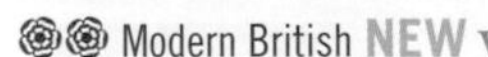

---

tel: 01926 853 840 **16 New Steet CV8 2EZ**
email: enquiries@thecrosskenilworth.co.uk
dir: *Phone for directions*

Modern British dining in revamped old pub

This former inn dating from the 19th century has had a new lease of life under the auspices of regional big-hitter Andreas Antona. Refurbishment has made the best of the original features while introducing a smart and traditional decor that is entirely in keeping with the mood of the place. The menu has its roots in classic Pan-European cooking and delivers a touch of refinement in this relaxed setting. Kick off with three-scallop ravioli with an accompanying fennel compôte and a frothy tomato sauce, before some Wiltshire pork belly with velvety mash and smoked onions, or cod with spiced brown shrimps and lentil dhal.

Chef Adam Bennett **Seats** 74, Pr/dining room 12 **Times** 12-2/6.30-10, Closed 25-26 Dec, 1 Jan, D Sun **Prices** Fixed L 2 course £21-£25, Fixed D 2 course £21, Tasting menu £65-£85, Starter £9.50-£12, Main £12-£32 **Wines** 48 bottles under £30, 20 by glass **Parking** 25 **Notes** Sunday L £30, Children welcome

LEA MARSTON Map 10 SP29

Lea Marston Hotel & Spa

---

tel: 01675 470468 **Haunch Ln B76 0BY**
email: info@leamarstonhotel.co.uk **web:** www.leamarstonhotel.co.uk
dir: *From M42 junct 9/A4097 signed Kingsbury Hotel, 2nd turning right into Haunch Lane. Hotel 200yds on right*

Modern seasonal cooking in a golf and spa hotel

The modern Lea Marston Hotel sits in tranquil Warwickshire countryside buffered by 54 acres of grounds. There's a spa, of course, a golf course, and good eating at The Adderley Restaurant. Decked out in shades of aubergine and grey, it's a swish, low-lit and romantic space with an unbuttoned vibe. The kitchen deals in unpretentious contemporary ideas, with a clear focus on seasonal, local ingredients. Pink and tender pigeon is balanced thoughtfully by raspberry vinaigrette and orange salad and makes a fine precursor to wild sea bass with scallops, peas and vanilla foam. Finish with a wobbly coconut pannacotta partnered with pineapple and vanilla salsa and cardamom ice cream.

LEAMINGTON SPA (ROYAL) **Map 10 SP36**

The Brasserie at Mallory Court

Modern British V

tel: 01926 453939 & 330214 **Harbury Ln, Bishop's Tachbrook CV33 9QB**
email: thebrasserie@mallory.co.uk
dir: *M40 junct 13 N'bound left, left again towards Bishop's Tachbrook, right onto Harbury Ln after 0.5m. M40 junct 14 S'bound A452 to Leamington, at 2nd rdbt left onto Harbury Ln*

Casual brasserie dining in an elegant hotel

As well as the main dining room, Mallory Court boasts a more contemporary-looking brasserie a short stroll from the main house. No mere adjunct to the main action, this is a fine venue in its own right, with clean, art deco-style lines, glass-topped wicker tables, soothing neutral decor, and a backdrop of gentle jazz. Dishes are given careful consideration, so that skilful technique produces crispy chicken and rabbit croquette with lovage mayonnaise, followed by pan-roasted cod with cocoa beans, chorizo, and brown butter and thyme chicken jus. For dessert, there's spiced carrot cake with yogurt ice and vanilla yogurt mousse.

Chef Jim Russell **Seats** 80, Pr/dining room 24 **Times** 12-2.30/6.30-9.30, Closed D Sun **Prices** Fixed L 3 course £19.50-£21.50, Fixed D 3 course £19.50-£21.50, Starter £5.25-£12, Main £12.50-£24.95, Dessert £6-£7.25 **Wines** 39 bottles over £30, 34 bottles under £30, 12 by glass **Parking** 100 **Notes** Sunday L £22.50, Children welcome

The Dining Room at Mallory Court Hotel

Modern British V NOTABLE WINE LIST

tel: 01926 330214 **Harbury Ln, Bishop's Tachbrook CV33 9QB**
email: reception@mallory.co.uk **web:** www.mallory.co.uk
dir: *M40 junct 13 N'bound. Left, left again towards Bishop's Tachbrook. 0.5m, right into Harbury Ln. M40 junct 14 S'bound, A452 for Leamington. At 2nd rdbt left into Harbury Ln*

Stunning seasonal cookery with views of rolling Warwickshire

The Rosette award for this establishment has been suspended due to a change of chef. Reassessment will take place in due course under the new chef. The ivy-clad manor house stands in 10 acres of sumptuous grounds, including its own kitchen garden, a little outside Royal Leamington Spa. Through the arched doorway, you will come across a charming mixture of art deco and Lutyensesque styling indoors, attended by supremely professional staff, the main dining room a restful place with wood panelling and floral drapes framing small windows. The full repertoire of multi-course tasters (five or seven), a seasonal carte and daily-changing prix-fixe deals is offered, and the food continues to represent a modern outlook on seasonally based British cooking. A slow-cooked duck egg with mushroom ketchup and crumbled bacony duck skin might open the bidding, or there may be roast cod cheek dressed in sweet-and-sour dill with a crispy cod cracker. Main courses accord the spotlight to pedigree prime materials such as Salisbury Plain fallow deer, served with seed and grain risotto, a parmesan fritter and black garlic, or opalescent wild sea bass, offset with a brandade of smoked eel and braised kombu. Finish with Yorkshire rhubarb variations and whipped egg custard, which comes with the further treat of a piece of ginger cake, or the technical artifice of aerated white chocolate with passionfruit ice cream.

Seats 56, Pr/dining room 14 **Times** 12-1.45/6.30-8.45, Closed L Sat **Prices** Fixed L 2 course fr £25, Fixed D 3 course £47.50, Tasting menu £70 **Wines** 200 bottles over £30, 25 bottles under £30, 12 by glass **Parking** 100 **Notes** Tasting menu 7 course, Sunday L £39.50, Children welcome

Queans Restaurant

Modern European

tel: 01926 315522 **15 Dormer Place CV32 5AA**
email: laura@queans-restaurant.co.uk
dir: *Phone for directions*

Charming restaurant with well-sourced menu

This is a delightful establishment with a good deal of genteel charm, where a smartly neutral decor meets an appealing menu of unpretentious dishes based on high-quality regional produce. You might start with a brie and hazelnut bake served with a smoky bacon jam. Clearly a dab hand at vegetarian cookery, chef can also turn out some impressive meat and fish options, too, such as a main-course grilled whole black bream (marinated in coriander and lime mustard), or roast loin of lamb with caramelised onion and fig stuffing. Finish with strawberry and pink champagne cheesecake.

Restaurant 23 & Morgan's Bar

Modern British

tel: 01926 422422 **34 Hamilton Ter CV32 4LY**
email: info@restaurant23.co.uk
dir: *M40 junct 13 onto A452 towards Leamington Spa. Follow signs for town centre, just off Holly Walk, next to police station*

Accomplished modern cookery in a handsome Victorian building

It's hard to miss this grand cream-coloured building with its portico entrance steps, while indoors neutral tones meet shocking pink for cushions and curtain linings in the dining room, where the soundly conceived modern food produces some definite hits. Salmon and crab tortellino reposes in lemongrass-scented bisque for a bracing opener, which may be followed by shoulder and braised cheek of good pork with earthy black pudding, tenderstem broccoli, a strong meaty jus and a slab of wonderful potato and pancetta terrine. For fish, there could be something as simple as fried plaice with leeks and shrimps in brown butter, while dessert brings on popcorn parfait with blackberry compôte and delectable ricotta sorbet.

Chef Peter Knibb **Seats** 60, Pr/dining room 25 **Times** 12-2/6.15-9.45, Closed 25-26 Dec, 1st 2 wks Jan, last 2 wks Aug, Sun-Mon **Prices** Tasting menu £55-£70, Starter £11-£16, Main £20-£29, Dessert £8-£10 **Wines** 200 bottles over £30, 26 bottles under £30, 11 by glass **Parking** On street opposite **Notes** Afternoon tea Tue-Sat, Tasting menu with wine £110, Vegetarian available, Children welcome

RUGBY Map 11 SP57

The WineGlass Restaurant

 Contemporay European NEW

tel: 01788 546100 **Brownsover Hall Hotel, Brownsover Ln, Old Brownsover CV21 1HU**
email: reservations@brownsoverhall.co.uk **web:** www.brownsoverhall.co.uk
dir: *M6 junct 1, A426 to Rugby. After 0.5m at rdbt follow Brownsover signs, right into Brownsover Rd, right again into Brownsover Ln. Hotel 250yds on left*

Fine dining and fine wines

The setting is a Victorian Gothic country house, whose dining room strikes a nice balance between traditional grandeur and clean modern lines, with cooking to match. Seasonal menus might open proceedings in autumnal mode via the route of scallops with bubble and squeak and spiced tomato concasse. Mains run from grilled brill with smoked garlic cassoulet, spinach purée and saffron potato to the emphatic flavours of saddle of venison with squash purée, banana shallots and wild blackberry jus. End with plum clafoutis or banana pudding with salted caramel sauce. In tune with the venue's name, more than 40 wines are available by the glass.

Chef Andrew Reeves, Richard Davies **Seats** 45, Pr/dining room 50 **Times** 12-3/6-9.30 **Prices** Fixed L 2 course fr £16.95, Starter £7-£9, Main £14-£24, Dessert £7-£9 **Wines** 24 bottles under £30, 18 by glass **Parking** 100 **Notes** Sunday L £19.95-£21.95, Vegetarian available, Children welcome

SHIPSTON ON STOUR Map 10 SP24

The Red Lion

 Traditional British

tel: 01608 684221 **Main St, Long Compton CV36 5JS**
email: info@redlion-longcompton.co.uk **web:** www.redlion-longcompton.co.uk
dir: *5m S of Shipston-on-Stour on A3400*

Cut-above British pub food in a Cotswold country inn

Built as a coaching stop in 1748, The Red Lion is a textbook country inn, right down to its inglenook fireplace, settles and eclectic furniture and artworks by locals. The cooking takes traditional pub food to a higher level, both in terms of preparation and presentation. A typical meal might start with spicy peanut chicken brochettes with sesame, spring onion and cucumber salad; then from the specials board a herb-crusted baked hake fillet, baby leaf spinach and tomato and chilli salsa. To finish, go for rhubarb and stem ginger fool with home-made ginger biscuits. A well-balanced wine list backs it all up.

Chef Sarah Keightley **Seats** 70 **Times** 12-2.30/6-9, Closed 25 Dec **Prices** Fixed L 2 course fr £13.50, Fixed D 3 course fr £16.50, Starter £5.50-£7.50, Main £14-£20, Dessert £6-£7.50 **Wines** 2 bottles over £30, 24 bottles under £30, 10 by glass **Parking** 70 **Notes** Prix fixe 2/3 course £13.50-£16.50 Mon-Fri before 7pm, Sunday L fr £14, Vegetarian available, Children welcome

STRATFORD-UPON-AVON Map 10 SP25

The Arden Hotel

 Modern British

tel: 01789 298682 **Waterside CV37 6BA**
email: enquiries@theardenhotelstratford.com **web:** www.theardenhotelstratford.com
dir: *M40 junct 15 follow signs to town centre. At Barclays Bank rdbt left onto High St, 2nd left onto Chapel Lane (Nash's House on left). Hotel car park on right in 40yds*

Enterprising modern cooking opposite the theatre

Just across the river from the theatres of the Royal Shakespeare Company, The Arden's contemporary brasserie dining room offers a champagne bar and enterprising modern cooking from a skilled team. Alscot Farm venison carpaccio with pickled girolle, red-wine-poached salsify and goats' cheese curd makes a stylish starter, while mains might offer a beautifully-presented and well balanced steamed cod pavé, wrapped in a banana leaf, with coconut lentil dhal, saffron pilau rice and south Indian-style green beans. The dark chocolate pavé with a deconstructed garnish of griottine cherries, cherry sorbet and Chantilly cream is a fashionable twist on a classic.

The Billesley Manor Hotel

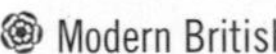 Modern British

tel: 01789 279955 **Billesley, Alcester B49 6NF**
email: billesleymanor.reservations@thehotelcollection.co.uk
web: www.thehotelcollection.co.uk
dir: *M40 junct 15, A46S towards Evesham. Over 3 rdbts, right for Billesley after 2m*

Modern British cooking in Tudor manor house

Billesley Manor is a charming mellow-stone Elizabethan mansion set in 11 acres of well-tended grounds deep in Shakespeare country. The Stuart Restaurant is split into two adjacent areas, one more like a minstrels' gallery, the other with oak panelling and a fireplace. The kitchen works around a slate of modern ideas, turning out an impressive starter of caramelised scallops on apple purée with black pudding hash and a crispy quail's egg. No less accomplished are main courses such as lamb cutlet and braised shoulder with pea purée, dauphinoise and mint jus. Finish with something like rich chocolate fondant with marshmallow and honeycomb ice cream.

The Falcon Hotel

 British, European

tel: 01789 279953 **Chapel St CV37 6HA**
email: reception.falcon@sjhotels.co.uk **web:** www.sjhotels.co.uk
dir: *From M40 junct 15 follow A46/A429 signs to Stratford. At rdbt take 1st exit A3400. Next rdbt take 1st exit onto High St*

Uncomplicated cooking in the town centre

Beyond the impressive half-timbered façade of this 16th-century former residence lie oak-beamed public areas and Will's Place, the hotel's opulent dining room, where the menu lists modern British dishes to satisfy most tastes. Start perhaps with an attractive starter of crisply crumbed boiled egg with sautéed wild mushrooms and a sherry dressing, before moving on to well-presented slow-roasted pork belly served with sticky red cabbage, fondant potato, pickled apples, apple purée, seared scallop and 'natural' jus. Desserts take a keep-it-simple approach with, for instance, warm treacle tart with clotted cream and a raspberry garnish. Traditional afternoon tea is served in the beautiful courtyard garden throughout the spring and summer.

Hallmark Hotel The Welcombe

Modern British, French

tel: 0330 028 3422 **Warwick Rd CV37 0NR**
email: welcombe@hallmarkhotels.co.uk **web:** www.hallmarkhotels.co.uk
dir: *M40 junct 15, A46 towards Stratford-upon-Avon, at rdbt follow signs for A439. Hotel 3m on right*

Updated country-house cuisine in elegant Victorian hotel

The formal garden outside this splendid Victorian house brings a stately presence to the Jacobean-style property. The restaurant matches the setting with its grandeur, with period features such as oak panels and huge windows. Start with a pre-dinner drink in the lounge and eat alfresco if the weather is up to snuff. The menu offers a contemporary take on classic country-house cuisine, so smoked salmon comes with a whizzy lemon jelly and pan-seared scallops are served with black pudding, celeriac and onion rösti, and parsnip and vanilla purée. Follow with cod wrapped in pancetta with red wine jus or rib-eye steak with triple-cooked chips, and finish with blood orange cheesecake.

Chef Gary Lissemore **Seats** 70, Pr/dining room 150 **Times** 12.30-2/7-10, Closed L Sat **Prices** Fixed L 3 course fr £35, Fixed D 3 course fr £35 **Wines** 10 bottles over £30, 10 bottles under £30, 8 by glass **Parking** 150 **Notes** Afternoon tea £18-£30, Pre-theatre D menu from 5.30pm, Sunday L fr £25, Vegetarian available, Children welcome

Macdonald Alveston Manor

Modern British

tel: 01789 205478 **Clopton Bridge CV37 7HP**
email: events.alvestonmanor@macdonald-hotels.co.uk
web: www.macdonald-hotels.co.uk/alvestonmanor
dir: *6m from M40 junct 15, (on edge of town) across Clopton Bridge towards Banbury*

Bright, modern cooking in a charming Tudor manor

A Tudor manor house only a few minutes' walk from the centre of the Shakespeare action in Stratford, Alveston brims with old-school charm. When you've wearied of minimalism in glass and steel, the gnarled oak beams and mullioned windows of the Manor dining room suddenly look luxurious. Traditional service from table-side trays is the vehicle for the kitchen's contemporary output. Kick off ham hock with pickled vegetables and apricot jam, or seared mackerel with spinach and chorizo, before moving on to pan-fried fillet of Scottish salmon with rösti wafer and dill velouté, or grilled rib-eye with traditional accompaniments.

Chef George Thomas **Seats** 110, Pr/dining room 40 **Times** 6-9.30, Closed L Mon-Sat **Prices** Prices not confirmed **Wines** 15 bottles under £30, 15 by glass **Parking** 120 **Notes** Pre-theatre menu, Sunday L, Vegetarian available, Children welcome

Mercure Stratford-upon-Avon Shakespeare Hotel

American, Italian

tel: 01789 294997 **Chapel St CV37 6ER**
email: h6630@accor.com **web:** www.mercure.com
dir: *Follow signs to town centre. Round one-way system, into Bridge St. At rdbt turn left. Hotel 200yds on left*

New York Italian food in Shakespeare country

The hotel named after the local genius is an appropriately antique-looking place. When it comes to dining, it fast-forwards a few centuries for Marco's New York Italian, in a smart room with a swish bar and terrace dining. Pastas, hand-made pizzas, burgers, steaks, ribs and seafood cover all bases, and the dishes are simple but deliver in terms of quality and flavour. Expect garlic and lemon prawns with rustic toast to start, or meatballs in penne, followed by a sterling burger topped with crispy prosciutto and mozzarella, olive-oiled grilled salmon on rocket, or sirloin fiorentina. Hit the high notes at dessert with affogato, tiramisù, or classic New York vanilla cheesecake.

The Stratford

Modern, Traditional British

tel: 01789 271000 **Arden St CV37 6QQ**
email: thestratfordreception@qhotels.co.uk **web:** www.qhotels.co.uk
dir: *A439 into Stratford. In town follow A3400/Birmingham, at lights left into Arden Street, hotel 150yds on right*

Creative, well-presented cooking in contemporary hotel dining room

The Stratford hotel, with its mod cons and business facilities, is home to Quills Restaurant, with its part-panelled walls and tones of purple, red and cream. The kitchen shows a degree of creativity in its contemporary combinations and has a keen eye for presentation. Pigeon breast with black pudding, blackcurrant jam and veal reduction is a well-considered starter, or go for smoked haddock fishcake with sauce gribiche. Main course hake fillet with Parma ham gets a Mediterranean spin with salsa verde, served with samphire and turmeric potatoes, or try duck confit with chorizo and cassoulet. For dessert, pear and thyme tarte Tatin comes with pear ice cream.

Chef Carl Weaver **Seats** 70, Pr/dining room 120 **Times** 5.30-9.30, Closed L all week **Prices** Starter £5.50-£11.50, Main £12.50-£29, Dessert £6.50-£9.50 **Wines** 12 bottles over £30, 18 bottles under £30, 16 by glass **Parking** 90 **Notes** Pre-theatre menu, Vegetarian available, Children welcome

WARWICK Map 10 SP26

The Brasserie

Modern British NEW

tel: 01926 843111 **Ardencote, The Cumsey, Lye Green Rd, Claverdon CV35 8LT**
email: hotel@ardencote.com **web:** www.ardencote.com
dir: *Off A4189. In Claverdon follow signs for Shrewley & brown tourist signs for Ardencote, approx 1.5m*

The all-day dining venue at Ardencote, The Brasserie, is another string to the bow of an establishment that already boasts a golf course, main restaurant, spa, and extensive conference and wedding facilities. Situated in an extension to the original grand Victorian house, and with a large outdoor terrace of its own, the modern and informal Brasserie is open for light lunches and sandwiches during the day, and ups the ante in the evening to deliver slow-cooked blade of beef with wild garlic pesto. Start with cider-braised pig's cheek and finish with strawberry mousse with cream tea ice cream. Afternoon tea on the terrace is a sunny day treat.

Chef Ian Buckle **Seats** 65 **Times** 12.30-2/7-10 **Prices** Starter £5.95-£8.95, Main £12.95-£16.95, Dessert £6.95-£8.95 **Wines** 37 bottles over £30, 38 bottles under £30, 12 by glass **Parking** 350 **Notes** All day bar & specials menus, Sunday L £19.95, Vegetarian available, Children welcome

WARWICK *continued*

Tailors Restaurant

Modern British V

tel: 01926 410590 **22 Market Place CV34 4SL**
email: info@tailorsrestaurant.co.uk
dir: *M40 junct 15. Follow A429 to Warwick, left into Swan St, 300mtrs on right in square*

Technically skilled deconstructions of the British heritage

In a pint-sized room centred on an old brick fireplace, the cooking is complex, with much technical skill. The seafood cocktail consists of prawns and brown shrimps, its Marie Rose dressing deep-fried in a breadcrumb coating, with red pepper purée and a gel of preserved lemon, a conceptual triumph. At main course, loin of fine local pork comes with a spring roll of the braised rib, toasted almonds, apricot and bitter coffee jelly, or there could be hot-smoked salmon with chestnut raviolo. Black Forest gâteau comes in for deconstruction too, its warm ganache encased in soft crumb, with freeze-dried sour cherries and smooth buttermilk ice cream boozed with Kirsch.

Chef Mark Fry, Dan Cavell **Seats** 28 **Times** 12-2/6.30-9.15, Closed Xmas, Sun-Mon **Prices** Fixed L 2 course £18-£23, Fixed D 3 course £25-£30 **Wines** 19 bottles over £30, 28 bottles under £30, 11 by glass **Notes** ALC 2/3 course £29.5/£39.50, Tasting menu L fr £32.50, Children 8 yrs+ L

WISHAW Map 10 SP19

The Belfry

Modern British NEW

tel: 0844 980 0600 *(Calls cost 7p per minute plus your phone company's access charge)* & 01675 477047 **B76 9PR**
email: enquiries@thebelfry.com **web:** www.thebelfry.com
dir: *At junct of A446 & A4091, 1m NW of M42 junct 9, adjacent to M6 toll junct T2*

Top golf resort with wide choice of places to eat

The Belfry resort has more than 300 bedrooms, a nightclub and four eating places, including its signature restaurant, the large and lively, three-roomed Ryder Grill. Diners can enjoy views across the famous Brabazon golf course, and in summer relax on its outdoor terrace. Steaks, chargrills and spit-roasts, fish and lobster are the stock in trade. A starter of nicely caramelised grilled scallops served with braised lentils, smoked bacon and apple and celeriac salad makes an ideal prelude to roasted loin of venison with dauphinoise potatoes, braised Savoy cabbage and blackberry jus. Cleanse the palate with apple and cinnamon delice with poached apples and cider yogurt sorbet.

Chef Glen Watson **Seats** 150, Pr/dining room 14 **Times** 6-10, Closed L all week **Prices** Fixed D 3 course £32.50-£40, Starter £6.50-£14.50, Main £19.50-£60, Dessert £7.25-£11.25 **Parking** 1000 **Notes** Sunday L £24.50-£32.50, Vegetarian available, Children welcome

WEST MIDLANDS

BALSALL COMMON Map 10 SP27

Nailcote Hall

 Traditional European

tel: 024 7646 6174 **Nailcote Ln, Berkswell CV7 7DE**
email: info@nailcotehall.co.uk **web:** www.nailcotehall.co.uk
dir: *On B4101 towards Tile Hill/Coventry, 10 mins from NEC/Birmingham Airport*

Flambéed steaks and modern cooking

Built on the eve of the Civil War, Nailcote is a stately home on a modest scale, with 15 acres of grounds containing what are reputedly some of England's oldest yew trees. Old-school service extends to tableside steak-flambéing, but otherwise the mood is modern, for contemporary classics such as scallops with puréed roasted cauliflower and Clonakilty black pudding, and appealing main dishes such as Gressingham duck breast with pak choi, sauce bigarade and an underlay of crunchy barley, or herb-crusted sea bass with red pepper and creamed leeks. For dessert, rhubarb and custard is reimagined as a parfait, topped with tangy apricot and ginger sorbet.

Chef Daniel Topa **Seats** 50, Pr/dining room 300 **Times** 12-2.30/7-9.30, Closed 31 Dec, L Sat, D 25 Dec **Prices** Fixed L 3 course £19.50-£21.50, Starter £5.90-£11.90, Main £14.50-£29.50, Dessert £6.50-£7.50 **Wines** 63 bottles over £30, 40 bottles under £30, 18 by glass **Parking** 200 **Notes** Fixed L Mon-Fri only, Afternoon tea daily, Sunday L £24.50-£32.50, Vegetarian available, Children welcome

BIRMINGHAM Map 10 SP08

Adam's

Modern British V

tel: 0121 643 3745 **New Oxford House, 16 Waterloo St B2 5UG**
email: info@adamsrestaurant.co.uk
dir: *In Birmingham city centre, 2 mins walk from New Street Station*

Dynamic contemporary cooking in the city centre

Adam and Nathasha Stokes moved their restaurant to a deliciously revamped premises around the corner from the original in early 2016. It's now spread over three floors, with a swanky bar at the front, a contemporary dining area and a large, funky kitchen (if you're into kitchens – in which case you might want to book the chef's table). Adam's cooking is confident and creative and he handles contemporary cooking techniques with a deft touch, maintaining the integrity of the ingredients at all times. Via a fixed-price carte, tasting menu and midweek lunch option, the kitchen turns out the likes of an impressively simple starter of purple sprouting broccoli, charred shallots and brown shrimps, with an ace béarnaise sauce on the side. Among main courses, a skilfully cooked piece of halibut arrives with celeriac, hazelnuts and crisp shards of air-dried ham, and, off the tasting menu, hare stars in a dish flavoured with Minus 8 vinegar and chocolate. Among desserts, sticky toffee pudding gets an extra dimension from its accompanying smoked lemon syrup. Everything from wonderful breads – served in a bespoke wooden box – to creative amuse-bouche such as beetroot and goats' cheese macaroons demonstrates attention to detail. One the city's best restaurants is even more exciting than before.

Chef Adam Stokes **Seats** 34, Pr/dining room 16 **Times** 12-2/7-9.30, Closed 2 wks summer, 3 wks Xmas, Sun-Mon **Prices** Fixed L 2 course £30, Tasting menu £85 **Wines** 84 bottles over £30, 6 bottles under £30, 19 by glass **Parking** On street **Notes** ALC menu 3 course £60, Children welcome

Carters of Moseley

Modern British V

tel: 0121 449 8885 & 449 2962 **2c Wake Green Rd, Moseley B13 9EZ**
email: enquiries@cartersofmoseley.co.uk **web:** www.cartersofmoseley.co.uk
dir: *B4217 Wake Green Rd off A435 Alcester Rd. On St Mary's Row slip road just past St Mary's Church*

Modern British food interpreted with simplicity and skill

The unassuming location amid a parade of shops belies this restaurant's ambition. Fixed-price menus tend to the lighter at lunch, perhaps for a soft-cooked duck's egg with butterscotch cap mushrooms in chicken gravy, followed by a tranche of roast cod in seaweed butter with a bundle of marine flora – sea-aster, sea cabbage and samphire. In the evening, the repertoire extends to hay-seared venison 'sashimi' with apple and smoked celeriac, sea bass with fermented garlic, and beef cheek with truffled polenta and a king oyster. You'll need a will of iron to resist sticky toffee pudding served in a Tate & Lyle Golden Syrup tin with Madagascar vanilla ice cream.

Chef Brad Carter **Seats** 35 **Times** 12-2/6.30-9.30, Closed Sun-Mon **Prices** Fixed L 3 course £32-£60, Tasting menu £60-£75 **Wines** 41 bottles over £30, 12 bottles under £30, 9 by glass **Parking** 4, 12 spaces outside **Notes** Tasting menu 6 course, wine pairing £50, Children 8 yrs+

Circle Restaurant Birmingham Hippodrome

Modern British

tel: 0844 338 9000 *(Calls cost 7p per minute plus your phone company's access charge)* & 0121 689 3181 **B5 4TB**
email: restaurantreservations@birminghamhippodrome.com
dir: *Phone for directions*

Show-stopping food for theatregoers

Pre-theatre dining doesn't get much closer to curtain-up than at this large, open-plan restaurant on the second floor of the Hippodrome. You can even save your dessert for the interval; a uniquely quirky touch. A contemporary room with crisp-white walls dotted with vibrant artwork and background music, service is friendly and the modern British cooking is confident. Seared tuna with green beans, lemon, black olives and confit tomatoes is one way to start, perhaps followed by a well-balanced main of Staffordshire pork belly fillet, crackling, bok choy, crispy potatoes, pineapple and curry oil. A well-presented Pina Colada pannacotta with pineapple, coconut and mint syrup is one of several enjoyable desserts.

Hotel du Vin & Bistro Birmingham

British, French

tel: 0121 200 0600 **25 Church St B3 2NR**
email: info@birmingham.hotelduvin.com **web:** www.hotelduvin.com
dir: *M6 junct 6/A38(M) to city centre, over flyover. Keep left & exit at St Chads Circus signed Jewellery Quarter. At lights & rdbt take 1st exit, follow signs for Colmore Row, opposite cathedral. Right into Church St, across Barwick St. Hotel on right*

Bistro dining in converted former eye hospital

In an imposing 1884 red-brick building in the right-on Jewellery Quarter, you can sip an aperitif in the Bubble Lounge Bar or head downstairs to the vaulted Pub du Vin before dining in the stylish restaurant, with its Gallic-inspired decor of bare floorboards and round-backed wooden chairs at polished tables. Kick off with Comté cheese soufflé or seared scallops with sauce vièrge before tucking into one of the plats principaux: roast cod fillet with braised Puy lentils, button onions and pancetta, say, or beef bourguignon on the bone. End with that English favourite of treacle tart with clotted cream ice cream or cross the Channel for tarte au citron.

Lasan Restaurant

Indian

tel: 0121 212 3664 & 212 3665 **3-4 Dakota Buildings, James St, St Paul's Square B3 1SD**
email: info@lasan.co.uk
dir: *Near city centre, adjacent to Jewellery Quarter*

Stylish Indian fusion cooking for the Jewellery Quarter

Set in the Jewellery Quarter, Lasan is a stylish contemporary Indian restaurant. A vibrant atmosphere pervades the light and spacious split-level dining room, where the menu takes a broad sweep across the subcontinent to deliver regional authenticity alongside modern fusion touches. Start with batair, which comprises quail breast in mango and cashew cream, the leg in date molasses and a Scotched egg. Main courses run to Mysore khatta jhinga, king prawns and wilted greens in curry-leafed coconut milk with green mango. Herefordshire beef cheek is braised overnight for a wonderfully tender and delicately spiced dish, and, to finish, there's gajar – carrot sponge with ginger ice cream and raisins.

Chef Aktar Islam, Gulsher Khan **Seats** 74 **Times** 12-2.30/6-11, Closed 25 Dec, L Sat **Prices** Fixed L 2 course £40-£55, Fixed D 3 course £50-£60, Tasting menu £54.95-£69.95, Starter £11.95-£23.95, Main £16.95-£24.95, Dessert £6.95 **Wines** 14 bottles over £30, 12 bottles under £30, 7 by glass **Parking** On street **Notes** Sunday L £40-£60, Vegetarian available, Children 10 yrs+

Malmaison Birmingham

Modern, Traditional

tel: 0121 246 5000 **1 Wharfside St, The Mailbox B1 1RD**
email: birmingham@malmaison.com **web:** www.malmaison.com
dir: *M6 junct 6, follow the A38 (city centre), via Queensway underpass. Left to Paradise Circus, 1st exit Brunel St, right T-junct, Malmaison directly opposite*

Buzzy setting and smart brasserie-style cooking

The Malmaison team bring their brand of boutique swagger to this place in the Mailbox, a swanky shopping and eating venue. The brasserie, with its floor-to-ceiling windows and contemporary finish, is a relaxed and lively spot offering a menu of globally inspired contemporary dishes. Kick off with moules marinière or sticky Thai-style chicken wings, and move on to a steak cooked on the grill (Black Angus New York strip). With the likes of Goan tiger prawn curry and a slate of burgers up for grabs, this place is all about 21st-century comfort food. The Malbar comes into its own in the evening when cocktails and champagne bring in the crowds.

Chef Brian Neath **Seats** 120, Pr/dining room 20 **Times** 12-2.30/6-10.30 **Prices** Starter £5-£12.50, Main £14-£49, Dessert £6-£9 **Wines** 36 bottles over £30, 14 bottles under £30, 30 by glass **Parking** Mailbox car park chargeable **Notes** Fixed 2/3 course, Sunday L £19.99-£29.95, Vegetarian available, Children welcome

BIRMINGHAM *continued*

Opus Restaurant

Modern British V

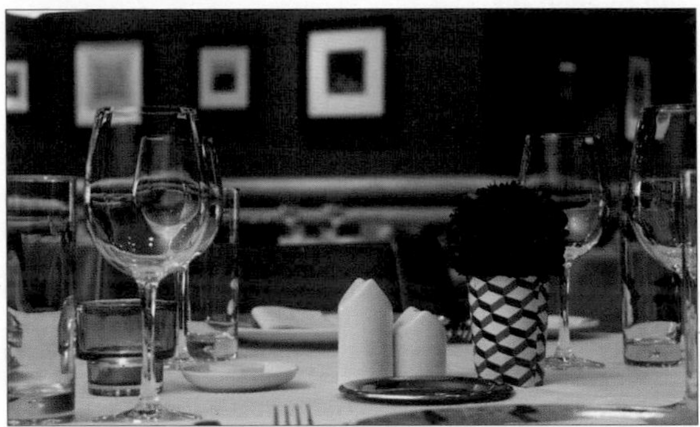

tel: 0121 200 2323 **54 Cornwall St B3 2DE**
email: restaurant@opusrestaurant.co.uk **web:** www.opusrestaurant.co.uk
dir: *Close to Birmingham Snow Hill railway station in the city's business district*

Smart city favourite for modern British cooking

Opus has bags of big-city attitude and a cosmopolitan vibe that suits its location in the city's financial quarter. Inside it's a stylish setting: darkwood floors, linen-clothed tables and jazzy wallpapers. Top-quality British produce anchors the whole operation. From the great-value market menu, a rich ballotine of chicken and wild mushrooms is offset by the summery lightness of broad bean and artichoke salad with watercress dressing, while roasted cod is partnered by crushed blue potatoes, and a spicy purée and crunchy tempura of cauliflower. If you're after something meaty, the carte might offer cottage pie poshed up with Wagyu beef and partnered by crushed root vegetables and spring greens.

Chef Ben Ternent **Seats** 85, Pr/dining room 32 **Times** 12-4/6-mdnt, Closed between Xmas & New Year, BHs, Sun, L Sat **Prices** Fixed L 2 course £20, Fixed D 2 course £20, Starter £5.50-£12.50, Main £13.50-£24, Dessert £2.25-£8 **Wines** 32 bottles over £30, 21 bottles under £30, 13 by glass **Parking** On street **Notes** Tasting menu 5 course, Kitchen table menu 5 course £75, Children welcome

Purnell's

Modern British NOTABLE WINE LIST

tel: 0121 212 9799 **55 Cornwall St B3 2DH**
email: info@purnellsrestaurant.com
dir: *Close to Birmingham Snow Hill railway station & junct of Church St*

Superbly accomplished and inventive cooking

The red-brick and terracotta site of Glynn Purnell's pace-setting city restaurant had an extensive new design job in 2015. Statement colours and counterpointing textures are in, with shades of aubergine and leafy green in the dining room, reached via an oak-shelved wine store. Jam jar lights illuminate the scene, a pillar box slot window affords kitchen peeps, while a soundtrack of rural noises accompanies your trip to the bathroom. It all makes a soothing context for the imaginative multi-course menus and 'Brummie tapas' where thoughtful combinations rule the roost. St Austell mussels with pickled cucumber and kohlrabi in dashi, followed by tuna sashimi and samphire in sour soy, are on-trend east Asia, but the compass needle swings westwards for principal dishes such as roast stone bass and pistachios with leeks in beurre noisette, or the majestic Balmoral venison bordelaise with pommes dauphinoise, red cabbage and black truffle. Winter might bring on something positively comforting such as a reimagined beef daube in sauce Albufera with duxelles and crisps, ahead of lemon meringue pie garnished with almonds and ginger powder. The tempting lunch deal might take in beetroot mousse with horseradish crumble, glazed pig cheek with treacle carrots, and dark chocolate tart with caramelised banana.

Chef Glynn Purnell **Seats** 45, Pr/dining room 12 **Times** 12-1.30/7-9, Closed 1 wk Etr, 2 wks late Jul-early Aug, Xmas, New Year, Sun-Mon, L Sat **Prices** Fixed L 3 course £35, Tasting menu £68-£88 **Wines** 208 bottles over £30, 6 bottles under £30, 16 by glass **Parking** On street, Snow Hill car park nearby **Notes** Tasting menu 6/12 course, Wine tasting fr £70, Vegetarian available, Children 10 yrs+

Simpsons

Modern British V NOTABLE WINE LIST

tel: 0121 454 3434 **20 Highfield Rd, Edgbaston B15 3DU**
email: info@simpsonsrestaurant.co.uk
dir: *1m from city centre, opposite St George's Church, Edgbaston*

Exceptional cooking in Edgbaston stalwart

Once a private house in leafy Edgbaston, chef-patron Andreas Antona's elegant restaurant with rooms has been at the forefront of Birmingham's gastronomic resurgence since 2004. The white Georgian house was extensively refurbished in 2015 to extend the main dining area and the conservatory extension overlooks the landscaped garden, which offers plenty of alfresco dining opportunities in the warmer months. Directing the day-to-day action in the kitchen is Nathan Eades, whose confident cooking delivers dishes displaying a high degree of finesse, an unwavering eye for detail and pin-sharp technical skills, all founded on the best ingredients available on the day. Crispy duck egg arrives with lentils, bacon, cep and chestnut, or you might start with cured trout teamed with buttermilk, pickled cucumber and smoked rye bread. Next up, ox cheek cooked in hay could be accompanied by onion purée, pearl barley, grapes and watercress. If you're up for fish, try the halibut with carrots, gingerbread, shrimps, buttermilk espuma and dill oil. Presentation remains impeccable through to a closing quince tarte Tatin with lemon thyme ice cream. As well as the carte and set-price lunch, there's a seven-course tasting menu with a veggie version and optional wine flight.

Chef Andreas Antona, Luke Tipping, Nathan Eades **Seats** 70, Pr/dining room 20 **Times** 12-2.30/7-9.30, Closed BHs, D Sun **Prices** Fixed L 3 course £45, Fixed D 3 course £55, Tasting menu £85 **Wines** 20 bottles over £30, 10 bottles under £30, 11 by glass **Parking** 12, On street **Notes** Tasting menu 7 course, Fixed L with wine, Sunday L, Children welcome

Turners

Modern British V

tel: 0121 426 4440 **69 High St, Harborne B17 9NS**
email: info@turnersrestaurantbirmingham.co.uk
dir: *Phone for directions*

Cooking up a gastronomic storm in a Birmingham suburb

The neat grey façade of Turners is unmistakable among the parade of shops on Harborne's high street. The modestly sized interior has had a new lick of paint and the addition of some chandeliers, but the wall mirrors etched with chef-patron Richard Turner's name remain, as do welcoming, friendly and attentive staff. The Simply Turners menu gives diners the flexibility of choosing up to six courses, which allows them the opportunity to sample the range of the kitchen's output. Richard follows a modern British approach, with some European flourishes, paying regard to flavour and texture combinations in his dishes, which means respecting his raw materials in terms of contrast and harmony. Mackerel with seaweed and horseradish may precede an impressive starter of langoustines with apple, celeriac and celery, followed in turn by the rich, forthright tastes of Anjou pigeon with duck liver, truffle, artichokes and watercress. Sea bass fillet is fashionably paired with oxtail and served with Yukon gold, salsify, chard and Jerusalem artichoke, and venison fillet with beetroot and accompanied by chervil root, pear and sprouts. Happy endings are guaranteed when there's raspberry and lemon verbena soufflé to go for. There's also a good-value set-price lunch and a tasting menu.

Chef Richard Turner **Seats** 28 **Times** 12-2.30/6-9.30, Closed Sun-Mon, L Tue-Thu **Prices** Prices not confirmed **Wines** 89 bottles over £30, 1 bottle under £30, 10 by glass **Parking** At rear **Notes** Children welcome

DORRIDGE **Map 10 SP17**

Hogarths Hotel

Modern British

tel: 01564 779988 **Four Ashes Rd B93 8QE**
email: reception@hogarths.co.uk **web:** www.hogarths.co.uk
dir: *M42 junct 4, exit onto A3400 Henley, 1st left onto Gale Ln, at T-junct left onto Four Ashes Rd*

Mediterranean-influenced brasserie food in a stylish setting

A little Midlands village is the setting for Hogarths, a picturesque location that also manages to be handy for the NEC and the airport. Fresh Mediterranean-influenced brasserie food is the bill of fare, with quality produce in simple preparations. A fig, walnut and blue cheese tart dressed in balsamic reduction packs a good flavour to begin with, as does treacle- and gin-cured salmon with sour cream and soda bread. The Inka charcoal grill works its magic for rib-eye steaks that come with the full set of onion rings, mushrooms and triple-cooked chips, or there's Spanish-themed hake on chorizo and saffron cassoulet. Try a citrussy take on baked Alaska to finish.

Chef Alex Alexandrov **Seats** 80, Pr/dining room 100 **Times** 12-3/6-10 **Prices** Fixed L 2 course £15-£32, Fixed D 3 course £25-£45, Starter £5-£9.60, Main £13-£28, Dessert £5-£8 **Parking** 120 **Notes** Afternoon tea, Sunday L £29-£35, Vegetarian available, Children welcome

HOCKLEY HEATH **Map 10 SP17**

Nuthurst Grange Hotel

 Modern British

tel: 01564 783972 **Nuthurst Grange Ln B94 5NL**
email: info@nuthurst-grange.co.uk **web:** www.nuthurst-grange.com
dir: *Exit A3400, 0.5m S of Hockley Heath. Turn at sign into Nuthurst Grange Lane*

Traditional and modern cooking amid private woodland

Nuthurst's long tree-lined avenue approach leads to a brick-built Victorian mansion in private woodland, so allow plenty of time for exploring. A judicious balance of culinary modernism and traditional ideas is evident on the menus, describing an arc from lobster and crab cocktail with tomatoes and brown bread to creamed sea trout and mascarpone terrine with Parma ham crisps and gingerbread among the starters. Dishes have a lot in them but manage not to look crowded, and might include duck breast with a pasty, roast parsnips, potato croquettes and roughly puréed trompette mushrooms in Madeira jus. Artfully arranged desserts include pineapple soufflé with Valrhona salted caramel chocolate mousse and nutty florentines.

MERIDEN **Map 10 SP28**

Best Western Plus Manor NEC Birmingham

Modern British, French

tel: 01676 522735 **Main Rd CV7 7NH**
email: reservations@manorhotelmeriden.co.uk **web:** www.manorhotelmeriden.co.uk
dir: *M42 junct 6, A45 towards Coventry then A452 signed Leamington. At rdbt take B4102 signed Meriden, hotel on left*

Smart upbeat cooking in a Midlands manor

The Regency Restaurant in this elegant hotel in the village of Meriden makes its mark with modern takes on classic dishes. It is an airy, traditionally styled space hung with paintings of English country scenes above smartly dressed tables. Assured and unpretentious modern British cooking is the order of the day, starting with crab and scallop ravioli teamed with samphire and prawn bisque, followed by a piggy trio of pork tenderloin medallions, smoked pig's cheek and a trotter bonbon partnered with apricot and sage compôte, carrots, dauphinoise potato and thyme jus. The show closes with another well-matched trio – salted caramel parfait, white chocolate popcorn and a mini crème brûlée.

Forest of Arden Marriott Hotel & Country Club

Modern British V

tel: 01676 522335 **Maxstoke Ln CV7 7HR**
email: ankush.sharma@marriotthotels.com **web:** www.marriottforestofarden.co.uk
dir: *M42 junct 6 onto A45 towards Coventry, over Stonebridge flyover. After 0.75m left into Shepherds Ln. Left at T-junct. Hotel 1.5m on left*

Good eating at a smart golfing hotel

A sprawling hotel with lots going on – golf and a spa for starters – the Forest of Arden Marriott is well-positioned for doing business in Brum, with the NEC and airport close to hand, and its Oaks Bar and Grill is a restaurant worth a trip in its own right. The kitchen deals in honest modern cooking without airs and graces, setting out with cider-steamed mussels with parsley and cream, followed by feather blade beef, braised to melting tenderness for six hours and served simply with mash and kale. To finish, apple and almond flapjack crumble is served with proper custard and apple crisps.

Chef Darcy Morgan **Seats** 192, Pr/dining room 18 **Times** 1-2.30/6.30-9.45 **Prices** Prices not confirmed **Wines** 16 by glass **Parking** 300 **Notes** Children welcome

OLDBURY Map 10 SO98

Saffron Restaurant

 Modern Indian

tel: 0121 552 1752 **909 Wolverhampton Rd B69 4RR**
email: info@saffron-online.co.uk
dir: *M5 junct 2. Follow A4123 (S) signs towards Harborne. Restaurant on right*

Smart modern setting for up-to-date Anglo-Indian fusion cooking

This contemporary Black Country Indian goes for a bold colour scheme involving scarlet and black chairs arranged in a chequerboard pattern at darkwood tables. The menu covers tandoori staples and classics (Punjabi saag gosht or chicken tikka masala, for instance) and more refined ideas built on quality, fresh ingredients. Catching the eye among starters is rabbit varuval, a South Indian speciality teaming tender rabbit with onion, curry leaves, mustard seeds and a palate-tingling hit of chilli. The signature dishes show a kitchen that's happy to innovate in the fusion style, with ideas such as pan-fried spiced red mullet with chickpea and spinach gâteau, sauced with cumin and coriander-scented beurre blanc.

Chef Sudha Shankar Saha, Avijit Mondol **Seats** 96, Pr/dining room 30 **Times** 12-2.30/5.30-11, Closed D 25 Dec **Prices** Prices not confirmed **Wines** 38 bottles under £30, 8 by glass **Parking** 25, On street **Notes** Sunday L, Vegetarian available, Children welcome

SOLIHULL Map 10 SP17

Hampton Manor

4 Rosettes – *see below*

SUTTON COLDFIELD (ROYAL) Map 10 SP19

The Oak Room Restaurant

2 Rosettes Modern British

tel: 0121 308 3751 **Moor Hall Hotel & Spa, Moor Hall Dr, Four Oaks B75 6LN**
email: mail@moorhallhotel.co.uk **web:** www.moorhallhotel.co.uk
dir: *A38 onto A453 towards Sutton Coldfield, right at lights into Weeford Rd. Hotel 150yds on left*

Elegant setting for a contemporary menu

A family-run country-house hotel set in parkland, Moor Hall's panelled Oak Room restaurant has a real sense of grandeur and lovely views over the grounds, including the golf course. Contemporary British cooking from a young kitchen team emphasises quality ingredients, on show in starters such as seared scallops with smoked cauliflower purée and black pudding crumb, or ham hock terrine with piccalilli, charred cucumber and crispy pig's ear. Mains might include saddle of rabbit with vanilla and celeriac purée and potato terrine, or wild mushroom, ale and salsify pie with truffle mash. Treacle tart is a traditional finish.

Chef Sean Byrne **Seats** 70, Pr/dining room 30 **Times** 12-2/7-9.30, Closed L Mon-Sat, D Sun **Prices** Tasting menu fr £49, Starter £6-£9.50, Main £16.50-£24.50, Dessert fr £5.50 **Wines** 13 bottles over £30, 38 bottles under £30, 10 by glass **Parking** 170 **Notes** Carvery open L only, Sunday L fr £22.95, Vegetarian available, Children welcome

Hampton Manor

SOLIHULL Map 10 SP17

Modern British V

tel: 01675 446080 **Swadowbrook Ln, Hampton-in-Arden B92 0EN**
email: info@hamptonmanor.com **web:** www.hamptonmanor.com
dir: *M42 junct 6 follow signs for A45 (Birmingham). At 1st rdbt, 1st exit onto B4438 (Catherine de Barnes Ln). Left into Shadowbrook Ln*

Imaginative contemporary cooking and bags of boutique style

You're only a couple of minutes down the line from the railway station for Birmingham airport, and yet, roaming the 45 acres of mature woodland in which Hampton is set, you'll find this is a thoroughgoing pastoral retreat. Quite the stately pile in fact, as inside is all relaxing elegance, the stylish guest rooms named after historic personages, including the founder of the modern police force, who is honoured in Peel's Restaurant. Overlooking the clock-tower gardens, this former dining room of the manor is a suitably impressive setting with its original oak panelling, grand fireplace, and stunning chinoiserie style wall friezes, with brilliant birds and floral motifs hand-woven in silk. The highly polished cookery to match comes from Rob Palmer, who takes a confident approach with dishes built on a few fine ingredients rather than an avalanche. Begin with a double act of crackled pork belly and langoustine, garnished with diced apple and leek in a ginger-inflected sauce. At main course, there may be halibut with mussels and Jerusalem artichoke purée, or beautifully rendered Muscovy duck breast in lavender oil with carrot variations – some purée, finely shredded shards with golden raisins, and one hefty great brute sitting there entire. A complex dessert construction offers chocolate crémeux, hazelnut ice cream, PX sherry and nitro-frozen chocolate, or there could be a passionfruit creation with bubbled white chocolate and liquorice. Incidentals, from architecturally inventive canapés to petits fours, both of which are served on flat stones, are equally stunning.

Chef Rob Palmer **Seats** 26, Pr/dining room 14 **Times** 6.30-9, Closed Sun-Mon, L all week **Prices** Tasting menu £55-£75, Starter £10-£15, Main £20-£34, Dessert £11-£14 **Wines** 122 bottles over £30, 26 bottles under £30, 13 by glass **Parking** 30 **Notes** D 4 course £35, Afternoon tea, Children welcome

Restaurant at New Hall

Modern British

tel: 0121 378 2442 **Walmley Rd B76 1QX**
email: newhall@handpicked.co.uk **web:** www.handpickedhotels.co.uk/newhall
dir: *On B4148, E of Sutton Coldfield, close to M6 & M42 junct 9*

Modern fine dining in historic house

It's hard to believe but before Birmingham's suburban sprawl engulfed the village of Sutton Coldfield, this 800-year-old moat house stood in empty countryside. Nowadays, it's cushioned from the hurly-burly of modern Brum by 26 acres of fabulous grounds. The Bridge Restaurant is the top-end dining option, where mullioned stained-glass windows blend with a gently modern neutral decor. Ham hock and goose liver terrine is matched with poached cherries and chamomile jelly, ahead of crisp-skinned stone bass with spiced aubergine, fennel, sunblushed tomatoes and lemon, and a crab beignet. A vibrant finale delivers glazed lemon tart with raspberry sorbet, meringue and fresh raspberries.

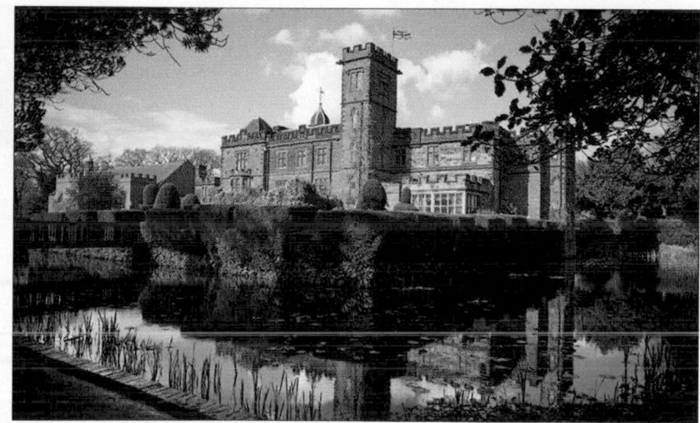

Chef Matthew Warburton **Seats** 52, Pr/dining room 12 **Times** 12-2.30/7-9.30, Closed L Mon-Sat **Wines** 21 bottles under £30, 14 by glass **Parking** 60 **Notes** Sunday L £25-£35, Vegetarian available, Children welcome

WALSALL Map 10 SP09

Fairlawns Hotel & Spa

Modern British V

tel: 01922 455122 **178 Little Aston Rd, Aldridge WS9 0NU**
email: reception@fairlawns.co.uk **web:** www.fairlawns.co.uk
dir: *Outskirts of Aldridge, 400yds from junct of A452 (Chester Rd) & A454*

Modern cooking in a characterful family-run hotel

Well placed to reach virtually anywhere in the West Midlands, the spa hotel near Walsall is family-owned and a refreshing antidote to corporate anonymity. The stylish dining room is decorated with vivid paintings, wooden blinds and globe light fittings. An extensive Market Menu of modern British ideas might open with a trio of potted rabbit meat, loin and cutlets with salt-baked carrots, baby gem and radish. Mains bring on the likes of venison loin and bolognese with kale, pumpkin and elderberries. Indulge yourself at the finishing line with date and raisin pudding served with clotted cream ice cream, smoked caramel sauce and toffee popcorn.

Chef Paul Soczowka **Seats** 80, Pr/dining room 100 **Times** 12-2/7-10, Closed 25-26 Dec, 1 Jan, Good Fri, Etr Mon, May Day, BH Mon, L Sat **Prices** Fixed L 2 course fr £17.50, Fixed D 3 course fr £33.95 **Wines** 20 bottles over £30, 40 bottles under £30, 12 by glass **Parking** 120 **Notes** Afternoon tea £19.95, Sunday L fr £22.50, Children welcome

WOLVERHAMPTON Map 10 SO99

Bilash

Indian, Bangladeshi

tel: 01902 427762 **2 Cheapside WV1 1TU**
email: m@thebilash.co.uk
dir: *Opposite Civic Hall & St Peter's Church*

A happy mix of new and old ideas in longstanding Indian

Bilash has been pushing beyond the confines of mere curry since 1982. The stylishly clean-cut interior works a colourful decor, with high-backed seats at wooden tables and walls hung with modern Indian-themed prints, a smart contemporary setting that reflects the kitchen's creative roll call of Bangladeshi and Indian dishes. Start with jalpari kebab – saffron-flavoured fish rolls stuffed with prawns – or spicy chicken patties, then follow with palak gosht (spiced lamb with spinach), hot Bengali-style fish curry, or chicken tikka in spicy tomato sauce. Vegetarian dishes, among them bhindi bhaji, and sundries like naan are well up to the mark, and don't miss out on a pudding.

Chef Sitab Khan **Seats** 48, Pr/dining room 40 **Times** 12-2.30/5.30-10.30, Closed 25-26 Dec, 1 Jan, Sun **Prices** Fixed L 2 course £9.95-£15.95, Fixed D 3 course £24.95-£34.95, Tasting menu £39.95-£55.95, Starter £5.90-£7.95, Main £10.90-£22.90, Dessert £6.90-£8.90 **Wines** 4 bottles over £30, 12 bottles under £30, 5 by glass **Parking** 15, Civic car park **Notes** Pre-theatre D, Tasting menu with wine, Vegetarian available, Children welcome

The Mount Hotel and Conference Centre

Modern European

tel: 01902 752055 & 752400 **Mount Rd, Tettenhall Wood WV6 8HL**
email: sales@themount.co.uk **web:** www.themount.co.uk
dir: *M54 junct 5, follow A41 down to Yew Tree Lane which becomes Mount Road, left at lights*

Buzzy brasserie cooking stately house style

In a stately Victorian mansion overlooking the canal, the dining room wears a more understated modern look. Expect brasserie buzz rather than a country-house whispering gallery, and food that satisfies most modern tastes. Spiced crab and saffron tortellini with brown crab aïoli in shellfish bisque has an array of appetising flavours in it, while pickled quince and raisin purée sharpen up a slice of chicken liver pâté. Lamb two ways presents braised shoulder and fried rump on quinoa with a thoroughgoing Moroccan-spiced jus, though grilled steaks are the principal main-course draw. Chocolate and raspberry delice sprinkled with amaretti crumbs is a classy finisher.

Chef Craig Thomas **Seats** 38, Pr/dining room **Times** 12-3/6-10 **Wines** 8 bottles over £30, 16 bottles under £30, 9 by glass **Parking** 120 **Notes** Sunday L £17.95-£19.95, Vegetarian available, Children welcome

WILTSHIRE

BEANACRE Map 4 ST96

Beechfield House Restaurant

Modern British

tel: 01225 703700 **SN12 7PU**
email: reception@beechfieldhouse.co.uk **web:** www.beechfieldhouse.co.uk
dir: *M4 junct 17, A350 S, bypass Chippenham, towards Melksham. Hotel on left after Beanacre*

Contemporary country-house dining

Built in 1878 in the Venetian style, Beechfield House has been gently updated for 21st-century requirements. Soft classical music is just right for the handsome restaurant, with its chandelier, rug on the wooden floor, large gilded mirror above the mantelpiece and Roman blinds at the windows. The cooking follows a contemporary theme and keeps things fairly simple, serving up breast and confit leg of quail with English asparagus and watercress purée, then chargrilled rump of local lamb with smoked aubergine, peas and broad beans. There's a dab hand at desserts too, sending out baked vanilla cheesecake with blueberry compôte, and apple and orange sorbet.

Seats 70, Pr/dining room 20 **Times** 12-2/7-9.30, Closed 23-26 & 31 Dec, 1 Jan **Prices** Fixed L 2 course £15, Starter £6.50-£10.50, Main £16-£24.50, Dessert £6.50-£9.50 **Wines** 24 bottles over £30, 29 bottles under £30, 10 by glass **Parking** 70 **Notes** Sunday L £19.50-£22.50, Vegetarian available, Children welcome

BOX Map 4 ST86

The Northey Arms

British, European

tel: 01225 742333 **Bath Rd SN13 8AE**
email: thenorthey@ohhcompany.co.uk **web:** www.ohhpubs.co.uk
dir: *Between juncts 17 & 18 of M4, on A4 between Bath & Corsham*

Comforting pub grub with a local flavour

Looking rather swish after top-to-toe renovation, this old stone-built inn has been brought up to full 21st-century spec with seagrass chairs and boldly-patterned wallpaper in the split-level dining area. Locally-reared 32-day-aged steaks get star billing – perhaps a 14oz T-bone if you're feeling peckish – and come chargrilled with mushrooms, vine tomatoes, triple-cooked chips, and a choice of classic sauces. Otherwise, kick off with fishcakes with mango and chilli salsa, followed by pan-roasted lamb rump with ratatouille, rosemary potatoes, spinach and red wine jus. Fish is brought daily from Looe to appear in ideas such as red mullet matched with saffron mash, glazed baby onions and roast red pepper sauce.

Chef Chris Alderson **Seats** 70 **Times** 12-10, All-day dining, Closed 25-26 Dec, D 31 Dec, 1 Jan **Prices** Prices not confirmed **Wines** 19 bottles over £30, 38 bottles under £30, 17 by glass **Parking** 40 **Notes** Sunday L, Vegetarian available, Children welcome

BRADFORD-ON-AVON Map 4 ST86

The Muddy Duck

Modern British

tel: 01225 858705 **Monkton Farleigh BA15 2QH**
email: dishitup@themuddyduckbath.co.uk **web:** www.themuddyduckbath.co.uk
dir: *M4 junct 18/A46 Batheaston/A363 to Bradford on Avon then turning to Monkton Farleigh & follow road to village*

Flying high pub/restaurant in pretty village

This is a switched-on dining pub. Still very clearly 17th-century, as its walk-in inglenook, exposed beams and wooden floors testify in a bar that remains happy to serve pints and nibbles, it serves hearty, modern pub grub. Try a starter of full-flavoured butternut squash soup with diced chorizo and parmesan, followed by a really good rib-eye steak with herb and parmesan fries, Portobello mushrooms and mixed dressed leaves. Or go for Goan fish curry with lime pickle and toasted flatbread. Desserts can be as simple as good old home-made sticky toffee pudding with honeycomb and vanilla ice cream.

Chef Josh Roberts **Seats** 70 **Times** 12-2.30/6-9.30, Closed Xmas, D Sun **Prices** Starter £5.50-£9.95, Main £13.50-£28, Dessert £6.95-£8.95 **Wines** 19 bottles over £30, 32 bottles under £30, 12 by glass **Parking** 30 **Notes** Sunday L, Vegetarian available, Children welcome

The Three Gables

Modern Mediterranean V NOTABLE WINE LIST

tel: 01225 781666 **St Margaret St BA15 1DA**
email: info@thethreegables.com
dir: *M4 junct 18, A46 towards Bath, A363 Bradford-on-Avon, restaurant over Tower Bridge*

Modern Med in a contemporary setting

Opposite the town bridge, this old greystone building has been extensively restored in a sleek contemporary style. Eat in the upstairs dining room (which features the eponymous gables) or alfresco in summer. Dishes have modern Mediterranean feel, so you might want to start with ragout of ox cheek with a crispy hen egg, or Cornish crab fingers. Main courses might include poached guinea fowl with wild mushroom risotto and oyster mushrooms, or glazed fillet of sea bass with creamed cauliflower, onion bhaji and curry oil. Caramel pannacotta with mandarin ice cream brings things to a satisfying close.

Chef Giacomo Carrera **Seats** 55 **Times** 12-2/6.30-10, Closed 1-12 Jan, 1-15 Aug, Sun-Mon **Prices** Fixed L 2 course fr £14, Tasting menu fr £48, Starter £8.25-£14.50, Main £18.75-£26.50, Dessert fr £7.75 **Wines** 200 bottles over £30, 50 bottles under £30, 16 by glass **Parking** Public car park **Notes** Children welcome

CALNE Map 4 ST97

The White Horse

Modern British

tel: 01249 813118 **Compon Bassett SN11 8RG**
email: info@whitehorse-comptonbassett.co.uk
web: www.whitehorse-comptonbassett.co.uk
dir: *M4 junct 16 onto A3102, after Hilmarton village turn left to Compton Bassett*

A warm welcome and local produce

This charming old inn dates from the early 18th century and has had a long history of serving the community as bakery, grocery shop and, of course, the village pub. The menu may well be unpretentious, but it is not unimaginative. Free-range chicken liver parfait, for example, arrives with a Sauternes and chamomile jelly and brioche, while a main course fillet of sea bass is partnered by sweet Muscat risotto. There is a 'pub classics' menu, too, where home-made steak and kidney pie rubs shoulders with the house burger. For dessert, wild berry millefeuille with raspberry sorbet looks as pretty as a picture, and Sunday lunch is a traditional affair.

Chef Danny Adams **Seats** 45, Pr/dining room 45 **Times** 12-9, All-day dining, Closed D Sun **Prices** Prices not confirmed **Wines** 7 bottles over £30, 34 bottles under £30, 14 by glass **Parking** 45 **Notes** Sunday L, Vegetarian available, Children welcome

CASTLE COMBE — Map 4 ST87

The Bybrook at The Manor House, an Exclusive Hotel & Golf Club

Modern British V 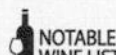

tel: 01249 782206 **SN14 7HR**
email: enquiries@manorhouse.co.uk **web:** www.manorhouse.co.uk
dir: *M4 junct 17, follow signs for Castle Combe via Chippenham*

Confident cooking in a pretty medieval village

Surveying the surroundings on a clear day, you could be forgiven for thinking that time has ground to a halt around these parts. The Manor House has stood here since the 14th century, the focal point of a feudal holding known as the Barony of Combe, only finally dissolved just after the last war. The village itself is endearing enough, but the house, now a grand country hotel where the grounds lend themselves readily to period film locations, is an immaculately maintained treasure. Tall green table vases add a splash of century-old moderne to the backdrop of armorially decorated mullioned windows in the Bybrook dining room. Robert Potter, the new chef here, has clear sense of purpose and clarity of thought and execution, underpinned by classic training, but which delivers punchy food in a smooth and effortless way. Start, perhaps with Cornish mackerel in marinated beetroot with a Porthilly oyster fritter, potato and horseradish mousse and then move on to a roasted loin of Brecon venison, potato compression, chestnut purée and roast baby parsnip. To finish, Amalfi lemon tart is hard to resist, delivering a perfect balance of sweetness and zest.

Chef Robert Potter **Seats** 60, Pr/dining room 100 **Times** 12.30-2/7-9.30, Closed L Mon-Sat **Wines** 300 bottles over £30, 25 bottles under £30, 20 by glass **Parking** 100 **Notes** Tasting menu 7 course, Sunday L £35, Children 11 yrs+

COLERNE — Map 4 ST87

The Brasserie

Modern British

'el: 01225 742777 **Lucknam Park Hotel & Spa SN14 8AZ**
'mail: brasserie@lucknampark.co.uk
lir: *M4 junct 17, A350 towards Chippenham, then A420 towards Bristol for 3m. At Ford eft to Colerne, 3m, right at x-rds, entrance on right*

;mart brasserie in majestic country-house hotel

'he Brasserie is the less formal dining option at Lucknam Park. Located within the valled garden, with a wall of glass of its own, it has a classy finish and serves up :lassy food from its open kitchen and a wood-burning oven. Start with crisp armesan beignets with tomato salsa, avocado and herbs, or a Brinkworth Blue heese mousse with parsnip fritters, pear and walnut salad, and truffled honey 'inaigrette. Slow-cooked pork belly might come in a main course with cumin auerkraut, carrot purée, roast apple and sage. To finish, there's the likes of atsuma, mango and pistachio in a creative trifle, or local farmhouse cheeses.

The Park Restaurant

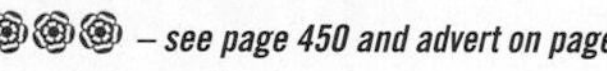
– see page 450 and advert on page 451

CORSHAM — Map 4 ST87

Guyers House Hotel

Modern European, British

tel: 01249 713399 **Pickwick SN13 OPS**
email: enquiries@guyershouse.com **web:** www.guyershouse.com
dir: *A4 between Pickwick & Corsham*

Dazzling creativity in a much-changed Wiltshire farmhouse

An elegant country house in handsome grounds (including kitchen garden and orchard) with a relaxing dining room patrolled by friendly staff, and menus with a real sense of creative elan. Begin with a fungal homage in the form of wild mushroom consommé with pickled girolles and mushroom jelly, glinting with gold leaf, or beetroot-cured salmon with orange and shallot salad. A dazzling fish course is perfectly timed brill fillets with smoked haddock raviolo, samphire, truffled cauliflower purée and a tuile dyed black with squid ink, while meat could be pork steak on merguez and bean cassoulet. The all-important chocolate and salted caramel combination comes as fondant and ice cream.

The Methuen Arms

British, Italian

tel: 01249 717060 **2 High St SN13 OHB**
email: info@themethuenarms.com **web:** www.themethuenarms.com
dir: *M4 junct 17 onto A350 towards Chippenham, at rdbt exit onto A4 towards Bath. 1m past lights, at next rdbt turn sharp left onto Pickwick Rd, 0.5m on left*

Destination restaurant in Georgian inn

In 1805 the former Red Lion took the Methuen family's name when it was rebuilt in Bath stone with three storeys and a fine portico. Inside are elm floorboards, rugs, log fires and neutral walls hung with local prints and etchings. The food boasts British roots with strong Italian influences. Try pork and pigeon terrine with fig and port purée and pecan and shallot salad. Then head for pan-fried cod, braised gem lettuce, samphire, potato and tarragon gnocchi and shellfish sauce. An Italian influence might reappear at dessert with affogato, or stay English with baked vanilla and custard cheesecake, poached rhubarb and rhubarb sorbet.

Chef Piero Boi **Seats** 60, Pr/dining room 20 **Times** 12-3/6-10, Closed 25-26 Dec **Prices** Fixed L 2 course fr £17.50, Fixed D 3 course fr £21.50, Starter £6-£10.50, Main £16.50-£25, Dessert fr £6.50 **Wines** 29 bottles over £30, 37 bottles under £30, 14 by glass **Parking** 40 **Notes** Party menu 3 course £29.50, Early supper £17.50-£21.50, Sunday L £22.50-£26.50, Vegetarian available, Children welcome

The Park Restaurant

COLERNE Map 4 ST87

Modern British V NOTABLE WINE LIST

tel: 01225 742777 **Lucknam Park Hotel & Spa SN14 8AZ**
email: reservations@lucknampark.co.uk
web: www.lucknampark.co.uk
dir: *M4 junct 17, A350 to Chippenham, then A420 towards Bristol for 3m. At Ford left towards Colerne. In 4m right into Doncombe Ln, then 300yds on right*

Enjoy skilful, individualist cooking from a vastly experienced chef

The approach down a tree-lined drive through the grounds – some 500 acres in total – raises expectations that are well and truly met when the glorious Palladian house comes into view. It's a stunner – grand, but not too imposing, just a beautiful house with a triple gable and portico entrance. Facilities such as a luxurious spa, equestrian centre and cookery school mark it out as one of the UK's top country-house experiences. There's a brasserie, but the main eaterie is The Park Restaurant, headed up by Hywel Jones for 10 years, which is one of the region's most compelling dining destinations. The restaurant is rich with period detail and is formally dressed – swagged curtains, chandeliers, and precise table settings. The impeccable service team seem full of pride, and it's the kind of place where you feel the need to dress up (smart casual is fine though). The kitchen gets full use of the kitchen garden and what isn't home grown is sourced from trusted suppliers, many of whom are certified organic. The setting may be formal and genteel, but the cooking is modern and creative. Things start with a roster of thrilling canapés and amuse-bouche including a sublime scallop and a fun yuzu lolly. The first course proper might see poached fillet of Devonshire rose veal with glazed sweetbreads, marinated salsify and Wiltshire truffles, or go for duck foie gras two ways. Among main courses, loin of Bwlch Farm venison comes with chocolate jelly and a hint of cumin, and braised fillet of turbot is partnered with Cornish crab, hand-rolled macaroni and Wiltshire truffle butter. The technical precision and accuracy of the cooking continues with desserts such as croustillante of roast pineapple with rum and raisin parfait.

Chef Hywel Jones **Seats** 70, Pr/dining room 28 **Times** 12.30-2.30/7-10, Closed Mon, L Tue-Sat **Prices** Fixed D 3 course fr £80, Tasting menu fr £105 **Wines** 270 bottles over £30, 30 bottles under £30, 12 by glass **Parking** 80 **Notes** Breakfast £19/£25, Sunday L fr £39, Children 5 yrs+

1720
LUCKNAM PARK
HOTEL & SPA, BATH

CRICKLADE Map 5 SU09

The Red Lion Inn

 Modern British

tel: 01793 750776 **74 High St SN6 6DD**
email: info@theredlioncricklade.co.uk **web:** www.theredlioncricklade.co.uk
dir: *Just off A419 between Swindon & Cheltenham*

Hearty food in a beer-oriented inn

A 17th-century inn with cosy beams, log fires and real ales from its own Hop Kettle microbrewery. Food is taken as seriously as the beer – the pub rears its own pigs, and veggies come from locals' allotments. Choose the bar for pub grub done right, or the contemporary country-chic dining room where the kitchen turns out dishes such as pan-fried local wood pigeon with beetroot carpaccio, smoked potato purée and chervil, ahead of a three-way serving of wild rabbit (loin, confit leg and faggot) with celeriac purée, dauphinoise potato and baby vegetables. For pud, perhaps chocolate and griottine cherry sponge with chocolate sauce and home-made cookie dough ice cream.

Chef James Maulgue **Seats** 40, Pr/dining room 16
Times 12-2.30/6.30-9, Closed 25-26 Dec, L all week, D Sun-Mon **Prices** Prices not confirmed **Wines** 7 bottles over £30, 24 bottles under £30, 9 by glass **Parking** On street **Notes** Sunday L, Vegetarian available, Children welcome

DEVIZES Map 4 SU06

The Peppermill

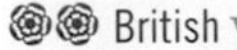 British V

tel: 01380 710407 **40 Saint John's St SN10 1BL**
email: philip@peppermilldevizes.co.uk **web:** www.peppermilldevizes.co.uk
dir: *In market place of town centre, opposite Santander Bank*

Unpretentious modern food in a lively venue

This family-run restaurant with rooms impresses with its contemporary, feel-good menu. In the evening you might start with BBQ-infused slow-roasted pork belly with carrot 'slaw', or potted shrimps with home-made brioche. Move on to a perfectly timed piece of swordfish with buttered cod cheeks and celeriac and vanilla purée, or 10oz rib-eye steak with triple-cooked chips and a choice of sauce. For dessert, the chocolate pot with home-made vanilla shortbread and sticky toffee pudding are just the job. At lunchtime, there are open sandwiches and wraps plus salads and light bites, plus steaks, salmon and chicken cooked on the grill. It is a popular place so it's worth booking ahead.

Chef Costinel Velicu **Seats** 60, Pr/dining room 12 **Times** 12-2.30/6-9, Closed D Sun **Prices** Fixed L 2 course £15-£20, Starter £5-£9, Main £12-£28, Dessert £5-£7 **Wines** 40 bottles over £30, 30 bottles under £30, 12 by glass **Parking** On street, Station Rd car park **Notes** Tue steak night £15, Thu fish night £15, Sunday L £50, Children welcome

FONTHILL BISHOP Map 4 ST93

The Riverbarn

 Modern British

tel: 01747 820232 **SP3 5SF**
email: info@theriverbarn.org.uk **web:** www.theriverbarn.org.uk
dir: *1m off A303 signed to Fonthill Bishop, on B3089 between Chilmark & Hindon*

Local produce in a charming rural setting

Some parts of the cottagey Riverbarn date back 600 years or so and the place has served the community in various ways over the centuries. The idyllic riverside setting plays its part in setting the mood, as does the charming service, with the simple decor and relaxed atmosphere recalling similar places across the Channel. Local produce and evident modernity appear in the construction of dishes in starters such as mullet céviche with crispy mullet and pickled ginger, for example. Roast rump of Wilshire lamb is a fine main course, cooked just right, or go for hake from south western waters. Finish with limoncello parfait with English raspberries and mint syrup.

Chef Jonny & Tom Sutcliffe **Seats** 40 **Times** 12-2.30/6.30-9, Closed Xmas & New Year, Mon, D Sun, Tue & Wed (ex for B&B guests) **Prices** Fixed L 2 course £20, Fixed D 3 course £25, Tasting menu £70, Starter £6-£9, Main £15-£22, Dessert £6-£8.50 **Wines** 13 bottles over £30, 17 bottles under £30, 12 by glass **Parking** 30 **Notes** Sunday L £22-£30, Vegetarian available, Children welcome

FOXHAM Map 4 ST97

The Foxham Inn

 Modern British

tel: 01249 740665 **SN15 4NQ**
email: info@thefoxhaminn.co.uk **web:** www.thefoxhaminn.co.uk
dir: *Off B4069 between Sutton Benger & Lyneham*

Local pub with imaginative menu based on local produce

Dinner is served in both the small bar and the purpose-built restaurant at this red-brick country inn. There's variety aplenty on the enticing menu, with starters running from snails with noodles in a light soya broth to sautéed lamb's sweetbreads in a creamy rosemary sauce spiked with sherry. Dishes have clear, distinct flavours: ham hock roasted with honey and mustard, say, with free-range eggs and chips, or roast poussin in mushroom sauce with creamed potatoes and green beans. Fish might appear as fillet of sea bass with white wine sauce, mash and spinach. Conclude with a theme on lemon (pannacotta, drizzle cake and ice cream).

Chef Neil Cooper **Seats** 60 **Times** 12-2.30/7-11, Closed 1st 2 wks Jan, Mon, D Sun **Prices** Prices not confirmed **Wines** 9 bottles over £30, 27 bottles under £30, 10 by glass **Parking** 16 **Notes** Sunday L, Vegetarian available, Children welcome

HORNINGSHAM Map 4 ST84

The Bath Arms at Longleat

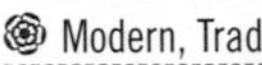 Modern, Traditional British

tel: 01985 844308 **Longleat Estate BA12 7LY**
email: enquiries@batharms.co.uk **web:** www.batharms.co.uk
dir: *A36 Warminster. At Cotley Hill rdbt 2nd exit (Longleat), Cleyhill rdbt 1st exit. Through Hitchcombe Bottom, right at x-rds. Hotel on the green*

Charming boutique hotel with accomplished cooking

A creeper-covered stone building, The Bath Arms is in a picturesque village within the Longleat Estate. The kitchen takes pride in sourcing produce from within 50 miles of the estate and in keeping within broadly British parameters. Ham hock and chicken terrine with piccalilli or beetroot-cured salmon with horseradish mousse may precede game and ale pie in rich gravy with seasonal vegetables or pan-fried sea bream with sunblush tomatoes, samphire, rocket and sautéed potatoes, all technically correct and full of distinct flavours. Breads are made in-house, as are puddings such as rhubarb and coconut crumble with coconut ice cream, or Earl Grey pannacotta with blood orange sorbet.

LITTLE BEDWYN Map 5 SU26

The Harrow at Little Bedwyn

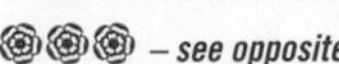 – *see opposite*

The Harrow at Little Bedwyn

LITTLE BEDWYN **Map 5 SU26**

Modern British V NOTABLE WINE LIST

tel: 01672 870871 **SN8 3JP**
email: office@theharrowatlittlebedwyn.com
web: www.theharrowatlittlebedwyn.com
dir: *Between Marlborough & Hungerford, well signed*

A shining beacon of quality food and wine in deepest Wiltshire

Little Bedwyn is a delightful village on the Wiltshire/Berkshire border, complete with a charming variety of thatched cottages, a 12th-century church, and the Kennet and Avon canal. The Harrow fits in comfortably – from the outside it's a classic Victorian red-brick country pub, creeper-clad and traditional, and one might be forgiven for expecting an equally traditional gastropub experience within. However one would be wrong. The dining rooms are smartly contemporary, warmed in cooler months by a double-sided wood-burner, and giving a relaxed feel with pale walls, elegantly clothed tables and comfortably upholstered seating. Chef-patron Roger Jones' enthusiasm and knowledge make the keenly-priced wine list a real feature, with pairings available for every dish on the menu, and this attention to detail is apparent throughout. Clearly believing that a chef is nothing without his suppliers he has spent years locating the very best producers and allowing their ingredients to inspire him to ever more creative combinations. Every element of every dish works together to best advantage, whether on the set menus or six- or eight-course tasting menus. (Vegetarians will be delighted with their own eight course option – the Tor goats' cheese and foraged sea herbs with smoked Isle of Wight tomatoes and Puy lentils with chestnuts being the sort of dishes that might even tempt the omnivores.) A five-course lunch might kick off with olives and sourdough, before taking in foie gras and salted caramel macaroon, moving on to seared tuna with pistachio and coriander and grilled Cornish cod with chorizo oil and winter cabbage, while a winter tasting menu might have lobster and truffle macaroni followed by line-caught wild turbot, fennel and squid, and fillet of roe venison with a quail and black pudding bonbon. Finish with cherry soufflé.

Chef Roger Jones, John Brown **Seats** 34
Times 12-3/7-11, Closed Xmas & New Year, Sun-Tue **Prices** Tasting menu £50 **Wines** 750 bottles over £30, 250 bottles under £30, 20 by glass **Parking** On street **Notes** Fixed L 5 course £30, Gourmet menu 8 course £75, Children welcome

LOWER CHICKSGROVE Map 4 ST92

Compasses Inn

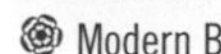 Modern British

tel: 01722 714318 **SP3 6NB**
email: thecompasses@aol.com **web:** www.thecompassesinn.com
dir: *Off A30 signed Lower Chicksgrove, 1st left onto Lagpond Ln, single-track lane to village*

Broadly appealing menu in an ancient inn

This thatched 14th-century inn is a charming place, with its low beams, standing timbers and menus more cosmopolitan than the surroundings would suggest. A highly professional brigade at the stoves delivers starters ranging from grilled pickled mackerel with radish and fennel salad and dill dressing to a canonical version of foie gras and chicken liver terrine with apricot and ginger chutney. There are 'traditionals', such as beer-battered hake with chips and tartare sauce, but there is adventure elsewhere, for example in duck breast in a Szechuan pepper glaze with basmati rice. Imaginative desserts stretch to ricotta and orange tart with cherry sorbet, and chocolate torte with mango ice cream.

Chef Dan Cousins, Ian Chalmers **Seats** 50, Pr/dining room 14
Times 12-3/6-11, Closed 25-26 Dec, L Mon (Jan-Mar) **Prices** Starter £5.50-£8.75, Main £8.50-£19.50, Dessert £6.25 **Wines** 2 bottles over £30, 28 bottles under £30, 8 by glass **Parking** 35 **Notes** Sunday L £9.95-£18.95, Vegetarian available, Children welcome

MALMESBURY Map 4 ST98

Whatley Manor Hotel and Spa

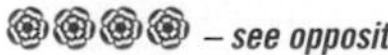 *– see opposite*

PEWSEY Map 5 SU16

Red Lion Freehouse

 British

tel: 01980 671124 **East Chisenbury SN9 6AQ**
email: enquiries@redlionfreehouse.com **web:** www.redlionfreehouse.com
dir: *Exit A303, at rdbt take A345 to Enford, right into East Chisenbury. Pub located on right*

Top-class produce handled with great skill

Dating from the Tudor period, this thatched pub has retained the look and feel of a traditional country inn, with sturdy unclothed wooden tables and a wood-burning stove in an inglenook and an informal, laid-back atmosphere. It might be in a tiny village on the edge of Salisbury Plain, but it's very much a destination restaurant. Virtually everything is made in-house, from smoked meats to ketchup, with kitchen gardens providing vegetables and everything else from local suppliers. The Mannings run a sure-footed kitchen, its output marked by dishes that can seem complex without being ostentatious, all elements working well together. A starter of well-timed tagliatelle with soft ox cheek in a red wine sauce with crispy bacon and breadcrumbs has impressed with its intense flavours. Imaginative and successful main courses have run from roast salmon fillet with beetroots, pickled apple, crispy kale and horseradish beurre blanc, to the full-on flavours of haunch of venison in red wine sauce with port-braised onions, glazed chicory and parsnip purée. Puddings might be as familiar as crème brûlée and as highly wrought as Valrhona and chestnut bombe, which comes as a shiny dome of chocolate encasing light chocolate mousse studded with pieces of chestnut accompanied by peat-smoked poached orange.

Chef Guy & Brittany Manning **Seats** 45, Pr/dining room 16
Times 12-2.30/6-9, Closed D 24-25 Dec **Prices** Fixed L 2 course fr £18, Starter £7-£10, Main £12.50-£30, Dessert £7-£10 **Wines** 35 bottles over £30, 19 bottles under £30, 20 by glass **Parking** 14 **Notes** Prix fixe menu Mon-Fri, Sunday L £20-£25, Vegetarian available, Children welcome

PURTON Map 5 SU08

The Pear Tree at Purton

Modern British

tel: 01793 772100 **Church End SN5 4ED**
email: stay@peartreepurton.co.uk **web:** www.peartreepurton.co.uk
dir: *From M4 junct 16, follow signs to Purton. Turn right at Best One shop, hotel 0.25m on right*

Conservatory dining in a former vicarage

Not a village pub as the name might suggest, but in fact a former vicarage turned into a country-house hotel. There's no shortage of global flavours on the menu – as is the modern British way – so starters run to smoked chicken timbale fired up with wasabi and pickled ginger, or a chicken breast served satay style. There's a refinement to the kitchen's output: the anything-but-humble pear and celeriac soup (with horseradish cream and sage oil), and main-course roasted loin of cod with an accompanying rösti enriched with fresh crab. Finish with a nicely tart glazed lemon tart. Check out the cuvée daughter Alix produces on the owners' own vineyard.

Chef Adam Conduit **Seats** 50, Pr/dining room 50 **Times** 12-2/6.30-9, Closed 26 Dec, D 25 Dec **Prices** Starter £5-£7.50, Main £12-£26, Dessert £5-£9 **Wines** 8 bottles over £30, 22 bottles under £30, 9 by glass **Parking** 30 **Notes** Afternoon tea £15, Sunday L £25, Vegetarian available, Children until 8.30

RAMSBURY Map 5 SU27

The Bell at Ramsbury

Modern British, European

tel: 01672 520230 **The Square SN8 2PE**
email: reservations@thebellramsbury.com **web:** www.thebellramsbury.com
dir: *M4 junct 14, A338 to Hungerford. B4192 towards Swindon. Left to Ramsbury*

Ambitious cooking in made-over country inn

An old village boozer reinvented as a smart food-oriented inn. The Shaker-style tea room does cakes and snacks, while a pint of Ramsbury Brewery's finest complements the daily pies, burgers, and beer-battered fish and chips in the bar. Trade up to the more formal restaurant for ambitious dishes such as leek and mussel pâté with crisp breaded mussels and braised red peppers preceding venison (from the Ramsbury Estate) with celeriac mash, red cabbage and roasted carrots, or pan-fried duck breast with a bonbon of spiced leg meat, roasted tomatoes and couscous. For dessert, golden syrup adds depth to a crème brûlée paired with caramelised puff pastry and mandarin sorbet.

Chef Jonas Lodge **Seats** 42, Pr/dining room 22 **Times** 12-3/6-9.30, Closed 25 Dec, D Sun **Parking** 25 **Notes** Sunday L £19.50-£24.50, Vegetarian available, Children welcome

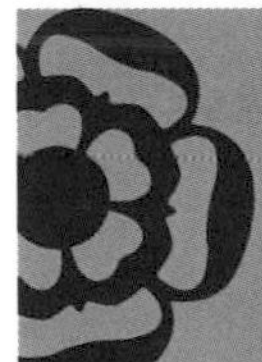

Who has won our Chef of the Year award? Find out on page 10

Whatley Manor Hotel and Spa

MALMESBURY **Map 4 ST98**

Modern French V NOTABLE WINE LIST

tel: 01666 822888 **Easton Grey SN16 0RB**
email: reservations@whatleymanor.com
web: www.whatleymanor.com
dir: *M4 junct 17, follow signs to Malmesbury, continue over 2 rdbts. Follow B4040 & signs for Sherston, hotel 2m on left*

Technically brilliant cooking in a luxury spa hotel

The manor house is late-Victorian and was originally part of the farmland estate of a rear admiral and his family. Its winning good looks made it perfect for transformation into a magnificent country-house hotel. There's a strong sense of stepping back in time as you pass through the huge doors, although the principal dining room is an understated modern place, with cream walls, bare floors and a measure of space around each table. Formidable culinary pyrotechnics await: Martin Burge has worked with some big-name players over the years, including a stint as Raymond Blanc's right-hand man at Le Manoir, and has been leading the line here since 2003, so you can expect supremely skilled cooking that delivers dishes full of complexity and intensity of flavour, presented with elegance. The evening format is a six-course tasting menu, opening perhaps with honey-glazed duck breast accompanied by Ibérico ham, foie gras and puréed pistachios, ahead of a sublime fish combination of lightly seared scallop, John Dory and battered cod cheek napped in bouillabaisse consommé. The main meat might be gloriously gamey venison loin with its own sausage and confit chestnuts in peppered brandy sauce, before the famous cheese presentation of deep-fried crottin and creamed Roquefort with black truffle ice cream and candied walnuts. A pair of desserts offers liquorice pannacotta, blackberry granité and pear sorbet, followed by the rousing finale of apple and maple syrup cheesecake with caramelised pecans. The extras, from a variety of breads and palate-priming canapés to intricate petits fours, all help to create a complete package. The pre-arranged wine flight with dinner is well worth the extra outlay.

Chef Martin Burge **Seats** 40, Pr/dining room 30
Times 7-10, Closed Mon-Tue, L all week **Prices** Tasting menu £110-£175 **Wines** 350 bottles over £30, 5 bottles under £30, 16 by glass
Parking 120 **Notes** Tasting menu additional 10% service charge, Children 12 yrs+

ROWDE Map 11 SP75

The George & Dragon

Modern British, Mediterranean V

tel: 01380 723053 **High St SN10 2PN**
email: restaurant@thegeorgeanddragonrowde.co.uk
web: www.thegeorgeanddragonrowde.co.uk
dir: *On A342, 1m from Devizes towards Chippenham*

Tudor inn with Cornish seafood and more

This Tudor coaching inn stands on the main road through the unassuming village of Rowde, and has a strong reputation as a destination dining venue for the area. The attractively traditional and rustic country finish is part of its charm, while the daily-changing menu of modern pub food makes a fitting speciality of seafood hauled in from the boats at St Mawes in Cornwall. Scallops and black pudding arrive on skewers, spicy fishcakes come with hollandaise sauce, and lemon sole is cooked on the bone to perfection, but there are impressive meaty options too, such as roast chicken with curried bubble and squeak.

Chef Christopher Day **Seats** 35 **Times** 12-3/6.30-11, Closed D Sun **Prices** Fixed L 2 course fr £16.50, Fixed D 3 course fr £19.50, Starter £7-£10, Main £12-£25, Dessert £6 **Wines** 4 bottles over £30, 4 bottles under £30, 9 by glass **Parking** 14 **Notes** Sunday L £19.50, Children welcome

SALISBURY Map 5 SU12

Salisbury Seafood & Steakhouse

Modern, Traditional International

tel: 01722 417411 & 424110 **Milford Hall Hotel, 206 Castle St SP1 3TE**
email: info@salisburyseafoodandsteakhouse.co.uk
web: www.salisburyseafoodandsteakhouse.co.uk
dir: *From A36 at rdbt on Salisbury ring road, right onto Churchill Way East. At St Marks rdbt left onto Churchill Way North to next rdbt, left in Castle St*

More than surf 'n' turf in a stylish setting

The restaurant is part of the Milford Hall Hotel, an extended Georgian mansion in pretty gardens. It's a smartly appointed room, with a blond wood floor, brown and cream high-backed dining chairs and one wall occupied by bottles of wine. You can dine very well on a seafood starter of house-cured gravad lax (in vodka, dill and orange as it happens), before tucking into one of the 28-day dry-aged Wiltshire steaks (10oz sirloin, say), served with triple-cooked chips. Barbecue ribs are glazed in Jack Daniels, seafood stew is flavoured with basil and chilli, and to finish there might be chocolate and hazelnut parfait.

Chef Chris Gilbert **Seats** 55, Pr/dining room 20 **Times** 12-2/6-10 **Prices** Starter £6-£9.95, Main £12-£21, Dessert £5.95-£7.95 **Wines** 2 bottles over £30, 32 bottles under £30, 11 by glass **Parking** 60 **Notes** Sunday L £9.95-£19.95, Vegetarian available, Children welcome

SWINDON Map 5 SU18

Chiseldon House Hotel

Modern European, British

tel: 01793 741010 **New Rd, Chiseldon SN4 ONE**
email: welcome@chiseldonhouse.com **web:** www.chiseldonhouse.com
dir: *M4 junct 15, A346 signed Marlborough. After 0.5m turn right onto B4500 for 0.25m, hotel on right*

Unfussy fine dining in a Regency manor house

The grand Regency manor house is a popular wedding venue, with the Marlborough Downs and attractive gardens providing a stunning backdrop, and the M4 nearby. The restaurant is a bright space with crisp white linen on the tables and a cheerful service team. The cooking takes a fine-dining stance, with lots going on and an eye for presentation. A starter of potted duck liver parfait comes with black truffle butter, piccalilli and Melba toast, then main-course pressed belly of pork is served with chorizo hash, apple fritter and black mustard seed dressing. For dessert: baked apple crumble cheesecake with pistachio brittle and lemon curd ice cream.

Chef Paul Suter **Seats** 100, Pr/dining room 32 **Times** 12-2/7-9 **Prices** Prices not confirmed **Wines** 7 by glass **Parking** 40 **Notes** Brunch served BHs, Champagne afternoon tea £25, Sunday L, Vegetarian available, Children welcome

TOLLARD ROYAL Map 4 ST91

King John Inn

British NEW

tel: 01725 516207 **SP5 5PS**
email: info@kingjohninn.co.uk **web:** www.kingjohninn.co.uk
dir: *From A354 or A350 onto B3081, 7m E Shaftesbury*

Hearty flavours in a village inn

You might expect a Victorian country inn on the Wiltshire-Dorset border to be a good bet for hearty English food built on a bedrock of game and local produce, and the King John obliges. The chef is there all the way from field to plate, shooting most of the game himself, and it's all served up in a country-chic setting with quarry tile floors and a solid oak bar. Local chalk stream trout is fresh enough to turn up as sashimi with soy sauce and wasabi, while venison haunch of outstanding quality comes with green beets, carrots and bacon. The wine list is a real corker too.

Chef Lloyd Bartlett **Seats** 50 **Times** 12-2.30/7-9 **Prices** Fixed L 2 course fr £15, Starter £5.95-£11.95, Main £12.95-£31, Dessert £3.95-£8.95 **Wines** 20 by glass **Notes** Sunday L £13.95-£22.95, Vegetarian available, Children welcome

WARMINSTER Map 4 ST84

The Bishopstrow Hotel & Spa

Modern British V

tel: 01985 212312 **Borenam Rd BA12 9HH**
email: info@bishopstrow.co.uk **web:** www.bishopstrow.co.uk
dir: *From Warminster take B3414 (Salisbury). Hotel signed*

Modern British cooking in a light-filled elegant Regency house

Surrounded by 27 acres of grounds alongside the River Wylye, this creeper-clad Regency mansion is now a glossy country-house hotel with a cool contemporary spa. The mood is airy and elegant, with neutral tones and light from full-length windows suffusing the dining rooms. The kitchen team creates vibrant contemporary menus, supported by top-class ingredients from the estate and local area. Garlicky pigeon Kiev with mulled wine syrup, golden raisins and candied walnuts is a typical starter. The main course sees pork tenderloin and belly matched with fondant potato, quince, apples, crackling and sweet cider jus. Baileys cheesecake with chocolate fondue provides a luscious finale.

Chef Jon Los **Seats** 65, Pr/dining room 30 **Times** 12-2/7-9.30 **Prices** Prices not confirmed **Wines** 50 bottles over £30, 5 bottles under £30, 8 by glass **Parking** 70 **Notes** Sunday L, Children welcome

WORCESTERSHIRE

ABBERLEY — Map 10 SO76

The Manor Arms

Modern International NEW V

tel: 01299 890300 & 890453 **The Village WR6 6BN**
email: enquiries@themanorarms.co.uk **web:** www.themanorarms.co.uk
dir: *N of Worcester on A443, follow brown tourist signs for The Manor Arms. From Ombersley, A443 towards Tenbury. After Great Witley, right onto B4202. Right into Netherton Ln, on right*

Charming pub with a real buzz

Originally dating from the 17th century, today's pub is a valuable part of the community, appreciated by locals and visitors alike (note the six classy bedrooms). The traditional decor inside is entirely in keeping and the finish is smart but informal. Lunch focuses more on pub classics – fish pie, say, or the varied delights of the farmhouse board – while in the evening you might start with ballotine of rabbit with pickled vegetables and move on to Dover sole with champagne sauce. There are also crowd pleasers such as Thai red duck curry and sausage and mash available in the evening.

Chef Liam Courage **Seats** 90, Pr/dining room 36 **Times** 12-2.30/6-9, Closed D Sun **Prices** Starter £7-£8, Main £10-£22, Dessert £6-£7 **Wines** 15 bottles over £30, 29 bottles under £30, 14 by glass **Parking** 30 **Notes** Sunday L, Children welcome

BEWDLEY — Map 10 SO77

The Mug House Inn

Modern British

tel: 01299 402543 **12 Severnside North DY12 2EF**
email: drew@mughousebewdley.co.uk **web:** www.mughousebewdley.co.uk
dir: *B4190 to Bewdley. On river, just over bridge on right*

Inventive modern British pub cookery

This Georgian inn is an entirely pleasing place, with hanging baskets adorning the white façade, and views of river traffic on the Severn. Lively ideas start with king prawns dressed in crisp vodka-and-tonic-infused batter and spiked with sautéed shallots, chilli, garlic-smoked salt and sweet chilli and lime dipping sauce. They continue in a main-course assiette of pork that features roast loin, slow-roasted belly, pulled pork croquettes flavoured with sage and apple, and home-made black pudding served with onion and thyme purée, mustard mash, warm slaw and a red wine reduction. To finish, 'Pimm's Mess' is a mash-up of meringue, cream, Pimm's syrup, strawberries, mint and cucumber sorbet.

Chef Drew Clifford, Mark Rhoden **Seats** 26, Pr/dining room 12 **Times** 12-2.30/6.30-9, Closed D Sun **Prices** Fixed D 3 course £16.50-£17.50, Starter £5.25-£6.95, Main £13.95-£29.95, Dessert £5.25-£7.95 **Wines** 1 bottle over £30, 26 bottles under £30, 10 by glass **Parking** Car park 100mtrs along river **Notes** Fixed D Mon-Thu only, Sunday L £9.95-£18.95, Vegetarian available, Children 10 yrs+

Royal Forester Country Inn

Modern European

tel: 01299 266286 **Callow Hill DY14 9XW**
email: royalforesterinn@btinternet.com **web:** www.royalforesterinn.co.uk
dir: *Phone for directions*

Contemporary dining in medieval inn

This historic inn has ancient beams and plenty of nooks and crannies, but with boutique bedrooms and an on-trend bar, it chimes with our times. The restaurant is the setting for a menu of classically-inspired dishes featuring Cornish seafood and some items foraged by the chef himself. Start with seared king scallops with local black pudding and cauliflower purée before moving on to spiced duck breast with a honey and anise jus. Steaks cooked on the grill are served with hand-cut chips, or find a willing accomplice and go for the roast rib of beef on the bone. Finish with a light lemon tart with Chantilly cream.

Chef Steven Patten **Seats** 60, Pr/dining room 18 **Times** 12-3/6-9.30 **Prices** Fixed L 2 course £13.99-£18.99, Starter £5.95-£9.95, Main £15-£25, Dessert £5.95 **Wines** 14 bottles over £30, 34 bottles under £30, 6 by glass **Parking** 25 **Notes** Gourmet menu with wine £30 1st Tue of month, Sunday L £10-£25, Vegetarian available, Children welcome

BROADWAY — Map 10 SP03

The Broadway Hotel

Traditional British

tel: 01386 852401 **The Green, High St WR12 7AA**
email: info@broadwayhotel.info **web:** www.cotswold-inns-hotels.co.uk/broadway
dir: *Follow signs to Evesham, then Broadway. Left onto Leamington Rd, hotel just off village green*

Nifty modern cooking in an atrium

The Broadway Hotel, overlooking the village green, has its roots in the 16th century, so Tattersall's Brasserie, in a contemporary light-filled atrium, is in sharp contrast to its traditional surroundings. The kitchen focuses on quality seasonal produce and has an assured sense of what will work, turning out appealing starters such as seared scallops with spiced cauliflower and pickled cucumber kimchi. Main courses maintain the momentum with Todenham pork, the pancetta-wrapped loin and twice-cooked belly with an apple and black pudding faggot in Bramley sauce. Ambition doesn't falter in desserts of caramelised pear tart with blackberry compôte, poached pear, toasted almonds and crème fraîche.

Chef Eric Worger **Seats** 60 **Times** 12-3/7-9.30 **Prices** Fixed L 2 course fr £15.50, Starter £6.25-£8.75, Main £16.50-£19.25, Dessert £6.50-£7.95 **Wines** 22 bottles over £30, 42 bottles under £30, 17 by glass **Parking** 15 **Notes** Prix fixe 2/3 course £15.50/£18.50, Breakfast £8.50-£16.50, Sunday L £19.50-£22.50, Vegetarian available, Children welcome

Dormy House Hotel

Modern British V

tel: 01386 852711 **Willersey Hill WR12 7LF**
email: reservations@dormyhouse.co.uk **web:** www.dormyhouse.co.uk
dir: *2m E of Broadway off A44, at top of Fish Hill turn for Saintbury/Picnic area. In 0.5m turn left, hotel on left*

Creative cooking in an impressive Cotswold house

Up on the hill above Broadway, that epitome of Cotswold charm, Dormy House is a delightfully cosy 17th-century former farmhouse, all golden stone, beams and panelling. The airy modern dining room enjoys fab garden views, and you can expect nicely constructed, thoughtful dishes from the modern British menu. Dinner might begin with lobster ravioli, Cornish crab, tomato and sea vegetables, or Tamworth pig with sage and onion, Bramley apple and crackling, before taking in squab pigeon with kohlrabi, cavolo nero and quince, or an onion tarte Tatin. Duck egg custard with Yorkshire rhubarb, oats and yogurt finishes things off nicely.

Chef Ryan Swift **Seats** 75, Pr/dining room 14 **Times** 12.30-2.30/7-9.30, Closed L Mon-Sat **Prices** Fixed D 3 course fr £45, Tasting menu fr £65 **Wines** 125 bottles over £30, 65 bottles under £30, 30 by glass **Parking** 70 **Notes** Sunday L fr £28, Children welcome

BROADWAY *continued*

The Fish

British NEW

tel: 01386 858000 & 852711 **Farncombe Estate WR12 7LJ**
email: reception@thefishhotel.co.uk **web:** www.thefishhotel.co.uk
dir: *Follow A44 to Moreton-in-Marsh then follow signs to Evesham & Broadway. Take Saintbury turn by Broadway Tower, estate on the left*

Relaxed contemporary dining with bucolic views

The sea is miles away, no river flows past, for The Fish is named after the hill on which it stands, because monks once cured fish in caves on the hillside. Part of a 400-acre estate, today's contemporary boutique hotel has an informal Scandi-chic style restaurant. A table on the terrace is a fair-weather treat. The kitchen's output matches the modern mood of the place, so you might start with scallops with smoked duck ham and cauliflower a couple of ways, move onto classic fish and chips, slow-roasted pork belly or a Med-inspired seared salmon with tapenade and salsa verde.

Chef Carl Holmes **Times** 12-2.30/6.30-9.30 **Prices** Starter £5-£11, Main £5-£26.50, Dessert £6-£8.50 **Wines** 43 bottles over £30, 32 bottles under £30, 11 by glass **Notes** Sunday L £19.50-£24.50, Vegetarian available, Children welcome

Russell's

Modern British

tel: 01386 853555 **20 High St WR12 7DT**
email: info@russellsofbroadway.co.uk **web:** www.russellsofbroadway.co.uk
dir: *A44 follow signs to Broadway, restaurant on High St opposite village green*

Modern cooking in a paradise of honey-coloured stone

In a prime spot on the High Street of this pretty, touristy village, Russell's is smartly decked out in contemporary style. Pressed pig's head terrine, its meat falling apart at the touch of a fork, is a well-executed starter, served with warm red wine jus and chunks of salsify and turnips braised in red wine, an alternative to seared scallops with celeriac, prunes and Parma ham. Roast breast and confit leg of duck is a fine main course, accompanied by juniper sauce, spicy pear and blackcurrant crumble and fondant potato. Puddings get heads turning: a light plum soufflé, say, with subtle Earl Grey pannacotta, poached plums and frothy almond foam.

Chef Neil Clarke **Seats** 60, Pr/dining room 14 **Times** 12-2.15/6-9.15, Closed BH Mon, 1 Jan, D Sun **Prices** Fixed L 2 course £18, Fixed D 3 course £22, Starter £6-£14, Main £15-£29, Dessert £7-£8 **Wines** 42 bottles over £30, 17 bottles under £30, 12 by glass **Parking** 7 **Notes** Sunday L £25-£29, Vegetarian available, Children welcome

BROMSGROVE **Map 10 SO97**

The Vernon

Modern European, British

tel: 01527 821236 **Droitwich Rd, Hanbury B60 4DB**
email: info@thevernonhanbury.co.uk **web:** www.thevernonhanbury.co.uk
dir: *A38 onto B4091 Hanbury Road, on junct with B4090*

Enticing cooking in classy 18th-century inn

While fully respecting its listed status, the 18th-century Vernon is now a sleek, contemporary 21st-century inn with boutique rooms. Lightwood furniture looks good in the bar, while the four-roomed dining area sports wooden chairs upholstered in coloured fabrics; outside, tables shelter under huge green umbrellas. Relaxed but attentive service will bring you modern European/British dishes such as citrus-cured salmon, chilli and lime crab, avocado purée and caviar; assiette of lamb, carrot purée, dauphinoise potatoes and rosemary jus; and chocolate tart, caramel pecans, and banana and lime ice cream. The wine list echoes The Vernon's style.

Chef Richard Felton **Seats** 73, Pr/dining room 24 **Times** 12-3/6-9.30 **Prices** Starter £4.50-£8.50, Main £10.50-£28.50, Dessert £4.50-£7.50 **Wines** 11 bottles over £30, 31 bottles under £30, 13 by glass **Parking** 80 **Notes** Light menu, Sunday L £10.50-£14.50, Vegetarian available, Children welcome

CHADDESLEY CORBETT **Map 10 SO87**

Brockencote Hall Country House Hotel

Modern British V

tel: 01562 777876 **DY10 4PY**
email: info@brockencotehall.com **web:** www.brockencotehall.com
dir: *A38 to Bromsgrove, off A448 towards Kidderminster*

Authoritative modern cookery in a grand Victorian manor house

With the Malvern and Cotswold hills within striking distance, Brockencote lacks for nothing in terms of location, and the house itself – a Victorian country manor and then some – reposes in 70 acres of luxuriant parkland, including an expansive lake. The sweeping pastoral views are best appreciated from either a seat in the Colonial lounge-bar or a table in the Chaddesley dining room, or preferably one after the other. In these lavish settings, Adam Brown's cooking steps up to the mark, with a precise and skilful interpretation of modern thinking in dishes that balance a certain robustness with unusual and unexpected flavours. An opener of dressed Cornish crab offers a tian of white meat with kombu seaweed jelly and preserved grapes dressed in verjus. That might be the prelude to braised blade of beef resting on kale-laced creamy truffled mash with roasted roots in a rich cep jus. The seven-course tasting menu takes off into the culinary stratosphere, soaring from scallop, kohlrabi and smoked ox tongue to Brillat-Savarin bonbon with wild strawberry sorbet, ending with superb English and French artisanal cheeses. Otherwise, chocolate aficionados need look no further than Manjari ganache with praline cream and an ice cream of goats' milk.

Chef Adam Brown **Seats** 40, Pr/dining room 16 **Times** 12-2/6.45-9.45 **Prices** Fixed L 2 course fr £23.50, Fixed D 3 course £45-£59.95, Tasting menu fr £75 **Wines** 120 bottles over £30, 16 bottles under £30, 12 by glass **Parking** 50 **Notes** Afternoon tea £22.50, Sunday L fr £32.50, Children welcome

EVESHAM **Map 10 SP04**

Wood Norton Hotel

Modern British

tel: 01386 765611 **Wood Norton WR11 4YB**
email: info@thewoodnorton.com **web:** www.thewoodnorton.com
dir: *M42 junct 3. Follow A435 towards Alcester, A46 Evesham. At Evesham Football Club rdbt 2nd exit onto A46. Evesham Country Park rdbt follow A44 Worcester, over 2 rdbts hotel on right*

Focused modern cooking in fabulous Victorian house

The hall was built in the late 19th century as an upmarket hunting lodge to attract European royalty. Interiors are fabulously rich, with chandeliers and wood panelling everywhere, and the dining room looks over the south terrace towards Bredon Hill and beyond. Dishes combine sharply focused flavour and thoughtful combination from the intricate likes of a starter of monkfish carpaccio with scallops, crispy seaweed and caramelised baby gem, to the assured simplicity of loin and belly of pork with apple purée, baby carrots and Savoy cabbage. Chocolate and cherry variations at dessert bring on chocolate crumble and poached cherries.

Chef Paul Hudson **Seats** 60, Pr/dining room 140 **Times** 7-9.30, Closed L all week (ex special occasions) **Prices** Prices not confirmed **Wines** 35 bottles over £30, 35 bottles under £30, 9 by glass **Parking** 70 **Notes** Vegetarian available, Children welcome

KIDDERMINSTER Map 10 SO87

The Granary Hotel & Restaurant

Modern British

tel: 01562 777535 **Heath Ln, Shenstone DY10 4BS**
email: info@granary-hotel.co.uk **web:** www.granary-hotel.co.uk
dir: *On A450 between Worcester & Stourbridge. 2m from Kidderminster*

Smart, seasonal contemporary cooking in a boutique hotel

Close to the Midlands motorways, yet nicely set in the countryside, the boutique-style Granary Hotel boasts a market garden to supply the kitchen with low-mileage fruit and veg. The key players in the kitchen brigade have worked together for a decade, developing a contemporary style to bring great seasonal ingredients together in well-considered compositions. A starter of confit duck comes with a zesty salad of orange and chestnuts with sherry vinaigrette. Main course brings a well-balanced combination of roast monkfish with spiced lentils, butternut squash and lime and coriander dressing. To finish, apples star in an assiette of Bramley apple cake, mousse, jelly, crisp and sauce.

Chef Anthony Phillips **Seats** 60, Pr/dining room 16 **Times** 12-2.30/7-11, Closed L Mon, Sat, D Sun **Prices** Fixed L 2 course £12.50-£14.50, Fixed D 3 course £22-£25, Starter £7-£10.50, Main £15-£22.50, Dessert £5.25 **Wines** 6 bottles over £30, 28 bottles under £30, 17 by glass **Parking** 95 **Notes** Light menu available all week, Sunday L £17.95-£18.95, Vegetarian available, Children welcome

Stone Manor Hotel

Traditional

tel: 01562 777555 **Stone DY10 4PJ**
email: enquiries@stonemanorhotel.co.uk
web: www.hogarths.co.uk/hogarths-stone-manor
dir: *2.5m from Kidderminster on A448, hotel on right*

Modernist dishes and old-fashioned flambé shows

In its newly refurbished Fields restaurant, Stone Manor makes space for appealing modern brasserie food. Flambé dishes cooked before your delighted eyes have been productively revived, so that beef fillet or chicken breast can be set alight with vodka or brandy. Before that, the more modernist likes of pork belly terrine with kiwi, raisins and sweet potato crisps in cider and ginger glaze might have set things on a course that continues with grey mullet and mussels with lemon and redcurrant couscous in saffron and parmesan cream. Finish with spiced plum crumble, served with sweet plum gnocchi, honeycomb and cinnamon crème fraîche.

Chef Paul Harris **Seats** 70, Pr/dining room 26 **Times** 12-2.30/6-10 **Prices** Fixed L 2 course fr £17, Fixed D 3 course fr £27, Starter £6-£10.50, Main £7.50-£29.50, Dessert £6.50-£8 **Wines** 16 bottles over £30, 18 bottles under £30, 13 by glass **Parking** 300 **Notes** Sunday L £15.95-£19.95, Vegetarian available, Children welcome

MALVERN Map 10 SO74

L'Amuse Bouche Restaurant

Modern French V

tel: 01684 572427 **The Cotford Hotel, 51 Graham Rd WR14 2HU**
email: reservations@cotfordhotel.co.uk **web:** www.cotfordhotel.co.uk
dir: *From Worcester follow signs to Malvern on A449. Left into Graham Rd signed town centre, hotel on right*

Gentle French modernity with an episcopal past

Built in the mid-19th century as a summer bolt-hole for the Bishop of Worcester, the Cotford Hotel is still in the rest-and-recreation business, its chapel now L'Amuse Bouche restaurant, an attractive room with russet and gold wallpaper. Loch Fyne scallops are flamed in anisette and served on a bed of wild mushrooms, samphire and tarragon with powdered pancetta, while mains deliver cider-braised pork belly stuffed with black pudding or, for the veggies, cranberry, apple and chestnut tart with cashews in basil cream sauce. To finish, dark chocolate mousse is laced with Amaretto and covered in raspberry foam, while banana Tatin is scented with rosemary and is served with clotted cream ice cream.

Chef Christopher Morgan **Seats** 40 **Times** 12-1.30/6-8.30, Closed L Mon-Sat **Prices** Prices not confirmed **Wines** 10 bottles over £30, 26 bottles under £30, 10 by glass **Parking** 12 **Notes** Pre-theatre menu, Sunday L, Children welcome

The Cottage in the Wood

Modern British

tel: 01684 588860 **Holywell Rd, Malvern Wells WR14 4LG**
email: reception@cottageinthewood.co.uk **web:** www.cottageinthewood.co.uk
dir: *From N, M5 junct 7 A449 to Malvern Wells. 3rd right after Railway Pub & before left B4209. Signed. From S, M5 junct 8, M50 junct 1. A38 (Worcester) for 3m, left to A4104, right after river bridge to B4211 for 1.5m. Left to B4209 Malvern Wells for 4m. Right at T-junct, immediately left*

Refined cooking and magnificent views

This delightful Georgian property has a panoramic view across the Severn Valley from its position high up on a wooded hillside. The aptly named Outlook Restaurant makes the best of its situation (get a window table if you can) while the kitchen's rather refined classically inspired output is a distraction in itself. A first-course crab verrine delivers good depth of flavour and looks pretty on the plate, while main-course pork belly pressé is partnered with pulled ham croquettes and glazed apples. A fishy main course might be herb-crusted cod with caviar and clam chowed, and, to finish, mango pannacotta comes with a zingy passionfruit and mango compôte.

Chef Dominic Pattin **Seats** 70, Pr/dining room 20 **Times** 12.30-2/7-9.30 **Prices** Starter £6-£10.50, Main £13-£28, Dessert £3-£12 **Wines** 359 bottles over £30, 86 bottles under £30, 10 by glass **Parking** 40 **Notes** Separate ALC L menu, Sunday L £21.95-£25.95, Vegetarian available, Children welcome

The Malvern

Modern British

tel: 01684 898290 **Grovewood Rd WR14 1GD**
email: enquiries@themalvernspa.com **web:** www.themalvernspa.com
dir: *A4440 to Malvern. Over 2 rdbts, at 3rd turn left. After 6m, left at rdbt, over 1st rdbt, hotel on right*

Contemporary brasserie dining in the Malvern Hills

The Malvern, the first spa resort in the town, opened in 1910. Its brasserie is a fresh-looking space of neutral tones, wooden tables and a tiled floor. The menu follows a bright and breezy format, and you might start with Indian flavours of pan-fried scallops on squash purée with an onion bhaji, coriander cress and curry oil, or Scotch egg with bacon jam and black pudding crumble. Main courses are just as varied: try sea bass fillets with lemongrass risotto, crab wontons and pak choi, or rump steak with peppercorn sauce. End with pear frangipane tart with vanilla ice cream and caramel sauce.

Chef Steve Rimmer **Seats** 52, Pr/dining room **Times** 12-3/7-9.30 **Prices** Starter £4.95-£9.75, Main £13-£16.25, Dessert £6.35-£9.25 **Wines** 8 bottles over £30, 12 bottles under £30, 9 by glass **Parking** 82 **Notes** Sun brunch, Themed menus, Vegetarian available, No children

OMBERSLEY Map 10 SO86

The Venture In Restaurant

@@ British, French

tel: 01905 620552 **Main Rd WR9 0EW**
dir: *From Worcester N towards Kidderminster on A449 (approx 5m). Left at Ombersley turn. Restaurant 0.75m on right*

Exceptional cooking in a crooked medieval house

Behind the half-timbered façade of this 15th-century property is a small bar with a welcoming open fire, comfortable sofas and low tables and a restaurant with bags of ancient character from its ceiling beams and standing timbers. Chef-patron Toby Fletcher stamps his style on a modern Anglo-French repertoire, carefully sourcing quality produce and handling it confidently and imaginatively. Pan-fried pigeon with a bubble and squeak galette and smoked mushroom jus is a typically effective, well-balanced combination, followed by pheasant breast paired with a fricassée of leg meat with buttered spinach and game jus. Moreish puddings include warm treacle tart with Bramley apple ice cream.

Chef Toby Fletcher **Seats** 32, Pr/dining room 32 **Times** 12-2/7-9.30, Closed 25 Dec-1 Jan, 2 wks summer & 2 wks winter, Mon, D Sun **Prices** Fixed L 2 course fr £27, Fixed D 3 course fr £41 **Wines** 38 bottles over £30, 35 bottles under £30, 6 by glass **Parking** 15, On street **Notes** Sunday L, Vegetarian available, Children 12 yrs+ D

UPTON UPON SEVERN Map 10 SO84

White Lion Hotel

@ Traditional British

tel: 01684 592551 **21 High St WR8 0HJ**
email: info@whitelionhotel.biz **web:** www.whitelionhotel.biz
dir: *From A422 take A38 towards Tewkesbury. After 8m take B4104 for 1m, after bridge turn left to hotel*

Historic hotel with a contemporary feel and flavour

Henry Fielding put up here while writing *Tom Jones*, and the White Lion also played a booze-fuelled part in the Civil War, but fascinating as the history may be, the place is in tune with current trends. The interior works a cheerfully updated look in the Pepperpot Brasserie, blending black timbered walls with bare chunky oak tables. Food-wise, the deal is straightforward combinations and big-hearted flavours: seared scallops come with an onion bhaji in minted yogurt dressing, ahead of a hearty plate of chicken breast with a potato pancake and roasted and puréed shallots in thyme jus. White chocolate and blueberry millefeuille is a properly indulgent dessert.

Chef Jon Lear **Seats** 45 **Times** 12-2/7-9.15, Closed 31 Dec-1 Jan, L few days between Xmas & New Year, D 24 Dec **Prices** Fixed L 2 course £14, Starter £4.95-£10, Main £11-£25, Dessert £6.45 **Wines** 2 bottles over £30, 20 bottles under £30, 7 by glass **Parking** 16 **Notes** Sunday L, Vegetarian available, Children welcome

EAST RIDING OF YORKSHIRE

BEVERLEY Map 17 TA03

The Pipe and Glass Inn

@@ Modern British V NOTABLE WINE LIST

tel: 01430 810246 **West End, South Dalton HU17 7PN**
email: email@pipeandglass.co.uk
dir: *Just off B1248*

Superior modern cooking in stylish country inn

The rustic bar has a smart finish with Chesterfield chairs and sofas, and a wood-burning stove, while the restaurant is dominated by horse-themed prints and chunky wooden tables. The industrious and creative team in the kitchen deliver arresting options such as a starter cheesecake made with Yellison goats' cheese and partnered with beetroot macaroon, golden beets and candied walnuts. It all seems entirely in keeping with the setting and chimes with the times. Carry on with slow-cooked, crispy shoulder of lamb (with devils on horseback and burnt onion purée) and finish with warm treacle tart with egg nog ice cream and nutmeg custard. The wine list is a cracker, too.

Chef James Mackenzie **Seats** 100, Pr/dining room 28 **Times** 12-2/6-9.30, Closed 25 Dec, 2 wks Jan, Mon (ex BHs), D Sun **Prices** Prices not confirmed **Wines** 54 bottles over £30, 37 bottles under £30, 13 by glass **Parking** 60 **Notes** Sunday L, Children welcome

GOOLE Map 17 SE72

The Burlington Restaurant

@ Modern British

tel: 01405 767999 **The Lowther Hotel, Aire St DN14 5QW**
email: info@lowtherhotel.co.uk **web:** www.lowtherhotel.co.uk
dir: *M62 junct 36, 3rd exit at rdbt, then 1st exit at rdbt onto A614. Right onto Boothferry Rd, right onto Mariners St, left onto Stanhope St. At rdbt take 4th exit onto North St, right onto Aire St*

Modern cooking in a resurrected Regency hotel

Head for the Burlington Restaurant – a snappy modern brasserie-style space in tones of red and cream, setting the tone for straightforward up-to-date food. Built around good-quality seasonal ingredients that the kitchen sources from local farms and trusted suppliers, a starter of rainbow trout is served with caper mayonnaise, smoked pea purée and chervil, followed by Gressingham duck breast with pearl barley, beetroot, carrot, shallots and celeriac. If you're in the mood for fish, monkfish might come with purple kale, samphire, cauliflower purée and Parma ham. Dessert is a satisfying confection involving rhubarb and ginger cheesecake, orange sponge and gel, and rhubarb sorbet.

Chef Scott Braithwaite, Luke Hoggard **Seats** 32, Pr/dining room 30 **Times** 12-2/5-9, Closed D Sun **Prices** Starter £3.95-£5.95, Main £10.95-£14.95, Dessert £3.95-£5.95 **Wines** 6 bottles over £30, 15 bottles under £30, 3 by glass **Parking** 15 **Notes** Themed menus (Pudding Club), Once mthly tasting menu, Sunday L fr £8.95, Vegetarian available, Children welcome

WILLERBY Map 17 TA03

Best Western Willerby Manor Hotel

Modern European

tel: 01482 652616 **Well Ln HU10 6ER**
email: willerbymanor@bestwestern.co.uk **web:** www.willerbymanor.co.uk
dir: *M62/A63, follow signs for Humber Bridge, then signs for Beverley until Willerby Shopping Park. Hotel signed from rdbt next to McDonald's*

Solid brasserie cooking with broad appeal

Willerby Manor is a thoroughly modern establishment where dining takes place in a contemporary room and a blackboard menu lists the many specials. The core of the operation is solid brasserie cooking and feel good flavours. Sandwiches and wraps are inveigled in between starters – salmon and asparagus quiche with champagne-dressed salad, or creamy mushroom pâté and Yorkshire Blue butter – and the main business. The last might be Cajun-rubbed pork medallions with couscous, battered courgettes and pineapple salsa. Tropical flavours pour forth from a dessert of lychee bavarois with coconut ice cream and passionfruit jelly.

Chef David Roberts, Ben Olley **Seats** 40, Pr/dining room 40 **Times** 10-9.15, All-day dining, Closed 25 Dec **Prices** Starter £6.10-£7, Main £6.80-£19.50, Dessert £4.65-£5.40 **Wines** 1 bottle over £30, 18 bottles under £30, 14 by glass **Parking** 200 **Notes** Sunday L, Vegetarian available, Children welcome

NORTH YORKSHIRE

ALDWARK Map 19 SE46

Aldwark Manor Golf & Spa Hotel

Traditional NEW

tel: 01347 838146 **YO61 1UF**
email: aldwarkmanor@qhotels.co.uk
web: www.qhotels.co.uk/our-locations/aldwark-manor-golf-spa-hotel-york
dir: *From A1, A59 towards Green Hammerton, then B6265 towards Little Ouseburn, follow signs Aldwark Bridge/Manor. A19 through Linton on Ouse to Aldwark*

Satisfying brasserie food in a Victorian country house

When you're all done with golf and pampering, the contemporary, split-level brasserie of this grand Victorian manor in 120 acres of parkland will see you right on the gastronomic front. The kitchen pulls together some tasty combinations, setting out with game terrine wrapped in Parma ham with truffle cream and toasted brioche, followed by a big-hearted main of slow-cooked belly pork with bubble and squeak, celeriac purée, roasted apple and red wine jus. A deconstructed mandarin cheesecake with mandarin jelly and dark chocolate sauce ends the show, and the deal is sealed by the bustling vibe and attentive and engaging staff.

Chef James Cooper **Seats** 85, Pr/dining room **Times** 6.30-9.30 **Prices** Starter £5-£7.50, Main £10-£29, Dessert £5.50-£8.50 **Wines** 31 bottles over £30, 17 bottles under £30, 14 by glass **Parking** 200 **Notes** Vegetarian available, Children welcome

ARKENGARTHDALE Map 18 NY90

Charles Bathurst Inn

British

tel: 01748 884567 **DL11 6EN email:** info@cbinn.co.uk **web:** www.cbinn.co.uk
dir: *B6270 to Reeth, at Buck Hotel turn N to Langthwaite, pass church on right, inn 0.5m on right*

Seasonal contemporary menus in a Dales inn

The CB – to its friends – is in Arkengarthdale – a tributary valley of celebrated Swaledale. It's named after a Georgian parliamentarian, and the beamed dining room is done out with pale wood and generously spaced tables. Local farmers and fishermen supply its seasonally-changing menus of modern Yorkshire cooking. This is shown off to best effect on the Mirror Menu, where pan-seared scallops come with Parma ham, and apple and sage purée. After that, there's a heartily sustaining trio of pork, comprising belly, fillet and cheek, with purple sprouting broccoli, boulangère potatoes, and apple and cider jus. Make space for classic custard tart with vanilla ice cream.

Chef Gareth Bottomley **Seats** 70, Pr/dining room 60 **Times** 12-2.30/6-9, Closed 25 Dec **Prices** Prices not confirmed **Wines** 15 bottles over £30, 20 bottles under £30, 10 by glass **Parking** 25 **Notes** Sunday L, Vegetarian available, Children welcome

ASENBY Map 19 SE37

Crab Manor

British, French V

tel: 01845 577286 **Dishforth Rd YO7 3QL**
email: enquiries@crabandlobster.co.uk **web:** www.crabandlobster.co.uk
dir: *A1(M) junct 49, on outskirts of village*

Long-running non-minimalist seafood dining

The Crab & Lobster restaurant offers various settings in which to dine, from a garden terrace to a room hung with a profusion of fishing nets and pots. Traditional seafood specialities cooked with flair include fresh plump blue-shelled mussels in a hearty marinière, or you might go Belgian with a preparation of cabbage, bacon and ale. Mains run to roast stone bass in bouillabaisse broth with chargrilled courgettes and baby fennel, or lobster thermidor that incorporates scallops and prawns. Ox cheek in port and Madeira pacifies the meat constituency, and it all ends with shortcrust lemon tart served with lemon curd ice cream, with orange and pink grapefruit segments.

Chef Steve Dean **Seats** 85, Pr/dining room 16 **Times** 12-2.30/7-9 **Prices** Prices not confirmed **Wines** 12 bottles over £30, 27 bottles under £30, 8 by glass **Parking** 80 **Notes** Sunday L, Children welcome

AUSTWICK Map 18 SD76

The Traddock

 Modern British

tel: 01524 251224 **Settle LA2 8BY**
email: info@thetraddock.co.uk **web:** www.thetraddock.co.uk
dir: *From Skipton take A65 towards Kendal, 3m after Settle turn right signed Austwick, cross humpback bridge, hotel 100yds on left*

Modern British with Mediterranean undercurrents

The Yorkshire Dales extend gloriously all around the characterful stone house, where a vigorous rendition of British modernism is the stock-in-trade, with overlays of various Mediterranean traditions. A white-truffled pumpkin and chestnut risotto is one way to start, or there might be salmon three ways – tartare, herbed ballotine and a gravad lax spin cured in beetroot, vodka and dill – garnished with Keta caviar. Pedigree meats for main include braised herb-stuffed shoulder of Old Spots pork with dauphinoise and roasted vegetables in sweet tomato sauce, while fish might be baked halibut in lemon and caper butter. Finish with properly rich sticky toffee pudding and vanilla ice cream.

Chef John Pratt **Seats** 36, Pr/dining room 16 **Times** 12-3/6.30-11 **Prices** Starter £4.95-£7.95, Main £16.75-£21.50, Dessert £6-£7.95 **Wines** 24 bottles over £30, 26 bottles under £30, 9 by glass **Parking** 20, On street **Notes** Afternoon tea, Sunday L £9.95-£17.95, Vegetarian available, Children welcome

Yorebridge House

BAINBRIDGE **Map 18 SD99**

Modern British V NOTABLE WINE LIST

tel: 01969 652060 **DL8 3EE**
email: enquiries@yorebridgehouse.co.uk
web: www.yorebridgehouse.co.uk
dir: *A648 to Bainbridge. Yorebridge House N of centre on right before river*

Refined cuisine and great wines

A solid-looking grey-stone property on the edge of Bainbridge, this boutique hotel occupies what was a school, built in 1848, and headmaster's house (1850). It's on the River Ure, with the River Bain forming the boundary of its five-acre grounds within the stunning backdrop of the Yorkshire Dales National Park. The owners have given a clean, uncluttered look to the interior decor and furnishings, with the oak-floored restaurant kitted out in chocolate and grey tones, with simply appointed bare wooden tables and an open pass into the calm and controlled kitchen. The atmosphere is relaxed and unpretentious, helped along by hospitable, service-minded staff. Dan Shotton is a confident chef who's not averse to experimentation, turning out neatly conceived dishes. Pig's head terrine, for instance, comes with two plump scallops under a fold of pleasantly rich, fatty lardo, along with pickled and puréed raisins, pickled shallots and pieces of crispy pork fat, slices of deep-fried breadcrumbed eel adding a pungent, smoky element: an involved dish, but all the flavours complement each other. Dishes are balanced in their conception and construction, and technical aspects are impressive, seen in a main course of roast fillet of halibut, moist and translucent, lifted by boneless chicken wings and accompanied by baby leeks, chanterelles, onion purée and fondant potato, all flaked with grated truffle and mushroom consommé poured at table. Meat-eaters could go for the full-on flavours of beef fillet and oxtail with confit shallots and kale. Breads are excellent and incidentals are well up to the mark, from canapés – among them perhaps goats' cheese and ham rolls with onion purée – to petits fours with coffee, while a pre-dessert sets the tone for the real thing: perhaps pretty-looking chocolate mousse with an orange gel centre accompanied by crisp chocolate 'soil', candied peel and blood orange sorbet.

Chef Daniel Shotton **Seats** 35, Pr/dining room 18 **Times** 12-3/7-9 **Prices** Fixed D 3 course £55, Tasting menu £75 **Wines** 80 bottles over £30, 20 bottles under £30, 20 by glass **Parking** 30 **Notes** Sunday L £17.50-£22.50, Children welcome

AYSGARTH Map 19 SE08

The Aysgarth Falls

Modern British V

tel: 01969 663775 **DL8 3SR**
email: info@aysgarthfallshotel.com **web:** www.aysgarthfallshotel.com
dir: *On A684 between Leyburn & Hawes, at junct with turning to Aysgarth Falls*

Imaginative cooking in traditional village inn

When you're exploring the Yorkshire Dales, schedule a pitstop at this traditional pub with rooms in the pretty village of Aysgarth, whether it's for a pint of locally brewed Black Sheep ale or a meal in the contemporary restaurant overlooking the lovely garden. Start with a well-timed line-caught east coast mackerel fillet with pickled kohlrabi, radish, cucumber and squid ink cracker, following on with a vibrant and well-executed main course of pan-roast venison, potato purée, swede and carrot, turnip, haggis fritter, beetroot, blackberry and heritage potatoes. Finish, perhaps, with forced Yorkshire rhubarb served with Earl Grey crème brûlée, poached rhubarb, rhubarb granita, red vein sorrel and ginger snap biscuit.

Chef Gavin Swift **Seats** 45, Pr/dining room 14 **Times** 12-2.30/6-8.45 **Wines** 1 bottle over £30, 22 bottles under £30, 5 by glass **Parking** 25 **Notes** Sunday L £11-£19, Children welcome

BAINBRIDGE Map 18 SD99

Yorebridge House

– see opposite

BOLTON ABBEY Map 19 SE05

The Burlington Restaurant *– see below*

The Devonshire Brasserie & Bar

Traditional British

tel: 01756 710710 & 710441 **The Devonshire Arms Hotel BD23 6AJ**
email: res@devonshirehotels.co.uk
dir: *On B6160, 250yds N of junct with A59*

Smart brasserie cooking in a top-class country hotel

The Devonshire Arms has a lot going for it, from its fabulous position on the 30,000-acre estate, the luxe bedrooms and the high-end restaurant, but don't forget about the Brasserie & Bar. The menu deals in upscale modern brasserie food, with a Yorkshire flavour, so you might tuck into ham hock terrine with salt-baked beetroot and red wine mustard dressing, before cod with chorizo and crushed new potatoes, or fine pork belly with creamed sprouts and mash. There's creativity in desserts, too: perhaps set Yorkshire yogurt with apple compôte, cinnamon crumble and apple sorbet, or a version of rhubarb crumble with toasted almond ice cream.

Chef Sean Pleasants **Seats** 60 **Times** 12-2.30/6-9.30 **Prices** Fixed L 2 course fr £18, Starter £5-£11, Main £16-£24, Dessert £6-£8 **Wines** 30 bottles over £30, 30 bottles under £30, 16 by glass **Parking** 40 **Notes** Sunday L £24-£28, Vegetarian available, Children welcome

The Burlington Restaurant

BOLTON ABBEY Map 19 SE05

Modern British

tel: 01756 710441 & 718111 **The Devonshire Arms Hotel BD23 6AJ**
email: res@devonshirehotels.co.uk **web:** www.thedevonshirearms.co.uk
dir: *On B6160 to Bolton Abbey, 250 yds N of junct with A59 rdbt*

Innovative Yorkshire Dales cooking

The Rosette award for this establishment has been suspended due to a change of chef. Reassessment will take place in due course under the new chef. Surrounded by the rolling hills of the Duke of Devonshire's Bolton Abbey estate, on the fringes of the Yorkshire Dales National Park, The Devonshire Arms is a gem of a 17th-century property with a luxe spa in a converted ancient barn, immaculate lawns, landscaped grounds, and an opulent interior that manages to seem both traditional and contemporary. The vibrant Brasserie is an appealing dining option, but the star attraction is the refined, chandeliered Burlington Restaurant with its charming conservatory extension. Here, fine Yorkshire produce – including the fruits of the kitchen garden – are used to deliver well-crafted plates of contemporary food rooted in classical culinary thinking. A starter of sautéed duck liver has at its core superbly tender and flavoursome livers, served with caramelised spiced pears, little gingerbread tuiles, vanilla-infused pear purée, and caramelised walnuts: a classy dish. Next up, Yorkshire grouse with pickled elderberries gets a dash of luxury in the shape of a caramelised apple filled with foie gras, or go for East Coast turbot with lettuce and lobster cream. There's more creativity at dessert stage, where a mango sphere filled with buttermilk ganache and a wonderfully sharp lime centre is a technical tour de force. The service team show flawless communication to keep it all going along swimmingly. The attention to detail here includes stellar canapés such as a small duck burger with tamarind ketchup, and stonking petits fours that actually come with a menu.

Seats 70, Pr/dining room 90 **Times** 12-4/7-9.30, Closed Xmas, New Year, Mon **Prices** Prices not confirmed **Wines** 2000 bottles over £30, 20 bottles under £30, 30 by glass **Parking** 100 **Notes** ALC menu D, Vegetarian available, Children welcome

BOROUGHBRIDGE Map 19 SE36

The Crown Inn

 Modern British V

tel: 01423 322300 **Roecliffe YO51 9LY**
email: info@crowninnroecliffe.co.uk **web:** www.crowninnroecliffe.co.uk
dir: *A1(M) junct 48, follow brown sign*

Old coaching inn with up-to-date cooking

In this 16th-century coaching inn you'll find stone-flagged floors, roaring log fires, fashionably mismatched furniture and a kitchen that churns out generous, satisfying dishes with unmistakably French accents. A springtime meal begins with home-made ravioli stuffed with local rabbit and tarragon, supported by a glossy wild mushroom sauce and pecorino cheese, ahead of rump of new-season lamb with crisp and buttery pommes Anna and a punchy pesto of capers and wild garlic. If you hanker for fish, how about hake steamed with king prawns over a stock of tomato, chorizo and mussels? For pudding, there's a textbook rendition of classic tarte Tatin with home-made vanilla ice cream.

Chef Steve Ardern **Seats** 60, Pr/dining room 20 **Times** 12-3.30/6-11 **Prices** Fixed L 2 course fr £18.95, Starter £4.95-£9.41, Main £13.97-£23.95, Dessert £6.89 **Wines** 20 bottles over £30, 20 bottles under £30, 19 by glass **Parking** 30 **Notes** Sunday L £18.95-£21.95, Children welcome

BURNSALL Map 19 SE06

The Devonshire Fell

 Modern British

tel: 01756 729000 **BD23 6BT**
email: manager@devonshirefell.co.uk **web:** www.devonshirefell.co.uk
dir: *On B6160, 6m from Bolton Abbey rdbt A59 junct*

Simple modern cooking in a chic Dales hideaway

This place presents a sober face to the world, but inside, a contemporary boutique makeover displays vibrant shades of lilac and blue, sensuous fabrics and attractive artwork in the funky bar and conservatory bistro. Informal, friendly service feeds into the easy-going vibe, while please-all menus are driven by quality ingredients, with simple pubby classics such as fish and chips or steaks thrown into the mix. Otherwise, ham hock terrine with black pudding beignet and mustard mayonnaise might precede a piggy trio of pork fillet, cheek and belly with chive mash and carrots, or sea bream with ratatouille and salsa verde.

ESCRICK Map 16 SE64

The Parsonage Country House Hotel

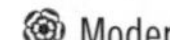 Modern British NEW V

tel: 01904 728111 **York Rd YO19 6LF**
email: reservations@parsonagehotel.co.uk **web:** www.parsonagehotel.co.uk
dir: *From A64 take A19 Selby. Follow to Escrick. Hotel on right of St Helen's Church*

Country-house comforts and appealing food

Built in the 1840s, the Parsonage comes up with the traditional country-house goods, including six acres of primped gardens, a spa, a pub for casual dining and the more formal Lascelles Restaurant. The place exudes a warm-hued, gently modernised style, matched by cooking that deals in comfort and familiarity. Come for chicken and mushroom terrine with tomato and tarragon relish, ciabatta croûtons and heirloom tomatoes, followed by roast pork fillet with a pressing of confit belly, potato fondant and sage jus. Rhubarb cheesecake with a ginger biscuit base and the textural contrasts of rhubarb sorbet, purée and jelly makes a fitting finale.

Chef Darren Davis **Seats** 60, Pr/dining room 24 **Times** 6.30-9, Closed L all week **Prices** Fixed D 3 course £26.95-£29.95 **Wines** 5 bottles over £30, 16 bottles under £30, 9 by glass **Parking** 70 **Notes** Children welcome

GILLING EAST Map 19 SE67

The Fairfax Arms

Classic British NEW

tel: 01439 788212 **Main St YO62 4JH**
email: info@thefairfaxarms.co.uk **web:** www.thefairfaxarms.co.uk
dir: *From A170 turn right onto B1257, right again onto B1363 to Gilling East*

A country inn in looks and character

Popular with the local farming community, The Fairfax guards the village crossroads, one of which leads to Gilling Castle, prep school for the well-known Ampleforth College. The pub's black-beamed open-plan bar and dining area leads out to a beer garden bordered by a stream. The menu presents classic British choices, typified by pan-fried king scallops with carrot and cumin purée, garden pea gel and Serrano crisp as a starter, and a main of slow-cooked belly and cheek of pork with black pudding mash, kale and cider jus. It might be hard to resist finishing with sticky toffee pudding, butterscotch sauce and cinder toffee ice cream.

Chef Ben Turner **Seats** Pr/dining room 20 **Times** 12-2/6-9 **Prices** Starter £5.25-£7.25, Main £11.95-£21.95, Dessert £4.95-£7.25 **Notes** Vegetarian available

GOATHLAND Map 19 NZ80

Mallyan Spout Hotel

 Modern British NEW

tel: 01947 896486 **YO22 5AN**
email: info@mallyanspout.co.uk **web:** www.mallyanspout.co.uk
dir: *A169 Pickering to Whitby. Turn left to Goathland, after 2.5m hotel on left opp St Mary's Church*

Fine dining in the North Yorks Moors

Named after the tumbling 70-ft waterfall behind the hotel, the Mallyan Spout clings comfortingly to a traditional style of furnishing and decor – textured wallpaper, large mirrors, high-backed upholstered chairs, that sort of thing. In the restaurant polite and helpful black-clad staff attend your fresh-rose-dressed, candlelit, bare table, taking your order for, say, pan-fried scallops, butternut squash and pea risotto with parmesan tuile and white truffle, followed by pan-roasted duck breast with duck cottage pie, blueberry sauce and vegetable garnish, finishing with caramel tart, lemon cream peanut butter and lemon jelly. Old and New World wines are well balanced on the 50-bin list.

Chef K C Crawley **Seats** 50, Pr/dining room 12 **Times** 12-9, All-day dining, Closed 25-26 Dec **Prices** Prices not confirmed **Wines** 45 bottles under £30, 11 by glass **Parking** 30 **Notes** Sunday L, Vegetarian available, Children welcome

GOLDSBOROUGH Map 19 SE35

Goldsborough Hall

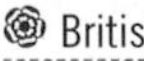 British

tel: 01423 867321 **Church St HG5 8NR**
email: info@goldsboroughhall.com **web:** www.goldsboroughhall.com
dir: *5 min E of Harrogate, just off A59 between Harrogate and A1(M)*

Stately surroundings for contemporary and classic British cooking

Princess Mary, one of the Queen's aunts, lived in this 1620s stately home until 1929. The Dining Room is small with large, widely spaced, formally laid tables. In one corner sits a baby grand, antique furniture is dotted around, and the marble fireplace is a corker. White-gloved staff serve from the informal Garden menu, a seven-course taster, or the carte, the source of inspiration for a typical meal of, say, salad of Whitby crab with Indian mango and tempura fennel, crispy ballotine of chicken with sunblushed tomato, asparagus and tarragon jus, and rhubarb pannacotta with poached rhubarb and ginger parkin. Meals may also be taken in the Princess Mary Drawing Room.

Chef Jamie Gill **Seats** 26, Pr/dining room 110 **Times** 12-10, All-day dining **Prices** Fixed L 3 course £45, Fixed D 3 course £45, Tasting menu £75, Starter £6-£12, Main £9.95-£25, Dessert £6-£9.75 **Wines** 40+ bottles over £30, 18 bottles under £30, 10 by glass **Parking** 50 **Notes** Fixed D 5 course £55, Afternoon tea, Sunday L, Vegetarian available, Children welcome

GRASSINGTON **Map 19 SE06**

Grassington House

Modern British

tel: 01756 752406 **5 The Square BD23 5AQ**
email: bookings@grassingtonhousehotel.co.uk **web:** www.grassingtonhousehotel.co.uk
dir: *A59 into Grassington, in town square opposite post office*

Modern European cooking amid the limestone hills

This stone-built Georgian house boasts a new state-of-the-art, eco-friendly kitchen producing modern food with the accent on sharply etched flavours. First up might be a pairing of rare-breed pork belly and seared king scallops in toffee apple jus, or perhaps one of the sharing slates of nibbles. The main menu deals in the likes of roast lamb rump with lamb-fat roasties, griddled aubergine and cumined pumpkin, or butternut and chestnut lasagne served with a leafy salad and parmesan. Imaginative side orders take in roast courgettes in honey, garlic and chilli, and desserts include classic apple Tatin with vanilla cream, or chocolate fondant with salted caramel ice cream.

Chef John Rudden **Seats** 40 **Times** 12-2.30/6-9.30 **Prices** Fixed L 2 course £14.50-£18.50, Fixed D 3 course £17.50-£19.50, Tasting menu £45, Starter £4.50-£7.95, Main £12.95-£25.50 **Wines** 17 bottles over £30, 28 bottles under £30, 12 by glass **Parking** 20 **Notes** Fixed D 4 course Sun-Mon £45 per couple, Sunday L £17.50-£19.50, Vegetarian available, Children welcome

GUISBOROUGH **Map 19 NZ61**

Gisborough Hall

Modern British

tel: 01287 611500 **Whitby Ln TS14 6PT**
email: general.gisboroughhall@macdonald-hotels.co.uk **web:** www.gisborough-hall.co.uk
dir: *A171, follow signs for Whitby to Waterfall rdbt then 3rd exit into Whitby Lane, hotel 500yds on right*

Well-crafted interesting dishes in a Victorian mansion

The hall is an imposing creeper-covered country-house hotel in well-kept grounds, and Chaloner's restaurant occupies a large space with pillars and a fireplace in what was once the billiard room. The kitchen creates interesting dishes such as a 'plate of pork' that comprises tender braised cheek and fillet wrapped in sage and pancetta together with black pudding, apple purée, mash, spinach and red wine sauce. Fish appears as roast cod loin with curried mussel chowder, with starters along the lines of ham hock terrine with pea mousse, pea salsa and sourdough wafers. Puddings include chocolate marquis with raspberries, pretzel crumb and honey ice cream.

HAROME **Map 19 SE68**

The Star Inn

Modern British V

tel: 01439 770397 **YO62 5JE**
email: reservations@thestaratharome.co.uk
dir: *From Helmsley take A170 towards Kirkbymoorside, after 0.5m turn right towards Harome. After 1.5m, inn 1st building on right*

Exhilarating Yorkshire-inspired cooking in a thatched country inn

This thatched pub in a moorland village boasts a rustic bar, a dining room with chunky tables, a real fire and knick-knacks galore, and a more modern restaurant. Andrew Pern's country cooking places a high premium on big, rugged flavours, seen in a starter of game haslet complemented by sharp pickled damsons, fiery ginger gel and a chestnut brioche. That might be followed by grilled fillet of John Dory with Jerusalem artichoke purée, salsify, a lobster fritter, a poached egg yolk and celeriac ash, or roast pheasant breast forestière with giblet juices. Cap them off with rhubarb burnt cream with black treacle ice cream and parkin.

Chef Andrew Pern, Steve Smith **Seats** 70, Pr/dining room 10 **Times** 11.30-3/6.30-11, Closed L Mon, D Sun **Prices** Fixed L 2 course £20, Fixed D 3 course £25, Tasting menu £55-£85, Starter £8-£15, Main £18-£28, Dessert £6-£12 **Wines** 64 bottles over £30, 22 bottles under £30, 20 by glass **Parking** 30 **Notes** Tasting menu 6-8 course with wine, Sunday L £19-£50, Children welcome

HARROGATE **Map 19 SE35**

Hotel du Vin & Bistro Harrogate

British, French, European

tel: 01423 856800 **Prospect Place HG1 1LB**
email: reception.harrogate@hotelduvin.com
web: www.hotelduvin.com/locations/harrogate
dir: *A1(M) junct 47, A59 to Harrogate, follow town centre signs to Prince of Wales rdbt, 3rd exit, remain in right lane. Right at lights into Albert St, right into Prospect Place*

Fine food and wine in chic Georgian townhouse setting

The Harrogate outpost of the HdV chain occupies a luxuriously converted terrace of eight Georgian townhouses opposite the 200-acre Stray Common. With hops around the windows and mustard-coloured walls, the place bears the group's corporate stamp, and the kitchen makes a virtue of simplicity and restraint in its standard French bistro repertoire, leaving the quality and freshness of the ingredients to speak for themselves. Classic moules marinière is a generous piping-hot bowlful, and there's no stinting on main courses either, such as rabbit in creamy cider sauce with a serving of pasta. Gooey tarte Tatin with crème normande makes a fitting finish.

Chef Walter Marskamp **Seats** 86, Pr/dining room 60 **Times** 12-2/5.30-10 **Prices** Fixed L 2 course £14.95, Fixed D 3 course £16.95-£19.95, Starter £5.95-£12.95, Main £14-£17.50, Dessert £6.95 **Wines** 60+ bottles over £30, 10 bottles under £30, 24 by glass **Parking** 33 **Notes** Afternoon tea, Sunday L £22.95-£24.95, Vegetarian available, Children welcome

HARROGATE *continued*

Nidd Hall Hotel

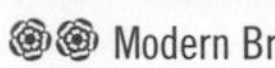 Modern British

tel: 01423 771598 **Nidd HG3 3BN**
web: www.warnerleisurehotels.co.uk
dir: *A1(M) junct/A59 follow signs to Knaresborough. Continue through town centre & at Bond End lights turn left, then right onto B6165 signed Ripley & Pateley Bridge. Hotel on right in approx 4m*

Graceful modern cooking in a grand late-Georgian manor house

Built in the 1820s, Nidd Hall is a glorious hodge-podge of architectural and stylistic references that take in everything from stained window panels to Tuscan columns. The fine-dining option of the Terrace restaurant manages a light decorative tone in keeping with the graceful version of modern British cooking on offer. Expect to find mandarin and chamomile fragrancing the confit duck and foie gras terrine, and then crispy noodles in seafood broth as a medium for main-course sea bass with mussels. Desserts are just as inventive, serving date and port clafoutis with an apple and brandy shot, rum and raisin ice cream and mint foam.

Rudding Park Hotel, Spa & Golf

Modern British

tel: 01423 871350 **Rudding Park, Follifoot HG3 1JH**
email: reservations@ruddingpark.com **web:** www.ruddingpark.co.uk
dir: *A61 at rdbt with A658 follow signs 'Rudding Park'*

Brasserie menu in an elegant Regency era hotel

Rudding Park boasts a golf course, glossy spa and kitchen garden, with food that's worth a detour in the Clocktower Restaurant. It's all vibrant, colourful spaces, from the long limestone bar to the grand conservatory with its Catalonian olive tree, and a dining room complete with eye-catching pink glass chandelier. The kitchen team delivers skilful modern British cooking in a brasserie-style menu, starting with seared scallops and tiger prawn satay with pak choi in minty lime dressing. Next comes pork fillet with robustly constructed wild boar tortellini and parsnip purée, sauced with cider, then chocolate praline mousse with smoked chocolate and gloriously tangy blackberry sorbet.

Chef Eddie Gray **Seats** 110, Pr/dining room 14 **Times** 12-3/6-10 **Prices** Fixed L 2 course fr £30.50, Fixed D 3 course fr £40, Starter £9.50-£13.50, Main £21-£28, Dessert fr £9.50 **Wines** 91 bottles over £30, 27 bottles under £30, 11 by glass **Parking** 350 **Notes** Food & Flicks menu every Mon (must pre-book), Sunday L £32.50-£37, Vegetarian available, Children welcome

Studley Hotel

 Pacific Rim

tel: 01423 560425 **28 Swan Rd HG1 2SE**
email: info@studleyhotel.co.uk **web:** www.orchidrestaurant.co.uk
dir: *Adjacent to Valley Gardens, opposite Mercer Gallery*

Smart hotel restaurant giving culinary tour of Asia

In the Studley Hotel's Orchid restaurant, a multinational brigade of chefs delivers authentic regional flavours in an eclectic Pan-Asian melting pot of cuisines. Mango and darkwood interiors divided by Japanese lattice-style screens make for a classy contemporary setting. A starter of sui yuk partners roasted belly pork with crunchy crackling and a sweet and savoury dip of yellow bean and honey, ahead of fried sea bass fillet with a spicy curry of Thai herbs, shredded lime leaves and coconut cream. Stick with the exotic theme for a dessert of Thai-style steamed banana and sticky rice cake cooked in a banana leaf and served with coconut ice cream.

Chef Kenneth Poon **Seats** 72, Pr/dining room 20 **Times** 12-2/6-10, Closed 25-26 Dec, L Sat **Prices** Fixed L 2 course £12.95, Fixed D 3 course £25.90-£33.50, Starter £5.20-£7.90, Main £8.40-£16.60 **Wines** 16 bottles over £30, 25 bottles under £30, 12 by glass **Parking** 18, On street **Notes** Sunday L £16.95, Vegetarian available, Children welcome

White Hart Hotel

Classic British

tel: 01423 505681 **2 Cold Bath Rd HG2 0NF**
email: reception@whiteharthotelharrogate.com **web:** www.whiteharthotelharrogate.com
dir: *A59 to Harrogate. A661 3rd exit on rdbt to Harrogate. Left at rdbt onto A6040 for 1m. Right onto A61. Bear left down Montpellier Hill*

Modern dishes in a Georgian landmark

The White Hart is a Harrogate landmark, having provided bed and sustenance to travellers since the Georgian era. The recently refurbished Fat Badger Grill is its main eating space, serving classic British food with a contemporary twist, including the chef's own style 'surf n turf' menu that focuses on fresh local produce. Starters might include ox cheek cannelloni with tomato and olives or pan-seared king scallops with sweet pepper risotto and chorizo. The grill has much to offer, including a 10oz North Yorkshire rib-eye, or there's the 'catch of the day' from the fish menu. Alternatively, you might like 'A Big Bowl of Fishes' bouillabaisse.

Chef Richard Ferebee **Seats** 100, Pr/dining room 90 **Times** 6-10, Closed L Mon-Sat **Prices** Starter £5.95-£9.95, Main £12-£4.50, Dessert £6.50 **Wines** 17 bottles over £30, 38 bottles under £30, 18 by glass **Parking** 80 **Notes** Sun open 12-9pm, Sunday L £15.95-£19.95, Vegetarian available, Children welcome

HAWES Map 18 SD88

The Four Fells Restaurant

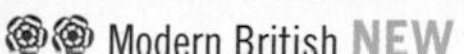

Modern British NEW V

tel: 01969 667255 **Simonstone Hall Hotel, Simonstone DL8 3LY**
email: enquiries@simonstonehall.com **web:** www.simonstonehall.com
dir: *1.5m N of Hawes on road signed Muker & Buttertubs*

Robust country-house hotel with contemporary dining

An old stone manor house, built to last, Simonstone Hall is these days a country-house hotel with a few contemporary surprises in store. The rural aspect may well be timeless, and the decor soothingly traditional, but in its evening-only restaurant the culinary mode is very much of our times. Pig's head terrine comes with fashionable spikes of acidity and sweetness, salt marsh lamb arrives with a bit of dry ice theatre, and there are flavours of miso and lime amid the raspberry and dark chocolate to finish. There's a market tasting menu, too, while the hotel's brasserie (open lunch and dinner) takes a more familiar gastronomic approach.

Chef Craig Wanless **Seats** 18, Pr/dining room 22 **Times** 6-9, Closed Sun-Mon, L all week **Prices** Tasting menu £72.50-£82.45 **Wines** 38 bottles over £30, 29 bottles under £30, 12 by glass **Parking** 20 **Notes** Tasting 9 course, Market tasting 6 course £45-£54.95, Children 12 yrs+

HAWNBY Map 19 SE58

The Inn at Hawnby

Modern British

tel: 01439 798202 **YO62 5QS**
email: info@innathawnby.co.uk **web:** www.innathawnby.co.uk
dir: *From the S, A1 to Thirsk & Teeside exit A19/A168 for Scarborough onto A170. 1st left through Felixkirk. Through Boltby into Hawnby*

Local cooking in an old grey moorland inn

The Youngs' old greystone country inn near Helmsley has the sweeping majesty of the North York Moors all around it, an inspiringly remote setting for walkers and gastronomes. A homely village pub atmosphere, complete with log fire, makes a cheering prospect, while the dining room offers a degree of refinement. The kitchen makes good use of local ingredients and the resulting dishes show a good amount of contemporary flair. A first-course roast pork belly arrives with scallop and black pudding, with the flavour of tamarind running through, with main courses extending to roast lamb neck served with carpaccio of shoulder meat. Finish with chocolate nemesis.

Chef Jason Reeves **Seats** 32, Pr/dining room 30 **Times** 12-2/7-9, Closed 25 Dec, L Mon-Tue (limited opening Feb-Mar please phone) **Prices** Starter £5-£9, Main £10-£22, Dessert £6-£9 **Wines** 15 bottles over £30, 11 bottles under £30, 12 by glass **Parking** 22 **Notes** Sunday L £5-£18, Vegetarian available, Children welcome

HELMSLEY Map 19 SE68

Black Swan Hotel

– see page 468

Feversham Arms Hotel & Verbena Spa

Modern British V

tel: 01439 770766 **1-8 High St YO62 5AG**
email: info@fevershamarmshotel.com **web:** www.fevershamarmshotel.com
dir: *A1 junct 49 follow A168 to Thirsk, take A170 to Helmsley. Turn left at mini rdbt then right, hotel on right past church*

Modern spa hotel with equally modern culinary ideas

Sophisticated cooking built on fine regional ingredients is the order of the day here. Seared scallop with warm apple jelly, black pudding and smoked roe emulsion seems entirely appropriate for a hotel in an affluent market town, and there might also be veal sweetbread with turnip and wood sorrel. Flavour combinations are well considered, seen in fillet of turbot served with an oxtail ravioli and Judas's ear (a mushroom), and fillet of pork Wellington with wild cabbage and a Taylor's tea and prune purée. There are 32-day aged steaks, too, served with triple-cooked chips, with good breads also part of the package. Tempting desserts have included chocolate and banana millefeuille.

Chef Norman Mackenzie **Seats** 65, Pr/dining room 32 **Times** 12-2.30/6.45-9.15 **Prices** Fixed D 3 course £48, Tasting menu £60, Starter £10-£17, Main £25-£32, Dessert £10-£14.50 **Wines** 120 bottles over £30, 12 bottles under £30, 18 by glass **Parking** 50 **Notes** Tasting menu 6 course whole tables only, Sunday L £19.50-£25.50, Children welcome

The Pheasant Hotel

Modern British V

tel: 01439 771241 **Mill St, Harome YO62 5JG**
email: reservations@thepheasanthotel.com **web:** www.thepheasanthotel.com
dir: *Exit A170 signed Harome, hotel opposite church*

Skilful cooking by the village duck pond

The Pheasant has been carved out of a blacksmith's, village shop and barns, all set around a courtyard. The flagstone-floored conservatory is mainly used for dining, and the cooking style is an updated British version of the classical French repertory, with an expert's skill behind judicious combinations. At lunchtime, expect devilled lamb's kidneys with fried bread and watercress ahead of fish pie with a shrimp and caper salad. Dinner might kick off with fennel-cured salmon with beetroot and rosemary and proceed to pan-fried stuffed partridge with mulled pears, spelt and roast parsnips. Tempting puddings include white chocolate parfait with hazelnut ice cream and a chocolate pencil.

Chef Peter Neville **Seats** 60, Pr/dining room 30 **Times** 12-2/6.30-9, Closed D 25 Dec **Prices** Fixed L 2 course fr £22.50, Fixed D 3 course fr £40, Tasting menu fr £65, Starter £10-£16, Main £20-£27, Dessert £9 **Wines** 67 bottles over £30, 20 bottles under £30, 12 by glass **Parking** 15 **Notes** Afternoon tea, Sunday L £28.50-£34, Children welcome

Black Swan Hotel

HELMSLEY Map 19 SE68

Modern British V

tel: 01439 770466 **Market Place YO62 5BJ**
email: enquiries@blackswan-helmsley.co.uk
web: www.blackswan-helmsley.co.uk
dir: *A170 towards Scarborough then Helmsley, hotel at end of Market Place, just off mini-rdbt*

Art on a plate in a gallery restaurant

The old Helmsley Highflyer, which used to link Leeds and York on the Victorian coaching route, doesn't run through here any longer, but you can still make it on the moorland steam train. Your destination is a delightful architectural dog's dinner, with a stone-built Elizabethan-style inn and a building done in herringbone half-timbering flanking a more sober-looking small Georgian house. Inside, a showcase for local artworks doubles as the Gallery restaurant, with paisley-patterned and plain blue walls the setting for the award-winning new head chef Alan O'Kane who joined the Black Swan as this guide was going to print. With a background at The Savoy and The Capital and Gilpin Lodge, he brings with him a wealth of experience and a classical/modern British style. Early indications are of impeccably contemporary food with the emphasis on counterpointing flavours and textures, perhaps starting with seared scallops with a parfait of their roe, sticky black rice, and apple and yuzu gel, with retro nods here and there, as when beef carpaccio arrives with a Marie Rose-dressed crab and tomato cocktail, or in main-course duck à l'orange 70s style, with Bull's Blood (the salad leaf, not the wine) and parsnip purée. Fish may be sea bass with clam chowder and samphire, while a version of Mont Blanc, the chestnut mousse dessert, with vanilla parfait and mandarin pulp is worth forsaking the chocolate creations for. English and European cheeses come arrayed in full fig, grape and quince.

Chef Alan O'Kane **Seats** 65, Pr/dining room 50
Times 12.30-2/7-9.30, Closed L Mon-Sat **Prices** Fixed D 3 course fr £45, Tasting menu fr £65 **Wines** 166 bottles over £30, 39 bottles under £30, 19 by glass **Parking** 40 **Notes** Tasting menu 6 course, Sunday L fr £29.95, Children welcome

HETTON **Map 18 SD95**

The Angel Inn

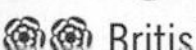 British

tel: 01756 730263 **BD23 6LT**
email: info@angelhetton.co.uk **web:** www.angelhetton.co.uk
dir: *6m N Skipton, follow B6265 towards Grassington, left at duck pond & again at T-junct. The Angel is up the hill on right*

Forthright British cooking in a heritage country inn

A 500-year-old inn with food at the heart of everything, The Angel was among the first pubs to break away from the chips-with-everything mentality back in the 1980s. It remains a dining destination to this day. The creeper-covered building is home to a Bar Brasserie and a smart restaurant with linen-clad tables and pretty, country-style decor. The kitchen offers a gently contemporary repertoire including butternut squash and sage risotto to start, followed perhaps by pan-roasted haunch of venison with celeriac remoulade and suet pudding filled with wild mushrooms. Finish with blackberry mousse with white chocolate and tarragon ice cream.

Chef Bruce Elsworth **Seats** 65, Pr/dining room 24 **Times** 12-2.30/6-10, Closed 25 Dec & 1 wk Jan, L Mon-Sat, D Sun **Prices** Tasting menu £55, Starter £7.98-£10.18, Main £15.35-£29.65, Dessert £7.65 **Wines** 107 bottles over £30, 21 by glass **Parking** 40 **Notes** Sat D 4 course £45, Sunday L £28, Vegetarian available, Children welcome

KNARESBOROUGH **Map 19 SE35**

General Tarleton Inn

Modern British

tel: 01423 340284 **Boroughbridge Rd, Ferrensby HG5 0PZ**
email: gti@generaltarleton.co.uk **web:** www.generaltarleton.co.uk
dir: *A1(M) junct 48 at Boroughbridge, take A6055 to Knaresborough. 4m on right*

Modern Yorkshire food with ambition

Not far from the castle, and with Harrogate barely five miles away, the GT is a country inn with character. When the chef entitles his menus 'Food with Yorkshire Roots' here, he means it. Twice-baked Wensleydale soufflé with tomato relish is a regionally unimpeachable starter option. Suckling pig appears in many guises on one plate – loin, belly, shoulder and black pudding with pear and dauphinoise – while the sole fish possibility on a meaty roll call of mains might be seared sea bass with truffle gnocchi and marinated artichoke. To round things off, treacle tart is served with clotted cream, Horlicks ice cream and peanut butter.

Chef John Topham, Marc Williams **Seats** 64, Pr/dining room 40 **Times** 12-1.45/6-9.15, Closed D 25-26 Dec, 1 Jan **Prices** Fixed L 2 course £14.95, Fixed D 3 course £18.50, Starter £7.95-£12, Main £13.95-£26.95, Dessert £4.95-£7.95 **Wines** 30 bottles over £30, 14 bottles under £30, 9 by glass **Parking** 40 **Notes** Sunday L £13.75-£18.95, Vegetarian available, Children welcome

MALTON **Map 19 SE77**

The Talbot Hotel

 British

tel: 01653 639096 **Yorkersgate YO17 7AJ**
email: reservations@talbotmalton.co.uk **web:** www.talbotmalton.co.uk
dir: *A46 Malton*

Distinctive modern cooking born and bred in Malton

Equidistant from Castle Howard and the Yorkshire Arboretum, The Talbot showcases contemporary cooking of distinctive flair. Dressing a Whitby crab involves adding lardo, fennel pollen and a sorrel sorbet as well as the more usual avocado, while a seasonal main course of Dales grouse is roasted in hay, accompanied by its confit leg, mulled red cabbage, salt-baked veg and a bramble and juniper jus. A seafood pairing to conjure with offers wreckfish and crayfish with crispy buckwheat in a rich bisque sauce. The resourceful technical range extends into entertaining desserts such as milk chocolate ganache with rapeseed oil and aerated chocolate, damson sorbet and a caramelised plum.

Chef Dan Graham **Seats** 40, Pr/dining room 40 **Times** 12.30-2.30/6.30-9.30 **Prices** Starter fr £8.50, Main fr £15.95, Dessert fr £7.95 **Wines** 71 bottles over £30, 34 bottles under £30, 10 by glass **Parking** 40 **Notes** Sunday L £20-£25, Vegetarian available, Children welcome

MASHAM **Map 19 SE28**

Samuel's at Swinton Park

Modern British

tel: 01765 680900 **Swinton HG4 4JH**
email: enquiries@swintonpark.com **web:** www.swintonpark.com
dir: *Phone for directions*

Dynamic modern cooking in a glorious country estate

Swinton Park makes quite an impression, with its solid-looking tower and castellated walls hung with creeper. The interior boasts antiques and family portraits (the Cunliffe-Listers have owned the property since the 1880s), that enhance the feeling of being in a stately home. The dining room is particularly grand, with its high carved ceilings, gilt-framed mirrors and plush drapes at the windows. This is where to experience Simon Crannage's modern British cooking, each dish carefully considered in terms of mixing and matching various components, with seasonality to the fore. A winter salad (all from the four acres of kitchen garden), raw, pickled and cooked, is accompanied by goats' cheese and truffle cream sauce to make an appealing starter, or there might be flame-cooked mackerel and tartare balanced by apple and dill-flecked cucumber purée. Ingredients are of the first order and the kitchen's technical skill is apparent in main courses: pink venison loin (from the estate) comes with braised chicory, squash, buckwheat adding additional textural contrast and a rich jus added at table, or accurately timed roast halibut fillet with mussels, fennel, samphire, chard, jeera and poached potato. Go out on light, smooth chocolate marquise complemented by the savoury flavours of parsnip purée and ice cream.

Chef Tom Pickard, Simon Crannage **Seats** 60, Pr/dining room 20 **Times** 12.30-2/7-9.30, Closed 2 days Jan, L Mon-Fri **Prices** Fixed L 2 course fr £22, Fixed D 3 course fr £58, Tasting menu fr £70 **Wines** 111 bottles over £30, 33 bottles under £30, 13 by glass **Parking** 80 **Notes** Sunday L £28-£40, Vegetarian available, Children 8 yrs+ D

MASHAM *continued*

Vennell's

Traditional British

tel: 01765 689000 **7 Silver St HG4 4DX**
email: info@vennellsrestaurant.co.uk
dir: *8m from A1 Masham exit, 10m N of Ripon*

Another of Masham's many assets

Jon Vennell's self-named neighbourhood eatery has become a destination for out-of-towners. Four dinners and one lunch a week keep things on a tight rein, and a meal might begin with a serving of lightly poached salmon in an array of shoots and croûtons, alongside lemon jelly and a blob of chived crème fraîche, before mains bring on fine prime cuts such as rare-breed confit pork with beans and chorizo stewed in Pinot Noir, or turbot fillet with brown shrimps and capers in beurre blanc. Some of the local ale goes into a majestic suet pudding of beef and mushrooms, and desserts maintain the pace with lemon cheesecake in raspberry coulis.

Chef Jon Vennell **Seats** 30, Pr/dining room 16 **Times** 12-4/7.15-12, Closed 26-29 Dec, 1-14 Jan, 1 wk Aug, Mon-Tue, L Wed-Sat, D Sun **Wines** 27 bottles over £30, 28 bottles under £30, 11 by glass **Parking** On street & Market Sq **Notes** ALC 2 course £28.50, Sunday L £22.75-£27.50, Vegetarian available, Children 4 yrs+

MIDDLESBROUGH **Map 19 NZ41**

Chadwicks Inn Maltby

Modern British V

tel: 01642 590300 **High Ln, Maltby TS8 0BG**
email: info@chadwicksmaltby.co.uk
dir: *A19-A174(W)/A1045, follow signs to Yarm & Maltby, left at the Manor House, inn 500yds on left through village*

Ambitious modern cooking in a moorland country inn

Food is very much a focus at this traditional 19th-century inn on the edge of the moors. Dine either in the bar, with its wood-burner and sofas, or in the comfortable restaurant. The dinner menu is a slate of ambitiously enterprising dishes straight out of the 21st-century school. Start with salmon ballotine with dressed crab and cucumber and go on to rib-eye steak with peppercorn sauce and traditional accompaniments. Or reverse the order: rare beef salad with horseradish, carrots and shallots, then pan-roast sea bream fillet with French-style peas and dauphinoise. Either way, end with lemon tart with raspberries, raspberry sorbet and sorrel.

Chef Steve Lawford **Seats** 47 **Times** 12-2.30/5-9.30, Closed 26 Dec, 1 Jan, Mon, D Sun **Prices** Fixed L 2 course £13.95, Fixed D 3 course £27.50, Starter £5.95-£9.95, Main £19.50-£32, Dessert £4.95-£7.95 **Wines** 26 bottles over £30, 25 bottles under £30, 7 by glass **Parking** 50 **Notes** Steak & wine night from £35 for 2, Bistro menu L & early eve, Sunday L £14.95-£22.95, Children welcome

MIDDLETON TYAS **Map 19 NZ20**

The Coach House

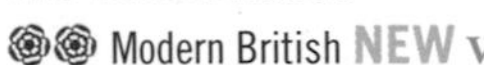

Modern British NEW V

tel: 01325 377977 **Middleton Lodge DL10 6NJ**
email: info@middletonlodge.co.uk **web:** www.middletonlodge.co.uk
dir: *A1 junct 56, follow signs towards Barton, 2nd right onto Kneeton Lane, 2 mins on left*

Contemporary flair on a Georgian country estate

Unshouty hues of cream and baby blue, stone floors and chunky wood tables beneath a soaring, heavy-beamed roof set the tone in this rustic-chic eatery on a 200-acre country estate. The kitchen takes a modernist approach, using calender-correct regional produce and treatments to deliver a starter of crab with sweet-and-sour apple, yuzu purée, pickled mooli radish and sea fennel, ahead of pork belly and pig's cheek matched with langoustine, caramelised cauliflower purée and braised spring onions. Dessert is an opportunity to show a bit of ambitious technique, delivered via a deconstructed passionfruit cheesecake with coconut ice cream, passionfruit sorbet and coconut crumble.

Chef Gareth Rayner **Seats** 80, Pr/dining room 24 **Times** 12-2.30/6-9 **Prices** Prices not confirmed **Wines** 47 bottles over £30, 43 bottles under £30, 13 by glass **Parking** 100 **Notes** Sunday L, Children welcome

OLDSTEAD **Map 19 SE57**

The Black Swan at Oldstead

– see opposite

OSMOTHERLEY **Map 19 SE49**

The Cleveland Tontine

Modern European

tel: 01609 882671 **Staddlebridge DL6 3JB**
email: bookings@theclevelandtontine.co.uk **web:** www.theclevelandtontine.co.uk
dir: *Phone for directions*

Modern cooking in revamped roadside restaurant with rooms

Once an overnight stop for travellers using the London to Sunderland mail coach, this has been an iconic restaurant for the past four decades. Now modernised for contemporary diners, the candlelit dining room oozes atmosphere with its stone fireplace and rustic carvings. The culinary style might be described as modern British-meets-French-bistro, opening effectively with ham hock ravioli, pea soup, crisp pancetta, followed by loin of rose veal, braised baby gem lettuce, sweet bread tortellini, sage and pine nut butter sauce. At dessert stage, apple jelly and custard is accompanied by blueberry ice cream and a cinnamon doughnut.

Chef Paul Bussey **Seats** 88, Pr/dining room 50 **Times** 12-2.30/6.30-9, Closed D 25-26 Dec, 1 Jan **Prices** Fixed L 2 course £16.95-£20, Fixed D 3 course £20-£25, Starter £6.95-£11.95, Main £14.95-£33, Dessert £6.95-£9.95 **Wines** 48 bottles over £30, 39 bottles under £30, 16 by glass **Parking** 40 **Notes** Afternoon tea, Sunday L £20-£25, Vegetarian available, Children welcome

PICKERING **Map 19 SE78**

Fox & Hounds Country Inn

Modern British

tel: 01751 431577 **Main St, Sinnington YO62 6SQ**
email: fox.houndsinn@btconnect.com **web:** www.thefoxandhoundsinn.co.uk
dir: *In Sinnington centre, 3m W of Pickering, off A170*

Well-wrought pub food on the edge of the Moors

This stone-built country inn at the hub of its own little Yorkshire community is all cosiness and cheer within, from the snug bar with its wood-burner to the dining room that looks onto the back garden. Well-wrought pub food based on fine prime materials, with chef's specials on the blackboard, embraces fried sea bass on pine nut fettuccine to start, or a twice-baked Lincolnshire Poacher soufflé with sweet-and-sour cherry tomatoes, and then gird your loins for three servings of lamb – a mini-rack, braised shoulder and a pie with tomatoes and rosemary – served with creamy, garlicky dauphinoise. Treacle tart and custard comes with a garnishing of kumquat.

Chef Mark Caffrey **Seats** 36, Pr/dining room 10 **Times** 12-2/6.30-9, Closed 25-27 Dec **Prices** Starter £5.25-£8.25, Main £12.75-£23.95, Dessert £5.95-£7.25 **Wines** 7 bottles over £30, 28 bottles under £30, 9 by glass **Parking** 35 **Notes** Early D menu Sun-Fri 5.30-6.30pm £9.95, Light L wknd £9.95, Sunday L £25-£30, Vegetarian available, Children welcome

The Black Swan at Oldstead

OLDSTEAD **Map 19 SE57**

Modern British V NOTABLE WINE LIST

tel: 01347 868387 **YO61 4BL**
email: enquiries@blackswanoldstead.co.uk
web: www.blackswanoldstead.co.uk
dir: *A1 junct 49, A168, A19 S (or from York A19 N), then Coxwold, Byland Abbey, Oldstead*

Dazzling intrepid modern cooking on a family farmstead

An appealing stone-built country house out on the North York Moors, The Black Swan has become a coveted destination restaurant in the region, a remarkable achievement for having been brought about without TV appearances or even a book. Whether or not Tom Banks chooses to head along the media route, nothing can detract from the creative energy currently driving the place. Members of his team work at least one day a week in the 2.5-acre kitchen garden (established in 2015 and now producing nearly all their fruit and veg), which helps deepen their understanding of how dishes are composed, and how flavours work together. The bar is cosy with its roaring log fire, oak tables and stone-flagged floor, and serves a proper pint of local real ale, along with some excellent wines by the glass, plus novel cocktails scented with herbs and extracts from fir trees in the local woods to emphasise the connection with the landscape from the off. The cooking is all about freshness, pleasing contrasts and surpassing simplicity, as in a starter of butter-poached new carrots, fennel, cobnuts and goats' curd. Another example from the standard five-course menu is lightly cooked trout in crystal-clear tomato consommé, served with langoustines and floral garnishes of nasturtiums and flowering borage. Main course could be superb crisp-skinned chicken breast with roasted leek and oyster mushrooms, garnished by pickled elderberries and crisp lovage leaves. A pre-dessert of macerated strawberries scented with woodruff precedes a quenelle of heather-fragrant mousse adorned with wisps of honey meringue and shards of honeycomb. The tasting menus expand into eight courses but retain that essential link with the surrounding earth and the passing seasons, perhaps centring on turbot with razor clams and broccoli, before partridge with red cabbage and pearl barley.

Chef Tommy Banks **Seats** 40, Pr/dining room 12
Times 12-2/6-9, Closed L Mon-Sat **Prices** Fixed L 3 course £38-£60, Fixed D 3 course £60, Tasting menu fr £85 **Wines** 90 bottles over £30, 2 bottles under £30, 81 by glass **Parking** 20 **Notes** Sunday L £38-£60, Children 10 yrs+

PICKERING *continued*

The White Swan Inn

 Modern British

tel: 01751 472288 **Market Place YO18 7AA**
email: welcome@white-swan.co.uk **web:** www.white-swan.co.uk
dir: *Just beyond junct of A169/A170 in Pickering, turn right off A170 into Market Place*

Proud Yorkshire produce in a Tudor coaching inn

A venerable stone-built Tudor coaching inn where the kitchen philosophy is all about good Yorkshire produce. Rare-breed meats from the celebrated Ginger Pig butcher in nearby Levisham, local cheeses, fish from Whitby and veg from the allotment all feature proudly. Expect to start with ham hock terrine with a quail's egg, piccalilli and chargrilled toast, or potted crab with celeriac remoulade. Main course could be shallow-fried stone bass with kale and smoked salmon cream sauce, or rack of lamb with a Jersey Royal potato cake, minted new carrots and caper sauce. Puddings might be sticky toffee pudding or lemon meringue with pannacotta and lemon and poppy seed tuile.

Chef Darren Clemmit **Seats** 50, Pr/dining room 30 **Times** 12-2/6.45-9 **Prices** Starter £5.95-£10.95, Main £11.95-£25.95, Dessert £6.95-£10.95 **Wines** 31 bottles over £30, 32 bottles under £30, 19 by glass **Parking** 45 **Notes** Fixed L/D menu on request, Sunday L, Vegetarian available, Children welcome

RICHMOND Map 19 NZ10

The Frenchgate Restaurant and Hotel

 Modern British

tel: 01748 822087 & 07921 136362 **59-61 Frenchgate DL10 7AE**
email: info@thefrenchgate.co.uk **web:** www.thefrenchgate.co.uk
dir: *From A1 (Scotch Corner) to Richmond on A6108. After lights, 1st left into Lile Close (leading to Flints Terrace) for hotel car park. Or for front entrance continue to 1st rdbt, left into Dundas St. At T-junct left into Frenchgate*

Technical artistry on the plate and on the walls

Compounded of two original townhouses in photogenic Richmond, The Frenchgate is a modern boutique hotel with bags of character. Concentrated technical artistry is on show in a starter of quail's ballotine filled with wild mushroom mousse, alongside a pile of Puy lentils and a morel jelly with a quail egg set in it. Mains cover a spectrum from stone bass with razor clams in an emulsion sauce of brown crab, to mustard-crusted fillet and belly of local pork, appetisingly set off with crisp-fried kale and creamed Savoy, as well as mustard mash. Peach mousse with caramelised peach in its own coulis is a late-summer treat, served with thyme ice cream.

Chef Lisa Miller **Seats** 24, Pr/dining room 24 **Times** 12-2/6-9.30 **Prices** Fixed D 3 course £34-£39 **Wines** 50 bottles over £30, 18 bottles under £30, 12 by glass **Parking** 12 **Notes** Pre-theatre menu, Tasting menu, Matching wine flights, Sunday L £15-£19, Vegetarian available, Children welcome

SCARBOROUGH Map 17 TA08

Lanterna Ristorante

 Italian

tel: 01723 363616 **33 Queen St YO11 1HQ**
email: ralessio@lanterna-ristorante.co.uk
dir: *Phone for directions*

Convivial long-running Italian with classic cooking

It has been honoured by Italian newspaper La Stampa as 'the English temple of Italian cuisine', which seems an extraordinary accolade for an unassuming, albeit heartily convivial restaurant. Chef-patron, the tireless Giorgio Alessio, oversees a venue done out in colour schemes of reds and oranges, and sunny yellow and sky-blue, in the two dining rooms. The menu features simple, well-handled Italian cooking of the classic school: velvet crab with spaghetti and a creamy sauce, ravioli filled with ricotta and spinach in a tomato and basil sauce, and meaty options such as medallions of fillet steak served rare with garlic butter. Finish with pannacotta flavoured with rum.

Chef Giorgio Alessio **Seats** 35 **Times** 7-9.30, Closed 2 wks Oct, 25-26 Dec, 1 Jan, Sun, L all week **Prices** Prices not confirmed **Wines** 35 bottles over £30, 36 bottles under £30, 5 by glass **Parking** On street, car park nearby **Notes** Vegetarian available, Children welcome

Palm Court Hotel

 Modern British

tel: 01723 368161 **St Nicholas Cliff YO11 2ES**
email: generalmanager@palmcourt-scarborough.co.uk
web: www.palmcourtscarborough.co.uk
dir: *In Scarborough town centre*

Modern dining in a Victorian hotel

This grand old Victorian hotel has a modern decor that sits comfortably beside its elegant period features. Dinner is served in the elegant, neutral-toned restaurant, where tables swathed in floor-length linen sit beneath chandeliers. The kitchen relies on top-class local produce allied with tried-and-true culinary principles for its effect. Ham hock terrine with plum chutney and toasted brioche is a capably executed starter, followed by the simple comforts of roast belly pork with red cabbage, grain mustard mash and honey-glazed parsnips. Or there might be locally-landed cod matched with chorizo and red pepper vinaigrette, seafood pudding and spinach. Dessert is a refreshing duo of lemon tartlet and lemon curd sorbet.

SCAWTON Map 19 SE58

The Hare Inn

@@@ Modern British V

tel: 01845 597769 **YO7 2HG**
email: info@thehare-inn.com **web:** www.thehare-inn.com
dir: *1m from A170 between Helmsley & Thirsk*

Creative modern cooking in an old village inn

The Hare is a 21st-century restaurant in a 13th-century inn, and although there may well be local ales at the pumps, it's really all about the dazzling cooking of Paul Jackson. It certainly looks the part of an old moorland inn, with a rugged exterior painted in pristine white, and indoors there's plenty of character in the form of original features and some quirky fixtures and fittings. Mr Jackson seeks out the very best ingredients that abound in this part of the world and offers them up in creative ways via fixed-price menus. Things get going with an amuse-bouche such as smoked cod roe and miso-flavoured mayonnaise atop a piece of crispy cod's skin, and breads include a mini loaf flavoured with parmesan and truffle. The meal proper might start with a prettily presented dish of bream, the perfectly timed fish loaded up with wild flowers and three succulent mussels, before a meat course of Sutton Bank Dexter beef (from just down the road) arrives pink, tender and full of flavour. Next up, local grouse is served with textures of beetroot and goats' cheese, followed by a dessert such as the invitingly titled milk and honey. Each dish has a recommended accompaniment from the compact wine list.

Chef Paul Christopher Jackson **Seats** 22 **Times** 12-2.30/6-9, Closed 22 Nov-3 Dec, 4-28 Jan, 20-28 Jun, Mon-Tue, D Sun **Wines** 20 bottles over £30, 8 bottles under £30, 12 by glass **Parking** 12 **Notes** Tasting menu L 4/5 course £20/£35, D 4/6/8 course £25-£65, Sunday L £15-£35, Children welcome

WEST WITTON Map 19 SE08

The Wensleydale Heifer

@ Modern British V

tel: 01969 622322 **Main St DL8 4LS**
email: info@wensleydaleheifer.co.uk **web:** www.wensleydaleheifer.co.uk
dir: *On A684 (3m W of Leyburn)*

Top-notch seafood and more in the heart of the Yorkshire Dales

Dining on super-fresh fish and seafood isn't the first thing that comes to mind when you're in the heart of the beautiful Yorkshire Dales National Park, but this chic 17th-century inn with boutique rooms draws foodies from far and wide for its piscine pleasures. The wide-ranging menu offers something for all comers: king prawns are given an Asian spin with sweet chilli, sesame, coriander, crispy shallots, cashews, toasted coconut and Japanese yakiniku dipping sauce. Next up, salmon and crab are baked in a banana leaf and matched with Thai peanut curry sauce. It's not all about fish, either: the kitchen pleases carnivores too, with prime slabs of locally-reared beef.

Chef David Moss **Seats** 70 **Times** 12-2.30/6-9.30 **Prices** Fixed L 2 course £19.75, Fixed D 3 course £23.75, Tasting menu £65, Starter £8.75-£12.50, Main £16.75-£39.50, Dessert £7.50-£8 **Wines** 91 bottles over £30, 46 bottles under £30, 13 by glass **Parking** 30 **Notes** Vegan menu, Tapas menu, Sunday L £21.75-£24.75, Children welcome

WHITBY Map 19 NZ81

Estbek House

@@ Modern British

tel: 01947 893424 **East Row, Sandsend YO21 3SU**
email: info@estbekhouse.co.uk **web:** www.estbekhouse.co.uk
dir: *From Whitby follow A174 towards Sandsend. Estbek House just before bridge next to Hart Inn*

Fresh seafood by the sea near Whitby

Overlooking the North Sea just north of Whitby, Estbek House is perfectly positioned to source its materials from the chilly waters out front and the rolling moors behind. It all takes place in a handsome Regency house that operates as a restaurant with rooms of considerable charm. Start with pan-seared scallops (from Shetland, but they grow 'em good up there) with pea purée and crisp Parma ham, and then lemon sole, expertly filleted and served with watercress sauce (or another sauce if you prefer) and dauphinoise potatoes and mixed veg. There's fish pie, too, plus local fillet steak glazed with Shiraz, and, for dessert, plum soup with ginger sorbet.

YARM Map 19 NZ41

The Conservatory

Modern British V NOTABLE WINE LIST

tel: 01642 789000 **Judges Country House Hotel, Kirklevington Hall TS15 9LW**
email: enquiries@judgeshotel.co.uk **web:** www.judgeshotel.co.uk
dir: *1.5m from junct W A19, take A67 towards Kirklevington, hotel 1.5m on left*

Country-house cooking in glorious grounds

The Rosette award for this establishment has been suspended due to a change of chef. Reassessment will take place in due course under the new chef. Dating from 1881, the Judges Country House Hotel occupies a magnificent edifice within 22 acres of well-maintained grounds that include a walled kitchen garden. The dining room is furnished and decorated in keeping with the age and the style of the property, with a patterned dark green carpet, striped wallpaper, double-clothed tables set with silver cutlery and fresh flowers, and large windows as standard in the conservatory area. Service is on the formal side, but staff are friendly and keen to engage with diners. First-class ingredients underpin the kitchen's output, with Loch Duart salmon and Wye Valley rhubarb appearing in an opener with garnishes of Avruga caviar and Granny Smith apple and a scent of lemon verbena, while main courses run to Yorkshire lamb loin and pressed shoulder alongside wild garlic mash and capers, or a marine combination of east coast cod, brown shrimps and cockles with potato and leeks. Classic steak and sauce pairings with triple-cooked chips, the meat salt-aged for at least 35 days, will please traditionalists, and desserts look to savoury seasonings for coconut parfait with wasabi sorbet and coriander, or crème brûlée with textured strawberries and tarragon. The short Market Menu is particularly good value in the opulent circumstances.

Seats 30, Pr/dining room 50 **Times** 6.30-9.30, Closed Sun-Mon, L all week **Prices** Starter £11.95, Main £34.50, Dessert £11.95 **Wines** 107 bottles over £30, 28 bottles under £30, 12 by glass **Parking** 110 **Notes** Children welcome

Crathorne Hall Hotel

Modern British

tel: 01642 700398 & 0845 072 7440 *(Calls cost 7p per minute plus your phone company's access charge)* **Crathorne TS15 0AR**
email: crathornehall@handpicked.co.uk
web: www.handpickedhotels.co.uk/crathorne-hall
dir: *Off A19, 2m E of Yarm. Access to A19 via A66 or A1, Thirsk*

Contemporary British style with clever combinations

While the decor and furnishings of the Leven Restaurant are all early 20th century – oak half-panelled walls, heavy drapes at tall windows, oil paintings, and a gilt-edged coffered ceiling – it's fast forward to today in the kitchen. Here the style tends towards modern British sensibilities, with sound, classical technique on display. Start with perfectly-timed scallops matched with chorizo, compressed apple and caper dressing. Next up, there might be pan-fried sea bass with red wine risotto, garlic purée and samphire. Puddings continue to show carefully considered combinations of flavour and texture, delivering velvety bitter chocolate tart with chocolate soil, pistachio ice cream and cherries.

YORK Map 16 SE65

Best Western Plus Dean Court Hotel

Modern British

tel: 01904 625082 **Duncombe Place YO1 7EF**
email: sales@deancourt-york.co.uk **web:** www.deancourt-york.co.uk
dir: *City centre, directly opposite York Minster*

Contemporary Yorkshire cooking next to the Minster

Sitting on the corner of Petergate, Dean Court is an amalgam of Victorian buildings originally put up to house clergy at the Minster. Today the DCH dining room is a clean-lined, light-coloured contemporary space. The modern styling gives a clue to the orientation of the cooking, where Yorkshire produce is put to effective use in offerings such as nettle risotto with goats' cheese bonbon, followed by venison loin with potato fondant, wild mushrooms, Chantenay carrots, parsnip crisps and game jus. The show might close with a pairing of chocolate fondant and mint clotted cream ice cream.

Chef Benji Thornton **Seats** 60, Pr/dining room 40 **Times** 12-3/6-9.30, Closed D 25 Dec **Prices** Fixed L 2 course £15-£20, Starter £4.25-£9.25, Main £11.50-£24.95, Dessert £4.50-£9.50 **Wines** 36 bottles over £30, 43 bottles under £30, 13 by glass **Parking** Pay & display car park nearby **Notes** Sunday L, Vegetarian available, Children welcome

The Churchill Hotel

 Modern British

tel: 01904 644456 **65 Bootham YO30 7DQ**
email: info@churchillhotel.com **web:** www.churchillhotel.com
dir: *On A19 (Bootham), W from York Minster, hotel 250yds on right*

Imaginative food and piano music

The set-up is rather civilised in this Georgian mansion, which blends its airy period elegance with the look of a contemporary boutique city hotel. The dining room looks through vast arching windows into the garden, where the trees are spangled in fairy lights. Laid-back music floats from a softly-tinkling baby grand piano as the soundtrack to cooking that delivers imaginative modern ideas. Pressed pork belly is paired with scallop and apple-and-chorizo jam, while main course sees juniper-smoked loin of lamb pan-fried and served with roast garlic, girolles and sea aster. To finish, there's a deconstructed take on lemon meringue pie with raspberry sorbet.

Le Cochon Aveugle

 French V

tel: 01904 640222 **37 Walmgate YO1 9TX**
email: booking@lecochonaveugle.uk **web:** www.lecochonaveugle.uk
dir: *Next to St Denys Church on Walmgate*

Contemporary French bistro that's a cut above

Even with a newly opened additional floor almost doubling the covers to 30, this converted shop still deserves its 'small but perfectly formed' tag, serving up a fixed-price six-course tasting menu. The flavours may be classical, but the execution is thoroughly modern, as demonstrated in an arresting starter of grilled Yorkshire asparagus, quail's egg, lemon jam and parmesan. Mains are equally punchy – blow-torched mackerel turns up with salmon roe and a cauliflower farotto that uses spelt rather than traditional risotto rice, while spring lamb is paired with a light bean cassoulet and hazelnut crumble. For dessert, there may be Brillat-Savarin cheesecake, meringue and strawberry sorbet.

Chef Joshua Overington **Seats** 30, Pr/dining room 12 **Times** 5.45-9, Closed 3 wks Jan, Sun-Mon, L all week **Prices** Prices not confirmed **Wines** 30 bottles over £30, 20 bottles under £30, 12 by glass **Parking** On street, George St car park **Notes** Tasting menu 6/9 course, Children 8 yrs+

The Grand Hotel & Spa, York

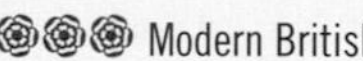 Modern British

tel: 01904 380038 **Station Rise YO1 6HT**
email: dining@thegrandyork.co.uk **web:** www.thegrandyork.co.uk
dir: *A1 junct 47, A59 signed York, Harrogate & Knaresborough. In city centre, near station*

Grand railway hotel with contemporary dining

This grand old Edwardian property by the city's ancient walls was built as the HQ of the North Eastern Railway and its fine features and generous proportions made it an ideal candidate for the hotel business. Today's luxurious establishment has stylish bedrooms, a glamorous spa, and a restaurant that catches the eye. Hudson's muted colour scheme, comfy upholstered chairs and linen-clad tables gives the room a sophisticated sheen, with formal and professional service to match. Head chef Craig Atchinson and his team turn out a contemporary repertoire with a local flavour and modern cooking techniques to the fore, with suppliers name-checked on the menu. Start with roast Norfolk quail glazed in Minus 8 vinegar, Jerusalem artichokes, toasted quinoa and a little pot of punchy wild garlic sauce on the side, or go for smoked sea trout with smoked heritage beetroots and watercress cream. Fillet and cheek of pork comes with a sharp elderberry jus and moreish squash and lemon caramel (like a purée), while a fishy main course might be East coast halibut with mussel sauce. Finish with a sophisticated carrot cake or Medjool date sponge with roasted Granny Smith apple. A tasting menu is up for grabs and afternoon tea is a real treat.

Chef Craig Atchinson **Seats** 60, Pr/dining room 32 **Times** 12.30-2.30/6.30-10 **Prices** Tasting menu £60-£95, Starter £8.50-£15.50, Main £17.95-£30.95, Dessert £7.50-£9 **Wines** 150 bottles over £30, 29 bottles under £30, 12 by glass **Parking** NCP Tanner Row **Notes** Sunday L £26, Vegetarian available, Children welcome

The Grange Hotel

Modern

tel: 01904 644744 **1 Clifton YO30 6AA**
email: info@grangehotel.co.uk **web:** www.grangehotel.co.uk
dir: *A19 (York/Thirsk road), approx 400yds from city centre*

Classy cooking in a city-centre hotel

A classic 1829 townhouse with a designer-led interior of some panache, with inviting sofas and open fires. The cooking makes an impact, with the kitchen clearly taking a broad-based attitude, moving with the times and picking up ideas from near and far. How about 'pastrami' of salmon with wild garlic and micro salad, or another well-balanced starter of sliced smoked duck with figs, radishes and maple dressing? Diehards could go for a grilled steak as main course; others could opt for lamb loin and sweetbreads offset by pickled tomatoes and herby couscous. End with an attractively plated pudding such as hot chocolate fondant with white chocolate chip ice cream.

Chef Will Nicol **Seats** 60, Pr/dining room 70 **Times** 12-2/6-9.30 **Prices** Fixed L 2 course £16.50, Fixed D 3 course £30, Starter £6.50-£9.50, Main £14.50-£29.95, Dessert £5.95-£7.25 **Wines** 18 bottles over £30, 34 bottles under £30, 6 by glass **Parking** 22, Marygate **Notes** Sunday L £16.50-£21.50, Vegetarian available, Children welcome

Guy Fawkes Inn

British

tel: 01904 466674 **25 High Petergate YO1 7HP**
email: reservations@guyfawkesinnyork.com **web:** www.guyfawkesinnyork.com
dir: *A64 onto A1036 signed York & inner ring road. Over bridge into Duncombe Place, right into High Petergate*

Historic city-centre inn serving classic British food

The gunpowder plotter was born here in 1570, in the shadow of York Minster. It is a darkly atmospheric den with an interior akin to stepping into an 'old master' painting, with log fires, wooden floors, gas lighting, cosy nooks and crannies, and cheerful service that suits the buzzy vibe. Menus keep step with the seasons and chalkboard specials follow a hearty modern pub-grub course, their down-to-earth simplicity apparent in a porcine plateful of roast belly and tenderloin of pork with a pig's cheek, home-made black pudding, apple purée and confit root veg. For afters, it's baked blueberry and vanilla cheesecake with fig compôte.

Chef Adrian Knowles **Seats** 34 **Times** 12-9.45, All-day dining **Prices** Fixed L 2 course £10, Starter £3.95-£6.95, Main £9.95-£21.95, Dessert £5.95-£7.95 **Wines** 8 bottles over £30, 20 bottles under £30, 11 by glass **Parking** Marygate car park **Notes** Sunday L £11.95, Vegetarian available, Children welcome

Hotel du Vin & Bistro York

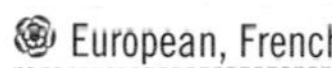 European, French

tel: 01904 557350 **89 The Mount YO24 1AX**
email: info.york@hotelduvin.com **web:** www.hotelduvin.com
dir: *A1036 towards city centre, 6m. Hotel on right through lights*

Sturdy French domestic fare from HdV

The York billet of the HdV group is a late Georgian townhouse in the vicinity of the Minster's Gothic splendour and the city racecourse. Bare tables and floor fit in with the unbuttoned ethos, and the menu offers sturdy French domestic fare with minimal flounce. Dressed crab on toasted baguette with radish in peppery mayonnaise might be the prelude to a robust fish main course such as roast cod on braised Puy lentils with button onions and pancetta, or calves' liver and bacon with mash, or the successful duck version of shepherd's pie. Lemon tart is perhaps a little sturdy, though offset with a decent raspberry sorbet.

The Judge's Lodging

Modern British

tel: 01904 638733 & 639312 **9 Lendal YO1 8AQ**
email: relax@judgeslodgingyork.co.uk **web:** www.judgeslodgingyork.co.uk
dir: *10 min walk from York train station*

All-day menu in a range of different spaces

The Georgian townhouse hard by the Minster has been reinvented as a modern hotel with a plethora of eating and drinking options. Dining can be elegantly panelled or domestic-cosy, and the all-day menus offer a wide range of international favourites. To start, try mushrooms fried with garlic and herbs in hollandaise, or chicken liver parfait wrapped in prosciutto with apricot and orange chutney. Choose your main act from a creative burger, the house fish pie (salmon, haddock and tiger prawns under cheesy mash), or succulent, accurately timed rib-eye in béarnaise with fat chips and rocket. To finish, few will pass up a chocolate brownie with salted caramel ice cream.

Chef James Peyton **Seats** 100 **Times** 7.30am-10pm, All-day dining **Prices** Starter £4.95-£6.95, Main £12.95-£26.95, Dessert £5.25-£6.50 **Wines** 11 bottles over £30, 29 bottles under £30, 14 by glass **Parking** NCP, Marygate **Notes** Sunday L, Vegetarian available, Children welcome

YORK *continued*

Lamb & Lion Inn

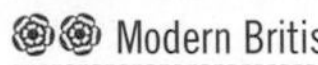 Modern British

tel: 01904 654112 & 612078 **2-4 High Petergate YO1 7EH**
email: reservations@lambandlioninnyork.com **web:** www.lambandlioninnyork.com
dir: *A64 onto A1036. 3.5m, at rdbt 3rd exit, continue on A1036. 2m, right into High Petergate*

Solid English tradition with cosmopolitan touches in the old city walls

Seamlessly grafted into the ancient city walls of medieval York, the Lamb & Lion pleases all comers, young and old, locals and visitors. The undisputed classic of the kitchen is a steak pie to be proud of, and Sunday roasts offer topside or pork loin with Yorkshires and proper stock-pan gravy. Elsewhere, things get more cosmopolitan, with starters of red mullet on crab and coriander risotto, or crackled pork belly in cider vinegar caramel. Then comes coley fillet on paella, or pot-roasted duck breast with herbed pommes Anna, braised red cabbage and a multitude of cherries. To finish, there's crème brûlée, given an old-English touch with quince.

Chef Katie Hoskins **Seats** 40 **Times** 12-3/5-9 **Prices** Starter £5.25-£6.95, Main £11.50-£21.95, Dessert £4.95-£6.95 **Wines** 4 bottles over £30, 21 bottles under £30, 11 by glass **Parking** Marygate car park **Notes** Sunday L £12.95, Vegetarian available, Children welcome

Middlethorpe Hall & Spa

Traditional British NOTABLE WINE LIST

tel: 01904 641241 **Bishopthorpe Rd, Middlethorpe YO23 2GB**
email: info@middlethorpe.com **web:** www.middlethorpe.com
dir: *A64 exit York West. Follow signs Middlethorpe & racecourse*

Seasonal modern British cooking in a 17th-century mansion

This majestic old building stands in 20 acres of gardens and parkland. Inside, there's a classy 18th-century look, plus a modern spa. The kitchen offers a fashionable surf 'n' turf combination of diver-caught roasted scallop with sticky pork belly, kohlrabi and apple purée among first courses, or poached and roasted quail with truffles. Next up, there is an optional sorbet. Among main courses, pan-fried fillet of stone bass comes with cauliflower in various forms and Ebène caviar, and, to finish, Bramley apple soufflé is served with crumble and apple ice cream. The cracking wine list offers good advice on food and wine matching.

Chef Ashley Binder **Seats** 60, Pr/dining room 56 **Times** 12.30-2/6.30-9.45, Closed 25 Dec, L 1 Jan, D 24 & 31 Dec **Prices** Fixed L 2 course £21, Fixed D 3 course £43, Tasting menu £69, Starter £11-£16.50, Main £23-£31.50, Dessert £8-£14 **Wines** 194 bottles over £30, 38 bottles under £30, 15 by glass **Parking** 70 **Notes** Gourmet menu 6 course, Sunday L £30, Vegetarian available, Children 6 yrs+

Oxo's on The Mount

 Modern European V

tel: 01904 619444 **The Mount Royale Hotel, 119 The Mount YO24 1GU**
email: info@oxosrestaurantyork.com **web:** www.oxosrestaurantyork.com
dir: *W on A1036, 0.5m after racecourse. Hotel on right after lights*

Cobbled together from a pair of Regency-era houses, The Mount Royale Hotel brings a country-house atmosphere to the city. The kitchen celebrates Yorkshire produce, beginning with ham hock and parsley terrine with a quail's egg, and Wensleydale cheese and pineapple salad pointed with honey and mustard dressing. For mains, a prime piece of turbot is poached in butter and supported by Whitby crab and tarragon gnocchi, peas, samphire, and champagne butter sauce. Local meat fans might go for rump of Yorkshire lamb with dauphinoise potatoes, red wine-braised baby onions, butternut squash and redcurrant and rosemary jus. To finish, crème brûlée comes with raspberry and saffron, macadamia shortbread and raspberry coulis.

Chef Russell Johnson **Seats** 70, Pr/dining room 18 **Times** 6-9.30, Closed L Mon-Sat **Prices** Fixed L 2 course £17.95, Starter £5.95-£12.95, Main £15.50-£28.95, Dessert £7.50-£8.95 **Wines** 6 bottles over £30, 30 bottles under £30, 16 by glass **Parking** 15 **Notes** Sunday L £17.95-£21.95, Children welcome

The Park Restaurant@Marmadukes Town House Hotel

Modern, Traditional British V

tel: 01904 540903 & 640101 **4-5 St Peters Grove, Bootham YO30 6AQ**
email: admin@theparkrestaurant.co.uk
web: www.marmadukestownhousehotelyork.com
dir: *Phone for directions*

Contemporary dining in a townhouse hotel

Adam Jackson may have been here for less than two years but this smartly refurbished conservatory-style restaurant, part of a Victorian townhouse hotel not far from the city centre, has already made a name for itself as somewhere to find sharp contemporary cooking. An intimate space, it is only open for dinner, allowing everyone involved to concentrate on delivering the ambitious menu exactly as the chef intends. It's a friendly and informal setting, while still having an air of switched-on professionalism. The eight-course tasting menu changes regularly and Jackson, a Yorkshireman born and bred, makes the very best use of the wonderful produce available in this neck of the woods. You can take the menu either with or without the suggested wine pairings, and there is no flowery verbiage on the menu – descriptions, in fact, are quite terse – 'mushrooms, sorrel, gnocchi', for example, is followed by 'beetroot, salmon, apple', and then a main course of 'duck, foie gras, artichoke and hazelnut'. Never fear, however – you're in safe hands with a thoughtful, imaginative chef who knows exactly what he's doing as he guides you on a journey of taste, texture and aroma.

Chef Adam Jackson **Seats** 25, Pr/dining room 25 **Times** 7-8, Closed 25-29 Oct, Sun-Mon, L all week **Prices** Tasting menu £55 **Wines** 20 bottles over £30, 9 bottles under £30, 13 by glass **Parking** 12

SOUTH YORKSHIRE

ROTHERHAM Map 16 SK49

Hellaby Hall Hotel

Modern British

tel: 01709 702701 **Old Hellaby Ln, Hellaby S66 8SN**
email: reservations@hellabyhallhotel.co.uk **web:** www.hellabyhallhotel.co.uk
dir: *0.5m off M18 junct 1, onto A631 towards Maltby. Hotel in Hellaby (NB do not use postcode for Sat Nav)*

Enterprising modern British cooking in a tasteful hotel

This hotel in pretty gardens has at its core a 17th-century manor, while its Carnelly Restaurant is spacious and airy, with a vaulted ceiling. A grounding in the classical French repertoire is apparent, with the kitchen following a modern British route. Chicken and tarragon mousse is a first-rate rendition, complemented by pickled radish and cucumber ribbons, while another starter is seared scallops with crispy bacon and pea velouté. Clearly defined flavours are a hallmark, seen in main courses of braised pork belly with brown onion jus, cauliflower purée and shallots, or duck breast with raspberry gel, fondant potato and baby vegetables. End with deconstructed lemon meringue pie.

Chef Russ Mountford **Seats** 62, Pr/dining room 12 **Times** 6-9.15, Closed L all week **Prices** Fixed D 3 course £26.95, Starter £6.50-£8.95, Main £10.95-£21.95, Dessert £5.50-£7.95 **Wines** 4 bottles over £30, 8 bottles under £30, 4 by glass **Parking** 268 **Notes** Vegetarian available, Children welcome

SHEFFIELD Map 16 SK38

Nonnas

Modern Italian NOTABLE WINE LIST

tel: 0114 268 6166 **535-541 Ecclesall Rd S11 8PR**
email: sheffield@nonnas.co.uk
dir: *From city centre onto Ecclesall Rd, large red building on left*

Italian mini-chain with exceptional modern cooking

Nonnas is a bustling, good-natured Italian restaurant with friendly staff, café-style marble-topped tables and green walls. This is an imaginative kitchen turning out properly cooked, highly original dishes. Rigatoni is sauced with duck leg braised in vin santo, with sausage and sage, and linguine with crab, chilli and fennel. Among accomplished secondi there might be the vivid combinations of Merlot-braised oxtail with beetroot mash and horseradish canederli (bread dumplings) and grilled sea bass fillet with borlotti bean and tomato stew and rosemary aïoli. Inspired puddings have included chocolate and beetroot cake with sweet beetroot and balsamic ripple ice cream alongside classic tiramisù.

Chef Ross Sayles **Seats** 80, Pr/dining room 30 **Times** 12-3.15/5-9.30, Closed 25 Dec, 1 Jan **Prices** Starter £3.50-£7, Main £10-£25, Dessert £5.50-£7 **Wines** 25 bottles over £30, 29 bottles under £30, 20 by glass **Parking** On street **Notes** Sun brunch, fresh pasta offer Sun-Fri £5.95, Vegetarian available, Children welcome

Rafters Restaurant

Modern British, European

tel: 0114 230 4819 **220 Oakbrook Rd, Nethergreen S11 7ED**
email: bookings@raftersrestaurant.co.uk **web:** www.raftersrestaurant.co.uk
dir: *5 mins from Ecclesall road, Hunters Bar rdbt*

Creative, modern cooking and leafy views

Rafters continues to deliver the goods after 20-odd years as a dining hotspot. Located on the first floor of a shop in a leafy neighbourhood, there are verdant views and some seriously good cooking to be enjoyed. The room is smart, the cooking is modern and the menu is packed with interesting combinations. A starter of pheasant, partridge and ham hock terrine comes with pickled shallots and a medley of beetroots in various guises. Main courses team an immaculately handled loin of cod with brown shrimps, crushed potatoes, buttered kale and dill butter sauce. Finish with chocolate crémeux with salted caramel and popcorn ice cream.

Chef Thomas Lawson **Seats** 38 **Times** 12-2/7-8.30, Closed 1-10 Jan, 22-30 Aug, 25-26 Dec, Mon-Tue, L Wed-Sat **Prices** Fixed D 3 course £43-£50, Tasting menu £60 **Wines** 52 bottles over £30, 16 bottles under £30, 12 by glass **Parking** On street **Notes** Vegetarian tasting menu with 48hrs notice, Sunday L £28-£37, Vegetarian available, Children 5 yrs+

Whitley Hall Hotel

Modern British

tel: 0114 245 4444 **Elliott Ln, Grenoside S35 8NR**
email: reservations@whitleyhall.com **web:** www.whitleyhall.com
dir: *A61 past football ground, then 2m, right just before Norfolk Arms, left at bottom of hill. Hotel on left*

Imaginative British cooking in a stunning country hotel

Surrounded by rolling countryside, Whitley Hall is a solid stone mansion dating from the 16th century, set in 20 acres of immaculate grounds. The restaurant may have a whiff of formality, but the kitchen keeps ahead of the game with a thoroughly modern menu. A slice of chicken and pistachio terrine with roasted shallot mousse and apple swipe is a confident opener before a bravura main course of seared salmon and mussels with chorizo and tagliatelle. Originality doesn't dry up among puddings, either: try lemon chiboust tart with matching ice cream adorned with edible flowers, or poppy seed meringue filled with passionfruit mousse.

WORTLEY Map 16 SK39

The Wortley Arms

Modern British V

tel: 0114 288 8749 **Halifax Rd S35 7DB**
email: enquiries@wortley-arms.co.uk
dir: *M1 junct 36. Follow Sheffield North signs, right at Tankersley garage, 1m on right*

Contemporary and classic food in a Georgian pub

The Wortley Arms is an appealing spot for a pint of local ale and some modern gastropub cooking. Timeless staples (beer-battered fish and chips with home-made tartare sauce, or gammon steak with griddled pineapple) rub shoulders with up-to-date ideas, starting with pan-fried belly pork with pig's cheek and butternut squash purée or goats' cheese pannacotta with pickled beetroot and beetroot crisp. Mains focus on prime local materials, such as roast rack of lamb served with a hot pot of shoulder meat, parsnips and roast shallots, or venison haunch with Puy lentils, creamed cabbage and a shepherd's pie croquette. A comforting conclusion might be sticky toffee pudding with pistachio ice cream.

Chef Andy Gabbitas **Seats** 80, Pr/dining room 12 **Times** 12-2.30/5-9, Closed D Sun **Prices** Prices not confirmed **Wines** 5 bottles over £30, 24 bottles under £30, 8 by glass **Parking** 30 **Notes** Sunday L, Children welcome

WEST YORKSHIRE

ADDINGHAM Map 19 SE04

Craven Heifer

Modern British

tel: 01943 830106 **Main St LS29 0PL**
email: info@thecravenheifer.com **web:** www.thecravenheifer.com
dir: *Follow Addingham signs. At major rdbt turn onto B6160. Hotel visable from following junct*

Switched-on cooking in an ambitious gastropub

An old stone village inn, the Craven Heifer offers compelling contemporary food on the fringes of the Yorkshire Dales. Seven-course taster and à la carte menus showcase the ambition of the kitchen's output. Start with 'cheese & pickle' (a ravioli of peppered goats' cheese served with scorched baby gem lettuce and a sherry reduction) or 'ox salad' with its smoked beef and oxtail fritter. Move on to North Yorkshire red deer with home-made black pudding and candied ginger, or a fishy number combining butter-roasted stone bass with sea vegetables and Shetland mussel stew. Dessert might be 'apple & custard' – an Earl Grey pannacotta, poached Granny Smith and cinder toffee.

Chef Lee Unthank **Seats** 41, Pr/dining room 16 **Times** 12-2/6-9 **Prices** Fixed L 2 course £10, Fixed D 3 course £13, Tasting menu £39-£54, Starter £5-£10, Main £10-£24, Dessert £5-£10 **Wines** 10 bottles over £30, 32 bottles under £30, 14 by glass **Parking** 20 **Notes** Early bird menu 2/3 course £10/£13, All day dining Sun, Sunday L £15-£20, Vegetarian available, Children welcome

BRADFORD Map 19 SE13

Prashad

Indian Vegetarian V

tel: 0113 285 2037 **137 Whitehall Rd, Drighlington BD11 1AT**
email: info@prashad.co.uk
dir: *Follow A650 Wakefield Road then Whitehall Road*

Indian vegetarian food of the highest order

There is strong competition in Bradford when it comes to authentic Indian cooking, but Prashad's meat-free repertoire ensures a loyal local following. A wall mural depicting a tumultuous Indian street scene provides a bright, vibrant look to the place, which has its roots in the vegetarian cuisine of the Gujarat. Exemplary breads are cooked to order and might be utilised to mop up a chickpea curry with tomato, bay and cinnamon. Before that, crisp, fried balls of root ginger and mint mashed artichokes with tamarind chutney is a starter with well-defined flavours. Spicing is spot-on throughout.

Chef Minal Patel **Seats** 75, Pr/dining room 10 **Times** 5-11, Closed Mon, L Tue-Fri **Prices** Prices not confirmed **Wines** 4 bottles over £30, 24 bottles under £30, 6 by glass **Parking** 26 **Notes** All-day dining Sat-Sun, Children welcome

CLIFTON Map 16 SE12

The Black Horse Inn Restaurant with Rooms

Modern British, Mediterranean

tel: 01484 713862 **Westgate HD6 4HJ**
email: mail@blackhorseclifton.co.uk
dir: *M62 junct 25, Brighouse, follow signs*

Bold British flavours in a Yorkshire inn

This rambling 17th-century inn has two dining rooms, one with darkwood furniture under a beamed ceiling, the other with double-clothed tables. The kitchen aims high delivering ambitiously creative dishes without ignoring old favourites like beer-battered haddock with traditional accompaniments. Seared scallops are partnered b a ham hock, pork and leek pie along with pea shoots, tomato and broad bean salad, plus bacon and tomato jam. Follow that with something like a winter warmer of ox cheek pie under a mash topping with root vegetable crisps, braised red cabbage and blueberry jus. Finish with a labour-intensive pudding such as strawberry and champagne jelly with basil pannacotta and foam and strawberry soup.

HALIFAX Map 19 SE02

Holdsworth House Hotel

Traditional British

tel: 01422 240024 **Holdsworth Rd, Holmfield HX2 9TG**
email: info@holdsworthhouse.co.uk **web:** www.holdsworthhouse.co.uk
dir: *From Halifax take A629 (Keighley road), in 2m right at garage to Holmfield, hotel 1.5m on right*

Secluded manor house with well-crafted cooking

Built during the reign of Charles I, Holdsworth House looks fit for a king with its handsome creeper-covered façade and charming period interior. Partridge off the Dales may find themselves potted in a first course with plum compôte, while Jerusalem artichokes are roasted in hay and served with goats' curd, winter truffle and trumpet mushrooms. The grill cooks up steaks, lamb rump, pork chop and the like, or go for roast monkfish tail with pommes Anna. For dessert, the kitchen's styl is summed by a dish of warm ginger beer cake with popcorn ice cream and spiced plums. Sunday lunches are classic affairs, and afternoon tea is the real deal.

Chef Martin Henley **Seats** 45, Pr/dining room 120 **Times** 12-2/7-9.30, Closed D 25-26 Dec **Prices** Prices not confirmed **Wines** 29 bottles over £30, 47 bottles under £30, 11 by glass **Parking** 60 **Notes** Tasting menu 5 course, Sunday L, Vegetarian available, Children welcome

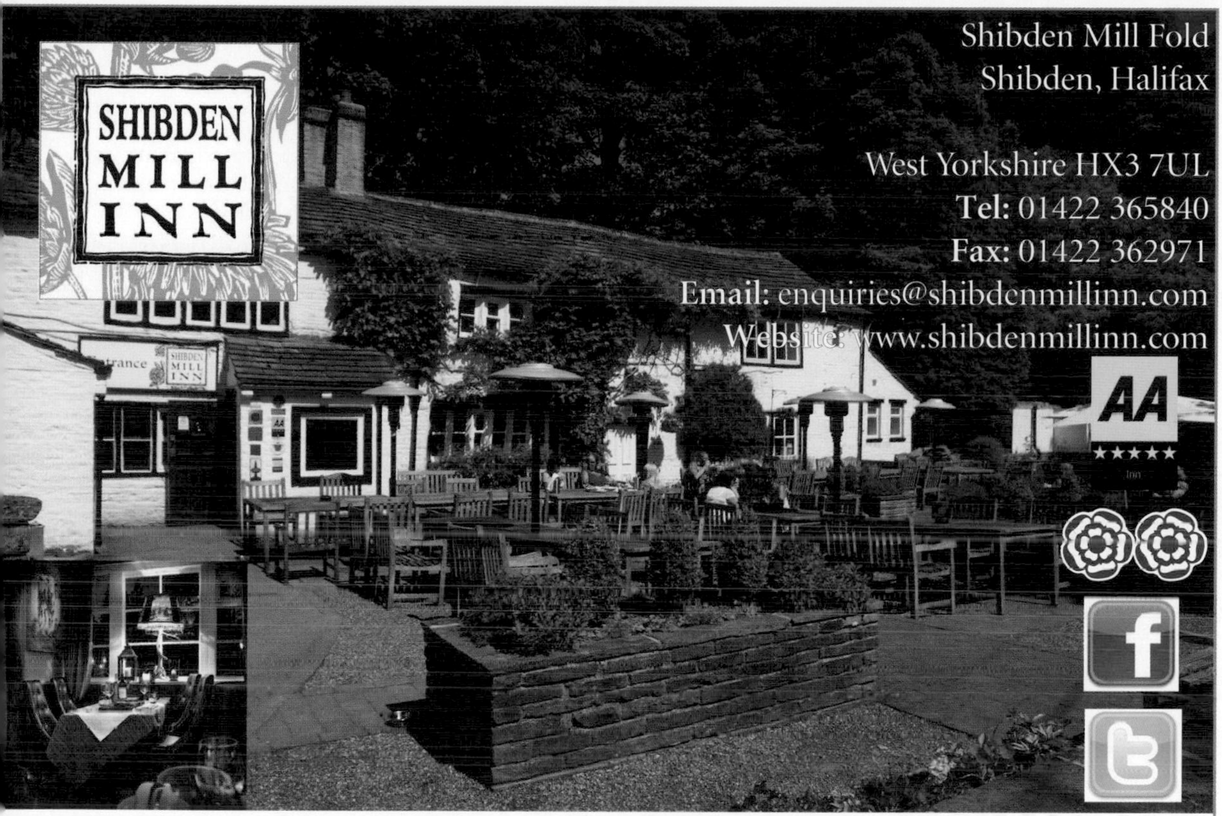

For over 350 years *The Shibden Mill Inn* has been at the heart of life in West Yorkshire's Shibden Valley. It's a magical place where generation after generation of locals have enjoyed time well spent with friends and family, sharing in life's special moments and shaping memories to last a life time.

The Inn's reputation for warm hospitality, premier 2 Rosette gastro dining and 5 Star Inn accommodation draws people to the Shibden Valley from far and wide, and the Mill has naturally become a popular choice for those wishing to savour a sumptuous weekend break or mid-week stay.

Stunning countryside walks are in easy reach, as too the bright lights and city centre shopping on offer in Leeds. From its unique location, The Shibden Mill offers easy access to the very best to be found in this delightful part of West Yorkshire.

Opening times for breakfast, morning coffee & cake, afternoon teas, lunch and dinner can be found on the food page of the website www.shibdenmillinn.com

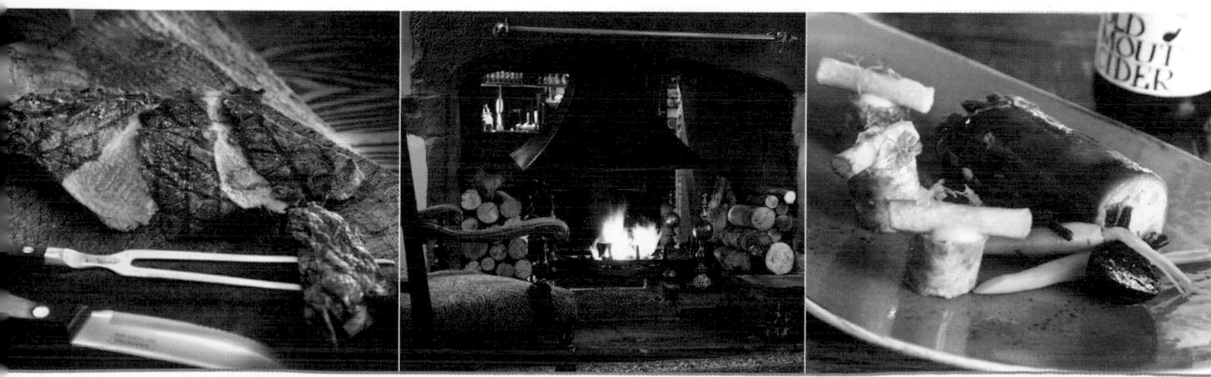

HALIFAX *continued*

Shibden Mill Inn

Modern British V

tel: 01422 365840 **Shibden Mill Fold, Shibden HX3 7UL**
email: enquiries@shibdenmillinn.com **web:** www.shibdenmillinn.com
dir: *From A58 into Kell Lane, after 0.5m left into Blake Hill. Inn at bottom of hill on left*

Adventurous flavours in a renovated corn mill

This 17th-century inn, once a mill, is an atmospheric old place with open fires, low beams and friendly but professional staff. The kitchen turns out some inspired and complex dishes. Crab with beetroot, pickled carrots and courgettes, burned lime and crackers is impressive, as is a main course of rolled and poached saddle of wild rabbit (cooked to perfection) served with langoustines, five spice, roast carrots, aged ham and light Jersey Royal soufflé. Seasonal game is a strength – partridge and chestnut pie, roast pheasant – and vegetarians are well looked after too. To finish, lemon tart with orange meringue, blood orange, pistachio and sorrel delivers great flavours.

Chef Darren Parkinson **Seats** 50, Pr/dining room 12 **Times** 12-2/6-9.30, Closed Xmas, D 24-26 Dec, 1 Jan **Prices** Fixed L 2 course fr £13.50, Fixed D 3 course fr £16.50, Starter £6-£9, Main £12-£25, Dessert £4-£6 **Wines** 32 bottles over £30, 54 bottles under £30, 22 by glass **Parking** 60 **Notes** Sunday L, Children welcome

See advert on page 479

HOLMFIRTH **Map 16 SE10**

The Spiced Pear

Traditional British V

tel: 01484 683775 **Sheffield Rd, New Mill HD9 7TP**
email: info@thespicedpearhepworth.co.uk **web:** www.thespicedpearhepworth.co.uk
dir: *Phone for directions*

Switched-on modern food in a trendy venue

This trendy contemporary package comprises a cocktail bar, restaurant and 1940s-themed tea shop. Bare wooden tables, leather chairs and piano music drifting in from the bar set the scene, and you can expect traditional British cooking that delivers plenty of big flavours. Things start with a full-bore duo of pan-seared scallops and crispy pig's cheek balanced by tart apple purée, a soy and chicken reduction, and Waldorf salad. Next up, venison haunch steak is marinated with blackberry and juniper, pan-seared and served up with a crisp venison-packed filo 'cigar', parsley root purée, spring veg and a cracking Pontefract liquorice sauce. Dessert is a zingy lemon tart and posset with raspberries.

Chef Timothy Bilton, Chris Kelly **Seats** 80 **Times** 11-5/6-9.30, Closed D variable **Prices** Tasting menu £45-£80 **Wines** 40 bottles over £30, 40 bottles under £30, 17 by glass **Parking** 50 **Notes** Breakfast, Afternoon tea, Tasting Sat D only, Children welcome

HUDDERSFIELD **Map 16 SE11**

315 Bar and Restaurant

Modern V

tel: 01484 602613 **315 Wakefield Rd, Lepton HD8 0LX**
email: info@315barandrestaurant.co.uk **web:** www.315barandrestaurant.co.uk
dir: *M1 junct 38 to Huddersfield*

Ambitious city-smart cooking in a reborn Yorkshire pub

This place brings a touch of metropolitan chic to Huddersfield. The menu bursts with bright, modern ideas such as crab and lobster mousse wrapped in nori with ginger, lime and coriander dressing to start. Main courses are no less original: fillet of sea bass, timed to the second, is served on a ginger-spiked compôte of rhubarb and white crabmeat with saffron potatoes and wilted lettuce, and duck breast on roast beetroot with blackberries, fondant potato and celeriac purée. Puddings are attractively presented, among them raspberry millefeuille on a base of lemon cake and cream topped with white chocolate, and chocolate cup filled with cherry compôte with brandy sabayon.

Chef Jason Neilson **Seats** 90, Pr/dining room 115 **Times** 12-9, All-day dining, Closed D Sun **Prices** Fixed L 2 course £15, Starter £5-£7.50, Main £12.50-£23.50, Dessert fr £6.25 **Wines** 18 by glass **Parking** 97 **Notes** Sunday L £17.50-£19.95, Children welcome

ILKLEY Map 19 SE14

Box Tree

 Modern, Traditional French V 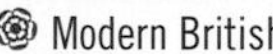

tel: 01943 608484 **35-37 Church St LS29 9DR**
email: info@theboxtree.co.uk
dir: *On A65 from Leeds through Ilkley, main lights approx 200yds on left*

Yorkshire culinary excellence since the early 1960s

In a property dating from 1720, the Box Tree has been on the restaurant scene since the early 1960s. The elegant interior has a timeless look, with deep sofas, dining chairs covered in rich fabrics, pictures in gold frames on the walls and antiques dotted around. Formally dressed staff, professional but unstuffy, keep the wheels turning. Simon Gueller's menus have their roots in the classical French repertory and combine traditional and contemporary ideas. Daube of beef in braising jus is a textbook example, accompanied by pommes purée, baby onions, mushrooms and lardons. There might also be a sea-fresh tranche of halibut topped with grated black truffle served with parsley and parsnip purées and salt-baked vegetables, all distinct flavours having an impact on the palate, with crispy smoked pancetta adding a further textural contrast. Among starters is a neat, even slice of galantine of chicken, duck and ham, bursting with flavour, cut by fig chutney served with wafer-thin toasted sourdough, and ham hock beignets with foie gras juxtaposed by smoked eel and apple purée. Puddings, too, showcase high technical skill: a signature blackcurrant soufflé, light and fluffy, with clotted cream ice cream, for instance. Canapés and breads are of the highest order, as are the petits fours with coffee.

Chef Simon Gueller, Mark Owens **Seats** 50, Pr/dining room 20 **Times** 12-2/7-9.30, Closed 27-31 Dec, 1-7 Jan, Mon-Tue, L Wed-Thu, D Sun **Prices** Fixed L 3 course £32.50-£37.50, Fixed D 3 course £45-£65, Tasting menu £75 **Wines** 11 bottles over £30, 12 bottles under £30, 7 by glass **Parking** NCP, Ilkley town car park **Notes** Fixed L Fri-Sat, Sunday L, Children 10 yrs+ D

LEEDS Map 19 SE23

Jamie's Italian, Leeds

Italian

tel: 0113 322 5400 **35 Park Row LS1 5JL**
email: leeds@jamiesitalian.com
dir: *300mtrs from station up Park Row, on left*

Italian tradition à la Jamie in a bank-turned-warehouse

A thoroughgoing makeover has transformed a once-grand banking temple into a warehouse eatery in the modern idiom, its original features still visible amid the bordering, tiling and brickwork. A bowl of wild truffle risotto with aged parmesan is beautifully timed, while local lamb ragù is slow-cooked for 20 hours in red wine and rosemary and mixed into what the menu calls 'wriggly' pappardelle. With planks of antipasti, chillified arancini, or baked salmon with balsamic-roasted veg, there is plenty of versatility to the range, and nobody minds deserting Italian tradition to finish with a lump of chocolate brownie, Amaretto ice cream and caramelised amaretti popcorn.

Malmaison Leeds

Modern British

tel: 0113 398 1000 & 0844 693 0654 *(Calls cost 7p per minute plus your phone company's access charge)* **1 Swinegate LS1 4AG**
email: leeds@malmaison.com **web:** www.malmaison.com
dir: *City centre. 5 mins walk from Leeds railway station. On junct 16 of loop road, Sovereign St & Swinegate*

Vibrant cooking with global influences in a stylish city brasserie

The Malmaison group's Leeds branch is decorated and furnished to a high standard after refurbishment and the brasserie is no exception, with plush leather booths and open fireplaces under its elegant ceiling. The cooking is built on quality ingredients, and talented professionals are clearly at work. So chicken liver parfait, rich and flavoursome, with figs might be followed by properly timed sea bass fillet with sautéed chorizo, black olives, mussel vinaigrette and new potatoes. Influences have been gathered from around the globe to add to the broad appeal, so veal bolognese with rigatoni might appear next to another main course of chicken tikka masala. End with a classic vanilla crème brûlée.

Chef Simon Silver **Seats** 85, Pr/dining room 12 **Times** 12-2.30/6-10 **Prices** Fixed L 2 course £19.95, Fixed D 3 course £24.95, Starter £5-£12.50, Main £14-£49, Dessert £6 **Wines** 07 bottles over £30, 32 bottles under £30, 26 by glass **Parking** Criterion Place car park, Q Park **Notes** Sunday L £19.95, Vegetarian available, Children welcome

The Man Behind The Curtain

Modern European NEW

tel: 0113 243 2376 **68-78 Vicar Ln, Top Floor Flannels LS1 7JH**
email: info@themanbehindthecurtain.co.uk **web:** www.themanbehindthecurtain.co.uk
dir: *Phone for directions*

Thrilling modern dining with bags of style

Not the latest John le Carré adaptation, but a quote from *The Wizard of Oz*, and a clue that this establishment above Flannels clothes store, brainchild of Michael O'Hare, is as idiosyncratic as they come. The minimalist decorative style is sharply contemporary, and chefs in Cuban-heeled shoes deliver the food to the tables. A 10-course tasting menu is the only way to go (a shorter Menu Rapide is available at lunch), and prepare for an opener served on a serpent-shaped silver spoon – a fabulous 'hand massaged' octopus with caper lemon butter and paprika emulsion. The full armoury of modern cooking techniques comes into play in a menu full of bold ideas within a broadly European spectrum. Galician beef of outstanding quality, 15-years-old, comes in an inspiring course with olive juice and rendered fat, adding a deep and satisfying depth to the finished dish. Sea urchin bolognese is another brilliant idea and a neat visual trick, resembling the Italian classic when a sea urchin sauce is poured on at the table. The excitement continues... black cod with dashi, veal sweetbreads in Chinese XO sauce with hot-and-sour beef consommé, and among sweet courses, a stunning-looking milk chocolate mousse with violet ice cream and warm potato custard (among other things).

Chef Michael O'Hare **Times** 12.30-2/6.30-8.30, Closed 21 Dec-13 Jan, Sun-Mon, L Tue-Thu **Prices** Tasting menu £75-£120 **Notes** L menu £45-£60

LEEDS *continued*

Salvo's Restaurant & Salumeria

Italian

tel: 0113 275 5017 & 275 2752 **115 Otley Rd, Headingley LS6 3PX**
email: dine@salvos.co.uk
dir: *On A660 2m N of city centre*

Popular Italian with a salumeria (deli-café)

Salvo's is a lively, family-friendly and family-run restaurant that will sort you out for some rustic and hearty Italian cooking. If you come for a pizza or a plate of pasta, you are spoiled for choice and won't leave disappointed. But there's much more besides: antipasti such as sea-fresh scallop gratin topped with a light cheese, lemon and parsley crumb, say, followed by fillet of cod with caponata and garlic aïoli. Meat is handled equally well, taking in pâté della casa with orange marmalade, and ox cheek with pancetta, roasted silverskins, oyster mushrooms and creamed potato. Citrus polenta cake with fruit compôte is a good way to finish.

Chef Geppino Dammone, Mo Zanoubi **Seats** 88, Pr/dining room 20 **Times** 12-2/5.30-10.30, Closed 25-26 Dec, 1 Jan, L BHs **Prices** Fixed L 2 course £10.95, Fixed D 2 course £14.95, Starter £4-£8.50, Main £8.50-£25, Dessert £5.95-£8.50 **Wines** 9 bottles over £30, 33 bottles under £30, 6 by glass **Parking** On street, pay & display nearby **Notes** Sunday L £14.95, Vegetarian available, Children welcome

Thorpe Park Hotel & Spa

Modern British

tel: 0113 264 1000 **Century Way, Thorpe Park LS15 8ZB**
email: thorpepark@shirehotels.com **web:** www.restaurant-and-bar.co.uk/leeds/
dir: *M1 junct 46, follow signs off rdbt for Thorpe Park*

Unfussy contemporary cooking near the M1

Close to the M1 and with quick access into Leeds or out into the countryside, the modern Thorpe Park Hotel is a handy base for exploring the area. The open-plan and split-level dining room has a contemporary finish with pale wooden floor, artwork on the walls, and black leather-type chairs. The populist menu offers feel-good stuff such as crispy duck salad to start, or share an antipasti sharing plate. Move on to tiger prawn linguine, Yorkshire lamb shepherd's pie with pickled red cabbage and beetroot, or a steak cooked on the grill. Desserts are equally as comforting – warm treacle tart, say, with Pedro Ximénez and clotted cream.

Town Hall Tavern

Modern British

tel: 0113 244 0765 **17 Westgate LS1 2RA**
email: info@townhalltavernleeds.co.uk
dir: *In city centre, opposite the Law Courts*

Refined pub fare in the city centre

This bustling city-centre pub looks like any old boozer from the outside, but the interior is stylish and an all-day menu offers a wide choice of appealing ideas. Grilled king prawns are served in tomato and garlic sauce on top of a slice of toasted bread, and could precede pan-fried pork fillet on thyme jus with a notably good hash cake of pig's cheek, accompanied by contrasting sour cherries and poached apples. Pan-fried salmon fillet on rösti with prawns and creamy herb sauce is one of the signature dishes. Desserts are taken seriously too: home-made peanut butter ice cream is the perfect foil for a chocolate brownie.

Chef Guy Claringbould **Seats** 26 **Times** 11.45-9, All-day dining, Closed 25-26 Dec, BH Mon **Wines** 18 bottles under £30, 8 by glass **Parking** On street at rear **Notes** Sunday L £9.95-£11.95, Vegetarian available, Children welcome

LIVERSEDGE — **Map 16 SE12**

Healds Hall Hotel & Restaurant

Modern British

tel: 01924 409112 **Leeds Rd WF15 6JA**
email: enquire@healdshall.co.uk **web:** www.healdshall.co.uk
dir: *M1 junct 40, A638. From Dewsbury take A652 signed Bradford. Left at A62. Hotel 50yds on right*

International favourites in a historic, family-owned hotel

This stone-built, family-owned hotel is definitely worth leaving the M62 for, in order to dine in either the open-plan Bistro or its conservatory extension, furnished with wicker-style chairs and tables with tea lights. There's a more formal restaurant, which fills up on busy evenings. Shared by both, the modern British menu ranges widely to offer seared king scallops with Spanish black pudding, apple, chervil, celeriac and sherry reduction as a starter, as well as indubitably English roast Gressingham duck breast and leg meat, rosemary crust, crispy potatoes, roast garlic, watercress purée and veal stock reduction. Puddings include glazed blackcurrant tart with liquorice ice cream and pistachio crumb.

Chef Andrew Ward, Simon Beaumont **Seats** 46, Pr/dining room 30 **Times** 12-2/6-10, Closed 27-29 Dec, 1 Jan, BHs, L Sat, D Sun (ex residents) **Prices** Fixed L 2 course fr £11.95, Fixed D 3 course fr £23.95, Starter £4.95-£9.95, Main £13.95-£26.95, Dessert £5.95-£8.95 **Wines** 14 bottles over £30, 34 bottles under £30, 13 by glass **Parking** 50 **Notes** Sunday L £16.95-£18.95, Vegetarian available, Children welcome

OTLEY — **Map 19 SE24**

Chevin Country Park Hotel & Spa

Modern British

tel: 01943 467818 **Yorkgate LS21 3NU**
email: gm.chevin@crerarhotels.com **web:** www.crerarhotels.com
dir: *A658 towards Harrogate. Left at 1st turn towards Carlton, 2nd left towards Yorkgate*

Modern cooking in a Scandinavian-style log cabin

Surrounded by 44 acres of woodland and lakes, this spa hotel is styled like an Alpine log cabin, a theme that extends to the Lakeside Restaurant. The industrious kitchen creates a daily-changing tasting menu as well as a carte, and there's also a steak and grill menu. Crab with avocado, parmesan beignets and gazpacho precede main courses ranging from traditional rump of lamb with ratatouille and garlicky potatoes to seared sea bass fillet with crayfish emulsion accompanied by new potatoes, peas, broad beans and baby onions. Close attention is paid to desserts too, among which are individual coconut and cardamom pannacottas wit tangy clementine sorbet.

PONTEFRACT — **Map 16 SE42**

Wentbridge House Hotel

Modern British V NOTABLE WINE LIST

tel: 01977 620444 **The Great North Rd, Wentbridge WF8 3JJ**
email: info@wentbridgehouse.co.uk **web:** www.wentbridgehouse.co.uk
dir: *4m S of M62/A1 junct, 0.5m off A1*

Multi-influenced cooking in a Yorkshire manor house

Set in 20 acres of landscaped grounds in a West Yorkshire conservation village, Wentbridge is a stone-built grand manor house from the turn of the 18th century. There's a degree of glossy formality, not least in the Fleur de Lys dining room, wher candy-coloured upholstery creates a light, bright effect, and the cooking reaches out in all directions for its references. First up might be warm salad of hoi sin duck with preserved orange, watermelon and chill, followed by fillet of Tancred Farm po wrapped in Parma ham, butternut squash and harissa risotto, or a steak cooked on the chargrill. Finish with sticky toffee pudding.

Chef Ian Booth **Seats** 60, Pr/dining room 24 **Times** 7.15-9.30, Closed L Mon-Sat, D Sun, 25 Dec **Prices** Fixed L 2 course £15.95, Starter £6.50-£12.95, Main £15.95-£29.95, Dessert £6.95-£10.95 **Wines** 100 bottles over £30, 30 bottles under £30, 10 by glass **Parking** 100 **Notes** Sunday L £28.50, Children welcome

WAKEFIELD **Map 16 SE32**

Waterton Park Hotel

Modern, Traditional British V

tel: 01924 257911 **Walton Hall, The Balk, Walton WF2 6PW**
email: info@watertonparkhotel.co.uk **web:** www.watertonparkhotel.co.uk
dir: *3m SE off B6378. Exit M1 junct 39 towards Wakefield. At 3rd rdbt right for Crofton. At 2nd lights right & follow signs*

Sound flavour-packed cooking by a huge lake

This Georgian hotel stands on an island in a 26-acre lake, with a modern extension on the shore accessed via a bridge, which explains how the attractive Bridgewalk restaurant was named. Dishes are admirably understated and flavours are to the fore, with starters taking in ham hock terrine with rhubarb relish, piccalilli purée and soused vegetables. Main course could bring on peppered venison steak with Jerusalem artichoke Lyonnaise and dark chocolate sauce, or monkfish wrapped in Parma ham served with samphire and white wine beurre blanc. Bow out on a high note with puddings such as Yorkshire rhubarb crème brûlée with vanilla ice cream.

Chef Armstrong Wgabi **Seats** 50, Pr/dining room 40 **Times** 7-9.30, Closed D Sun **Prices** Prices not confirmed **Wines** 10 by glass **Parking** 200 **Notes** Afternoon tea, Sunday L, Children welcome

WETHERBY **Map 16 SE44**

Wood Hall Hotel & Spa

Modern British V

tel: 01937 587271 & 0845 072 7564 *(Calls cost 7p per minute plus your phone company's access charge)* **Trip Ln, Linton LS22 4JA**
email: woodhall@handpicked.co.uk **web:** www.handpickedhotels.co.uk/woodhall
dir: *From Wetherby take A661 (Harrogate road) N for 0.5m. Left to Sicklinghall/Linton. Cross bridge, left to Linton/Woodhall, right opposite Windmill Inn, 1.25m to hotel (follow brown signs)*

Classy cooking using local produce in an elegant country-house hotel

High on a hill with fine views, the Georgian Wood Hall retains much of its original detailing. Its dining room is an elegant, relaxing space where a rigorous dedication to Yorkshire produce – beef from local farms, moorland lamb, produce from the garden – is observed, and the cooking is marked by clear, distinct flavours. Crab and chervil tortellini seasoned with lime and wasabi offers a productive mixture of messages, while a main-course plate is laden with pork fillet, black pudding, Scotch egg, baby carrots, mash, and more besides. Finish on a more straightforward note with chocolate truffle, served with salted caramel and peanut ice cream.

Chef David Humphreys **Seats** 40, Pr/dining room 100 **Times** 12-2.30/7-9.30, Closed L Mon-Sat **Prices** Fixed L 3 course £25, Fixed D 3 course £39, Starter £9-£15, Main £17-£25.50, Dessert £8.50 **Wines** 50 bottles over £30, 10 bottles under £30, 18 by glass **Parking** 100 **Notes** Sunday L £25, Children welcome

CHANNEL ISLANDS

GUERNSEY

CASTEL **Map 24**

Cobo Bay Hotel

Modern, Traditional

tel: 01481 257102 & 07781 156757 **Coast Rd, Cobo GY5 7HB**
email: reservations@cobobayhotel.com **web:** www.cobobayhotel.com
dir: *From airport turn right, follow road to W coast at L'Erée. Turn right onto coast road for 3m to Cobo Bay. Hotel on right*

Superb views and admirable use of local produce

The main focus of the hotel's elegant dining room, with its flagged floor and stylish mirrors, is straight out to sea, and there's also an outdoor terrace. Seafood is a strong suit, presented in contemporary combinations along with a cornucopia of top-quality produce. Start with fishcakes with salad and sweet chilli dip, or seared scallops with crisp pancetta and tomato and onion salsa, ahead of sea bass fillet with tomato and shellfish broth and a potato cake laced with chorizo and spring onions. Carnivores may prefer chargrilled chicken breast with Madeira sauce, fondant potato, spinach and mushrooms. To finish, lemon crème brûlée with plums is the real deal.

ST MARTIN **Map 24**

The Auberge

Modern British, French

tel: 01481 238485 **Jerbourg Rd GY4 6BH**
email: dine@theauberge.gg
dir: *End of Jerbourg Rd at Jerbourg Point*

Locally led menu on a Guernsey clifftop

A clifftop position overlooking the neighbouring islands draws people to this sleek contemporary restaurant near St Peter Port. The menu is big on fish and seafood, as in seared scallops with aromatic twice-cooked pork belly, or main course pan-roasted brill with warm tartare sauce and mussels deep-fried in panko breadcrumbs. Steak boards include onglet, fillet and Angus rump (served with chunky chips or French fries), or the whopping côte de boeuf for two to share. The fixed-price menu offers value at lunchtime and midweek evenings. Finish with a clever take on Eton Mess – a toffee and apple version with apple compôte, meringue, caramel brittle, Guernsey cream and toffee sauce.

Chef Daniel Green **Seats** 70, Pr/dining room 20 **Times** 12-2/6.30-10, Closed 25-26 Dec, 1 Jan, D Sun **Prices** Fixed L 2 course £17.80-£40, Fixed D 3 course £22.80-£50, Starter £5.80-£8.95, Main £12.80-£18.95, Dessert £6.60 **Wines** 30 bottles over £30, 26 bottles under £30, 12 by glass **Parking** 25 **Notes** Sunday L £12.80-£22.80, Vegetarian available, Children welcome

ST MARTIN *continued*

La Barbarie Hotel

Traditional British

tel: 01481 235217 **Saints Rd, Saints Bay GY4 6ES**
email: reservations@labarbariehotel.com **web:** www.labarbariehotel.com
dir: *At lights in St Martin take road to Saints Bay. Hotel on right at end of Saints Rd*

Unpretentious country-house cooking in a charming setting

This former priory is now a comfortable hotel with a soothing vibe and a restaurant using the peerless fresh produce – fish, seafood, meat, cream and butter – of Guernsey's coasts and meadows. The kitchen looks to the French mainland for inspiration in their repertoire of simply cooked and presented dishes. A simple pairing of pan-fried scallops with black pudding, pancetta and apple sauce gets things off the blocks, followed by a classic combo of roast rack of new-season lamb with shallot, port and rosemary sauce, dauphinoise potatoes, and fine green beans. Caramelised apple tart with a sharp palate-refreshing green apple sorbet brings things to a zingy close.

Bella Luce Hotel, Restaurant & Spa

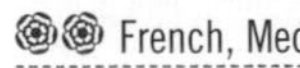
French, Mediterranean

tel: 01481 238764 **La Fosse GY4 6EB**
email: wakeup@bellalucehotel.com **web:** www.bellalucehotel.com
dir: *From airport, turn left to St Martin. At 3rd set of lights continue 30yds, turn right, straight on to hotel*

Sharp, modern cooking in a classy boutique hotel

With its 12th-century granite walls, period charm and luxe boutique finish, Bella Luce is a class act. The culinary action takes place in the romantic restaurant, where there's some sharp, contemporary European cooking built on a good showing of local produce and a good deal of skill in the execution of dishes. Get the show on the road with beef carpaccio with truffled egg dressing, parmesan and shaved cauliflower. Follow with roast fillet of cod with squid and mussels, butternut squash, braised leeks and saffron sauce or go for a rib-eye of Aberdeen Angus beef from the grill. End with a tasting of chocolate.

Hotel Jerbourg

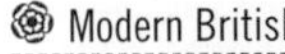
Modern British

tel: 01481 238826 **Jerbourg Point GY4 6BJ**
email: stay@hoteljerbourg.com **web:** www.hoteljerbourg.com
dir: *From airport turn left to St Martin, right at filter, straight on at lights, hotel at end of road on right*

Ocean views and classic seafood dishes

Magnificent views are a major pull at this modern hotel in lovely grounds. With the Atlantic all around, thoughts are bound to turn to fish, so you will not be disappointed to see that the repertoire is weighted in that direction. The kitchen lets the sheer freshness and quality of prime piscine produce do the talking, serving breaded calamari with lemon and herb mayonnaise, ahead of roast sea bass with herb butter and seasonal vegetables, or moules et frites. Chargrilled steaks or something like lamb cutlets marinated in garlic and basil should keep the carnivores quiet. End with classic Normandy apple tart.

ST PETER PORT Map 24

The Absolute End

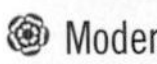
Modern, Traditional

tel: 01481 723822 **St Georges Esplanade GY1 2BG**
email: reservations@absoluteend.com
dir: *Less than 1m from town centre. N on seafront road towards St Sampson*

Italian-accented fish restaurant overlooking the harbour

When you're above the harbour just outside St Peter Port you should be in the market for spanking-fresh fish and seafood, and this unpretentious restaurant in converted fishermen's cottages comes up trumps. Reliable renditions of seared scallops with pea purée and crispy pancetta, and mains such as pan-fried brill fillet with potted mussels, crushed new potatoes and chives, all pass muster. Meat-eaters are not forgotten: herb-crusted rack of lamb, sauced with rosemary and red wine and served with dauphinoise potatoes, or chargrilled beef fillet with béarnaise and proper chips should keep them happy. Desserts such as sticky toffee pudding with butterscotch sauce will put a smile on everyone's face.

Best Western Hotel de Havelet

Traditional British, International V

tel: 01481 722199 **Havelet GY1 1BA**
email: stay@dehaveletguernsey.com **web:** www.dehaveletguernsey.com
dir: *From airport follow signs for St Peter Port through St Martins. At bottom of 'Val de Terres' hill turn left at top of hill, hotel on right*

Sea views and classic no-nonsense cooking

The Georgian hotel is surrounded by trees with sea and castle views, and picture windows in the two restaurants make the most of the vista. Both are in the converted coach house, with the Havelet Grill on the ground floor and the Wellingtor Boot above. The latter is the main event, and it deals in classical cooking with its feet on the ground. Start with pan-seared scallops with cauliflower and crispy chorizo. Next up, lamb fillet comes with herb and spinach couscous, grilled courgettes and plum sauce, and with the French coast close by, classic apple tarte Tatin provides a suitably Gallic finale.

Chef Mohammed Ekamy **Seats** 100, Pr/dining room 20 **Times** 12-2/7-9.30, Closed L Mon-Sat **Prices** Fixed D 3 course £20.95, Starter £4.95-£6.95, Main £12.95-£21.95, Dessert £5.95-£8.95 **Wines** 10 bottles over £30, 20 bottles under £30, 5 by glass **Parking** 35 **Notes** Sunday L £16.50-£19.50, Children welcome

Mora Restaurant & Grill

Modern Mediterranean

tel: 01481 715053 **The Quay GY1 2LE**
email: eat@mora.gg
dir: *Facing Victoria Marina*

Quayside seafood cooking with a Med twist

The old place on the quay has been given a real decorative boost. There's a happy buzz from strong local custom, which pours in for the likes of charred piquillo peppers filled with herbed ricotta in roast garlic dressing, or plates of local crab and prawns with Scottish smoked salmon. Seafood mains wrap cod in chorizo and accompany it with artichoke and tomato gnocchi, or team monkfish medallions wit aubergine purée and green tapenade. The fish component of fish and chips encompasses bass, brill, scallops and battered prawns. Meat includes grilled steaks, with indulgent desserts like vanilla cheesecake and chocolate ice cream, o lemon tart and raspberry sorbet, to finish.

Chef Trevor Baines **Seats** 90 **Times** 12-2.30/6-10, Closed 26 Dec-21 Jan **Prices** Fixe L 2 course fr £15, Starter £5.50-£9.25, Main £13.75-£25.95, Dessert £5.95-£6.95 **Wines** 30 bottles over £30, 40 bottles under £30, 11 by glass **Parking** On pier **Notes** Brasserie menu, Tapas Menu, Vegetarian available, Children welcome

The Old Government House Hotel & Spa

Modern French V

tel: 01481 724921 & 738604 **St Ann's Place GY1 2NU**
email: fandb@theoghhotel.com **web:** www.theoghhotel.com
dir: *At junct of St Julian's Av & College St*

Fine dining at the old governor's residence

The beautiful white Georgian building was once the island governor's harbourside residence, though it was converted into a hotel as long ago as 1858. Among several dining options at the hotel, The Brasserie is the place to be, offering fresh Guernsey fish as part of the menu at lunch and dinner. As you sit in the spacious conservatory, overlooking private gardens and St Peter Port harbour, your starter might be a ham hock ballontine, followed by a main course of sea bass with potato and asparagus. Lemon meringue turns up to finish the meal off.

Chef Simon McKenzie **Seats** 60, Pr/dining room 12 **Times** 12-2/6.30-9.30, Closed 25 & 31 Dec **Prices** Starter £11, Main £22, Dessert £7 **Wines** 94 bottles over £30, 31 bottles under £30, 26 by glass **Parking** Odeon car park **Notes** Sunday L £27.50

ST SAVIOUR Map 24

The Farmhouse Hotel

Modern British, International

tel: 01481 264181 **Route des bas Courtils GY7 9YF**
email: enquiries@thefarmhouse.gg **web:** www.thefarmhouse.gg
dir: *From airport turn left. Approx 1m left at lights. 100mtrs, left, around airport runway perimeter. 1m, left at staggered junct. Hotel in 100mtrs on right*

Boutique hotel with resourceful cooking

The family has owned this 15th-century farmhouse for three generations. Beams, stone floors and granite are reminders of the property's antiquity, superimposed today with a clean-cut contemporary look. The restaurant is in the oldest part of the building, and eating outside is an attractive proposition during the balmy months. Twice-baked leek and parmesan soufflé with lemon butter sauce and red onion marmalade is a typical opener, followed by game in winter – perhaps a duo of venison comprising pan-seared loin and ragout of haunch with braised red cabbage and herby mashed potato. Go for a finale of dark chocolate and Kirsch cake with Chantilly cream.

HERM

HERM Map 24

White House Hotel

European, Traditional British

tel: 01481 750000 **GY1 3HR**
email: hotel@herm.com **web:** www.herm.com
dir: *Close to harbour. Access by regular 20 min boat trip from St Peter Port, Guernsey*

Creative cooking and sea views in an island retreat

If you hanker for a simpler, slower pace of life, how about the pocket-sized, car- and pollution-free island of Herm? The island's only hotel is a real time-warp experience, dispensing with TVs, phones and clocks. Every table has a sea view in the Conservatory Restaurant, where pin-sharp technique and peerless raw materials combine to impressive effect in the contemporary European menu. Start with braised lamb with garden pea salsa, cucumber and caraway seed, before curried cod teamed with saffron and lemon fondant, cauliflower textures and spiced mussel cream. To finish, there's dark chocolate tart with pink peppercorn ice cream and kaffir lime jelly.

JERSEY

GOREY Map 24

The Moorings Hotel & Restaurant

Traditional

tel: 01534 853633 **Gorey Pier JE3 6EW**
email: reservations@themooringshotel.com **web:** www.themooringshotel.com
dir: *At foot of Mont Orgueil Castle*

Local food on the quayside

Smack on Gorey's picturesque harbour front, The Moorings has a continental feel with its pavement terrace overlooking the sea and the ruins of Mont Orgueil Castle. With the smell of the sea in the air, it's no surprise to see plenty of local seafood on the menu. Start with diver-caught scallops with truffled potatoes and pancetta crisp, followed by roast duck breast, glazed with marmalade and served with fondant potatoes and port jus. Fishy ideas might include pan-fried fillet of sea bass with crushed potatoes, scallops and sauce vièrge, and for pudding, a classic vanilla crème brûlée is done just right.

Chef Simon Walker **Seats** 65, Pr/dining room 35 **Times** 12-2/7-8.30 **Prices** Prices not confirmed **Wines** 26 bottles over £30, 36 bottles under £30, 8 by glass **Notes** Sunday L, Vegetarian available, Children welcome

Sumas

Modern British V

tel: 01534 853291 **Gorey Hill JE3 6ET**
email: info@sumasrestaurant.com **web:** www.sumasrestaurant.com
dir: *From St Helier take A3 E for 5m to Gorey. Before castle take sharp left. Restaurant 100yds up hill on left (look for blue blind)*

Inventive cooking and harbour views

Terrace tables at Sumas look out on boats bobbing in the harbour – or, at low tide, locals digging for clams in the sands of Gorey Bay. There's a good amount of seafood on the menu and a classic fish soup with croûtons and rouille is a great way to start. The main course delivers roast loin of lamb wrapped in Serrano ham along with glazed sweetbreads, dauphinoise potato, pea purée and red wine sauce. For dessert, almond and vanilla pannacotta with green apple sorbet, salted caramel and vanilla sablé wraps things up on a high note, or you might finish with an entente cordiale of French and English cheeses.

Chef Patrice Bouffaut **Seats** 40 **Times** 12-2.30/6-9.30, Closed late Dec-mid Jan (approx), D Sun **Prices** Fixed L 2 course £18-£20, Fixed D 3 course £23-£25, Starter £7-£12, Main £15-£26, Dessert £6-£9.50 **Wines** 31 bottles over £30, 29 bottles under £30, 12 by glass **Parking** On street **Notes** Breakfast Sat-Sun, Sunday L £20-£25, Children welcome

ROZEL Map 24

Château la Chaire

Traditional British, French

tel: 01534 863354 **Rozel Bay JE3 6AJ**
email: res@chateau-la-chaire.co.uk **web:** www.chateau-la-chaire.co.uk
dir: *From St Helier NE towards Five Oaks, Maufant, then St Martin's Church & Rozel. 1st left in village, hotel 100mtrs*

Locally based cooking at the Pulpit

The interiors of this 1840s property are all lush Victorian rococo, with mouldings sporting cherubs and walls of oak panelling in what are now the bar and dining room. The best of local materials – scallops, crab, pork, rabbit – are the kitchen's stock-in-trade, with the menus squarely in the modern British mainstream. Those scallops turn up pan-fried and served with dhal, apple and coriander cress before roast fillet of sea bass with shellfish ravioli, a salsify emulsion and vegetables, or perhaps stuffed roast saddle of lamb with mushroom cassoulet and baby root vegetables. End on a traditional note with rice pudding with red berries and sorbet.

Chef Marcin Ciechomski **Seats** 60, Pr/dining room 28 **Times** 12-2/7-9.30 **Prices** Starter £7.95-£10.95, Main £15.95-£21.95, Dessert £6.95 **Wines** 24 bottles over £30, 18 bottles under £30, 7 by glass **Parking** 30 **Notes** Tasting menu with/out wines, Sunday L £27.95, Vegetarian available, Children welcome

ST BRELADE Map 24

L'Horizon Beach Hotel and Spa

Modern British

tel: 01534 743101 **St Brelade's Bay JE3 8EF**
email: lhorizon@handpicked.co.uk **web:** www.handpickedhotels.co.uk/lhorizon
dir: *From airport right at rdbt towards St Brelade & Red Houses. Through Red Houses, hotel 300mtrs on right in centre of bay*

Creative cooking and a touch of luxury on the beach

The wonderful view over the bay is a big draw at this hotel, but the Grill restaurant really puts the place on the map. It's a smart room with neutral colours and white napery, and a menu making excellent use of the island's bounty, with plenty of seafood in evidence, in bright, modern dishes. This is creative stuff, with first courses such as a terrine of suckling pig and pressed hock counterbalanced by piccalilli vegetables and apple gel. Among main courses, sea bass fillet is served with a crab bonbon, Jerusalem artichoke and crab butter sauce, and for pudding try lemon tart with limoncello syrup.

Chef Andrew Soddy **Seats** 44, Pr/dining room 300 **Times** 6.30-10, Closed L Mon-Sat **Prices** Fixed D 3 course £37, Starter £9.50-£11.50, Main £21.50-£28.50, Dessert £8.50-£15 **Wines** 33 bottles under £30, 19 by glass **Parking** 100 **Notes** Afternoon tea £17, Sunday L £21, Vegetarian available, Children welcome

Hotel La Place

 Modern British

tel: 01534 744261 & 748173 **Route du Coin, La Haule JE3 8BT**
email: andy@hotellaplacejersey.com **web:** www.hotellaplacejersey.com
dir: *Off main St Helier/St Aubin coast road at La Haule Manor (B25). Up hill, 2nd left (to Red Houses), 1st right. Hotel 100mtrs on right*

Modern bistro cooking near the harbour

Tucked away in a tranquil corner of Jersey close by St Aubin's harbour, the hotel started life as a huddle of rustic cottages around an original 17th-century farmhouse. The cuisine is a harmonious blend of uncomplicated classics and gently modern European ideas built on plenty of the island's peerless produce. Start with a tried-and-true pairing of pan-fried scallops and crispy pancetta pointed up with tomato and red onion concasse. For mains, try the subtly spicy Portuguese chicken piri piri with French fries and a vibrant salad. To finish, white chocolate and orange add a lush veneer to a crème brûlée.

Ocean Restaurant at The Atlantic Hotel

– see opposite

Oyster Box

Modern British

tel: 01534 850888 **St Brelade's Bay JE3 8EF**
email: eat@oysterbox.co.uk
dir: *On the beach just E of Fishermen's chapel*

A beachside setting for spankingly fresh seafood and more

The views of St Brelade's Bay are unbeatable from the Oyster Box, whether you're dining on the terrace or in the cool, contemporary dining room. A starter of Jersey rock oysters from the Royal Bay of Grouville is hard to beat and carnivores will find rabbit, smoked ham hock and foie gras terrine alongside seared tuna sashimi with toasted sesame, white radish and piquillo peppers. If you can resist grilled lobster with garlic butter and chancre crab with mayonnaise, there may be brill 'chop' served on the bone with spinach, Jersey Royals and brown shrimp béarnaise. For pudding, blood orange sorbet adds zip to a classic vanilla crème brûlée.

Chef Tony Dorris **Seats** 100 **Times** 12-2.30/6-9.30, Closed 25-26 Dec, Mon (Jan-Mar), L Mon, D Sun (winter only) **Prices** Fixed L 3 course £26, Fixed D 3 course £26, Starter £7.50-£12.50, Main £12.50-£28, Dessert £6.95-£8.50 **Wines** 55 bottles over £30, 50 bottles under £30, 25 by glass **Parking** Car park opposite **Notes** Sunday L, Vegetarian available, Children welcome

ST CLEMENT Map 24

Green Island Restaurant

British, Mediterranean

tel: 01534 857787 **Green Island JE2 6LS**
email: info@greenisland.je
dir: *Phone for directions*

Great local seafood in bustling beach café

This laid-back beach café and restaurant claims to the most southerly eatery in the British Isles, so kick back and bask in sun-kissed views over the sandy bay. The emphasis is on fish and shellfish, and the kitchen has the nous to treat them with a light touch to let the freshness and quality do the talking. Try a simple starter of crab, prawn and spring onion risotto with mascarpone. Next up, perhaps brill fillet with parmesan polenta, chargrilled Mediterranean vegetables, asparagus and sauce vièrge and to finish, a classic crème brûlée with sablé biscuits strikes a suitably Gallic note.

Chef Paul Insley **Seats** 40 **Times** 12-2.30/7-9.30, Closed Xmas, New Year, Jan-Feb, Mon, D Sun **Prices** Fixed L 2 course £16.50-£19.50, Fixed D 3 course £26.50, Starter £8.75-£9.50, Main £18.75-£26.95, Dessert £5.95-£9.25 **Wines** 20 bottles over £30, 20 bottles under £30, 5 by glass **Parking** 20, Public car park adjacent **Notes** Fixed D £23.50 Tue-Thu, Sunday L, Vegetarian available, Children welcome

Ocean Restaurant at The Atlantic Hotel

ST BRELADE **Map 24**

Modern British V 

tel: 01534 744101 **Le Mont de la Pulente JE3 8HE**
email: info@theatlantichotel.com
web: www.theatlantichotel.com
dir: *A13 to Petit Port, turn right into Rue de la Sergente & right again, hotel signed*

Top-class Jersey produce treated with skill

Clocking up almost half a century since it opened in 1970, the Atlantic is looking pretty swish: with its clean art deco-ish lines, white colonial-style shutters and a deep-blue pool straight out of a Hockney painting, you could be in 1930s Miami. Its Ocean Restaurant is the real draw for gastronomes, though, since the exciting cooking of Mark Jordan has turned this place into a real Channel Islands destination. Having served his time with a stellar cast of mentors in top-drawer restaurants, he produces contemporary food that isn't intended to startle, but is meticulously crafted and fizzes with great ideas, and it's all delivered in a soft-focus setting of blue, white and beige, with modern artwork on the walls and soothing views of the gardens. There's a seasonal à la carte and daily-changing set menus, including a seven-course taster and, at the other end of the spectrum, a spectacular value lunch menu, and vegetarians get a fair crack of the whip, with a dedicated carte and tasting option. Whichever you choose, each is chock-full of splendid Jersey produce, starting, perhaps with Jersey beef tartare supported by the luxury of foie gras mousse, oyster ceviche and watercress mayonnaise. Whether you go for a fish or meat main course, you can be sure that the materials are all of exemplary quality – grilled fillet of Jersey turbot, for example, served in a coat of crispy potato scales and matched with silky mussel cream. On the meat front, honey-roasted breast of Gressingham duck comes with earthy celeriac purée, compressed apple and vanilla jus. Jordan's dexterity really shines with desserts too – how about coconut pannacotta with exotic fruit soup, passionfruit and mango sorbet to end on an exhilarating note? Service is perfectly pitched, and the sommelier will guide the way through a list of thoroughbred wines teeming with quality.

Chef Mark Jordan **Seats** 60, Pr/dining room 60
Times 12.30-2.30/7-10, Closed Jan **Prices** Fixed L 2 course £20, Fixed D 3 course £55, Tasting menu £85 **Wines** 459 bottles over £30, 30 bottles under £30, 32 by glass **Parking** 60 **Notes** Fixed ALC 2/3 course £55/£65, Tasting menu 7 course, Sunday L £30, Children welcome

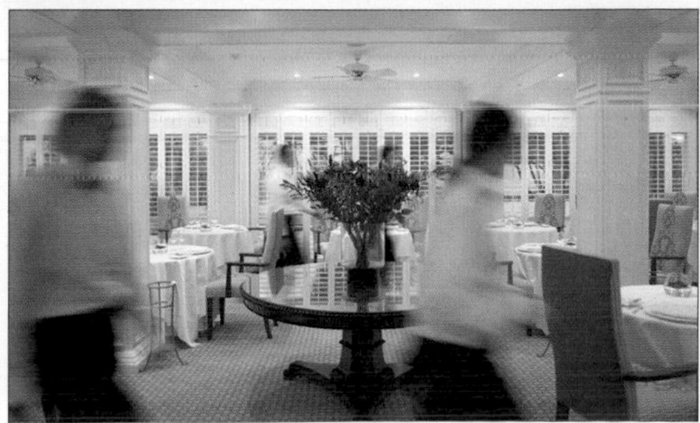

ST HELIER Map 24

Best Western Royal Hotel

Modern European

tel: 01534 726521 **David Place JE2 4TD**
email: manager@royalhoteljersey.com **web:** www.morvanhotels.com
dir: *Follow signs for Ring Rd, pass Queen Victoria rdbt keep left, left at lights, left into Piersons Rd. Follow one-way system to Cheapside, Rouge Bouillon, at A14 turn to Midvale Rd, hotel on left*

Trendily presented food in a smart hotel

In the hotel's Seasons restaurant, a predominantly white colour scheme, with lightwood flooring, flowers on the tables and comfortable leather chairs, creates a coolly elegant atmosphere, appropriate surroundings for some polished cooking. Pink slices of duck breast fanned on a reduced jus, served with earthier leg confit, parsnip purée and roasted vegetables, is a well-considered main course, and could follow something like grilled mackerel fillets, moist and bursting with flavour, cut by pickled vegetables. A decent choice of bread, all made on the premises, is offered, and puddings include nicely presented vanilla pannacotta flavoured with lavender accompanied by seasonal berries.

Bohemia Restaurant

– *see below*

Hampshire Hotel

Mediterranean

tel: 01534 724115 **53 Val Plaisant JE2 4TB**
email: info@hampshirehotel.je **web:** www.hampshirehotel.je
dir: *Phone for directions*

Contemporary setting and a local flavour

The Hampshire Hotel has a contemporary restaurant sporting a colonial look with rattan chairs, ceiling fans and pot plants. Among starters, seared scallops (local ones from Bouley Bay, cooked just right) come with spring pea purée and wild rock samphire, or there might be local mussels cooked à la crème. Rack of spring lamb combines with minted and crushed Jersey Royals and wild garlic pesto in a winning combination, and wild duck (breast and confit leg) arrive in the creative company of a red cabbage mousse. There are simple steak options, too, and a terrific value daily menu, with desserts running to the likes of sticky toffee pudding.

Bohemia Restaurant

ST HELIER Map 24

Modern French, British V
tel: 01534 880588 & 876500 **The Club Hotel & Spa, Green St JE2 4UH**
email: bohemia@huggler.com **web:** www.bohemiajersey.com
dir: *In town centre. 5 mins walk from main shopping centre*

Free-thinking creative cooking at a boutique spa hotel

The Club Hotel & Spa is a sophisticated boutique hotel as sharp and contemporary as any slick big-city operation. The restaurant is an exercise in pared-back contemporary chic, with burnished wood panelling, chrome, toffee-hued leather chairs, and tables swathed in crisp white linen. Chef Steve Smith reveals prodigious talent and creativity with dynamic dishes delivered via multi-course tasting menus and accompanying wine flights – although those with an eye for staggering value should go for the two- or three-course lunch menu. Descriptions are minimal, but the service team are entirely up to speed to help. Among the tasting options, the 'pescatarian' puts glorious Jersey seafood in the spotlight, using langoustine with sweetcorn, chanterelle and purslane, and a signature combination of scallop, celeriac, apple, smoked eel and truffle to build up to a main event involving turbot with textures of cauliflower, oyster and seaweed. It's exciting, modern stuff, but Smith's cooking maintains a solid grasp of flavour combinations, and his forays into creativity are firmly rooted in a sound understanding of what works with what. Asian influence runs through output such as a dish combining mango and coriander with local crab custard and tart. Everything turns up looking beautiful on the plate, and it's always followed through with head-spinning depth of flavour, particularly in meaty main courses such as lamb loin and braised shoulder matched with Jerusalem artichoke and black garlic. The impressive, highly detailed dishes keep coming at dessert stage, perhaps bringing together roast pear with sticky toffee cake and brown butter, or an intriguing partnership of mango, Douglas fir and blueberry.

Chef Steve Smith **Seats** 60, Pr/dining room 24
Times 12-2.30/6.30-10, Closed 24-30 Dec, Sun (ex Mother/Father's Day), BH Mon
Prices Fixed L 2 course fr £19.95, Tasting menu £75-£85, Starter fr £17.50, Main fr £30, Dessert fr £15 **Wines** 200 bottles over £30, 19 bottles under £30, 30 by glass **Parking** 20, Opposite on Green Street **Notes** ALC 3 course £59, Surprise L/D menu 6 course £45/£49, Children welcome

Restaurant Sirocco@The Royal Yacht

ST HELIER **Map 24**

Modern British

tel: 01534 720511 **The Weighbridge JE2 3NF**
email: reception@theroyalyacht.com **web:** www.theroyalyacht.com
dir: *Adjacent to Weighbridge Park overlooking Jersey Harbour*

Bright Jersey cooking with harbour view

A starkly modern hotel with acres of plate glass facing the harbour, The Royal Yacht has copious balconies shaped like waves to echo its maritime location. It most definitely isn't an actual yacht. The contemporary vibe continues on the inside, too, where there is a host of dining and drinking opportunities, the pick of the bunch being the snazzy Restaurant Sirocco with its huge terrace affording views over the harbour. The stylish, smart, and colourful space is the setting for some creative modern food based firmly around the island's superb natural resources. Dishes arrive looking pretty as a picture, a starter of succulent butter-poached lobster, say, with cocoa butter, parsnip and caviar, while another opener sees smoked foie gras partnered with blood orange. Top-notch Jersey lamb arrives in a well-judged main course, with potato terrine, peas, lambs lettuce and onion while the island's beef is showcased as succulent fillet and tender cheek, served with morels and asparagus. Among desserts, an apple crumble soufflé is light and full of flavour, as is its accompanying apple sorbet, or if you're feeling indecisive go for a delightfully well-tempered chocolate sphere with salted caramel and honeycomb.

Chef Steve Walker **Seats** 65, Pr/dining room 20
Times 12-4/7-10, Closed L Mon-Sat **Prices** Prices not confirmed
Wines 108 bottles over £30, 49 bottles under £30, 20 by glass
Parking Car park **Notes** Tasting menu, Wkly rotating table d'hôte menu, Sunday L, Vegetarian available, Children welcome

ST HELIER *continued*

Ormer

Modern European V NOTABLE WINE LIST

tel: 01534 725100 **7-11 Don St JE2 4TQ**
email: book@ormerjersey.com
dir: *Phone for directions*

Shaun Rankin's sophisticated St Helier venture delivers the goods

The 2015 redesign of Ormer, largely the work of in-demand restaurant designer Martin Brudnizki, is something to be seen. Shaun Rankin's town centre venue is topped by an overgrown roof garden and cigar terrace, a must for balmy Jersey nights. In the ground-floor restaurant, mustard-yellow armchairs face royal blue sofas at tables equipped with small lamps, against a backdrop of walls in delicately striped panels with sconces. Island produce pours forth from menus of intricately worked dishes, where the combinatorial arts are explored with gusto and every element earns its place. A piece of seared foie gras is scattered with sea salt and served with dried grapes and hazelnuts, the final touch an opulent velouté of Beaufort cheese poured at the table. Main may be pine nut-crusted turbot on puréed cauliflower, another clever textural exercise, with samphire and sea purslane to emphasise the maritime mood, or perhaps venison with chocolatey beetroot purée, macerated blackberries and chestnut granola. Torn between cheese and dessert, you could opt for the ingenious compromise of ripe Camembert drizzled with orange marmalade, accompanied by salt caramel, pecans and milk foam. Home-made breads are impressive, and when the appetiser is chorizo and parmesan custard coated in panko, you're in for a memorable experience.

Chef Shaun Rankin **Seats** 70, Pr/dining room 14
Times 12-2.30/6.30-10, Closed 25 Dec, Sun **Prices** Fixed L 2 course £19, Tasting menu £75-£124, Starter £13-£18, Main £27-£35, Dessert £9 **Wines** 196 bottles over £30, 48 bottles under £30, 15 by glass **Parking** On street, Sand Street car park **Notes** Spring market D menu 3 course, Children welcome

Restaurant Sirocco@The Royal Yacht

– see page 489 and advert opposite

Tassili

British, French V

tel: 01534 722301 **Grand Jersey, The Esplanade JE2 3QA**
email: reception.grandjersey@handpicked.co.uk
web: www.handpickedhotels/grandjersey
dir: *On St Helier seafront*

Refined Anglo-French cooking in a historic bayfront hotel

The white-fronted Grand Jersey Hotel lords it over the island capital's seafront, with St Aubin's Bay laid out in sparkling array before it. Full of elegance and swagger since it opened in 1890, it was used as headquarters by Nazi occupation forces during the war and, despite much of its furniture being burned for fuel, emerged on VE Day with its dignity intact. The principal dining room, Tassili, is done in chic contemporary style, with textured abstract paintings and a sober dark grey colour scheme, a setting where Nicolas Valmagna has brought the cooking to a high pitch of modern Anglo-French refinement, as befits the location. Dishes are carefully structured but not overworked, leaving an overall impression of lightness and grace. A serving of moist crabmeat in bisque dressing with yuzu gel and crab espuma is a brilliant overture, as is the adventurous seared foie gras that comes with white balsamic jelly and sweetcorn ice cream. A signature main dish of truffled pork – comprising belly, braised cheek and black pudding with compressed apple and a cider cracker – is a textural triumph, or there may be gently cooked turbot with subtly assertive saffron risotto, cockles and sea veg. Bringing up the rear, textures of orange are offset with the mega-richness of 67% Madagascar chocolate ganache and tonka ice cream.

Chef Nicolas Valmagna **Seats** 24 **Times** 7-10, Closed 25 Dec, 1 Jan, Sun-Mon, L all week **Prices** Tasting menu £67-£87 **Wines** 70 bottles over £30, 14 bottles under £30, 12 by glass **Parking** 32, NCP **Notes** Children welcome

ST PETER — Map 24

Greenhills Country Hotel

Mediterranean, British, French

tel: 01534 481042 **Mont de L'Ecole JE3 7EL**
email: reception@greenhillshotel.com **web:** www.greenhillshotel.com
dir: *A1 signed St Peters Valley (A11). 4m, turn right onto E112*

Gently contemporary cooking of Jersey's fine produce

There is much to like about this relaxed country hotel with its riotously colourful gardens, heated outdoor pool and bags of traditional charm. The kitchen team turns out a wide-ranging menu taking in everything from a classic straight-up combo of fillet steak with wild mushrooms, chunky chips and grilled tomato, to more ambitious ideas along the lines of poached salmon fillet and prawns with vegetable paella and lobster and Noilly Prat sauce. Preceding this, Jersey scallops come in a tried-and-tested alliance with pancetta, capers and cauliflower purée. For pudding, that 1970s favourite tipple – advocaat – turns up in crème anglaise to go with sticky toffee pudding.

Chef Lukasz Pietrasz **Seats** 90, Pr/dining room 40 **Times** 12.30-2/7-9.30, Closed 22 Dec-14 Feb **Prices** Fixed L 2 course fr £14, Fixed D 3 course fr £32, Starter £7.50-£12.50, Main £15.50-£35, Dessert £3.50-£4.95 **Wines** 19 bottles over £30, 62 bottles under £30, 8 by glass **Parking** 45 **Notes** ALC specialities, Sunday L £23-£25, Vegetarian available, Children welcome

Mark Jordan at the Beach

Anglo French

tel: 01534 780180 **La Plage, La Route de la Haule JE3 7YD**
email: bookings@markjordanatthebeach.com
dir: *A1 W from St Helier, left mini-rdbt towards St Aubins, follow sign 50mtrs on left*

Anglo-French fish dishes next to the beach

A pleasant white-walled space with wicker chairs and fish pictures, which gives you a clue as to what the forte is. The style is contemporary Anglo-French, as befits the location, seen in a starter of duck terrine with fig chutney and toasted brioche. Next up, a splendid piece of pan-fried cod, the flesh properly opalescent, is left to speak for itself, alongside crushed new potatoes, spinach, and beurre Nantais foam. You won't be neglected if you're set on meat, with the likes of honey-roasted duck breast with griottine cherries, caramelised red cabbage and fondant potato up for grabs. Dessert brings a perfectly risen mint chocolate chip soufflé and chocolate ice cream.

Chef Mark Jordan, Tamas Varsanyi **Seats** 50 **Times** 12-2.30/6-9.30, Closed 7-22 Nov, Mon (winter) **Prices** Fixed L 2 course £19.50, Fixed D 3 course £27.50, Starter £7.50-£13.50, Main £14.50-£35, Dessert £6-£9.50 **Wines** 35 bottles over £30, 26 bottles under £30, 20 by glass **Parking** 16 **Notes** Seasonal special offers, Sunday L £27.50, Vegetarian available, Children welcome

ST SAVIOUR — Map 24

Longueville Manor Hotel

Modern Anglo-French V NOTABLE WINE LIST

tel: 01534 725501 **JE2 7WF**
email: info@longuevillemanor.com **web:** www.longuevillemanor.com
dir: *From St Helier take A3 to Gorey, hotel 0.75m on left*

Accomplished country-hotel cooking in an ancient house

There was a house on the present site in the early 14th century, when it was used on the judicial circuit to try local cases. Rescued from disrepair in the 1940s, it has been painstakingly nurtured by successive generations of the Lewis family, from being the first hotel on Jersey to have en suite rooms and a swimming pool to the present personally run, luxuriously appointed hotel. Dining extends from the dark-panelled Oak Room into a lighter space overlooking the gardens, and the jewel in the culinary crown here is the long residency of Andrew Baird, who continues to blend classical and contemporary modes with distinctive skill. A typical example of his approach is the opening butter-poached lobster, which comes with a dim sum-style shumai dumpling of lobster mousse in a light Asian broth of coconut milk, enoki mushrooms and ginger. Exemplary technique also shines forth from a main course of grilled Angus fillet with oxtail tortellini, served with tartiflette potatoes, puréed butternut and béarnaise, with the added bonus of a richly truffled jus. The apposite finish might then be a Valrhona chocolate sphere with Baileys ice cream, hazelnut mousse and banana, or for something lighter, look to passionfruit soufflé with raspberry ripple sorbet.

Chef Andrew Baird **Seats** 65, Pr/dining room 22 **Times** 12.30-2/7-10 **Prices** Fixed L 3 course £25-£30, Fixed D 3 course £60-£66 **Wines** 300 bottles over £30, 69 bottles under £30, 25 by glass **Parking** 45 **Notes** Discovery menu £80-£110, ALC 2/3 course £52.50/£60, Sunday L £40-£46, Children welcome

SARK

SARK — Map 24

La Sablonnerie

Modern, Traditional International

tel: 01481 832061 **Little Sark GY10 1SD**
email: reservations@sablonneriesark.com **web:** www.sablonneriesark.com
dir: *On southern part of island. Horse & carriage transport to hotel*

Uncomplicated ways with home-grown produce on a special island

Reaching this small hotel is an adventure: a horse-drawn carriage collects guests arriving on the ferry. The building itself is pretty ancient, with beams and stone walls as evidence. Seafood draws the attention, from lobster (thermidor, say, or grilled with a lime and ginger butter glaze) to grilled fillets of sea bass served simply with bisque and croquette potatoes, or monkfish braised in sherry vinegar with brown shrimps and bacon. A meat dish might be caramelised duck breast with Sarladaise potatoes and a sage and green peppercorn jus. To start try perfectly seared scallops with pancetta and cauliflower purée, and to finish there is almond mousse with poached pears and caramel sauce.

Chef Colin Day **Seats** 39 **Times** 12-2.30/7-9.30, Closed mid Oct-Etr **Prices** Prices not confirmed **Wines** 16 bottles over £30, 50 bottles under £30, 6 by glass **Notes** Vegetarian meal on request, Sunday L, Vegetarian available, Children welcome

Stocks Hotel

 Modern British

tel: 01481 832001 & 832444 **GY10 1SD**
email: reception@stockshotel.com **web:** www.stockshotel.com
dir: *From Jersey or Guernsey via ferry to Sark harbour. Transfer to hotel approx 20 mins by foot, bicycle or carriage*

Seriously good cooking in a secluded valley

Sitting in a quiet and picturesque valley, Stocks is a smart hotel built around an 18th-century farmhouse. It's done out in a traditional manner, and that goes for the fine-dining main restaurant too, which delivers plenty of local ingredients in deftly wrought modern dishes. Hand-dived Sark scallops come with scallop mousse, cauliflower, white chocolate gel and liquorice foam, and main course showcases local lamb (herb-crusted best end, braised neck and shoulder) partnered with fondant potato, butternut squash, spinach balls and lamb jus. Deconstructed Black Forest cleverly plays on the delights of cherries and chocolate. There's also a bistro by the swimming pool and an atmospheric bar.

Chef Richard Smache **Seats** 60, Pr/dining room 12 **Times** 12-2.30/7-9, Closed 2 Jan-1 Mar **Prices** Fixed L 2 course £20-£35, Fixed D 3 course £35-£45, Tasting menu £75-£90, Starter £6.50-£10.50, Main £15.50-£25.50, Dessert £7.50-£12.50 **Wines** 57 bottles over £30, 24 bottles under £30, 6 by glass **Parking** 36, Bicycle spaces only **Notes** Champagne afternoon tea £49.50 for 2, Ride & dine £85 for 2, Sunday L £20-£35, Vegetarian available, Children welcome

Scotland

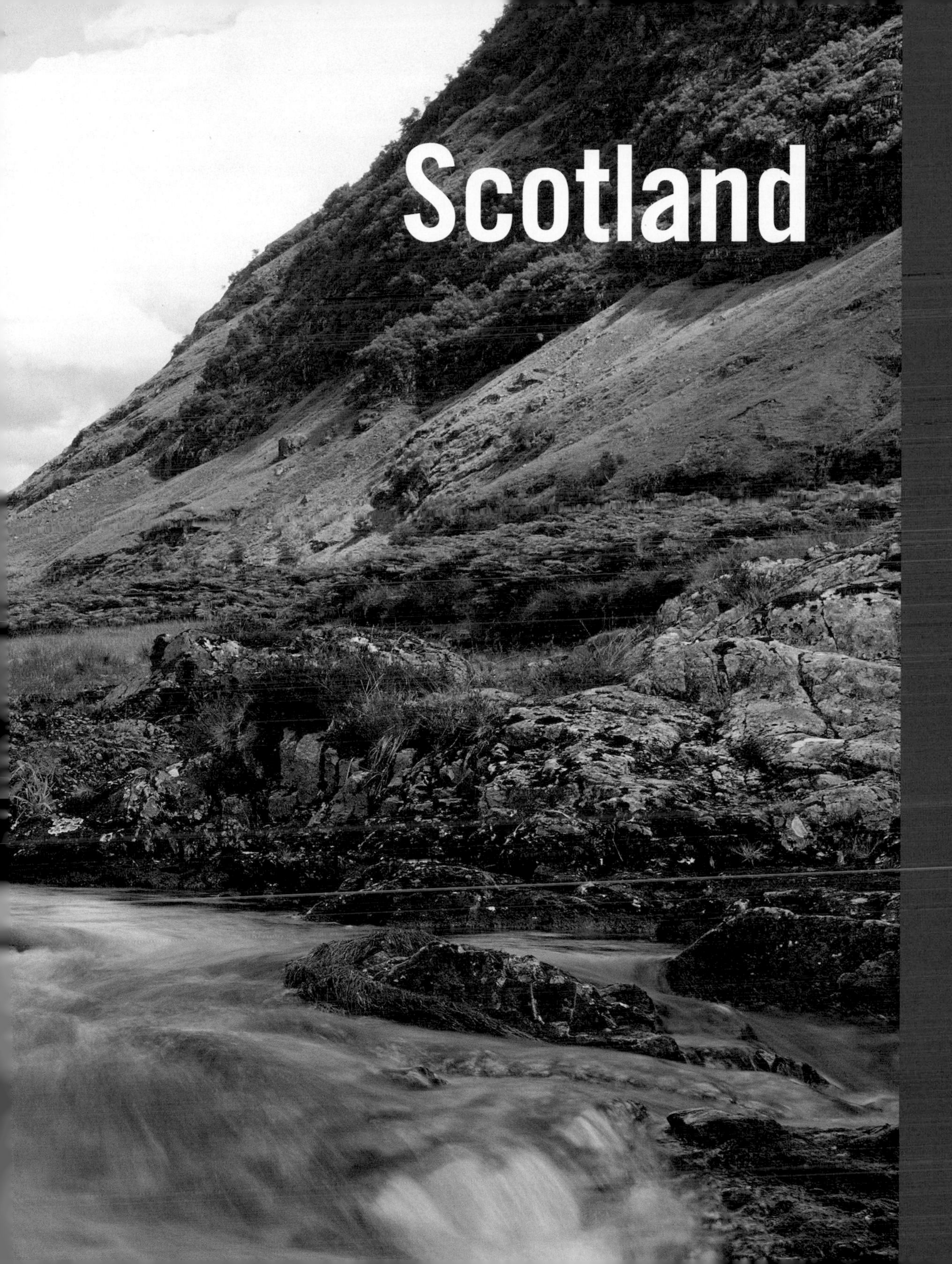

CITY OF ABERDEEN

ABERDEEN Map 23 NJ90

The Adelphi Kitchen

Modern Smoked Meat, Seafood

tel: 01224 211414 & 589109 **28 Adelphi AB11 5BL**
email: hello@theadelphikitchen.co.uk
dir: *Off Union St*

Switched-on barbecue restaurant with an upbeat vibe

An open-pit barbecue in the kitchen of this restaurant delivers impeccably sourced meat and seafood cooked 'dirty' – directly on the hot charcoal – with clear influences from those ol' stateside barbecue-meisters and their racy Tex-Mex flavours. The kitchen sends out the likes of pastrami-spiced chicken thighs and boneless meat on buttermilk purée and a quenelle of tomato and chilli jam, followed by crispy monkfish cheek and bite-sized pieces of spiced fish with garlic mash, mixed beetroots, and lemon and thyme yogurt. For dessert, blueberry sorbet and chutney are clever foils to cut through the richness of vanilla cheesecake.

Chef Chris Tonner, Murray Dawson **Seats** 37 **Times** 12-2.30/5-9.45, Closed 24-25 Dec, 1 Jan **Prices** Starter £5.50-£12, Main £14-£32, Dessert £5.50-£7 **Wines** 11 bottles over £30, 12 bottles under £30, 7 by glass **Parking** On street **Notes** Taster tray for 2 Tue £45, Vegetarian available, Children welcome

Fusion

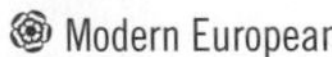

Modern European

tel: 01224 652959 **10 North Silver St AB10 1RL**
email: dining@fusionbarbistro.com **web:** www.fusionbarbistro.com
dir: *Phone for directions*

Funky spot for fizz and switched-on cooking

Blurring the line between bar and restaurant, Fusion's upstairs Gallery restaurant is a chic spot to see and be seen in with its lime green seats, wooden floors and stencilled white walls. The creative modern British menu suits the upbeat vibe and kicks off with loin of hare combined with pheasant and thyme mousse and pointed up with cranberry mustard and herb brioche crumbs. A main-course duo of pork matches loin and confit belly with prune purée, sweet potato croquettes, silverskin onions and cider jus. Sloe gin pannacotta with pear sorbet and blueberry compôte is a good way to finish. Smiley staff keep it on the boil with pin-sharp service.

Chef Steven Murray **Seats** 50, Pr/dining room 25 **Times** 12-2.30/5-9.30, Closed Xmas (4 days), New Year (4 days), Sun-Mon, L Tue-Fri **Prices** Fixed D 3 course £29.95-£42.95, Tasting menu £45-£75 **Wines** 11 bottles over £30, 17 bottles under £30, 11 by glass **Notes** Early supper/Sat L, Vegetarian available, Children welcome

IX Restaurant

Modern Scottish NEW

tel: 01244 327777 **The Chester Hotel, 59-63 Queens Rd AB15 4YP**
email: enquiries@chester-hotel.com **web:** www.chester-hotel.com
dir: *From Aberdeen Airport follow sign to Perth A90, at Queens Rd rdbt take first exit left. Hotel is on the right*

Slick contemporary grill with ambition

The kitchen team behind this glossy contemporary grill are on a mission to be one of Aberdeen's top restaurants, and their switched-on menu is heading straight for that target. Happily, the food is about great flavours rather than ego, and a starter of smoked duck and venison with grated foie gras, pickled vegetables and truffle mayonnaise achieves the required results, as does main-course poached Gigha halibut in a pine nut crust with creamed potatoes, crispy mussels and shellfish marinière. If you're up for an unreconstructed meat-fest, the Josper oven imparts its smoky magic to prime slabs of Scottish beef.

Chef Kevin Dalgleish **Seats** 85, Pr/dining room 22 **Times** 12-2/7-10, Closed D Sun **Prices** Fixed L 2 course fr £25.50, Starter £8-£17, Main £16.50-£26, Dessert £9-£15 **Wines** 73 bottles over £30, 34 bottles under £30, 20 by glass **Notes** Sun brunch £29.95, Vegetarian available, Children welcome

Malmaison Aberdeen

Modern British

tel: 01224 327370 **49-53 Queens Rd AB15 4YP**
email: info.aberdeen@malmaison.com **web:** www.malmaisonaberdeen.com
dir: *A90, 3rd exit onto Queens Rd at 3rd rdbt, hotel on right*

Cool contemporary brasserie with theatre kitchen

Built from the solid granite that gives the city its moniker, the Aberdeen branch of the Malmaison group is suitably dashing, with boutique allure and a cool industrial-chic finish. The brasserie is at the heart of the operation, with an open-to-view kitchen revealing the Josper grill, the source of a good deal of what follows. Start with ahi tuna tartare with avocado, wasabi, pickled ginger and soy dressing, followed by something meaty from that Josper: a perfectly timed rib-eye steak perhaps, served with whichever sauce floats your boat. Other options include roast Atlantic cod with shellfish vinaigrette and samphire. Finish your meal with lemon meringue cheesecake.

Chef John Burns **Seats** 120, Pr/dining room 30 **Times** 12-2.30/5.30-10.30 **Prices** Prices not confirmed **Wines** 26 bottles over £30, 16 bottles under £30, 27 by glass **Parking** 30 **Notes** Brunch £29.95, Prix fixe menu 2/3 course £19.95/£24.95, Sunday L, Vegetarian available, Children welcome

Mercure Aberdeen Ardoe House Hotel & Spa

Modern Scottish, French

tel: 01224 860600 **South Deeside Rd, Blairs AB12 5YP**
email: h6626-dm@accor.com **web:** www.mercure.com
dir: *4m W of city off B9077*

Smartly updated Victorian building, modern Scottish cooking

The Scots certainly knew how to build grand houses in the 1870s. This once-staid old pile in 30 acres of grounds three miles from the city centre is now a smart hotel and spa with a jazzy contemporary look that extends to the sleekly designed Blair's Restaurant. Among the modern Scottish dishes are the starter of corned beef and Aberdeen Angus terrine, piccalilli purée, cornichons and rye bread cubes, and the main dish of hake gremolata crust, spinach and leek risotto, and chorizo velouté. A juicy tarte Tatin with Calvados ice cream dessert is perhaps more conformist.

Chef Richard Yearnshire **Seats** 100, Pr/dining room 25 **Times** 12.30-2.30/6.30-9.30 **Prices** Starter £5-£15, Main £15-£25, Dessert £10-£15 **Wines** 15 bottles over £30, 15 bottles under £30, 17 by glass **Parking** 90 **Notes** Afternoon/high tea, Sunday L £25, Vegetarian available, Children welcome

Moonfish Café

Modern British NEW

tel: 01224 644166 **9 Correction Wynd AB10 1HP**
email: info@moonfishcafe.co.uk
dir: *Phone for directions*

Inventive food, sharply executed

Chef-patron Brian McLeish was a finalist on *MasterChef: The Professionals* a few years back, although his Moonfish Café has been on the local foodie radar since 2004. It's a relaxed set-up, its pared-back looks enlivened by changing artworks and fish motifs on the large windows. There's plenty of sharp technique in the cooking, opening with mackerel fillets matched with chicory marmalade, Jerusalem artichoke purée and tarragon, ahead of pan-fried guinea fowl with celeriac purée and remoulade, pickled mushrooms and caramelised shallot. It ends on a high, courtesy of poached rhubarb with shortbread, vanilla cream, meringue and pistachio. The gin list is worth a visit, too.

Chef Brian McLeish **Times** 12-2/6-9, Closed Sun-Mon **Prices** Fixed D 3 course £37.95, Starter £3.95-£5.95, Main £7.95-£9.95, Dessert £5.95 **Wines** 5 bottles over £30, 13 bottles under £30, 17 by glass **Notes** D 4 course £43.95, Vegetarian available, Children until 8pm

Norwood Hall Hotel

 Modern British

tel: 01224 868951 **Garthdee Rd, Cults AB15 9FX**
email: info@norwood-hall.co.uk **web:** www.norwood-hall.co.uk
dir: *Off A90, at 1st rdbt cross Bridge of Dee, left at rdbt onto Garthdee Rd (B&Q & Sainsburys on left) continue to hotel sign*

Victorian mansion showcasing fine Scottish produce

The interior of this 1881-built mansion is stunning; all ornate fireplaces and stained-glass windows, while cuisine is contemporary with a strong Scottish element. Ham hock terrine with red peppers and pineapple chutney is a strident starter, while Marie Rose sauce gains a shot of whisky for crayfish, prawns and langoustines. Prime ingredients are carefully handled, as in rack of local lamb (three- or seven-bone), cooked to pink, served with red wine jus, dauphinoise, spinach and carrot purée, and in well-timed roast fillet of halibut in a parmesan crust with mussels, peas and warm tartare-style sauce. Puddings follow the route of lemon tart with caramel ice cream and Seville orange syrup.

The Silver Darling

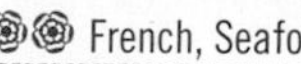 French, Seafood

tel: 01224 576229 **Pocra Quay, North Pier AB11 5DQ**
email: silverdarling@hotmail.co.uk
dir: *At Aberdeen Harbour entrance*

Interesting ways with superbly fresh seafood

As befits its location at the mouth of Aberdeen harbour, The Silver Darling focuses on seafood, and you can watch the trawlers come and go from the conservatory-style restaurant atop a stocky granite building. The kitchen produces menus of French-accented contemporary ideas with the odd foray into Far Eastern flavours. Smoked ham hock and foie gras terrine with fig chutney and pickled vegetables gets things off to a flying start, and might be followed by monkfish poached in red wine served on pancetta and cabbage fricassee with celeriac mousseline and a black pudding croquette. Desserts are impressive too: try mango and passionfruit cheesecake with chocolate sorbet.

Chef Didier Dejean **Seats** 50, Pr/dining room 8
Times 12-1.45/6.30-9.30, Closed Xmas-New Year, Sun, L Sat **Prices** Fixed L 2 course fr £20.50, Starter £7.50-£15, Main £18-£28.50, Dessert £8.50-£11.50 **Wines** 26 bottles over £30, 14 bottles under £30, 9 by glass **Parking** On quayside **Notes** ALC D only, Vegetarian available, Children welcome

ABERDEENSHIRE

BALLATER **Map 23 NO39**

Loch Kinord Hotel

Traditional Scottish

tel: 01339 885229 **Ballater Rd, Dinnet AB34 5JY**
email: stay@lochkinord.com **web:** www.lochkinord.com
dir: *Between Aboyne & Ballater, on A93, in Dinnet*

Classical cooking in Royal Deeside

Built in granite in Victorian times, Loch Kinord has homely lounges with real fires, a small bar and a dining room done out with tartan wallpaper and plush red and gold carpets. There's a classical leaning to the kitchen's output and a good showing of regional produce to inject a sense of place. Start on game terrine with red onion marmalade and toasted brioche, followed by rack of lamb with mustard and herb crust, the meat perfectly pink and tender, served with braised red cabbage and black pudding mash. Chocolate fondant oozes in all the right places and comes with a scoop of intensely flavoured vanilla ice cream.

BALMEDIE Map 23 NJ91

Cock & Bull

Modern Scottish, British V

tel: 01358 743249 **Ellon Rd, Blairton AB23 8XY**
email: info@thecockandbull.co.uk **web:** www.thecockandbull.co.uk
dir: *6m N of Aberdeen on A90*

Big flavours at a distinctive country inn

The Cock & Bull is a low-slung establishment full of 19th-century character with wooden beams and real fires, but there's nothing stuck in the past about this gastropub: modern food and local artworks ensure that. Eat in the conservatory dining room, cosy lounge in front of the fire, or the main restaurant, where there's an all-day menu of enticing, up-to-date ideas. Try scallops with sweetcorn and coriander salsa, followed by slow-cooked pork belly with Stornoway Black Pudding, burnt apple purée, and Granny Smith apple and spinach salad. For dessert, go for dark chocolate mousse with honeycomb ice cream.

Chef Ryan Paterson **Seats** 80, Pr/dining room 30 **Times** 10.30am-late, All-day dining, Closed 26 Dec, 2 Jan **Prices** Prices not confirmed **Wines** 11 bottles over £30, 24 bottles under £30, 7 by glass **Parking** 50 **Notes** Sunday L, Children welcome

BANCHORY Map 23 NO69

The Falls of Feugh Restaurant

Scottish, French NEW

tel: 01330 822123 **Bridge of Feugh AB31 6NL**
email: enquiries@thefallsoffeugh.com
dir: *Phone for directions*

Riverside dining with a refined, local flavour

In a bucolic spot by the river, surrounded by trees, the sound of running water is particularly evocative if you're sitting on the small terrace. There's a charming café, but the main draw is the modern French- and Scottish-inflected food on offer in the restaurant. Blond wood floors add a contemporary touch to the homely decor, while the cheerful service team are all smiles. Local ingredients get a good showing on a menu that offers classic flavour combinations in up-to-date preparations. Presse of smoked ham hock and parsley is well matched with spiced green tomato chutney and apple purée, followed perhaps by perfectly cooked hake with shellfish sauce.

Chef John Chomba **Seats** 96, Pr/dining room 40 **Times** 12-12, All-day dining, Closed Mon & Tue (Jan-Mar), Tue (Apr-Dec), D Mon-Wed, Sun **Prices** Fixed L 2 course £14.95-£16.95, Fixed D 3 course £37.50-£45, Tasting menu £55-£70, Starter £6-£10, Main £12-£28, Dessert £6-£10 **Wines** 19 bottles over £30, 26 bottles under £30, 9 by glass **Parking** 20, Car park opposite with 100 spaces **Notes** Afternoon tea £13.95 (with champagne £20.95), Sunday L £22-£28, Vegetarian available, Children welcome

ELLON Map 23 NJ93

Eat on the Green

British, Scottish, European

tel: 01651 842337 **Udny Green AB41 7RS**
email: enquiries@eatonthegreen.co.uk
dir: *A920 towards Udny Green/Ellon. Or B999 from Bridge of Don to Tarves*

Refurbed for stylish modern fare

It's all change at Eat on the Green, with a new chef and a refurbishment of the restaurant. They've even moved the bar, and there's a new garden/champagne lounge, all demonstrating how seriously they take things here. The kitchen turns out stylish modern dishes from top Scottish ingredients. Start with Portsoy smoked salmon and haddock tartare with a soft-poached egg, and follow that with braised cheek of Oldmeldrum beef with pommes purée and pickled beetroot, or maybe pan-fried Orkney monkfish and scallops, served with spiced split pea dhal and curried mussels. Finish with a Cox apple and caramel tart.

Chef Mateusz Majer, Craig Wilson **Seats** 48, Pr/dining room 16 **Times** 12-2/6-9, Closed 1 wk Jan, Mon-Tue, L Sat **Prices** Fixed L 2 course fr £24.95, Tasting menu £80-£120, Starter £6.95-£9.95, Dessert £6.95-£9.95 **Wines** 42 bottles over £30, 26 bottles under £30, 9 by glass **Parking** 7, On street **Notes** Sat D 4 course £59, Tasting 8 course Wed-Sun 48hrs notice, Sunday L, Vegetarian available, Children welcome

INVERURIE Map 23 NJ72

The Green Lady

Modern British NEW

tel: 01467 621643 **Thainstone House AB51 5NT**
email: thainstone@crerarhotels.com **web:** www.crerarhotels.com/thainstone-house
dir: *A96 from Aberdeen. Pass by-pass to Kintore. Entrance to hotel at 1st rdbt Thainstone Rdbt. Take 1st left then sharp right to hotel*

Country-house elegance and excellent food

The phrase '18th-century elegance' perfectly sums up the setting of Wedgwood-green walls, chandeliers and white linen in Thainstone House's fine-dining restaurant (it's named after one of the hotel's ghosts). The food, however, is distinctly modern British stuff, delivering smart contemporary dishes full of vibrancy and bold strokes. Pan-seared wood pigeon with beetroot carpaccio and celeriac purée opens the show, followed by a main course that showcases the quality of locally-sourced produce: breast of Gartmore chicken with skirlie bonbons, carrot purée, crispy kale and tarragon jus. Desserts also dazzle, especially rhubarb pannacotta served up with star anise syrup, lavender shortbread and frozen yogurt.

Chef Paul Grant **Seats** 45, Pr/dining room 16 **Times** 12.30-2.30/6.30-9, Closed L Mon-Sat **Prices** Tasting menu £35, Starter £7.95-£10.95, Main £16.50-£22.95, Dessert £7.95-£10.95 **Wines** 26 bottles over £30, 29 bottles under £30, 9 by glass **Parking** 100 **Notes** Sunday L £17.95-£19.95, Vegetarian available, Children welcome

Macdonald Pittodrie House

Modern, Traditional Scottish

tel: 01467 622437 **Chapel of Garioch, Pitcaple AB51 5HS**
email: pittodrie@macdonald-hotels.co.uk **web:** www.macdonald-hotels.com/pittodrie
dir: *From A96 towards Inverness, pass Inverurie under bridge with lights. Turn left & follow signs*

Gently modern cooking in a pastoral setting

A few miles off the main road, Pittodrie House has a wonderfully peaceful position, plus 2,000 acres to call its own. Inside all is rich, warm decor and period detail, including the restaurant with its classical proportions and large oil canvases on the walls. It's a smart, classical setting for gently modern Scottish cuisine. Start with West Coast wild salmon and lobster tortellini with a frothy lobster bisque and spinach dressed with lobster oil. Follow on with loin of Highland venison, the meat pink and tender, and served with celeriac both roasted and puréed, plus chestnuts and silky juniper-flavoured jus. Finish with blackberry parfait or a selection of British cheeses.

KILDRUMMY Map 23 NJ41

Kildrummy Inn

Modern Scottish

tel: 01975 571227 **AB33 8QC**
email: enquiries@kildrummyinn.co.uk **web:** www.kildrummyinn.co.uk
dir: *From Aberdeen inn on A97, 2m past Mossat junct, en-route to Cairngorm National Park*

Confident modern cooking in a rural inn

Kildrummy Inn has an authenticity that appeals to tourists and locals, while the output from its dynamic kitchen has put it on the foodie map. Menus reveal classical sensibilities and a contemporary touch. Start with a terrine made with rillettes of confit chicken, looking pretty as a picture on a vibrant apricot purée, and topped with a crispy black pudding bonbon. Next up, beef appears fashionably in two ways – sirloin and slow-cooked featherblade – in a dish that marries flavours and textures. Flavours hit the mark when it comes to desserts, too, with a pannacotta alongside tropical fruit salsa and a suitably sharp lime sorbet.

Chef David Littlewood **Seats** 30, Pr/dining room 12 **Times** 6-9, Closed Jan, Tue, L Mon, Wed-Sat **Prices** Fixed L 2 course £19, Fixed D 3 course £35 **Wines** 6 bottles over £30, 20 bottles under £30, 9 by glass **Parking** 20 **Notes** Sunday L, Vegetarian available, Children welcome

OLDMELDRUM Map 23 NJ82

Meldrum House Country Hotel & Golf Course

Modern Scottish

tel: 01651 872294 **AB51 0AE**
email: enquiries@meldrumhouse.com **web:** www.meldrumhouse.com
dir: *11m from Aberdeen on A947 (Aberdeen to Banff road)*

Smart country-house hotel with a local flavour

Even if you're not nifty with a niblick, Meldrum House is a good place to marinate in the luxury of a turreted baronial pile. The deeply traditional country-house hotel has 350 acres of wooded parkland and its dining room makes a grand setting for modern Scottish country-house cooking, with ancestral portraits, real fire and burnished darkwood tables. Start on a rich note with smoked hare loin paired with confit leg fritter and celeriac textures, then progress to North Sea halibut with a tapenade crust, vegetable spaghetti and spring onion and potato sauce. To finish, pear soufflé and ice cream marry perfectly with Cognac caramel.

Chef David Murray **Seats** 40, Pr/dining room 16 **Times** 12-2/6.30-9 **Prices** Prices not confirmed **Wines** 8 by glass **Parking** 70 **Notes** Afternoon tea, Sunday L, Vegetarian available, Children welcome

PETERHEAD Map 23 NK14

Buchan Braes Hotel

Modern Scottish, European

tel: 01779 871471 **Boddam AB42 3AR**
email: info@buchanbraes.co.uk **web:** www.buchanbraes.co.uk
dir: *From Aberdeen take A90, follow Peterhead signs. 1st right in Stirling signed Boddam. 50mtrs, 1st right*

Bright modern cooking in a contemporary hotel

The low-slung Buchan Braes won't win any architectural prizes, but it's a splendid contemporary hotel with a rural aspect and up-to-date wedding and conference facilities. There's also the Grill Room restaurant, with its open kitchen and warmly colourful decor. The modern Scottish cooking isn't all about the grill, although you might opt for a chargrilled steak or hunk of salmon. The kitchen also turns out Cullen skink terrine with balsamic glaze and parmesan, followed by rack of lamb with minted pea purée and honeyed carrots in roasting juices, or seared king scallops in spiced lentils and garlic butter. For dessert, try toffee and honeycomb vacherin.

Chef Gary Christie **Seats** 70, Pr/dining room 80 **Times** 12-2/6-9.30 **Prices** Prices not confirmed **Wines** 10 bottles over £30, 24 bottles under £30, 9 by glass **Parking** 100 **Notes** Sunday L, Vegetarian available, Children welcome

STONEHAVEN Map 23 NO88

The Tolbooth Restaurant

Modern British, Seafood

tel: 01569 762287 **Old Pier, Stonehaven Harbour AB39 2JU**
email: enquiries@tolbooth-restaurant.co.uk
dir: *15m S of Aberdeen on A90, in Stonehaven harbour*

Speciality seafood restaurant overlooking the harbour

There can't be many better spots than this for tucking into seafood: it's right on the harbour wall, with a museum on the ground floor and the upstairs restaurant giving sea views. What you eat depends on what's been landed that day. To start, steamed mussels come in a broth flavoured with ginger, chilli and coriander, and there might be crab soup. Main-course grilled fillet of cod is spiked with chorizo and served with ratatouille, sage and salsa verde, and seared halibut fillet is glazed in ponzu and accompanied by shrimp and spring onion butter. End strongly with pineapple tarte Tatin with cherry sorbet.

Chef Craig Somers **Seats** 46 **Times** 12-4/6-12, Closed 1st 3 wks Jan, Mon-Tue (winter), Mon (summer), D Sun (winter) **Prices** Fixed L 2 course £15, Starter £7-£10.95, Main £17-£25, Dessert £6.50-£9 **Wines** 21 bottles over £30, 13 bottles under £30, 6 by glass **Parking** Public car park, 100 spaces **Notes** Sunday L £21.50-£26.50, Vegetarian available, Children welcome

ANGUS

FORFAR Map 23 NO45

Drovers

Modern Scottish

tel: 01307 860322 **Memus By Forfar DD8 3TY**
email: info@the-drovers.com
dir: *Forth Road bridge onto A823 then M90. Dundee through to Forfar onto A90, then B9128 Memus, Cortachy, The Glens*

Country inn serving rustic modern Scottish cooking

Surrounded by beautiful glens, The Drovers is the kind of wild place you want to be stranded when the weather closes in. Although a modern pub in many ways, the walls of antlers remind you this rustic bolt-hole has been around for many years. In the buzzy restaurant, the menu makes good use of what lives and grows locally and turns these fine ingredients into modern Scottish food. Chargrilled king scallops with pea purée, pancetta, apple and beetroot dressing might precede a main course of roast rump of lamb with sauté rosemary potatoes, roasted garlic, minted peas and smoked bacon.

INVERKEILOR Map 23 NO64

Gordon's

Modern Scottish

tel: 01241 830364 **Main St DD11 5RN**
email: gordonsrest@aol.com **web:** www.gordonsrestaurant.co.uk
dir: *From A92 exit at signs for Inverkeilor (between Arbroath & Montrose)*

Striking modern Scottish cookery in a coastal hamlet

If it was once the fate of Inverkeilor to be overlooked by travellers hurtling towards nearby Arbroath, but, over a 30-year period, Gordon and Maria Watson have brought it firmly into the Scottish spotlight. Sadly, Gordon passed away in June 2016, but the restaurant remains a fitting testament to his exemplary culinary standards. Set beside peaceful Lunan Bay, this coastal village is home to this warmly relaxing restaurant with rooms, some of the warmth provided by a traditional log burner, the rest by a thoroughly welcoming front-of-house approach. Gordon's son, Garry Watson, oversees the kitchen for a mixture of simple regional and more high-toned classical cooking, and the drill is a fixed-price menu of four courses at dinner, with a silky velouté soup such as carrot and orange with smoked eel often cropping up at second stage. Prior to that, there could be a well-executed twice-baked soufflé of Mull Tobermory cheddar, or a trend-conscious pairing of scallops and crispy chicken wings with Jerusalem artichoke and hazelnuts. For mains, quality Scottish meat and fish is showcased, perhaps in best end cutlets and confit shoulder of Forfar lamb with minted pea ravioli and butternut squash in tomato jus, or fennel seed-crusted monkfish with spiced couscous. At the close, divine Angus raspberries (whole and in sorbet) almost upstage a wildly rich Valrhona parfait garnished with cocoa nib tuile.

Chef Garry Watson **Seats** 24, Pr/dining room 8 **Times** 12.30-1.45/7-9, Closed Jan, Mon, L Sat, Tue, D Sun (in winter) **Prices** Fixed L 3 course fr £34 **Wines** 11 bottles over £30, 33 bottles under £30, 5 by glass **Parking** 6 **Notes** All bookings essential, 5 course D £57, Vegetarian available, Children 12 yrs+

ARGYLL & BUTE

ARDUAINE Map 20 NM71

Loch Melfort Hotel

 Modern British

tel: 01852 200233 **PA34 4XG**
email: reception@lochmelfort.co.uk **web:** www.lochmelfort.co.uk
dir: *On A816, midway between Oban & Lochgilphead*

Ambitious contemporary cooking and magnificent views

Tranquilly set in 17 acres of gardens, this country-house hotel was built in the late 19th century slap-bang on the shore of Asknish Bay with jaw-dropping views over to Jura and other islands. Pheasant, duck, quail and black pudding go into a terrine set off by a port reduction and pear and saffron chutney, followed perhaps by braised shin of beef with pan-fried mignon of fillet served with girolles, roast shallots, potato cakes and red wine jus. Resourceful seafood dishes include grilled mackerel fillet with barigoule and fennel purée, and pan-fried fillet of sea bass with saffron potatoes, mussels, spinach and tapenade. To finish, fly the Scottish saltire with cranachan.

Chef Michael Knowles **Seats** 60, Pr/dining room 14 **Times** 6.30-9, Closed mid 2 wks Jan, midwk Nov-Mar, 1st 2wks Dec, L all week, D Tue-Wed (Nov-Mar) **Prices** Starter £8.95-£11.95, Main £12.95-£23.50, Dessert £6.95-£8.95 **Wines** 21 bottles over £30, 54 bottles under £30, 8 by glass **Parking** 65 **Notes** 4 course D £39.50, Vegetarian available, Children welcome

COVE Map 22 NG89

Knockderry House Hotel

Modern Scottish NEW

tel: 01436 842283 & 842404 **Shore Rd G84 0NX**
email: info@knockderryhouse.co.uk **web:** www.knockderryhouse.co.uk
dir: *A82 to Lochlomondside, left onto A817 signed Garelochhead, through Glen Fruin to A814. Follow Coulport signs. At Coulport left at rdbt, 2m to hotel*

Lochside location for multi-layered modern Scottish cooking

Standing on the shore of Loch Long, this much-altered Victorian house is a period treat inside, with a billiard room, intricate wood panelling and magnificent stained windows in the dining room. Gloved staff serve modern Scottish food that embraces modern techniques, from a starter of a circlet of chicken roulade in Parma, crispy chicken wing, a seared king prawn and some roasted celeriac and its purée, to a main dish of beautifully complementary turbot and chorizo, alongside scallop tortellino, baby turnips and broccoli foam. Similar multi-layering informs desserts such as chocolate marquise scattered with candied jasmine, with honey and almond ice cream on lavendered chocolate crumb.

Chef David Toward **Seats** 30, Pr/dining room 50
Times 12.30-2.30/7.15-8.45, Closed 12-28 Dec **Prices** Fixed L 2 course £12.95, Fixed D 3 course £39 **Wines** 17 bottles over £30, 23 bottles under £30, 8 by glass **Parking** 15 **Notes** Early D menu 3 course £19.95, Sunday L £22.95, Vegetarian available, Children welcome

KILCHRENAN Map 20 NN02

The Ardanaiseig Hotel

Modern British V NOTABLE WINE LIST

tel: 01866 833333 **by Loch Awe PA35 1HE**
email: jamie@ardanaiseig.com **web:** www.ardanaiseig.com
dir: *From A85 at Taynuilt onto B845 to Kilchrenan. Left in front of pub (road very narrow) signed Ardanaiseig Hotel & No Through Road. Continue for 3m*

A creative menu and high comfort in a stunning lochside hotel

Located in lush gardens with a backdrop of Ben Cruachan rising from the waters of Loch Awe, the hotel's interior is traditional with a contemporary spin and a touch of Gothic charm. The restaurant – candlelit in the evening – is a stylish space with striking artworks and tables dressed in pristine white-linen cloths. The kitchen turns out modern dishes such as fillet of wild sea bass with textures of apple and celeriac remoulade, followed by slow-cooked Angus beef partnered with braised oxtail and a piece of seared foie gras. Finish with a deconstructed version of banoffee pie, or hot chocolate fondant with pistachio ice cream.

Chef Colin Cairns **Seats** 40, Pr/dining room 20 **Times** 12-6.30/7-11 **Prices** Fixed L 2 course £12-£32, Tasting menu £60, Starter £6.50-£13.50, Main £15.50-£26, Dessert £7-£14 **Wines** 76 bottles over £30, 14 bottles under £30, 9 by glass **Parking** 20 **Notes** ALC L menu £2-£25, Tasting menu 8 course, Sunday L £25, Children 5 yrs+

Taychreggan Hotel

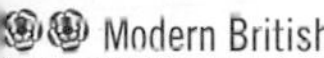

Modern British

tel: 01866 833211 & 833366 **PA35 1HQ**
email: info@taychregganhotel.co.uk **web:** www.taychregganhotel.co.uk
dir: *W from Crianlarich on A85 to Taynuilt, S for 7m on B845 (single track) to Kilchrenan*

Ambitious cooking with sublime loch views

The whitewashed 17th-century hotel lies a short drive from Oban on a peninsula jutting into Loch Awe, framed by timeless Highland landscapes. The kitchen delivers five-course set dinner menus beginning with a soup – courgette, with perch and tarragon oil – ahead of a colourful composition involving tomato terrine with home-cured salmon, carrot purée, caviar, pickled cucumber, quail's egg and ruby chard. The main event stars Highland beef (roasted sirloin and slow-braised ox cheeks) with pearl barley, dauphinoise potato, wilted spinach, chargrilled courgettes and a rich red wine jus. Then it's strawberries with vanilla pannacotta, mascarpone, puff pastry and crème fraîche sorbet before a finale of oak-smoked brie on toast.

LUSS Map 20 NS39

The Lodge on Loch Lomond

Modern British, International

tel: 01436 860201 **G83 8PA**
email: res@loch-lomond.co.uk **web:** www.loch-lomond.co.uk
dir: *N of Glasgow on A82*

Fine modern British dining above the loch

Situated on the edge of Loch Lomond, The Lodge occupies a peaceful woodland setting. The unbeatable loch views and sense of tranquillity in the balcony restaurant give the impression that you are floating on water. From the open-view kitchen, the modern British food is underpinned by classic technique. Chicken liver parfait served with pear chutney and toasted brioche makes for a well-made starter and might be followed by slow-braised pork belly with spiced apple compote, sauté potatoes and apple jus. Desserts such as white chocolate and kirsch parfait, mango purée and orange sorbet are impressive.

Chef David McCulloch, Graham Harrower **Seats** 100, Pr/dining room 100 **Times** 12-5/6-9.30 **Prices** Prices not confirmed **Wines** 11 bottles over £30, 28 bottles under £30, 11 by glass **Parking** 70 **Notes** Afternoon tea, Sunday L, Vegetarian available, Children welcome

OBAN Map 20 NM82

Coast

Modern British

tel: 01631 569900 **104 George St PA34 5NT**
email: coastoban@yahoo.co.uk
dir: *On main street in town centre*

Vivacious brasserie cooking in a converted bank building

Next door to the art gallery, Coast is the very image of a modern brasserie, with a seasonally changing menu of vivacious dishes. Start with home-made chicken liver parfait with apple chutney, or enjoy the simplicity of chargrilled local langoustine dressed with garlic butter. Move on to pan-fried fillet of red gurnard (landed at Tarbert) with a mix of veg including salsify and fennel, anchovy fritter and chervil cream sauce, or haunch of Argyll venison with spiced red cabbage, pickled walnuts and a mash fired up with truffle and chives. Finish with apple and honeycomb parfait with toffee ice cream or a ginger sponge pudding with spiced pears.

Chef Richard Fowler **Seats** 46 **Times** 12-2/5.30-9.30, Closed 25 Dec, 2 wks Jan, Sun (Nov-Mar), L Sun **Prices** Fixed L 2 course £14.50, Fixed D 3 course £17.50, Starter £4.50-£10.95, Main £10.50-£25, Dessert £5.95 **Wines** 13 bottles over £30, 33 bottles under £30, 5 by glass **Parking** On street **Notes** Vegetarian available, Children until 8pm

OBAN *continued*

The Hawthorn Restaurant

Modern British NEW

tel: 01631 720777 **5 Keil Crofts, Benderloch PA37 1QS**
email: info@hawthorn-restaurant.co.uk **web:** www.hawthorn-restaurant.co.uk
dir: *From Oban N on A85 towards Connel, cross Connel Bridge, continue on A828 to Benderloch. Left before Lochnell Primary School. Restaurant 0.5m on right, next to Hawthorn B&B*

Sharp cooking on a 300-year-old croft

A short drive from Oban, this relaxed restaurant occupies a low-slung building on a 300-year-old working croft. Inside, an almost Nordic sparseness – darkwood floors, bare tables and exposed stone – is the backdrop to the smart menu of old favourites and gently contemporary ideas. Isle of Mull scallops come tempura-style, with caramelised leek purée and soy and lime jelly bringing a balance of salt-and-sour notes. Main course delivers a piggy trio of slow-cooked belly, fillet and a croquette of pulled pork and potato matched with carrot and thyme purée and creamy Calvados sauce. Finish with sticky toffee pudding with brandy-soaked prunes and gingerbread ice cream.

Chef Kevin Hanlon **Seats** 42 **Times** 12-2/5.30-9, Closed Nov-Mar, L Mon-Thu **Prices** Starter £4.95-£8.50, Main £10.95-£25, Dessert £4.99-£8.50 **Wines** 5 bottles over £30, 14 bottles under £30, 8 by glass **Parking** 16 **Notes** Vegetarian available, Children welcome

Manor House Hotel

Scottish, European

tel: 01631 562087 **Gallanach Rd PA34 4LS**
email: info@manorhouseoban.com **web:** www.manorhouseoban.com
dir: *Follow MacBrayne Ferries signs, pass ferry entrance for hotel on right*

Traditional country-house dining by Oban harbour

Built for the Duke of Argyll in 1780, the Manor House sits in a commanding position overlooking the harbour at Oban. Half-panelled walls and original oils set a heightened tone in the dining room, where a lighting level to encourage intimacies prevails. Fine regional Scottish produce is celebrated in menus that aim for a soft-focus country-hotel approach rather than anything too offbeat. First up might be sweet potato tortellini with carrot and orange purée in cumin butter, then roast brill with cauliflower fritters and dried grapes, or guinea-fowl in bacon and thyme sauce with champ. Iced lemon meringue parfait with raspberry sorbet delivers a big finishing hit.

Chef Shaun Squire **Seats** 34 **Times** 12-2/6.45-8.45, Closed 25-26 Dec **Prices** Prices not confirmed **Wines** 20 bottles over £30, 60 bottles under £30, 6 by glass **Parking** 20 **Notes** ALC L only, Fixed L(book)/D 4/5 course £31/£42, Sunday L, Vegetarian available, Children 12 yrs+

PORT APPIN **Map 20 NM94**

Airds Hotel and Restaurant

Modern Scottish V 

tel: 01631 730236 **PA38 4DF**
email: airds@airds-hotel.com **web:** www.airds-hotel.com
dir: *From A828 (Oban to Fort William road), turn at Appin signed Port Appin. Hotel 2.5m on left*

Accomplished modern seasonal cooking by Loch Linnhe

Port Appin is a peaceful hamlet in a beautiful setting on the shore of Loch Linnhe with the Morven mountains in the background. Airds, a whitewashed converted ferry inn, just across a narrow road from the loch, is a modestly proportioned (just 11 bedrooms) boutique-style hotel with bags of class – a perfect retreat. Entry is through a small flower-filled conservatory, with two lounges beyond in which to enjoy a wee dram on one of the deep soft furnishings in front of the fire or in the whisky bar, which is purpose-built in American walnut. The restaurant, candlelit at night, is a stylish room, with views over the loch from large picture windows. The seasonal menus show a kitchen taking a gently contemporary approach, with nothing too startling. A platter of smoked salmon and crab, served with garden beetroot and horseradish, or foie gras terrine with blood orange, are the sort of starters to expect. Pin-point timing and seasoning are hallmarks, with loin of lamb cooked to pink and accompanied by garlic, goats' cheese gnocchi and black olives. Not surprisingly, seafood gets a strong showing: perhaps pan-seared sea bass fillet with an oyster emulsion, clams and lemongrass cream. End indulgently with dark chocolate delice with bitter orange purée and mandarin sorbet.

Chef Chris Stanley **Seats** 30 **Times** 12-1.45/7.15-9.15 **Prices** Fixed L 3 course £18.95, Tasting menu £74, Starter £3-£7, Main £7.50-£21, Dessert £4-£6 **Wines** 225 bottles over £30, 10 bottles under £30, 12 by glass **Parking** 20 **Notes** 5 course D £55, Tasting menu 7 course, Sunday L £18.50, Children 8 yrs+

The Pierhouse Hotel

Seafood

tel: 01631 730302 & 730622 **PA38 4DE**
email: reservations@pierhousehotel.co.uk **web:** www.pierhousehotel.co.uk
dir: *M8, A82 to Crianlarich & Fort William. At Ballachulish take A828 towards Oban. Turn right in Appin for Port Appin & Lismore Ferry*

Top-notch fish and seafood with stunning views

Tucked away on a quiet arm of Loch Linnhe, this waterside restaurant is a simple, magnolia-painted space – there's no point fretting over interior design when all eyes are turned towards the peaks marching across the skyline above the loch. Oysters are hand-picked from the Lismore oyster beds, mussels and langoustines come from Loch Linnhe, and lobsters are kept in creels at the end of the pier where day boats drop off fish. Who could resist seared scallops with artichoke purée and Stornoway Black Pudding to start? The glorious simplicity and freshness of the seafood platters is hard to ignore, and there's Drambuie crème brûlée to send you home happy.

RHU Map 20 NS28

Rosslea Hall Hotel

Modern International

tel: 01436 439955 **Ferry Rd G84 8NF**
email: sales@rossleahallhotel.co.uk **web:** www.rossleahallhotel.co.uk
dir: *From Erskine Bridge A82 to Dumbarton to junct with A814, follow to Helensburgh. Along waterfront 2m on left*

Well-executed modern dishes and wonderful Clyde views

Views over the Firth of Clyde offer a stunning backdrop to this substantial Victorian mansion, now a comfortable, stylish hotel. In the smart restaurant, friendly but informed staff cut through any hint of formality, and the kitchen works around a tranche of modern ideas, producing a starter of smoked cured beef with chargrilled asparagus and a vegetable spring roll. Next up, roast rump of lamb comes with pea and mint purée and potato rösti. Fish appears in the shape of baked whole sea bream with potatoes and olives, coriander salad and tartare sauce. To close, there's chocolate and raspberry torte with milk chocolate ice cream.

Chef James Quinn **Seats** 48, Pr/dining room 40 **Times** 12.30-4.30/6.30-9.30 **Prices** Starter £5.50-£6.95, Main £15.50-£24.50, Dessert £4.95-£6.95 **Wines** 18 bottles under £30, 7 by glass **Parking** 60 **Notes** Afternoon tea fr £9.95, Sunday L £12.95-£19.95, Vegetarian available, Children welcome

STRACHUR Map 20 NN00

AA RESTAURANT OF THE YEAR FOR SCOTLAND 2016–17

Inver Restaurant

Modern Scottish NEW v

tel: 01369 860537 **Strathlachlan PA27 8BU**
email: ask@inverrestaurant.co.uk
dir: *A83, at Cairndow take A815. In Strachur right onto A886. After 2m right onto B8000. Restaurant is signed*

Creative ideas and heavenly views

The uplifting setting on the shores of Loch Fyne is in itself worth the trip out to this unassuming little restaurant in a whitewashed cottage done out with Scandinavian minimalism and a dose of cool, retro styling. Chef Pam Brunton has done time in the renowned kitchen of foodie-mecca Noma in Copenhagen, so it's no surprise to see on-trend Nordic influences appearing in the food too, where foraged ingredients and some eye-opening combinations combine to great effect. Eclectic influences and a creative mind deliver a knockout starter of chanterelle mushroom soup with seared chicken hearts, smoked egg yolk and baked chervil root. Main course brings a head-to-tail serving of pheasant involving confit leg meat in a richly savoury porridge, blood buns topped with a gamey liver partait, and pink-roasted breast with cavolo nero and hispi cabbage, bacon fat emulsion and parsley powder. The kitchen also shows its class with fish – marinated mackerel with baked beetroot, oyster emulsion, crispy seaweed and horseradish cream is a medley of superbly balanced, crystal-clear flavours. Baked quince with buttermilk curds, pink peppercorns, rosehip ice cream and shards of meringue makes a lively, textural finish. The details are spot-on too: excellent sourdough bread and butter are made in-house.

Chef Pamela Brunton **Seats** 35, Pr/dining room 20 **Times** 12-2.30/6.30-9, Closed Xmas, Jan-Feb, Mon-Tue (ex BHs) **Prices** Tasting menu £42-£49, Starter £4.50-£11, Main £12.50-£27, Dessert £5-£7 **Wines** 7 bottles over £30, 9 bottles under £30, 4 by glass **Parking** 20 **Notes** Dinner & Disco/Music & Meal monthly Fri, Steak night monthly, Sunday L £15-£35, Children welcome

TAYNUILT Map 20 NN03

The Taynuilt

Fresh Gastro NEW

tel: 01866 822437 **PA35 1JN**
email: enquiries@taynuilthotel.co.uk **web:** www.taynuilthotel.co.uk
dir: *In Taynuilt, on A85*

A roadside gem offering big flavours

It's not just the colonnaded entrance that makes a good first impression at this white-painted coaching inn. The simplicity of the menu hides some serious skills from the kitchen, whose dishes are big on flavour. Add great local sourcing, including foraging and home smoking, and a real passion from the chef-proprietor and you'll find you've discovered a little gem. Home-made duck liver pâté, for example, comes with Cointreau jelly and home-made sourdough bread, and a leg of Aberdeenshire lamb arrives with home-cured pancetta as well as pea shoots and wild leeks. To finish, forced rhubarb souffle, rhubarb and thyme ice cream and rhubarb anglaise delivers a wonderful intensity of flavour.

Chef John McNulty **Seats** 88, Pr/dining room 18 **Times** 12-9, All-day dining **Prices** Tasting menu £55-£75, Starter £5-£10, Main £10-£26, Dessert £6-£8.50 **Wines** 15 bottles over £30, 44 bottles under £30, 10 by glass **Parking** 14 **Notes** Vegetarian available, Children welcome

NORTH AYRSHIRE

DALRY Map 20 NS24

Braidwoods

Modern Scottish

tel: 01294 833544 **Drumastle Mill Cottage KA24 4LN**
email: keithbraidwood@btconnect.com
dir: *1m from Dalry on Saltcoats road*

Creative cooking in an all-action hotel

In a cottage in the middle of a field near Dalry, this small, unpretentious restaurant has two rooms split by a central fireplace, and an informal, relaxed atmosphere. Open with beetroot-cured gravad lax on beetroot and clementine salad with a potato cake. Main courses impress with their timing and presentation, such as melt-in-the-mouth roast local lamb on wilted spinach, with a mound of cauliflower purée topped with confit neck fillet and a square of dauphinoise, all complemented by rosemary jus. The canapés are great, and puddings impress too, among them Valrhona truffle cake with prune and Armagnac ice cream.

SOUTH AYRSHIRE

AYR Map 20 NS32

Enterkine Country House

 Modern British V

tel: 01292 520580 **Annbank KA6 5AL**
email: mail@enterkine.com **web:** www.enterkine.com
dir: *5m E of Ayr on B743*

Well-crafted contemporary cooking in an elegant country house

Dating from the 1930s, Enterkine is approached via a tree-lined avenue running through its 300 acres. Three sides of Browne's restaurant have huge windows with views of the estate. It's a handsome room, with high-backed upholstered chairs at clothed tables, a polished floor and swagged curtains. The kitchen adds a gently contemporary spin to classic country-house fare, producing starters like goats' cheese soufflé with Meaux mustard sauce and red pepper compôte, while well-conceived main courses see Orkney beef fillet served alongside beef cheek, parsnip purée, spinach and shallots. Puddings make a satisfying conclusion: perhaps iced honey parfait with granola crumble, toffee sauce and golden raisins.

Chef Paul Moffat **Seats** 40, Pr/dining room 14 **Times** 12-2/7-9 **Prices** Fixed L 2 course fr £16.95, Fixed D 3 course £39 **Wines** 7 bottles over £30, 18 bottles under £30, 13 by glass **Parking** 20 **Notes** Sunday L £16.95-£20.95, Children welcome

Fairfield House Hotel

 Modern International

tel: 01292 267461 **12 Fairfield Rd KA7 2AS**
email: reservations@fairfieldhotel.co.uk **web:** www.fairfieldhotel.co.uk
dir: *From A77 to Ayr South. Follow signs for town centre. Left into Miller Rd. At lights turn left, then right into Fairfield Rd*

Modern Scottish food overlooking the Firth of Clyde

A Glasgow tea merchant built Fairfield House as a seaside retreat affording views over the firth towards the Isle of Arran. Confident modern Scottish cooking is the kitchen's forte, with pedigree Scots produce used as the bedrock of an appealing menu of big flavours. Cairngorm grouse is a good bet, particularly in a starter comprising roast breast and a slow-cooked croquette partnered by celeriac and pearl barley risotto and girolles. Mains are equally eye-catching compositions, perhaps another two-way serving – venison this time – its roast loin matched with a steamed pudding, alongside root vegetable Parisienne and creamed potatoes. Finish with a chocolate fondant with coconut sorbet, tuile and jelly.

BALLANTRAE Map 20 NX08

Glenapp Castle

 Modern British V

tel: 01465 831212 **KA26 0NZ**
email: info@glenappcastle.com **web:** www.glenappcastle.com
dir: *S through Ballantrae, cross bridge over River Stinchar, 1st right, castle gates in 1m; use entry system*

Country-house cooking in the baronial style

Round the final corner of the long, narrow driveway and witness the true majesty of the Scottish baronial-style castle, with its battlements and towers, manicured and tiered gardens creating a stunning backdrop. The opulent interior meets all expectations too, with large, high-ceilinged lounges and the dining room done out in rich reds, thick carpeting feeling like cushions underfoot. Tyron Ellul is a master of the art of the modern country-house style, his gently innovative ideas arousing interest without going too far. Timings and seasoning are spot on, and high-end ingredients are the norm. A set six-course dinner menu is the formula, with no choice before the main course. A soup – perhaps garlicky potato velouté with a quail's egg – normally kicks off before something like smoked ham hough 'sausage roll' with piccalilli. Something fishy follows: crisp-skinned seared fillet of sea bass with salade Niçoise, say. The main event could well be honey-basted duck breast, nicely pink, on a smear of date purée with a pastry parcel of confit leg. A pre-dessert precedes the real McCoy, which could be chocolate ganache atop a slab of chocolate in a comb pattern with a scoop of smooth milk ice cream, the plate dotted with salted caramel.

Chef Tyron Ellul **Seats** 34, Pr/dining room 20 **Times** 12.30-2/6.30-9.30 **Prices** Fixed L 3 course £29.50-£39.50, Fixed D 3 course £45, Tasting menu £65 **Wines** 115 bottles over £30, 9 by glass **Parking** 20 **Notes** Tasting menu D 6 course, Sunday L £29.50-£39.50, Children 5 yrs+

TROON Map 20 NS33

Lochgreen House Hotel

Modern French

tel: 01292 313343 **Monktonhill Rd, Southwood KA10 7EN**
email: lochgreen@costley-hotels.co.uk **web:** www.lochgreenhouse.com
dir: *From A77 follow Prestwick Airport signs, take B749 to Troon, hotel on left, 1m from junct*

Modern cooking in a stunningly restored manor house

Whichever way you come at it, Lochgreen is enviably located – not far off the M77, handy for Prestwick airport, next to the greens of Royal Troon, and with spellbinding views over the Ayrshire coast. Well-tended gardens add to the allure, while the Tapestry restaurant with its tartan carpeting and partly timbered ceiling is the first choice among various eating options. Executive chef Andrew Costley's menus are easy to comprehend, with simplicity of presentation allowing the prime materials their full value. That can be seen in a starter of slow-cooked pork belly in mushroom consommé garnished with langoustines, or a salad of dressed crab and home-smoked trout with avocado. Dazzling Scottish produce occupies centre-stage again at main, when Highland venison loin appears with a light suet pudding and pear variations, in a sauce of dark chocolate and blackcurrant, while Anster cheddar is crumbled onto the smoked haddock and leek risotto that partners a fillet of cod. Finish with a citrus trio comprising lemon posset, orange jelly and lime macaroon, or consider the attractions of a cranberry and orange parfait served with honeycomb, dressed in Drambuie. Local and continental cheeses roll around on a trolley, and there are smartly turned-out canapés and petits fours to fill in the details.

Chef Andrew Costley, Iain Conway **Seats** 80, Pr/dining room 40 **Times** 12-2/7-10 **Prices** Prices not confirmed **Wines** 70 bottles over £30, 40 bottles under £30, 11 by glass **Parking** 90 **Notes** Afternoon tea, Sunday L, Vegetarian available, Children welcome

MacCallums of Troon

International, Seafood

tel: 01292 319339 **The Harbour KA10 6DH**
dir: *Phone for directions*

Simple, fresh seafood on the harbourside

There should really only be one thing on your mind when dining at the Oyster Bar. It's all about the bass, the turbot, the sole... for this is a seafood restaurant in a glorious harbourside setting within a converted pump house. The fish does the talking in a first-course tempura turbot, with suitably thin and crisp batter and a perky garlic mayo to dip them into, and in a main-course dish of lemon sole with two plump langoustines and garlic butter. It is simple stuff cooked with care, which is also true of desserts such as steamed date sponge pudding with salted caramel and hazelnut ice cream.

TURNBERRY Map 20 NS20

Turnberry Resort, Scotland

@@ Traditional French

tel: 01655 331000 **Maidens Rd KA26 9LT**
email: turnberry@luxurycollection.com **web:** www.turnberryresort.co.uk
dir: *From Glasgow take A77, M77 S towards Stranraer, 2m past Kirkoswald, follow signs for A719/Turnberry. Hotel 500mtrs on right*

Classical dining at renowned coastal golf resort

The 1906 restaurant at this luxurious golf-centric hotel, with sweeping views across greens and fairways to the hump of Ailsa Craig, is named after the year it opened. The setting resembles a giant wedding cake, and the kitchen puts a luxury modern spin on Escoffier's classics. Foie gras gets its own section, starting perhaps with a brûlée with Sauternes-poached fruit, pumpernickel granola and gingerbread, then follow that with something from Escoffier's recipe book – perhaps honey-glazed duck suprême with braised chicory, baby turnips and pan juices. For a spot of table-side theatre, finish with a Grand Marnier-flambéed crêpe Suzette with orange and vanilla ice cream.

DUMFRIES & GALLOWAY

AUCHENCAIRN Map 21 NX75

Balcary Bay Hotel

@@ Modern French, European

tel: 01556 640217 & 640311 **Shore Rd DG7 1QZ**
email: reservations@balcary-bay-hotel.co.uk **web:** www.balcary-bay-hotel.co.uk
dir: *On A711 between Dalbeattie & Kirkcudbright. In Auchencairn follow signs to Balcary along shore road for 2m*

Modern country-house cooking on the Solway coast

The solid-looking white hotel stands on the shore of the Solway Firth with views across the water to Heston Isle and the Lake District beyond. Soak up the views from the restaurant, a pleasant environment in which to enjoy some snappy cooking. The hotel might be in a secluded spot, but the kitchen team proves to be a forward-looking lot, turning out starters of sea bass with fennel and orange salad, followed by Scottish salmon with herb cream, or pan-fried loin of local lamb enriched with port sauce. Finish with dark chocolate torte served with chocolate sauce and raspberry sorbet.

Chef Craig McWilliam **Seats** 55 **Times** 12-2/7-8.30, Closed Dec-Jan, L Mon-Sat **Wines** 54 bottles over £30, 43 bottles under £30, 12 by glass **Parking** 50 **Notes** D 4 course £46.75, Sunday L £26.25, Vegetarian available, Children welcome

GATEHOUSE OF FLEET Map 20 NX55

Cally Palace Hotel

@ Traditional V

tel: 01557 814341 **Cally Dr DG7 2DL**
email: info@callypalace.co.uk **web:** www.callypalace.co.uk
dir: *From A74(M) take A75, at Gatehouse take B727. Hotel on left*

Country-house dining using Scottish produce on the Solway coast

Old-school opulence, playing golf from dawn til dusk and upmarket pampering sessions are the watchwords in this Georgian country manor in 150 acres of parkland on the Solway coast, where a pianist tinkling away in the background adds a softer note to proceedings in the formal restaurant. The kitchen delivers gently-modernised country-house cooking built on soundly-sourced Scottish produce, setting off with crispy confit duck leg with Puy lentil cassoulet and Bramley apple purée, followed by pan-fried venison haunch matched with dauphinoise potatoes, green beans, celeriac purée and grand veneur sauce. End with caramelised banana with passionfruit syrup and a lime tuile.

Chef Jamie Muirhead **Seats** 110, Pr/dining room 25 **Times** 12-1/6.45-9, Closed 3 Jan-early Feb **Prices** Tasting menu fr £32.50, Starter £3.95-£6.95, Main £10.95-£18.95, Dessert £4.95-£6.95 **Wines** 35 bottles over £30, 55 bottles under £30, 11 by glass **Parking** 70 **Notes** Afternoon tea £15.95, Sunday L, Children welcome

GRETNA Map 21 NY36

Smiths at Gretna Green

@@ Modern British, International

tel: 01461 337007 **Gretna Green DG16 5EA**
email: info@smithsgretnagreen.com **web:** www.smithsgretnagreen.com
dir: *From M74 junct 22 follow signs to Old Blacksmith's Shop. Hotel opposite*

Imaginative cooking in sexy surroundings

Smiths certainly extends the options for those fleeing here with marriage on their minds, and makes a stylish stay to celebrate a landmark anniversary. The imaginative menus are especially good at game, seen in a starter of heather-smoked hare with pickled pear purée and beetroot pannacotta, perhaps followed by venison loin with a faggot, a strip of liver, roasted celeriac and puréed chestnuts. Nori-wrapped salmon in crab and white bean chowder is one of the fish possibilities. Try carrot cake with cinnamon ice cream, and don't miss the excellent bread, which comes in a plant pot.

Chef Phillip Woodcock **Seats** 60, Pr/dining room 18 **Times** 12-9.30, All-day dining, Closed 25 Dec **Prices** Prices not confirmed **Wines** 31 bottles over £30, 37 bottles under £30, 12 by glass **Parking** 115 **Notes** Tea time menu 3 course £10.95 4.30-6pm, Sunday L, Vegetarian available, Children welcome

MOFFAT Map 21 NT00

Brodies

@ Modern British

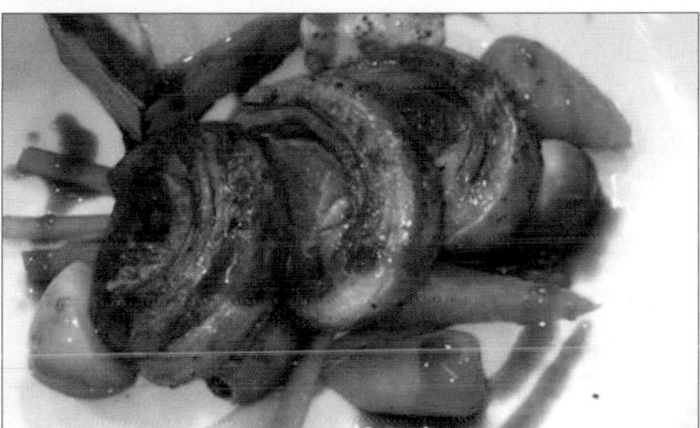

tel: 01683 222870 **Holm St DG10 9EB**
email: whatscooking@brodiesofmoffat.co.uk **web:** www.brodiesofmoffat.co.uk
dir: *M74 junct 15 towards Selkirk, take 2nd right turn*

Bistro-style cooking in a contemporary setting

Just off the high street, there's a contemporary sheen to Brodies that really pays off in the evening when it becomes quite a smart dining spot. The bistro-style menu offers some interesting stuff made with high-quality ingredients. Kick off with a rustic tomato tarte Tatin, say, with melting goats' cheese and basil dressing, or a double-baked Lockerbie cheddar soufflé, and move on to a main course of smoked haddock with Parisienne potatoes. Pan-fried rib-eye arrives with chips stacked Jenga-style, plus onion rings, pea purée and mushroom fricassée, while a honey mascarpone pannacotta passes the wobble test. Sunday lunch is a classic affair.

Chef Russell Pearce **Seats** 40 **Times** 10am-11pm, All-day dining, Closed 25-27 Dec, D Tue-Wed (Oct-Mar) **Prices** Prices not confirmed **Wines** 2 bottles over £30, 21 bottles under £30, 18 by glass **Parking** On street **Notes** Early doors menu 5.30-7pm, Sunday L, Vegetarian available, Children welcome

PORTPATRICK Map 20 NW95

Knockinaam Lodge

 Modern Scottish V 

tel: 01776 810471 **DG9 9AD**
email: reservations@knockinaamlodge.com **web:** www.knockinaamlodge.com
dir: *From A77, follow signs to Portpatrick, then tourist signs to Knockinaam Lodge*

Well-judged cooking in splendid Galloway isolation

When you're after that elusive away-from-it-all experience, Knockinaam Lodge fits the bill like few other places around the UK. The drive along the single-track lane through beautiful countryside helps to create a sense of anticipation before the former Victorian hunting lodge comes into view. Set in 30 acres of lush grounds, the place has its own private pebble beach and views across to Ireland on a fine day. It's so out-of-the way that Churchill and Eisenhower met here secretly during WWII. Kick off with canapés and a snifter in one of the lounges before heading into the genteel, traditional dining room, where the no-choice daily menu begins with an amuse-bouche of rich devilled kidney. The kitchen's modern Scottish repertoire delivers grilled fillet of halibut with pickled fennel and an orange and coriander reduction, followed by hazelnut-crusted roast loin of Lochmaben roe deer with spiced carrot purée, baked baby beetroot and juniper, thyme and port sauce. Cappuccino of leek and thyme with truffle oil might intervene between starter and main course, and a trenchant lime sorbet paves the way for a finale of caramel pannacotta with poached William pears and honeycomb. At the end, log fires and an oak-panelled bar stocked with more than 120 malts await.

Chef Anthony Pierce **Seats** 32, Pr/dining room 18 **Times** 12-1.15/7-9 **Wines** 350 bottles over £30, 30 bottles under £30, 7 by glass **Parking** 20 **Notes** Fixed L 4 course £40, D 5 course £67.50, Sunday L £32.50, Children 12 yrs+

SANQUHAR Map 21 NS70

Blackaddie House Hotel

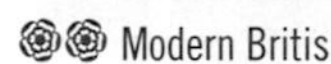 Modern British

tel: 01659 50270 **Blackaddie Rd DG4 6JJ**
email: ian@blackaddiehotel.co.uk **web:** www.blackaddiehotel.co.uk
dir: *300mtrs off A76 on north side of Sanquhar*

Scottish country cooking with fish a strong suit

This stone-built house on the east bank of the River Nith is in the perfect location for sourcing top-drawer produce. Salt-cod brandade with French beans in shallot vinaigrette is the powerful, simple opener to a Gourmet Menu that might roll on with a fricassée of mussels, prawns and shrimps with leeks and caviar. Firm classical underpinnings produce a Scotch beef study that combines sautéed fillet, a sticky ragoût and beef terrine with accompanying greens, while salmon comes with roast chicory and crushed new potatoes in chive cream. To finish, lemon posset appears with raspberries, pistachios, honeycomb and meringue, and the selection of impeccable Scottish cheeses is served with home-made oatcakes.

Chef Ian McAndrew **Seats** 20, Pr/dining room 20 **Times** 12-2/6.30-9 **Prices** Fixed L 2 course £29.75, Tasting menu £75 **Wines** 53 bottles over £30, 14 bottles under £30, 12 by glass **Parking** 20 **Notes** Gourmet tasting menu 7 course, Fixed D 4 course £55, Sunday L £29.75-£36, Vegetarian available, Children welcome

STRANRAER Map 20 NX06

Corsewall Lighthouse Hotel

 Modern Scottish

tel: 01776 853220 **Corsewall Point, Kirkcolm DG9 0QG**
email: info@lighthousehotel.co.uk **web:** www.lighthousehotel.co.uk
dir: *Take A718 from Stranraer to Kirkcolm, then follow B718 signed Lighthouse*

Magical location for Scottish-influenced food

Corsewall is a hotel, restaurant and still, following automation in 1994, an essential beacon for shipping in the Irish Sea. Perched high above the waves, it's reached via a winding, single-track road. With candlelit, dark wooden tables, the maritime-themed restaurant occupies what used to be living quarters and stores. The daily changing menu keeps things relatively simple, so you might start with Kirkcudbright 'hot-smoked' peppered mackerel, before roast Braehead Estate guinea fowl supreme and venison sausage. Finish with richly flavoured treacle and almond tart with vanilla ice cream and brandy-scented cream swirls. Only one red and white wine is available by the glass.

THORNHILL Map 21 NX89

The Buccleuch and Queensberry Arms Hotel

 Modern Scottish V

tel: 01848 323101 & 330215 **112 Drumlanrig St DG3 5LU**
email: info@bqahotel.com **web:** www.bqahotel.com
dir: *On A76 in centre of Thornhill*

Hotel dining with a local flavour

The BQA to its friends, this family-run hotel has undergone an extensive refurbishment and emerged looking good and fit for purpose in the 21st century. There's a satisfying Scottish-ness to the place, which extends to the culinary output. The region's produce figures large on menus that show Pan-European leanings and no lack of ambition. Pancetta-wrapped scallops with cauliflower purée and roasted spring onion might set the ball rolling, ahead of main-course halibut with leeks, kale and seafood sauce. To finish, a wee dram of whisky adds backbone to sticky toffee pudding with vanilla ice cream, or you could go savoury with local cheeses, oatcakes and chutney.

Chef Will Pottinger **Seats** 52, Pr/dining room 22 **Times** 12-10, All-day dining **Prices** Starter £4-£9, Main £9-£25, Dessert £1.95-£9 **Wines** 22 bottles over £30, 16 bottles under £30, 9 by glass **Parking** 100 **Notes** Brunch Sat-Sun, Gluten-free menu, Sunday L £14, Children welcome

WEST DUNBARTONSHIRE

BALLOCH Map 20 NS38

The Cameron Grill

Modern British

tel: 01389 722582 & 755565 **Cameron House on Loch Lomond G83 8QZ**
email: reservations@cameronhouse.co.uk **web:** www.cameronhouse.co.uk
dir: *M8 (W) junct 30 for Erskine Bridge. A82 for Crainlarich. 14m, at rdbt signed Luss, hotel on right*

Classy lochside steak venue

In a splendid location on the banks of Loch Lomond, Cameron House is a stylish blend of tartans and luxurious contemporary looks. The steaks here are truly exceptional, cooked on a Josper grill from locally reared Ayrshire beef. A 28-day aged rib-eye with onion rings, roasted shallots, plum tomato, blue cheese sauce and triple-cooked chips should satisfy. Otherwise, start with chicken liver and foie gras parfait and pickled veg, then move on to cannon and sweetbreads of lamb with crisped risotto. Finish with Valrhona chocolate ganache with whisky ice cream and raspberries. The hotel is also home to the fine-dining Martin Wishart at Loch Lomond

Martin Wishart at Loch Lomond

Modern French V NOTABLE WINE LIST

tel: 01389 722504 **Cameron House on Loch Lomond G83 8QZ**
email: info@mwlochlomond.co.uk
dir: *M8 (W) junct 30 for Erskine Bridge. A82 for Crainlarich. 14m, at rdbt signed Luss, hotel on right*

Refined, intelligent cooking on the shores of Loch Lomond

Interpreting Wishart's contemporary take on French classics here is head chef Graeme Cheevers, who keeps faith with the house style of razor-sharp, refined modern cooking. What a setting he has: the stately castellated mansion of Cameron House is the base for a lochside restaurant looking over the banks of Loch Lomond. It's worthy of a glossy interiors magazine, delivering five-star treatment and everything from a chic spa and posh lodges tucked away in the countryside to a handsome contemporary dining room that looks rather dashing with lime-green banquettes and Regency stripes. There's a bargain three-course lunch deal, but otherwise it's six- or eight-course tasters with dedicated veggie versions. From the six-course menu, you might start with marinated sea bream with avocado, radish and bergamot dressing, with subsequent courses bringing on pressed foie gras and smoked eel with balsamic, beetroot and horseradish. Flavours ring clear and true and there's finely-judged precision in the execution. Saddle of roe deer arrives with celeriac, black garlic and caramelised onion jus. Among desserts, Valrhona milk and dark chocolate is matched with praline, Williams pear and salted caramel, while the selection of pasteurised and unpasteurised cheese is well worth checking out. Be sure to give the impressive Francophile wine list the attention it deserves.

Chef Graeme Cheevers **Seats** 40 **Times** 12-2.30/6.30-10, Closed 25-26 Dec, 1 Jan, Mon-Tue, L Wed-Fri **Prices** Fixed L 3 course £32.50, Fixed D 3 course £75 **Wines** 240 bottles over £30, 12 bottles under £30, 12 by glass **Parking** 150 **Notes** Tasting menu 6/8 course, Du Jour L 3 course, ALC menu £75, Sunday L £32.50, Children welcome

CLYDEBANK **Map 20 NS47**

Golden Jubilee Conference Hotel

Modern British

tel: 0141 951 6000 **Beardmore St G81 4SA**
email: hotel@goldenjubilee.scot.nhs.uk **web:** www.goldenjubileehotel.com
dir: *M8 junct 19, follow signs for Clydeside Expressway to Glasgow road, then A814 (Dumbarton Road), then follow Clydebank Business Park signs. Hotel on left*

Intimate dining in a conference hotel

A hotel and conference centre next to the Jubilee hospital, the Golden Jubilee Conference Hotel is a multi-purpose hub for business meetings, fitness workouts and aspirational dining. A newish spin on a modern classic produces a trio of scallops with crisp pancetta and three matching pyramids of a rather salty cauliflower pannacotta amid the terrines and ballotines of the starter listing. The main event might be pork loin poached in sage butter alongside garlicky mash and apple purée in raisin-dotted jus, or cod with sautéed potatoes and confit fennel. Ecclefechan tart with toffee ice cream is a fine regional speciality, or there may be three variations on apple – Tatin, pannacotta and sorbet.

Chef Iain Ramsay **Seats** 36, Pr/dining room 200 **Times** 6.30-10, Closed Sun, L all week **Prices** Starter £5.95-£8.75, Main £10-£27.50, Dessert £6-£9 **Wines** 12 by glass **Parking** 300 **Notes** Seasonal menu, Vegetarian available, Children welcome

CITY OF DUNDEE

DUNDEE **Map 21 NO43**

Castlehill Restaurant

Modern Scottish

tel: 01382 220008 **22-26 Exchange St DD1 3DL**
email: enquire@castlehillrestaurant.co.uk
dir: *From High St, travel down Castle St. Left into Exchange St. On left*

Modern dining down a cobbled lane

Close to the city's booming waterfront, Castlehill is a sophisticated spot with a decorative style evoking the colours and textures of Scotland. There's a real sense of place to the menu, too, with Scottish ingredients to the fore, while the cooking is thoroughly modern and creative. A starter of wild rabbit with an artichoke pearl barley risotto allows the central ingredients to shine, or go for the more cutting-edge duck egg cooked precisely at 63° and served with pineapple. Among the main coursess, wild halibut with gnocchi and coconut competes for your attention with Highland venison, and, to finish, blood orange soufflé is matched with liquorice root ice cream.

Chef Graham Campbell **Seats** 40 **Times** 12-2.30/5.30-10, Closed Sun-Mon **Prices** Fixed L 2 course £15, Fixed D 3 course £36, Tasting menu £55-£75 **Wines** 14 bottles over £30, 9 bottles under £30, 13 by glass **Parking** On street **Notes** Vegetarian available, Children welcome

Malmaison Dundee

British, French

tel: 01382 339715 **44 Whitehall Crescent DD1 4AY**
email: brasseriemgr.dundee@malmaison.com **web:** www.malmaison.com
dir: *Phone for directions*

Modern brasserie cooking in boutique style

The Dundee branch of the chain is a majestic old hotel with a domed ceiling above a central wrought-iron staircase, with the Malmaison trademark sexy looks, which run through to the candlelit brasserie's darkly atmospheric colour scheme. The menu plays the modern brasserie game too, setting out with mussels cooked in beer with pancetta, served with rustic bread. A main course might be surf and turf consisting of tender beef and tempura prawns with bacon, gruyère, onion rings and shallot mayonnaise, while red meat fans will be overjoyed that there's a Josper grill for those dry-aged steaks. Valrhona chocolate cheesecake wraps things up in style.

Chef Michael Fames **Seats** 90, Pr/dining room 12 **Times** 12-10.30, All-day dining, Closed D 25 Dec **Prices** Prices not confirmed **Wines** 25 bottles over £30, 16 bottles under £30, 41 by glass **Parking** Greenmarket multi-storey **Notes** Sunday L, Vegetarian available, Children welcome

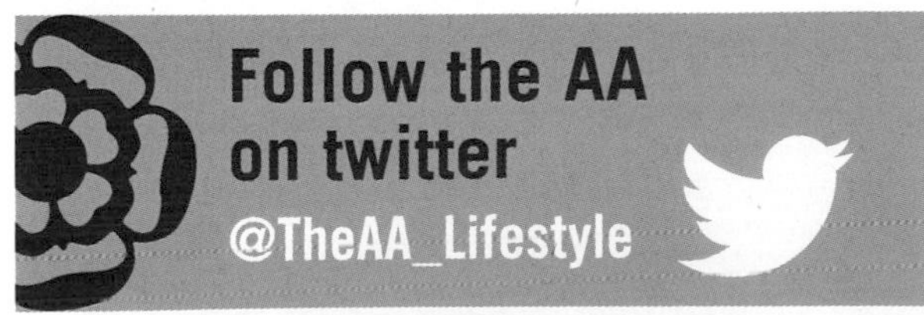

The Tayberry Restaurant

594 Brook Street, Broughty Ferry, DD5 2EA

Bookings & Enquiries T: +44 (0)1382 698 280

info@tayberryrestaurant.com

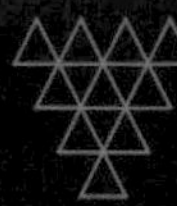

THE TAYBERRY

Opening Hours

Tuesday - Saturday: Lunch 12:00pm - 2:00pm

Dinner 6:00pm - 9:00pm

Sunday Lunch 12:00pm - 4:00pm

Inspired by his love of food and his desire to raise Tayside's profile on the culinary map, Chef Proprietor, Adam Newth opened The Tayberry Restaurant in November 2015. Situated in a beautiful coastal setting, overlooking the Mouth O' The Tay in Broughty Ferry, Dundee, The Tayberry Restaurant offers a contemporary dining experience, using a combination of modern and classic techniques to showcase the best of Scotland's natural larder by offering a variety of innovative and seasonal menus, changing regularly to reflect the seasonality of the produce available.

"Team Tayberry" is at the heart of all that The Tayberry Restaurant strives to achieve. Led and nurtured by Chef Proprietor, Adam Newth, his fresh and dynamic team reflect his dedicated work ethic and ambition to take The Tayberry from strength to strength.

Adam is passionate about discovering new talent and developing it for the future and is always keen to hear from aspiring Chefs and Front of House staff with an interest in a career in hospitality.

The Tayberry Restaurant offers a relaxed, contemporary Scottish fine dining experience set across two levels in a beautiful coastal setting, overlooking the Mouth O' The Tay. The décor is neutral and subtly Scottish, accented in purple tones, giving a nod to our namesake, the tayberry - a soft fruit, akin to a black raspberry, which was first cultivated in the Dundee area in 1979 and named after the River Tay.

DUNDEE *continued*

The Tayberry

Scottish NEW

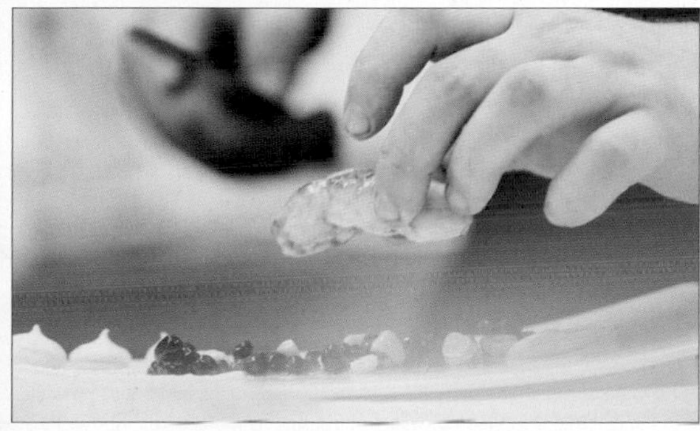

tel: 01382 698280 **594 Brook St, Broughty Ferry DD5 2EA**
email: info@tayberryrestaurant.com **web:** www.tayberryrestaurant.com
dir: *From Dundee City follow A92 & signs for Broughty Ferry. At Brook St follow towards the Esplanade. Restaurant at end of street overlooking the beach*

Up-and-coming eatery with river views

This relaxed, contemporary operation has made quite a splash on the local culinary scene. Spread over two floors, its purple-toned decor is a nod to the namesake berry, and views across the River Tay from the first floor are a real bonus. Focused, modern dishes allow local produce to shine, setting out with foraged mushroom gnocchi, flavoured with rosemary and served with cauliflower purée, parmesan crisps and foam. Next up, pork belly and crackling comes with creamed potato and a sharp pickled walnut sauce to balance the richness of the pork, while dessert brings poached pear with chocolate ganache, Parma violet sweets and caramelised hazelnuts.

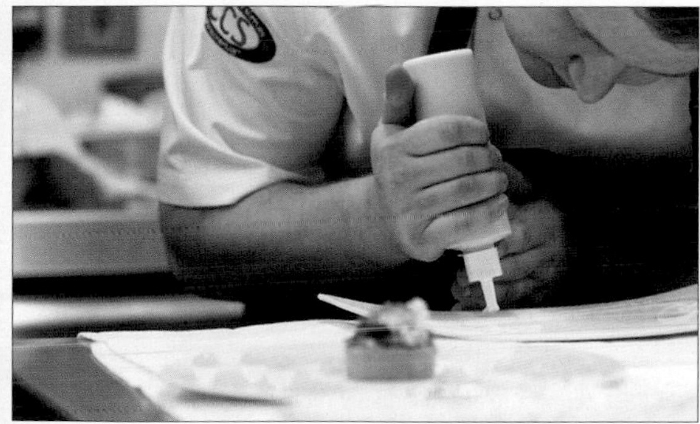

Chef Adam Newth **Seats** 36, Pr/dining room 16 **Times** 12-2/6-9, Closed 25-27 Dec, Mon, D Sun **Prices** Fixed L 2 course £18, Fixed D 3 course £36-£40, Tasting menu £55-£60 **Wines** 14 bottles over £30, 4 bottles under £30, 7 by glass **Parking** On street **Notes** Dish of the day + glass of wine £12.95, Sunday L £18-£22, Vegetarian available, Children until 8pm

See advert opposite

CITY OF EDINBURGH

EDINBURGH Map 21 NT27

Acanthus

Modern Scottish

tel: 0131 550 4500 **Macdonald Holyrood Hotel, Holyrood Rd EH8 8AU**
email: holyrood@macdonald-hotels.co.uk **web:** www.macdonaldhotels.co.uk
dir: *Parallel to Royal Mile, near Holyrood Palace*

Stylish dining option in a modern hotel

In Edinburgh's historic old town and just a couple of minutes from Royal Mile and the Scottish Parliament, this modern hotel is well positioned and the elegant, brasserie-style Acanthus restaurant is a destination in itself. The kitchen makes good use of prime Scottish ingredients in the contemporary European dishes. Flying the Scottish flag, a robust starter of cullen skink made with peat-smoked haddock is a nod to tradition, with a main of 24-hour cooked beef steak, root vegetable mash and thyme jus bringing things bang up to date. Finish with the glazed lemon tart and raspberry sorbet.

The Atelier

Modern European

tel: 0131 629 1344 **159-161 Morrison St EH3 8AG**
email: info@theatelierrestaurant.co.uk
dir: *In the centre of Haymarket, 0.2m from station*

Informal urban dining with concentrated flair

The Atelier is a culinary partnership of two ambitious and much-travelled chefs, whose output demonstrates accuracy, balance and flair. First up could be crisped pork belly bedded on deep-fried shredded leek, with braised chicory and red pepper jelly. Sturdy hunks of meat such as venison haunch or 10oz rib-eye seem to have raided the tuckshop for their accompaniments – cocoa nibs in the jus for the former, a revamped béarnaise of white chocolate and prosecco for the steak. If you've held off from chocolate thus far, choose a chai-scented opéra gâteau and dark choc ice cream to finish, or else go for nougat parfait full of glorious chewy bits.

Chef Maciek Zielinski **Seats** 32 **Times** 12-2.30/5.30-10.30, Closed 25-26 Dec, 2 wks Jan, Mon, L 1 Jan **Prices** Fixed L 2 course £14.90, Fixed D 3 course £17.90-£18.90, Tasting menu £50-£60, Starter £4.50-£9.90, Main £14-£19.90, Dessert £7.20-£10.50 **Wines** 13 bottles over £30, 23 bottles under £30, 14 by glass **Notes** Sunday L £14.90-£18.90, Vegetarian available, Children 5yrs+

Bia Bistrot

British, French

tel: 0131 452 8453 **19 Colinton Rd EH10 5DP**
email: info@biabistrot.co.uk
dir: *From city centre at Holy corner turn right onto Colinton Rd*

Classy bistro fare that is tasty and well-crafted

The 'Bia' element of the name is the Gaelic for food, the 'Bistrot' part more self-evident, and it's the winning setting for the cooking of husband-and-wife team Roisin and Matthias Llorente. Their Irish/Scottish and French/Spanish backgrounds are apparent in well-crafted and satisfying food in a charming and easy-going environment with wooden tables and smart leather seats. Things get off to a flying start with smoked pork belly and celeriac and apple remoulade, then mains bring hake fillet with smoked haddock velouté, spinach and potato. Finish with chocolate and polenta cake with orange and cardamom cream. There's a good-value set lunch and early-evening menu, too.

Chef Roisin & Matthias Llorente **Seats** 60, Pr/dining room 24
Times 12-2.30/5-10, Closed 1st 2 wks Jan, 2nd wk Jul, Sun-Mon **Prices** Prices not confirmed **Wines** 8 bottles over £30, 16 bottles under £30, 9 by glass **Notes** Pre-theatre menu 5-6pm, Vegetarian available, Children welcome

EDINBURGH *continued*

Bistro Provence

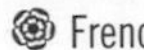 French

tel: 0131 344 4295 **88 Commercial St EH6 6LX**
email: reservations@bistroprovence.co.uk
dir: *Phone for directions*

Traditional Provençal cooking on the waterfront

Provençal native Michael Fons left a post at Gidleigh Park, Chagford, to open a restaurant homage to his native region in the Scottish capital. The waterfront venue has a wide-windowed frontage and is stylishly modern, with unclothed tables making a neutral background for the food. Fish soup with rouille and garlic croûtons has a reassuring place on the menu, and you might find confit pork belly with rosemary mash and apple and Calvados sauce or stuffed guinea fowl with smoked cauliflower purée among the mains. To finish, there's traditional crème brûlée or Muscat and olive oil cake with poached berries.

Chef Michael Fons **Seats** 45, Pr/dining room 12 **Times** 12-3/6-10.30, Closed 1-15 Oct, Mon **Prices** Fixed L 2 course fr £12.95, Fixed D 3 course fr £27.50, Tasting menu fr £39 **Wines** 16 bottles over £30, 11 bottles under £30, 11 by glass **Parking** 20 **Notes** Tasting menu 4 course, Special offer L menu £10.50, Sunday L £10.50-£27, Vegetarian available, Children welcome

The Bon Vivant

Contemporary European

tel: 0131 225 3275 **55 Thistle St EH2 1DY**
email: info@bonvivantedinburgh.co.uk
dir: *Phone for directions*

Vibrant small-plate dining in a trendy spot

Tapas-style grazing and sharing is the drill at this trendy cocktail bar and eatery. The kitchen takes its inspiration mainly from the Med, but global accents pop up here and there, so get started with crab cake with spicy seafood bisque mayonnaise, crispy squid with chilli jam, or crispy pork belly glazed with soy. The small-plate format isn't compulsory: larger servings deliver guinea fowl marinated in North African spices with tabbouleh, coriander yogurt, rose harissa and pomegranate, or perhaps salmon with crab-crushed potatoes and cucumber and basil sauce vièrge. Finish with salted caramel and chocolate tart with passionfruit ice cream.

Chef Martin Collins **Seats** 30 **Times** 12-10, All-day dining, Closed 25 Dec, 1 Jan **Prices** Starter £4-£6, Main £13-£18 **Wines** 19 bottles over £30, 21 bottles under £30, 40 by glass **Notes** Vegetarian available, Children 5 yrs+

Britannia Spice

Indian, Thai, Bangladeshi NEW v

tel: 0131 555 2255 **150 Commercial St EH6 6LB**
email: info@britanniaspice.co.uk
dir: *Near to Ocean Terminal*

A taste of Asia in the docks

Named after the famous ship that is docked a short distance away, the award-winning Britannia Spice occupies a former whisky warehouse, with some nautical themed adornments adding to the seafaring vibe. That said, it's a simple and stylish place, with burnished wooden tables and some banquette seating. The menu contains lots of dishes that might be considered curry-house classics, but there's a lot more besides, with the culinary cultures of Thailand, Bangladesh, Nepal and Sri Lanka among those explored within its pages. Start with macher bhorta, for example, which is baked fish mixed with onions, mushrooms and green chillies, or chicken pakora, moving on to murgh musallam or Thai sesame chicken.

Chef Abu Zaman **Seats** 130 **Times** 12-2.15/5-11.15, Closed L Sun **Prices** Fixed L 2 course £9.95, Fixed D 3 course £19.95-£24.95, Tasting menu £9.95, Starter £3.95-£5.95, Main £8.95-£17.95, Dessert £2.25-£4.25 **Wines** 1 bottle over £30, 17 bottles under £30, 2 by glass **Notes** Children welcome

Café Royal

Modern Scottish

tel: 0131 556 1884 **19 West Register St EH2 2AA**
email: info@caferoyal.org.uk
dir: *Just off Princes St, close to Waverley Station, opposite Balmoral Hotel*

Victorian baroque grand dining

The Café Royal's Victorian-baroque interiors simply cry out to be the scene of grand dining with their gilt pillars, panelled ceilings and stained windows. These days, traditional Scots fare mingles with modern thinking on menus that open with oysters on mounds of crushed ice, but get into their stride with mussels in Thai broth, and a sweetly alluring main course of duck breast and confit leg on sticky red cabbage with sweet potato purée in port jus. Fish might be straightforward baked cod with asparagus in hollandaise, or monkfish in Goan-style coconut curry. A layered torte of salted caramel on chocolate biscuit base is well complemented by its benchmark vanilla ice.

Calistoga Restaurant

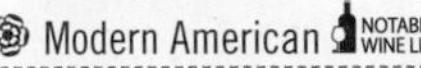
Modern American NOTABLE WINE LIST

tel: 0131 225 1233 **70 Rose St, North Ln EH2 3DX**
email: bookings@calistoga.co.uk
dir: *In North Lane off Rose St, between Frederick St & Castle St*

West Coast eating and drinking in a cobbled back alley

Calistoga is a shrine to California's dynamic wine scene. Wine references and bottles abound, as does a suitably laid-back West Coast mood, the menus naturally following suit with the likes of corn chowder and flat-iron steaks. That chowder is rich and creamy, with carrots, butter beans, celery and potato floating about amid the sweetcorn, and might be followed by chilli-battered pollack with aubergine and sweet potato bake in dill sauce. Dessert may be vanilla pannacotta with praline or there's a peanut butter and chocolate blondie with toffee sauce up for grabs. The wine list is an extended reminder of the versatility and ambitious reach of American viticulture.

Chef Marco Cavallaro **Seats** 45, Pr/dining room 32 **Times** 12-2.30/5-10, Closed 26 Dec **Prices** Fixed L 2 course £12-£14, Fixed D 3 course fr £27, Tasting menu fr £78, Starter £6-£12, Main £16-£28, Dessert £6.50-£10 **Wines** 38 bottles over £30, 75 bottles under £30, 14 by glass **Notes** Pre-theatre 2 course 5-6pm £12, Sunday L fr £12, Vegetarian available, Children welcome

Castle Terrace Restaurant

 Scottish, French V  NOTABLE WINE LIST

tel: 0131 229 1222 **33-35 Castle Ter EH1 2EL**
email: info@castleterracerestaurant.com
dir: *Close to Edinburgh Castle, at the bottom of Lady Lawson St on Castle Terrace*

Creative cooking with panache near the Castle

Castle Terrace underwent a £1m facelift at the start of 2016, which included a full refurbishment of the kitchen and restaurant and the creation of a new private dining room, chef's table and wine cellar. Opened in 2010 by Dominic Jack and Tom Kitchin, this thoroughly contemporary place mirrors the same 'from nature to plate' cooking ethos as Kitchin's eponymous restaurant nearby. Using classic French techniques, the modern cooking produces unpretentious dishes that excite with their technical flair and dazzling presentation. Scottish raw materials may be the cornerstone of the kitchen but the chefs are not afraid of giving produce from Rungis market in Paris star billing. From the à la carte menu, begin with seared hand-dived Orkney scallop served with a light curry sauce, or a velouté of celeriac with Dunsyre Blue cheese ravioli. Follow with roasted darne of monkfish with a ragout of haricot coco beans, mussel and anchovy, or saddle of venison with celery, celeriac, apple and caramelised walnuts. Desserts are no less irresistible: mango and lime marshmallow, say, with pistachio cream and mango sorbet. A range of menus includes a set lunch option and a 'land and sea' tasting version. The international wine list includes an excellent choice by the glass.

Chef Dominic Jack **Seats** 75, Pr/dining room 16 **Times** 12-2.15/6.30-10, Closed 20 Dec-19 Jan, Sun-Mon **Prices** Fixed L 3 course £29.50, Tasting menu fr £75, Starter £13-£19, Main £26-£42, Dessert £12-£15 **Wines** 330 bottles over £30, 4 bottles under £30, 29 by glass **Parking** NCP Castle Terrace **Notes** Children 5 yrs+

Chop Chop

Traditional Chinese

tel: 0131 221 1155 & 440 4708 **248 Morrison St, Haymarket EH3 8DT**
email: yin@chop-chop.co.uk
dir: *From Haymarket Station, restaurant 150yds up Morrison St*

Dumplings a go-go at a charming Chinese café

Jian Wang opened Chop Chop in 1997 with the intention of supplying jiaozi, the traditional dumplings of her native Dongbei (in northeast China) to an unsuspecting UK public. Essentially a dim sum format, the menus feature little bites full of savoury intensity, textural variety and spice. Fried pork and prawn guo tie (pot-stickers) are wonderful dipped in rice vinegar and soy, while the boiled items include beef and chilli, lamb and leek, and chicken. Other successful orders are crispy squid in sesame seeds and lemongrass, cumin-seeded lamb, and sides such as gingery bean sprout salad, and garlic-fried aubergine. Finish with Mongolian fried dumplings, non-traditionally filled with chocolate ice cream.

Chef Xuwei Yu **Seats** 80 **Times** 12-2/5.30-10 **Prices** Prices not confirmed **Wines** 11 bottles under £30, 8 by glass **Parking** On street, NCP **Notes** Banquets L £8.50, Pre-theatre £11.95, D £20.95, Sunday L, Vegetarian available, Children welcome

Divino Enoteca

Modern Italian, International NOTABLE WINE LIST

tel: 0131 225 1770 **5 Merchant St EH1 2QD**
email: info@divinoedinburgh.com
dir: *Near National Museum of Scotland and The Grassmarket*

Exemplary Italian cooking and wines

A hip and happening venue with contemporary artworks on the walls, exposed brickwork and displays of wine bottles wherever you look: it's dark, moody, and a lot of fun. The kitchen's Italian output includes an excellent range of antipasti plus the more modern pan-fried scallops with smoked paprika polenta. Pasta options include ravioli of the day, or go for gnocchi with pancetta, clams and sautéed samphire. Pan-fried monkfish cheeks are served with salt-cod baccalà, confit lemon and braised leeks, grilled steak arrives in red wine sauce, and vegetarians can tuck into lasagne made with pumpkin and gorgonzola. Finish with white and dark truffles served with a glass of Pedro Ximenez.

Chef Francesco Ascrizzi **Seats** 50, Pr/dining room 14 **Times** 5.30-11, Closed Sun, L Mon-Fri **Prices** Prices not confirmed **Wines** 200 bottles over £30, 40 bottles under £30, 34 by glass **Parking** On street **Notes** All-day dining Sat, Vegetarian available, Children welcome

The Dungeon Restaurant at Dalhousie Castle

Traditional European NOTABLE WINE LIST

tel: 01875 820153 **Bonnyrigg EH19 3JB**
email: info@dalhousiecastle.co.uk **web:** www.dalhousiecastle.co.uk
dir: *From A720 (Edinburgh bypass) take A7 south, turn right onto B704. Castle 0.5m on right*

Creative cuisine in a truly unique setting

Dalhousie Castle is a 13th-century fortress in wooded parkland on the banks of the River Esk, so you know you're in for something special when you head for The Dungeon Restaurant. The cooking here has its roots in French classicism and a bedrock of top-class Scottish ingredients and it doesn't rely on the setting for effect: it's all brought together with skill and clever contemporary creativity. Smoked duck and foie gras cromesquis is matched with spiced bread and pear, ahead of pan-fried halibut and pork belly with parsley root purée and apple chutney. Dessert is a winning confection of white chocolate and vanilla parfait with pistachio sponge, meringue and griottine cherries.

Chef Francois Giraud **Seats** 45, Pr/dining room 100 **Times** 7-10, Closed L all week **Prices** Prices not confirmed **Wines** 52 bottles over £30, 43 bottles under £30, 10 by glass **Parking** 150 **Notes** ALC 5 course £49.50, Vegetarian available, Children welcome

Edinburgh Larder Bistro

Modern Scottish, British NEW

tel: 0131 225 4599 **Alva St EH2 4PH**
email: bistro@edinburghlarder.co.uk
dir: *West End, 10 mins from Haymarket train station*

Simple, on-trend cooking in a rustic West End bistro

The sun-trap conservatory comes as quite a surprise in this basement bistro in the West End Village. The decor is rough-and-ready rustic, with lobster-creel lightshades, and the kitchen takes a suitably fuss-free approach, setting out its stall with the likes of pan-fried crayfish tails with salsify and wild garlic. Follow with oven-baked witch sole paired with spinach, purple broccoli and wild leek, or perhaps roast chicken leg with crushed potatoes, Savoy cabbage with chorizo, and green beans. The propensity to throw less common flavours into the mix continues at dessert, when woodruff might appear with salted caramel in a lush cheesecake.

Chef Caoimhe McShane **Seats** 55, Pr/dining room 20 **Times** 12-2.30/5.30-9.30, Closed 24-26 Dec, 1 Jan, Sun-Mon **Prices** Fixed L 2 course fr £12, Fixed D 3 course fr £19, Starter £5-£6.50, Main £14-£20, Dessert £5.50-£8 **Wines** 7 bottles over £30, 20 bottles under £30, 10 by glass **Parking** On street **Notes** Vegetarian available, Children welcome

EDINBURGH *continued*

L'Escargot Bleu

French, Scottish

tel: 0131 557 1600 **56 Broughton St EH1 3SA**
email: contact@lescargotbleu.co.uk **web:** www.lescargotbleu.co.uk
dir: *On Broughton St, near Omni Centre*

French classics done right

L'Escargot Bleu is indeed blue – on the outside at least, and snails are present and correct among les entrées. The bilingual menu deals in classic bistro dishes such as those snails, which come from Barra in the Outer Hebrides, and there's a Scottish flavour to much of the kitchen's output. Start with seared scallops (from Skye) with spicy Puy lentils and crispy bacon, and move on to casserole of venison and beef cheeks with a rich red wine sauce, or pan-fried sea bass with Jerusalem artichokes and hollandaise. Desserts are as traditional as the crème brûlée which arrives without adornment. The restaurant's two-course lunch and early-evening menu is a bargain.

La Favorita

Modern Italian, Mediterranean

tel: 0131 554 2430 **325-331 Leith Walk EH6 8SA**
email: dine@la-favorita.com
dir: *On A900 from Edinburgh to South Leith*

Vibrant Leith Italian venue with more than just pizzas

The Vittoria group's Leith pizzeria provides upscale Italian food for a vibrant crowd seated at booth tables. The deal is a compendious list of pizzas – caprino e porri (topped with goats' cheese, leeks, roast spring onions and pancetta) to name but one – and platters of cured meats, multi-ingredient pasta dishes and risottos to broaden the choice. Kick off with salt cod fishcakes with tapenade and saffron mayonnaise, move on to classic pollo alla Milanese – breadcrumbed corn-fed chicken breast – and end with dark chocolate torte with orange marmalade sauce. Cocktail pitchers help the party mood, and there's a bargain weekday set-price lunch.

Chef Jarek Splawski **Seats** 120, Pr/dining room 30 **Times** 12-11, All-day dining, Closed 25 Dec **Prices** Fixed L 2 course £10, Fixed D 2 course £25, Starter £4.25-£6.75, Main £8.95-£22.50, Dessert £3.15-£11.95 **Wines** 4 bottles over £30, 26 bottles under £30, 7 by glass **Parking** On street **Notes** Sunday L £10.50-£25, Vegetarian available, Children welcome

Field

Scottish NOTABLE WINE LIST

tel: 0131 667 7010 **41 West Nicolson St EH8 9DB**
email: dine@fieldrestaurant.co.uk
dir: *From Waverley Station, right onto Princes St, right onto South Bridge for 0.5m, then right onto West Nicolson St*

Refined contemporary cooking in a minimalist setting

With just seven tables, this dinky restaurant with its minimalist colour scheme offers modern Scottish food of some refinement. Begin with some scallops (from this part of the world of course), seared and served with a lightly spiced pumpkin purée, black pudding, gingerbread and pomegranate. Move on to a maple-glazed duck breast with Savoy cabbage enriched with pancetta and a duck sausage roll, or home-smoked sea trout with curried mussels. For dessert, the chocolate fondant oozes in all the right places, and comes with burnt marshmallow ice cream. There's a fixed-price menu available at lunchtimes and a pre-theatre one in the evening.

Chef Byron Kennedy **Seats** 22 **Times** 12-2/5.30-9, Closed Mon **Prices** Fixed L 2 course £12.95, Starter £4.95-£8.50, Main £10.95-£22.50, Dessert £5.95-£6.50 **Wines** 20 bottles over £30, 21 bottles under £30, 10 by glass **Parking** On street **Notes** Pre-theatre menu 1/2/3 course £9.50/£12.95/£15.95, Sunday L £9.50-£15.95, Vegetarian available, Children 5 yrs+

G&V Royal Mile Hotel

Italian NOTABLE WINE LIST

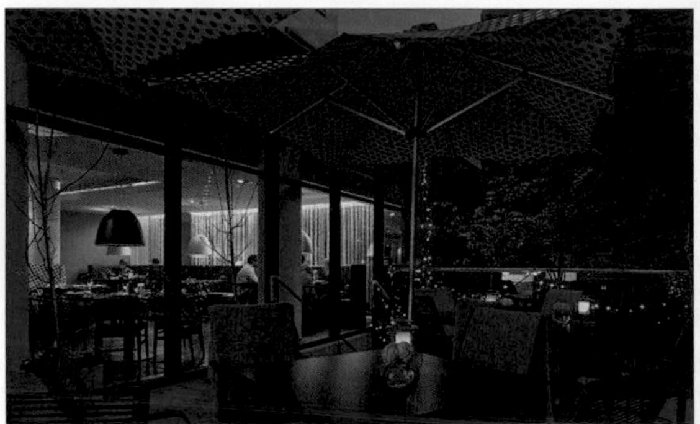

tel: 0131 220 6666 & 240 1666 **1 George IV Bridge EH1 1AD**
email: info@gandvhotel.com **web:** www.quorvuscollection.com
dir: *At corner of Royal Mile & George IV Bridge*

Modern Italian cucina in a glamorous Royal Mile hotel

In the Cucina restaurant, colourful abstracts hang on vivid blue walls and modern, seasonal Italian cooking is the order of the day. Tagliatelle with pork ragù is a nicel balanced starter, or wander into the unknown with buffalo mozzarella with chocolate, prunes and candied chillies. Accurate cooking is the norm, with main courses never so complex as to muddy flavours. Pan-fried guinea fowl breast with Savoy cabbage and pancetta, mixed mushroom, potato fondant makes a decent main course, and a freshly baked tiramisù with sweet whipped cream and a dusting of cocoa finishes things off nicely.

Chef Mattia Camorani **Seats** 90, Pr/dining room 40 **Times** 12.30-3/6-10, Closed D 25 Dec **Prices** Fixed L 2 course £15.95, Tasting menu £50, Starter £7-£13, Main £13-£34, Dessert £6-£13.50 **Wines** 67 bottles over £30, 15 bottles under £30, 14 by glass **Notes** Pre-theatre 2/3 course 6-7pm £17/£21, Sunday L, Vegetarian available, Children welcome

Galvin Brasserie de Luxe

French

tel: 0131 222 8988 **The Caledonian, A Waldorf Astoria Hotel, Princes St EH1 2AB**
email: brasserie.reservations@waldorfastoria.com
dir: *On Rutland St, off Lothian Rd, at Caledonian Hotel*

Timeless French brasserie dishes à la Galvin

The luxurious Caledonian Waldorf Astoria is the home of the Galvin brothers in Edinburgh, and this iteration of their cross-Channel classicism pleases diners with its Parisian brasserie-styled looks: darkwood flooring and tables around a circular island seafood bar, and waiting staff in time-honoured black-and-white uniforms. As for the food, it's all you'd expect and more, start with perfectly cooked hand-rolled pappardelle, ragout of Highland hare and aged pecorino, or Berwick crab mayonnaise, and then take in duck cassoulet, perhaps, or breast of Perthshire pheasant with Puy lentils and Alsace bacon. Finish with the signature apple tarte Tatin and crème fraîche.

Chef Jamie Knox **Seats** 150, Pr/dining room 24 **Times** 12-2.30/6-10 **Prices** Fixed L 2 course £16, Starter £6.50-£19, Main £12-£22, Dessert £6.50-£7.50 **Wines** 24 bottles over £30, 13 bottles under £30, 12 by glass **Parking** 42 **Notes** Prix fixe menu before 7pm, Sunday L £17, Vegetarian available, Children welcome

The Gardener's Cottage

British

tel: 0131 558 1221 **1 Royal Terrace Gardens, London Rd EH7 5DX**
email: eat@thegardenerscottage.co
dir: *Access from London Road. Opposite No 1 Hillside Cresent*

Carefully sourced Scottish garden cooking

With its blackboard menu in the gravel outside, this restaurant with full-on royal connections is an oasis of pastoral calm in the bustling city. Cosy up in wicker chairs at big communal tables for Scottish cooking that takes pride in its carefully sourced prime materials. That's clear from a starter of mutton and roe-deer meatballs in maltagliati pasta bound in rich creamy sauce with chopped nuts, and from a seafaring main course of turbot with winkles, strongly cured smoked bacon, apple and celeriac and a smoked yogurt dressing. Moist, substantial hazelnut cake comes with poached rhubarb and light sherry ice cream.

Chef Edward Murray, Dale Mailley **Seats** 30, Pr/dining room 10
Times 12-2.30/5-9.30, Closed Xmas & New Year, Tue **Prices** Prices not confirmed
Wines 13 bottles over £30, 9 bottles under £30, 19 by glass **Parking** On street (charges apply 8.30-5) **Notes** Fixed 7 course £40, Paired wines £40, ALC L, Vegetarian available, Children welcome

La Garrigue

Traditional French, Mediterranean NOTABLE WINE LIST

tel: 0131 557 3032 **31 Jeffrey St EH1 1DH**
email: reservations@lagarrigue.co.uk **web:** www.lagarrigue.co.uk
dir: *Halfway along Royal Mile towards Holyrood Palace, turn left at lights into Jeffrey St*

Charming bistro with authentic South of France menu

La Garrigue is the name given to the wild, herb-scented scrubland in Provence and Languedoc in the south of France. Chef-patron Jean-Michel Gauffre (who hails from down that way) has brought the region's honest rustic cooking to his smart neighbourhood restaurant in Edinburgh's old town. Expect regional cooking delivering full-bore flavours, starting with pork, rabbit and apple terrine with celeriac remoulade, then fish of the day might be red snapper with aïoli lentils. Gauffre was born in the heartlands of cassoulet so his take on the rich stew of belly pork, duck confit, Toulouse sausage and white beans is the real deal.

Chef Jean-Michel Gauffre **Seats** 48, Pr/dining room 11
Times 12-3/6.30-10.30, Closed 26-27 Dec, 1-2 Jan **Prices** Fixed L 2 course £14.50, Fixed D 3 course £25, Starter £4.75-£7.25, Main £14.50-£26.50, Dessert £4.75-£8.50 **Wines** 33 bottles over £30, 30 bottles under £30, 12 by glass **Parking** On street, NCP **Notes** Sunday L £14.50-£17, Vegetarian available, Children welcome

Hadrian's

Modern Scottish

tel: 0131 557 5000 & 557 2414 **The Balmoral Hotel, 1 Princes St EH2 2EQ**
email: hadrians.balmoral@roccofortehotels.com
dir: *Follow city-centre signs. Hotel at east end of Princes St, adjacent to Waverley Station*

Classy brasserie in landmark hotel

This large, bustling brasserie-style restaurant is within The Balmoral Hotel. A cool, modern vibe is created by walnut flooring, darkwood tables and a colour scheme of lime green and heather, while a mirror-lined wall reflects the light. Scottish classics range from haggis, neeps and tatties to whisky pannacotta. Pork belly with a scallop on a bed of tapenade is a masterly starter, and might be followed by a relatively simple main course of golden-skinned seared sea bream fillet on braised chicory with ratatouille. Sourdough bread is so good as to be moreish, and puddings run to visually attractive lemon meringue pie with grapefruit sorbet, crushed pistachios and an orange tuile.

EDINBURGH *continued*

Harajuku Kitchen

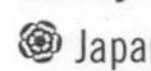 Japanese NEW V

tel: 0131 281 0526 **10 Gillespie Place EH10 4HS**
email: kaori@harajukukitchen.co.uk
dir: *Phone for directions*

Fresh Japanese bistro cooking

Named after an area of Tokyo, this bistro offers authentic Japanese dishes with a touch of panache in an informal café-like atmosphere of chunky wood chairs and bare tables. The menu is a mix of small plates and signature main dishes, with tempura mixes, stir-fried noodles and regulation sushi and sashimi. Deep-fried items such as karaage chicken in daikon sauce, tempura king prawns, and panko-crumbed tonkatsu pork curry are appealing, and the maki rolls are full of zippy freshness. Miso soup is made with good dashi stock, and you might conclude with dorayaki, a kind of Japanese crêpe flavoured with vanilla and filled with green tea ice cream.

Chef Kaori Simpson, Seiji Itogawa **Seats** 30 **Times** 12-3/5-10, Closed 25 Dec, 1 Jan **Prices** Fixed L 2 course fr £12.95, Starter £3.95-£12.95, Main £8-£24.95, Dessert £4.50 **Wines** 1 bottle over £30, 6 bottles under £30 **Notes** Pre-theatre menu, Sunday L £3.95-£24.95, Children welcome

Harvey Nichols Forth Floor Restaurant

British, Modern European, International NOTABLE WINE LIST

tel: 0131 524 8350 **30-34 St Andrew Square EH2 2AD**
email: forthfloor.reservations@harveynichols.com
web: www.harveynichols.com/restaurants
dir: *On St Andrew Square at east end of George St, 2 min walk from Princes St*

City views and sharp modern Scottish cooking

With views of the castle and the Forth Bridge, the top floor of Harvey Nic's Edinburgh restaurant serves up the city on a plate. The restaurant is a slick contemporary space with white linen on the tables, burgundy-coloured leather seats and a smart line in seasonal dishes combining contemporary finesse with Scottish ingredients. Aberdeenshire pork and ham rillettes with roast plums, piccalilli and truffle mayonnaise is a creative first course. Next up, red wine-poached halibut is supported by garlic mash, spinach, roast butternut squash and salsify. Finish with a 'Mont Blanc' confection of meringue, Cognac-infused stewed prunes and chestnut purée and ice cream.

Chef Robert Meldrum **Seats** 47, Pr/dining room 14 **Times** 12-3/6-10, Closed 25 Dec, 1 Jan, D Sun-Mon, 24 & 26 Dec, 2 Jan **Prices** Fixed L 2 course £25, Fixed D 3 course £30, Starter £8-£9, Main £17-£25, Dessert £8-£9 **Wines** 305 bottles over £30, 45 bottles under £30, 15 by glass **Parking** On street, Q park **Notes** Afternoon tea fr £20, Sunday L, Vegetarian available, Children welcome

The Honours

 Modern French

tel: 0131 220 2513 **58a North Castle St EH2 3LU**
email: info@thehonours.co.uk **web:** www.thehonours.co.uk
dir: *In city centre*

Classic French brasserie food Wishart-style

Martin Wishart is a shining star of the Scottish restaurant firmament, his self-named restaurant in Leith his flagship. Here, he's brought his dedication to high quality and his attention to detail to French brasserie classicism. There's a contemporary sheen to the place and a dedication to Scottish produce that proves the Auld Alliance is alive and well. A starter of sea bass tartare with cucumber jelly and saladings is a bracing opener. For main, there are charcoal-grilled steaks, as well as rabbit in mustard with sauté potatoes, or blanquette de veau with pilaf, and then Tatin for two or soufflé du jour pour finir.

Chef Paul Tamburrini **Seats** 65 **Times** 12-2.30/6-10, Closed Xmas, 1-3 Jan, Sun-Mon **Prices** Fixed L 2 course £18.50, Fixed D 3 course £22.50 **Wines** 34 bottles over £30, 22 bottles under £30, 20 by glass **Parking** On street **Notes** Fixed D Tue-Fri 5.30-7pm, Vegetarian available, Children welcome

Hotel du Vin Edinburgh

Modern British, French

tel: 0131 247 4900 **11 Bristo Place EH1 1EZ**
email: reception.edinburgh@hotelduvin.com **web:** www.hotelduvin.com
dir: *M8 junct 1, A720 (signed Kilmarnock/W Calder/Edinburgh W). Right at fork, follow A720 signs, merge onto A720. Take exit signed A703. At rdbt take A702/Biggar Rd. 3.5m. Right into Lauriston Pl which becomes Forrest Rd. Right at Bedlam Theatre. Hotel on righ*

Bags of HdV style and sound brasserie cooking

The former city asylum is the setting for HdV's Edinburgh outpost. These days the setting is considerably more cheerful thanks to the group's trademark gentleman's-club look of well-worn leather seats and woody textures. There's a splendid tartan-clad whisky snug, plus a buzzy mezzanine bar overlooking the bistro, which offers the usual nods to France with its wine-related paraphernalia and hearty, rustic contemporary brasserie cooking that the group specialises in everywhere from Roya Tunbridge Wells to the Scottish capital. A classic soupe à l'oignon is an appropriately Gallic starter, followed by roast salmon with braised Puy lentils, button onions and pancetta. Finish with zesty lemon tart.

Chef Gavin Lindsay **Seats** 88, Pr/dining room 26 **Times** 12-2.30/5.30-10.30, Closed 25 Dec **Prices** Fixed L 2 course fr £16.95, Fixed D 3 course fr £19.95, Starter £5.95-£12.95, Main £12.50-£29.50, Dessert £6.95-£9.95 **Wines** 150 bottles over £30, 75 bottles under £30, 20 by glass **Parking** NCP **Notes** Sun 4 course brunch, Sunday L fr £22.95, Vegetarian available, Children welcome

The Kitchin

EDINBURGH Map 21 NT27

WINNER OF THE AA WINE AWARD FOR SCOTLAND 2016–17

Scottish, French V NOTABLE WINE LIST

tel: 0131 555 1755 **78 Commercial Quay, Leith EH6 6LX**
email: info@thekitchin.com
dir: *In Leith, off Commercial St, opposite Scottish Executive building*

Benchmark modern Scottish cooking of great impact

A former whisky warehouse in Leith's regenerated docklands is home to a chef whose name seems to have predestined him for his trade: Tom Kitchin is one of Scotland's most dynamic chefs, and his reputation has gathered momentum since he (and wife Michaela) opened here in 2006. With a run of TV appearances playing their part and cookery books to spread the word, it's fair to say that he has played a leading part in positioning Edinburgh among the UK's top dining destinations. Recent renovation and expansion into the neighbouring premises has resulted in a stylish space that combines the cast-iron girders of the building's industrial heritage with shades of heather and marine blue, and textures of slate and oak echoing the natural environment that inspires the cooking. The place is a good fit with the 21st-century zeitgeist – smart but not starchy, serious but not pretentious. Having trained with such luminaries of classical French cuisine as Pierre Koffmann and French super-chef Alain Ducasse, you can be sure that Kitchin's technical skills are out of the top drawer and a passion for fine Scottish ingredients is reflected in the restaurant's 'nature to plate' philosophy that delivers dishes of refinement and astonishing precision. There is art in the presentation, too, with everything looking gorgeous on the plate, but never at the expense of flavour. It's all delivered via a seasonal à la carte, with a trio of tasting options (including a veggie version) and accompanying wine flights available if the whole table is up for it, plus a set lunch menu that offers remarkable value for food of this level. From the carte, an opening dish called 'rock pool' is rich with the finest, freshest fish and seafood, pointed up with foraged seaweed and finished with a punchy shellfish consommé. Or there could be boned and rolled pig's head in a harmonious composition with roast langoustine, crispy pig's ear salad to add textural variety, and gribiche cream. Next up, perhaps a splendid piece of roasted monkfish, landed at Scrabster, stuffed with spinach and served with winkles, lardons and an intense red wine sauce, while a meaty main course brings roasted breast of mallard with confit leg meat, carrot Tatin and an orange sauce. A typically seasonal dessert might showcase rhubarb, poached and sorbet alongside a crowdie cheesecake. Another unites chocolate and pumpkin in a light-as-air soufflé and in a ripple ice cream. The trolley laden with perfectly ripened British cheeses is hard to pass by, while the wine list majors in France without ignoring the rest of the world and the selection by the glass offers some rather good stuff without the need to tackle a whole bottle.

Chef Tom Kitchin **Seats** 75, Pr/dining room 20
Times 12.15-2.30/6.30-10, Closed Xmas, New Year, 1st 2 wks Jan, Sun-Mon **Prices** Fixed L 3 course £29.50, Tasting menu £75, Starter £15-£29, Main £30-£45, Dessert £12-£15 **Wines** 330 bottles over £30, 30 by glass **Parking** 30, On site parking evening only, all day Sat **Notes** Tasting menu 6 course, Celebration of the season menu, Children 5 yrs+

EDINBURGH *continued*

The Howard

Traditional British, French

tel: 0131 557 3500 **34 Great King St EH3 6QH**
email: reception@thehoward.com **web:** www.thehoward.com
dir: *E on Queen St, 2nd left, Dundas St. Through 3 lights, right, hotel on left*

Quality Scottish cooking in an intimate hotel dining room

Edinburgh's New Town was so well planned in Georgian times that, together with the Old Town, it's a UNESCO World Heritage Site. Built in the 1820s as three townhouses, the Howard has a small restaurant, the Atholl, with a marble fireplace, smartly-dressed tables and fresh flowers. It only seats 14, so do book. The food often declares its provenance, as in Arbroath Smokies, horseradish mousse with rustic oatcakes, and Newtonmore venison loin, braised red cabbage, honey-roast parsnips, mash and whisky jus. Some things travel from south of the border, like the Maldon sea salt that accompanies apple pie, caramel sauce and vanilla ice cream.

Chef William Poncelet **Seats** 14 **Times** 12-2/6-9.30 **Prices** Fixed L 2 course £22.50-£31.50, Fixed D 3 course £22.50-£31.50, Tasting menu £65-£105, Starter £8.50-£10.75, Main £17.50-£28.95, Dessert £7.90-£10.25 **Wines** 50 bottles over £30, 10 bottles under £30, 10 by glass **Parking** 10 **Notes** Pre-theatre menu, Sunday L £16.50-£35, Vegetarian available, Children welcome

The Indian Cavalry Club

Indian

tel: 0131 220 0138 **22 Coates Crescent EH3 7AF**
email: info@indiancavalryclub.co.uk
dir: *Few mins walk from Haymarket Railway Station & the west end of Princes St*

The West End's Indian star serving authentic flavours

Just a few minutes from the city's hub, this Indian restaurant has been going strong since 1986. It's a comfortable, good-looking place with a contemporary decor of creamy tones and a wooden floor, and the kitchen deploys sound techniques and quality ingredients to produce full-bore flavours. A careful hand with spicing and seasoning means a classic tandoori mixed kebab bursts with flavour, priming the palate for chargrilled fillet of sea bass with a Keralan-style sauce of lime, coconut, tamarind and green chillies. Vegetarian options, among them paneer palak (spinach and cottage cheese), get the thumbs up, as do naan and light and fluffy pilau rice.

Chef M D Qayum **Seats** 120, Pr/dining room 50 **Times** 12-2/5.30-11.30 **Prices** Prices not confirmed **Wines** 9 bottles over £30, 23 bottles under £30, 2 by glass **Parking** On street **Notes** Sunday L, Vegetarian available, Children welcome

Kanpai Sushi

Japanese

tel: 0131 228 1602 **8-10 Grindlay St EH3 9AS**
dir: *Joined to Lothian Road behind Usher Hall*

Classic Japanese food in Edinburgh's culture zone

Just around the corner from the Usher Hall and the Traverse Theatre, Kanpai is a diminutive but elegant sushi place with an open kitchen counter where you can watch its well-drilled artistry take place. Attention to fine detail, and exemplary freshness are the hallmarks of wakame salad with soy and seaweed dressing, seared tuna in home-made miso, delicately battered squid tempura, melt-in-the-mouth nigiri scallops, white snow crab with onions in ponzu, and the moreish Kanpai special roll. This is an artfully presented king prawn wrapped in sticky rice, with sweet bean curd and avocado. Make sure to check out the list of sake and shochu spirits.

Chef Max Wang **Seats** 45, Pr/dining room 8 **Times** 12-2.30/5-10.30, Closed Mon **Prices** Starter £2-£9.90, Main £7.90-£20.90, Dessert £4.50-£6.50 **Wines** 3 bottles over £30, 8 bottles under £30, 9 by glass **Parking** On street **Notes** Vegetarian available, Children 6 yrs+

The Kitchin

– see page 515

Locanda De Gusti

Italian, Mediterranean, Seafood

tel: 0131 346 8800 **102 Dalry Rd EH11 2DW**
dir: *5-min walk from Haymarket station*

A Neapolitan trattoria transported

Translating loosely as 'inn of taste', this Haymarket award-winner has more than a hint of an Italian domestic kitchen about it. The mixed Scottish seafood feast is a starter full of the freshest squid, king prawns, langoustines, scallops and more, with white wine and a kiss of chilli. Or there's a main course of linguine with grilled half lobster, Vesuvian and sun-dried tomatoes and, again, a hint of chilli. From chef-patron Rosario's birthplace comes Neapolitan meatloaf stuffed with egg, parmesan, smoked mozzarella and ham, drowned (his word) in a rich tomato passata and basil sauce. Finish with cannolo Siciliano – crispy pastry filled with sweet cheese, infused with icing sugar.

Chef Rosario Sartore **Seats** 30 **Times** 12.30-2.15/5.30-9.45, Closed Sun, L Mon-Wed **Prices** Fixed L 3 course £12.95, Tasting menu £27-£50, Starter £5.95-£9.95, Main £8.95-£24.95, Dessert £4.95 **Wines** 10 by glass **Parking** On street **Notes** Business L Thu-Fri, ALC Sat, Vegetarian available, Children welcome

Malmaison Edinburgh

British, French

tel: 0131 468 5000 **One Tower Place, Leith EH6 7BZ**
email: edinburgh@malmaison.com **web:** www.malmaison.com
dir: *A900 from city centre towards Leith, at end of Leith Walk through 3 lights, left into Tower St. Hotel on right at end of road*

Dockside brasserie in the Mal boutique style

This Edinburgh hotel was the first opening for the Malmaison chain, housed in a renovated seamen's mission on the Forth waterfront in the old part of Leith, and is nowadays the grande dame of the boutique chain. A brasserie-style operation with brown leather seating, unclothed tables and candles, the restaurant overlooks the docks and there's a terrace for alfresco dining when the sun shines. The globally influenced menu might start with Goan mussels, coriander and coconut cream before a Mediterranean main of cod with shellfish vinaigrette and samphire. Look to Italy for a dessert of tiramisù with pistachio and orange biscotti.

The Mumbai Mansion

Modern Indian NEW V

tel: 0131 229 7173 **250 Morrison St EH3 8DT**
email: dine@themumbaimansion.com
dir: *0.5m walk from Haymarket train station, Hilton Hotel & Premier Inn*

Creative Indian dining in stylish room

Mumbai Mansion is an Indian restaurant, under new ownership since 2015, where both the interior design and menu take a glamorous and contemporary approach. A statement chandelier, plum-coloured columns and chairs, and chunky wooden designer tables make for an appealing space, watched over by a smartly turned-out service team. Monkfish tikka manages to take on the flavours of its marinade without overpowering the fish, while main-course breast of duck shows the same subtle hand, served in a well flavoured coconut-based sauce. Whole leg of Scottish lamb is cooked in the tandoor, and, to finish, an Indian trio includes carrot halwa.

Chef Pramod Kumar Nawani **Seats** 85 **Times** 12-2/5.30-11 **Prices** Fixed L 2 course £9.95-£12.90, Fixed D 3 course £24.65-£33.90, Tasting menu £21.95-£32.95, Starter £4.50-£8.95, Main £10.95-£24.95, Dessert £4.95-£5.95 **Wines** 7 bottles over £30, 27 bottles under £30, 5 by glass **Parking** On street **Notes** Sunday L, Children welcome

Norton House Hotel & Spa

Modern Scottish, French

tel: 0131 333 1275 & 0845 072 7468 *(Calls cost 7p per minute plus your phone company's access charge)* **Ingliston EH28 8LX**
email: nortonhouse@handpicked.co.uk
web: www.handpickedhotels.co.uk/nortonhouse
dir: *M8 junct 2, off A8, 0.5m past Edinburgh Airport*

Outstanding modern Scottish cooking near the airport

A stone-built manor house dating from the early Victorian era, Norton House was once home to the Usher family, beer brewers and distillers of the Glenlivet single malt. The family lends its name to the principal dining room, a compact space with just seven tables, done in white and adorned with narrow framed casts of architectural features from the original Usher Hall, an interesting feature. Graeme Shaw cooks modern Scottish food led by impeccable regional ingredients, in presentations that heap the components of each dish together rather than islanding each one in lonely isolation. A home-made boudin of white pudding interleaved with foie gras comes with balled apple, salt-baked celeriac and pickled kohlrabi under a yeasty, appley foam, while another foam, this time redolent of shellfish, covers a construction of smoked langoustines in cannelloni with spinach. At main, there may be Scrabster monkfish with oysters and kale, or a serving of no fewer than four cuts of Border lamb – belly, back, loin and crumbed sweetbreads – with assertive garnishes of fennel, olives and goats' cheese in mustard sauce. A fascinating marshmallow-textured parfait of calvados with intense apple sorrel sorbet, puréed prunes and frangipane ends things with a flourish. Incidentals, including brilliant breads, are equally captivating.

Chef Graeme Shaw, Glen Bilins **Seats** 22, Pr/dining room 40
Times 7-9.30, Closed Jan-Feb, Sun-Tue, L all week **Prices** Tasting menu fr £65, Starter £9.50-£12.50, Main £26.50-£38, Dessert £7.50-£8.95 **Wines** 80 bottles over £30, 15 bottles under £30, 12 by glass **Parking** 100 **Notes** Tasting menu 8 course, Vegetarian available, Children welcome

Number One, The Balmoral

– see below

Number One, The Balmoral

EDINBURGH **Map 21 NT27**

Modern Scottish V NOTABLE WINE LIST
tel: 0131 557 6727 **1 Princes St EH2 2EQ**
email: numberone.balmoral@roccofortehotel.com
web: www.roccofortehotels.com
dir: *Follow city-centre signs. Hotel at east end of Princes St, adjacent to Waverley Station*

Exquisite modern cooking in a majestic hotel

In a city not short of a landmark building or two, The Balmoral is high on the status list, with the clock on its looming tower above Waverley station set three minutes fast to motivate those heading for a train. The imposing interior harks back to the days of the railway era, when a railway hotel was a grand beast indeed. The main dining option is the Number One restaurant, a classy space with dove-grey and gold banquettes and contemporary artworks on loan from the Royal College of Art on red lacquered walls. Jeff Bland has been executive chef for over a dozen years, with Brian Grigor leading the line at the stoves day-to-day, and together they deliver a creative and intelligent output that has a true sense of Scottishness. Begin with hand-dived scallops and peat-smoked haddock, or cured foie gras parfait with gingerbread and the contrasting sweet and acidic notes of hibiscus jelly, fresh apple and apple purée in a visually thrilling dish that reveals the kitchen's astute understanding of the balance of flavours and textures. Follow with wild turbot – a perfectly cooked piece of fish – partnered with the robust flavours of smoked bacon and oxtail ravioli, or the earthy satisfaction of Inverurie hogget, its loin, neck and belly served with baby gem lettuce, peas, mint and yogurt. For dessert, Brillat-Savarin cheesecake is another stunner, with poached rhubarb and blood orange to offset any richness. The wine list does justice to the wonderful food, as does the highly professional service team.

Chef Jeff Bland, Brian Grigor **Seats** 60 **Times** 6.30-10, Closed 2 wks Jan, L all week **Prices** Fixed D 3 course £70, Tasting menu £79-£110 **Wines** 350 bottles over £30, 30 by glass **Parking** NCP & on street **Notes** Tasting menu 7/10 course, D 4 course £75, Children welcome

Restaurant Mark Greenaway

EDINBURGH **Map 21 NT27**

Modern British NOTABLE WINE LIST

tel: 0131 226 1155 **69 North Castle St EH2 3LJ**
email: bookings@rmgedinburgh.com
web: www.markgreenaway.com
dir: *Phone for directions*

Tautly controlled, imaginative dishes from a Scottish food ambassador

A sophisticated dining room in an elegant Georgian building, all calming blue-grey walls and white-clothed tables. Light enters through large sash windows and the dramatic fanlight above the doors that lead onto the plant-filled terrace. Having represented Scotland on The Great British Menu, and cooked at such high-flying establishments as One Devonshire Gardens, Glasgow, and Kilcamb Lodge, Strontian, Mark Greenaway is one of the prime movers and shakers north of the border. He's also a proud supporter of local produce and suppliers, and his carefully constructed menus demonstrate exactly what's best in the seasonal larder. Options include the seriously good-value lunchtime and early-evening Market Menu, with three choices at each course, the standard carte or, if everyone on your table can agree, the eight-course tasting menu. This gives the kitchen a chance to show what they're really about, but whatever you choose there's plenty going on to keep you interested. Things might kick off with a pressing of Perthshire pheasant, with carrot and ginger gel, sweet cicely mayonnaise, bread tuile, boudin blanc and baby carrot, or 'cannelloni' of Loch Fyne crab with smoked cauliflower custard, herb butter and baby coriander, a collection that goes well together, helped along by lemon pearls to mitigate the richness. Greenaway's dishes brim with flair and imagination, and everything feels tautly controlled and cohesive – Parma ham-wrapped monkfish, for example, with crispy chicken wings, baby turnip, confit carrots and brown butter jus, or the 11-hour slow-roasted Clash Farm belly pork with pork cheek 'pie', blackened fillet, sweetcorn and toffee apple jus. As for dessert, frozen rhubarb mousse comes with ginger and hibiscus jelly, pressed candy floss, popcorn toffee and Amaretti meringue.

Chef Mark Greenaway **Seats** 60, Pr/dining room 16
Times 12-2.30/5.30-10, Closed 25-26 Dec, 1-2 Jan, Sun-Mon
Prices Fixed L 2 course fr £20, Fixed D 3 course fr £24.50, Tasting menu fr £65.50, Starter £8-£13, Main £22-£32, Dessert £8-£10
Wines 67 bottles over £30, 25 bottles under £30, 13 by glass
Notes Vegetarian available, Children 5 yrs+

EDINBURGH *continued*

Ondine Restaurant

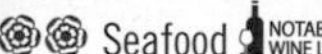

Seafood NOTABLE WINE LIST

tel: 0131 226 1888 **2 George IV Bridge EH1 1AD**
email: enquiries@ondinerestaurant.co.uk
dir: In Edinburgh City Centre, just off the Royal Mile

Contemporary seafood restaurant with an ethical outlook

Ondine has earned a loyal following in a few short years, and it's not hard to see why: just off the Royal Mile, on George IV Bridge, it's a contemporary space with great views out over the old town. But sustainable seafood served amid an atmosphere of cheerful bustle is the main draw, and the ecological ethos is not empty marketing speak. You could take a high seat at the central horseshoe-shaped crustacean bar, or park on a stripy banquette and get things under way with oysters – four types, no less, either as they come or cooked tempura-style with Vietnamese dipping sauce – or something like a classic fish and shellfish soup with the time-honoured accompaniments of rouille, gruyère and croûtons. Chef Roy Brett takes a sensibly restrained approach, so nothing is overworked and every molecule of flavour is extracted from the first-class piscine produce at his disposal. Thus main course brings wild Cornish sea bass with squid peperonata and whipped artichoke, or meat fans might tackle a rib of Orkney beef served on the bone with bordelaise sauce and pied de bleu mushrooms. Finish with good old treacle tart, lifted with a zesty hit of lemon and served with clotted cream.

Chef Roy Brett **Seats** 82, Pr/dining room 10 **Times** 12-3/5.30-10, Closed Sun **Prices** Prices not confirmed **Wines** 68 bottles over £30, 21 bottles under £30, 31 by glass **Parking** On street or Castle Terrace car park **Notes** Pre-theatre menu 2/3 course £21.95/£25.95 5.30-6.30pm, Vegetarian available, Children welcome

One Square

Modern British

tel: 0131 221 6422 **Sheraton Grand Hotel & Spa, 1 Festival Square EH3 9SR**
email: info@onesquareedinburgh.co.uk **web:** www.onesquareedinburgh.co.uk
dir: *Off Lothian Road. Entrance to hotel from Festival Square*

Modern regional cooking in a trendy setting

The views of Edinburgh Castle certainly give a sense of place to this slick, modern dining option in the Sheraton Grand Hotel. The restaurant and bar have floor-to-ceiling windows and a cool, classy finish. The lunch and dinner menus have a sharp focus on Scotland's fine produce in their crowd-pleasing medley of modern ideas. A fine version of chicken liver pâté comes with blood orange jelly, while Gressingham duck breast is partnered with a faggot of braised leg meat, celeriac fondant, sprout leaves and bramble jus. Finish with a creative combo of gin consommé with liquorice ice cream, lemon cream and bitter salted chocolate.

Chef Craig Hart **Seats** 90, Pr/dining room 40 **Times** 7am-11pm, All-day dining **Prices** Fixed L 2 course £16.95, Fixed D 3 course £20.95, Tasting menu £120-£160, Starter £7.50-£11.50, Main £16-£31, Dessert £4-£10.50 **Wines** 41 bottles over £30, 19 bottles under £30, 21 by glass **Parking** 125 **Notes** Unique dining experiences at The Pass or The Kitchen Table, Sunday L £29, Vegetarian available, Children welcome

Pompadour by Galvin

Modern French V

tel: 0131 222 8975 & 222 8777 **Waldorf Astoria Edinburgh, The Caledonian, Princes St EH1 2AB**
email: pompadour.reservations@waldorfastoria.com **web:** www.galvinrestaurants.com
dir: *On west end of Princess St, on Rutland St & Lothian Rd*

Haute cuisine Galvin-style comes to Edinburgh

This entirely glamorous establishment is part of a splendid Victorian railway hotel, the Waldorf Astoria Edinburgh – The Caledonian, and has been the last word in over-the-top opulence since opening in 1925. The Leith docks have been rejuvenated out of all recognition, but still nothing looks quite as extravagant as the Galvin brothers' Edinburgh outpost, which offers views of the Castle, hand-painted panelling and intricate plaster detailing. When they call it 'one of Edinburgh's most magnificent dining rooms' they're really not kidding. The staff are charmingly efficient, ensuring that everything runs smoothly as you work your way through the focused, classically French menus, where everything is perfectly considered and constructed with skill and panache. Perhaps begin with carpaccio of Orkney beef, Périgord truffle, aubergine purée, pickled mushrooms and horseradish, or roast Mull scallops with rhubarb, ginger and vanilla, and then choose breast of Perthshire pheasant, creamed cabbage, roast parsnip and chestnut purée, say, or poached filled of Peterhead cod, Beaufort and thyme crust, leeks, trompette and red wine jus. The dessert menu might offer more rhubarb, in a cheesecake accompanied by rhubarb and ginger beer sorbet, or go for the truffled brie de meaux with heather honey, dried pears and oatcake.

Chef Fraser Allan **Seats** 60, Pr/dining room 20 **Times** 12-2.30/6-10, Closed 2 wks Jan, Sun-Mon, L Tue-Thu, Sat **Prices** Fixed D 3 course £35, Tasting menu £68-£120, Starter £16.50-£24.50, Main £26.50-£36, Dessert £6.50-£11 **Wines** 135 bottles over £30, 3 bottles under £30, 10 by glass **Parking** 42 **Notes** Tasting menu 7 course, Children welcome

Restaurant Mark Greenaway

– see opposite

Restaurant Martin Wishart

– see page 520

EDINBURGH *continued*

Rhubarb at Prestonfield House

Traditional British NOTABLE WINE LIST

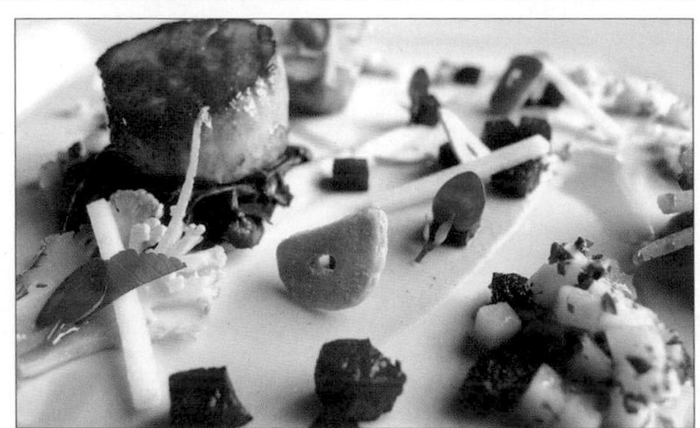

tel: 0131 225 1333 **Priestfield Rd EH16 5UT**
email: reservations@prestonfield.com **web:** www.rhubarb-restaurant.com
dir: *Exit city centre on Nicholson St, onto Dalkeith Rd. At lights turn left into Priestfield Rd. Prestonfield on left*

Opulent surroundings for high-impact cooking

One of the city's most visually impressive dining rooms, Rhubarb at Prestonfield House is a real stunner. Classical preparations mix with contemporary ideas in a menu with broad appeal. New-season's asparagus star in a first course with morels and squat lobsters from Mull, while another combines Gressingham duck meat and foie gras in a terrine with lime brioche and macerated blueberries. Among main courses, Peterhead cod is served en papillote with cider and tamarind paste and curried celery (plus some crabmeat), and guinea fowl with its leg meat in an accompanying pastilla. There are classic Scottish steaks, too. For dessert, go for tarte Tatin for two.

Rhubarb at Prestonfield House

Restaurant Martin Wishart

EDINBURGH **Map 21 NT27**

Modern French V NOTABLE WINE LIST
tel: 0131 553 3557 **54 The Shore, Leith EH6 6RA**
email: info@martin-wishart.co.uk
dir: *Off the A199*

Contemporary cooking from Scotland's culinary darling

Martin Wishart's restaurant led the charge in the transformation of Leith's dilapidated docklands into a trendy foodie quarter. His pedigree CV takes in stints with the great and the good of the British culinary scene and his style is anchored in modern French cuisine. A slick team of immaculately presented and consummately professional staff provide thoughtful, unobtrusive service. Those with a nose for a bargain should come for lunch Tuesday to Friday, otherwise there's a trio of six-course tasting menus – seafood and veggie versions alongside the regular one – and a concise fixed-price carte. Exquisite canapés – perhaps warm cauliflower beignet subtly fired up by curry oil, or a squid ink cracker with smoked salmon and avocado – pave the way for luxurious starters such as sautéed foie gras matched intelligently with carrot, apricot and cinnamon. Another sees langoustine and veal sweetbreads roasted in buckwheat and thyme and partnered with braised endive, curry and Sauternes sauce. Among main courses, turbot poached in red wine comes in a harmonious composition with braised pig's trotter, young leeks, new potatoes and red wine sauce. Fish fans will find much to love in ideas such as Dover sole in a picturesque medley with oyster and caviar, fregola, squid and herbs. There's no let up in the creativity and technical whizz bangs at dessert. Try spiced Valrhona chocolate mousse with macerated pineapple, cocoa tuile and the astringent contrast of clementine juice, or lemon and bergamot crémeux with yogurt sorbet and pink grapefruit meringue. The wine list is a class act, and a selection of very fine examples is available by the glass.

Chef Martin Wishart, Joe Taggart **Seats** 50, Pr/dining room 10
Times 12-2/6.30-10, Closed 25-26 Dec, 1 Jan, 2 wks Jan, Sun-Mon **Prices** Fixed L 3 course £28.50, Tasting menu £80 **Wines** 250 bottles over £30, 9 bottles under £30, 24 by glass **Parking** On street **Notes** Tasting menu 6 course, ALC 3 course £75, Children welcome

Timberyard

EDINBURGH **Map 21 NT27**

Modern British V 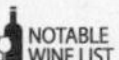 NOTABLE WINE LIST

tel: 0131 221 1222 **10 Lady Lawson St EH3 9DS**
email: eat@timberyard.co
web: www.timberyard.co
dir: *From Princes St, Lothian Rd (A700) left onto Castle Terrace, right at rdbt, left onto Lady Lawson St, restaurant on right*

Creative modern cooking in a cool, casual setting

Timberyard was built in the 19th century as a warehouse for props and costumes and then became – yes – a timber yard. Some original features remain in the shape of a rough boarded floor and pillars supporting the ceiling, but its restaurant incarnation has brought in high stools at a painted brick bar, a sofa in front of a wood-burning stove, and tartan throws over some of the chairs at wooden-topped tables. Outside is a south-facing courtyard, some of it covered over, with a silver birch and tables and chairs for alfresco dining. The place is run with enthusiasm, energy and great aplomb by five members of the Radford family, with Ben heading up the stoves. He sources his supplies from local artisan producers and foragers, has an in-house smokery and butchery, and grows herbs, flowers, vegetables and fruit on site in raised beds. He also turns his hand to producing exciting, whizz-bang dishes that bear his own individual, highly original hallmark. Sampling one of the Bite, Small or Large dishes is a good way into the style, taking in anything from crab with dill, crème fraîche, fennel and rye, to salmon fillet with brown butter, tarragon, potato and broccoli. Or go mainline with four to six courses at lunch and four to eight at dinner, with bookends of perhaps mackerel fillets with horseradish, buttermilk, cucumber, apple and dill, and apple with sorrel, yogurt and a brioche. Quality raw materials, some rarely encountered, are carefully prepared, and combinations result in zingingly flavourful dishes. Main courses include properly timed halibut fillet with mussels, onion, wild leek, crow garlic (ask one of the staff) and potatoes, and lamb cutlets with celeriac, black garlic, shallots, carrots and kale. There are separate pescatarian and vegetarian menus.

Chef Ben Radford **Seats** 72, Pr/dining room 10
Times 12-2/5.30-9.30, Closed 1 wk Apr, Oct, Xmas, Sun-Mon
Prices Tasting menu £60-£75, Starter £7-£15, Main £14-£25, Dessert £6-£10 **Wines** 234 bottles over £30, 12 bottles under £30, 12 by glass **Parking** Castle Terrace NCP, On street **Notes** L&D 4/6 course £55/£65, Tasting menu 8 course, Children 8 yrs+ D

EDINBURGH *continued*

The Scran & Scallie

Traditional Scottish NOTABLE WINE LIST

tel: 0131 332 6281 **1 Comely Bank Rd EH4 1DT**
email: info@scranandscallie.com
dir: *In Stockbridge behind Inverleith Park & Botanical Gdns*

Classy pub food from two stellar chefs

Tom Kitchin and Dominic Jack's pub is done out in fashionable shabby-chic, just the right sort of setting for a menu of modern classics combined with traditional preparations that might unjustly have fallen out of favour. First up might be a solidly stuffed raviolo parcel of ham in watercress soup, or the bracing simplicity of half-a-dozen oysters. Main-course roasted monkfish swaddled in pancetta with Puy lentils is another classy little number, as an alternative to versions of pot-au-feu or the house fish pie. The feel-good factor continues into desserts such as sponge-topped apple tart with a rich crème anglaise served cold, or chocolate brioche pudding with pistachio ice cream.

Chef James Chapman, Tom Kitchin, Dominic Jack **Seats** 70 **Times** 12-3.30/6-10.30, Closed 25 Dec **Prices** Fixed L 3 course £15, Starter £7.50-£13, Main £9.50-£21, Dessert £4.50-£11.50 **Wines** 37 bottles over £30, 22 bottles under £30, 40 by glass **Parking** On street **Notes** Breakfast Sat-Sun, All-day dining Sat-Sun 12-10pm, Sunday L £9.50-£17.50, Vegetarian available, Children welcome

The Stockbridge Restaurant

Modern European

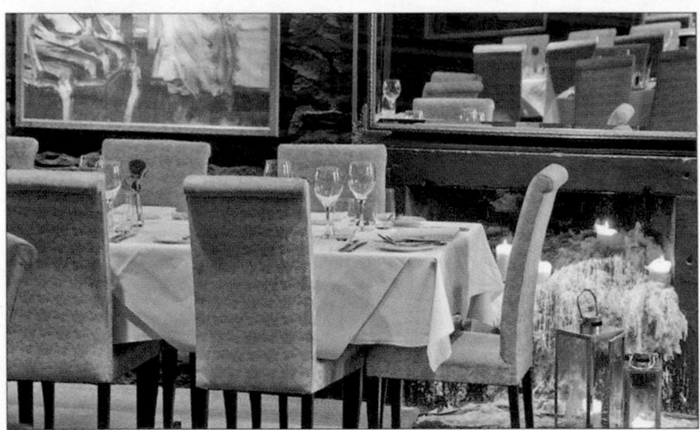

tel: 0131 226 6766 **54 Saint Stephen St EH3 5AL**
email: jane@thestockbridgerestaurant.com **web:** www.thestockbridgerestaurant.com
dir: *From A90 towards city centre, left Craigleith Rd B900, 2nd exit at rdbt B900, straight on to Kerr St, turn left onto Saint Stephen St*

Spirited flavours and assured cooking in distinctive surroundings

The Stockbridge is a charming restaurant where the walls are hung with vivid modern artwork and mirrors, and spotlights in the low ceiling create pools of light on crisply clothed tables. The cooking goes from strength to strength, producing consistently well-conceived dishes from fine Scottish produce. Seared cod with a scallop and crab boudin in langoustine bisque is one starter. A lot goes into main courses, but an assured touch means flavours are clean and well-defined, as with venison loin in port, with poached pear, celeriac purée, kale and chocolate oil. A pre-dessert arrives before the real thing, perhaps banana Tatin with butterscotch sauce.

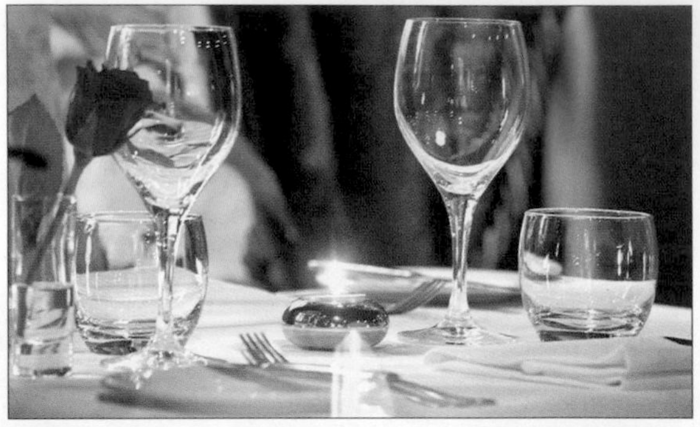

The Stockbridge Restaurant

Chef Jason Gallagher **Seats** 40 **Times** 7-9.30, Closed 24-25 Dec, 1st 2 wks Jan, Mon, L all week (open on request only min 6 people) **Prices** Fixed L 2 course £18.95, Fixed D 3 course £31.95-£36.95, Starter £8.45-£12.95, Main £20.95-£24.95, Dessert £4.95-£9.95 **Wines** 34 bottles over £30, 18 bottles under £30, 7 by glass **Parking** On street **Notes** Vegetarian available, Children until 8pm

Ten Hill Place Hotel

Modern, Traditional British

tel: 0131 662 2080 **10 Hill Place EH8 9DS**
email: reservations@tenhillplace.com **web:** www.tenhillplace.com
dir: *Phone for directions*

On a cobbled street overlooking a quiet square

Can there be another hotel that uses its profits to help train the world's would-be surgeons? That is what this part-Georgian, part-new hotel owned by The Royal College of Surgeons of Edinburgh does. If you're thinking of trying Scotland's classic dish for the first time, then head for the elegantly decorated and furnished restaurant for a starter of haggis pastilla with neep (turnip) fondant, mashed potato and whisky jelly. Follow with braised and pressed pork belly with red onion purée, buttered mash and black pudding, or seared Scottish salmon with smoked haddock foam, Jersey Royals, burnt pickles and onions. Finish with vanilla pannacotta, rhubarb sorbet and jelly.

Chef Alan Dickson **Seats** 54 **Times** 5-9.30, Closed Xmas, L all week **Prices** Fixed D 3 course £30, Starter £4.50-£7.50, Main £14.25-£23.50, Dessert £6.50-£8.25 **Wines** 1 bottle over £30, 22 bottles under £30, 21 by glass **Parking** 6, On street **Notes** Vegetarian available, Children welcome

Timberyard

– see page 521

21212

– see opposite

The Witchery by the Castle

Traditional Scottish V NOTABLE WINE LIST

tel: 0131 225 5613 **Castlehill, The Royal Mile EH1 2NF**
email: mail@thewitchery.com **web:** www.thewitchery.com
dir: *Top of Royal Mile at gates of Edinburgh Castle*

Confident Scottish cooking in magnificent surroundings

This 16th-century merchant's house by the gates of the castle makes a strikingly atmospheric, even Gothic-looking restaurant. The cooking follows a contemporary route built on Scottish traditions, with the kitchen using quality native produce. Start with partridge with grilled potato terrine and burned onion mayonnaise and follow that with beef Rossini with Madeira jus, pommes Anna and spinach. Seafood gets a strong showing, from seared scallops with Ibérico ham and garlic butter to monkfish poached in olive oil with grilled kohlrabi, cumin-spiced lentils and curry velouté. Puddings are worth a punt: perhaps pineapple tarte Tatin with rum-flavoured caramel and coconut ice cream.

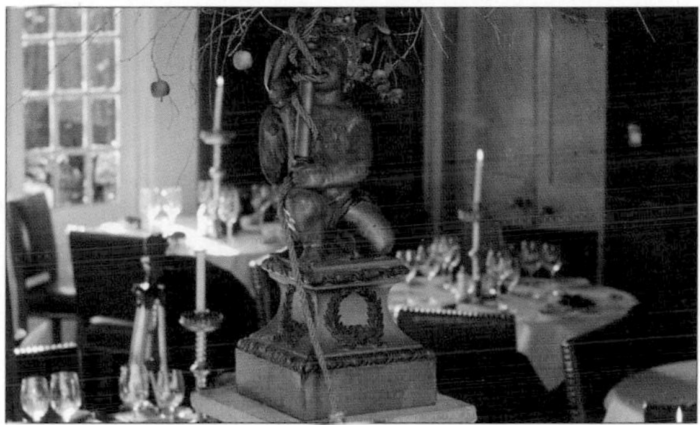

The Witchery by the Castle

Chef Douglas Roberts **Seats** 110, Pr/dining room 60 **Times** 12-11.30, All-day dining, Closed 25 Dec **Prices** Fixed L 2 course £18.95, Fixed D 3 course £35, Starter £8.50-£15, Main £23-£40, Dessert £6.50-£8.50 **Wines** 12 by glass **Notes** Pre/post-theatre 2 course £18.95, Sunday L, Children 6 yrs+

21212

EDINBURGH **Map 21 NT27**

Modern French NOTABLE WINE LIST

tel: 0131 523 1030 & 0845 222 1212 *(Calls cost 7p per minute plus your phone company's access charge)* **3 Royal Ter EH7 5AB**
email: reservation@21212restaurant.co.uk **web:** www.21212restaurant.co.uk
dir: *Calton Hill, city centre*

Intense flavours and fun from a true culinary genius

The classical exterior of this listed Georgian townhouse conceals a profusion of luxurious rooms. There's a sumptuously furnished first-floor drawing room for drinks, two private dining rooms, one with an image of Caravaggio's 'The Seven Works of Mercy', and four bedrooms as well as the restaurant, with its abundance of designer furnishings and elegantly set tables, ornate plasterwork and an open kitchen with the team fully on view. The name refers to the number of choices per course on the five-course lunch menu, with the number jumping up to 31313 at dinner. Paul Kitching is one of the most inventive chefs around, and eating here brings one delight and surprise after another. Dinner might open with oriental scallops with battered smoked haddock, the accompaniments of rhubarb, coriander, beetroot and ginger adding bursts of pungent and sweet flavours, followed by a vegetable soup in three layers: purée, then chunks, topped with foam, spicy popcorn and a brittle crisp. 'Pork pickle ploughman's' has appeared as the main event, delicate pork loin of staggering flavour with various styles and textures of ham, black pudding and crackling, crowned with a crisp of pickle, with a second plate of hot, crisp vegetables. A fish alternative could be halibut ratatouille with tuna mayo, spinach, caviar, pine nuts and feuillette. Next up is cheese, before the finale, perhaps the playfully described 'mustn't grumble, just a humble crumble': crumble topped with apples and pears, a couple of concentrated cherries and Drambuie-spiked custard, with a separate plate of whole and crushed brazil nuts and dried and fresh fruit.

Chef Paul Kitching **Seats** 36, Pr/dining room 10 **Times** 12-1.45/6.45-9.30, Closed 2 wks Jan, 2 wks summer, Sun-Mon **Prices** Fixed L 2 course £22, Fixed D 3 course £55 **Wines** 245 bottles over £30, 7 by glass **Parking** On street **Notes** 4/5 course L £42/£55, D £62/£70, Sat D 5 course only, Vegetarian available, Children 5 yrs+

RATHO Map 21 NT17

The Bridge Inn at Ratho

Modern British NEW

tel: 0131 333 1320 **27 Baird Rd EH28 8RA**
email: info@bridgeinn.com **web:** www.bridgeinn.com
dir: *Phone for directions*

Classic canal-side inn with seasonal menu

Right by the Union Canal, with views over the water from both garden and restaurant, The Bridge Inn is the perfect spot for watching the passing boats. If the canal-side action doesn't float your boat, fear not, for there are cask ales, regional whiskies, and an appealing menu on board. The restaurant is as traditional and soothing as the view, with everything from comforting old favourites such as fish and chips to more ambitious options such as butter-seared scallops with local carrot and stem ginger purée, followed by loin of Perthshire venison. A kitchen garden down the towpath ensures a fresh supply of seasonal goodies.

Chef Ben Watson **Seats** 72, Pr/dining room 12 **Times** 12-3/5-9.30, Closed 25 Dec **Prices** Starter £4.25-£8, Main £13-£29, Dessert £5-£9 **Wines** 9 bottles over £30, 30 bottles under £30, 34 by glass **Parking** 50 **Notes** All day dining at wknds, Sunday L £14.50, Vegetarian available, Children welcome

FALKIRK

BANKNOCK Map 21 NS77

Glenskirlie House & Castle

Modern British V

tel: 01324 840201 **Kilsyth Rd FK4 1UF**
email: macaloneys@glenskirliehouse.com **web:** www.glenskirliehouse.com
dir: *Follow A803 signed Kilsyth/Bonnybridge, at T-junct turn right. Hotel 1m on right*

Labour-intensive dishes in the modern British style

A castle for the 21st century, Glenskirlie is a bright white pile, kitted out with a conical-roofed turret here, a little step-gabling there. Set in central Scotland, it's a country retreat that welcomes the wedding trade and has a range of eating options. Start with the like of seared scallops with crab and lime mousse, pickled watermelon, lemon-rind purée and Jerusalem artichoke. Mains are no less labour-intensive, partnering venison loin with braised venison and potato terrine, celeriac fondant, smoked apple purée and wilted spring greens in red wine jus. Desserts spin variations on apple, or fashion banana into a parfait alongside caramelised banana, cinnamon pain perdu and nutty ganache.

Chef Daryl Jordan **Seats** 54, Pr/dining room 150 **Times** 12-2/6-9, Closed 26-27 Dec, 1-4 Jan **Prices** Fixed L 2 course £19.99, Fixed D 3 course £29.99, Starter £8.25-£13.95, Main £23.99-£28.99, Dessert £8.25-£9.95 **Wines** 50 bottles over £30, 25 bottles under £30, 11 by glass **Parking** 100 **Notes** Afternoon tea £15, Champagne tea £22.50, Sunday L £24.99, Children welcome

POLMONT Map 21 NS97

Macdonald Inchyra Hotel and Spa

Modern, Traditional

tel: 01324 711911 **Grange Rd FK2 0YB**
email: inchyra@macdonald-hotels.co.uk **web:** www.macdonald-hotels.co.uk
dir: *2 mins from M9 junct 5*

Brasserie-style cooking in a popular hotel

The solid-stone Inchyra is a smart hotel with a plush spa and all mod cons. It's also home to The Scottish Steak Club, a brasserie-style dining option done out in swathes of rich leather, animal prints and darkwood. The menu is a foray into brasserie-land, so prawn cocktail or shallot and goats' cheese tart might kick things off. Next up, rib-eye on the bone, perhaps, served with the classic accompaniments of fat-cut chips, vine tomatoes, watercress and a béarnaise sauce. There are plenty of non-steak options such as pie of the day, jumbo scampi, or burgers. Finish with sticky toffee pudding or suchlike.

Seats 90, Pr/dining room **Times** 12-9.45, All-day dining **Prices** Prices not confirmed **Wines** 32 bottles over £30, 13 bottles under £30, 15 by glass **Notes** Sunday L, Vegetarian available, Children welcome

FIFE

ANSTRUTHER Map 21 NO50

The Cellar

Modern British

tel: 01333 310378 **24 East Green KY10 3AA**
email: thecellarrestaurant@outlook.com
dir: *Behind Scottish Fisheries Museum*

Inventive modern cooking in an intimate setting

Tucked away behind the Scottish Fisheries Museum, this 17th-century house may not get the waterside views of Anstruther's harbour front but its intimacy and character more than makes up for it. Accessed via a pretty cobbled courtyard, the building was once a cooperage and smokery so chef-patron Billy Boyter is continuing half a century of tradition here, with plenty of smoked ingredients on the menu. A sizzling fire and the soft glow of candles illuminate the dining room with its ancient beams and stone walls. The classy modern British menu offers dishes steeped in classical technique. Beef shoulder is cooked with great skill and served with hay-baked celeriac, charred baby gem and smoked onion. For a restaurant so close to the harbour, it comes as no surprise that fish cookery is also note-perfect – a precisely timed stone bass turning up with brown shrimps, sprouting broccoli, quinoa and lemon butter sauce. Before this, pork belly is paired with an oyster tempura, parsley and pickled fennel, or you could kick off with beetroot, vintage Gouda custard and smoked apple jelly. Finish with coconut parfait, chocolate crémeux, mint and cacoa ice cream or Crowdie mousse, parsnip cake, maple oats and lemon thyme.

Chef Billy Boyter **Seats** 28 **Times** 12.30-1.45/6.30-9, Closed 25-26 Dec, 1 Jan, Mon-Tue, L Wed **Prices** Fixed L 3 course £25, Tasting menu £48 **Wines** 46 bottles over £30, 10 bottles under £30, 21 by glass **Parking** On street **Notes** No children under 10yrs L and 12yrs D, Sunday L £25, Vegetarian available

CUPAR Map 21 NO31

Ostlers Close Restaurant

Modern British V

tel: 01334 655574 **Bonnygate KY15 4BU**
email: ostlersclose@btconnect.com
dir: *In small lane off main street, A91*

Fabulous seasonal produce and skilled hand in the kitchen

Down an alley off the main street, this one-time scullery of a 17th-century Temperance hotel has been a popular destination since 1981. With red-painted walls and linen-clad tables, it's an intimate space run with charm and enthusiasm. Concise handwritten menus showcase produce from the garden and wild mushrooms from local woods. Dishes are packed with flavour, the ingredients given room to shine. Typical examples are well-timed halibut with lobster in a buttery leek sauce to start, then roast saddle, confit shoulder and sautéed kidneys of local lamb on ratatouille in a strong stock reduction. Mirabelle plum tart with raspberry ripple ice cream makes a satisfying finale.

Chef James Graham **Seats** 26 **Times** 7-9.30, Closed 25-26 Dec, 1-2 Jan, 2 wks Apr, 2 wks Oct, Sun-Mon, L all week **Prices** Fixed D 3 course £30, Starter £8-£13, Main £23-£26, Dessert £8 **Wines** 23 bottles over £30, 44 bottles under £30, 6 by glass **Parking** On street, public car park **Notes** Fixed D 3 course Tue-Fri, Nov-May, Children 5 yrs+ D

ELIE Map 21 NO40

Sangsters

Modern British

tel: 01333 331001 **51 High St KY9 1BZ**
dir: *From St Andrews on A917 take B9131 to Anstruther, right at rdbt onto A917 to Elie. (11m from St Andrews)*

Modern cooking on the village high street

Bruce and Jackie Sangster regularly wow diners with finely crafted modern Scottish cooking that includes apples and herbs from the back garden. It all takes place in a smart dining room, furnished with crisply dressed tables and high-backed chairs. Dinner perhaps kicks off with seared Ross-shire scallops in a cauliflower and bacon purée with black pudding crumble and bacon crisps. Main course might be a seared breast of Gressingham duck with puy lentils, a creamy-rich gratin potato, and a port wine sauce, while a beautifully rich orange gel cuts through a melt-in-the-mouth chocolate-glazed banana delice to make a lovely end to the meal.

Chef Bruce & Jacqueline Sangster **Seats** 28 **Times** 12.30-1.30/7-8.30, Closed 25-26 Dec, Jan, 1st wk Nov, Mon (also Tue winter), L Tue-Sat, D Sun **Prices** Fixed D 3 course £42 **Wines** 8 by glass **Parking** On street **Notes** Pre-order vegetarian options, Fixed D 4 course £47.50, Sunday L £29, Vegetarian available, Children 12 yrs+

NEWPORT-ON-TAY Map 21 NO42

The Newport Restaurant

Modern British NEW

tel: 01382 541449 **1 High St DD6 8AB**
email: info@thenewportrestaurant.co.uk **web:** www.thenewportrestaurant.co.uk
dir: *Phone for directions*

Passion on a plate from *MasterChef: The Professionals* winner

There's not much better publicity than winning *MasterChef: The Professionals*, so 2014 winner Jamie Scott got off to a flyer when he opened his own restaurant. Cheerful and enthusiastic service and a breezy contemporary decor make for a relaxed dining experience, while pin-sharp contemporary cooking from Scott and his team make it a hot ticket. Choose between the small plates or go for a pre-ordained tasting menu, and expect the likes of a glorious veggie number with violet artichoke, goats' curd and pickled carrots. The ingredients impress throughout – local hogget, say, with aubergine prepared three ways, or sea trout with a divine mussel emulsion. One to watch.

Chef Jamie Scott **Times** 12-2.30/6-9.30, Closed Mon, L Tue, D Sun **Prices** Tasting menu £45-£65, Dessert £7-£9 **Notes** Tasting menu 5/8 course, Wknd brunch, Sunday L £30, Children welcome

PEAT INN Map 21 NO40

The Peat Inn

Modern British

tel: 01334 840206 **KY15 5LH**
email: stay@thepeatinn.co.uk **web:** www.thepeatinn.co.uk
dir: *At junct of B940/B941, 6m SW of St Andrews*

Virtuoso skills in village institution

Geoffrey and Katherine Smeddle celebrated a decade at this 18th-century inn in 2016, proudly continuing a tradition of 250 years of hospitality and making this tiny Fife village a suitable destination for any serious foodie. The Peat Inn is everything one looks for in a restaurant with rooms – the comfortable, welcoming suites being the perfect place to retire to after an indulgent evening in the restaurant. All three softly lit dining areas are comfortable and the thoughtfully constructed, seasonally-influenced menus are inspired by local produce. The style is contemporary, with classic French techniques and a comforting lack of gimmickry. There are tasting (including a vegetarian version) and à la carte menus, and you can expect dishes along the lines of quails eggs Benedict, langoustines and saffron brioche, or home-smoked monkfish with oyster mousse, cauliflower couscous and cucumber to begin, followed by crisp confit pork cheek, pickled red cabbage, and potatoes braised with buttered shallots and caramelized apple, or slow braised daube of veal with smoked mashed potato, shallot and balsamic purée and red wine sauce. Finish with Scottish farmhouse cheeses, or something more exotic – hot mango and passionfruit soufflé with rum and chocolate sauce, perhaps. The wine list is well worth investigating.

Chef Geoffrey Smeddle **Seats** 50, Pr/dining room 14
Times 12.30-2/6.30-9, Closed 25-26 Dec, 1-14 Jan, Sun-Mon **Prices** Fixed L 3 course fr £19, Fixed D 3 course fr £50, Tasting menu fr £70, Starter £19, Main £28, Dessert £10.50 **Wines** 350 bottles over £30, 10 bottles under £30, 16 by glass **Parking** 24 **Notes** Tasting menu 6 course D, Chef's menu 4 course L, Vegetarian available, Children welcome

ST ANDRESS Map 21 NO51

The Adamson

 Modern

tel: 01334 479191 **127 South St KY16 9UH**
email: info@theadamson.com
dir: *Phone for directions*

Confident cooking in a classy modern brasserie

Once home to photographer and physician Dr John Adamson (hence the name), the handsome building is a cool restaurant with exposed bricks, darkwood tables and a bar serving up nifty cocktails. The menu brings vim and vigour to the brasserie format with oodles of contemporary style and high-quality ingredients. Slow-roast tomato risotto with red pepper, pesto mozzarella and basil is a winning starter, ahead of new season lamb shoulder, which stars in a main course with lamb bacon, gem lettuce and deep-fried potato and sunblushed tomato gnocchi. The standard remains high with desserts such as banana parfait teamed with bitter chocolate, caramel and cherries.

Chef Stewart MacAulay **Seats** 70 **Times** 12-3/5-10, Closed 25-26 Dec, 1 Jan **Prices** Fixed L 2 course £13.90-£24, Starter £4.95-£9.50, Main £11.50-£32.50, Dessert £5.75-£7.50 **Wines** 21 bottles over £30, 18 bottles under £30, 12 by glass **Parking** On street **Notes** Chateaubriand to share £69, Sun L 2 sharing £29.50, Sunday L fr £15, Vegetarian available, Children welcome

Ardgowan Hotel

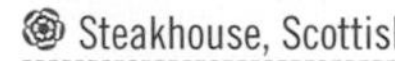 Steakhouse, Scottish

tel: 01334 472970 **2 Playfair Ter, North St KY16 9HX**
email: info@ardgowanhotel.co.uk **web:** www.ardgowanhotel.co.uk
dir: *A91 onto A917. 100 mtrs from rdbt on left*

Accomplished cooking in a golfing hotel

The Playfair's Restaurant and Steakhouse is located under the reception area, below street level, and the configuration means that diners can often find themselves eating close to drinkers using the bar. It all makes for a relaxed atmosphere, although the linen-clothed tables in the restaurant add a touch of formality to proceedings in a room dotted with deer skulls and other county pursuit objets d'art. High-quality ingredients are treated simply and with confidence to conjure modern Scottish dishes. Among starters might be local pigeon breast with Stornaway Black Pudding, chutney and pomegranate dressing, while main courses bring on grilled Loch Tay salmon with a mushroom garni and truffled hollandaise sauce.

Chef Duncan McLachlan **Seats** 45 **Times** 12-5/6-10, Closed Xmas, New Yr **Prices** Starter £3.95-£9.99, Main £9.95-£34.95, Dessert £5.95-£9.95 **Wines** 8 bottles over £30, 23 bottles under £30, 7 by glass **Parking** On street **Notes** Vegetarian available, Children welcome

Hotel du Vin St Andrews

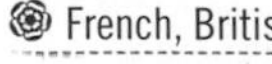 French, British

tel: 01334 472611 **40 The Scores KY16 9AS**
email: reception.standrews@hotelduvin.com **web:** www.hotelduvin.com
dir: *M90 junct 3, A92, A914, A91 to St Andrews. Left onto Golf Place, take first right*

Classic bistro dining in the old town

The latest outpost of the HdV brand has the usual broad appeal with its compelling mix of stylish boutique rooms, lively and informal bistro and stonking wine list. The kitchen delivers the trademark menu of French impressionism, where Gallic and British classics sit side by side: Toulouse sausage and mash, or haddock and chips? Shetland scallops might arrive as a first course dressed with sauce vièrge, and when it comes to main courses, the Josper oven turns out 28-day aged rib-eye (served with frites and a choice of sauce). Desserts show the same allegiances with treacle tart with clotted cream ice cream competing with tarte au citron. The wine list is renowned.

Chef Ross Edgar **Seats** 45, Pr/dining room 27 **Times** 12-2.30/5.30-10 **Prices** Fixed L 2 course £16.95, Fixed D 3 course £19.95, Starter £5.95-£9.50, Main £12.50-£29.50, Dessert £6.95-£9.95 **Wines** 105 bottles over £30, 41 bottles under £30, 22 by glass **Parking** 5, On street **Notes** Sun brunch 4 course with French market table, Sunday L £22.95, Vegetarian available, Children welcome

Road Hole Restaurant

– *see opposite*

Rocca Restaurant

Modern Scottish, Italian V

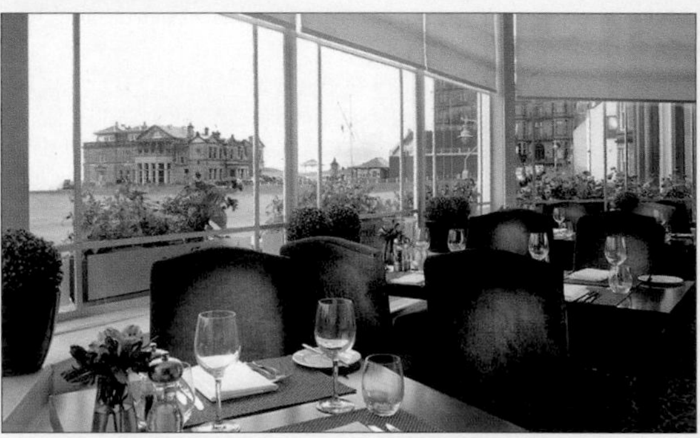

tel: 01334 472549 **Macdonald Rusacks Hotel, Pilmour Links KY16 9JQ**
email: info@roccarestaurant.com **web:** www.roccarestaurant.com
dir: *M90 junct 8, A91 to St Andrews. Turn left onto Golf Place, then right onto the links. Within Macdonald Rusacks Hotel*

Ingenious Scots-Italian food with ringside views of the golf

There are a number of fine-dining establishments offering wonderful vistas of the Old Course at St Andrews but only Rocca provides unparalleled views of the world-famous 18th hole – window seats here are hotly contested by those wishing to overlook the fairway. The cooking at the Rusacks Hotel combines Italian simplicity with inventive Scottish modernism conjured from top-drawer produce sourced from Fife and Perthshire. The ingredients shine throughout a meal that might kick off with perfectly timed hand-dived West Coast scallops, their sweet freshness accentuated by acorn-fed black ham, a robust orange purée and added textural contrast from hazelnuts and chicory. At main course, impressively tender Goosnargh duck appears with crisp and golden sarladaise potatoes, sweet and full-flavoured heritage carrots, rhubarb and gingerbread. Another second course sees Anstruther lobster teamed with a tagliatelle of herbs and sauce vièrge. A dessert of dark chocolate pavé delivers a bitterness that is perfectly complemented by the light and creamy dulce de leche and crunch of the hazelnuts. The well-constructed wine list, featuring a fair few meaty Italians, offers a generous number by the glass. The hotel's One Under gastropub offers simpler bistro fare.

Chef Davey Aspin **Seats** 70, Pr/dining room 35 **Times** 12.30-2.30/6.30-9.30, Closed Sun-Mon (Nov-Mar), L all week (Oct-Apr), D all week (Oct-Apr) **Prices** Fixed L 2 course £21.50, Tasting menu £65-£100, Starter £9.95-£14.50, Main £27.50-£32, Dessert £7.50-£10.95 **Wines** 100 bottles over £30, 7 bottles under £30, 16 by glass **Parking** 23 **Notes** Children welcome

Road Hole Restaurant

ST ANDREWS Map 21 NO51

Modern European

tel: 01334 474371 **The Old Course Hotel, Golf Resort & Spa KY16 9SP**
email: reservations@oldcoursehotel.co.uk
web: www.oldcoursehotel.co.uk
dir: *M90 junct 8 then A91 to St Andrews*

Stylish modern Scottish cooking overlooking the 17th hole

There is no shortage of five-star hotels on the Scottish golfing circuit, but the famous Old Course overlooks the cradle of the game at the world-renowned links at St Andrews, specifically the hallowed Road Hole of the 17th green, and that's a hard-to-beat location. As you'd expect, the interior bears the elegant trappings of a top-class hotel, all swish drapes, squishy sofas and deluxe appointments, with the Road Hole Restaurant, with panoramic views across the stick-swinging action, Swilcan Bridge and West Sands Beach, done out in shades of gold. There are set-lunch, tasting and dégustation menus as well as the carte, with the kitchen working around a modern Scottish style. Given the surroundings it's no surprise to find luxuries of foie gras and lobster among the starters, the former in a pavé of foie gras with confit leg cromesquis, the richness cut by caramelised orange and cocoa granola – a well-conceived dish of top-class ingredients all perfectly prepared – the latter as a deeply flavoured dish of lobster gratin with parsley purée and hollandaise. Timings and techniques never falter and dishes are not too complex, witness tender loin of venison with smoked rosemary spätzle, carrot gratin and broccoli, or a robust partnership of Black Isle beef fillet and curried oxtail with cauliflower purée, Roscoff onion and red wine salsify. Fish treatments are pretty robust all round, as is seen in monkfish served with with persillade noisette, a langoustine, Morteau sausage and leeks. Breads are of the same high standards, canapés are a delight, and puddings include the appealing balance of flavours in caramelised bananas with blonde Dulcey crème and salted toffee. Staff contribute to a memorable experience with their clued-up, correct but unfussy and friendly manner.

Chef Craig McAllister **Seats** 70, Pr/dining room 16 **Times** 12.30-2/7-9.30, Closed Mon-Tue, L Thu-Sun (Apr-Sep), Fri-Sun (Oct-Mar) **Prices** Fixed L 3 course £19.50-£21.50, Tasting menu £55-£80, Starter £10-£22.50, Main £18-£38, Dessert £8.50-£11 **Wines** 15 bottles under £30, 11 by glass **Parking** 100 **Notes** Tasting menu 5/8 course, Sunday L £19.50-£21.50, Vegetarian available, Children welcome

ST ANDREWS *continued*

Rufflets Country House

Modern British, European NOTABLE WINE LIST

tel: 01334 472594 **Strathkinness Low Rd KY16 9TX**
email: reservations@rufflets.co.uk **web:** www.rufflets.co.uk
dir: *1.5m W of St Andrews on B939*

Family-owned hotel in exquisite grounds

The creeper-covered turreted mansion on the outskirts of the city has been in the same family ownership since 1952, sitting in 10 acres of exquisite gardens. Its name refers to the 'rough flat lands' that once comprised the local landscape. The cooking is as modern as can be, trying out interesting approaches to top-drawer prime materials. First up might be ham hough terrine garnished with sticks of apple, mango salsa and cider jelly. Main course might bring on vividly tinted saffron-poached cod in herb and pancetta crust with cauliflower foam. Dessert may well be damn fine pecan pie with cinnamon ice cream and caramelised banana.

Russell Hotel

Scottish, International

tel: 01334 473447 **26 The Scores KY16 9AS**
email: enquiries@russellhotelstandrews.co.uk **web:** www.russellhotelstandrews.co.uk
dir: *From A91 left at 2nd rdbt into Golf Place, right in 200yds into The Scores, hotel in 300yds on left*

Scottish-Italian cooking in an intimate hotel dining room

A Victorian terraced townhouse overlooking the bay makes a relaxing bolt hole for anyone, though golfing fanatics relish its proximity to the Old Course. The small dining room sports a mixture of sober grey and thistled wallpaper, with framed prints of the local scenery, and low lighting in the evenings. The cooking is modern Scottish with Italian inflections. Smoked haddock with leek and goats' cheese croquettes and a salad of rocket, basil and walnuts is a gentle opener. Main courses include lemon- and herb-crusted cod in garlicky tomato sauce, pot-roasted pheasant with chestnut mushrooms and lardons, or roast loin of Grampian venison with pearl barley risotto, shaved parmesan and pesto.

St Andrews Bar and Grill

Scottish NEW

tel: 01334 837000 **Fairmont St Andrews, Scotland KY16 8PN**
email: standrews.scotland@fairmont.com **web:** www.fairmont.com/standrews
dir: *1.5m outside St Andrews on A917 towards Crail*

Spectacular views and modern comfort food

A free shuttle bus takes you from the Fairmont Hotel to this dining option in the clubhouse, but it is a lovely walk. Spectacularly situated on a promontory overlooking St Andrew Bay – it's like you're floating above the sea – St Andrews Bar and Grill offers sandwiches, burgers and such like at lunchtime, while the evening sees the seafood bar and grill come into their own. Begin with a Perthshire chicken liver and foie gras parfait with orange gel, or dressed crab, move on to local lobster or 28-day aged Black Isle beef cooked on the grill. Finish with poached pineapple with pistachio sponge, coconut sorbet and lime gel.

Chef Alan Matthew **Times** 12-5/6-9 **Prices** Fixed D 3 course £35, Tasting menu £69, Starter £5-£6, Main £14-£21, Dessert £2-£7 **Wines** 16 bottles over £30, 10 bottles under £30, 10 by glass **Notes** ALC L only, Seafood Bar £7-£60, Grill £19-£70, Vegetarian available, Children welcome

Sands Grill

Steak, Seafood

tel: 01334 474371 & 468228 **The Old Course Hotel, Golf Resort & Spa KY16 9SP**
email: reservations@oldcoursehotel.co.uk
dir: *M90 junct 8 then A91 to St Andrews*

Locally inspired brasserie-style cooking

Overlooking the world-famous golf course and the coast beyond, The Old Course Hotel occupies a desirable position and offers a wide range of dining options. The Sands Grill is the more informal option, a contemporary brasserie run by slick, unstuffy staff. The kitchen looks around the globe for influence and a meal could begin with maple syrup-glazed pork ribs, smoked pepper chutney and coleslaw before a main course of Thai-style crab cake with sea bass, Asian salad and Oriental dressing. Sticky toffee pudding with clotted cream ice cream brings a meal to a more traditional British finish.

The Seafood Restaurant

Modern Seafood

tel: 01334 479475 **Bruce Embankment KY16 9AB**
email: standrews@theseafoodrestaurant.com
dir: *On A917 turn left along Golf Place*

Uncomplicated fish cookery between golf and sea

Enjoying an enviable waterfront position 200 yards from the Old Course at St Andrews, the restaurant sits precariously balanced over the edge of the sea wall. With waves crashing on the rocks below, the decor does nothing to distract the eye from the nearby marine activity. From the open kitchen, the fish and seafood dishes are as enlivening as the sea spray itself. The freshness of the produce is encapsulated in a starter of sashimi (sea bream, tuna, salmon) served with wasabi, while a fillet of cod with borlotti beans, chorizo, squid and red pepper sauce is a robust main.

ST MONANS Map 21 NO50

raig Millar@16 West End

Modern Scottish NOTABLE WINE LIST

el: 01333 730327 **16 West End KY10 2BX**
mail: craigmillar@16westend.com
ir: *Take A959 from St Andrews to Anstruther, then W on A917 through Pittenweem. In St Ionans to harbour then right*

clectic cooking with sweeping harbour views

weeping views of the Firth of Forth and St Monans harbour can get dramatic when vinter waves surge over the sea wall, but the proximity of the sea is a reminder of ne business here: serving seafood with an exciting modern spin. Chef-patron Craig Iillar applies well honed techniques to his produce to deliver precise, Asian- and uropean-influenced dishes. Sea trout with oyster soup and miso caramel might be ollowed by cod fillet with saffron and mussel broth and gnocchi. The short menus lso offer some meat dishes – perhaps a main course of braised veal cheek with nash and spring onions – and puddings include pannacotta with strawberries and uff candy'.

hef Craig Millar **Seats** 35, Pr/dining room 25 **Times** 12.30-2/6.30-9, Closed 25-26 ec, 1-2 Jan, 2 wks Jan, Mon-Tue **Prices** Prices not confirmed **Wines** 77 bottles over 30, 11 bottles under £30, 7 by glass **Parking** 10 **Notes** Sunday L, Vegetarian vailable, Children 12 yrs+ D

CITY OF GLASGOW

GLASGOW Map 20 NS56

lythswood Square

Modern British NOTABLE WINE LIST

l: 0141 248 8888 **11 Blythswood Square G2 4AD**
mail: reserve@blythswoodsquare.com **web:** www.blythswoodsquare.com
r: *Phone for directions*

ontemporary and classic cooking in former automobile headquarters

uilt in 1821 as the grand headquarters for the Royal Scottish Automobile Club, is building has been injected with a good dollop of boutique style, plus a xurious 21st-century spa, resulting in a hotel of real verve. The restaurant in the rmer ballroom mixes contemporary decor with high ceilings and ornate asterwork – a setting that says switched-on and modern, with food to follow suit. eared scallops with curried pumpkin purée and pickled butternut squash set the ne, while pork belly from the Josper grill comes with mash, black pudding and pple sauce. To finish, there's sticky toffee pudding with candied pecans and ourbon ice cream.

a Bonne Auberge

French, Mediterranean

l: 0141 352 8310 & 352 8300 **Holiday Inn Glasgow, 161 West Nile St G1 2RL**
nail: theatreland@labonneauberge.co.uk **web:** www.labonneauberge.co.uk
r: *M8 junct 16, follow signs for Royal Concert Hall, hotel opposite*

arisian style with imaginative menu in theatreland

is ever-popular venue is kitted out like a French brasserie, with a predominantly d decor, lamps on wooden tables, banquettes and attentive and friendly staff. gin with a rich chicken live pâté flavoured with garlic and port, served with iced pear compôte and toasted brioche, before moving on to pork fillet wrapped in ncetta and partnered with white beans and chorizo. Meats including BBQ pork in and rib-eye steak are cooked on the grill. The lunchtime special might be croque monsieur followed by chocolate profiteroles, and is terrific value for money. For dessert, coconut and raspberry tart with pistachio ice cream hits the spot.

Chef Gerry Sharkey **Seats** 90, Pr/dining room 100 **Times** 12-2.15/5-10 **Prices** Fixed L 2 course fr £16.95, Fixed D 3 course £23.95-£25.95, Starter £5-£9.95, Main £12-£29, Dessert £5-£8 **Wines** 7 bottles over £30, 21 bottles under £30, 14 by glass **Parking** NCP opposite **Notes** Pre-theatre menu £18.95 from 5pm, Sunday L, Vegetarian available, Children welcome

Cail Bruich

Modern British

tel: 0141 334 6265 **752 Great Western Rd G12 8QX**
email: info@cailbruich.co.uk
dir: *Phone for directions*

Skilful contemporary cookery using top-notch regional produce

Brothers Paul and Chris Charalambous recently celebrated a decade since they opened their slick bistro in Glasgow's bohemian West End, adjacent to the city's world-famous Botanical Gardens. Cail Bruich means 'eat well' and it would be hard not to at this family-run restaurant where artisan producers supply the kitchen with seasonal, predominantly local ingredients. A recent refurbishment with low-slung copper lights, red leather banquettes and unclothed darkwood tables has also resulted in a new kitchen that is open to the dining room, adding to the theatre of a meal here. The modern European cooking is delivered via a trio of menu formats, from a well-priced market formula, upgrading to the carte and tasting menu with optional wines to match. Whichever route you take, there's vibrant, inventive cooking and sound technique, as demonstrated in a memorable starter of salmon with its accompanying crab, cucumber, baked lemon and avocado. Next up, a honey-glazed breast and crispy leg of Gressingham duck is in the company of spiced date and chicory, or, if fish is your thing, a precisely cooked fillet of stone bass appears alongside violet artichokes, fennel, shrimp and brown butter. Dessert brings rhubarb cheesecake, pink peppercorn, yogurt and sorrel.

Chef Chris Charalambous **Seats** 48 **Times** 12-2.30/5.30-9.30, Closed Xmas, New Year, L Mon-Tue **Prices** Fixed L 2 course £16, Fixed D 3 course £25, Tasting menu £39-£55, Starter £8-£12, Main £16-£24, Dessert £7-£12 **Wines** 31 bottles over £30, 12 bottles under £30, 16 by glass **Parking** On street **Notes** Sunday L fr £25, Vegetarian available, Children welcome

Chop Chop Glasgow

Chinese **NEW**

tel: 01412 219799 **43 Mitchell St G1 3LN**
email: chopchop.glasgow@gmail.com
dir: *Phone for directions*

Vibrant setting for cracking Chinese cuisine

Having made a name for itself in Edinburgh, Chop Chop has opened a branch 40 miles to the west, in Glasgow's Mitchell Street. The large and brightly decorated dining room gets even more colour from four artificial blossom trees that take centre stage, with the staff adding to the sunny atmosphere. North Eastern China is the focus of the menu, so check out the excellent dumplings (pork and coriander jiaozi, say), but the deliciously sticky pork ribs shouldn't be missed either. Dishes come in small and large plates (sharing is encouraged) – coley in black bean sauce, crispy Northern beef, and, to finish, sugar string apple.

Chef Vijay Kate **Seats** 110 **Times** 12-2.30/6-10 **Prices** Prices not confirmed **Parking** NCP **Notes** Vegetarian available, Children welcome

GLASGOW *continued*

The Fish People Café

Modern Seafood NEW

tel: 0141 4298787 **350a Scotland St G5 8QF**
email: thefishpeoplecafe@hotmail.co.uk
dir: *Directly opposite Shields Road & underground, across from Scotland St museum*

Terrific seafood in an unassuming eatery

A lively little fish restaurant run by the fishmonger next door sounds an irresistible proposition, and the skilled team in the kitchen know how to handle the peerless piscine produce, turning out uncomplicated dishes with pin-sharp technique and timings. Super-fresh yellowfin tuna carpaccio is helped along by garlic olive oil and balsamic, while a whole grey sole is grilled to perfection and served on the bone, together with classic brown shrimp butter with lemon, peas and spring cabbage. There's no going wrong with the fish stew either, which delivers generous chunks of fish in a deeply flavoured sauce with saffron rouille, croûtons and gruyère.

Chef John Gillespie **Seats** 39 **Times** 12-8.45, All-day dining, Closed 25-26 Dec, 1st wk Jan (incl 1 Jan), Mon **Prices** Fixed L 2 course £13, Starter £5-£9.50, Main £9.50-£19.50, Dessert £5.50 **Wines** 1 bottle over £30, 12 bottles under £30, 7 by glass **Parking** Multistorey or park & ride **Notes** Sunday L, Vegetarian available, Children welcome

Gamba

Scottish, Seafood

tel: 0141 572 0899 **225a West George St G2 2ND**
email: info@gamba.co.uk
dir: *On corner of West Campbell St & West George St, close to Blythswood Sq*

Top-notch vibrant fish and seafood in the West End

This perennial favourite enjoys a well-deserved reputation as the go-to place for top-notch fish and seafood. The kitchen is passionate about sourcing the best seasonal produce, with fish from sustainable stocks cooked with simplicity and style. The menu might get under way with one of its original ideas – perhaps a glass of tartare of sea bass mixed with pieces of goats' cheese, chives, sesame seeds and tomato and basil sorbet – and go on to halibut fillet on crabmeat with smoked haddock, asparagus, coral cream and tarragon. No less impressive are desserts: perhaps carrot pudding with citrus cream cheese and marmalade ice cream.

Chef Derek Marshall **Seats** 66 **Times** 12-2.15/5-9.30, Closed 25-26 Dec, 1st wk Jan, L Sun **Prices** Fixed L 2 course £19, Fixed D 3 course £22, Starter £7-£14.50, Main £11.50-£28, Dessert £6.50-£10.50 **Wines** 21 bottles over £30, 14 bottles under £30, 6 by glass **Parking** On street **Notes** Pre-theatre menu £19-£22, 3 course market menu with wine £30, Vegetarian available, Children welcome

The Gannet

 Modern Scottish

tel: 0141 204 2081 **1155 Argyle St G3 8TB**
email: info@thegannetgla.com
dir: *Phone for directions*

Buzzing contemporary venue with Scottish flavour

The guys behind The Gannet looked to the wild and rugged Hebridean coastline for inspiration before opening here in Glasgow's West End, focusing on the fabulous ingredients those islands and the rest of Scotland have to offer. They've created one of the city's hottest addresses. The pared-back interior suits the mood of our times with its urban/rustic finish of exposed bricks, natural woods, simple furniture and minimal decorative touches – it's cool, contemporary and very, very popular. Grab a stool at the front bar and tuck into a small plate (warm cured salmon confit with herb purée and crisp capers, say) and a cocktail such as the evocatively named Wild Lady. The à la carte offers the likes of lamb's sweetbreads – supremely tender and velvety – with a deeply satisfying chicken sauce and Jerusalem artichokes in various forms, followed perhaps by plaice landed at Peterhead and served up with slow-cooked pork cheek, leeks (braised and scorched), and potato purée. The unwaveringly seasonal menu also extends to red deer matched with pickled blackberries and a glossy port and red wine sauce, while perfectly executed desserts might include treacle tart, which arrives with a scoop of vanilla ice cream. There are some interesting Scottish beers to be had, plus a short and appealing wine list.

Chef Peter McKenna, Ivan Stein **Seats** 45, Pr/dining room 14 **Times** 12-2.30/5-9.45, Closed 25-26 Dec, 1st wk Jan, Mon **Prices** Starter £7-£9, Main £15-£23, Dessert £6-£9 **Wines** 28 bottles over £30, 13 bottles under £30, 8 by glass **Parking** On street **Notes** Small plate menu 12-2.30 & 5-7pm £5-6.50, Sunday L £30, Vegetarian available, Children welcome

The Hanoi Bike Shop

Vietnamese V

tel: 0141 334 7165 **8 Ruthven Ln G12 9BG**
email: pho@hanoibikeshop.co.uk **web:** www.hanoibikeshop.co.uk
dir: *Phone for directions*

Stirring Vietnamese street food

This vibrant venture displays the machines alongside hanging lanterns to bring vivid colour, and is the brainchild of the people behind the Ubiquitous Chip and its sister restaurant, Stravaigin. Over two buzzing floors, staff in branded T-shirts work like troopers, and the chilled-out, canteen-style vibe suits the authentic street food menu of dazzling Vietnamese flavours. The menu gives the Vietnamese names of dishes followed by an English translation, thus ga loi xa lach is salt-and-chilli pheasant thigh – packed with flavour – and ga muong BBQ is barbecued chicken with pickled cucumber and morning glory. There are classic pho dishes, too.

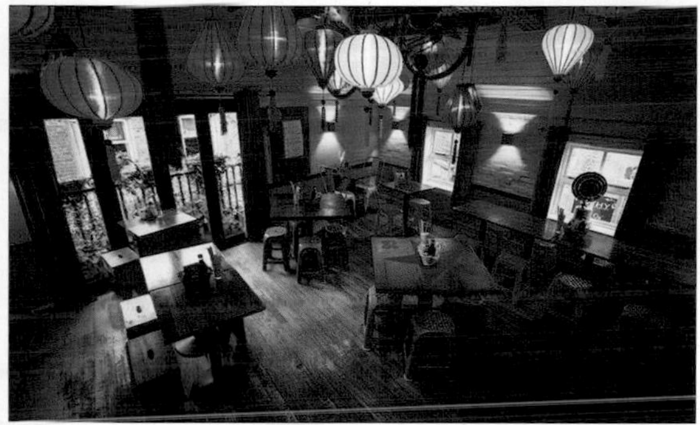

Chef Jesse Stevens **Seats** 75, Pr/dining room 35 **Times** 12-12.30, All-day dining, Closed 25 Dec, 1 Jan, L 26 Dec **Prices** Prices not confirmed **Wines** 2 bottles under £30, 4 by glass **Parking** On street **Notes** Sun brunch (Yum Cha), Phat Phuc monthly event, Sunday L, Children welcome

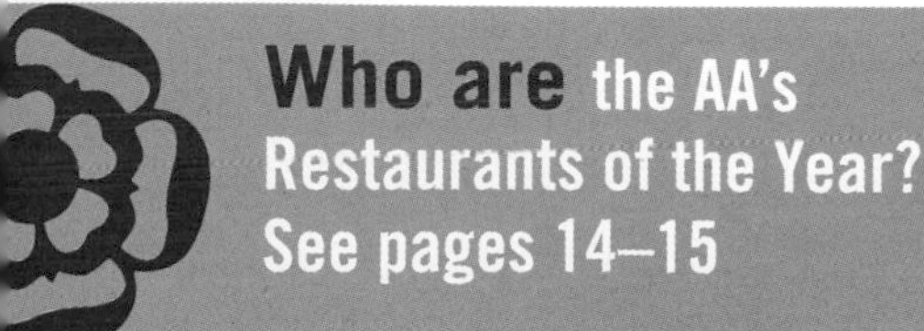

Who are the AA's Restaurants of the Year? See pages 14–15

Hotel du Vin at One Devonshire Gardens

French, European

tel: 0141 339 2001 **1 Devonshire Gardens G12 0UX**
email: bistromer.glasgow@hotelduvin.com **web:** www.hotelduvin.com
dir: *M8 junct 17, follow signs for A82, after 1.5m turn left into Hyndland Rd*

Smart, creative cooking in an elegant townhouse hotel

The crown of the HdV group rests fittingly on one of its northerly extremities, in the West End of Glasgow, in a supremely elegant Victorian terrace hotel. Discreet freshening of the interior decor has produced a set of dining rooms where sparkling new chandeliers light up uncovered floors and upholstery matches the building's stone facade. Barry Duff heads up the kitchens, which aim to soar above the core bistro offering of Hotel du Vin. Visual dazzle is guaranteed by the vivid green pea velouté with smoked ham hock, into which a lightly poached egg bursts in gold, or there could be chicken and leek terrine in truffled vinaigrette. Scottish prime materials are sourced with pride, as for the Ayrshire lamb that comes as loin with ratatouille, puréed white beans, aubergine caviar and tapenade, and some of the shoulder meat bound into a rich potato cake. For another stunning optical display, monkfish is painted in squid ink and served with saffron noodles and mussels in coconut broth. Finish with delicate banana soufflé and toffee ice cream.

Chef Barry Duff **Seats** 78, Pr/dining room 70 **Times** 12-2/5.30-10, Closed D 25 Dec **Prices** Fixed L 2 course £21.95, Tasting menu £38.50-£59, Starter £10.50-£14.95, Main £18.50-£32.50, Dessert £8.50-£9 **Wines** 200+ bottles over £30, 10 bottles under £30, 12 by glass **Parking** On street **Notes** Tasting 4/6 course, Pre-theatre 2/3 course £21.95/£26.95, Sunday L £24.95, Vegetarian available, Children welcome

Malmaison Glasgow

Modern French

tel: 0141 572 1001 **278 West George St G2 4LL**
email: info@thehonoursglasgow.co.uk **web:** www.malmaison.com
dir: *From George Square take St Vincent St to Pitt St. Hotel on corner with West George St*

Brasserie cooking in a former church

The Glasgow Mal has made its home in a deconsecrated Greek Orthodox church. A mix of traditional and modern French brasserie cooking is the draw, with crab Marie Rose to start, alongside less mainstream offerings such as a tartare constructed of sea bream, anchovies, red pepper and crème fraîche. Select breeds and cuts of thoroughbred beef are the backbone of main courses, but useful diversions include the sharply distinctive curry-dusted fillets of John Dory with leeks in a mussel-infused buttery sauce and Sauternes foam. Soufflé du jour is worth a look at dessert.

Mother India

Indian

tel: 0141 221 1663 & 221 1832 **28 Westminster Ter, Sauchiehall St G3 7RU**
email: info@motherindia.co.uk
dir: *From Kelvingrove Museum located on corner of Sauchiehall St & Kelvingrove St*

Long-running Indian landmark serving smart, interesting curries

This landmark restaurant continues to draw the crowds with its inventive, flavour-packed Indian food. Spread over three floors, Mother India avoids cliché in its decor with prints of the city on the walls and panelling in the first-floor room. The menu takes a step away from curry-house standards to deliver broadly appealing dishes. Start with haddock pakoras – pieces of deep-fried fish marinated in ginger and chilli – served with spicy mixed beans, and follow with fall-apart lamb karahi in a rich pepper sauce. Desserts don't let the side down either.

GLASGOW *continued*

Number Sixteen

Modern International NEW

tel: 0141 339 2544 & 07957 423615 **16 Byres Rd G11 5JY**
dir: *2 mins walk from Kelvinhall tube station, at bottom of Byres Rd*

Buzzy neighbourhood venue mixing interesting flavour combinations

This dinky neighbourhood restaurant has a strong local following. It's an elbow-to-elbow sort of place with a pocket-sized downstairs area, and a mini-mezzanine above, all decorated with colourful artwork, and kept ticking over by casually dressed, on-the-ball staff. The chefs beavering away in the open-to-view kitchen aren't scared to experiment with a vibrant barrage of flavours, without losing sight of the seasons, thus seared partridge breast might appear with roast pear, forced rhubarb, Jerusalem artichoke purée and brown butter, before cod fillet with seared spinach, skirlie potato cake and seafood cassoulet. Pudding might be yogurt pannacotta with passionfruit foam and oatmeal flapjack.

Chef Gerard Mulholland **Seats** 36, Pr/dining room 17
Times 12-2.30/5.30-9, Closed 25-26 Dec, 1-2 Jan **Prices** Fixed L 2 course £14.95, Starter £4.95-£9.50, Main £13.50-£17.50, Dessert £6.50-£8.95 **Wines** 8 bottles over £30, 25 bottles under £30, 6 by glass **Parking** On street **Notes** Pre-theatre 2/3 course £15.95/£19.95, Sunday L £15.95-£18.95, Vegetarian available, Children welcome

111 by Nico

Modern European NEW V

tel: 0141 334 0111 **111 Cleveden Rd, Kelvinside G12 0JU**
email: dine@111bynico.co.uk
dir: *Phone for directions*

Smart city cooking with a philanthropic angle

Nico Simeone's altruism in employing youngsters who didn't get the best start in life is thoroughly commendable. Together, they produce contemporary cooking for a city-smart audience, the kind that appreciates ingenious duck leg croustillants with textures of parsnip including an Indian-spiced purée, scattered with pomegranate seeds, with perhaps a main pairing of mackerel and squid on a stew of white beans, chorizo and butternut, the dish dressed in freshly squeezed lemon. To finish, cheesecake is ritually taken apart for quenelles of lime cream cheese with a separate thyme-scented crumble, poached pear and lime gel.

Chef Nico Simeone, Modou Diagme **Times** 12-2.30/5-10, Closed Mon **Prices** Fixed L 2 course £19, Fixed D 3 course £22, Tasting menu £30-£60 **Wines** 15 bottles over £30, 23 bottles under £30, 18 by glass **Notes** Tasting menu 5 course, Wknd all day dining

Opium

Chinese, Oriental fusion

tel: 0141 332 6668 **191 Hope St G2 2UL**
email: eat@opiumrestaurant.co.uk
dir: *Phone for directions*

Asian fusion from a Hong Kong masterchef in the heart of the city

A pin-sharp, contemporary-styled Asian-fusion restaurant in the pulsing heart of Glasgow. Big picture windows allow light to flood into a slick space where communal tables with high chairs share the space with conventional restaurant seating. Kwan Yu Lee has honed an on-trend mix of classical and modern Asian fusion dishes. An array of dim sum showcases basic skills, with steamed salmon, fennel and chive dumplings with a ginger dipping sauce full of evocative aromas. Next up, try a bowl of noodles such as one packed with tenderloin of pork, fine beans and bean sprouts, flavoured with Shaoxing wine and oyster sauce. Finish with mango jelly with coulis and cream.

Chef Kwan Yu Lee **Seats** 54 **Times** 12-2.30/5-10 **Prices** Prices not confirmed **Wines** 2 bottles over £30, 19 bottles under £30, 11 by glass **Notes** Pre-theatre 2/3 course menu, Sunday L, Vegetarian available, Children welcome

Ox and Finch

Modern British V

tel: 0141 339 8627 **920 Sauchiehall St G3 7TF**
email: hello@oxandfinch.com
dir: *500mtrs E of Kelvingrove Art Gallery & Museum, near Hydro & SECC*

Hip, go-to spot on Sauchiehall Street

Tapas-size portions are the deal at this buzzing venue. Bare brick walls, roughly painted wooden floors, banquette and booth seating and unbuttoned service create a casual, laid-back atmosphere. The menu is divided into such headings as 'snacks' and 'raw, cured and cold', and guests are advised to order two or three dishes. Layers of rabbit, ham hock and foie gras in a terrine with pistachios, served with gingerbread and pear, is a stunning prelude to, perhaps, spiced scallops with dhal, pickled cucumber and yogurt, and Italian sausage with gnocchi, squash, rosemary and chilli. Don't stint on puddings: lemon and Earl Grey baked Alaska is a masterpiece.

Chef Daniel Spurr **Seats** 70, Pr/dining room **Times** 12-12, All-day dining, Closed 25-26 Dec, 1-2 Jan **Prices** Main £4-£9.50, Dessert £5-£8.50 **Wines** 15 bottles over £30, 29 bottles under £30, 15 by glass **Parking** On street **Notes** Children welcome

La Parmigiana

Italian, Mediterranean

tel: 0141 334 0686 **447 Great Western Rd, Kelvinbridge G12 8HH**
email: info@laparmigiana.co.uk **web:** www.laparmigiana.co.uk
dir: *Next to Kelvinbridge underground*

West End institution serving superior Italian fare

The blue-painted exterior of this West End stalwart conceals a calm and refined interior of red walls, bare wooden floor and purple-padded wooden seats at white-clothed tables, with friendly and knowledgeable staff adding to the congenial atmosphere with endearing touches of flamboyance. Classics such as aubergine Parmigiana are well made and home-made pasta options like langoustine tagliatelle with courgettes and tomato are highly reliable, while for main there could be venison scaloppine with salsiccia and polenta croutons in a rich red wine ragù. Then wave the Italian flag with desserts like amaretto tiramisù and cappuccino ice cream.

Chef Peppino Camilli **Seats** 50 **Times** 12-2.30/5.30-10.30, Closed 25-26 Dec, 1 Jan, D Sun **Prices** Prices not confirmed **Wines** 35 bottles over £30, 15 bottles under £30,

8 by glass **Parking** On street **Notes** Pre-theatre 2/3 course 5.30-7pm £17.10/£19.90, Sunday L, Vegetarian available, Children welcome

Rogano

Scottish, Seafood V

tel: 0141 248 4055 **11 Exchange Place G1 3AN**
email: info@roganoglasgow.com
dir: *Phone for directions*

Abidingly popular Glasgow institution

Glasgow's longest serving restaurant became an octogenarian in 2015, having provisioned the city with fish and shellfish since luxury liner Queen Mary began her life on the Clyde. An often starry clientele returns for platters of fruits de mer, langoustines in garlic butter, and perhaps sea-and-land main courses such as seared scallops and slow-roast pork belly with cauliflower purée in curry oil. Meatier appetites might go for roast venison loin with braised red cabbage in bramble jus. More unusual starters might encompass blue cheese brûlée with beetroot salsa and poached figs, and it all concludes with cardamom-spiced white chocolate tart in cherry brandy syrup.

Chef Gordon Provan **Seats** 70, Pr/dining room 16 **Times** 12-2.30/6-10.30, Closed 1 Jan **Prices** Fixed L 2 course £16.50, Fixed D 3 course £21.50, Tasting menu £45, Starter £6.50-£12, Main £20-£40, Dessert £6.50-£14 **Wines** 100 bottles over £30, 30 bottles under £30, 14 by glass **Parking** NCP car parks **Notes** Tasting menu 4 course with wine £80, Sunday L, Children welcome

Shish Mahal

Indian

tel: 0141 339 8256 **60-68 Park Rd G4 9JF**
email: reservations@shishmahal.co.uk
dir: *From M8/A8 take exit towards Dumbarton. On Great Western Rd 1st left into Park Rd*

Longstanding Indian in a quiet part of the city

A Glaswegian institution since the 1960s, there's a smart modern feel to this restaurant's colour scheme, with leather seating, linen-clad tables and friendly and knowledgeable service. The extensive menu explores familiar regional variations, taking in old favourites from the madras, vindaloo and bhuna stables, but there are plenty of intriguing new ideas. Lamb karahi is full of tender meat and vibrant, complex flavours, strong chilli heat as well as sweetly caramelised onion, coriander seed and garlic, and might be the follow-up to generously packed chicken pakoras in gram flour batter with raita and chutney, or prawns in garlic butter with pineapple. Finish with stickily satisfying gulab jamon in cardamom syrup.

Chef I Humayun **Seats** 95, Pr/dining room 14 **Times** 12-2/5-11, Closed 25 Dec, L Sun **Prices** Prices not confirmed **Wines** 2 bottles over £30, 18 bottles under £30, 1 by glass **Parking** Side street, Underground station car park **Notes** Fixed L 4 course, Vegetarian available, Children welcome

Stravaigin

Modern International

tel: 0141 334 2665 **28-30 Gibson St, Kelvinbridge G12 8NX**
email: stravaigin@btinternet.com **web:** www.stravaigin.com
dir: *Next to Glasgow University. 200yds from Kelvinbridge underground*

Popular eatery with creative, multi-national flavour

The 'Think global, eat local' tagline of this switched-on stalwart of the Glasgow foodie scene sums up its culinary ideology. Spread over two floors of café-bar and a basement restaurant, the quirky venue features modern art set against rough stone walls. The kitchen unites Scotland's magnificent produce with an eclectic approach to global cuisine. Slow-cooked ox cheek might come with pea purée, sautéed mushrooms and sweetcorn, while rack and braised neck of lamb with spiced channa dhal and mint and coriander raita makes a similarly full-frontal attack on the taste buds. For dessert, there's apple and Muscovado bread pudding with caramelised plums and crème fraîche ice cream.

Chef Kenny Mackay **Seats** 62 **Times** 11-11, All-day dining, Closed 25 Dec, 1 Jan, L 26 Dec **Prices** Prices not confirmed **Wines** 18 bottles over £30, 30 bottles under £30, 14 by glass **Parking** On street, car park 100yds **Notes** Breakfast, Wknd brunch, Vegetarian available, Children welcome

GLASGOW *continued*

Turnip & Enjoy Restaurant

Modern European, Scottish NEW V

tel: 0141 334 6622 **393-395 Great Western Rd, Kelvinbridge G4 9HY**
email: hello@turnipandenjoy.co.uk **web:** www.turnipandenjoy.co.uk
dir: *2 min walk after Kelvinbridge going from west end towards city centre*

Just turn up and enjoy modern Scottish cooking

When the Enjoy Café's owner decided to upgrade it to a restaurant, he thought he'd call it Turn Up & Enjoy. But Turnip won the day. The compact, simply decorated interior features pale wood furniture, exposed brick, a large clock, mirrors and a small bar. Begin with monkfish cheeks, smoked oyster cream, nero spaghetti and fennel, or Stornoway Black Pudding with duck egg and chorizo crumble. Then how about slow-cooked pork belly, celeriac and vanilla, sticky pork rib purée, baked quince and spinach? Finish the meal with pecan butter parfait, cocoa nib bourbon biscuit, banana and Pedro Ximenez sherry ice cream. Naturally, turnips usually feature somewhere.

Chef Martin Connor **Seats** 40 **Times** 12-3/5-10, Closed 26 Dec, 1 Jan, Mon, L Tue **Prices** Fixed L 2 course £13.95-£15.95, Fixed D 3 course £19.95-£21.95, Tasting menu £35, Starter £6.50-£9.50, Main £14.95-£25, Dessert £6.50-£8.50 **Wines** 10 bottles over £30, 23 bottles under £30, 10 by glass **Parking** On street **Notes** Sunday L £13.95-£16.95, Children welcome

Ubiquitous Chip

Scottish V NOTABLE WINE LIST

tel: 0141 334 5007 & 334 7109 **12 Ashton Ln G12 8SJ**
email: reservations@ubiquitouschip.co.uk **web:** www.ubiquitouschip.co.uk
dir: *In West End, off Byres Rd. Adjacent to Hillhead underground station*

Iconic address for modern Scottish cooking

The Chip has been in business since 1971, its success due in part to its talent for keeping in step with the times without becoming a fickle follower of fashion. The cooking is imaginative but always clear-headed and based on superb Scottish ingredients. Chickpea and roast garlic cake is pepped up with raisin salsa and toasted pistachios, while a hearty main course of wild pheasant breast gains depth from a flageolet bean cassoulet and buttered kale. If you're up for fish, lythe fillet (that's pollack to folk from south of the border) comes with samphire, smoked ham and spring onion velouté. For dessert, there's malt pannacotta with dark chocolate ganache.

Ubiquitous Chip

Chef Andrew Mitchell **Seats** 110, Pr/dining room 45 **Times** 12-2.30/5-11, Closed 25 Dec, 1 Jan, L 26 Dec **Prices** Fixed L 2 course £16.95, Fixed D 3 course £20.95, Starter £6.45-£13.95, Main £15.95-£35, Dessert £6.45-£15 **Wines** 215 bottles over £30, 58 bottles under £30, 37 by glass **Parking** Lillybank Gardens (50mtrs) **Notes** Pre-theatre 2/3 course 5-6.30pm Sun-Fri £15.95/£19.95, Children welcome

Urban Bar and Brasserie

Modern British

tel: 0141 248 5636 **23-25 St Vincent Place G1 2DT**
email: info@urbanbrasserie.co.uk
dir: *In city centre between George Sq & Buchanan St*

Updated and interesting brasserie fare in a former bank

This sleek, modern bar-brasserie capitalises on the grandiose architecture of a former bank, throwing in brown leather banquettes, smartly laid tables and huge canvases of modern art. Add black-clad staff wearing long white aprons, and a bustling vibe, and you might be in Paris. The menu is Scotland-meets-Mediterranean ideas sprinkled with Asian flavours, a starter of smoked salmon with Thai jelly, cornichons and capers being typical of the style. Main courses can be as traditional as grilled lemon sole with tartare sauce and chips and as full-on as braised beef cheeks with parsnip purée, star anise gravy and crispy fennel. To finish, the addition of liquorice rejuvenates a crème brûlée.

Chef David Clunas **Seats** 120, Pr/dining room 20 **Times** 12-10, All-day dining, Closed 25 Dec, 1 Jan **Prices** Fixed L 2 course £15.95-£18.95, Starter £6-£12, Main £12-£29, Dessert £6-£8 **Wines** 20 bottles over £30, 20 bottles under £30, 8 by glass **Parking** NCP West Nile St **Notes** Pre-theatre menu, Sunday L, Vegetarian available, Children 14 yrs+

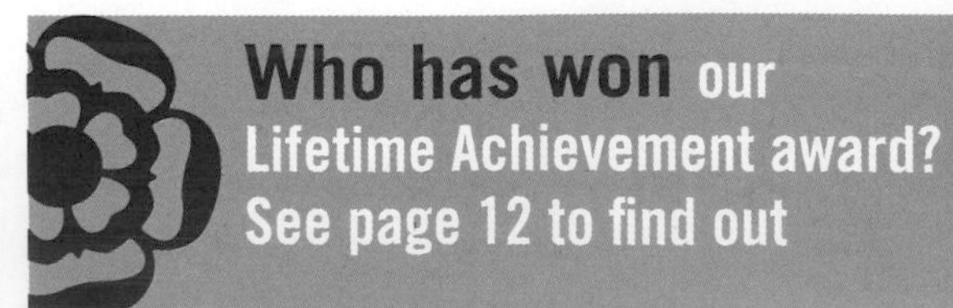

Wee Lochan

Modern Scottish

tel: 0141 338 6606 **340 Crow Rd, Broomhill G11 7HT**
email: eat@an-lochan.com
dir: *Phone for directions*

Contemporary cooking in the leafy West End

The black frontage gives a distinguished look to a neighbourhood restaurant in the quiet, leafy reaches of the West End, its wide terrace allowing pleasant outdoor dining in summer. The contemporary Scottish cooking scores a hit with precise, defined flavours. Start with a quartet of seared scallops with sliced chorizo, sauced with a buttery ribbon of herbs, lime and chilli, as a prelude to golden-skinned roast breast of guinea fowl garnished with a crisp bacon rasher, honey-glazed parsnips and mash in thyme-scented cider sauce. Desserts play to the gallery with an array of favoured flavours: perhaps dark chocolate delice, orange cake, hazelnut praline and honeycomb ice cream in orange anglaise.

Chef Rupert Staniforth, Bob Storrie **Seats** 50 **Times** 12-3/5-10, Closed 25 Dec, 1-2 Jan **Prices** Fixed L 2 course £13.95, Starter £4.50-£5, Main £12-£18, Dessert £4.50-£6.20 **Wines** 12 bottles over £30, 30 bottles under £30, 18 by glass **Parking** On street (no charge) **Notes** Pre-theatre fixed menu, Sunday L £15.95-£18.95, Vegetarian available, Children welcome

HIGHLAND

CROMARTY Map 23 NH76

The Factor's House

Modern British

tel: 01381 600394 **Denny Rd IV11 8YT**
email: stay@thefactorshouse.com **web:** www.thefactorshouse.com
dir: *A832 to Cromarty. Left after 30mph sign. If pass the "Welcome to Cromarty" sign then gone too far*

Daily-changing home-grown menu in a coastal hotel

This attractive red sandstone house on a coastal inlet features a wood-floored dining room with walls in burgundy and grey. A daily-changing four-course dinner menu, including Scottish cheeses, is the offering, and there is real personality to the dishes. First up might be an odd but successful construction of smoked haddock and leek lasagne topped with a gratinated cheddar soufflé, to be followed by a much simpler, intensely flavoured rolled pork loin stuffed with spinach, accompanied by garlicky dauphinoise and a mound of braised red cabbage and apple. The dessert could then be rhubarb frangipane tart with poached home-grown rhubarb and a brandy snap basket of ginger ice cream.

Chef Fiona Deakin **Seats** 10, Pr/dining room 10 **Times** 7-10, Closed 15 Dec-5 Jan, L all week **Prices** Prices not confirmed **Parking** 4 **Notes** Fixed D 4 course + coffee £37.50, Vegetarian available, Children 5 yrs+

DORNOCH Map 23 NH78

Dornoch Castle Hotel

Modern Scottish

tel: 01862 810216 **Castle St IV25 3SD**
email: enquiries@dornochcastlehotel.com **web:** www.dornochcastlehotel.com
dir: *2m N of Dornoch Bridge on A9, turn right to Dornoch. Hotel in village centre opp Cathedral*

Medieval castle hotel with a true Scottish flavour

A 15th-century castle makes romantic setting for a hotel, and here a sympathetic updating and modernisation has managed to preserve original features. The kitchen works a modern vein without losing sight of regional traditions. Beautifully pan-fried pigeon breast is served in a stew of pancetta and Puy lentils to make a memorable starter. Scotland's lochs and coastline are the source of seafood – perhaps a cold mixed platter, or salmon fillet with braised fennel and lemony herb butter – while carnivores could try a well-composed dish of chargrilled pork chop on apple purée with a black pudding and potato cake, plus honey-roast carrots and parsnips. Finish with classic tarte Tatin.

Chef Brian Sangster **Seats** 75, Pr/dining room 25
Times 12-2.30/6.30-9, Closed 25-26 Dec, 2nd wk Jan **Prices** Starter £6.95-£9.95, Main £14.95-£21.95, Dessert £7.50-£8.95 **Wines** 10 bottles over £30, 20 bottles under £30, 6 by glass **Parking** 12, On street (free) **Notes** Early D special menu, Sunday L £12.95-£18.95, Vegetarian available, Children welcome

Links House at Royal Dornoch

Classic Scottish NEW

tel: 01862 810279 **Links House, Golf Rd IV25 3LW**
email: info@linkshousedornoch.com **web:** www.linkshousedornoch.com
dir: *From A9 onto A949 into Dornoch. From Castle St, right into Church Street then left into Golf Rd. House at junct of Golf Rd & Kennedy Ave*

French-based cooking and lots of golf

Links House is single-mindedly devoted to the pursuit of golf and pictures of fairways and bunkers adorn the dining room, where a peat-burning fireplace is a feature. Modern European cooking with a firm French foundation is the name of the game, with traditional technique underpinning a fantastic maple-cured ham and Arran mustard terrine garlanded with little flowers and some celeriac remoulade, before a confit leg of Gressingham duck arrives on butterbean and chorizo cassoulet. A fish option might be seafood risotto garnished with scallops, confit tomato and spinach, and the deal is closed with dark chocolate mousse and matching ice cream, with honeycomb and Italian meringue.

Chef Jon-Paul Saint **Times** 12.30-2.30/6.30-close, Closed L Mon-Sat **Notes** D 4 course £55, Afternoon tea £20-£29, Sunday L £35

FORT AUGUSTUS Map 23 NH30

Station Road

Modern British V

tel: 01456 459250 **The Lovat, Loch Ness, Loch Ness Side PH32 4DU**
email: info@thelovat.com **web:** www.thelovat.com
dir: *On A82 between Fort William & Inverness*

Dynamic, stimulating cooking with loch views

A hotel since 1869, the Lovat has been run by the Gregory family for the past 12 years and it remains a landmark hotel in the Highlands. Located a brisk uphill walk from the southern end of Loch Ness, the Lovat offers stylish accommodation but it has retained much of the building's Victorian appeal. Whether you choose the brasserie or Station Road Restaurant, you can be sure of some gastronomic fireworks along the way. Chef Sean Kelly is a master of ambitious and innovative cooking, but it's all executed with a degree of playfulness. The hotel's environmentally friendly ethos extends to the kitchen, where food miles and provenance are taken very seriously. With views over the loch, the oak-panelled dining room provides a refined setting for dynamic food delivered via a five-course tasting menu (including a vegetarian version). The menu descriptions are terse and often cryptic but the presentation of each dish is designed to excite and surprise. An amuse-bouche of duck liver, beetroot and muesli might kick things off before a starter of seafood carbonara.
A main course of Highland beef might make way for a spirited dessert of garden rhubarb, lemon and toast. A closing 'Kinder Surprise' displays solid technical skills.

Chef Sean Kelly **Seats** 24, Pr/dining room 50 **Times** 7-9, Closed Nov-Mar, Sun-Tue, L all week **Prices** Tasting menu £45-£55 **Wines** 25 bottles over £30, 35 bottles under £30, 13 by glass **Parking** 30 **Notes** Children 8 yrs+

FORT WILLIAM Map 22 NN17

Inverlochy Castle Hotel

 Modern French NEW V 

tel: 01397 702177 **Torlundy PH33 6SN**
email: info@inverlochy.co.uk **web:** www.inverlochycastlehotel.com
dir: *3m N of Fort William on A82, just past Golf Club, N towards Inverness*

Dining chez Roux in a grand castle

Now under the auspices of a couple of culinary legends, father and son Albert and Michel Roux, the restaurant is now billed as 'Albert and Michel Roux Jr at Inverlochy Castle'. Inverlochy is the quintessential Victorian baronial castle, all castellated stone walls and turrets surrounded by 500 green acres overlooking its own loch. Pretty impressive then, and inside it gets better: luxuriant furnishings and fittings, paintings, crystal chandeliers and open fires all add to an ambience of grandeur and opulence. Queen Victoria was particularly taken with the place, and some of the furniture in the three dining rooms was a gift from the King of Norway, maintaining the royal connections. You feel the need to put on the glad rags for dinner, and in any case, dining here without a jacket and tie, gentlemen, is not permitted. Expect a menu of modernised, classically inspired dishes and high-quality ingredients sourced from this bountiful part of the country. Loch Creagan oysters find their way into a terrine served with red and white chicory, loin of Highland venison is partnered with braised red cabbage and sauce poivrade, and, to finish, there might be pistachio financier with caramel pears.

Chef Andrew Turnbull **Seats** 40, Pr/dining room 20 **Times** 6-10, Closed L all week **Prices** Tasting menu £67-£79 **Wines** 240 bottles over £30, 4 bottles under £30, 11 by glass **Parking** 20 **Notes** Children 8 yrs+

GLENFINNAN Map 22 NM98

The Prince's House

 Modern British

tel: 01397 722246 **PH37 4LT**
email: princeshouse@glenfinnan.co.uk **web:** www.glenfinnan.co.uk
dir: *From Fort William N on A82 for 2m. Turn left on to A830 Mallaig Rd for 15m to hotel*

Regionally based cooking in a gorgeous historic region

Kieron and Ina Kelly's white-fronted house has charm in bucket loads. The dining room is hung with a fine art collection and the small conservatory has ravishing views over the glen. Kieron Kelly's cooking steps up to the regional plate in four-course set menus that might start with wild mushroom ravioli with grilled mushrooms and a truffle emulsion, before poached oysters with salsify, dittander (foraged peppergrass), red wine shallots and chorizo. The main event might star local lamb with gratin dauphinoise and Maderia and thyme jus, ending with a sunny combo of caramelised pineapple in passionfruit syrup, alongside lime and ginger sorbet and candied chillies.

Chef Kieron Kelly **Seats** 30 **Times** 7-9, Closed Xmas, Oct-Mar, L all week **Prices** Prices not confirmed **Wines** 40 bottles over £30, 30 bottles under £30, 5 by glass **Parking** 18 **Notes** 5 course D £48, Vegetarian available, Children welcome

INVERGARRY Map 22 NH30

Glengarry Castle Hotel

 Scottish, International

tel: 01809 501254 **PH35 4HW**
email: castle@glengarry.net **web:** www.glengarry.net
dir: *1m S of Invergarry on A82*

Traditional fare in a grand lochside hotel

The Glengarry, overlooking Loch Oich, is a typical slice of Victorian Scottish baronial, built in the 1860s and furnished in the grand manner. Spotless white linen and quality glassware glow beneath the chandelier in the opulent dining room, where lightly modernised traditional fare is the order of the day. Haggis, neeps and tatties with whisky and redcurrant sauce makes an appropriate starter and could be the prelude to rack of lamb with onion and oatmeal stuffing, sweet onion jus and château potatoes. Desserts are of the likes of pear frangipane tart with pannacotta ice cream flavoured with raspberry and vanilla.

Chef John McDonald **Seats** 40 **Times** 12-1.45/7-8.30, Closed mid Nov-mid Mar **Prices** Prices not confirmed **Wines** 14 bottles over £30, 35 bottles under £30, 9 by glass **Parking** 30 **Notes** Vegetarian available, Children welcome

INVERGORDON Map 23 NH77

Kincraig Castle Hotel

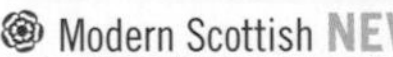

Modern Scottish NEW

tel: 01349 852587 **IV18 0LF**
email: info@kincraig-castle-hotel.co.uk **web:** www.kincraig-castle-hotel.co.uk
dir: *Off A9, past Alness towards Tain. Hotel is 0.25m on left past church*

A modern Scottish flavour in a traditional setting

Pretty gables and wee turrets give this former ancestral seat of Clan MacKenzie a bit of gravitas, while its lush lawn sweeps down towards the Cromarty Firth. The house is decorated to suit the grand baronial setting, and the traditional and smart Alexander Restaurant matches the mood. The kitchen shows a sense of place in its output, with fine Scottish ingredients peppering the menu. Begin with Moray pork prepared in a modern style (crispy rib and pulled pork). Move on to slow-roasted rump of hogget with home-made haggis, or grilled sole with corn chowder and capers. Finish with a contemporary take on rhubarb and custard.

Chef Stuart Thomson **Seats** 30, Pr/dining room 50 **Times** 12-2/6-9 **Prices** Starter £6-£7, Main £15-£22.50 **Wines** 27 bottles over £30, 27 bottles under £30, 6 by glass **Parking** 40 **Notes** Sunday L £15.95, Vegetarian available, Children welcome

INVERNESS Map 23 NH64

Bunchrew House Hotel

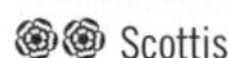

Scottish

tel: 01463 234917 **Bunchrew IV3 8TA**
email: welcome@bunchrewhousehotel.com **web:** www.bunchrewhousehotel.com
dir: *3m W of Inverness on A862 towards Beauly*

A touch of Scottish baronial splendour

Bunchrew House is a magnificent 17th-century mansion, complete with turrets and a pink façade, on the water's edge of the Beauly Firth. An updated version of traditional Scottish cooking is the kitchen's view of its culinary world. The daily-changing menu might open with smooth, light chicken liver parfait alongside a dollop of fruity chutney and small pieces of excellent home-made soda bread. Follow that with wonderfully fresh and moist hake fillet topped with glossy chive butter on smooth mash flecked with pancetta along with black pudding wrapped in pancetta, cauliflower purée and grilled asparagus. For finale, choose layers of strawberries, cream and shortcake with refreshing basil ice cream.

Contrast Brasserie

Modern British V

tel: 01463 223777 **Glenmoriston Town House Hotel, 20 Ness Bank IV2 4SF**
email: reception@glenmoristontownhouse.com **web:** www.glenmoristontownhouse.com
dir: *2 mins from city centre, on river opposite theatre*

City-centre brasserie in a tree-lined riverside terrace

Now relocated as the Glenmoriston's main restaurant, Contrast's single window doesn't let in much daylight, but in the evening, with a pianist playing soft, funky music, the low lighting and modern decor, the atmosphere is rather romantic. Scottish produce is used here in, for example, Shetland mussels and seared carpaccio of Ardgay venison, but overall we're talking modern British cooking. Look for smoked ham hough (hock) and rabbit terrine, black pudding bonbon and spiced piccalilli, or pan-fried loin of red deer, hazelnuts, beetroot, truffled pommes purées and red wine jus. To finish warm chocolate and salted caramel fondant, served with raspberry ice cream and topped with a chocolate tuille.

Chef Luke Webber **Seats** 56, Pr/dining room 90 **Times** 12-2.30/5-10 **Prices** Fixed L 2 course £10.95, Fixed D 3 course £35-£55, Starter fr £4.50, Main fr £13, Dessert fr £5 **Wines** 10 bottles over £30, 15 bottles under £30, 8 by glass **Parking** 45 **Notes** Early bird 2/3 course £12.95-£15.95, Children welcome

Loch Ness Country House Hotel

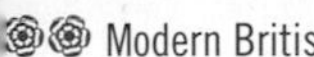

Modern British

tel: 01463 230512 **Loch Ness Rd IV3 8JN**
email: info@lochnesscountryhousehotel.co.uk **web:** www.lochnesscountryhousehotel.co.uk
dir: *On A82 (S), 1m from Inverness town boundary*

Asian influenced modern cooking for the monster-hunters

This creeper-covered Georgian house in lovely grounds is not actually on Loch Ness, and is three miles outside Inverness. The classy interiors are all stripes and tartan, with three dining rooms, each with only a few tables, decorated in restrained greys and browns. The short menu suggests smoked eel risotto with bacon crumb, warm apple jelly and basil oil, followed by Ibérico black presa pork, pork belly, black pudding, braised Puy lentils, fried quail's egg, crispy pancetta and maple jus. The inventiveness continues in desserts such as basil pannacotta on gingerbread crumble with spiced toffee apple chunks and a ginger beer sorbet.

Chef Adam Dwyer **Seats** 42, Pr/dining room 24 **Times** 12-9, All-day dining **Prices** Fixed L 2 course £14-£15.95, Fixed D 3 course £30-£40, Tasting menu £55-£69, Starter £5-£12, Main £13-£32, Dessert £6-£10 **Wines** 12 bottles over £30, 22 bottles under £30, 9 by glass **Parking** 70 **Notes** Afternoon tea, Sunday L £9.95-£18.95, Vegetarian available, Children welcome

The New Drumossie Hotel

Modern Scottish

tel: 01463 236451 **Old Perth Rd IV2 5BE**
email: stay@drumossiehotel.co.uk **web:** www.drumossiehotel.co.uk
dir: *From A9 follow signs for Culloden Battlefield, hotel on left after 1m*

Confident, seasonal cooking at an art deco hotel

A few miles out of Inverness, the hotel is a sparkling-white art deco beauty in acres of well-tended grounds framed by the Scottish Highlands. Its charm is due in no small part to the staff who treat guests with engaging politeness and feed them in a setting of well-oiled serenity in the Grill Room, where intricately presented modern Scottish dishes are built on top class raw materials. Begin with a creative combination of seared king scallops with eel, barley risotto and langoustine bisque, then follow on with slow-cooked beef cheek or fillet of wild halibut with octopus carpaccio. Finish with a modern take on rhubarb and custard.

Chef Stewart Macpherson, Euan Walker **Seats** 90, Pr/dining room 30 **Times** 12.30-2/7-9.30 **Wines** 69 bottles over £30, 16 bottles under £30, 13 by glass **Parking** 200 **Notes** Sunday L £17.95-£21.95, Vegetarian available, Children welcome

Rocpool

Modern European

tel: 01463 717274 **1 Ness Walk IV3 5NE**
email: info@rocpoolrestaurant.com **web:** www.rocpoolrestaurant.com
dir: *On W bank of River Ness close to the Eden Court Theatre*

Riverside setting and smart modern cooking

This buzzy brasserie on the banks of the River Ness, and sweeping windows open up floodlit views of the river and castle at night. The interior is an exercise in contemporary design flair featuring lots of wood and natural tones. An appealing cast of modern European dishes built on top-class Scottish produce opens with Cromarty crab with curried mayonnaise, Granny Smith apple, fennel and shallot dressing, and creamed avocado and lime. Next up, roast venison loin wrapped in Parma ham is matched with black pudding, creamed parsnips, wild mushrooms with garlic, thyme and crisp fried potatoes. Finish off with an exemplary vanilla crème brûlée.

Chef Steven Devlin **Seats** 55 **Times** 12-2.30/5.45-10, Closed 25-26 Dec, 1-3 Jan, Sun **Prices** Fixed L 2 course fr £15.95, Fixed D 2 course fr £17.95, Starter £3.95-£12.95, Main £12.95-£25.95, Dessert £6.95-£8.90 **Wines** 18 bottles over £30, 24 bottles under £30, 11 by glass **Parking** On street **Notes** Early D 5.45-6.45pm 2 course £17.95, Vegetarian available, Children welcome

KINGUSSIE Map 23 NH70

The Cross

 Modern Scottish V 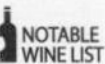

tel: 01540 661166 **Tweed Mill Brae, Ardbroilach Rd PH21 1LB**
email: relax@thecross.co.uk **web:** www.thecross.co.uk
dir: *From lights in Kingussie centre along Ardbroilach Rd, 300yds left onto Tweed Mill Brae*

Modern Scottish cooking in an old mill

A former tweed mill alongside the River Gynack, The Cross has long been a regional dining hotspot and since taking over in 2012, Derek and Celia Kitchingman have continued to build on its reputation. The stunning setting within the Cairngorm National Park doesn't change, of course, and remains as peaceful and uplifting as ever. Expect stylish public rooms, pretty bedrooms and a smart, traditional restaurant – think darkwood ceiling, whitewashed stone walls, and a striking yellow and black carpet. In the kitchen, David Skiggs delivers creative modern food via a three-course fixed-price menu or signature tasting option (lunch must be booked in advance), with seasonal and local ingredients to the fore. A tasting dish of duck arrives on a glass plate, the silky parfait, smoked breast and confit leg looking pretty as a picture, followed by loin of George Gow's lamb with a fabulous jus gras served in a little glass teapot. A fish option might be line-caught sea bass with crispy chicken wing and tortellini filled with hazelnut and parsnip. For dessert, 'variations of apple' includes a candied apple-infused sponge and sorbet, with a clever ginger custard espuma on the side. The owners take a hands-on approach front of house, and if you've room, let them talk you through the dessert trolley.

Chef David Skiggs **Seats** 30 **Times** 12-2.30/7-8.30, Closed Xmas & Jan (ex New Year) **Prices** Fixed L 3 course £25, Tasting menu £60 **Wines** 92 bottles over £30, 41 bottles under £30, 7 by glass **Parking** 12 **Notes** Afternoon tea £17, ALC D 3 course £55, Tasting menu 6 course, Sunday L, Children welcome

LOCHALINE Map 20 NM64

The Whitehouse Restaurant

Modern British, Scottish

tel: 01967 421777 & 07884 361545 **PA80 5XT**
email: info@thewhitehouserestaurant.co.uk **web:** www.thewhitehouserestaurant.co.uk
dir: *Take Corran Ferry on A82, on disembarking left towards Lochaline.*

Vibrant, ingredient-led modern Scottish cooking

This must be one of the remotest restaurants in Scotland, reached via a single track road. The kitchen cooks whatever its suppliers have provided on the day, with blackboards revealing all. This local bounty is turned into dishes that maintain integrity through simplicity, so flavours are to the fore. Start with stunning-looking delicately smoked ham hough terrine wrapped in Parma ham with dill dressing and piccalilli, and move on to exemplary best end of lamb with haggis, sherry sauce and an array of vegetables. Top them with delicate vanilla and lavender pannacotta topped with strawberry sorbet surrounded by intense strawberry soup.

Chef Michael Burgoyne, Lee Myers **Seats** 26 **Times** 12-2.30/6-9.30, Closed Nov-Mar, Sun-Mon **Prices** Fixed L 2 course £16.99-£19.99, Starter £6.90-£11, Main £15.90-£25, Dessert £6.90-£12.50 **Wines** 9 bottles over £30, 17 bottles under £30, 5 by glass **Parking** 10 **Notes** Fixed D only before 5pm, Vegetarian available, Children welcome

MUIR OF ORD Map 23 NH55

Ord House Hotel

British, French

tel: 01463 870492 **Ord Dr IV6 7UH**
email: admin@ord-house.co.uk **web:** www.ord-house.co.uk
dir: *Off A9 at Tore rdbt onto A832. 5m, through Muir of Ord. Left towards Ullapool (A832). Hotel 0.5m on left*

Comforting bistro cooking in a 17th-century house

Built for a laird in the 17th century, Ord House sits in 40 acres of woodland and gardens. The small-scale restaurant is on the first floor: pink carpet, polished wooden tables and elevated views over the grounds. The cooking leans towards the straightforward, just spot-on flavours and fresh ingredients. Expect starters such as a salad of ham and cheddar with mixed leaves, tomatoes, a hard-boiled egg and croûtons, or smoked salmon pâté, then poached chicken breast stuffed with haggis in white wine sauce, or king prawn linguine in Mediterranean-style garlic sauce. Cap things off with classic crème brûlée or rich, sticky ginger pudding with ginger and brandy sauce.

Chef Eliza Allen **Seats** 26 **Times** 12-2/7-9, Closed Nov-end Feb **Prices** Starter £5.50-£10.50, Main £15-£23.50, Dessert £5.25-£6.95 **Wines** 9 bottles over £30, 37 bottles under £30, 4 by glass **Parking** 24 **Notes** Vegetarian available, Children welcome

NAIRN Map 23 NH85

Boath House

– see opposite

Golf View Hotel & Spa

Modern Scottish

tel: 01667 452301 **Seabank Rd IV12 4HD**
email: golfview@crerarhotels.com **web:** www.golfviewhotel.co.uk
dir: *Off A96 into Seabank Rd & continue to end*

Modern Scottish cooking with golfing and sea views

In case you get the impression there's only golf to look at, this hotel's seaside location looks out over the Moray Firth. The Fairways Restaurant is a half-panelled room with chandeliers, serving a six-course fixed-price menu of modern Scottish food as well as the carte. This may kick off with goats' cheese and sun-dried tomato profiteroles, continue through pan-fried scallops with black pudding and tomato and fennel purée, and on to a soup. The main event may bring on roast duck breast and confit leg with cabbage, pancetta and Cognac jus, and a dessert such as poached pear with Amaretto ice cream precedes cheese with redcurrant jelly.

SPEAN BRIDGE Map 22 NN28

Russell's at Smiddy House

Modern Scottish

tel: 01397 712335 **Roy Bridge Rd PH34 4EU**
email: enquiry@smiddyhouse.com web: www.smiddyhouse.com
dir: *In village centre, 9m N of Fort William, on A82 towards Inverness*

Seasonal cooking amid elegant pastoral surroundings

Occupying a corner spot on the main road through Spean Bridge, the low-roofed, whitewashed building offers four smart bedrooms so you can stop over and spoil yourself with top seasonal cooking. Russell's is in the 'Smiddyhouse', once the village blacksmith's, and is an intimate, candlelit spot with crisp linen-clothed tables decked with sparkling glasses and fresh flowers. Well-presented modern Scottish cuisine makes good use of top-notch local materials, as in a starter of salmon and prawn roulade with citrus fruits and crème fraîche, followed by herb-crusted salmon with fish velouté, or perhaps some seasonal Highland game. Chocolate and hazelnut profiteroles make for a comforting finale.

Chef Glen Russell **Seats** 38 **Times** 6-9, Closed 2 days a week (Nov-Apr), L Mon-Sat **Prices** Prices not confirmed **Wines** 14 bottles over £30, 20 bottles under £30, 7 by glass **Parking** 15 **Notes** Sunday L, Vegetarian available, Children welcome

STRONTIAN Map 22 NM86

Kilcamb Lodge Hotel

Modern European, Scottish, Seafood V

tel: 01967 402257 **PH36 4HY**
email: enquiries@kilcamblodge.co.uk web: www.kilcamblodge.co.uk
dir: *Take Corran ferry off A82. Follow A861 to Strontian. 1st left over bridge after village*

Traditional seafood specialities and modern Scottish cooking

A new departure at this Georgian house with Victorian additions is the speciality seafood menu, a daily changing offering bought from a fishing-boat operating out of Tiree. Cracked crab claws with a dip, split langoustines in garlic butter and seared trout with mustard mash are among its strengths, while the main menu deals in shredded duck leg with spiced onion, pak choi and a fried duck egg, followed by twice-cooked pork belly with burnt apple purée in whisky sauce. Finish with date and toffee pudding and caramelised banana, or with the lighter option of pannacotta served with orange and star anise sorbet and chillified tropical fruit salsa.

Chef Gary Phillips **Seats** 40 **Times** 12-2/5.30-9.30, Closed 1 Jan-1 Feb **Prices** Tasting menu £69, Starter £6.50-£14, Main £16.50-£24, Dessert £8 **Wines** 53 bottles over £30, 16 bottles under £30, 10 by glass **Parking** 28 **Notes** Afternoon tea, Sunday L £21.50, Children 5 yrs+

Boath House

NAIRN Map 23 NH85

Modern British V NOTABLE WINE LIST

tel: 01667 454896 **Auldearn IV12 5TE**
email: wendy@boath-house.com web: www.boath-house.com
dir: *2m E of Nairn on A96 (Inverness to Aberdeen road)*

Astonishing culinary intricacy in a restored Georgian manor

Boath House offers a taste of aristocratic life: the porticoed front door opens onto a plush interior of deep sofas, antiques and paintings and sculptures, and there are 22 acres of pretty gardens, pristine lawns, wild woodland, a trout lake and walled gardens. Don and Wendy Matheson restored it in the 1990s, making it one of Scotland's finest dining destinations, with Charlie Lockley at the stoves combining the very best regional produce with foraged ingredients and the seasonal bounty supplied by the walled garden and the orchards. Things get off the blocks with canapés in the elegant lounge. The circular dining room, like everywhere else, is pretty classy: French doors look out over the lawn to the lake, and the spaces has a contemporary feel. Lockley's cooking is thrillingly contemporary, and the technical skill on show is impressive. Daily-changing fixed-price lunch and dinner menus come in three- or six-course options (there's a bargain two-course deal at lunch) whose tight-lipped descriptions belie the labour-intensive results. Opening the show might be a sweet parsnip soup with parsnip crisps and spiced oil, a gentle overture to a dish of lamb with parsley root and mint that sings with clear natural flavours and clever contrasts. Next up is a seafood course with langoustine, amaranth and hazelnut, while local game could show up as red deer with salsify and truffle. Sweet courses might include nutmeg custard served with quince and mandarin, or an impressive composition involving chocolate, pistachio and tonka bean. Excellent cheeses come with interesting accompaniments – perhaps Lanark Blue served with plum pudding, or Morangie brie with quince.

Chef Charles Lockley **Seats** 28, Pr/dining room 10 **Times** 12-1.30/7-close, **Prices** Fixed L 2 course £24, Fixed D 3 course £45, Tasting menu £70 **Wines** 120 bottles over £30, 20 bottles under £30, 15 by glass **Parking** 25 **Notes** Tasting menu 6 course, Afternoon tea, Sunday L £24-£30, Children welcome

TAIN Map 23 NH78

The Glenmorangie Highland Home at Cadboll

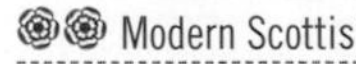 British, French

tel: 01862 871671 **Cadboll, Fearn IV20 1XP**
email: relax@glenmorangie.co.uk **web:** www.theglenmorangiehouse.com
dir: *N on A9, at Nigg Rdbt turn right onto B9175 (before Tain) & follow signs for hotel*

Dinner-party dining in a magnificent Highland location

Set in fantastic grounds with a walled garden and a private beach, The Glenmorangie has appeal in spades, while the nearby distillery makes it a whisky lover's paradise. The French-influenced cuisine is top-drawer stuff. Guests dine dinner-party-style, tackling four-course, no-choice menus at a long oak table. Langoustine with spiced mango and avocado salsa partnered with apricot and plum sauce might precede black pepper-crusted beef fillet marinated in Glenmorangie Quinta Ruban malt, matched with ginger, pak choi, pumpkin gnocchi and mushroom consommé. Dessert brings another Glenmorangie malt in the crème anglaise accompanying passionfruit and Valrhona chocolate tart with coffee bean and chocolate ice cream.

Chef David Graham, John Wilson **Seats** 30, Pr/dining room 12
Times 8-close, Closed Jan, L ex by prior arrangement **Prices** Prices not confirmed **Wines** 43 bottles over £30, 10 bottles under £30, 15 by glass **Parking** 60 **Notes** 4 course D £55, D single sitting guests seated 7.30 for 8pm, Vegetarian available, Children 18 yrs+

THURSO Map 23 ND16

Forss House Hotel

Modern Scottish

tel: 01847 861201 **Forss KW14 7XY**
email: anne@forsshousehotel.co.uk **web:** www.forsshousehotel.co.uk
dir: *On A836, 5m outside Thurso*

Gentle country cooking in a Highland Georgian hotel

You can't get much further away from urban bustle in the mainland British Isles than the northern Highlands, where this Georgian country-house hotel luxuriates in splendid tranquillity below a waterfall on the River Forss, amid 20 acres of woodland. Plenty of pedigree Highland produce is on parade, naturally, starting with Tain cheddar and leek tart, its richness offset with lemon vinaigrette, while main course sees loin of Caithness lamb teamed with crispy tongue, artichoke and fondant potato, or perhaps roasted Scrabster monkfish with curried pumpkin and Puy lentils. Finish up with an intensely lemony trio, comprising drizzle cake, iced parfait and a meringue.

Chef Billy Steele **Seats** 26, Pr/dining room 14 **Times** 7-9, Closed 23 Dec-4 Jan, L all week **Prices** Starter £6.50-£7.50, Main £12.50-£24.50, Dessert £6.50-£7.50 **Wines** 7 bottles over £30, 18 bottles under £30, 4 by glass **Parking** 14 **Notes** Vegetarian available, Children welcome

TORRIDON Map 22 NG95

The Torridon Restaurant

 British, French V NOTABLE WINE LIST

tel: 01445 791242 **By Achnasheen, Wester Ross IV22 2EY**
email: info@thetorridon.com **web:** www.thetorridon.com
dir: *From Inverness take A9 N, follow signs to Ullapool (A835). At Garve take A832 to Kinlochewe, take A896 to Torridon. Do not turn off to Torridon Village. Hotel on right after Annat*

A piece of lochside Highland luxury

The Earl of Lovelace did well when he chose the site of his 1887 shooting lodge (some lodge: it's actually a substantial property with a clock tower and turret) at the end of Loch Torridon within 58 acres surrounded by magnificent Highland scenery. Highland cattle roam the fields beside the hotel, chickens and Tamworth pigs are raised on the estate, and fruit and vegetables flourish in the two-acre kitchen garden. Within, Victorian features are overlaid with a classy decor and furnishings, there's an unusual zodiac ceiling in the drawing room, more than 350 whiskies await in the bar, and the restaurant is panelled, with an ornately plastered ceiling and draped windows giving Highland views. David Barnett is doing great things in the kitchen, using top-end Scottish produce in ambitious, well-conceived and technically accurate dishes. His five-course menu might open with wild garlic velouté and proceed to seared scallops with spicy aubergine, cauliflower and mango. Main courses are compellingly devised and short of fuss, so flavours are clear and clean-cut, seen in chicken with a ham crumb, orange and shallots, and fillet of local turbot with mushrooms, parmesan and parsley. Mango cheesecake might be a sweet taster before prunes, honey and oatmeal in whisky parfait, then coffee and petits fours in the drawing room.

Chef David Barnett **Seats** 38, Pr/dining room 16 **Times** 12-2/6.45-9, Closed 2 Jan for 5 wks **Prices** Prices not confirmed Tasting menu £60-£75 **Wines** 8 by glass **Parking** 20 **Notes** Tasting menu 4/7 course, Children 10 yrs+

WICK Map 23 ND35

Mackay's Hotel

Modern Scottish V

tel: 01955 602323 **Union St KW1 5ED**
email: info@mackayshotel.co.uk **web:** www.mackayshotel.co.uk
dir: *Opposite Caithness General Hospital*

Local produce in a cheerful hotel bistro

Mackay's is home to the No. 1 Bistro, a gently contemporary restaurant with a relaxed vibe. The kitchen makes good use of quality local ingredients, and there's a definite modernity to the output. Take an attractive starter of pan-fried hand-dived scallops, for example, which arrive in the company of smoked cauliflower purée, haggis bonbon and pickled shallots. Next up, baked Scrabster cod is an altogether more straightforward dish, with the flavoursome fish on creamy mash surrounded by herb and shellfish broth. Dessert brings a light iced passionfruit parfait with chocolate crumb and coconut and lime cream. There's a buzzy bar for real ales, cocktails and a terrific range of whiskies.

Chef Steve Martin **Seats** 40, Pr/dining room 30
Times 12-2.30/5.30-9.30, Closed 24-25 Dec, 1-2 Jan **Prices** Fixed L 2 course £13-£19.50, Fixed D 3 course £30-£40, Tasting menu fr £45, Starter £4-£10, Main £12-£24, Dessert £5-£9 **Wines** 5 bottles over £30, 57 bottles under £30, 20 by glass **Notes** Sunday L £17-£28, Children welcome

NORTH LANARKSHIRE

CUMBERNAULD Map 21 NS77

The Westerwood Hotel & Golf Resort

Modern Scottish

tel: 01236 457171 **1 St Andrews Dr, Westerwood G68 0EW**
email: jabercrombie@qhotels.co.uk **web:** www.qhotels.co.uk
dir: *A80 junct signed Dullatur, from junct follow signs for hotel*

Confident modern cooking and top-drawer service

A sharply modern construction of brick and glass, Westerwood House's restaurant – Flemings – matches the contemporary mood of the hotel and its colour scheme recalls the natural Scottish landscape. A modern-minded menu delivers the likes of céviche of halibut with candied lime and passionfruit pearls among first courses, followed by baked pork belly with honey-glazed figs and prunes soaked in Armagnac, or go for the simplicity of chargrilled Cairn Hill rib-eye. There's a tasting menu, too, with wine flight option. The creativity continues into desserts such as rhubarb crème brûlée matched with a liquorice ice cream, or another that combines orange and passionfruit in a soufflé.

Chef Joe Queen **Seats** 180, Pr/dining room 60 **Times** 6.30-9.30, Closed Jan, Sun-Mon, L all week **Prices** Starter £5.25-£9.50, Main £13.50-£28, Dessert £5.50-£7.95 **Wines** 21 bottles over £30, 23 bottles under £30, 12 by glass **Parking** 250 **Notes** Vegetarian available, Children welcome

SOUTH LANARKSHIRE

EAST KILBRIDE Map 20 NS65

Macdonald Crutherland House

British

tel: 01355 577000 **Strathaven Rd G75 0QZ**
email: general.crutherland@macdonald-hotels.co.uk **web:** www.macdonald-hotels.co.uk
dir: *Follow A726 signed Strathaven, straight over Torrance rdbt, hotel on left after 250yds*

Elegant hotel dining room with accomplished cooking

Dating from the early 1700s, Crutherland House stands in nearly 40 acres of peaceful grounds. The hotel keeps things traditional, not least in the restaurant, with its panelled walls, paintings and burnished darkwood tables. The menu takes a classical approach to things, with plenty of Scottish ingredients on show, starting with twice-baked Mull of Kintyre cheddar soufflé with red onion marmalade. Among main courses there are steaks cooked on the grill (21-day hung Scottish rib-eye, maybe), or Gressingham duck breast with a leg-meat croquette, carrot and orange purée and five spice sauce. For dessert, there's marshmallow Pavlova with raspberry sorbet.

STRATHAVEN Map 20 NS74

Rissons at Springvale

Modern Scottish V

tel: 01357 520234 & 521131 **18 Lethame Rd ML10 6AD**
email: info@rissons.co.uk **web:** www.rissonsrestaurant.co.uk
dir: *M74 junct 8, A71, through Stonehouse to Strathaven*

Modern Scottish bistro cooking in a comfortable restaurant with rooms

Centrally located near Strathaven's main shopping area, this restaurant with rooms is a popular dining destination. The restaurant, looking over the well-manicured garden, is smartly done out, a bright room with wooden floors, dark leather chairs and plain wooden tables. Crisp-coated fishcake, moist and tasty within, is complemented by strips of soft dill-marinated mackerel and some pickled vegetables to make an enjoyable starter. Follow perhaps with pork belly on braised red cabbage surrounded by red wine sauce, accompanied by three haggis bonbons, parsnip purée and roast potatoes, or pan-fried salmon fillet with kedgeree. Cheeses are Scottish, and dessert might be excellent vanilla crème brûlée with home-made berry jam.

Chef Scott Baxter, Euan Munro **Seats** 40 **Times** 6-9.30, Closed New Year, 1 wk Jan, 1st wk Jul, Mon-Tue, L Wed-Sat, D Sun **Prices** Fixed D 3 course £18.95, Starter £4.50-£10, Main £12.50-£22.50, Dessert £5.50-£7 **Wines** 2 bottles over £30, 20 bottles under £30, 6 by glass **Parking** 10 **Notes** Early evening menu Wed-Fri, Small plate menu Wed-Thu, Sunday L £15.95-£18.95, Children welcome

EAST LOTHIAN

ABERLADY Map 21 NT47

Ducks Inn

Modern British NOTABLE WINE LIST

tel: 01875 870682 **Main St EH32 0RE**
email: info@ducks.co.uk **web:** www.ducks.co.uk
dir: *A1 (Bankton junct) take 1st exit to North Berwick. At next rdbt 3rd exit onto A198 signed Longniddry, left towards Aberlady. At T-junct, facing river, right to Aberlady*

Creative cooking in smart restaurant with rooms

Located in the heart of a small village, Ducks Inn covers all the bases with its bar-bistro, restaurant and smart accommodation. The good-looking dining area, recently refurbished, is matched by the attractiveness of what arrives on the plate. The kitchen turns out appealing combinations like honey-roasted carrot and cumin veloute with cashew nuts and, for mains, perhaps, moves on to fillet of seabream, tarragon linguini, salsify, cumin and mussels or spiced pork belly, braised red cabbage, potato rösti, Brussel sprouts and chestnuts. Dessert might be a crème caramel with macerated pineapple. There's also more than 200 wines to choose between.

Chef Michal Mozdzen **Seats** 22, Pr/dining room 22 **Times** 12-3/6-10, Closed 25 Dec, Mon-Tue, L Wed-Thu **Prices** Starter £10-£14, Main £26-£35, Dessert £6.50-£8.50 **Wines** 121 bottles over £30, 48 bottles under £30, 9 by glass **Parking** 15 **Notes** Sunday L £25-£35, Vegetarian available, Children welcome

GULLANE Map 21 NT48

La Potinière

 Modern British

tel: 01620 843214 **Main St EH31 2AA**
dir: *5m from North Berwick on A198*

Well-considered cooking on the high street

A double-act operation with Mary Runciman and Keith Marley at the stoves. Menus change regularly and the deal is just a couple of choices per course, kicking off with courgette and rosemary soup with apple crème fraîche, or twice-baked cheese soufflé with chives and tomato cream. A high level of skill is evident in main courses: perhaps braised salmon partnered by crushed new potatoes with spring onion and smoked salmon, and tarragon and tomato sauce, or guinea fowl, its poached and seared breast teamed with confit leg, dauphinoise potatoes and a guinea fowl and mushroom jus. For dessert, vanilla pannacotta is contrasted with poached nectarine, raspberry sorbet and shortbread.

Chef Mary Runciman, Keith Marley **Seats** 24 **Times** 12.30-1.30/7-8.30, Closed Xmas, Jan, BHs, Mon-Tue, D Sun **Prices** Fixed L 2 course fr £20, Fixed D 3 course fr £38 **Wines** 31 bottles over £30, 26 bottles under £30, 7 by glass **Parking** 10 **Notes** Fixed D 4 course £43, Sunday L, Vegetarian available, Children welcome

NORTH BERWICK Map 21 NT58

Macdonald Marine Hotel & Spa

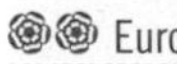 European

tel: 01620 897300 **Cromwell Rd EH39 4LZ**
email: sales.marine@macdonald-hotels.co.uk **web:** www.macdonaldhotels.co.uk/marine
dir: *From A198 turn into Hamilton Rd at lights then 2nd right*

Impressive Victorian pile with confident and accomplished cooking

The Marine Hotel is an upscale Grade II listed Victorian manor overlooking the East Lothian golf course. The Craigleith Restaurant surveys the action through sweeping bay windows, while oak panelling, plush fabrics and chandeliers suspended from lofty ceilings convey a sense of occasion. The kitchen follows contemporary culinary style, while showing respect for classical thinking. Braised pork belly with white bean and chorizo casserole has a well-balanced richness, followed by an impeccably-timed fillet of sea bass partnered with king prawn and sweetcorn broth. To finish, classic crème brûlée is served with mango sorbet, or there might be the deep comfort of warm treacle tart with clotted cream.

WEST LOTHIAN

LINLITHGOW Map 21 NS97

Champany Inn

 Traditional British

tel: 01506 834532 & 834388 **Champany Corner EH49 7LU**
email: reception@champany.com
dir: *2m NE of Linlithgow. From M9 (N) junct 3, at top of slip road turn right. Champany 500yds on right*

Quality steakhouse in a characterful old mill

Close to Linlithgow Palace, this cluster of buildings dates from the 16th century and the candlelit restaurant occupies a former flour mill complete with bare stone walls and vaulted roof. Open for more than 30 years, the Champany Inn is less than a mile from the M9 and a the destination of choice for fans of properly-hung, expertly-butchered slabs of top-quality meat, much of it from herds of prime Aberdeenshire cattle. A starter of hot-smoked salmon from the Champany smokepot will invariably precede your favourite cut of beef – T-bone, porterhouse, rib-eye, Chateaubriand and all points in between – cooked to your liking on the charcoal grill.

Chef C Davidson, D Gibson **Seats** 50, Pr/dining room 30 **Times** 12.30-2/7-10, Closed 25-26 Dec, 1-2 Jan, Sun, L Sat **Prices** Fixed L 2 course £24.50, Fixed D 3 course £42.50, Starter £9.90-£17.50, Main £29-£49.90, Dessert £8.95 **Wines** 450 bottles over £30, 24 bottles under £30, 8 by glass **Parking** 50 **Notes** Vegetarian available, Children 8 yrs+

Livingston's Restaurant

Modern British, European V

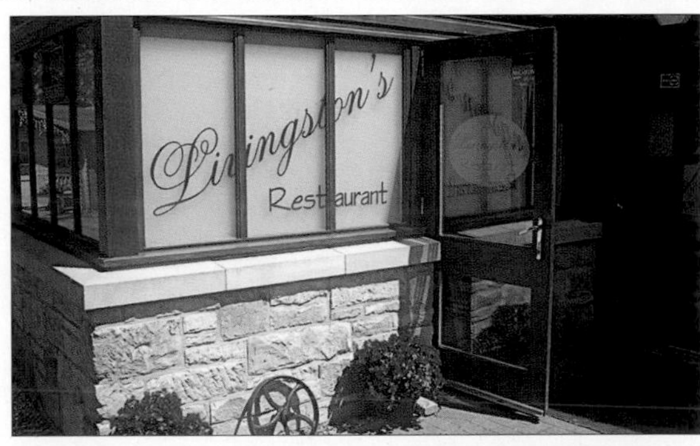

tel: 01506 846565 **52 High St EH49 7AE**
email: contact@livingstons-restaurant.co.uk **web:** www.livingstons-restaurant.co.uk
dir: *On high street opposite old post office*

Classic and modern cookery in tranquil backwater

Accessed via a narrow alleyway just off Linlithgow's bustling high street, this family-run restaurant has a surprisingly tranquil setting with gardens and a clean-lined look of whitewashed walls and tiled floor. The small kitchen team combines modern and classic cookery with an emphasis on local produce. A starter of pan-roasted sea scallops with cauliflower (a caramelised purée and a carpaccio) and caviar dressing might be followed by roast saddle of Perthshire venison, fondant potatoes and game and wild berry jus. Desserts take in white chocolate parfait with raspberry sorbet and whisky gums, or thoroughbred Scottish cheeses.

Chef Derek Livingston **Seats** 60, Pr/dining room 15 **Times** 12-2.30/6-9.30, Closed 2 wks Jan, Mon, D Sun **Prices** Prices not confirmed **Wines** 32 bottles over £30, 29 bottles under £30, 6 by glass **Parking** NCP Linlithgow Cross, on street **Notes** Midwk menu offer 3 course £25, Sunday L, Children welcome

UPHALL Map 21 NT07

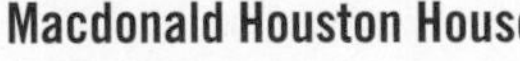

Macdonald Houston House

 Traditional British, Modern Scottish

tel: 01506 853831 **EH52 6JS**
email: houstoun@macdonald-hotels.co.uk
web: www.macdonaldhotels.co.uk/our-hotels/macdonald-houstoun-house
dir: *M8 junct 3 follow Broxburn signs, straight over rdbt then at mini-rdbt turn right towards Uphall, hotel 1m on right*

Scottish cooking in an atmospheric tower restaurant

The white-painted house, surrounded by 22 acres of woodlands, dates from the 16th century. The restaurant – Jeremy Wares at Houstoun House – sports deep burgundy walls, chandeliers and elegant unclothed tables. The kitchen relies heavily on quality Scottish ingredients and presents them in a modern, unfussy style. Start with smoked duck ham hock press with sauce gribiche and pickles, or poached salmon fillet with beetroot, pickled cucumber and horseradish, before moving on to mixed grill of seafood with farfalle, ratatouille and shellfish sauce, or roast chicken breast with haggis, roast vegetables and tarragon sauce. Finish patriotically with clootie dumpling with vanilla ice cream and custard.

Chef Jeremy Wares **Seats** 65, Pr/dining room 30 **Times** 6.30-9.30, Closed L all week **Prices** Starter £6.50-£9.95, Main £16.50-£24, Dessert £6.95-£9 **Wines** 60 bottles over £30, 16 bottles under £30, 13 by glass **Parking** 200 **Notes** Vegetarian available, Children welcome

MIDLOTHIAN

DALKEITH Map 21 NT36

The Sun Inn

Modern, Traditional

tel: 0131 663 2456 & 663 1534 **Lothian Bridge EH22 4TR**
email: thesuninn@live.co.uk **web:** www.thesuninnedinburgh.co.uk
dir: *Opposite Newbattle Viaduct on the A7 near Eskbank*

Winning menus in a popular gastropub

'Eat, drink, relax' is the motto of this gastropub, and it's made easy by boutique bedrooms and a dose of rustic-chic style with the original oak beams, exposed stone and panelling. Expect welcoming log fires, a bright patio in summer, and Scotland's larder forming the backbone of the kitchen's output. An eclectic menu delivers pub classics as well as contemporary offerings such as braised pig's cheek with black pudding, apple and parsnip purée and crisp Serrano ham. Mains could bring venison loin with date purée, poached blackberries, celeriac dauphinoise and roast peanut crumb. Beer from Stewart's of Edinburgh and a well-chosen wine list complete the picture.

Chef Ian Minto, Barry Drummond **Seats** 90 **Times** 12-2/6-9, Closed 26 Dec, 1 Jan **Prices** Starter £5-£9, Main £11-£25, Dessert £5 **Wines** 15 bottles over £30, 17 bottles under £30, 19 by glass **Parking** 75 **Notes** Early bird 2/3 course £11/£14 served 6-7pm, Sunday L, Vegetarian available, Children welcome

MORAY

ELGIN Map 23 NJ26

Mansion House Hotel

Traditional Scottish NEW

tel: 01343 548811 **The Haugh IV30 1AW**
email: reception@mhelgin.co.uk **web:** www.mansionhousehotel.co.uk
dir: *In Elgin turn off A96 into Haugh Rd, hotel at end of road by river*

Contemporary dining in a grand baronial house

The cossetting grounds of Mansion House may give the impression that this glorious 19th-century baronial property is a rural idyll, but it's only a short stroll from the centre of Elgin. The River Lossie flowing by enhances the sense of tranquillity. The formal restaurant maintains the period feel of the building, and is the sort of place where a drink in the lounge is all part of the occasion. The kitchen delivers a modern British menu that might take you from goats' cheese with port-infused shallots, glazed parmesan crisp and burnt onion powder to chocolate indulgence, via main-course oven-roasted loin of venison with balsamic jus.

Chef Barry Milne **Seats** 40, Pr/dining room 30 **Times** 12-2/6-9, Closed Xmas, New Yr **Prices** Fixed L 2 course £28.50, Fixed D 3 course £34 **Wines** 8 bottles over £30, 23 bottles under £30, 7 by glass **Parking** 40 **Notes** Sunday L £28.50-£34, Vegetarian available, Children welcome

FORRES Map 23 NJ05

Cluny Bank

Traditional European

tel: 01309 674304 **69 St Leonards Rd IV36 1DW**
email: info@clunybankhotel.co.uk **web:** www.clunybankhotel.co.uk
dir: *From Forres High St turn down Tolbooth St beside Clocktower. At rdbt take 2nd exit (B9010), 500yds on left*

Sophisticated classical cooking and warm hospitality in a smart setting

A substantial Victorian mansion in lush gardens, Cluny Bank has traditionally styled decor and a small, smart restaurant called Franklin's. There is a lot of period charm to the restaurant and a definite air of sophistication, while the menu name-checks the local Moray suppliers. You might kick off with Asian-inspired wok-fried king prawns and monkfish cheeks, or home-cured rollmops with celeriac remoulade, followed by new-season grouse – a superb local bird – with red cabbage and game jus. Chef likes to come out of the kitchen and his bonhomie is very welcome indeed, as are his desserts, such as chocolate parfait with Madeira-soaked raisins and biscuit crumb.

Chef Lloyd Kenny **Seats** 24 **Times** 6.30-8.45, Closed Sun, L all week **Prices** Starter £4.95-£10, Main £18.95-£28, Dessert £6.25-£7.95 **Wines** 29 bottles over £30, 41 bottles under £30, 7 by glass **Parking** 10 **Notes** Vegetarian available, Children 8 yrs+

PERTH & KINROSS

AUCHTERARDER Map 21 NN91

Andrew Fairlie@Gleneagles

– *see page 544*

The Strathearn

British, French NOTABLE WINE LIST

tel: 01764 694270 **The Gleneagles Hotel PH3 1NF**
email: gleneagles.restaurant.reservations@gleneagles.com **web:** www.gleneagles.com
dir: *Off A9 at exit for A823 follow signs for Gleneagles Hotel*

Classical and modern cooking in art deco dining room

The Strathearn is a splendid art deco room with columns and moulded ceilings. The number of trolleys wheeled to the tables (roast meats are carved, Dover sole is taken off the bone and so on) may create the impression that the restaurant is in some time warp, but the kitchen embraces the contemporary as well as the classics. Start with seared scallops with turnip purée, radish and apple salad and sauce nero. Dishes are appealingly composed, main courses ranging from duckling with tortellini, parsnips, cherry gel and mushrooms to lobster thermidor. Puddings could run to classical crêpe Suzette, flambéed at the table.

Chef Jonathon Wright **Seats** 322 **Times** 12.30-2.30/7-10, Closed L Mon-Sat **Prices** Fixed D 3 course fr £62.50 **Wines** 15 by glass **Parking** 300 **Notes** Sunday L fr £45, Vegetarian available, Children welcome

COMRIE Map 21 NN72

Royal Hotel

 Traditional Scottish

tel: 01764 679200 **Melville Square PH6 2DN**
email: reception@royalhotel.co.uk **web:** www.royalhotel.co.uk
dir: *In main square, 7m from Crieff, on A85*

Luxury small hotel with confident modern cooking

The 18th-century stone building on the main street of this riverside village is now a plush small-scale luxury hotel, with a restaurant split into two areas linked by double doors. The seasonally-changing menu might open with fettuccine, cooked al dente, with a sauce of butternut squash, mushrooms and chestnuts, served with sage butter and parmesan shavings, or reassuringly familiar potted shrimps. Trustworthy sourcing is clear in pink slices of venison, of excellent quality, with black pudding clapshot, buttery spring greens and a port and redcurrant sauce, and in sea bass fillet with tomato tagliatelle. Standards are well maintained in puddings of vanilla pannacotta with chopped pineapple, and Eton Mess.

FORTINGALL Map 20 NN74

Fortingall Hotel

Modern Scottish

tel: 01887 830367 & 829012 **PH15 2NQ**
email: enquiries@fortingall.com **web:** www.fortingall.com
dir: *B846 from Aberfeldy for 6m, left signed Fortingall for 3m. Hotel in village centre*

Well-balanced menu in Arts and Crafts village

Fortinghall is very much a tourist destination, many of whom end up at this Victorian country-house hotel. Dining takes place in two rooms, the main one done out in Arts and Crafts style, with a red carpet, an open fire, paintings on the walls and tartan-effect curtains. Dinner might open with skilfully made chicken and duck liver pâté served with home-made chutney and melba toast, before a main course such as rump of lamb sliced on tasty provençale vegetables with dauphinoise and a flavour-packed Madeira jus. Canapés are offered, breads are freshly baked and to finish there may be a glass of silky white chocolate mousse topped with local raspberries.

Chef David Dunn **Seats** 30, Pr/dining room 30 **Times** 12-2/6.30-9, Closed Jan, Mon-Fri (Feb & Nov) **Prices** Fixed L 2 course £22, Fixed D 3 course £39, Starter £5.95-£11.95, Main £11.50-£28, Dessert £5.95-£7.50 **Wines** 15 bottles over £30, 20 bottles under £30, 12 by glass **Parking** 20 **Notes** Sunday L £15-£20, Vegetarian available, Children welcome

---

Andrew Fairlie@Gleneagles

AUCHTERARDER Map 21 NN91

Modern French V NOTABLE WINE LIST
tel: 01764 694267 **The Gleneagles Hotel PH3 1NF**
email: reservations@andrewfairlie.co.uk
dir: *Off A9 at exit for A823 follow signs for Gleneagles Hotel*

Thrilling cooking at the glossy heart of an iconic golfing hotel

This vast pile has the look of a French chateau beamed into 850 acres of prime Perthshire, and Andrew Fairlie's restaurant makes it a world-class dining destination. The glamorous dining room boasts gold-framed artworks on black walls and sumptuous gold-hued fabrics, and completely turns its back on the fairways (there are no windows), offering nothing to distract from the culinary fireworks. The tasting menu delivers the full-works experience with a wine-flight option if all of the table are up for it, while the à la carte offers some half-dozen choices per course. A first-course duo of roast pheasant and seared foie gras, their richness cut with pickled pear and Calvados jus, shows the style, while in another first course, scallops are roasted and partnered with slow-cooked pork, parsnip and apple purée. The technical dexterity and pin-point accuracy continues with main courses such as roast and slow-cooked lamb with aubergine caviar and parmesan, or a dish of turbot, say, is matched with marine mustard, oyster and champagne velouté in another winning combination of flavours and textures. The trolley of hummingly ripe cheese trundles along before dessert, as is the French way. Everything looks picture-perfect on the plate, through to desserts such as apple crumble soufflé with cinnamon ice cream and vanilla sauce, or another that sees milk chocolate mousse partnered with dark chocolate crémeux and redcurrant. Running to 300 bins, the pedigree wine list is big on Burgundy, Bordeaux and champagne, while the service is slick and professional from start to finish.

Chef Andrew Fairlie, Stephen McLaughlin **Seats** 54 **Times** 6.30-10, Closed 24-25 Dec, 3 wks Jan, Sun, L all week **Prices** Tasting menu £125, Starter £31-£41, Main £46, Dessert £18 **Wines** 220 bottles over £30, 16 by glass **Parking** 300 **Notes** ALC 3 course £95, 8 course degustation £125, Children 12 yrs+

KILLIECRANKIE Map 23 NN96

Killiecrankie Hotel

Modern British V

tel: 01796 473220 **PH16 5LG**
email: enquiries@killiecrankiehotel.co.uk **web:** www.killiecrankiehotel.co.uk
dir: *Off A9 at Pitlochry, hotel 3m along B8079 on right*

Satisfying country-house cooking in tranquil Perthshire

Built for some blessed church minister back in 1840, the views across the Pass of Killiecrankie and the River Garry will soothe the troubled soul of any visitor. The kitchen delivers a fixed-price à la carte that comes with suggestions for accompanying wines. A tian of crayfish makes a classic opener, with avocado, pink grapefruit and crème fraîche, or go for a twice-baked goats' cheese brûlée with micro basil and red onion marmalade. Follow on with pan-fried fillet of Highland venison with a damson plum jus, or a salad of poached salmon and prawns with lemon and herb mayonnaise. Plum and stem ginger tarte Tatin is a winning dessert.

Chef Mark Easton **Seats** 30, Pr/dining room 12 **Times** 6.30-8.30, Closed Jan-Feb, L all week **Prices** Fixed D 3 course £42 **Wines** 32 bottles over £30, 47 bottles under £30, 9 by glass **Parking** 20 **Notes** Pre-theatre menu from 6.15pm Mon-Sat, 4 course D £42, Sunday L £17.50-£19.50, Children welcome

KINCLAVEN Map 21 NO13

Ballathie House Hotel

Classic

tel: 01250 883268 **PH1 4QN**
email: info@ballathiehousehotel.com **web:** www.ballathiehousehotel.com
dir: *From A9, 2m N of Perth, take B9099 through Stanley & follow signs, or from A93 at Beech Hedge follow signs for Ballathie, 2.5m*

Modern country-house cooking by the Tay

This privately owned, turreted mansion overlooking the River Tay hosts a restaurant that impresses with its dedication to local ingredients. The dining room has a classical elegance, with plenty of space between tables and views across the verdant countryside. Traditional flavours combine with a moderated degree of invention to create dishes that seem entirely in keeping with the setting. Try pan-fried breast of partridge with little crumbed balls of confit leg meat and foie gras mousse, followed by roast rump of lamb with haggis bonbon and mint and parsley salsa, or grilled halibut with herb crust and an aromatic chowder. Finish with dark chocolate cake with brown bread ice cream.

PERTH Map 21 NO12

Deans Restaurant

Modern Scottish

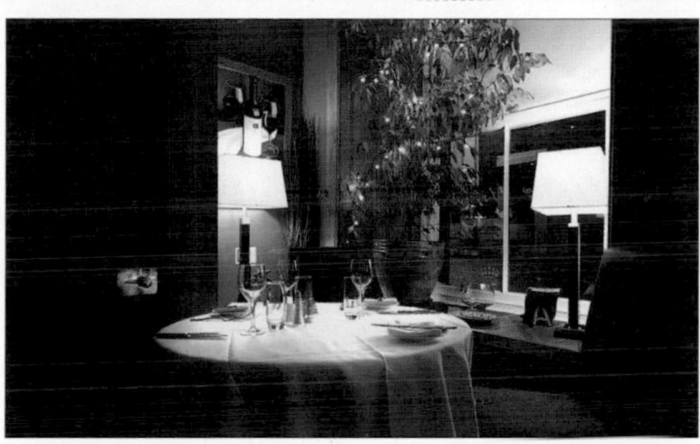

tel: 01738 643377 **77-79 Kinnoull St PH1 5EZ**
email: deans@letseatperth.co.uk **web:** www.letseatperth.co.uk
dir: *On corner of Kinnoull St & Atholl St, close to North Inch & cinema*

Dazzling cooking in stylish restaurant

Right in the centre of town, the family-run, recently-refurbished Deans is ever-popular. Here you'll find modern Scottish flavours in a vibrant, easy-going atmosphere. Willie Deans is a highly accomplished chef and his kitchen turns out skilfully executed, elegant dishes such as a first-course cassoulet of slow-cooked pork, pink venison loin and chargrilled potatoes. A main-course dish of fillet of lemon sole, with grilled king prawn, lemon-poached leeks, tomato braised potatoes and lobster cream, is delicate and subtle. For dessert, check out the chocolate and Armagnac soufflé cake, with ginger syrup and cherry ice cream.

Chef Willie Deans **Seats** 70 **Times** 12-3/6-10, Closed 1st 2 wks Jan, Mon **Prices** Fixed L 2 course £12.50, Fixed D 3 course £25, Starter £4.95-£10.50, Main £13.50-£26, Dessert £6.50-£8.95 **Wines** 23 bottles over £30, 36 bottles under £30, 14 by glass **Parking** Multi-storey car park (100 yds) **Notes** Pre-theatre menu Tue-Fri 6-9pm, Sunday L £16.50-£22, Vegetarian available, Children welcome

Murrayshall House Hotel & Golf Course

Modern British

tel: 01738 551171 **New Scone PH2 7PH**
email: info@murrayshall.co.uk **web:** www.murrayshall.co.uk
dir: *From Perth A94 (Coupar Angus) turn right signed Murrayshall before New Scone*

Polished cooking amid the rolling Lowland acres

With not one but two golf courses, Murrayshall doesn't do anything by halves. The main dining option is the Old Masters restaurant, a series of elegant spaces with views over the green Perthshire landscape. The menu is rich with Scottish ingredients, from salmon to scallops, and haggis to steaks, while cooking techniques combine both contemporary and traditional elements. Start with pork, cider and foie gras pie, which is really a terrine, served with pickled vegetables, and move on to braised veal with turnip and haggis mash, or a clever chicken creation with tattie scone and mushroom and red wine sauce. Dessert could be Amaretto crème brûlée with almond shortbread.

Chef Craig Jackson **Seats** 55, Pr/dining room 40
Times 12.30-2.30/6.30-9.30, Closed 26 Dec, L Sat-Mon **Prices** Fixed L 2 course £20, Fixed D 3 course £35, Starter £6.50-£7.50, Main £15.95-£24.50, Dessert £6.50-£7.95 **Wines** 17 bottles over £30, 27 bottles under £30, 8 by glass **Parking** 120 **Notes** Sunday L £25, Vegetarian available, Children welcome

PERTH *continued*

Pig'Halle

 French

tel: 01738 248784 **38 South St PH2 8PG**
email: info@pighalle.co.uk
dir: *Beside Salutation Hotel*

Pork, and more, in a buzzy French bistro

Pig'Halle has a Parisian look, with a map of the Metro embossed on a large mirror, wine memorabilia, brown banquette seating and red-upholstered chairs. It's atmospheric and buzzy, and pork is a theme on the France-inspired menu, from a starter of belly with scallops and black pudding, to a main course of shoulder steak from Pata Negra pork. Elsewhere, seek out Gallic classics such as fish soup, followed by confit de canard with redcurrant jus, fondant potato and steamed greens, or go for warm goats' cheese in filo with roast beetroot and toasted walnuts, then seafood risotto. Desserts might include Amaretto parfait with pear purée.

Chef Herve Tabourel **Seats** 40 **Times** 12-3/5.30-9.30 **Prices** Fixed L 2 course £11.90-£17.90, Fixed D 3 course £21-£57, Starter £4.90-£8, Main £11.90-£32.50, Dessert £5-£9 **Wines** 6 bottles over £30, 26 bottles under £30, 11 by glass **Parking** Canal St car park **Notes** Pre-theatre 5.30-6.45pm 2/3 course £13.90/£16.90, Sunday L £11.90-£25, Vegetarian available, Children welcome

The Roost Restaurant

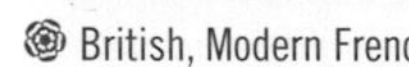 British, Modern French

tel: 01738 812111 **Forgandenny Rd, Bridge of Earn PH2 9AZ**
email: enquiries@theroostrestaurant.co.uk
dir: *M90 junct 9, Bridge of Earn. Follow brown tourist signs*

Modern French cooking with fine Scottish ingredients

Resembling a farmyard outhouse, The Roost is smart as can be inside, with crisply clad tables and a plethora of pictures and mirrors. Thoroughbred Scottish ingredients include some from the Roost's own kitchen gardens and starters of seared Rougié foie gras with hibiscus purée and grape jam, or a salad of pigeon, bacon and boudin noir with artichoke crisps in Marsala dressing, set the scene. At main, there could well be sensitively handled halibut with saffron tagliatelle, brown shrimps, baby fennel and samphire in shellfish sauce, or perhaps loin of red deer with a shallot tart in medlar and juniper jus. Finish with rhubarb vacherin adorned with pistachios.

Chef Tim Dover **Seats** 24 **Times** 12-2/6.45-9, Closed 25 Dec, 1-18 Jan, Mon, D Tue-Wed, Sun **Prices** Starter £6-£12, Main £14-£25, Dessert £6.50-£8 **Wines** 19 bottles over £30, 20 bottles under £30, 10 by glass **Parking** 6 **Notes** ALC L menu, Tasting menu with wine £100, Sunday L, Vegetarian available, Children welcome

63@Parklands

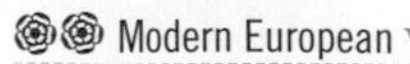 Modern European V

tel: 01738 622451 **Parklands Hotel, 2 St Leonards Bank PH2 8EB**
email: info@63atparklandshotel.com **web:** www.63atparklands.com
dir: *Adjacent to Perth station, overlooking South Inch Park*

Taking up the slack when Tay Street is closed

In a manor house in fine gardens overlooking South Inch Park, the format is a five-course fixed-price menu, with two or three choices at most stages. Proceedings might open with grilled smoked mackerel with Beaufort cheese crumble in winter minestrone, or more robustly with wild hare in celeriac velouté, before an intervening soup turns up. A three-way option for main might encompass halibut fillet with roast chicken and scallop cream and fragrant rice, Highland venison with haggis cannelloni, bittersweet cabbages and neeps, or the standby classic, Angus beef fillet in béarnaise. Cheeses precede the dessert alternatives, which could be poached rhubarb in pink peppercorn sabayon with white chocolate mousse.

Chef Graeme Pallister **Seats** 32, Pr/dining room 22 **Times** 7-9, Closed 25 Dec-5 Jan, Tue-Wed, L all week **Prices** Tasting menu £39.50 **Wines** 30 bottles over £30, 45 bottles under £30, 8 by glass **Parking** 25 **Notes** Children welcome

63 Tay Street

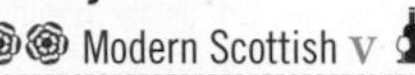 Modern Scottish V NOTABLE WINE LIST

tel: 01738 441451 **63 Tay St PH2 8NN**
email: info@63taystreet.com
dir: *In town centre, on river.*

Attractive, imaginative cooking by the River Tay

Graeme Pallister's restaurant occupies part of the ground floor of an imposing stone building on the Tay. Portholes and fishy hanging fabric create a maritime feel, while a tartan carpet adds a touch of luxury underfoot. 'Local, honest, simple' is the aim, although the kitchen adds a pleasing degree of complexity, evident in a stunning-looking starter of chicken-of-the-wood mushrooms with haggis and a fried egg, and a main course of baked hake fillet with a mustard crumb, Jersey Royals and mussel broth, both providing many layers of flavours. Puddings are another strength, judging by wobbly chocolate fondant with white chocolate mousse and Baileys ice cream.

Chef Graeme Pallister **Seats** 38 **Times** 12-2/6-9, Closed Xmas, New Year, 1st wk Jul, Sun-Mon, L Tue-Wed **Prices** Fixed L 2 course £19-£27.50, Fixed D 3 course £42-£46.50, Tasting menu £55 **Wines** 125 bottles over £30, 49 bottles under £30, 7 by glass **Parking** On street **Notes** Pre-theatre, express menu Tue-Thu 2/3 course £17/£22, Children welcome

Tabla

 Indian V

tel: 01738 444630 **173 South St PH2 8NY**
email: thirmalreddy@yahoo.com
dir: *Phone for directions*

Zesty Indian home cooking in the city centre

At the Kumar family's central Perth eaterie the ambience has more personality than many a formula Indian restaurant, with exposed stone walls, full-drop windows and a glass panel looking into the kitchen. Indian music featuring the eponymous tabla drums plays softly. A vegetable pakora of crisp potato nuggets filled with carrots, peas and coriander seeds served with a tomato salsa-style dressing, is an appetiser for a classic main course of murgh balti, a delicate, fragrantly-spiced dish of tender chicken in a sauce of tomato, chickpeas, ginger and garlic. A full listing of vegetarian dishes is prominent on the menu. Finish with sticky gulab jamon dumplings flavoured with cardamom and rose water.

Chef Praveen Kumar **Seats** 42 **Times** 12-2.30/5-10.30, Closed L Sun **Prices** Fixed L 2 course £9.95, Fixed D 3 course £20-£25, Starter £5-£8, Main £10-£15, Dessert £5 **Wines** 4 bottles over £30, 4 bottles under £30, 3 by glass **Parking** On street **Notes** Pre-theatre 2 course fr £13.95, Tapas menu L £9.95, D £14.95, Children welcome

PITLOCHRY Map 23 NN95

Fonab Castle Hotel & Spa

Modern Scottish V

tel: 01796 470140 **Foss Rd PH16 5ND**
email: reservations@fonabcastlehotel.com **web:** www.fonabcastlehotel.com
dir: *Pitlochry A9 take Foss Rd junct. Hotel 1st on left*

Innovative Scottish cooking in a magical setting

With its conical corner turret and handsome gables, this magical, castellated pile of reddish stone wouldn't look out of place in a film adaptation of a Sir Walter Scott novel. Built around a core of sweeping staircases and panelled interiors, Fonab's refurbishment has conjured a contemporary country-house hotel and spa from the place, with glassed-in views over Loch Faskally from both the Brasserie and the upmarket restaurant Sandemans, named in honour of the port-shipping family who once lived here. Chef Paul Burns' culinary style suits the setting with its strikingly modern approach, creating dishes that are full of bold combinations but avoiding flamboyance. A six course tasting menu, with optional wine matches, offers a wide-ranging tour of Burns' abilities. An appetiser may lead may lead on to ham hock tian, celeriac remoulade, apple, quail egg, caper and a Sandeman's Amontillado gel. Then the main business arrives in the form of a perfectly poached and roasted beef fillet, shoulder-blade beignet, chervil root purée, salsify and fondant potato. You might then move on to a dazzling dessert of Valrhona chocolate tart with salted caramel ice cream and textures of chocolate and coffee.

Chef Paul Burns **Seats** 60, Pr/dining room 40 **Times** 12-2.30/5-9 **Prices** Fixed L 2 course fr £19.95, Fixed D 3 course fr £40, Tasting menu fr £65 **Wines** 114 bottles over £30, 36 bottles under £30, 15 by glass **Parking** 50 **Notes** Tasting menu 6 course, Pre-theatre menu, Sunday L, Children welcome

Knockendarroch

Modern Scottish

tel: 01796 473473 **Higher Oakfield PH16 5HT**
email: bookings@knockendarroch.co.uk **web:** www.knockendarroch.co.uk
dir: *On entering town from Perth, 1st right (East Moulin Road) after railway bridge, then 2nd left, last hotel on left*

Resourceful cooking at an elegantly appointed hotel

A handsome sandstone house in a wooded setting, Knockendarroch has country-house comforts and a diminutive restaurant delivering daily-changing menus of classy modern Scottish food. It's very traditional within, with warming fires in the cooler months, ornate cornicing, chandeliers and the like, while genuine hospitality runs right through the place. Well-crafted and refined dishes include a starter of wood pigeon with chicory salad, pickled pear, beetroot, and heather honey and mustard dressing, while main courses could see loin Highland venison loin partnered with tarragon mash, squash purée, wild mushroom ragoût and juniper jus. For dessert, perhaps chilled rhubarb consommé with strawberries, blueberries and ginger beer sorbet.

Chef Graeme Stewart **Seats** 24 **Times** 5.30-8.30, Closed mid Nov-mid Jan, L all week **Prices** Fixed D 3 course £42 **Wines** 8 bottles over £30, 25 bottles under £30, 5 by glass **Parking** 12 **Notes** Pre-theatre D Jun-Oct, Vegetarian available, Children 10 yrs+

ST FILLANS Map 20 NN62

The Four Seasons Hotel

Modern British V

tel: 01764 685333 **Loch Earn PH6 2NF**
email: info@thefourseasonshotel.co.uk **web:** www.thefourseasonshotel.co.uk
dir: *From Perth take A85 W, through Crieff & Comrie. Hotel at west end of village*

Breathtaking loch views and appealing modern cooking

Perched on the edge of Loch Earn, The Four Seasons has breathtaking views over the water and wooded hills. In the waterside Meall Reamhar restaurant, those stunning views complement the modern British menu, built on spectacular Scottish ingredients. Kick off with (perfectly) seared hand-dived scallops matched with crisp air-cured bacon, Granny Smith jam, smoked morcilla black pudding and cauliflower pannacotta. Next up, Pata Negra pork and pig's cheek is served with truffled mash and a chilli and sherry vinegar sauce, and seared turbot and king scallop come in the company of pea and pancetta risotto. Finish with a creative mango and chilli parfait with coconut truffle and punch sorbet.

Chef Ben Mailer **Seats** 40, Pr/dining room 20 **Times** 12-2.30/6-9.30, Closed Jan-Feb & some wkdays Mar, Nov & Dec **Prices** Fixed D 2 course fr £32 **Wines** 61 bottles over £30, 52 bottles under £30, 8 by glass **Parking** 30 **Notes** 4 course D £42-£49.95, Sunday L £15.95-£20.95, Children welcome

SPITTAL OF GLENSHEE Map 23 NO16

Dalmunzie Castle Hotel

Modern British NEW V

tel: 01250 885224 **PH10 7QG**
email: reservations@dalmunzie.com **web:** www.dalmunzie.com
dir: *On A93 at Spittal of Glenshee, follow signs to hotel*

Simple flavours in Baronial splendour

The castle was built in the 1920s in the Scottish Baronial style, turrets et al, while the Dalmunzie Estate itself (all 6,500 acres of it) dates from the early 1500s. Today's country-house hotel, at the end of a mile-long drive, has a restaurant that reflects the traditional setting and offers a menu with some contemporary touches. Thus cured mackerel is served with pickled raspberries in a simple but effective first course, while roast chicken with fondant potato, baby carrots and tempura broccoli is brought together by a flavoursome, glossy jus. Perthshire strawberry soufflé is the star of a summer dinner, partnered with white chocolate ice cream topped with sorrel and biscuit crumb.

Chef Noel Breaks **Seats** 36, Pr/dining room 16 **Times** 12-2.30/7-9, Closed 1-23 Dec **Prices** Fixed L 2 course £15-£18, Fixed D 3 course £50 **Wines** 43 bottles over £30, 29 bottles under £30, 4 by glass **Parking** 20 **Notes** Children welcome

SCOTTISH BORDERS

KELSO Map 21 NT73

The Cobbles Freehouse & Dining

Modern British

tel: 01573 223548 **7 Bowmont St TD5 7JH**
email: info@thecobbleskelso.co.uk
dir: *A6089 from Edinburgh, turn right at rdbt into Bowmont St. Restaurant in 0.3m*

Modern menu in a lively pub setting

Tucked just off the town's main square, this old inn has successfully negotiated the pub/restaurant dynamic. There are bar snacks such as wraps and burgers on offer, but in the dapper restaurant you'll find Scottish-inspired dishes that really impress. West Coast scallops come with a pecan crumb, black pudding and cauliflower purée, plus dinky shallot rings, while a main-course confit pork belly number hits all the right buttons. There are steaks, too, sourced from Scottish herds, and served with a host of accompaniments including caramelised vegetables and garlic mushrooms. Finish with an ace dark chocolate fondant with cherry purée and an almond streusel.

Chef Daniel Norcliffe **Seats** 35, Pr/dining room 30 **Times** 12-2.30/5.45-9, Closed 25 Dec **Prices** Prices not confirmed **Wines** 7 bottles over £30, 20 bottles under £30, 9 by glass **Parking** Free parking behind restaurant **Notes** Early supper deal, Sunday L, Vegetarian available, Children welcome

The Roxburghe Hotel & Golf Course

British, French V

tel: 01573 229250 & 450331 **Heiton TD5 8JZ**
email: hotel@roxburghe.net **web:** www.roxburghe.net
dir: *From A68, 1m N of Jedburgh, take A698 for 5m to Heiton*

Impressive country setting for fine modern cooking

Owned by the Duke of Roxburghe, this turreted Jacobean country-house hotel is tucked in woodland close to the River Teviot. The dining room delivers ducal finery in spades, with plush fabrics, horse-racing prints, crisp linen tablecloths and a tartan carpet. The kitchen, run by an Albert Roux enterprise, turns out modernist ideas, starting with chicken terrine with soused tomatoes and herb salad, followed by seared stone bass with red pepper butter sauce and a ragout of lobster and sweetcorn, with a meat option of smoked venison saddle with cider-braised onions, confit potatoes and Calvados and game jus. To finish, try seasonal summer pudding with clotted cream.

Chef Lee Pattie **Seats** 40, Pr/dining room 16 **Times** 12-2/6.30-9.30 **Prices** Fixed L 2 course £17.25-£24, Fixed D 3 course £29.50, Starter £8-£12, Main £18-£23.50, Dessert £7-£13 **Wines** 149 bottles over £30, 21 bottles under £30, 17 by glass **Parking** 150 **Notes** Afternoon tea, Children welcome

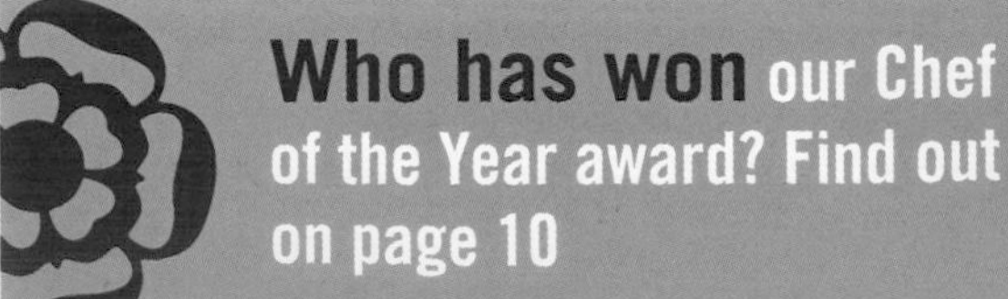

MELROSE Map 21 NT53

Burts Hotel

Modern Scottish, British

tel: 01896 822285 **Market Square TD6 9PL**
email: enquiries@burtshotel.co.uk **web:** www.burtshotel.co.uk
dir: *A6091, 2m from A68, 3m S of Earlston. Hotel in market square*

Contemporary cooking at an old favourite

Owned and run by the Henderson family for more than 40 years, this handsome 18th-century inn is rooted into Melrose life. The kitchen turns out modern Scottish dishes prepared from quality local produce. Yellow split pea and ham soup is a heart-warming classic, or seared scallops with confit potato, truffle mayonnaise and pancetta sauce. This being Scotland, you're never far from game, so follow with venison served with boulangère potatoes, spiced red cabbage and pearl vegetable jus, or pan-fried salmon fillet with chorizo and tiger prawn risotto and herb salad. Finish with an assiette of apple, comprising a nutty crumble, a moist sponge, apple strudel ice cream and vanilla crème anglaise.

Chef Trevor Williams **Seats** 50, Pr/dining room 25 **Times** 12-2/7-9, Closed 26 Dec, L Mon-Fri **Prices** Starter £4.50-£9.95, Main £13.95-£25.50, Dessert £7.50-£8.50 **Wines** 33 bottles over £30, 27 bottles under £30, 8 by glass **Parking** 40 **Notes** Sunday L £18.95-£40, Vegetarian available, Children 10 yrs+

STIRLING

ABERFOYLE Map 20 NN50

Macdonald Forest Hills Hotel & Resort

Modern Scottish

tel: 01877 389500 **Kinlochard FK8 3TL**
email: general.foresthills@macdonald-hotels.co.uk
web: www.macdonald-hotels.co.uk/foresthills
dir: *4m from Aberfoyle on B829*

Modern cooking in a happening resort hotel

Twenty-five acres of mature gardens run down to the shore of Loch Ard at this white-painted mansion, where 'keep it simple' might be the kitchen's mantra and flavours are undiluted by an over-abundance of ingredients. Brie and red onion tart with herb salad is an effective starter, contrasting with the relative complexity of seared cod fillet atop a pancake rolled around creamed smoked mackerel. Braised lamb shoulder, of beautifully tender meat, comes with rosemary jus, buttery mash, cabbage and baby onions, alongside another sensibly composed main course of seared salmon fillet with ratatouille and wilted spinach. Finish with satsuma crème brûlée with decadent chocolate chip cookies.

Chef Scott Swift **Seats** 78, Pr/dining room 20 **Times** 12-2.30/6.30-9.30, Closed L Mon-Sat **Prices** Prices not confirmed **Wines** 80 bottles over £30, 10 bottles under £30, 14 by glass **Parking** 50 **Notes** Sunday L, Vegetarian available, Children welcome

CALLANDER Map 20 NN60

Roman Camp Country House Hotel

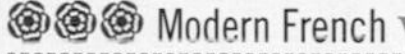 Modern French V

tel: 01877 330003 **FK17 8BG**
email: mail@romancamphotel.co.uk **web:** www.romancamphotel.co.uk
dir: *N on A84 through Callander, Main St turn left at East End into drive*

Modernist cooking of inventive energy

This early 17th-century manor house was built for the Earls of Moray and has been a hotel since the 1930s. It's jam-packed with period furnishings and has a traditional and formal atmosphere. Despite the fact it is in the centre of Callander, once inside the property it is all too easy to forget about the outside world and imagine you're miles from anywhere. The two smart dining rooms match the formal mood, while the kitchen's output is much more modern-minded than you might imagine. Whether you go for the carte or four-course fixed-price menu, expect well-judged dishes that show classical good sense and creative flair. Begin with seared scallops, which arrive with a potato terrine and smoked haddock sauce, or monkfish tail with crispy oxtail and squid. Organic salmon might turn up in a main course with cep gnocchi and verjus sauce, while, on the fixed-price menu, loin of Borders lamb is partnered with an aubergine tart and caramelised sweetbreads, dressed with a thyme jus. Among desserts, dark chocolate and peanut butter cake is served with gingerbread ice cream, with farmhouse cheeses an alternative, served with fig and walnut toast and membrillo.

Chef Ian McNaught **Seats** 120, Pr/dining room 36 **Times** 12-2/7-9 **Prices** Fixed L 3 course fr £28.50, Starter £11.50-£20.90, Main £28.50-£29.90, Dessert £10.90-£13 **Wines** 180 bottles over £30, 15 bottles under £30, 16 by glass **Parking** 80 **Notes** Fixed D 4 course £55, Sunday L, Children welcome

DUNBLANE Map 21 NN70

Cromlix and Chez Roux

French NEW NOTABLE WINE LIST

tel: 01786 822125 **Kinbuck FK15 9JT**
email: enquiries@cromlix.com **web:** www.cromlix.com
dir: *From A9 take B8033 (Kinbuck), through village, 2nd left after small bridge*

Classical French cooking in historic, luxury country-house hotel

When tennis superstar Andy Murray decided to give something back to his home area (he grew up in nearby Dunblane) by attracting more visitors, his eyes alighted on this turreted country house hotel. Already rather swish, it's even more so now. It emerges from the trees at the end of a long, single-track drive through an estate partly owned by the Eden family (think Sir Anthony, the 1950s, prime minister). The Chez Roux restaurant, overseen by the legendary Albert, and run by award-winning executive head chef Darin Campbell, is in a glass-walled conservatory, with an open kitchen to one side, added in Andy's time. The menu, listing dishes in both French and English, changes frequently to offer, say, hand-dived Mull scallops with British rose veal sweetbreads and smoked red pepper purée to start, while a main might be Gigha (the most southerly Hebridean island) halibut, with new-season asparagus, grapes, garden mint gnocchi, white asparagus and verjus velouté; and ballotine of French rabbit with Scottish wild mushrooms, garden tarragon mousse, fondant potato, carrot purée and rabbit jus. In the spring, look for Perthshire strawberry soufflé and sorbet. That the hotel has a tennis court should be no surprise, but its purple and green surface, Wimbledon's house colours, might well be.

Chef Albert Roux, Darin Campbell **Seats** Pr/dining room 28 **Times** 12-2/7-9.30 **Prices** Fixed L 3 course £28.50, Fixed D 3 course £31.50, Starter £8-£14, Main £19.50-£22.50, Dessert £8-£12.50 **Notes** Vegetarian available

FINTRY Map 20 NS68

Culcreuch Castle Hotel & Estate

Traditional Scottish V

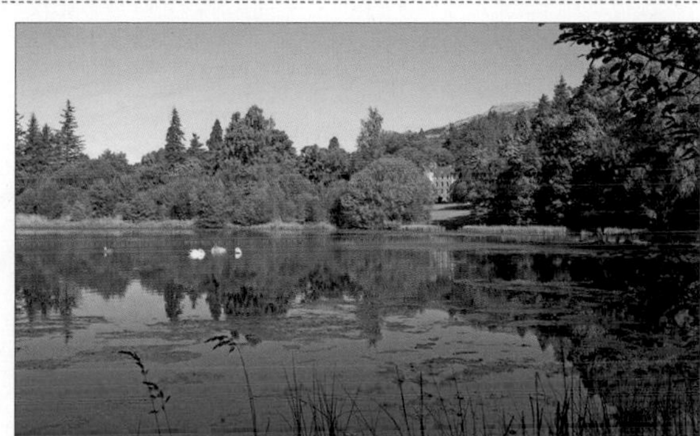

tel: 01360 860555 **Kippen Rd G63 0LW**
email: info@culcreuch.com **web:** www.culcreuch.com
dir: *Phone for directions*

Dining room or dungeon dining at an ancestral castle

Standing in 1600 acres of grounds, including a picturesque loch, Culcreuch Castle has all the medieval accoutrements that could be desired. Country-house cooking with some imaginative touches is the approach. For example, a dish of pan-seared scallops next to a small crispy-skinned and boned chicken wing and piece of crackling that hides a small column of charred soft leek is a lovely take on the classic 'Cock-a-Leekie'. Elsewhere, a deceptively complex Culcreuch lamb with peas, mint and sheeps' milk showcases the estate's produce and a caramel chocolate sphere with quenelle of coconut ice cream makes for a wonderful end to a meal.

Chef Paul O'Malley **Seats** 22, Pr/dining room 30 **Times** 12-2.30/5-9, Closed 25-26 Dec, 1st 2wks Jan **Prices** Fixed D 3 course £36-£40, Starter £4-£8.50, Main £10.50-£19.50, Dessert £4-£6.50 **Wines** 5 bottles over £30, 21 bottles under £30, 7 by glass **Parking** 60 **Notes** Children welcome

STIRLING Map 21 NS79

The Stirling Highland Hotel

British, European

tel: 01786 272727 **Spittal St FK8 1DU**
email: stirling@thehotelcollection.co.uk **web:** www.thehotelcollection.co.uk
dir: *In road leading to Stirling Castle, follow Castle signs*

Commanding valley views and confident cooking in an old school

A grand old Victorian property just down the hill from Stirling's historic castle, The Stirling Highland Hotel was built in the 1850s as a school. The eating takes place in three third-floor dining rooms of generous Victorian proportions. The menu takes a modern approach to some familiar ideas, so a first-course smoked haddock kedgeree is breaded and deep-fried, and served with curried mayonnaise and a quail's egg, and main-course guinea fowl arrives filled with prune mousse and partnered with a fondant potato, Savoy cabbage and butternut squash purée. There's a similarly contemporary approach to desserts, as when rhubarb gets the trio treatment – crumble, fool and sorbet.

STRATHYRE Map 20 NN51

Creagan House

@@ French, Scottish

tel: 01877 384638 **FK18 8ND**
email: eatandstay@creaganhouse.co.uk **web:** www.creaganhouse.co.uk
dir: *0.25m N of village, off A84*

17th-century Trossachs farmhouse with good food

The views alone make a visit to this 17th-century farmhouse worthwhile. Gordon and Cherry Gunn have been welcoming guests to 17th-century Creagan House for 30 years. Gordon does all the cooking himself. Dinner is served in the grandly vaulted baronial-style dining room. The short contemporary menu makes the most of the fantastic local ingredients. Start with breast of new-season grouse on bacon and mushroom skirlie with redcurrant sauce, before taking in a main-course collop of local venison saddle, venison pie, Worcester berry and cassis sauce. Desserts are home-made, or go for the selection of well-kept Scottish cheeses.

Chef Gordon Gunn **Seats** 15, Pr/dining room 6 **Times** 7.30-8.30, Closed 26 Oct-6 Apr, Wed-Thu, L all week (ex parties) **Prices** Prices not confirmed **Wines** 44 bottles over £30, 27 bottles under £30, 7 by glass **Parking** 15 **Notes** Vegetarian available, Children 10 yrs+

SCOTTISH ISLANDS

ISLE OF HARRIS

TARBERT (TAIRBEART) Map 22 NB10

Hotel Hebrides

 Modern Scottish, Seafood

tel: 01859 502364 **Pier Rd HS3 3DG**
email: stay@hotel-hebrides.com **web:** www.hotel-hebrides.com
dir: *To Tarbert via ferry from Uig (Isle of Skye); or ferry from Ullapool to Stornoway, A859 to Tarbert; or by plane to Stornoway from Glasgow, Edinburgh or Inverness*

Seafood specialities overlooking the incoming ferries

The modern boutique hotel is the focal point of a village of some 500 souls on the Isle of Harris. In the Pierhouse seafood restaurant, a bare boarded look keeps things simple. Fish and shellfish are strong suits, ranging from bowls of generously crammed chowder to mains of seared megrim sole in citrus and caper beurre blanc with samphire, and rainbow trout with kale in salsa verde. Meat sticklers might set a course via fried chicken livers on toasted brioche in blackberry and rosemary jus to roast Hebridean lamb rack with minted mash, before all are reunited for biscuit-based Belgian chocolate torte, served with Amaretto cream streaked with berry coulis.

ISLE OF MULL

FIONNPHORT Map 20 NM32

Ninth Wave Restaurant

@ Modern Pacific Rim V

tel: 01681 700757 **PA66 6BL**
email: enquiries@ninthwaverestaurant.co.uk **web:** www.ninthwaverestaurant.co.uk
dir: *Near end of Ross of Mull, just before village of Fionnphort (A849) where the ferry to Iona departs, turn off signed*

Creative cooking in a remote island location

On the southern tip of Mull where ferries leave for Iona, John and Carla Lamont's pocket-sized restaurant is about as remote as they come. The dinner-only affair seats just 18 lucky diners, who can expect skilfully cooked menus full of inventive ideas. To start, langoustine and crab won ton dumplings come in a spicy Thai-style coconut milk and kaffir lime broth, while pan-fried sea bream is partnered creatively by a deep-fried courgette blossom stuffed with fish and sea urchin. Elsewhere, crab and smoked Applewood cheese are united in a soufflé-style cheesecake, and to finish, blackberries from the croft turn up in a dark chocolate tart with bramble jelly and semi-freddo.

Chef Carla Lamont **Seats** 18 **Times** 7-12, Closed Mon-Tue, L all week **Prices** Fixed D 3 course £46 **Wines** 14 bottles over £30, 18 bottles under £30, 2 by glass **Parking** 10 **Notes** 4/5 course D £54/£64, Children 12 yrs+

TOBERMORY Map 22 NM55

Highland Cottage

 Modern Scottish, International

tel: 01688 302030 **24 Breadalbane St PA75 6PD**
email: davidandjo@highlandcottage.co.uk **web:** www.highlandcottage.co.uk
dir: *Opposite fire station. Main St up Back Brae, turn at top by White House. Follow road to right, left at next junct into Breadalbane St*

Inspired local cooking in a charming island hotel

Enjoying a stunning elevated location overlooking Tobermory harbour, this salmon-hued hotel close to the fishing pier is a jewel of a place. The homely interiors are a delight and the place is cleverly laid out to lead you from the bar and conservatory into the suavely furnished dining room. Chef Jo Currie does a fine job of showcasing Mull produce, with local crab cakes served with rocket and a zingy chilly caper sauce making for a satisfying starter. A precisely cooked roast saddle of Ardnamurchan venison with haggis parcel, dauphinoise potatoes and juniper gravy is a typical main course.

Chef Josephine Currie **Seats** 24 **Times** 7-9, Closed Nov-Mar, L all week **Prices** Tasting menu £42.50 **Wines** 12 bottles over £30, 21 bottles under £30, 11 by glass **Parking** On street in front of establishment **Notes** Vegetarian available, Children 10 yrs+

SHETLAND

SCALLOWAY **Map 24 HU43**

Scalloway Hotel

◎◎ Modern Scottish V

tel: 01595 880444 **Main St ZE1 0TR**
email: info@scallowayhotel.com **web:** www.scallowayhotel.com
dir: *7m from Lerwick on west mainland on A970*

Creative cooking in an unpretentious setting in the far north

An unpretentious place that opens its arms to all-comers, from oil-rig workers to passing ships' crews, making the bar a convivial haunt for casual dishes along the lines of fish pie with parsley mash or haddock and chips done right. The restaurant has linen tablecloths, quality glasses and a seasonal menu that showcases the islands' produce – local lamb, for starters, its seared belly and crisp lamb 'bacon' served with Jerusalem artichoke purée, followed by lemon sole with crushed Shetland Black potatoes, caramelised salsify, and crab and tarragon butter sauce. Desserts are no-less creative: pear tarte Tatin with five spice ice cream and almond shards, for example.

Seats 36 **Times** 12-3/5-9.30, Closed Xmas, New Year **Prices** Starter £7.50-£9.50, Main £16-£27.50, Dessert £7 **Wines** 23 bottles over £30, 22 bottles under £30, 10 by glass **Parking** 10 **Notes** Sunday L, Children welcome

ISLE OF SKYE

COLBOST **Map 22 NG24**

The Three Chimneys & The House Over-By

◎◎◎ – *see page 552*

ISLEORNSAY **Map 22 NG71**

Duisdale House Hotel

◎◎ Modern Scottish

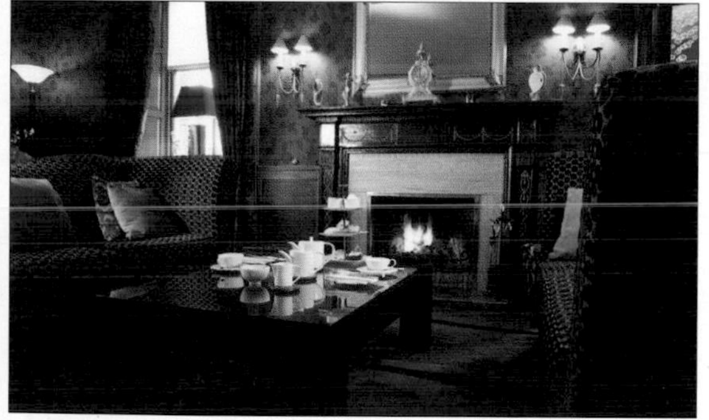

tel: 01471 833202 **Sleat IV43 8QW**
email: info@duisdale.com **web:** www.duisdale.com
dir: *7m N of Armadale ferry & 12m S of Skye Bridge on A851*

Modern Scottish seasonal cooking in remotest southern Skye

With bags of boutique style and a dreamy location by the Sound of Sleat, Duisdale House has a lot going for it. The garden is a treat, especially if you're a fan of rhododendrons, and the conservatory restaurant boasts stylish looks. Expect modern cooking based on seasonal, regional ingredients, starting with wood pigeon partnered by Puy lentils, Jerusalem artichoke purée and a Stornoway Black Pudding bonbon. Breast of guinea fowl appears in an equally satisfying construction, with pearl barley risotto, celeriac purée and a rich, glossy red wine sauce. To finish, comforting custard and nutmeg tart is served with coffee and hazelnut ice cream.

Chef Brian Ross **Seats** 50 **Times** 12-2.30/6.30-9 **Prices** Fixed L 2 course fr £15 **Wines** 30 bottles over £30, 30 bottles under £30, 6 by glass **Parking** 30 **Notes** Sunday L £15.50-£35, Vegetarian available, Children welcome

Hotel Eilean Iarmain

◎ Traditional Scottish with French influences

tel: 01471 833332 **Sleat IV43 8QR**
email: hotel@eileaniarmain.co.uk **web:** www.eileaniarmain.co.uk
dir: *At Mallaig, cross by ferry to Armadale, 8m to hotel or via Kyle of Lochalsh*

Spectacular sea views and consummate cooking

The hotel is very much a part of this small community, with Gaelic spoken and regular ceilidh nights, while the owners also run a small distillery and art gallery next door. The restaurant has tables dressed in white linen and flickering candles, while the culinary output is rather more contemporary than you might imagine. Start with a savoury pannacotta (goats' cheese, garlic and chive) with beetroot purée and pickled carrots, before moving on to oven roasted loin of estate venison with mini fondant potato, sautéed kale and a glossy red wine sauce. Finish with a dark chocolate sphere with white chocolate and honey ganache, Cointreau mousse, raspberry jelly and honeycomb crumble.

Chef Philip Bertand **Seats** 40, Pr/dining room 22 **Times** 12-2.30/6.30-9 **Prices** Starter £5-£9, Main £12-£18, Dessert £5-£6 **Wines** 10 bottles over £30, 9 bottles under £30, 5 by glass **Parking** 10 **Notes** Afternoon tea on request, Sunday L, Vegetarian available, Children welcome

Kinloch Lodge

◎◎◎ French, Scottish V NOTABLE WINE LIST

tel: 01471 833214 & 833333 **Sleat IV43 8QY**
email: reservations@kinloch-lodge.co.uk **web:** www.kinloch-lodge.co.uk
dir: *1m off main road, 6m S of Broadford on A851, 10m N of Armadale*

Accomplished Scottish cooking in the Macdonald ancestral home

The white-painted house is handsome enough – the ancestral home of the high chief of the Clan Donald no less – while the setting is awesome, overlooking the waters of na Dal sea loch. The current laird, Godfrey Macdonald (the 8th Lord Macdonald), lives at Kinloch with Lady Claire, the well-known cookery writer. They have created a glorious retreat with an unassuming elegance, cosy fires, and a restaurant that really packs a punch. Head chef Marcello Tully and his team deliver an inspiring repertoire of French influenced modern Scottish fair, with superb regional ingredients at the heart of everything. The formal dining room is adorned with imposing historic portraits. After an opening 'soupçon' of roast butternut squash comes west coast scallops, served up with a warm mousse made with the roes, and the flavours of citrus and ginger. Next up, 'Marcello's special', which might be Mallaig hake with some subtle Indian spicing, followed by the necessity to make a decision – meat or fish. The former could be Speyside beef with Strathdon blue cheese mousse and rich brandy sauce. To finish, choose between dark chocolate melt with vanilla espuma and crème de menthe or Scottish and French cheeses from the trolley, or have both.

Chef Marcello Tully **Seats** 55, Pr/dining room 12 **Times** 12-2.30/6.30-9 **Prices** Fixed L 3 course £32.99, Tasting menu £80-£160 **Wines** 165 bottles over £30, 5 bottles under £30, 19 by glass **Parking** 50 **Notes** Fixed L 4 course £37.99, Fixed D 5 course £70, Sunday L £32.99-£37.99, Children welcome

The Three Chimneys & The House Over-By

COLBOST **Map 22 NG24**

Modern Scottish NOTABLE WINE LIST

tel: 01470 511258 **IV55 8ZT**
email: eatandstay@threechimneys.co.uk
web: www.threechimneys.co.uk
dir: *5m W of Dunvegan take B884 signed Glendale. On left beside loch*

Exceptional cooking in a wild, romantic setting

Eddie and Shirley Spear's restaurant has played a considerable part in building Skye's gastronomic reputation over the past 30 years. Not a place to stand still, this iconic restaurant has seen quite a few changes in the past year or so, with a refurbishment, a change of chef and a rethink that goes right down to the bespoke ceramics and crockery. A remote, whitewashed cottage with views of loch and land, the decor reflects a strong sense of place. This same respect for the island's identity is mirrored by the inventive cooking, which draws from the Scottish and Nordic heritage of the highlands and Islands and allows tip-top raw materials (many grown within walking distance of the kitchen) the opportunity to speak for themselves, truly living up to the ethos of 'the best of sky, land and sea'. Many traditional techniques are employed including salt-curing, smoking and, for the current year, cooking root vegetables in a salt and ash crust. The cooking is all delivered via concise menus (three options per course) alongside an eight-course tasting extravaganza ideal for those planning to stay in one of the restaurant's charming bedrooms. You might kick off with a crisp-coated egg (sourced from a croft behind the restaurant) teamed with summer vegetables, pickled cauliflower and toasted hazelnuts, or an impressive oyster number that sees the bivalves served in tempura batter, dressed to thrill and as they come. 'Head to tail' Black Isle beef (cheek, tongue, blade and oxtail) with shallot tart and potato fondant is a flawless main course of perfect balance. Creative talent is behind a dessert offering 'temperatures and textures' of bitter chocolate complemented by caramel, popcorn and Skye sea salt, and another that brings together those comforting bedfellows rhubarb and custard in an imaginative manner.

Chef Scott Davies **Seats** 40 **Times** 12.15-1.45/6.30-9.30, Closed 12 Dec-13 Jan, L 23 Mar-27 Nov **Prices** Tasting menu fr £90 **Wines** 140 bottles over £30, 14 by glass **Parking** 12 **Notes** ALC 3 course £65, Tasting menu 7 course, Fixed L £38, Sunday L, Vegetarian available, Children 5yrs L/8yrs D

ISLEORNSAY *continued*

Toravaig House Hotel

Modern Scottish

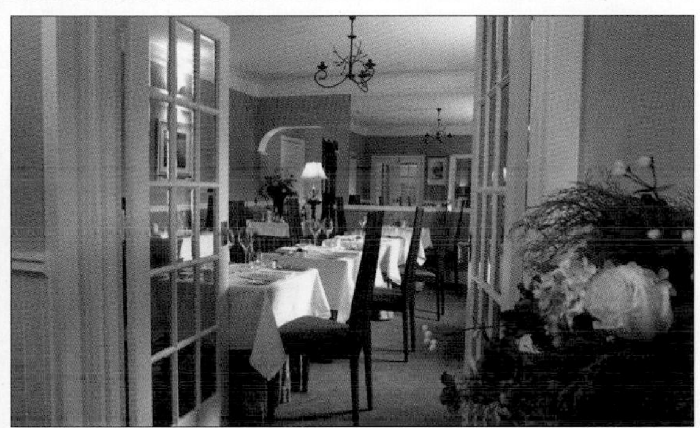

tel: 01471 820200 **Knock Bay, Sleat IV44 8RE**
email: info@toravaig.com **web:** www.toravaig.com
dir: *From Skye Bridge, left at Broadford onto A851, hotel 11m on left. Or from ferry at Armadale take A851, hotel 6m on right*

Plush island retreat with modern Scottish cooking

With views over Knock Castle and the Sound of Sleat, the whitewashed Toravaig House serves up an enviable Skye vista. The hotel has classy interiors, with high-quality fixtures and fittings, and its restaurant is a smart candlelit space. The cooking takes a modern Scottish path, in keeping with the majestic surroundings, and produces well-crafted plates of food. Island scallops come in a creative combination with confit carrot, mustard dressing and smoked cheddar. There's a nifty wild mushroom velouté next, followed by a main course such as Barbary duck breast with pearl barley and caramelised shallots. Finish with Blairgowrie raspberries with white chocolate and oregano oil.

Chef Finn Wood **Seats** 25 **Times** 12.30-2.30/6.30-9.30 **Prices** Fixed L 2 course fr £15, Fixed D 3 course £49 **Wines** 40 bottles over £30, 25 bottles under £30, 6 by glass **Parking** 20 **Notes** Sunday L, Vegetarian available, Children 10 yrs+

PORTREE Map 22 NG44

Cuillin Hills Hotel

Traditional Scottish

tel: 01478 612003 **IV51 9QU**
email: info@cuillinhills-hotel-skye.co.uk **web:** www.cuillinhills-hotel-skye.co.uk
dir: *0.25m N of Portree on A855*

Creative and classic dining with breathtaking views

The restaurant at this country-house hotel looks out over Portree Bay to the Cuillin mountains – no wonder it's called 'The View'. A single menu offers creative modern dishes alongside some updated classics, and an excellent showing of regional seafood. A first-course terrine of confit chicken is pointed up by an array of pickled vegetables and silky apricot purée, while another purée of blood orange accompanies Barbary duck breast. Portree Bay langoustines, Carbost oysters and Loch Eishort mussels are the very best the local waters have to offer. For traditionalists, there's all the comfort of breaded haddock with tartare sauce and the burger with Orkney cheddar. Finish with a sharp lemon posset with raspberry gel.

Chef Daniel Flemming **Seats** 40, Pr/dining room 20 **Times** 12-2/6-9 **Prices** Prices not confirmed **Wines** 25 bottles over £30, 36 bottles under £30, 8 by glass **Parking** 56 **Notes** Sunday L, Vegetarian available, Children welcome

STEIN Map 22 NG25

Loch Bay Restaurant

British Seafood, Traditional Scottish, French

tel: 01470 592235 **Macleods Ter IV55 8GA**
email: info@lochbay-restaurant.co.uk
dir: *4m off A850 by B886*

Franco-Scottish cookery by the bay

With room only for a couple of dozen diners at a time, Loch Bay is a diminutive institution around these parts, a place of simplicity and integrity, and its position right by the loch shore, in a row of 18th-century fishermen's cottages, is a magical one. Under new ownership this year, it now offers traditional Scots cooking with a French accent. Start with mussel and oatmeal soup, or ox tongue and black pudding with celeriac remoulade, as preludes to classic fish-packed bourride, or Glendale venison with ceps and cocoa gravy. A clootie dumpling and whisky cream ends things on a high.

Chef Michael Smith **Seats** 23 **Times** 12.15-2/6.15-9, Closed Mon, L Tue, D Sun **Prices** Fixed L 2 course fr £21, Fixed D 3 course fr £37.50, Tasting menu fr £55 **Wines** 10 bottles over £30, 30 bottles under £30, 8 by glass **Parking** 6 **Notes** Sunday L fr £21, Vegetarian available, Children 8 yrs+ D

STRUAN Map 22 NG33

Ullinish Country Lodge

Modern Scottish NEW Y

tel: 01470 572214 **IV56 8FD**
email: ullinish@theisleofskye.co.uk **web:** www.theisleofskye.co.uk
dir: *9m S of Dunvegan on A863*

Classy, contemporary cooking in a Skye hideaway

The breathtaking views alone make the considerable effort of travelling to Ullinish worthwhile, with lochs on three sides and the rugged beauty of the Black Cuillins and MacLeod's Tables marching across the skyline. The white-painted restaurant (plus six guest rooms) dates from the 18th century, and is done out in a traditional style with tartan carpet in the intimate restaurant, where service is relaxed, friendly and polished. A daily 'link van' collects meat, seafood and garden produce from a network of the island's small suppliers and delivers them to the kitchen. Start with hand-dived scallops served with squid ink tortellini and saffron cream sauce, or Perthshire wood pigeon matched with flavours and textures of brambles and beetroot. Among main courses, fillet of Speyside beef is finished with a red wine jus, while a fish option might be Scrabster cod with chive gnocchi, white onion purée and a fashionably charred lettuce (romaine in this instance). The cheese course is a little out of the ordinary, offering up something local, Clava brie, say, with onion chutney, venison salami and a croissant – and it is served before dessert. To finish, tonka bean flavours a pannacotta, and rhubarb parfait keeps company with the more exotic mango.

Seats 22 **Times** 7.30-8.30, Closed 24 Dec-31 Jan, L all week **Prices** Prices not confirmed **Wines** 36 bottles over £30, 40 bottles under £30, 16 by glass **Parking** 10 **Notes** 5 course D £55, Children 16 yrs+

Wales

ISLE OF ANGLESEY

BEAUMARIS Map 14 SH67

Bishopsgate House Hotel

Traditional Welsh

tel: 01248 810302 **54 Castle St LL58 8BB**
email: hazel@bishopsgatehotel.co.uk **web:** www.bishopsgatehotel.co.uk
dir: *From Menai Bridge onto A545 to Beaumaris. Hotel on left in main street*

Reliable cookery on the Beaumaris waterfront

The mint-green façade of Bishopsgate House stands out on its Georgian terrace overlooking Beaumaris Green and Snowdonia across the Menai waterfront, while the intimate, low-ceilinged restaurant is full of old-world charm. Straightforward menus start out with braised pork belly with apple purée and white pudding, while brandy and herbs add interest to a chicken liver pâté served with onion marmalade and brioche. Next up, a fresh piece of hake is crusted with lemon and herbs and served with creamed leeks, or there might be pan-fried loin of lamb with a mustard and herb crust and honey and rosemary jus. Finish with pecan tart and honeycomb ice cream.

The Bull – Beaumaris

– see opposite

Château Rhianfa

Modern French NEW

tel: 01248 713656 **LL59 5NS**
email: hello@chateaurhianfa.com **web:** www.chateaurhianfa.com
dir: *On Glyngarth Road between Menai Bridge & Beaumaris*

Country house cooking in a posh Welsh château

Oak panels and a grand fireplace certainly make for an impressive dining room, but one would expect nothing less in this swanky 19th-century French chateau-style hotel surveying Snowdonia's peaks across the Menai Strait. The kitchen doesn't pull any left-field tricks, sticking to hearty country-house dishes. Thus a spring dinner gets going with Anglesey asparagus matched with smoked cheddar beignets and cheddar sauce, as a prelude to roast rump and pressed shoulder of lamb with raisin and caper purée and braised local vegetables. For dessert, rhubarb arrives in a shot glass with ginger beer, as well as poached and puréed, alongside pecan buttermilk pudding and buttermilk ice cream.

Chef Paul Wenbourne **Seats** 30, Pr/dining room 12 **Prices** Fixed L 2 course £15-£25, Fixed D 3 course £26-£41, Tasting menu £45-£75, Starter £6-£10, Main £14-£22, Dessert £6-£9 **Parking** 20 **Notes** Sunday L £25-£35, Vegetarian available, Children welcome

LLANFACHRAETH Map 14 SH38

Black Lion Inn

Modern, Traditional British

tel: 01407 730718 **Llanfaethlu LL65 4NL**
email: mari.faulkner@blacklionanglesey.co.uk **web:** www.blacklionanglesey.com
dir: *From A55 junct 3, signed A5 Valley. Right at lights onto A5025 for 6m*

Revamped pub with a local flavour

The gloriously rural 17th-century Black Lion was derelict before new owners took over. Today's whitewashed inn features slate floors and Welsh fabrics ensuring a sense of place. There are real ales on tap, but it's very much a dining pub, with the kitchen using local supplies and home-grown salads and veg. Y Cwt Caws goats' cheese and red pepper pannacotta has just the right amount of wobble, served with a balsamic reduction and peppery leaves, and main courses include beer-battered haddock and chips, or soft and melting pork belly with black pudding fritter and maple cream sauce. Finish with Welsh cheeses or a seasonal fruit tart.

Chef Wayne Roberts **Seats** 80, Pr/dining room 30 **Times** 12-2.30/6-8.30, Closed 10 days Jan, Mon-Tue (Nov-Apr), L Wed **Prices** Starter £5.25-£10.95, Main £12.95-£22.95, Dessert £6.50-£8.95 **Wines** 3 bottles over £30, 18 bottles under £30, 7 by glass **Parking** 30 **Notes** Sunday L fr £13, Vegetarian available, Children welcome

MENAI BRIDGE Map 14 SH57

Sosban & The Old Butcher's Restaurant

Modern V

tel: 01248 208131 **Trinity House, 1 High St LL59 5EE**
email: eat@sosbanandtheoldbutchers.com
dir: *A55 E, junct 9 straight on, Britannia Bridge. Exit A55 at junct 8a, right at T-junct A5 to Menai Bridge. At rdbt 2nd exit onto B5420. Left at x-rds, A545 High St*

Progressive contemporary dining on the high street

Wall tiles are reminders that this unprepossessing double-fronted shop was once a butcher's, now a modest restaurant with plain wooden tables and chairs. It's in a village at the end of Thomas Telford's suspension bridge, which seems an unlikely place for a destination restaurant. But booking a table means a long wait, not only due to the limited number of covers and the fact that the place is open for only three evenings a week: word has spread about Stephen Stevens's innovative, often experimental cooking. He offers no choice, or even a menu, although diners are asked about preferences when they book. His cooking is characterised by bold, unconventional combinations in well-presented dishes. Wild mushroom purée is dotted with grains of cereal and golden raisins, and might be followed by celeriac risotto topped with pieces of apple and coffee. A fish course could bring on salted cod with yeasted cauliflower sprinkled with dried ox heart, followed by a main course of a piece of venison, from Snowdonia, with roasted pears, parsnips and smoked yogurt. Eating here involves well-defined, exciting flavours, even when it comes to puddings – such as a sphere of bitter chocolate filled with passionfruit, with peanut sauce poured over it, and a final palate-cleanser of lemon posset flavoured with liquorice and mint.

Chef Stephen Owen Stevens **Seats** 16 **Times** 12.30-1.30/7-11, Closed Xmas, New Year, Jan, Sun-Wed, L Thu-Fri **Prices** Fixed L 3 course £27-£30, Tasting menu £50 **Wines** 15 bottles over £30, 18 bottles under £30, 10 by glass **Parking** On street, car park **Notes** Children 12 yrs+

The Bull – Beaumaris

BEAUMARIS **Map 14 SH67**

Modern British

tel: 01248 810329 **Castle St LL58 8AP**
email: info@bullsheadinn.co.uk
web: www.bullsheadinn.co.uk
dir: *Town centre, main street*

Dynamically detailed cooking in a historic inn

Dating from the 15th century, the inn stands just a stone's throw from the walls of Beaumaris Castle and comes with a serious weight of history, having provided lodgings for parliamentary forces when Cromwell's General Mytton requisitioned the place during the Civil War, as well as less belligerent illustrious patrons, including diarist Dr Samuel Johnson and Charles Dickens. It underwent numerous transformations over the years, and now offers swanky boutique accommodation for the style-conscious 21st-century traveller, as well as bang-up-to-date dining possibilities, running from a traditional pub to an elegant bistro, as well as the flagship first-floor Loft restaurant, where sloping ceilings and a fawn colour scheme are enlivened by swirly patterns on the walls, friendly engaging service, and the confident modern Welsh stylings of Hefin Roberts. Excellent breads, including chive brioche and caraway focaccia, are memorable accompaniments, and being so close to the sea, fish and shellfish are a notable strong point, evident in a dinner that progresses from smoked sea bass with spiced raisin purée, asparagus and sweet grapes to accurately seasoned seared turbot with brown shrimps and puréed celeriac, a main dish built around the ingenious note of caramelised fermented cabbage fired up with ginger and chilli. For meaty fare, look to roast loin, smoked kidney and crispy shoulder of Anglesey lamb partnered with fondant potato, parsnip purée and wild garlic. A technically dazzling layered cheesecake comprising lime and apple sections, served with creamy basil ice cream and cider-soaked apple, is a concluding triumph, or you might opt for Welsh cheeses with bara brith and turmeric crackers.

Chef Hefin Roberts **Seats** 45 **Times** 7-9.30, Closed 25-26 Dec, 1 Jan, Sun-Tue, L all week **Prices** Prices not confirmed **Wines** 74 bottles over £30, 27 bottles under £30, 4 by glass **Parking** 10
Notes Vegetarian available, Children 7 yrs+

CARDIFF

CARDIFF Map 9 ST17

Bully's

French, European

tel: 029 2022 1905 **5 Romilly Crescent CF11 9NP**
email: info@bullysrestaurant.co.uk
dir: *5 mins from city centre*

Lively modern cooking and eclectic surrounds

Bully's is a busy-looking restaurant, virtually every inch of its walls covered with pictures, mirrors and other paraphernalia. The kitchen relies on Welsh providers for its materials and devises menus that show a clear grounding in the French repertoire while pulling in ideas from near and far. Starters could see pan-fried foie gras cut by the tang of quince and cranberry, and sauces are well considered: perhaps port and thyme to bolster a main course of chargrilled Welsh beef fillet with chervil root, purple sprouting broccoli and crispy shallots. Puddings are worth a punt too, among them guava pannacotta with pineapple and toasted coconut.

Chef Christie Matthews **Seats** 40 **Times** 12-2/6.30-9, Closed 24-26 Dec, 1 Jan, D Sun **Prices** Fixed L 2 course £12, Fixed D 3 course £20, Tasting menu £21-£35, Starter £7.50-£9.50, Main £15-£26, Dessert £6.50-£9.50 **Wines** 33 bottles over £30, 29 bottles under £30, 12 by glass **Parking** On street **Notes** Tasting 5 course, Bi-monthly gourmet 7 course, Sunday L £12.50-£19.50, Vegetarian available, Children welcome

Moksh

Indian V

tel: 029 2049 8120 **Ocean Building, Bute Crescent CF10 5AN**
email: enquiries@moksh.co.uk
dir: *M4 junct 33, A4232, exit Cardiff Bay before Butetown tunnels. 1st exit rdbt. In Mermaid Quay*

Creative techno-cooking, Indian style

Contemporary Indian fusion cooking is nothing new, but this kitchen throws elements of molecular wizardry into the mix. 'Einstein in India' starts things off by throwing the kitchen sink at a dish comprising whisky smoke-scented king prawn tikka, a sous-vide Lucknowi lamb chop with 'candy floss', Hyderabadi mince cupcake and a chicken kebab with tikka masala spheres and 'disappearing' Bombay mix. By comparison, Ratnagiri mango lamb is almost mainstream, the lamb cooked in a balanced sweet and spicy sauce of coconut milk and mango pulp. Dessert is another innovative idea – a crisp tikka masala samosa alongside white chocolate and saffron mousse cake with coconut ice cream and applewood smoke.

Chef Stephen Gomes **Seats** 53 **Times** 12-2.30/6-11, Closed 25 Dec **Prices** Tasting menu £40-£60, Starter £6-£9, Main £12-£19, Dessert £3-£6 **Wines** 6 bottles over £30, 19 bottles under £30, 5 by glass **Parking** Mermaid Quay car park **Notes** Vegetarian tasting menu £33-£53, Children welcome

Park House

British, International NOTABLE WINE LIST

tel: 029 2022 4343 **20 Park Place CF10 3DQ**
email: enquiries@parkhouserestaurant.co.uk **web:** www.parkhouserestaurant.co.uk
dir: *Opposite Cardiff Museum*

Contemporary cooking in a Gothic-revival architectural masterpiece

Housed in a Gothic architectural extravagance and overlooking the gardens of the National Museum of Wales, the restaurant is done out in hues of pink and peach. Kick off with a starter of lobster and crab ravioli with spiced chilli ketchup and lemongrass-scented tea. Next up, Cornish turbot is sent out in the bracing company of Hafod cheddar leeks, buttered spinach, morel mushroom cream and smoked bacon gnocchi, while caramelised Kelmscott pork might appear with brown shrimp, Bramley apples and summer cabbage. A chocolate platter involving a rich pavé and 'pulled' chocolate with a peppermint macaroon and spearmint sorbet rounds off a polished act.

See advert opposite

CARMARTHENSHIRE

LAUGHARNE Map 8 SN31

The Corran Resort & Spa

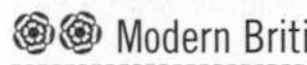 Modern British, Welsh

tel: 01994 427417 **East Marsh SA33 4RS**
email: info@thecorran.com **web:** www.thecorran.com
dir: *Phone for directions*

Welsh coastal cooking in a boutique spa hotel

Amid the coastal marshland of Carmarthenshire, The Corran is a stylish spa hotel within three miles of Laugharne Castle. Salmon cured in black treacle with pickles and salad vies for attention with generously stuffed short-rib ravioli in mushrooms and Marsala to begin. After those come Indian-styled John Dory with sag aloo in curried velouté, topped with coconut foam, fried Dover sole with fennel in Pernod butter, or else a beef study comprised of fillet, cheek and hot pot, given extra dimension with rich artichoke purée. A combination of chocolate ganache, passionfruit curd and honeycomb is full-on sweet temptation, or there may be textbook Bakewell tart with clotted cream.

Chef Chris Lovell **Seats** 185, Pr/dining room 30 **Times** 12-9, All-day dining **Prices** Fixed L 2 course £17.95-£21.95, Starter £6.50-£10, Main £14.95-£24.95 **Wines** 6 bottles over £30, 24 bottles under £30, 10 by glass **Parking** 30 **Notes** Afternoon tea, Sunday L £12.95-£19.95, Vegetarian available, Children welcome

LLANELLI Map 8 SN50

Sosban Restaurant

British, French

tel: 01554 270020 **The Pumphouse, North Dock SA15 2LF**
email: rhys@sosbanrestaurant.com
dir: *Phone for directions*

Informal brasserie cooking in a former hydraulic station

The Victorian pump-house building on Llanelli's North Docks has been reinvented as a powerhouse on the local culinary scene. The team toiling away at the stoves inside an open-to-view kitchen turns carefully-conceived, on-trend dishes – flavour-packed pork rillettes, paired with sweet pear chutney, pickles and crisp toast to start, followed by roast loin of Gower lamb with the Mediterranean glow of ratatouille, pesto and tomatoes. Otherwise, fish fans might go for turbot with the defiantly Welsh accompaniments of cockles, laverbread sauce and curly kale. To finish, a textbook chocolate fondant with raspberry ripple ice cream hits the spot, or you might have a savoury ending with the all-Welsh cheeseboard.

Chef Karl Summerfield, Chris Price **Seats** 90, Pr/dining room 20 **Times** 12-2.45/6-9.45, Closed 25 Dec, 1 Jan, Mon, D Sun **Prices** Fixed L 2 course fr £15.90, Fixed D 3 course fr £18.90, Starter £6-£9.50, Main £14-£28, Dessert £5-£9 **Wines** 49 bottles over £30, 34 bottles under £30, 14 by glass **Parking** 100 **Notes** Sunday L £12.90-£23.90, Vegetarian available, Children welcome

LLANSTEFFAN Map 8 SN31

Mansion House Llansteffan

Modern French NEW

tel: 01267 241515 **Pantyrathro SA33 5AJ**
email: info@mansionhousellansteffan.co.uk **web:** www.mansionhousellansteffan.co.uk
dir: *From Carmarthen on B4312 towards Llansteffan, follow brown signs*

Estuary views and contemporary Welsh cooking

If you like striking contemporary surroundings and estuary views, the restaurant of this bijou Victorian mansion is the place to be. The kitchen's general approach is fresh and modern. Starter might be an open-seared pigeon pie with puréed spinach and a side jug of pouring carrot jus. As you'd hope, fish is deftly handled: line-caught sea bass is paired with a prawn raviolo, fennel purée and a white wine reduction. An apple-centric dessert presents the fruit in the form of iced 'lipstick', sponge, doughnut, profiterole and sorbet. It's all delivered via daily market menus and a seasonal carte.

Chef Paul Owen **Seats** 32 **Times** 12-2.30/6-9, Closed D Sun **Prices** Fixed L 2 course £12.95-£14.95, Fixed D 3 course £14.95-£17.95, Starter £4.75-£9.25, Main £15.50-£26, Dessert £4.95-£9.95 **Wines** 5 bottles over £30, 20 bottles under £30, 5 by glass **Parking** 50 **Notes** Sunday L £10.95-£18.95, Vegetarian available, Children welcome

NANTGAREDIG Map 8 SN42

Y Polyn

Modern British

tel: 01267 290000 **SA32 7LH**
email: ypolyn@hotmail.com
dir: *Follow brown tourist signs to National Botanic Gardens, Y Polyn signed from rdbt in front of gardens*

Unpretentious cooking from an industrious country-pub kitchen

A hospitable country pub where the owners deserve plaudits for their single-minded commitment to hard graft. The menu invites a lip-smacking start with crispy ham hock bonbons in a pool of vividly flavoursome parsley sauce with a poached egg and shards of Carmarthen ham. Main course stars pan-fried brill fillet with a supporting cast of pea purée, wilted baby spinach and brown butter breadcrumbs or there could be rump and confit breast of splendid salt marsh lamb with celeriac purée and onion soubise. At the end comes a skilfully-made blackberry baked Alaska, or fine Welsh cheeses served with wheat wafers and walnut chutney.

Chef Susan Manson **Seats** 100, Pr/dining room 40 **Times** 12-2/7-9, Closed Mon, D Sun **Prices** Fixed L 2 course £13.50, Fixed D 3 course £35, Starter £6-£9, Main £13.50-£18.50, Dessert £7.50 **Wines** 25 bottles over £30, 51 bottles under £30, 9 by glass **Parking** 35 **Notes** ALC prices for L only, Sunday L £20-£25, Vegetarian available, Children welcome

CEREDIGION

EGLWYS FACH — Map 14 SN69

Gareth Ward at Ynyshir Hall

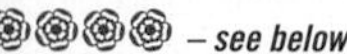 *– see below*

LAMPETER — Map 8 SN54

The Falcondale Hotel & Restaurant

 Modern British V

tel: 01570 422910 **Falcondale Dr SA48 7RX**
email: info@thefalcondale.co.uk **web:** www.thefalcondale.co.uk
dir: *1m from Lampeter take A482 to Cardigan, turn right at petrol station, follow for 0.75m*

Fine Welsh produce cooked in a lovely rural setting

An Italianate mansion built in verdant countryside, Falcondale has 14 acres all to itself. It's the kind of country-house hotel that delivers peace and quiet and that getting-away-from-it-all vibe. The dining room has a traditional finish, but a dash of contemporary style. The cooking reveals classical roots, but this is gently modernised stuff, and good use is made of the regional bounty. Home-cured salmon is served as a starter with fennel and beets, while among main courses there might be the classically combination of calves' liver with mashed potato and bacon, or a veggie saffron-flavoured risotto with leeks and caramelised onion jam.

Chef Justin Heasman **Seats** 36, Pr/dining room 20 **Times** 12-2/6.30-9 **Prices** Prices not confirmed **Wines** 67 bottles over £30, 56 bottles under £30, 18 by glass **Parking** 60 **Notes** Tasting menu 7 course (pre-booked), Sunday L, Children welcome

TREGARON — Map 9 SN65

Y Talbot

Modern British NEW V

tel: 01974 298208 **The Square SY25 6JL**
email: info@ytalbot.com **web:** www.ytalbot.com
dir: *Phone for directions*

Classics and more from Welsh sources

Drovers of old began their long treks to Midlands and London markets from Tregaron, no doubt first fortifying themselves in this part-17th-century inn. Through the pillared front doorway there's a bar one side and a restaurant the other, with chunky oak tables and bilingual, wide-choice menus. Fried scallops, fennel purée and orange and cardamom caramel is an excellent starter. Then try roast fillet of hake with confit potatoes, baby gem lettuce, smoked bacon velouté and crisp pancetta, or maybe braised Welsh lamb neck and root vegetable shepherd's pie with braised red cabbage. And finally, a lightish egg custard and griottine cherry tart with dark chocolate sorbet.

Chef Dafydd Watkin **Seats** 40, Pr/dining room 8 **Times** 12-2.30/6-9 **Prices** Starter £6-£12, Main £10-£19, Dessert £6 **Wines** 25 bottles under £30, 8 by glass **Parking** 8, On street **Notes** Sunday L £15-£30, Children welcome

Gareth Ward at Ynyshir Hall

EGLWYS FACH — Map 14 SN69

Modern British V NOTABLE WINE LIST

tel: 01654 781209 **SY20 8TA**
email: ynyshir@relaischateaux.com **web:** www.ynyshir-hall.co.uk
dir: *On A487, 6m S of Machynlleth*

Daring contemporary cooking amid birdsong and ancient trees

Plas Ynyshir was once owned by Queen Victoria, who had many trees planted on the estate, and birdsong floats around the splendid gardens within a 1,000-acre RSPB reserve. Rob and Joan Reen have established it as one of the foodie destinations of Wales, while Rob's vibrant sheep-themed paintings adorn the lavender-hued dining room walls. Head chef Gareth Ward completed a three-year stint at Sat Bains in Nottingham before heading west to continue weaving intricate interplays of flavours, texture and temperature. It's all delivered via daily-changing five-course lunch and dinner menus and minimally-worded eight and 11-course tasting options, founded on ingredients of the highest possible order: Welsh lamb and Wagyu beef, fish from Cardigan Bay and local rivers, produce from the gardens and foraged wild ingredients. Opening the show, the signature 'Not French onion soup' is made from Japanese dashi stock flavoured with onion oil, diced tofu, pickled shallots, sea vegetables, onion and miso purée and brown butter croûtons. Sea-fresh mackerel arrives in a creative medley with apple, bramble and pork back fat, duck liver comes with Cox's apple, eel and spelt, while elder and bitter chocolate could be used as accompaniments to roast grouse. Melt-in-the-mouth Welsh Wagyu beef features in complex multi-part presentations: in a 'burger' with shallots and sesame seeds, perhaps, or glazed with soy sauce and Marmite and matched with pickled shiitaki mushrooms, and in a deeply-flavoured beef 'fudge'. Then Tunworth cheese with carrot, cumin and rye provides a crossover dish before desserts such as a deconstructed tiramisù, or an exotic chocolate and banana composition counterpointed by the bracing flavours of miso, lime and coriander.

Chef Gareth Ward **Seats** 30, Pr/dining room 16 **Times** 12-2/7-9, Closed Jan **Prices** Tasting menu £55-£120 **Wines** 277 bottles over £30, 19 bottles under £30, 18 by glass **Parking** 15 **Notes** Fixed L 5/8 course £39.50/£80, Fixed D 8/11 course £80/£90, Sunday L £39.50-£120, Children welcome

CONWY

ABERGELE Map 14 SH97

Brasserie 1786

Modern British NEW

tel: 01745 832014 **The Kinmel, St George's Rd LL22 9AS**
email: reception@thekinmel.co.uk **web:** www.thekinmel.co.uk
dir: *A55 junct 24, hotel entrance on rdbt*

Seasonal approach with a modern edge

After a hard day in the Kinmel's spa, the hotel's bright, contemporary Brasserie 1786 is the place to head for some plain-speaking food. Despite the chic, minimalist looks, the place has been around for a while, in the hands of five generations of the same family since, well, the clue's in the name. The menus work with the seasons, so turn up in autumn and there may be duck breast and bonbons with plum and pickled ginger to set the ball rolling, followed by seared loin and shepherd's pie of venison with sticky red cabbage, wild mushrooms and juniper. Dessert might be elderberry soufflé.

Chef Robert Brown **Seats** 48, Pr/dining room 30 **Times** 12-2/6-9 **Prices** Fixed L 2 course £17.50, Fixed D 3 course £30-£33 **Wines** 10 bottles over £30, 29 bottles under £30, 12 by glass **Parking** 84 **Notes** Sunday L £13-£19, Vegetarian available, Children 12 yrs+ D

The Kinmel Arms

 Modern British, French

tel: 01745 832207 **The Village, St George LL22 9BP**
email: info@thekinmelarms.co.uk **web:** www.thekinmelarms.co.uk
dir: *From A55 junct 24a to St George. E on A55, junct 25. 1st left to Rhuddlan, then 1st right into St George. Take 2nd right*

Energetically creative coastal cooking

A stone-built village inn at St George on the north Wales coast, about 15 minutes' drive from Llandudno, The Kinmel has an elegant dining room arrayed in crisp linen, gleaming stemware and candlelight, where pigeon breasts and salt-baked parsnip with granola, or mackerel with beetroot variations, pickled mooli, and oyster and cucumber sauce, are among the alluring ways to begin. Roll on with breast and pressed leg of guinea fowl with choucroute in sauce allemande, or perhaps a relatively traditional serving of sea bass in vermouth with sprouting broccoli and puréed celeriac. Dessert could be as straightforward as a regally risen passionfruit soufflé.

Chef Chad Huges, Heddwen Wheeler **Seats** 70, Pr/dining room 10 **Times** 12-3/6-11.30, Closed 25 Dec, 1-2 Jan, Sun-Mon **Prices** Fixed L 2 course £15, Fixed D 3 course £19, Starter £7.50-£12, Main £15-£26, Dessert £5-£7 **Wines** 37 bottles over £30, 52 bottles under £30, 15 by glass **Parking** 60 **Notes** Vegetarian available, Children welcome

BETWS-Y-COED Map 14 SH75

Craig-y-Dderwen Riverside Hotel

 Traditional, International

tel: 01690 710293 **LL24 0AS**
email: info@snowdoniahotel.com **web:** www.snowdoniahotel.com
dir: *A5 to Betws-y-Coed, cross Waterloo Bridge, take 1st left*

Modern Welsh cooking in a beautiful riverside setting

Built in the 1890s for an industrialist, the partly timbered house became a favourite bolt-hole for Sir Edward Elgar. A hotel since the 20s, it has been carefully restored to offer the full country-house package, complete with conservatory dining-room views of a riverside teeming with wildlife (do look out for the otters). Begin with sardines with a hollandaise sauce and tomato brioche, or cockles and mussels in a creamy leek sauce, and move on to confit duck leg with dauphinoise potatoes and an orange and Cointreau sauce. To finish, pecan tart arrives in the company of rum and raisin ice cream, while the cheese selection is a slate of Welsh options.

Chef Paul Goosey **Seats** 60, Pr/dining room 40 **Times** 12-2.30/6.30-9, Closed 2 Jan-1 Feb **Prices** Prices not confirmed **Wines** 50 bottles over £30, 60 bottles under £30, 7 by glass **Parking** 50 **Notes** Sunday L, Vegetarian available, Children welcome

Llugwy River Restaurant@Royal Oak Hotel

Modern British, Welsh

tel: 01690 710219 **Holyhead Rd LL24 0AY**
email: royaloakmail@btopenworld.com **web:** www.royaloakhotel.net
dir: *On A5 in town centre, next to St Mary's church*

Former coaching inn with quality Welsh cuisine

Cappuccino-coloured walls with yellow sconces and ceiling chandeliers characterise the restaurant at this Victorian coaching inn. The kitchen supports local suppliers and the concise menu buzzes with interest. Starters include butter-poached rabbit loin with pear and hazelnut salad, while mains see pan-fried grey mullet with new potatoes, chorizo and roasted red peppers. Game shows up in season – perhaps wild mallard with root vegetable gâteau, sticky red cabbage and damson jus – and to end there may be pistachio and olive oil cake with Pants-y-Gawen organic goats' cheese and black olive ice cream and roasted figs.

Chef Dylan Edwards **Seats** 60, Pr/dining room 20 **Times** 12-3/6.30-9, Closed 25-26 Dec, Mon-Tue, L Wed-Sat, D Sun **Prices** Fixed D 3 course £25-£35 **Wines** 6 bottles over £30, 28 bottles under £30, 11 by glass **Parking** 100 **Notes** Sunday L £13.95-£15.95, Vegetarian available, Children welcome

CAPEL CURIG Map 14 SH75

Bryn Tyrch Inn

Modern Welsh

tel: 01690 720223 & 07855 762791 **LL24 0EL**
email: info@bryntyrchinn.co.uk **web:** www.bryntyrchinn.co.uk
dir: *On A5 at top end of village*

Charming old inn with mountain views

The old whitewashed roadside inn with a stunning Snowdonia backdrop offers sanctuary to walkers, climbers and families. The interior has plenty of charm and you can eat in the bar or the terrace dining room and expect simple, homely stuff based on a good amount of regional produce. There's some modernity in the kitchen's output, with tempura king prawns with a Japanese-style chilli sauce on offer, or go local with smoked salmon, trout and mackerel roulade served with pickled vegetables and melba toast. Main-course Welsh rump steak is served in th classic manner, while Anglesey sea bass comes with locally-grown cauliflower and samphire and chive potatoes. Finish with lemon posset.

Chef Paul Ryan, Daniel Demetriou **Seats** 100, Pr/dining room 20 **Times** 12-9, All-day dining, Closed 15-27 Dec **Prices** Starter £5.50-£8, Main £16-£20, Dessert £5.50-£8 **Wines** 10 bottles over £30, 20 bottles under £30, 8 by glass **Parking** 40 **Notes** Sunday L, Vegetarian available, Children welcome

COLWYN BAY Map 14 SH87

Bryn Williams at Porth Eirias

 British NEW

tel: 01492 577525 **The Promenade LL29 8HH**
email: reservations@portheirias.com
dir: *A55 junct 22, follow signs for promenade. Turn left and restaurant on right*

Lively cooking and bay views

The modern steel-and-glass building stands out on the seafront, with floor-to-ceiling windows offering sweeping views of Colwyn Bay, and exposed steelwork, pendant lights and industrial-chic looks that smack of a hip, big-city eatery. The man whose name is above the door made his bones with big-name chefs and has been chef-patron of Odette's in London's Primrose Hill since 2008, so you can expect sharp modern British bistro ideas built on prime materials. Melt-in-the-mouth lamb breast comes with aubergine, cumin and yogurt, while main-course roast cod is partnered by chorizo, confit carrot and lentils. Finish with buttermilk pannacotta served with poached plums.

Chef Bryn & Richard Williams **Seats** 66 **Times** 12-8.45, All-day dining, Closed 25 Dec **Prices** Starter £4.95-£13, Main £8-£19, Dessert £4.95-£7.95 **Wines** 17 bottles over £30, 26 bottles under £30, 8 by glass **Parking** 25 **Notes** Vegetarian available, Children welcome

CONWY Map 14 SH77

Castle Hotel Conwy

Modern British

tel: 01492 582800 **High St LL32 8DB**
email: mail@castlewales.co.uk **web:** www.castlewales.co.uk
dir: *A55 junct 18, follow town centre signs, cross estuary (castle on left). Right then left at mini rdbts onto one-way system. Right at Town Wall Gate, right onto Berry St then High St*

Modern British dining in a local landmark

Conwy is a UNESCO World Heritage Site and, when it comes to matters of history, the town's Castle Hotel can hold its own. Dawsons Restaurant & Bar, with its courtyard garden and stylish decor, offers modern British menus that deliver brasserie-style dishes and classic comfort options. Start with a sharing plate of charcuterie or smooth chicken liver parfait with rich prune chutney, and move on to twice-cooked sticky pork belly (with caramelised apples and red onions), or Conwy mussels in cider and spring onion sauce. There are posh fish and chips, burgers and steaks, too, and desserts such as apple and brandy tarte Tatin. A slate of Welsh cheeses includes Perl Las and Caws Llyn, served with savoury palmiers and red grape and sultana chutney.

Chef Andrew Nelson **Seats** 70 **Times** 12-9.30, All-day dining, Closed D 25 Dec **Prices** Starter £4.85-£9.95, Main £12.95-£22.95 **Wines** 19 bottles over £30, 25 bottles under £30, 16 by glass **Parking** 36 **Notes** Small plates menu spring & summer, Sunday L, Vegetarian available, Children welcome

DEGANWY Map 14 SH77

Quay Hotel & Spa

Modern European

tel: 01492 564100 & 564165 **Deganwy Quay LL31 9DJ**
email: reservations@quayhotel.com **web:** www.quayhotel.com
dir: *M56, A494, A55 junct 18, straight across 2 rdbts. At lights bear left into The Quay. Hotel/Restaurant on right*

Modern cooking and views of Snowdonia

Beautifully located on the Conwy estuary, with views across the marina to the castle, this is a stylish, modern boutique hotel. The smart Grill Room offers a relatively informal setting for straightforward European cooking. Locally-landed fish and seafood feature, maybe in a first course of Great Orme crab with pink grapefruit, avocado purée and caraway crispbread. Main-course seared breast of guinea fowl comes rolled and tied with bacon, accompanied by smooth parsnip purée, honey roast parsnip, boulangere potatoes and red cabbage. Warm Bakewell tart, with vanilla sauce and black cherry and amaretto ice cream, is a good place to finish.

LLANDUDNO Map 14 SH78

Bodysgallen Hall and Spa

Modern British V NOTABLE WINE LIST

tel: 01492 584466 **LL30 1RS**
email: info@bodysgallen.com **web:** www.bodysgallen.com
dir: *A55 junct 19, A470 towards Llandudno. Hotel 2m on right*

Grand National Trust property with suitably elegant cooking

John Williams spent four years in the kitchens at Bodysgallen before running his own restaurants but April 2015 marked his return to the hotel after eight years away. This National Trust-owned 17th-century stately home is shielded from the real world by 200 acres of parkland and immaculate rose gardens, and the memorable view sweeps across the skyline to Snowdonia, Conwy Castle and the Isle of Anglesey. Despite rooms and corridors lined with antiques, oil paintings, dark oak panelling and stone-mullioned windows, this is no stuffy country house, thanks to the efforts of obliging and courteous staff. Located in the Main Hall, the dining room is an elegant and rarified space, with period character and the unbuttoned approach means that, while smart dress is favoured, jacket and tie is not obligatory. The cooking matches the grand setting with its aspiration and finesse, and there is a modernity to starters such as a soy and maple glazed belly pork, paired with caramelised chestnuts, smoked apple and black pudding. The main event might be roasted breast of Gressingham duck, confit cabbage, smoked carrot purée and spiced plum dressing. Bold desserts such as poached rhubarb, custard pannacotta and thyme biscuit end the show. The noble wine list does justice to the tremendous cooking.

Chef John Williams **Seats** 60, Pr/dining room 40
Times 12.30-1.45/7-9.30, Closed 24-26 Dec, L Mon **Prices** Fixed L 2 course £21-£43, Fixed D 3 course £55 **Wines** 6 bottles under £30, 8 by glass **Parking** 40 **Notes** Pre-theatre D, Tasting menu on request, Sunday L £28, Children 6 yrs+

LLANDUDNO *continued*

Dunoon Hotel

Traditional British

tel: 01492 860787 **Gloddaeth St LL30 2DW**
email: reservations@dunoonhotel.co.uk **web:** www.dunoonhotel.co.uk
dir: *Exit promenade at War Memorial by pier onto Gloddaeth St. Hotel 200 yds on right*

Local ingredients and unpretentious British cooking

The restaurant here is full of old-world charm, with oak-panelled walls, brass fittings and chandeliers, flowers and linen napery on the tables and a cooking style that's more likely to reassure than to startle with modernism, with the kitchen quite rightly keeping its customer base happy. Dishes are technically accurate and nicely presented without being showy, starting with crisp pork belly with white bean purée, chorizo, apple jelly and a crispy quail's egg. Main course brings salmon fillet with a crab and spring onion patty, sweet potato dauphinoise, buttered samphire, roast beetroot and white wine cream. For pudding, look no further than strawberry pannacotta with shortbread.

Chef Rob Kennish **Seats** 80 **Times** 12-2/6.30-8.30, Closed mid Dec-1 Mar **Wines** 23 bottles over £30, 97 bottles under £30, 8 by glass **Parking** 20 **Notes** ALC menu 5 course £29.50, Pre-theatre D menu, Sunday L £15.95-£18.95, Vegetarian available, Children welcome

Imperial Hotel

Modern, Traditional British

tel: 01492 877466 **The Promenade, Vaughan St LL30 1AP**
email: reception@theimperial.co.uk **web:** www.theimperial.co.uk
dir: *A470 to Llandudno*

Grand hotel cooking with views of the sea

The wedding-cake stucco façade of the Imperial is a landmark on Llandudno's seafront. On a balmy day, alfresco dining on the terrace with a splendid backdrop of the bay is on the cards. The kitchen turns out menus of classically-inflected modern cooking featuring a sound showing of fine Welsh produce: slow-braised ham hock with pear and cider jelly, salt-and-pepper crackling and home-made herb brioche might open the show, while labour-intensive mains run to loin of Welsh lamb wrapped in leek mousse and prosciutto with crispy lamb breast, pea purée, pommes Anna and rosemary jus. Desserts bring on classic crème brûlée with roasted pineapple.

Chef Arwel Jones, Joanne Tucker, Leighton Thoman **Seats** 150, Pr/dining room 30 **Times** 12.30-3/6-9.30 **Prices** Starter £6.50-£8.50, Main £19.50-£25.75, Dessert £6.50-£8.50 **Wines** 37 bottles over £30, 87 bottles under £30, 15 by glass **Parking** 20, Promenade pay & display **Notes** Sunday L £18-£23, Vegetarian available, Children welcome

The Lilly Restaurant with Rooms

Modern Welsh

tel: 01492 876513 **West Pde, West Shore LL30 2BD**
email: thelilly@live.co.uk **web:** www.thelilly.co.uk
dir: *Just off A546 at Llandudno, follow signs for the Pier, beach front on right*

Modern Welsh cooking overlooking the sea

Located in the sedate West Shore part of the town, and with unrestricted views over the coastline and restless sea, The Lilly can offer snacks and grills in its Madhatters Brasserie, or the Full Monty in the flamboyantly decorated restaurant. With only 10 tables, the restaurant is the setting for menus that combine creativity with comforting familiarity. Kick off with scallops with a crab Scotch egg and sweetcorn purée, and move on to a duo of Welsh lamb (rump and braised shoulder), or go for posh fish and chips with tartare dressing. There's fillet steak, too with traditional accompaniments, and, for dessert, a classic lemon tart delivers a satisfying sharpness.

St George's Hotel

Modern, Traditional, Welsh

tel: 01492 877544 & 862184 **The Promenade LL30 2LG**
email: info@stgeorgeswales.co.uk **web:** www.stgeorgeswales.co.uk
dir: *A55, exit at Glan Conwy for Llandudno. A470 follow signs for seafront (distinctive tower identifies hotel)*

Patriotic Welsh cooking in a grand seafront hotel

Llandudno's prom is the place to be for splendid sunsets and sweeping views across the bay, and St George's Hotel sits centre stage. The place is a timeless slice of Victorian wedding-cake grandeur, with an irresistible terrace and floor-to-ceiling windows in the restaurant to enjoy the view all year. The kitchen turns out modern starters such as pan-roasted scallops with scallop 'dust', crispy ham and sweet potato purée, or belly of pork with an oriental glaze. Next up, loin of cod is matched with Welsh rarebit, and, to finish, a firm pannacotta comes with rum-infused compressed pineapple.

Chef Gwyn Roberts **Seats** 110, Pr/dining room 12 **Times** 12-2.30/6.30-9.30 **Prices** Fixed L 2 course £15-£25, Fixed D 3 course £22-£40, Starter £6-£10, Main £12-£20, Dessert £7-£10 **Wines** 10 bottles over £30, 10 bottles under £30, 10 by glass **Parking** 36 **Notes** Pre-theatre menu, Sunday L £18-£30, Vegetarian available Children welcome

LLANDUDNO JUNCTION Map 14 SH77

Queens Head

Traditional British, Seafood NEW

tel: 01492 546570 **Glanwydden LL31 9JP**
email: enquiries@queensheadglanwydden.co.uk **web:** www.queensheadglanwydden.co.uk
dir: *From A55 Expressway, take Llandudno exit onto A470. At 3rd rdbt, right towards Penrhyn Bay. After 1.5m (approx), 2nd right into Glanwydden*

Generous cooking in a homely pub

When you want a pub that's as traditional as they come – rustic beams, stone fireplace, cosy vibes and a sincere welcome – look no further than the Queens Head. And the food fits the bill, aiming straight for the comfort zone with a starter of chicken liver parfait with sticky onions and toasted brioche. Mains stick to please-all territory, pairing king scallops with crispy belly pork, crunchy crackling, pea purée and roasted tomatoes, or you might up the hearty factor with braised shoulder of Welsh lamb with root vegetables, creamed leeks, root vegetables and redcurrant and rosemary gravy. Finish in comfort with brioche bread-and-butter pudding.

Chef Barry Edwards **Seats** Pr/dining room 36 **Times** 12-9, All-day dining, Closed 25 Dec **Prices** Prices not confirmed **Wines** 10 bottles over £30, 54 bottles under £30, 1 by glass **Notes** Sunday L, Vegetarian available, Children welcome

DENBIGHSHIRE

RUTHIN Map 14 SJ15

ʀuthin Castle Hotel

Modern British

el: 01824 702664 **Castle St LL15 2NU**
mail: reservations@ruthincastle.co.uk **web:** www.ruthincastle.co.uk
ir: *From town square take road towards Corwen for 100yds*

'an-European influenced cooking beneath chandeliers

ı its 750-year existence, Ruthin Castle has been many things including a clinic for reating obscure internal diseases. In the early 60s it was incorporated into today's ichly furnished hotel. Enjoy a pre-dinner drink in the octagonal, panelled Library ɜar (which offers its own menu, by the way), then aim for Bertie's restaurant, amed after Edward VII, a frequent visitor. Don't expect a huge choice, for the menu sts only four dishes for each course. Nonetheless this still permits plenty of ermutations, one being braised rabbit boudin, followed by grilled fillet of cod with moked bacon and potato chowder, and a rhubarb and custard dessert. Themed nedieval dinners are popular.

hef Michael Cheetham **Seats** 70, Pr/dining room **Times** 12-3/6-9 **Prices** Fixed L 2 ourse fr £19.95, Fixed D 3 course fr £29.95, Starter fr £5.95 **Wines** 57 bottles over 30, 27 bottles under £30, 15 by glass **Notes** Afternoon tea £17.50, Sunday L 19.95-£29.95, Vegetarian available, Children before 7pm

GWYNEDD

ABERDYFI Map 14 SN69

'enhelig Arms

British NEW

ɘl: 01654 767215 **Terrace Rd LL35 0LT**
eb: www.penheligarms.com
ir: *Phone for directions*

elaxed dining on Snowdonia's southern edge

riginally a collection of fishermen's cottages on the Dyfi estuary, the Penhelig Arms verlooks what centuries ago was a shipbuilding harbour. Its two blue-themed ining areas – the Fisherman's Bar and the restaurant – share a menu, backed up / specials. The maritime location might suggest launching with flash-fried alamari, lemon mayo and dressed leaves, followed perhaps by pork two ways – st-pink loin cutlet and slow-roasted belly – with green beans, Pembrokeshire new otatoes, roasted apple and sage. The Bakewell tart owes little to school dinners of esteryear: surely it was never served, as here, with toasted almonds, raspberry oulis and vanilla pod ice cream?

mes 12-2.30/6.30-10 **Prices** Starter £4.95-£6.95, Main £8.50-£24.95, Dessert 4.95-£5.95 **Wines** 3 bottles over £30, 26 bottles under £30, 23 by glass **otes** Afternoon tea fr £7.95, Sunday L, Vegetarian available, Children welcome

ABERSOCH Map 14 SH32

The Dining Room

British Bistro NEW

tel: 01758 740709 & 07772 301973 **4 High St LL53 7DY**
email: eat@thediningroomabersoch.co.uk
dir: *A499 to Abersoch, onto one-way system. On left opposite St Tudwall Inn*

Pint-sized local bistro with appealing food

In pole position among the buzzy bars and hip surfie shops of trendy Abersoch's main drag, this low-key bistro with a tea-shop frontage and mismatched chairs and tables is building a loyal fan base for its warm hospitality and confidently executed food with its roots in the Welsh countryside. Crisp lamb's tongue is neatly balanced with pickled shallots and a tart gribiche sauce spiked with mint, while perfectly-timed sea bass from Cardigan Bay stars in a main course with crisp ham, confit tomato and a vibrant dressing of brown shrimps and laverbread. To finish, honeycomb ice cream is a heavenly match with rosemary burnt cream.

Chef Si Toft **Seats** 24 **Times** 7-mdnt, Closed days vary due to seasonal location, L all week **Prices** Prices not confirmed **Wines** 4 bottles over £30, 20 bottles under £30, 5 by glass **Parking** On street, public car park 200yds away **Notes** Vegetarian available, Children 12 yrs+

Porth Tocyn Hotel

Modern British NOTABLE WINE LIST

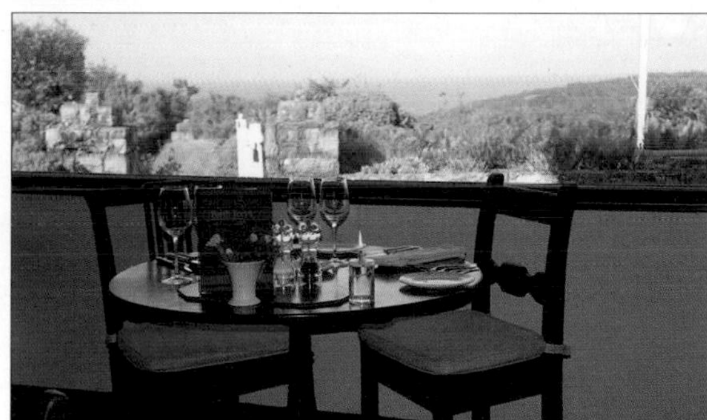

tel: 01758 713303 **Bwlchtocyn LL53 7BU**
email: bookings@porthtocynhotel.co.uk **web:** www.porthtocynhotel.co.uk
dir: *2m S of Abersoch, through Sarn Bach & Bwlchtocyn. Follow brown signs*

Well-established country house with first-class cooking

The Fletcher-Brewer family converted a terrace of lead miners' cottages into the comfortable, relaxed and unstuffy place we see today. Inside are antique-filled lounges and a smart restaurant, where picture windows give spectacular views over Cardigan Bay to Snowdonia. Louise Fletcher-Brewer oversees the kitchen with assurance, her repertoire combining traditional values and more modern sensibilities. Start with chicken and foie gras galantine with Waldorf salad dressed with blue cheese, and go on to grilled sea bass fillet with a warm salad of rocket, artichokes, tomatoes and red onion, pearl potatoes and a herb dressing. End with comforting cheesecake with cherry compôte and vanilla ice cream.

Chef L Fletcher-Brewer, Ian Frost **Seats** 50 **Times** 12.15-2.30/7.15-9, Closed mid Nov, 2 wks before Etr, occasional low season **Prices** Fixed D 3 course £47 **Wines** 26 bottles over £30, 71 bottles under £30, 6 by glass **Parking** 50 **Notes** Light lunches Mon-Sat, Sunday L £25.50, Vegetarian available, Children 6 yrs+ D

CAERNARFON — Map 14 SH46

Seiont Manor Hotel

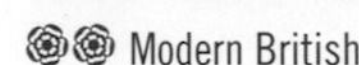
Modern British V

tel: 01286 673366 & 0845 072 7550 *(Calls cost 7p per minute plus your phone company's access charge)* **Llanrug LL55 2AQ**
email: seiontmanor@handpicked.co.uk **web:** www.handpickedhotels.co.uk/seiontmanor
dir: *From Bangor follow signs for Caernarfon. Leave Caernarfon on A4086. Hotel 3m on left*

Compelling cooking in farmhouse hotel

Positioned between Snowdonia National Park and the Menai Strait, Seiont Manor has upscaled rather dramatically since its days as a working farmstead. A first course delivers the taste of the sea in the shape of lobster bisque with seared scallop, buttered langoustine and a salmon samosa, while main-course venison comes in the inventive company of smoked potato and chocolate sauce. There are good cooking skills on show and a creative take on regional ingredients; local sewin trout, for example, prepared confit-style with vanilla, and served with fennel purée and garlic 'whizz'. A dessert of pistachio and orange cake ends things on a high.

Seats 55, Pr/dining room 30 **Times** 12-2/7-9.30 **Prices** Fixed D 3 course £37 **Wines** 104 bottles over £30, 6 bottles under £30, 18 by glass **Parking** 60 **Notes** ALC 3 course £49, Sunday L £21.95, Children welcome

CRICCIETH — Map 14 SH53

Bron Eifion Country House Hotel

Modern British, Welsh

tel: 01766 522385 **LL52 0SA**
email: enquiries@broneifion.co.uk **web:** www.broneifion.co.uk
dir: *A497, between Porthmadog & Pwllheli*

Modern Welsh cooking in a Victorian summer residence

Built in 1883, the creeper-clad house has the dual charm of ravishing gardens and stone's-throw proximity to Criccieth's beach. A majestic staircase, oak panelling and comfortable country-house furniture give the right impression, though the Garden Room restaurant offers a more contemporary experience, with bare tables and Modern Welsh cooking. An inventive roll call of dishes runs from pan-fried scallops with spiced pork belly, and fennel and cider apple salad, to mains such as Welsh lamb rib with aubergine, wild garlic, anchovy dressing and Jersey Royal salad. End on a high with peanut butter parfait, served with ginger crumb, banana tart and chocolate.

Chef David Spencer **Seats** 150, Pr/dining room 24 **Times** 12-2/6.30-9 **Prices** Fixed L 2 course fr £16.95, Fixed D 3 course fr £30, Starter £5.95-£8.95, Main £13.95-£24.95, Dessert £6.95-£8.95 **Wines** 20 bottles over £30, 28 bottles under £30, 6 by glass **Parking** 50 **Notes** Gourmand menu 8 course £65, Sunday L £16.95-£19.95, Vegetarian available, Children welcome

DOLGELLAU — Map 14 SH71

Bwyty Mawddach Restaurant

Modern British

tel: 01341 421752 **Pen Y Garnedd, Llanelltyd LL40 2TA**
email: enquiries@mawddach.com
dir: *A470 Llanelltyd to A496 Barmouth, restaurant 0.2m on left after primary school*

Confident modern British cooking in barn conversion

As barn conversions go, this one is rather impressive. Ifan Dunn turned the old granite building on the family farm into a snazzy modern restaurant with views over the Mawddach Estuary and the slopes of Cader Idris through a glass wall. The cool, contemporary interior, spread over two levels, has a vaulted ceiling upstairs and slate floors below. The cooking demonstrates bright ideas, taking in celeriac soup with Granny Smith apple and Perl Las organic blue cheese, then roast hake fillet with corn chips, cauliflower sauce, curry oil, curly kale and gremolata. For dessert, perhaps warm ginger cake with salted caramel ice cream.

Chef Ifan Dunn **Seats** 35 **Times** 12-2.30/6.30-9, Closed 26 Dec, 1 wk Jan, 1 wk Apr, 2 wks Nov, Mon-Wed **Prices** Starter £6.50-£9, Main £14.50-£22.50, Dessert £7-£8 **Wines** 8 bottles over £30, 19 bottles under £30, 7 by glass **Parking** 20 **Notes** Sunday L £20.95-£23.95, Vegetarian available, Children welcome

Penmaenuchaf Hall Hotel

Modern British NOTABLE WINE LIST

tel: 01341 422129 **Penmaenpool LL40 1YB**
email: relax@penhall.co.uk **web:** www.penhall.co.uk
dir: *From A470 take A493 (Tywyn/Fairbourne), entrance 1.5m on left by sign for Penmaenpool*

Modern British cooking in a Snowdonia garden room

The greystone Victorian hall, in 21 acres, gives spectacular views to Cader Idris and the Mawddach Estuary. Within, oak floors, panels, artwork and fresh flowers give a real sense of age and quality. The menu pays homage to indigenous produce, and there's no lack of contemporary creative flair. Crab salad comes spiked with chilli and ginger complemented by grapefruit jelly and herbs. Then there might be pink-roast rump of lamb with fondant potato, summer vegetables and red wine jus. A fish option may be seared sea bass fillet with saffron potatoes and a red pepper and fennel bouillon, while, to finish, try pineapple mousse with roasted pineapple and coconut cream.

Chef J Pilkington, T Reeve **Seats** 36, Pr/dining room 20 **Times** 12-2/7-9.30 **Prices** Fixed L 2 course fr £20.50, Fixed D 3 course fr £27.50, Starter £9-£11, Main £27-£33, Dessert £9-£13.25 **Wines** 52 bottles over £30, 67 bottles under £30, 6 by glass **Parking** 36 **Notes** Sunday L fr £22.50, Vegetarian available, Children 6 yrs+

PORTHMADOG Map 14 SH53

Royal Sportsman Hotel

Modern British, Welsh

.el: 01766 512015 **131 High St LL49 9HB**
:mail: enquiries@royalsportsman.co.uk **web:** www.royalsportsman.co.uk
lir: *At rdbt junct of A497 & A487*

Contemporary cooking in a buzzy old coaching inn

The four-square hotel has been holding court on this spot since 1862, when it made ts debut as a coaching inn. Today it's very much a 21st-century version of the same, with smart bedrooms, buzzy bar and a restaurant that delivers some rather good stuff. In the traditionally decorated dining room, regional ingredients form the basis of the contemporary cuisine (there's a 'classics' menu too). Monkfish sashimi brings an Asian spin to proceedings, while main courses such as slow-cooked pork belly or roast rack of Welsh lamb have a more regional flavour. Strawberry Arctic roll s a modern interpretation of an old favourite.

Chef Russell Croston **Seats** 60 **Times** 12-2.30/6-9 **Wines** 4 bottles over £30, 20 bottles under £30, 11 by glass **Parking** 17, On street **Notes** Sunday L £10.95-£19.95, Vegetarian available, Children welcome

PORTMEIRION Map 14 SH53

The Hotel Portmeirion

Modern Welsh

el: 01766 770000 & 772324 **Minffordd LL48 6ET**
mail: hotel@portmeirion-village.com **web:** www.portmeirion-village.com
ir: *Off A487 at Minffordd*

Lively modern Welsh cooking in a fantasy Italianate village

he fantasy Italianate village on the north Wales coast, created by Sir Clough Williams-Ellis, was conceived around the ruin of what is now the hotel. When the whole place began to materialise in 1926, the hotel became its focal point, its gracefully curving dining room being added in 1931. Fresh, lively, modern Welsh cooking enhances the whole experience no end, in the form of starters such as tomato tarte fine with goats'-milk ricotta and iced avocado, while the main course delivers a turbot and chicken wing duo with pea purée in smoked chicken jus. Finish with a regal blueberry soufflé alongside chocolate and lavender ice cream.

Chef Mark Threadgill **Seats** 100, Pr/dining room 36
Times 12-2.30/6.30-9.30, Closed 2 wks Nov **Prices** Fixed D 3 course £30-£40, Tasting menu £45-£55 **Wines** 45 bottles over £30, 38 bottles under £30, 17 by glass **Parking** 130 **Notes** Sunday L £23.95, Vegetarian available, Children welcome

PWLLHELI Map 14 SH33

Plas Bodegroes

Modern British

tel: 01758 612363 **Nefyn Rd LL53 5TH**
email: gunna@bodegroes.co.uk
dir: *On A497, 1m W of Pwllheli*

Seasonal cooking in a scene of pastoral contentment

The Chowns' restaurant with rooms has been a fixture of the northwest Wales dining scene since the 1980s. The dining room is a fresh, airy space with mint-green walls hung with artworks, a barewood floor and elegant high-backed chairs. A fine smoked haddock tart with lemon-dressed fennel and watercress salad is an appealing opener, its pastry excellent, the filling beautifully balanced. Main courses might deliver sea bass in the Asian style, with crab, ginger and pak choi in lemongrass sauce. A satisfying chocolate trio to finish comprises dark mousse, a chocolate-pastried tart and a quenelle of white chocolate ice cream.

MONMOUTHSHIRE

ABERGAVENNY Map 9 SO21

Angel Hotel

Modern, Traditional British, International

tel: 01873 857121 **15 Cross St NP7 5EN**
email: mail@angelabergavenny.com **web:** www.angelabergavenny.com
dir: *From A40 & A465 junct follow town centre signs, S of Abergavenny, past stations*

Old inn with a brasserie-style menu

This hotel in the heart of the town was a posting inn in the first half of the 19th century, and its Georgian façade and spacious interiors are in fine fettle today. The same brasserie-style menu is up for grabs in the Foxhunter Bar or Oak Room restaurant, with lunchtime sandwiches and steaks cooked on the grill. Why not try a fresh crab and mango salad or Tuscan bean and pasta soup to start, followed by rack of lamb – pink and tender – served with a little pan of shepherd's pie, or tiger prawns piri-piri style. Finish with a simple chocolate pot with pistachios and vanilla ice cream.

Chef Wesley Hammond **Seats** 80, Pr/dining room 120
Times 12-2.30/6-9.30, Closed 25 Dec, D 24-26 Dec **Prices** Fixed L 3 course fr £25, Fixed D 3 course fr £25, Starter £5.50-£12, Main £14-£28, Dessert £5-£8 **Wines** 47 bottles over £30, 47 bottles under £30, 10 by glass **Parking** 30 **Notes** Breakfast, Afternoon tea £21.80, Sunday L £17-£25, Vegetarian available, Children welcome

ABERGAVENNY *continued*

The Hardwick

Modern British NOTABLE WINE LIST

tel: 01873 854220 **Old Raglan Rd NP7 9AA**
email: info@thehardwick.co.uk
dir: *Phone for directions*

Compellingly simple cooking in revamped country pub

Hard at work in a revamped old inn just outside Abergavenny is Stephen Terry, a chef with a wealth of experience at the sharp end of the restaurant biz. The food is unpretentious, mood-enhancing stuff such as a starter of meatloaf (made from Welsh pedigree pork) with melted Swiss cheese, onion marmalade and pickles, or a salad of hot chorizo and Castelfranco radicchio. Dry-aged rib-eye is a superb piece of meat cooked just right (served with triple-cooked chips and melting Hardwick butter), while another main course matches shoulder of Brecon lamb with deep-fried polenta and salsa verde. Set lunches and Sunday lunch are a cut above the norm.

Chef Stephen Terry **Seats** 100, Pr/dining room 50 **Times** 12-3/6.30-10, Closed 25 Dec **Prices** Prices not confirmed **Wines** 42 bottles over £30, 30 bottles under £30, 11 by glass **Parking** 50 **Notes** Sunday L, Vegetarian available, Children welcome

Llansantffraed Court Hotel

Modern British, Welsh NOTABLE WINE LIST

tel: 01873 840678 **Old Raglan Rd, Llanvihangel Gobion, Clytha NP7 9BA**
email: reception@llch.co.uk **web:** www.llch.co.uk
dir: *M4 junct 24/A449 to Raglan. At rdbt take last exit to Clytha. Hotel on right in 4.5m*

Ambitious Welsh modernism in a William and Mary mansion

A handsome brick-built William and Mary house in rural Monmouthshire, LLCH (as the web address has it) stands in 20 acres of trimly kept lawns with mature trees and a walled kitchen garden, within sight of the Tudor church of St Bridget's. A page of proudly attributed local suppliers inspires confidence. The results can be seen in seared langoustines with a 'risotto' of diced potato and smoked bacon, followed by roast breast and confit leg of Gressingham duck supported by roasted baby beetroot and beetroot purée, parsnips (roasted and crisps), and wild mushrooms. To finish, there's tangerine soufflé and jelly with confit peel, almonds and candied citrus ice cream.

Chef Tim McDougall **Seats** 50, Pr/dining room 35 **Times** 12-2/7-9 **Prices** Fixed L 2 course £15, Fixed D 3 course £32.50, Tasting menu £55-£75, Starter £8-£14, Main £16-£29, Dessert £8-£12 **Wines** 78 bottles over £30, 52 bottles under £30, 130 by glass **Parking** 300 **Notes** Tasting menu 7 course with matched wines £95, Sunday L £30, Vegetarian available, Children welcome

Restaurant 1861

Modern British, European V

tel: 01873 821297 **Cross Ash NP7 8PB**
web: www.18-61.co.uk
dir: *On B4521, 9m from Abergavenny, 15m from Ross-on-Wye, on outskirts of Cross Ash*

Modern European cooking in a converted Victorian pub

After beginning his career with the Roux brothers, Simon King has gone native in Wales, and 1861 celebrates what the region has to offer, including fine vegetables grown by Kate King's dad. The culinary style applies classic techniques in unmistakably appealing modern combinations. A first course of game terrine and melba toast or duo of seared scallops and pumpkin purée with chicken juices might be followed by seared skirt of beef with wild mushroom coulis, or fillet of brill, poached in red wine. It's worth the wait for the hot desserts, perhaps apple tarte Tatin with stem ginger ice cream.

Chef Simon King **Seats** 40 **Times** 12-2/7-9, Closed 1st 2 wks Jan, Mon, D Sun **Prices** Fixed L 2 course fr £22, Fixed D 3 course fr £35, Tasting menu fr £60, Starter £8-£14.50, Main £21-£25, Dessert £7.25-£8.50 **Wines** 39 bottles over £30, 39 bottles under £30, 7 by glass **Parking** 20 **Notes** Tasting menu 7 course, Sunday L £22-£25, Children welcome

The Walnut Tree Inn

– see opposite and advert on page 570

The Walnut Tree Inn

ABERGAVENNY **Map 9 SO21**

Modern British NOTABLE WINE LIST

tel: 01873 852797 **Llanddewi Skirrid NP7 8AW**
email: mail@thewalnuttreeinn.com
web: www.thewalnuttreeinn.com
dir: *3m NE of Abergavenny on B4521*

Blissfully unfussy and focused cooking by a true culinary mastermind

The whitewashed, slate-roofed old inn is an unassuming-looking property, and there's nothing flashy about the interior either, with its wooden tables, plain walls hung with artwork and flower arrangements adding flashes of colour. But the Walnut Tree has been a foodie beacon for a couple of generations, first under Franco Taruschio and now under Shaun Hill. He cut his teeth at Robert Carrier's Islington restaurant (and pays tribute to the late, great chef with his starter of Robert Carrier's pâté aux herbes with piccalilli) and put Ludlow on the gastronomic map when he ran Merchant House there. Shaun still 'shakes the pans', as he describes his work, something we can all be grateful for. He follows no particular culinary path, preferring to treat his top-class produce on an ad hoc basis to produce compelling, appetising dishes. Starters on the daily-changing menus can be a mixed bunch. Fillet of red mullet, for instance, comes in a dashi broth with spring onions and ginger, and veal sweetbreads with sauerkraut and mustard dressing, with a vegetarian option like asparagus with scrambled duck eggs and morels. There's plenty of skill and imagination in evidence, as well as technical prowess, with little flummery or extraneous garnishes disguising the quality of ingredients, so flavours are clearly defined. Main courses include the full-blooded meaty tastes of cassoulet of goose, lamb, pork and sausage, as well as a mutton and potato pie to accompany rack of lamb. Fish makes an impact too: perhaps halibut fillet in a hazelnut crust with clams and the contrast of bacon, or Dover sole with shrimps, parsley and capers. Puddings close proceedings memorably, from mango parfait with lime and ginger sorbet, to pistachio and cherry cheesecake with cherry sorbet.

Chef Shaun Hill **Seats** 70, Pr/dining room 26
Times 12-2.30/7-10, Closed 1 wk Xmas, Sun-Mon **Prices** Prices not confirmed **Wines** 50 bottles over £30, 40 bottles under £30, 8 by glass **Parking** 30 **Notes** Vegetarian available, Children welcome

THE WALNUT TREE

A famous inn and restaurant since the early 60's, The Walnut Tree sits two miles east of Abergavenny. It offers proper dining and drinking in an informal setting. There are around 20 tables simply laid. The restaurant seats up to 70 diners and we open from Tuesday to Saturday, lunchtime and evening.

The food is an eclectic mix, based on Shaun Hill's personal taste, paired with sound cooking techniques; rather than a particular country's cuisine. A unifying feature is the core of excellent ingredients.

Together The Art Shop and The Walnut Tree promote works by contemporary artists, established and emerging. Work is always available through The Art Shop and Gallery. The Walnut Tree's interior and exterior paints are from Farrow and Ball, also available from The Art Shop.

LLANDDEWI SKIRRID, ABERGAVENNY, MONMOUTHSHIRE, WALES NP7 8AW UK

MONMOUTH Map 10 SO51

#7 Church Street

Modern British NEW

tel: 01600 712600 **7 Church St NP25 3BX**
email: enquiries@pregomonmouth.co.uk **web:** www.pregomonmouth.co.uk
dir: *Travelling N A40 at lights left turn, T-junct left turn, 2nd right, hotel at rear of car park*

Friendly town-centre bistro

The owners of #7 have rebranded the former Bistro Prego, which is squeezed into a traffic-free, town-centre street of interesting shops and galleries. The restaurant is fairly narrow, with white walls, some exposed brickwork and a wooden floor. Modern British menus offer plenty of scope, represented well by seared scallops, caramelised onion purée and rocket; lamb three ways – seared loin, pan-fried liver, breast fritter – with celeriac purée and roast onions; and baked lemon cheesecake with pistachios. Worthy alternatives are baked monkfish in Italian speck, mashed potatoes, grilled asparagus, roast artichoke and black olive tapenade, or pappardelle pasta, grilled asparagus, roast red onion, olive oil and parmesan.

Chef Mark Turton, Adam Penfold **Seats** 66 **Times** 12-2.15/6.30-9.30, Closed 25-26 Dec **Prices** Starter £5-£8, Main £14-£22, Dessert £5.50 **Wines** 15 bottles over £30, 30 bottles under £30, 15 by glass **Parking** Pay & display at rear of restaurant **Notes** Light L £5-12.50, Pre-theatre from 6pm bookings only, Sunday L £14-£22, Vegetarian available, Children welcome

ROCKFIELD Map 9 SO41

The Stonemill & Steppes Farm Cottages

Modern British

tel: 01600 716273 **NP25 5SW**
email: bookings@thestonemill.co.uk **web:** www.thestonemill.co.uk
dir: *A48 to Monmouth, B4233 to Rockfield. 2.6m from Monmouth town centre*

Clearly focused modern cooking in a 16th-century cider mill

A beautifully converted barn in a 16th-century mill complex with self-catering cottages provides an impressive setting for accomplished cooking. Inside it's a riot of oak beams and vaulted ceilings, with chunky rustic tables around an ancient stone cider press. The kitchen uses fresh regional produce to deliver accurately cooked and simply presented modern dishes. A starter of seared scallops comes with soy, ginger and leek broth and black onion seeds, followed by slow-cooked pork belly and white hogs pudding with potato gratin, pickled walnuts, and apple and beetroot tea. A combo of nougat cheesecake, honey and almond brittle and amaretti ice cream brings things to a close.

Chef Mark Lane, Jordan Simons **Seats** 56, Pr/dining room 12 **Times** 12-2/6-9, Closed 25-26 Dec, 2 wks Jan, Mon, D Sun **Prices** Fixed L 2 course £15.95, Fixed D 3 course £21.95, Starter £6.75-£8.95, Main £16.95-£24.95, Dessert fr £6.50 **Wines** 10 bottles over £30, 36 bottles under £30, 7 by glass **Parking** 40 **Notes** Sunday L £17.50-£19.50, Vegetarian available, Children welcome

The Whitebrook

WHITEBROOK Map 4 SO50

WINNER OF THE AA WINE AWARD FOR WALES 2016–17

Modern British, French V NOTABLE WINE LIST

tel: 01600 860254 **NP25 4TX**
email: info@thewhitebrook.co.uk **web:** www.thewhitebrook.co.uk
dir: *From Monmouth take B4293 towards Trellech, in 2.7m left towards Whitebrook, continue for 2m*

Modern metropolitan cooking in the Wye Valley

A former drovers' inn surrounded by soaring trees in the lush Wye Valley, The Whitebrook is a restaurant with rooms with a genuine sense of place. Authenticity runs through it from the sincerity of the welcome, the respectful revamp of the interior, to the seasonally- and locally-minded cooking of chef-patron Chris Harrod. Time spent at Le Manoir with Raymond Blanc has helped to inform Chris's cooking with genuine craft and precision, and the local environment provides the final ingredient to create one of the region's top dining experiences. The restaurant itself is simple and stylish, with clever retention of original features, neutral and natural colours, and plenty of room between the smartly-laid, linen-clad tables. Passion for foraging and uncommon plants is evident on fixed-price menus that show well-measured creativity. Cornish crab gets a hit of heat from charlock (a wild mustard plant), and horseradish foam, or try smoked feather blade of Longhorn beef with Herefordshire snails, beer barley and nettle purée. Main-course suckling pig – rack and belly – comes with a fine piece of crackling, caramelised celeriac, and pear to cut through the richness and lamb's sorrel, while Gigha halibut is served with parsley root and nasturtium tubers. There's equal craft and creativity among desserts, where excellent quality chocolate encases an intense apple filling, with a little kick from Ty Gwyn cider and a soothing hit of cinnamon. The lunch menu is an absolute bargain, while the full-on tasting menu gives the opportunity to go the whole hog. The wine list is sorted by style and includes organic and biodynamic options.

Chef Chris Harrod **Seats** 32 **Times** 12-2/7-9, Closed 1st 2 wks Jan, Mon, L Tue **Prices** Fixed L 2 course fr £25, Fixed D 3 course fr £54, Tasting menu fr £67 **Wines** 98 bottles over £30, 32 bottles under £30, 15 by glass **Parking** 20 **Notes** Sunday L £29-£67, Children 12 yrs+

USK Map 9 SO30

Newbridge on Usk

Traditional British

tel: 01633 451000 & 410262 **Tredunnock NP15 1LY**
email: newbridgeonusk@celtic-manor.com **web:** www.celtic-manor.com
dir: *A449 to Usk exit through town & turn left after bridge through Llangibby. After approx 1m Cwrt Bleddyn Hotel on right, turn left opposite hotel up lane. Drive through village of Tredunnock, down hill, inn on banks of River Usk*

Pastoral riverside setting for contemporary cooking

On a bend in the Usk, with river views, this restaurant with rooms is surrounded by well-tended gardens. The property dates back 200 years, so expect the usual beams and fireplaces, while the two-level restaurant has a rustic charm. The kitchen is assiduous about its sourcing and its menu ticks some cosmopolitan boxes. To start, crab mayonnaise is partnered with peanut brittle and chilli jelly, while two can share a seafood platter. Main courses include stimulating fish options such as brill with curried lentils or Cornish pollack with charred leek and mussel chowder, or go for slow-roasted 28-day aged flat rib of Welsh beef.

Chef Adam Whittle **Seats** 90, Pr/dining room 16 **Times** 12-2.30/6.30-10 **Prices** Fixed L 2 course fr £15.95, Starter £5.95-£11.25, Main £15.95-£45, Dessert £6.25-£7.95 **Wines** 20 bottles over £30, 20 bottles under £30, 9 by glass **Parking** 60 **Notes** Sunday L £24.95, Vegetarian available, Children welcome

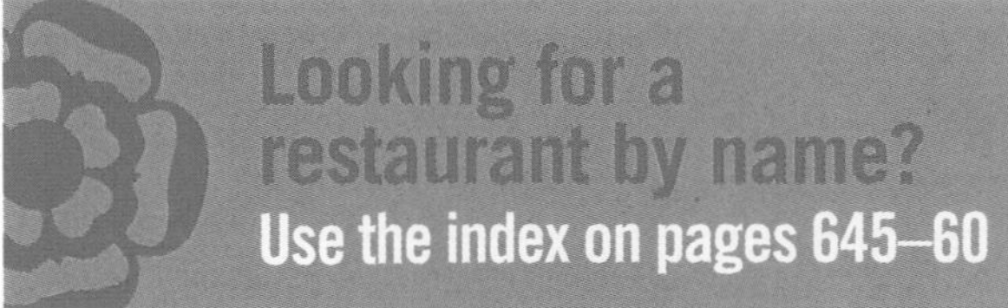

The Three Salmons Hotel

Modern Welsh

tel: 01291 672133 **Bridge St NP15 1RY**
email: general@threesalmons.co.uk **web:** www.threesalmons.co.uk
dir: *M4 junct 24/A449, 1st exit signed Usk. On entering town hotel on main road*

Brasserie cooking of appealing simplicity

The Three Salmons is one of those places that runs its own kitchen garden, and the rest of the produce is sourced just as discerningly for brasserie cooking that highlights its quality. An opening dish of ham hock with black pudding, apple and a Scotch quail's egg makes that clear. Mains might follow on with a suitably robust treatment of hake, which comes with confit chicken wing, a giant oyster mushroom and dauphinoise in lemon butter. Calves' liver is tenderly timed, and matched with crisp smoked bacon, spinach and creamy mash, and meals end in populist fashion with chocolate fondant and ginger ice cream, or crème caramel with poached pear.

Chef Edward Lawrence **Seats** 55, Pr/dining room 80 **Times** 12-2.30/6.30-9.30, Closed D Sun **Wines** 39 bottles over £30, 61 bottles under £30, 14 by glass **Parking** 80 **Notes** Afternoon tea £18, Sunday L £12-£24, Vegetarian available, Children welcome

WHITEBROOK Map 4 SO50

The Whitebrook

– *see page 571*

NEWPORT

NEWPORT **Map 9 ST38**

The Epicure Experience by Richard Davies

Modern British NOTABLE WINE LIST

tel: 01633 413000 **The Celtic Manor Resort, Coldra Woods NP18 1HQ**
email: epicure@celtic-manor.com **web:** www.celtic-manor.com
dir: *M4 junct 24, take B4237 towards Newport. Hotel 1st on right*

Fine-tuned modern cooking at a world-class golfing hotel

With over 2,000 acres of panoramic parkland, three 18-hole championship golf courses and other sporting facilities, Celtic Manor is an impressive set-up. There's a plethora of drinking and dining venues, with this the top-end choice. Elegant and contemporary, it features modern artworks, walnut flooring, cascading crystal-bead chandeliers, high-backed ivory leather chairs, and linen-clad tables served by formal, attentive staff. Richard Davies started out here in the 1990s before striking out to hone his talent in a succession of stellar kitchens. He's back to regale us with the finely-tuned modern British cooking showing the flair, imagination, balance and depth of flavour one expects of a high-calibre restaurant, delivered via the wide-ranging carte, a six-course tasting menu, or great value three-course lunch. Start with a torchon of foie gras, its richness balanced by rhubarb, orange and gingerbread, and follow with a duo of pork, the belly meat rich and well rendered, the cheek wrapped in crisp potato, served with textures of carrot and a hit of Szechuan spice. The food is meticulously worked and hewn from a classical mould, thus fish courses might see turbot paired with ceps, celeriac and pancetta. To finish, there's an impressive semi-fredo of lemon and meringue enhanced by the grown-up notes of anise and liquorice.

Chef Richard Davies **Seats** 50, Pr/dining room 12
Times 12-2.30/7-9.30, Closed 1-14 Jan, Sun-Mon, L Tue-Thu **Prices** Fixed L 3 course fr £32.50, Tasting menu fr £75 **Wines** 195 bottles over £30, 40 bottles under £30, 12 by glass **Parking** 1000 **Notes** ALC 3 course £65, Tasting menu 6 course, Vegetarian available, Children 16 yrs+

Rafters

Modern British

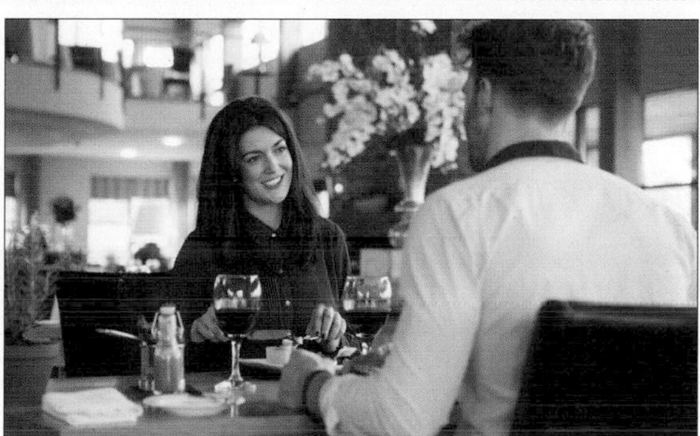

tel: 01633 413000 **The Celtic Manor Resort, Coldra Woods NP18 1HQ**
email: bookings@celtic-manor.com **web:** www.celtic-manor.com
dir: *M4 junct 24, B4237 towards Newport. Hotel 1st on right*

Grill classics at the 19th hole

There are views over the Ryder Cup course from Rafters, a classy grill restaurant on the Celtic Manor Resort. It's within the Twenty Ten Clubhouse (2010 being when the cup came to town), and with its high cedar-beamed ceiling, smart, modern look and those views, there's much to like. Welsh ingredients take centre stage and, this being a grill restaurant, there are locally reared, 21-day-aged steaks as the star attraction – who could resist steak Diane flambéed at the table with shallots, Dijon mustard, brandy and double cream? Kick off with chicken liver parfait with toasted brioche, hazelnuts and tomato chutney, and finish with Indian rice pudding with mango sorbet.

Chef Gareth Pembridge **Seats** 80, Pr/dining room 96 **Times** 12-5.30/6-9.45 **Prices** Fixed L 2 course fr £15.95, Starter £6.95-£9.50, Main £15.95-£36.50, Dessert £6.50-£9.55 **Parking** 115 **Notes** Sunday L fr £24.95, Vegetarian available, Children welcome

Steak on Six

Modern British NEW

tel: 01633 413000 **The Celtic Manor Resort, Coldra Woods NP18 1HQ**
email: postbox@celtic-manor.com
dir: *M4 junct 24, take B4237 towards Newport. Hotel 1st on right*

Prime Brit produce in a contemporary steakhouse

The 'Six' in question is the sixth floor of the upmarket, golf-centric Celtic Manor Resort, where this stylish, contemporary steakhouse looks out over Coldra Woods. When the culinary proposition is this straightforward, the quality of the raw materials is key, and the pedigree meat here proudly flies the flag for prime British protein. That's not to say that things lack subtlety, as in a starter of cauliflower textures – mousse, soused and charred – with pan-fried scallop and crunchy granola. Next up, an expertly-executed English rib-eye comes with a beef cheek croquette, béarnaise sauce, watercress and potato gratin, before a zingy key lime pie wraps things up in style.

Chef Michael Bates, Simon Crockford **Seats** 60 **Times** 1-2.30/6-9.30, Closed Tue-Wed, L Mon, Thu-Sat **Prices** Starter £8.25-£12.55, Main £24-£58, Dessert £7-£7.95 **Wines** 25 bottles over £30, 11 bottles under £30, 16 by glass **Notes** Sunday L £32.50, Vegetarian available, No children

PEMBROKESHIRE

HAVERFORDWEST Map 8 SM91

Slebech Park Estate

Modern British, French NEW

tel: 01437 752000 & 752002 **SA62 4AX**
email: enquiries@slebech.co.uk **web:** www.slebech.co.uk
dir: *Follow A40 from Carmarthen to Haverfordwest. At Slebech, take left signed Picton Castle & The Rhos. After 1m turn left after gateway lodge to Slebech Park Estate. Follow drive for 1.3m & signs to reception*

Upscale hotel in a national park

The castellated, 18th-century manor house of Slebech Park is surrounded by 600 acres of parkland bordering the 'hidden waterway' of the Eastern Cleddau River. The restaurant, a naturally lit, modern addition with a river view, draws people from all over Pembrokeshire for local fish, shellfish, lamb and beef on a daily changing dinner menu. Highlights include smooth chicken liver parfait with red onion compôte, walnut crumb and aged port reduction, followed by olive-oil-poached fresh cod, Caerphilly cheese mash, air-dried ham, purple sprouting broccoli and lobster cream sauce. Choose molten white chocolate fondant, bitter chocolate delice, ice cream, chocolate soil and passionfruit to finish.

Seats 40, Pr/dining room 20 **Times** 12-2/7-9 **Prices** Fixed L 2 course £14-£20, Fixed D 3 course £30, Starter £8-£11, Main £17-£28, Dessert £8-£9 **Wines** 24 bottles over £30, 25 bottles under £30, 8 by glass **Parking** 40 **Notes** Afternoon/high tea, Sunday L £17.50-£25, Vegetarian available, Children welcome

Wolfscastle Country Hotel

Modern British, Welsh

tel: 01437 741225 **Wolf's Castle SA62 5LZ**
email: info@wolfscastle.com **web:** www.wolfscastle.com
dir: *From Haverfordwest take A40 towards Fishguard. Hotel in centre of Wolf's Castle*

Modern classic cooking in a historic location

Welsh rebel leader Owain Glyndwr may be buried in the field alongside this old stone country hotel where the principal restaurant offers unclothed tables and a menu of modern classics. A double act of pork belly and scallop with puréed cauliflower in chicken jus is a well-rendered version of the familiar dish, or there might be potted pulled duck with red onion marmalade and cornichons. Accurately cooked fillet and short rib of Welsh Black beef is served with roast garlic mash and puréed spinach, while hake appears Spanish-style with prawn and chorizo paella and charred fennel. Finish with chocolate fondant, served with salted caramel ice cream and orange jelly.

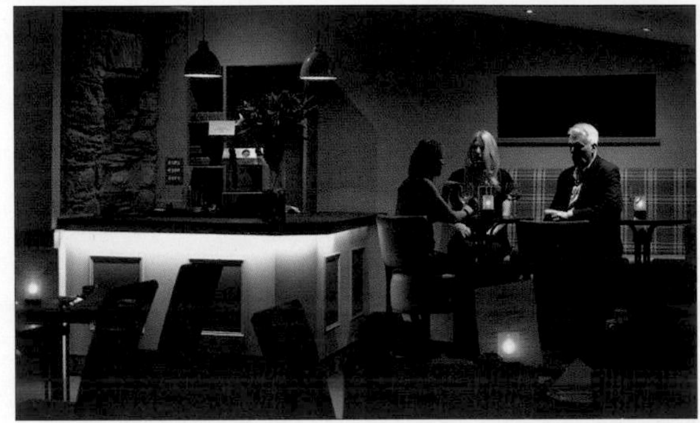

Wolfscastle Country Hotel

Chef Leon Fitzgerald **Seats** 55, Pr/dining room 32 **Times** 12-2/6.30-9, Closed 24-26 Dec **Prices** Fixed L 2 course £13.95, Starter £5.50-£10.95, Main £13.95-£24.95, Dessert £5.95-£7.95 **Wines** 21 bottles over £30, 29 bottles under £30, 13 by glass **Parking** 75 **Notes** Sunday L £11.50-£19.50, Vegetarian available, Children welcome

NARBERTH Map 8 SN11

Grove

– see opposite and advert on page 576

NEWPORT Map 8 SN03

Llys Meddyg

British

tel: 01239 820008 & 821050 **East St SA42 OSY**
email: info@llysmeddyg.com **web:** www.llysmeddyg.com
dir: *A487 to Newport, on Main St, through centre of town*

Accomplished cooking in a former coaching inn

The handsome Georgian townhouse is in the centre of Newport village: converted from a coaching inn, it is now a smartly-done-out restaurant with rooms. There's a cosy stone-walled cellar bar, a lovely kitchen garden for pre-dinner drinks, and an elegant restaurant hung with art. The kitchen champions local produce, and goes foraging to boost the repertoire, perhaps adding hedgerow sorrel to the mash that accompanies main-course sea bass, enoki mushrooms, sea beet and cockle jus. Bookending that, perhaps, peppered lamb sweetbreads with a juniper glaze and wild salad, and, to finish, vanilla pannacotta with salted lemon, spiced pineapple, almonds and mango sorbet.

Chef Ashley Butt **Seats** 30, Pr/dining room 14 **Times** 6-9, Closed L all week (ex summer L kitchen garden) **Prices** Starter £6.50-£8, Main £14.50-£22, Dessert £7.95-£9.95 **Wines** 15 bottles over £30, 18 bottles under £30, 5 by glass **Parking** 8, On street **Notes** Vegetarian available, Children welcome

Grove

NARBERTH **Map 8 SN11**

Modern British V 

tel: 01834 860915 **Molleston SA67 8BX**
email: info@thegrove-narberth.co.uk
web: www.thegrove-narberth.co.uk
dir: *From A40, take A478 to Narberth. Continue past castle & Herons Brook, turn right bottom of hill*

Tireless attention to detail in a beautifully restored country house

A Plantagenet longhouse, where family and livestock rubbed along together side by side, was once all there was here. It still stands, but was supplemented by a L-shaped Restoration manor eventually, itself much extended by a Victorian owner. It's an architectural historian's paradise, and perhaps another sort of heaven to those looking for a country-house refuge. Smartly attired with botanical wallpapers, elegant furniture and a mellow decorative tone in the dining room, it aims to soothe at every turn. Staff contribute to the restful demeanour of the place, and Allister Barsby's arrival as executive chef in early 2016 guarantees that culinary imagination remains the principal driver. Dishes of impeccable modernity flow forth: veal sweetbreads with caramelised cauliflower, confit lemon, gremolata and sherry foam to start, or perhaps scallops in yogurt with vanilla-scented chicken jus and raisin vinaigrette. East Asian notes are never too distant in the new British cooking, so don't be surprised to find soy-spiked shiitake purée, bok choy salad and lemongrass foam with the poached sea bass, while Welsh lamb receives its due celebration in a main course that combines the Provençal elements of red pepper, courgette and confit fennel with tangy sheep's curd. A veggie main course may be parmesan and rosemary gnocchi with wild garlic, dressed in egg yolk vinaigrette and rosemary foam. At dessert, there could be something as unabashedly classical as a pistachio soufflé with its own ice cream and bitter chocolate sauce, as well as more obviously contemporary trends in the shape of roast pineapple with kaffir lime, mango sorbet and chilli syrup. English, Cornish and Welsh cheeses served with tomato jelly are from the top drawer, and so is the wondrous wine list, which offers a world of exploration, opening with 11 fine selections by the glass.

Chef Peter Whaley, Allister Barsby **Seats** 70, Pr/dining room 25 **Times** 12-2.30/6-9.30 **Prices** Fixed L 3 course £29, Fixed D 3 course £59, Tasting menu £89 **Wines** 250 bottles over £30, 23 bottles under £30, 18 by glass **Parking** 42 **Notes** ALC 3 course £54, Tasting menu 7 course, Sunday L £29, Children welcome

PORTHGAIN Map 8 SM83

The Shed

Fish, Traditional British, Mediterranean

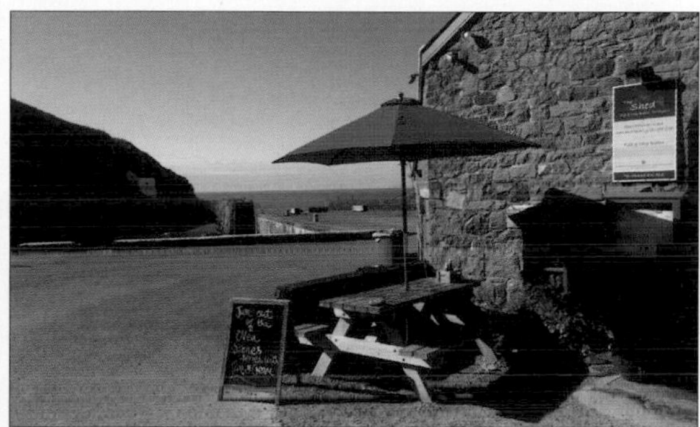

tel: 01348 831518 **SA62 5BN**
email: caroline@theshedporthgain.co.uk **web:** www.theshedporthgain.co.uk
dir: *7m from St Davids. Off A487*

Fresh seafood and laid-back ambience on the harbour

Seafood is king at this simple beach hut-style 'fish and chip bistro' right on the quayside in the dinky fishing village of Porthgain. The place sells its own-caught and local sustainable fresh fish and seafood from a counter during the warmer months, and sitting outdoors with a glass of wine, you couldn't ask for a more delightfully unaffected venue. Proper beer-battered fish and chips gets its own menu, otherwise tiger prawns are pan-fried with lashings of garlic butter and parsley, then spanking-fresh hake is matched with poppy seeds, cucumber pickle salad and coriander yogurt. End with dark chocolate and Tia Maria torte with coffee crunch ice cream and espresso sauce.

Chef Rob & Caroline Jones **Seats** 50 **Times** 12-3/5.30-9, Closed Mon-Tue (Nov-Mar only) **Prices** Starter £5.50-£7.95, Main £10.50-£21.50, Dessert £4.95-£6.95 **Wines** 2 bottles over £30, 24 bottles under £30, 7 by glass **Parking** On village street **Notes** Sunday L, Vegetarian available, Children welcome

ST DAVIDS Map 8 SM72

Cwtch

Modern British

:el: 01437 720491 **22 High St SA62 6SD**
email: info@cwtchrestaurant.co.uk
ir: *A487 St Davids, restaurant on left before Cross Square*

Big taste of Wales in the smallest city

'he name is pronounced 'cutsh' and it has all the cosseting connotations of hug, snug and cosy. Three small dining rooms spread over two floors are done out with he simplicity of whitewashed stone walls and sturdy beams. The cooking takes a imilarly restrained approach, opening with a chunky terrine of ham, chicken and horizo with home-made piccalilli and sourdough toast, followed by a soul-soothing nain course of rolled lamb shoulder with Molly Parkin parsnips and red wine jus. Round things off with puddings that fly the red dragon, such as Merlyn liqueur hocolate mousse with nut brittle and Chantilly cream.

hef Nic Mascall **Seats** 50, Pr/dining room 18 **Times** 6-10, Closed 25-26 Dec, Jan, Mon-Tue (Nov-Mar), L Mon-Sat (Oct-Apr), D Sun (Oct-Apr) **Prices** Fixed D 3 course 26-£32 **Wines** 7 bottles over £30, 25 bottles under £30, 11 by glass **Parking** On treet, car park **Notes** Early evening offer 6-6.45pm 2/3 course £22/£26, Sunday L 20-£24, Vegetarian available, Children welcome

SAUNDERSFOOT Map 8 SN10

Coast Restaurant

Modern British V NOTABLE WINE LIST

tel: 01834 810800 **Coppet Hall Beach SA69 9AJ**
email: reservations@coastsaundersfoot.co.uk **web:** www.coastsaundersfoot.co.uk
dir: *Phone for directions*

Emblematic modern building on the Pembrokeshire shoreline

This purpose-built wooden structure stands on the shore, with picture windows giving unrivalled views, and simple furnishings of bare tables and banquettes. The seafood-strong menu is of the moment too. A starter of crab comes with avocado purée, white tomato mousse and semi-dried tomatoes, or there might be confit rabbit ballotine with carrot and pea salad and tarragon mayonnaise. Imaginative main courses range from John Dory fillet with gingerbread crumb, white beans, saffron emulsion and artichokes to roast turbot fillet with samphire, mash and lobster sauce, with perhaps poached chicken breast for meat-eaters. Puddings maintain the momentum: try raspberry frangipane tart with ripple ice cream.

Chef Will Holland **Seats** 64 **Times** 12-2.30/6-9.30, Closed 25-26 Dec, Mon-Tue (Nov-Mar) **Prices** Tasting menu fr £65, Starter £11-£15, Main £17-£27, Dessert £9-£10 **Wines** 29 bottles over £30, 9 bottles under £30, 17 by glass **Parking** Pay & display before 6pm **Notes** Tasting menu 6 course, Market menu autumn/winter only, Children welcome

SAUNDERSFOOT *continued*

St Brides Spa Hotel

 Modern British

tel: 01834 812304 **St Brides Hill SA69 9NH**
email: reservations@stbridesspahotel.com **web:** www.stbridesspahotel.com
dir: *A478 onto B4310 to Saundersfoot. Hotel above harbour*

Pleasingly unfussy food and fabulous sea views

The coastal views of Saundersfoot harbour and Carmarthen Bay from its clifftop perch are reason enough to pay this laid-back spa hotel a visit, and the kitchen provides a brace of wide-ranging menus. Plump for the outdoor terrace in fine weather, but when the Welsh climate does its thing, there's the Gallery bar for a menu of simple classics, and the Cliff Restaurant, where the chefs deliver vibrant, unpretentious cooking. A combo of chorizo with roasted potato cake and charred red pepper starts things off, followed by halibut wrapped in pancetta with roasted garlic mash and parsley jus. To finish, roasted figs come with mascarpone ice cream and cinnamon toast.

Chef Toby Goodwin **Seats** 100, Pr/dining room 50 **Times** 11-close, All-day dining **Prices** Starter £6.50-£8, Main £16-£28, Dessert £6.25-£7.25 **Wines** 104 bottles over £30, 79 bottles under £30, 14 by glass **Parking** 60 **Notes** All day Gallery menu, Sunday L £25-£30.75, Vegetarian available, Children welcome

SOLVA Map 8 SM82

Crug Glâs Country House

Modern British

tel: 01348 831302 **Abereiddy SA62 6XX**
email: janet@crug-glas.co.uk **web:** www.crug-glas.co.uk
dir: *From St Davids take A487 to Fishguard. 1st left after Carnhedryn, house signed*

Unflashy cooking in a country restaurant with rooms

Owners Janet and Perkin Evans have renovated 12th-century Crug Glâs using local materials to achieve smart modernity without trampling on the house's history. At the end of the day, kick off the walking boots and settle into the formal Georgian dining room for Janet's traditional country-house cooking. Pembrokeshire's finest produce forms the backbone of menus that aim to comfort rather than challenge. Cream of celeriac and apple soup gets a lift from curry oil and parsnip crisps, followed by pan-fried pheasant breast with chestnut-stuffed cabbage, dauphinoise potatoes, parsnip purée and an aromatic sauce of apple and Black Mountain liqueur. Finish with a salted caramel and chocolate slice.

POWYS

BRECON Map 9 SO02

Peterstone Court

Modern British, European

tel: 01874 665387 **Llanhamlach LD3 7YB**
email: info@peterstone-court.com **web:** www.peterstone-court.com
dir: *1m from Brecon on A40 to Abergavenny*

Excellent local food on the edge of the Brecon Beacons

Georgian proportions and its position in the Brecon Beacons make Peterstone Court an ideal base for exploring the landscape, but, it's also a lovely bolt-hole for a bit of pampering. There's a contemporary feel to the place and the classy finish includes a swish bar and a spa. Best of all, there's nifty modern food in the Conservatory Restaurant. A starter of pork brawn with tarragon mayonnaise and grain mustard dressing shows the way. Main courses include herb-crusted salt marsh lamb and sweetbreads with mash, white beans, and tomato and herb casserole. Finish with panettone bread-and-butter pudding with brandy-infused custard.

Chef Glyn Bridgeman **Seats** 30 **Times** 12-2.30/6-9.30 **Prices** Fixed L 2 course fr £16.50, Starter £6-£8, Main £11.50-£21, Dessert £5-£8.50 **Wines** 15 bottles over £30, 33 bottles under £30, 9 by glass **Parking** 40 **Notes** Afternoon tea, Sunday L £14.50-£22.50, Vegetarian available, Children welcome

BUILTH WELLS Map 9 SO05

Caer Beris Manor Hotel

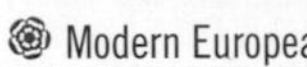 Modern European

tel: 01982 552601 **LD2 3NP**
email: caerberis@btconnect.com **web:** www.caerberis.com
dir: *From town centre follow A483/Llandovery signs. Hotel on left on edge of town*

Innovative modern cooking in a Welsh feudal estate

This timber-framed country-house hotel sits in 27 acres of parkland bordered by the River Irfon. Dining takes place in the conservatory or the panelled dining room, where a large stone fireplace is a focal point. The kitchen gives a contemporary European spin on country-house cooking, confidently handling some beguiling combinations. A starter of rump of lamb is accompanied by saffron pannacotta, pomegranate and spiced aubergine, and a main course of John Dory with cauliflower purée, orange-glazed fennel and curry oil, and beef fillet comes with morcilla sausage, chanterelles and red wine reduction. End with mocha torte with espresso syrup and salted caramel ice cream.

Chef Christian Naylor **Seats** 40, Pr/dining room 100 **Times** 12-2.30/6.30-9.30 **Prices** Tasting menu fr £59, Starter £7.95-£9.50, Main £16.50-£24.95, Dessert £7.50-£7.95 **Wines** 9 bottles over £30, 25 bottles under £30, 7 by glass **Parking** 50 **Notes** Sunday L £10.95-£13.95, Vegetarian available, Children welcome

CRICKHOWELL Map 9 SO21

The Bear

Modern British, International

tel: 01873 810408 **High St NP8 1BW**
email: bearhotel@aol.com **web:** www.bearhotel.co.uk
dir: *Town centre, off A40 (Brecon road). 6m from Abergavenny*

Vibrant modern cooking in a medieval pub

The old stagecoach doesn't run past here any more, but an enduring testament to the last time it did comes with a Victorian timetable in the bar. The Bear goes back further than that, to the reign of Henry III in the 1430s. Its traditional interiors and ancient arched cellar where the beers are kept are all part of the deal, as is vibrant modern food with the emphasis on regionally sourced ingredients. Start with Cajun-spiced fishcake with lemon and chilli dip, before going on to prime Welsh steak with port and Stilton sauce. Simple but effective desserts include rice pudding with winter berry compôte.

Chef Adam Littlewort **Seats** 60, Pr/dining room 30 **Times** 12-2.15/6.30-9.30, Closed 25 Dec, L Mon-Sat, D Sun **Prices** Prices not confirmed **Wines** 6 bottles over £30, 45 bottles under £30, 10 by glass **Parking** 40 **Notes** Sunday L, Vegetarian available, Children 7 yrs+

Manor Hotel

Modern British

tel: 01873 810212 **Brecon Rd NP8 1SE**
email: info@manorhotel.co.uk **web:** www.manorhotel.co.uk
dir: *On A40, 0.5m from Crickhowell*

Farm-fresh food in a sparkling-white valley hotel

The sparkling-white hotel stands on a thoroughly enthralling spot under Table Mountain in a valley of the Brecon Beacons National Park. The relaxing dining room with tall plants and elegant furniture has views out towards the hills, and its bistro-style menu hauls in most of its prime materials from the family farm seven miles away in Llangynidr. Get going with chicken, parsley and mushroom roulade with Melba toast and pickled carrot, then move on to pheasant breast wrapped in bacon, served with bubble and squeak, braised red cabbage and gamey red wine jus. End with a Black Forest meringue ice cream bombe with Kirsch syrup.

Chef Glyn Bridgeman **Seats** 54, Pr/dining room 26 **Times** 12-2.30/6-9.30 **Prices** Fixed L 2 course fr £15.95, Starter £5.50-£7, Main £11-£19, Dessert £5.50-£8 **Wines** 4 bottles over £30, 31 bottles under £30, 9 by glass **Parking** 200 **Notes** Sunday L £16.95-£18.95, Vegetarian available, Children welcome

HAY-ON-WYE Map 9 SO24

Old Black Lion Inn

Modern British, Italian

tel: 01497 820841 **26 Lion St HR3 5AD**
email: info@oldblacklion.co.uk **web:** www.oldblacklion.co.uk
dir: *1m off A438. From TIC car park turn right along Oxford Rd, pass NatWest Bank, next left (Lion St), hotel 20yds on right*

Well-judged, appealing cooking in a historic inn

Dating from the 17th century, the whitewashed inn has bags of character, with beams in low ceilings and stone fireplaces. You can eat in the bar or in the dining room. A starter of partridge pâté with a port-enriched blackberry sauce sounds straightforward enough, but the kitchen puts thought and effort into all its output, so it may also present main courses of fillet of monkfish wrapped in Parma ham with potatoes crushed with red pesto and salad, and a winter dish of slowly cooked venison shoulder with celeriac mash and seasonal vegetables. End memorably with vanilla pannacotta with coffee and frangelico syrup.

KNIGHTON Map 9 SO27

Milebrook House Hotel

Modern, Traditional V

tel: 01547 528632 **Milebrook LD7 1LT**
email: hotel@milebrookhouse.co.uk **web:** www.milebrookhouse.co.uk
dir: *2m E of Knighton on A4113 (Ludlow)*

Quality British food on the Welsh-English border

An idyllic Georgian mansion in the Marches hills much-loved by shooting parties, with a handy kitchen garden to provide fresh seasonal fruit and veg, and a skilled hand in the kitchen to track down the best local suppliers and deliver country-house classics cooked with flair and imagination. Seared breast of local pigeon with crispy chorizo, caramelised apple and watercress is the sort of thing to expect, followed by pan-fried pork fillet wrapped in prosciutto with potato purée, sautéed courgettes and honey and wholegrain mustard sauce. Desserts such as lemon posset with whimberry jelly hit the spot, or there are artisan cheeses from both sides of the border.

Chef Katie Marsden **Seats** 40, Pr/dining room 16 **Times** 12-2/6.30-9, Closed L Mon **Prices** Fixed L 2 course £18-£20, Fixed D 3 course £33-£36 **Wines** 6 bottles over £30, 36 bottles under £30, 8 by glass **Parking** 24 **Notes** Sunday L, Children 8 yrs+

LLANDRINDOD WELLS Map 9 SO06

Metropole Hotel & Spa

Modern British V

tel: 01597 823700 **Temple St LD1 5DY**
email: info@metropole.co.uk **web:** www.metropole.co.uk
dir: *In centre of town off A483, car park at rear*

Stylish spa hotel with sound modern cooking using regional fare

In the same family for more than 170 years, this imposing building in the centre of Llandrindod Wells has long been a local landmark. The hotel offers a couple of dining options, with a brasserie and the more formal Radnor and Miles Restaurant. There's a regional accent to the menu, with plenty of game in season, and local meat cooked on the grill. Pressed ham hock terrine, Granny Smith apple, fine beans, black pudding and chorizo is a full-flavoured starter. It might precede a main of sea bass, confit potatoes, pancetta, vanilla-braised fennel and date and raisin purée.

Chef Nick Edwards **Seats** 46, Pr/dining room 250 **Times** 12-2.15/6-9.30 **Prices** Prices not confirmed **Wines** 4 bottles over £30, 29 bottles under £30, 9 by glass **Parking** 150 **Notes** Sunday L, Children welcome

LLANFYLLIN Map 15 SJ11

Seeds

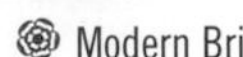 Modern British

tel: 01691 648604 **5-6 Penybryn Cottages, High St SY22 5AP**
dir: *In village centre. Take A490 N from Welshpool, follow signs to Llanfyllin*

Accurate cooking in an intimate, relaxed setting

When you don't require your food to push culinary boundaries or feature froths and gels, try Seeds, a little bistro with just 20 seats, run by an amiable husband-and-wife team. Mellow jazz floats around the artworks and curios decorating the low-beamed, slate-floored dining room as chef-patron Mark Seager turns out simple, tasty classic bistro dishes at the stoves of a bijou kitchen. Starters can be as simple as grilled sardines with salt and lemon, while mains take in rack of Welsh lamb with Dijon mustard and herb crust. Desserts follow the comfort theme – perhaps treacle tart with cream, or classic crème brûlée.

Chef Mark Seager **Seats** 18 **Times** 11-2/7-9, Closed 24-25 Dec, 1 wk Oct, Sun-Tue (Sun-Wed winter), may vary **Prices** Fixed D 3 course £27.95-£31.90, Starter £4.95-£6.95, Main £12.95-£19.95, Dessert £5.45-£6.95 **Wines** 14 bottles over £30, 74 bottles under £30, 3 by glass **Parking** Free town car park, on street **Notes** Pre-music festival menu Jun-Jul, Vegetarian available, Children welcome

LLANWDDYN Map 15 SJ01

Lake Vyrnwy Hotel & Spa

Modern British

tel: 01691 870692 **Lake Vyrnwy SY10 OLY**
email: info@lakevyrnwyhotel.co.uk **web:** www.lakevyrnwy.com
dir: *On A4393, 200yds past dam turn sharp right into drive*

Interesting menus, breathtaking views

Bird-watching, fishing and hill-walking are all possibilities at this stylish Victorian hotel with lovely views over the lake. Local produce is the backbone of the kitchen's output, some from the estate itself. You might begin with a full-bore partnership of pan-fried quail breast with apple and brandy purée, candied walnuts and balsamic, followed by roast duck breast with cider-braised potato, baby gem lettuce, sweet caramelised onions and a red cabbage purée full of mulled fruit spiciness. Fish is handled deftly, perhaps roast halibut with samphire, pink grapefruit and basil sauce, buttered spinach and a prawn raviolo. Pudding might be lemon curd tart with sweet basil mousse.

Chef David Thompson **Seats** 85, Pr/dining room 220 **Times** 12-2/6.45-9.15 **Prices** Fixed D 3 course £35 **Wines** 29 bottles over £30, 55 bottles under £30, 10 by glass **Parking** 80 **Notes** Sunday L £22.50, Vegetarian available, Children welcome

LLANWRTYD WELLS Map 9 SN84

Lasswade Country House

Modern British

tel: 01591 610515 **Station Rd LD5 4RW**
email: info@lasswadehotel.co.uk **web:** www.lasswadehotel.co.uk
dir: *Exit A483 into Irfon Terrace, right into Station Rd, 350yds on right*

Organic focus in an Edwardian country house

Run with great charm by owners Roger and Emma Stevens, this Edwardian house offers 360-degree views of the Cambrian Mountains and Brecon Beacons. It's a soothing spot made even more inviting by the chef-proprietor's skilled cooking. Driven by a passion for sourcing organic and sustainable produce from Wales and the Marches area, Roger keeps combinations straightforward, timings accurate, and interweaves flavours intelligently in daily-changing dinner menus. Get going with ham hock terrine with onion marmalade, followed by a plate of that splendid Cambrian mountain lamb, comprising roast, herb-crusted rack, confit shoulder and a mini shepherd's pie with a rich Madeira wine jus.

Chef Roger Stevens **Seats** 20, Pr/dining room 20 **Times** 7.30-9.30, Closed 25-26 Dec, L all week **Prices** Fixed D 3 course £34 **Wines** 3 bottles over £30, 17 bottles under £30, 4 by glass **Parking** 6

LLYSWEN Map 9 SO13

Llangoed Hall

Modern British V

tel: 01874 754525 **LD3 OYP**
email: enquiries@llangoedhall.co.uk **web:** www.llangoedhall.co.uk
dir: *On A470, 2m from Llyswen towards Builth Wells*

Refined contemporary dining in a grand country house

A fabulous country-house hotel with all the traditional features and period details you could hope for. The original Jacobean hall was rebuilt in the early 20th century by Clough Williams-Ellis, who also designed and built Portmeirion. There's an air of comfortable Edwardian glamour, with fine furniture, impressive fireplaces, and 17 acres of lawns, gardens and grounds – they even have a maze. The stylish Wedgwood blue and white restaurant is a smart, airy space, and head chef Nick Brodie can be confident in the provenance of his ingredients – much of the produce comes from the estate and kitchen garden. Diners can choose either the four course menu offering multiple choices on each course or a prestige menu of nine courses (there's a vegetarian version as well) offering a series of carefully constructed and elegantly conceived dishes. Menus offer simple descriptions, and might move from gnocchi, ham, tomato through scallop ceviche, caviar and English wasabi, foie gras, smoked eel and puffed rice, to Wagyu beef, black bean and mushroom, finishing with meringue, rhubarb, sorrel and pineapple. It's impressive cooking of the modern British school, every element pays its way and it all looks stunning on the plate.

Chef Nick Brodie **Seats** 40, Pr/dining room 80 **Times** 12-2/7-9 **Prices** Tasting menu £75-£95 **Parking** 150 **Notes** Prestige & Vegetarian menu 9 course, Sunday L £75, Children welcome

RHONDDA CYNON TAFF

PONTYCLUN Map 9 ST08

La Luna

Modern International

tel: 01443 239600 **79-81 Talbot Rd, Talbot Green CF72 8AE**
email: info@la-lunarestaurant.com
dir: *M4 junct 34, follow signs for Llantrisant, turn left at 2nd lights*

Relaxed bistro dining near the shops

The family-run La Luna has an easy-going atmosphere and a contemporary finish, which fits the kitchen's sunny Med-style, brasserie-inspired output. A starter of chargrilled king prawns with samphire and slow-roasted tomatoes and peppers shows the style, with the simplicity of seafood cocktail, pasta options, and Welsh steaks cooked on the grill adding to its broad appeal. Medallions of Welsh sirloin might find their way into a stroganoff, with confit potatoes, parsnips and onions. Desserts run to the likes of raspberry crème brûlée or bread-and-butter pudding with rum and toffee sauce. There's an early evening menu, too, and some fair-weather outside tables.

PONTYPRIDD Map 9 ST08

Llechwen Hall Hotel

Modern Welsh

tel: 01443 742050 **Llanfabon CF37 4HP**
email: reservations@llechwenhall.co.uk **web:** www.llechwen.co.uk
dir: *A470 N towards Merthyr Tydfil. 3rd exit at large rdbt then 3rd exit at mini rdbt, hotel signed 0.5m on left*

Scenic, historical setting for unfussy cooking

The low-ceilinged, heavily beamed restaurant has plenty of atmosphere with its whitewashed walls hung with oils and candles flickering on bare wooden tables. The kitchen is ahead of the game when it partners pan-fried and sautéed scallops with confit chorizo cassoulet and aïoli and turns out a main course of roast rump of local lamb with honey-roast salsify, herby and garlicky mash and delightful, sticky onion jus. Another well-considered main course might be pan-fried sea bass fillet with seafood bisque and crushed potatoes. Conclude with bara-brith-and-butter pudding with Penderyn whisky-infused custard, or baked Welsh cake cheesecake with strawberry preserve.

Chef Paul Trask **Seats** 60, Pr/dining room 300 **Times** 12-2/7-9 **Prices** Prices not confirmed **Wines** 2 bottles over £30, 30 bottles under £30, 4 by glass **Parking** 100 **Notes** Sunday L, Vegetarian available, Children welcome

SWANSEA

REYNOLDSTON Map 8 SS48

Fairyhill

Modern British V 

tel: 01792 390139 **SA3 1BS**
email: postbox@fairyhill.net **web:** www.fairyhill.net
dir: *M4 junct 47, take A483 then A484 to Llanelli, Gower, Gowerton. At Gowerton follow B4295 for approx 10m*

Elegant country-house hotel with food showcasing local flavours

A charming Georgian mansion, Fairyhill is in a secluded position within 24 acres. The smart restaurant makes excellent use of local produce and delivers a refined experience that isn't in the least stuffy. The modern British cooking may start with duck liver parfait with pear and apple chutney, or smoked haddock beignets with hazelnut and citrus salad, ahead of chicken ballotine with chard (from the kitchen garden), rösti and tarragon sauce, or fillet of sea bass with laverbread sauce, broccoli and baby potatoes. Puddings can be as familiar as spotted dick and as novel as green tea pannacotta with hibiscus sorbet and poached rhubarb.

Chef Paul Davies, David Whitecross **Seats** 60, Pr/dining room 40 **Times** 12-2/6.30-9.30, Closed 26 Dec, 1-25 Jan, Mon-Tue (Nov-Mar) **Prices** Fixed L 2 course £20, Fixed D 3 course £49.50 **Wines** 120 bottles over £30, 50 bottles under £30, 10 by glass **Parking** 45 **Notes** Afternoon tea £20-£27.50, Sunday L £27.50, Children 8 yrs+

SWANSEA Map 9 SS69

Hanson at the Chelsea Restaurant

Modern Welsh, French

tel: 01792 464068 **17 St Mary St SA1 3LH**
email: andrew_hanson@live.co.uk
dir: *In small lane between St Mary Church & Wine St*

Appealing bistro cooking in a popular city-centre venue

Andrew Hanson's unassuming-looking restaurant resembles a classic modern bistro inside with clothed tables pressed in cheek by jowl, blackboard menus and small framed pictures against a delicate yellow colour scheme. The cooking is an appealing mix of local produce and French influences, with the emphasis on fish and seafood, but not forgetting fine Welsh lamb. Potted chicken rillettes matched with pistachio and thyme butter, fig chutney and toasted sourdough makes for a hearty opener, followed by a time-honoured main-course combination of calves' liver, button mushrooms, shallots, Alsace bacon and Madeira sauce, and potato purée. Finish with vanilla pannacotta with raspberry coulis, or brioche bread-and-butter pudding with honey and whisky.

Chef Andrew Hanson, Gareth Sillman, Nathan Kirby **Seats** 50, Pr/dining room 20 **Times** 12-2/7-10, Closed 25-26 Dec, BHs, Sun **Prices** Fixed L 2 course £13.95-£17.95, Tasting menu £35, Starter £4.50-£9.95, Main £11.95-£23.50, Dessert £5.75 **Wines** 8 by glass **Notes** Tasting menu 6 course, Vegetarian available, Children welcome

TORFAEN

CWMBRAN Map 9 ST29

The Parkway Hotel & Spa

Modern European

tel: 01633 871199 & 486312 **Cwmbran Dr NP44 3UW**
email: enquiries@theparkwayhotel.co.uk **web:** www.parkwayhotelandspa.com
dir: *M4 junct 25a & 26, A4051 follow Cwmbran-Llantarnam Park signs. Right at rdbt, right for hotel*

Modern hotel with unfussy menu and carvery

The single-storey Parkway has a whopping 70 bedrooms and spa facilities aplenty. You can come here for afternoon tea, bar meals served in the lounge and à la carte and carvery options in the Ravellos Restaurant. The warmly decorated dining room is the setting for simple dishes like smooth duck liver pâté with date and grape compôte, or Perl Las cheese with pickled pear and candied walnuts. Move on to roast salmon with a bouillabaisse garnish, or a roast carved to order and served with roast potatoes and a choice of vegetables. Finish with chocolate cheesecake with cookie crumb or vanilla pannacotta partnered with an orange jelly and dark chocolate.

Chef Clive Williams **Seats** 85, Pr/dining room **Times** 6.30-10, Closed L Mon-Sat **Prices** Fixed D 3 course £21.95, Starter £4.50-£7.50, Main £12-£21.50, Dessert £5.25-£6.95 **Parking** 250 **Notes** Sunday L £14-£22, Vegetarian available, Children welcome

VALE OF GLAMORGAN

HENSOL Map 9 ST07

Llanerch Vineyard

Modern British

tel: 01443 222716 **CF72 8GG**
email: info@llanerch-vineyard.co.uk **web:** www.llanerch-vineyard.co.uk
dir: *M4 junct 34, follow brown tourist signs to Llanerch Vineyard*

Local produce and home-grown wine

Around 22 acres of south-facing slopes of the Ely Valley have been planted with vines since 1986, and you can raise a glass to the industrious owners while dining in their restaurant or bistro. The latter offers simple fare such as Welsh rarebit, sandwiches or a gourmet burger, while in the evening restaurant there's celeriac soup, say, with poached pears and watercress, or pan-seared pollack with fennel velouté. Welsh meats figure large – Duffryn Bach lamb rump with an accompanying Wellington, or haunch of Bwlch venison with orange-scented red cabbage – and desserts run to a zesty glazed pineapple number. To wash it down – what else? – Welsh wine.

Chef Michael Hudson **Seats** 40 **Times** 12-5/6.30-9, Closed 25-26 Dec, D Sun **Prices** Fixed L 2 course £11.95-£31.95, Fixed D 3 course £24.50-£41.45, Starter £6-£8.50, Main £14.50-£20.50, Dessert £4-£6.95 **Wines** 32 bottles over £30, 36 bottles under £30, 13 by glass **Parking** 400 **Notes** Afternoon tea £15, Sunday L £18.50-£22.50, Vegetarian available, Children welcome

The Vale Resort

Modern British

tel: 01443 667800 **Hensol Park CF72 8JY**
email: sales@vale-hotel.com **web:** www.vale-hotel.com
dir: *M4 junct 34, exit signed Pendoylan, turn 1st right twice, then 1st left before white house on bend. Hotel on right*

Huge valley resort with plenty of options

The Resort luxuriates in 650 acres of the Vale of Glamorgan, but is only 15 minutes' drive from Cardiff. A bright airy room, the Vale Grill, with white walls and well-spaced tables is one dining option, or there's a linen-clad restaurant, La Cucina, as well as a champagne bar. Up-to-date British cooking is the draw in the Grill, moving from a pairing of marbled ham hock and black pudding roulade in mustard from twin dressings of remoulade and vinaigrette, to roast pheasant breast with braised red cabbage and a savoury bread pudding in redcurrant jus. A smooth-textured cheesecake to finish gains depth from mulled wine syrup and cinnamon ice cream.

Chef Daniel James **Seats** 80, Pr/dining room 50 **Times** 6.30-11, Closed L all week **Prices** Prices not confirmed **Parking** 500 **Notes** Sunday L, Vegetarian available, Children welcome

PENARTH Map 9 ST17

AA RESTAURANT OF THE YEAR FOR WALES 2016–17

Restaurant James Sommerin

Modern British V

tel: 029 2070 6559 **The Esplanade CF64 3AU**
email: info@jamessommerinrestaurant.co.uk
web: www.jamessommerinrestaurant.co.uk
dir: *Phone for directions*

Dazzling displays of contemporary cuisine

James Sommerin's latest berth is this multi-hued timbered building on the esplanade at Penarth, a boutique spot for elegant relaxation with soothing sea views, and the nerve-centre for an ambitious culinary operation that extends to chef's demonstrations, an on-view kitchen, and a range of menu deals. These include a full carte as well as the six- and nine-course surprise tasters, together with the option of a chef's table and afternoon tea if you're in the mood for a scone. Sommerin's cooking is full of technical panache and inventive energy, using modern classic ideas in fascinating ways. An opening assemblage of roast beetroot with pine nuts, goats' cheese and pickle looks dramatic, while scallops get a runout with Jerusalem artichoke, mushrooms and fennel seed. At main course, gentle cooking brings all the expressive depth out of a cut of 32-day aged sirloin, partnered with oxtail and puréed parsnips in red wine, or there may be sea bass with butternut squash and fennel in spiced butter, or locally caught cod glammed up in squid ink with samphire. Fruit-based desserts are fragrant and satisfying, as when a cherry soufflé appears with marzipan ice cream, or exotic kalamansi is seasoned with black sesame and orange blossom.

Chef James Sommerin **Seats** 65, Pr/dining room 12
Times 12-2.30/7-9.30, Closed 1 wk Jan, Mon **Prices** Tasting menu £60-£140, Starter £7.50-£12, Main £18-£28, Dessert £9-£12 **Wines** 100+ bottles over £30, 15 bottles under £30, 14 by glass **Parking** On street **Notes** Tasting menu 6/9 course, Chef's table £150, ALC Tue-Thu, Children welcome

WREXHAM

LLANARMON DYFFRYN CEIRIOG — Map 15 SJ13

The Hand at Llanarmon

Modern European

tel: 01691 600666 **Ceiriog Valley LL20 7LD**
email: reception@thehandhotel.co.uk **web:** www.thehandhotel.co.uk
dir: *Leave A5 at Chirk onto B4500 signed Ceiriog Valley, continue for 11m*

Modern pub cooking in a whitewashed Marches inn

A whitewashed country inn buried in the sumptuous Ceiriog Valley, The Hand makes a concerted effort to come up to rustic expectations inside, with dozing dogs toasting themselves before the open fires, plenty of chunky furniture and brass ornaments, and a stuffed fox standing sentinel in the hallway. The kitchen turns out impressive renditions of classic and modern pub food, beginning in time-honoured style with chicken liver pâté with fruit chutney and hot toast, and continuing with honey-roasted duck with tomato ragoût and red wine sauce. Finish in heart-warming fashion with a dark chocolate and rum crème brûlée, or Welsh cheeses and oatcakes.

Chef Grant Mulholland **Seats** 40 **Times** 12-2.30/6.30-8.45 **Prices** Starter £4.50-£6.50, Main £9.50-£24.50, Dessert £5.75-£7.25 **Wines** 17 bottles over £30, 29 bottles under £30, 7 by glass **Parking** 15 **Notes** Sunday L £15-£21.50, Vegetarian available, Children welcome

ROSSETT — Map 15 SJ35

Best Western Hallmark Chester Llyndir Hall

Traditional British

tel: 01244 571648 **Llyndir Ln LL12 0AY**
email: llyndirhallhotel@feathers.uk.com **web:** www.feathers.uk.com
dir: *Phone for directions*

Country-house hotel with gently modern menus

A country-house hotel with space for weddings and events, Llyndir Hall is a handsome house with five acres of landscaped gardens: check out the sculptures as you take a stroll. The hotel is home to a bright and contemporary restaurant looking out over the grounds. Expect classic dishes and a modern twist along the way. Slow-braised pork cheek is soft and tender in a first course with carrot and caraway purée and chargrilled asparagus, with main courses running to pan-seared sea bass with sautéed scallops and salsa verde, plus steaks cooked on the grill and served with classic sauces. For dessert, strawberry millefeuille has plenty of full-on fruity flavour.

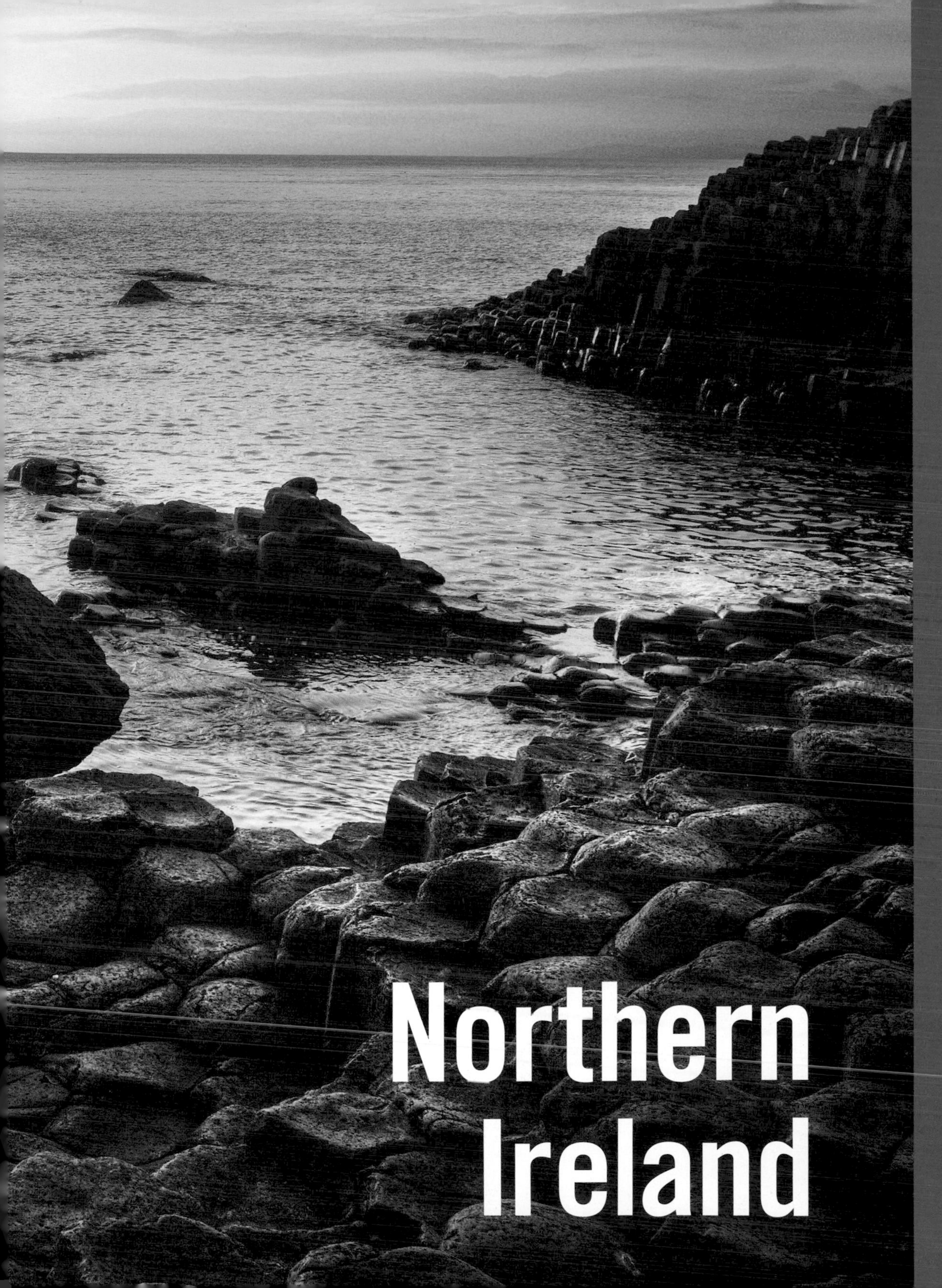

Northern Ireland

COUNTY ANTRIM

BALLYMENA Map 1 D5

Galgorm Resort & Spa

– see opposite and advert on page 588

BUSHMILLS Map 1 C6

Bushmills Inn Hotel

Modern Irish V

tel: 028 2073 3000 **9 Dunluce Rd BT57 8QG**
email: mail@bushmillsinn.com **web:** www.bushmillsinn.com
dir: *2m from Giant's Causeway on A2 in Bushmills after crossing river*

Confident cooking in the heart of whiskey country

For centuries a coaching inn at the heart of this world-famous whiskey village, this is now an upmarket boutique hotel. The peat fires may remain from the days when guests arrived by horse but modern-day visitors are more likely to arrive via helipad. In the restaurant, the menu is packed with attention-grabbing ideas, among them salt-and-chilli squid, pak choi, chilli jam, wasabi mayo, soy and ginger dip, followed perhaps by crispy pork belly, cauliflower purée, savoy cabbage and cider-soaked golden raisins. End with salted caramel and chocolate tart, vanilla ice cream and pistachio brittle.

Chef Donna Thompson **Seats** 120 **Times** 12-5/6-9.30 **Prices** Starter £5.35-£9.50, Main £16.95-£23.50, Dessert £5.95-£7.85 **Wines** 47 bottles over £30, 39 bottles under £30, 8 by glass **Parking** 70 **Notes** Sunday L £13.85, Children welcome

BELFAST

BELFAST Map 1 D5

Buskers

Modern Mediterranean, Irish V

tel: 028 9020 2290 **44 University Rd BT7 1NJ**
email: buskersreception@gmail.com
dir: *Adjacent to Queens University*

Modern bistro food in the university district

Located in the university district, this Victorian-era townhouse restaurant has a pre-theatre menu for anyone on a budget or in a rush for curtain up, and a bespoke veggie menu if required. The menu casts a wide net with dishes that show a Pan-European approach and a few Asian influences. Start, say, with wonderfully tender crispy beef with curried lentils and spiced tomato relish, or smoked cod with a soft egg and black pudding beignet. Next up, there's more curry flavour in a roast monkfish dish (served with a shellfish wonton). Round it all off with pecan pie with Chantilly cream.

Chef Jim McCarthy **Seats** 75, Pr/dining room 25
Times 12.30-3/5-10.30, Closed 24-26 Dec, 1 Jan, Etr, Mon, L Tue-Sat **Prices** Starter £4-£6, Main £10-£19, Dessert £5 **Wines** 6 bottles over £30, 25 bottles under £30, 4 by glass **Parking** On street **Notes** Pre-theatre 5-7pm £14.95, 6 course £40, ALC wknd brunch, Sunday L £8-£18.50, Children welcome

Café Vaudeville

French

tel: 028 9043 9160 **25-39 Arthur St BT1 4GQ**
email: info@cafevaudeville.com
dir: *Phone for directions*

Big-flavoured brasserie dishes in a historic city-centre building

The city-centre building was once a bank, but Café Vaudeville is now a glamorous bar and restaurant with a touch of Art Nouveau bling. In the restaurant, coloured lights change to set the mood. The menu deals in modern Irish small plates and sharing options alongside traditional main courses, with punchy flavours on offer. Baby back ribs are marinated with chilli and tamarind, slow-cooked and finished on the chargrill, followed by a rib-sticking main course of pork belly slow-cooked for 18 hours with Guinness, served with potato mash, chorizo baked beans and apple purée. Finish with perfectly executed chocolate fondant cake with a liquid centre, served with honeycomb ice cream.

Deanes at Queens

Modern British V

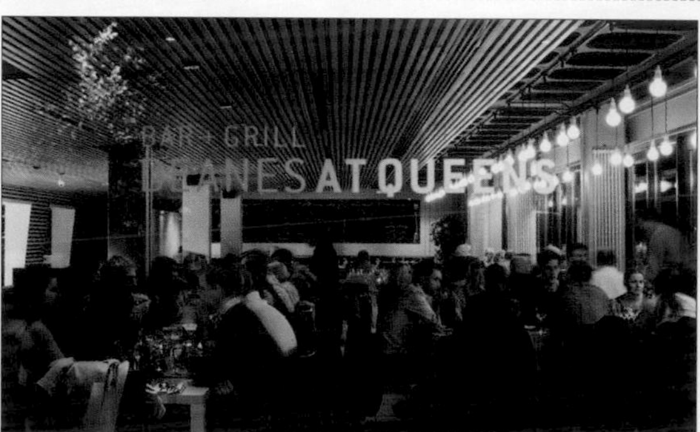

tel: 028 9038 2111 **1 College Gardens BT9 6BQ**
email: deanesatqueens@michaeldeane.co.uk
dir: *From city centre towards Queens University then 1st left onto College Gardens, restaurant 1st on right*

Vibrant brasserie dining near the university

In a stylish, contemporary space of chrome and glass, the cooking matches the modernity of the setting, delivering a genuine Irish flavour and some creative combinations. An opener of roast cauliflower and aged parmesan risotto is partnered with Ryan's Farm black pudding and tarragon, while another sees Portavogie crab paired with warm whiskey maple-cured salmon in a bouillabaisse. For mains, try roast duck breast with vanilla and butternut squash and an orange and port sauce or perhaps a crisp confit duck leg in poached Armagh pear with blue cheese and salted walnuts. To finish, choose from a range of desserts, or go savoury with the French and Irish cheeses.

Chef Chris Fearon **Seats** 120, Pr/dining room 44 **Times** 12-3/5.30-10, Closed 25-26 Dec, D Sun **Prices** Fixed L 2 course £17-£18, Fixed D 3 course £20, Starter £6.50-£9, Main £10.50-£20, Dessert £5-£6.50 **Wines** 17 bottles over £30, 24 bottles under £30, 12 by glass **Parking** On street **Notes** Prix fixe menu 3 course £20, Sunday L, Children welcome

Galgorm Resort & Spa

BALLYMENA **Map 1 D5**

Modern Irish V NOTABLE WINE LIST

tel: 028 2588 1001 **136 Fenaghy Rd, Galgorm BT42 1EA**
email: reservations@galgorm.com
web: www.galgorm.com
dir: *1m from Ballymena on A42, between Galgorm & Cullybackey*

Ambitious contemporary cooking and river views

Galgorm is a luxury hotel with the River Maine running through its 160-plus acres of glorious parkland, not far from the spectacular scenery of the north Antrim coast. There's a lot going on here, with extensive meetings, conference and wedding facilities, a number of spa and treatment areas, including a Thermal Village, a champagne and gin bar, a pub and live entertainment. The whole of the interior is beautifully furnished and decorated, and a glossy sheen of opulence hangs over the place, not least in the River Room Restaurant, where floor-to-ceiling windows look over the fast-flowing river, romantically floodlit after dark. The kitchen has at its disposal the estate's own kitchen garden, sourcing everything else from local artisan producers (listed on the menus), so seasonality is to the fore on the daily-changing menus. Canapés with drinks are a promising foretaste of what follows, borne out by well-considered starters such as sea trout céviche with radish, oyster, cucumber and buttermilk, or the earthier flavours of carpaccio with marrowbone, blue cheese and mushrooms. The kitchen's approach to its modern style rests on classical, well-honed techniques, with main courses thankfully not too cluttered, and combinations chosen with flavours in mind. Duck breast, for instance, is accompanied by a Madeira jus, Savoy cabbage and beetroot, and halibut fillet with beurre noisette, cockles, pearl barley and cauliflower. As to be expected in the context, a few luxuries can be spotted, with shavings of truffle added to humble potato and leek velouté with croûtons, and a textbook rendition of tournedos Rossini among main courses. Puddings maintain the kitchen's innovative approach, among them perhaps buttermilk pannacotta with rhubarb, elderflower, white chocolate and honeycomb, and chocolate delice with burnt citrus, passionfruit and pistachio nuts.

Chef Israel Robb, Jonnie Boyd **Seats** 50 **Times** 1-4/6.30-9.30, Closed Mon-Tue, L Wed-Sat **Prices** Tasting menu £55-£65, Starter £9-£10.50, Main £22-£27, Dessert £7.50-£8.50 **Wines** 200 bottles over £30, 54 bottles under £30, 12 by glass **Parking** 200 **Notes** Sunday L £27.95-£31.95, Children 12 yrs+

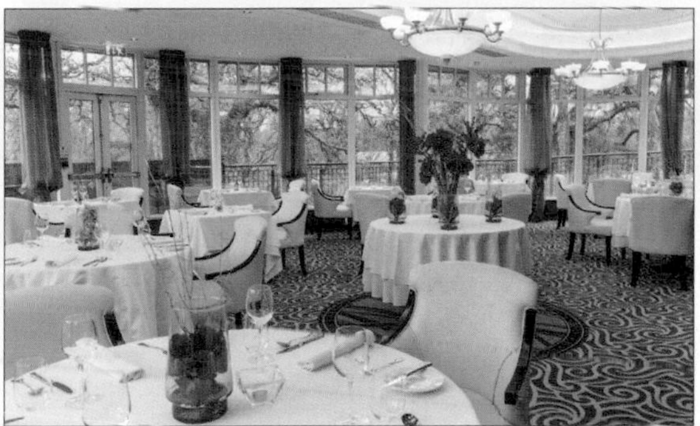

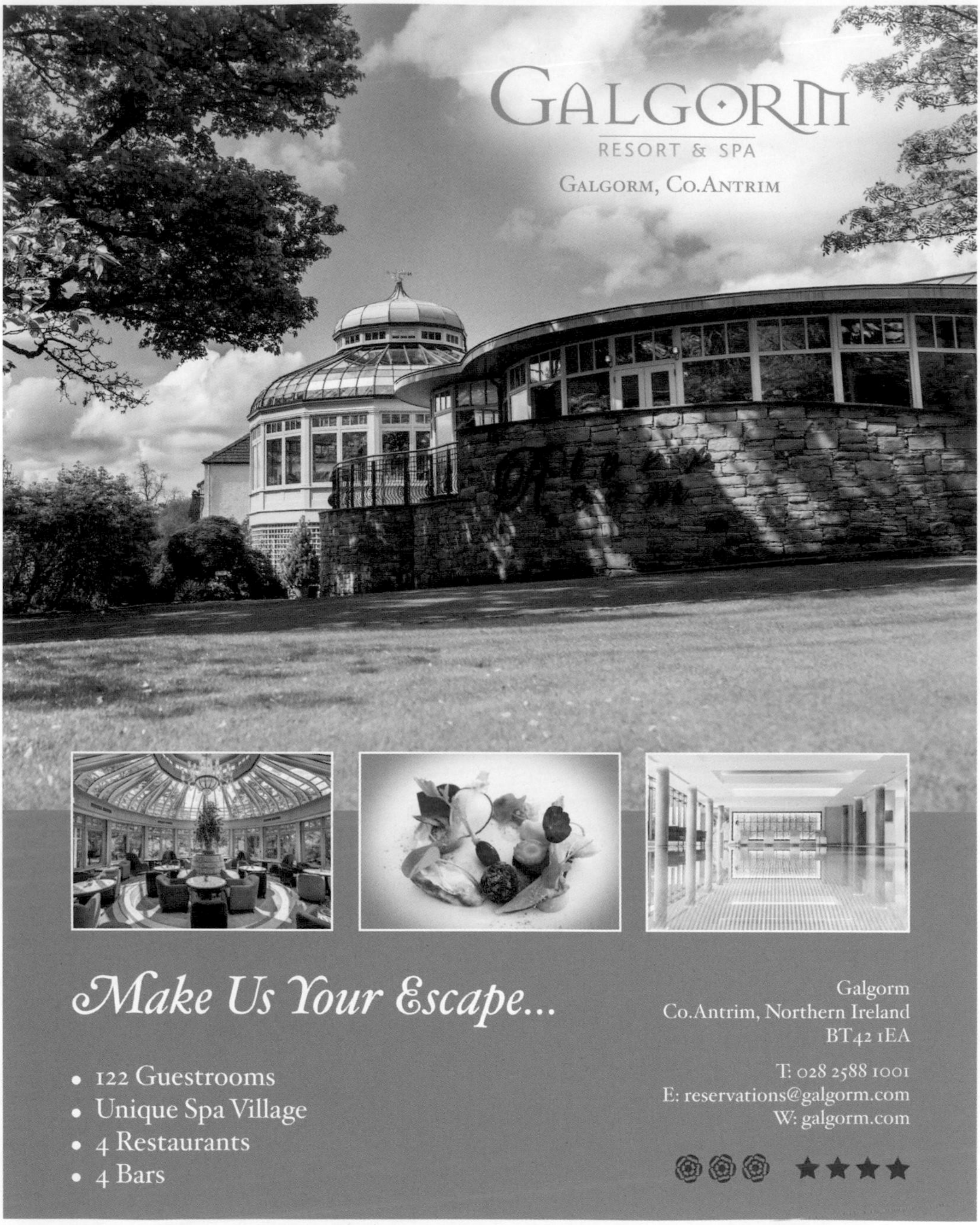
GALGORM
RESORT & SPA
GALGORM, CO.ANTRIM
Make Us Your Escape...
• 122 Guestrooms
• Unique Spa Village
• 4 Restaurants
• 4 Bars
Galgorm
Co.Antrim, Northern Ireland
BT42 1EA
T: 028 2588 1001
E: reservations@galgorm.com
W: galgorm.com

Deanes EIPIC

◎◎◎ Modern European V

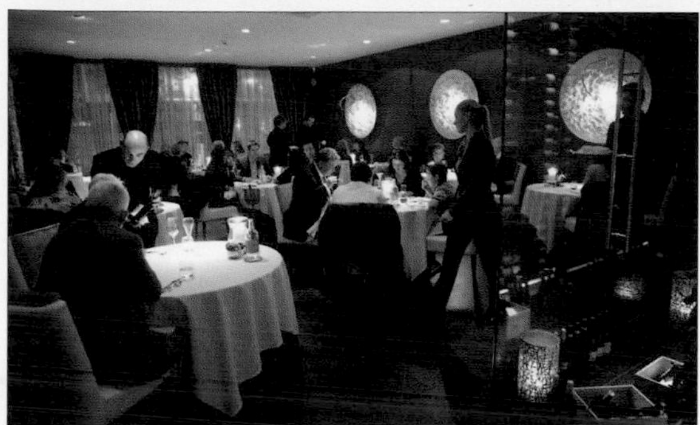

tel: 028 9033 1134 **36-40 Howard St BT1 6PF**
email: info@michaeldeane.co.uk
dir: *At rear of City Hall. Howard St on left opposite Spires building*

Classy and confident cooking chez Michael Deane

As well as EIPIC, restaurateur Michael Deane owns a chain of notable restaurants around the city (Deanes Meat Locker, Deanes Love Fish, Deanes Deli Bistro & Vin Café, Deanes At Queens and Deane & Decano), providing something that will appeal to all sectors of the community. This one is a high-flying sort of place, with a predominantly grey decor, upholstered dining chairs at clothed tables, heavy drapes at the windows and spotlights in the ceiling. Danni Barry heads up the stoves and she's the driving force behind some exciting, progressive cooking built on fresh local produce. Her set-price menus are sensibly short and to the point, opening with something straightforward like onion tart, or smoked haddock with parsley and potatoes. There's nothing too showy or highfalutin about the cooking, so flavours are clear and precise: BBQ pork fillet with cabbage, turnips and pickled mustard seeds, or haunch of venison with cocoa, Jerusalem artichoke and pickled cabbage. Accurate technique is a hallmark, seen notably in fish main courses, among them perhaps grilled monkfish with a meaty though delicate sauce based on a reduction of roast bones, accompanied by celeriac and leeks. To finish, poached rhubarb is imaginatively partnered by sweet cheese and pink peppercorns, or there might be rhubarb and buttermilk yogurt.

Chef Michael Deane, Danni Barry **Seats** 30, Pr/dining room 50
Times 12-3/5.30-10, Closed 18-27 Dec, 20-29 Mar, 10 Jul-2 Aug, Sun-Tue, L Wed-Thu, Sat **Prices** Fixed L 3 course £40-£60, Tasting menu £40-£60 **Wines** 76 bottles over £30, 25 bottles under £30, 8 by glass **Parking** On street (after 6pm), car park Clarence St **Notes** Children welcome

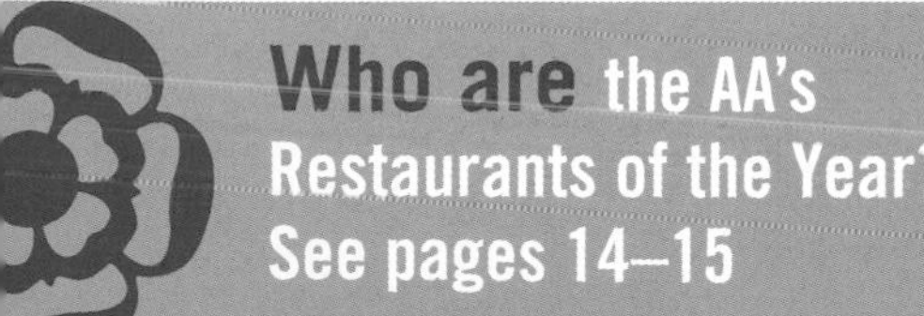

Who are the AA's Restaurants of the Year? See pages 14–15

James Street South Restaurant & Bar

◎◎ Modern European

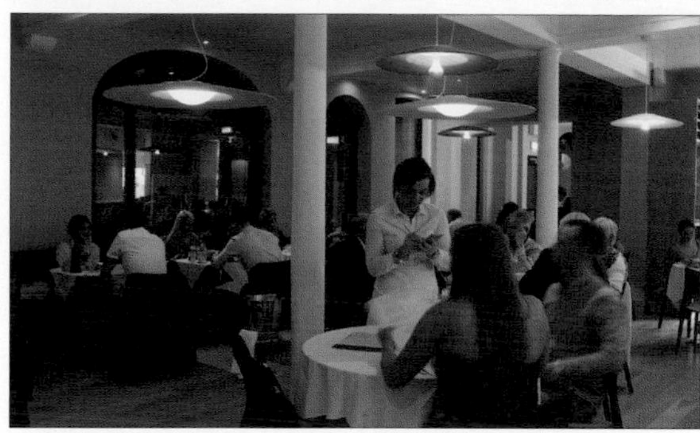

tel: 028 9043 4310 **21 James Street South BT2 7GA**
email: info@jamesstreetsouth.co.uk **web:** www.jamesstreetsouth.co.uk
dir: *Between Brunswick St & Bedford St*

Serious city-slicker cooking in a sharp venue

Tucked away behind City Hall, this capacious red-brick former linen mill makes a serene and understated setting for refined, French-accented food, as witnessed in a starter of coffee-roasted carrots pointed up with crème fraîche and tarragon vinegar caramel. Regional ingredients take a leading role, such as the local monkfish, John Dory and hake in a signature Irish Sea bouillabaisse, or the Baronscourt Estate venison that is partnered with turnip and a mushroom 'cottage pie'. Bargain lunch and pre- and post-theatre options keep things affordable, and there are tasting menus with matching wines if you're going for broke. To finish, dark chocolate and black cherries make an intense version of clafoutis.

Chef David Gillmore **Seats** 60, Pr/dining room 40
Times 12-2.45/5.45-10.45, Closed 1 Jan, Etr Mon, 12-15 Jul, 25-26 Dec, Sun, L Mon **Prices** Fixed L 2 course £15.50, Fixed D 3 course £18.50, Tasting menu £40-£70, Starter £4-£11, Main £15.50-£24, Dessert £4-£9.50 **Wines** 35 bottles over £30, 40 bottles under £30, 11 by glass **Parking** On street **Notes** Pre-theatre menu Mon-Sat 2/3 course, Vegetarian available, Children welcome

The Merchant Hotel

◎◎ Modern European

tel: 028 9023 4888 **16 Skipper St, Cathedral Quarter BT1 2DZ**
email: thegreatroom@merchanthotel.com **web:** www.themerchanthotel.com
dir: *In city centre, 2nd left at Albert clock onto Waring St. Hotel on left*

Magnificent grand setting for inventive contemporary cooking

The former headquarters of Ulster Bank is a grand building and these days the beneficiaries are those that rock up for lunch or dinner. The kitchen delivers a classical-meets-modern repertoire where tip-top regional produce is treated with respect. Portavogie lobster and scallops might provide the filling for first-course ravioli, paired with poached langoustine and shellfish bisque, while seared foie gras comes with fig marmalade, fresh almonds and brioche. Next up, perhaps seared wild venison loin with glazed chicory, roast swede and sour cherry marmalade, or roast cod fillet with white crab bonbon, buttered curly kale and salt-cod brandade. To finish, try Valrhona dark chocolate and peanut fondant with banana sorbet.

BELFAST *continued*

OX

Modern Irish

tel: 028 9031 4121 **1 Oxford St BT1 3LA**
email: info@oxbelfast.com
dir: *Near Queensbridge Beacon of Hope statue in Belfast city centre*

Skilful modern cooking in stunning riverside location

Overlooking the River Lagan in the heart of Belfast, OX is a collaboration between local boy Stephen Toman and Frenchman Alain Kerloc'h. The cooking's light, modern touch keeps things simple and fresh, as seen in a delicate starter of scallops, white bean bisque and lemongrass. A spring meal might feature a well-judged rump of Mourne lamb teamed with chicory, black olive and spinach, before ending with a wonderfully fresh jasmine crème brûlée with plum sorbet. For those diners eager to sample more dishes, the tasting menus – including one for vegetarians – are a popular choice for the table. A conscientiously chosen wine list adds gloss to this quality operation.

Chef Stephen Toman **Seats** 40 **Times** 12-2.30/6-9.30, Closed Last 2 wks Jul, Xmas, New Year, BHs, Sun-Mon **Prices** Fixed L 2 course £16, Tasting menu £45, Starter £8.50-£9.50, Main £15.50-£24, Dessert £7 **Wines** 43 bottles over £30, 18 bottles under £30, 12 by glass **Parking** Car park nearby **Notes** Tasting menu 5 course, Vegetarian available, Children welcome

Shu

 Modern Irish

tel: 028 9038 1655 **253-255 Lisburn Rd BT9 7EN**
email: eat@shu-restaurant.com
dir: *From city centre take Lisburn Rd (lower end). Restaurant in 1m, on corner of Lower Windsor Avenue*

Contemporary Irish cooking with a buzz and good service

Situated in a Victorian terrace, the airy space with an open-to-view kitchen is served by a smartly turned-out team. One or two dishes on the menu have an Asian flavour – witness a starter of salt-and-chilli squid served with classic dipping sauces of sweet chilli, wasabi mayonnaise, and soy, garlic and chilli. Otherwise, start with something like foie gras and chicken liver parfait with apple and chilli jelly, and toasted walnut and raisin bread. Main-course wood pigeon is scented with smoky Lapsang Souchong, and comes with celeriac purée, deep-fried kale, and beetroot. For pudding, vanilla cheesecake is matched with textures of blood orange and almond praline.

Chef Brian McCann **Seats** 100, Pr/dining room 24 **Times** 12-2.30/6-10, Closed 25-26 Dec, 1 Jan, 12-13 Jul, Sun **Prices** Fixed L 2 course £13.25, Fixed D 3 course £28, Tasting menu £45, Starter £4.75-£9, Main £12.50-£26.50, Dessert £6 **Wines** 33 bottles over £30, 45 bottles under £30, 21 by glass **Parking** 4, On street **Notes** Vegetarian available, Children welcome

COUNTY DOWN

BANGOR **Map 1 D5**

The Boathouse Restaurant

Modern International

tel: 028 9146 9253 **1a Seacliff Rd BT20 5HA**
email: info@theboathouseni.co.uk
dir: *Down Main St just after the marina & below the pier*

Inventive fusion cooking by the marina

Set across two floors of a stone-built Victorian harbourmaster's office, this diminutive marina restaurant continues to reel in roving gourmets from far and wide. Vaulted ceilings, local art on whitewashed stone walls and views of yachts bobbing outside add to the buzz of this vibrant place run by the Castel brothers. Dutch chef Joery Castel turns out bold European dishes that combine top-class local produce with displays of great technical skill, delivered via daily-changing menus inspired from far and wide. Things might get off the mark with a comforting crab thermidor comprising a crab croquette, Comte cheese, pickled mushroom, black truffle purée, rocket and wholegrain mustard, or perhaps pastrami-style wood pigeon, toasted hazelnut, plum, gingerbread toast, foie gras, pickled Jerusalem artichoke and cress. Next up, the influence may be from the Far East in the shape of a fragrant main of glazed pork belly, Malaysian-style steamed bun, cucumber, coriander, kumquat gel and spiced coconut, or plaice accompanied by salsify, wild mushrooms, lightly smoked potato mousseline and mushroom consommé. Dessert returns to the realms of fusion cooking with spiced pumpkin pannacotta, glazed walnuts, compressed apple, confit butternut squash and spiced biscotti, or a playful tonka bean rice pudding with cherries, sorrel and marshmallows.

Chef Joery Castel **Seats** 36 **Times** 12.30-2.30/5.30-9.30, Closed 1 Jan, Mon-Tue **Prices** Fixed L 2 course £12-£18, Fixed D 3 course £32.50-£35, Tasting menu £40-£50, Starter £5-£8.50, Main £9.50-£20, Dessert £5-£9 **Wines** 23 bottles over £30, 18 bottles under £30, 10 by glass **Parking** Public car park **Notes** Sunday L £12.50-£15.50, Vegetarian available, Children welcome

COMBER **Map 1 D5**

The Old Schoolhouse Inn

Modern British NEW V

tel: 028 9754 1182 **100 Ballydrain Rd BT23 6EA**
email: info@theoldschoolhouseinn.com **web:** www.theoldschoolhouseinn.com
dir: *Phone for directions*

Lively modern Irish inspiration by the Lough

Ensconced in the Down countryside by Strangford Lough, The Old Schoolhouse turns out modern cooking that's full of lively inspiration. Seafood is a strong suit, perhaps for crab with a smoked mackerel fishcake, beetroot and apple, or in scallops teamed with pork belly, Alsace bacon and butter beans. Duck from a local farm is served as breast and a roll of confit leg and shredded potato, with creamed cabbage and puréed carrot aromatised with star anise, while mussels are given a main-course marinière spin with Armagh cider, shallots and buckwheat. The signature dessert is high-powered chocolate marquise with intense vanilla ice cream, cocoa nibs and honeycomb.

Chef Will Brown **Seats** 50, Pr/dining room 30 **Times** 12-10.30, All-day dining, Closed Mon **Prices** Fixed L 2 course fr £14.95, Fixed D 3 course fr £18.95, Tasting menu fr £45 **Wines** 26 bottles over £30, 27 bottles under £30, 11 by glass **Parking** 30 **Notes** Wine & Dine 3 course Wed-Fri £55 per couple, Sunday L £20-£25, Children welcome

CRAWFORDSBURN Map 1 D5

The Old Inn

Modern European

tel: 028 9185 3255 **15 Main St BT19 1JH**
email: info@theoldinn.com **web:** www.theoldinn.com
dir: *From Belfast along A2, past Belfast City Airport. Continue past Holywood & Belfast Folk & Transport museum. 2m after museum left at lights onto B20 for 1.2m*

Revamped restaurant in a historical old inn

A busy dining venue, drawing people with its decor and its modern European-style cooking built on prime local produce. Scallops, as fresh as can be, are served with no more than wilted salad and mayonnaise to make a delightful starter, or there might be the earthier flavours of Clonakilty black pudding with crispy pancetta, a poached egg and roast tomatoes. Timings are impeccable, seen in chicken breast with artichokes, root vegetables and a well-considered sauce, and monkfish dusted in black olives with chorizo, spinach and sunblush tomato fettuccine. Canapés and breads are of a standard, as are puddings along the lines of chocolate delice with salted caramel ice cream.

DUNDRUM Map 1 D5

Mourne Seafood Bar

Seafood

tel: 028 4375 1377 **10 Main St BT33 0LU**
email: bob@mourneseafood.com
dir: *On main road from Belfast to The Mournes, on village main street*

Fresh fish and shellfish at the foot of the Mourne mountains

With a sister establishment in Belfast, the Dundrum branch of Mourne Seafood is in a refreshingly peaceful location. At the foot of the Mourne mountains, with a nature reserve close by, it's dedicated, of course, to fish and shellfish, much of which comes from the proprietors' own seafood beds. The daily-changing menu offers its wares in a broad range of styles, from scallops in linguine with wilted greens and chilli-garlic oil to start, and then temptations such as smoked haddock with a potato cake, creamed leeks and a soft-poached egg. If you're not of the fish persuasion, look to grilled chicken breast with asparagus and mushroom risotto.

Chef Cally Colleran **Seats** 75, Pr/dining room 20 **Times** 12.30-9.30, All-day dining, Closed 25 Dec, Mon-Thu (winter) **Prices** Starter £4-£7, Main £9-£16, Dessert £4.50 **Wines** 6 bottles over £30, 12 bottles under £30, 5 by glass **Parking** On street **Notes** Fixed D menu Sat only, Sunday L £6-£18, Vegetarian available, Children welcome

NEWCASTLE Map 1 D5

Brunel's Restaurant at The Anchor Bar

Modern Irish

tel: 028 4372 3951 **9 Bryansford Rd BT33 0HJ**
email: reservations@brunelsrestaurant.co.uk
dir: *Top of Main St, follow road to right. Restaurant immediately on right above The Anchor Bar, accessed via red front door*

Modern Irish brasserie food with bracing sea views

Brunel's is a first-floor venue above the ever-popular Anchor Bar, just off the Newcastle seafront. Craft beers and a decent wine list are among the attractions, the star turn being the modern Irish brasserie food, with seafood a trump card. Start with butter-poached langoustines and roast carrots, garnished with buttermilk froth and gingerbread crumb, and follow perhaps with roast coley and chorizo risotto, with capers and pine nuts in a sherry dressing. Rump of Mourne mountain lamb is a fine cut that doesn't need the distraction of hazelnut purée, but gains from its accompaniments of sea beets and samphire. Chocolate fondant comes with the sharpening touch of black cherry sorbet.

NEWTOWNARDS Map 1 D5

Balloo House

Modern British

tel: 028 9754 1210 **1 Comber Rd, Killinchy BT23 6PA**
email: info@balloohouse.com **web:** www.balloohouse.com
dir: *A22 from Belfast, through Dundonald, 6m from Comber*

Lively bistro and serene dining room in a venerable old house

A major refurbishment in late 2014 accentuated Balloo House's original historical features, while the additions of darkwood panelling and peacock-blue and tan leather booth seating create an intimate atmosphere. When it comes to the menu, the roast Kilmore pigeon, apple & celeriac remoulade, hazelnut and red wine vinegrette gets the ball rolling, before moving on to Finnebrogue venison liver with a creamy mash and crispy onions or, perhaps, Portavogie prawn stuffed sole, potato gnocchi, wilted spinach and watercress veloute. Dessert might be cranberry bakewell with salted orange caramel and gingerbread ice cream or a chocolate panacotta with passionfruit sorbet, curd and chocolate tuile.

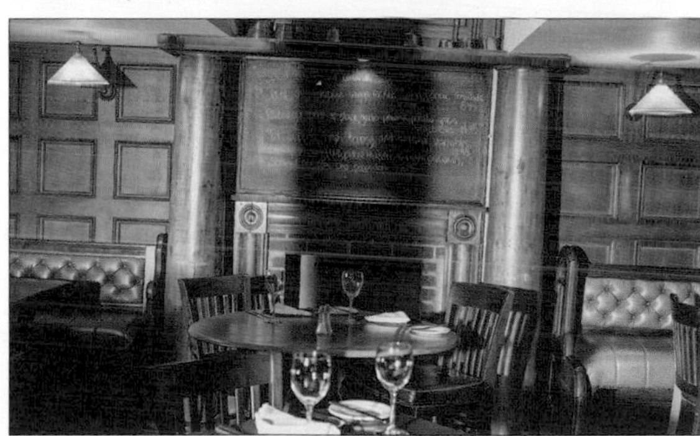

Chef Danny Millar, Grainne Donnelly **Seats** 80, Pr/dining room 30 **Times** 12-9, All-day dining, Closed 25 Dec **Prices** Fixed L 2 course £14.95, Fixed D 3 course fr £18.95, Starter £3.25-£6.95, Main £10.95-£24.95, Dessert £3.50-£6.95 **Wines** 15 bottles over £30, 45 bottles under £30, 9 by glass **Parking** 60 **Notes** Sunday L £22.95, Vegetarian available, Children welcome

COUNTY FERMANAGH

ENNISKILLEN Map 1 C5

Lough Erne Resort

Modern, Traditional V 

tel: 028 6632 3230 **Belleek Rd BT93 7ED**
email: info@lougherneresort.com **web:** www.lougherneresort.com
dir: *A46 from Enniskillen towards Donegal, hotel in 3m*

Dynamic modern Irish cooking at a luxury resort hotel

In an absolutely stunning location on Lough Erne, set expansively in 60 acres on its own peninsula, this is a truly indulgent five-star treat. From the golf course (due to be home to the 2017 Irish Open) to the Thai spa to the restaurant, there's no messing around at this purpose-built hotel. Fine dining takes place in the spacious, vaulted Catalina restaurant with views across the lough and golf course. Noel McMeel's kitchen is working at the top of its game, producing thoughtful, exuberant modern Irish cuisine. Vegetarians will be delighted with their own menu, and the standard à la carte is just as considered. A starter of Liscanner crab comes with equally local scallop, from Ballycastle, Rathlin Island seaweed, samphire, and fresh lemon curd. Mains might include rump of Glenhoy lamb with potato and onion gratin, black garlic, grape and red wine mustard, carrot purée and red wine jus, or the signature Lough Erne Pork Dish – fillet of pork, pork cheek, ham hock, black pudding palmier and pork belly. Have a lemon tart with raspberry sorbet and croquant tuile to finish, or creamed rice pudding with poached plums and white chocolate ice cream, or else choose from the cheese menu.

Chef Noel McMeel **Seats** 75, Pr/dining room 30 **Times** 1-2.30/6.30-10, Closed L Mon-Sat **Prices** Fixed D 3 course £45, Tasting menu £75 **Wines** 70 bottles over £30, 36 bottles under £30, 13 by glass **Parking** 200 **Notes** Sunday L £19.50-£24, Children welcome

Manor House Country Hotel

Irish, European

tel: 028 6862 2200 **Killadeas BT94 1NY**
email: info@manorhousecountryhotel.com **web:** www.manorhousecountryhotel.com
dir: *On B82, 7m N of Enniskillen*

Contemporary cooking and lough views

The colonel who rebuilt this old manor in the 1860s brought craftsmen over from Italy to spruce up the interior, evidence of which can still be seen. The fine-dining action takes place in the Belleek Restaurant, housed in a conservatory extension that gets the very best of the view of the lough. The menu has a genuine local flavour and a contemporary European spin, as seen in seared Donegal Bay scallops with gremolata and a parsnip and vanilla purée, or roast rack of Fermanagh lamb partnered with lemon-glazed sweetbreads and colcannon. Sunday lunch is a traditional affair, while desserts are a creative bunch.

Chef Rory Carville **Seats** 90, Pr/dining room 350 **Times** 12.30-3/6-10, Closed L Mon-Fri, D Sun **Prices** Prices not confirmed **Wines** 20 bottles over £30, 40 bottles under £30 **Parking** 300 **Notes** Sunday L, Vegetarian available, Children welcome

COUNTY LONDONDERRY

LIMAVADY Map 1 C6

The Lime Tree

Traditional Mediterranean

tel: 028 7776 4300 **60 Catherine St BT49 9DB**
email: info@limetreerest.com
dir: *Enter Limavady from Derry side. Restaurant on right on small slip road*

Long-running restaurant showcasing the pick of the province

The Lime Tree is a pint-sized neighbourhood restaurant in the town centre, its simply painted walls hung with vibrant artwork. Main courses have taken in seafood thermidor (nuggets of plaice, monk, salmon, hake and cod in a rich cheese and brandy sauce) and fillets of lemon sole stuffed with crabmeat in creamy chive sauce, preceded perhaps by a signature starter of crab cakes. Meat-eaters, meanwhile, can choose chicken liver pâté with Cumberland sauce, then duck confit cut by classic orange sauce served with champ. Themed evenings, such as Spanish, are successes, and puddings can be as decadent as gooey chocolate brownie with creamy vanilla ice cream and chocolate sauce.

Chef Stanley Matthews **Seats** 30 **Times** 12-1.30/5.30-9, Closed 25-26 Dec, 12 Jul, Sun-Mon, L Sun-Wed **Prices** Fixed L 2 course fr £10, Fixed D 3 course £20-£25, Starter £4.75-£7.95, Main £17-£22.50, Dessert £5.50-£5.95 **Wines** 8 bottles over £30, 24 bottles under £30, 5 by glass **Parking** On street **Notes** Early bird menu 2/3 course 5.30-7pm £17.50-£20, Vegetarian available, Children welcome

Roe Park Resort

Modern, Traditional

tel: 028 7772 2222 **BT49 9LB**
email: reservations@roeparkresort.com **web:** www.roeparkresort.com
dir: *On A6 (Londonderry-Limavady road), 0.5m from Limavady. 8m from Derry airport*

Traditional dining in a relaxed resort hotel

Built as a country mansion in the 18th century and surrounded by 150 acres of grounds beside the River Roe, Roe Park has been extended into a vast modern golfing and leisure resort. Just one of several dining options here, Greens Restaurant is a stylish, split-level space offering mostly traditional cooking with the odd modern twist. Start with duck liver and pistachio pâté with rosemary brioche and tomato chutney, moving on to marinated lamb rump with Puy lentil ragoût, vegetable rondelles and mint jus. Puddings take the comfort route with warm chocolate brownie pie served with vanilla ice cream and chocolate sauce.

Chef Frank Kivlehan **Seats** 160, Pr/dining room 50 **Times** 12-3/6.30-9 **Prices** Prices not confirmed **Wines** 8 by glass **Parking** 250 **Notes** Sunday L, Vegetarian available, Children welcome

LONDONDERRY Map 1 C5

Browns Restaurant and Champagne Lounge

Modern Irish V

tel: 028 7134 5180 **1 Bonds Hill, Waterside BT47 6DW**
email: eat@brownsrestaurant.com
dir: *Phone for directions*

On-the-money modern Irish cooking

Situated on the edge of the city centre by Lough Foyle, Browns has built a local following since 2009. Get in the mood with some bubbly in the champagne lounge, then head for one of the white linen-swathed tables in the sleek, contemporary dining room. The kitchen turns out an appealing roll call of modern Irish ideas, with fish and seafood strong suits. Scallop mousse could appear with leek, smoked caviar and polenta, ahead of roast fillet of monkfish matched with crispy chicken, curried cream sauce and samphire. To finish, the flavours of orange, tarragon and bergamot put an intriguing spin on custard tart.

Chef Ian Orr **Seats** 60 **Times** 12-3/5.30-10, Closed 3 days Xmas, Mon, L Sat, D Sun **Prices** Fixed L 2 course £12-£14.95, Fixed D 3 course £21.95-£24.90, Tasting menu £40-£65 **Wines** 42 bottles over £30, 62 bottles under £30, 14 by glass **Parking** On street **Notes** Tasting menu 6 course, Early bird £21.95 Tue-Sat, Sunday L £17.95-£24.90, Children welcome

MAGHERA Map 1 C5

Ardtara Country House

Irish NEW V

tel: 028 7964 4490 **8 Gorteade Rd BT46 5SA**
web: www.ardtara.com
dir: *Phone for directions*

Country-house dining with a local flavour

Built in the 19th century by a linen magnate, Ardtara is a country-house hotel set in glorious grounds. It's a particularly engaging spot for afternoon tea on a warm day, and the restaurant, with its real fireplaces and oak panels, is a smart backdrop for the bright, contemporary cooking on offer. A local flavour is ensured by the use of home-grown and locally foraged ingredients. A starter of tender pork belly arrives with piccalilli to cut through its inherent richness, and is followed by hake served in the company of Portavogie prawns and a light champagne sauce. To finish, passionfruit soufflé shows a touch of class.

Chef Ian Orr **Seats** 50, Pr/dining room 25 **Times** 12-3/5-9, Closed 25-26 Dec **Prices** Prices not confirmed **Notes** Sunday L, Children welcome

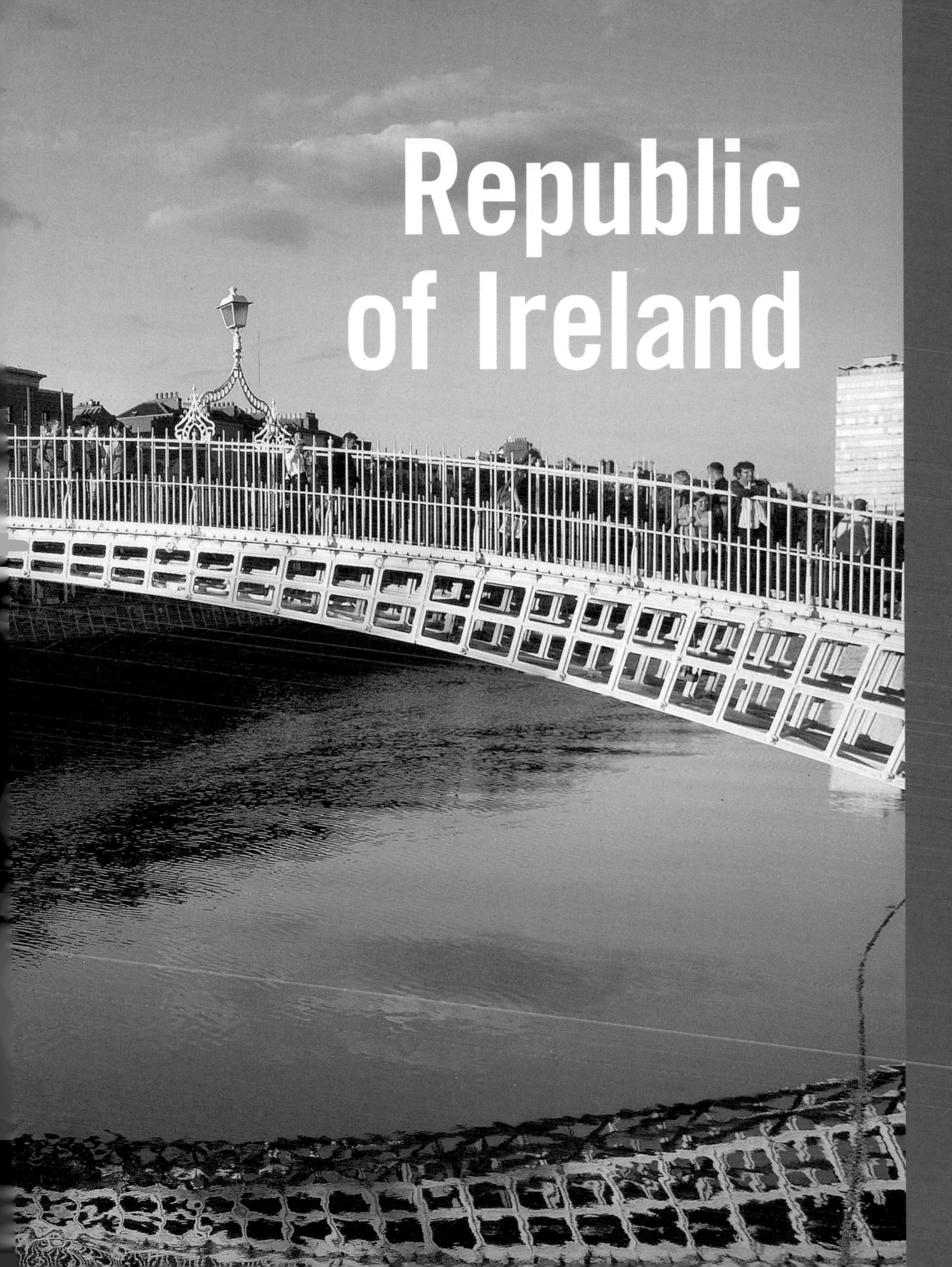

Republic of Ireland

COUNTY CARLOW

BORRIS Map 1 C3

1808 Brasserie

Modern British NEW

tel: 059 9773209 **Step House Hotel, Main St**
email: info@stephousehotel.ie **web:** www.stephousehotel.ie
dir: *M50 exit 9 to Kildare. M9 to R448 in Carlow. M9 exit 6. R705 to R702. On left*

Impressive local food and Georgian comforts

This Georgian mansion has morphed into a swish hotel with a brasserie, which despite its subterranean location actually looks over the gardens. Dining on the terrace is also an option, weather permitting. The menu is a tribute to local produce and follows the seasons with mainly British-influenced dishes. A fish plate with tempura of sole with chilli jam, pineapple salsa, cured trout, lemon and lime emulsion, potted Kilmore crab and croûte opens the show, then roast breast of chicken, twice-cooked leg of chicken with butternut squash and thyme purée served with a truffle-scented pomme mousseline. To finish, mango parfait, raspberries, honeycomb and raspberry sorbet.

Times 12.30-close, All-day dining **Prices** Starter €6-€10, Main €15-€27, Dessert €6-€7 **Notes** Early bird Mon-Fri 5-7.30pm 2/3 course €22/€27, Sunday L €21-€27

LEIGHLINBRIDGE Map 1 C3

Lord Bagenal Inn

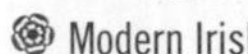
Modern Irish

tel: 059 9774000 **Main St**
email: info@lordbagenal.com **web:** www.lordbagenal.com
dir: *M9 junct 6, R448 left onto R705, hotel on right*

Unpretentious dining in a riverside hotel

Back in 1979, the original roadside restaurant was almost killed off by the advent of a new motorway, but the enterprising owners built a hotel on the site. The place is distinctly contemporary these days, with its Signature Restaurant and bar revamped to create an open-plan space with darkwood tables and modern artworks on the exposed brick walls. The menu covers the globe to offer up local Duncannon crab with fennel and chilli alongside crisp hoisin duck wrap among first courses, before classic fish and chips, chicken curry with rice and poppadum, or pan-seared venison partnered with braised red cabbage.

Chef Shein Than, George Kehoe **Seats** 85, Pr/dining room 60
Times 12-2.30/6-9.30, Closed 25-26 Dec **Wines** 70 bottles over €30, 30 bottles under €30, 8 by glass **Parking** 100 **Notes** Sunday L €25-€30, Vegetarian available, Children welcome

TULLOW Map 1 C3

Mount Wolseley Hotel, Spa & Country Club

Modern European

tel: 059 9180100 & 9151674
email: info@mountwolseley.ie **web:** www.mountwolseley.ie
dir: *N7 from Dublin. In Naas, take N9 towards Carlow. In Castledermot left for Tullow*

Modern Irish cooking on an ancestral estate

The Wolseleys of Staffordshire came to Ireland in the 17th century and fought on King William's side in 1690. In keeping with the chic surroundings, the place encompasses a stylish split-level dining room overlooking a garden courtyard, where smartly attired staff attend at equally well turned-out tables. Seafood is a forte, as is demonstrated by a starter of gin-cured salmon with pickled cucumber and a wasabi and cucumber emulsion. Meatier appetites are assuaged by a main course of roast chicken breast with butternut squash purée, fondant potato, and chorizo and barley jus. Finish with the signature lemon posset, served alongside confit orange and shortbread.

COUNTY CAVAN

CAVAN Map 1 C4

Cavan Crystal Hotel

Modern Irish NEW

tel: 049 4360600 **Dublin Rd**
email: info@cavancrystalhotel.com **web:** www.cavancrystalhotel.com
dir: *On outskirts of Cavan town, N3, straight over rdbt, hotel immediately on left*

A crystal manufacturer's modern eatery

Sharing the same site as its factory, Ireland's second oldest crystal manufacturer also has a smart contemporary hotel, a leisure club and the clean-lined Opus One restaurant. It's a relaxed spot done out with hardwood floors, buttoned banquettes and food that chimes in tune with the setting: confident, modern and uncomplicated. Smoked salmon roulade stuffed with crabmeat and served with a baby leaf salad and capers is a simple opening gambit that works well, before pan-fried hake partnered with salsify purée and confit, and champagne cream sauce. Dessert offers the familiar comforts of apple crumble with crème anglaise and vanilla ice cream.

Chef Dolores Reilly **Times** 12.30-3.30/6-9.30, Closed Mon-Thu, L Fri-Sat, D Sun **Prices** Fixed D 3 course €30 **Notes** Sunday L

Radisson Blu Farnham Estate Hotel

European, Modern International

tel: 049 4377700 **Farnham Estate**
email: info.farnham@radissonblu.com **web:** www.farnhamestate.com
dir: *From Dublin take N3 to Cavan. From Cavan take Killeshandra road for 4km*

Irish produce, French-influenced cooking

With lakes, rivers and ancient oak forests all over the 1,300-acre, 16th-century estate, it's easy to work up an appetite at this historic stately home that is now an upmarket country hotel. Clever use of plush drapes and screens softens the capacious space of the Botanica Restaurant, and the kitchen treats local ingredients with French-inspired flair. Spicy tiger prawns, orange and dill-infused salmon, and smoked mackerel rillettes make up a seafood platter, then roast rack and slow-cooked rump of local lamb is delivered with aubergine caviar and buttery potato mash. Dessert could be a riff on lemon, in the shape of a zesty tart, madeleines, and jelly.

COUNTY CLARE

BALLYVAUGHAN Map 1 B3

Gregans Castle

Modern Irish, European

tel: 065 7077005
email: stay@gregans.ie **web:** www.gregans.ie
dir: *On N67, 5km S of Ballyvaughan village*

Outstanding contemporary food at a little house in The Burren

The distinctive limestone rock of The Burren creates something of the look of a lunar landscape, and Ireland's smallest National Park makes an impressive backdrop for this luxurious Georgian country-house hotel. The magical setting inspired Tolkein and C S Lewis by all accounts. It's not a 'castle', but it is a charming creeper-covered house in neat gardens with views to Galway Bay. Well-turned out staff look after proceedings in the smart, formal restaurant, where daylight views stretch across to the bay and candles flicker on elegantly dressed tables in the evening. It's a captivating setting for the pin-sharp contemporary cooking of David Hurley, with the food on the plate matching the view for visual impact. Barbecued smoked eel arrives as a starter with textures of Jerusalem artichoke and apple, or go for the luxe lobster raviolo with fennel salad and toast consommé. Regional ingredients figure large on a menu that puts together wild local rabbit with a boudin of the slow-cooked leg meat, plus black pudding, variations of carrot, and a chanterelle jus. Local seafood figures large, too – pan-roasted halibut with glazed chicken and leek, say – and, to finish, a blackcurrant soufflé comes with sorbet, compôte, and a wee jug of warm buttermilk custard.

Chef David Hurley **Seats** 50, Pr/dining room 30 **Times** 6-9, Closed Nov-mid Feb, Sun, Wed (ex Sun BHs), L all week **Prices** Fixed D 3 course €72 **Wines** 58 bottles over €30, 14 bottles under €30, 11 by glass **Parking** 20 **Notes** Vegetarian available, Children 7 yrs+

DOOLIN Map 1 B3

Cullinan's Seafood Restaurant & Guest House

Modern French

el: 065 7074183
mail: info@cullinansdoolin.com **web:** www.cullinansdoolin.com
ir: *In Doolin town centre R479*

rtistically presented seafood and meat by the River Aille

n an unquestionably charming setting, chef-proprietor James Cullinan's skilful rench-influenced modern cooking might bring forth a rich and creamy chowder, ollowed by butter-roasted hake topped with gremolata, and matched with sparagus fricassée, mussels and scallion, and smoked haddock velouté. If you're noving on to meat for main, you might encounter roasted rack and mini shepherd's ie of superlative Burren lamb, served with baby peas, roast garlic and thyme jus, r Irish beef fillet with beer-braised onions, mushroom duxelles, French beans and a urgundy wine reduction. Finish self-indulgently with a choc-fest trio of chocolate, range and pistachio marquise, chocolate millefeuille and ice cream.

ENNIS Map 1 B3

Legends Restaurant

Modern International NEW V

tel: 065 6823300 **Temple Gate Hotel, The Square**
email: info@templegatehotel.com **web:** www.templegatehotel.com
dir: *Exit N18 onto Tulla Rd for 0.25m, hotel on left*

Assured cooking in a former convent

Set in a former convent, the fine dining restaurant of the Temple Gate Hotel is an impressive space with its soaring hammerbeam roof and striking contemporary decor. There's a capable hand in the kitchen, and daily specials mean that seasonal produce is well represented. A starter of goats' cheese tartlet with roast peppers, squash, smoked salmon, basil and pine nuts is a little over-elaborate, and it's the simpler ideas that work best – the likes of beef sirloin with glazed shallots and green peppercorn sauce, and Baileys-filled profiteroles with butterscotch sauce for dessert.

Chef Paul Shortt **Seats** 100, Pr/dining room 60
Times 12.30-2.30/6-9.30, Closed 25-26 Dec **Prices** Prices not confirmed **Wines** 7 bottles over €30, 10 bottles under €30, 6 by glass **Parking** 50 **Notes** Early bird menu, Sunday L, Children welcome

LAHINCH Map 1 B3

Moy House

Modern French V

tel: 065 7082800
email: moyhouse@eircom.net **web:** www.moyhouse.com
dir: *1km from Lahinch on Miltown Malbay road*

Seasonal cooking with panoramic views of the bay

Standing proud in 15 acres of grounds overlooking the bay at Lahinch, Moy House is full of period character, though the dining room with its minimalist chandeliers and panoramic views is more contemporary. As is the food, which draws on unimpeachable local supply lines for five-course seasonal dinner menus. First up might be goats' cheese agnolotti with rainbow chard, pine nuts and raisins, with a fish course of poached fillet of hake with coconut and garam masala, followed by pan-roast fillet of Irish beef, shallot purée, asparagus and girolles. Pear tarte Tatin with clotted cream is a satisfying ending.

Chef Matthew Strefford **Seats** 35, Pr/dining room 22 **Times** 7-8.30, Closed Nov-Mar, Sun-Mon (off peak) **Prices** Tasting menu €60 **Wines** 4 bottles under €30, 4 by glass **Parking** 50 **Notes** Fixed D 5 course €60 (reservation req), Children welcome

LISDOONVARNA Map 1 B3

Sheedy's Country House Hotel

Modern Irish

tel: 065 7074026
email: info@sheedys.com **web:** www.sheedys.com
dir: *20m from Ennis on N87*

Flavour-led cooking in a small rural hotel

This small-scale country-house hotel exudes the sort of family-run, unpretentious tradition that keeps fans returning. John Sheedy has long-established local supply lines, and the kitchen garden provides fresh herbs and vegetables to supplement local organic meat and fish landed at nearby Doolin. Expect full-on, clearly defined flavours in a repertoire of uncomplicated modern dishes, such as crab claws in garlic and parsley cream, or ham hock terrine with celeriac and apple slaw, followed by baked fillets of hake on chive sauce with crab and leeks, or caramelised belly pork with cider sauce and mushroom mash. Classic lemon posset with fruit is a house speciality.

Chef John Sheedy **Seats** 28 **Times** 6.30-8.30, Closed mid Oct-mid Mar, 1 day a wk (Mar-Apr) **Prices** Starter €9.50-€12.50, Main €20-€29, Dessert €7.80-€8.50 **Wines** 10 bottles over €30, 8 bottles under €30, 2 by glass **Parking** 25 **Notes** Vegetarian available, Children 8 yrs+

Wild Honey Inn

Modern Irish, French

tel: 065 7074300 **Kincora**
email: info@wildhoneyinn.com **web:** www.wildhoneyinn.com
dir: *N18 from Ennis to Ennistymon. Continue through N67 from Ennistymon towards Lisdoonvarna, on right at edge of town*

Simple cooking done right

Wild Honey has been around since 1860, and despite a smart contemporary makeover, this family-run inn oozes character. Driven by the splendid larder of the rugged West Coast, the culinary emphasis is on wild, free-range and seasonal ingredients. The kitchen delivers well-defined flavours, whether it's a starter of scallops with crispy chicken wings, roasted carrots and carrot purée, or wild halibut served with cockles and mussels, peas, broad beans, and fennel velouté. Meatier fare might run to marinated lamb neck fillet with pearl barley, root vegetables, wild garlic, and red wine jus, while desserts such as warm toffee pudding with toffee sauce and salted caramel ice cream complete the picture.

Chef Aidan McGrath **Seats** 50, Pr/dining room 40 **Times** 5.30-9, Closed Nov-Feb, Tue **Prices** Fixed L 2 course €35-€45, Fixed D 2 course €70-€80, Starter €7-€11.90, Main €19.10-€27.90, Dessert €8.50 **Wines** 42 bottles over €30, 11 bottles under €30, 6 by glass **Notes** Restricted opening Oct & Mar-Apr, Vegetarian available, Children 12 yrs+

NEWMARKET-ON-FERGUS Map 1 B3

Dromoland Castle Hotel

Traditional Irish, European V

tel: 061 368144
email: sales@dromoland.ie **web:** www.dromoland.ie
dir: *From Ennis take N18, follow signs for Shannon/Limerick. 7m follow Quin. Newmarket-on-Fergus sign. Hotel 0.5m. From Shannon take N18 towards Ennis*

Classical haute cuisine in a spectacular castle

As well as a golf course and spa, you'll find turrets and ramparts at this fabulous country-house hotel. Formal dining takes place in the Earl of Thomond restaurant, a spectacular room filled with antiques, oak-panelled period character and a resident harpist. The cooking fits the bill with its unmistakably French accent and top-notch produce, from the estate and local suppliers. Service is formal and everything looks wonderful on the plate. You might start with wild mushroom and celeriac risotto and then perhaps try the roast wild duck breast with apple and vegetable quinoa and calvados sauce. Opt for a brown bread soufflé with Bailey's ice cream to finish.

Chef David McCann **Seats** 80, Pr/dining room 40 **Times** 7-10, Closed L all week (ex private bookings) **Prices** Tasting menu €90-€130, Starter €15-€18, Main €34-€38, Dessert €10-€16 **Wines** 184 bottles over €30, 7 bottles under €30, 6 by glass **Parking** 140 **Notes** Priority/Group L can be booked, Children welcome

COUNTY CORK

BALLINGEARY Map 1 B2

Gougane Barra Hotel

Irish, French

tel: 026 47069 **Gougane Barra**
email: info@gouganebarrahotel.com **web:** www.gouganebarrahotel.com
dir: *Off R584 between N22 at Macroom & N71 at Bantry. Take Keimaneigh junct for hotel*

Tried-and-true country cooking in hauntingly beautiful setting

The Cronin family has owned property in hauntingly beautiful Gougane Barra since Victorian times, when its potential as an idyllic retreat was first fully realised, though the present hotel dates back to the 1930s. Those views over the lake towards the mountains of Cork look especially magnificent from the ample windows of the dining room, where fine seasonal artisan produce takes centre stage. There are no airs and graces on a menu that runs from grilled Clonakilty black pudding with Bramley apple purée and crispy bacon, to grilled local sirloin steak or monkfish with scallops and seafood chowder.

Chef Katy Lucey **Seats** 70 **Times** 12.30-2.30/6-8.30, Closed 20 Oct-10 Apr **Prices** Fixed L 2 course €23.70-€33.10, Fixed D 3 course €29.95-€40.60, Starter €6.25-€8.15, Main €17.45-€24.95, Dessert €6.25-€7.50 **Wines** 7 bottles over €30, 28 bottles under €30, 6 by glass **Parking** 40 **Notes** Pre-theatre menu 3 course €29.95, Sunday L €23.70-€29.95, Vegetarian available, Children welcome

BALLYLICKEY Map 1 B2

Seaview House Hotel

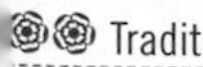 Traditional V

tel: 027 50073 & 50462
email: info@seaviewhousehotel.com web: www.seaviewhousehotel.com
dir: *3m N of Bantry towards Glengarriff, 70yds off main road, N71*

Polished cooking in a smart country-house hotel

The grand white-painted Seaview has the promised vista over Bantry Bay, glimpsed through the trees in the pretty gardens, while the restaurant comprises three rooms including a conservatory. There's much local produce on the menu – crabs out of the bay, lamb from west Cork – and everything is handled with care. Start with a light and flavourful scallop mousse, served with a vermouth sauce and topped with the scallop roe. Next up, a superb piece of sole, grilled on the bone, which is removed before service, and partnered with a caper butter served in a pot, plus mashed potatoes, wilted spinach, broccoli and cauliflower.

Chef Damian O'Sullivan **Seats** 50 **Times** 12.30-1.45/7-9.30, Closed Nov-Mar, L Mon-Sat **Prices** Fixed D 3 course €35-€40, Starter €5-€7.50, Main €17.50-€22.50, Dessert €6.50 **Wines** 10 by glass **Parking** 32 **Notes** Sunday L €30, Children welcome

BALTIMORE Map 1 B1

Rolf's Country House

French, European

tel: 028 20289
email: info@rolfscountryhouse.com web: www.rolfscountryhouse.com
dir: *Into Baltimore, sharp left, follow restaurant signs, up hill*

Regional produce in a heavenly spot

Set in beautiful sub-tropical gardens overlooking Baltimore Harbour to Roaringwater Bay and Carbery's 100 islands, it is hardly surprising that the Haffner family have put down roots at their delightful 10-room hotel since 1979. The kitchen makes good use of produce that is locally grown, reared and caught, organic whenever possible, and all pastries and breads are home-baked. The beamed and stone-walled restaurant provides a smart setting for a repertoire that runs to seared wild pigeon fillets with a zippy red grape and chilli salsa, followed by rack of Slaney Valley lamb, or king scallops flambéed in Cognac and cream.

Chef Johannes Haffner **Seats** 50, Pr/dining room 14 **Times** 6-9.30, Closed Xmas, Mon-Tue (winter) **Prices** Starter €4.50-€13, Main €20-€29.50, Dessert €6.50-€9.50 **Wines** 21 bottles over €30, 16 bottles under €30, 12 by glass **Parking** 45 **Notes** Vegetarian available, Children welcome

CORK Map 1 B2

Maryborough Hotel & Spa

Modern International V

tel: 021 4365555 **Maryborough Hill, Douglas**
email: info@maryborough.ie web: www.maryborough.com
dir: *From Jack Lynch Tunnel take 2nd exit signed Douglas. Right at 1st rdbt, follow Rochestown road to fingerpost rdbt. Left, hotel on left 0.5m up hill*

Contemporary country-house cooking in a luxury hotel

There's a whiff of glamour at this Georgian country-house hotel, with later additions tacked on, surrounded by 14 acres of well-maintained gardens and woodland. The bar and restaurant, Bellini's, provide a modern glossy sheen. Fresh, locally-sourced produce is the kitchen's stock in trade and bright, modern ideas win the day. Maple-glazed pork belly with a Calvados reduction is one way to begin, followed by wild Irish pheasant (breast and confit leg) with herb polenta cake, or roast halibut fillet with sous vide fennel and blood orange. There's creativity among desserts, too, with passionfruit and mango baked Alaska arriving with tropical fruit foam and mango salsa.

Chef Getta Murphy **Seats** 170, Pr/dining room 60 **Times** 12.30-10, All-day dining, Closed 24-26 Dec **Prices** Fixed L 3 course €30-€38, Fixed D 3 course €40-€45 **Wines** 15 bottles over €30, 13 bottles under €30, 8 by glass **Parking** 300 **Notes** Sunday L, Children welcome

DURRUS Map 1 B2

Blairscove House & Restaurant

Modern European

tel: 027 61127
email: mail@blairscove.ie web: www.blairscove.ie
dir: *R591 from Durrus to Crookhaven, in 1.5m restaurant on right through blue gate*

Buffet dining in a converted barn

Blairscove brims with charm, on a promontory overlooking peaceful Dunmanus Bay. The main house is Georgian, and the accommodation and restaurant occupy a pretty development facing a pond, in what were the piggery, stables and barn. The dining room is full of character, not least from striking modern artworks. Stroll to the buffet, cruise-ship fashion, and help yourself to hors d'oeuvres before ordering from the main menu for the principal dish. That could be peppered medallions of wild venison, served with celeriac gratin and redcurrant compôte, or fillet of hake with an oriental spin. Then it's back to serve yourself for puddings.

Chef Ronald Klötzer **Seats** 75, Pr/dining room 48 **Times** 6.30-9.30, Closed Nov-17 Mar, Sun-Mon, L all week **Prices** Fixed D 3 course €60 **Wines** 14 bottles over €30, 27 bottles under €30, 5 by glass **Parking** 30 **Notes** Advance reservations recommended, Vegetarian available, Children welcome

GOLEEN Map 1 A1

The Heron's Cove

Traditional Irish

tel: 028 35225 **The Harbour**
email: suehill@eircom.net web: www.heronscove.com
dir: *In Goleen village, turn left to harbour*

Unbroken sea views and unpretentious menu

This delightful restaurant with rooms sits in an idyllic spot on Goleen harbour near to Mizen Head, where the lonely Fastnet Rock lighthouse beams out across the Atlantic. This is an exceptionally easy-going, friendly place, where you can eat out to sublime sea views on the balcony in summer, and the kitchen takes time to source the best local ingredients that are the backbone of its output. The menu is as straightforward and unfussy as its surroundings; West Cork smoked sprats, say, followed by pork chop rack with champ and apricot sauce, or tempura-style monkish. To finish, iced coffee soufflé is fuelled up with rum.

Chef Irene Coughlan **Seats** 30 **Times** 7-9.30, Closed Xmas, Oct-Apr (only open for pre-bookings), L all week (ex private functions) **Prices** Fixed D 3 course €30, Starter €5.50-€12.50, Main €17.25-€29.50, Dessert €6.95 **Wines** 25 bottles over €30, 35 bottles under €30, 2 by glass **Parking** 10 **Notes** Vegetarian available, Children welcome

KINSALE Map 1 B2

The White House

Traditional, International

tel: 021 4772125 **Pearse St, The Glen**
email: info@whitehouse-kinsale.ie **web:** www.whitehouse-kinsale.ie
dir: *In town centre*

Broadly appealing menu in a gastronomic hub

The White House occupies a prime site in the centre of a town that holds a Gourmet Festival every autumn, so there's plenty to live up to in the gastronomic stakes. The kitchen triumphs with a resourceful repertoire of modern Irish dishes taking inspiration from far and wide, but is also a dab hand at Irish stews, fish pies and the like. Baked cod fillet is coated in Cajun spices for a satisfying main course accompanied by ratatouille topped with melted cheese. Local mussels make a fine starter, with a creamy dressing of white wine, garlic and lemongrass, and puddings take in passionfruit and mango cheesecake.

MALLOW Map 1 B2

Springfort Hall Country House Hotel

Modern, Irish

tel: 022 21278 & 30620
email: stay@springfort-hall.com **web:** www.springfort-hall.com
dir: *N20 onto R581 at Two Pot House, hotel 500mtrs on right*

Modern dining in a Georgian country house

This is an immaculately-preserved Georgian country house where the enthusiastic kitchen team don't cut corners – meat and fish is smoked in-house and everything is made from scratch. In the palatial Lime Tree Restaurant all the detail of the original ornate plasterwork is picked out in gold paint and a crystal chandelier hangs above pristine white linen-clothed tables. Dishes are broadly modern Irish in style – salmon gravadlax with pickled cucumber on a chive cream cheese crostini might be followed a rosemary and garlic chicken supreme with an apricot and sausage stuffing. Finish with an apple and blackberry crumble.

Chef Viktor Bosz **Seats** 60, Pr/dining room 40 **Times** 12-9.30, All-day dining, Closed 24-26 Dec **Prices** Prices not confirmed **Wines** 38 by glass **Parking** 250 **Notes** Sunday L, Vegetarian available, Children welcome

SHANAGARRY Map 1 C2

Ballymaloe House

 Traditional, European NOTABLE WINE LIST

tel: 021 4652531
email: res@ballymaloe.ie **web:** www.ballymaloe.com
dir: *From R630 at Lakeview rdbt, left onto R631, left onto Cloyne. Continue for 2m on Ballycotton Rd*

Farm-fresh food in a classic country-house setting

The Allens were ahead of the curve 50 years ago when they opened a restaurant in their farmhouse. Now there's a cookery school and hotel, and the idea of fresh produce brought to the table in double-quick time seems the happy norm. The restaurant is supplied by the farm and walled garden, and the kitchen team has a wealth of superb produce to work with. Smoked mackerel rillettes with beetroot relish might start things off, while another opener offers garden chicory in an anchovy- and parmesan-dressed salad. Main-course Ballycotton monkfish comes with sprouting cavolo nero, or there could be peppered venison haunch with Jerusalems in red wine.

Chef Gillian Hegarty, Rory O'Connell **Seats** 110, Pr/dining room 50
Times 1-1.30/7-9.30, Closed Xmas, 6 Jan-6 Feb, Mon-Tue (Feb), L Wed (Feb), D Sun (Feb) **Prices** Fixed L 2 course €32, Fixed D 2 course €50 **Wines** 300 bottles over €30, 20 bottles under €30, 18 by glass **Parking** 100 **Notes** Fixed D 5 course €70-€75, Sunday L €45, Vegetarian available, Children 7 yrs+ D

SKIBBEREEN Map 1 B2

Kennedy Restaurant

Modern, Traditional Irish NEW

tel: 028 21277 **West Cork Hotel, Ilen St**
email: info@westcorkhotel.com **web:** www.westcorkhotel.com
dir: *N71 into Bridge St, with Baby Hannah's pub on left, right into Ilen St, hotel on right. From Cork Road, N71 to Schull, left at next rdbt towards town centre, hotel on left*

Hotel dining with a local flavour

This riverside hotel's restaurant offers a carvery at lunchtime with a dessert buffet, while in the evening the à la carte focuses on locally sourced ingredients to ensure a sense of place. It all takes place in a simply stylish room with a buzzy atmosphere and lots of mirrors, bevelled glass and ceiling lanterns. Kick off with crab cakes served up with pea purée and crème fraîche, garnished with dressed leaves from a nearby organic farm. Next up, grilled hake, cooked just right, with potato and leek gratin and a light, frothy garlic foam, and, for dessert, a simple lemon posset with berry compôte.

Chef Christian Pozimski **Seats** 60, Pr/dining room 300
Times 12.30-2.30/5.30-9, Closed 25-27 Dec, D 24 Dec **Wines** 4 bottles over €30, 17 bottles under €30, 10 by glass **Parking** 50 **Notes** Sunday L €12.95-€25, Vegetarian available, Children welcome

COUNTY DONEGAL

BALLYLIFFIN Map 1 C6

Jacks Restaurant

Modern European NEW

tel: 074 9378146 & 9378200 **Ballyliffin Lodge & Spa, Shore Rd**
email: info@ballyliffinlodge.com **web:** www.ballyliffinlodge.com
dir: *From Derry take A2 towards Moville, exit for Carndonagh at Quigleys Point. Ballyliffin 10km*

Generous cooking and quality ingredients

Ballyliffin Lodge has ditched the 'faine daining' approach in Jacks Restaurant, and the new look – brown leather seats and banquettes, bare tables and darkwood floors – backed by a pubby bar and an unbuttoned menu are a hit with the guests. There's a clear penchant for oriental accents in starters such as Thai salmon fishcakes, but there's a strong showing of regional flavours too: pan-seared fillet of local beef, say, with caramelised onion mash, wild mushrooms and pancetta jus, or pork fillet with apricot and pine nut stuffing and apple and Calvados cream. Round off with milk chocolate and lavender crème brûlée.

Chef Janusz Kilinski **Seats** 64, Pr/dining room 400
Times 12-close/6-9.30, Closed 24-25 Dec **Prices** Fixed L 2 course €16, Fixed D 3 course €30, Starter €6.50-€7, Main €17.50-€26.95, Dessert €6-€6.95 **Wines** 6 bottles over €30, 21 bottles under €30 **Parking** 100 **Notes** Sunday L €18.95, Vegetarian available, Children welcome

DONEGAL Map 1 B5

Harvey's Point Hotel

Modern, Irish

tel: 074 9722208 **Lough Eske**
email: stay@harveyspoint.com **web:** www.harveyspoint.com
dir: *From Donegal 2m towards Lifford, left at Harvey's Point sign, follow signs, take 3 right turns to hotel gates*

Contemporary Irish cooking overlooking Lough Eske

It was the heavenly setting that brought the Swiss family Gysling here to the shore of Lough Eske to build their luxurious hotel complex in the late 1980s. The kitchen uses pedigree Irish produce in imaginative contemporary dishes. Lobster opens proceedings in a relatively traditional mode, delivering the luxurious crustacean encased in tortellini topped with shaved parmesan, truffle and lobster foam. Main-course grilled sea trout comes with a crab croquette and pearl barley in parsley sauce, or there may be venison loin with broccoli purée, red wine-braised salsify and poached plum. Proceedings close with a tasting of orange, comprising a moist Tunisian orange cake with orange sorbet and millefeuille.

Chef Chris McMenamin **Seats** 120 **Times** 12.30-9.30, All-day dining, Closed Sun-Tue (Nov-Apr), Sun, Wed (Jun-Oct) **Prices** Fixed D 3 course €55 **Wines** 70 bottles over €30, 17 bottles under €30, 17 by glass **Parking** 200 **Notes** Sunday L €29-€35, Vegetarian available, Children welcome

The Red Door Country House

Modern, Traditional European

tel: 074 9360289 **Fahan, Inishowen**
email: info@thereddoor.ie **web:** www.thereddoor.ie
dir: *In Fahan village, church on right, The Red Door is signed on left*

Confident modern Irish cooking by a lough

If it's a deal breaker, the front door is indeed red. With views over Lough Swilly, this country house has a restaurant run by a hands-on team. The series of dining rooms – including a sun room – have polished teak tables and smart linen napery. The menu shows a passion for local produce, along with sound classical training and bright modern thinking. Seared scallops with Haven Smokehouse salmon comes with pickled cucumber, cumin-scented beetroot and courgette jelly in a smart first course, followed by rack of Donegal lamb with ratatouille and boulangère potatoes. To finish, strawberry and white chocolate mousse, or tarte Tatin with apple parfait and crème anglaise.

DUNFANAGHY Map 1 C6

Arnolds Hotel

Traditional

tel: 074 9136208 **Main St**
email: enquiries@arnoldshotel.com **web:** www.arnoldshotel.com
dir: *On N56 from Letterkenny, hotel on left on entering the village*

Good Irish cooking in a pretty coastal village

Overlooking Sheephaven Bay, a stroll away from Killahoey Beach, Arnolds is not far short of its centenary. It's a friendly, comfortable place, with open fires and lots of windows in Seascapes Restaurant to capitalise on the coastal views. The kitchen takes a fuss-free approach to starters like oriental beef salad with chilli, ginger and soy. Fish, as you would expect, is well handled, as borne out by herb-crusted baked cod, Donegal Bay mussels, champ and French beans; a meat alternative could be honey-glazed roast half Monaghan duckling served on rösti with rich orange sauce. Try pannacotta with berry compôte, one of the home-baked desserts.

LETTERKENNY Map 1 C5

Radisson Blu Hotel Letterkenny

Modern Irish

tel: 074 9194444 **Paddy Harte Rd**
email: info.letterkenny@radissonblu.com **web:** www.radissonblu.ie/hotel-letterkenny
dir: *N14 into Letterkenny. At Polestar Rdbt take 1st exit, to hotel*

Unpretentious cooking in a modern hotel

A modern hotel of glass and steel, this outpost of the Radisson Blu group has a brace of dining options. In the smart TriBeCa Restaurant a large screen shows kitchen action, which whets the appetite for the likes of duck confit with braised red cabbage and apple and cinnamon purée. The menu embraces modern brasserie cooking to deliver the likes of salad of Clonakilty black pudding with sauté potatoes and poached egg, followed by glazed rump of Slaney Valley lamb (with roasted sweet potatoes and pea purée), or sirloin steak with an accompanying red onion tarte Tatin. Finish with white chocolate crème brûlée or Irish cheeses.

MOVILLE Map 1 C6

Redcastle Hotel, Golf & Spa Resort

Modern, International

tel: 074 9385555 **Inishowen Peninsula**
email: info@redcastlehotel.com **web:** www.redcastlehotel.com
dir: *On R238 between Derby & Greencastle*

Traditionally based Irish cooking with loughside views

The Redcastle estate can trace its lineage all the way back to a 16th-century proprietor called Cathal O'Doherty. At one point, it was owned by a Pennsylvania farming family, but today it makes a superbly located northwestern seafront hotel in the modern boutique style. A terrace overlooking Lough Foyle is a covetable place for a sundowner, informal eating is offered in the Captain's Bar, or repair to the Edge dining room for some traditionally-based Irish cooking with modern flourishes. Start with Cashel Blue and asparagus quiche, move on to daube of beef braised in Guinness, or risotto of beetroot and feta with candied walnuts.

Chef Gordon Smyth **Seats** 120 **Times** 12-4/6-9.30, Closed 25 Dec **Wines** 16 bottles over €30, 11 bottles under €30, 6 by glass **Parking** 360 **Notes** Early bird offer off-peak, Sunday L €23-€27, Vegetarian available, Children welcome

DUBLIN

DUBLIN Map 1 D4

Ashling Hotel, Dublin

Irish, European

tel: 01 6772324 **Parkgate St**
email: info@ashlinghotel.ie **web:** www.ashlinghotel.ie
dir: *Close to River Liffey, opposite Heuston Station*

Skilfully turned-out modern cooking near Dublin Zoo

The Ashling is a large, modern and glitzy hotel near Phoenix Park and Dublin Zoo, where Chesterfields Restaurant occupies a spacious, softly lit room with plushly upholstered dining chairs and a busily patterned carpet. The kitchen takes a modern tack with its combinations of flavours and textures, sending out pan-seared wood pigeon with spiced red cabbage, bacon, quince and red wine reduction. Then comes a duo of turbot and langoustine partnered with crabmeat bonbons, chargrilled lemon and champagne velouté. Prime native produce is the stock-in-trade, so Irish farmhouse cheeses bring up the rear alongside puddings such as chocolate and Baileys bavarois with Amaretto cream.

Chef Gary Costello **Seats** 180 **Times** 12.30-2.30/6-9.30, Closed 24-26 Dec **Wines** 8 bottles over €30, 8 bottles under €30, 6 by glass **Parking** 80 **Notes** Sunday L €7.95-€16.95, Vegetarian available, Children welcome

Balfes at The Westbury

Contemporary Irish

tel: 01 6463353 **Grafton St**
email: reserve@balfes.ie
dir: *Phone for directions*

Buzzy all-day dining venue with creative menu

With its own street entrance, and pavement tables, Balfes is an affable place with white walls, dark leather seats and a long bar-counter down one end. Kick off in the morning with an omelette or blueberry pancakes with maple syrup or pop in for a lunch of roast sea trout with yuzu salt, asparagus and citrus hollandaise. The Josper oven turns out grilled gambas, served with harissa aïoli, and breast of free-range chicken partnered with chorizo and white bean cassoulet. A long list of cocktails appeals at any time of day. For dessert, Josper-grilled pineapple with coconut competes for your attention with chocolate fondant with almond ice cream.

Chef Jorge Ballester **Seats** 140 **Times** 12-10.30, All-day dining, Closed 25 Dec, Good Fri **Prices** Prices not confirmed **Wines** 24 bottles over €30, 4 bottles under €30, 8 by glass **Parking** St Stephen's Green **Notes** Sunday L, Vegetarian available, Children welcome

Bang Restaurant

Modern European NEW V

tel: 01 400 4229 **11 Merrion Row**
email: info@bangrestaurant.com **web:** www.bangrestaurant.com
dir: *Just off St Stephen's Green*

Lively spot for contemporary dining

The slick and stylish Bang is handy for the National Concert Hall, with a pre-theatre menu to ensure that you don't miss a note, but there's also a tasting menu, which is worth sticking around for. Contemporary artworks fit the bill in a split-level space that positively buzzes with life much of the time. A modern approach in the kitchen means the sea trout is smoked in hay and comes with buttermilk and sorrel picada and a soft-boiled hen's egg gets a dusting of grated foie gras. Next up, sea bream arrives with a boneless, crispy chicken wing, and slow-cooked beef in a more traditional pairing with champ and fresh horseradish.

Chef Nial O'Sullivan **Seats** 90, Pr/dining room 40 **Times** 5.30-10.30, Closed Xmas, BHs, L all week **Prices** Fixed D 3 course fr €34.95, Tasting menu fr €69, Starter €6-€17, Main €22-€33, Dessert €7-€13 **Wines** 45 bottles over €30, 15 bottles under €30, 14 by glass **Parking** On street **Notes** Pre-theatre menu, Children welcome

Castleknock Hotel & Country Club

European, International

tel: 01 6406300 **Porterstown Rd, Castleknock**
email: info@chcc.ie **web:** www.castleknockhotel.com
dir: *M50 from airport. Exit at junct 6 (signed Navan, Cavan & M3) onto N3, becomes M3. Exit at junct 3. At top of slip road 1st left signed Consilla (R121). At T-junct left. 1km to hotel*

Contemporary dining in a country-club setting

Just 15 minutes from Dublin, Castleknock has plenty of pizazz. The pick of its eating and drinking choices is the elegantly finished Park Restaurant. There are floor-to-ceiling windows with swagged curtains, richly-coloured walls and large artworks. Steak is the mainstay of the kitchen's output, but there is plenty more besides, and a heap of regional produce to ensure a local flavour. Confit of wild Wicklow rabbit with apple gel, hazelnuts, Granny Smith apple and watercress is a creative first course, followed by roast rump of Cooley lamb – a fine piece of meat, soft and tender – served with broad beans, feta and a warm potato salad.

The Cellar Restaurant

Modern Irish

el: 01 6030600 & 6030630 **Merrion Hotel, Upper Merrion St**
mail: info@merrionhotel.com
ir: *Top Upper Merrion Street, opp Government buildings*

Modern Irish cooking down below

Down below the gleaming-white expanses of the Merrion Hotel, The Cellar is the place for modern Irish cooking. Begin with dashi-seasoned calamari with fennel salad and citrus aïoli, and then wheel out the big guns of tradition for 28-day dry-aged rib-eye in Café de Paris butter with broccoli hollandaise, or a whole black sole from Kilmore Quay with garlicky spinach in lemon and caper beurre noisette. Or mix it up modern-style for seared halibut with lardo, charred cauliflower, salsify and broad beans in beurre rouge. Desserts with attitude include a chocolate-orange crémeux made with Valrhona, along with hazelnuts and a buttermilk and coconut sorbet.

Coppinger Row Restaurant

Mediterranean, Modern Irish NEW

el: 01 672 9884 **off South William St**
mail: info@coppingerrow.com
ir: *Just off Grafton St*

Hip venue with a Med flavour

With its no-booking policy (unless you're six or more), open kitchen and raft of cool cocktails and quirky gin preparations, Coppinger Row is a fashionable address. The chefs take inspiration from the Mediterranean countries, but most of what turns up on the plate is sourced from hereabouts. Kick off with garlic and chilli prawns cooked a la plancha – a dozen of them served in their shells – or spinach and ricotta gnocchi, before stepping up to generous grilled swordfish (a daily special), or Moroccan-spiced lamb shank. Vanilla pannacotta with poached black cherries hobbles in all the right places.

hef Edward Daly **Seats** 60 **Times** 12-4/6-10, Closed 25-27 Dec, 1 Jan **Prices** Starter 7-€14, Main €19.50-€29.50, Dessert €6.50-€8.50 **Wines** 4 bottles over €30, 4 ottles under €30, 6 by glass **Parking** 100 yds **Notes** Early bird Sun-Wed 5.30-7pm, egetarian available, Children welcome

Crowne Plaza Dublin Northwood

Asian Fusion

l: 01 8628888 **Northwood Park, Santry Demesne, Santry**
mail: info@crowneplazadublin.ie **web:** www.cpdublin.crowneplaza.com
ir: *M50 junct 4, left into Northwood Park, 1km, hotel on left*

East-West fusion food near the airport

The Crowne Plaza sits amid 85 acres of mature woodland in Northwood Park. The whole place is done in swish contemporary style, including the Touzai restaurant, where east-meets-west for a menu of creative fusion cooking. That could mean prawn and rice noodle salad in Thai dressing to start, and then nasi goreng with chicken and seafood, or pork ribs with spring onion dressing and champ. Wok dishes come as starters or mains, but if you're determined to stay west, look to ham hock terrine with sourdough bread and piccalilli, and cod gratinated in mozzarella with saffron orzo. Try lemongrass brûlée and vanilla ice cream for dessert.

hef Logan Irwin **Seats** 156, Pr/dining room 15 **Times** 5.30-10, Closed 25 Dec, L all eek **Prices** Fixed D 3 course €25.95, Starter €8.95-€14.95, Main €12.95-€29.95, essert €6.95-€7.95 **Wines** 34 bottles over €30, 17 bottles under €30, 15 by glass **arking** 360 **Notes** Vegetarian available, Children welcome

Crowne Plaza Hotel Dublin – Blanchardstown

Italian, European, International

tel: 01 8977777 **The Blanchardstown Centre**
email: info@cpireland.crowneplaza.com **web:** www.cpireland.ie
dir: *M50 junct 6 (Blanchardstown)*

Italian dining in a buzzy modern hotel venue

The Blanchardstown branch of the Crowne Plaza empire is a short hop from the district's glitzy shopping centre. Its Forchetta restaurant works a loud and proud contemporary look with bold floral wallpaper and bare darkwood tables, a buzzy, breezy setting that suits the modern Italian menu. The usual suspects from the world of pizza and pasta are present and correct, or you might start with suppli di riso, fried rice balls with crab and mozzarella in lemony salsa verde, and follow with pan-roasted Kerry lamb chump with celeriac purée and pickled beetroot in thyme jus. Puddings are Italian classics, including nutty torta della nonna.

Chef Jason Hayde **Seats** 100, Pr/dining room 45 **Times** 12-2.30/6-9.30, Closed 24-25 Dec **Prices** Prices not confirmed **Wines** 20 bottles over €30, 27 bottles under €30, 6 by glass **Parking** 200 **Notes** Carvery L served Sanctuary Bar, Vegetarian available, Children welcome

Fahrenheit Restaurant

Modern Irish

tel: 01 8332321 & 8523263 **Clontarf Castle Hotel, Castle Av, Clontarf**
email: mwoods@clontarfcastle.ie **web:** www.clontarfcastle.ie
dir: *From Dublin city. O'Connell St, south onto O'Connell St Lower, left onto Abbey St Lower, continue onto R105, at Clontarf Rd left onto Castle Ave, left after 500mtrs*

Modern Irish cookery in a boutique castle

The Fahrenheit is the destination restaurant of Dublin's Clontarf Castle Hotel, a beguiling mix of the ancient (12th-century roots) and modern boutique luxiness, and it's a dramatic showcase for some striking modern Irish cooking. Kick off with beetroot-cured wild salmon with smoked salmon mousse, beetroot gel and horseradish, and move on to loin of Wicklow lamb, cooked pink and served atop garlic risotto, with slow-roast belly, roasted onions, carrots and fondant potato, or perhaps loin of venison with dark chocolate jus, grilled leeks and mushrooms. Conclude happily with braised rhubarb topped with fruit and nut crumble, mascarpone and chunks of meringue.

Chef Stuart Heeney **Seats** 90, Pr/dining room 20 **Times** 5.30-10, Closed L all week (private pre-booked only) **Prices** Fixed D 3 course €27.95-€39, Starter €6.95-€9.50, Main €17.95-€33.50, Dessert €6.95-€9 **Wines** 15 bottles over €30, 38 bottles under €30, 13 by glass **Parking** 200 **Notes** Early bird 2/3 course €23.95/€27.95, Table d'hôte 3 course, Sunday L €24.99-€29.99, Vegetarian available, Children welcome

DUBLIN *continued*

The Marker

Modern International NEW

tel: 01 687 5100 **Grand Canal Square**
email: info@themarker.ie **web:** www.themarkerhoteldublin.com
dir: *M50 junct 1, 2nd exit North Wall Quay. Right onto Commons St, right onto Mayor St, right on Guild St, over Samuel Beckett Bridge, left onto Sir John Rogerson's Quay. Right onto Forbes St, right onto Hanover Quay*

Modern food in the Docklands

Set in a cool, contemporary canalside hotel in the rejuvenated Docklands zone, this sleek brasserie is making quite a splash on the local dining scene, and celebrates the pick of Irish produce in its ambitious modernist food. Global accents abound, starting with crispy lamb croquettes matched with houmous, cucumber foam and smoked tomato ketchup, followed by spatchcock poussin jump-started with za'atar herbs and spices and served with sweetcorn and chorizo ragout, confit tomato and Provençal dressing. Applause, too, for the deeply-flavoured cherry and pistachio millefeuille with cherry gelato. If you're heading for a show in the Bord Gàis theatre, book early for the popular pre-theatre session.

Chef Gareth Mullins **Seats** 130, Pr/dining room 250 **Times** 12-2/5-10, Closed 24-25 Dec, Jan, L Sat, Mon, D Sun, Mon **Prices** Fixed L 2 course €26, Fixed D 3 course €33, Starter €9-€14, Main €18-€35, Dessert €9-€14 **Wines** 53 bottles over €30, 9 bottles under €30, 19 by glass **Parking** 40, Chimney Q-Park **Notes** Sun brunch with live DJ, Pre-theatre 5-7pm, Sunday L €13-€22, Vegetarian available, Children welcome

One Pico Restaurant

Modern NEW

tel: 01 6760300 & 6760411 **Molesworth Place, off St. Stephens Green**
email: info@onepico.com
dir: *Down from the Shelbourne hotel on Kildare St, 1st lane on left*

Creative modern cooking in an old coach house

The Rosette award for this establishment is unconfirmed at the time of going to print. Down a narrow lane, a revamped 18th-century coach house is the setting for some of the most diverting contemporary cooking in Dublin. In a soothingly refined dining room with a mellow colour scheme, velour seats, modern art and closely-packed tables dressed up to the nines, Ciaran McGill and his team turn out classically inspired dishes with an up-to-date edge. Lincolnshire eel keeps fashionable company with crispy chicken skin and charred leeks in a first course, while another might see confit quail packed into ravioli and served with Alsace bacon and potato consommé. Among main courses, tender rump of lamb is matched with a croquette of slow-cooked belly and a burnt aubergine purée, and a fishy option might be John Dory with Wye Valley asparagus, morels and a flavourful bisque. There's further evidence of appreciation of French classical ways in a dessert of Poire Williams soufflé, served with milk and honey ice cream, with a more exotic option being passionfruit posset with pineapple sorbet and frozen yogurt. A slate of Irish and French cheeses arrives with spiced pear chutney and crackers. There's also a two-course pre-theatre menu available for anyone heading for a show or looking to save a few Euros.

Chef Ciaran McGill **Seats** 70, Pr/dining room 45 **Times** 12-2.45/5.30-10, Closed BHs **Prices** Fixed L 2 course €25, Fixed D 3 course €49 **Wines** 137 bottles over €30, 10 bottles under €30, 25 by glass **Parking** Dawson car park **Notes** Sat & Sun 2 course lunch €27, Sunday L €27, Vegetarian available, Children welcome

Pichet

Modern Bistro NEW

tel: 01 677 1060 **14-15 Trinity St**
email: info@pichetrestaurant.ie
dir: *Phone for directions*

A vibrant update on the bistro theme

The name should be enough of a pointer to the Gallic inspiration for this buzzy 'modern take on a classic bistro', and the place ticks all the right style boxes with its chequerboard floor, blue leather seats and open-to-view kitchen. A technically astute kitchen team produces fine-tuned food from splendid ingredients, leading the charge with duck rillettes paired with a poached egg, hollandaise sauce and crunchy French beans. Next up, pan-fried sea bream comes with crabmeat and a cassoulet-style stew of white beans, tomato, basil, chorizo and shrimp. A luscious dessert of Muscovado cream and crisp with ginger crumb and coffee granita is a reminder that sugar is not always bad news.

Chef Stephen Gibson **Times** 12-3/6-9.30, Closed 1 wk after Xmas, Sun, L Sat **Prices** Starter €8-€12, Main €19-€30

Radisson Blu St Helens Hotel

Traditional Italian, International

tel: 01 218 6000 & 218 6032 **Stillorgan Rd**
email: talavera@radissonblu.com **web:** www.radissonblu.ie/sthelenshotel-dublin
dir: *On N11 Stillorgan dual carriageway*

Regional and classic Italian cooking in a grand house

This grand old house dates from the mid-17th century but has all the expected mo[illegible] cons. The Talavera restaurant serves up smart Italian food – especially from Lombardy – in a series of rooms with either traditional country-house decor or mor[illegible] contemporary chic. There's a tasting menu with a risotto and maybe osso buco as the star attraction. Otherwise start with a classic carpaccio, or spaghetti with tomato sauce and a generous amount of seafood. Move on to noisettes of lamb wit[illegible] a fresh mint dressing and chorizo-flavoured mash, or pan-fried brill with asparag[illegible] confit, tomatoes and capers. Finish with rhubarb tart or tiramisù.

Restaurant Patrick Guilbaud

– *see opposite*

Roganstown Hotel and Country Club

European

tel: 01 8433118 **Naul Rd, Sword**
email: info@roganstown.com **web:** www.roganstown.com
dir: *Phone for directions*

Modern cooking in a golfing resort

Golf, spa and conference facilities all feature at this large resort, but for dinner you'll be wanting the impressive, wood-panelled McLoughlins Restaurant. There's plenty of room between the well-dressed tables, and the kitchen seeks out first-class ingredients and delivers an ambitious, contemporary menu. A first-course terrine of smoked ham hock and vegetable piccalilli comes with candied beetroot, radish and crispy shallots, while main courses include braised daube of beef with baby Irish carrot and leeks or fillet of turbot with confit potato and Jerusalem artichoke purée and truffle jus. Opt for a lemon posset to finish.

Chef Iain McFadden **Seats** 100, Pr/dining room 30
Times 12.30-4.30/5-10, Closed Xmas, L Mon-Sat **Prices** Fixed D 3 course €24.95-€32.50 **Wines** 4 bottles over €30, 24 bottles under €30, 10 by glass **Notes** Sunday [illegible] €19.95-€32.50, Vegetarian available, Children welcome

Restaurant Patrick Guilbaud

DUBLIN **Map 1 D4**

Modern French V

tel: 01 6764192 **Merrion Hotel, 21 Upper Merrion St,**
email: info@restaurantpatrickguilbaud.ie
web: www.restaurantpatrickguilbaud.ie
dir: *Opposite government buildings, next to Merrion Hotel*

Outstanding service and French cooking at the pre-eminent Dublin address

The elegant Merrion Hotel has been home to Restaurant Patrick Guilbaud since the late 1990s, but this grande dame of the Dublin dining scene first opened at a different address in 1981. Admirable longevity indeed, but perhaps the most remarkable thing is that the winning team of Patrick and his head chef, Guillaume Lebrun, have been running the place that entire time. Restaurant manager Stéphane Robin has been here since 1986. This dedication and consistency is reflected in every element of this business, from the supply lines bringing the country's best produce to the doorstep, the professionalism and charm of the service, and the pin-sharp contemporary French cooking on offer. It all takes places in a well-dressed space with bold modern artworks and a colourful carpet which is a work of art itself. The kitchen's output keeps faith with many of the constructs of classic French cooking, but there's nothing dated about it, and the food is captivating, contemporary and creative. Pan-roasted duck foie gras arrives with pineapple to cut through its splendid richness, and dark rum caramel to take it to another level, while another starter brings together fabulous Castletownbere scallops with a zesty fennel escabèche and spicy guacamole. Among main courses, turbot arrives in another inspired dish, poached in aromatic milk, with yuzu hollandaise, or go for a meat option such as mellow spiced Wicklow lamb with Basque pepper stew and bergamot condiment. Grand Marnier soufflé is a suitably inspiring and Gallic finale. The wine list covers the whole world while ensuring that France stays centre stage.

Chef Guillaume Lebrun **Seats** 80, Pr/dining room 25 **Times** 12.30-2.15/7.30-10.15, Closed 25 Dec, 1st wk Jan, Sun-Mon **Prices** Fixed L 2 course €45, Tasting menu €98-€185 **Wines** 1200 bottles over €30, 20 by glass **Parking** In square **Notes** ALC menu 2/3/4 course €98/€105/€130, Children welcome

DUBLIN *continued*

The Shelbourne Dublin, a Renaissance Hotel

Traditional Irish, European

tel: 01 6634500 **27 St Stephen's Green**
email: rhi.dubbr.dts@renaissancehotels.com **web:** www.theshelbourne.ie
dir: *M1 to city centre, along Parnell St to O'Connell St towards Trinity College, 3rd right into Kildare St, hotel on left*

Grand modern hotel with seafood, steaks and modernist dishes too

This grand modern hotel is in a prime location on St Stephen's Green, and offers a range of eating and drinking options culminating in the tip-top Saddle Room. Here a menu of modern brasserie dishes specialises in seafood (including generously loaded platters) and majestic 32-day aged beef (two of you might set about a pound of Chateaubriand). Modernists might consider the likes of seared foie gras in Banyuls with fig compôte, or Knockdrinna goats' cheese with pickled courgette in beetroot emulsion. There's a five-course taster showcasing the more adventurous dishes, while puddings take a traditional line for rhubarb crumble, or blackberry mousse with caramelised apple.

Chef Garry Hughes **Seats** 120, Pr/dining room 20 **Times** 12.30-2.30/5.45-10.30 **Prices** Fixed L 2 course €22.95-€25.95, Fixed D 3 course €45, Tasting menu €80-€120, Starter €9-€21, Main €20-€38, Dessert €9-€12 **Wines** 100 bottles over €30, 10 bottles under €30, 12 by glass **Parking** Valet parking **Notes** Pre-theatre menu 2/3 course 6-7pm, Sunday L €24.95-€30.95, Vegetarian available, Children welcome

The Talbot Hotel Stillorgan

Modern Fusion

tel: 01 2001800 & 2001822 **Stillorgan Rd**
email: info@talbotstillorgan.com **web:** www.talbothotelstillorgan.com
dir: *On N11 follow signs for Wexford, pass RTE studios on left, through next 5 sets of lights. Hotel on left*

Gently modern cooking in a spa hotel

A hotel with a spa and wedding packages among its attractions, the Talbot at Stillorgan Park is also home to the Purple Sage restaurant, with its breezy air and contemporary finish. The menu has a gently conceived modern fusion tack, offering crab cake with mango, cucumber and watermelon in lemon emulsion, or sweet potato and cumin velouté with a Cashel Blue croûton, to open. Then it takes off with Parma-wrapped chicken breast with sun-dried tomato risotto and puréed spinach, or perhaps grilled cod with spinach and fennel peperonata and a tandoori-spiced beurre blanc. For dessert, expect bread-and-butter pudding made with croissants.

Chef Tommy Butler **Seats** 140, Pr/dining room 60
Times 12-2.30/5.45-10.15, Closed 25 Dec, L Sat, D Sun-Mon **Prices** Fixed L 2 course €14.35-€17.50, Fixed D 3 course fr €25, Starter €5.50-€9.50, Main €12-€28, Dessert €6-€9 **Wines** 5 bottles over €30, 20 bottles under €30, 14 by glass **Parking** 300 **Notes** Early bird menu 2/3 course €21/€25, Sunday L €14.35-€19.25, Vegetarian available, Children welcome

The Westbury

Modern Irish

tel: 01 6791122 **Grafton St**
email: westbury@doylecollection.com **web:** www.doylecollection.com
dir: *Adjacent to Grafton St, halfway between Trinity College & St Stephen's Green*

Crowd-pleasing cooking in a swish hotel

This prestigious city-centre hotel has a fine-dining restaurant dedicated to Oscar Wilde. The kitchen showcases the cream of Ireland's produce in a starter of Carlingford Lough oysters or Irish smoked salmon with caper berries and lemon crème fraîche. Staying in seafood mode, main course delivers well-timed stone bass matched with sauce vièrge and baby fennel, or you might go for meaty mains – perhaps a steak or herb-crusted rack of lamb from the grill, or duck confit with pickled Puy lentils and parsnip purée. Puddings are a strong suit when they include an authentic rendition of classic crema Catalana, or vanilla pannacotta with poached rhubarb.

COUNTY DUBLIN

KILLINEY Map 1 D4

Fitzpatrick Castle Hotel

Modern European

tel: 01 2305400
email: info@fitzpatricks.com **web:** www.fitzpatrickcastle.com
dir: *From Dun Laoghaire port turn left, on coast road right at lights, left at next lights. Follow to Dalkey, right at Ivory pub, immediate left, up hill, hotel at top*

Country-house cooking with views over Dublin Bay

The castellated house was built in the 18th century, and despite having something of a martial career, now offers a range of hospitable dining venues including the Grill, housed in the former dungeon, where wine-red banquettes and exposed stone walls are the background for a menu of well-wrought modern brasserie cooking. There's no wild experimentation here, just good honest preparations of prime materials. Expect rosemary-scented seared scallops on an underlay of wilted spinach as the prelude to pistachio-crusted rack of lamb on champ, or monkfish with minted pea purée in saffron sauce. Finish with frozen winter berries and coconut ice cream.

Chef Phil Whittal **Seats** 75 **Times** 5.30-9.30, Closed 25 Dec, L all week **Prices** Fixed D 3 course €30, Starter €5.95-€12, Main €14.50-€29, Dessert €6-€8.50 **Wines** 7 bottles over €30, 12 bottles under €30, 11 by glass **Parking** 200 **Notes** Vegetarian available, Children welcome

COUNTY GALWAY

BARNA Map 1 B3

The Pins at The Twelve

International, Modern Irish

tel: 091 597000 **Barna Village**
email: enquire@thetwelvehotel.ie
dir: *Coast road Barna village, 10 mins from Galway*

Eclectic dining in a design-led venue

Part of the boutique-style Twelve Hotel, The Pins is an unusual amalgam of bar, bakery, bistro and pizzeria, the latter being authentic Neapolitan-style thin and crispy pizzas made in a Vesuvian stone oven. There's also a modern gastro pub menu of championing regional suppliers. Start with something like a terrine of pork belly, pistachio and black pudding with pear compôte, followed by pan-seared hake with gratinated oyster, fondant potato, creamed leeks and prawn bisque, or slow-braised lamb shank with coriander couscous, grilled vegetables, apricot purée and toasted almonds. Dessert might be bread-and-butter pudding with caramel sauce. For more ambitious contemporary cooking, trade up to the Upstairs@West Restaurant (see next entry).

Chef Martin O'Donnell **Seats** 140, Pr/dining room 20 **Times** breakfast-10, All-day dining **Prices** Prices not confirmed **Wines** 300 bottles over €30, 60 bottles under €30, 35 by glass **Parking** 120 **Notes** BBQ menu options private functions, Pre-theatre menu, Sunday L, Vegetarian available, Children welcome

Jpstairs@West, The Twelve

Modern Irish NOTABLE WINE LIST

el: 091 597000 **Barna Village**
mail: west@thetwelvehotel.ie **web:** www.thetwelvehotel.ie
ir: *Coast road Barna village, 10 mins from Galway*

/ell-conceived modern dishes in a seaside hotel

boutique hotel with bags of contemporary swagger, The Twelve is in a coastal rea a short distance from the town centre. There's a lot going on: a cool bar, a akery selling artisan breads and cakes, and a pizza place, but the main dining ction takes place in the Upstairs restaurant, which is focused on seasonal egional produce, kicking off perhaps with garden pea and wild garlic risotto. Mains eliver appealing hang-on flavours with a contemporary flourish – try pork belly and callops with saffron-braised potato and puréed apple. Finish with rhubarb and ingerbread crumble and rhubarb ripple ice cream, or Irish cheeses.

hef Martin O'Donnell **Seats** 94, Pr/dining room 100 **Times** 1-4/6-10, Closed Mon-ue, L Wed-Fri **Prices** Prices not confirmed **Wines** 300 bottles over €30, 60 bottles nder €30, 35 by glass **Parking** 120 **Notes** Gourmet menu 5 course with wine, Wine torials, Sunday L, Vegetarian available, Children welcome

CASHEL Map 1 A4

ashel House

Traditional Irish, French

l: 095 31001
nail: sales@.cashelhouse.ie **web:** www.cashelhouse.ie
r: *S of N59. 1m W of Recess*

heavenly location and top-notch regional produce

anding at the head of Cashel Bay in 50 acres of delightful gardens, Cashel House a gracious 19th-century country pile that has belonged to the McEvilly family nce 1968. The restaurant offers French-accented classics, served in either an airy nservatory extension, or a polished traditional setting amid antiques and tworks. Local materials are handled simply and with confidence. Pan-fried dneys on toast with wholegrain mustard sauce sets the ball rolling before a sorbet soup, then Dover sole, grilled on the bone, comes with herb butter, or there could Connemara lamb shank with chilli and tomato. Finish with classic crème brûlée.

ef Arturo Tillo **Seats** 70, Pr/dining room 20 **Times** 12.30-2.30/6.30-9, Closed 2 n-12 Feb **Prices** Fixed L 2 course €6.50-€15.50, Fixed D 3 course €32, Starter €6-2.75, Main €15.50-€38, Dessert €7.50 **Wines** 5 by glass **Parking** 30 **Notes** Fixed D course €55, Sunday L, Vegetarian available, Children welcome

CLIFDEN Map 1 A4

Abbeyglen Castle Hotel

French, International

tel: 095 21201 **Sky Rd**
email: info@abbeyglen.ie **web:** www.abbeyglen.ie
dir: *N59 from Galway towards Clifden. Hotel 1km from Clifden on Sky Rd*

Fresh local produce in a charming old property

The crenellated Victorian fantasy of Abbeyglen Castle basks in sweeping views, but is just a five-minute walk from the bustle of Clifden village. The decor is bold and bright with artworks on cherry-red walls, crystal chandeliers, and a pianist tinkles away. Expect classic cooking built on excellent local materials. Fish and seafood stars – fresh oysters, seafood chowder, or poached salmon with hollandaise – while meat could turn up as slow-roasted suckling pig teamed with braised belly pork, apple chutney, celeriac crisps and a grain mustard reduction. Puddings finish slap in the comfort zone with the likes of chocolate bread-and-butter pudding or rhubarb crumble with crème anglaise.

GALWAY Map 1 B3/4

Ardilaun Bistro

Modern Irish NEW

tel: 091 521433 **Taylor's Hill**
email: info@theardilaunhotel.ie **web:** www.theardilaunhotel.ie
dir: *1m from city centre, towards Salthill on west side of city, near Galway Bay*

Ambitious, complex Irish bistro food

Formerly Glenarde House, the Ardilaun was built in 1840 for the Persse family, Galway landowners of some grandeur. It was launched as a modern hotel in 1962, and the Bistro is its venue for dynamic modern Irish cooking of vaulting ambition. Dishes are complicated but make an impact, as when cider-cured sea trout arrives with avocado purée, sea-salted egg yolk shavings and horseradish crème fraîche. That might precede hot-smoked pheasant with its leg en pithivier, alongside cavolo nero and bacon in a smoked garlic and thyme jus. Sweet potato beignets are a dessert, as you might guess from their accompaniments of espresso mousse and clementine.

Chef David O'Donnell **Seats** 90 **Times** 12-9, All-day dining, Closed 25-26 Dec, D 24 Dec **Prices** Fixed L 2 course €6.70-€23.75, Fixed D 3 course €29.45-€41.50, Starter €4.50-€9.50, Main €16.25-€25.50, Dessert €5.50-€9.50 **Wines** 62 bottles over €30, 9 bottles under €30, 9 by glass **Parking** 250 **Notes** Sunday L, Vegetarian available, Children welcome

The G Hotel

 Modern Irish

tel: 091 865200 **Wellpark, Dublin Rd**
email: info@theg.ie **web:** www.theghotel.ie
dir: *Phone for directions*

Modern Irish brasserie cooking in a postmodern experience hotel

This is a Force 10 postmodern experience hotel. Hard reflective surfaces are offset by pillbox views of the wild western coast, while Gigi's restaurant boasts full-throttle collisions of purple and pink, green and blue. The food is contemporary Irish brasserie fare, with sharing boards of charcuterie or seafood, or starters such as king scallops with smoked bacon and caper noisette. Outstanding mains include Wexford beef rib-eye with oxtail cannelloni, or roast sea bass in clam and mussel broth with saffron whipped potatoes. Sign up for Dinner and A Movie, and glide through to the cinema after enjoying cookies and cream cheesecake with winter berry and star anise compôte.

GALWAY *continued*

Glenlo Abbey Hotel

 Modern French

tel: 091 519600 **Kentfield, Bushypark**
email: info@glenloabbey.ie **web:** www.glenloabbeyhotel.ie
dir: *2m from Galway city centre on N59 to Clifden*

Country-house dining in Pullman carriages from the Orient Express

As if this grandiose country house built in the early Georgian era didn't have architectural diversion enough, its dining room has been fashioned from a pair of railway carriages from the Orient Express. It's a splendid design concept, and makes an elegant setting for the traditionally based European cooking on offer. A seafood path might take you from seared king scallops on onion soubise with watercress pesto to potato-scaled turbot en papillote in a capered white wine sauce. Otherwise, go for Bluebell Falls goats' cheese mousse with beetroot, then venison loin with wild mushrooms and rowanberries. For afters, the rich chocolate pudding is well matched with a sharp-tasting blackcurrant sorbet.

Chef Alan McArdle **Seats** 66, Pr/dining room 30 **Times** 1-3.30/6.30-9.30, Closed Sun-Tue (Oct-Apr), L Mon-Sat **Prices** Fixed D 3 course €59 **Wines** 50 bottles over €30, 28 bottles under €30, 12 by glass **Parking** 150 **Notes** Sunday L €35, Vegetarian available, Children welcome

Park House Hotel & Restaurant

 Modern Irish, International

tel: 091 564924 **Forster St, Eyre Square**
email: restaurant@parkhousehotel.ie **web:** www.parkhousehotel.ie
dir: *In city centre/Eyre Sq*

An appealing menu in a bustling city-centre hotel

Standing just off Eyre Square and built of striking pink granite, Park House has offered high standards of food and accommodation for well over 35 years. Its celebrated Park Restaurant – where paintings of old Galway help keep the past alive – fairly bustles at lunchtime and mellows in the evening. Endearing classical design – in reds and golds with banquette seating and chairs at closely-set tables – suits the surroundings. The traditionally-inspired cooking lets the produce speak for itself in an assiette of Galway seafood, followed by a whole baked Dover sole served with champagne beurre blanc. Things stay classic to the end, with a textbook crème brûlée.

Chef Robert O'Keefe, Martin Keane **Seats** 145, Pr/dining room 45 **Times** 12-3/6-10, Closed 24-26 Dec **Prices** Prices not confirmed **Wines** 12 bottles over €30, 43 bottles under €30, 7 by glass **Parking** 40, Adjacent to hotel **Notes** Early evening menu 3 course with tea/coffee €33, Sunday L, Vegetarian available, Children welcome

RECESS (SRAITH SALACH) Map 1 A4

Lough Inagh Lodge

Irish, French

tel: 095 34706 & 34694 **Inagh Valley**
email: inagh@iol.ie **web:** www.loughinaghlodgehotel.ie
dir: *From Galway take N344. After 3.5m hotel on right*

Spectacular scenery and Irish country-house cooking

This boutique hotel in a lovely spot on the Lough shore has an oak-panelled bar, a library with a log fire, and a restaurant where silver and glassware reflect candlelight and an oval window gives wonderful views. Chatty and attentive staff help you choose from the set-price dinner menu, which might open with air-dried lamb and beef with a warm chickpea croquette and red onion marmalade. Main courses are commendably free of frills and flounces: precisely-cooked duck breast comes in a sauce of plum purée hinting of star anise with fondant potato and well-timed seasonal vegetables. End with luscious chocolate pudding with raspberry sorbet and slices of poached orange.

COUNTY KERRY

DINGLE (AN DAINGEAN) Map 1 A2

Coastguard Restaurant

 Modern Irish

tel: 066 9150200 **Dingle Skellig Hotel**
email: reservations@dingleskellig.com **web:** www.dingleskellig.com/restaurant
dir: *N86 from Tralee (30km). Hotel on harbourside on left*

Modern Irish cooking and Dingle Bay views

It isn't possible to get much further west on the European continent than here. The Dingle Skellig is a sprawling establishment right on the coast with glorious views all round, best enjoyed from the Coastguard restaurant with its capacious picture windows. The kitchen draws on excellent regional produce, with locally landed fish and Kerry lamb among the highlights. Its modern Irish repertoire runs to salmon cured in Dingle whiskey with radish, cucumber and crème fraîche, followed by honey-roast duck breast with griottes and bok choy, or roast hake with samphire, squash and preserved lemon in white wine cream. Finish with praline, pistachio and white chocolate cheesecake.

Chef John Ryan **Seats** 120 **Times** 6.30-9, Closed Jan **Prices** Prices not confirmed **Wines** 35 bottles over €30, 14 bottles under €30, 14 by glass **Parking** 150 **Notes** Vegetarian available, Children welcome

Gormans Clifftop House & Restaurant

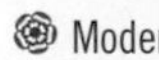 Modern, Traditional

tel: 066 9155162 & 083 0033133 **Glaise Bheag, Ballydavid (Baile na nGall)**
email: info@gormans-clifftophouse.com **web:** www.gormans-clifftophouse.com
dir: *R559 to An Mhuirioch, turn right at T-junct, N for 3km*

Clifftop cracker with splendid local produce

The stone-built house perching on the clifftops above Smerwick harbour has been owned by the Gorman family since the 18th century. Simplicity is the key to this delightful restaurant with rooms: there's nothing to get in the way of the dining room's sweeping views across the Atlantic, produce is spankingly fresh and the concise menu offers five choices at each stage. Start with locally-smoked organic salmon served with a simple salad and horseradish cream, and follow with a hear Kerry lamb stew with root vegetables and potatoes, or pan-fried hake fillet with roasted cherry tomatoes, lemon butter and fresh herbs. To finish, try mango parfai with passionfruit and mango syrup.

KENMARE Map 1 B2

Park Hotel Kenmare

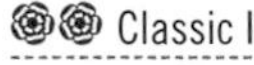 Classic Irish

tel: 064 664 1200
email: info@parkkenmare.com **web:** www.parkkenmare.com
dir: *Phone for directions*

Classy cooking in opulent surroundings

Set against a backdrop of the Cork and Kerry Mountains, with stunning views over Kenmare Bay, this landmark Victorian hotel dates from 1897. Top-notch ingredien sourced from the surrounding area dominate the menu, starting with attractively presented Kenmare Bay scallops teamed with pork cheek croquette and spiced carrot. Main course might bring a super-fresh fillet of halibut accompanied by roasted cauliflower, brown shrimps, bulgar wheat, brown butter and a sweet and fruity caper and raisin purée. A well-flavoured dessert of 'Kir Royale' blackcurrant nousse and champagne sorbet is one satisfying way to end a meal. A carefully hosen and comprehensive wine list offers some notable bottles at prices to match.

hef James Coffey **Seats** 70 **Times** 7-9, Closed 27 Nov-23 Dec, 2 Jan-26 Feb, Sun, L ll week **Prices** Prices not confirmed **Wines** 450 bottles over €30, 6 by glass **arking** 60 **Notes** Table d'hôte 5 course D €70, Vegetarian available, Children velcome

heen Falls Lodge

Modern European V

el: 064 6641600 **Sheen Falls Lodge**
mail: info@sheenfallslodge.ie **web:** www.sheenfallslodge.ie
r: *From Kenmare take N71 to Glengarriff. Take 1st left after suspension bridge. 1m from enmare*

rench, European cooking by cascading waters

ot far from the Rings of both Kerry and Beara, Sheen Falls maintains a refined ne in its La Cascade restaurant, enhanced by informed staff. Home-smoked almon, superb seafood and organic produce distinguish the output. This takes a assical French line with soft-textured duck liver parfait to start, copiously arnished with caramelised figs, quince and red fruit compôte, before main courses at might feature perfectly timed fish, perhaps roast halibut with provençale egetables in bouillabaisse sauce. Meats might include rack and shoulder of Kerry mb with mint foam and gnocchi. Irish farmhouse cheeses or shortbread-based mon tart with blackcurrant sorbet close the deal.

hef Philip Brazil **Seats** 120, Pr/dining room 40 **Times** 7-9.30, Closed 2 Jan-1 Feb, L l week **Prices** Prices not confirmed **Wines** 16 by glass **Parking** 75 **Notes** Children elcome

KILLARNEY Map 1 B2

he Brehon Killarney

Modern European V

l: 064 663 0700 & 662 3920 **The Brehon Hotel, Muckross Rd**
nail: info@thebrehon.com **web:** www.thebrehon.com
r: *Enter Killarney follow signs for Muckross Road (N71). Hotel on left 0.3m from town ntre*

old contemporary cooking showing vim and vigour

ehon was the name for the ancient body of law that governed Ireland. It gave its bjects an obligation of hospitality, so is a logical name for a hotel. The kitchen st-forwards us to the present day with contemporary Irish cooking of impressive pth. That translates as organic Clare Island salmon cured in orange and vodka, companied by salmon tartare, ribbons of pickled cucumber and horseradish eam, before pinkly seared lamb rump in a jus infused with Douglas fir needles, rved with a dollop of buttery colcannon threaded with vivid green kale and asoned with smoked paprika. Finish with a faithful interpretation of crème brûlée th home-made biscotti.

ef Mr Chad Byrne **Seats** 100, Pr/dining room 100 **Times** 6.30-9, Closed L all week **ices** Fixed D 3 course €35-€40, Tasting menu €40-€45, Starter €6.50-€9.50, Main 0-€28, Dessert €8-€10 **Wines** 6 bottles over €30, 21 bottles under €30, 8 by glass **rking** 250 **Notes** Children welcome

The Lake Hotel

Traditional European V

tel: 064 6631035 **On the Shore, Muckross Rd**
email: info@lakehotel.com **web:** www.lakehotelkillarney.com
dir: *2km from town centre on N71 Muckross Rd*

Traditional European cooking with lough and mountain views

On the shore of Killarney's lower lake, Lough Lein, the hotel has been in the Huggard family for more than a century. Although the original house is much extended since 1820, Castlelough Restaurant retains its Georgian high ceilings, while its wide windows reveal one of those splendid views in which Ireland specialises. Expect local place names on the menu, as in Dingle Bay crab starter with apple and ginger mayonnaise, mango salsa, yogurt and cardamom purée. Try caramelised scallops with Annascaul pudding, squash purée, chorizo oil and shallot foam as a main course. Red wine-poached pear, citrus sorbet, Muscovado jelly and honeycomb tuile is a typical dessert.

Chef Noel Enright **Seats** 100, Pr/dining room 65 **Times** 6-9, Closed Dec-Jan, L all week **Prices** Fixed D 3 course €35-€43, Starter €10-€15, Main €20-€32, Dessert €9-€12 **Wines** 30 bottles over €30, 19 bottles under €30, 6 by glass **Parking** 150 **Notes** Children welcome

KILLORGLIN Map 1 A2

Carrig House Country House & Restaurant

Modern Irish, European

tel: 066 9769100 **Caragh Lake**
email: info@carrighouse.com **web:** www.carrighouse.com
dir: *N70 to Killorglin*

Fine dining with expansive lough views

Carrig is a lovingly restored Victorian country manor in acres of colourful woodland gardens with views across Caragh Lake to the Kerry Mountains. Inside, the genteel house is done out in period style, with turf fires sizzling in cosy, chintzy lounges, while the dining room is the very image of 19th-century chic, with William Morris wallpapers, swagged curtains, polished floorboards, and formally laid tables. The cooking takes a more up-to-date approach. Crab could get a fashionable three-way treatment as ravioli, soup and pasty, and might be followed by Skeaghanore duck breast with vanilla and lime potato purée, and sweet port and brandy jus. Finish with prune and Armagnac crème brûlée.

TRALEE Map 1 A2

Ballyseede Castle

Traditional European

tel: 066 7125799
email: info@ballyseedecastle.com **web:** www.ballyseedecastle.com
dir: *On N21 just after N21/N22 junct*

Appealing well-conceived food in a castle hotel

This 16th-century castle surrounded by 30 acres of woodland is now a deluxe hotel. Its O'Connell Restaurant is a gracefully curved room with luxurious drapes at the windows, and columns, oil paintings and a chandelier. The kitchen takes a contemporary outlook, with starters such as breaded monkfish cheeks and prawns with home-made tomato and caraway seed ketchup and tartare sauce. Top-quality native produce is used throughout, evident in well-conceived, unfussy main courses: perhaps pan-fried salmon fillet with a creamy sauce of leeks, peas, dill and saffron, or roast duck confit glazed in honey and orange with a jus of port, grapes and orange. End with chocolate parfait and butterscotch sauce.

COUNTY KILDARE

STRAFFAN Map 1 C/D4

The K Club

Traditional French

tel: 01 6017200 **River Room**
email: sales@kclub.ie **web:** www.kclub.ie
dir: *From Dublin take N4, exit for R406, hotel on right in Straffan*

Classy, contemporary food in a five-star hotel

Once home to the Barton wine family, this luxurious hotel has the look of a French château and there are dining options aplenty, not least of which is the River Restaurant, with its impressive views of the Liffey. The cooking is built around classic technique but there is a pronounced regional influence when it comes to ingredients. Irish buffalo mozzarella teamed with a punchy Bloody Mary jelly and basil custard might precede a full-flavoured main of Achill Island blackface lamb with goats' cheese fondue, mint and wild garlic oil. Rhubarb parfait with poached fruit makes for a satisfying finale.

Chef Finbar Higgins **Seats** 110, Pr/dining room 30 **Times** 7-9.15, Closed L all week **Prices** Fixed D 3 course €63-€93.50, Starter €18-€30, Main €35-€53.50, Dessert €12.50 **Wines** 250 bottles over €30, 10 by glass **Parking** 300 **Notes** Vegetarian available, Children welcome

COUNTY KILKENNY

KILKENNY Map 1 C3

Lyrath Estate

Modern Irish, European NEW V

tel: 056 7760088 **Old Dublin Rd**
email: restaurant@lyrath.com **web:** www.lyrath.com
dir: *M9 junct 8 signed Kilkenny. 1st exit at both 1st & 2nd rdbts, hotel 1km*

Ambitious modern cooking in top-end hotel

The hotel and spa occupies an imposing 17th-century property set in 170 acres of parkland that includes lakes and ornamental gardens. La Perla, a large room overlooking the rose garden, is the gem among the dining options. The kitchen works around a modern Irish repertory, producing dishes of multiple flavours without over-elaboration. Seared breast of wood pigeon on crushed potato, for instance, is paired with a pot of braised leg in rich mushroom sauce, and might be followed by grilled hake fillet with saffron butter, chorizo, a curried croûton, quinoa and poached clams and mussels. Finish on praline parfait with caramel sauce and coconut sorbet.

Chef Andy Kreczmer **Seats** 150, Pr/dining room 30
Times 12.30-3/6-10.30, Closed 21-26 Dec, D Sun, Tue, Thu **Prices** Fixed L 2 course €24.50, Fixed D 3 course €35-€45, Tasting menu €45-€65, Starter €8-€13, Main €22-€29, Dessert €8-€15 **Wines** 48 bottles over €30, 6 bottles under €30
Parking 420 **Notes** Early bird fr €24.50, Sunday L €24.50-€29.50, Children welcome

THOMASTOWN Map 1 C3

Kendals Brasserie

French, European

tel: 056 7773000 **Mount Juliet Hotel**
email: info@mountjuliet.ie
dir: *M7 from Dublin, N9 towards Waterford, exit at junct 9/Danesfort for hotel*

A taste of France beside the golf course

Kendals is housed in a converted stable block of Mount Juliet Hotel, a light-filled, airy space under a pitched wooden ceiling. The kitchen concentrates on French brasserie classics with some input from other cuisines, so goats' cheese mousse appears with pistachios, black grapes, beetroot and raisins, while chicken parfait is partnered by duck rillettes and accompanied by salted grapes and watercress. Main courses follow in similar mould: fillet of hake with bean cassoulet, a chorizo and leek sausage and mussels, and pan-fried pork cutlet with apple jus, black pudding, kale and pommes purée. Menus are bilingual, so among puddings expect cheesecake à la vanille with blood orange jelly and sorbet.

Chef Peter Culvehouse **Seats** 70 **Times** 6-9.30, Closed Mon & Wed (seasonal) **Prices** Fixed D 3 course €20-€45 **Wines** 38 bottles over €30, 25 bottles under €30, 10 by glass **Parking** 200 **Notes** Early bird menu 6-7pm 3 course €28, Vegetarian available, Children welcome

The Lady Helen Restaurant

Modern Irish V

tel: 056 7773000 **Mount Juliet Hotel**
email: info@mountjuliet.ie **web:** www.mountjuliet.com
dir: *M7 from Dublin, N9 towards Waterford, exit at junct 9/Danesfort for hotel*

Cooking of artistry and impact in a manor-house hotel

Woodland strolls, fishing, archery and shooting: if you always fancied a life as landed gentry, this is the place to play out such dreams. Throw in a spa and a golf course designed by Jack Nicklaus and the sprawling Mount Juliet estate offers every modern comfort, while the dining room in this handsome Georgian manor house is an elegant space with elaborately stuccoed ceilings and splendid views of the estate sweeping down to the River Nore. Wild game from the estate and named local producers get full credit, whether you order from the carte or loosen your belt for the tasting menus. The tersely-written menu descriptions don't really tell the full story of the intricate dishes. A starter of poached and pan-fried veal sweetbreads appears with sautéed artichoke hearts and caramelised shallots, the red wine jus enhanced with a luxurious slice of fresh truffle and a parmesan foam. Precisely cooked squab pigeon makes an appearance at main course with oyster mushrooms, gently foaming almond milk and a subtle liquorice jus that doesn't overpower. A labour-intensive dessert of brown sugar tart, hazelnut and chocolate tuile and mandarin sorbet displays pin-point accuracy in both presentation and flavour balance.

Chef Ken Harker **Seats** 60, Pr/dining room 80 **Times** 6.30-9.45, Closed Sun & Tue, L all week **Prices** Prices not confirmed **Wines** 10 by glass **Parking** 200
Notes Children welcome

COUNTY LAOIS

BALLYFIN Map 1 C3

3allyfin Demesne

Traditional European V

el: 057 875 5866
mail: info@ballyfin.com **web:** www.ballyfin.com
ir: *M7 junct 18, follow signs to Mountrath. In Mountrath turn right at lights, follow 3allyfin Rd for 8km. Entrance gate on left via intercom*

)azzling French-inspired cooking amid Regency opulence

n possibly Ireland's most opulent Regency house, the high-ceilinged dining room azes out towards a temple where a water feature cascades. A walled garden upplies the kitchen with plenty of produce, as do the resident bees, and lucky umans are regaled with French-inspired contemporary cooking of considerable azzle. A trio of scallops comes with soused and puréed cauliflower in a caper-otted shellfish dressing to start, prior to salted cod with langoustine cannelloni n truffled beurre blanc, or magisterial Kilkenny duck with date purée, roasted arrots and spinach in a glossy orange jus. The signature dessert is a traditional utmegged egg custard tart garnished with shards of meringue and hubarb sorbet.

hef Michael Tweedie **Seats** 39, Pr/dining room 39 **Times** 6.30-9.30, Closed Jan-14 eb, L all week **Prices** Fixed D 3 course €105, Tasting menu €125 **Parking** Valet arking **Notes** I residents only, Fixed D 5 course €115, Tasting 8 course, Children 9 rs+

COUNTY LIMERICK

LIMERICK Map 1 B3

'imerick Strand Hotel

Irish Contemporary

el: 061 421800 **Ennis St**
mail: info@strandlimerick.ie **web:** www.strandlimerick.ie
ir: *On Shannon side of Sarsfield Bridge, on River Shannon*

:ontemporary Irish brasserie food by the river

new-build riverside hotel with all mod cons, including a bright, airy dining room. ourcing from within the county supplies a menu of populist brasserie dishes, with n Irish contemporary gloss on international ideas. Start with two slices of duck oulade zinged up with five spice on ginger- and sesame-dressed saladings with umquat marmalade. That could lead to a brace of sea bass fillets saltimbocca-tyle, wrapped in Parma ham and sage leaves, or chicken breast with truffle-oiled ash in wild mushroom and tarragon cream. The chocolate marquise packs a ighty punch, and is nicely offset with a sharp raspberry sauce. Good breads come ith intensely anchovied tapenade.

COUNTY LOUTH

CARLINGFORD Map 1 D4

Ghan House

Modern Irish

tel: 042 9373682
email: info@ghanhouse.com **web:** www.ghanhouse.com
dir: *M1 junct 18 signed Carlingford, 5mtrs on left after 50kph speed sign in Carlingford*

Creative dining by the lough

Perched on the water's edge within a pretty walled garden complete with veg patch to fuel the kitchen, Ghan House's restaurant has views over the Mourne Mountains. Just about everything is made in-house. Local sea scallops might turn up in the company of white beans, chorizo from the Gubbeen smokehouse and mojo verde, or you could go for the warming comfort of roast parsnip soup with curried crème fraîche. Among main courses, saddle of Wicklow venison is partnered with celeriac and beetroot, with a kick of ginger, and rump of Slane Valley lamb with a sage and bacon rissole and onion ash. Finish with Grand Marnier parfait and chocolate tart.

Chef Stephane Le Sourne **Seats** 50, Pr/dining room 34
Times 1-3/6-9.30, Closed 24-26 & 31 Dec, 1-2 Jan, 1 day a wk (varies), L Mon-Sat (open by arrangement & most Sun), D 1 day a wk (varies) **Prices** Tasting menu €33 €55 **Wines** 14 bottles over €30, 40 bottles under €30, 14 by glass **Parking** 24
Notes Tasting menu 6 course Mon-Thu 6-7.45pm, D 4 course €45, Sunday L €29.50, Vegetarian available, Children welcome

DROGHEDA Map 1 D4

Scholars Townhouse Hotel

Modern Irish

tel: 041 9835410 **King St**
email: info@scholarshotel.com **web:** www.scholarshotel.com
dir: *Follow West St (Main St) to St Lawrences Gate. Turn left, up the hill. On left*

Lively modern cooking in a Victorian former monastery

Originally built as a Christian Brothers monastery in 1867, ceiling frescoes of the Battle of the Boyne in the interlinked dining rooms furnish a historical note that's a contrast to the modern Irish cooking. Start with salt-and-vinegar lemon sole and crispy mussels with smoked potato salad, or maybe foie gras parfait with pistachio butter and chocolate oil, before pedigree main-course meats bring on rump and braised shoulder of Kerry lamb dressed with garlic purée and mint jelly in red wine jus, or chicken breast and maple-syrup wings with sage and onion polenta and truffled feta terrine. Praline soufflé with pumpkin ice cream and hazelnuts is an interesting way to finish.

COUNTY MAYO

BALLINA **Map 1 B4**

Belleek Castle

International V

tel: 096 22400 & 21878 **Belleek**
email: info@belleekcastle.com **web:** www.belleekcastle.com
dir: *In Belleek woods N of Ballina*

Irish regional cooking with a foothold in tradition

Built in the 1820s on the site of a medieval abbey, Belleek is more manor house than castle, but altogether splendid even so. The style is sophisticated, but retains a foothold in tradition, offering first the house pie of pork in pork-fat pastry with orange and ginger marmalade, or a bowl of forest and hedgerow soup, all wild mushrooms, nettle pesto and garlic. Seafood could be Mulranny trout in lemon and dill, or turbot in capers and champagne, while the beef fillet in flamed in Jameson's and served with a peppery jus. At the end comes caramel cheesecake with peanut ice cream and blueberries, or lemon and passionfruit tart.

Chef Stephen Lenahan **Seats** 55, Pr/dining room 30 **Times** 5.30-9.30, Closed Xmas & Jan **Prices** Prices not confirmed **Wines** 57 bottles over €30, 7 bottles under €30, 5 by glass **Parking** 90 **Notes** Early bird menu 3 course €29.50, Tasting menu 5/8 course, Sunday L, Children welcome

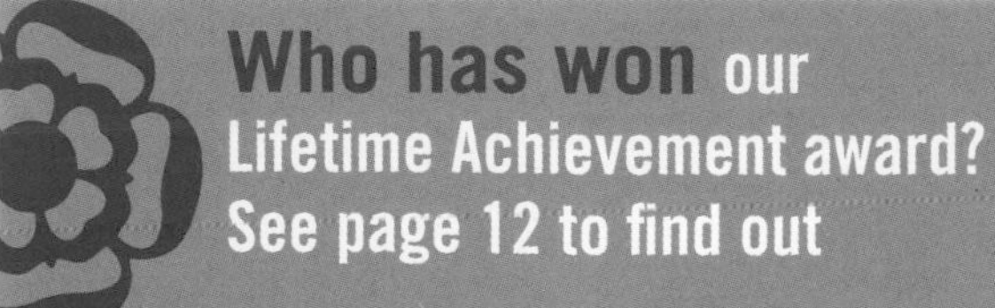

Mount Falcon Estate

Traditional

tel: 096 74472 **Foxford Rd**
email: info@mountfalcon.com **web:** www.mountfalcon.com
dir: *On N26, 6m from Foxford & 3m from Ballina. Hotel on left*

Polished cooking using exemplary local materials

The restaurant at this grand baronial-style hotel on the River Moy is the Kitchen Restaurant, which occupies the original kitchen and pantry area, looking good with its linen-clad tables and food-related prints on the walls. There's a definite French classicism to the kitchen's output, as well as an appreciation of top-quality materials. Start perhaps with oxtail ravioli, or textures of prawn with rouille and sea lettuce. Main courses might deliver beef fillet with swede purée and pearls, mushrooms, carrots and port and thyme jus, or more adventurous-sounding spicy monkfish fillet with pickled radish, cauliflower purée, crispy fennel pollen, tomato and sumac velouté and lobster oil.

Chef Daniel Willimont **Seats** 70, Pr/dining room 30 **Times** 6.30-9, Closed 25 Dec, L Mon-Sat **Prices** Prices not confirmed **Wines** 12 by glass **Parking** 100 **Notes** Sunday L, Vegetarian available, Children welcome

BELMULLET **Map 1 A5**

The Talbot Hotel

Modern Irish

tel: 097 20484 **Barrack St**
email: info@thetalbothotel.ie **web:** www.thetalbothotel.ie
dir: *Phone for directions*

Contemporary cooking amid boutique glamour

Once a pub but now a hip boutique hotel, The Talbot has a stylish look and a friendly attitude with live music in the bar at weekends. The plush Barony Restaurant is the main dining option here and there's a small terrace for alfresco lunch or early dinner. The kitchen seeks out good regional ingredients and delivers a menu that matches the tone of the place for contemporary attitude. A strong link with local fishermen is evident with a starter of seafood chowder, which might lead on to turbot with mussels and saffron. For dessert, try the apple tasting plate.

Chef Brendan Conmy **Seats** 60, Pr/dining room 12 **Times** 6.30-9 **Prices** Prices not confirmed **Parking** On street **Notes** Reduced hrs out of season, Sunday L, Vegetarian available, Children welcome

CONG **Map 1 B4**

The George V Dining Room

Traditional European, International V NOTABLE WINE LIST

tel: 094 9546003 **Ashford Castle**
email: ashford@ashfordcastle.com **web:** www.ashfordcastle.com
dir: *In Cross, left at church onto R345 signed Cong. Left at hotel sign & continue through castle gates*

Great Irish produce in a splendid location

Once home to the Guinness family, Ashford Castle dates from the 13th century and sits grandly on the shores of Lough Corrib, amid 350 acres of parkland. The dining room was built to host a reception for the Prince of Wales in 1906 – hence its name. You'll find Waterford crystal chandeliers, oak panelling and classic dishes from the new head chef. Home-smoked Skeaghanore duck with heritage carrots, black garlic and fennel jam might be a good place to start, followed by scallops with seaweed gnocchi, or venison with duck foie gras. There's a tasting menu, too.

Chef Philippe Farineau **Seats** 166, Pr/dining room 44 **Times** 7-9.30, Closed L all week **Prices** Prices not confirmed **Wines** 347 bottles over €30, 5 bottles under €30, 24 by glass **Parking** 115 **Notes** Children welcome

The Lodge at Ashford Castle

Contemporary Irish V

tel: 094 9545400 **Ashford Estate**
email: reception@thelodgeatashfordcastle.com **web:** www.thelodgeatashfordcastle.com
dir: *Phone for directions*

Creative Irish cooking and lough views

The original Victorian building hosts the Quay Bar and Brasserie and the main dining option, Wilde's, which offers glorious views over Lough Corrib from its first-floor setting. The kitchen aims to impress with its ambitious contemporary output (including a tasting menu) and local suppliers are name-checked on the menu. Killary Fjord mussels are cooked in squid ink batter and matched with a liquorice mayonnaise, while beef tartare comes with a hen's egg, wood sorrel and horseradish. 'Wilde's Wild Fish' is a main-course dish of turbot with monk's beard and Caesar sauce, and, to finish, rum baba gets a hit from its accompanying wasabi ice cream.

Chef Jonathan Keane **Seats** 60, Pr/dining room 50 **Times** 1-3/6.30-9.30, Closed 24-26 Dec, L Mon-Sat **Prices** Tasting menu €60, Starter €12-€16, Main €23-€30, Dessert €10 **Wines** 40 bottles over €30, 3 bottles under €30, 6 by glass **Parking** 50 **Notes** Sunday L €28, Children welcome

MULRANY **Map 1 A4**

Mulranny Park Hotel

Modern

tel: 098 36000
email: info@mulrannyparkhotel.ie **web:** www.mulrannyparkhotel.ie
dir: *R311 from Castlebar to Newport onto N59. Hotel on right*

Country-house splendour on the Atlantic coast

Once the station hotel for Mulranny, opened by Great Western Railways in the 1890s, this is now a sumptuous country-house with sweeping views over the Atlantic. A duo of Keem Bay smoked salmon and barbecued fresh salmon with honey-mustard aïoli, pickled cucumber and red onion dressing might start proceedings, with complex but effective main dishes extending from seared duck magret with black pudding mousse, braised spiced red cabbage and puréed parsnips in veal jus to roast Curran blue trout with chorizo and baby leek orzo and sauce gribiche. Tempting finishers include pear and almond frangipane tart, served warm with crème anglaise and rum and raisin ice cream.

Chef Chamila Manawatta **Seats** 100, Pr/dining room 50 **Times** 6.30-9, Closed Jan **Prices** Prices not confirmed **Wines** 6 bottles over €30, 14 bottles under €30, 3 by glass **Parking** 200 **Notes** Vegetarian available, Children welcome

WESTPORT **Map 1 B4**

Hotel Westport Leisure, Spa & Conference

Modern Irish, British, European

tel: 098 25122 **Newport Rd**
email: reservations@hotelwestport.ie **web:** www.hotelwestport.ie
dir: *N5 to Westport. Right at end of Castlebar St, 1st right before bridge, right at lights, left before church. Follow to end of street*

Exemplary local produce at a riverside hotel

Heavenly scenery frames this expansive family-run hotel and spa set in seven acres of mature woodland. Miles of walking and cycling on the Great Western Greenway close by are more reasons to bring a keen appetite to the restaurant, which has an ornate ceiling and timeless views over the Carrowbeg River. Expect a bedrock of straightforward modern ideas – sautéed scallops and Dublin Bay prawns with cauliflower purée and lemon and chive aïoli, followed by roast loin of lamb with potato gratin and tomato and mint relish. Finish with a plate of rhubarb, served stewed, as jelly and in a tart with home-made biscotti.

Chef Stephen Fitzmaurice **Seats** 120, Pr/dining room 45 **Times** 1-2.30/6-9.30 **Prices** Fixed D 3 course €35-€38, Tasting menu €35-€45, Starter €5-€11, Main €8.50-€28.50, Dessert €5-€6.50 **Wines** 20 bottles over €30, 31 bottles under €30, 10 by glass **Parking** 220 **Notes** Afternoon tea, Sunday L €25.50-€26.50, Vegetarian available, Children welcome

Knockranny House Hotel

Modern International

tel: 098 28600
email: info@khh.ie **web:** www.knockrannyhousehotel.ie
dir: *On N5 (Dublin to Castlebar road), hotel on left before entering Westport*

Inventive modern Irish cooking in the tranquil west

This tranquil spa hotel makes the most of its Mayo situation, with stunning views every which way. Inside comes with all the accoutrements of an upscale hotel, including a full-dress dining room, La Fougère, which eschews modern minimalism in favour of immaculate table linen and glassware. The kitchen draws on thoroughbred west Irish produce, including saladings from Knockranny's own organic garden, and the team in the kitchen are adept at the art of combining tastes and textures. Start with salt-cod croquette with pickles and chive beurre blanc, follow up with local mountain lamb with rosemary mousseline, and finish with passionfruit pannacotta with mango ice cream.

Chef Seamus Commons **Seats** 90, Pr/dining room 120 **Times** 6.30-9.30, Closed 23-26 Dec, L Mon-Sat (open selected Sun) **Prices** Fixed D 3 course €52 **Wines** 196 bottles over €30, 30 bottles under €30, 6 by glass **Parking** 200 **Notes** Table d'hôte menu €52, Sunday L €25.50-€35, Vegetarian available, Children welcome

COUNTY MEATH

DUNBOYNE **Map 1 D4**

Dunboyne Castle Hotel & Spa

Modern European

tel: 01 8013500
email: cdiaz@dunboynecastlehotel.com **web:** www.dunboynecastlehotel.com
dir: *In Dunboyne take R157 towards Maynooth. Hotel on left*

Classy contemporary European cooking in a regal setting

At this regal hotel with its sprawling outbuildings, the elegant Ivy Restaurant offers seared quail breast with duck foie gras, a deep-fried quail's egg, soubise and orange gel for starters, or there might be cured mackerel with lemon crème fraîche, pickled carrot, pear and mustard relish and a potato crisp. Next up could be loin of venison wrapped in Parma ham with bitter chocolate and port sauce, red cabbage, salsify, candied beetroot and potato gratin. Turbot luxuriates in a parmesan crust with lime and coriander oil, curried cauliflower, cauliflower and coconut purée and potato noodles. Tarte Tatin with custard and vanilla ice cream brings down the curtain in style.

Chef John Nagle **Seats** 154 **Times** 1-3/6.30-9.30, Closed L Mon-Sat **Prices** Prices not confirmed **Wines** 30 bottles over €30, 29 bottles under €30, 12 by glass **Parking** 360 **Notes** Early bird Sun-Thu all evening & Fri 6-7.30pm €21.95/€26.95, Sunday L, Vegetarian available, Children welcome

NAVAN Map 1 D4

Bellinter House

@@ Modern European

tel: 046 9030900
web: www.bellinterhouse.com
dir: *M3 junct 7 Dublin to Cavan. Follow Kilmessa signs, straight over 2 rdbts left at Tara Na Ri pub*

Sharp modern food in a Palladian mansion

A country-house hotel that is popular on the wedding scene, its interior combining period charm with 21st-century boutique glamour. Down in the vaulted basement there's a slick contemporary finish to the space and a menu to match. The kitchen's output is focused on regional produce and there's evident technical ability on show. Dublin Bay prawns make an appearance alongside a tomato and chilli aïoli, snappy sesame tuile and punchy pickled cucumber, with main courses running to a rack of tender Slaney lamb with a nicely judged salsa and pommes Anna, or baked fillets of sea bass. Finish with a good-looking Pina Colada millefeuille.

Chef Robert Krawczyk **Seats** 70 **Times** 12.30-3.30/6-9, Closed 3 days Xmas, Mon-Tue, L Wed-Sat **Prices** Fixed L 2 course €25, Tasting menu €70, Starter €11.50-€14.50, Main €29.50-€39.50, Dessert €11.50-€12 **Wines** 46 bottles over €30, 21 bottles under €30, 7 by glass **Notes** 3 course menu for larger groups €35, Tasting menu 7 course, Sunday L €25-€35, Vegetarian available, Children welcome

SLANE Map 1 D4

Conyngham Arms Hotel

@ Modern Irish

tel: 041 988 4444 **Main St**
email: info@conynghamarms.ie **web:** www.conynghamarms.ie
dir: *M1 junct 10, N51 (Navan-Slane road) for 15 mins to Slane village. Hotel on main street*

Smart village inn with unfussy food

This 18th-century coaching inn is home to a smart brasserie-style restaurant offering straightforward food from breakfast through to dinner. There's a decent amount of Irish produce on the menu, including goods from the owners' bakery and coffee shop in the village. Chicken liver parfait is made in-house and arrives encased in butter with lightly pickled cucumber and carrot to cut through the richness. Next up, lamb shanks come with creamy mash and a red wine jus, and locally-sourced chicken is chargrilled and served atop a well-made asparagus risotto. There's a burger or sirloin steak, too, and desserts extend to a nicely tart lemon tart or chocolate fudge cake.

Chef Killian O'Donohoe **Seats** 35, Pr/dining room 30 **Times** 12-9, All-day dining **Prices** Fixed D 3 course €27.50, Starter €5.50-€8.50, Main €10.50-€23.50, Dessert €6 **Wines** 18 bottles under €30, 10 by glass **Parking** On street **Notes** Sunday L €22.50-€27.50, Vegetarian available, Children welcome

Tankardstown

@@ Modern Irish

tel: 041 9824621
email: info@tankardstown.ie **web:** www.tankardstown.ie
dir: *M1 junct 10, N51 (Navan-Slane road), take turn directly opposite main entrance to Slane Castle, signed Kells. Continue for 5km*

Modern Irish cooking in a classy rustic setting

In the restaurant situated in the one-time cow shed, expect a smart rustic finish with exposed stonework, a central fireplace and pretty terrace. The kitchen calls on the walled organic garden for supplies, and a newly installed smoker brings a potent aroma to proceedings. The menu is filled with dishes that reflect modern ideas and cooking techniques. Start with house-cured bacon and radish tops with celeriac and ash, and move on to fillet of hake with cauliflower, pollen and squid ink. A meaty main course might be hay-smoked duck breast with a mini Wellington, and finish with a deconstructed classic such as poached apple with crumble, sorbet and cider sabayon.

COUNTY MONAGHAN

CARRICKMACROSS Map 1 C4

Shirley Arms Hotel

@ Modern Irish V

tel: 042 9673100 **Main St**
email: reception@shirleyarmshotel.ie **web:** www.shirleyarmshotel.ie
dir: *N2 to Derry, take Ardee Rd to Carrickmacross*

Irish brasserie food in a handsome Georgian house

The market town of Carrickmacross is home to this handsome stone-built hotel, once called White's, a name that lives on in its principal dining room, which is kitted out in checkered upholstery with wood dividers and big floral pictures. Here, the style is modern Irish brasserie food that sweeps over a broad arc from Thai beef salad with peanuts and julienne veg, or prawn and courgette risotto dressed in lemon and chilli, to start, closely followed by the likes of herb-crusted hake fillet on ratatouille in basil velouté, lamb shank with mustard mash in red wine jus, or a classic surf 'n' turf pairing of fillet steak and lobster in garlic butter.

Chef Micheál Muldoon **Seats** 90, Pr/dining room 150 **Times** 12-3/5-9.30, Closed Good Fri, 25-26 Dec **Prices** Prices not confirmed **Wines** 2 bottles over €30, 10 bottles under €30, 3 by glass **Parking** 150 **Notes** Fixed seasonal menu Mon-Thu, Sunday L, Children welcome

GLASLOUGH Map 1 C5

Snaffles Restaurant

@@ Traditional Irish, International

tel: 047 88100 **The Lodge, Castle Leslie Estate**
email: info@castleleslie.com **web:** www.castleleslie.com
dir: *M1 junct 14 N Belfast signed Ardee/Derry. Follow N2 Derry Monaghan bypass, then N12 to Armagh for 2m, left N185 to Glaslough*

Contemporary country-house cooking in splendid isolation

The Castle Leslie Estate extends over 1,000 acres and boasts two plush bolt-holes – the Castle and the Lodge – operating as separate country-house hotels. The boutique-style Lodge comes with Snaffles, a stylish contemporary restaurant with hand-carved ceiling, oak beams and sweeping countryside views. The kitchen keeps its finger on the pulse, turning out up-to-date country-house cooking. Haddock bavarois on smoked mackerel gets things under way, matched intelligently with Jerusalem artichoke crisps in coriander-lemon dressing. Then the estate venison gets a workout, arriving as loin and confit shoulder with celeriac, a port-poached pear and puréed blackberries. For dessert, try lime crème brûlée garnished with tropical fruits.

Snaffles Restaurant

Chef Andrew Bradley **Seats** 110, Pr/dining room 50 **Times** 6-9.30, Closed 24-27 Dec, L all week **Prices** Prices not confirmed **Wines** 27 bottles over €30, 37 bottles under €30, 14 by glass **Parking** 200 **Notes** Tasting menu, Vegetarian available, Children welcome

COUNTY ROSCOMMON

ROSCOMMON — Map 1 B4

Kilronan Castle Estate & Spa

Modern French

tel: 071 9610000 & 086 0210542 **Ballyfarnon**
email: enquiries@kilronancastle.ie **web:** www.kilronancastle.ie
dir: *M4 to N4, exit R299 towards R207 Droim ar Snámh/Drumsna/Droim. Exit R207 for R280, turn left Keadue Road R284*

Modern country-house cooking amid Victorian Gothic grandeur

Kilronan certainly looks like an authentic medieval castle, complete with crenallated turret, but it actually dates from the early 19th century. Perhaps unsurprisingly, given the grand setting, the kitchen looks to French classicism for its inspiration, spiked here and there with oriental notes. A starter of quail Benedict sees a brace of quail breasts served atop wilted spinach on a toasted muffin and pointed up with a well-made hollandaise sauce, while main-course sea bass fillets come with Dublin Bay prawns, prawn mousseline, and a deeply-flavoured reduction of fish stock and dry Vermouth. Dessert is an elaborate millefeuille layered with creamy 'pannacotta' parfait.

COUNTY SLIGO

ENNISCRONE — Map 1 B5

Waterfront House

Modern European

tel: 096 37120 **Sea Front, Cliff Rd**
email: relax@waterfronthouse.ie **web:** www.waterfronthouse.ie
dir: *Phone for directions*

Globetrotting seafood cookery plus sunsets

Situated on the 'wild Atlantic way' that is the Sligo coast, dining takes place in a light-filled, wood-floored room with views over miles of beach and often-spectacular sunsets. Start with panko-crumbed calamari and spiced houmous with coconut-sumac dressing if you will, and there are Spanish and east Asian stylings too. Otherwise, a serving of sautéed mushrooms with St Tola goats' cheese on toast might precede accurately cooked whole Dover sole fillets with crab, scallops and prawns in nut butter, or Mayo lamb rump in port and redcurrants. Finish with mint Pavlova sandwiching chocolate ganache, a scoop of orange ice cream on the side.

SLIGO — Map 1 B5

Radisson Blu Hotel & Spa Sligo

Modern Irish, Mediterranean

tel: 071 9140008 & 9192400 **Rosses Point Rd, Ballincar**
email: info.sligo@radissonblu.com **web:** www.radissonblu.ie/sligo
dir: *From N4 into Sligo to main bridge. Take R291 on left. Hotel 1.5m on right*

Technically ambitious cooking for the Yeats fans

A classy modern hotel designed with plenty of vivid colour, notably reds and purples in the Classiebawn dining room. Here, the bill of fare is contemporary Irish cooking of notable technical ambition. Try a deconstructed egg for starters, the yolk crisped, the breadcrumbed white poached in red ale, dressed in horseradish crème fraîche. That might lead on to Ballinasloe lamb, the rack smoked over turf and heather, the shoulder herb-crusted, served with polenta and garlicky mash in minted jus with a jelly of Sheep Dip Irish whiskey. End with an inventive dessert such as gingerbread and candied peel crème brûlée with a baby pear poached in mulled wine.

Sligo Park Hotel & Leisure Club

Modern Irish

tel: 071 9190400 **Pearse Rd**
email: sligo@leehotels.com **web:** www.sligopark.com
dir: *On N4 to Sligo, junct 52 (Sligo S) Carrowroe/R287. Follow signs for Sligo (R287), 1m on right*

Simple Irish fare in a contemporary hotel restaurant

Covering all the bases, Sligo Park's full-on leisure facilities and surrounding verdant countryside, means there's plenty of opportunity to build up an appetite. The dining option is the Hazelwood Restaurant, which has a warm contemporary finish of fuchsia and mauve. The kitchen stays true to Irish produce and delivers classic dishes with a few modern touches. A dressed crab and pineapple roll, for example, comes with goats' cheese beignet and sweet tomato salsa, and there's an oriental flavour to a main-course honey-glazed duck breast. Dry-aged steak comes with hand-cut chunky chips, crispy onion tempura and a whiskey cream sauce and desserts might offer up a classic crème brûlée.

Chef Chris Friel **Seats** 120 **Times** 1-2.15/6.30-9, Closed L Mon-Sat **Prices** Prices not confirmed **Wines** 7 bottles over €30, 19 bottles under €30, 5 by glass **Parking** 200 **Notes** Sunday L, Vegetarian available, Children welcome

COUNTY TIPPERARY

CLONMEL — Map 1 C3

Hotel Minella

Traditional

tel: 052 612 2388
email: reservations@hotelminella.ie **web:** www.hotelminella.com
dir: *S of river in town*

Country cooking in an extended Georgian hotel

The garden runs down to the banks of the River Suir and the Comeragh Mountains loom in the background – it's a charming spot. The restaurant is in the original Georgian house, so has plenty of character and a traditional, period feel, and the kitchen keeps things simple. Two crisp and golden fishcakes might get the ball rolling, packed with fish and herbs, and served with home-made tartare sauce and dressed salad leaves. Next up, roast rack of lamb comes nicely pink and in the company of a redcurrant and rosemary sauce, plus accurately cooked vegetables. For dessert, a wobbly pannacotta is flavoured with a mix of berries.

THURLES Map 1 C3

Inch House Country House & Restaurant

Irish

tel: 050 451348 & 51261
email: mairin@inchhouse.ie **web:** www.inchhouse.ie
dir: *6.5km NE of Thurles on R498*

Splendid ingredients cooked simply in a Georgian manor

Inch House is the hub of a working farm run by the Egan family, and is not only a rather lovely country-house hotel, but a hive of activity. Needless to say the land provides a lot of the ingredients – they make their own black pudding, among much else – and what isn't home-grown won't have come far. Warm Gortnamona goats' cheese with a walnut and crumb crust is a simple enough starter, the cheese gently warmed through and served with salad from the garden and the house's red onion marmalade. Next up, suprême of chicken wrapped in bacon with a mushroom sauce, and for dessert, a berry crème brûlée.

COUNTY WATERFORD

ARDMORE Map 1 C2

Cliff House Hotel

– see below

WATERFORD Map 1 C2

Bianconi Restaurant

Traditional NEW

tel: 051 305555 **Granville Hotel, The Quay**
email: stay@granville-hotel.ie **web:** www.granville-hotel.ie
dir: *Take N25 to waterfront in city centre, opposite Clock Tower*

Waterfront views and appealing food

Occupying pole position on Waterford's river quay, the Georgian Granville Hotel's genteel Bianconi Restaurant makes the most of those views over the River Suir and the marina from decorous linen-clad tables beneath a coffered ceiling. The kitchen displays a feel for what's right on the plate, and seasonal ingredients obviously play their part, from home-made terrine of chicken liver and pork with Cumberland sauce to loin of pork with wild mushroom and cider sauce, served with comforting, creamy mash and purple sprouting broccoli. Desserts follow the same uncomplicated path, for example, pairing perfectly wobbly buttermilk pannacotta with buttery shortbread.

Chef Stephen Hooper **Seats** 140, Pr/dining room 36 **Times** 5-9.30, Closed 25-26 Dec, L Mon-Sat **Prices** Fixed D 3 course €32.50, Starter €6.95-€7.50, Main €16.95-€26.50, Dessert €6.95 **Wines** 2 bottles over €30, 20 bottles under €30, 6 by glass **Parking** Opposite hotel car park **Notes** Sunday L €25, Vegetarian available, Children welcome

Cliff House Hotel

ARDMORE Map 1 C2

Modern Irish V

tel: 024 87800 & 87803
email: info@thecliffhousehotel.com **web:** www.thecliffhousehotel.com
dir: *N25 to Ardmore. Hotel at the end of village via The Middle Road*

Tirelessly innovative Irish cooking overlooking the ocean

Almost as if sculpted into the cliff face, Cliff House has been in situ since the 1930s, but a revamp saw it reopen in 2008 as the luxe hotel we see today. There are pampering opportunities aplenty, swanky bedrooms with terraces overlooking Ardmore Bay, and, when it comes to dining, a restaurant that reaches for the stars. The kitchen is led by Martijn Kajuiter, a Dutchman with an evident passion for Irish ingredients and who has embraced contemporary cooking techniques. Expect excellent presentation and some creative ideas. Take a starter of West coast lobster and chicken, for example, which has three distinct elements that combine to create a highly impressive whole – poached chicken wrapped in nori, lobster served on a warm stone with lobster jelly, and a stunning lobster 'Bloody Mary'. Follow that with a dish based around McGrath's Suffolk lamb that has as much going on as the first course, or go for wild halibut landed locally, served as loin and a nifty pie, plus a black olive crumb and saffron jus. Among desserts, peaches get a workout with one such fruit poached in red wine alongside a smooth sorbet, pieces of jelly, and some delightfully chewy semi-dried shards. There's a tasting menu as you might expect, while the impressive wine list – check out the glass-walled wine cellar – includes a range of sakes and bottled beers.

Chef Martijn Kajuiter, Stephen Hayes **Seats** 64, Pr/dining room 20 **Times** 6.30-10, Closed Xmas, Sun-Mon (occasional Tue), L all week **Prices** Tasting menu €95 **Wines** 100 bottles over €30, 7 bottles under €30, 20 by glass **Parking** 30 **Notes** Tasting menu 8 course, ALC menu 3 course €75, Children welcome

Bistro at the Tower

🏵 Modern Irish, European

tel: 051 862300 **The Mall**
email: events@thw.ie **web:** www.towerhotelwaterford.com
dir: *City centre, main N25. Located at end of Merchants Quay*

Seafood-led menu at a smart city-centre hotel

Part of an Irish-Spanish group of upmarket venues, the Tower is a smart hotel and leisure centre on the Mall in Waterford. Its principal dining room, the Bistro, has a vividly colourful design, and fish and seafood are strong suits. You might start with seafood chowder, or fishcakes in Thai sweet chilli sauce, to whet the appetite for salmon fillet with egg noodles and stir-fried veg, or a mixed grill of seafood with chorizo in lemon butter. Meatheads might choose grilled Irish Angus steak of impeccable pedigree, with garlic potatoes in Jameson's and peppercorn sauce. Finish with chocolate fondant, served with fudge sauce and honeycomb ice cream.

Chef John Moore, Ray Kelly **Seats** 80, Pr/dining room 70
Times 12.30-2.30/6.30-9.30, Closed 25-26 Dec, L Mon-Sat (open on request)
Prices Fixed L 2 course €15.50-€18.50, Fixed D 3 course €55-€65, Starter €5-€6.95, Main €17-€22, Dessert €5.95-€7.95 **Wines** 19 bottles over €30, 19 bottles under €30, 4 by glass **Parking** 90 **Notes** Pre-theatre menu with wine 2 people €65, Sunday L €14-€23.50, Vegetarian available, Children welcome

Faithlegg House Hotel & Golf Resort

🏵🏵 Modern Irish, French

tel: 051 382000 **Faithlegg**
email: reservations@fhh.ie **web:** www.faithlegg.com
dir: *From Waterford follow Dunmore East Rd then Cheekpoint Rd*

Modern country-house cooking in an 18th-century hotel

The original mansion was built in the 1780s and is immaculately restored, while the high-ceilinged restaurant overlooks the garden from what was a pair of drawing rooms. The cooking is based on native produce and a range of neat ideas, and it really makes an impact. One novel and effective starter is trout gravad lax, rillette and smoked trout velouté with pickled cucumber. Move on to a tasting plate of duck – breast, confit leg and a tranche of foie gras – with cherry sauce and a side plate of broccoli, asparagus and mashed potato. Finish with orange cake with a matching ice cream and a poached pear.

The Munster Room Restaurant

🏵🏵 Irish, International NEW V

tel: 051 878203 **Waterford Castle Hotel, The Island**
email: info@waterfordcastleresort.com
dir: *From city centre turn onto Dunmore Rd for 2km. At hospital take exit for Dunmore Rd. Left at 3rd set of lights*

Modern Irish cooking on a private island

With its dark oak panelling, intricate plasterwork ceiling and ancestral portraits, the Munster Room is exactly what you'd expect from the dining room of a luxe hotel set on its own private 300-acre island. It's a jacket-and-tie affair with a pianist adding to the old-school ambience. The modern Irish cooking is underpinned with French classical roots. So the daily-changing menu might start with a savoury éclair filled with smoked potato mousse with shimeji mushrooms, granola and beurre noisette, followed by plaice with nori, broad beans, samphire, crab cream and soy gel. To finish, there's dark and white chocolate mousse matched with mango and passionfruit.

Chef Michael Thomas **Seats** 60, Pr/dining room 24 **Times** 6.30-8.30 **Prices** Fixed D 3 course €55 **Wines** 90 bottles over €30, 4 bottles under €30, 10 by glass **Parking** 50 **Notes** Private Sun L for 10+, Sun Afternoon tea, Children welcome

COUNTY WEXFORD

GOREY Map 1 D3

Amber Springs Hotel

🏵 Irish NEW

tel: 053 9484000 **Wexford Rd**
email: info@amberspringshotel.ie **web:** www.amberspringshotel.ie
dir: *500mtrs from Gorey by-pass at junct 23*

First-rate steaks from their own farm

A modern hotel with a spa and host of dining opportunities, the Farm Steakhouse is the latest addition and makes perfect sense given that the owners keep several hundred head of Angus cattle on their nearby farm. It's a smart dining room done out in dark, moody shades. Start with seafood platter or highly-flavoured beef tea, while an alternative to steak among main courses might be rump of Wicklow lamb or 'poisson du jour'. Those steaks are dry-aged for 36 days and come with vegetables from the farm, Pont Neuf potatoes and a sauce such as béarnaise – tender roast prime rib, say, cooked just right.

Chef William Miller **Seats** Pr/dining room 80 **Times** 12.30-3.30/6-9, Closed L Mon-Sat, D Wed-Thu, Sun **Prices** Prices not confirmed

Ashdown Park Hotel

🏵 Mediterranean, European

tel: 053 9480500 **Station Rd**
email: info@ashdownparkhotel.com **web:** www.ashdownparkhotel.com
dir: *On approach to Gorey town take N11 from Dublin. Take left signed for Courtown. Hotel on left*

Crowd-pleasing menu in an elegant setting

This modern hotel on a grand scale, within walking distance of Gorey, has 22 acres of grounds to explore before a trip to its Rowan Tree Restaurant. Here tables are dressed up in crisp white linen, and the kitchen turns out pleasingly straightforward dishes using local ingredients. Start with a Caesar salad with croûtons, smoked bacon and parmesan, or prawn and pineapple skewers with an Asian dressing. Next, rump of Wexford lamb is roasted and served with buttered cabbage and thyme jus, or there might be a duo of cod and rainbow trout with braised leeks and almond and dill butter. Move on to mango cheesecake with blackcurrant coulis.

Clonganny House

🏵🏵 Contemporary Irish NEW

tel: 053 9482111 **Ballygarrett**
email: info@clonganny.com **web:** www.clonganny.com
dir: *Phone for directions*

Confident classic French cooking in charming Georgian house

A handsome creeper-covered Georgian house at the end of a tree-lined drive, Cloganny has a refined, traditional interior. The highly experienced French chef-patron cooks with confidence and delivers a classically-inspired repertoire via a short bilingual carte. An impressive opener might be steamed fillet of salmon and mussels in a flavourful saffron sauce, before roast fillet of John Dory with another fab sauce (tarragon this time), or go for a meat option such as herb-crusted rack of lamb with dauphinoise potatoes and basil jus. Among desserts, a perfect tarte Tatin shows off the chef's skills. Kick off with drinks and canapés in the charming drawing room.

Chef Phillipe Brillant **Times** 7-7.30, Closed L all week **Prices** Prices not confirmed **Wines** 44 bottles over €30, 14 bottles under €30, 5 by glass **Notes** D 4 course €50 Fri-Sat only for non-residents

GOREY *continued*

Marlfield House

 Classical

tel: 053 9421124 **Courtown Rd**
email: info@marlfieldhouse.ie **web:** www.marlfieldhouse.com
dir: *N11 junct 23, follow signs to Courtown. Turn left for Gorey at Courtown Road Rdbt, hotel 1m on the left*

Grand hotel dining in the heart of Wexford

This opulent Regency home is now a smart and luxurious hotel whose dining room consists of several handsomely decorated spaces, leading into an impressive conservatory. Murals and mirrors are interspersed with huge windows opening onto the immaculate garden. The kitchen garden delivers first-rate seasonal produce, and the chefs do the rest. The contemporary Mediterranean-inflected fare starts with crab and lemon crumble with roast beetroot salad, or pan-roasted quail with ragoût of fennel, peppers and thyme jus. Next up, seared North Atlantic monkish with a cassoulet of saffron potatoes, or pan-fried rib-eye of Wexford beef, and for dessert, buttermilk pannacotta with Wexford berries, sesame seed tuile and toasted almond flakes.

Seafield Golf & Spa Hotel

 Modern Irish, French

tel: 053 942 4000 **Ballymoney**
email: reservations@seafieldhotel.com **web:** www.seafieldhotel.com
dir: *M11 exit 22*

Smart contemporary cooking in a modern spa hotel

We've Italian designers to thank for the super-cool finish within this luxe spa and golf hotel on the cliffs. The high-end finish extends to the restaurant, where a huge bronze female centaur keeps watch, lighting and music are soft, and the decor is cool black. The food matches this modernity and creativity, partnering poached mackerel fillets with rhubarb (poached, gel and a tart), and white chocolate-covered capers. There's real technical proficiency in a main course showcasing lamb – rack, sweetbreads and shoulder – with wild garlic pommes Dauphine and goats' cheese jus. Dessert brings strawberries in another multi-faceted workout involving purée, sorbet, salsa, macaroon and vanilla pannacotta.

Chef Susan Leacy **Seats** 90, Pr/dining room 40 **Times** 6-9.30, Closed Xmas, L all week **Prices** Prices not confirmed **Wines** 36 bottles over €30, 6 bottles under €30, 12 by glass **Parking** 100 **Notes** Vegetarian available, Children welcome

ROSSLARE **Map 1 D2**

Beaches Restaurant at Kelly's Resort Hotel

 Traditional European

tel: 053 9132114
email: info@kellys.ie **web:** www.kellys.ie
dir: *From N25 take Rosslare/Wexford road signed Rosslare Strand*

Beachside resort hotel with modern cooking

Beaches restaurant sits on the golden sands in Rosslare, and is set up to capitalise on the views, bathed in light through good-sized windows, and with restful pastel hues, white linen on the tables, and a mini gallery of original artworks on the walls. The kitchen lets the quality of local produce do the talking in simple contemporary dishes. Confit duck arrives in an unfussy combo with spiced pears and baked plums with five spice, while local goose from an artisan producer is roasted and pointed up with chestnut stuffing, braised ham, caramelised pear and glazed pearl onions. For desserts, yogurt and lime pannacotta with raspberry sorbet provides a refreshing finale.

La Marine Bistro

 Modern

tel: 053 9132114 **Kelly's Resort Hotel & Spa**
email: info@kellys.ie
dir: *From N25 take Rosslare/Wexford road signed Rosslare Strand*

Bistro-style cooking at a smart seaside resort hotel

The more casual stand-alone restaurant of Kelly's Resort Hotel is an easy-going venue with an open kitchen. The shipshape French bistro theme suits the beachside setting, as does its menu, which is built on the eminently solid foundations of spankingly fresh local produce. Top-class fish and seafood comes a short way from Kilmore Quay to be treated simply and sent out in ideas such as monkfish medallions with warm saffron and garlic mayonnaise, or scallops with creamy spiced Puy lentils and coconut crème fraîche. Meat can enjoy roast rack of lamb with gratin dauphinoise and redcurrant sauce. To finish, try pear, chocolate and almond pithivier or well-chosen local cheeses.

WEXFORD **Map 1 D3**

Aldridge Lodge Restaurant and Guesthouse

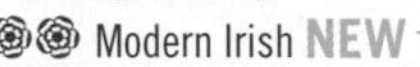 Modern Irish NEW V

tel: 051 389116 **Duncannon**
email: info@aldridgelodge.com **web:** www.aldridgelodge.com
dir: *From New Ross or Wexford follow R733 to Duncannon, restaurant 2km outside village on L8100*

Ingredient-driven cooking near the coast

With its fashionably pared-back looks – wood floors, bare tables and black high-backed seats – chef-patron Billy Whitty's restaurant with rooms achieves a stylish informality. It has also become something of a hot spot on the local foodie scene thanks to its sharply-executed dishes that deliver the finest local ingredients at their seasonal best. Dishes arrive looking rustically attractive and full of flavour – perhaps pan-fried turbot with crispy pork belly, carrot purée and butter crumb to start, followed by roast venison loin with hazelnuts, turnip purée, wild mushrooms and port jus. Desserts include lemon posset with raspberry and vodka sorbet.

Chef Billy Whitty **Seats** 37 **Times** 6.30-9.30, Closed 3 wks from 6 Jan, Mon-Tue, L all week **Prices** Fixed D 3 course €40, Tasting menu €35 **Wines** 20 bottles over €30, 15 bottles under €30, 7 by glass **Parking** 30 **Notes** Children welcome

COUNTY WICKLOW

DELGANY **Map 1 D3**

Glenview Hotel

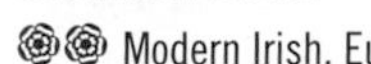 Modern Irish, European V

tel: 01 2873399 **Glen O' the Downs**
email: sales@glenviewhotel.com **web:** www.glenviewhotel.ie
dir: *From Dublin city centre follow signs for N11, past Bray on N11 S'bound, exit 9. From airport, M50 S onto N11 S, junct 9*

Imaginative seasonal cooking and lush valley views

The Woodlands Restaurant at this hotel is on the first floor to maximise the view over the Glen o' the Downs, with arched windows looking down the valley. Inside, a[ll] is soothing pastels and sparkling glassware. The style is what is loosely termed modern Irish. A starter of pan-fried scallops and crispy pork belly is a winning combination, served with rhubarb chutney. Follow with seared beef fillet partnered by a corned beef croquette, sautéed mushrooms, spinach purée and red wine jus, o[r] pan-fried sea bass fillet with lemon rice, vegetable ribbons and a lemongrass and coconut emulsion. For dessert, try minted Baileys crème brûlée.

Chef Sandeep Pandy **Seats** 80, Pr/dining room 36
Times 12.30-2.30/5.30-9.30, Closed L Mon-Sat **Prices** Fixed D 3 course €32-€36
Wines 20 bottles over €30, 19 bottles under €30, 13 by glass **Parking** 150
Notes Sunday L, Children welcome

ENNISKERRY Map 1 D3

Powerscourt Hotel

Modern European

tel: 01 2748888 **Powerscourt Estate**
email: info@powerscourthotel.com **web:** www.powerscourthotel.com
dir: *N11 to R117 Enniskerry, follow signs for Powerscourt Gardens*

Upscale dining in a Palladian hotel

With a sweeping Palladian mansion at its heart, the Powerscourt resort has two golf courses, a luxurious spa and an Irish pub, but the main event food-wise is the glamorous Sika Restaurant. There are glorious mountain views from its third-floor dining room, a glossy space with an upscale finish and a chef's table. Skilfully cooked modern dishes start with pan-fried scallops with pigs' head croquette, creamed leeks and lardo di Colonnata, followed by a rib-eye and glazed cheek of veal with caramelised onion mash, purple sprouting broccoli, wild leeks and blanquette sauce. Dessert is a creative and well-crafted Guanaja chocolate soufflé with malted barley ice cream.

MACREDDIN Map 1 D3

BrookLodge Hotel & Macreddin Village

Modern Irish Organic

tel: 0402 36444
email: info@brooklodge.com **web:** www.brooklodge.com
dir: *N11 to Rathnew, R752 to Rathdrum, R753 to Aughrim, follow signs to Macreddin Village*

Dramatic dining venue with organic and wild food

This luxurious country-house hotel is the heart of purpose-built Macreddin Village. The Strawberry Tree is its blue-riband dinner option, an opulent setting spreading through three grand rooms with mirrored ceilings reflecting twinkling chandeliers and gilt-framed mirrors on midnight-blue walls. Being Ireland's first certified organic restaurant, provenance of seasonal ingredients is king, with herbs and soft fruit grown in the Village's walled garden. The kitchen brings this peerless produce together confidently in dishes such as home-smoked salmon, cucumber, pickled wild samphire, crispy duck yolk and smoked chilli aïoli followed by seared wild sika loin, red cabbage, pear, vanilla Jus. To finish, perhaps an organic chocolate plate.

Chef Evan Doyle, James Kavanagh **Seats** 120, Pr/dining room 50
Times 7-9.30, Closed 24-26 Dec, Mon, L all week **Prices** Prices not confirmed
Wines 82 bottles over €30, 41 bottles under €30, 25 by glass **Parking** 200
Notes Fixed D 5 course €65, Vegetarian available, Children welcome

NEWTOWNMOUNTKENNEDY Map 1 D3

Druids Glen Resort

Modern European V

tel: 01 2870800
email: reservations@druidsglenresort.com **web:** www.druidsglenresort.com
dir: *M50 south from airport then M11/N11 through Kilmacanogue, junct 12 signed Newtown Mount Kennedy, follow signs*

Simple brasserie dishes and two golf courses

Druids Glen boasts the full package of spa, golf and leisure facilities with the Wicklow hills thrown in as a backdrop. Stylishly revamped in muted hues, with a feature fire set in a huge granite hearth, the main dining room is Hugo's Restaurant, an impressive arena for the kitchen's French-accented modern Irish repertoire. Tee off with a three-way treatment of salmon – confit, rillettes and a smoked brûlée with avocado foam, cucumber jelly and shaved fennel – then follow on with fillet of Atlantic cod with lobster ravioli, celeriac boulangère, and a fennel and lobster emulsion. Finish with strawberry crème brûlée with wild strawberry sorbet.

Chef Tim Daly **Seats** 170, Pr/dining room 22 **Times** 1-2.30/5.30-10, Closed L Mon-Sat **Prices** Fixed D 3 course €50, Starter €7-€12.95, Main €19.75-€34, Dessert €8-€13 **Wines** 59 bottles over €30, 10 bottles under €30, 16 by glass **Parking** 400 **Notes** Afternoon tea, Sunday L €26-€32, Children welcome

RATHNEW Map 1 D3

Hunter's Hotel

Traditional Irish, French

tel: 0404 40106 **Newrath Bridge**
email: reception@hunters.ie **web:** www.hunters.ie
dir: *N11 exit at Wicklow/Rathnew junct. 1st left onto R761. Restaurant 0.25m before village*

Classical Irish cooking in an ancestral family hotel

Barely half an hour from the Dun Laoghaire ferry, Ireland's oldest coaching inn sits in riotously colourful gardens, its dining room a vision of crisp linen, mahogany and fine living. Expect daily-changing menus of classically informed Irish cooking, starting with spanking-fresh crab tian in dill mayonnaise, and progressing via an intermediate course (perhaps leek and potato soup or lime and ginger sorbet) to the likes of crisply roasted breast and leg of duckling with blueberry sauce and pommes purée. Strawberry pannacotta to finish comes in a cocktail glass, lifted with a portion of balsamic-marinated strawberries, or you might be tempted by a selection of Ireland's latest artisan cheeses.

Tinakilly Country House

Modern Irish

tel: 0404 69274
email: reservations@tinakilly.ie **web:** www.tinakilly.ie
dir: *From Dublin Airport follow N11/M11 to Rathnew. Continue on R750 towards Wicklow. Hotel entrance approx 500mtrs from village on left*

Modernised country-house cooking overlooking the Irish Sea

A distinguished Italianate Victorian mansion is the diverting setting for the modernised country-house cooking on offer. The timing and seasoning of dishes does them justice, as does an opening pairing of scallops and the famous Clonakilty black pudding from County Cork, with butternut purée and pea shoots. Mains offer fine local meats such as herb-crusted Wicklow lamb rack in a provençale medium of chargrilled ratatouille veg and tomato fondue, or freshest fish such as Parma ham-wrapped cod with braised fennel, baby leeks and champ. A tarte Tatin variant made with pineapple is a success, the triumph ratified by its accompanying unabashedly boozy rum and raisin ice cream.

KEY TO ATLAS

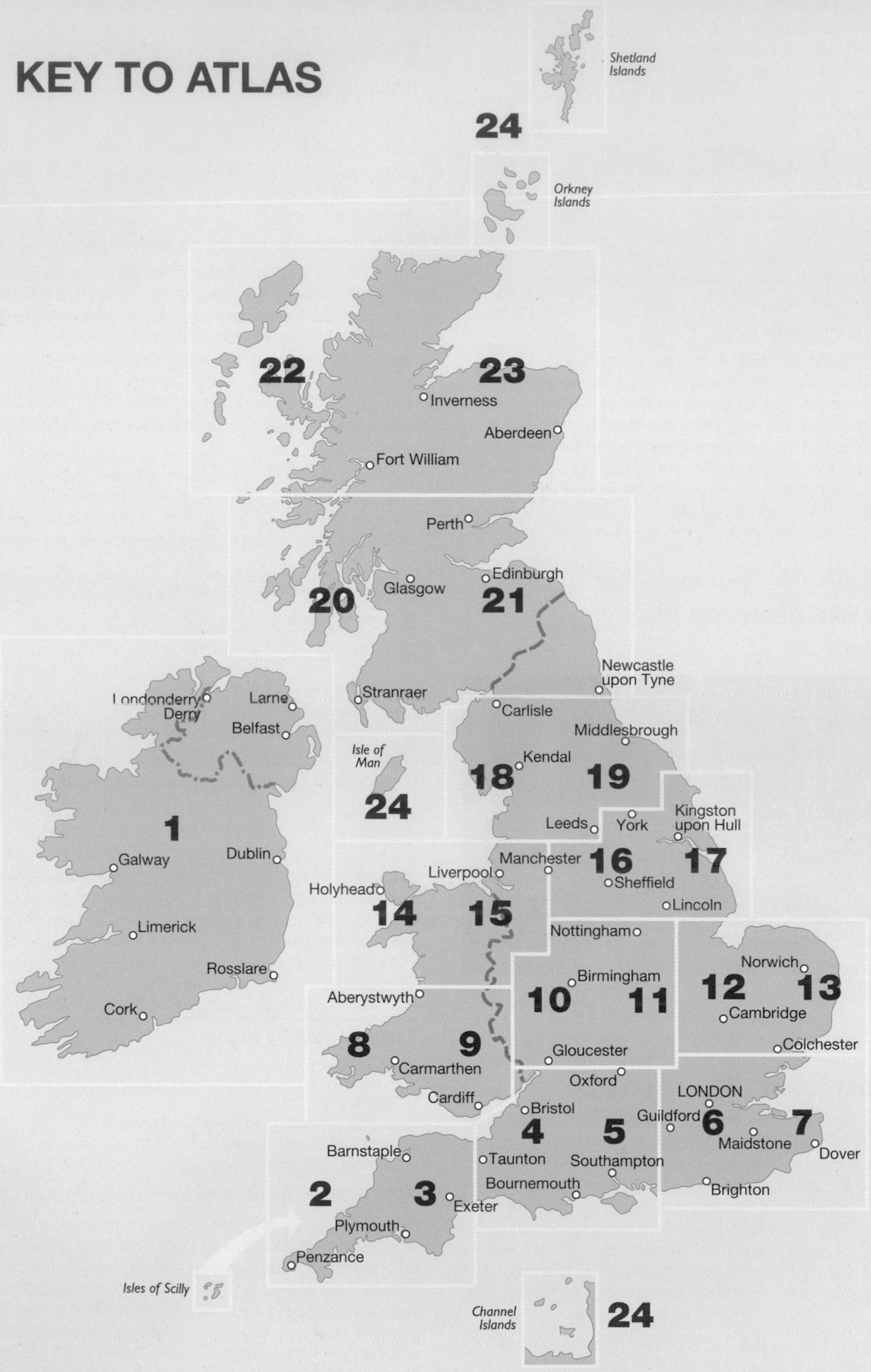

Shetland Islands
24
Orkney Islands
22
23
Inverness
Aberdeen
Fort William
Perth
Edinburgh
Glasgow
20
21
Newcastle upon Tyne
Stranraer
Londonderry Derry
Larne
Belfast
Carlisle
Middlesbrough
Isle of Man
Kendal
18
19
24
1
Leeds
York
Kingston upon Hull
Galway
Dublin
Manchester
16
17
Liverpool
Sheffield
Holyhead
14
15
Lincoln
Limerick
Nottingham
Rosslare
Norwich
Birmingham
12
13
Aberystwyth
10
11
Cork
Cambridge
8
9
Gloucester
Colchester
Carmarthen
Oxford
LONDON
Cardiff
Bristol
Guildford
6
7
4
5
Maidstone
Dover
Barnstaple
Taunton
Southampton
Bournemouth
Brighton
2
3
Exeter
Plymouth
Penzance
Isles of Scilly
Channel Islands
24

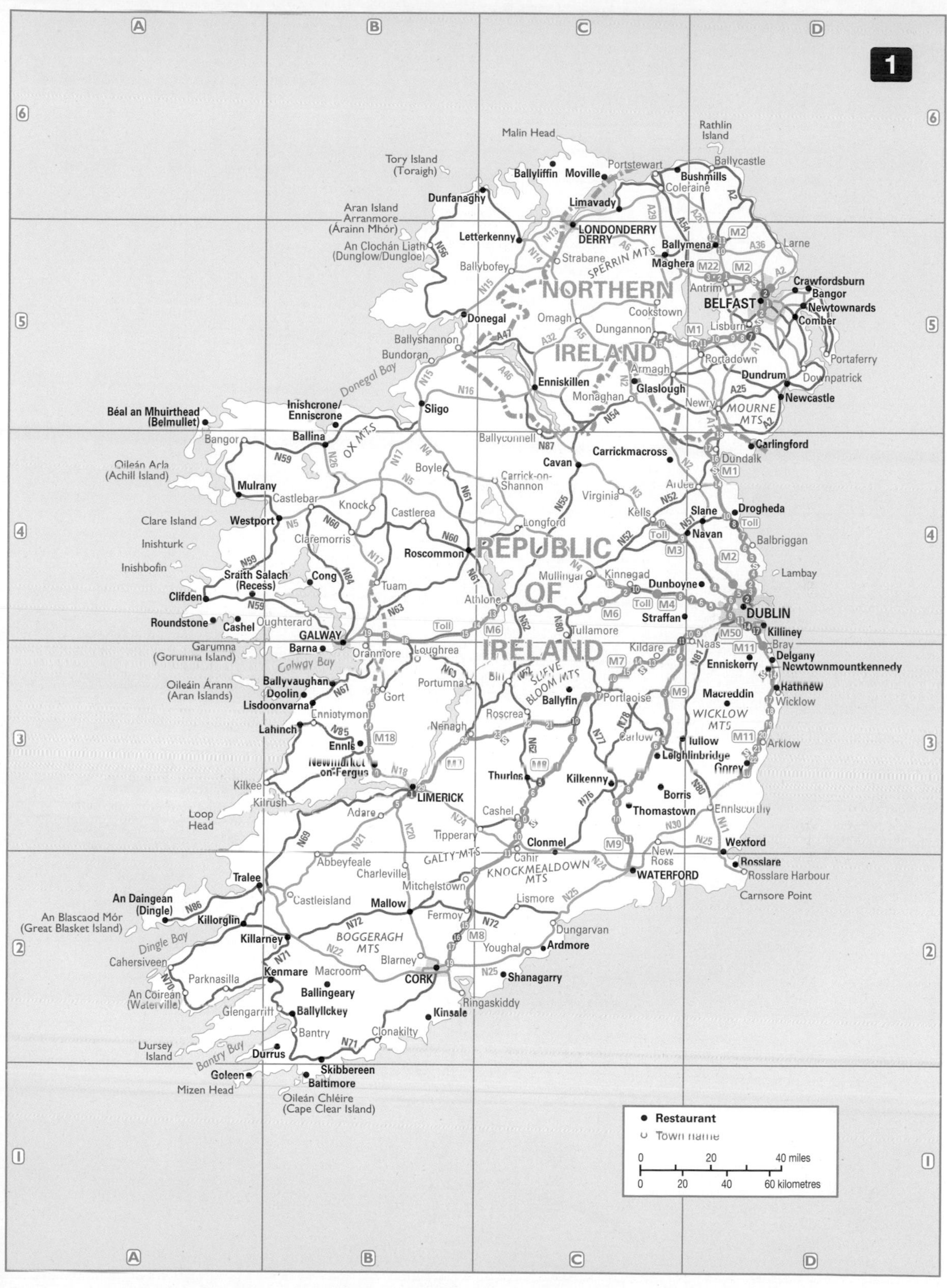
1
A
B
C
D
6
5
4
3
2
1
Malin Head
Rathlin Island
Tory Island (Toraigh)
Ballyliffin
Moville
Portstewart
Ballycastle
Bushmills
Coleraine
Dunfanaghy
Limavady
Aran Island Arranmore (Árainn Mhór)
An Clochán Liath (Dunglow/Dungloe)
Letterkenny
LONDONDERRY DERRY
Ballymena
Larne
Strabane
SPERRIN MTS
Maghera
Ballybofey
Antrim
Crawfordsburn
Bangor
NORTHERN
BELFAST
Newtownards
Comber
Cookstown
Donegal
Omagh
Dungannon
Lisburn
Ballyshannon
Bundoran
IRELAND
Portadown
Portaferry
Donegal Bay
Armagh
Dundrum
Downpatrick
Enniskillen
Glaslough
Monaghan
Newcastle
Béal an Mhuirthead (Belmullet)
Inishcrone/ Enniscrone
Sligo
Newry
MOURNE MTS
Bangor
Ballina
OX MTS
Ballyconnell
Carlingford
Oileán Acla (Achill Island)
Cavan
Carrickmacross
Dundalk
Boyle
Carrick-on-Shannon
Mulrany
Castlebar
Knock
Ardee
Virginia
Kells
Slane
Drogheda
Clare Island
Westport
Castlerea
Longford
Navan
Balbriggan
Inishturk
Claremorris
Roscommon
REPUBLIC
Inishbofin
Lambay
Sraith Salach (Recess)
Cong
Tuam
Mullingar
Kinnegad
Dunboyne
Clifden
OF
Athlone
DUBLIN
Straffan
Roundstone
Cashel
Oughterard
GALWAY
Tullamore
Killiney
Garumna (Gorumna Island)
Barna
Oranmore
Loughrea
IRELAND
Kildare
Naas
Bray
Delgany
Galway Bay
Newtownmountkennedy
Enniskerry
Oileáin Árann (Aran Islands)
Ballyvaughan
Doolin
Lisdoonvarna
Gort
Portumna
SLIEVE BLOOM MTS
Ballyfin
Portlaoise
Rathnew
Macreddin
Wicklow
Ennistymon
Roscrea
WICKLOW MTS
Lahinch
Ennis
Nenagh
Carlow
Arklow
Tullow
Leighlinbridge
Gorey
Newmarket-on-Fergus
Thurles
Kilkenny
Kilkee
LIMERICK
Borris
Kilrush
Cashel
Thomastown
Enniscorthy
Loop Head
Adare
Tipperary
Clonmel
Wexford
New Ross
Abbeyfeale
GALTY MTS
Cahir
Rosslare
Charleville
KNOCKMEALDOWN MTS
WATERFORD
Rosslare Harbour
Tralee
Mitchelstown
Carnsore Point
An Daingean (Dingle)
Castleisland
Mallow
Lismore
An Blascaod Mór (Great Blasket Island)
Killorglin
Fermoy
Dungarvan
Dingle Bay
Killarney
BOGGERAGH MTS
Youghal
Ardmore
Cahersiveen
Blarney
Kenmare
Macroom
Parknasilla
CORK
Shanagarry
An Coirean (Waterville)
Ballingeary
Ringaskiddy
Glengarriff
Ballylickey
Kinsale
Bantry
Clonakilty
Dursey Island
Bantry Bay
Durrus
Skibbereen
Goleen
Baltimore
Mizen Head
Oileán Chléire (Cape Clear Island)
Restaurant
Town name
0
20
40 miles
0
20
40
60 kilometres

For continuation pages refer to numbered arrows

BRISTOL CHANNEL
SUPER-MARE
3
9
4
Bleadon
Winscombe
Blagdon
Bridgwater Bay
Berrow
Brent Knoll
Biddisham
Sedgemoor
Draycott
Mark
Wedmore
Burnham-on-Sea
Highbridge
Bleadney
Meare
Glastonbury
Ashcott
Walton
Middlezoy
Othery
Somerton
Langport
Curry Rivel
Long Sutton
Ilchester
Martock
South Petherton
Montacute
Ilminster
Crewkerne
Chard
Winsham
Misterton
Mosterton
Broadwindsor
Beaminster
Lynmouth
Lynton
Brendon
Porlock Weir
Porlock
Minehead
Dunster
Blue Anchor
Watchet
Kilve
Stogursey
West Huntspill
Ilfracombe
Combe Martin
Lee
Mortehoe
Woolacombe
Kentisbury
Parracombe
EXMOOR
Wootton Courtenay
Carhampton
Williton
Georgeham
Challacombe
NATIONAL
PARK
Croyde
Saunton
Braunton
Muddiford
Bratton Fleming
Simonsbath
Exford
Wheddon Cross
Monksilver
Crowcombe
Elworthy
QUANTOCK HILLS
Nether Stowey
Cannington
Bridgwater
Goathurst
North Petherton
Barnstaple or Bideford Bay
Barnstaple
Withypool
Winsford
Brompton Regis
Appledore
Instow
Northam
Westward Ho!
Bideford
Horns Cross
South Molton
North Molton
Dulverton
Wiveliscombe
Fitzhead
Bishops Lydeard
Taunton
Lyng
North Curry
Fivehead
Hatch Beauchamp
Corfe
Staple Fitzpaine
Horton
Milverton
Petton
Exebridge
Knowstone
Bampton
Wellington
Sampford Arundel
Taunton Deane
Culmstock
Hemyock
Upottery
SS
ST
SOMERSET
Monkleigh
Umberleigh
Chittlehamholt
Great Torrington
Little Torrington
Stibb Cross
Rackenford
Burrington
Beaford
Merton
Dolton
Chulmleigh
Chawleigh
Witheridge
Tiverton
Halberton
Uffculme
Willand
Cullompton
Bickleigh
Bradworthy
Milton Damerel
Shebbear
Black Torrington
Sheepwash
Meeth
Winkleigh
Eggesford
Lapford
Morchard Bishop
Cheriton Fitzpaine
Hatherleigh
Highampton
Halwill Junction
Beaworthy
Copplestone
Crediton
Silverton
Yarcombe
Tytherleigh
Honiton
Wilmington
Fenny Bridges
Axminster
Shute
Colyton
Colyford
Uplyme
Charmouth
Bridport
North Chideock
Lyme Regis
West Bay
Burton Bradstock
Seaton
Axmouth
Beer
Branscombe
Sidmouth
Otterton
Budleigh Salterton
Lyme Bay
Ashwater
Okehampton
Bratton Clovelly
DEVON
Tedburn St Mary
Newton St Cyres
Stoke Canon
Broadclyst
Whimple
Rockbeare
Ottery St Mary
EXETER
South Zeal
Whiddon Down
Crockernwell
Drewsteignton
Sourton
Bridestowe
Chagford
Dunsford
Doddiscombsleigh
Clyst St Mary
Topsham
Exminster
Kennford
Kenton
Exmouth
Lifton
Lydford
DARTMOOR
Moretonhampstead
Milton Abbot
Lamerton
Mary Tavy
Postbridge
Widecombe in the Moor
Haytor Vale
Bovey Tracey
Chudleigh
Ideford
Tavistock
Two Bridges
Ilsington
Chudleigh Knighton
Bishopsteignton
Dawlish
Teignmouth
Shaldon
Princetown
Kingsteignton
Gunnislake
Callington
Horrabridge
Hexworthy
Ashburton
Newton Abbot
Kingskerswell
Maidencombe
Dousland
Yelverton
Holne
Buckfastleigh
Ipplepen
Bere Alston
St Mellion
Pillaton
Bere Ferrers
Shaugh Prior
Dartington
TORQUAY
Paignton
Tor Bay
Landrake
Cornwood
South Brent
Totnes
Stoke Gabriel
Wrangaton
Saltash
Plympton
Ivybridge
Harbertonford
Dittisham
Churston Ferrers
Brixham
Torpoint
PLYMOUTH
Ugborough
Halwell
Ermington
Kingswear
Crafthole
Millbrook
Brixton
Yealmpton
Modbury
Dartmouth
Cawsand
Heybrook Bay
Wembury
Holbeton
Aveton Gifford
Stoke Fleming
Newton Ferrers
Slapton
Strete
SX
SY
Bigbury-on-Sea
Bigbury Bay
Kingsbridge
Chillington
Thurlestone
Start Bay
Hope
Torcross
Malborough
Salcombe
Beesands
Start Point
East Prawle
M5
A39
A361
A30
A38
A35
A303
A358
A386
A388
A377
A396
A379
A380
A381
A385
A3072
A3124
A3052
A375
A373
0 10 miles
0 10 20 kilometres

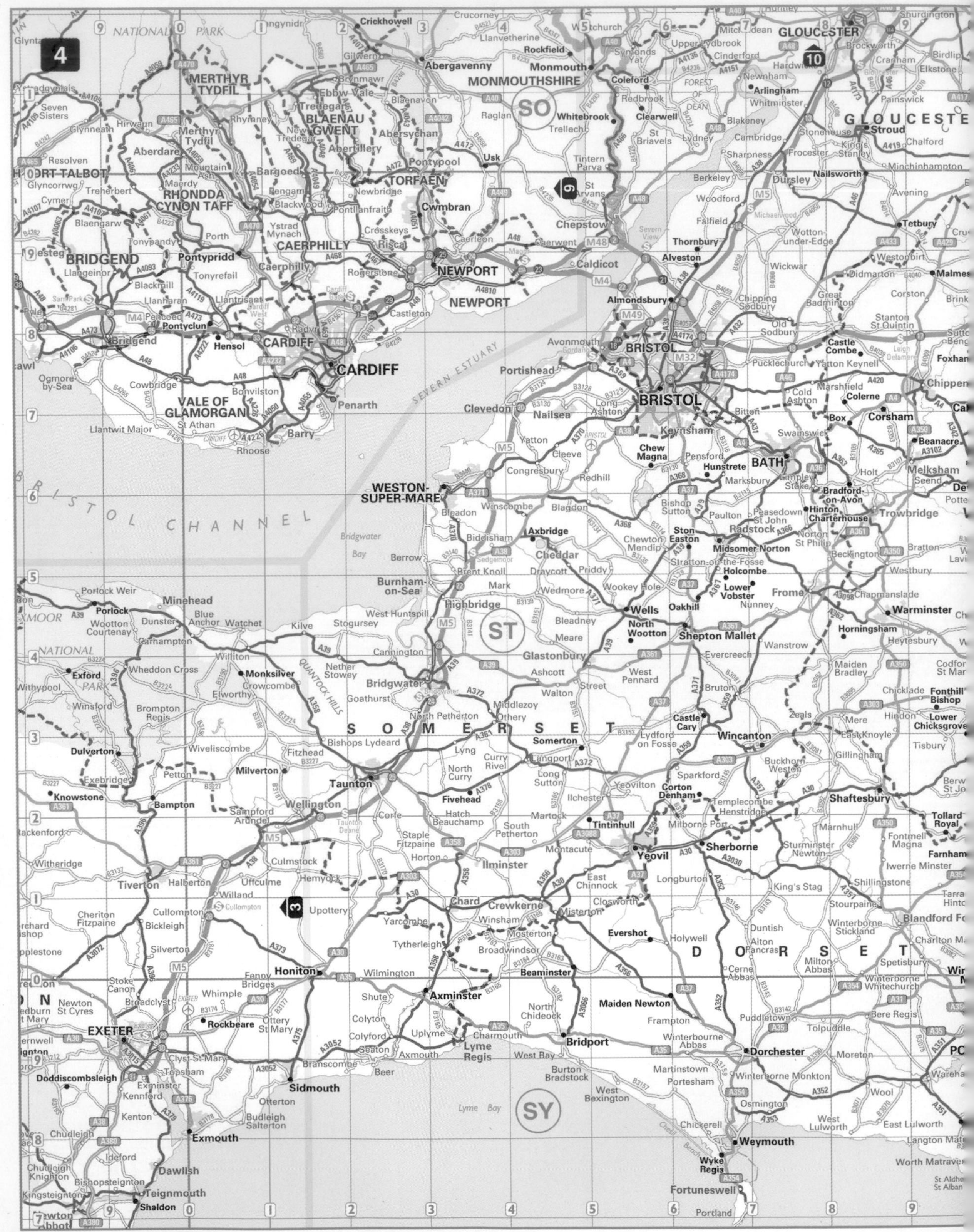

For continuation pages refer to numbered arrows

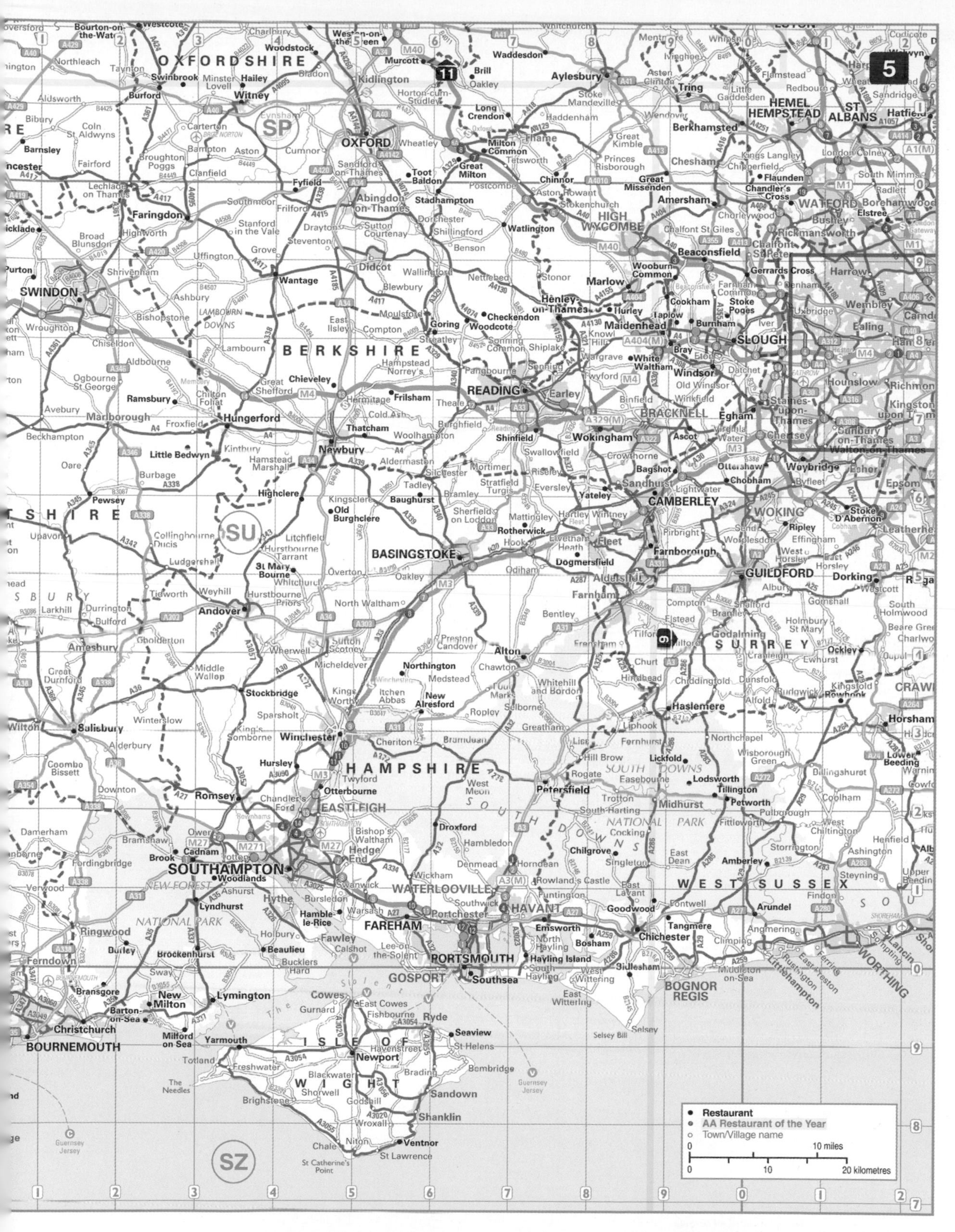
5
OXFORDSHIRE
Bourton-on-the-Water
Westcote
Charlbury
Woodstock
Weston-on-the-Green
Whitchurch
Northleach
Taynton
Swinbrook
Minster Lovell
Hailey
Witney
Bladon
Kidlington
Murcott
Brill
Oakley
Waddesdon
Aylesbury
Aldsworth
Burford
Horton-cum-Studley
Long Crendon
Stoke Mandeville
Haddenham
Wendover
Tring
Aston Clinton
Ivinghoe
Little Gaddesden
Flamstead
Redbourn
Harpenden
Wheathampstead
Sandridge
HEMEL HEMPSTEAD
ST ALBANS
Hatfield
Bibury
Coln St Aldwyns
Carterton
Brize Norton
SP
OXFORD
Wheatley
Thame
Berkhamsted
Barnsley
Bampton
Aston
Cumnor
Milton Common
Great Kimble
Princes Risborough
Chesham
Kings Langley
Chipperfield
London Colney
Cirencester
Fairford
Broughton Poggs
Clanfield
Sandford-on-Thames
Toot Baldon
Great Milton
Tetsworth
Chinnor
Great Missenden
Flaunden
South Mimms
Lechlade on Thames
Fyfield
Postcombe
Aston Rowant
Amersham
Chandler's Cross
Radlett
Faringdon
Southmoor
Frilford
Abingdon-on-Thames
Stadhampton
Stokenchurch
Chorleywood
WATFORD
Borehamwood
Elstree
Bushey
Cricklade
Broad Blunsdon
Highworth
Stanford in the Vale
Drayton
Sutton Courtenay
Dorchester
Shillingford
Watlington
HIGH WYCOMBE
Chalfont St Giles
Rickmansworth
Steventon
Benson
Grove
Uffington
Beaconsfield
Chalfont St Peter
Purton
Shrivenham
Wantage
Didcot
Wallingford
Nettlebed
Stonor
Marlow
Wooburn Common
Gerrards Cross
Harrow
SWINDON
Ashbury
Blewbury
Henley-on-Thames
Denham
Farnham Common
Stoke Poges
Wembley
Cookham
Hurley
Taplow
Burnham
Uxbridge
Ealing
Lambourn Downs
Bishopstone
Moulsford
Checkendon
Woodcote
East Ilsley
Compton
Goring
Streatley
Maidenhead
Knowl Hill
Iver
SLOUGH
Wroughton
Chiseldon
Lambourn
BERKSHIRE
Sonning Common
Shiplake
Bray
Eton
Aldbourne
Hampstead Norrey's
Wargrave
White Waltham
Windsor
Datchet
Ogbourne St George
Membury
Great Shefford
Chieveley
Pangbourne
Sonning
Twyford
Old Windsor
Hounslow
Richmond
Ramsbury
Chilton Foliat
Hermitage
Frilsham
Theale
READING
Earley
Binfield
Winkfield
Staines-upon-Thames
Kingston upon Thames
Avebury
Marlborough
Hungerford
Froxfield
Cold Ash
Thatcham
Burghfield
Shinfield
Wokingham
BRACKNELL
Egham
Virginia Water
Sunbury-on-Thames
Beckhampton
Woolhampton
Chertsey
Walton-on-Thames
Little Bedwyn
Kintbury
Newbury
Hamstead Marshall
Aldermaston
Swallowfield
Crowthorne
Ascot
Oare
Burbage
Silchester
Mortimer
Riseley
Bagshot
Ottershaw
Weybridge
Esher
Pewsey
Highclere
Tadley
Bramley
Stratfield Turgis
Eversley
Sandhurst
Lightwater
Chobham
Byfleet
Epsom
Yateley
Kingsclere
Baughurst
Old Burghclere
Sherfield on Loddon
Mattingley
Hartley Wintney
CAMBERLEY
WOKING
Stoke D'Abernon
Leatherhead
Ripley
Cobham
WILTSHIRE
Upavon
Collingbourne Ducis
SU
Litchfield
Hurstbourne Tarrant
Rotherwick
Hook
Elvetham Heath
Fleet
Pirbright
Send
Worplesdon
Effingham
BASINGSTOKE
Dogmersfield
Farnborough
West Horsley
East Horsley
Ludgershall
St Mary Bourne
Overton
Oakley
Whitchurch
Odiham
Aldershot
GUILDFORD
Dorking
Westcott
Salisbury Plain
Tidworth
Weyhill
Hurstbourne Priors
Larkhill
Durrington
Bulford
Andover
North Waltham
Farnham
Albury
Gomshall
Shalford
Compton
Elstead
Bramley
Holmbury St Mary
South Holmwood
Beare Green
Bentley
Amesbury
Cholderton
Sutton Scotney
Preston Candover
Alton
Frensham
Tilford
Milford
Godalming
SURREY
Charlwood
Ockley
Wherwell
Micheldever
Chawton
Cranleigh
Ewhurst
Great Durnford
Middle Wallop
Northington
Medstead
Churt
Hindhead
Chiddingfold
Dunsfold
Whitehill and Bordon
Kingsfold
Rowhook
Rudgwick
Crawley
Stockbridge
Itchen Abbas
New Alresford
Four Marks
Selborne
Alfold
Kings Worthy
Winchester
Ropley
Haslemere
Horsham
Winterslow
Sparsholt
Greatham
Liphook
Wilton
Salisbury
King's Somborne
Cheriton
Bramdean
Liss
Fernhurst
Northchapel
Alderbury
Hill Brow
Lickfold
Wisborough Green
Lower Beeding
Coombe Bissett
Hursley
HAMPSHIRE
Rogate
SOUTH DOWNS
Billingshurst
Warninglid
Twyford
West Meon
Easebourne
Lodsworth
Downton
Otterbourne
Petersfield
Tillington
Cowfold
Romsey
Chandler's Ford
EASTLEIGH
Trotton
Midhurst
Petworth
Coolham
Bishop's Waltham
Droxford
South Harting
NATIONAL PARK
Fittleworth
Pulborough
West Chiltington
Damerham
Bramshaw
Ower
Hambledon
Cocking
Henfield
Cadnam
Totton
Hedge End
Chilgrove
Storrington
Ashington
Fordingbridge
Brook
SOUTHAMPTON
Denmead
Horndean
Singleton
East Dean
Amberley
Upper Beeding
Woodlands
Wickham
Rowland's Castle
Steyning
Verwood
NEW FOREST
Ashurst
Swanwick
WATERLOOVILLE
Funtington
WEST SUSSEX
Findon
Lyndhurst
Hythe
Bursledon
Southwick
HAVANT
East Lavant
Fontwell
Arundel
Hamble-le-Rice
Warsash
Portchester
Goodwood
NATIONAL PARK
Ringwood
Holbury
Fawley
FAREHAM
Emsworth
Chichester
Tangmere
Angmering
Lancing
Shoreham
Burley
Beaulieu
Calshot
Lee-on-the-Solent
North Hayling
Bosham
Clymping
Sompting
Ferndown
Brockenhurst
PORTSMOUTH
Hayling Island
Ferring
East Preston
WORTHING
Sway
Bucklers Hard
GOSPORT
Southsea
South Hayling
West Wittering
Sidlesham
Middleton-on-Sea
Rustington
Littlehampton
Bransgore
New Milton
Lymington
The Solent
Cowes
East Cowes
East Wittering
BOGNOR REGIS
Barton-on-Sea
Gurnard
Fishbourne
Ryde
Christchurch
Milford on Sea
Yarmouth
Seaview
Selsey
Selsey Bill
BOURNEMOUTH
ISLE OF WIGHT
Havenstreet
St Helens
Newport
Totland
Freshwater
Bembridge
The Needles
Blackwater
Brading
Guernsey Jersey
Shorwell
Brighstone
Godshill
Sandown
Shanklin
Wroxall
Chale
Niton
Ventnor
St Lawrence
St Catherine's Point
SZ
Restaurant
AA Restaurant of the Year
Town/Village name
10 miles
20 kilometres

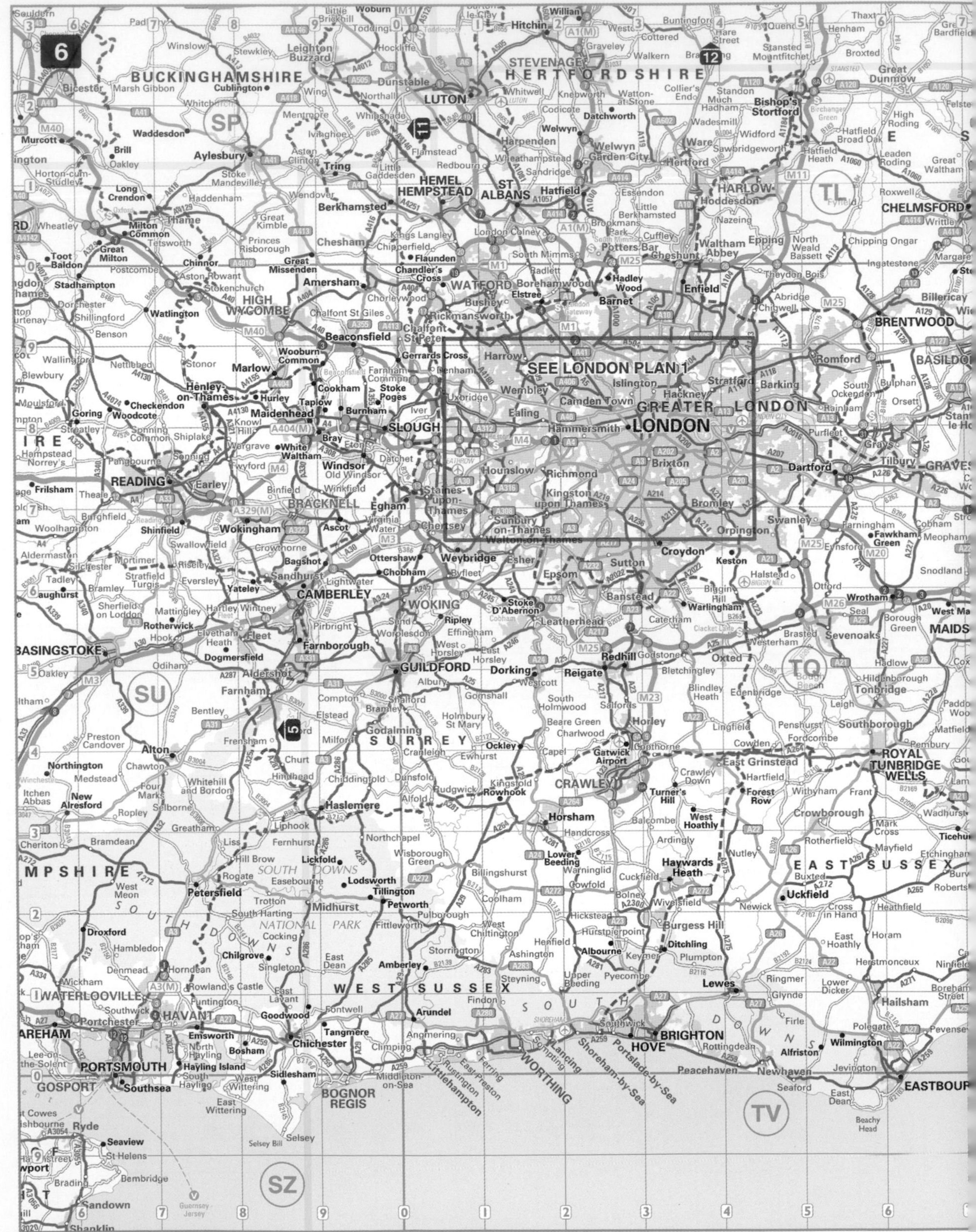

For continuation pages refer to numbered arrows

COLCHESTER
Harwich
Ardleigh
Wix
Tendring
Thorpe-le-Soken
Walton on the Naze
Frinton-on-Sea
Little Clacton
Thorrington
St Osyth
CLACTON-ON-SEA
Brightlingsea
West Mersea
Earls Colne
Aldham
Marks Tey
Coggeshall
Copford Green
Wivenhoe
Elmstead Market
Silver End
Kelvedon
Tiptree
Witham
Great Totham
Tolleshunt D'Arcy
Goldhanger
Tollesbury
Maldon
River Blackwater
Bradwell-on-Sea
Steeple
Cold Norton
Latchingdon
Southminster
South Woodham Ferrers
Burnham-on-Crouch
Hockley
Rayleigh
Rochford
Great Wakering
SOUTHEND-ON-SEA
Canvey Island
TM
Grain
Sheerness
Minster
Eastchurch
Leysdown-on-Sea
Isle of Sheppey
Iwade
Sittingbourne
Teynham
Faversham
Ospringe
Bredhurst
Whitstable
Herne Bay
Reculver
MARGATE
Broadstairs
Ramsgate
Sarre
Upstreet
Minster
Sturry
Hersden
Blean
Boughton Street
Fordwich
Ash
Sandwich
Canterbury
Wingham
Eastry
Doddington
Hollingbourne
Stalisfield Green
Lenham
Chilham
Chartham
Bridge
Aylesham
Deal
Challock
Charing
Sutton Valence
Crafty Green
Egerton
KENT
Wye
Kingsdown
St Margaret's at Cliffe
Headcorn
Pluckley
Smarden
Ashford
Bethersden
Elham
Densole
Alkham
DOVER
Lyminge
Hawkinge
CHANNEL TUNNEL TERMINAL
Sellindge
Biddenden
High Halden
Kingsnorth
Sissinghurst
Woodchurch
Benenden
Tenterden
Lympne
Hythe
FOLKESTONE
Rolvenden
Hamstreet
Wittersham
Appledore
Brookland
Brenzett
Dymchurch
St Mary's Bay
Northiam
New Romney
Peasmarsh
Rye
Camber
Lydd
Brede
Winchelsea
Dungeness
Westfield
Guestling Green
Fairlight
HASTINGS
St Leonards
STRAIT OF DOVER
TR
Restaurant
AA Restaurant of the Year
Town/Village name
10 miles
20 kilometres

For continuation pages refer to numbered arrows

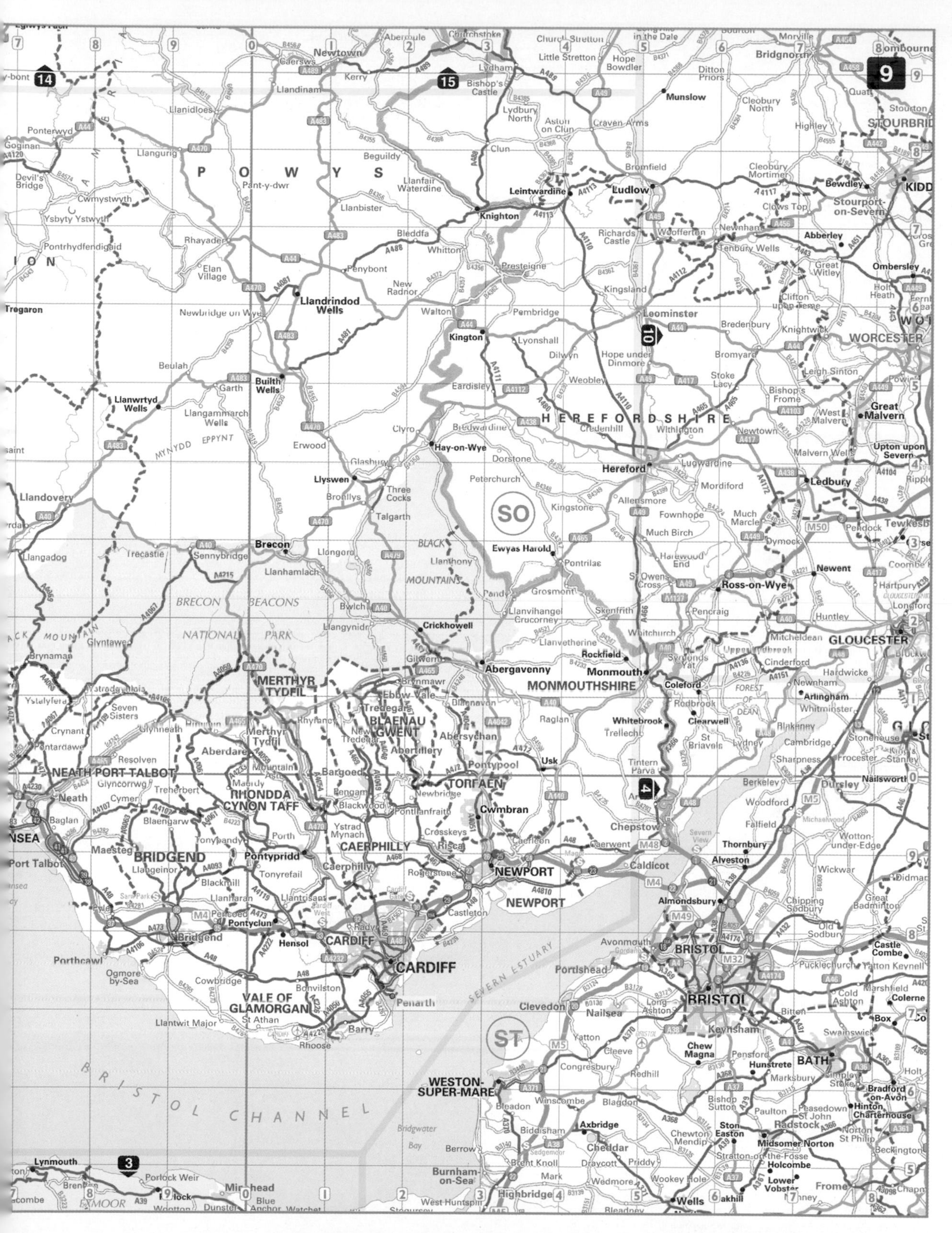

9
14
15
10
4
3
Newtown
Churchstoke
Church Stretton
Little Stretton
Hope Bowdler
Morville
Bridgnorth
Caersws
Kerry
Lydham
Bishop's Castle
Llandinam
Llanidloes
Lydbury North
Aston on Clun
Craven Arms
Munslow
Ditton Priors
Cleobury North
Highley
Quatt
Stourton
STOURBRIDGE
Ponterwyd
Goginan
Devil's Bridge
Cwmystwyth
Ysbyty Ystwyth
Pontrhydfendigaid
Llangurig
P O W Y S
Pant-y-dwr
Beguildy
Llanfair Waterdine
Clun
Bromfield
Cleobury Mortimer
Bewdley
Leintwardine
Ludlow
Stourport-on-Severn
Clows Top
Llanbister
Knighton
Rhayader
Bleddfa
Whitton
Richards Castle
Woofferton
Newnham
Tenbury Wells
Abberley
Ombersley
Elan Village
Penybont
New Radnor
Presteigne
Kingsland
Great Witley
Holt Heath
Clifton upon Teme
Tregaron
Llandrindod Wells
Newbridge on Wye
Walton
Pembridge
Leominster
Bredenbury
Knightwick
WORCESTER
Kington
Lyonshall
Dilwyn
Hope under Dinmore
Bromyard
Leigh Sinton
Beulah
Garth
Builth Wells
Eardisley
Weobley
Stoke Lacy
Bishop's Frome
Great Malvern
Llanwrtyd Wells
Llangammarch Wells
Clyro
Bredwardine
H E R E F O R D S H I R E
Credenhill
Withington
West Malvern
Newtown
Upton upon Severn
MYNYDD EPPYNT
Erwood
Hay-on-Wye
Dorstone
Glasbury
Hereford
Lugwardine
Malvern Wells
Ledbury
Llyswen
Peterchurch
Mordiford
Llandovery
Bronllys
Three Cocks
Talgarth
Allensmore
Kingstone
Fownhope
Much Marcle
Tewkesbury
SO
Much Birch
Dymock
Pendock
BLACK MOUNTAINS
Llangadog
Trecastle
Sennybridge
Brecon
Llangorse
Llanthony
Ewyas Harold
Pontrilas
Harewood End
Newent
Coombe Hill
Llanhamlach
St Owens Cross
Ross-on-Wye
Hartpury
BRECON BEACONS NATIONAL PARK
Bwlch
Pandy
Grosmont
Skenfrith
Pencraig
Huntley
Llanvihangel Crucorney
Crickhowell
Llangynidr
Whitchurch
Mitcheldean
GLOUCESTER
Glyntawe
Brynaman
Gilwern
Abergavenny
Llanvetherine
Rockfield
Monmouth
Symonds Yat
Cinderford
Hardwicke
MERTHYR TYDFIL
Brynmawr
Ebbw Vale
Blaenavon
MONMOUTHSHIRE
Coleford
Newnham
Arlingham
Ystradgynlais
Ystalyfera
Seven Sisters
Tredegar
BLAENAU GWENT
Rhymney
Raglan
Whitebrook
Trellech
Ruardean
Clearwell
St Briavels
FOREST OF DEAN
Whitminster
Blakeney
Lydney
Stonehouse
Crynant
Glynneath
Merthyr Tydfil
New Tredegar
Abersychan
Abertillery
Cambridge
Frocester
Pontardawe
Resolven
Aberdare
Mountain Ash
Bargoed
Pontypool
Usk
Tintern Parva
Sharpness
Kings Stanley
NEATH PORT TALBOT
Glyncorrwg
Treherbert
Maerdy
RHONDDA CYNON TAFF
TORFAEN
Berkeley
Dursley
Nailsworth
Neath
Cymer
Bengam
Blackwood
Newbridge
Pontllanfraith
Cwmbran
Woodford
Baglan
Blaengarw
Ystrad Mynach
Crosskeys
Falfield
Porth
Tonypandy
Chepstow
SWANSEA
Maesteg
BRIDGEND
Pontypridd
CAERPHILLY
Risca
Caerleon
Caerwent
Thornbury
Wotton-under-Edge
Port Talbot
Llangeinor
Caerphilly
Rogerstone
NEWPORT
Caldicot
Alveston
Wickwar
Blackmill
Tonyrefail
Didmarton
Llanharan
Llantrisant
Castleton
NEWPORT
Almondsbury
Chipping Sodbury
Great Badminton
Pyle
Pencoed
Pontyclun
Radyr
Old Sodbury
Bridgend
Hensol
CARDIFF
Avonmouth
BRISTOL
Castle Combe
Porthcawl
Ogmore-by-Sea
Cowbridge
CARDIFF
SEVERN ESTUARY
Portishead
Pucklechurch
Yatton Keynell
Bonvilston
Marshfield
VALE OF GLAMORGAN
Penarth
Clevedon
Nailsea
Long Ashton
BRISTOL
Cold Ashton
Colerne
Llantwit Major
St Athan
Barry
Keynsham
Bitton
Box
Rhoose
ST
Yatton
Cleeve
Chew Magna
Pensford
BATH
Swainswick
BRISTOL CHANNEL
Congresbury
Redhill
Hunstrete
Marksbury
Limpley Stoke
Holt
WESTON-SUPER-MARE
Bradford-on-Avon
Bleadon
Winscombe
Blagdon
Bishop Sutton
Paulton
Peasedown St John
Hinton Charterhouse
Bridgwater Bay
Biddisham
Axbridge
Cheddar
Chewton Mendip
Ston Easton
Radstock
Norton St Philip
Berrow
Brent Knoll
Draycott
Priddy
Midsomer Norton
Beckington
Lynmouth
Porlock Weir
Burnham-on-Sea
Stratton-on-the-Fosse
Holcombe
Brendon
Mark
Wedmore
Wookey Hole
Lower Vobster
Frome
EXMOOR
Minehead
Highbridge
Oakhill
Wells
Mells
Blue Anchor
Watchet
West Huntspill
Dunster
Wootton

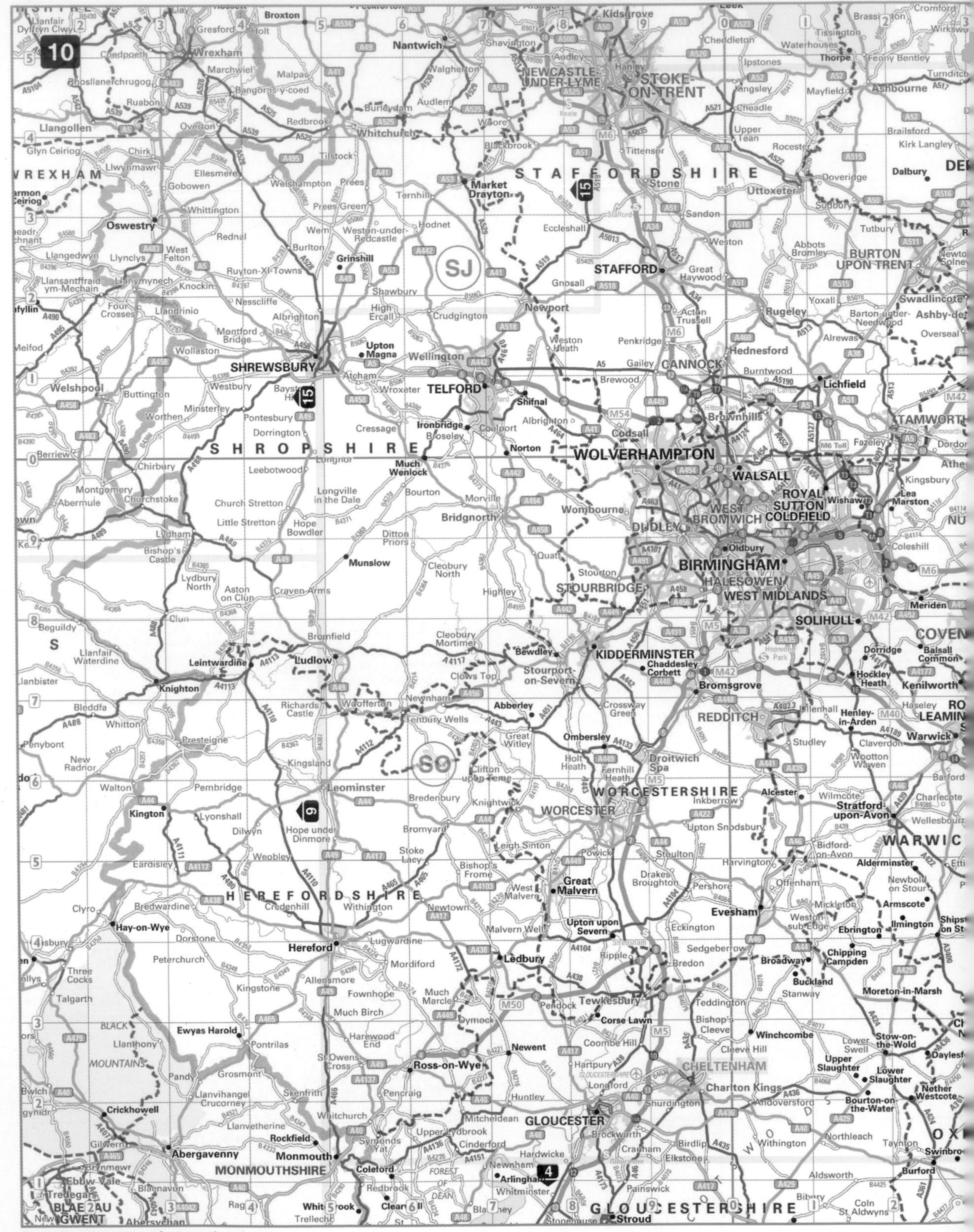

For continuation pages refer to numbered arrows

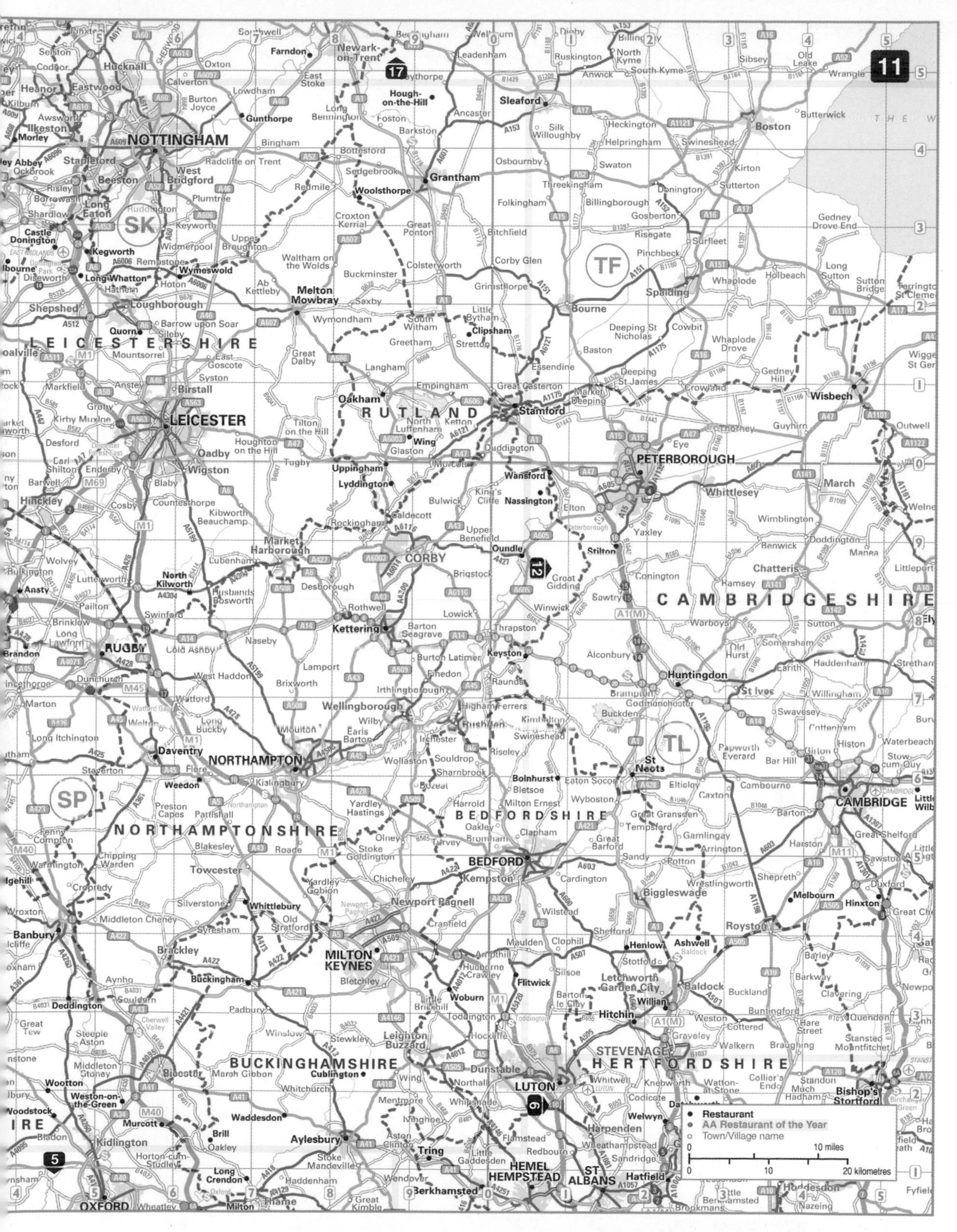
11
NOTTINGHAM
LEICESTER
PETERBOROUGH
CAMBRIDGE
NORTHAMPTON
BEDFORD
MILTON KEYNES
LUTON
OXFORD
CORBY
STEVENAGE
HEMEL HEMPSTEAD
ST ALBANS
LEICESTERSHIRE
RUTLAND
NORTHAMPTONSHIRE
BEDFORDSHIRE
BUCKINGHAMSHIRE
HERTFORDSHIRE
CAMBRIDGESHIRE
SK
TF
TL
SP
Newark-on-Trent
Grantham
Sleaford
Boston
Spalding
Bourne
Stamford
Oakham
Uppingham
Melton Mowbray
Loughborough
Hinckley
Market Harborough
Kettering
Wellingborough
Rugby
Daventry
Banbury
Huntingdon
St Ives
St Neots
Wisbech
March
Whittlesey
Oundle
Bicester
Aylesbury
Buckingham
Towcester
Newport Pagnell
Leighton Buzzard
Dunstable
Hitchin
Letchworth Garden City
Baldock
Royston
Biggleswade
Harpenden
Tring
Berkhamsted
Bishop's Stortford
Hatfield
Welwyn
Kidlington
Wing
Clipsham
Woolsthorpe
Wymeswold
Kegworth
Long Whatton
Gunthorpe
Farndon
Hough-on-the-Hill
Lyddington
Wansford
Nassington
Keyston
Stilton
Bolnhurst
Weedon
Whittlebury
Woburn
Flitwick
Henlow
Ashwell
Melbourn
Hinxton
Waddesdon
Brill
Long Crendon
Murcott
Cublington
Wootton
Weston-on-the-Green
Deddington
Milton
Ansty
● Restaurant
● AA Restaurant of the Year
○ Town/Village name
0 10 miles
0 10 20 kilometres

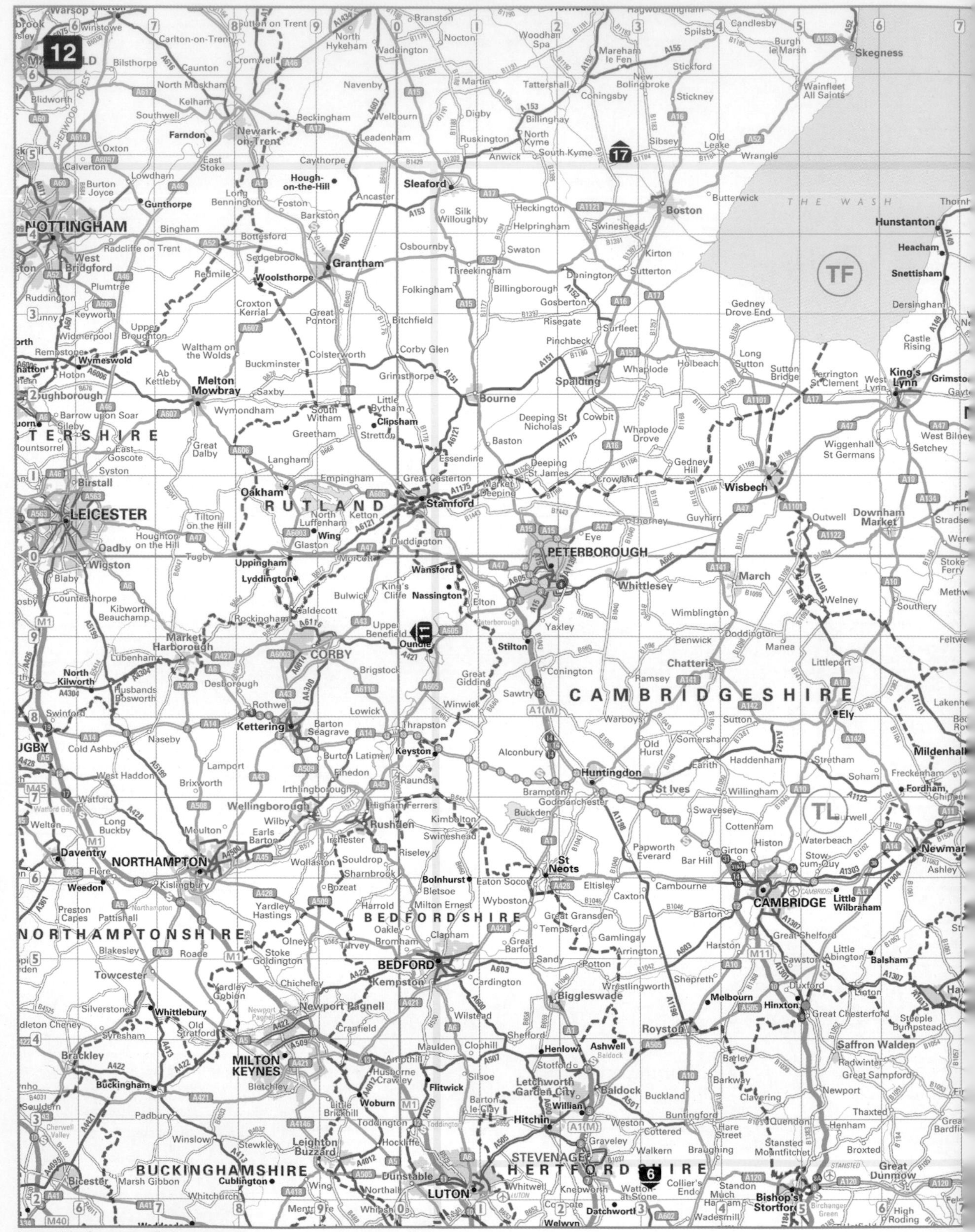

For continuation pages refer to numbered arrows

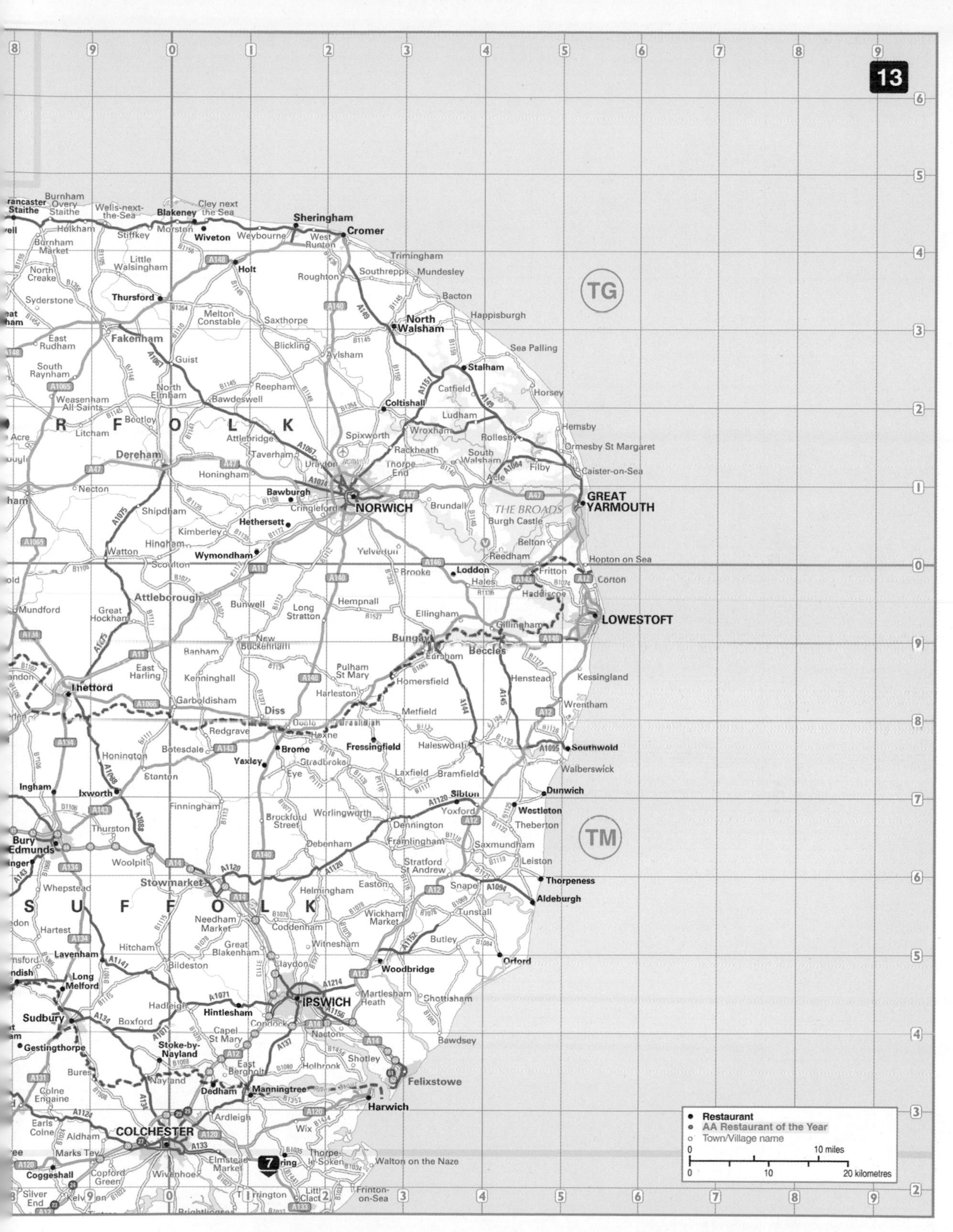

13
TG
TM
NORFOLK
SUFFOLK
Burnham Overy Staithe
Wells-next-the-Sea
Blakeney
Cley next the Sea
Sheringham
Cromer
Holkham
Stiffkey
Morston
Wiveton
Weybourne
West Runton
Burnham Market
Little Walsingham
Holt
Trimingham
North Creake
Roughton
Southrepps
Mundesley
Syderstone
Thursford
Bacton
Melton Constable
Saxthorpe
Happisburgh
North Walsham
East Rudham
Fakenham
Blickling
Aylsham
Sea Palling
South Raynham
Guist
Stalham
North Elmham
Reepham
Catfield
Horsey
Weasenham All Saints
Bawdeswell
Coltishall
Ludham
Bootley
Litcham
Attlebridge
Spixworth
Wroxham
Hemsby
Rollesby
Ormesby St Margaret
Dereham
Taverham
Rackheath
South Walsham
Drayton
Thorpe End
Acle
Filby
Caister-on-Sea
Honingham
Necton
Bawburgh
NORWICH
GREAT YARMOUTH
Brundall
THE BROADS
Cringleford
Shipdham
Hethersett
Burgh Castle
Kimberley
Belton
Hingham
Watton
Wymondham
Yelverton
Reedham
Scoulton
Hopton on Sea
Brooke
Loddon
Fritton
Hales
Corton
Haddiscoe
Attleborough
Mundford
Great Hockham
Bunwell
Long Stratton
Hempnall
Ellingham
Gillingham
LOWESTOFT
New Buckenham
Bungay
Banham
Beccles
Earsham
East Harling
Pulham St Mary
Kenninghall
Homersfield
Henstead
Kessingland
Thetford
Harleston
Garboldisham
Diss
Metfield
Wrentham
Redgrave
Hoxne
Honington
Botesdale
Brome
Fressingfield
Halesworth
Southwold
Yaxley
Stradbroke
Eye
Stanton
Laxfield
Bramfield
Walberswick
Ingham
Ixworth
Dunwich
Sibton
Westleton
Finningham
Yoxford
Brockford Street
Worlingworth
Theberton
Thurston
Dennington
Framlingham
Saxmundham
Debenham
Bury St Edmunds
Woolpit
Leiston
Stratford St Andrew
Whepstead
Stowmarket
Easton
Snape
Thorpeness
Helmingham
Aldeburgh
Wickham Market
Needham Market
Tunstall
Coddenham
Hartest
Butley
Hitcham
Great Blakenham
Witnesham
Lavenham
Bildeston
Claydon
Woodbridge
Orford
Long Melford
Martlesham Heath
Chattisham
Hadleigh
IPSWICH
Sudbury
Hintlesham
Boxford
Copdock
Nacton
Capel St Mary
Bawdsey
Gestingthorpe
Stoke-by-Nayland
Shotley
East Bergholt
Holbrook
Bures
Nayland
Felixstowe
Colne Engaine
Dedham
Manningtree
Harwich
Earls Colne
Ardleigh
Aldham
COLCHESTER
Wix
Marks Tey
Elmstead Market
Thorpe-le-Soken
Walton on the Naze
Coggeshall
Copford Green
Wivenhoe
Frinton-on-Sea
Silver End
Kelvedon
Restaurant
AA Restaurant of the Year
Town/Village name
0
10 miles
0
10
20 kilometres

For continuation pages refer to numbered arrows

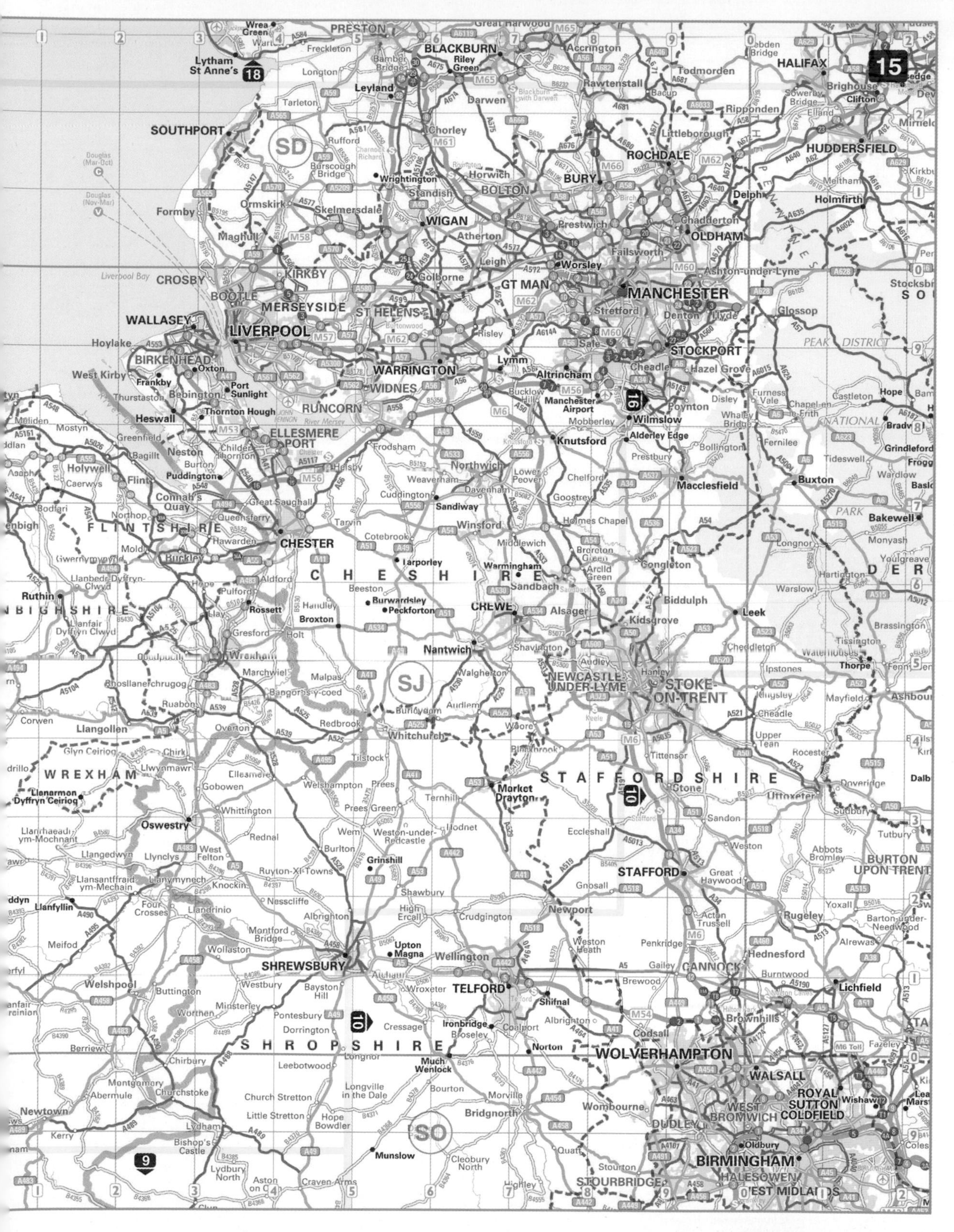

15
PRESTON
BLACKBURN
Accrington
Lytham St Anne's
18
Freckleton
Riley Green
Rawtenstall
Todmorden
HALIFAX
Brighouse
Leyland
Darwen
Tarleton
Ripponden
Littleborough
SOUTHPORT
SD
Chorley
Rufford
ROCHDALE
HUDDERSFIELD
Burscough Bridge
Wrightington
Horwich
BURY
Ormskirk
Skelmersdale
Standish
BOLTON
Delph
Holmfirth
Formby
WIGAN
Prestwich
Chadderton
OLDHAM
Maghull
Atherton
Liverpool Bay
CROSBY
KIRKBY
Leigh
Worsley
Failsworth
BOOTLE
Golborne
GT MAN
MANCHESTER
Ashton-under-Lyne
MERSEYSIDE
ST HELENS
Stretford
WALLASEY
LIVERPOOL
Denton
Hyde
Glossop
Hoylake
Risley
PEAK DISTRICT
BIRKENHEAD
Oxton
Sale
STOCKPORT
West Kirby
Frankby
WARRINGTON
Lymm
Altrincham
Cheadle
Hazel Grove
Bebington
Port Sunlight
WIDNES
Thurstaston
RUNCORN
Manchester Airport
Poynton
Disley
Hope
Heswall
Thornton Hough
Wilmslow
Castleton
Mostyn
Mobberley
Chapel-en-le-Frith
ELLESMERE PORT
Knutsford
Alderley Edge
Greenfield
Neston
Frodsham
Prestbury
Bollington
Bagillt
Holywell
Flint
Northwich
Tideswell
Puddington
Weaverham
Chelford
Macclesfield
Buxton
Connah's Quay
Great Saughall
Cuddington
Sandiway
Goostrey
Queensferry
Tarvin
Winsford
Holmes Chapel
Bakewell
FLINTSHIRE
Hawarden
CHESTER
Cotebrook
Middlewich
Buckley
Tarporley
Congleton
Mold
CHESHIRE
Sandbach
Ruthin
Rossett
Beeston
Burwardsley
Peckforton
CREWE
Alsager
Biddulph
Leek
Broxton
Kidsgrove
Gresford
Holt
Wrexham
Nantwich
Cheddleton
Marchwiel
Malpas
SJ
NEWCASTLE-UNDER-LYME
STOKE-ON-TRENT
Thorpe
Ruabon
Bangor-is-y-coed
Audlem
Mayfield
Corwen
Llangollen
Overton
Redbrook
Whitchurch
Woore
Cheadle
Chirk
Tilstock
Tittensor
Rocester
WREXHAM
Ellesmere
STAFFORDSHIRE
Llanarmon Dyffryn Ceiriog
Gobowen
Welshampton
Prees
Market Drayton
Stone
Uttoxeter
Whittington
10
Oswestry
Hodnet
Eccleshall
Sandon
Tutbury
Wem
Weston-under-Redcastle
Llangedwyn
West Felton
Burlton
Grinshill
Abbots Bromley
BURTON UPON TRENT
Ruyton-XI-Towns
STAFFORD
Llansantffraid-ym-Mechain
Knockin
Gnosall
Great Haywood
Llanfyllin
Nesscliffe
Shawbury
Four Crosses
Albrighton
High Ercall
Crudgington
Newport
Rugeley
Acton Trussell
Meifod
Montford Bridge
Wollaston
Upton Magna
Penkridge
Alrewas
SHREWSBURY
Wellington
Gailey
CANNOCK
Hednesford
Welshpool
Westbury
Bayston Hill
TELFORD
Wroxeter
Brewood
Lichfield
Buttington
Shifnal
Minsterley
Pontesbury
Albrighton
Brownhills
Worthen
Dorrington
Cressage
Ironbridge
Coalport
Codsall
Berriew
Broseley
SHROPSHIRE
Norton
WOLVERHAMPTON
Chirbury
Longnor
Much Wenlock
WALSALL
Montgomery
Abermule
Churchstoke
Leebotwood
Bourton
Morville
ROYAL SUTTON COLDFIELD
Wishaw
Newtown
Church Stretton
Longville in the Dale
Little Stretton
Hope Bowdler
Bridgnorth
Wombourne
WEST BROMWICH
DUDLEY
Kerry
Lydham
SO
Oldbury
Bishop's Castle
9
Munslow
Cleobury North
Quatt
Stourton
BIRMINGHAM
Lydbury North
Aston on Clun
Craven Arms
Highley
STOURBRIDGE
HALESOWEN
WEST MIDLANDS
M6
M6 Toll
M54
M56
M62
M60
M65
M61
M58
M57
M53

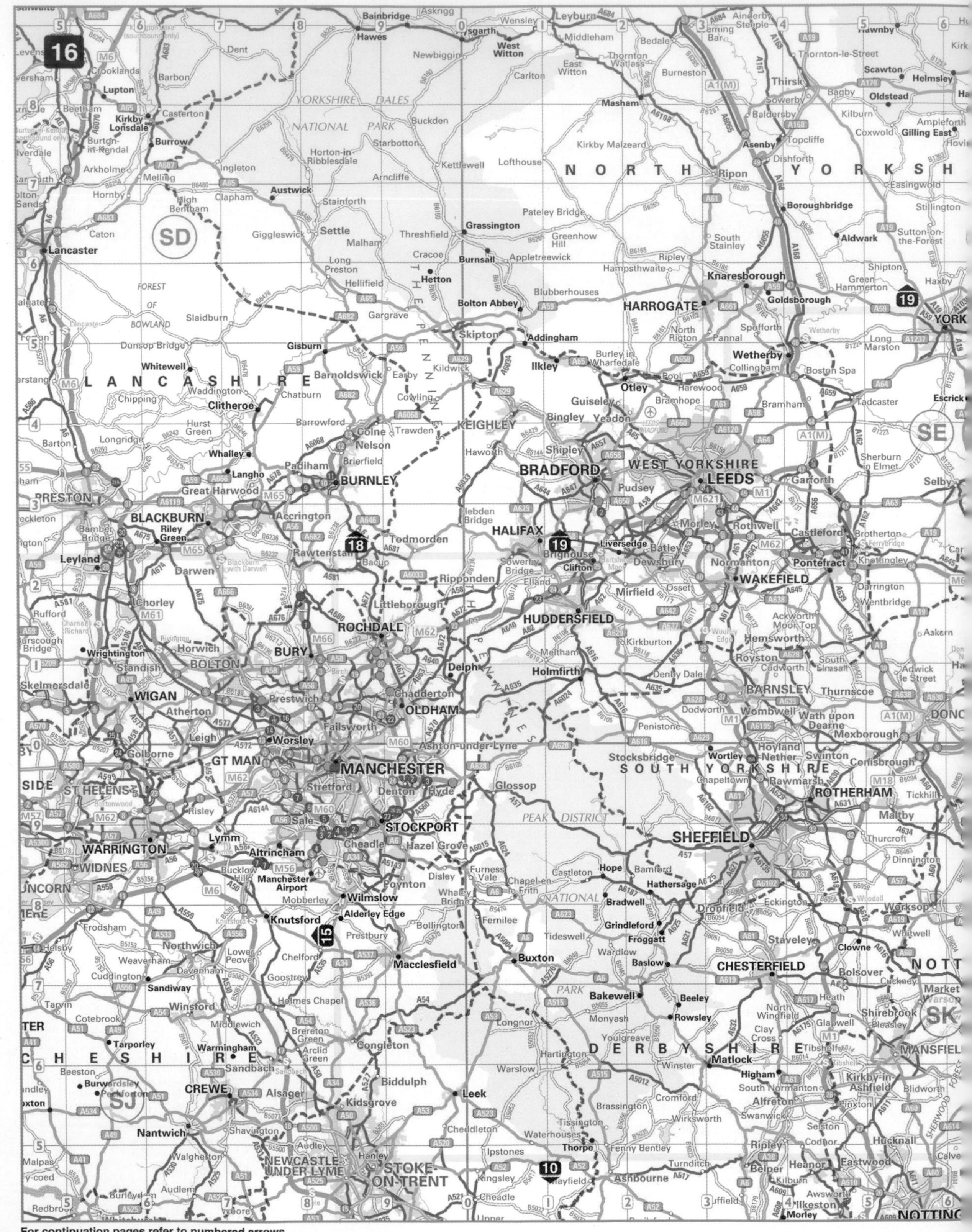

For continuation pages refer to numbered arrows

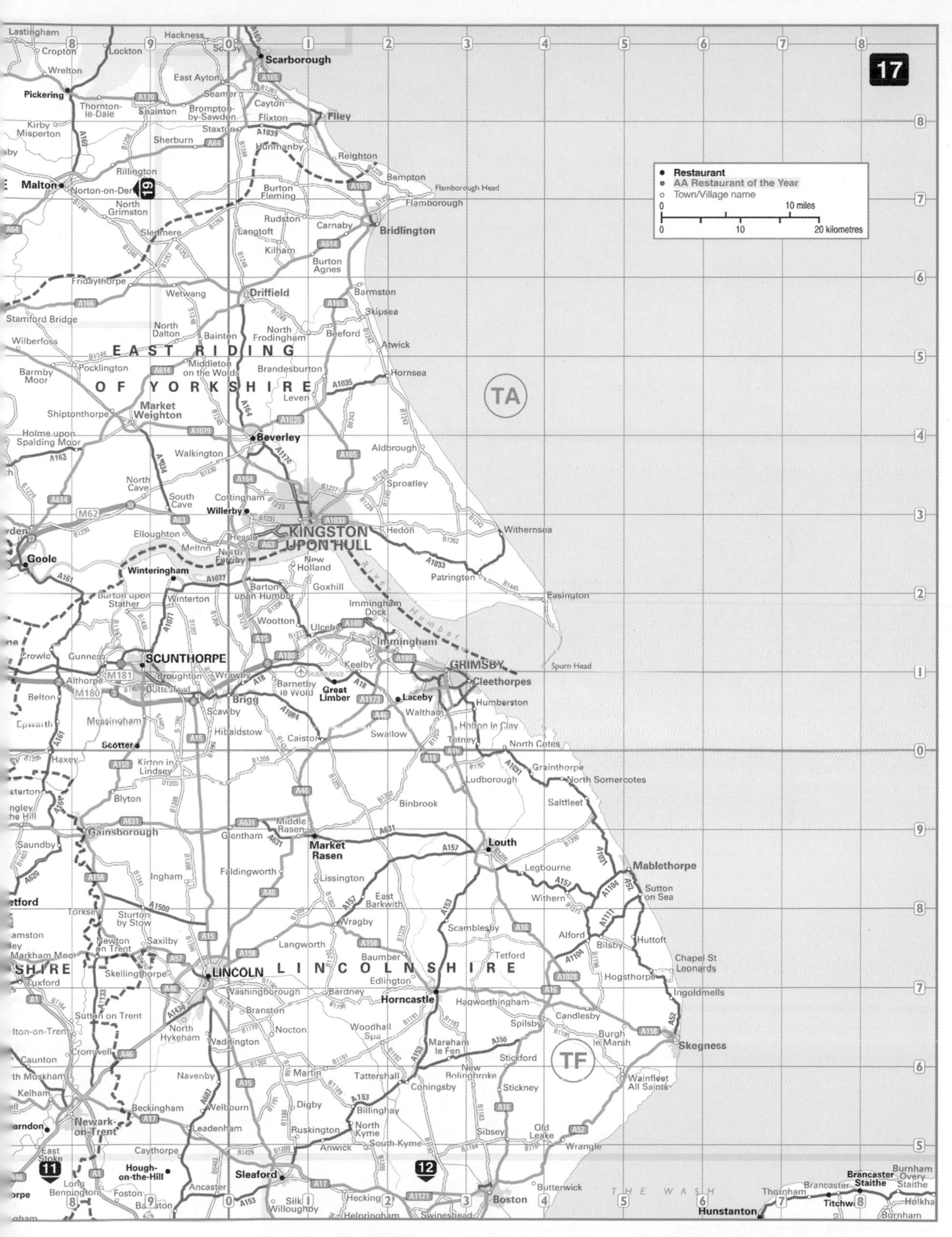

17
Restaurant
AA Restaurant of the Year
Town/Village name
0
10 miles
0
10
20 kilometres
TA
TF
EAST RIDING OF YORKSHIRE
LINCOLNSHIRE
Scarborough
Filey
Flamborough Head
Flamborough
Bempton
Reighton
Hunmanby
Bridlington
Carnaby
Burton Agnes
Kilham
Rudston
Burton Fleming
Langtoft
Driffield
Barmston
Skipsea
Beeford
Atwick
Hornsea
Brandesburton
Leven
Aldbrough
Sproatley
Withernsea
Hedon
Patrington
Easington
Spurn Head
KINGSTON UPON HULL
Beverley
Cottingham
Willerby
Hessle
North Ferriby
Melton
Ellougnton
Walkington
Market Weighton
Shiptonthorpe
Pocklington
Middleton on the Wolds
North Dalton
Bainton
North Frodingham
Wetwang
Fridaythorpe
Sledmere
North Grimston
Malton
Norton-on-Derwent
Rillington
Sherburn
Staxton
Brompton-by-Sawdon
Snainton
Thornton-le-Dale
Pickering
Wrelton
Cropton
Lastingham
Lockton
Hackness
Scalby
East Ayton
Seamer
Cayton
Flixton
Kirby Misperton
Stamford Bridge
Wilberfoss
Barmby Moor
Holme upon Spalding Moor
North Cave
South Cave
Goole
Winteringham
Burton upon Stather
Winterton
Barton-upon-Humber
New Holland
Goxhill
Immingham Dock
Immingham
Ulceby
Wootton
Humber
SCUNTHORPE
Gunness
Crowle
Althorpe
Belton
Epworth
Broughton
Bottesford
Wrawby
Brigg
Barnetby le Wold
Great Limber
Keelby
Laceby
GRIMSBY
Cleethorpes
Humberston
Waltham
Holton le Clay
Tetney
North Cotes
Swallow
Caistor
Scawby
Hibaldstow
Messingham
Scotter
Kirton in Lindsey
Haxey
Blyton
Gainsborough
Glentham
Middle Rasen
Market Rasen
Binbrook
Grainthorpe
North Somercotes
Saltfleet
Ludborough
Louth
Legbourne
Mablethorpe
Sutton on Sea
Withern
Alford
Huttoft
Bilsby
Chapel St Leonards
Hogsthorpe
Ingoldmells
Skegness
Burgh le Marsh
Candlesby
Spilsby
Hagworthingham
Tetford
Scamblesby
Horncastle
Baumber
Wragby
East Barkwith
Lissington
Faldingworth
Ingham
Saundby
Sturton by Stow
Torksey
Saxilby
Newton on Trent
Skellingthorpe
LINCOLN
Langworth
Edlington
Bardney
Washingborough
Branston
Nocton
Woodhall Spa
Mareham le Fen
Stickford
Stickney
New Bolingbroke
Wainfleet All Saints
Tattershall
Coningsby
Martin
Waddington
North Hykeham
Navenby
Welbourn
Digby
Billinghay
North Kyme
South Kyme
Ruskington
Anwick
Sibsey
Old Leake
Wrangle
Leadenham
Caythorpe
Hough-on-the-Hill
Ancaster
Sleaford
Silk Willoughby
Heckington
Helpringham
Swineshead
Boston
Butterwick
THE WASH
Hunstanton
Thornham
Brancaster
Brancaster Staithe
Titchwell
Burnham Overy Staithe
Burnham
Newark-on-Trent
Beckingham
Sutton on Trent
Cromwell
Caunton
Kelham
Tuxford
Markham Moor
Foston
Long Bennington
East Stoke
Balderton
19
11
12

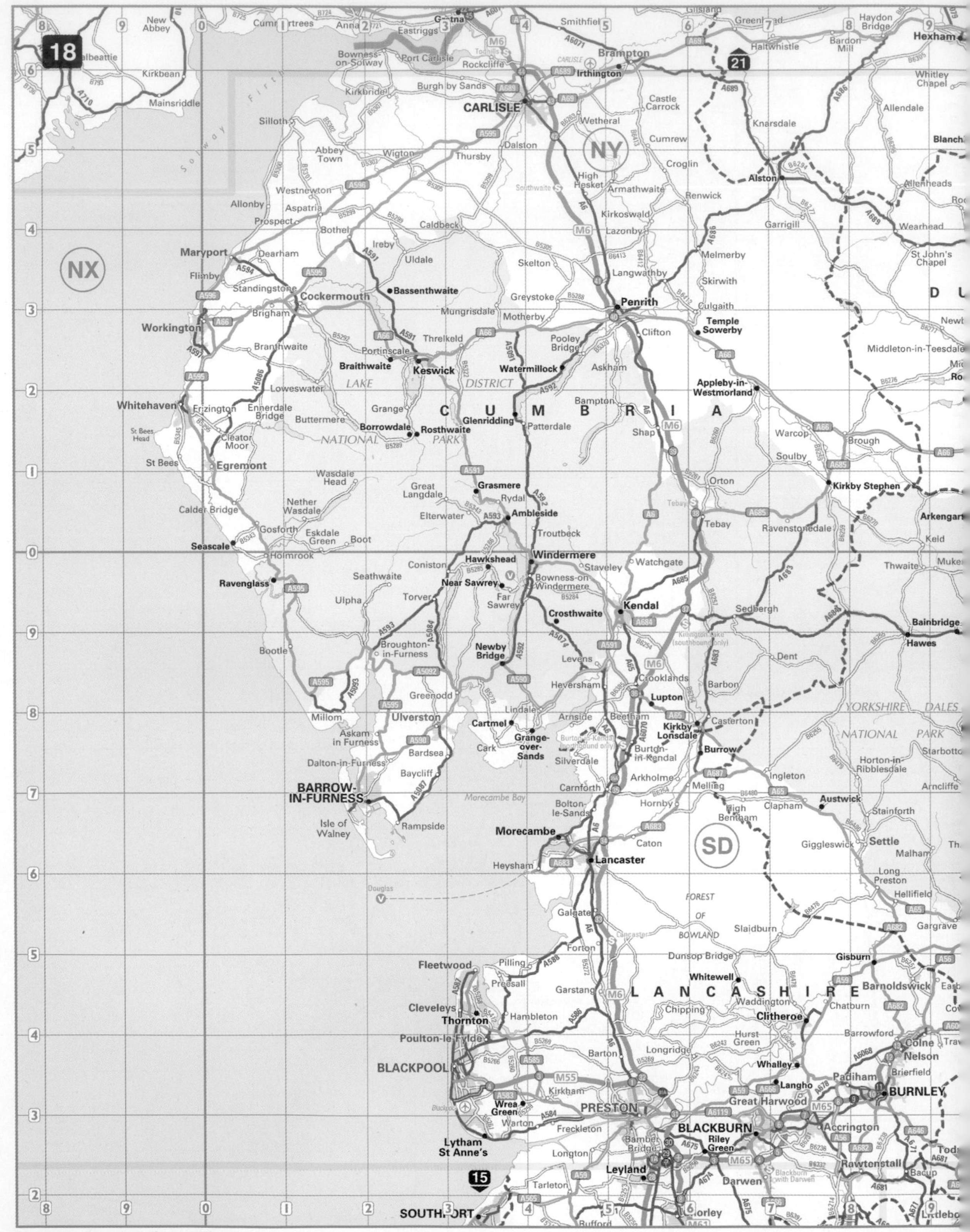

For continuation pages refer to numbered arrows

19
Restaurant
AA Restaurant of the Year
Town/Village name
0
10 miles
0
10
20 kilometres
NZ
SE
TA
NEWCASTLE UPON TYNE
GATESHEAD
SOUTH SHIELDS
TYNE AND WEAR
SUNDERLAND
WASHINGTON
Horsley
Prudhoe
Blaydon
Whickham
Rowlands Gill
Burnopfield
Birtley
Ebchester
Stanley
Leadgate
Annfield Plain
Consett
Chester-le-Street
Lanchester
Houghton-le-Spring
Seaham
Easington
Durham
Brandon
Thornley
Peterlee
Tow Law
Crook
Wingate
Trimdon
HARTLEPOOL
Spennymoor
Ferryhill
Bishop Auckland
Witton le Wear
Toft Hill
Sedgefield
West Auckland
Shildon
Rushyford
Copley
Newton Aycliffe
Wolviston
Billingham
Redcar
Marske-by-the-Sea
Saltburn-by-the-Sea
Staindrop
STOCKTON-ON-TEES
MIDDLESBROUGH
Brotton
Staithes
Skelton
Loftus
Hinderwell
Eston
Gainford
Barnard Castle
Piercebridge
DARLINGTON
Guisborough
Lythe
Greta Bridge
Hutton Magna
Hurworth-on-Tees
Yarm
Great Ayton
Sandsend
Whitby
Newsham
Stokesley
Kildale
Ruswarp
Barton
Crathorne
Castleton
Egton Bridge
Sleights
Middleton Tyas
Gilling West
Scotch Corner
Great Smeaton
West Rounton
Robin Hood's Bay
Richmond
Seave Green
NORTH YORK MOORS
Goathland
Ravenscar
Hipswell
Catterick
Osmotherley
Scotton
Northallerton
Rosedale Abbey
Cloughton
NATIONAL PARK
Leyburn
Ainderby Steeple
Lastingham
Hackness
Wensley
Leeming Bar
Hutton-le-Hole
Scalby
Middleham
Hawnby
Cropton
Lockton
West Witton
Bedale
Kirkbymoorside
Scarborough
Thornton Watlass
Thornton-le-Street
Wrelton
East Ayton
Carlton
East Witton
Burneston
Scawton
Helmsley
Pickering
Seamer
Thirsk
Cayton
Masham
Sowerby
Bagby
Oldstead
Harome
Thornton-le-Dale
Snainton
Brompton-by-Sawdon
Filey
Flixton
Baldersby
Kilburn
Oswaldkirk
Kirby Misperton
Staxton
Ampleforth
Kirkby Malzeard
Coxwold
Gilling East
Hovingham
Slingsby
Sherburn
Hunmanby
Asenby
Topcliffe
Reighton
Lofthouse
Dishforth
Rillington
NORTH YORKSHIRE
Ripon
Easingwold
Malton
Norton-on-Derwent
Burton Fleming
North Grimston
Sheriff Hutton
Boroughbridge
Stillington
Sledmere
Rudston
Carnaby
Pateley Bridge
Langtoft
Greenhow Hill
South Stainley
Aldwark
Sutton-on-the-Forest
Strensall
Kilham
Burton Agnes
Appletreewick
Ripley
Hampsthwaite
Shipton
Fridaythorpe
Knaresborough
Green Hammerton
Wetwang
Driffield
Barmston
Blubberhouses
Goldsborough
Haxby
Skipsea
HARROGATE
Stamford Bridge
North Dalton
Bainton
North Frodingham
Beeford
YORK
Spofforth
Wilberfoss
Addingham
North Rigton
Pannal
Long Marston
EAST RIDING OF YORKSHIRE
Burley in Wharfedale
Wetherby
Pocklington
Middleton on the Wolds
Brandesburton
Ilkley
Collingham
Elvington
Barmby Moor
Boston Spa
Otley
Harewood
Leven
Guiseley
Bramhope
Escrick
Shiptonthorpe
Market Weighton
Bramham
Tadcaster
Bingley
Yeadon
Holme upon Spalding Moor
Beverley
Shipley
Sherburn in Elmet
Walkington
North Cave
BRADFORD
WEST YORKSHIRE
LEEDS
Garforth
Bubwith
Pudsey
Selby
Cliffe
South Cave
Cottingham
Willerby
Morley
Rothwell
Howden
Castleford
KINGSTON UPON HULL
ALIFAX
Brotherton
Ellougton
Hessle
Liversedge
Batley
Ferrybridge
Melton
North Ferriby
Brighouse
Carlton
Goole
Clifton
Dewsbury
Normanton
Pontefract
Knottingley
Winteringham
New Holland
WAKEFIELD
Ossett
Darrington
Barton-upon-Humber
Goxhill
Burton upon Stather
Winterton
Immingham Dock
Wootton

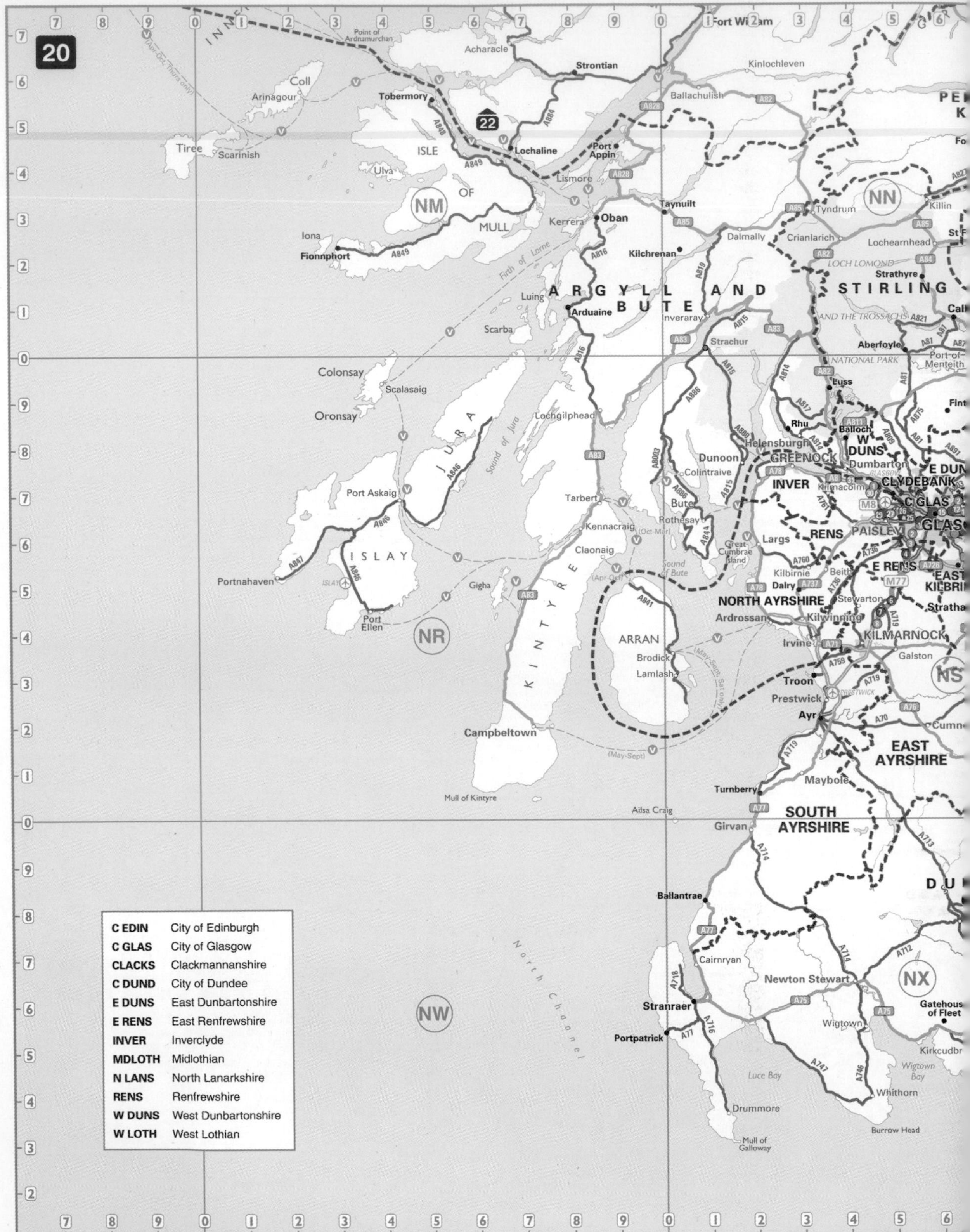

For continuation pages refer to numbered arrows

21
Restaurant
AA Restaurant of the Year
Town/Village name
0
10
20 miles
0
10
20
30 kilometres
ANGUS
NO
NT
NU
NY
NZ
NORTH
SEA
Spittal of Glenshee
Blair Atholl
Pitlochry
Kirriemuir
Brechin
Montrose
Inverbervie
Inverkeilor
Forfar
Arbroath
Blairgowrie
Rattray
Coupar Angus
Kinclaven
SIDLAW HILLS
DUNDEE
Carnoustie
Newport-on-Tay
Perth
Crieff
St Andrews Bay
Newburgh
St Andrews
Auchtermuchty
Cupar
Auchterarder
Glenfarg
Peat Inn
FIFE
Fife Ness
Crail
Falkland
Kinross
Anstruther
St Monans
Elie
Glenrothes
Leven
CLACKS
Alloa
Kincardine
Kirkcaldy
DUNFERMLINE
North Berwick
Gullane
FIRTH OF FORTH
Aberlady
East Linton
Dunbar
Polmont
Linlithgow
FALKIRK
EDINBURGH
W LOTH
Uphall
Ratho
LIVINGSTON
Haddington
EAST LOTHIAN
St Abb's Head
Eyemouth
Dalkeith
MDLOTH
LAMMERMUIR HILLS
Penicuik
PENTLAND HILLS
Duns
Berwick-upon-Tweed
Lauder
Greenlaw
Holy Island
Biggar
Peebles
Coldstream
Cornhill-on-Tweed
Bamburgh
Innerleithen
Galashiels
Melrose
St Boswells
Kelso
Selkirk
Wooler
Chathill
SCOTTISH BORDERS
Jedburgh
Hawick
UPLANDS
CHEVIOT HILLS
NORTHUMBERLAND
Alnwick
Amble
Moffat
Thornhill
Annandale Water
NATIONAL PARK
Longhorsley
NORTHUMBERLAND
Ashington
Morpeth
Blyth
Bedlington
Lochmaben
Lockerbie
Langholm
Dumfries
Matfen
Longtown
NEWCASTLE UPON TYNE
Tynemouth
Annan
Gretna
Corbridge
SOUTH SHIELDS
Dalbeattie
Irthington
Brampton
Hexham
GATESHEAD
TYNE AND WEAR
Kirkbean
SUNDERLAND
CARLISLE
18
19
23
WASHINGTON
Blanchland
Consett
Solway Firth
Wigton
Chester-le-Street
Seaham
Alston
Southwaite
Durham
Peterlee
Maryport
CUMBRIA
Crook
HARTLEPOOL
Bassenthwaite
DURHAM
Bishop Auckland
Workington
Cockermouth
Penrith
Temple Sowerby
Newton Aycliffe
Braithwaite
Billingham
Redcar
Keswick
Watermillock
Appleby-in-Westmorland
Romaldkirk
STOCKTON-ON-TEES
Whitehaven
Glenridding
Barnard Castle
MIDDLESBROUGH
LAKE DISTRICT
DARLINGTON
St Bees Head
Egremont
Brough
Guisborough

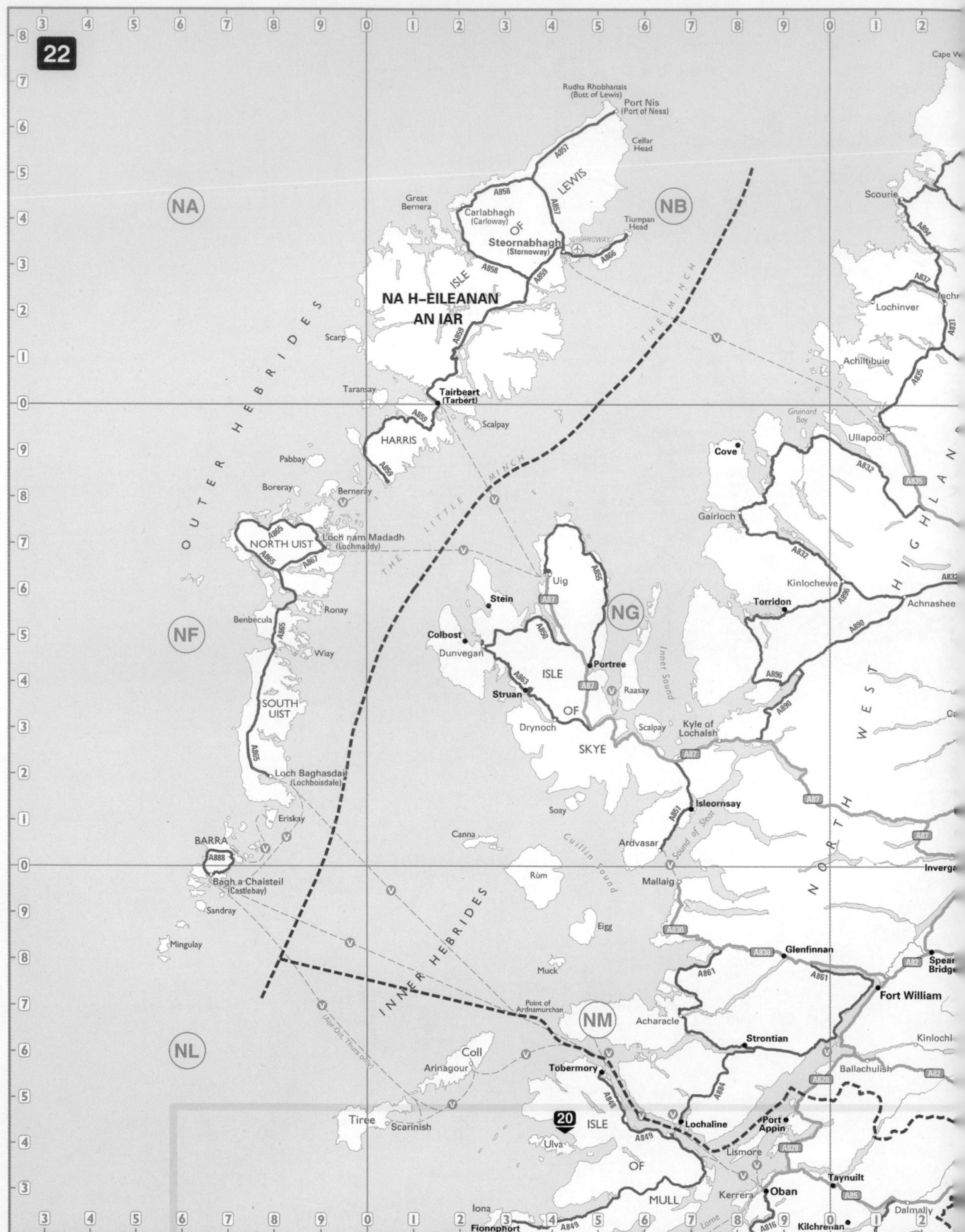

For continuation pages refer to numbered arrows

Restaurant
AA Restaurant of the Year
Town/Village name
0 10 20 miles
0 10 20 30 kilometres
NC
ND
NH
NJ
NK
NN
NO
PENTLAND FIRTH
Stromness
Dunnet Head
St Margaret's Hope
Duncansby Head
John o' Groats
Gills
Scrabster
Strathy Point
Thurso
Tongue
Bettyhill
Melvich
Wick
Lybster
Dunbeath
Altnaharra
Helmsdale
Lairg
Golspie
Brora
Bonar Bridge
Dornoch
Tain
GHLAND
Alness
Invergordon
Cromarty
MORAY FIRTH
Dingwall
Fortrose
Nairn
Forres
Muir of Ord
INVERNESS
MORAY
Lossiemouth
Elgin
Buckie
Cullen
Portsoy
Banff
Fraserburgh
Rothes
Keith
Aberchirder
Turriff
Peterhead
Aberlour
Dufftown
Huntly
Grantown-on-Spey
Carrbridge
Tomintoul
Ellon
Oldmeldrum
Inverurie
Kintore
Balmedie
Dyce
Kirkwall
Lerwick
Kildrummy
Alford
CITY OF ABERDEEN
ABERDEEN
Monadhliath Mountains
Aviemore
CAIRNGORMS
CAIRNGORM MOUNTAINS
NATIONAL
PARK
ABERDEENSHIRE
Kingussie
Newtonmore
Peterculter
Aboyne
Ballater
Banchory
Braemar
Stonehaven
GRAMPIAN MOUNTAINS
Laurencekirk
Inverbervie
Spittal of Glenshee
Blair Atholl
ANGUS
Killiecrankie
Pitlochry
Brechin
Montrose
PERTH AND KINROSS
Kirriemuir
Aberfeldy
Forfar
Inverkeilor
Fortingall
Kenmore
Blairgowrie
Rattray
Coupar Angus
Kinclaven
SIDLAW HILLS
Arbroath
Killin
Carnoustie
C DUNDEE
DUNDEE
Newport-on-Tay
St Fillans
Perth
Crieff
Comrie
St Andrews Bay
21

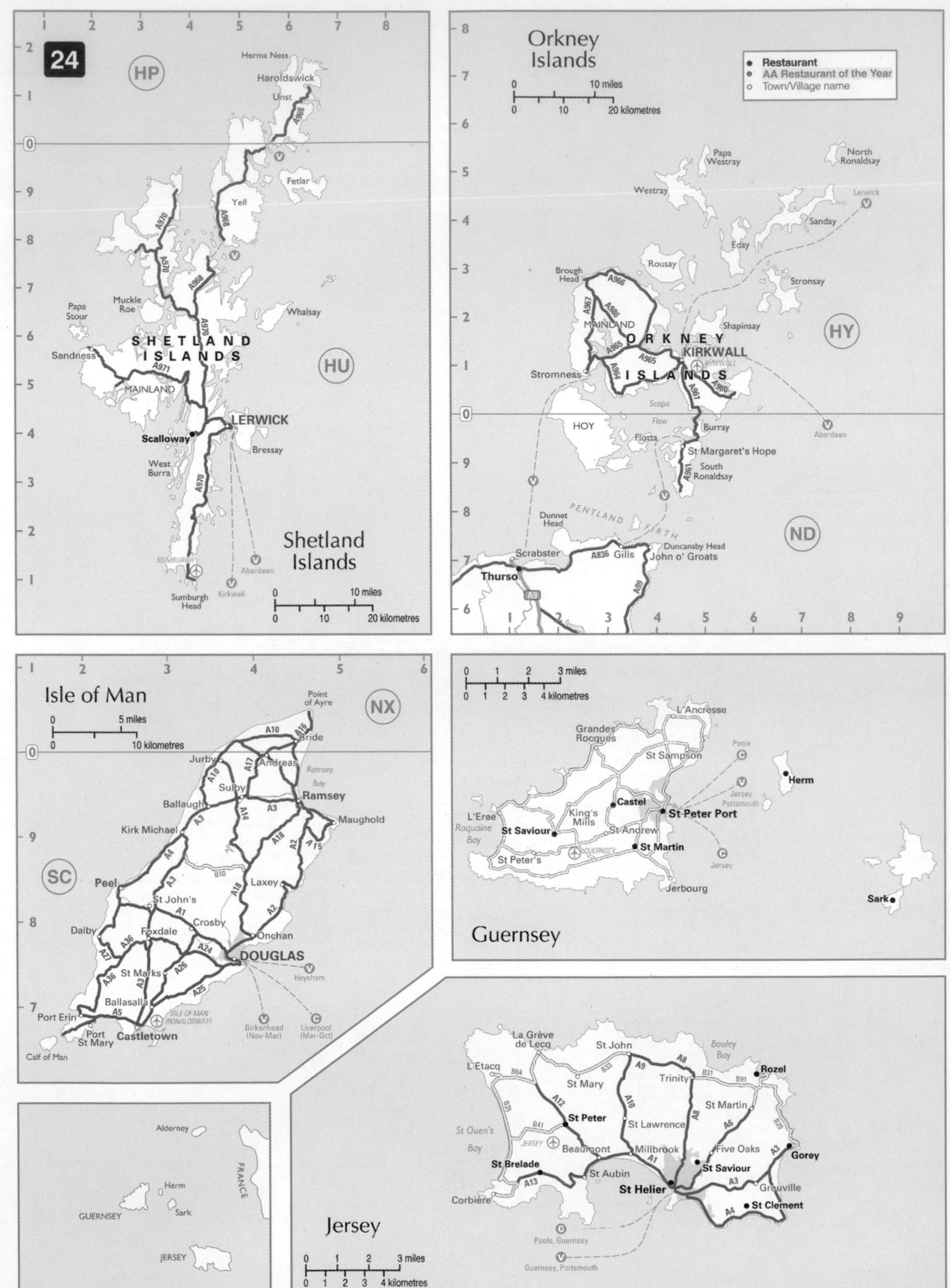
24
Shetland Islands
Herma Ness
Haroldswick
Unst
Fetlar
Yell
Whalsay
Papa Stour
Muckle Roe
SHETLAND ISLANDS
Sandness
MAINLAND
LERWICK
Scalloway
Bressay
West Burra
Sumburgh Head
Kirkwall
Aberdeen
Orkney Islands
Restaurant
AA Restaurant of the Year
Town/Village name
Papa Westray
North Ronaldsay
Westray
Sanday
Eday
Rousay
Stronsay
Brough Head
Shapinsay
ORKNEY ISLANDS
KIRKWALL
Stromness
Scapa Flow
HOY
Flotta
Burray
St Margaret's Hope
South Ronaldsay
Dunnet Head
PENTLAND FIRTH
Scrabster
Thurso
Gills
Duncansby Head
John o' Groats
Isle of Man
Point of Ayre
Bride
Jurby
Andreas
Ramsey Bay
Sulby
Ramsey
Ballaugh
Maughold
Kirk Michael
Peel
Laxey
St John's
Crosby
Dalby
Foxdale
Onchan
DOUGLAS
Heysham
St Marks
Ballasalla
Port Erin
Port St Mary
Castletown
Calf of Man
Birkenhead (Nov-Mar)
Liverpool (Mar-Oct)
Guernsey
L'Ancresse
Grandes Rocques
St Sampson
Poole
Jersey Portsmouth
Herm
Castel
St Peter Port
L'Eree
Rocquaine Bay
St Saviour
King's Mills
St Andrew
St Martin
St Peter's
Jersey
Jerbourg
Sark
Alderney
FRANCE
GUERNSEY
JERSEY
La Grève de Lecq
St John
Bouley Bay
L'Etacq
St Mary
Trinity
Rozel
St Ouen's Bay
St Peter
St Lawrence
St Martin
Beaumont
Millbrook
Five Oaks
Gorey
St Brelade
St Aubin
St Saviour
St Helier
Grouville
Corbière
St Clement
Poole, Guernsey
Guernsey, Portsmouth

Index of Restaurants

C

D

F

I

M

N

P

Q

R

S

T

W

X

Y

Z

Acknowledgments

The Automobile Association wishes to thank the following photographers and organisations for their assistance in the preparation of this book.

Abbreviations for the picture credits are as follows – (t) top; (b) bottom; (l) left; (r) right; (c) centre; (AA) AA World Travel Library.

Front & Back Cover A. Astes / Alamy; 3 Courtesy of riverstation, Bristol; 4 Courtesy of Abode, Exeter; 6 Courtesy of The Holbeck Ghyll Country House Hotel, Windermere; 8 Courtesy of Goodfellows, Somerset; 10 Courtesy of Simon Rogan; 11 Courtesy of L'Enclume - Copyright Kendall & Simms Ltd ; 12 Courtesy of Pierre Koffmann; 13 Courtesy of The Ritz, London; 14l Courtesy of Lumière, Cheltenham; 14r Courtesy of Sosharu, London; 15l Courtesy of Inver Restaurant, Strachur; 15r Courtesy of Restaurant James Sommerin, Penarth; 16 Johner Images / Alamy; 18 Courtesy of Sketch, London; 19l Courtesy of The Kitchin, Edinburgh; 19r Courtesy of The Whitebrook, Monmouthshire; 20-23 AA College Rosette Awards Feature: Copyright People 1st; 26 Courtesy of Deans Place, East Sussex; 30-31 AA/A Burton; 216-217 AA/ J Tims; 493 AA/P Trenchard; 494-495 AA/S Anderson; 554-555 AA/M Bauer; 584-585 AA/C Hill; 594-595 AA/K Blackwell.

Every effort has been made to trace the copyright holders, and we apologise in advance for any unintentional omissions or errors. We would be pleased to apply any corrections in a following edition of this publication.

Readers' Report Form

Please send this form to:–
Editor, The Restaurant Guide,
Lifestyle Guides,
AA Media,
Fanum House,
Basingstoke RG21 4EA

e-mail: lifestyleguides@theAA.com

Please use this form to recommend any restaurant you have visited, whether it is in the guide or not currently listed. Feedback from readers helps us to keep our guide accurate and up to date. Please note, however, that if you have a complaint to make during your visit, we strongly recommend that you discuss the matter with the restaurant management there and then, so that they have a chance to put things right before your visit is spoilt.

Please note that the AA does not undertake to arbitrate between you and the restaurant management, or to obtain compensation or engage in protracted correspondence.

Date

Your name (BLOCK CAPITALS)

Your address (BLOCK CAPITALS)

Post code

E-mail address

Restaurant name and address: (if you are recommending a new restaurant please enclose a menu or note the dishes that you ate.)

Comments

(please attach a separate sheet if necessary)

Please tick here ☐ if you DO NOT wish to receive details of AA offers or products

PTO

Readers' Report Form *continued*

Have you bought this guide before? ☐ YES ☐ NO

Please list any other similar guides that you use regularly

What do you find most useful about The AA Restaurant Guide?

Please answer these questions to help us make improvements to the guide:

What are your main reasons for visiting restaurants? (tick all that apply)

Business entertaining ☐ Business travel ☐ Trying famous restaurants ☐ Family celebrations ☐

Leisure travel ☐ Trying new food ☐ Enjoying not having to cook yourself ☐

To eat food you couldn't cook yourself ☐ Because I enjoy eating out regularly ☐

Other (please state)

How often do you visit a restaurant for lunch or dinner? (tick one choice)

Once a week ☐ Once a fortnight ☐ Once a month ☐ Less than once a month ☐

Other (please state)

Do you use the location atlas? ☐ YES ☐ NO

Do you generally agree with the Rosette ratings at the restaurants you visit in the guide?

(If not please give examples)

Who is your favourite chef?

Which is your favourite restaurant?

Which type of cuisine is your first choice e.g. French?

Which of these factors is the most important when choosing a restaurant? (tick one choice)

Price ☐ Service ☐ Location ☐ Type of food ☐

Awards/ratings ☐ Decor/surroundings ☐

Other (please state)

What elements of the guide do you find most useful when choosing a restaurant? (tick all that apply)

Description ☐ Photo ☐ Rosette rating ☐ Price ☐

Other (please state)

Readers' Report Form

Please send this form to:–
Editor, The Restaurant Guide,
Lifestyle Guides,
AA Media,
Fanum House,
Basingstoke RG21 4EA

e-mail: lifestyleguides@theAA.com

Please use this form to recommend any restaurant you have visited, whether it is in the guide or not currently listed. Feedback from readers helps us to keep our guide accurate and up to date. Please note, however, that if you have a complaint to make during your visit, we strongly recommend that you discuss the matter with the restaurant management there and then, so that they have a chance to put things right before your visit is spoilt.

Please note that the AA does not undertake to arbitrate between you and the restaurant management, or to obtain compensation or engage in protracted correspondence.

Date

Your name (BLOCK CAPITALS)

Your address (BLOCK CAPITALS)

Post code

E-mail address

Restaurant name and address: (if you are recommending a new restaurant please enclose a menu or note the dishes that you ate.)

Comments

(please attach a separate sheet if necessary)

Please tick here ☐ if you DO NOT wish to receive details of AA offers or products

PTO

Readers' Report Form *continued*

Have you bought this guide before? ☐ YES ☐ NO

Please list any other similar guides that you use regularly

What do you find most useful about The AA Restaurant Guide?

Please answer these questions to help us make improvements to the guide:

What are your main reasons for visiting restaurants? (tick all that apply)

Business entertaining ☐ Business travel ☐ Trying famous restaurants ☐ Family celebrations ☐

Leisure travel ☐ Trying new food ☐ Enjoying not having to cook yourself ☐

To eat food you couldn't cook yourself ☐ Because I enjoy eating out regularly ☐

Other (please state)

How often do you visit a restaurant for lunch or dinner? (tick one choice)

Once a week ☐ Once a fortnight ☐ Once a month ☐ Less than once a month ☐

Other (please state)

Do you use the location atlas? ☐ YES ☐ NO

Do you generally agree with the Rosette ratings at the restaurants you visit in the guide?
(If not please give examples)

Who is your favourite chef?

Which is your favourite restaurant?

Which type of cuisine is your first choice e.g. French?

Which of these factors is the most important when choosing a restaurant? (tick one choice)

Price ☐ Service ☐ Location ☐ Type of food ☐

Awards/ratings ☐ Decor/surroundings ☐

Other (please state)

What elements of the guide do you find most useful when choosing a restaurant? (tick all that apply)

Description ☐ Photo ☐ Rosette rating ☐ Price ☐

Other (please state)